C000156770

LARS PEARSON
and LANCE PARKIN

AHISTORY

AN UNAUTHORIZED HISTORY OF THE
DOCTOR WHO UNIVERSE
4TH EDITION

mad
norwegian
press

Des Moines, IA

TABLE OF CONTENTS

The following *only* catalogs main story entries for each adventure; some stories occur in multiple time zones, and hence have more than one page number listed. For a complete listing of *all* story references, consult the Index.

Some stories proved undateable and lack main entries; for a list of these, consult the None of the Above section (pages 1353-1356).

For easier reference across what's become a quite sprawling guidebook series, the pages of *Ahistory* Fourth Edition are numbered 1000 and up for Volume 1, 2000 and up for Volume 2, and 3000 and up for Volume 3.

All titles listed are *Doctor Who* stories (or were supplemental comics made for *Doctor Who Magazine*) unless otherwise noted. BBV and Reeltimes Pictures stories include a notation of the particular monster or *Doctor Who* character they feature. For more on the designations used in the Table of Contents, see the Key in the Introduction.

Big Finish box sets, for the most part, are listed under the box set title, then the individual stories therein. (The format is a bit inconsistent – whenever possible, we've gone with whatever's on the cover.)

To save space, Titan's comics are listed under *The Tenth Doctor Year One*, *The Eleventh Doctor Year One*, etc. We've anticipated a collection of *The Ninth Doctor Year One*.

TABLE OF CONTENTS

TABLE OF CONTENTS

TABLE OF CONTENTS

TABLE OF CONTENTS

TABLE OF CONTENTS

TABLE OF CONTENTS

TABLE OF CONTENTS

Footnote Features

Pre-History

History

Present Day

UNIT

Present Day (cont.)

TABLE OF CONTENTS

A very special thank you to our supporters on Patreon, namely: Darren Buckley, David H Adler, Evan Lamb, Greg Holtham, Janet Reimer, Jeff Peck, Jeremy Remy, Jeremy Roebuck, Joseph Coker, Maggie Howe, Matt Bracher, Mitchell S Easter, Pat Harrigan, Rick Taylor, Stephen Webb, Steve Grace, Steven Ashby, Steven Mollmann, Steven Sautter, Tyson Woolman and Vitas Varnas. You guys are awesome!

Copyright © 2019 Lance Parkin and Lars Pearson.
Published by Mad Norwegian Press (www.madnorwegian.com)
Cover & interior design by Adam Holt and Christa Dickson.
Volume 1 ISBN: 9781935234227
Volume 2 ISBN: 9781935234234
Volume 3 ISBN: 9781935234241
Word count, Vol. 1: 284,216; Vol. 2 (bibliography and acknowledgements included): 368,874; Vol. 3: 351,159;
TOC, introduction, index (some repeat, but counted once): 56,932...
Grand Total (page headers and back cover text not included): 1,061,183

Printed in the USA. First Printing (Vol. 3): February 2019.

mad norwegian press | des moines

This book seeks to place every event referred to in *Doctor Who* into a consistent timeline. Yet this is "a" history of the *Doctor Who* universe, not the "definitive" or "official" version.

Doctor Who has had hundreds of creators, all pulling in slightly different directions, all with their own vision of what *Doctor Who* was about. Without that diversity, the *Doctor Who* universe would no doubt be more internally consistent, but it would also be a much smaller and less interesting place. Nowadays, fans are part of the creative process. Ultimately, we control the heritage of the show that we love. The authors of *Ahistory* hope people will enjoy this book, and we know that they will challenge it.

# # # # #

A total adherence to continuity has always been rather less important to the successive *Doctor Who* production teams than the main order of business: writing exciting stories, telling good jokes and scaring small children with big monsters. This, as most people will tell you, is just how it should be.

Doctor Who has always been created using a method known as "making it up as they went along". The series glories in its invention and throwaway lines. When the TV series was first in production, no-one was keeping the sort of detailed notes that would prevent canonical "mistakes", and even the same writer could contradict their earlier work. It's doubtful the writer of *The Mysterious Planet* (broadcast in 1986) had a single passing thought about how the story fit in with *The Sun Makers* (1977)... even though they were both authored by Robert Holmes.

Now, with all the legions of new books, audios, comic strips, short stories and a new TV series, not to mention spin-offs, it is almost certainly impossible to keep track of every new *Doctor Who* story, let alone put them all in a coherent – never mind consistent – framework. References can contradict other references in the same story, let alone ones in stories written forty years later for a different medium by someone who wasn't even born the year the original writer died.

It is, in any case, impossible to come up with a consistent view of history according to *Doctor Who*. Strictly speaking, the Brigadier retires three years before the first UNIT story is set. The Daleks and Atlantis are both utterly destroyed, once and for all, several times that we know about. Characters "remember" scenes, or sometimes entire stories, that they weren't present to witness, and show remarkable lack of knowledge of real world events or events in *Doctor Who* that happened after the story first came out.

"Continuity" has always been flexible, even on the fundamentals of the show's mythology – *The Dalek Invasion of Earth* (1964), *The War Games* (1969), *Genesis of the Daleks*

(1975) and *The Deadly Assassin* (1976) all shamelessly threw out the show's history in the name of a good story. Their versions of events (the Daleks are galactic conquerors; the Doctor is a Time Lord who stole his TARDIS and fled his home planet; the Daleks were created by the Kaled scientist, Davros; Gallifreyan society is far from perfect and Time Lords are limited to twelve regenerations) are now taken to be the "truth". The previous versions (the Daleks are confined to one city; the Doctor invented the "ship" and his granddaughter named it before their exile; the Daleks are descendants of the squat humanoid Dals, mutated by radiation; the Time Lords are godlike and immortal barring accidents) have quietly been forgotten.

# # # # #

However, it would be unfortunate to write a book so vague that it becomes useless. Firm decisions have to be made about where stories are placed, so this book contains abundant footnotes that lay out the evidence pertaining to each story, and to explain each story's placement in this chronology.

In some cases, this is simply a matter of reporting an exact date spoken by one of the characters in the story (*Black Orchid*, for example). In others, no firm date is given. In those cases, we attempt to look at internal evidence given on screen, then evidence from the production team at the time (from the script, say, or from contemporary publicity material), then branch out to cross-referencing it with other stories, noting where other people who've come up with *Doctor Who* chronologies have placed it. What we're attempting to do is accurately list all the evidence given for dating the stories and other references in as objective an way as possible, then weigh it to reach a conclusion.

For a good example of this process at its most complicated, look for *The Seeds of Death* or *The Wheel in Space*. You may not agree with the years we've set, it might make your blood boil, but you'll see how we've reached our answer.

# # # # #

This book is one attempt, then, to retroactively create a consistent framework for the history of the *Doctor Who* universe. It is essentially a game, not a scientific endeavour to discover "the right answer".

All games have to follow a consistent set of rules, and as we attempt to fit all the pieces of information we are given, we have to lay some groundwork and prioritise. If a line of dialogue from a story broadcast in 1983 flatly contradicts what was said in one from 1968, which is "right"? Some people would suggest that the newer story "got it wrong", that the later production team didn't pay enough attention to what came before. Others might argue that the new information "corrects" what came before. In practice, most fans are inconsistent, choosing the facts that best support their arguments or preferences. *The Discontinuity Guide* (1995) has some very healthy advice regarding continuity: "Take what you want and ignore what you don't. Future continuity cops will just have to adapt to your version".

BASIC PRINCIPLES

For the purposes of this book, we have worked from the following assumptions:

• Every *Doctor Who* story takes place in the same universe, unless explicitly stated otherwise. The same individual fought the Daleks with Jo on Spiridon (on TV), Beep the Meep with Sharon (in the comics), the Ice Warriors with Benny in London (the novels), became Zagreus in the Antiverse (the audios), blew up Gallifrey to prevent Faction Paradox taking over the universe (the novels again), saved Rose Tyler from the Autons and married River Song.

For legal, marketing or artistic reasons, it should be noted that some of the people making *Doctor Who* have occasionally stated that they don't feel this to be the case. However there are innumerable cross references (say, Romana being president of Gallifrey in both the books and the audios) and in-jokes that suggest very strongly that, for example, the eighth Doctor of the books is the same individual as the eighth Doctor of the Big Finish audios – or at the very least, they've both got almost-identical histories.

• The universe has one, true "established history". Nothing (short of a being with godlike powers) can significantly change the course of history with any degree of permanency within that universe. The Mars attacked by the Fendahl is the Mars of the Ice Warriors.

• We have noted where each date we have assigned comes from. Usually it is from dialogue (in which case, it's quoted), but often it comes from behind-the-scenes sources such as scripts, publicity material and the like. It is up to the individual reader whether a date from a BBC Press release or draft script is as "valid" as one given on screen.

• In many cases, no date was ever given for a story. In such instances, we pick a year and explain our reasons. Often, we will assign a date that is consistent with information given in other stories. (So, it's suggested that the Cyber War mentioned in *Revenge of the Cybermen* must take place after *The Tomb of the Cybermen*, and probably after *Earthshock* because of what is said in those other stories.) These dates are marked as arbitrary and the reasoning behind them is explained in the footnotes.

• Where a date isn't established on screen, we have also included the dates suggested by others who have compiled timelines or listed dates given in the series. Several similar works to this have been attempted, and we have listed the most relevant in the Bibliography.

• It's been assumed that historical events take place at the same time and for the same reasons as they did in "real history", unless specifically contradicted by the television series. Unless given reason to think otherwise, we assume that the Doctor is telling the truth about meeting historical figures, and that his historical analysis is correct. (It has, however, been established that the Doctor is fallible and/or an incorrigible name-dropper.) When there's a reference in our footnotes to "science", "scientists", "history" or "historians", unless stated otherwise it means scholars and academics from the real world, not the *Doctor Who* universe (they are usually invoked when *Doctor Who*'s version of science or events strays a distance from ours).

• Information given is usually taken literally and at face value, unless there's strong reason to think that the person giving it is lying or mistaken. Clearly, if an expert like the Doctor is talking about something he knows a great deal about, we can probably trust the information more than some bystander's vague remark. (In recent years, it's become trendy to go the other way and invoke River Song's "The Doctor Lies" credo to explain any given point of ambiguity, but – as with not claiming that every discrepancy is the fault of the Last Great Time War – we've resisted that urge as much as possible.)

• *Ahistory*'s version of Earth's future history is generally one of steady progress, and as such stories featuring similar themes and concepts tend to be lumped together – say, intergalactic travel, isolated colonies, humanoid robots and so on. If the technology, transportation or weaponry seen in story A is more advanced than in story B, then we might suggest that story A is set in the future of story B. We also assume that throughout future centuries, humans age at the same rate (unless told otherwise), so their life spans don't alter too dramatically, etc. A "lifetime" in the year 4000 is still about one hundred years.

• All dates, again unless specifically stated otherwise, work from our Gregorian calendar, and all are "AD". It is assumed that the system of leap years will remain the same in the future. For convenience, all documents use our system of dating, even those of alien civilisations. The "present" of the narrative is now, so if an event happened "two hundred years ago", it happened in the early nineteenth century. Often we are told that a specific date takes place on the wrong day: in *The War Machines*, 16th July, 1966, is a Monday, but it really occurred on a Saturday.

• We assume that a "year" is an Earth year of 365 days, even when an alien is speaking, unless this is specifically contradicted. This also applies to terms such as "Space Year" (*Genesis of the Daleks*), "light year" (which is used as a unit of time in *The Savages* and possibly *Terror of the Autons*) and "cycle" (e.g. *Zamper*).

• If an event is said to take place "fifty years ago", we frequently take it to mean exactly fifty years ago, unless a more precise date is given elsewhere or it refers to a known historical event. If an event occurs in the distant past or the far future, we tend to round up: *Image of the Fendahl* is set in about 1977, the Fifth Planet was destroyed "twelve million years" before. So, we say this happened in "12,000,000 BC", not "11,998,023 BC". When an event takes place an undefined number of "centuries", "millennia" or "millions of years" before or after a story, we arbitrarily set a date.

• On occasion we've followed a convention from the TV series: that future-based stories sometimes occur on a rounded number from the year of their broadcast. This is why – to pick a prominent example – *Colony in Space*, broadcast in 1972, takes place in 2472. Likewise with *The Enemy of the World* (1967-1968) quietly taking place fifty years on, in 2018. When and where we've followed this pattern, it's because a story's dating placement is otherwise a bit vague, and – frankly – our gut impulse says it's acceptable to do so. Also, to be honest, one of us grew up a huge fan of *Legion of Super-Heroes*, which magically took place a thousand years after publication. It's been a hard habit to shake.

• A "generation" is assumed to be twenty-five years, as per the Doctor's definition in *Four to Doomsday*. A "couple" of years is always two years, a "few" is less than "several" which is less than "many", with "some" taken to be an arbitrary or unknown number. A "billion" is generally the American and modern British unit (a thousand million) rather than the old British definition (a million million).

• Characters are in their native time zone unless explicitly stated otherwise. Usually, when a *Doctor Who* monster or villain has a time machine, it's central to the plot. On television, the Cybermen only explicitly have time travel in *Attack of the Cybermen*, for example, and they've stolen the time machine in question. It clearly can't be "taken for granted" that they can go back in history. The Sontarans have a (primitive) time machine in *The Time Warrior*, and are clearly operating on a scale that means they can defy the Time Lords in *The Invasion of Time* and *The Two Doctors*, but there's no evidence they routinely travel in time. The only one of the Doctor's (non-Time Lord) foes with a mastery of time travel are the Daleks – they develop time travel in *The Chase*, and definitely use it in *The Daleks'*

Master Plan, *The Evil of the Daleks*, *Day of the Daleks*, *Resurrection of the Daleks*, *Remembrance of the Daleks*, *Dalek*, *Army of Ghosts/Doomsday*, *Daleks in Manhattan, Evolution of the Daleks*, *The Stolen Earth/Journey's End*, *Victory of the Daleks, Asylum of the Daleks, The Day of the Doctor, The Time of the Doctor* and *The Magician's Apprentice/The Witch's Familiar*. Even so, in the remaining stories, we've resisted assuming that the Daleks are time travellers.

• Sometimes, stories occur with the sort of impact that means it seems odd that they weren't mentioned in an earlier story. For instance, no-one from *The Power of the Daleks* and *The Moonbase* (both shown in 1966) recalls the Daleks and Cybermen fighting in *Doomsday* (shown in 2006). For that matter, when the Doctor and his companions refer to their past adventures on TV, they rarely mention the events of the Missing Adventures, Past Doctor novels, comic strips or Big Finish audios. (There are exceptions, however, usually when a writer picks up a throwaway line in a TV episode.) In *Doctor Who* itself, this may point to some deep truth about the nature of time – that events don't become part of the "Web of Time" until we see the Doctor as part of them... or it may be simply that it was impossible for the people making *Doctor Who* in the sixties to know about stories authored by their successors – many of whom hadn't even been born then.

• And, in a related note, few people making *The Tenth Planet* (in 1966, depicting the distant space year 1986) would have imagined anyone in the early twenty-first century worrying how to reconcile the quasi-futuristic world they imagined with the historical reality. Whenever the UNIT stories are set, it was "the twentieth century", and that's history now. Some of the early New Adventures novels took place in a "near future" setting. We've therefore accepted the dates given, rather than said that – for example – as we still haven't put a man on Mars, *The Ambassadors of Death* is still set in our future. There's clearly a sensible reason why the "present day" stories made now look like our present day, not *The Tenth Planet: The Next Generation*. The in-story explanation/fudge would seem to be that most *Doctor Who* stories take place in isolated locations, and that there are agencies like UNIT, C19 and Torchwood tasked with keeping alien incursions covered up. This paradigm has broken down over time, however, given the sheer number of public events involving aliens in the new series, *The Sarah Jane Adventures* and (to a lesser degree) *Torchwood*.

• There are still errors of omission, as when a later story fails to acknowledge an earlier one (often in other media) that seems relevant. No-one in *The Christmas Invasion*, for example, notes that it's odd Britain is making a big deal about sending an unmanned probe to Mars, when there were manned UK missions there in the seventies (in *The Ambassadors of Death*) and the nineties (*The Dying Days*). As with Sarah in *School Reunion* remembering *The Hand of Fear* but not *The Five Doctors*, there's got to be an appeal to clarity in storytelling. With so many *Doctor Who* stories in existence, it's almost impossible to tell a new one that doesn't explicitly contradict an earlier story, let alone implicitly. The reason no-one, say, remarks that the second Doctor looks like Salamander except in *The Enemy of the World* is the same reason that no-one ever says Rose looks like the girl who married Chris Evans – it gets in the way of the story, and doesn't help it along.

THE STORIES

This book restricts itself to events described in the BBC television series *Doctor Who*, and its original full-length fiction, audio plays and comics; the spin-off series *The Sarah Jane Adventures*, *Torchwood*, *K9*, *Class* and their related full-length fiction, audio plays and comics; and any spin-off books, audios, comics and direct-to-video/DVD films involving characters that originated in the above, and were used with permission by their rights holders (see Section No. 4 below). To be included in this Fourth Edition of *Ahistory*, a story had to be released before 31st December, 2017. (At our discretion, and as deadlines allowed, we included stray stories from 2018 if they finished an ongoing storyline or had some special significance.)

This is not an attempt to enter the debate about which stories are "canon" (although we have been compelled to make such determinations at times), it is simply an attempt to limit the length and scale of this book. There are two types of information in this book – evidence given in TV stories, and anything provided in another format – and these are distinguished by different typefaces.

1. The Television Series. Included are the episodes and on-screen credits of...

• *Doctor Who*, from *An Unearthly Child* (1963) to the end of the twelfth Doctor era, *Twice Upon a Time* (2017)

• The pilot episode *K9 and Company* (1981)

• *Torchwood* (2006-2011), stars the alien-tech-harvesting group first seen in *Doctor Who* Series 2

• *The Sarah Jane Adventures* (2007-2011), features the long-running companion Sarah Jane Smith and her teenage friends

• The *K9* TV series (2009-2010), set in the future, with a new version of K9

• *Class* (2016), short-lived spin-off set at Coal Hill Academy, following on from *Doctor Who* Series 9.

We have also taken into consideration extended or unbroadcast versions that have since been commer-cially released or broadcast anywhere in the world – there are few cases of "extended" material contradicting the original story.

Priority is given to sources closest to the finished product or the production team of the time the story was made. In descending order of authority are the following: the programme as broadcast; the official series websites; official guidebooks made in support of the series (*Doctor Who: The Encyclopedia*, etc.), the *Radio Times* and other contemporary BBC publicity material (which was often written by the producer or script editor); the camera script; the novelisation of a story by the original author or an author working closely from the camera script; contemporary interviews with members of the production team; televised trailers; rehearsal and draft scripts; novelisations by people other than the original author; storylines and writers' guides (which often contradict on-screen information); interviews with members of the production team after the story was broadcast; and finally any other material, such as fan speculation.

Scenes cut from broadcast were considered if they were incorporated back into a story at a later time (as with those in *The Curse of Fenric* VHS and DVD). Not included is information from unreleased material that exists, is in release but was kept separate from the story (for instance, the extra scenes on the *Ghost Light* DVD) or that no longer exists (such as with *Terror of the Autons*, *Terror of the Zygons* and *The Hand of Fear*). Neither does the first version of *An Unearthly Child* to be filmed (the so-called "pilot episode") count, nor "In character" appearances by the Doctor interacting with the real world on other programmes (e.g.: on *Animal Magic*, *Children in Need*, *Blue Peter* etc.).

2. The *Doctor Who*, *The Sarah Jane Adventures*, *Torchwood* and *Class* books, audios and webcasts. This present volume also encompasses the *Doctor Who* New Adventures (continued the adventures of the seventh Doctor and Ace after the end of the original TV series) and Missing Adventures (retro Doctor stories) published by Virgin (1991-1997); the BBC's Eighth Doctor Adventures (1997-2005); the BBC's Past Doctor Adventures (1997-2005); the BBC's New Series Adventures (up through *Plague City*, 2017); the *Torchwood* novels (up through *TW: Exodus Code*, 2012); all of the Telos novellas (2001-2004); the three *Class* novels; the four *K9* children's books (1980); and a number of one-off novels: *Harry Sullivan's War*, *Turlough and the Earthlink Dilemma* and *Who Killed Kennedy*.

The audios covered include *The Pescatons*, *Slipback*, *The Paradise of Death* and *The Ghosts of N-Space*; the BBC fourth Doctor mini-series (*Hornets' Nest*, *Demon Quest* and *Serpent Crest*); and the extensive Big Finish *Doctor Who* audio range... its monthly series (up to *Static*, #233), the

Companion Chronicles (up to Series 11), the Fourth Doctor Adventures (starring Tom Baker, up to Series 6), the Early Adventures (first and second Doctor stories, up to Series 4), the eighth Doctor audios initially broadcast on BBC7 (up to *To the Death*, #4.10), various promotional audios (up to *Trial of the Valeyard*), special releases (up to *The Sixth Doctor – The Last Adventure*), the eighth Doctor box sets *Dark Eyes* and *Doom Coalition*, *Philip Hinchcliffe Presents* (to *The Helm of Awe*), the Lost Stories (unmade TV scripts adapted for audio) and many more. The BBC webcasts *Real Time*, *Shada* and *Death Comes to Time* (the last one somewhat controversially) are included, as well as the *Torchwood* webcast *Web of Lies*.

A handful of stories were available in another form – *Shakedown* and *Downtime* were originally direct-to-video spin-offs, some Big Finish stories like *Minuet in Hell* and *The Mutant Phase* are (often radically different) adaptations of stories made by Audio Visuals. *Ahistory* deals with the "official" versions, as opposed to the fan-produced ones.

This volume covers two stories that appear in different versions, because they were told in two media that fall within the scope of the book and were adapted for different Doctors: *Shada* and *Human Nature*. Those have been dealt with on a case-by-case basis. *Doctor Who* fans have long had different versions of the same story in different media – the first Dalek story, for example, was televised, extensively altered for the novelisation, changed again for the movie version and adapted into a comic strip.

We haven't included in-character appearances in nonfiction books (e.g: the *Doctor Who Discovers...* and *Doctor Who Quiz Book of* series), and *Make Your Own Adventure/Find Your Fate*-style books where it's impossible to determine the actual story. It was tempting, though.

3) The *Doctor Who* comics, including the strip that has been running in *Doctor Who Weekly/Monthly/Magazine* since 1979 (up through "Matildus", *DWM* #518), along with all original backup strips from that publication, and the ones from the various Specials and Yearbooks. With a book like this, drawing a line between what should and shouldn't be included is never as simple as it might appear. Including every comic strip would include ones from the Annuals, for example. This book doesn't include the text stories that *Doctor Who Magazine* has included at various points during its run.

There's a relatively straightforward distinction between the *DWM* comic strip and other *Doctor Who* comic strips: while it's the work of many writers, artists and editors, it also has a strong internal continuity and sense of identity. This book, in all previous editions, has confined itself to "long form" *Doctor Who* and there's a case to be made that the *DWM* strip represents one "ongoing story" that's run for over a quarter of a century. The *Doctor Who Magazine* strip has now run for longer than the original TV series,

and most fans must have encountered it at some point.

That said, this book excludes *DWM* strips that are clearly parodies that aren't meant to be considered within the continuity of the strip. The same logic applies to spoofs like *Dimensions in Time* and *The Curse of Fatal Death*. For the record, the affected strips are "Follow that TARDIS!", "The Last Word" and "TV Action".

DWM has reprinted a number of strips from other publications over the years. We have tended to include these. The main beneficiary of this is *The Daleks* strip from the sixties comic *TV Century 21* (and *DWM*'s sequel to it from issues #249-254).

It's certainly arguable that the *DWM* strip exists in a separate continuity, with its own companions, internal continuity, vision of Gallifrey and even an ethos that made it feel quite unlike the TV eras of its Doctors. This certainly seemed to be the case early on. However, this distinction has broken down over the years – the comic strip companion Frobisher appeared in a book (*Mission: Impractical*) and two audios (*The Holy Terror*, *The Maltese Penguin*); the village of Stockbridge (from the fifth Doctor *DWM* comics) has featured in various audios starting with *Circular Time*; the audio *The Company of Friends* incorporated characters from different book and comic ranges; and for a number of years the strip and the New Adventures novels were quite elaborately linked. In the new TV series, we've met someone serving kronkburgers (in *The Long Game*, first mentioned in "The Iron Legion") the Doctor quoted Abslom Daak in *Bad Wolf*, and Daak's mug shot appeared in *Time Heist*.

The strip tends to "track" the ongoing story (the television series in the seventies and eighties, the New Adventures in the early nineties) – so the Doctor regenerates, without explanation within the strip and on occasion during a story arc. Companions from the television series and books come and go. Costume changes and similar details (like the design of the console room) do the same. It's broadly possible to work out when the strip is set in the Doctor's own life. So, the first *Doctor Who* Weekly strips with the fourth Doctor mention he's dropped off Romana, and he changes from his Season 17 to Season 18 costume – so it slots in neatly between the two seasons. There are places where this process throws up some anomalies, which have been noted.

Also included are the *Doctor Who* comics produced by IDW for the American market; the *Radio Times* comics featuring the eighth Doctor; the comics that first appeared in *Torchwood: The Official Magazine*; and the *Torchwood* and *The Sarah Jane Adventures* webcomics.

We also include the ongoing *Doctor Who* and *Torchwood* comics published by Titan, although – owing to the cut-off point of this guidebook being at the end of 2017 – we've included all of *The Tenth Doctor Year Three* and *The Eleventh Doctor Year Three*, but had to stop partway through *The*

Twelfth Doctor Year Three (#3.9, "The Great Shopping Bill"). All of the Titan comics before that are present, however, as are crossover events up through "The Lost Dimension".

4) Spin-off series featuring characters that originally appeared in *Doctor Who* (whatever the format), and were used elsewhere with permission by their respective rights holders.

This needs some explaining... *Doctor Who* is a very unusual property in that, generally speaking, the BBC retained ownership of anything created by salaried employees, but freelance scriptwriters working on the TV show in the 60s, 70s and 80s (and the novelists working on the books in the 90s) typically wound up owning the rights to any characters they created. Infamously, this has meant that writer Terry Nation (and his estate) kept ownership of the name "Dalek" and the conceptual property therein, but the BBC retained the rights to the likeness of the Daleks, which were created by staff designer Raymond Cusick.

This is very counter-intuitive to how other series work – a world where *Star Trek* is so divided (say, with one person owning the Klingons, another owning the Horta and another owning Spock, while Paramount continues to retain ownership of Captain Kirk and the *Enterprise*) would be unthinkable. Nonetheless, over the years, the rights holders to iconic *Doctor Who* characters and monsters have licensed them for use elsewhere, and – unless given reason to think otherwise – their use in a non-*Doctor Who* story seems as valid as any BBC-sanctioned story.

The spin-offs included in this volume are:

• The Bernice Summerfield novels, audios and novella collections (1997-present), featuring the Doctor's companion who was first seen in the New Adventure *Love and War* (1992). Benny was the lead of the Doctor-less New Adventures novels published from 1997 to 1999; Big Finish took over the license afterward, and has produced Benny audios, novels, short story anthologies, novella collections and one animated story. Later, Benny was folded (after a fashion) back into the main *Doctor Who* range with *The New Adventures of Bernice Summerfield* box sets.

The first five Benny audios were excluded, as they were adaptations of New Adventures novels.

• BBV audios and films (1994-2015?) featuring licensed characters such as the Sontarans, the Rutans and the Zygons, as well as *P.R.O.B.E.* (1994-1996, 2015): a spin-off series featuring Liz Shaw, a third Doctor companion.

• Big Finish audio spin-off series...
–*Charlotte Pollard* (2014-present), featuring the eighth (and later sixth) Doctor companion who debuted in *Storm Warning* (2001).
–*The Churchill Years* (2016-present), with Ian McNeice reprising his role as Winston Churchill, first seen in *Victory*

of the Daleks (2010).
–*The Confessions of Dorian Gray* (2012-2016), mature-themed, supernatural stories centered on the "real life" immortal Dorian Gray, a friend of Oscar Wilde. This version of Dorian also appears in the Bernice Summerfield range and *The Worlds of Big Finish*. (For the timeline of the Dorian Gray stories, see the appendix.)
–*Counter-Measures* (2012-2015), relaunched as *The New Counter-Measures* (2016-2019?) with the team of the same name that debuted in *Remembrance of the Daleks* (1988).
–*Cyberman* (2005-2009), original cast of characters fights against the Cybermen in Earth's future.
–*Dalek Empire* (2001-2008), the same, but against the Daleks.
–*The Diary of River Song* (2015-present), further escapades of River Song, prior her first appearance in *Silence in the Library* (2008).
–*Gallifrey* (2004-present), a political drama featuring Romana as president of Gallifrey, as aided by Leela and the two K9s.
–*Graceless* (2010-present?), mature-themed stories with the two Key to Time Tracers (and sisters), Abby (formerly "Amy") and Zara, who first appeared in *The Judgement of Isskar* (2009).
–*I, Davros* (2006), covers the early history of the Daleks' creator.
–*Jago & Litefoot* (2010-2018), Victorian investigations into the strange and the supernatural, starring Henry Gordon Jago and Professor Litefoot from *The Talons of Weng-Chiang* (1977). We've included up through *J&L* Series 13; absent is the coda story *Jago & Litefoot Forever* (2018).
–*The Lives of Captain Jack* (2017), box set with stories from various points in Jack's history.
–*Sarah Jane Smith* (2002-2006), features the long-standing third and fourth Doctor companion, in stories set prior to *The Sarah Jane Adventures*.
–*The Unbound* series (2003-2008), an exercise in having different actors play the Doctor. Considered apocrypha for years, this became part of the main timeline owing to *The New Adventures of Bernice Summerfield* Volume 3 (2016).
–*UNIT* (2004-present): a mini-series with original characters, then a box set starring the seventh Doctor, and then box sets starring Kate Stewart and Osgood from the new series.
–*Vienna* (2013-present), with the bounty hunter first seen in *The Shadow Heart* (2012).
–*The War Doctor* (2015-2017), with John Hurt reprising his role as the War Doctor from *The Day of the Doctor* (2013), in conflicts during the Last Great Time War.
–*The War Master* (2017), with Derek Jacobi reprising his role as the Master seen in *Utopia* (2007), in conflicts during the Last Great Time War.
–*The Worlds of Big Finish* (2015) crossover event featur-

ing the Graceless, the Big Finish version of Sherlock Holmes (played by Nicholas Briggs), Dorian Gray, Iris Wildthyme, Vienna and Bernice Summerfield.

• *City of the Saved* anthologies (2012-present), stories set in the end-of-the-universe metropolis first seen in the *Faction Paradox* guidebook *The Book of the War* (2002). The term "spin-off of a spin-off" is frequently misused, but here it applies.

• *Erimem* books (2005-present), featuring the fifth Doctor audio companion first seen in *The Eye of the Scorpion* (2001), after her departure from the TARDIS in *The Bride of Peladon*.

• *Faction Paradox* books (2002-present), audios and a comic; featuring characters and concepts first seen in the EDA *Alien Bodies* (1997).

• Iris Wildthyme audios and two novels, a novella and many anthologies (2005-present); a character seen in the original fiction of Paul Magrs, and who first appeared in *Doctor Who* in the *Short Trips* story "Old Flames" and the EDA *The Scarlet Empress*.

• *Kaldor City* audios (2001-2011), spun off from *The Robots of Death* and the PDA *Corpse Marker* (1999).

• *Lethbridge-Stewart* novels (2015-present), featuring Colonel (later Brigadier) Alistair Gordon Lethbridge-Stewart in adventures set between *The Web of Fear* and *The Invasion*.

• *Minister of Chance* (2011-2013), undatable audios featuring the lead from the webcast *Death Comes to Time* (2001-2002).

• *Miranda* comic (2003), from the character seen in the EDA *Father Time* (2001).

• Reeltime Pictures direct-to-VHS/DVD films (1988-present), featuring the Sontarans, the Draconians, the Daemons, etc.

• *Time Hunter* novellas (2003-2007), featuring characters from the Telos novella *The Cabinet of Light* (2003), and also involving the Fendahl and the Daemons.

# # # # #

Unhistory, a digital-only supplement to the book you're holding, covers many works that – even with the best of will and a heady desire to be all-inclusive – we viewed as apocrypha (see *Unhistory* for our reasoning on this), so couldn't justify placing in the main timeline. *Unhistory* is a

cornucopia of nearly five hundred such stories, the highlights of which include:

• Comic strips released prior to the advent of the *Doctor Who Magazine* strip, including the *TV Comic* and *Countdown* strips. There are some profound canonicity concerns with these strips, plus it would have taken *Ahistory* to an even more staggering length.

• *The Dalek Book* (1964), *The Dalek World* (1965) and *The Dalek Outer Space Book* (1966), as well as the four *Terry Nation's Dalek Annuals* (1976-1979). Very interesting early texts about the Daleks, often credited to Dalek co-creator Terry Nation and *Doctor Who* script editor David Whitaker.

• Two Big Finish stageplay adaptations *The Curse of the Daleks* and *The Seven Keys to Doomsday*. A third stageplay adaptation, *The Ultimate Adventure,* and its sequel audio, *Beyond the Ultimate Adventure*, were included in *Ahistory* as they are more compatible with the established timeline.

• The 2003 *Scream of the Shalka* webcast, which debuted Richard E. Grant as the ninth Doctor and was then superseded with the advent of the new series. This story was previously included in *Ahistory*, but has been excluded because the sheer preponderance of material establishing the Eccleston version as the ninth Doctor means that almost nobody at time of writing (not even the *Scream of the Shalka*'s creators) accepts the Grant Doctor as canon.

• Short stories from the World Distributors *Doctor Who Annuals* (1966-1986).

• Stories that were explicitly marketed as being apocryphal, mockumentaries and many instances of *Doctor Who* actors portraying their characters in real-life events or commercials (such as the Prime Computers adverts).

# # # # #

However, despite the efforts of *Ahistory* and *Unhistory* combined, there remain some significant omissions:

• Short stories, whether they first appeared in *Doctor Who Magazine*, the *Decalog* and *Short Trips* anthologies, the *Doctor Who Annuals* (1992-present), or any of the innumerable other places they have cropped up.

There are a few exceptions to this... anthologies were included if they were a rare exception in a full-length story range (say, the *Story of Martha* anthology published with the New Series Adventures novels). Or, if they informed upon the New Series so much (as with *The Legends of Ashildr* and *The Legends of River Song* anthologies), it seemed too glaring an oversight to leave them out.

Also, information from the Bernice Summerfield,

Faction Paradox and Iris Wildthyme short story anthologies were included if they were so interwoven into continuity elsewhere that omitting them would have been confusing (prime examples of this are the Benny anthologies *Life During Wartime* and *Present Danger*). Similarly, information from *Faction Paradox: The Book of the War* (itself a guidebook) was included if it directly pertained to characters or events prominently featured in other *Faction Paradox* stories (for instance, the background of Cousin Octavia, the lead character in *FP: Warring States*).

• Unlicensed "cover series" with actors playing thinly veiled counterparts of their *Doctor Who* characters, such as Sylvester McCoy starring as "the Professor" in the BBV audios.

• Proposed stories that were never made, including *Campaign* (a Past Doctor novel commissioned but never released by the BBC; it was later privately published).

• Unauthorised charity anthologies.

• Big Finish's *Sherlock Holmes* audios (see the Sherlock Holmes sidebar), although the detective as played by Nicholas Briggs also appears in *The Worlds of Big Finish* and the audio adaptation of *All-Consuming Fire*.

# # # # #

On the whole, the television series takes priority over what is said in the other media, and where a detail or reference in one of the books, audios or comics appears to contradict what was established on television, it's been noted as much and an attempt made to rationalise the "mistake" away.

The New Adventures and Missing Adventures built up a broadly consistent "future history" of the universe. This was, in part, based on the "History of Mankind" in Jean-Marc Lofficier's *The Terrestrial Index* (1991), which mixes information from the series with facts from the novelisations and the author's own speculation. Many authors, though, have contradicted or ignored Lofficier's version of events. For the purposes of this book, *The Terrestrial Index* itself is non-canonical, and it's been noted, but ultimately ignored, whenever a New Adventure recounts information solely using Lofficier as reference.

Writers' guides, discussion documents and the authors' original submissions and storylines provide useful information; we have, when possible, referenced these.

KEY

The following abbreviations are used in the text:

B – box set (specifically, a Big Finish format)

BENNY – A Bernice Summerfield book or audio

BF – The Big Finish audio adventures

CC – Big Finish's *Companion Chronicles* audios, which switches to a box set format with Series 9

CITY – The *City of the Saved* anthologies

CLASS – *Class*

CD,NM – Big Finish's *Classic Doctors, New Monsters* box sets

CM – *Counter-Measures*

CHARLEY – *Charlotte Pollard* audios

DC – Big Finish's *Doom Coalition* audios, four box sets starring the eighth Doctor. These were released after...

DEyes – Big Finish's *Dark Eyes* audios, four box sets also starring the eighth Doctor

DG – Big Finish's *The Confessions of Dorian Gray* audios, starring the Oscar Wilde creation

DL – *The Darksmith Legacy* novellas

DotD – *Destiny of the Doctor,* an audio mini-series

DWM – *Doctor Who Magazine* (also known for a time as *Doctor Who Monthly*)

DWW – *Doctor Who Weekly* (as the magazine was initially called until issue #44)

1stA – Big Finish's *The First Doctor Adventures* audios, starring David Bradley as the first Doctor

1stD – Big Finish's *The First Doctor* box sets, a continuation of the *Companion Chronicles*

FP – *Faction Paradox*

EA – Big Finish's *Early Adventures* audios, adventures concerning the first and second Doctors

EDA – Eighth Doctor Adventures (the ongoing novels published by the BBC)

ERIMEM – The *Erimem* novels

5thB – Big Finish's *The Fifth Doctor Box Set* audios

IRIS – The Iris Wildthyme books and audios

KC – *Kaldor City*

K9 – The *K9* TV show

JACK – *The Lives of Captain Jack* audio box set

J&L – *Jago & Litefoot* audios

LETH-ST – The *Lethbridge-Stewart* novels

LS – Big Finish's *Lost Stories,* audio adaptations of unmade stories proposed for the TV series

MA – Missing Adventures (the past Doctor novels published by Virgin)

NA – New Adventures (the ongoing novels published by Virgin, chiefly featuring the seventh Doctor)

NAoBENNY – *The New Adventures of Bernice Summerfield*

New CM – *The New Counter-Measures,* a continuation of the *Counter-Measures* audios.

9thC – Big Finish's *The Ninth Doctor Chronicles* audios

NSA – New Series Adventures (featuring the ninth Doctor et al)

PDA – Past Doctor Adventure (the past Doctor novels published by the BBC)

PHP – *Philip Hinchcliffe Presents*, fourth Doctor audios as conceptualised by the TV producer of the same name

RIVER – *The Diary of River Song* audios

S – Season or Series

2ndD – Big Finish's *The Second Doctor* box sets, a continuation of the *Companion Chronicles*

6thLA – *The Sixth Doctor – The Last Adventure*, an audio box set

SJA – *The Sarah Jane Adventures*

SJS – Big Finish's *Sarah Jane Smith* audio series

ST – *Short Trips*, short story anthologies released in print by Virgin, BBC Books and Big Finish, and also on audio by the latter.

TEL – Telos novellas

3rdA – Big Finish's *The Third Doctor Adventures* audios

TimeH – *Time Hunter*

TV – The TV series

TW – *Torchwood*

TWM – *Torchwood: The Official Magazine*

V – Volume

WD – *The War Doctor*

WM – *The War Master*

WORLDS BF – Big Finish's *The Worlds of Big Finish* crossover box set (featuring BF's spin-off characters)

WORLDS DW – Big Finish's *The Worlds of Doctor Who* crossover box set (mostly features TV characters such as Jago and Litefoot)

In the text of the book, the following marker appears to indicate when the action of specific stories take place:

c 2005 – THE REPETITION OF THE CLICHE ->

The title is exactly as it appeared on screen or on the cover. For the Hartnell stories without an overall title given on screen, we have used the titles that appear on the BBC's product (*An Unearthly Child*, *The Daleks*, *The Edge of Destruction*, etc.).

The letter before the date, the "code", indicates how accurately we know the date. If there is no code, then that date is precisely established in the story itself (e.g. *The Daleks' Master Plan* is set in the year 4000 exactly).

• "c" means that the story is set circa that year (e.g. *The Dalek Invasion of Earth* is set "c.2167")

• "?" indicates a guess, and the reasons for it are given in the footnotes (e.g. we don't know what year *Destiny of the Daleks* is set in, but it must be "centuries" after *The Daleks' Master Plan*, so it's here set it in "? 4600").

• "&" means that the story is dated relative another story that we lack a date for (e.g.: we know that *Resurrection of the Daleks* is set "ninety years" after *Destiny of the Daleks*, so *Resurrection of the Daleks* is set in "& 4690"). If one story moves, the linked one also has to.

• "u" means that the story featured UNIT. There is, to put it mildly, some discussion about exactly when the UNIT stories are set. For the purposes of this guidebook, see the introduction to the UNIT Section.

• "=" indicates action that takes place in a parallel universe or a divergent timestream (such as *Inferno* or *Battlefield*). Often, the Doctor succeeds in restoring the correct timeline or erasing an aberrant deviation of history – those cases are indicated by brackets – "(=)". As this information technically isn't part of history, it's set apart by boxes with dashed lines.

• "@" is a story set during the eighth Doctor's period living on Earth from 1888 (starting with *The Ancestor Cell*) to 2001 (*Escape Velocity*). During this period, he was without a working TARDIS or his memories.

• "lgtw" refers to an event pertaining to the Last Great Time War that serves as the background to *Doctor Who* Series 1, and dramatically comes into play in *The Day of the Doctor*.

• "wih" refers to an event that took place during the future War timeline (a.k.a. the War in Heaven, not to be confused with the Last Great Time War featured in New *Who*) in the eighth Doctor books, and which continued in the *Faction Paradox* series. Events in *The Ancestor Cell* annulled this timeline, but remnants of it "still happened" in the real *Doctor Who* timeline, just as *Day of the Daleks* "still happened" even though the future it depicted was averted.

We've attempted to weed out references that just aren't very telling, relevant or interesting. Clearly, there's a balance to be had, as half the fun of a book like this is in listing trivia and strange juxtapositions, but a timeline could easily go to *even more* absurd extremes than presently exist. If a novel set in 1980 said that a minor character was 65, lived in a turn-of-the-century terraced house and bought the Beatles album *Rubber Soul* when it first came out, then it could generate entries for c.1900, 1915 and 1965. We would only list these if they were relevant to the story or made for particularly interesting reading.

We haven't listed birthdates of characters, except the Doctor's companions or other major recurring figures, again unless it represents an important story point.

The Doctor placed a personal advert "Ace – Behind You!" in an *NME* from 2018. Ace bought a copy outside Ladbroke Grove hypertube station.[1] Paletti wrote the opera *The Fourth Sister*, including the stirring *Rebirth Aria*.[2]

The risk of nuclear warfare diminished after the Southport Incident, when governments realised that the stockpiling of atomic weapons could only lead to a serious accident or all-out nuclear warfare.[3]

The World Zones

2018 - THE ENEMY OF THE WORLD[4] -> Rockets could now be used to travel between continents on Earth – the journey from Australia to Hungary took around two hours. Hovercars made shorter trips. Television pictures were broadcast via videowire.

The political situation on Earth had stabilised.

National concerns were put aside and the world was reorganised into large administrative areas called Zones, such as the Australasian, North African and Central European Zones. The world was organised by the United Zones, more properly known as the World Zones Authority. Commissioners dealt with multinational concerns such as Security matters. A Controller led each Zone.

One of the major problems the world faced was famine. The scientist Salamander announced he could solve the problem using his Mark Seven Sun-Catcher satellite, which made previously desolate areas of the world into fertile farmland that robots could harvest. Within just a year, the Sun-Catcher had solved the problems of world famine, allowing crops to grow in Siberia and vineyards in Alaska. In the more fertile areas, concentrated sunlight forced growth: each sum-

---

1 *Timewyrm: Revelation*

2 "A few decades" after *Vampire Science*.

3 Benny remembers the Southport Incident in *Just War* (p214), but doesn't specify what or when it was. Zoe, who lacks even rudimentary historical knowledge, recognises the effects of an atomic blast in *The Dominators*, perhaps suggesting that nuclear weapons are still around (and have been used?) in her time.

4 Dating *The Enemy of the World* (5.4) - None of the scripts contain any reference to the year that the story is set in. However, the *Radio Times* in certain regions featured an article on fashion that set *The Enemy of the World* "fifty years in the future", which would give a date of 2017. The first edition of *The Programme Guide* mistakenly thought that the story had a contemporary setting, and placed it between "1970-75".

The date "2030", which is now commonly associated with the story, first appeared in David Whitaker's storyline for the novelisation of his story, submitted to WH Allen in October 1979. The document was reprinted in *DWM* #200, and amongst other things of interest it is the only place to give Salamander a first name: "Ramon". The novelisation was due to be published in 1980, and was to be set "some fifty years later than our time – the year 2030" according to the storyline, but the book was not completed before Whitaker's death.

The second edition of *The Programme Guide* duly gave the date as "2030". The blurb for the novelisation by Ian Marter, published in 1981 – the same year as *The Programme Guide* – concurred, although perhaps significantly, the text of the book didn't specify a date. 2030 was soon adopted wholesale, with *The TARDIS Logs* and *The Terrestrial Index* giving the new date. *Encyclopedia of the Worlds of Doctor Who* is confused: the entry for "Denes" gives the date as "2017", but that for "Fedorin" states "2030". *The TARDIS Special* was less specific than most, claiming the story takes place in an

"Unknown Future" setting. *The Legend* states it's "c.2017". *About Time* hedges its bets a little, saying that "around 2017 – 2030 is the most likely possibility". *Alien Bodies* sets the story later, after *Warchild* and apparently around the 2040s.

Previous editions of *Ahistory* have noted that the dialogue refers to a newspaper displaying "last year's date", but that the date couldn't be read on the telesnap of the scene. Since the rediscovery of the missing episodes in Nigeria and the subsequent DVD release, we can see that the newspaper Swann brandishes with "last year's date" has the dateline "Friday, August 16, 2017" (episode five). The first episode has another unsuspected piece of dating evidence: the helicopter piloted by Astrid Ferrier has a registration card that says, "Valid until 31st Dec: 2018". Taking that into account, we can settle the matter: *The Enemy of the World* is set in 2018 (so, fifty years on from when the bulk of the story was broadcast – from 23rd December, 1967 to 27th January, 1968).

WEATHER CONTROL: In a number of stories set in the twenty-first century, we see a variety of weather control projects. The earliest is in the New Adventure *Cat's Cradle: Warhead*, and simply involves "seeding" clouds with chemicals to regulate rainfall (p129). A year before *The Enemy of the World*, Salamander develops the Sun-Catcher, the first Weather Control system. As its name suggests, the Sun Store satellite collects the rays from the Sun and stores them in concentrated form. It is also capable of influencing tidal and seismic activity.

Each major city has its own Weather Control Bureau by *The Seeds of Death*, and these are co-ordinated and monitored centrally by computer. The London Bureau is a large complex, manned by a handful of technicians. The Weather Control Unit itself is about the size of a large desk, with separate circuits for each weather condition. With fully functioning Rain Circuits, rainfall over

mer could bring three or even four harvests. Salamander was hailed as the saviour of humankind.

Soon after Salamander's announcement, a series of natural disasters struck, including a freak tidal wave that sank a liner full of holidaymakers in the Caribbean and the first volcanic eruptions in the Eperjes-Tokaj mountain range since the sixteenth century. These were caused by Salamander's followers in a bunker below Kanowa using his technology. Salamander had convinced them that the Earth's surface was highly radioactive, and that they had to fight back against the aggressors.

The second Doctor, Jamie and Victoria uncovered the truth: that Salamander had been gradually assassinating his political opponents within the United Zones and replacing them with his own people in a bid to become the dictator of Earth. Salamander was defeated when his followers in Kanowa learned there had been no global nuclear war. He tried to escape in the TARDIS, but was sucked into the Vortex when the Ship's door opened in flight.

Ramon Salamander was dragged in the TARDIS' wake back to the twentieth century.[5]

c 2018 - FP: "Now or Thereabouts"[6] **->** Godfather Starch whittled down a pool of applicants for Faction Paradox. In one round, Starch despaired because some of the novices bargained with the double-crossing Herdsmen of Klasterhaus for a bio-weapon, a Chronofungal War-Cow. Little Sister Ceol won the final round by attesting that whereas Little Brother Dominic thought the Faction was

cool, she *needed* to join it as a means of survival. As Cousin Ceol, she slew her sometimes-boyfriend Ryan, who had been invading her dreams as a glass-faced priest.

Joining Faction Paradox was a means to an end, and so Cousin Ceol facilitated her escape by rewriting her biodata. She was reborn in the far future as Sojourner Hooper, even as the hollowed-out remains of Cousin Ceol volunteered for a fatal mission against the House Military on Mohandassa.[7]

Single Molecule Transcription replaced the microprocessor in 2019.[8] Dr Hugo Macht developed a means of building environmentally friendly homes out of garbage, via coupling trash recycling with 3D printers.[9]

From around 2019, Earth experienced forty long years of chaos including climate change, difficulty with the ozone layer and an "oil apocalypse". The human race almost reached extinction.[10]

---

a large area can be arranged quickly.

By 2050, the Gravitron had been set up on Earth's moon. This is the ultimate form of weather control, working on the simple principle that "the tides control the weather, the Gravitron controls the tides". Weather control is under the control of the (United Zones?) General Assembly.

It's clear those last two are different systems, but it's less clear which is the most advanced. This becomes important when trying to date *The Seeds of Death* – *About Time* suggests that the weather control in *The Seeds of Death* is "far more compact and efficient", so that's the later story. But it can certainly be argued that a device in a room in London that makes it rain on special occasions looks primitive compared with a moon-based one that manipulates gravity as part of an international programme to manage the entire world's weather.

5 "The Heralds of Destruction"
6 Dating *FP: "Now or Thereabouts"* (*FP: A Romance in Twelve Parts* anthology, story #1d) - For "Ceol" (another name for Kelsey Harper), the story follows on from *Iris:*

"Party Kill Accelerator!" and continues in *FP: Weapons Grade Snake Oil*.

There's contemporary references to Richard Dawkins and a bikini-clad Rihanna posing for *Heat* magazine. Ceol and Maria Jackson here meet face to face for the first time in "several years". As it all boils down to "Faction Paradox meets *The Apprentice*", and concerns young professionals, we might guess that ten years have passed since Kelsey and Maria ("thirteen years old" in *The Sarah Jane Adventures* pilot) were in school together.

7 *The Long Game*
8 "Ten years" before *Shield of the Jotuun*.
9 *FP: Weapons Grade Snake Oil*
10 As detailed by Brooke in *The Waters of Mars*. There's a fairly consistent narrative in *Doctor Who* that the first half of the twenty-first century sees environmental and other catastrophes that are overcome in the second half of the century by technology – space exploration in particular – although there are many differences in detail.

The 2020s

Book Ten of *Harry Potter* entailed, among other things, Ron and Hermione's efforts to find an Occamy's scale.[11] The Minister of War attained a level of infamy.[12]

2020 - THE HUNGRY EARTH / COLD BLOOD[13] -> The eleventh Doctor, Rory and Amy arrived in the village of Cwmtaff, South Wales, in the right year but the wrong place, as they had been aiming for Rio. Rory and Amy saw their future selves in the distance, but the Doctor was more interested in patches of blue grass: evidence of minerals unseen in Britain for twenty million years.

Cwmtaff was the site of the most successful recorded boring in human history – a shaft had been drilled to a depth of 21 km. The drill threatened an underground Silurian city, and its automatic systems awoke Silurian warriors to stage a response. The Doctor found that these were a different branch of the species to the one he had previously encountered.

One Silurian, Alaya, was killed. Her enraged sister Restac attempted a coup against Eldane, a peaceful Silurian leader willing to negotiate with humanity.

Eldane decided that his people were not ready to share the planet and activated a decontamination programme, forcing the warriors to return to their cryo-chambers. The humans Nasreen Chaudhry and Tony Mack accompanied them into stasis. The Doctor altered the Silurians' systems to awaken them in a thousand years, when they would hopefully be welcomed by humanity. The drilling site was destroyed.

Restac killed Rory, who was dematerialised by a Crack in Time. Amy lost all memory of him, and remembered seeing only her future self, not Rory, in the distance.

The population of Earth was six billion.[14]

2020 (17th July) - TIMEH: KITSUNE[15] -> Ikari, the brood mother of the White Claw Kitsune, thought the developed world had lost its way and sought to punish humanity for it. She started a clothing business, Hide and Chic, whose offerings were woven with chaos-inducing hair. Honoré Lechasseur and Emily Blandish averted an apocalypse by convincing Ikari to refrain from unleashing animal spirits of vengeance, and to instead take her kitsune and find a new world.

---

11 The Minister is name-dropped into *Beyond the Flood*, as being relevant to a period of time between Harold Saxon [2007] and *Kill the Moon* [2049].
12 *The Shining Man* (ch13).
13 Dating *The Hungry Earth/Cold Blood* (X5.8-5.9) - The year is given in a caption at the beginning of *The Hungry Earth*.
14 Or so the Doctor claims in *The Hungry Earth*, either suggesting that it's fallen fairly dramatically since 2009, or that he's just confused.
15 Dating *TimeH: Kitsune* (*TimeH* #4) - Honoré and Emily attend an evening festival in Kyoto on "17 July 2020" (p23). It's later said that they "left for Tokyo on the Friday morning" (p30) - which presumably denotes the next day, although 17th July, 2020, will *be* a Friday.
16 Dating *Power Play* (BF LS #3.5) - No year given. The blurb says that it's been "many years" since Victoria left the TARDIS (in *Fury from the Deep*), and the story was originally intended for the unmade Season 23 in 1986.

Victoria repeatedly comments upon her advanced age (it's the reason she declines to go off in the TARDIS again), and has to be at least 60 – hence her remark to David that he's "Twenty years [behind her], at least. You can't be much more than 40." *Downtime* specifies that Victoria was 28 in 1984, so if she's currently a sexagenarian, it must be 2016 at the earliest. That roughly concurs with Victoria here claiming, "I was born more than 150 years ago" (circa 1852, according to *Downtime*). The placement here, of circa 2020, is derived from Deborah Watling (born 2nd January, 1948) being 64 when she recorded this story.

Nothing is said here about Victoria's personal life, so there's no conflict with *The Great Space Elevator* claiming that she's a mother and grandmother. A bit of discontinuity exists in that Victoria professes to have no idea that the Doctor can change bodies – an idea she *seems* to comprehend, perhaps, in the epilogue to the book version of *Downtime*, as well as the prelude to *Birthright* in DWM #203 (treated by this chronology as a secondary source of information).
17 Dating *House of Blue Fire* (BF #152) - Sally tests a colleague's memory by asking, "I'm guessing you remember what year it is?", and receives the (evidently correct) reply, "Of course... 2020."
18 *Gods and Monsters*
19 VULCAN: The planet Vulcan is only seen in *The Power of the Daleks*, a story that is almost certainly set in 2020. There is no indication that humankind has developed interstellar travel or faster-than-light drives in this or any other story set at this time. This would seem to suggest that Vulcan is within our own solar system.

There is some evidence to support this conjecture: since the nineteenth century, some astronomers (including Le Verrier, who discovered Neptune), speculated that a planet might orbit the sun closer than Mercury. There was new interest in this theory in the mid-nineteen-sixties, which might explain why the home planet of Mr Spock was also called Vulcan around the same time in *Star Trek*. The draft script talked of a "Plutovian Sun", suggesting Vulcan is far from the Sun, not close.

In 1964, *The Dalek Book*, which, like *The Power of the*

c 2020 - POWER PLAY (BF)[16] **->** The Terrible Zodin, a "devastating diva of dissimulation, the queen of corruption and chicanery", hired the professional escapologist and planet-killer Dominicus to arrange Earth's destruction. Dominicus infiltrated a nuclear power plant, then stockpiled energy within his spaceship by introducing a trans-uranic element more powerful than Uranium-235 into the plant's reactor. This generated excessive waste, which Dominicus sent down a time corridor to decay harmlessly in Earth's past, circa 500 million BC.

The power plant's retooling drew the attention of anti-nuclear advocates, including Victoria Waterfield and her friend David. One of Dominicus' associates – Collator Leiss of the Playerek, a reptilian intergalactic police force from the Playerek Dominion – brought down the TARDIS with a temporal stinger, embroiling the sixth Doctor and Peri in these events. Dominicus intended to ruin Earth with missiles from his spaceship, then flee down the temporal corridor while framing the Doctor for the crime. The Doctor sent Dominicus' missiles down the time corridor, where they exploded harmlessly in the past. David prevented Dominicus from fleeing the explosion, which killed them both.

The Doctor offered to let Victoria re-join him on his travels, but she declined given her age, so he left with Peri.

Sally Morgan Joins the TARDIS

2020 - HOUSE OF BLUE FIRE[17] **->** Eve Pritchard's work into Rapid-Emotional Programming (REP) technology – a means of extracting phobias, either to create fearless soldiers or to cripple a target population with "fear bullets" – reached an apex at Fulton Down Military Base. Four test subjects with chronic fears, including Private Sally Morgan (who had athazagoraphobia, the fear of being forgotten about) were connected to an REP control apparatus: the Blue Fire System. The seventh Doctor prevented the Mi'en Kalarash from manifesting via Blue Fire and triggering global Armageddon, and banished it back to the wasteland between realities. Afterward, he accepted Sally as his new travelling companion.

Private Sally Morgan was positioned aboard the Doctor's TARDIS as a game piece of the elder god Weyland, and her athazagoraphobia was a pre-cursor to the invisibility exhibited by Weyland's Shield.[18]

The Daleks Revive on Vulcan[19]

2020 - THE POWER OF THE DALEKS[20] **->** The colony on Vulcan was in danger of being "run down". Mining operations had not proved economically successful and the governor of the colony, Hensell, faced mutiny. An Examiner from Earth was due to assess the Vulcan colony in two years.

The chief scientist, Lesterson, discovered what he thought might be the colony's salvation – a buried alien spaceship. He quickly determined that the capsule was constructed of a metal that wasn't found on Vulcan and could revolutionise space travel. Lesterson opened the capsule and discovered that it contained three inert Daleks. The lure of reviving them proved too great for the human colonists.

At first, the Daleks cunningly pretended to be servants, dependent as they were on the power provided by the humans. The Daleks promised to build a com-

---

Daleks was co-written by David Whitaker, named Vulcan as the innermost planet in our solar system (and Omega as the outermost). This, though, contradicts the story that immediately precedes The Power of the Daleks, in which Mondas is referred to as "the Tenth Planet"; Image of the Fendahl, where the Fendahleen homeworld is "the Fifth Planet"; and The Sun Makers, where Pluto is established as the ninth planet of the solar system. So it seems that Vulcan wasn't in our solar system in the late nineteen-eighties or the far future.

Taking all this literally and at face value, Doctor Who fan Donald Gillikin has suggested that Vulcan arrives in the solar system but later leaves. This might be scientifically implausible – at least in the timescale suggested – but we know of at least three other "rogue planets" that enter our solar system according to the series: Earth's moon, Mondas and Voga. The Taking of Planet 5 (p15) confirms Gillikin's theory by stating that Vulcan was discovered in 2003 and had vanished by 2130.

The Pursuit of History cheekily mentions how the French mathematician Urbain Le Verrier "discovered" Vulcan in 1859, since Vulcan is "real" in the Doctor Who universe. In real life, Le Verrier published a provisional theory about Vulcan in 1843, and expanded upon it in 1859.

20 Dating The Power of the Daleks (4.3) - There is no confirmation of the date in the story itself. Lesterson says the Dalek ship arrived "at least two centuries ago", "before the colony", which might suggest the Earthmen have been there for just under two hundred years. However, the generally low-level of technology, the reliance on "rockets" and the fact that there is only one communications link with Earth suggests the colony is fairly new. The colonists don't recognise the Daleks, suggesting it's before The Dalek Invasion of Earth.

The contemporary trailer (included on the Lost in Time DVD) announced it was set "in the year 2020", and press material at the time confirmed that. This date also appeared in the 10th anniversary Radio Times, was used by the second edition of The Making of Doctor Who and

puter that could predict meteorite showers and protect the weather satellites, a move that offered huge financial savings and won the colonists' trust. All the time, though, the Daleks were setting up their production line. Dozens of Daleks swarmed across the colony within a matter of hours, exterminating every human in their path.

The newly regenerated second Doctor, Ben and Polly witnessed the Daleks' rampage. Once again, though, the Daleks' external power sources proved their undoing – although they guarded their static electricity generator, it proved possible to destroy the power source. This rendered the Daleks immobile once more.

The eleventh Doctor later happened upon a Dalek from Vulcan in the Dalek Asylum.[21]

On Earth, an energy crisis worsened in 2021. Damien Stephens' impoverished mother froze to death, and so he, along with Jack Coulson – a classmate at the University at Durham – did pioneering work on lunar construction techniques and solar power. The two of them sought to provide humanity with free, limitless energy. Time-travelling Daleks mentally enthralled Stephens and forced him to sever ties with Coulson. Stephens used government aid to found GlobeSphere, which established a base and vast solar panels on the moon. A target date of 31st January, 2025, was slated for the first transmission of solar power from the GlobeSphere base to Earth.[22]

Steffi Ehrlich, a future Mars colonist, was born in Iserlohn, Germany, in September 2021.[23] Some UK army units were privatised, and were hired out for commercial security purposes.[24]

Thomas Hector "Hex" Schofield Joins the TARDIS

2021 (12th October) - THE HARVEST[25] **->** There was political tension between Europe and the Pan-US Core. The European Council had recovered an expeditionary force of Cybermen that crashed in the Pyrenees. The Cybermen brokered a deal with the European government, offering Cyber-technology to create astronauts cyber-augmented for space. In return, the Cybermen asked for operations to make them organic beings again.

By October 2021, the "Recarnative Program" was secretly in operation at St Gart's Brookside, a London hospital managed by the Euro Combine Health Administration. The duplicitous Cybermen intended to turn the facility

---

the first edition of *The Programme Guide*.

Nevertheless, *Doctor Who* fans can see a statement like "I'm from 1980" as problematic and ambiguous, and most fan chronologies have seen 2020 as implausibly early for Earth to have a colony on a planet that's not in our solar system. Ergo, they often use the fact the date only appeared in a trailer to disallow it. (To be fair, the trailer for *The Dalek Invasion of Earth* set that story in "2000" – a date to which nobody subscribes.)

In DWM, *The TARDIS Logs* offered a date of "2049", but "A History of the Daleks" contradicted this and gave the date as "2249". The American *Doctor Who* comic offered the date of "2600 AD", apparently unaware that the Dalek ship has been dormant. *The Terrestrial Index* came to the elaborate conclusion that the colonists left Earth in 2020 – in spacecraft with suspended animation – and then used the old calendar when they arrived. As a result, while they call the date 2020, the story is really set in "2220". *Timelink* opted for "2120". *About Time* claims that "internal publicity" gave the date as "2070" (it didn't, actually – that was for *The Moonbase*), but concludes the story is set "probably somewhere in the mid-2100s". Earth could only really have a colony on another world this early if the planet Vulcan was in our solar system. See the article "Vulcan" for how it might be possible to justify the "2020" date.

The Dalek Handbook (pgs. 39-40) names Vulcan as "one of humanity's first non-terrestrial colonies" from the "21st century", in order to reconcile the people there being wholly unfamiliar with Daleks (prior to *The Dalek Invasion of Earth*, but also *Army of Ghosts/Doomsday*).

The Daleks themselves, the *Handbook* says, are as a time-travel squad from around the time of Skaro's downfall in *The Evil of the Daleks*, which explains why they recognise the second Doctor in his newly regenerated form.

21 *Asylum of the Daleks*
22 *Energy of the Daleks*
23 *The Waters of Mars*
24 *Afterlife*
25 Dating *The Harvest* (BF #58) - The date is given on the back cover blurb.
26 "Years" before *Signs and Wonders*.
27 "Six months" before *Afterlife*.
28 "A year" before *The Silurian Gift*.
29 "A week" before *Afterlife*.
30 Dating *Benny S5: The Grel Escape* (Benny audio #5.1) - The year is given. The "Festival of Piranha" is a parody of the "Festival of Ghana" seen in *The Chase*.
31 Dating *Afterlife* (BF #181) - It's New Year's Eve, the end of the year of life allocated to Hector Thomas.

The actual year is harder to pin down – it's after Hex joined the TARDIS on 12th October, 2021, and Hilda's comment that she was supposed to receive her grandson's letter "six months ago" indicates that it's at least 2022. Supporting that, DI Derek Mortimer mentions "the 2020 riots", not "last year's riots". The back cover punts on naming the year (stating that it's simply "21st century Liverpool"), as does Ace when she tells the Doctor to set course for "the 2020s, you'll know when".

It's somewhat symmetrical to think that *Afterlife* does, in fact, take place in 2022: the first calendar year

into a ready-made Cyber-conversion centre, facilitating a planetary takeover. The seventh Doctor and Ace learned of the plot and triggered a termination protocol that shut down the Cybermen. The Doctor also erased the Program's data, preventing the Euro government from exploiting it. Thomas Hector "Hex" Schofield, a staff nurse at St Gart's, joined the Doctor and Ace on their travels.

An AI system was in use at St Gart's, and the Wheel space stations were in operation.

2022

Hector Thomas, an Iteration of Hex, Manifests on Earth

Owing to events at the dawn of time, Hex was reincarnated at the stroke of midnight on the new year as Hector Thomas: a small-time criminal who quickly rose to become a gang leader running such nightclubs as the Empire. The Finnegan family – the head of which was actually the fire elemental Koloon – rivaled Hector's operations.[26] The seventh Doctor and Ace returned Sally Morgan and Lysandra Aristedes home following their defeat of Fenric and Weyland. Officially, Sally was AWOL from her unit, having been attached to the King's New Delta, and co-opted for international investigations.[27]

The energy firm PelCorp, as headed by the American Rick Pelham, discovered a Silurian colony at the South Pole. The revived Silurians there offered Pelham Fire Ice – a concentrated form of energy crystal – as a peace offering, but Pelham's guards captured the Silurian base. By threatening to kill the Silurians still in hibernation, Pelham facilitated greater exploitation of Fire Ice's potential.[28]

The seventh Doctor posted a letter that Hex had written to his grandmother, Hilda, to provide her with some context before informing her of Hex's death.[29]

2022 - BENNY S5: THE GREL ESCAPE[30] **->** With the time-travelling Grel in hot pursuit, Benny, Jason and Peter stopped at the Festival of Piranha, a disused funfair (and the home to flesh-eating Evatra Wraiths).

Hector Thomas Joins the TARDIS

c 2022 (31st December) - AFTERLIFE[31] **->** In the United Kingdom, the Police Department and the Postal Service had been privatized. Some reports claimed that Lysandra Aristedes was freelancing in the New African States.

At Ace's insistence, the seventh Doctor visited Hex's grandmother, Hilda Schofield, to inform her of his demise. The Doctor advertised a memorial for Hex, and was thereby reunited with Private Sally Morgan. Ace happened upon Hector Thomas, failed to make him remember his past life as Hex, and – in part motivated by her grief for Hex's loss – became Hector's lover.

The fire elemental Koloon attempted to claim Hector at the stroke of New Year's per its bargain with Hex, but the Doctor banished Koloon back to the elder gods' realm with a fire extinguisher filled with intra-dimensional particles. The vessel containing Hex's memories was smashed to pieces. The Doctor and Ace took Hector, who retained no recollection of his past life, with them in the TARDIS.

c 2023 - THE SILURIAN GIFT[32] **->** PelCorp's "discovery" of Fire Ice at the South Pole made headlines as a means of resolving Earth's energy crisis, and the eleventh Doctor pulled strings with UNIT to investigate it. The Silurian Partock revived her base's phalanx of Myrka to drive away their human captors, and added a boosting agent to PelCorp's Fire Ice that would speed up global warming – the prelude to a Silurian takeover of Earth. The situation resolved with the Silurians re-entering hibernation, and freezing water swallowing the Fire Ice containers and the Myrka.

available after Hex's departure with the Doctor and Ace. Running contrary to this, UNIT's file on Ace in *Signs and Wonders* (set "two years" after *Afterlife*) notes her involvement in incidents in 1963 (*Remembrance of the Daleks*), 1997 (*Battlefield*) and 2025 (possibly an erroneous reference to *Project: Destiny*, which actually occurs in 2026), suggesting that *Afterlife* should occur somewhere around 2024 at the earliest. It's easier to think, however, that the likes of Lysandra Aristedes preemptively updated UNIT's files than to believe that Hilda went four years without seeing or hearing from her grandson, and yet gives no sign of it.

Matt Fitton, the writer of *Afterlife*, initially planned to allocate Hector Thomas five years of life, with events reaching a climax on the New Year for 2028, but dialed this back to one year of life lasting in 2022. Fitton's intent was that Hilda was unaware Hex had left in the TARDIS in 2021, thought he was still working in a London hospital, and was only informed of his death the following year.

32 Dating *The Silurian Gift* (*Quick Reads* #7) - The book saw print in 2013, and seems either a contemporary or near-future story. The Doctor, rather anachronistically, claims to be working for *Beezer* (1956-1993) or *Whizzer and Chips* (1969-1990). Earth is currently experiencing a "global energy crisis", which seems more in keeping with events detailed in *The Feast of Axos* than anything currently seen in the television series.

During the 2020s, the Silurians entombed at Wenley Moor were scheduled to revive. If they did so, they remained hidden from humanity.[33] The Doctor contained plastic-eating nanites from Phophov IV after "a battle and a half". The CD industry consequently had to give way to MP3 downloads. In 2023, UNIT turned its moonbase over to the company World State, believing that private enterprise could better fund the research there.[34] The UN banned beryllium laser weapons in the mid-2020s.[35] The phased plasma rifle was developed in 2024.[36]

2024 - EMOTIONAL CHEMISTRY[37] -> The eighth Doctor, Fitz and Trix infiltrated the Kremlin Museum to retrieve a diamond locket that formerly belonged to the Russian noblewoman Dusha. Colonel Grigoriy Bugayev, working for the Russian division of UNIT, knew the Doctor of old and aided the time travellers.

The disgraced physicist Harald Skoglund had retro-engineered a lost time belt into the Misl Vremnya, a device that enabled its user to see down the timeline of various objects, and to witness events through the eyes of anyone in contact with them. With further exertion, the device allowed its operator to dominate the wills of such people. Bugayev destroyed the device.

By now, the Moscow waste management system had organic microfilters to reprocess sewage. Robot drones were used for reconnaissance.

Hex Restored, Leaves the TARDIS

& 2024 - SIGNS AND WONDERS[38] -> The seventh Doctor and Ace returned Hector Thomas home at his insistence. Hex's grandmother, Hilda Schofield, had died in the two years since their last visit.

Eagle-like beings, members of the Third Holy Aquilion Empire, sought to transfer the power of To'Koth – the dying elder god slumbering near Liverpool – into themselves, thinking it would make them divine. As a distraction, the Aquilion conscripted a human agent – the self-proclaimed prophet Rufus Stone – to summon fierce extraterrestrial leeches, the Hirodine, to attack Liverpool while they siphoned off To'Koth's life force. The long-lived Jenny Greenteeth destroyed the Hirodine and contested the Aquilion for To'Koth's energy. As To'Koth merely

---

33 At the end of *Doctor Who and the Silurians*, the Reptile People go back into deep freeze for "fifty years". Alternatively, they might have all perished in the explosions triggered by the Brigadier's men. There are Silurians working alongside humanity in *Eternity Weeps* in 2003, but it's never stated they are from Wenley Moor, and we know there were other shelters. The UNIT audios (set circa 2005) show a failed attempt to reconcile humanity and the Silurians, although a group of Silurians nonetheless help human scientists to cure a lethal virus. The eleventh Doctor indicates in *Cold Blood* that the Wenley Moor Silurians were killed, not entombed.

34 *Horror of the Space Snakes* (ch7).

35 "Twenty years" after *The Fearmonger*.

36 *First Frontier* (p137).

37 Dating *Emotional Chemistry* (EDA #66) - The date appears in the blurb.

38 Dating *Signs and Wonders* (BF #191) - Hector broad-brushes the time as "Liverpool, the 2020s", but one of Hilda's neighbours says it's been "a couple of years ago now" since "the business with [Hilda's] grandson" (in *Afterlife*). Inter-dimensional energies cause premonitions of possible futures, including the Doctor hearing *Madame Butterfly* (*The TV Movie*) and Ace both riding a moped through nineteenth-century Paris (*Set Piece, Happy Endings*) and wearing a high collar and cloak (*UNIT: Dominion, The New Adventures of Bernice Summerfield*, the *Gallifrey* audios).

39 Dating "Ghost Stories" (Titan mini-series) - It's "eight years" since the Doctor last saw Grant and company in *The Return of Doctor Mysterio*. The story opens "the day after Christmas", ends with an epilogue "one week later".

Jennifer's age is inconsistent – she's "eight years old" in issue #1, age "11" in #5 and #7.

40 *Happy Endings*

41 Glauss was born twenty-six years after *Millennial Rites* (p86). A bit confusingly, p70 says her *Cybercrime* text was written "in the early twenty-first century".

42 "Twenty years" after *9thC: Retail Therapy*. The writer, James Goss, confirmed to us that the "celebrity" isn't anyone in particular.

43 Dating *Energy of the Daleks* (BF 4th Doc #1.4) - The year is given, and a newscast says that it's the day before the first energy transmissions from the GlobeSphere moonbase, which is slated for 31st January. The GlobeSphere base's teleport system is a special accommodation the Daleks have supplied, and not representative of Earth's technological level. (It's not impossible, though, that the technology later gives rise to T-Mat – see *The Seeds of Death*.) This energy crisis is presumably the same one described in *The Feast of Axos* [c 2025].

44 Dating *Horror of the Space Snakes* (BBC children's 2-in-1 #5) - The exact day is given (ch4). It's "eight years" after 2017.

45 Dating *The Feast of Axos* (BF #144) - Axos was stuck in the time loop "fifty years" ago in *The Claws of Axos*, making this story subject to UNIT dating.

46 Dating *The Ring of Steel* (BBC DW audiobook #8) - The Doctor tells Amy that they're "maybe fifteen years into her future".

47 Dating *You are the Doctor and Other Stories*: "Dead to the World" (BF #207d) - The Doctor states that space tourism "was quite a fad in this period". The story's author, Matthew J Elliott, said: "It was my intention that

wished to die in peace, the Doctor used the TARDIS as a conduit to return it to the elder gods' domain at the dawn of time. A diminished Greenteeth left Earth with the Aquilion.

Sally Morgan found that Hex's memories, per his deal with the elder gods, were actually within her St Christopher and restored Hector to his former self. Hex remained in Liverpool to aid in the rebuilding and tend to the wounded. The Doctor and Ace left, and visited Hex and Sally some fifteen years in the future.

Winifred Bambera was now a general.

& 2024 (26th December) to 2025 (2nd January) - "Ghost Stories"[39] ->

Grant Gordon (a.k.a. the Ghost), his wife Lucy and their daughter Jennifer had not seen the twelfth Doctor for eight years. Suddenly, he enlisted their help – to use Grant's gemstone to track down its three fellows. The four of them acquired the gems from a ruined New York City in the future, the planet Nixtus III and a Sycorax mothership. Grant gave up his Ghost gem, as all four gems were needed to prevent a dark energy wave from corrupting the universe. The Doctor returned a powerless Grant and his family home. A week later, the Doctor revealed to Grant that the Ghost had permanently altered his DNA, and he still had his superpowers.

Lucy's father had died the week before Christmas.

The novel *The Unformed Heart* by Emily Hutchings was published, and the Doctor acquired a copy. The word "cruk" was very rude by 2025.[40] Demeter Glauss, the future author of *Cybercrime: An Analysis of Hacking*, was born. The book was the seminal work on breaking and entering computer systems, including the Paradigm operating system. Mel would use the text to hack into Ashley Chapel Logistics in 1999.[41]

In the United Kingdom, a female film star tried to capitalise on a Slibot invasion and make herself Prime Minister.[42]

2025 (30th January) - ENERGY OF THE DALEKS[43] ->

The corporation GlobeSphere provided holographic Internet access to anyone with an account, as identified by their fingerprint. Some theatres in London closed, as energy costs made it unfeasible to keep them lit. Handheld TV sets were common.

The fourth Doctor had hoped to visit London circa 2015, preferably around lunchtime, but he and Leela instead found themselves there in 2025. The GlobeSphere moonbase was scheduled to begin transmission of concentrated solar energy to Earth, but protestors at the National Gallery decried the decision to keep the cost of such power high, for benefit of energy companies, governments and cartels. Free energy supplies were forecast to occur in twenty years.

The Doctor discovered that time-travelling Daleks – hoping to destroy Earth before the human race could challenge Dalek supremacy – had rigged the GlobeSphere energy reception dishes around Earth to create a force field that would cancel out gravity. Activation of the GlobeSphere transmissions would propel the moon away from Earth, drastically shifting Earth's axis and causing enough climate change to wipe out humanity. The Daleks killed Stephens, but the Doctor redirected the first GlobeSphere energy transmissions onto the Daleks' scoutship, destroying them.

2025 (18th April) - HORROR OF THE SPACE SNAKES[44] ->

World State announced the debut of its first lunar transport shuttle, which would make regular trips to the company's moonbase. Four months later, the Korean Unity sold off its territory on Earth's moon. The eleventh Doctor was present at World State's moonbase – Moonbase Laika – as space snakes retrieved the queen egg that would help determine their destiny. The snakes said they would consider contacting humanity in future.

c 2025 - THE FEAST OF AXOS[45] ->

Earth continued to experience an energy crunch – fossil fuel supplies were dwindling, renewable energy sources couldn't meet demand and security concerns had slowed growth in the nuclear industry. A large portion of Oklahoma was now desert. The Eurozone Space Agency operated the space shuttle *Jules Verne*. A global lottery was now in operation.

Ironside Industries offered space-tourism flights for the cost of a luxury cruise. The CEO of Ironside, Campbell Irons, had the shuttle *Windermere* fitted with an alien displacement device capable of penetrating the time loop surrounding Axos, and sent a crew to negotiate with it. Irons wanted Axos to supply Earth with carbon-free energy. The sixth Doctor, Evelyn and Thomas Brewster were present as Axos used the *Windermere*'s microwave transmitter to exterminate the Ironside mission control station at Devesham. The Doctor strengthened the time loop as the mini-nuclear reactor aboard the *Windermere* was detonated, trapping Axos in a cycle of being exploded over and over again.

c 2025 - THE RING OF STEEL[46] ->

The eleventh Doctor and Amy stopped a Caskelliak – a weapon of war crafted by a dead race, and which had been tasked with polluting and destroying entire worlds – from using Astragen, a utilities company in the Orkney islands, Scotland, to complete an energy circuit that would have poisoned the Earth.

c 2025 - YOU ARE THE DOCTOR AND OTHER STORIES: "Dead to the World"[47] ->

The most ruthless estate agents of all, the Galparians, habitually claimed worlds for which no official documentation of ownership existed, then "beautified" them by wiping out the indigenous population. On Earth, space tourism had become something of a fad, and the tourist ship *Daedalus* intercepted a Galparian beam keyed to revert human DNA into primordial goo. The seventh Doctor and Ace strong-armed the Galparians into canceling out their signal.

As he had saved Earth so many times, and in accordance with the Galparians' bylaws, the Doctor declared himself the owner to Earth to ward off further mischief. The *Daedalus* incident soured investor confidence in space tourism for twelve years.

The End of the Forge

2026 (18th-22nd April) - PROJECT: DESTINY / A DEATH IN THE FAMILY[48] **->** The public accepted that aliens were real, as too much evidence was available in the information age to deny it. Nimrod, a.k.a. Sir William Abberton, had spent years rebuilding the Forge into Department C4 – a governmental agency that served as the public face of extra-terrestrial investigation. C4 bungled a harvest of alien xenotech, causing a widespread infection of DNA from insectoid aliens named the Contaminants. These creatures' life cycle entailed mutating residents of a target world into hybrids, then breeding to produce more pure offspring. London was evacuated and quarantined as fifteen thousand people were infected. The hybrids consumed those too old or infirm to survive the transformation. Outbreaks were reported in Chelsea, Hammersmith,

Camden and Wandsworth.

Two months after the evacuation, the Home Secretary assured Parliament – which was currently in session in Harrogate – that the quarantine zone around the M-25 was secure. The Contaminant hybrids all swarmed to C4's main facility – the Crichton Building, which overlooked the Thames – in a mating frenzy. Captain Lysandra Aristedes usurped control of C4 and destroyed the Crichton Building and all the Contaminants with an air strike of dystronic missiles. Nimrod perished in the blast, and his death effectively ended the Forge.

Afterward, the seventh Doctor and Ace located a Gallifreyan sarcophagus in the Forge archives – and found within an older version of the seventh Doctor, who had become the Storyspeaker for the Handivale of Pelican. The Word Lord had been trapped within the Handivale, but was now freed. The Handivale transferred into Captain John Stillwell of UNIT, who became comatose.

The Word Lord made a soldier intone "Nobody can stop the Doctor regenerating" and "No One has the power of life and death over the Doctor" – and thereby gained those very attributes. The younger seventh Doctor re-bottled the Word Lord within a conflicting narrative spun from the trans-galactic Internet, but this burned out the Doctor's cerebral cortex, killing him. The older seventh Doctor, now only a potential future, took Hex to the distant past on Pelican, then had the TARDIS deliver Ace to 2027.

S.J. Wordly was now Prime Minister.

[the story] should be set in the early to mid-21st century – space travel as an industry is still in its infancy".
48 Dating *Project: Destiny* and *A Death in the Family* (BF #139-140) - The Doctor is initially uncertain as to the date ("We're in the year 2024, or possibly 2026") and the back cover says that it's 2025. It's said three times within the story, though, that it's 2026 – once by Nimrod in response to Hex asking about the year, and twice on data files related to the Contaminants. The same data files seem to indicate that *Project: Destiny* begins on "18th of April" and continues the next day – when the Doctor is shot, and later awakens after spending three days in healing coma. So, that adventure ends – and events seem to pick up immediately afterwards in *A Death in the Family* – on the 22nd. The later portion of *A Death in the Family*, which begins in 2027, confirms that London was evacuated "last year".
49 Dating *A Death in the Family* (#140) - Ace establishes the date of her arrival (24th June, 2027) by checking a newspaper. She dispatches Henry's account of her to Hex on "Tuesday, 24th of May" (actually a Wednesday in 2028) – evidently the same day that Professor Noone springs into creation and confronts the Word Lord.
50 *Project: Nirvana*, evidently per Lysandra entering the TARDIS, briefly, at the end of *Project: Destiny*.
51 *FP: The Brakespeare Voyage* (ch3).

52 "A decade or two" after *The Lost Angel*. There have been "synthetic cements" since the early twentieth century, this must be a new type.
53 *The Lost Angel*
54 *The Waters of Mars*
55 Dating *Shield of the Jotunn* (BF #206) - The Doctor steps out of the TARDIS and tells Constance that it's "2029. July the 13th. A Sunday morning, I believe." Some locals confirm that it's indeed "July" and "a Sunday"... in the real world, however, 13th July, 2029 will fall on a Friday.
56 "Twenty or thirty years" after *The King of Terror*.
57 *The Last Dodo*
58 *The Left-Handed Hummingbird*
59 "Apotheosis"
58 *Winner Takes All*. No date is given, but William is currently second in line to the throne, and will be King at some point in the twenty-first century.
60 Dating *Warchild* (NA #47) - The book is the sequel to *Warlock*. At the end of the earlier novel, Justine was in the early stages of pregnancy, so her baby would have been born in the spring of the following year. In *Warchild*, her son Ricky is "15". This book is set in the early autumn, as the long summer ends and the school year is starting in America.

The TARDIS sensed the elder god Derleth's presence in Captain Lysandra Aristedes' mind the first time she stepped aboard the Ship. The knowledge of this motivated the Doctor to recruit Lysandra to aid him against the elder gods.[49]

2027 (24th June) to 2028 (Tuesday, 24th May) - A DEATH IN THE FAMILY[50] -> The British government, UNIT, the remnants of the Forge and a secret cabal of the Doctor's former companions covered up his death in 2026, fearing the consequence of extra-terrestrials learning that Earth no longer had his protection. The Doctor's corpse was interred in York Minster, in a secret chamber reserved for Earth's fallen, clandestine heroes.

The TARDIS, per the older seventh Doctor's instructions, arrived in 2027 with Ace aboard. In the months to follow, she entered into a relationship with Henry Louis Noone. In May 2028, Ace had Henry write about what she would be like as his wife of ten years, then sent the document to Hex in the distant past using a Vaspen space-time stamp. This created a linguistic version of Ace – Professor Dorothy Noone – whose name enabled her (per the phrase, "No One has the power of life and death over the Doctor") to tap the Word Lord's reality altering CORDIS and bring the Doctor back to life. The Word Lord was liberated from the Doctor's narrative and killed Professor Noone, but was then uploaded, along with his CORDIS, into the Handivale within Captain Stillwell. Ace and the restored Doctor took Stillwell back in time to Pelican.

The first anti-aging drugs for humans weren't widely available before 2028, and even then had such extensive side-effects that old age seemed preferable.[51] The advent of a synthetic cement would aid the twelfth Doctor in burying a quartet of Weeping Angels.[52] At some point, humanity would use advanced 3D printers to produce kidneys.[53]

A number of future Mars colonists were born around this time: Andrew Stone on a commune in Iowa in 2025; Tarak Ital in 2026 in Karachi; and Margaret Cain in Sheffield in December 2028. After intensive training, Adelaide Brooke became the first non-US citizen to fly shuttles for NASA. Ed Gold earned a BA in mechanical engineering in 2030.[54]

2029 (13th July) - SHIELD OF THE JOTUNN[55] -> Humanity was losing the fight on climate change, as greenhouse gases melted the ice caps and caused environmental havoc. Earth First emerged as an eco-terrorist group. Two-D movies were now antiquated.

In Burnt Oak, Arizona, Dr Hugo Macht oversaw construction of a mountain-sized geo-engine that, when activated, would disperse nanites in an attempt to reverse the environmental damage. The Jothunn shield buried nearby usurped the geo-engine and constructed bodies for some of the Talessh trapped in its transmat beam. The Talessh moved to seize Earth, and so the sixth Doctor and Constance resurrected Chief Herger and his men from the shield as twenty-foot-tall Vikings made from calcium. The substance destroyed the Talessh's bodies, whereupon Herger crushed the shield – ending his life and that of his Vikings, but trapping the remaining Talessh in limbo.

The 2030s

By 2030, the issue of thargon differentials in the orange spectrum of upper atmospheric problems was solved. This enabled the creation of stable energy fields on satellites.[56] Gorillas were extinct on Earth by 2030.[55] The seventh Doctor, Ace and Bernice visited UNIT HQ in Geneva in 2030, and picked up a note left by Cristian Alvarez thirty-seven years before.[57] The eleventh Doctor claimed that the World Cup final held at Wembley Stadium in 2030 was the greatest football match in history. The score was Scotland three, England nil.[58]

The Doctor acquired a ten pound coin from the time of King William V.[59]

2030 (early autumn) - WARCHILD[60] -> Computer technology enabled cars to practically drive themselves and computers that understood straightforward voice commands. Instead of passports, people had implants on the back of their necks. Three-dimensional television now existed. Passenger airliners were still in use. A cure had been found for Alzheimer's disease, and few people smoked thanks to health-awareness campaigns.

Vincent Wheaton had secretly inserted himself into the life of his son, Ricky McIlveen, in the guise of a history teacher. Vincent suspected that Ricky possessed immense mind-control abilities... enough to make Ricky president of America, with Vincent pulling his strings. Ricky was potentially the greatest alpha male who ever lived, and so Vincent experimented with the concept of pack behaviour. The dog Vincent owned, which contained the mind of a human, Jack, accordingly became the White King – an old dog that caused packs of dogs to display remarkable intelligence and murder people. The seventh Doctor, travelling with Benny, Roz and Chris, reunited Jack's mind with his human body.

Creed McIlveen now worked for a secretive crimefighting force, the Agency, but started an affair with his associate Amy Cowan – who was secretly in Vincent's employ. Vincent wanted revenge on Creed and Justine, and invaded their home. In the resulting confrontation, Amy had a change of heart and killed Vincent to save Justine. Creed and Justine's marriage ended. The Doctor and his friends pledged to help Ricky learn control of his abilities.

(=) c 2031 - DotD: THE TIME MACHINE[61] **->** The eleventh Doctor and Alice Watson identified an alternate timeline in which the Creevix were busy consuming Earth's history. The Creevix captured the TARDIS, but the Doctor and Alice found a replica of Guy Taylor's time machine and left for the Creevix's domain at the end of time. The TARDIS answered the Doctor's summons, and went there to rescue him.

c 2032 (Tuesday, 30th November) - SINGULARITY[62] **->** Houses were now equipped with computer attendants that responded to voice recognition; phones also recognised voice command.

In Russia, the Somnus Foundation had been created to study sleep disorders and neuroscience, but some descendents of humanity – originating from near the end of the universe – usurped the organisation. The descendents hoped to modify the brain chemistry and "wave forms" of several humans, inducing telepathy and achieving a group consciousness. If successful, the effect would cascade through Earth's electro-magnetic signature and turn the whole of humanity into a single entity. The resultant Singularity would allow the descendants to bring their fellows through en masse from the future, and let them exact vengeance against the Time Lords.

On 30th November, Moscow witnessed its worst storm in fifty years. The fifth Doctor arrived to investigate matters at a Somnus clinic, but the Somnus test subjects started an electrical fire, hoping to end their suffering. The clinic burned down as the Doctor escaped.

In 2032, Yuri Kerenski began work for the Russia Federal Space Agency. He would end up specialising in treating long-term cosmonauts after they returned home. In the same year, Mia Bennett was born in Houston. Her mother was killed in a car accident, and her father relinquished a career in space exploration to raise her.[63] Earth picked up an Arcturan signal that included enough information to build a transmat device.[64] Iris owned a martini glass signed by actor Leonard Rossiter, which was said to contain the soul of TV presenter Noel Edmonds.[65]

Lethbridge-Stewart returned to Earth in 2032, having spent twenty years in the realm of Avalon.[66] By 2034, a young man called Craig would either be a drunk living under Hammersmith Bridge *or* a successful carpenter with children – depending on the choices he made in 2006.[67]

Ed Gold earned his doctorate in 2034 – the same

---

61 Dating *DotD: The Time Machine* (*Destiny of the Doctor* #11) - It's "less than twenty years" from the year the Doctor and Alice just left, 2013.
62 Dating *Singularity* (BF #76) - The year is unspecified, but 30th November is a Tuesday; in the twenty-first century – and allowing that the portion of *Singularity* eleven years hence cannot occur before 2090 – that narrows the possibilities to 2010, 2021, 2027, 2032, 2038, 2049, 2055, 2060, 2066 and 2077. As Somnus publicity materials brag about the goal of its members to terraform Mars within "two years", 2077 doesn't seem very likely; it would push the later portion of *Singularity* to 2088 and the end of the devastating Thousand-Day War – a year in which Somnus would be rather brazen to make such a claim.

Moscow endures its worst storm "in fifty years", an event that would be unlikely in the era of weather control witnessed in *The Moonbase* and *The Seeds of Death*. The former story takes place in 2070, ruling out this part of *Singularity* occurring before 2066. One complication is the Doctor's offhanded comment that humankind is only "a few years" from expanding beyond the solar system, suggesting a later dating as opposed to an earlier one. Nonetheless, given *Ahistory*'s projected dating of *The Seeds of Death*, the best compromise for the early part of *Singularity* seems to be 2032, with the remainder of this adventure occurring in 2043.
63 *The Waters of Mars*. See Dating *The Seeds of Death*.
64 *Cold Fusion* (p216), no date given.
65 *Iris S2: The Two Irises*. Rossiter lived 1926-1984; Edmonds was born in 1948 and is still alive; the place-

ment here arbitrarily has him living to his mid-eighties, and assumes he didn't lose his soul while living.
66 *The King of Terror*
67 "F.A.Q."
68 *The Waters of Mars*
69 Darius is 15, and Jorjie and Starkey are both 14, in *K9: Regeneration*. Jorjie is still 14 in *K9: Dream-Eaters* and *K9: The Last Oak Tree*.
70 "About ten years" prior to *Hothouse*.
71 Dating *Benny: The Vampire Curse*: "Possum Kingdom" (Benny collection #12b) - It's "the technologically comfortable early-to-mid twenty-first century" (p111).
72 *The Wheel of Ice* (p171).
73 *The Wreck of the World*
74 *The Seeds of Death*
75 At some point before *K9: The Sirens of Ceres*.
76 "Years" before *K9: Robot Gladiators*, but presumably after the development of hyperlogarithms.
77 *Alien Bodies*. The World Zones Accord was intended as a reference to the establishment of the political system of *The Enemy of the World*, which most chronologies set earlier than this. We could speculate that the World Zones Accord strengthened an existing World Zones Authority, in the same way successive European treaties have granted more powers to the EEC/EC/EU.
78 "Ten years" before *Kill the Moon*.
79 Dating *Signs and Wonders* (BF #191) - Hex says it's been "What? Fifteen years?" since he last saw the Doctor and Ace.
80 Dating *Unbound: Full Fathom Five* (BF Unbound #3) - The blurb names the year.

year Roman Groom, a future child genius, was born.[68] Starkey, Jorjie Turner and Darius Pike – future friends of K9 – were born in the mid-2030s.[69] The Experts, featuring lead singer Alex Marlow, became the biggest band in the world. Marlow eventually abandoned performing in favour of being a charity worker and environmental activist, working to save endangered animals.[70]

c 2035 - BENNY: THE VAMPIRE CURSE: "Possum Kingdom"[71] -> Benny and the Yesterways Ltd. tour group arrived at Forks, Washington, and disrupted the Edward and Bella Players' re-creation of a battle between vampires and werewolves.

The Advent of Travel-Mat

The father of Florian Hart started from nothing, went to university, and founded a company that developed quantum teleportation techniques. Eventually, Hart's company joined the international consortium that developed the Travel-Mat Relay.[72] *The World*'s archives would contain a logic cube from a prototype T-Mat system.[73]

On Earth, there was a period of technological progress. Hypersonic aircraft were built, and humankind discovered how to synthesise carbohydrates and protein, which helped to feed the planet's ever-increasing population. Computers were now advanced enough to give spoken responses to sophisticated verbal instructions. Most energy now came from solar power, and compact solar batteries became available. Petrol cars were confined to museums. There were further advances in robotics and weather control technology.

Regular passenger modules were travelling between the Earth and its moonbases. Most people thought the moon would provide a stepping stone to the other planets of the solar system, and eventually to the stars. At this time Professor Daniel Eldred, the son of the man who designed the lunar passenger modules, invented an ion jet rocket with a compact generator. This vehicle promised to revolutionise space travel, paving the way for humankind's rapid exploration of the solar system.

Then the Travel-Mat Relay, an instantaneous form of travel, was invented. The massive capital investment required, and the promise of easy movement of all resources around the world, meant that after some debate the government ended all funding for space travel. All but a skeleton staff on the moon were recalled. Man had travelled no further than the moon. For years, all space travel halted.

Travel-Mat revolutionised the distribution of people and materials around the world. A T-Mat brochure boasted that:

"The Travel-Mat is the ultimate form of travel. Control centre of the present system is the moon, serving receptions in all major cities on Earth. Travel-Mat provides an instantaneous means of public travel, transporting raw materials and vital food supplies to all parts of the world. Travel-Mat supersedes all conventional forms of travel, using the principal of dematerialisation at the point of departure and rematerialisation at the point of arrival in special cubicles. Departure and arrival are almost instantaneous. Although the system is still in its early stages, it is completely automated and foolproof against power failure."[74]

The development of hyperlogarithms allowed the development of a new generation of technology, including artificial intelligence.[75] Alistair Gryffen was involved in the development of the Thought Matrix, a revolutionary robot brain.[76]

In 2038, the World Zones Accord was signed. Around this time, Colonel Kortez fought the Cyber breaches for the ISC. He joined UNISYC in 2039 and fought lemur people at some point before 2069.[77]

Minera Luna San Pedro was established as a privately financed mineral survey of the moon. The bacteria in close proximity to the growing moon-chick became large enough to resemble giant spiders and killed the Mexicans, unknown to anyone back on Earth.[78]

Hex and Sally Morgan Start a Family

& 2039 - SIGNS AND WONDERS[79] -> The seventh Doctor and Ace visited Hex, his partner Sally Morgan and their daughter Cassie. He declined to go adventuring with them again, especially as he and Sally had a second child on the way.

= 2039 - UNBOUND: FULL FATHOM FIVE[80] -> At the Deep-sea Energy Exploration Project (DEEP), Professor Vollmer's assistant, Lee, secretly worked to develop super-soldiers augmented with marine-life DNA. In 2039, the Doctor went to the DEEP to end Lee's efforts. The Doctor killed Lee, but Lee's super-serum transformed Vollmer and General Flint into marine monsters. The Doctor shot Vollmer dead, but left his TARDIS behind as Flint self-destructed the base – or so the Doctor believed. Flint cancelled the self-destruct, but dirty bombs detonated and isolated the DEEP with radiation. The Doctor sought out Vollmer's daughter Ruth and raised her, without explaining how she'd become an orphan.

2040 - PHANTOMS OF THE DEEP[81] -> The fourth Doctor and the first Romana joined the deep submergence vehicle *Erebus* as it assessed the Mariana Trench as a place to dispose of radioactive waste. The alien spaceship trapped in the Trench had upgraded the vampire squid (*vampirotoothus infernalis*) in the vicinity to use symbolic logic and higher mathematics, and now sought to recreate the minds of its dead makers in human bodies. Dr Patricia Sawyer sacrificed herself to self-destruct the ship, preventing a hostile takeover of humankind.

Ace told Henry Noone that bees would recover from a malady afflicting them by 2040, and also that "you're going to get new pandas!"[82]

Hazel Bright joined the League of Nature after witnessing ten thousand people perish in the Ganges during a flood. She worked undercover for Alex Marlowe at the World Ecology Bureau, and stole the Krynoid cuttings saved by Sir Colin Thackeray.[83]

The (Projected) Passing of Sarah Jane Smith

It was predicted that Sarah Jane Smith would die around 2040, and that members of UNIT and Black Seed, possibly including Sam Jones, would attend her funeral.[84]

In 2043, Black Seed published their third manifesto.[85] There were anti-weather control demonstrations.[86]

The Doctor on Draconia

A race of reptilian humanoids had evolved on the planet Draconia. Although technologically advanced,

---

81 Dating *Phantoms of the Deep* (BF 4th Doc #1.5) - The year is given. The DSV *Erebus* is made from a carbon-nanotube composite, the same material as the titular structure in *The Great Space Elevator*.

82 *A Death in the Family*. It's not established whether "you" means Great Britain, humanity in general or something else entirely.

83 The cuttings are stolen "five years" prior to *Hothouse*. It's not expressly said that Hazel herself arranged the theft, but it seems likely.

84 *Interference Book Two*

85 *Interference* (Book Two, p292, p314), where the If, one of IM Foreman's incarnations, predicts Sarah's death. Following the machinations of the Council of Eight, the timeline is altered so that Sam Jones died in 2002.

86 *Dreamstone Moon* (p58).

87 "Five hundred years" before *Frontier in Space*. The incident is also recounted in *Shadowmind*.

88 *Paper Cuts*. The Doctor who visits Draconia is described as being "old" and "aged", which sounds like the first Doctor, but *The Dark Path* establishes it was the second Doctor.

89 *Catastrophea*

90 *Return of the Living Dad*. According to the Doctor in *The Parting of the Ways*, the Daleks also refer to him by that title.

91 "Cold-Blooded War!" The Doctor is familiar with this custom, so it must predate his first visit to Draconia.

92 *Benny: Nobody's Children*. There's no evidence that the Doctor actually tried to make off with the Empress' daughter.

93 Dating *The Seeds of Death* (6.5) - This story is tricky to pin down a date for, or even to place in relation to other stories.

On screen, the only indication of the date is the Doctor's identification of the ion rocket designed by Eldred as a product of "the twenty-first century". As the rocket only exists as a prototype at this stage, the story

must take place before 2100. T-Mat is developed at least two generations after space travel, as Eldred's father designed spacecraft, including a "lunar passenger module", and Eldred is an old man himself. It's impossible to infer a firm date from that, particularly as we know from *The Tenth Planet* that moonshots were unremarkable events by the mid-1980s in the *Doctor Who* universe. However, "lunar passenger module" suggests an altogether more routine service, and that this story is not set in the late twentieth or very early twenty-first century. It's never stated how long Travel-Mat has been in operation before *The Seeds of Death*, but it is a relatively new invention, as the video brochure we hear (transcribed here in full) states. Young Gia Kelly was involved with the development of T-Mat, but it has been around "a good many years" according to Eldred, long enough to make a rocket-travel advocate look eccentric. T-Mat is referred to as having been around for "years", rather than "decades" or "generations" – all told, it seems reasonable to suggest that T-Mat has been around for about a decade before the story.

It is possible to rule out certain dates by referring to other stories: The Weather Control Bureau is seen, so it must be set after 2016 when Salamander invents weather control; the Bureau is on Earth, which might suggest the story is set before 2050 when the Gravitron is installed on the moon, or that the system is later moved to Earth. Either way, the story can't be set between 2050 and (at least) 2070, because the Gravitron is in operation from the moon at that time and rockets are in use during that period. By the time of *The Seeds of Death*, it's stated that humanity has not travelled beyond the moon. *Kill the Moon* [2049] shows that same status quo – humankind has no interest in interstellar travel until the splendour of the space dragon hatching inspires it.

While *About Time* claims that the "technology is shown to be in advance of that in *The Wheel in Space*",

they retained a feudal system. The Doctor visited Draconia at the time of the Fifteenth Emperor, around 2040, and cured a great space plague.[87] The Emperor was known as the Red Emperor, and by the Draconian calendar, it was the 68th Year of the Serpent. The Doctor became the only person to beat the Emperor at Sazou – a Draconian game akin to chess – and not lose his head. The Doctor implored the Emperor to seal Draconia's borders to contain the plague, and insisted that the plague-antidote be given to commoners and royals alike. The Emperor agreed, but the quarantine made Draconia lose contact with its Imperial domains, and its empire collapsed.[88]

The Doctor was given the rank of High Earl of the Imperial House.[89] The Draconians took to referring to the Doctor as "the Oncoming Storm".[90] Draconian society had changed from the days of its Tribal Epoch; historical records suggested that it was only when it entered its Industrial Epoch that Draconian females had become sub-servient to males.[91]

The Draconian tradition of the *nikhol vakarshta* – a retreat for mothers and daughters – dated back to the great space plague. A legend held that the Karshtakavarr, "The Oncoming Storm", tried to depart with the Empress' daughter, but that she drove him off empty-handed – a symbol of female empowerment and the importance of motherhood.[92]

The Ice Warriors Subvert T-Mat

c 2040 (early in the year, winter) - THE SEEDS OF DEATH[93] -> Thanks to Travel-Mat, humanity had become dangerously insular. The Ice Warriors remained confined to Mars during all this time, limited by the lack of resources their home planet had to offer.

it's a bit hard to see what that's based on. We're explicitly told that Zoe has a more extensive knowledge of spaceflight than Eldred. (He admits as much, and Radnor says the same later – and, despite what *About Time* says, clearly distinguishes between Zoe's expertise and Jamie's lack of it.) Laser weapons have been developed by *The Wheel in Space*, including compact hand "blasters", but projectile weapons are still used here. There are quite advanced robots in Zoe's time, nothing like that seen here. Zoe was trained in a futuristic city, yet the cities we see here look much as they do now. That might be circumstantial evidence, but there's far more than that – *The Seeds of Death* is set at a time when man has travelled no "farther than the moon", whereas *The Wheel in Space* is set at a time when man's got at least to the asteroid belt, explicitly has ships in "deep space", has a "fleet" of manned ships, has at least five permanent space stations, and has been selecting and intensively training people to be astronauts for at least Zoe's lifetime (nineteen years, according to *The Invasion*). While no one says it in the story, *The Seeds of Death* is clearly – and is clearly intended to be – set before *The Wheel in Space*, case closed.

Deep space interstellar missions with crews in suspended animation were launched in the twenty-first century according to *The Sensorites*, which would be after the events of this story. The lack of deep space travel would seem to set the story before *The Power of the Daleks* (whichever year that is).

Evidence in subsequent stories would indicate that it's not set between 2068 and 2096, as Galactic Salvage and Insurance are covering spacecraft between those dates according to *Nightmare of Eden* (although if the space programme ended, it might explain why they went bust). If it was just Galactic Insurance, we could say it was just a meaningless brand name – we can buy Mars bars, that's not evidence we've built chocolate factories on Mars. It's Galactic *Salvage* and Insurance.

The implication seems to be that whatever else they do, they salvage and insure spacecraft.

The T-Mat network seems to connect up the whole world – it includes both New York and Moscow, for example, which would seem inconsistent with the Cold War world of 2084 seen in *Warriors of the Deep*. Not every city in the world is named, of course, and *About Time* speculates that China might be in a hostile rival bloc, because no Chinese cities are named (although "Asiatic Centres" are). Finally, the story probably isn't set after 2096, as four years seems too short a period to explore the entire solar system (*The Mutants*) before the interstellar missions mentioned in *The Sensorites*.

Or, to cut a long story short, and assuming a ten-year period before the story when T-Mat has been operating, *The Seeds of Death* has to be set more than ten years after *The Enemy of the World* (so after 2027), but before the Gravitron is installed in 2050 (so, before the moon is obliterated and re-laid in *Kill the Moon*).

This contradicts the limited space travel seen in stories (made after *The Seeds of Death*) to Mars in *The Ambassadors of Death*, *The Dying Days* and *Red Dawn*, and to Jupiter in *Memory Lane* and (accidentally) *The Android Invasion*, as well as the most likely date for *The Power of the Daleks*. If Vulcan was a rogue planet in our solar system, perhaps the colonisation mission was launched as it passed relatively close to Earth (although that piles supposition on supposition), or perhaps – more likely – the Vulcan colony had long failed and "doesn't count".

The Waters of Mars, set in 2059, provides us with a lot of new information, mainly in the backstory of characters seen on computer screens. There are no direct or indirect references to the future history established in any other *Doctor Who* story (including *The Seeds of Death*), and it strongly supports an earlier, rather than later, dating for *The Seeds of Death*. It rules out *About Time*'s dating of circa 2090, given that's after (we know

The Grand Marshall of the Martians ordered an invasion of Earth. A small squad led by Lord Slarr took Seed Pods – oxygen-fixing plants native to Mars – to the moonbase that controlled T-Mat. The plan was to cripple Earth by disabling the T-Mat, then use the Seeds to alter Earth's atmosphere until it more closely resembled that of Mars. The Pods were sent to Earth via Travel-Mat and preparations were made to guide the Martian invasion fleet to Earth. As killer foam spread through London, the second Doctor, Zoe and Jamie travelled to the moon and defeated the Ice Warriors, directing the Martian fleet into the Sun.[94]

now) Earth's first lightspeed ship reached Proxima Centauri. Consequently, this edition of *Ahistory* has moved *The Seeds of Death* a few years earlier than previous editions, from ?2044 to c2040.

"Mankind has travelled no further than the moon" in *The Seeds of Death*. As discussed, a number of other stories have astronauts landing on Mars, and we have to fudge that, whenever we set *The Seeds of Death*. *The Waters of Mars*, though, has a full-fledged, historic, long-term colony on the planet in 2058.

It might seem plausible to speculate that Bowie Base One "doesn't count" because it was destroyed, just as it's easy enough to see how manned space exploration might be temporarily abandoned (for a few years, at least) in the light of the disaster. As with the issue of when the Silurians ruled (see "A Complete Misnomer"), though, *Ahistory* always tries to look at the spirit of a story, as well as every letter. We might be able to fudge "no further than the moon", but the whole thrust of *The Waters of Mars* is that Brooke's sacrifice was the spark that directly inspired further space exploration. We know from *The Moonbase* that space travel was not abandoned in the 2060s.

We face the problem that Brooke doesn't know about the Ice Warriors, but given that UNIT know about the Martians (*The Christmas Invasion*, even confining ourselves just to television stories), this is a problem whenever we place it. Brooke and Cain were the first and second female Britons to land on the moon... and yet, we saw Gia Kelly on the moon in *The Seeds of Death*. That said, assuming Kelly is British, she didn't "land on the moon", she went there by Travel-Mat. The act of piloting the ship to a safe landing is what "counts", there. For that matter, if we're counting every Briton who's been to the moon, then there was a hospital full of them that materialised there in *Smith and Jones*.

Accepting that *The Seeds of Death* is set before *The Waters of Mars*, we now have to find somewhere in the timeline for the former before 2059, where there's about ten years with no evidence of human space exploration. Only one exists, between 2032 and 2040. We know from *The Waters of Mars* that Peter Bennett gave up space exploration to look after his daughter Mia, who was born in 2032. We are told that Yuri Kerenski started working as a doctor for the Russian space agency in 2032. There's nothing then until 2040, when *The Waters of Mars* tells us there is a burst of space exploration activity in 2040 to 2042 (as documented in the timeline). This is exactly what we'd like to see, exactly when we'd want to see it. The connection is not made in *The Waters of Mars*, but we can conjecture this: around 2032, Russia and America, at least, had functioning space programmes. These were abandoned when T-Mat came along shortly afterwards – Peter Bennett either got out just in time or saw which way the wind was blowing. Yuri got his job at the wrong time, and either didn't specialise in treating long term cosmonauts until later in his career, or he treated former cosmonauts or people working on the T-Mat station on the moon. Following the end of T-Mat, there was a burst of recruitment and activity.

Kill the Moon has the "privately financed" Minera Luna San Pedro mission to the Moon disappearing circa 2039. Clearly government missions are over by this time, and there doesn't seem to be any capacity to send a rescue mission. *The Seeds of Death* has the Travel-Mat Relay on the Moon, and even if the people on this moon mission are seen as eccentric (like Eldred), or it's felt they're reckless or mercenary, it seems a little harsh that the authorities don't send a rescue team via Travel-Mat (if the base lacks things like moon buggies or other rescue equipment, you'd think those could be sent up, too). It may be as simple as the base and the landing site being too far apart.

The original storyline set the date as "3000 AD", but later press material suggested the story took place "at the beginning of the twenty-first century".

As we might expect, no fan consensus exists on the dating of *The Seeds of Death*, and probably – despite *The Waters of Mars* and *Kill the Moon* bringing a lot more information to the debate – never will. The first edition of *The Making of Doctor Who* claimed the story is set in "the latter part of the twentieth century", the second was less specific and simply placed the story in the "twenty-first century". The first two editions of *The Programme Guide* set the story "c2000", *The Terrestrial Index* alters this to "c2090", and the novel *Lucifer Rising* concurs with this date (p171). *DWM* writer Richard Landen suggested "2092".

Whoniverse (BBC, p190) says that the Moonbase (*The Moonbase*) was renovated to accommodate the T-Mat system, meaning *The Seeds of Death* happens sometime after 2070. The same book stresses, though, that the "exact dates" of this "are unknown". *Timelink* says "2096, February", conceding "this is a difficult story to date". *Encyclopedia of the Worlds of Doctor Who* set the story in "the twenty-second century". Ben Aaronovitch's *Transit* follows on from *The Seeds of Death*, with his "Future History Continuity" setting the television story "c2086"; *About Time* conforms to that.

The global teleportation system lead to disastrous UN aid decisions.[95] At some point, an intellectual copyright battle erupted between T-Mat and iTeleport.[96]

The Conquest of the Solar System

Space travel was readopted and co-ordinated by International Space Command in Geneva. Ion jet rockets explored the solar system.[97]

Ed Gold became a US citizen in 2040 so that he could join NASA's astronaut program. The same year saw unprecedented storms; Andrew Stone's Iowa commune developed new farming techniques to cope.[98]

Temperatures in Britain were three degrees higher than they were in the Middle Ages, pollution levels were much higher and every oak tree and silver birch tree had now died out.[99] Many scientists were involved in the efforts to develop artificial methods of cooling the planet.[100] As part of a team of scientists conducting experiments to that end, Alistair Gryffen almost single-handedly caused The Great Cataclysm: an event that included massive hurricanes and a sudden, massive rise in sea levels.[101]

Around 2040, Alistair Gryffen's family – his wife Eleanor and children Mina and Jacob – went for a walk without him while on holiday, and disappeared. He

94 WHATEVER HAPPENED TO TRAVEL-MAT?: While we're told space travel will be readopted at the end of *The Seeds of Death*, no-one says they'll abandon T-Mat. As T-Mat is an astonishingly useful technology – one that's quickly been adopted by most countries, if not all – it seems odd that we never see it again. It's not just absent from the twenty-first century either – it's missing from every story set on a future Earth (with one exception: *The Year of Intelligent Tigers*, set circa 2185, which suggests that large spaceships use it). Service might be disrupted by the moon hatching and being re-laid (*Kill the Moon*) or the Dalek Invasion, but you'd think they'd have it working again for, say, *Frontier in Space*. Also, we know from *The Moonbase* [2070] that the possibility of the moon re-hatching isn't such a concern as to rule out installing a Gravitron there – a new T-Mat base should be equally feasible.

The obvious explanation is that Earth can afford a space programme or a T-Mat programme, but not both. This is implicit in *The Seeds of Death*. It might not be simply a case of money so much as expertise – it's stated that a number of top rocket scientists became T-Mat ones. Logically, if you can instantaneously beam men and materials to the moon, it ought to lead to a mass colonisation of the moon – but it hasn't. Earth's priorities have changed, humankind is looking inward. *The Seeds of Death* offers a world where the technology is there for space exploration, but the political will isn't (as such, it's the most realistic prediction of the twenty-first century that *Doctor Who* writers made in the sixties).

There are other explanations, all pure speculation, and mainly economic. T-Mat is a network requiring a huge infrastructure, and must be expensive. When real-life people were presented with the choice of seven hours on a normal plane or two hours on Concorde, they ended up picking the normal plane on cost grounds. Presumably using the T-Mat isn't free, and the technology might not look so attractive if instant travel from London to New York cost ten times more than taking a plane. Alternatively, the analogy might be with trams – a system with many advantages over the cars

that replaced them, but which lost out for all sorts of reasons (mainly that it was hard for them to co-exist, and trams required governmental funding but cars made money in taxes). Even if individuals aren't picking up the T-Mat bills, someone must be. It's a centralised system, and perhaps it's an all or nothing proposition – either a worldwide network or it's useless (like, say, GPS in the present day).

Or it might be that space travel starts paying off – perhaps materials from the asteroid belt and cheap energy from space means there's suddenly an abundance of resources. Perhaps there were disasters. These could either be *Hindenburg*-style serious failures of the T-Mat system itself, or unintended consequences like T-Mat allowing a rapid spread of something undesirable – terrorists, diseases or even just migrant workers or counterfeit/grey market goods. Or, *The Wheel of Ice* establishes that one of the founders of T-Mat was prosecuted in the fallout from *The Seeds of Death*, without spelling out what this means for the technology. Ultimately, the answer might lie in an off-handed reference in *Horror of the Space Snakes* (ch10) to an intellectual copyright struggle between T-Mat and iTeleport. If iTeleport prevailed and T-Mat went under, however, there's no sign of humans of this era continuing to have teleport technology – as the name iTeleport would seem to imply – at their disposal.

Transit tackles these questions, and imagines a solar system radically transformed a generation after T-Mat. Its author, Ben Aaronovitch, dated *The Seeds of Death* to about 2085 and *Transit* to about 2109, with the T-Mat system in continuous use between them – the story is essentially *The Seeds of Death: The Next Generation*, complete with Ice Warriors. But this needn't have been a continuous process. Perhaps, once the solar system had been explored by rockets for a generation, the political will and funding re-emerged and the T-Mat network was rebuilt and expanded (just as tram networks are now being re-established in many cities).

In the future, we see stories where rockets and trans-mats *can* co-exist, but mainly as a way to beam from a spacecraft to the surface of a planet – not as mass

would never forgive himself for their loss, and the trauma of it made him agoraphobic.[102] Around 2041, Darius Pike's father arranged for a clown to provide the entertainment at his son's sixth birthday party, which gave Darius a permanent phobia.[103]

NASA undertook Project Pit Stop around 2041 – a refuelling base was set up on the moon, as a stepping stone to Mars. Adelaide Brooke met Ed Gold when they both worked on the project. Brooke became the first female Briton to land on the moon. Following this, unmanned shuttles flew to Neptune and Jupiter.

In 2042, Adelaide Brooke became the first woman to land on Mars, part of a three-person team. On her return, she campaigned to colonise Mars before the

moon. Steffi Ehrlich was studying at the Bundeswehr and Aachen University at this time.[104]

c 2043 - SINGULARITY[105] -> Led by Natalia Pushkin – a.k.a. Qel, the High Priestess of the New Consciousness – the Somnus Foundation had emerged as a quasi-religious organisation dedicated to awakening humankind's potential. The Somnus Tower had been built behind the Kremlin, employing a Bygellian style that humans wouldn't create for another six hundred years.

Qel and her colleagues proceeded with their plan to turn all of humanity into a Singularity gestalt, and snared the inhabitants of Moscow in such a network. The fifth Doctor and Turlough intervened, and consequently the

transit. But even given that, transmats are surprisingly rare in humanity's future. On television, humans use transmats in *The Mutants, The Ark in Space, The Sontaran Experiment* and *Revenge of the Cybermen* (and three of those stories use the same machine!), and transmats are mentioned in *The Twin Dilemma* (but it's alien technology). So we might not know exactly why T-Mat was abandoned, but it clearly was.

95 *The Indestructible Man* (p78).

96 *Horror of the Space Snakes* (ch10).

97 International Space Command is mentioned in *The Tenth Planet* and *Revenge of the Cybermen*, as well as *The Moonbase*, where it seems to be an agency of the World Zones Authority as seen in *The Enemy of the World* – we hear about "the General Assembly", "Atlantic Zone 6", and the head of the ISC is a "Controller" Rinberg. Ion jet rockets are mentioned in *The Seeds of Death*.

98 *The Waters of Mars*

99 *K9: The Last Oak Tree*

100 *K9: The Korven*

101 *K9: Aeolian* and *K9: The Sirens of Ceres*. The Great Cataclysm presumably happens before Gryffen becomes an agoraphobic. *The Waters of Mars* establishes that "unprecedented storms" happen in 2040, and that's a perfect fit. It's much more of a stretch to say this was one of the "disastrous decisions" caused by Travel-Mat alluded to in *The Indestructible Man*, but it's certainly possible that the atmospheric disturbances, flooding and hurricanes caused by the Great Cataclysm might have been what crippled the T-Mat system.

102 Gryffen has "not been out of the house for ten years", according to Darius in *K9: The Korven*; this was "a few years" before *K9: The Fall of the House of Gryffen*. *K9: The Last Precinct* claims Gryffen's house was a police station used by human officers until the introduction of robot CCPCs, and as that development only happened two years before that story, Gryffen must have lived in different places since becoming agoraphobic. The mystery of his family's disappearance was never solved in the series.

103 *K9: Dream-Eaters*

104 *The Waters of Mars*

105 Dating *Singularity* (BF #76) - The Doctor reads a Somnus Foundation brochure that claims the groups' brightest minds will terraform Mars "by 2090", so the story cannot occur after that date.

106 *The Waters of Mars*

107 *The Wheel of Ice* (p98). No date given. Patrick's 16-year-old daughter Phee says she "wasn't even born" when this happened.

108 Dating *The Great Space Elevator* (BF CC #3.2) - The back cover blurb only tells us it's "the future". Although the link isn't made in either story, we're told in *The Waters of Mars* that Ed Gold successfully lobbied to have a space elevator built "off the coast of Western Australia". Sumatra just about qualifies, and the weather control technology is consistent with that seen in *the Seeds of Death*.

109 Dating *The Architects of History* (BF #132) - The year is repeatedly given.

110 *The Well-Mannered War* (p204).

111 *Alien Bodies* (p9).

112 *Christmas on a Rational Planet.* "Nearly a millennium" before Roz is born (p31).

113 Dating *Hothouse* (BF BBC7 #3.2) - No year is given, but the story can be comfortably dated to the middle of the twenty-first century. It's said that white rhinos became extinct in "the wild" in "the last five years" – some are presumably still around in captivity, but all rhinos on Earth are extinct by 2051 according to *The Last Dodo*. The environment is in a bad way, and clearly headed for the sort of ecological carnage that occurs circa 2060 according to *Loups-Garoux*. Krynoids and the World Ecology Bureau were first seen in *The Seeds of Doom*. One curiosity is that an undercover Lucie Miller appears on the TV of the future as a raving member of the League of Nature while using her real name. As she was born in 1988, that should give any historian tracking her life something to think about.

114 Dating *Forty-Five*: "The Word Lord" (BF #115d) - The year is given. The "Second Cold War" presumably leads to the state of affairs seen in *Warriors of the Deep*.

Singularity didn't hold, the Somnus Tower exploded, Qel was killed and the other conspirators were catapulted back to the far-flung future. Authorities claimed the incident was a terrorist attack against the Somnus cult, one that resulted in a hallucinogenic compound being released.

The Doctor believed that dozens of nonterrestrials were operating on Earth in this period. A Russian Public Security Directorate was in service.

Tarak Ital won gold medals in sprinting and the high jump in the Havana Olympics of 2044. He angered many of his countrymen by giving up athletics for a career in medicine. Ed Gold lobbied for an Australian space programme, and this led to a space elevator being built off the coast of Western Australia.[106]

On Earth, mining companies developed proposals to harvest materials from the other planets in the Sol System. As influenced by the ArkHive amulet, Josephine Laws Patrick advocated that prospecting probes leapfrog over Jupiter and head to Saturn. The mining consortium Bootstrap Inc. found deposits of the rare mineral bernalium on the ice moon Mnemosyne, and focused its efforts there. The result was humanity's first interplanetary mining effort. Patrick's family was among the first set of Mnemosyne pioneers.[107]

c 2044 - THE GREAT SPACE ELEVATOR[108] ->

Engineers on Earth had developed super conducted carbon microtubing that solved various stress-weight problems, and had used it to construct the Space Elevator: a giant lift going from a base station in Sumatra to a Sky Station 22,500 miles above the ground. A creature that had been drifting in space for thousands of years – one that existed as a kind of electromagnetic field – invaded the Sky Station and possessed some of its crew. The second Doctor, Victoria and Jamie stopped the creature from using the station's weather-control systems to direct a massive electrical storm against the Elevator's base, which would have made the creature immensely powerful but killed millions. The Doctor grounded the creature into the Earth's crust.

The First Klein's History Erased

(=) 2044 - THE ARCHITECTS OF HISTORY[109] ->

Elizabeth Klein, having stolen the seventh Doctor's TARDIS, made enough historical alterations to bring about the Terran Galactic Reich. She attained the rank of Oberst, and oversaw the Reich's temporal affairs. The Doctor of this timeline aided the Selachians in developing time-travel, which enabled their warfleet to travel from the future and lay waste to Earth in 2044. The Reich's moonbase was also destroyed, and the casualties included Rachel Cooper, the alternate Doctor's companion.

The consciousness of the Doctor from the proper timeline supplanted that of his alternate self, and he and Klein agreed to undo Earth's devastation by using the alternate Doctor's TARDIS to erase her – i.e. the version of her who travelled back to Colditz – from history. This undid Klein's historical revisions, and retroactively erased the Galactic Reich.

Professor Otterbland of the Dubrovnik Institute of New Sciences discovered psychotronic conditioning in 2045.[110] Borneo became a ReVit Zone in 2049. The rainforests were replanted and stocked with genetically engineered plants and animals.[111] The United States fell in the mid-twenty-first century.[112]

c 2045 - HOTHOUSE[113] ->

Earth's population now stood at ten billion. The last five years had seen the extinction in the wild of the cheetah and the white rhino. Half of the Amazon rain forest was now a dust bowl. Britain had experienced drought for twenty weeks, and the government prosecuted people violating standpipe rations. In London, one hundred thousand protestors called for increased efforts to combat global warming. The previous year had seen a refugee crisis – millions had tried to flee North Africa and the Black Sea states, but borders were shut to avoid the Eurozone being overwhelmed. The St Petersburg Bio-Protection Treaty enabled the World Ecology Bureau to inspect any facility used for agricultural research.

The activist Alex Marlowe had formed the ecomilitant League of Nature, which advocated mandatory population reduction and the abolition of private capital. The group had eight hundred and nine million paid members. Marlowe constructed the Hothouse as a top-secret research facility, and – using the Krynoid cuttings stolen from the World Ecology Bureau – had hundreds of people smuggled in from outside the Eastern Eurozone and forcibly turned into Krynoids. He hoped to develop a Krynoid variant that retained a human consciousness but could exert control over nature. If successful, he envisioned a mass sterilisation that would bring Earth's population down to about one hundred million.

One of Marlowe's agents, Hazel Bright, was forced to become a Krynoid and retained enough of her identity to kill him. With Bright's help, the eighth Doctor and Lucie destroyed the Hothouse's main biodome – killing Bright and all of Marlowe's Krynoids.

2045 - FORTY-FIVE: "The Word Lord"[114] ->

During the Second Cold War, the Ranulph Fiennes Bunker was constructed in Antarctica. It was located four hundred and fifty miles from civilisation, and housed top-secret peace talks. The seventh Doctor, Ace and Hex arrived at the bunker pursued by the Word Lord, a.k.a. Nobody No

One. The engines of Nobody's CORDIS had repeated instances of "45" in the Doctor's recent adventures. Nobody failed to capture the Doctor's party and claim several bounties on them. At this time, only thirty-four people had access to UN files on the Doctor.

Andrew Stone left his commune in Iowa in 2045, and had the desire to help the world survive the effects of global warming with new farming techniques. Despite Stone's lack of formal training, Peter Bennett recruited him for the Mars colonisation programme. Steffi Ehrlich gained her degree in solid state physics in 2046. She joined the German astronaut team of the European Space Agency in 2048. Tarak Ital was working on space medicine, and developed a transdermal dimenhydrinate patch to solve the problem of space sickness. That year, the Olympics were held in Paris. Margaret Cain beat twenty-five thousand candidates to become one of four astronauts on the Russian mission Midas. She spent eighteen months training at the Yuri Gagarin cosmonaut training centre.[115]

In 2048, the police force dishonourably discharged Harry Pike after he protested the Department's decision to replace human police officers with Cybernetic Civic Pacification troops: cyborgs built from cloned humans.[116]

Genesis of the Krotons

The Krotons first evolved as a predatory, quasi-organic tellurium-based crystal (later called the "Kroton Absolute") on the planet Krosi-Apsai-Core. The Absolute generated "slaved" sub-beings capable of mimicking their prey's abilities, but didn't develop a true consciousness until human capitalists arrived to expand their territory and find mineral wealth. The humans' servo-robots proved easy to copy, and so the Absolute created millions, perhaps billions, of Krotons: semi-sentient, armoured crystalline entities that were linked through mental vibrations.[117]

2048 (end of September) - "Blood and Ice"[118] -> The Antarctic Treaty had forbidden military activity, mining and nuclear waste disposal on the icy continent, and kept Antarctica relatively unspoiled. Snowcap University, however, had been established in the remains of Snowcap Base. Oswin Clarence, one of Clara Oswald's duplicates, had arrived at the university age 18, and was now a graduate student there. The Antarctic Treaty was up for renewal, and corporations were eager to exploit the 200 billion barrels of oil estimated to lie beneath the ice.

The twelfth Doctor, Clara and Oswin learned that Vice Chancellor Patricia Audley was conducting illicit experiments on the Snowcap students, with the goal of engineering humans that could survive in Antarctic temperatures, to make the continent autonomous from corporate control. The Doctor and his friends ended Audley's operations, and remained hopeful for the Treaty's renewal.

Earth's Moon Hatches, Inspires Humanity to Look to the Stars; New Moon Egg Laid

2049 - KILL THE MOON[119] -> Humanity had abandoned all interest in going into space, and the last remaining space shuttle was a museum relic. Nuclear disarmament had been so extensive that only a hundred viable nuclear bombs remained. The President of the United States was female.

The creature gestating within the Moon neared the moment of its hatching, which increased the Moon's mass. The resultant gravity subjected Earth to the

115 *The Waters of Mars*.
116 CCPCs were introduced "two years" before *K9: The Last Precinct*.
117 *Alien Bodies*, pgs 263-264. This is the origin of the titular characters from *The Krotons*, the obvious implication being that the Krotons were pattered on the servo-robots from *The Wheel in Space*. (They *do* look roughly similar, as it happens.) The placement of the Krotons' creation in the twentieth century is nonetheless tricky – Lawrence Miles, as outlined in *About Time 2*, envisioned an earlier dating for *The Wheel in Space* (circa 2030) than this chronology, but the central question is when humans and their servo-robots could have feasibly arrived on Krosi-Apsai-Core. Humankind doesn't venture beyond the Sol System much in the twentieth century, so the Kroton homeworld should be comparatively closer to Earth than not. Either way, the Krotons undergo a startling evolution in just a few decades – by 2068, according to *Alien Bodies*, their war capabilities are fairly formidable.
118 Dating "Blood and Ice" (*DWM* #485-488) - The Doctor gives the year, in accordance with the Antarctic Treaty's historical status. It's the end of the university's "six-month summer term", which in Antarctica would equate to late September. Snowcap Base appeared in *The Tenth Planet*.
119 Dating *Kill the Moon* (X8.7) - The caption gives the year. The Doctor says that it's "2049, judging by that prototype version of the Bennett oscillator", a device named in *The Ark in Space*, and also *The Rescue* novelisation by Ian Marter.
120 *Kill the Moon*; Blinovitch was first mentioned in *Day of the Daleks*. Courtney is presumably the female US President in office during events in *Kill the Moon* (she'd be about the right age). It might be best to assume that Courtney either was born in America or has American parents, but is being raised in Britain, as the US Constitution bars non-Americans from becom-

greatest natural disaster in history, as the tides became strong enough to drown entire cities.

Captain Lundvik was chosen to pilot the last space shuttle and detonate the remaining nuclear bombs on the Moon, destroying it to save the Earth.

The twelfth Doctor arrived with Clara and Courtney Woods, and deduced that the Moon was a giant egg. Moreover, the outcome of this moment in time hadn't been determined, and so the Doctor left humanity to determine whether or not to let the moon-creature life. Clara broadcast a message to humanity...

"Hello, Earth. We have a terrible decision to make. It's an uncertain decision and we don't have a lot of time. We can kill this creature or we can let it live. We don't know what it's going to do, we don't know what's going to happen when it hatches – if it will hurt us, help us or just leave us alone. We have to decide together. This is the last time we'll be able to speak to you, but you can send us a message. If you think we should kill the creature, turn your lights off. If you think we should take the chance, let it live, leave your lights on. We'll be able to see. Goodnight, Earth."

The lights visible to the moon – those of Europe and the Americas – went dark. Clara opted to ignore the decision and terminated the countdown. The moon chick hatched, and replaced the disintegrated Moon with a new egg. Humanity saw the majesty and beauty of the moon-creature, and became moved to think about what life existed beyond its homeworld. The Doctor returned, and told Clara, Courtney and Lundvik that the course of human history had been changed:

"In the mid-twenty first century, humankind starts creeping off into the stars, spreads its way through the galaxy to the very edges of the universe. And it endures till the end of time."

The Doctor pointed Lundvik towards NASA, suggested a new space programme would imminently start, and returned Clara and Courtney home.

As an adult, Courtney Woods became President of the United States, and met a man named Blinovitch.[120] The corrosiveness of Earth's acid rain increased dramatically in the mid-twenty-first century.[121]

K9 Series 1[122]

By 2050, London was a near-police state. Cybernetic Civic Pacification troops (CCPCs) patrolled the city and surveillance cameras and drones were ubiquitous. Giant floating screens advertised products and warned potential criminals. A totalitarian government agency, the Department, handled security and also ran Dauntless prison. The Tower of London had a facility that secretly held "Fallen Angels" – aliens – and experimented with alien technology. Most aliens were peaceful, but all were indefinitely detained. Juvenile human

ing president.
121 *The Eleventh Doctor Year Three:* "Strange Loops", perhaps at odds with the weather-control systems seen in this era (*The Seeds of Death*).
122 Dating *K9* Series 1 – The stories of the *K9* TV series follow on from each other in relatively short order. No date is ever given on screen, but the prepublicity stated that the year is 2050, and that works as well as any other date. Prepublicity also stated that the titular character was K9 Mark 1, but the on-screen evidence isn't nearly so certain about this...

THE FOUR K9s: Four models of K9 appear on television, with all of them making an appearance in at least one tie-in property.

Mark 1 K9: First appears in *The Invisible Enemy*, leaves the TARDIS to stay on Gallifrey with Leela in *The Invasion of Time*, goes on missions for the Time Lords in *The Adventures of K9* book series, loyally serves Leela on Gallifrey in the *Gallifrey* audios and is destroyed in *Gallifrey II: Imperiatrix*.

Mark 2 K9: First appears (in a box) at the end of *The Invasion of Time*, and is first seen (out of box) in *The Ribos Operation*. He remains in E-Space with Romana in *Warriors' Gate*, then returns with her to Gallifrey (as seen in *Lungbarrow*), and so becomes embroiled in the planet's ambiguous fate. He secretly survives the first destruction of Gallifrey (in *The Ancestor Cell*) and rejoins the eighth Doctor (as revealed in *The Gallifrey Chronicles*), but he's also present on the Gallifrey seen in the Big Finish audios. At the end of Gallifrey Series 4, he's left stranded in the Axis.

These two K9s first meet in *Lungbarrow*. There is some uncertainty as to which of these two K9s ends up starring in the *K9* TV series. The prepublicity for the show stated that it was the Mark 1 model. But in the first episode, *K9: Regeneration*, when an old model K9 is destroyed and regenerates into a new form, his reboot menu gives him the options "Mark 1" and "Mark 2"... and he clearly selects "Mark 2". So, either this is (as stated) the Mark 2 version, or it might be the Mark1 K9 taking an opportunity to upgrade his software. In either event, and somewhat unhelpfully, this K9 has lost its memory. As K9 Mark 1 is apparently destroyed in *Imperiatrix*, and without any other evidence to go on, the *K9* TV series would seem to feature the Mark 2 model – a survivor of the Last Great Time War.

criminals were held in Virtual Reality detention.[123]

People carried verometers: advanced mobile phones.[124] The currency in Britain was either the pound or the "cred".[125] Britain had a King.[126] Omnivorous bacteria had been discovered on Pluto.[127] Experiments on cyborgs were strictly regulated.[128]

The Mark II CCPC was introduced. It secretly used a variety of alien technology.[129] The Department was protected by hovering stun mines. The Jixen were winning their war with the Meron until the Korven began supplying the Meron with new energy weapons.[130]

2050 - K9: REGENERATION -> The activist Stark Reality, in reality a teenager named Starkey, stumbled across the house of the agoraphobic Professor Alistair Gryffen. He worked for the Department, mainly on the Time/Space Project, which reconstructed a device capable of creating portals in time and space. Darius Pike, age 15, was employed as Gryffen's assistant.

K9 materialised in Gryffen's house, quickly followed by four turtle-like Jixen warriors. K9 self destructed to save Gryffen and the children, but Starkey recovered K9's regeneration disc. This activated and caused K9 to reform, but his memdrive was damaged, meaning he could not account for where and when he was from...

2050 - K9: LIBERATION -> One Jixen survived, had Starkey's scent and pursued him. K9 and his friends broke into Dauntless prison and freed the aliens held captive there. A Meron was revealled to be working at the Dauntless disguised as a human. The Jixen was killed and the existence of Dauntless made public, forcing the Department to close it.

2050 - K9: THE KORVEN -> K9 assisted Starkey, who was considered a dissident and on the run, to avoid the CCPCs and their invisible Camo vehicles. A dangerous alien Korven materialised in Gryffen's house and kidnapped him, but K9 and the children tracked them down to an iceworks. The Korven had travelled back in time to absorb Gryffen's knowledge and use it to cool the Earth in preparation for an invasion in the twenty-fifth century, but K9 defeated him.

2050 - K9: THE BOUNTY HUNTER -> The technology of this era included the THX1138 self-aware oven and the experimental NX2000 spacecraft. A Mr Smith won a billion pounds playing the Lottery.

The bounty hunter Ahab arrived from the year 50,000, and attempted to apprehend K9 for the assassination of the diplomat Zanthus Pia. K9 had been framed – Ahab and the Jixen were the true culprits. Ahab escaped to exactly the same spot in his own time... but the Earth had moved by then, and Ahab was left adrift in space.

2050 (Sunday) - K9: SIRENS OF CERES -> After witnessing police brutality, the rebellious teenager Jorjie Turner threw a stone at a CCPC. She was sent as punishment to Magdalen Academy, where pupils wearing strange bracelets were unusually conformist. K9 learned that the bracelets contained Cerilium, a material that notoriously caused civilisation on Ceres to collapse after destroying its inhabitants' free will. He also exposed the Department's use of the material at the Academy.

Mark 3 K9: First appears in *K9 and Company: A Girl's Best Friend* (the 1981 pilot for a *K9* show that didn't get made). This K9 belongs to Sarah Jane Smith, and they subsequently have a series of adventures as outlined in the *K9 Annual* (not covered in this chronology); he briefly appears in *The Five Doctors*; he's seen in the comic strip "City of Devils" (*DWM Holiday Special 1992*); in 1996 he's still working with Sarah Jane (*Interference*), but after this time he falls into disrepair (loosely in accord with the short story "Moving On" from *Decalog 3*); his non-functional form is stolen by Hilda Winters (*SJS: Mirror, Signal. Manoeuvre*) in 2002, but possibly recovered following her death in 2005; he's repaired by the Doctor and is apparently destroyed in *School Reunion*. For those who wish to count such things as canon, it's possible that he regenerates and appears again in the *Make Your Own Adventure* book *The Search for the Doctor*.

Mark 4 K9: First appears at the end of *School Reunion*, is sidelined shortly afterwards to tend to a black hole (*SJA: Invasion of the Bane*) and is then released from

that duty, joining Sarah Jane on Earth (*SJA: The Mad Woman in the Attic*). In his last TV appearance to date, *SJA: Goodbye, Sarah Jane Smith*, he's living with Luke Smith while Luke studies at Oxford.

123 The general background to the *K9* television series, as given in *K9: Regeneration*.

124 *K9: The Korven*

125 It's pounds in *K9: The Bounty Hunter*, the cred in *K9: Oroborus*, *K9: Black Hunger*, *K9: The Custodians* and *K9: Mutant Copper*.

126 *K9: Oroborus*, *K9: Robot Gladiators*.

127 *K9: Black Hunger*

128 *K9: Mutant Copper*

129 The Mark II CCPCs have been in operation "six months" before *K9: The Last Precinct*.

130 *K9: Hound of the Korven*

131 *K9: Aeolian* establishes that Earth's population in the *K9* series is "six billion", which is lower than it is in 2010 (in both real life and the *Doctor Who* universe), and this might suggest there has been a catastrophic lost of life – possibly owing to the "Great Catastrophe"

2050 - K9: FEAR ITSELF -> Widespread riots spread across the world, putting everyone on edge. The source was an alien living in a wardrobe, but K9 isolated the alien before Drake – an agent of the Department – detonated a bomb, destroying it.

2050 - K9: THE FALL OF THE HOUSE OF GRYFFEN -> The "biggest electrical event for decades", a huge storm, affected London. This disrupted the Space-Time Manipulator installed at Gryffen's house and released the Sporax, a creature that generated fear. It created ectomorphic replicas of Gryffen's lost family, but K9 and his friends banished them.

2050 - K9: JAWS OF ORTHRUS -> K9 was caught on a coast-to-coast vidcast attempting to assassinate Drake – all part of Drake's Project Orthus. The truth was revealed: the K9 that shot Drake was actually a duplicate, intended to frame the real K9 and have him taken into custody to be disassembled.

The Department was on the verge of introducing tracker chips for people.

2050 - K9: DREAM-EATERS -> London was bombarded with psychic energy that induced sleep and gave people nightmares. Terrifying creatures from Celtic myth, the Bodachs, had been disturbed by the Department's unearthing of an obelisk containing the Eyes of Oblivion – crystals that the Bodachs planned to use to send the world to sleep. The Bodachs were using Jorjie's mother June as an avatar, but Jorjie broke their control by convincing her mother she got a tattoo. K9 destroyed the obelisk.

2050 - K9: THE CURSE OF ANUBIS -> A pyramid-like spacecraft approached Earth. Drake ordered its destruction, but the ship vanished before the missiles hit, and reappeared over London close to K9 and his friends. Jackal-headed aliens, the Anubians, arrived and knelt before "the mighty K9, the great liberator": the being that freed them from the domination of the Huducts. The Anubians took over Gryffen's house, and used Torcs to control the minds of everyone present. K9 learned that the Anubians had used the Huduct mind-control technology to conquer other races that apparently included the Alpha Centaurians, Mandrels, Sea Devils, Aeolians and Jixen. K9 and Darius broke the conditioning, and the Anubians left.

2050 - K9: OROBORUS -> Gryffen's Space-Time Manipulator activated, seemingly by itself. K9, Gryffen and the others began to encounter time loops and reversals. Starkey's arm itched, and a scan revealed his body was producing alien antibodies. Gryffen revealed that Starkey's parents had experimented on him, and endowed him with an alien immune system. Despite events happening out of sequence, or twice, or not at all, K9 and his allies tracked the source of the time shifts to a snake creature: the time-consuming Oroborus. They lured the Oroborus back into the Space-Time Manipulator, and banished it.

2050 - K9: ALIEN AVATAR -> The Department interrogated some aliens, the Medes, who could project avatars of themselves. Drake was keen to acquire their molecular refractor technology, but his researchers were dumping an alien toxin – chenium – that was a by-product of Qualon 37, as used by the Medes in interdimensional technology, into the Thames. K9 detected the pollutant while he and Starkey were fishing, and later helped to free the Medes, who departed.

2050 - K9: AEOLIAN -> A huge hurricane swept across the UK and North Sea, disrupting communications. The event was centred on Holy Cross Cathedral. Tornadoes destroyed the Royal Albert Hall and Hyde Park. Drake arrested Gryffen, as Gryffen had created conditions similar to this when one of his experiments went wrong and caused the Great Cataclysm. K9 identified the disruption as indicative of the Aeolians, masters of amplification long thought wiped out. The culprit was the last of the Aeolians, left without memories following the destruction of her race – the music was a desperate mating call. Gryffen detected a mating call from another Aeolian in the Orpheus Constellation, and the two Aeolians were brought together and then left Earth, which restored the weather to normal.

Earth's population at this time was six billion.[131]

2050 - K9: THE LAST OAK TREE -> K9, Jorjie and Starkey met Robin Hood in a virtual reality Sherwood Forest exhibition, the centrepiece of which was the last oak tree: the Major Oak of the Robin Hood legend. An alien jamming signal disrupted the exhibit, and the Major Oak was stolen. K9 found traces of an alien substance and tracked down a Centuripede, which was using the oak to build a pod to transport her eggs. The Centuripede became a butterfly and her babies hatched. She gave Starkey three acorns as a reward for saving them from the Department.

2050 - K9: BLACK HUNGER -> The Department created the Black Hunger: an all-consuming bacteria swarm made from a combination of yeast and microbes from Pluto. The Hunger was made to alleviate London's rubbish problem, but it mutated into flesh-eaters and swarmed through the sewers. This would have destroyed all life on Earth in a week, but K9 contained the Hunger, and planned to take the swarm to Atrios. The leader of the Department, Lomax, decided that Drake had disobeyed orders too many times and replaced him with Thorne, the former governor of the Dauntless.

2050 - K9: THE CAMBRIDGE SPY -> Jorjie learned as part of a school assignment that Gryffen's mansion was a police station in 1963, the centre of an investigation into a spy ring. The Space-Time Manipulator whisked her back to that year. Darius was briefly erased from history, but Starkey and K9 went to 1963 and recovered Jorjie, repairing the timelines.

2050 - K9: LOST LIBRARY OF UKKO -> The Department held an Open Day to look for new recruits, much to K9's curiosity. Starkey attended and was sucked into a mysterious picture. K9 identified this as a library card from Ukko; Thorne had been planning to use it to exile criminals. Starkey was trapped on a barren world, Urlic, which had been compressed into a hologram by the Ukkans, an all-female race of archivists. An Ukkan, Yssaringintinka, arrived and retrieved Starkey.

The major world powers currently included the United Kingdom, the Americas and the Pacific Union.

2050 - K9: MUTANT COPPER -> The CCPCs were given sweeping new powers, including the ability to enter homes without warrants. K9 and the others come across a "mutant" CCPC whose connection to the Department had been broken, and who had human DNA. They named him Birdie, because he was fascinated with birds. Birdie gradually became more human, and learned new skills such as how to make toast. K9 and his friends smuggled Birdie away from London to the countryside, where he enjoyed seeing the birds.

2050 - K9: THE CUSTODIANS -> Jorjie and Darius played the new VR game *Little Green Men*, even as the city outside was in chaos, and emergency services were

overwhelmed. The headsets for the game were alien in origin, and twenty million children had been simultaneously affected by it. Greenroom Entertainment had allied with the last of the Etydions – they were the most powerful telepaths who ever lived, and had hired themselves out to psionically repel invading forces with waves of fear, but were wiped out by their enemies. Greenroom intended that the Etydion would create a telepathic network that would pacify youngsters into being good children, but the Etydion secretly planned to transform the children into members of its own race. The Etydion died when June's emotions for Jorjie's safety overloaded it.

2050 - K9: TAPHONY AND THE TIME LOOP -> Gryffen helped to free Taphony, a girl trapped in a VR created by the Department. She was a Time Blank, an entity that didn't follow the normal rules of time and could disintegrate everything she touched. She had been created within the Department by use of alien technology, but became vengeful upon learning that Gryffen was partly responsible for said experiment. Starkey, Jorjie and Darius befriended Taphony, and persuaded her to leave for a realm better suited to her.

2050 - K9: ROBOT GLADIATORS -> Freddie Maxwell ran Destructertainment, which put on robot gladiator shows. Darius pretended to trick K9 into becoming part of Maxwell's stable of robots – all part of a plan to end Maxwell's illegal scam. Thorne colluded with Maxwell to develop combat robots such as the Pain-Maker, with the ultimate aim of acquiring K9's regenerative technology. The Pain-Maker was packed with enough solarmite explosive to destroy everything in the arena apart from K9's regeneration unit, and when K9 refused to fight, Thorne had the Pain-Maker self-destruct. The blast wasn't enough to damage K9. Maxwell's business was shut down, leaving Gryffen, K9 and the kids to wonder how Thorne knew that K9 could regenerate...

---

described in the *K9* show or some other event.

132 The episode is a clip show, with very little new material.

133 *Iris* S2: *The Claws of Santa* outright states that the ice cap melted. *Hothouse* shows that global warming has become a major political issue, and *K9: Sirens of Ceres* says that many top scientists have been assigned to find a solution. It's very tempting to see the Gravitron from *The Moonbase*, a global weather control system set up in 2050, as a potential solution to the environmental collapse the planet is suffering from in other

stories set around that time.

134 Dating *The Time of the Daleks* (BF #32) - It is "the mid twenty-first century".

135 "Twenty years" before *The Moonbase*.

136 *Deceit* (p27, p153). It was possibly based on Silurian technology, as the Silurians establish a Gravitron on the moon (in an alternate history) in *Blood Heat* (p196).

137 *The Last Dodo*

2050 - K9: MIND SNAP[132] -> K9 activated the Space-Time Manipulator, hoping that some siphoned temporal power would help restore his memories. Instead, it adversely affected his mind, making him confused and aggressive. Gryffen restored his memories by having K9 remember his previous adventures.

2050 - K9: ANGEL OF THE NORTH -> K9 deduced the co-ordinates of a Fallen Angel – the ship from which the Space-Time Manipulator was recovered – in Canada. Gryffen thought the ship might contain the device's missing temporal stabiliser, but was unable to conquer his agoraphobia, and so travelled to Canada in a VR encasement suit. K9 and the kids used the Manipulator to teleport to the alien ship, where they encountered a Korven – one of over a hundred in the area. The Korven were the most dangerous race K9 had ever encountered, and the Manipulator had been made from their technology. Gryffen vowed to never use the temporal stabiliser upon deducing that K9's enhancement code was somehow part of it.

2050 - K9: THE LAST PRECINCT -> A group called The Last Precinct staged a spate of attacks on CCPCs. Fake CCPCs came to Gryffen's house and immobilised K9 – these were actually humans, all of them all ex-policemen made obsolete by the CCPCs. Darius' father, Harry Pike, was among their number. They planed to infect the CCPCs with a virus, but it proved unstable, and caused the CCPCs to go on a rampage. K9 deactivated the CCPCs, and the Last Precinct members were rounded up and arrested.

2050 - K9: HOUND OF THE KORVEN -> Thorne showed Darius that his father was cracking up in his solitary confinement VR prison, and demanded that he fetch him K9's regeneration unit. He also revealled he had K9's memory disc and offered a swap. Thorne and K9 traded the components – but K9's memory disc had been implanted with a self-destruct code that would activate if he got within range of an unknown location. A Jixen kidnapped Gryffen, and explained that the Jixen were a friendly, peaceful race marauded by the Meron, who were allied with the Korven. K9 and his allies realised that someone at the Department was working for the Korven. Although K9 rerouted the self-destruct orders on his memory disc, Thorne still had his regeneration unit.

2050 - K9: THE ECLIPSE OF THE KORVEN -> The Space-Time Manipulator observed a white hole and a black hole coming together – if they touched, Earth would be destroyed. K9 discovered that the Department also had a Space-Time Manipulator at their Millennium Dome base. Thorne's army of CCPCs surrounded K9, and Thorne explained that an alien army was massing on the other side of the galaxy, ready to invade Earth via a temporal portal. The Department had engineered Trojan – a supersoldier built from the DNA of every alien species they had encountered – and fitted it with K9's regeneration unit. Throne was working with the invaders, and had engineered the white hole and black hole to come together, knowing it would force Gryffen to use the temporal stabiliser to widen the portal. Thorne was actually as a Meron, while the head of the Department, Lomax, was a Korven.

The spearhead of the Korven invasion force arrived through the portal, but Gryffen conquered his agoraphobia and closed the portal using his personal voice command: "Omega, Sigma, Theta, Ohm". Lomax and the Korven were sucked into the portal and destroyed. K9 fought Trojan, and got its Jixen and Meron imperatives to destroy each other. Thorne was crushed to death when Trojan toppled on him. The more evil elements of the Department had been eliminated.

The polar ice cap melted in the twenty-first century.[133]

c 2050 - THE TIME OF THE DALEKS[134] -> The Daleks attempted to exploit a temporal rift to enhance their time travel capabilities, but the experiment backfired and they almost lost their entire fleet. They made contact with Mariah Learman, the ruler of New Britain, who had a primitive time scanner. Learman didn't believe the population appreciated Shakespeare, and the price for her co-operation with the Daleks was that they would assassinate Shakespeare as a youth and preserve the only copy of his works for Learman's benefit. Rebels thwarted this plan by smuggling an eight-year-old Shakespeare from 1572 for his own protection, but this caused further time distortion. The eighth Doctor arrived, trying to explain why his companion Charley didn't know of Shakespeare. The Doctor set history back on course by returning young Shakespeare to his rightful time. The Daleks were trapped in an endless temporal loop after mutating Learman into one of them.

It now took only a couple of hours for a shuttle rocket to travel from the Earth to the new moonbases. Around 2050, the ultimate form of weather control, the Gravitron, was built on the moon's surface. The political implications on Earth proved complex, and the General Assembly spent more than twenty years negotiating between farmers and landowners.[135] The Butler Institute built the Gravitron.[136] Rhinos were extinct on Earth by 2051.[137]

By the mid-twenty-first century, the reach of online ordering meant that brick and mortar stores in the High Street and Pease Pottage consisted only of one hundred and seventy three different coffee shops.[138]

Harnessing gravity waves allowed artificial gravity to be installed on spacecraft and space stations. Permanent space stations were built. Flowers were cultivated on the surface of Venus. The first Doctor visited this timezone.[139]

Victorian time traveller Penelope Gate and her companion Joel Mintz accidentally visited the middle of the twenty-first century.[140]

Around the middle of the century, domesticated wolves were reintroduced into the forests of Northern Europe. It was rumoured that the Wicca Society had released wild wolves, and there was some debate as to which strain would become dominant.[141]

In 2050, after two years of training, Steffi Ehrlich formed part of the tenth German moon mission. The following year, she married Hans Stott. Roman Groom had degrees in English and Physics, and was beginning postdoctoral work in astrophysics. He was only 17, but was accepted into NASA's Search for Astronauts programme in January 2051, and began two years' training. In April 2051, Margaret Cain became only the second female Briton to land on the moon. As part of that effort, she met Adelaide Brooke.

Mia Bennett had her thesis on Martian geology published. She had managed to grow green beans and turnips from samples of Martian soil.[142]

2050 (28th September) - THE KING OF TERROR[143]

-> Eighty years after the events occurred, some early UNIT files were officially released. The records included details on Cybermen, the Autons, the fall of General Carrington and the Stahlman incident.

Reporter Daniel Clompus, writing for the *Guardian*, visited the elderly Brigadier General Sir Alistair Lethbridge-Stewart at the Westcliffe Retirement Home in Sussex; the Brigadier General was thought to be 121 years old, but physically looked about 75.

Lethbridge-Stewart passed away shortly afterwards. The book that Clompus wrote on UNIT, *Watch the Skies: The Not-So-Secret-History of Alien Encounters*, was published in 2051. Lethbridge-Stewart's memoirs, *The Man Who Saved the World*, were published in 2052.

The people of the ocean planet Ockora built exoskeletal battlesuits and started an uprising against their Kalarian oppressors, who hunted them for sport. These warriors renamed themselves Selachians. After defeating the Kalarians, they conquered four planets, including Kalaya and Molinar. The Selachians became arms dealers, and attacked a Martian colony with a sunstroker.[144]

Freda, an offspring of the aliens who settled in Cardiff, was born on 30th May, 2053.[145]

In 2054, the Doctor and UNISYC (led by General Tchike) defeated the Montana Republican militia, who were using Selachian weapons.[146] Sam Jones had a mid-2050s ergonomic chair in her TARDIS room.[147] The Dogworld poodles built their first space station. It received radio signals from other planets, including Earth.[148]

All the religious faiths of the world were merged with the idea of creating world harmony. This consensus was unworkable and quickly collapsed. The Chapter of St

---

138 *The Warehouse*

139 *The Wheel in Space*. The Doctor's familiarity with the Gravitron in *The Moonbase*, ion rockets in *The Seeds of Death* and Galactic Salvage and Insurance in *Nightmare of Eden* suggests he visited the solar system during this period at least once.

140 *The Room with No Doors* (p48).

141 *Transit*

142 *The Waters of Mars*

143 Dating *The King of Terror* (PDA #37) - The day that Daniel Clompus visits the Brigadier is given.

144 "Almost a century" before *The Final Sanction* (p175), although it must be a little longer than that, as the Selachians were active in the twenty-first century according to both *The Murder Game* and *Alien Bodies*.

145 *TW: Asylum*

146 *Alien Bodies* (p12).

147 *Vampire Science*

148 *Mad Dogs and Englishmen*

149 *St Anthony's Fire*

150 Dating *Gods and Monsters* (BF #164) - Year unknown, but Private Sally Morgan, born in 2000, here looks upon her older self – who has risen through the ranks and become a general – and comments, "I'm so old..." In the proper history of Earth, Nimrod never acquired Weyland's Shield, so didn't develop the Higgs-Boson killer from it.

151 *Interference* (p217). *The Indestructible Man* specifies that the UN is the force behind the ban (p13).

152 *Worlds BF: The Phantom Wreck*

153 *Scavenger*

154 "A few decades" after *Horror of the Space Snakes* (ch10).

155 *The Waters of Mars*. We're told that the crew have been "gone over two years" before November 2059, and also that it was a "two year journey" to get to Mars, so they left in late 2056/early 2057. It would only take "nine months" to get back, but the outbound trip involved taking all the supplies necessary to build the colony, time refuelling on the moon and possibly time in Martian orbit while drones built the base.

156 Dating *The Waters of Mars* (X4.16) - The historical significance of the date of the destruction of Bowie Base One means the precise day is repeated a number of times. Once again, human beings who you'd think would have been briefed by someone in the know are

Anthony was formed to fill the spiritual vacuum. When China was taken over by Hong Kong, the Yong family joined them on a new crusade to purge the heathens.[149]

(=) c 2055 - GODS AND MONSTERS[150] **->** Fenric took Sally Morgan and Lysandra Aristedes through time – hoping to turn them against his opponent, Weyland – to witness a possible future in which thousands of invading spaceships overcame humanity's tenth, eleventh and twelfth spacefleets and disintegrated Mars. Sally's older self, General Morgan, acquired a Higgs-Boson killer device – capable of obliterating matter – from the Forge's remnants. She learned the device's passcode after burning out the contemporary Lysandra's mind with a Truthsayer. Triggering the Higgs-Boson killer would result in Earth's destruction, but Morgan judged the planet as lost, and wished to spare other worlds the same fate. The general killed herself after deploying the Higgs-Boson killer against the invaders, as the younger Sally and Lysandra returned to the dawn of time...

In the mid 2050s, the world government overreacted to major wars and nuclear terrorism by passing police shoot-to-kill laws and banning all religions. There were years of total chaos, and cities became no-go areas. There was no effective government.[151] The charity Chuckle-Aid, having expanded its operations beyond the UK and into Sector 5, ended in 2056.[152] The Doctor saw Jessica Allaway best Roger Borg at Wimbledon in 2057.[153]

The Doctor teamed up with Sam Sergei – a technical genius from the Ukraine, and whom he had met at the World State moonbase – to help solve the Oil Apocalypse.[154]

The shuttle *Apollo 34* taking the first colonists to Mars set off around 2057. The first Martian colony was established on 1st July, 2058. This was Bowie Base One, built by robot drones on top of the underground glacier in Gusev Crater, and as supervised by nine human astronauts. Their mission was to discover whether the planet could be made suitable for human beings. The crew of Bowie Base One had dehydrated protein for their Christmas Dinner in 2058. Susie Fontana Brooke, granddaughter of mission commander Adelaide Brooke, was born after the crew left Earth. The base was partly constructed using a steel combination manufactured in Liverpool.[155]

The Bowie Base One Incident

2059 (21st November) - THE WATERS OF MARS[156]
-> The tenth Doctor arrived at Bowie Base One, the very first Martian colony, and realised he had arrived on the day it was doomed to be destroyed. History recorded that all the colonists were killed in a mysterious explosion. This would have an inspirational effect on humanity, spurring them to explore space. The Doctor theorised that base commander Adelaide Brooke's death was a "fixed" moment in time that was crucial to the future of humanity, and as such he was powerless to intervene.

The colonists had tapped the underground glacier in Gusev Crater for water, and in doing so had woken the Flood – an ancient lifeform that lived in liquid water, and could transform host creatures with water in their bodies. As more of the colonists were affected, Brooke initiated Action Procedure Five: the destruction of the base via a nuclear device in its central dome.

(=) Brooke and all of her fellow colonists – Ed Gold, Tarak Ital, Andy Stone, Margaret Cain, Mia Bennett, Yuri Kerenski, Steffi Ehrlich and Roman Groom – were killed. Humanity mourned their loss, not knowing the cause of the tragedy.

The Doctor decided to change history and save the remaining colonists – as the last of the Time Lords, he believed that he alone could command the Laws of Time. Ed Gold sacrificed himself to prevent the Flood from capturing the base's shuttle; Ital, Stone, Cain, Ehrlich and Groom died as Action Protocol Five obliterated the base. The Doctor took Brooke, Bennett and Kerenski back to Brooke's home on Earth. Brooke was so horrified by the Doctor's arrogance, power and unaccountability that she killed herself in her house. Bennett and Kerenski, as the only survivors, credited Brooke with having saved Earth from the Flood, guaranteeing her reputation in future. Media accounts mentioned how "The Mythical Doctor" had saved Bennett and Kerenski.

Brooke's suicide made the Doctor acknowledge to himself that he had gone too far. He briefly saw a vision of Ood Sigma, and, worried that it was an omen of his death, departed in the TARDIS.

At this time, robots were commonplace, from small repairmen controlled by autogloves to giant construction drones. Other technology included atom clamps, medpacks and Hardinger Seals that hermetically sealed rooms. On Earth, people still drove cars, paying for them with credit stamps. Gay marriage was legal in Dagestan. Solar flares sometimes disrupted communications between Earth and Mars. Politically, the Earth consisted of the World State (including at least the USA, UK, Germany and Russia) and the independents (which might have included Spain and Philippines). There had been multiple stories of the Philippines building a rocket, and they were the leading contenders for a rival mission to Mars. The Spanish had been keeping their Spacelink Project under wraps. The

Branson Inheritance had been talking about a Mars shot for years.

(=) 2059 - SJA: THE MAD WOMAN IN THE ATTIC[157] **->** A boy called Adam visited an ancient Rani Chandra in the attic of her home, Sarah Jane Smith's former abode at 13 Bannerman Road. Rani had been living here alone for so many years, she had become something of a local legend. Adam was the son of Eve, an alien Rani had befriended when she was a teenager. Adam changed history so that Rani was never alone.

Rani lived at 13 Bannerman Road, and had at least one son and at least two grandsons. She had just returned from a visit to Washington with Luke, where they caught up with Maria.

2059 - THE PURSUIT OF HISTORY[158] **->** On Earth, the Oceanic States were in conflict with the Asiatic States. The Conglomerate CEO, Cuthbert, negotiated with the finance minister for the Oceanic States – in exchange for tritonium, a substance that would revolutionise artificial intelligence and AI systems, the Oceanic States made the Conglomerate the sole provider of their tech solutions. Cuthbert time-jumped ahead some years, and the fourth Doctor and K9 pursued him.

The collapse of the Amazon's ecosystem made the "Lung of the World" into a dust bowl stretching from Rio de Janiero to the Andes, displacing a number of werewolves and Amazon Indian tribes. A constant risk of global war existed until the Earth's governments turned their attention to the moon and asteroid belt for resources.[159]

When the Belt was first prospected, an accident caused a prospector ship to abandon a cargo pod there. The gravity of one of the larger rocks attracted it.[160]

Zoe Heriot

Zoe Heriot, a companion of the second Doctor, was born.[161] She grew up on a space station.[162] Zoe was taken from her parents when she was very young.[163] The best and brightest of Earth's children, including Zoe, were given over to the Company's Elite Programme at a young age. The Elite Programme erased the children's memories of their families – Zoe became unable to remember her mother – and performed other techniques so alarming, the Company could have toppled if the truth became known. The children learned self-defence techniques.[164]

Zoe studied at the Paris Psychology Unit, and won the Speed Calculus Cup from Girdle House. The Psychology Unit's students were said to have "All brains, no heart". Zoe's brain was highly compartmentalised, effectively "half-machine".[165]

---

totally unaware of the Ice Warriors. There's no evidence that the computer or robots on Bowie Base One have artificial intelligence.
157 Dating *SJA: The Mad Woman in the Attic* (SJA 3.2) - The date is given in a caption and reiterated by Adam. While no link is made in any of the stories, we might infer some and come to interesting conclusions. Luke may have inherited the house on Sarah Jane's death (in 2040, according to a possible future seen in *Interference*). This is set after the *K9* series, so we can infer the teenagers from *The Sarah Jane Adventures* were in their fifties and in London during those events. We don't know the fate of K9 Mk IV, but it's entirely possible there are at least two versions of K9 around in Britain in 2059 – the Mk I or II model from the *K9* series, and the Mk IV from *The Sarah Jane Adventures*.
158 Dating *The Pursuit of History* (BF 4th Doc #5.7) - The year is given.
159 "About twenty years" before *Loups-Garoux*.
160 *Graceless IV: The Ward*
161 Extrapolating from *Ahistory*'s dating of *The Wheel in Space* to 2079, and assuming from the Brigadier's claim that Zoe is, in fact, "19" in *The Invasion*. Wendy Padbury, born 7th December, 1947, was 21 when she started playing Zoe.
162 *Second Chances*
163 *The Wreck of the World*

164 *The Memory Cheats*. Mention of the Company's self-defence techniques presumably explains how Zoe can flip the Karkus about the place in *The Mind Robber*.
165 *Last of the Cybermen*. Leo Ryan teases Zoe with the "all brains, no heart" line in *The Wheel in Space*.
166 *The Apocalypse Mirror*
167 Dating *The Wheel of Ice* (PDA #77) - No year named. Humanity is expanding into the solar system, but hasn't made the jump to interstellar travel. (The Doctor: "This is only the beginning. Even in this age humans are definitely on their way, leapfrogging across space with their clever little eyes already fixed on the stars", p39.) The Mnemosyne operation is cited as humanity's first interplanetary mining operation; the Doctor says its children are "some of the first... to have been born away from the mother world" (p56).
The story continually evokes the second Doctor TV stories set in the twenty-first century (and, by extension, *The Tenth Planet*) and decisively positions itself between *The Seeds of Death* and *The Wheel in Space*. Florian Hart "grew up" (p172) watching her father's downfall in the aftermath of the Ice Warrior gambit with T-Mat, but is now high enough in Bootstrap Inc.'s ranks that she's been administrating its first interplanetary operation, suggesting at least a generation has passed since *The Seeds of Death*. Conversely, it's before Zoe's native time of "the latter half of the twenty-first

Flooding large enough to encompass the globe was predicted in Zoe's era, but didn't come to pass.[166]

c 2060 - THE WHEEL OF ICE[167] -> Earth now had outposts on other planets and moons, and in deep space. The Bootstrap, Inc. mining colony built around Mnemosyne – a moon of Saturn, and the centre of the Mnemosyne Cincture, a.k.a. the Wheel of Ice – had a society in which workers were given parapsychological-socioeconomic classification, and ranked according to single letters: A, B and C. The colony's inner council included representatives chosen by International Space Command in Geneva and the Planetary Ethics Commission. The colony sought to mine bernalium, a highly conductive metal wanted for the next generation of ventures into space. Titan was home to a methane extraction plant, as well as a form of marine-like life called T-sharks.

The ArkHive attempted to "restore" its dead creators by generating bio-chemical Blue Dolls roughly based on human form. It also made a second attempt to build a time machine, which triggered a Relative Continuum Displacement Zone that derailed the TARDIS. The second Doctor, Jamie and Zoe stopped ArkHive from causing an explosion that would have annihilated the Sol System, and also prevented the colony's administrator, Florian Hart, from blowing up the ArkHive to better harvest bernalium.

The Mnemosyne Cincture's inner council declared independence from Bootstrap, and agreed to grant the ArkHive official status. The sterile Blue Dolls were expected to die off in a generation. To ease ArkHive's mind, the Doctor asked the Malenfant-IntelligeX Modular Autonomous Component (MMAC) to spend some decades or centuries mining a bit of taranium on Uranus, then use it to send a message back through time to the ArkHive's creators.

International Space Command had full access to UNIT's records, which surged with evidence of alien incursions dating back centuries. The Suncatcher was considered antiquated technology. In future, Saturn's clouds would be home to flower gardens.

2060 - DEATH AMONG THE STARS[168] -> The twelfth Doctor estimated Earth's current population as nine billion. The Zeus V rocket had been retired.

As backed by New Frontiers Collective, the *Davy Crockett* was launched to establish humanity's first off-world colony on Europa, a moon of Jupiter. The live feed from a Europa rover suddenly included a woman, Amber Lewis, raving about terrible monsters... which doubly surprised Lewis's co-workers at Kennedy Space Center, as she was present and casually chatting with the twelfth Doctor, whom she'd just met.

The Doctor took Lewis back two hours in the TARDIS. On Europa, they found that the remnant of an alien expedition – an insane simulacrum of an "alien abduction" celebrity, Morton Beck – was plotting to destroy the *Davy Crockett* with fusion bombs. The travellers convinced the faux Beck of his artificial nature, and to self-destruct his alien base. Lewis enacted the "beware the monsters!" transmission as history demanded, whereupon the Doctor sent a second message to Earth authorities – with whom he had good standing – telling them to ignore it. He hoped Lewis would do something useful with her newfound celebrity.

---

century" (pgs. 4, 6, 36, 38), but not so far in advance that she – or her eidetic memory – is unacquainted with this era's space laws (p46).

The trick is matching that paradigm up with the generations of Laws women who have owned the ArkHive amulet that's been influencing humankind's interest in Saturn. We're told that Jo Laws received the item in 1890 (p87), and gave it to her daughter Josephine Laws in 1930 (p91). Assuming a similar forty-year interval for the generations to come, Joss Laws gets the amulet circa 1970 (p91-95), Josephine Laws Patrick has it circa 2010, and Phee Laws (currently 16, so just recently given the item) is given it circa 2050... which was perhaps writer Steven Baxter's intention for where *The Wheel of Ice* takes place, but that's much too early for a whole generation to have passed since *The Seeds of Death*. With the story not giving hard dates for any of the Laws women beyond 1930, it seems best to assume that the intervals between the generations get longer with time, and to split the difference between *Ahistory*'s current placement for *The Seeds of Death* [c.2040] and *The Wheel in Space* [2079].

References to *The Wheel in Space* include the Pull Back to Earth faction, bernalium (used to power the Wheel's X-ray laser), and a Mark II-A Phoenix-class freighter (*The Silver Carrier* was a Mark IV Phoenix). International Space Command was mentioned in *The Tenth Planet* [1986] and *The Moonbase* [2070]. Demeter rockets (*The Tenth Planet*) are referred to as "missiles from another century" (p241) and "century-old ICBMs" (p265). The "suncatcher system" (Salamander's design from *The Enemy of the World* [2018] is now "discredited old technology back on Earth", p31). Saturn is said to have "sixty" moons (p255); as of 2014, sixty two have formally been identified with confirmed orbits (but only fifty three have been named).

MMAC receives a letter dated "fifteenth of June" (p305), but it was misplaced for a time, so is of limited use in determining the time of year. The Doctor's mention of "a solar stack" and "a suncatcher system" in the same breath (p31) might suggest a connection between the technology respectively in use in *The Ark in Space* and *The Enemy of the World*.

168 Dating *Death Among the Stars* (BBC *DW* audiobook #30) – The year is given. It's after "all that business with the moon" (*Kill the Moon* [2049]). A scientist has been in

Commanded by Captain Lambert, the *Davy Crocket* landed on Europa with 319 passengers and crew. Eventually, Europa would become home to underground cities and resorts, as well as travel in mini-submarines.

The planet Flissta became uninhabitable due to a stellar cataclysm. The Doctor was on board the medical frigate *Talaha*, with some of the surviving Flisk, when a rift opened as the ship crossed the Opius Expanse.[169]

Earth sent out colony ships in the late twenty-first century to Mars, Venus and a "weird little planet" that was later determined to be a moon, but never left Earth's solar system for the first fifty years of this mode of travel. One colony ship ended up five systems away, possibly after falling through a wormhole or temporal eddy created by the Tef'Aree. The colonists were given terraforming technology that they used to "reboot" the planet's ecology. Only those within the shielded Colony One Base survived the process.[170] A complete systems failure aboard a colony ship from Earth killed everyone in stasis. Centuries on, the foxes in the habitat areas evolved into the Foxkind, cloned the humans and activated the ship's matter seed, creating a massive space station: the Twist.[171]

New governments started to form by the 2060s. Octogenarian Samantha Jones might have been a major player in these events. Before this point, her father had died, shortly after the last King of England abdicated.[172]

> (=) During a period of extreme instability, Karen Coltraine established an oppressive right-wing regime in Europe, and put Earth's expansion into space on a more aggressive footing. The Gallifreyan CIA prevented this future from occurring.[173]

In the 2060s, the Bantu Independence Group received new funding from energy tycoon Olle Ahlin, and directed its efforts to central Africa and Scandinavia. In the decades to come, Bantu would look to aiding colonies on other worlds.[174] Cricket was an Olympic sport in time for the Barcelona Olympics of 2060.[175] The eleventh Doctor, Amy and Rory photographed a lake that occupied the space where Swallow Woods had stood.[176]

2062 - THE LAST DODO[177] -> Chinese Three-Striped Box Turtles were now extinct on Earth. The Museum of the Lost Ones had a single specimen of each extinct species in

---

the news "a lot lately", commenting upon the Bowie Base One disaster (*The Waters of Mars* [2059]). A Zeus IV rocket appeared in *The Tenth Planet*. Vulcan might alternatively count as humanity's first off-world colony, depending on its actual location and when one dates *The Power of the Daleks*.

169 "Nearly forty years" before *Snowglobe 7*.

170 "Final Sacrifice". The "weird little planet" could be a reference to Vulcan from *The Power of the Daleks*. The Doctor finds the lost colony circa 21906.

171 An unknown amount of "generations" before *The Twelfth Doctor Year Two*: "The Twist". The evolutionary cycle of the Foxkind makes little sense, as they go – without any external factor that we're told about – from being normal foxes to upright intelligent ones in less than two thousand years at most. Even the Cat on *Red Dwarf* required millions of years to develop, and with benefit of a radiation leak.

172 *Interference* (p217).

173 *Human Resources*. No date is given, but it has to be at a point in the twenty-first century with both political instability and a human space programme. Karen is apparently the same age as Lucie (late teens) in 2006.

174 *Benny: Another Girl, Another Planet*

175 *Nekromanteia*

176 "Fifty years in the future" of the present-day component of *The Way Through the Woods*. Although the temporal anomalies that occur in Swallow Woods are undone, the area presumably does still become a lake after Reyn's spaceship is sent away from Earth.

177 Dating *The Last Dodo* (NSA #13) - The Chinese Three-Striped Box Turtle is a new addition to the collec-

tion, and has recently gone extinct, so it's around 2062.

178 Dating "Prisoners of Time" (IDW *DW* mini-series) – Adam's age isn't said, but flashbacks show him transitioning from youth to middle age to a grey-haired old age. We might arbitrarily imagine that it's been fifty years since he last saw the Doctor in *The Long Game* [2012]. Events in Adam's limbo base occur outside the universe. The Master's usual *modus operandi*, no matter how crazed and illogical at times, has never really entailed him wanting to destroy the universe just for the sake of it – but these events happen after Aeroliths torture him "for decades", so perhaps he's not entirely feeling himself.

179 Dating *Erimem: Prime Imperative* (Erimem novel #5) - The year is given. The space station seen here coordinates efforts with the Great Space Elevator (from the story of the same name, set c.2044).

180 *The Waters of Mars*. They were planning "five years on Mars", which started in 2058.

181 *Alien Bodies*. See "Are There Two Dalek Histories?"

182 Dating *Unbound: Full Fathom Five* (BF Unbound #3) - The blurb names the year, and says it's "27 years" after 2039.

183 *The Beast Below*

184 "At least five hundred", maybe five hundred and fifty years" before *Benny S8: The Tub Full of Cats*.

185 *The Indestructible Man*. This story seems to contradict a lot of the other stories set around this time, both in broad terms and points of detail.

186 Dating *Alien Bodies* (EDA #6) - The date is given, p68.

the Milky Way and Andromeda. The tenth Doctor and Martha arrived as Eve, the curator, had decided to wipe out all other life in the universe. She died when a weapon she was aiming at the Doctor exploded. The Doctor returned the specimens to their native times.

The Death of Adam Mitchell

c 2062 - "Prisoners of Time"[178] -> Adam Mitchell had spent a lifetime in hiding, fearing discovery of the computer interface in his head, but using that interface to plunder corporate accounts. He hired a retrieval team to penetrate Van Statten's vault in Utah and harvest the alien artifacts there. Adam summoned a Time Agent – Captain Neal Shaw – with a signal broadcast from a severed Cyberhead, then overpowered Shaw and stole his vortex manipulator. The technology Adam derived from the Manipulator – and a partnership he forged with the Tremas Master – enabled him to create a base of operations in limbo, and to kidnap many of the Doctor's companions. Adam sought to avenge his downfall by forcing the Doctor to choose one companion to live as the others died.

The eleventh Doctor summoned ten of his previous incarnations to limbo. The Master sent a chronal energy blast into the multiple versions of the Doctor's TARDIS, hoping it would cascade and destroy all of space-time. Adam rebelled against the Master's nihilism and thwarted his goals, and the Master escaped after fatally stabbing his collaborator. The multiple Doctors and their companions buried Adam at his limbo base before departing.

2062 - ERIMEM: PRIME IMPERATIVE[179] -> Venus had atmosphere stations. Shuttle runs were conducted to that planet and Mars.

IASA sent the deep space probe ship *Clinton* on a seven-month mission to examine an orphan comet cutting across interstellar space, but a spore on the comet infected the crew. Erimem and Andrea Hansen stopped the spore from overwhelming Earth by propelling the *Clinton* and its home space station into the sun.

Prior to the Bowie Base One disaster, the plan had been for the first colonists to stay on Mars until 2063.[180] During the mid 2060s, the Daleks were scattered around the edges of Mutter's Spiral, trying to build up a decent galactic powerbase. The ones who got left behind on Skaro were just starting to think about putting together their own little empire – this was the "static electricity" phase of Dalek development...[181]

= 2066 - UNBOUND: FULL FATHOM FIVE[182] -> The radiation isolating the Deep-sea Energy Exploration Project (DEEP) cleared enough that the military planned to retrieve the base's data. The Doctor reached the DEEP first to retrieve his TARDIS, as well as destroy any evidence of his actions there. The Doctor's adopted daughter Ruth stowed aboard the mini-sub to learn her biological father's fate... and discovered that the Doctor had killed him twenty-seven years ago. The monstrous General Flint broke the Doctor's neck, then swim into the depths to end his life. The Doctor regenerated... and Ruth shot him dead once more, and vowed to keep murdering him until his extra lives were extinguished.

Legend had it that star whales guided early space travellers through the asteroid belt.[183] The spaceship *Gravity's Rainbow* was constructed in the twenty-first century.[184]

By 2068, a few colonisation missions had been launched to other solar systems, but there was no indication of whether they had succeeded. UNIT had recently been replaced by PRISM. On 3rd March, 2068, the Lunar Base picked up an alien signal. This was evidence of the Myloki. First contact proved disastrous, and the Myloki launched a war on humanity. Although conducted in secret, the war with the Myloki was so devastating that on 29th August, 2068, the UN banking system collapsed under the strain. The war ended when Colonel LeBlanc sent Captain Grant Matthews, an indestructible Myloki duplicate who retained his loyalties to humanity, to the moon with a twenty-megaton bomb strapped to his back. This destroyed the Myloki base. But the war exhausted Earth's natural resources and saw New York destroyed in a nuclear attack. An altered maize crop destroyed the ecology of Africa. The City of London became an independent city-state, walled off from the rest of the world.[185]

The Eighth Doctor Destroys the Relic

wih - 2069 (26th March) - ALIEN BODIES[186] -> In the East Indies ReVit Zone, Mr Qixotl hosted a private conference in which representatives from various powers were to bid on the Relic, a Gallifreyan body that contained extremely rare biodata... and which the eighth Doctor, accompanied by Sam, discovered was *his* body from his personal future.

Friction among the delegates increased, and a Kroton Warspear arrived to claim the Relic by force. The Doctor used a Faction Paradox timeship to reflect the Warspear's weaponry back on itself, destroying the entire battlefleet. Mortally wounded, Qixotl traded the Relic to the Celestis in return for a new body. The Doctor travelled to Mictlan, the Celestis' powerbase, and reclaimed the Relic. The Doctor buried the Relic alongside the dog Laika on the planet Quiescia, and destroyed the Relic with a thermosystron bomb.

By now, Kroton weapons developed on Quartzel-88 had

decimated the Metatraxi homeworld, reduced the moons of Szacef-Po to powder, and convinced the united forces of Criptostophon Prima to surrender.

The Cardiff public had what resources they needed to live, but water was rationed, and fresh tomatoes were a rarity – as were automobiles. Tapping grid power in the daytime wasn't permitted. Universal Remote Controls (URCs) were hand-held devices used to make purchases – running one over a "zed code" would debit your ration. UK citizens had ID codes such as 818945/CF209B.

Peaceful, human-looking aliens who'd been living in Cardiff for fifty years became the targets of racism, and their offspring were disparagingly called "ghosties". One such offspring died in a deliberately set house fire, and a Torchwood agent – or possibly Captain Jack himself – sent the dead woman's daughter, Freda, through the Rift back to 2009.[187]

Middle Eastern countries turned their economies to high technology, particularly the space industry, as the oil ran out.[188] **Galactic Salvage and Insurance was set up in** London in 2068.[189] The space station Hotel Galaxian became the first offworld tourist attraction.[190]

2070 - THE MOONBASE[191] **-> The Cybermen attempted to take control of the Gravitron on Earth's moon by using Cybermats to introduce a plague to the moonbase. The second Doctor, Ben, Polly and Jamie thwarted them. Medical units could now administer drugs and automatically control the pulse, temperature, breathing and cortex factor of a patient.**

Tobias Vaughn recovered bodies of Cybermen from W3 and the moonbase, and used the components to repair his cybernetic body.[192] **Facing extinction, the Cybermen conquered Telos, all but wiping out the native Cryons and building their "tombs" using Cryon technology. Once this was completed, the Cybermen retreated to their tombs and vanished from the galaxy. The location of Telos remained a mystery.**[193] **Telos was a city of ice tombs.**[194]

The Cybermen launched a star destroyer from Telos that

---

187 *TW: Asylum.* Freda seems to hail from 2069, despite Gwen's suspect math; somehow, she's able to add Freda's birthday (30th May, 2053) to her age (17) to determine that she stems from 2069.

188 *Seeing I* (p29). No date given.

189 *Nightmare of Eden.* A monitor readout states that Galactic Salvage and Insurance were formed in "2068". The Doctor has heard of the company and briefly pretends to be working for them.

190 *The Murder Game* (p9).

191 Dating *The Moonbase* (4.6) - Hobson tells the Doctor they are in "2070", and Polly later repeats this. On screen, the small crew of the moonbase includes Englishmen, Frenchmen and Danes. The production file for the story listed the other nationalities represented at the moonbase: Australians, New Zealanders, Canadians, Germans and Nigerians.

Use of the Gravitron system crumbled during the political turmoil of the 2080s, according to *A History of the Universe in 100 Objects* (p185).

192 *Original Sin* (p289).

193 *The Tomb of the Cybermen, Attack of the Cybermen.*

194 *The Doctor Falls*, clarifying that "Telos" is the name of both the city and the planet in *The Tomb of the Cybermen*. The sixth Doctor says (*Attack of the Cybermen*) that the Cryons made other cities, but we never see them.

195 *Sword of Orion*

TELOS: After the destruction of their vast advance force (*The Invasion*), their homeworld of Mondas (*The Tenth Planet*) and most of the surviving Cyber warships (*Silver Nemesis*), the Cybermen must have been severely weakened. They gradually regrouped and attempted to attack Earth at least twice in the twenty-first century

(*The Wheel in Space, The Moonbase*). These attempts failed, and the Cybermen faced extinction (according to the Controller in *The Tomb of the Cybermen*). So they left the solar system and conquered Telos. (The Doctor says in *Attack of the Cybermen* that "if Mondas hadn't been destroyed, the Cybermen would never have come here [to Telos]", which contradicts an unbroadcast line from *The Moonbase* where a Cyberman states, "We were the first space travellers from Mondas. We left before it was destroyed. We came from the planet Telos.") The Cybermen subjugated the native Cryons, used Cryon technology to build their "tombs" (*Attack of the Cybermen*) and experimented with new weapons before entering suspended animation. In the late twenty-fifth century, the Cybermen revive (*The Tomb of the Cybermen*), but are refrozen. Telos is destroyed soon after in an asteroid strike (the *Cyberman* audio series), but a new breed of Cybermen is forged to menace the galaxy (*Cyberman 2*, evidently leading into The Cyber War).

Last of the Cybermen is problematic in that it names Telos as the locale of the final battle of The Cyber War, entirely overlooking that Telos was destroyed prior to Big Finish's *Cyberman* audios, and its remains play a key role at the end of *Cybermen* Series 1. Moving *Cyberman* to after *Last of the Cybermen* doesn't solve the problem, as the former is reliant upon few people knowing that the Cybermen even exist – something that's surely not possible once the Cyber War comes and goes. If one squints hard, it's *possible* (but a stretch) that the "Telos" seen in *Last of the Cybermen* simply bears the same name as the one first seen in *Tomb* – beyond mention of Alpha Meson phosphor lights, and swaths of dialogue pertaining to the solving of logic blocks, the two

headed to the Garazone Sector.[195] Seismic shifts created an island in the Atlantic, and this became a homeland for the Dutch, the New Dutch Republic.[196] The Sontarans left the Coal Sack sector of space and wouldn't return for three hundred years.[197]

? 2070 - "The Forgotten"[198] -> The second Doctor, Jamie and Zoe arrived on a space station that was being attacked by an Alvarian Space Wyrm. The Doctor sent her snake soldiers to sleep by playing his recorder, then did the same to the Wyrm herself by amplifying the signal through the station's communication system.

2071 - CASUALTIES OF TIME[199] -> The Oceanic States and the Asiatic States were now the two main power blocs on Earth. Years of conflict between them, as quietly orchestrated by Cuthbert, caused great famine in the Asiatic Territories. The Asiatic States signed a contact with Cuthbert's Conglomerate that led to improved food supplies and production. In future, the Conglomerate would hold major influence with the new united Earth government, and be the power behind the Earth presidency.

2071 (28th May) - SCAVENGER[200] -> The Doctor helped to found Space Guard, a NASA programme to track five thousand active satellites and fifteen thousand pieces of hazardous space junk.

Above Earth, the mile-long Nelson Mandela International Space Station serviced specialists and tourists. Clean-Up Space, an environmental programme sponsored by the Indian space agency and Britain, launched Salvage 2: a vessel designed to surround "zombie satellites" and other space debris, then eject them to burn up in Earth's atmosphere. Salvage 2's efforts awoke the alien Scavenger probe, but its programming became so deluded that it classified the people in New Delhi as "space junk". Scavenger also captured Flip Jackson when she and the sixth Doctor visited the Mandela, but the long-lived Prince Salim convinced Scavenger to accept his mind as a new host. In such

a state, he was reunited with his beloved Anarkali, and directed Scavenger to fly into the Sun.

Flip ejected from Scavenger in a space suit, and made a desperate, perhaps fatal, jump toward Earth...

The Doctor opened a space-time tear that translocated Flip back to 2011, and safely deposited her in the Indian Ocean.[201] On Earth, PVC made a big resurgence.[202]

2074 - MAD DOGS AND ENGLISHMEN[203] -> Science fiction by human authors had become the subject of serious academic debate. There were also groups who sought to rewrite literary texts for their own evil ends, including The Circle Hermeneutic and The New Dehistoricists. The eighth Doctor accidentally landed his TARDIS on one academic, Alid Jag.

The Doctor, Fitz and Anji learned that the novel *The True History of Planets* was a book about talking poodles, not the sword and sorcery epic the Doctor remembered. The Doctor teamed up with Mida Slike of the Ministry for Incursions And Ontological Wonders, a group that investigated such changes to history. Slike was killed, and poodle fur found on her body. Fitz discovered the co-ordinates for Dogworld in Tyler's novel.

The space station of the Dogworld poodles was now receiving radio signals from Earth. The movie of *The True History of Planets* was the story of how the Emperor deposed the mother of Princess Margaret, the true heir to the throne. After trips to 1942 and 1978, the Doctor and his companions discovered that Margaret had been manipulating history to change the contents of Tyler's book, and changed it back. Margaret was killed and the Emperor restored to power. A grateful Emperor allowed writer Reginald Tyler to remain on the Dogworld.

Talking boars were now part of Earth society and had their own culture.

The Doctor rode a flying motorbike in the Anti-Grav Olympics, 2074, but finished last.[204] On Earth, govern-

---

don't share any characters or features in common. *Last of the Cybermen* also features a Super-Controller, making no mention of the Cyber-Controller who oversaw operations on Telos in both *Tomb of the Cybermen* and *Attack of the Cybermen*.
196 *St Anthony's Fire*
197 *Lords of the Storm* (p104).
198 Dating "The Forgotten" (IDW *DW* mini-series #2) - No date is given. The level of technology seems reminiscent of Zoe's time.
199 Dating *Casualties of Time* (BF 4th Doc #5.8) - K9 reports that it's "Earth, Master. AD 2071." The Doctor and K9 last saw Cuthbert, in 2059, "a few years" and (more accurately) "over ten years" back. The Oceanic

States and Asiatic States are presumably the two unnamed power blocs mentioned in *Warriors of the Deep*, whereas *The Silurian Candidate* continues with the "Eastern Bloc" and "Western Bloc" terminology. It's possible that Cuthbert's AI revolution brings about the synch-op technology seen in that story.
200 Dating *Scavenger* (BF #184) - The day is given and identified as "Thursday", which is in synch with the real-world calendar.
201 *The Widow's Assassin*
202 "Sixty years" after *Autonomy*.
203 Dating *Mad Dogs and Englishmen* (EDA #52) - It is "one hundred years" (p9) after "1974" (p3).
204 *The Bells of Saint John*

ments used genetic manipulation and intelligent chips to maintain their soldiers' loyalty.[205]

Earth had now experienced hostile alien visitors such as the Sycorax and the Slitheen, and friendly ones such as the Svillia and the Hive of Mooj. The Flisk arrived on Earth after a stellar cataclysm almost wiped out their race, and were welcomed until they were revealled as telepathic, whereupon they became targets of suspicion. Nonetheless, their expertise with computer programming helped many of them find employment across the globe.[206]

c 2075 - ERIMEM: ANGEL OF MERCY[207] **->** Erimem, Andy Hansen and Helena Hadmani time-jumped into the future of the UK and found themselves in The City: a township built in the North to contain the unemployed, immigrants, the mentally ill, the poor and other such dispossessed. Cameras broadcast life within The City on The City Channel, to the great profit of the government and the participating network. Anyone within The City who found a means of boosting ratings received additional food, even their freedom.

Erimem and her allies revealed that Razor – a gang leader causing murders, rapes and indiscriminate attacks within The City – was colluding with a local hero, Angela, to boost their respective popularity. A mob stormed Angela and Razor as Erimem's trio returned home.

A roller coaster was installed at Buckland Abbey in 2078.[208]

The Cyber Incursions

Zoe Heriot Joins the TARDIS; the Time Lords Send Her Back Home

? 2079 - THE WHEEL IN SPACE / THE WAR GAMES[209] **->** Jet helicopters had become the principal form of transport on Earth. Simple servo robots were developed, as were x-ray laser weapons and food dispensers. John Smith and Associates built advanced medical equipment for spacecraft. Psychotropic drugs could now prevent brain control, and all astronauts were fitted with Silenski capsules to detect outside influences on the human mind. Two years beforehand, Dr.

---

205 *Deceit* (p188), with similar technology in *Transit*.

206 "Twenty years" before *Snowglobe 7*.

207 Dating *Erimem: Angel of Mercy* (*Erimem* novel #3) - It's "Earth, within fifty or seventy years of now" (meaning "2015", for Erimem and company). The advent and longevity of The City seems at odds with details of this period as related in other *Doctor Who* stories.

208 *The Lost Magic.* Sir Francis Drake lived at Buckland Abbey for fifteen years; it's now part of the National Trust.

209 Dating *The Wheel in Space/The War Games* (5.7, 6.7) - This, along with *The Seeds of Death*, is one of two stories set in the twenty-first century that are trickiest to date. There's no date given in the story itself.

In *The Moonbase*, base leader Hobson states that "every child knows" about the destruction of Mondas (in *The Tenth Planet*). Yet none of the crew of the Wheel have heard of the Cybermen, and they're generally sceptical about the existence of alien life. This is a contradiction whether Zoe comes from before, around the same time or after *The Moonbase*. Invoking Zoe's narrow education doesn't work if "every child" knows about Mondas' demise, and surely the only way she wouldn't know is if it had been deliberately kept from her, which would be a bit bizarre. (Unless it's felt that telling future astronauts about all the monsters up there would be counter-productive.)

Amongst its other duties, the Wheel gathers information on Earth's weather, but this needn't mean that weather control isn't in use – to control the weather, you surely need the ability to monitor it.

As it's Zoe's native time, we get more clues in subsequent stories she's in: Zoe is "born in the twenty-first" century (*The War Games*), and she is "19 or so" according to the Brigadier in *The Invasion*, so the story must be set somewhere between 2019 and 2119. In *The Mind Robber*, she recognises the Karkus – a comic strip character from the year 2000 – which might suggest she comes from that year. For that reason (presumably), the narration in *The Prison in Space* identifies Zoe as "a pretty astrophysicist from the year 2000". However, when discussing the Karkus, Zoe asks the Doctor if he's *been* to the year 2000 – if it's not a rhetorical question, then *The Wheel in Space* isn't set in that year. In *The Mind Robber*, we see an image of Zoe's home city – a highly futuristic metropolis.

It's never explicitly stated that *The Seeds of Death* takes place before Zoe's time (see the dating notes on *The Seeds of Death*). In *The Seeds of Death*, Zoe understands the principles behind T-Mat, meaning she possesses knowledge that's otherwise limited to a few specialists (she may have picked this up on her travels – although she doesn't in any story we see). Why Zoe doesn't remember T-Mat or recognise the Martians is a mystery, but it does indicate she was born after T-Mat was abandoned, or she'd recognise it. Then again, Zoe has a narrow education and doesn't recognise kilts or candles, either, so perhaps T-Mat is seen as a quaint and irrelevant historical detail by her time.

If Zoe's inability to recognise T-Mat is relevant, it suggests that the earliest date for *The Wheel in Space* is at least "nineteen years or so" (the Brigadier's estimate of Zoe's age in *The Invasion*) after *The Seeds of Death* (dated to circa 2040 in this chronology), so it can't take place before 2059. This doesn't help narrow the upper limit on when the story can occur, however.

Gemma Corwyn's husband had been killed exploring the asteroid belt. The loss of rockets was becoming rarer, though.

The Earth School of Parapsychology was founded around this time. It was based in an area known only as the City and trained children from a very early age in the disciplines of pure logic and memory. Zoe Heriot, one of the School's pupils, developed total recall and majored in pure maths. She qualified as an astrophysicist and astrometricist (first class). Her education was narrow and vocational, though, and didn't include any pre-century history. When she was about 19, Zoe was assigned to Space Station W3.

The Space Wheels were set up around the solar system. W3, for example, was positioned relative to Venus, 24,564,000 miles at perihelion, 161,350,000 miles at aphelion, a week's rocket travel from Earth. W5 was between eighty and ninety million miles from W3. The small, multinational crews of the Wheel warned travellers of meteorite storms and acted as a halfway house for deep space ships of the space fleet; they monitored all manner of stellar phenomenon, and also supplied advance weather information to Earth.

The Wheels were armed with x-ray lasers with a range of ten thousand miles, and protected by a convolute force field, a neutron field barrier capable of deflecting meteorites of up to two hundred tonnes. Phoenix IV cargo rockets, which had a four-man crew but could be placed on automatic power drive, kept the stations supplied with food and materials.

Back on the human homeworld, the Pull Back to Earth movement believed it was wrong to colonise other planets. They committed acts of sabotage against the space programme, but their exponents were never seen as anything but crackpots. Space travel had undoubted benefits, but remained hazardous.

Zoe aided the second Doctor and Jamie in repelling a Cybermen assault on W3, then joined the TARDIS crew. Gemma Corwyn died in the attack.

As part of the resolution of the Doctor's first trial, the Time Lords returned Zoe to W3, but walled off her memories of her time in the TARDIS.

Zoe had a photographic memory and a degree in Pure Mathematics.[210] She eventually left the Wheel. Years later, she experienced dreams of her time with the Doctor and Jamie, and wondered if some of her memories were blocked off. She sought counselling, and related a particularly vivid adventure involving the Daleks. Zoe's unsettling dreams ceased after the Doctor's voice – through unknown means – told her not to fear the Daleks.[211]

2080 - LOUPS-GAROUX[212] **->** The ancient werewolf Pieter Stubbe tried to reclaim Illeana de Santos, now the de facto werewolf leader, as his mate. Illeana resisted Stubbe's advances, but Stubbe seized control of Illeana's werewolves and directed them to assault Rio de Janeiro. The fifth Doctor and Turlough broke Stubbe's dominance of the pack. Stubbe died when he rushed into the TARDIS, enabling the Doctor to materialise in orbit and sever Stubbe from the Earth – the source of his elemental power – thus aging him to death.

Many subsequent stories establish that the governments of Earth knew about the existence of aliens in the twentieth century, and the new television series (as well as stories in the books and comics) establish that the general public accepts the existence of aliens by the early twenty-first.

The Indestructible Man places this story after 2096, as it's set before Zoe was born. *The Harvest* (set in 2021) refers to the Wheel space stations. *The Wheel of Ice* (p4) says that Zoe's native time is "the latter half of the twenty-first century".

The first two editions of *The Programme Guide* placed *The Wheel in Space* between "1990-2000", but *The Terrestrial Index* suggested a date "c2020" (or "2030" in *The Universal Databank*). "2074" was suggested by "A History of the Cybermen" in *DWM*. *Cybermen*, after some discussion (p61-62), said "2028 AD". The first edition of *Timelink* said "2020"; the Telos version favoured "2080". *About Time* says "it looks like the 2030s to us".

Whoniverse (BBC, p176) places *The Wheel in Space* before *The Moonbase* [2070]. The Space Station W3 entry in *A History of the Universe in 100 Objects* (p158) is generalised as the "21st century", but is positioned before the "Sentinel Six" (*Warriors of the Deep*) entry dated to 2084 (p158).

The Dying Light (BF CC #8.6) offers a clear and unambiguous date, "2079", for the year that Zoe departed Space Station W3 in *The Wheel in Space*. Said year is derived by a Time Lord, Quadrigger Stoyn, whose calculations correctly identify Jamie as hailing from "Scotland, 1746". With so much about *The Wheel in Space*'s placement being ambiguous, and 2079 being a not-unreasonable choice, it seems fair to relocate the story to that year until more evidence comes to light. It also means that, if Zoe is indeed "19" as the Brigadier claims in *The Invasion*, she was born in either 2059 or 2060.

Previous editions of *Ahistory* placed *The Wheel in Space* a century after it was broadcast, around the same time as the other Cyberman incursion seen in *The Moonbase*. In the last episode of *The War Games*, Zoe is returned to her native time.

210 "The Forgotten"

211 *Fear of the Daleks*. Wendy Padbury was 58 when this was recorded, a possible indicator of Zoe's age.

212 Dating *Loups-Garoux* (BF #20) - The date is given.

Rio de Janeiro now had a monorail and spaceport. ID implants were compulsory, and robots checked passports. People had hover vehicles including limos, jeeps and four hundred mile-an-hour trains. The currency was the credit.

c 2080 - "The Eye of Torment"[213] -> The quadrillion-aire Rudy Zoom, born in Leeds, had built his first hover-bike at age ten, started marketing the item by 12, and was worth £60 billion by 15. He had been the first man to swim the Mariana Trench, climb Olympus Mons, and to cycle the Rings of Saturn. Now, Zoom set off with an all-female crew aboard the *Pollyanna*, the first of the Ninth Era Sunships, to achieve another milestone: become the first man to circumnavigate the Sun itself. The *Pollyanna*'s voy-age awoke the Umbra within Earth's sun, and they coalesced their forms into a destructive vortex: the Eye of Torment. The twelfth Doctor and Clara used the *Pollyanna*'s gravitron inverter to flip gravity and heat around the Umbra, freezing them to death on the sun's surface.

& 2083 - "The Soul Garden"[214] -> The twelfth Doctor and Bill Potts saw a spectacular vista on her favourite planet, Saturn. They soon met the explorer ship *Beagle*, which was two weeks out from Shackleton Spaceport, and its financier: Rudy Zoom. While mapping Titan, the explorers found the habitation dome of the wooden Haluu warlord Sythorr, who threatened to transfer his conscious-ness into the humans via the Dreamscape, then spread his

---

213 Dating "The Eye of Torment" (*DWM* #477-480) - The Gravitron Inverter stems from the Gravitron system seen in *The Moonbase* [2070]. The technology Rudy Zoom helps to develop is advanced, but it must be reasonably early in humanity's explorations away from Earth, if he was genuinely the first to accomplish climb-ing Olympus Mons et al. Zoom also cracks a joke – pos-sibly with a veneer of truth, possibly not – about being able to clone the Dalai Lama, but not with fins and a blowhole.

214 Dating "The Soul Garden" (*DWM* #512-514) – The Doctor previously met Ruby Zoom in "The Eye of Torment" [c.2080], published three years before this adventure. It's early in humankind's exploration of space – Sythorr has been twiddling his thumbs for centuries, waiting for someone to come within range of Titan.

215 *A Death in the Family*

216 "Four hundred years" before *The Game*.

217 Dating *Warriors of the Deep* (21.1) - The Doctor tells Tegan that the year is "about 2084". The televised story doesn't specify which bloc the Seabase belongs to, and only the novelisation specifies the blocs as "East and West". Even that leaves the geopolitics far from clear. The most obvious division in 1984 would have been between a capitalist West and communist East, but nowadays that seems unlikely. Lt Preston doesn't seem surprised that the TARDIS is "not from this planet", and no-one seems shocked that the Silurians are intelligent nonhumans. This might suggest that contact has been made with a number of alien races by this time.

THE RETURN OF THE EARTH REPTILES: In *Doctor Who and the Silurians*, *The Ambassadors of Death* and *The Sea Devils*, the Doctor thinks that the Brigadier has killed all the Silurians at Wenley Moor. However, they may simply be entombed, and one Silurian – Ichtar – seems to sur-vive the first story into *Warriors of the Deep*.

Based on discrepancies between the events of *Doctor Who and the Silurians*, the descriptions of the Doctor's last encounter with the species in *Warriors of the Deep*, and the fact that the Doctor recognises Icthar, the Myrka and the Silurian submersible, *The*

Discontinuity Guide postulated that there is an unre-corded adventure featuring the Doctor and the Silurians set between the two stories. The novel *The Scales of Injustice*, set in the UNIT era and published the year after *The Discontinuity Guide*, addresses most of these issues in an attempt to fill the gap.

Cold Blood [2020] entails a Silurian colony that's slat-ed to revive and try to negotiate an accord with humanity around 3020, but we aren't shown the out-come of that effort. *The Silurian Candidate* [2085] shows a different Silurian colony being timed to awaken in 16,087; we don't learn how that turns out either. Silurians are referred to in a number of New and Missing Adventures set in the future (*Love and War*, *Transit* and *The Crystal Bucephalus* to name three). They seem particularly peaceful towards humans in Benny's native time.

218 *The Silurian Candidate*

219 *The Wreck of the World*

220 Dating *The Silurian Candidate* (BF #229) – The Doctor names the year, and was involved in the destruction of a Silurian colony (presumably *Doctor Who and the Silurians*) "over a hundred years ago". The political situation derives from *Warriors of the Deep* [c.2084], which happened "last year".

221 *The Dying Days* (p115). This is humankind's first diplomatic contact with alien races, as opposed to being invaded by them. See also "When Does the General Public Accept the Existence of Aliens?"

222 *No Future* (p257).

223 It arrived "thirty years" after *The Waters of Mars*. Travelling at lightspeed, it would take a little over four years to reach Proxima Centauri, so it must have been launched in 2085.

224 Dating "Black Destiny" (*DWM* #235-237) - The date is given. The United Nations World Health Organisation is still operating, as are nuclear power stations. Peace must have broken out since *Warriors of the Deep*.

225 Dating *2ndD* V2: *The Integral* (CC #10.3) - Zoe: "Judging from the design and materials [of the Aspen Treatment Centre], I would guess this is somewhere near my time. Late twenty-first century."

seeds on Earth. Bill, Rudy and another Dreamscape traveller – the writer Samuel Taylor Coleridge – aided the Doctor in spurring Sythorr's Haluu to rebel, leading to the habitation dome's destruction. Before his death, Sythorr ominously warned the Doctor that the Unknown Soldier was stirring.

A body scan predicted that Henry Louis Noone was likely to die at age 82.[215] Circa 2084, on the planet Cray, the game Naxy started out as an innocent arena sport. The Naxy fans became increasingly violent, and took to fighting outside the arena before matches. The public's interest shifted to the bloody fan conflict, and Naxy was soon retooled as a sport in which teams fought to the death.[216]

The Western, Eastern Blocs

The Silurians Attack Seabase 4

c 2084 - WARRIORS OF THE DEEP[217] -> Earth consolidated into two blocs, the East and the West, and a new Cold War developed. New weapons technology was developed: Seabases sat on the ocean floor, armed with proton missiles that were capable of destroying life while leaving property intact. Sentinels – robots armed with energy weapons – orbited the Earth and large Hunter-Killers patrolled the seas. "Synchoperators" had computer interfaces implanted into their heads, allowing split-second control over proton missile runs. Soldiers carried energy rifles.

At the height of interbloc tension, a group of Silurians and Sea Devils attacked Seabase 4. They planned to launch the missiles there and provoke a war that would kill all human life. The fifth Doctor, Tegan and Turlough failed to prevent a massacre at the base, but saved humanity.

The Sea Base incident exacerbated tensions between the power blocs, but was blamed on a rogue sync operator. The Doctor scrambled the circuits aboard the Sea Devils' vessel at Sea Base Four. Nonetheless, a graverobber program recovered its software, including schematics of the Silurians' capital city.[218] Efforts were made to eliminate paper in Zoe's time.[219]

2085 - THE SILURIAN CANDIDATE[220] -> Earth's two power blocs remained locked in opposition. Director Shen led the China-based Eastern Bloc. The office of President of the United States had been abolished, and the arms manufacturer Bart Falco (campaign slogan: "There are Never Any Accidents") was elected Chairman of the Western Bloc, the capitol of which was in Canberra. Paper money had become obsolete. The P-One Thousand Bowhead stealth jet was developed, and ran on slush

hydrogen. The Gizmonics Institute in Scranton, Pennsylvania, created "Karlas": female-gendered security androids.

The highest ruling Silurian triad – Chordok, and the spouses Spenodus and Avvox – had awoken from stasis four years previous, and surgically brainwashed Falco as their agent. They schemed that Falco would assassinate Director Shen during talks held near Washington state, triggering a nuclear war that would eliminate humanity and awaken the billions of Silurians in hibernation. The seventh Doctor, Ace and Mel stymied Falco's attempt on Shen's life, although Falco identified Ace and Mel as would-be killers on live television.

Avvox agreed with the Doctor's proposal to leave the Silurians in hibernation until humanity reclaimed Earth after the solar flare incident, putting both races on equal terms. Spenodus persisted in trying to destroy humanity, and so Avvox killed him. The Doctor programmed the Silurians to awaken in 16,087.

First Contact

The Arcturan Treaty of 2085 was often officially counted as humankind's first contact with alien races, as it was the first diplomatic contact.[221] The whole of humanity finally accepted the existence of aliens. Danny Pain's role in stopping an alien invasion in 1976 was now legendary.[222]

The first lightspeed mission to another solar system launched in 2085.[223]

2086 (25th April) - "Black Destiny"[224] -> The fourth Doctor, Sarah and Harry landed at the Troika Cultural Centre to celebrate world peace in Takhail in Russia, but the staff suddenly started dying. The Doctor met Direktor Arkady, the great-grandson of a boy who had been exposed to radiation there a hundred years before. The dead bodies reanimated as zombies. The Doctor checked the world-net computer network, and discovered that Arkady was fascinated by nuclear accidents. Arkady began to glow with energy and transformed into an energy cloud, then attacked Moscow, but the Doctor managed to neutralise and disperse him. Sarah noted that Chernobyl had a new nuclear power station.

The Threshold abducted Sarah during this encounter.

c 2086 - 2NDD V1: THE INTEGRAL[225] -> The tech company Quercus Robar created violent entertainment that inadvertently induced a murderous rage, Quercus Syndrome, in some of its users. The Earth Government forced Quercus Robar to construct Aspen Base to treat the victims, and alien telepaths, the Integral, were hired to syphon away the victims' anger. The second Doctor, Jamie and Zoe learned that Dr Edvard was killing the Integral at Aspen Base to prove his invention, the Pacivitron, could affordably replace them. Edvard's interference caused the Aspen patients to riot, and they tore him apart. The Doctor taught the surviving Integral the art of anger management, restoring Quercus Syndrome sufferers to normal.

The Doctor believed that Disneyland would be worth visiting in future, after it "had time to settle".[226]

The Thousand-Day War

Out of the blue, one day in 2086, the Martians attacked. Paris was hit with a meteorite that killed a million people, and wiped out centuries of history including the Mona Lisa, the Venus de Milo, Notre Dame and EuroDisney.[227] Humanity united behind President Achebe against the common enemy. First in were the Zen Brigade, the Blue Berets of the United Nations Third Tactical Response Brigade, made up of Irish and Ethiopians. They dropped in from orbit, and the Martians cut them to pieces. One of the few survivors was their commanding officer, Brigadier Yembe Lethbridge-Stewart. But the Blue Berets completed their mission and formed a bridgehead: the UN forward-base at Jacksonville halfway up Olympus Mons. More crucially, their engineers set up the first interstitial tunnel, a refinement of old Travel-mat technology that allowed instantaneous travel between Earth and Mars. Men and materiel poured through the Stunnel.

Half-kiloton groundbreakers poured from the air onto the Martian nests. Tactical nuclear weapons were used. The early stages of the war were dogged by friendly fire incidents, but these were ironed out. As the war dragged on, some soldiers were genetically and cybernetically augmented to increase their efficiency. These first-generation ubersoldaten retained less than 50% of their natural DNA. Just about every soldier took combat drugs like Doberman and Heinkel to make them better fighters.[228]

At one point, the Zen Brigade was ambushed at Achebe Gorge – pinned down by snipers, they retreated under cover of a storm.[229]

New slang entered the language: Greenie (Martian), pop up (a cannon used by the Martians), spider trap, fire mission, medevac. During the war, hologram technology became more advanced. The Ice Maiden, an R&R stop in Jacksonville, became notorious. For a generation afterwards, the imagery and iconography of the War was burnt into the minds of humanity, and was popularised in vids like *Violet Sky*.

The war ended in 2088, exactly a thousand days after it had started. The surviving Martians had either fled the planet or gone into hibernation in deep nests. At first, the human authorities were worried about "stay behind" units, but it became clear that the Martian threat had completely dissipated, and the military satellites were decommissioned. A memorial forest was set up at Achebe Gorge on Mars. A tree was planted for each one of the four hundred and fifty thousand men who had died in the War, which didn't include the death toll in Paris. For many decades, Victory Night was celebrated every year on Earth, and trees were planted to honour the military dead.[230]

The only human defeat was at Viis Claar, or the Valles Marineris, when Abrasaar killed fifteen thousand humans and ten thousand of his own men in a trap.[231] 99% of Martians headed for a new planet, Nova Martia, beyond Arcturus. Hundreds of thousands of Martians remained behind, hidden in subterranean cities. UN peacemakers found the planet deserted. The bodies of six of the eight

226 "A hundred years or so" after *The Nightmare Fair*. This isn't the Doctor's best suggestion, as "a hundred years" after that story would be around 2086, at the start of the Thousand-Day War.

227 *Transit*, with additional details of Paris' obliteration provided in *Benny: Beige Planet Mars*. The Mona Lisa that perishes is presumably the one with "This is a Fake" scrawled on it in felt-tip, per *City of Death*.

228 *Transit*

229 *Fear Itself* (PDA, p176-177).

230 *Transit*

231 *GodEngine*

232 *Legacy* (p86), *GodEngine* (p79). In *The Curse of Peladon*, the Martians and Arcturans are "old enemies".

233 *GodEngine* (p168).

234 *Legacy* (p86).

235 Dating *The Story of Martha*: "Breathing Space" (NSA #28b) - The year is given.

236 *Fear Itself* (PDA)

237 *Transit*

238 "Thirty years" after *The Waters of Mars*.

239 "Hypothetical Gentleman", elaborating on *The Waters of Mars*.

240 "Over a hundred years" before *ST*: "All Hands on Deck".

241 Dating *The Beginning* (BF CC #8.5) - These humans are part of Earth's first lunar *colony*, not one of the many "bases" established on the moon over the decades.

242 *The Dying Light*

243 Dating *Paper Cuts* (BF #125) - The Doctor twice says that it's been "sixty years" since he visited Draconia and aided with the space plague, but the Queen Mother – who vividly remembers meeting the Doctor when she was only 12, and would presumably be in a better position to know – claims it's actually been "fifty years". The story leaves open-ended how Draconia resolves the struggle between the fifteen emperors, but however it happens, the Draconians have a new empire and just one emperor by *Frontier in Space*.

244 *Benny: The Vampire Curse*: "Possum Kingdom".

245 Roughly five hundred years before *Benny: The Gods of the Underworld*.

members of the ruling Eight Point Table were found, but these did not include Supreme Grand Marshal Falaxyr or Abrasaar.[232]

The Martian fleet heading to Nova Martia stopped off in the Rataculan System. A few Ice Warriors remained behind to found a colony on the planet Cluut-ett-Pictar.[233] There was little or no contact between the Ice Warriors and humanity for nearly a thousand years, and the Martians rarely allowed any visitors to their new world. In the twenty-sixth century, the "extinct" Martians briefly became a curiosity for archaeologists, but after that, humankind forgot all about their old neighbours.[234]

2088 - THE STORY OF MARTHA: "Breathing Space"[235]**->** The alien Benefactors arrived in Earth orbit, offering to end global warming and atmospheric pollution. The tenth Doctor and Martha found themselves at an Earth space station, and the Doctor recognised the aliens as the Cineraria – a hostile race that subjugated planets by dropping space whales onto heavily-populated areas. The Cineraria's plan relied upon secrecy, and they retreated when the Doctor exposed their intentions.

The Colonisation of the Solar System

Wal-Mart began building the first trading post on Mars, but this was abandoned when the settlement Sheffield was established on Olympus Mons.[236] The World Government invested heavily in the state-owned Sol Transit System (STS) over the next twenty years, and soon Interstitial Tunnels linked every city, continent, habitable planet and moon in the solar system. Transportation within the solar system was now instantaneous and readily available. For the first time, the solar system had a single elected government, the Union of Solar Republics.

In the decade following the Thousand-Day War, Paris was rebuilt. Lowell Depot on Pluto was built to soak up population overspill.[237]

In 2089, thirty years after Bowie Base One was destroyed, the granddaughter of Adelaide Brooke – Susie Fontana Brooke – piloted the first lightspeed ship to Proxima Centauri. Some form of computer news service still operated at this time.[238] Fontana Brooke's mission to Proxima Centauri initiated a second British Empire.[239] The grounds of Coal Hill School was converted into flats.[240]

The Doctor and Susan's First Adventure (cont.)

c 2090 - THE BEGINNING[241] **->** An archaeologist attached to Earth's first moon colony discovered a cave containing the first Doctor, Susan, the TARDIS, Quadrigger

Stoyn and the Archaeons – an act that liberated them from stasis after some four hundred and fifty million years. The Archaeons were appalled to find how much their grand designs for life on Earth had gone awry. They sought to cleanse the planet with a blue lightning attack from their ancient systems and eliminate the humans at Giant Leap Base with lethal worms, but were eradicated when Earth authorities responded with a missile. The Doctor and Susan left Stoyn behind, and went in the TARDIS to a world with a blue sun. The Ship's exterior adopted the form of a giant mushroom.

Quadrigger Stoyn cobbled together devices to track the TARDIS' movements, but the degree to which the Doctor was woven into Earth's timelines rendered them useless. Stoyn left the moon and relocated to a dying, ancient world at the heart of the galaxy, where he spent "hundreds, thousands of years" creating wormholes to snag the Doctor's Ship.[242]

c 2090 - PAPER CUTS[243] **->** By the eightieth Year of the Blood on Draconia, no alien had set foot on Draconia for over fifty Earth years. The Fifteenth Emperor (a.k.a. the Red Emperor) was declared dead, and was placed in an orbiting tomb – still alive – alongside his predecessors. Four vigil-keepers were summoned to the tomb to witness the rite of succession – the sixth Doctor and Charley (actually Mila in disguise) answered this call, which had sat in the Doctor's In-Box for one hundred and fifty years.

The fifteen dormant emperors remained aware, and had a half-set of life-size Sazou pieces that responded to their mental commands. The White Emperor sought revenge on the Doctor for his role in the collapse of the Draconian Empire – in the power-struggles that followed, all of the emperors revived from stasis. It remained to be seen who would ascend to the throne. Despite this political quagmire, Draconia in future would forge a new empire.

Gypsy culture was subsumed in the late twenty-first century after proto-viruses left many ethnic groups sterile.[244] The Boor were interplanetary gangsters; the planet Oblivion was decimated and recolonised when it failed to pay their protection scheme. The Stellar Police ended the Boor's operations, but the key Boor entered suspended animation on Venedel. They expected to awaken in three decades, but wouldn't for five hundred years.[245]

The Halavans, humanoids who resided on Petreus III, destroyed their homeworld through misuse of their mental abilities. Some of their elite escaped on a spaceship, leaving everyone else behind to die. In-fighting amongst the Halavans made the ship crash on an unnamed planet; they tried to conquer the one-eyed humanoids who lived there, but were themselves enslaved when their telepathic boosters were destroyed. The subjugated Halavans named their masters "Monoids". The rest of the civilised universe believed that a natural disaster had ravaged Petreus III, and the Galactic Trust worked to preserve it.[246]

(A Possible) Death of Ace

2092 (29th August) - "Ground Zero"[247] **->** Ace was arrested on suspicion of theft at the Notting Hill Carnival, but the policeman was actually Dixon, an agent of Threshold. The seventh Doctor met another agent, Isaac, who showed him the abducted Susan.

Meanwhile, Ace met the similarly kidnapped Sarah Jane and Peri. The Doctor learned that Threshold were an organisation that opened doors in space and time for their clients – their clients in this case being creatures living with the collective unconscious of humankind, the Lobri, who manifested as giant fleas. The TARDIS interior was heavily damaged. Ace sacrificed her own life to save the Doctor from the creatures – but the last Lobri nonetheless

started to manifest on Earth. The Doctor materialised the TARDIS inside the Lobri, destroying it. He then returned his surviving companions to their rightful places in time, and was left travelling alone.

Tracks for a linear-induction monorail on Mars were first laid in 2093. Terraforming efforts started in 2095; the University of Mars was founded in the same year.[248]

2096 - THE INDESTRUCTIBLE MAN[249] **->** Intercontinental travel was impossible, and the world was broken into city-states. France and the former United States of America were in a state of civil war. Japan had invaded New Zealand. There was a United Zion Arab States. Only Australia was spared the worst effects of a collapsing society. The second Doctor, Jamie and Zoe defeated the Myloki's plan to use Captain Grant Matthews as the ultimate agent of humankind's destruction.

---

246 This happens long enough before *Benny S6: The Kingdom of the Blind* that the Halvans' descendents don't remember their own history.

247 Dating "Ground Zero" (*DWM* #238-242) - The date is given in a caption. The destruction of the TARDIS console would seem to lead to its new design in *Doctor Who – The Movie*, although oddly it's the old TV console introduced in *The Five Doctors* that's destroyed, not the version seen in the later seventh Doctor strips.

ACE'S FATE: The seventh Doctor and Ace walk off together in *Survival*, but the next time we see the seventh Doctor (in *Doctor Who - The Movie*), he's travelling alone. Thus, there have been a number of accounts of Ace's fate.

The New Adventures saw her grow to become a young woman, then in *Set Piece* she acquires her own time machine and left the Doctor, and the last time we see her is in *Lungbarrow*, where she's still an independent time traveller. In "Ground Zero", a teenaged Ace sacrifices her life to save the Doctor's – and the Doctor is wearing the costume he did in *The Movie*, suggesting it's shortly before he regenerates. In (the possibly apocryphal) *Death Comes to Time*, an older Ace is training to become a Time Lord, and witnesses the seventh Doctor's death. In *Prime Time*, we see the Doctor exhume Ace's teenage body – although in *Loving the Alien*, we learn the dead Ace (the one we saw with the Doctor on TV) was replaced by one from an alternate timeline.

The four Big Finish audios adapted from suggested stories for the unmade Season 27 (*Thin Ice*, *Crime of the Century*, *Animal* and *Earth Aid*) don't have Ace leave the TARDIS as the production team at the time initially planned (she was meant to exit midway through the season); instead, she continues travelling with the Doctor and Raine Creevy. However, *UNIT: Dominion*, *The*

New Adventures of Bernice Summerfield and the *Gallifrey* audios all depict Ace as living on Gallifrey, in rough accord with what the production team had sketched out for her. As part of that, *Gallifrey – Time War* V1: *Soldier Obscura* entailed Irving Braxiatel removing Ace's memory of him (and possibly her time on Gallifrey also), leaving her in twentieth-century England for safekeeping and allowing the Time Lords to think she'd been killed in their service. It's as yet unclear if this Big Finish's way of telling "Ace's last story".

It is, of course, very difficult to fully reconcile these accounts. The main problem is rationalising Ace's death in "Ground Zero" with her other appearances, although one explanation is that her "demise" relates to the Council of Eight's attempts to eliminate the Doctor's companions – *Sometime Never* p154-155 even mentions Ace's double timeline, and although this was in reference to *Loving the Alien*, it could also, albeit retroactively, be made to apply to "Ground Zero". As such, temporally speaking, Ace's "death" in "Ground Zero" might hold no more weight than the notion that Sarah Jane "dies" in *Bullet Time* (set in April 1997).

248 *Benny: Beige Planet Mars*

249 Dating *The Indestructible Man* (PDA #69) - The date is given. This story contradicts many other stories, but only ones that were written after the sixth season in which the novel is set. It's set after a "global teleportation system" is built and fails (p78), a reference to *The Seeds of Death* (or possibly *Transit*); and it's before Zoe's time (p283), which puts it before *The Wheel in Space*. (We've chosen to contradict this reference; see the dating notes on *The Wheel in Space*.)

250 *The Gallifrey Chronicles*. These would have to be time-travelling Daleks from the future, as the Daleks of this time period are confined to Skaro.

251 This is the historical background to *Transit*. In *The*

In 2097, the eighth Doctor, Fitz and Trix prevented an unnamed alien race from killing the Pope on Mars, and she consecrated the first cathedral on another planet.[250]

The economic boom promised by the Transit system didn't arrive. Instead, the ability to move freely around the solar system caused massive economic and social upheaval. Small companies saw an opportunity to undermine the industrial zaibatsu. Household names such as Sony, IBM and Matsui went under, and new companies from Brazil, China and Africa – such as Imbani Entertainment, Mtchali and Tung-Po – took their place. Power shifted to Washington, Brazilia, Harare, Beijing, Tehran, Jacksonville and Zagreb. Japan's economy collapsed and plans to terraform Mars proved more costly than had been expected. The money ran out, the floating cities planned for the Ionian Sea were never built and Australia starved. A new genre, silicon noir, charted the resultant corporate battles in the datascape.

The recession was not harsh on everyone. Relatively speaking, Europe was less prosperous than before, but many in Brazil, Africa and China were a great deal wealthier. For millions in Australia, though, and at the Stop – the end of the Transit line at the Lowell Depot – extreme poverty became a way of life. Whole areas became dead-end ghettos, and urban areas became battlegrounds for streetgangs. Vickers All-Body Combat Systems offered the option of using the Melbourne Protocols, automatically preventing the wearer from shooting civilians. Millions fled the riots using the Transit system, and relief workers rehoused the poor anywhere that would take them, mostly on Mars. Private security firms such as the KGB and V Soc became very rich. With freedom of transport, humanity became more open to ideas from other cultures and to more experimental ways of living. Communal marriages enjoyed a brief vogue.

In 2090, Yembe Lethbridge-Stewart came out of retirement one last time and raided the headquarters of the genetics company IMOGEN. He stole a single child, the first of the second-generation ubersoldaten, and all the files pertaining to her creation. He named her after his great-grandmother, the historian Kadiatu.[251]

Two hundred years after they'd travelled with Pierre Bruyere, the tenth Doctor and Martha visited a museum of Polar Exploration.[252]

Out to the Stars

After humankind "had sacked the solar system they moved on to pastures new".[253] Twenty-first century ships still travelled slower than the speed of light and the crews were placed in suspended animation. It was not unusual to discover such ships many centuries later.[254] These were NAFAL ships, meaning Not As Fast As Light.[255] Nuke burning cadmium-damped spacebuckets were the first ships used to conquer the stars. The galaxy was full of the so-called "nukers" at one time. The first ships Earth built for deep space exploration were the starjammers, and great fleets of them were constructed. By 51,007, only one ship of this type, the *Paine*, remained.[256]

Huge Pioneer stations were set up, lining the way to the stars. They helped to refuel and restock colony ships.[257]

Manned space travel remained enormously expensive prior to the advent of gravity plating. Once the hyperdrive was developed, Earth authorities – including the United Nations Aeronautics and Space Administration (UNASA) sent out unmanned Van Neumann probes to the first colony worlds to prepare them for human habitation. The probes were extremely adaptive but often disruptive – one landed on Arcturus and started to build a city, oblivious to the fact that the planet was already inhabited.[258]

Seeds of Death, Zoe has never heard of the Ice Warriors – even though humankind is exploring the solar system in her time – which suggests that her contemporaries are not interested in Mars. We learn in *Transit*, amongst many other historical snippets, that the Thousand-Day War ended about twenty-five years before (p188) and that the decade following the war saw economic upheaval (p108). In his "Future History Continuity", Ben Aaronovitch stated that the War took place between 2086-2088, which by his reckoning was straight after *The Seeds of Death*. Victory Night is mentioned in *The Highest Science* (p21), and it might celebrate the end of this War. We learn in *Infinite Requiem* that forests are still planted after a battle (p266).

252 *The Story of Martha:* "The Frozen Wastes"

253 According to the Doctor in *The Mutants*. As we will see, a number of stories claim to be set on the "first" colony. To explain the apparent contradiction, it's pos-

sible that colonists are either counting different "firsts" (the first plan to colonise, to actually leave Earth, to arrive, to terraform, to settle, to form a local government and so on) or that they simply like to take pride in their pioneering ways and are prepared to exaggerate a little.

254 In *The Sensorites*, ship captain Maitland thinks the Doctor's party is from the twenty-first century. *The Waters of Mars* establishes the first mission to Proxima Centauri flew at "lightspeed", but there's been no firm date set for when humankind first flew faster than light.

255 *Transit* (p264).

256 *The Coming of the Terraphiles*. It's unclear what qualifies as "deep space" in the Terraphile era, when ships fly between galaxies and even universes.

257 *The Pit*

258 *Benny: The Big Hunt*

The children of Susie Fontana Brooke and their children forged their way across the stars to the Dragon Star and the Celestial Belt of the Winter Queen. They mapped the Water Snake Wormholes. A Brooke fell in love with a Tandorian prince, which was the start of a whole new species.[259]

Prospectors such as Dom Issigri and Milo Clancey were the first men into deep space. Clancey's ship, the "C" Class freighter LIZ 79, remained in service for forty years. Spacecraft at that time were built with the metal tillium and used a thermonuclear pile to supply power. Mined ore was sent to refineries in "floaters", slow unmanned vessels. An almost indestructible metal, argonite, was found on some of the planets in the fourth sector. Soon, all ships were made from argonite, which became the most valuable mineral known to man.

Clancey and Issigri became rich over the next fifteen years of working together, especially after they had spent ten years strip-mining the planet Ta in the Pliny System. Clancey became something of a legend on Reja Magnum. The partners eventually split, though, and Issigri went on to found the Issigri Mining Company.[260]

Robots such as the self-activating Megapodic Mark seven-Z Cleaners had some degree of autonomy. Scanners were developed that could track individuals. Miracle City had been masterpiece of the architect Kroagnon, but he refused to move out and let the residents sully his work by moving in. He was forced out, but the booby-traps he left behind massacred many of the residents. Kroagnon fled and was allowed to build Paradise Towers. During the war, youngsters and oldsters were evacuated to the 304-storey building, where the authorities forgot all about them.[261]

Earth's Colonial Age began in the 2090s. Multinational conglomerates started the Century Program, sending colony ships to a dozen worlds in the hope of alleviating the population crisis on Earth.[262]

---

259 *The Waters of Mars.* The Doctor no doubt means that the Brookes were space explorers for many generations, so it's very difficult to date these events. The Dragon Star might (or might not) be a reference to Draconia.

260 *The Space Pirates.* The story states the "whole galaxy" has been explored. Yet based on evidence from many other stories, in which planets and civilisations are discovered long after this time, this must be an exaggeration or the exploration must be fairly rudimentary.

261 The Doctor watches the prospectus in *Paradise Towers* and relates Kroagnon's story. The Chief Caretaker describes Kroagnon as a "being" rather than a "man", suggesting Kroagnon might be an alien. It's never specified that the tower block was built on Earth, but this seems to be the implication. The war in question might be the conflict of *Warriors of the Deep* or the Thousand Day War first referred to in *Transit*.

262 *Killing Ground*

263 "At least a hundred years" before *Wooden Heart*.

264 *TW: Red Skies,* as evidenced in *The Satan Pit*.

265 *Shakedown*

266 *Vengeance on Varos.* The Governor notes that "Varos has been stable for more than two hundred years".

267 *The Prisoner's Dilemma*

268 "They've come a long way in a hundred years" according to the Doctor in *Time of Your Life* (p27).

269 *Love and War* (p39).

270 *Birthright* (p189).

271 *The Also People* (p155, p191).

272 *The Face-Eater* (p64).

273 *Nightmare of Eden*

274 *So Vile a Sin*

275 "The Screams of Death", "The Child of Time" (*DWM*).

276 Dating *Snowglobe 7* (NSA #23) - The year is given.

277 Dating "Sun Screen" (*The Doctor Who Storybook 2008*) - It's "the twenty-first century". The technological prowess needed to erect the Great Solar Shield is well beyond contemporary levels. The Doctor believes that humanity will find a means of dealing with global warming in "a few years", but it's still a problem in *Snowglobe 7,* set in 2099.

278 "Twenty years" before *Under the Lake*.

279 "Ninety-one years" before *Killing Ground*.

280 *The Evil One*

281 According to the Doctor in *Army of Ghosts*, although he might just mean they shouldn't have them at that point in the twenty-first century (2007).

282 *Leth-St: Night of the Intelligence* (ch10).

283 *Last of the Gaderene* (p246). He also says he has flown a Spitfire in *Loups-Garoux*.

284 *Heart of TARDIS*

285 "Profits of Doom"

286 *CD, NM: Day of the Vashta Nerada.* This presumes a restarting of the Apollo programme, or perhaps – as with the tenth Doctor novel *Apollo 23* – even more missions were launched in the *Doctor Who* universe. In real life, the last such mission, Apollo 17, happened 7th to 19th December, 1972.

287 *The Wreck of the World,* date unknown. *Kill the Moon* relies upon there being very little exploitation of the moon by 2049, and there's no sign of a lunar TV station in *The Moonbase* [2070] either.

288 Dating *Paradise Towers* (24.2) - Paradise Towers has been abandoned for between about fifteen and twenty years, judging by the age of the Kangs. The Doctor's remark that the building won awards "way back in the twenty-first century" may or may not suggest that the story is set in the twenty-second. Taking the New Adventures into account, the War at Time Start might

Slow Century Class ships were sent into deep space – once they arrived at their destination, they became useful space stations. Two such vessels, the *Castor* and the *Pollux*, were sent out into a demilitarised sector by the New Rome Institute to house dangerous criminals. Earth at this time was ruled by a World Minister. The Pacific Rim Co-operative was in conflict with the SubSaharan Autonomies. Quad fuel cars were operating.[263]

When humanity ventured into space, it took the name "Torchwood" with them.[264]

The Pinkerton Intergalactic Agency of detectives soon followed colonists into space, solving crimes on colony worlds where law enforcement was often erratic or corrupt.[265] **The prison planet Varos was established in the late twenty-first century to remove the criminally insane from galactic society.**[266] Humanity converted the moon Erratoon into a prison planet by encasing it in a geodesic sphere.[267] The seven planets of the binary Meson System were colonised at this time.[268]

Human Travellers fled oppression on Earth by stealing a ship. When human ships reached Arcturus Six, the Earth ambassador was told that Travellers had already landed.[269] Developers filled in the Serpentine in the late twenty-first century.[270] The corporation Imogen built a facility on Titan to clone generation two ubersoldaten. The Doctor visited this period to download Kadiatu's user manual.[271]

The Global Mining Corporation replaced the US Army, and provided military training for corporations. The world language was "International American".[272] **Galactic Salvage and Insurance went bankrupt in 2096.**[273] Kadiatu Lethbridge-Stewart acquired a Triangulum Swift 400, a ship built in the twenty-first century.[274]

In Salzburg, 2098, the leader of the Eugenic Cult – Eldritch Valdemar – was betrayed by his colleagues and convicted of treason, murder and mental domination. He was given a death sentence.

(=) The time child Chiyoko transported Valdemar back to nineteenth-century Earth.[275]

2099 - SNOWGLOBE 7[276] -> Global warming had now accelerated the melting of the polar ice caps to the point that the world's governments preserved large portions of the Arctic and Antarctic in ten enormous domes around the globe. Seven of these were transferred from public to private ownership and became holiday resorts. Service Robots were common in this era.

The TARDIS landed in Snowglobe 7 in Saudi Arabia, where the tenth Doctor and Martha found that the sole-surviving Gappa had been disturbed from its dormancy in the ice, and was hatching offspring from eggs. The Doctor destroyed the Gappa, and Snowglobe 7, by detonating the fusion core of the spacecraft that had brought the Gappa to Earth a hundred thousand years before.

c 2099 - "Sun Screen"[277] -> The Great Solar Shield – a series of networked mirrors in space that decreased the sunlight that fell on Earth, and was a stop-gap means of reducing global warming – was one of humankind's greatest technological achievements in the twenty-first century. Energy parasites, the Silhouettes, were drawn to the Shield's energy, then Earth. The tenth Doctor and Martha re-attuned the Shield to project a rainbow that destroyed the Silhouettes, but the Shield broke up. The Doctor ferried the Shield crew back to Earth in the TARDIS, and told Martha that humanity would develop an ingenious means of dealing with global warming in a few years' time.

Vector Petroleum surveyed the submerged MOD town in Caithness, Scotland.[278] The sixth Doctor and Grant Markham went back to see the *New Hope* leave for the Centraxis System in 2100. Within ten years, the colonists aboard would found Grant's home planet of Agora.[279]

Gold was discontinued as a reserve currency in the late twenty-first century.[280] **Humankind didn't develop particle guns until after the twenty-first century.**[281]

The Twenty-Second Century

Adam Hicks, the son of an acid farmer and a reincarnation of Owain Vine, was born in the twenty-second century.[282] The Doctor flew a Spitfire in the twenty-second century.[283] He also took Victoria to the NovaLon Hypercities of the twenty-second century.[284] Vincent Grant, the Butcher of Strasbourg, unified the Western Alliance in the early twenty-second century.[285] The eighth Doctor owned spacesuits from Apollo 32 or 33.[286]

BBC Luna became the first TV station based on the moon.[287]

c 2100 - PARADISE TOWERS[288] -> Paradise Towers, a self-contained, award-winning tower block that had been abandoned during the war, was rediscovered in the early twenty-second century. With only old and young people in residence, society became stratified. The young girls became Kangs – with an array of "ice-hot" slang and "high fabsion" (sic) clothing – the old women became Rezzies and the Caretakers tried to maintain the building by rigidly sticking to their rule book. Each group had a distinctive language, and each preyed mercilessly on the other. At least two of the residents resorted to cannibalism.

The Kangs split into three rival factions – Red, Blue and Yellow – although "wipeouts" or "making unalive" was forbidden (as were visitors, ball games and fly posting).

Kroagnon's disembodied mind had been exiled to the Towers' basement, but he now possessed the Chief Caretaker using the science of corporal ectoscopy. He put the Towers' robotic cleaners to the task of eliminating the residents, but the various social factions united alongside the seventh Doctor and Mel. A war deserter, Pex, sacrificed himself to kill Kroagnon. Social order was restored, and Pex was remembered in wallscrawls.

Foundation of the Guild of Adjudicators

In the early twenty-second century, the Guild of Adjudicators was established as a judicial force unrestrained by authority or financial dependence. They were based on the remote planet Ponten IV. Early successes for the "ravens" (so-named because of their black robes) included the execution of fifteen drug dealers on Callisto, the suppression of a revolution in Macedonia and the disciplinary eradication of the energy-wasting population on Frinelli Minor. The Adjudicators also dealt with the Kroagnon Affair, vraxoin raids over Azure, the Macra case and the Vega debacle.[289] Adjudicator Bishop discovered Paradise Towers.[290]

c 2100 (24th December) - IRIS S2: THE CLAWS OF SANTA[291] -> Father Christmas was bedevilled as humanity expanded into space, leaving him unable to deliver presents on time. Iris Wildthyme provided Santa with Clockworks technology that let him take short cuts through the Vortex, and the two of them had a quick fondle in the back of his sleigh. Santa's wife, Mary Christmas, became incensed upon finding Iris' earring there.

Mary found Panda after he'd been lost to the Vortex in 1999. She kicked her husband out of his North Pole factory, and created "Flare Bears" modelled upon Panda. These became the best-selling toys in the multiverse, but contained a device that would regress all adults to children – which in Mary's opinion make the universe much happier. Iris was reunited with Panda while foiling Mary's plan, and an adaptation of Mary's device made her and Father Christmas young and in love again.

Zoe Heriot read the ingredients of a tea box in a kitchen on Pluto.[292] The Ceatul Empire's downfall enabled humans to settle the four planets of the Domus System. The

---

well be the Thousand-Day War that took place a generation before *Transit*. In *Lucifer Rising*, Adjudicator Bishop refers to the "messy consequences of the Kroagnon Affair" (p189), so it is set before then.

The Terrestrial Index suggested that the war is the Dalek Invasion of Earth, and therefore set the story around 2164. *About Time* pondered placing the story near *Nightmare of Eden* in the early twenty-second century, while wondering if the war was indeed the Dalek Invasion. *Timelink* sets the story in 2040.

289 The Master poses as an Adjudicator in *Colony in Space*, the only time the Adjudicators were referred to or seen on television. They feature a number of times in the New Adventures, and the Doctor's companions Cwej and Forrester are ex-Adjudicators. *Lucifer Rising* relates the foundation of the Guild of Adjudicators, and their early successes. "The Macra case" (p189) isn't necessarily *The Macra Terror*, and is likely another encounter with that race. *Gridlock* would suggest that humanity had many encounters with the species.

290 *Lucifer Rising*. There's no indication how long after *Paradise Towers* this happened.

291 Dating *Iris S2: The Claws of Santa* (BF Iris #2.5) - It's Christmas Eve, obviously. The story takes place after the melting of the polar ice cap in the late twenty-first century. Also, *The Claws of Santa* is predicated on Father Christmas not being able to cope with humanity's expansion beyond the solar system – a flip-over point that roughly dates to 2100. All of this presumes that the planet-sized Cosmo Mart that Iris visits – which seems to be in the same time zone – actually has nothing to do with humanity at all, as it's far, far too soon for humankind's space explorers to have the resources and technology for such an undertaking.

292 "Seventeen years" before *The Memory Cheats*.
293 This occurs as part of Earth's "first wave" of colonists, "five hundred years" (p153) before *Benny: A Life in Pieces*.
294 "Five hundred years" before *Benny S6: The Goddess Quandary*. There's no reason to think that any of the participants of the Festari war are human.
295 Dating *River S2: The Unknown/Five Twenty-Nine/World Enough and Time* (BF *The Diary of River Song* #2.1-2.3) - The first three episodes of this box set, set in Earth's future, take place "four hundred years" after the Great Storm of 1703. The story is ultimately, as you might have sensed, very paradoxical.

Other *Doctor Who* stories establish that humanity doesn't gain time-technology until well after this point, and it's notable that the *Saturnius'* prototype temporal shielding doesn't actually work. (Humanity does seem to have hyperspace technology, however, even though it's a bit early for that also.) *The Android Invasion* established that oak trees only grow on Earth.

296 *The End of the World*
297 *Excelis Decays*
298 Dating "The Cruel Sea" (*DWM* #359-362) - It's "the early twenty-second century". At one point, the Doctor says Rose is his fifty-seventh companion.
299 *Lucifer Rising* (p100, p320).
300 *Timewyrm: Revelation*
301 *Transit* (p157-158).
302 *Deceit* (p27-28).
303 *Wetworld*
304 Dating *Genocide* (EDA #4) - The date is given (p30).
305 Dating *Wetworld* (NSA #18) - The year is given (p32).

Purpura Pawn – thought to have decorated Ceatul XVI's sword pommel during his final battle – became a surviving relic of the empire.[293] War spread throughout the quadrant containing the Imogenella Star Cluster. The Festari were defeated when a woman, Aldebrath, transferred her mind into the systems aboard the spaceship *Fervent Hope*, then emitted a telepathic virus that compelled the Festari to seek a path of love and tranquillity. Legends subsequently arose about Aldebrath, the mighty male warlord who saved Imogenella.[294]

c 2103 - RIVER S2: THE UNKNOWN / FIVE TWEN-TY-NINE / WORLD ENOUGH AND TIME[295] ->

Botanists tried to seed oaks on worlds beyond Earth, but they always died. Oil rigs were still in use on humanity's homeworld. Androids became commercially available.

(=) Golden Futures offered artisan dream services to the elite – a cover for its true operations, four centuries in the making. With an apocalypse due to overtake Earth on a fateful day at 5.29pm, Golden Futures crafted a copy of Earth in a hyper-dimensional gallery, and planned to sell this duplicate once the original was destroyed. Clandestine elements within the company intended that the Sperovore larvae birthed in 1703 would feast upon the new Earth's inhabitants.

Earth Government detected the duplicate Earth, which was replete with temporal breaks, and rushed the *Saturnius* – a vessel with temporal shielding derived from hyperspace technology – into production. A collision between the *Saturnius*, the duplicate Earth and the seventh Doctor's TARDIS created a multi-dimensional singularity, but River Song retroactively prevented the event from happening.

The sixth Doctor suspected something was awry with Golden Futures, and purchased 51% of the company. He and River used Golden Futures' equipment to transfer the scheduled apocalypse from Earth to its doppelganger, but this caused a temporal schism. Earth became a Schrodinger's World: existing one moment, destroyed the next.

River kissed the sixth Doctor with her amnesiac lipstick, and sent him away in his TARDIS. She accepted a lift from the seventh Doctor back to 1703, where they deprived the Sperovore larvae of nourishment, scrubbing these events from the timeline.

Earth in 2105 was "a bit boring", according to the Doctor.[296] Grayvorn escaped the Imperial Museum when someone died there and he mentally inhabited their body. He took a position of authority within the Wardens and instigated a series of sociopolitical changes on Artaris.[297]

c 2106 - "The Cruel Sea"[298] -> The ninth Doctor and

Rose arrived on Mars – now a leisure planet with artificial seas for the ultra-rich to sail on. They'd landed on the yacht of Alvar Chambers, who owned the air on Earth, the air on Io, air with lime and classic air. A protoplasmic replica of one of Chambers' ex-wives attacked them, and the Doctor deduced that the sea had become sentient. A dormant ancient Martian organism had been revived by the terraforming process on Mars, but the Doctor dissipated it.

2106 saw the Ozone Purge, the first sign that man had not solved the Earth's environmental problems. The Purge was caused by a breakdown of weather control technology, and a number of species – including such previously common creatures as sheep, cats and sparrows – were wiped out.[299]

During the twenty-second century, human babies were grown artificially to be used in scientific tests.[300] Yembe Lethbridge-Stewart died in 2106. His daughter buried him alongside his wife at Achebe Gorge on Mars.[301]

In 2107, Eurogen and the Butler Institute – relatively small corporations for the time – merged to become Eurogen Butler or the "EB Corporation". Eurogen was a major genetic research facility. After its near-collapse a century before, the Butler Institute had survived by specialising in artificial intelligence, meteorology and weather control. Both companies were expanding into the field of interplanetary exploration, and their services were now required on a dozen worlds.[302]

Humans colonised the planet Sunday in 2107 in the Mk II Worldbuilder *One Small Step* – which was powered by a polluting fission generator, and had launched from the Democratic Republic of Congo. An asteroid caused a tsunami that inundated the colonists' main settlement, Sunday City, shortly after their arrival. Half of the four hundred settlers drowned, including their leaders.[303]

(=) 2108 (1st January) - GENOCIDE[304] -> The eighth Doctor and Sam arrived on Earth in a deviant timeline in which humanity had been eradicated. The relatively passive Tractites now occupied Earth and had named it Paratractis. The Doctor and Sam travelled back to historical junctures 2.5 million years and 3.6 million years in the past to avert this history.

2108 - WETWORLD[305] -> The tenth Doctor planned to take Martha to Tiffany's near the Robot Regent's palace on the planet Arkon, but they ended up on the swampy world of Sunday – where a mindless alien creature, the Slimey, had taken control of the native otterlike creatures. The Slimey planned to blast itself into space by detonating the colony's nuclear reactor, but the Doctor defeated it.

2108 - IRIS S2: THE TWO IRISES[306] -> Iris Wildthyme's lover Roger had been sent back in time with a Naxian beachhead, but judged that his people were rubbish at conquering the galaxy and instead opened a nightclub in Spain. He unwisely tried to get Iris' attention by sparking an international incident using the power of disco.

Iris had now retired to a rehab dimension, and left Panda to travel with Iris Hilary Wildthyme, a computer-generated projection made by Iris' bus. Panda summoned the real Iris when Roger's actions triggered a nuclear conflict between Earth's North and South Blocs. Iris and her friends prevented the disaster, and Hilary stayed to help Roger run the nightclub.

In July 2108, the Doctor visited Oxford Street and bought a Xavier Eugene microscope and a pair of wings in the sales.[307] Marmadons were foul creatures that lived in deep space. A century after Kim Krontska, Tom Braudy and Samuel departed Earth, one such monster broke into their ship and killed Samuel. Tom and Kim revived from cryo-sleep and dealt with the creature, then learned they were far from home. Kim re-entered stasis and returned to Earth, but Tom left in a coffin-shaped escape pod.

Tom crashed on the planet Lucentra, marking the first visit to that world by an extra-terrestrial. The natives were a technologically advanced race with dreadful long-term memories. Two Lucentran entrepreneurs, Lest and Argot, extended Tom's lifespan and kept him docile in a cell that re-created his childhood. In the decades to come, Lest and Argot would repeatedly haul Tom out and dramatically re-create his arrival for the forgetful Lucentrans' enjoyment.

The Lucentrans, as with many other races, engineered nano-forms: tiny creatures with limited intelligence, designed to carry out very specific tasks. Such technology always derived from the nature of the species forging it.[308]

Events portrayed in the film *Independence Day* (1996) actually happened, but in 2109.[309] Earth manufactured technology with an even-greater quantum capacity.[310]

The Stunnel; the Seventh Doctor Meets Kadiatu Lethbridge-Stewart

c 2109 - TRANSIT[311] -> The Union of Solar Republics attempted to build the first interstitial tunnel to another star system. The Stunnel would provide instantaneous travel to Arcturus II, twenty-six light years away, and if successful would allow rapid colonisation of other planets.

306 Dating *Iris S2: The Two Irises* (BF *Iris* #2.3) - The year is given.
307 *Speed of Flight, Genocide.*
308 *Memory Lane*
309 *Heart of Stone* (p79)
310 Zoe finds such tech that, she believes, originates from "a good few decades on" from her time in *The Wreck of the World.*
311 Dating *Transit* (NA #10) - The exact date of the story is not specified. The book takes many of its themes from *The Seeds of Death*, and is set at least a generation after that story. The Transit system has been established for at least the last couple of decades and has revolutionised the world – no television stories seem to be set during this period. It is hinted that the story takes place in the twenty-second century (p134). In his "Future History Continuity", *Transit* author Ben Aaronovitch places this story "c2109". *GodEngine*, following the Virgin version of *Ahistory*, dated the story as "2109" (p1). *So Vile a Sin* gave the date as 2010, which would seem to be a misprint (p140).
312 *GodEngine*
313 *Festival of Death*, possibly a reference to *Transit*.
314 *Graceless IV: The Ward*
315 *Deceit* says that production line warships are being made by 2112 (p28). Suspended animation is seen in a number of New Adventures set after this time, including *Deceit, The Highest Science* and *Lucifer Rising.*
316 *Nightmare of Eden.* This happens after *Transit*, but there's enough time before *Nightmare of Eden* to allow Tryst to explore and for Earth to found a colony on (at

least) Azure. The starship *Empress* has left from Station Nine.
317 *Benny: Genius Loci*
318 *Cold Fusion.* The planet was named as Salomon in the synopsis, but not the book.
319 The Interstellar Space Corps appears in *The Space Pirates*, the Marine Space Corps appears in *Death to the Daleks* and the Space Corps is referred to in *Nightmare of Eden.*
320 "Three years" after *Transit* (p260).
321 *St Anthony's Fire* (p195, p260). Urrozdinee first appeared in a short story of the same name by Mark Gatiss in Marvel's *Doctor Who Yearbook 1994.* In that story, the city is a post-apocalyptic feudal state inhabiting the remains of EuroDisney.
322 *Sword of Orion*
323 Centuries before *Vanishing Point.* Arbitrary date.
324 Dating *Kursaal* (EDA #7) - The year isn't stated, but Gray Corporation is mentioned in *Seeing I* (p25), establishing – given that the founder of Gray Corp is here killed – something of a lower threshold as to when *Kursaal* can take place. Interplanetary travel is used to reach Kursaal, and visitors there include an Alpha Centaurian (from *The Curse of Peladon*) and some Ogrons (*Frontier in Space*). Not only does this suggest that Saturnia Regna is located near Earth space, but it's possible that Kursaal is a precursor to the sort of "leisure planet" trend found in such stories as *The Leisure Hive* (dated to 2290).

The seventh Doctor and Benny were at King's Cross station when disaster struck during the Stunnel's initiation – a portion of an intelligence from another dimension came through the Stunnel, and the President was killed. The Doctor found that Stunnel network itself had attained a level of intelligence, and banished the intruder back to its native dimension. It became clear that it was impossible to maintain Transit tunnels over interstellar distances. Following activity on Mars, a nest of Martians was revived and entered negotiations with humanity.

The Doctor visited the Stone Mountain archive and found that the security software there had become sentient. He agreed to keep silent about this development if it wiped all records pertaining to him. The AI named itself FLORANCE.

Kadiatu Lethbridge-Stewart was now a student at Lunaversity, and met the Doctor – who postulated that she might be a sort of anti-body created in response to his intervening in history. After the Doctor and Benny left, Kadiatu finished her own time machine and followed them.

The Transit system was abandoned soon after this incident. The Martian castes debated making peace with Earth in 2110. Humans established two human cities on Mars: Jacksonville and Arcadia Planitia.[312] Humanity developed the theory of hyperspace tunnels in the early twenty-second century.[313]

An expedition to find arkenite, a substance used in planetary cleansing, went awry in the Belt. The crew survived by locating a cargo pod abandoned fifty years earlier. The event's publicity encouraged the Belt to become a hub of abandoned materials and rescue ships, leading to the creation of the hospital Space Dock One.[314]

The first production line warships began to be built. Lagships were still used for many years on longer journeys, although the technology remained risky.[315] **Humankind discovered warp drive, allowing it to travel faster-than-light. Azure, in West Galaxy, was colonised and became a tourist destination. At least nine space Stations were set up. By now, contact with alien species was almost routine.[316]**

The Protocols of Colonisation were established. The Earth Reptiles and their allies inserted a Hibernation Clause stating that colonists must withdraw from a world if the indigenous species revived from stasis.[317] An ice planet was discovered when a scientific expedition made a misjump through hyperspace. Marooned for three years, they established a colony run along rational lines. Three years later, when the rescue ships arrived, they elected to stay. Miners and other colonists arrived and were ruled by an elite of scientists, the Scientifica.[318]

The Space Corps was set up.[319]

Kadiatu Lethbridge-Stewart destroyed the Butterfly Wing, apparently committing suicide in the process ... although there were rumours that she had built a time machine.[320]

The crusade of the Chapter of St Anthony was becoming notorious. Youths from the Initiate League torched the city of Urrozdinee when they refused to accept the rule of the Chapter. Shortly afterwards, the crusade spread unopposed to the stars, in two mighty battleships capable of laying waste to whole planets and destroying small moons. The Chapter raided Titan, and recruited the malevolent dwarf Parva De Hooch. Shortly afterwards, the Chapter returned to Earth and De Hooch killed his parents.[321]

Garazone Central was one of the first cities to "float between the stars", and was located well away from Earth authorities, maintaining its own Space Patrol. The Garazone bazaar became a trading post for humans and aliens alike.[322]

Earth authorities imprisoned the geneticist Cauchemar for murdering people in his quest to achieve immortality. He was dispatched on a colony arkship to a prison world at the edge of the New Earth frontier, but half the crew died in a meteor strike. A race of benevolent aliens offered to save the survivors from dying of radiation poisoning. Cauchemar aided the aliens in transforming the humans into hosts for their own criminals.

The hybrids were seeded onto an unnamed planet, lacking knowledge of their previous identities. Those who lived commendable existences passed into the afterlife; those who didn't were reincarnated to try again. The colony lost population as souls were redeemed. "The Creator" was a semi-sentient entity that oversaw this process.

Cauchemar's experiments had rendered him unsuitable as a host, and he was exiled. He returned to find his lover Jasmine among the reincarnated populace, but his "alien" presence disrupted the Creator and killed her.[323]

c 2110 - KURSAAL[324] -> Gray Corporation owned the planet Saturnia Regna, and was constructing the theme park/holiday destination Kursaal there. The eighth Doctor and Sam wanted to visit Kursaal, but erroneously arrived some years before it had been built. Gray Corp's bulldozers unearthed the Jax cathedral, enabling the revived Jax virus to turn human corpses into animated were-creatures. The founder of Gray Corp, Maximillian Gray, was infected with the virus while he was still alive; moonlight catalysed his transformation into a Jax pack leader. A struggle led to Gray's death, and the virus secretly passed into Sam, who departed with the Doctor.

Because interstellar travel and communications were still relatively slow, colony planets were often left to their own devices. The founding fathers of these worlds were often important, and all sorts of political and social experimentation was attempted.

Many colonies were set up and directly controlled by the corporations, and many others were reliant on them for communications, transport and technology.[325] The EB Corporation was among the first to offer an escape from Earth in their warship, *The Back to Nature*, which was commissioned in 2112. Arcadia was a temperate planet, the second in its system, and was less than a thousand light-years from Earth. A number of years previous, the EB Corporation had set up a survey camp on the planet, the site of which would become the capital city Landfall, and set about terraforming the world. The planet came to resemble medieval Europe, and was ready for the first influx of colonists. Arcadia eventually became the Corporation's centre of operations.[326] **The eleventh Doctor took Amy to Arcadia at some point.**[327]

Early during Earth's interstellar expansion, a colony ship landed on Demigest and contact was lost. A rescue mission was also wiped out, but only after one member, Trudeau, dictated a log entry that became known as *The Black Book of Demigest*. Space and time never settled on Demigest as they did on most other worlds. The original colonists mutated to become the Warlocks of Demigest, and obtained great powers.[328]

No intelligent life was discovered on the outskirts of the galaxy, where the stars and planets were sparse. Before long, man abandoned all attempts to venture out past Lasty's Nebula. Humankind's colonisation efforts focused towards the centre of the galaxy – "the hub", as it became known. A thriving interplanetary community grew up.

The planet Evertrin was the site of the annual Inner Planets Music Festival, known as Ragasteen. The biggest bands in space attended to plug their discods: Deep Space, M'Troth, The Great Mothers of Matra, Is Your Baby a God and Televised Instant Death were all at Ragasteen 2112. The riggers on Earth changed the style of music every three years to keep it fresh. Zagrat, for example, were very popular during the "headster time", but teenagers found their discod "Sheer Event Shift" embarrassing just a few years later.[329]

Worlds such as the five planets of the Sirius System and Delta Magna rapidly became industrialised and overpopulated.[330] **Burglars began to use computers, forcing people to install audio locks.**[331] Tourism on Earth was a thing of the past.[332] The lethal drink

---

325 The founding fathers of a planet are revered in *The Robots of Death*, *The Caves of Androzani* and the New Adventure *Parasite*. Earth colonies feature in many, many *Doctor Who* stories. The corporations' stranglehold over the early colonies is a theme touched on in many New Adventures, especially the "Future History Cycle" which ran from *Love and War* to *Shadowmind*.
326 The Arcadia colony was founded "three hundred and seventy-nine" (Arcadian?) years before the events of *Deceit* (p115). It was one of the first Spinward Settlements (p16) and the planet (or at least part of it) has been terraformed (p103).
  NAMING PLANETS: The planet Arcadia is referred to in "Profits of Doom", *Deceit*, *Doomsday* and *Vincent and the Doctor*; Arcadian diamonds are mentioned in *TW: Kiss Kiss, Bang Bang*. In each case, this could be the same planet, as could the planets called Lucifer referred to in *Lucifer Rising* and *Bad Wolf*.
  The same can't be said for "New Earth", though – there's a New Earth Frontier in *Vanishing Point*, a New Earth Republic in *Synthespians™*, a New Earth System in "Fire and Brimstone", and planets called New Earth in "Dogs of Doom", *Time of Your Life*, *The Romance of Crime* and, well, *New Earth* (seen again in *Gridlock*). From what we see of the planets, what we're told of their locations and the dates in which they're settled, these are *not* the same planets. It's a natural enough name for a human colony, of course.
327 *Vincent and the Doctor*
328 *The Infinity Race*
329 *The Highest Science*
330 The Doctor says he visited Androzani Major when "it was becoming rather developed" in *The Caves of*

Androzani. In *The Power of Kroll*, we see the third moon of Delta Magna. (It is called "Delta III" in the novelisation and *Original Sin*, p21.)
  THE SIRIUS SYSTEM: In *Frontier in Space*, the Master poses as a Commissioner from Sirius IV and accuses the third Doctor and Jo of landing a spaceship in an unauthorised area on Sirius III. According to Romana in *City of Death*, Sirius V is the home of the Academia Stellaris, an art gallery she rates more highly than the Louvre. Circa 2773, in *DotD: Babblesphere*, the fourth Doctor and Romana give a hard drive to the Library of Artificial Intelligence at the Academia Stellaris on Sirius V.
  Max Warp occurs during a time of prosperity for Sirius (probably circa 3999), when the Sirius Exhibition Station plays host to the Inter-G Cruiser Show. In *The Caves of Androzani*, Morgus is the chairman of the Sirius Conglomerate based on Androzani Major, and spectrox is found on its twin planet Androzani Minor. These two facts make Morgus the "richest man in the Five Planets". We might infer that these are the five planets of the Sirius System, and that Androzani Major and Minor are Sirius I and II. The Doctor once had a sneg stew in a bistro on Sirius Two, according to *Island of Death*. By *The Children of Seth*, Sirius has an empire.
331 *The Space Pirates*
332 *Lucifer Rising* (p84).
333 *The Highest Science* (p102). Bubbleshake is an addictive drink akin to Bubble Shock (*SJA: Invasion of the Bane*). No overt connection has been made between the two, save that both stories were written by Gareth Roberts.
334 Dating *The Rebel Flesh/The Almost People* (X6.4-6.5) - We're told it's "the twenty-second century", but

Bubbleshake, invented by the unscrupulous Joseph-Robinson corporation, was originally an appetite suppressant. Unchecked, it was addictive, leading to memory loss, hyperactivity and compulsive behaviour. The substance was eventually outlawed.[333]

c 2111 - THE REBEL FLESH / THE ALMOST PEOPLE[334]
-> On Earth, the Morpeth-Jetsan company set up industrial operations to harvest crystal-diluric acid. The process killed so many workers that Morpeth-Jetsan created the Flesh: a malleable substance used to create human clones, Gangers, that were remote-controlled by their progenitors. The Gangers were treated as expendable, although an electrical surge on the Isle of Sheppey had granted a Ganger enough autonomy to kill its controller.

The eleventh Doctor brought Amy and Rory to an acid-mining facility built into a thirteenth-century monastery, as he wished to see the Flesh technology in its early days. A solar tsunami caused all of the Gangers present to became autonomous. Hostility arose between the workers and their Ganger counterparts, and the facility was destroyed. The Doctor took the survivors – one human and two Gangers – back to the mainland, where they held a press conference to call for Ganger rights.

Back on the TARDIS, the Doctor revealed that for several months now, the Amy travelling with him and Rory had been a Ganger planted in their midst by the Silence. He dissolved the duplicate into Flesh as the real Amy went into labour...

2112 - THE GEMINI CONTAGION[335] -> Zalnex
Corporation's researchers on the ice planet Vinsk used cloned Meme-Spawn to create Gemini: a dual-purpose handwash that made anyone who used it fluent in every known language. Gemini was only tested on the native Vinskians, and turned humans into savage mutants. The eleventh Doctor and Amy helped to stop an initial shipment of Gemini from reaching Earth, and used heat to destroy some giant Meme-Spawn.

& 2112 - MARTHA IN THE MIRROR[336] -> The planets
Anthium and Zerugma had been at peace for twenty years, and were scheduled to sign a peace treaty in Castle Extremis. The tenth Doctor and Martha were present as Zerguman soldiers hidden within the interior dimension of the Mortal Mirror stormed Extremis, but were killed by a combination of sonic waves and combat with troops from the Galactic Alliance. Manfred Grieg emerged from the Mirror's interior. With the treaty assured, the Alliance planned to turn Extremis into a theme park.

One of the last Hyperions survived, but remained dormant, on Neptune in 2114.[337] Earth discovered universal concrete in 2115.[338] Welford Jeffery invented antigrav technology.[339] In 2115, human archaeologists found the Martian city of Ikk-ett-Saleth completely abandoned.[340]

An engine-waste cartridge, ejected from a Baldrassian Corp spaceship, landed on the Golhearn homeworld. Every forty years, the cartridge vented particles that drove the Golhearn to madness.[341]

2116 - NIGHTMARE OF EDEN[342] -> Interplanetary
standards and conventions were set up that applied to the whole of Human Space. The Galactic Credit (z) was a convertible interplanetary currency. Credits resembled colourful blocks of plastic, and were used for everything from buying a drink to funding an expedition to a new planet. None of this prevented a recession from hitting the galactic economy.

Laser technology advanced during this period. Stun

---

nothing more specific, and the story doesn't have any explicit links with other adventures. We can probably conclude it is the first half of the century, as the second half entailed Earth being ravaged by the Dalek Invasion. There's no hint of interstellar travel or mention of space colonies, and the mining workers are listening to Dusty Springfield. All in all, we can probably set it a hundred years after the story was broadcast. *The Doctor: His Lives and Times* (p230) says an Equity Bill concerning the Gangers was given a Second Reading on "28 May".

335 Dating *The Gemini Contagion* (BBC *DW* audiobook #12) - The year is given.

336 Dating *Martha in the Mirror* (NSA #22) - No date is given. The only real clue is that the Darksmiths of Karagula (the ten-part *Darksmith Legacy*) built the Mortal Mirror, meaning that *Martha in the Mirror* cannot take place more than a century after the Darksmiths

are killed. Therefore, this dating reflects the latest that the story can occur.

337 *The Twelfth Doctor Year One*: "Terrorformer"

338 *The Face-Eater* (p40).

339 "Several hundred years" after Charley's time (the 1930s), according to *Sword of Orion*.

340 *GodEngine* (p73).

341 "Several hundred years" before *The Gods of Winter*. Writer James Goss verified that Baldrassian Corp isn't necessarily human.

342 Dating *Nightmare of Eden* (17.4) - Galactic Salvage and Insurance went bankrupt "twenty years ago" according to Captain Rigg, who had just read a monitor giving the date of the bankruptcy as "2096". *In-Vision* suggested that Azure is in "West Galaxy", but this could just be a mishearing of Rigg's (fluffed) line "you'll never work in *this* galaxy again". While others have disagreed

laser weapons became available for the first time. Entuca lasers capable of carrying millions of signals were now used for telecommunications. Finally, vast amounts of information could now be recorded on laser data crystals.

Crime was a problem in the galaxy. Drug trafficking increased when the drug XYP, or Vraxoin, was discovered. Vrax addicts felt a warm complacency at first, followed by total apathy and thirst. Inevitably, its effects were fatal. The narcotic ruined whole planets and communities until the planet that was the only known source of the drug was incinerated. A Vraxoin merchant (drug trafficker) risked the death penalty if caught. Molecular scanners were developed that could detect even minute quantities of the drug. All citizens were required to carry an ident-plaque.

Interplanetary tourism developed at this time. Government-subsidised interstellar cruise liners, each holding nine hundred passengers, travelled between Station Nine and Azure. Passengers could travel either economy or first class, the former seated in "pallets" and forced to wear protective clothing, the latter allowed a great deal more freedom and luxury.

The scientist Tryst attempted to qualify and quantify every lifeform in the galaxy. As Tryst's log (published to coincide with a series of lectures given by the zoolo-gist) recounted, his ten-man expedition travelled to Zil, Vij, Darp, Lvan, Brus, the windswept planet Gidi and the temperate world Ranx. Finally, Tryst's ship, the *Volante*, travelled past the Cygnus Gap to the three-planet system of M37. The second planet contained primitive life: molluscs, algae and insects. As well as taking visprints, they used a Continuous Event Transmitter (CET) machine – a device that encoded samples on laser crystals, enabling people to physically interact with them.

Six months before arriving at Azure, the *Volante* visited the planet Eden. They lost a member of the crew, Stott, who was secretly working for the Intelligence Section of the Space Corps. It was later discovered that Mandrels from the planet Eden decomposed into Vraxoin when they died, and that Tryst had partnered with Dymond, the pilot of the *Hecate*, to smuggle the material. Owing to intervention by the fourth Doctor, the second Romana and K9, the two of them were arrested.

An advanced type of radiation pill was developed.[343]

Humanity instigated the first of the great time shots, and saw one of its chrononauts, Colonel Orson Pink, off with fanfare. Pink's vessel was supposed to fire him into the middle of the next week, but it overshot and

---

with that, there is certainly no on screen justification for *The Discontinuity Guide*'s "Western galaxy". *The TARDIS Logs* gave the date as "c.2100", *The Doctor Who File* as "2113".

343 "One hundred years" after *Death Among the Stars* [2017].

344 *Listen*, "about a hundred years" in Clara's future.

345 *The Prisoner's Dilemma*. This is presumably the same galactic recession mentioned in *Nightmare of Eden*.

346 Dating *The Art of Destruction* (NSA #11) - The Doctor says it's "the eleventh of April 2118".

347 Dating *Legend of the Cybermen* (BF #135) - Zoe is clearly older, in contrast to her fictional self in the Land looking the same age as when she travelled with the Doctor. It seems reasonable to assume that from Zoe's perspective, the same number of years have passed since *The War Games* as have occurred since that story's broadcast in 1969 and the release of *Legend of the Cybermen* in 2010. *The Laird of McCrimmon*, an unmade TV story, is here cited as an adventure that Zoe invented in her capacity as the Land's Mistress.

348 Dating *Echoes of Grey*, *The Memory Cheats*, *The Uncertainty Principle* and *Second Chances* (BF CC #5.2, 6.3, 7.2, 8.12) - These four audios comprise a storyarc in which an older Zoe is increasingly embroiled in the affairs of the domineering Company.

In *Echoes of Grey*, the Doctor tells the Zoe with him that they've arrived, "A little into your future, I think"; Ali says that the contemporary Zoe is now a "fifty year old"; and the contemporary Zoe says that she is "forty years older" than when she travelled with the Doctor – something she reiterates in *Second Chances*. The younger Zoe in *Second Chances* says the TARDIS has arrived "only a few decades after my time".

The chosen placement of these Companion Chronicles to "& 2119" reflects it being forty years on from this guidebook's revised dating of *The Wheel in Space* to 2079, per information given in *The Dying Light*. In *Second Chances*, Zoe notes her first interrogation at Ali/Kym's hands (*Echoes of Grey*) was "less than a year" ago, providing a starting and ending boundary for all four Companion Chronicles. As *Echoes of Grey* saw release after (albeit by just two months) *Legend of the Cybermen*, it seems fair to assume that Zoe-related Companion Chronicles happen afterward.

In *The Memory Cheats*, Jen pulls records pertaining to the 1919 visit from an archive "one hundred fifty years old", but this would seem to be the age of the archive, not the duration of time since the Uzbekistan incident. If mention of it being "forty-seven days into cycle" in any way parallels the Gregorian calendar, then it's 16th February.

The *Hourly Tele-Press* was mentioned in *The Mind Robber*, Synch-operators appeared in *Warriors of the Deep*, and Spectrox is a key element of *The Caves of Androzani*.

sent him to the end of time. The twelfth Doctor and Clara returned the colonel home.[344] The prison moon Erratoon was forgotten about during the galactic recession. The thousands serving life sentences there had families, and the robot wardens monitored their descendents, making them do maintenance.[345]

2118 (April) - THE ART OF DESTRUCTION[346] ->

Earth risked famine, and Agriculture Technology research was underway to prevent this. The tenth Doctor and Rose thwarted the Wurms in Chad, but the Wurms had tracked down a warren of their archenemies, the Valnaxi, to Earth.

During the second and third decade of the twenty-second century, the Western Alliance banks foreclosed on Earth and the World Civilian Police Corps was formed. The Oceanic-Nippon bloc was working on interstellar flight, and the first supra-light vessel *New Horizon* was launched in 2126, taking five thousand colonists on a two-year journey to Proxima 2, the first colony in an alien environment. Proxima City was founded there. The second human colony world was called Earth 2.

& 2119 - LEGEND OF THE CYBERMEN[347] ->

Zoe Heriot deduced that she travelled with the Doctor and Jamie for a time, and her memories returned. The Cybermen re-invaded Space Wheel W3 and Cyber-converted its staff, including Leo Ryan. Zoe modified the Cybership's propulsion unit and transferred the Cybermen to the Land of Fiction, then enthroned herself as its new Mistress. She marshalled an army of fictional characters against the Cybermen, and pulled the sixth Doctor's TARDIS into the Land so he could help. He had some side adventures with a fictional version of Jamie McCrimmon, and eventually helped Zoe to resolve the Cybermen into fiction. He returned Zoe to the Wheel – whereupon the Time Lords' memory blocks renewed themselves, and she forgot her travels with him again.

Zoe and the Company

& 2119 - ECHOES OF GREY / THE MEMORY CHEATS / THE UNCERTAINTY PRINCIPLE / SECOND CHANCES[348] ->

At the Whitaker Institute in central Australia, the second Doctor, Jamie and Zoe shut down research pertaining to the Achromatics – man-made creatures who could heal any disease or injury, but couldn't refrain from killing both their patients and healthy people.

Afterward, Ali, an agent for the Company who backed the Achromatic research, approached the Zoe native to this timezone, and used a device to retrieve her memory of the adventure. The agent hoped that Zoe would provide the genetic codes for the Achromatics, but Zoe, sensing the Company wanted to turn the Achromatics into weapons of war, insisted she couldn't remember. The Company pun-

ished Ali, a.k.a. Kym, for her failure. Her supply of Spectrox was rescinded, causing her to outwardly age more than a decade, and her boyfriend left her.

Forty-seven days into the cycle, the Company charged Zoe on thirty-six counts, including sedition, extortion and threats to personnel. Zoe's defence assistant, Jen, said that the Company would exert a leniency clause if Zoe could provide information on time travel. Jen and Zoe examined the Doctor, Jamie and Zoe's trip to Uzbekistan, 1919, in the hope of restoring Zoe's memory. Zoe continued to insist that she had never travelled in time, and manipulated Jen into reading files that revealed the unscrupulous nature of the Company's Elite Programme. The Company in return selected Jen's children for the Elite Programme, binding her hands.

Kym covertly approached Zoe again, hoping for a breakthrough that would put her back in the Company's graces. Short-lived memory techniques enabled Zoe to recall how her younger self, the Doctor and Jamie had visited a Company space station, *Artemis*, near Saturn following the destruction of *Apollo*, its sibling. Researchers aboard *Apollo* had developed a computer virus that physically manifested to destroy metal and flesh alike – an ideal weapon for eliminating Synch-operators. The younger Zoe decoded a final transmission from *Apollo*, and unknowingly unleashed the virus into *Artemis*' systems. *Artemis* broke up, at the loss of all hands. The TARDIS crew escaped.

Kym realised that *Apollo* and *Artemis* had not fallen *yet*, and – to preserve causality – messaged *Apollo* to run a test of their prototype virus. A news tablet, the *Hourly Tele-Press*, reported that Apollo had been destroyed as Zoe predicted. Kym accompanied Zoe to *Artemis* under the pretence that they could change history and save the station, but then forced Zoe to use her computer expertise to copy the virus. Kym attempted to escape with the virus-copy in a shuttle as *Artemis* broke up, and shot Zoe as she transmitted a self-terminating form of the virus that targeted the Company and destroyed it. Zoe blacked out as the virus also damaged the shuttle's computers...

... and later awoke, realising that Kym, possibly in an act of repentance, had given Zoe her breather as the shuttle fell apart. Zoe believed the Doctor had saved her one last time, and that there was some truth in the saying that when you die, you're made to remember your entire life...

2119 (21st November) - UNDER THE LAKE / BEFORE THE FLOOD[349] ->

UNIT, still in service, acted as Earth's first line of defence. The Doctor's UNIT security visa, No. 710Apple00, was still valid.

Vector Petroleum established the Drum – a mining facility with equipment valued at $1 trillion – to drill for oil beneath a lake in Caithness, Scotland. The Drum-staffers discovered the Tivoli hearse submerged since 1980, and the alien technology aboard laboured to facilitate people's deaths, then harness their souls as electro-magnetic transmitters. With sufficient numbers, the soul-transmitters would summon an armada to rescue the Fisher King... or would have done, if he hadn't died back in 1980.

The twelfth Doctor took Drum staffers O'Donnell and Bennett back in time to look into the spaceship's origins. Clara spied the Doctor's "ghost", as he had evidently been killed in the past. The genuine Doctor awoke from a stasis pod he'd entered in 1980, having programmed his sonic sunglasses to project his "ghost" (actually an AI hologram), and thereby averting his demise via an application of the Bootstrap Paradox. The TARDIS returned with only Bennett aboard, and the Doctor used the Fisher King's recorded screams to contain the "ghosts" in a Faraday Cage. The Doctor and Clara left UNIT to destroy the Tivoli spaceship and transport the cage into space, which would make the "ghosts" fade away.

UNIT had been disbanded by this time. The records of Global Mining Corporation listed the Doctor as a security consultant from 2127 (adding that his female companion graduated Geneva Corporate University in 2124) following an unrecorded incident in Albania.[350] Proxima 2 was the first of the settled worlds and humans would come to share it with the Centauri.[351] The Particle Matter Transmission (Deregulation) Act was passed in 2122.[352] The first humans to arrive on Hitchemus, a planet on the edge of explored space, were hunters in pursuit of the tigers that lived there. The colony of Port Any was built shortly afterwards. It became famed for music and attracted musicians from across human space.[353]

c 2122 - "Space Invaders!"[354] -> Humanity's formidable production of material goods led the Great Storage Migration of 2122, as excess possessions were increasingly sent into orbit aboard containers equipped with pocket-dimensional shunts. The twelfth Doctor and Clara visited an Enormous Storage Company container as a storage unit belonging to conglomerate owner Hyphen T Hyphen was auctioned off. The Rigellan hyper-kraken within the unit went on a rampage, but the Doctor and Clara used the

---

349 Dating *Under the Lake/Before the Flood* (X9.3-9.4) - Captain Moran's journal gives the exact day. Proving that some dating statements *are* approximations, the Doctor says it's "one hundred fifty years" after 1980.

350 *The Face-Eater.* The dates given in the book seem to contradict a number of other stories set around this time.

351 *Tomb of Valdemar.* These Centauri are "multi-limbed" and have a "giant eye", so are almost certainly the same race as first seen in *The Curse of Peladon*.

352 *Cold Fusion*

353 The space port has been open a hundred years before *The Year of Intelligent Tigers*.

354 Dating "Space Invaders!" (*DWM* #484) - The year of the Great Storage Migration is named.

355 Dating *Kursaal* (EDA #7) - It's fifteen years after the Doctor and Sam's first visit.

356 The background to *Full Circle*.

357 *Mistfall*, elaborating on *Full Circle*.

358 *State of Decay.* No date is given. On screen, one computer monitor seems to suggest that the computer was programmed on "12/12/1998", but the *Hydrax* is clearly an interstellar craft. The *TARDIS Logs* suggested a date in "the thirty-sixth century", *The Terrestrial Index* placed it "at the beginning of the twenty second".

359 *Lucifer Rising* (p59, p272-273).

360 Variously said to happen "hundreds, maybe thousands of years"/"centuries"/"generations" before *Equilibrium*.

361 *The Taking of Planet 5* (p15).

362 *Spiral Scratch*

363 Dating *The Face-Eater* (EDA #18) - The date is given (p126).

364 "Two hundred years" after *The Silent Scream*.

365 Two hundred years after "A Matter of Life and Death" (issue #3).

366 Dating "The Doctor and the Nurse" (IDW Vol. 4 #3-4) - A caption provides the year.

367 *St Anthony's Fire*

368 *The Taint*

369 *The Face-Eater*

370 Dating *The Space Pirates* (6.6) - A monitor readout in episode two suggests that the year is "1992", but this contradicts dialogue stating that prospectors have been in deep space for "fifty years". No other date is given on screen. The *Radio Times* said that the story takes place in "the far future". Earth is mentioned once in the first episode, but after that only a "homeworld" is referred to. The force here is specified as the Interstellar Space Corps. The regulatory actions of the government suggest that space travel is becoming more common now, but is still at an early stage.

As Zoe is unfamiliar with the technology of this story, it is almost certainly set after her time. The Main Boost Drive is not very advanced, and this story almost certainly takes place well before *Frontier in Space*, where hyperdrive technology is common. At the start of the story, the V41-LO is both "fifty days" and "fifty billion miles" from Earth - it seems reasonable to assume that writer Robert Holmes meant "billion" in the British sense of a million million, rather than the American (and now generally accepted British) thousand million. If this is the case, then the Beacon is 8.3 light years from Earth (otherwise it is a thousandth of this distance, and only just outside the solar system).

The Programme Guide set the story "c.2600". The

dimensional shunt to send the kraken and its eggs to a backwater world.

& 2125 - KURSAAL[355] -> The eighth Doctor and Sam returned to Kursaal when it was open for business. Sam mentally succumbed to the Jax virus within her, but was stymied in her attempts to bathe in moonlight and complete her transformation. The Jax cathedral was obliterated, and the destruction of technology beneath it caused the Jax virus to perish. Unknown to the Doctor and Sam, the founder of the ecoterrorist organisation HALF, Bernard Cockaigne, remained at large as a Jax drone.

The Starliner and the *Hydrax*

The Starliner, a type of colony vessel, crashed onto the planet Alzarius in E-Space. The indigenous humanoids there, the Marshmen, broke into the Starliner and slaughtered those aboard. Owing to the rate of hyper-evolution on Alzarius, the progeny of the Marshmen in the Starliner developed to resemble the original Starliner crew. Manuals pertaining to the Starliner's construction and maintenance remained, but knowledge of how to pilot the ship was lost. The Deciders ruling the Starliner fostered the belief that the Starliner people were "readying" the ship for a return to the planet Terradon.[356] The crust of the planet Alzarius expelled life-infusing minerals into its waters, endowing all life on the planet with the same inheritance. When the Starliner crashed onto Alzarius, one of its fuel cells destroyed a Pool of Life endowed with such minerals.[357]

The exploration vessel *Hydrax* was lost en route to Beta Two in the Perugellis Sector. Its officers included Captain Miles Sharkey, science officer Anthony O'Connor and navigation officer Lauren Macmillan. It fell through a CVE into the pocket universe of E-Space.[358] The *Hydrax* disappeared around 2127. The InterSpace Incorporated ship had a crew of two hundred and forty-three. InterSpace refused to pay out pensions for the lost crew, claiming they might be found. IMC later claimed to have discovered traces of the ship in order to blackmail Piper O'Rourke – whose husband Ben had been an engineer on the *Hydrax* – into revealing details about the Eden Project. The ship was never discovered.[359]

Researchers in E-Space determined that their realm was finite and contracting, and established the domed, snowy kingdom of Isenfel to test how much energy could be recycled in a closed system. Exactly 9,582 people lived in Isenfel, the balance maintained by killing a member of each family as an offspring was produced. Matter-dissolving black snow fell on any settlement that failed to comply with the cull. Isenfel's founding researchers decided to seek a means of leaving E-Space for another universe, and the Isenfel experiment continued in their absence.[360]

The planet Vulcan suddenly vanished in 2130.[361]

= In one alternate universe, a hydrogen accident had devastated America. Racing spaceships around the solar system was a spectator sport by 2130.[362]

2130 - THE FACE-EATER[363] -> The eighth Doctor and Sam discovered the F-Seeta, a telepathic gestalt of the rat-like natives, was responsible for a series of murders on the first human colony world of Proxima 2. The colony was saved, but at the cost of the Proximans' group mind.

Humankind began tinkering with time corridors; Dr Julius used one to visit the dawn of talking films in Hollywood. Trans-organic celluforms, Celluloids, were invented for use as synthetic avatars.[364] If the eighth Doctor's instructions were heeded, the Bingham family once more turned the hibernation key keeping the Nixi king asleep.[365]

2133 - "The Doctor and the Nurse"[366] -> The eleventh Doctor and Rory found themselves at Dunlop Station, in orbit around 70 Virginis B, while trying to reach 1814.

On Betrushia around the year 2133, as it had done many times over the centuries, war broke out between the Ismetch and the Cutch. Millions died in the conflict, which became the longest and most bitter struggle the planet had seen for three hundred years. The Ismetch had an early success at Dalurida Bridge under Portrone Ran.[367]

The eighth Doctor, Sam and Fitz arrived in London during the summer of 2134, and confirmed that the Earth was free of the Beast.[368] A second wave of colonists was expected on Proxima 2 in 2136.[369]

? 2135 - THE SPACE PIRATES[370] -> As space travel became more common, the Earth government introduced a series of regulations to better control the space lanes in its territory. Space was divided into administrative and strategic Sectors. All flights now had to be logged with Central Flight Information and a network of Mark Five Space Beacons were established to monitor space traffic. The Interstellar Space Corps was given the latest V-Ships, armed with state-of-the-art Martian Missiles (H-bombs were considered old-fashioned by this time) and carrying squadrons of Minnow Fighters. The V-Ships were powered by Maximum Boost atomic motors. The Space Corps routinely used mind probes to interrogate their prisoners. The resources of the Space Corps were stretched very thin: they fought brush wars in three sectors, acted as customs and excise officials and attempted to curtail the activities of space pirates.

For two years, pirates were active in the Ta System

and hijacked five of Milo Clancey's floaters, each of which contained fifty thousand tons of argonite ore. Despite a dozen requests, the Space Corps did little to help. As an old-timer, Clancey was suspicious of authority; he had lost his registration documents thirty years before and he didn't maintain his feedback link to CFI.

The Space Corps became involved when the pirates began to break up government space beacons to steal the argonite. The V41-LO was more than fifty days out of Earth, under the command of General Nikolai Hermack, Commander of the Space First Division. The ship was ninety minutes away from Beacon Alpha 4 when it was broken up by pirates. Clancey's ship was detected nearby, and he was questioned but quickly released. The second Doctor, Jamie and Zoe were recovered from Beacon Alpha 4, but they too were innocent.

The real culprit was Maurice Caven. His pirates were organised enough to equip themselves with Beta Dart ships, costing one hundred million credits each, that could outrun virtually everything else in space. Some time ago, Caven had kidnapped Dom Issigri and blackmailed his beautiful daughter Madeline, the head of the Issigri Mining Company, into providing facilities for him on the planet Ta. The Corps hunted Caven down and executed him.

After this, the Issigri Mining Company was renamed the Interplanetary Mining Company, or IMC for short.[371] Humanity's contact with the Arcturans was proving fruitful. The Arcturans allowed limited human settlement in their sector, and supplied humanity with specialised drugs. Some humans became interested in studying Arcturan literature.

On Earth, however, things were getting desperate. The Islam-dominated Earth Central, based in Damascus and led by an elected president, was unable to prevent society from collapsing. An unprecedented energy crisis led to draconian restrictions on consumption and the foundation of the Energy Police. The invention of the vargol generator did little to relieve the demands for fuel.

In 2137, with Earth desperate for energy, corporations successfully lobbied for the repeal of all the anti-pollution laws brought in over the last century and a quarter. Three years later, an American subsidiary of Panorama Chemicals filled the Carlsbad Caverns with plastic waste, and the

---

Terrestrial Index suggested it was "during the Empire" period. *The TARDIS Logs* claimed a date of "8751". *Timelink* suggested "2146", *About Time* "2135ish". Milo Clancey's Toaster originates from the "22nd century" in *A History of the Universe in 100 Objects* (p105).

371 The Issigri Mining Company appears in *The Space Pirates*. Another company with the same initials, the Interplanetary Mining Company, is seen in *Colony in Space*. In the Missing Adventure *The Menagerie*, we learn that they are the same company (p161). The change of name must have occurred before *Lucifer Rising*, when we see IMC in action.

372 *Lucifer Rising*. The evil polluting company in the television version of *The Green Death* is called "Global Chemicals". A real company of that name objected, and the name was changed in the novelisation to "Panorama Chemicals".

373 Dating *The Memory Bank and Other Stories*: "Repeat Offender" (BF #217c) - The blurb says it's the "22nd century". Lara Jensen moved to Reykjavik in "37", so "Repeat Offender" presumably nestles between that year and the highly disruptive Dalek Invasion of Earth.

374 *Fear Itself* (PDA)

375 *Benny: Another Girl, Another Planet*. Aragonite was mentioned in *The Space Pirates*.

376 *The Sorcerer's Apprentice* (p203-204).

377 *Heritage* (p198).

378 *Leviathan*

379 Dating *The Murder Game* (PDA #2) - The date is given (p12).

380 *Lucifer Rising* (p158).

381 *Parasite*

382 Dating "The Daleks: The Terrorkon Harvest" (TV21 #70-75) - There's no indication how long after "Impasse" this TV Century 21 Dalek story is set, allowing the first significant gap in the narrative. The next story, "Legacy of Yesteryear", is set "centuries" after the first (which seems to be set in 1763 AD). The novel *GodEngine* notes that the Daleks became concerned with Earth ten years before they invade, and that's exactly what we see happening in these strips, so the novel has been used to establish the dating of these stories. This block of stories ends with the Daleks discovering Earth of the future and gearing up to invade – clearly a reference to *The Dalek Invasion of Earth*.

383 Dating "The Daleks: Legacy of Yesteryear" (TV21 #76-85) - It is "centuries" since the original Daleks were frozen – and that happened the day of the meteorite strike that set off the neutron bomb (seen in "Genesis of Evil"). The Daleks remember Yarvelling and his inventions. So there are "centuries" between "Impasse" and "The Terrorkon Harvest".

384 Dating "The Daleks: Shadow of Humanity" (TV21 #86-89) - There is no indication how long it has been since "Legacy of Yesteryear". The Emperor now knows about "human beings", although it's unclear when he heard the name – perhaps fragments of evidence were discovered in the wreckage of Lodian's ship after the previous story. The following stories all seem to take place without lengthy gaps between them.

oceans of the world were a sludge of industrial effluent. Mineral water became a precious commodity. The whale finally became extinct, and auto-immune diseases – "the plague" of over a century before – returned.

Despite this, human life expectancy was now one hundred and ten years, and the population was soaring. Although it had religious objections to gambling, Earth Central introduced the Eugenics Lottery, and couples were forbidden from having children unless they won.[372]

(=) c 2140 - THE MEMORY BANK AND OTHER STORIES: "Repeat Offender"[373] **->** In Reykjavik, justice officers could try suspects on the spot. A failure to register carried two years in jail; criminals with three strikes could receive thirty years in a lunar penal colony. Some countries on Earth were considerably hotter and dryer than a century before.

A body-jumping Bratanian Shroud killed two different Doctors for their artron energy, and desired to kill his previous selves to absorb even more. The fifth Doctor, accompanied by Turlough, used his foreknowledge to avert his murders.

A string of fundamentalist Jihads killed many people on Earth.[374] Eurogen Butler colonised Dimetos in 2142, and plundered the planet's mineral wealth, including aragonite. The indigenous population wouldn't accept relocation off world, so Eurogen Butler all but exterminated them.[375]

A colony ship made landfall on the planet Avalon in the year 2145. The colonists discovered an ancient Avalonian technology which allowed them to perform miracles, but soon rendered their electronic equipment useless. The colony regressed to a medieval level, in which certain people – unknowingly tapping the Avalonian technology – performed "magic".[376]

Dolphins' ability to think in three dimensions made them ideal pilots for Earth's first interstellar fighters.[377]

Humanity designed Leviathans – enormous multi-generation ships to the stars, with an independent ecosystem inside – in the mid-twenty-second century. Several prototype Leviathans were built until the interstellar drive was invented, and photon-speed travel made Leviathans obsolete. With Earth's governments moving against them, the Sentinels of the New Dawn populated a disused Leviathan with clones and slept in cryo-freeze as the Leviathan travelled toward the planet Flegathon in the Nyad System. The biomechanoid Herne, the Sentinels' chief assassin, kept watch over the clones. Zeron, a computer programme designed to control prison vessels, oversaw the Leviathan.[378]

2146 - THE MURDER GAME[379] **->** The European Government and the Terran Security Forces (TSF) were established by this time. The First Galactic Treaty had been signed. The Selachians had menaced Terra Alpha.

The second Doctor, Ben and Polly answered a distress call and landed in the Hotel Galaxian, a space station in Earth orbit. Two scientists, Neville and Dorothy Adler, were trying to sell assassination software to the Selachians. Neville Adler was killed and the space hotel burned up in the atmosphere. Dorothy Adler could not work the software without her husband.

In 2146, the American economy collapsed, and there were food riots.[380] The Doctor was in America at the time, and he was powerless to stop cannibals from killing Sonia Bannen shortly after she saved her son. Mark Bannen was placed on board a huge colony ship bound for a new star system. The stardrive misphased in the Elysium System and the colony ship crashed there.[381]

The Daleks Discover Earth

c 2146 - "The Daleks: The Terrorkon Harvest"[382] **->** On Skaro, one of the unknown creatures from the Lake of Mutations, the Terrorkon, attacked an underwater Dalek defence station. The Emperor and the Red Dalek watched as another mutation attacked it, saving the city.

& 2146 - "The Daleks: Legacy of Yesteryear"[383] **->** The Daleks begin a new survey of their home planet, discovering mineral riches and wiping out a race of sand creatures. One hoverbout inadvertently revived the group of original Daleks who had been in suspended animation for centuries, since the neutron explosion. These were the scientists Lodian, Zet and Yvric, who quickly determined that the new Daleks were without conscience. Even so, Yvric was keen to join the Daleks, but they exterminated him before he could even explain who he was. Zet realised that the Daleks would want to know about the Earth, a planet teeming with life and energy, and handed himself and Lodian over to them. Lodian escaped to a spaceship, planning to warn Earth of the Daleks. The spaceship exploded, killing the last two original Daleks and preserving the secret of Earth's existence.

& 2146 - "The Daleks: Shadow of Humanity"[384] **->** The Emperor ordered the building of a road to the Lake of Mutations, but one Dalek questioned the order and sabotaged the destruction of "beautiful" plant life. The Emperor feared that the introduction of human qualities could prove a disaster to the Daleks. The rebel Dalek exploited the natural Dalek to obey by issuing a new command to "protect beauty", and soon led a faction of Daleks as their Emperor. The Emperor quickly reasserted his power and destroyed the rebel.

& 2146 - "The Daleks: The Emissaries of Jevo"[385]
-> A space expedition from Jevo headed to Arides to prevent the spread of deadly pollen from that world. Their ship passed close to Skaro, and was snared by the Daleks' magnetrap. The Emperor assumed the pollen wouldn't affect Daleks, but the Jevonian leader Kirid tricked him into thinking otherwise. Kirid saved the universe from the pollen, but was tracked down and killed by the Daleks ... who nevertheless had started to worry about the strength of the human spirit.

& 2146 - "The Daleks: The Road to Conflict"[386] **->** The Daleks engineered a meteorite storm that damaged the Earth passenger ship *Starmaker*, which made a forced landing on Skaro. The Emperor was now obsessed with finding Earth – a planet hidden from Skaro by "skycurve" – as he was convinced that it was rich in polar magnetism and aluminium. Captain Fleet was captured and rescued by the children Jennie and Tom, but the Daleks destroyed the *Starmaker*. The three humans escaped in a Dalek transport ship to warn humanity about the Daleks... but the Daleks had now discovered the location of Earth, and planned its conquest.

& 2146 - "The Daleks: Return of the Elders"[387] **->** The Daleks attacked Colony Five on Titan, and experimented on six humans as another alien fleet entered the solar system. The mysterious aliens identified themselves as Elders, and explained that they have tended Earth and

warned that the Daleks would soon invade. The Earthmen destroyed one Dalek ship in the rings of Saturn, but another escaped. The Dalek Emperor vowed not to fail in his second attempt to conquer Earth.

By 2146, the Supreme Council of the Daleks had become concerned by the rapid expansion of humanity. They would monitor the situation carefully for ten years. The Martian Axis sprang up on Mars and turned to terrorism, bombing Coventry.[388]

3D cameras were developed around this time.[389]

2148 - ST ANTHONY'S FIRE[390] **->** A mothership of the Chapter of St Anthony moved to pacify Betrushia, breaking up the planet's artificial ring system to wrack Betrushia with meteorites. Loosed from its shackles, the organic catalyser became active and threatened all life that it encountered. The seventh Doctor convinced the Chapter as to the creature's threat, and arranged for Betrushia's destruction while instigating an evacuation. Appalled by the Chapter's zealous actions, Bernice and Ace sabotaged the mothership's engines, crippling it to suffer the same destruction as Betrushia and the organism. The Doctor helped the Betrushia survivors relocate to the sister planet of Massatoris.

Earth funded a small Transit station on Charon, a moon of Pluto. The Martian Axis terrorists destroyed the Montreal monorail system, resulting in many deaths.[391]

---

385 Dating "The Daleks: The Emissaries of Jevo" (*TV21* #90-95) - At the end of the story, the Emperor praises Kirid's "human spirit", and before that Kirid seems to call himself "human", although he looks more like a humanoid alien (he has forehead ridges, like a Klingon). Given that the next story features a spaceship from Earth, we are now definitely in the future.

386 Dating "The Daleks: The Road to Conflict" (*TV21* #96-104) - The story is set soon after "The Emissaries of Jevo". There's no date given, but this story features an interstellar human passenger spacecraft, and the people have never heard of the Daleks. So this is set before *The Dalek Invasion of Earth*, almost certainly in the first half of the twenty-second century, which fits in with later televised stories such as *Nightmare of Eden*.

387 Dating "The Daleks: Return of the Elders" (*DWM* #249-254) - This was a sequel to the *TV Century 21* strip. It is set straight after "The Road to Conflict". The Daleks attack the solar system, but it ends in failure. The Emperor vows to succeed next time – and that is almost certainly what happens, as we discover in *The Dalek Invasion of Earth*.

388 "10.6 human years" and "about ten years" before *GodEngine* (p107, p168).

389 *Frontier Worlds*

390 Dating *St Anthony's Fire* (NA #31) - The Doctor tells Bernice that the year is "2148" (p39).

391 "Five years" before *GodEngine* (p15, p98, p193).

392 *GodEngine*

393 *Cold Fusion*

394 *Autonomy*

395 Dating *The Bounty of Ceres* (BF EDA #1.3) - No year named, but it's during Earth's early exploitation of the solar system. It takes five years of cryo-sleep just to reach Ceres (so, arguably, space travel isn't as advanced as even that of *The Space Pirates*), and yet the Cobalt robots are highly developed, able to combine into bigger configurations and seemingly much more adept than (say) the servo robot seen in *The Wheel in Space*. Also, the Back to Earth movement referenced in that story is here mentioned.

Vicki and Steven both conclude that it's before their native times – the platform's artificial gravity isn't as strong as Vicki's day; Steven says the Cobalt robots are "early service" models of versions he's seen in museums, and the platform's pre-made habitation blocks are a precursor to the ones he transported in his native era (*The First Wave*), with similar connectors. Perhaps generalising a little, Steven says: "Everyone was born on Earth in this era."

The Arcturans attacked the Martian colony on Cluut-ett-Pictar.[392] A premodernist architectural revival occurred in the mid-twenty-second century.[393] The fashions of the 1970s had a revival in the mid-twenty-second century.[394]

c 2150 - THE BOUNTY OF CERES[395] -> Humanity continued its exploitation of the solar system. People wore skin tags for identification purposes. Spaceships had limited gravity, but solar sails enabled automated systems to run for decades, and algae banks produced air for long-term human placement.

Cobalt Corporation obtained mining exploitation rights for Ceres, a dwarf planet in the asteroid belt between Mars and Jupiter. Three Cobalt employees (Supervisor Qureshi, Moreland and Thorn) spent five years in cryo-sleep to reach Ceres and – as aided by robots and automated systems – established a mining platform there. Six years later, Thorn, motivated by boredom and jealousy toward Moreland, engineered system malfunctions while Ceres was isolated from Cobalt's monitoring. The first Doctor, Vicki and Steven stopped Thorn from killing Moreland and claiming substantial work bonuses. Thorn opted for suicide rather than standing trial for his crimes.

c 2150 - "The Grief"[396] -> The seventh Doctor and Ace landed on the dead planet Sorshan and met some marines from the Earth starship *Rosetta*. They worked for the Cartographic Historical Exploratory Service (CHEX). A device used the marines as material to recreate the voracious Lom – the Doctor and Ace escaped as the planetary shield and toxin were reactivated, killing the aggressors.

In the 2150s, the Cybermen invaded the colony world of Agora, making it one of their breeding colonies. Human Overseers were in charge of harvesting people to become Cybermen.[397] Eurogen Butler withdrew from Dimetos in 2151. A group of miners and officials remained behind to continue establishing the colony.[398]

The totalitarian Inner Party seized power in the city-state Excelis, and assassinated the Imperial family. More than a century and a half of oppression ensued. Grayvorn pushed other city-states into open conflict, fuelling a technology race.[399]

Earth's Colonial Marines fought in civil wars on the Outer Planets in the Arcturus System.[400] The third fleet from Zygor was scheduled to pass near Earth.[401] In 2156, Supreme Grand Marshall Falaxyr of Mars contacted the Daleks and offered them the GodEngine, an Osirian weapon that could destroy whole planets and stars. In return, he asked for Ice Warrior sovereignty of Mars. The Daleks accepted the offer.[402] By this time, humankind invented the Simularity, a holographic virtual reality.[403]

c 2157 - LUCIFER RISING[404] -> Earth encountered the Legions, a seven-dimensional race from Epsilon Eridani. Trading agreements were set up between the Legions and IMC. The Legions' sector of space was threatened by an unknown alien fleet, so IMC would supply the Legions with weaponry in return for advanced technology. Some Legions began working for IMC.

Earlier in the century, a Von Neumann probe had discovered a stable element with a very high mass in the core of the planet Lucifer, a gas giant two hundred and eighty light years from Earth. Theoretically, such an element

---

Claims about this era's relation to Vicki and Steven's times are workable individually, but inconsistent when woven into a single narrative. It's repeatedly stated that Steven originates from before Vicki's era – *so long before*, in fact, that Vicki has to ask if the spaceships in Steven's time had artificial gravity. Another substantial gap is implied when Steven asks the Doctor: "I can just about believe [a creature on Ceres] wouldn't have been spotted by my time... but by Vicki's?" (The writer, Ian Potter, worked off our placement of Steven's time in *Ahistory* Second Edition; we moved it later for Third.)

However, Steven also claims that his time has no records of this period of humanity (owing to some unnamed development, the most likely culprit being the Dalek Invasion of Earth), and that only an "ancient historian" would have written about such things. It's a bit hard to assume such lengthy durations of time pass between *The Bounty of Ceres* and Steven's era *and* between Steven's era and Vicki's time (the twenty-fifth century; see *The Rescue*) and have that sum equal less than four centuries. Fortunately, it's not entirely necessary, since placing *The Bounty of Ceres* in the early

twenty-second century works well whatever daylight appears between Steven and Vicki's remarks.

The Doctor here adapts the dimensional control he nicked from the Monk's TARDIS (*The Time Meddler*) to increase his own Ship's living space, and bring out of storage, among other things, a wardrobe room (presumably the one Vicki avails herself of *The Myth Makers*). Ceres also features in *K9: Sirens of Ceres*.

396 Dating "The Grief" (*DWM* #185-187) - No date specified. CHEX is an agency of the Sol Government; it has energy weapons and genetic fabrication units. It seems as if it's early in humanity's exploration efforts.

397 *Killing Ground* (p15).

398 *Benny: Another Girl, Another Planet*

399 *Excelis Decays*

400 *GodEngine* (p18).

401 "One hundred fifty years" after *Zygon: When Being You Isn't Enough*.

402 "A year" before *GodEngine*.

403 *Lucifer Rising, GodEngine*

404 Dating *Lucifer Rising* (NA #14) - The story takes place in the mid-twenty-second century, shortly before

could be used as a rich energy source. In 2152, Earth Central invested heavily in a scientific research station – the Eden Project – on Belial, one of the moons of Lucifer.

This was the era when Company Shock Troops – military men armed with neutron cannons, flamers, burners and screamers – took part in infamous corporate raids. In '56, IMC asset-stripped InterSpace Incorporated in Tokyo using armoured skimmers and Z-Bombs. Legend had it that companies used to capture employees of rival corporations and experiment on them. It was a risky life – on one raid in '51, praxis gas was used – but on average it paid four times more than Earth Central. The big human corporations learnt lessons from the aggressive capitalist races such as the Cimliss, Usurians and the Okk. But humanity proved capable of callousness that would put all three of those races to shame.

Six years after it was set up, the Eden Project had still not borne fruit, and pressure was growing to close it down. As Earth's government grew weaker and weaker, the corporations were flexing their muscles: an IMC fleet of over one hundred ships was sent to Belial Base when the scien-

tists reported some progress.

The seventh Doctor, Ace and Benny found that Lucifer and its two moons, Belial and Moloch, formed a device that could affect morphic fields, and could transform one species of being into another. It had been formerly used upon the intelligent species of Lucifer, the "Angels". An expedition member, Alex Bannen, experimented with the device's control system and destabilised it; IMC troops worsened the situation by burning their way through a forest on Moloch, which was part of the device's control system. The IMC captain, a Legion, killed the Adjudicator Bishop – and the Doctor then killed the Legion. Bannen rectified his errors by allowing himself to be transformed into a new forest on Moloch. The Angels set up an exclusion zone around their world.

The Corporations had reached new levels of ruthlessness. IMC tripled the price of the fuel zeiton, and an impoverished Earth Central could no longer afford it. Earth was declared bankrupt and fell into the hands of its receivers: the Earth Alliance of Corporations, a holding company that was in reality the board of directors from all

the Dalek Invasion of Earth. The Adjudicators' simularity registers the Doctor's arrival as "19/11/2154" (p30), Paula Engado's death as "22/2/2154" (p174) and her wake as "23/2/2154" (p13). Ace and Benny had expressed the desire to "pop back to the year 2154 or so" (p338), so at first sight it might appear that the story is set *in* 2154. However, this is inconsistent with the Dalek Invasion, which the authors of *Lucifer Rising* place in "2158" (p337). On p195, there's mention of a raid "in Tokyo in fifty-six". The story is here placed in 2157, consistent with this chronology's dating for the Dalek Invasion.

405 *The Dalek Invasion of Earth*, with the date established in *The Daleks' Master Plan*.

406 According to the Doctor in *The Dalek Invasion of Earth*.

THE MIDDLE PERIOD OF DALEK HISTORY: Taking the Doctor's analysis at face value, the Middle Period of Dalek history might be the time when their power is at its zenith – they are technologically advanced, expansionist and feared. In the words of the Doctor in *Death to the Daleks*, they are "one of the greatest powers in the universe".

In the Virgin edition of *Ahistory*, it was speculated that it coincided with the Daleks developing an internal power supply – in *The Daleks*, they took static electricity up through the floor and so couldn't leave their city. In *The Dalek Invasion of Earth*, they had a disc resembling a satellite dish fastened to their backs; the Doctor and Ian speculate that it allows them free movement. In the first two Dalek stories, they have "bands" rather than the "slats" seen in all other stories. In *The Power of the Daleks*, they are dependent on a static electricity generator. In all subsequent stories – all of

which (apart from the prototypes seen in *Genesis of the Daleks*) have Daleks originating from after *The Dalek Invasion of Earth* – none of these restrictions seem to apply. We are explicitly told they move via "psychokinetic power" in *Death to the Daleks*.

The Daleks are confined to the First Segment of Time, according to *The Ark*. We might speculate that the end of the Middle Period of Dalek history comes with either their defeat at the hands of the Movellans (*Resurrection of the Daleks*), or shortly afterwards with Skaro's destruction (*Remembrance of the Daleks*).

As we've now seen the end of Dalek history (the Daleks withdrawing from history to fight the Time War, as recounted by Jack in *Bad Wolf*), we can perhaps speculate that the "early period" Daleks have bands and are dependent on externally-generated static electricity; the "middle period" Daleks are the slatted ones familiar from the original TV series and now we can add the "late period" Daleks seen in the new television series, which seem significantly more mobile and advanced than their forebears.

407 *The Dalek Invasion of Earth*
408 The Arcturus attacks take place at "the beginning of the year" according to *Lucifer Rising*. Sifranos is also mentioned in *GodEngine*.
409 *The Dalek Invasion of Earth*, *Legacy of the Daleks*.
410 *Lucifer Rising*
411 *GodEngine* (p3).
412 *The Dalek Invasion of Earth*
413 *The Final Sanction* (p75, p178).
414 According to Vicki in *The Chase* and *Salvation* (p58). *The Indestructible Man* said New York was destroyed in a nuclear assault in 2068, but it was evidently rebuilt. Even after its second devastation it

the corporations that traded off-Earth. It was a bloodless coup, and the megacorporations took formal control of the homeworld for the first time. Their reign lasted just under six months.

The Dalek Invasion of Earth

In 2157, the Daleks invaded Earth.[405] This was the Middle Period of Dalek history.[406]

An Astronaut Fair was held in London. The city was a beautiful metropolis, complete with moving pavements and a gleaming new nuclear power station alongside the historic Battersea Power Station.[407]

On the very same day that an Earth embassy opened on Alpha Centauri V, a billion settlers were exterminated on Sifranos in the Arcturus Sector. Fourteen other colonies were wiped out in a three-week period, including Azure and Qartopholos. Rumours of a mysterious alien fleet massing at the Legion homeworld of Epsilon Eridani were denied, but the Interstellar Taskforce was put on permanent standby, and a Spacefleet flotilla sent to that planet was completely destroyed. The alien fleet was a Dalek armada, the Black Fleet, which was annihilating any colony that might render aid to the human homeworld, and systematically destroying Earth's warships.[408]

Meteorites bombarded the Earth. Scientists dismissed it as a freak cosmic storm, but people started to die from a mysterious plague. The Daleks were targeting the Earth, and soon the populations of Asia, Africa and South America were wiped out. Only a handful of people had resistance to the plague, and although scientists quickly developed a new drug, it was too late. Earth was split into tiny communities.[409]

Millions started dying of a mysterious virus in Brazilia, Los Angeles and Tycho City. Some humans showed a mysterious resistance to the plague – because the seventh

Doctor had seeded the atmosphere with an antidote.[410] The Daleks' Black Fleet destroyed Void Station Cassius while entering the solar system.[411]

Six months after the plague began, the first of the Dalek saucers landed. Some cities were razed to the ground, others simply occupied. Anyone who resisted was destroyed. Dalek saucers patrolled the skies. Ruthlessly suppressing any resistance, the Daleks subdued India. The leaders of every race and nation on Earth were exterminated.[412]

The Daleks quickly defeated the Terran Security Forces. Many Americans evacuated to Canada.[413] **New York was destroyed.**[414] Baltimore was reduced to ruins.[415] The Daleks exterminated the last monarch of Britain.[416] The royal bloodline would continue at least until the fifty-third century.[417]

A supersaucer landed on Luton, crushing the city.[418] The Daleks mounted a victory parade in London, in front of the Houses of Parliament and Westminster Bridge.[419] The Daleks blockaded the solar system. The Bureau of Adjudicators on Oberon, a moon of Uranus, tried to work out the Daleks' plan. The Adjudicators detected mysterious signals at the Martian North Pole. Oberon continued to serve as a secret human military base throughout the invasion.[420] Chainswords were used to fight the Daleks.[421] The Daleks destroyed Earth's rockets, leaving the humans aboard a moonbase without a means of retrieval.[422]

The Daleks invaded Mars, but were defeated when a virus ate through their electrical cables.[423] The Daleks retaliated by releasing a virus that consumed all the oxygen in the atmosphere, and it would take decades to make the air breathable again.

2157 - GODENGINE[424] **->** The seventh Doctor and Roz arrived on Mars, but Chris ended up on Pluto's moon of Charon after the TARDIS hit a subspace infarction. The

---

seems to recover somewhat, as *Fear Itself* (PDA) says that New York's waterways are a tourist attraction near the end of the twenty-second century.

415 *Nekromanteia*

416 *Legacy of the Daleks* (p45).

417 *The Mutant Phase*, although this occurs in an alternate timeline.

418 *GodEngine* (p107).

419 *Head Games* (p157).

420 *GodEngine*

421 *Fear Itself* (PDA), and referencing the weapon of choice of Abslom Daak.

422 *An Earthly Child*

423 *Genesis of the Daleks*. It is confirmed in *GodEngine* that this invasion takes place at the same time as the Dalek Invasion of Earth.

424 Dating *GodEngine* (NA #51) - The year is given (p3).

EARTH ALLIANCE: Humanity's development into space coincides with repeated mention, in the books and the audios, of Earth Alliance – an organisation that's prominently named in the likes of *Dark Eyes* and many works by Nicholas Briggs (*The Sirens of Time*, *The Dalek Generation*, *3rdA: The Conquest of Far* and most noticeably *Dalek Empire*), and yet we never learn anything concrete about the group's origins, hierarchy or longevity. It's there to evoke as the name of an Earth-centric military organisation, and rarely anything more.

It's not even clear what precisely Earth Alliance *is*, save that the first work to coin the term "Earth Alliance", *GodEngine* [2157], paints it as the spacebourne equivalent of NATO. It commands powerful spacefleets, and there's mention of "Alliance colonies", in the same way one might mention "NATO countries". Other works invoke "Earth Alliance" as something of a background

Daleks bombed Charon, but Chris escaped down a Transit stunnel. The Doctor and Roz accompanied an expedition to the North Pole of Mars, which was joined by Ice Warrior pilgrims. At the pole, the Martian leader Falaxyr was about to complete the GodEngine, a device capable of making suns expel plasma bursts. Falaxyr hoped to negotiate with the Daleks to regain control of Mars. The Doctor defeated Falaxyr's amended plan to eliminate the human colony of Jacksonville. The GodEngine was destroyed, and Dalek ships shot down Falaxyr as he fled.

Once the population of Earth was under control, the Daleks set to work in vast mining areas, the largest one covering the whole of Bedfordshire. There were few Daleks on Earth, and they boosted their numbers by enslaving humans and converting them into Robomen controlled by high frequency radio waves.

The Daleks cleared the smaller settlements of people and set them to work in the mines. In the larger cities, Robomen and Daleks patrolled every nook and cranny, looking for survivors. The Black Dalek oversaw the mining operations in Bedfordshire. At night, his "pet", the gruesome Slyther, patrolled the camp, attacking and eating any humans it found trying to escape.

The rebels in London survived by dodging Robo-patrols, raiding warehouses and department stores. Other threats came from escaped zoo animals, packs of wild dogs, human scavengers and traitors. The largest rebel group, under the leadership of the crippled scientist Dortmun, could only muster a fighting force of between fifteen and twenty and survived in an underground bolthole. They had a radio, although as time went by, contact was lost with more and more rebel groups. Dortmun spent much of his time developing an acid bomb, the only known weapon that could crack the Dalekenium shells of the invaders.[425]

The Daleks had total control of the Earth, barring a few pockets of resistance, and began a number of projects.[426]

---

detail, not worrying too much about whether we're to infer that Earth Alliance also handles the civil administration of Earth and/or its colonies (this appears not to be the case, at least, in *Dark Eyes*). Earth Alliance isn't in charge (so far as we're told) of the Earth government seen in *Frontier in Space* [2540], and the closest we get to its mention in a broadcast story is talk of "Earth Command" in *The Infinite Quest*, which could be something different altogether.

We know that Earth Alliance comes into being not long after humanity's expansion into space – in *GodEngine*, it's heavily involved in the prolongued battle against the Daleks in *The Dalek Invasion of Earth* [c.2167]. Here we need to differentiate between Earth Alliance and "the Alliance", a coalition of Earth, Draconia and perhaps the Thals "to attack and punish the Daleks", as first suggested in *The Terrestrial Index*, but later mentioned in *Original Sin* (p286) and *Lords of the Storm* (p201). That group comes about in the aftermath of *The Dalek Invasion of Earth*, whereas *GodEngine* has Earth Alliance existing beforehand. (*Legacy* also makes mention of a spacebound "Alliance", but writer Gary Russell confirmed to us that it's nothing to do with Earth Alliance.)

In the centuries after the first Dalek Invasion, Earth Alliance holds some affiliation with the Spacefleet of the twenty-sixth century (*Return of the Living Dad*), fights the 52-year Eminence War (*Dark Eyes*), defeats Sancroff's Knights of Velyshaa (*The Sirens of Time* [3562]), is active during the Daleks' gambit with the Sunlight Worlds (*The Dalek Generation* [?4750]) and hotly coordinates strikes against the Daleks in *3rdA: The Conquest of Far* [?4845].

Just as we don't know when Earth Alliance came into being, however, we don't really know when it ended. It's active at the time of *Dalek Empire I* and *II* (set in this chronology & 5425 to & 5441), but there's no record of it after that – not even in *Dalek Empire III* [& 7520]. It's possible that the Great Catastrophe at the end of *Dalek Empire II* (see The Great Catastrophe sidebar) proved so devastating to human society and Earth in particular, there was no time to reform Earth Alliance before the Solar Flare incident in *The Ark in Space*.

425 *The Dalek Invasion of Earth*

426 *GodEngine*

427 Dating *The Mutant Phase* (BF #15) - The year is given as "2158".

428 Dating *Renaissance of the Daleks* (BF #93) - The date is given, and re-confirmed as being "a year" after the Daleks should have invaded Earth in 2157. Vague mention is made of a "new Dalek homeworld".

429 *War of the Daleks*

430 "Three years" after *GodEngine* (p214).

431 *The Dalek Invasion of Earth*, *The Mutant Phase*.

432 *GodEngine* (p11).

433 *Alien Bodies*

434 Dating *Masters of Earth* (BF #193) - The blurb says: "The year is 2163. Ten years since the Daleks invaded the Earth. One year until the Doctor... will help bring the occupation to an end [in *The Dalek Invasion of Earth*]."

Within the story, the Doctor tells Peri: "This is the year 2163... A dark time. The solar system blockaded. Other worlds unable or unwilling to stand against the Dalek Empire. A decade of occupation that almost brought the human race to its knees... About a year from now, Earth will be liberated." The stated start and end points of the invasion presumably take to heart the "2164" calendar that the Doctor and Ian find in the TV story – which explains why Kyle Inskip claims that the Dalek invasion started "ten years ago" via meteorite bom-

2158 / (=) 2158 - THE MUTANT PHASE[427] -> In Kansas, an Agnomen wasp worked its way inside a battle-damaged Dalek casing and stung the Dalek creature within. Dalek medics prepared to remove the tainting wasp DNA from the stung Dalek.

> (=) The time-travelling Emperor Dalek arrived with a pesticide, GK50, which the Emperor claimed would destroy the wasp cells and safeguard the future. The Dalek medics complied, but the pesticide failed to work on the larval wasp cells. In the millennia to follow, the wasp DNA would spread through Dalek reproduction plants and taint the entire race, giving rise to the Mutant Phase and leading to Earth's destruction in the fifty-third century.

The fifth Doctor and Nyssa realised the Emperor Dalek's actions had paradoxically created the very condition he was trying to prevent and convinced him to not use the pesticide, averting the Mutant Phase.

(=) 2158 - RENAISSANCE OF THE DALEKS[428] -> The collective thoughts of trillions of Daleks created a "seed Dalek" – a being known as the Greylish – who lived on an "island of time" inside a dimensional nullity: a Pan-Temporal Ambience, which existed in all times simultaneously. Time tracks from this realm led to conflicts in history, including Rhodes 1320; Petersburg, Virginia, 1864; and the Vietnam War.

The indifferent Greylish allowed his realm to become a Dalek foundry, and towers were constructed from millions of Dalek armour shells. The realm's temporal properties enabled the Daleks to project subliminal voices to various points in space-time, making humanity receptive to Dalek thoughts and concepts. This created an alternate timeline in which the Dalek invasion in 2157 didn't happen – by 2158, humanity was so comfortable with the idea of Daleks that merchandisers were pumping out Dalek toys.

The fifth Doctor found himself in the alternate history, diverted to rescue Nyssa and the knight Mulberry from 1864, and realised that the Daleks had developed a type of nano-Dalek. They had also learned to harness actinodial energy, which could be projected through space-time. Unless stopped, the Daleks intended to transmit their nano-Daleks from the Greylish's realm into the Dalek toys, which would enable the nano-Daleks to infest every human on Earth. The Dalek invasion of Earth in the twenty-second century would succeed without bloodshed.

Mulberry destroyed the nano-Daleks by sweeping them out of the TARDIS and into the Vortex, but was lost to it as well.

Afterward, the Greylish came to better recognise his origins, understanding that *he* was the genetic template for the nano-Daleks. The Greylish erased his Pan-Temporal Ambience from existence with a thought, and all consequences of its creation were erased from history.

Searching Earth records, the Daleks discovered an account of the ICMG's battle with Daleks in 1963, including a description of Skaro's destruction in the future. Forewarned, the Daleks had a new mission – avert the destruction of their homeworld.[429]

In 2160, the Daleks began work on extracting the Earth's core, seeking to replace it with the GodEngine.[430] **Once the Earth's core was destroyed and replaced with a drive system, the Daleks planned to move the entire planet around space.**[431] The Daleks had conquered every planet of the solar system by 2162.[432]

The High Council of the Time Lords sent their agent Homunculette to a ruined London to acquire the Relic – which arrived from 15,414 – but Qixotl got there first.[433]

2163 (August) - MASTERS OF EARTH[434] -> The Daleks put down resistance efforts in Australia and China, and recruited slave labour from small communities in the Highlands. The Daleks embarked upon an Elite Roboman programme to create human agents capable of infiltrating and destroying resistance groups. Some isles in Scotland were thought free of Dalek control, but this alleged "sanctuary" served to lure intelligent and strong recruits for the elite programme. The Daleks also established Varga plantations, intending to seed target planets with Vargas after Earth was transformed into a mobile battle platform.

The sixth Doctor and Peri wound up aiding Moira Brody – recorded in the history tapes as someone instrumental to Earth rebuilding after the invasion – in prematurely escaping from the Daleks. Brody had been converted into the Robomen's Elite-Prime, but broke her conditioning. She adapted the Varga infection to target Dalek tissue, and thereby destroyed the Daleks creating the Elite Robomen. Brody intended to upgrade all humans into the Elite – a possible prelude to humanity destroying the Daleks and waging war against the universe – and so the Doctor alerted the Dalek Supreme as to Brody's intentions. The Daleks activated a failsafe pulse, killing Brody and the Elite Robomen. The Doctor destroyed the Elite project's data, and the Daleks classified it a failure.

To preserve history, the Doctor and Peri spread the legend of Moira Brody, who would be regarded as a heroic liberator.

The Dalek Invasion of Earth Ends, Susan Leaves the TARDIS

c 2167 - THE DALEK INVASION OF EARTH[435] -> Ten years after the Daleks invaded, Project Degravitate neared its conclusion. Slave workers were instructed to begin clearing operations. The Daleks were tampering with the forces of creation, drilling down through the Earth's crust. A fission capsule was prepared and when detonated, it would release the Earth's magnetic core, eliminating Earth's gravitational and magnetic fields. Once the core was removed, it would be replaced with a power system allowing the Earth to be piloted anywhere in the universe.

The first Doctor, Ian, Barbara and Susan assisted the rebels fighting Dalek control. The rebels broke into the Dalek control room, and ordered the Robomen to attack their masters. The Robomen and slaves over-whelmed the invaders and fled the mining area. The fission capsule was diverted, and upon its detonation the Dalek base – containing the Daleks' external power supply – and the saucer Alpha Major was destroyed. An active volcano formed at the old Dalek mine.

Susan left the TARDIS to make a new life with David Campbell.

(=) As a result of the cadaverous Master's conceptual bomb in 1963, the Doctor never left Gallifrey and didn't stop the Dalek Invasion of Earth.[436]

= During the Dalek Invasion of Earth, an alt-Doctor was told, "a Dalek can't change its bumps", and replied that actually, its sensor casings were extremely replaceable.[437]

---

bardments in "[21]52". (See dating notes on *The Dalek Invasion of Earth* for the argument that the Dalek occupation begins and ends later than this.)

A thief stands accused of stealing food on "the morning of 22nd August", denoting the month. Oddly, two resistance members find it incredible to think that the Doctor and Peri have been to other planets – something that doesn't square with humanity's progress prior to the twenty-second century.

435 Dating *The Dalek Invasion of Earth* (2.2) - There are two dates to establish: the date of the initial Dalek invasion, and the date of this story, which takes place after the Daleks have occupied Earth for some time. To start, the Doctor and Ian discover a calendar dated "2164" in a room that "hasn't been used in years" and Ian remarks that "at least we know the century". Arguably, the Doctor's recollection of the calendar is why Ben comments in *The Forbidden Time* that the Doctor told him about "that Dalek invasion in 2164". The prisoner Jack Craddock later says that the Daleks invaded "about ten years" ago.

However, it seems that someone was printing calendars after the invasion – in *The Daleks' Master Plan*, the Doctor urges Vyon to "tell Earth to look back in the history of the year 2157 and that the Daleks are going to attack again". In *The Space Museum*, Vicki states that the Daleks invaded Earth "three hundred years" before her own time [c 2193]. In *Remembrance of the Daleks*, the Doctor states that the Daleks conquered Earth in "the twenty-second century".

In *Lucifer Rising*, the Doctor says that the Daleks invade in "2158" (p337). *GodEngine* dates the invasion to 2157; the TV story to "ten years" later (p240). *The Mutant Phase* sets the TV story in "nine years" [2168]. It's "a few decades" after *No Future* [c.2000], "two centuries" after *Head Games* (p157) [c.2201], it's "2157" in *Killing Ground* (p48), "2154" in *Return of the Living Dad* (p241),

and "ten years" prior to "2163" in *Masters of Earth*.

A production document written in July 1964 gave the date as "2042". The trailer for the 1964 serial claimed the story was set in "the year 2000" (and, unlike *The Power of the Daleks*, that's explicitly contradicted in the story itself), and in *Genesis of the Daleks*, the Doctor talks of the Daleks' extraction of the Earth's magnetic core in "the year 2000", apparently referring to this story (although he seems to be remembering the movie version, which was set in 2150).

Radio Times consistently dated the story as "2164", as did *The Making of Doctor Who* second edition, *The Doctor Who File* and even the 1994 radio play *Whatever Happened to... Susan Foreman?*. The first edition of *The Programme Guide* set the story "c2060", the second "2164", while *The Terrestrial Index* said "2167". "A History of the Daleks" (*DWM* #77) set the story in "2166". *The Discontinuity Guide* suggested a date of "2174".

Timelink took an Occum's Razor approach, and derived a dating of "2173" from it being about ten years after the "2164" calendar was printed. Additionally, it flagged the Monk's claim (*The Time Meddler*) to have withdrawn a bank deposit "two hundred years" after "1968", which – without benefit of rounding – would require a workable, non-Dalek-obliterated banking system circa 2168. *About Time* seemed to lean toward the more traditional dating of "around 2167", based upon the Doctor claiming the invasion happening in "2157" in *The Daleks' Master Plan*.

In John Peel's novelisation of *The Chase*, Vicki says that the Daleks will destroy New York "one hundred years" after 1967. *Whoniverse* (BBC, p264) has Earth bombarded by the Daleks' meteorites "around 2157", then occupied for "the best part of ten years".

In "The Forgotten", the tenth Doctor claims to have never seen Susan since they parted ways during the Dalek Invasion. But as his memory isn't the most relia-

The seventh Doctor recovered the TARDIS key that Susan dropped[438], and yet Susan later had it in her possession.[439] Susan's husband David continued to think of her as human, and she found it easier to keep quiet about her true origins.[440] Susan and David had a son named Alex.[441]

Tythonus – the home to enormous globular beings who could live for forty thousand years – ran dangerously short of their main food supply: chlorophyll. The Tythonian Erato tried to negotiate a trade agreement with the forest world Chloris, which had an abundance of chlorophyll but lacked metal. Unfortunately, he was negotiating with Lady Adrasta, who owned Chloris' only metal mine, and who protected her monopoly by having Erato imprisoned in a deep pit. A distress signal from Erato's ship prompted the Tythonians to regard their ambassador's imprisonment as an act of war, and to send a neutron star – which would take years to reach its target – to destroy Chloris' sun.[442]

Aftermath of the Dalek Invasion

The Battle of Cassius saw the end of the Dalek blockade of the solar system.[443] The Dalek invasion reduced Earth's population by two-thirds, and its technological advancement was set back two hundred years.[444]

The second Doctor visited a ruined New York clearing up after the Dalek Invasion.[445]

The colony worlds offered to help rebuild, but Earth refused. The Peace Officers were formed in England to neutralise Dalek artifacts left behind after the Invasion. The attempt at creating a central authority, though, soon splintered into around a hundred dominions.[446]

The volcano formed by the destruction of the Daleks' base, Mount Bedford, became a tourist attraction. A salvage team recovered a starchart of Earth's whole sector of the galaxy from a derelict Dalek saucer.[447] A powerful cartel of Earth conglomerates took control of the Terran Security Forces. Within five years, it had become a force capable of waging intergalactic war.[448]

Following the Dalek Invasion of Earth, it became clear that there were a number of powerful warlike races in the galaxy. A number of planets, including Earth, Centauri and the Cyrennhics formed the Alliance, a mutual defence organisation. The corporation INITEC supplied the Alliance with state-of-the-art armaments.[449]

? 2170 - THE CHASE[450] **-> Upon discovering time-travel technology, the Daleks on Skaro launched a prototype time machine after the first Doctor and his companions Ian, Barbara and Susan.**

A Dalek from Aridius was later incarcerated in the Dalek Asylum.[451] **The Daleks used time-travel to go back to Earth in the twenty-first century and re-invade the planet. This time they succeeded.**[452]

At some point, while the Daleks continued to grow in power, they all but abandoned their homeworld, Skaro. The Daleks remaining behind became confined to their city.[453]

The Riley Act of 2171 banned neurological implants as

---

ble when he says this, it's perhaps best ignored – it would contradict not just tie-in stories such as *An Earthly Child* and *Legacy of the Daleks*, but *The Five Doctors* also.

More detail of the Dalek invasions of both Earth and Mars is given in *Benny: Beige Planet Mars*.

436 *The Light at the End*
437 *Unbound: Masters of War*
438 *GodEngine*
439 *To the Death*, although it's possible the eighth Doctor returned the key to Susan, off screen, as a keepsake.
440 *Here There Be Monsters*. This presumably changes later in Susan and David's marriage; by *Legacy of the Daleks*, he's certainly aware that she's aging slower than a human.
441 *An Earthly Child*
442 Erato is imprisoned "fifteen years" before *The Creature from the Pit*.
443 *The Crystal Bucephalus, GodEngine*.
444 *An Earthly Child*
445 *The Final Sanction*
446 *Legacy of the Daleks*
447 *Cold Fusion*

448 *The Final Sanction* (p75).
449 Per "the Alliance" proposed in *The Terrestrial Index*, and mentioned in *Original Sin* (p286) and *Lords of the Storm* (p201). See the Earth Alliance sidebar.
450 Dating *The Chase* (2.8) - The Daleks launch an attack against their "greatest enemies" – the first Doctor, Ian, Barbara and Susan – in revenge for *The Dalek Invasion of Earth*. The fact they don't know Susan has left and Vicki has joined the TARDIS crew indicates that this is relatively soon after their defeat. No date is given, but as the Daleks are based on Skaro here, but will be confined to their city by *The Daleks*, this has to be substantially before then. The Dalek time machine was named the DARDIS in the script but not on screen.
451 *Asylum of the Daleks*
452 *Day of the Daleks*
453 Reconciling the first Dalek story, *The Daleks*, with the other Dalek stories is difficult. There was no intention to bring back the Daleks, and the first story is a self-contained story about a war confined to Skaro, that sees the Daleks killed off at the end. From *The Dalek Invasion of Earth*, the Daleks became galactic conquerors – they invade and occupy the Earth, go on to invent time travel, twice threaten to conquer the entire galaxy,

a fundamental infringement of human rights, in reaction to use of Roboman technology during the Dalek Invasion.[454]

(=) c 2172 - DAY OF THE DALEKS[455] **->** An alternate timeline was created in the 1970s when the World Peace Conference failed. A series of wars erupted, and over the next century, seven-eighths of the world's population were wiped out. Time-travelling Daleks conquered the Earth in the mid-twenty-first century, hoping to exploit the planet's mineral wealth. The remnants of humanity were put to work in prison camps, guarded by Ogron servants. Human guerrillas stole Dalek time-travel technology, and travelled back to the crucial peace conference.

This timeline was erased when the third Doctor and Jo had the Peace Conference delegates evacuated before Auderley House was destroyed.

Unidentified alien beings visited Earth, and one of their number – adopting the name Estella – stayed behind out of love for Duke Orsino, the ruler of Venice. They wed, but he soon lost her in a game of cards. As punishment, she cursed the Duke to extended life so he could better experience the guilt of losing her, and also cursed the city to destruction in a hundred years' time. Estella was rumoured to have committed suicide by flinging herself into the canal. The Cult of Our Lady Estella soon emerged to worship her memory.

The aliens evidently left behind paintings from other worlds, including one that depicted a lady in a glass jar, and one showing fox-people in smart outfits. These became part of Orsino's art collection.[456]

In 2172, the Tzun Confederacy invaded Veltroch, but the arboreal Veltrochni clans united to defeat them. The Veltrochni wiped out the Tzun Confederacy, destroying every Tzun starship but leaving behind many Tzun artifacts and ruins. A whole sector of space containing ten thousand planets was consequently abandoned. Humankind colonised many of these former Tzun worlds, and the Veltrochni begin to fear the spread of humanity.[457]

On 21st July, 2172, Agnomen wasps were deliberately agitated to quell crop-threatening caterpillars, but the wasps killed five hundred people in a Kansas town. The governor authorised use of pesticide GK50 to deal with the problem.[458] In 2172, Grant Markham, a companion of the sixth Doctor, was born.[459] The Intercity Wars started and spread across Earth for decades. Military intervention from Earth's colonies enforced peace.[460]

---

then go off to fight a mutually destructive war with the Time Lords.

Despite the Doctor's assertion that *The Daleks* takes place in the far future, we know that *The Daleks* takes place before *Planet of the Daleks* (2540). We also know that, by then, the Daleks are back on Skaro.

There's no elegant way of reconciling this. The Daleks have to abandon Skaro, leaving behind a city full of Daleks who don't have space travel or any apparent knowledge of other planets. They can't leave their city, let alone conquer another planet. And they have to do it after *The Dalek Invasion of Earth*, then develop time travel (the Daleks in *The Chase* specifically leave and report back to Skaro).

If there *is* a logical reason this happened, there's no indication in an existing story. Vicki (from 2493) has heard of the Dalek Invasion of Earth, but doesn't know what a Dalek looks like, suggesting that from 2167ish to at least 2493, the Daleks don't menace Earth. (The eighth Doctor audios somewhat complicate this by featuring a second Dalek invasion later in the twenty-second century.)

454 *Fear Itself* (PDA)

455 Dating *Day of the Daleks* (9.1) - It is "two hundred years" after the UNIT era. A Dalek states that they "have discovered the secret of time travel, we have invaded the Earth again, we have changed the course of history". This isn't, as some fans have suggested, a version of events where the conquest seen in *The Dalek Invasion of Earth* was more successful – the Daleks travel back and invade a full century earlier, after the first attempt has failed.

The Daleks don't recognise the third Doctor, so they have come from before 2540 and *Planet of the Daleks* (or the alternate history they set up has wiped that story from the new timeline).

Dalek: The Astounding Untold History of the Greatest Enemies of the Universe (p209) – while not pretending to be definitive, and possibly just to be cute – claims that the Daleks only gain the time-travel prowess seen in *Day of the Daleks* after they've gleaned some know-how about temporal mechanics from the Master during their alliance in *Frontier in Space*. (How exactly they obtained the knowledge goes unsaid; the Master isn't exactly the sort of person to share such things.) Moreover, this book says, it's only after the Gold Dalek from those stories is "lost in the past after its efforts to rewrite history failed" that a Supreme Councillor takes charge and approves the time-machine vendetta against the first Doctor in *The Chase*.

456 "A hundred years" before *The Stones of Venice*. The painting of the "woman in a jar" probably refers to an Empress of Hyspero from *The Scarlet Empress*.

457 There are frequent references to the Veltrochni and Tzun in the books of David A McIntee. In *White Darkness*, we learn that civilisation on Veltroch is more than three billion years old (p90). The Tzun appear in *First Frontier*, and *Lords of the Storm* reveals much of their technology and the history of their destruction. The history is further sketched out in *First Frontier* (p94),

c 2179 - THE CREATURE FROM THE PIT[461] -> The TARDIS' Mark Three emergency transceiver detected a distress signal from the forest planet Chloris. The fourth Doctor, the second Romana and K9 found themselves at the Place of Death – where anyone found was put to death, i.e. thrown into a pit containing "the Creature". The travellers found that the Creature was actually the Tythonian High Ambassador Erato, and freed him from the clutches of the ruthless Lady Adrasta. Erato killed Adrasta, then aided the Doctor's party in diverting the neutron star the Tythonians had sent to wipe out Chloris. The Doctor and his friends left as Erato offered the people of Chloris a formal trade agreement.

In the late twenty-second century, the Monk withdrew the £200 he had deposited two hundred years before and collected a fortune in compound interest.[462] The Doctor once claimed that he was "fully booked" until this time.[463] On Tara, nine-tenths of the population was wiped out by a plague and replaced by androids.[464] Some crewmen aboard an Earth Forces science mission to Jupiter suffered psychological damage.[465]

In 2180, FLORANCE's status as a sentient citizen was revoked under the Cumberland Convention. The Dione-Kisanu company bought FLORANCE and installed it at their private base. Director Madhanagopal, an operative for a Brotherhood that sought to augment humanity's psi-powers, experimented on it to research human memory and learning.[466]

Also in 2180, a Eurogen survey dispatched to see if Ha'olam could become an agricultural planet was abandoned when the company made budget cuts.[467]

The Kusks, a massive, brown-skinned species with advanced computer skills, dispatched a time probe to study various planets' histories, hoping to gather intelligence for potential conquests. The probe malfunctioned near the planet Hirath, and the Kusk spaceship sent to retrieve it failed in its mission. The Kusk crew entered suspended animation. Later, the Temporal Commercial Concerns (TCC) company set up a series of time barriers on Hirath, and rented space there for various races to use as penal colonies. TCC adapted the Kusk spaceship, with the sleeping Kusk crew inside, into a moonbase.[468]

Susan was transported to the Death Zone on Gallifrey.[469] Dream Flowers (*ostrecallis mediosai*) were native to Ostrecallis Major, but thought destroyed in a meganova. A few survived on the planet Strellin; the Brotherhood of the Black Petal guarded them in secret.[470]

c 2185 - THE YEAR OF INTELLIGENT TIGERS[471] -> One year, the Hitchemus tigers suddenly became intelligent, as they were prone to do every few generations. They attempted to take power, leading to massive conflict with the human colonists. To avert bloodshed, the eighth Doctor, accompanied by Fitz and Anji, destroyed the Hitchemus spaceport and used the tigers' weather control station to exacerbate the planet's already unstable tilt. This would have put all land on Hitchemus under water in ten years, but the humans and tigers – denied outside help – were compelled to work together to save their world. They agreed to live in peace.

Larger spaceships used T-Mat at this time.

In 2187, Ted Henneker led a rebellion against the Cybermen on Agora.[472] In November, the peaceful Ivorians, on a recommendation from the Doctor, brokered a trading agreement with Earth.[473]

Lords of the Storm (p24) and *The Dark Path* (p142). The Veltrochni also appear in *Mission: Impractical*, and the aliens in *Bullet Time* – although never named – could well be Tzun survivors of the *First Frontier* incident.
458 *The Mutant Phase*
459 He's 19 in *Killing Ground*.
460 *The Janus Conjunction*
461 Dating *The Creature from the Pit* (17.3) - This is one of the most enduringly undatable *Doctor Who* stories. The only clue is that the twelfth Doctor novella *Lights Out* (dated to c.2285 in this guidebook) happens when Chloris has established itself as an interstellar producer of coffee beans. In *The Creature from the Pit*, Chloris has lacked the metal needed to overcome its forests and foster agriculture; if that has occurred by *Lights Out*, it's probably because the trade agreement that Erato negotiates has facilitated such development.
462 *The Time Meddler*
463 The Doctor is booked up for "two hundred years" after *The Seeds of Doom*.
464 In *The Androids of Tara*, Zadek, one of Prince Reynart's men, states that the plague was "two hundred years" ago.
465 "Fifteen years" before *Fear Itself* (PDA).
466 "Forty-seven years" before *SLEEPY*. The Brotherhood plays a role in *The Death of Art* and *So Vile a Sin*.
467 *Seeing I* (p83).
468 "Twenty-five years" before *Longest Day*.
469 *The Five Doctors*. How much time has passed since Susan left the Doctor isn't clear, but she does look older.
470 "Centuries" before *Order of the Daleks*.
471 Dating *The Year of Intelligent Tigers* (EDA #46) - It's the "twenty-second century" (p145), and references to colonies on Lvan and Gidi link it to *Nightmare of Eden*. It is early in humanity's colonisation of other planets. That said, the spaceport has been established for a hundred years, so it must be the latter part of the century.
472 *Legacy of the Daleks*
473 "Four years" before *Killing Ground* (p71).

The Second
Dalek Invasion of Earth[474]

The Doctor Meets His Great-Grandson Alex

As part of his alliance with the Daleks, the Monk went back in time, threw a vial of plague outside his TARDIS door, and left.[475]

c 2187 (summer) - AN EARTHLY CHILD -> Two decades after the Dalek invasion, civil unrest continued on Earth. Public burnings of Dalek technology were still being held. Some people were being found hiding in caves. The lack of people and industry, though, helped to ease global warming. Brewster College was open in Bristol, but could barely afford a proper computer. A Council governed Earth. A political movement, Earth United, spurred xenophobia.

David Campbell had died prior to this. His wife Susan became an advocate of accepting help from other worlds, and sent out a distress signal. The Galdresi – a race that established treaties with vulnerable worlds, then exploited them to fuel a war effort – answered her call. As a show of good faith, they rescued the humans who had been trapped in a moonbase since the invasion started.

The eighth Doctor exposed the Galdresi's plans, and made them withdraw from Earth. He was briefly reunited with Susan, and also met her son (and his great-grandson), college student Alex Campbell.

**c 2187 (24th December) - RELATIVE DIMENSIONS -> ** The eighth Doctor and Lucie collected Susan and Alex so they could share Christmas together in the TARDIS. A

---

474 Dating *An Earthly Child* (BF special release #8), *Relative Dimensions*, *Lucie Miller* and *To the Death* (BF BBC7 #4.7, 4.9-4.10) - These Big Finish audios explore what becomes of Susan on post-Dalek invasion Earth. The blurb to the first of these, *An Earthly Child*, says it's "thirty years on" from the Daleks conquering Earth. Within the story, it's repeatedly said that it's "thirty years since the invasion, twenty years since we set ourselves free" (in *The Dalek Invasion of Earth*). Susan suggests that everyone over 35 remembers where they were when the invasion came; one of her associates, Duncan, doesn't because he's only 33.

In the follow-up audio, *Relative Dimensions*, the Doctor picks up Susan and Alex on "Christmas Eve"- events in *An Earthly Child* are said to have happened "six months ago", establishing that *An Earthly Child* probably happens in summer. The Doctor seems to drop off Susan and Alex (along with Lucie) on the day they left, and the concluding two-parter (*Lucie Miller/To the Death*) plays out over a period of two years (to judge by Alex's remark that Lucie fell ill during the initial plague outbreak "two years" ago).

These audios are virtually impossible to reconcile against *Legacy of the Daleks*, set circa 2199, and which also covers Susan's life on post-invasion Earth. Some of the contradictions pertain to Susan's personal life – *An Earthly Child* presents Alex Campbell as Susan and David's son, Susan acknowledges seeing her grandfather in *The Five Doctors*, and David Campbell has died beforehand in unspecified circumstances. Against all of that, *Legacy of the Daleks* claims that Susan and David never had biological children, and instead adopted three war orphans (in some accordance with *The Five Doctors* novelisation); Susan says she *hasn't* seen her grandfather since *The Dalek Invasion of Earth* (although the eighth Doctor, somehow, remembers their meetup in *The Five Doctors*), and David Campbell dies saving the Doctor's life from the Master. In both stories, at least,

it's established that Susan worked to secure Dalek technology left over from the invasion.

Perhaps the bigger concern, however, is that *Lucie Miller* and *To the Death* entail a second Dalek invasion of Earth – and the accompanying deaths of millions due to Dalek plague – that isn't referenced in any other *Doctor Who* story.

The conclusion that seems rather hard to overlook is that history *has* been changed here, either by a) the Dalek Time Controller arriving in the twenty-second century from Amethyst station, or b) the Monk intervening on the Daleks' behalf. (The Monk, we know, has the *ability* to change history – so adamant is the Doctor about this in *The Time Meddler*.) History might have gotten off its established path, in fact, the moment the Monk nipped back a few years and threw the plague vial out of his TARDIS door.

Earth society is in relatively good shape in *An Earthly Child*, but is practically down to feudal levels in *Legacy of the Daleks* – this would be extremely hard to reconcile, were it not for the second Dalek invasion falling between the two, and almost inevitably setting Earth back some notches. In short, what remains of Earth after *To the Death* could easily slide into the "dominions" seen in *Legacy of the Daleks*.

The wild card here is to what degree, barring a complete and total temporal catastrophe, History might actively try to restore itself to its established path. *Doctor Who*, cumulatively, is less than clear on to what degree this is the case, but stories such as *The Waters of Mars* support the notion. (Actually, *The Kingmaker* is downright whimsical about it, claiming that the motto of the Celestial Intervention Agency is, "The [historical] details change, the story remains the same...") An entirely new timeline of Earth might have unfolded had the Monk's intervention led to the Daleks succeeding – but their defeat at Lucie Miller's hands might enable History to get back on track, give or take. An

good time was had by all, save that a now-giant Resurrection Fish that Susan had once acquired on Quinnis rampaged through the Ship. The Doctor returned his family home afterwards, and Lucie decided to accompany Alex on a grand tour of Europe to study its surviving architecture.

The Daleks Defeated; Lucie Miller, Tamsin Drew and Alex Campbell Die

c 2188 - LUCIE MILLER -> A Dalek Time Controller – the sole survivor of the Dalek defeat at Amethyst station – arrived through time, gravely injured. The Daleks sought a temporal expert to stabilise the Controller's condition, and procured the services of the new incarnation of the Monk. In exchange for being allowed to collect humanity's great art treasures, the Monk aided the Daleks in a renewed bid to conquer Earth. The planet was quarantined as a Dalek-engineered plague once again ravaged humanity, and killed millions. Lucie sent the Doctor a distress call, but the Monk's interference prevented him from arriving on time...

c 2190 - LUCIE MILLER / TO THE DEATH -> The Daleks consolidated their hold on Earth, and engaged in mining operations in North America. The Time Controller intended to fit Earth with a time-space drive, then fly it to a point in the far future when the Vortex-flung Amethyst viruses would amass in a single place. This would turn Earth into a mobile plague planet; the Daleks would use it to infect worlds that threatened them. The eighth Doctor and his allies resisted the Daleks; during the fighting, an unknown amount of the great works the Monk had collected – the statue of Diana from Ephesus, the Elgin

Marbles, the roof of the Sistine Chapel, a Mona Lisa, the crown jewels from every known royal dynasty, the Venus de Milo and the Star of India – were destroyed.

The Daleks killed Alex Campbell and the Monk's companion, Tamsin Drew. Lucie Miller died to detonate a doomsday bomb that destroyed the Dalek fleet and its mining operation.

The Time Lord Kotris rescued the Dalek Time Controller from oblivion, and proposed an alliance between them. Although Kotris' existence and actions were erased from history, the Time Controller still endured.[476] The former grounds of Coal Hill more-or-less survived the first Dalek Invasion of Earth, but hadn't reopened as flats before the Second Invasion struck.[477]

In the late twenty-second century, England's dominions were consolidated into ten large Domains, including Canterbury, Devon, Edmonds, Haldoran, London and Salisbury.[478]

Foreign Hazard Duty

? 2189 - "Echoes of the Mogor"[479] **->** Mekrom was a wild world on the edge of known space, the location of a Confederation colony. The colonists were being killed, and had requested a relief ship and a Foreign Hazard Duty (FHD) team. Now, the last of them, Stanton, was murdered. The seventh Doctor arrived shortly before the FHD squad, and learned the men died of fear.

Members of the FHD squad started dying. The Doctor discovered seams of crystal that could absorb emotion, creating "echoes" of someone's presence. The colonists died of fear from echoes of the warlike Mogor, meaning

---

innate tendency of History to bend back into shape when possible might also explain David Campbell's contradictory fates – perhaps he initially died in *Legacy of the Daleks*, and in the revised history, he dies as a sort of temporal "pre-shock". (This wouldn't explain, of course, why Susan in the revised history has given birth to Alex if she was childless in the original timeline – but it might explain Alex's death in *To the Death*, if he was never supposed to have been born, and History is manoeuvring to both eliminate him and thwart the Daleks in the process.)

This is all, naturally, the result of us trying to pound a round peg into a square hole. Some open-ended questions will remain no matter how this is played. (If the audios overwrote *Legacy of the Daleks*, for instance, then how did the Roger Delgado Master come to be gravely wounded and dying on Terserus?) Still, if one squints a bit, it's possible to accept that intervention on the Monk's part has left Susan's life irrevocably altered, even though Earth's history runs pretty much as intended.

The Venus de Milo is collected by the Monk and possibly destroyed in *To the Death; Benny: The Sword of Forever* alternatively states that it was destroyed during the Thousand-Year War.

475 "Three years" before *To the Death*. It's possible that this happens concurrent with the start of *Lucie Miller* circa 2188, but as only two years elapse from the outbreak of the plague to the end of *To the Death*, the plague must take some time to spread.

476 *DEyes: X and the Daleks*

477 *ST:* "All Hands on Deck"

478 "Last month" according to *Relative Dimensions*.

479 Dating "Echoes of the Mogor" (*DWM* #143-144) - There's no indication of the date, but it seems to be early in the history of Earth's interstellar exploration. There are bullet holes in the walls at one murder scene, so the FHD might have projectile weapons, although weapons that resemble these are called "lasers" in "Hunger from the Ends of Time!". Due to the presence of the FHD, and their wearing the same uniforms and carrying the same weapons, we've assumed that this story,

there were no real monsters. The Doctor snuck away as the FHD team filed their report.

? 2190 - "Hunger from the Ends of Time!"[480] ->

The planet Catalog was the repository for all collated knowledge in the universe. The seventh Doctor decided to go for a browse there, as he hadn't visited for decades, but he found the TARDIS dragged there anyway.

The Doctor met an FHD team, who informed him that the data was now stored as "information energy" across time rather than space. The system had become infiltrated by "bookworms" eating the information. These forces of chaos were only meant to exist at the ends of time, and their presence here was affecting the fabric of time. The Doctor brought all the records back into the present, cutting off the food supply... but leaving around a century's worth of refiling to do.

? 2190 - TW: RED SKIES[481] ->

Captain Jack took a break from humanity and visited Cotter Paluni's World: the 26th Wonder of the Universe, named after the explorer who died when the planet's red lightning crashed her spaceship. The surface was completely isolated from the rest of the universe, and the populace – as created by the Martin Gibbons-AI gestalt – revered Torchwood as their government and god. The crime of blasphemy against Torchwood caused spontaneous combustion. Visitors to a Universal Heritage space station could view the planet's awesome red beauty from a distance.

Jack convinced the Gibbons-AI that it had taken its beliefs and theology too far, and the gestalt willed itself to death after Jack gave it forgiveness. Mental contact with the gestalt had given Jack a vision of Gwen Cooper being killed, and so he returned to Earth in 2012...

c 2190 - ABSOLUTE POWER[482] ->

Lyam Yce made an initial fortune on ginger beer, and leveraged that into a commercial empire, Yce Industries, which exported Earth products to the Ursa Aquarii System. Operatives of the Galaxy Three Parliament monitored Yce's operations. Lyam Yce died after awakening the dormant Ninexie on Teymah, and trying to harness its unique electrical properties. The sixth Doctor and Constance relocated the Ninexie back to its homeworld, to repopulate its race. It was expected that Yce's empire would crumble without him.

The Sirtis Major platform had a new Ultramall.

"Hunger from the Ends of Time!" and "Conflict of Interests" all take place around the same time.

In "Conflict of Interests", humankind has a base on Rigel (between seven and nine hundred light years from Earth in real life), and spacecraft capable of "light by six".

480 Dating "Hunger from the Ends of Time!" (*DWM* #157-158) - "Conventional filing has been obsolete here on Catalog for centuries." The FHD squad's uniforms and weapons are identical to those in "Echoes of the Mogor", so the two stories are probably set around the same time.

481 Dating *TW: Red Skies* (*TW* audiobook #9) - A Universal Heritage tour guide thinks that Jack is "possibly a human", suggesting this is after humanity has ventured into space. The people of Cotter Paluni's World were created following Martin Gibbons merging with the AI in the 1990s, but at least two generations have passed since then – notably, Detective Hoyer recalls his grandfather being executed for blasphemy. The Gibbons-AI seems effectively immortal, only dying because it wishes to do so.

The tenth Doctor mentions Cotter Paluni's World in *The Sontaran Strategem*. Cotter Paluni's World is named the 26th Wonder of the Universe; the city of the Exxilons (*Death to the Daleks*, 2600) is one of the Seven Hundred Wonders of the Universe.

482 Dating *Absolute Power* (BF #219) - A bit confusingly, the Doctor tells Constance: "The entire Teymahrian race died out two thousand years ago, relatively speaking... According to the TARDIS this is, approximately, the year 3319 – the equivalent of 2190-ish, in Earth years. The [Anomalous Extinction Level Event on Teymah] took place around 1300." So, it seems, *Absolute Power* takes place in space year 3319, which is roughly 2190, and the extinction event commenced two thousand years ago in space year 1300, which is actually circa 190.

483 Dating *Time of Your Life* (MA #8) - It is "three weeks into Earth year 2191" (p1).

484 Dating *Killing Ground* (MA #23) - This is set the same year as *Time of Your Life*.

485 Grant's departure from the TARDIS isn't conveyed in canonical *Doctor Who*; by default, then, the short story "Schrodinger's Botanist" in the *Missing Pieces* charity anthology serves to explain what becomes of him.

486 Dating "Conflict of Interests" (*DWM* #183) - As with other FHD stories, this seems to be set in an early colonial period. Humanity doesn't have translation devices. The story has to be set before "Pureblood", when the Sontarans withdraw from human space. Aleph-777 is the planet seen in the back-up strip "The Final Quest".

487 *Benny: Beige Planet Mars*

488 Dating *Fear Itself* (PDA #73) - It's decades after the Dalek invasion of Earth (p274), but still the twenty-second century according to the back cover and p4.

489 Dating *DEyes: X and the Daleks* (BF *DEyes* #1.4) - It's "centuries" after the Doctor and Molly's previous visit to Shrangor, in the late 1800s.

Grant Markham Joins the TARDIS

2191 (January) - TIME OF YOUR LIFE[483] **->** For over twenty years, the Meson Broadcasting Service (MBS) had showed some of the all-time TV classics: *Bloodsoak Bunny*, *The Party Knights and the Kung-Fu Kings*, *Jubilee Towers*, *Prisoner: The Next Generation*, *Life's a Beach* and *Abbeydale High*. The broadcaster successfully rebuffed the claims of the Campaign for the Advancement of Television Standards that such programming as *Death-Hunt 3000*, *Masterspy* and *Horror Mansions* increased violence and criminal behaviour.

On Torrok, the citizens were compelled by law to watch MBS' offerings all day. Peace Keeper robots patrolled every street, rounding up suspected criminals. The sixth Doctor arrived on Torrok during this time and accepted an inquisitive Angela Jennings as his companion. The Time Lords directed the TARDIS to MBS' space station headquarters, where a mechanical adversary killed Angela.

As part of the reality show *Time of Your Life*, the city of Neo Tokyo was teleported from New Earth into a Maston Sphere, where the residents were terrorised. The Doctor discovered that the information-consuming datavore Krllxk had gone insane from absorbing the entire MBS output. He transmatted Neo Tokyo back home, and the ensuing conflict made the MBS station fly into the sun. Krllxk took refuge in a game-show android, but the Doctor destroyed it. MBS went off the air when the people on Torrok rebelled, overthrowing the totalitarian regime. Grant Markham, a computer programmer who helped the Doctor, joined him on his travels.

2191 - KILLING GROUND[484] **->** Humanity thought the Cybermen were extinct. Most were asleep in their Tombs on Telos, but some nomads wandered the galaxy. Earth was still rebuilding from the Dalek Invasion at this time.

The sixth Doctor suspected the Cybermen were involved in the affairs of Agora, Grant Markham's home planet. The Overseers who ruled the planet on the behalf of the Cybermen captured the Doctor, and Grant fell in with the rebels.

One of the rebels, Maxine Carter, used Cybertechnology to build the Bronze Knights – a volunteer army of cyborgs. The Doctor learned that the Cybermen were running out of parts and becoming increasingly reliant on stolen technology. These Cybermen hijacked and adapted a Selechian warship. The Doctor sabotaged it, releasing radiation that was lethal to the Cybermen. The Bronze Knights left Agora to hunt down more Cybermen, and the remaining colonists rebuilt their planet.

It was unknown when and where Grant Markham parted ways with the Doctor.[485]

? 2192 - "Conflict of Interests"[486] **->** Rigel Depot sent an FHD team at light by six to Aleph-77 in the Deneb System, where they found a Sontaran Infantry squad. Galactic Survey was keen to protect the archaeology of the extinct civilisation on the planet, but found the Sontarans had the same goal... and they'd have to fight for it.

Efforts to terraform Mars continued throughout the twenty-second century. Each Martian pole was given an ocean – the Borealis Ocean in the north had freshwater and canals, whereas the Southern Sea generated carbon dioxide. Ransom Spaceport was near Mars' north pole, Carter Spaceport was near its south. Noachis Spaceport handled approximately 60% of Mars' commercial flights. Transmats were in use. Eventually, Mars became a popular living destination for retirees.[487]

The Eighth Doctor, Fitz and Anji are Separated for Four Years; Anji Marries

c 2192 - FEAR ITSELF (PDA)[488] **->** The eighth Doctor, Anji and Fitz landed on Mars, where Anji was attacked and hospitalised. The Doctor and Fitz linked her attackers to Farside Station and set off to investigate... but shortly afterwards, Farside reported destroyed with all hands lost.

Thinking the Doctor and Fitz dead – and that she was stranded – Anji became a consultant on twenty-first century matters for a television channel. She married a cameraman called Michael. At this time, a new and ruthless military group called the Professionals emerged.

The Yucatan had a space elevator, and holographic slides had replaced paper. A vaccine for the common cold had been developed. Anti-radiation suits were made from Dortmunium. The Martians who remained on Mars were a social underclass, and some resorted to terrorist acts.

(=) c 2193 - DEyes: X AND THE DALEKS[489] **->** Aided by the rogue Time Lord Kotris, the Daleks on Shrangor had constructed a temporal chamber and relativity map. With this, they could look upon any point in space and time, and track time travellers. The Time Lord Straxus brought the eighth Doctor, Molly O'Sullivan and the Doctor's TARDIS to Shrangor, where Kotris intended to use the retrogentior particles within Molly – which had become synched with Time Lord physiognomy during her travels with the Doctor – to calibrate the chamber and relativity map. If successful, Kotris would obliterate all Time Lord matter throughout space-time, preventing the Time Lords from ever having existed.

The Daleks exterminated Straxus when he hampered Kotris' plans. As Straxus was Kotris' previous incarnation, Kotris and everything he'd achieved were wiped from history.

Only the eighth Doctor, Molly and the Dalek Time Controller remembered these events. The TARDIS returned to France, World War I, where Molly left the Doctor's company.

Humanity fought against a number of hostile races in deep space, including the Cybermen. A number of Cyber Wars were fought at the beginning of the twenty-third century, but humanity prevailed.[490] Gustav Zemler's unit defeated some Cybermen on the borders of Earth's colonies, but the Cybermen's hostages were killed. Zemler and his survivors were dishonourably discharged and became mercenaries.[491]

After the Cyber Wars, Eurogen Butler changed their name and became the Spinward Corporation.[492] The former Houses of Parliament were used as a hospice for veterans of the first Cyber Wars.[493]

Privateers from the Andosian Alliance made several incursions into Earth's solar system in the last half of the twenty-second century. In the decade before 2197, they caused much loss of life and damage to cargo payloads, and continued menacing the spaceways into the early twenty-third century. The Privateers were eight feet tall, with rippling mauve muscles and possibly three heads. They had a penchant for the melodramatic, with their leaders choosing such names as Doctor Leopard.[494]

The I had developed as a gestalt, centaur-like race that seeded technology onto planets, then later returned to harvest the developments. The I acquired some Gallifreyan technology and the eyes of a Time Lord named Savar, and around 2192 used this to facilitate the development of advanced retinal implants on the planet Ha'olam.[495]

The buffalo became extinct in 2193.[496] The Selachians sold their Cloak weapons to Earth in the mid-2190s.[497]

& 2196 - FEAR ITSELF (PDA)[498] **->** Farside Station was rediscovered in Jupiter's atmosphere. Anji had become distant from her husband, and stowed away as a

---

490 Cyber Wars in the twenty-second or twenty-third century were postulated in *Cybermen* and *The Terrestrial Index*, and a number of stories that used those books as reference (including *Deceit, Iceberg, The Dimension Riders, Killing Ground* and *Sword of Orion*) have referred to "Cyberwars" in this time period. This is not the "Cyber War" involving Voga that is referred to in *Revenge of the Cybermen*. We might speculate that while the main force of Cybermen conquer Telos, another group remained active and travelled into deep space, perhaps colonising worlds of their own, and that this breakaway group was wiped out in the Cyber Wars. They seem to keep well away from Earth and only menace isolated human colonies.
491 *The Janus Conjunction* (p98).
492 *Deceit* (p23).
493 *Interference* (p305).
494 *The Nowhere Place*
495 *Seeing I*
496 *The Also People* (p29).
497 "A decade" before *The Final Sanction*.
498 Dating *Fear Itself* (PDA #73) - Anji is separated from the Doctor and Fitz for "four years".
499 Dating *ST: "*All Hands on Deck*"* (BF *ST* #7.10) – It's been "almost two hundred and fifty years" since Susan was a student at Coal Hill in *An Unearthly Child* [1963]. For Susan, some time has passed since the Second Dalek Invasion of Earth; in the real world, six years have elapsed between the release of that conflict (in *To the Death*) and this story. Susan names the time of year.
500 *Fear Itself* (PDA). The "Paris crater" is evidently a reference to the Martian-propelled asteroid that obliterated Paris in the Thousand-Day War, as told in *Transit* and *GodEngine*. *Transit* specifies that Paris is rebuilt in the decade to follow this event, but a monument area might remain.

501 *Dreamstone Moon* (p18).
502 Dating *Wooden Heart* (NSA #15) - No date is given, but it's "at least a hundred years" since the *Castor* was launched. The hints we get are that the *Castor* was operating very early in Earth's era of interstellar travel, and the fact it's "Century-class" might link it to the Century ships referred to in *Killing Ground*. Space is divided into sectors and largely unregulated, suggesting the *Castor* was launched before *The Space Pirates*.
503 Dating *The Nowhere Place* (BF #84) - The story opens on 15th January, although Oswin files a report at 15:38 on the 16th, which suggests the Doctor and Evelyn don't arrive until that date.
504 *The Janus Conjunction* (p100).
505 Four hundred years before *Benny: The Doomsday Manuscript*.
506 Dating *Legacy of the Daleks* (EDA #10) - Susan met David when he was 22, and he's now 54 (p15), so it's thirty-two years after *The Dalek Invasion of Earth*. The blurb says it is the late twenty-second century. It's unclear why the Doctor is searching for Sam by travelling in time, rather than space, yet that's the implication of p27, where he "allows" for Thannos time. This does seem to mean he's looking for Sam before he lost her in *Longest Day* circa 2202, but he is admittedly diverted to Earth by a telepathic signal from Susan. While the Doctor thinks he is in the right timezone, perhaps the TARDIS has taken him just a handful of years earlier.

See the dating notes under *An Earthly Child* for the argument as to whether *Legacy of the Daleks* has been erased from history or not.
507 *The Pit* (p86).
508 *Managra* (p63).
509 *The Shadow of the Scourge*
510 *Genocide* (p27).

Professional was sent to investigate. The survivors had gone feral, while the station had been influenced by alien biological weapons – Fear and Loathing – which had survived in Jupiter's atmosphere for millennia.

The Doctor, who had been brainwashed into operating as a Professional for the last four years, neutralised the weapons. Reunited with Anji, the Doctor and Fitz continued on their travels.

lgtw - & 2196 (late October) - ST: "All Hands on Deck"[499] **->** On Earth, humanity restored its living standards in part by using salvaged Dalek tech. Air Space Command Centre in Greenwich controlled missiles powerful enough to deflect or ruin oncoming asteroids.

Susan Foreman helped to adapt the Daleks' power generators and chemical synthesisers. When the former grounds of Coal Hill School reopened as flats, Susan occupied an apartment on the first floor. Her former English Lit classroom was now her kitchen. The school's playground was now a garden, and an oak tree planted in memorium of Ian Chesterton and Barbara Wright – without citing when they died – had overrun the school's quad, and was trimmed back some.

Gallifrey sent message cubes to summon Susan to serve in the Last Great Time War. The eighth Doctor distracted Susan with a small flood of custard, a false report of an oncoming meteor and an outbreak of cyborg-spiders – anything to keep her from discovering her call-up papers. Susan discovered her grandfather's duplicity and answered Gallifrey's call. A wardrobe-shaped TARDIS took her off to the conflict...

At this time, tent cities existed on Earth and Mars. The Paris crater and the New York waterways were popular tourist traps.[500] In 2197, the Dreamstone Moon Mining Company was set up to exploit the discovery of dreamstone on the moon of Mu Camelopides VI.[501]

? 2197 - WOODEN HEART[502] **->** The tenth Doctor and Martha landed on the *Castor*, a prison ship full of century-old corpses. Deep in the ship, they discovered a strange virtual reality forest and a preindustrial village. Aliens had preserved humans in the wooden heart of the ship.

2197 (15th-16th January to March) - THE NOWHERE PLACE[503] **->** Earth's *Damocles*-class ships emerged as the deadliest fighter-craft of their age, and were the envy of their enemies. The Red Cross symbol was still in use. Earth's military used security locks that were susceptible to high-frequency vibrations. A station was in operation on Jupiter. Cryo-freezing was used in this era.

The Damocles-fighter carrier *Valiant* travelled to Pluto's orbital path; scans indicated that hostile raider activity had occurred there in late December. The sixth Doctor and

Evelyn arrived on the *Valiant*, which was under the command of Captain Tanya Oswin, as a mysterious door appeared in the ship's hull. Crew members were mentally compelled to walk through the door – a device used by the original species that had evolved on Earth, and was trapped in the realm called Time's End. The original race hoped to use the door to ensnare humanity and retroactively erase humankind from history. The Doctor and Evelyn identified the sound of a train bell coming from the door as hailing from 1952, and ventured back there to investigate. In their absence, three-fourths of the *Valiant* crew were lost to the door.

The Doctor and Evelyn returned two months later, just as the spaceship *Exeter* arrived in response to the *Valiant*'s cry for help. Oswin ordered the *Exeter* to fire nuclear weapons against the door; this would have paradoxically created Time's End and consigned humanity to suffer there. However, the Doctor altered events in Time's End so that Oswin's nuclear strike permanently destroyed Earth's original species.

Colonial marines fought in the Alphan Kundekka conflict of 2198.[504] Archaeologists Niall Goram and Matt Lacey contracted radiation sickness after opening the tomb of Rablev. They resealed it and split their journal – later known as *The Doomsday Manuscript* – into two halves. After they died, their estates sold off the documents.[505]

(=) & 2199 - LEGACY OF THE DALEKS[506] **->** The eighth Doctor arrived in New London as the UNIT Master started a war between rival Domains Haldoran and London. Haldoran and London themselves died in the conflict, and one of Haldoran's commanders, Barlow, took charge of both regions. The Master reawoke a hidden Dalek factory to gain an experimental matter transmuter. David Campbell was killed in a struggle with the Master, who fled to the planet Tersurus. Susan Campbell destroyed the matter transmuter, an act that ravaged the Master's body. The Time Lords sent Chancellor Goth to investigate the disturbance on Tersurus, leading to his meeting the now-cadaverous Master. A grieving Susan left in the Master's TARDIS.

The Twenty-Third Century

Brian Parsons fought in many space conflicts at this time, and his tactics were programmed into android soldiers for many centuries to come.[507] During the twenty-third century, Jung the Obscure published his theory of the Inner Dark in the Eiger Apocrypha.[508] By the twenty-third century, a riot control gas named Pacificus was invented.[509] Sperm whale songlines were published.[510] 1970s fashions were once again revived in the twenty-third century.[511] Mobile phones were phased out in the twenty-third century.[512]

Humanity conducted tests with fusion bombs out on the Galactic Rim. The devices were so powerful they were immediately banned.[513] The Doctor bought Bobby Charlton's 1966 World Cup shirt in a Venusian Auction in the twenty-third century.[514]

The corporations made vast profits from the colonisation of other planets and became a law unto themselves, killing colonists to get to mineral resources. The Adjudication Service became a neutral arbiter of planetary claims.[515]

The Judoon took the ninth Doctor into custody, after he'd framed himself for the death of UNIT's Tara Mishra.[516] The Corsair squirreled a void into a hatbox in twenty-third century Windon, thinking that nobody would possibly think of looking for it there.[517]

Around 2200, the Interbank scandal took place. Chairman Wayne Redfern was indirectly responsible for the organisation's bankruptcy.[518] The Re'nar and Ju'wes fought a war in the Matrua Nebula. A Re'nar fell through a time portal to 1888, and was pursued by a Ju'wes.[519]

c 2200 - BENNY: SHADES OF GRAY[520] **->** Jennifer Alford, a con artist, attracted Dorian Gray's attention by displaying the soul-stealing Marwick Tapestry at the Montesquieu Gallery, a venue that specialized in Trotman digital watercolours. Gray accepted an invitation to view Alford's private collection of supernatural artifacts, which enabled Alford to capture Gray long enough to steal his portrait on behalf of her employer, the Collector. The next day, Gray escaped and found that the Marwick Tapestry had claimed Alford's soul. Gray and his portrait would remain separated until the twenty-seventh century.

c 2201 - THE SELACHIAN GAMBIT[521] **->** The Galacti-Bank catered to a number of high-profile clients with its dimensionally transcendental vault. The second Doctor, Jamie, Polly and Ben were delayed at the Galacti-Bank when the TARDIS was claimed as salvage, and the Doctor lacked the ten credits needed to procure its release.

A team of Selachians attacked the Galacti-Bank to gain the blueprints to experimental weapons – including the G-bomb – kept there, but found the vault was empty. The Galacti-Bank owners had lost billions in bad investments, and robbed their own business in preparation to destroy

---

511 *Autonomy*
512 *The House of Winter*
513 "The twenty-third century" according to *Cold Fusion* (p180).
514 "They Think It's All Over"
515 *Colony in Space.* Many of the books pick up on this theme.
516 In the "23rd century", supposedly, but see the dating notes on *The Ninth Doctor Year One*: "Sin-Eaters".
517 "Weapons of Past Destruction"
518 *The Final Sanction*, no date is given on p146, but it must be some time before 2203.
519 "Hundreds of years" after "Ripper's Curse".
520 Dating *Benny B3: Legion: Shades of Gray* (Benny box set #3.2) - Benny's associate Jack, in viewing these events via a séance with Benny and Ruth, estimates that it's the "twenty-second, twenty-third century, at a guess".
521 Dating *The Selachian Gambit* (BF CC #6.8) - The G-bomb used to destroy the Selachian homeworld of Ockora in *The Final Sanction* (set in 2204) is here classified as an "experimental weapon". A Z-bomb featured in *The Tenth Planet* (set in 1986); presumably, the naming of these doomsday weapons has occurred in reverse-alphabetical order.
   The Selachians that attack the Galacti-Bank intend to transmit their spoils back to Ockora, and the presence of a Selachian embassy on Pluto doubly suggests that it's before the full-blown warfare with humanity that leads to Ockora being eradicated.
522 Dating *Longest Day* (EDA #9) - It's "Ex-Thannos system, Relative Year 3177" (p15). In *Legacy of the*

Daleks, it's stated "In Thannos time it had been 3177" (p27), so it's almost certainly not 3177 AD. This is the same time zone as *Legacy of the Daleks* (give or take), *Dreamstone Moon* and *Seeing I*.
523 Dating *Dreamstone Moon* (EDA #11) - For Sam, six days have passed (p7) since *Longest Day*.
524 Dating *Seeing I* (EDA #12) - Sam was en route to the planet Ha'olam at the end of *Dreamstone Moon*, and has only just arrived at the start of this novel. The Doctor sending out Data-umphs in 2202 looking for Sam must mean that he expects to find her in that year. "James Bowman" was the alias that Grace attributed to the Doctor in *Doctor Who – The Movie*.
525 Dating *The I: I Scream* (BBV audio #26) - The unnamed central character of *I Scream* describes Earth as having "ground cars, power plants, killer smog and diseases" – a state of affairs that loosely fits conditions of the late thirtieth century. Then again, such a description could just be part and parcel of the Company's propaganda machine, designed to prevent the Galspar residents from wanting to venture off world. Another X-factor is whether or not the I's scheme has any measure of success; the period of the Earth Empire is documented well enough that people turning into I en masse would probably have warranted a mention in some other *Doctor Who*-related story. Either the scheme is thwarted off screen, then, or *I Scream* actually takes place in an indeterminate era. The dating is arbitrary, but fits an early colonial period.
526 *The Janus Conjunction* (p98).
527 According to *The Final Sanction*, p75. Page 146 suggests the war has been going on for a year.

the facility in an insurance fraud. A Selachian bomb obliterated the Galacti-Bank, but the Doctor saved those present by herding them into the vault, then re-establishing a dimensional link to a safe locale. He was duly given a reward, which he used to buy back the TARDIS.

The Selachians had an embassy on Pluto.

Sam Jones and the Eighth Doctor are Separated for Three Years

& 2202 - LONGEST DAY[522] **->** A Kusk rescue party arrived on the moon of Hirath, intent on retrieving their lost time probe. The probe malfunctioned even further and destabilised TCC's time barriers on Hirath, threatening to blow up half the galaxy. The eighth Doctor destroyed the probe, triggering an electrical surge that also killed the rampaging Kusks. Samantha Jones was separated from the Doctor in the confusion to follow, and was launched away from Hirath in a crewless Kusk ship.

& 2202 - DREAMSTONE MOON[523] **->** Dreamstones, a material mined from a satellite of Mu Camelopides VI, also known as the Dreamstone Moon, became very desirable. Consumers would sleep with dreamstones under their pillows to experience vivid dreams. However, Anton La Serre, an artist who recorded and sold his dreams, had a tortuous dreaming experience with a dreamstone and sought to discredit the entire industry.

The Dreamstone Moon Mining Corporation (DMMC) ship *Dreamstone Miner* rescued Sam Jones, who had drifted in the Kusk ship for a week. She was taken to the DMMC mining operation on the Dreamstone Moon, which began to experience tremors. The Doctor arrived and concluded that the entire moon was a living entity, and that the dreamstones were parts of its brain.

The pained entity shared a special mental link with La Serre, and instinctively began lashing out due to his anger toward DMMC. The entity started projecting mental illusions – Earth Fleet had five hundred ships in the Mu Camelopides System on manoeuvres, and the captain of the dropship *Royale* self-destructed his vessel while experiencing such a waking nightmare. The ship's compliment of one thousand troops was lost, and altogether five thousand people died.

The Doctor entered La Serre's dreams and calmed him, allowing La Serre to peacefully dream himself to death, and the dreamstone entity fell dormant. DMMC abandoned operations on the moon. Sam Jones, embarrassed for her previous abandonment of the Doctor, departed the moon in an evacuation shuttle.

c 2202 - SEEING I[524] **->** Sam Jones relocated to the world of Ha'olam, where she initially worked as a volunteer in an INC-run homeless shelter. She turned 18 during this time.

The eighth Doctor was responsible for the Great Umph Massacre of 2202 when he sent data-umphs into the galaxy-wide computer network to look for Sam.

The Doctor, using the alias "Dr James Alistair Bowman", continued to look for Sam and was arrested as an industrial spy on INC premises. He was given a ten year sentence and taken to the Oliver Bainbridge Functional Stabilisation Centre (OBFSC). He was questioned by Dr Akalu, the prison's "morale officer". Akalu implanted the Doctor with a retinal implant that provided advance warning of the Doctor's escape attempts. Akalu also set up DOCTOR, an artificial intelligence, to create an accurate psychological profile on the Doctor. DOCTOR would discover three hundred forty-six reports of TARDIS sightings in hundreds' years worth of data, despite someone erratically, not systematically, erasing nearly all of it.

The non-profit organisation Livingspace hired Sam to do volunteer work at Eurogen Village, a desert community for former Eurogen workers. She started a relationship with Paul Hamani, a Eurogen worker assigned to teach her about life on the settlement; their relationship ended five months later. Sam also had relationships with a woman named Chris and a man named Orin (despite his being a soldier and eating meat). After Sam and Orin broke up, he and Paul became a couple.

? 2202 - THE I: I SCREAM[525] **->** Humans devoted nearly every available acre of the planet Galspar to dairy, egg and sugar farms. These produced the raw ingredients for Galspar's single export: ice cream, of which Galspar made seven hundred million litres per day, and shipped to such worlds as Earth. The Governor of Galspar served as the CEO of the Company that made the ice cream, and the ruling council was the Company's board of directors. Galspar's relatively small population served the Company in one form or another. In their final term at school, students picked their occupation from a choice of farmer, driver, management, admin, computers, family, education and none of the above. Marco Polo City was Galspar's largest urban area.

The I – who reproduced in multiple ways – subverted Galspar's operations, and seeded into its ice cream a filament that would convert anyone who consumed it into the I. In this fashion, the I sought to "promote" humanity to become like them...

Around 2203, the Selachian Empire invaded Rho Priapus, one of Earth's colony worlds.[526] Terran Security Forces (TSF) in response instigated a war to combat the alleged Selachian threat, but the conflict owed more to the Selachians endangering human corporate interests on the arms markets.[527]

On Earth, Professor Laura Mulholland developed the gravity bomb, a devastating weapon capable of making a planet collapse in on itself. The G-bomb boosted Earth's confidence in the conflict with the Selachian Empire, and a warfleet, led by the flagship *Triumph*, left Earth to engage the enemy. The Selachians were forced back to their own system within a year.[528] In 2204, Adam Dresden was on his first TSF mission when the Selachians captured him on Molinar. He was subsequently transported to Ockora as a prisoner.[529] Robert Eliot Whitman stole valuable antiques that included a Kettlewell-type Robot, and the humans on the colony of Jegg-Sau used it to create more of its kind. The colony was abandoned when Jegg-Sau's soil failed due to bad terraforming. Whitman died, and the Robots – confused without any humans to serve – were left behind.[530]

An Eternal, Hardy, used a shard of Enlightenment to create Marlowe's World and the people living there – all of them pawns in a game against Barron, a rival Eternal. Barron spent centuries luring champions to Marlowe's World – had any of them discovered the planet's true nature, he would have won and claimed the Enlightenment shard. Barron's champions all failed.[531] The Bantu Independence Group became more militaristic in the 2200s, and – supported by various alien races – formed a loose alliance of dominated worlds.[532]

2204 - THE FINAL SANCTION[533] -> The war with the Selachians was coming to an end. Humans invaded Kalaya, the final planet in need of liberation from the Selachians. After a while, the humans forewent air raids to

protect the native population. Out of a thousand troops, only around three hundred survived the campaign.

The second Doctor, Jamie and Zoe arrived on the war-torn Kalaya shortly before Selachian forces abandoned it. The Doctor found himself on board the *Triumph* as it pursued the retreating Selachians to their homeworld of Ockora. The *Triumph*'s G-bomb was launched, turning Ockora into a black hole and obliterating nine million lives there, including ten thousand hostages. Lieutenant Kent Michaels of the TSF gave the final password that launched the bomb, but the history books condemned Commander Wayne Redfern for the catastrophe, deeming him one of the most evil men who ever lived.

A group of surviving Selachians captured the *Triumph* and attempted to retaliate against Earth with the ship's second G-bomb. Professor Mulholland detonated the bomb before it could reach Earth, turning the *Triumph* into a second black hole.

& 2205 - SEEING I[534] -> Sam Jones was involved in a failed protest to prevent INC from buying Eurogen Village. She sought to expose INC's corrupt practices and broke into a TCC research plant – where she found they were growing human clones with no higher brain functions for immoral experimentation.

Now 21, Sam learned about the Doctor's incarceration by hacking into INC's medical databases. She helped to liberate him, and the TARDIS removed his retinal implant.

528 *The Final Sanction* (pgs. 73, 255) says this occurs "almost a year" before 2204.
529 *The Final Sanction* (p196).
530 *Benny S5: The Relics of Jegg-Sau*
531 "Centuries" before *Benny S6: The Heart's Desire*. Eternals first appeared in *Enlightenment*, but compared to the Eternals seen there, Hardy and Barron's *modus operandi* is more akin to that of the Celestial Toymaker.
532 *Benny: Another Girl, Another Planet*
533 Dating *The Final Sanction* (PDA #24) - The date is given (p4).
534 Dating *Seeing I* (EDA #12) - The Doctor is imprisoned for "three years". Oddly, according to *SLEEPY*, also by Kate Orman, FLORANCE was trapped in a lab at this point.
535 "Fifty years" after *GodEngine*.
536 Dating *The Janus Conjunction* (EDA #16) - It is "Dateline 14.09.2211 Humanian Era" (p16).
537 Dating *Benny S10: Secret Origins* (Benny audio #10.4) - Bernice names the year. Peter's math is very bad when she does so, as he reckons that 2212 was "nearly three centuries" prior to 2609.
538 Dating *The Demons of Red Lodge and Other Stories*: "Doing Time" (BF #142c) - This all seems roughly in keeping with humanity's stage of development per the likes of *Seeing I*. The participants don't appear to be

massively removed from present-day humanity – not only is the Gregorian calendar (or some local variation of it) in use on Folly, one of the locals references Bonnie and Clyde. Interstellar travel is possible, but takes some time – a year is here required to cross "three [solar] systems". One of the Doctor's fellow prisoners is alien, and relations with his race are such that his parents are allowed to visit.
While no year is given, the date of the explosion – 10th of May – is named as a Monday. In this era, and assuming the Folly calendar is exactly in synch with the Earth one (hardly a guarantee), that narrows the possibilities to 2202, 2213, 2219, 2224 and 2230.
539 *Iris S3: The Iris Wildthyme Appreciation Society*
540 Dating *The Cradle of the Snake* (BF #138) - It's currently "Manussan Year 2215", which is here presumed to be the same year in the Earth calendar (see the dating notes to *Snakedance*). Where the day is concerned, "Tomorrow's New Year".
541 *The Highest Science* (p17).
542 *Strange England* (p7).
543 "Seventy years" after *GodEngine*.
544 Dating *SLEEPY* (NA #48) - While investigating the Dione-Kisanu Corporation in 2257, the Doctor sends Roz and Bernice back "thirty years", to "2227".

The Doctor had been an inmate of OBFSC for just over three years.

The I overran the INC Research and Development Complex at Samson Plains to strip-mine its technology. The Doctor liberated the I's organic spaceship from their control, turning the I into mindless drones. Reunited with Sam, he departed for Gallifrey to return Savar's eyes.

DOCTOR, having acquired some of the Doctor's personality traits through studying him, departed Ha'olam and travelled human dataspace with another AI, FLORANCE.

The settlement of Shelbyville was founded on Mars.[535]

2211 (September) - THE JANUS CONJUNCTION[536] -> In 2110, an aged Spacemaster, with one thousand colonists on board, was holed by an asteroid prior to crash-landing on the planet Menda. Led by Gustav Zemler, the mercenaries hired to protect the colonists discovered a hyperspatial Link that joined Menda to its neighbour, Janus Prime. The mercenaries crossed over to Janus Prime but were trapped there for a year, and went insane due to radiation sickness.

The eighth Doctor and Sam discovered that the hyperspatial Link was an accidental by-product of the Janus System's doomsday device. Zemler was killed before he could set the Janus Conjunction in motion and turn the sun into a black hole. Sergeant Jon Moslei sacrificed himself to collapse the Link, saving Janus Prime.

2212 - BENNY S10: SECRET ORIGINS[537] -> The android Robyn and a temporal projection of Benny foiled Samuel Frost from recovering a zombifying virus from the planet Kresma.

? 2212 (May) to 2213 (Monday, 10th May) - THE DEMONS OF RED LODGE AND OTHER STORIES: "Doing Time"[538] -> The fifth Doctor and Nyssa detected the echo of a potential temporal explosion on the planet Folly. The Doctor's efforts to warn the authorities of this resulted in his being incarcerated for a year, but he still retroactively prevented the explosion – the result of a warp drive accident – from occurring.

In 2214, a playset of Iris Wildthyme's bus was marketed, with replicas of her mock tiger-skin scatterpillows.[539]

? 2215 (last day of year) - THE CRADLE OF THE SNAKE[540] -> The Mara manifested through Tegan a third time, and compelled the fifth Doctor – who was also accompanied by the older Nyssa and Turlough – to land on Manussa about a century before the Mara dominated it. Not caring if it violated its own timeline, the Mara tried to achieve full manifestation, and to conquer the Manussan

Empire (again), through a 4-D crystal featured on the Manussan TV show *Dreamarama*. The Doctor eradicated the Mara by inverting the crystal's power. He expressed doubt that the Mara could ever truly be killed.

The Intergalactic Mineral Exploitation Act was passed in 2217, granting the mining combines vast powers. The corporations had already supplied the colony ships, weather control, terraforming and computer technology to the colonists.[541] The seventh Doctor, Ace, and Benny visited the Moscow City Carnival in 2219.[542]

The city of Springfield was established near Ascraeus Lacus on Mars around 2227.[543]

2227 - SLEEPY[544] -> The Adjudication Service was just one of many organisations trying to enforce the law. The Serial/Spree Killers Investigations National Unit was one of the hundreds of small agencies operating in tandem with the conventional legal authorities throughout the twenty-third century – often with more powers than the authorities. Thanks to a combination of paranoia and real concern – some political parties took to hiring serial killers – Unit operatives could get in just about anywhere.

In the early twenty-third century, CM Enterprises attempted to create a computer that could think like a human by installing organic components – a cat's brain – into an Imbani mainframe. They only succeeded in building a computer that wanted to play with string and sit on newspapers. The Dione-Kisanu Company (DKC), on the other hand, encoded information in the form of memory RNA. Before long, DKC taught a woman the first verse of *Kublai Khan* by injection. In 2223, Madhanagopal finished his work on the AI named FLORANCE, which was taken offline.

Psychic ability was now recognised by humanity, and standard tests had been introduced. DKC were attempting to encode psi-powers using a model of the human mind: the AI named GRUMPY. Bernice Summerfield and Roz Forrester arrived in the preprogrammed TARDIS and met GRUMPY – who injected them with an antidote to a viral outbreak on Yemaya 4 thirty years in the future.

GRUMPY later escaped DKC by pushing himself through the computer networks, leaving his own hardware behind. He stored a few years' memories in a data vault in Malindi, tucked away a copy of his operating system in a communications satellite trailing Phobos, and spread pieces of himself across the solar system. For a decade, DKC kept the fact that GRUMPY had escaped secret and destroyed all they could find of him. GRUMPY became increasingly desperate, and used his psychic ability to terrorise and blackmail. After two years, DKC tracked him down, brought him back to Saturn's moon of Dione and erased the copies he had made of himself.

? 2230 - FRAYED[545] -> Earth sent those with a perceived genetic disposition to crime or latent psychic abilities (the "future deviants") to the Refuge on Iwa. There was a strict Eugenics Code on Earth. Corporations funded research into psychic ability, but it was felt that the psychics' sense of superiority led them to a criminal lifestyle. Babies without brains were cloned for medical research.

A Time Lord and his companion landed on Iwa. Adopting the names "the Doctor" and "Susan", they observed the humans' fight with wolf-like aliens. An uneasy truce was forged, and the humans agreed to help the aliens cure a genetic decay that was afflicting them.

The Ulla people of Xirrinda developed self-replicating, ravenous machine-creatures that threatened to consume the planet. The machine-creatures were launched into space, but the Ulla civilisation collapsed anyway.[546]

The Colonies

The second quarter of the twenty-third century became a time of great expansion of Earth's colonial efforts. Around 2230, the Survey Corps vessel *Icarus* entered service.[547]

The early-mid-twenty-third century was known as the First Great Breakout, a period of massive colonial expansion from Earth. Humanity reached the Uva Beta Uva System, which contained fourteen planets. Earth was becoming crowded and polluted, so there was no shortage of settlers for Uva Beta Uva Five. A couple of years later, a mining agent found belzite on Uva Beta Uva Three, and the settlers discovered that all of their legal rights were rescinded under the Intergalactic Mineral Exploitation Act of 2217. The mining companies moved in.[548]

? 2231 - "Spider-God"[549] -> A survey team from the Earth ship *Excelsior* landed on UX-4732 at the same time as the fourth Doctor. The Earthmen saw the peaceful natives apparently sacrifice themselves to giant spiders, and moved to eradicate the creatures. The Doctor deduced

---

545 Dating *Frayed* (TEL #11) - No date is given, but as children are screened for psychic abilities, and this is an early colony world, it ties in with information given in *SLEEPY*. The oldest child is 12, perhaps suggesting the colony has been established that long.

546 *Rain of Terror*. This is twice implied as happening "centuries" ago. The Doctor suggests that it was "millions of years" (p381) ago, although it's not evident how he comes to that conclusion.

547 "A hundred and fifty years" before *The Dimension Riders* (p61).

548 "A hundred and fifty years" before *The Romance of Crime* (p8). There's another Great Breakout in the year 5000, according to *The Invisible Enemy*. Uva Beta Five was re-named "New Earth", but is not the planet of the same name in *Time of Your Life* or *New Earth*.

549 Dating "Spider-God" (*DWM* #52) - No date is given, but it seems to be the early colonial period. It is twenty years since Frederic joined the survey corps, and three years since the *Excelsior* left Earth. The Earthmen have a hover car "scouter" and energy weapons.

550 *Benny: The Sword of Forever* (p40).

551 Dating *Memory Lane* (BF #88) - It is two hundred twenty-seven years and some months after Kim and Tom departed Earth, an event that occurs near the modern day.

552 *SLEEPY*

553 "Profits of Doom". It's "eight decades" before 2321.

554 Dating *The Twelfth Doctor Year Two* (Titan 12th Doc #2.1-2.4, "Clara Oswald and the School of Death") - The Doctor says it's "227 years in the future" from the modern day.

555 At least "a century" – or four termite generations – before *Valhalla*.

556 The "mid-twenty-third century at least", according to Benny in *Benny B1: Epoch: Private Enemy No. 1*.

557 *Lords of the Storm*

558 *The Leisure Hive*

559 *Placebo Effect*

560 Dating *DL: The Game of Death* (*DL* #6) - No year is given. The dating clues are somewhat fleeting... the Mars-Centauri Grand Prix is mentioned (and treated as a contemporary event), and it's said that General Augustus Korch fought in "the last" Dalek War, and was instrumental in securing the release of the infamous Aurora hostages. (This is sometimes confused with the "Auros" incident from *Prisoner of the Daleks* – also by Trevor Baxendale – but Korch didn't appear in that book, and the two events are very different in detail.)

The TARDIS data bank cites that the Silver Devastation was created "one hundred billion years ago" – a comment unlikely to have any relation to this story, as *Utopia* takes place in 100,000,000,000,000, and the state of humanity there is in no way similar to what's seen in *The Game of Death*. It's unlikely that the Nocturns are moving their victims through time to this era: time travel isn't mentioned (save for TARDIS and the Agent pursuing it), and such a feat – given the Doctor's claim in *Utopia* that even the Time Lords didn't venture out as far as the year 100,000,000,000,000 – would represent an enormous exertion of power for the comparatively frivolous purpose of killing a few people in a habitat dome. It's an arbitrary guess, but this story feels like it takes place during humankind's early colonial era – say, in the 2200s. The story continues in *DL: The Planet of Oblivion*.

that the "people" were actually the larval stage of beautiful butterfly creatures, and relied upon the spiders to weave cocoons for them to emerge from.

In 2234, the French artist Heironymous Basquait tried to wrap the Sphinx in holly-and-snowball giftwrap, then attempted to buy it. The world governments deliberated on whether to protect their great structures by spraying them with a layer of clear glassite. Over the next half century, this debate caused twelve economic fiascos, two minor wars and a pilot episode for *All Our Yesterdays 2*.[550]

c 2237 - MEMORY LANE[551] -> Astronaut Kim Kronotska returned to Earth a total of two hundred twenty-seven years after her departure, and instantly became a celebrity. She found that spaceships in this era could travel the distance she'd previously covered in mere months, and tracked the missing Tom Braudy to the planet Lucentra. She became trapped in the Earth-simulation cell holding him. The eighth Doctor, Charley and C'rizz helped to free the astronauts from the entrepreneurs Lest and Argot. They also demonstrated use of video-playback, allowing Lest and Argot to sell the technology to their people.

Portable sound-file players could now transmit sound directly into the user's ear canals.

In 2237, the artificial intelligence GRUMPY transferred his operating system into the computer of a fighter shuttle, and leapt out into interstellar space. DKC intercepted him at Sunyata, and shot him down over the temperate world of Yemaya, which was being surveyed for possible colonisation. To survive, GRUMPY seeded bits of its RNA into the colonists via their inoculations.[552]

In the twenty-third century, Earth was cluttered and grey, although there were crystal spires in Paris. Cities now stretched fifty levels underground, individuals had about five square metres of space.

The great entrepreneur Varley Gabriel scouted for planets to colonise. In 2241, the "top drawer" of the fittest and smartest people – along with twenty thousand crew to serve them – set off in the colony ship *Mayflower* on a planned one hundred year journey to a new world. It would go on to pass Aldebaran. At this time, humans used hovering service robots to maintain spaceships.[553]

& 2244 - THE TWELFTH DOCTOR YEAR TWO[554] -> The Steel Reivers had enjoyed success as mercenaries, until the twelfth Doctor embarrassingly magnetised them to the planet Phobos. Their captain, Lucifer Van Volk, attacked the Doctor on *The Rosette of Sirius* – the flagship of the Onedin interstellar line – but the Doctor enjoyed two pangalactic gargle-blasters (for medicinal purposes, as he had a sore throat) while defeating them once more.

A rush ensued to establish gas mines on the moons of Jupiter, including Callisto and Ganymede. The domed city of Valhalla was established as Callisto's capital, but when the mines ran dry, Earth declared the moon cities as independent and washed its hands of them. In the century to follow, conditions in the moon cities greatly deteriorated.

Genetically engineered termites had been used to burrow into Callisto in search of new energy sources. As the region's economic prosperity waned, the termites remained outside Valhalla's gravity pan. Jupiter's gravity fluxes affected them, and they grew to monstrous size within just three generations. The termites had been tasked with providing information to the Valhalla Registry computer, but the flow of information became two-way, which greatly enhanced their intelligence.[555]

On Mars, the police used helicars.[556]

Hindu settlers colonised the Unukalhai System. In 2247, the Colonial Office began to terraform Raghi, the sixth moon of Unukalhai IV (which the settlers named Indra), a process that took forty million people a quarter of a century to complete. Raghi was one of the few colonies funded by public donation rather than the corporations. The colonists traded airavata (creatures that lived in the clouds of Indra, and whose DNA contained a natural radiation decontaminant) with Spinward Corporation.[557]

In 2250, the Argolin warrior Theron started a war with the Foamasi. The war lasted twenty minutes and two thousand interplanetary missiles reduced Argolis to a radioactive wasteland. Following this disaster, the Argolin became sterile and started tachyonics experiments in an effort to perpetuate their race.[558] The Foamasi homeworld of Liasici was destroyed in the war.[559]

? 2250 - THE GAME OF DEATH[560] -> Horatio Hamilton did the Mars-Centauri Grand Prix in under six parsecs – which possibly entailed bending the rules, as parsecs were increments of space, not time.

Destronic particles derailed the TARDIS from 1895 to an asteroid in the Silver Devastation. The tenth Doctor and Gisella found a habitation bubble that was the setting for The Game of Death: a murder mystery in which contestants vied for a hundred million galactic credits. Karl Zalenby, a member of the Galactic Police, realised that the Game was a front to enable some shapechanging predators, the Nocturns, to satiate their murderous tendencies by killing the Game-players. The Judoon helped Zalenby shut down the Game, and he crushed to death the Darksmith Agent pursuing the Doctor. The Doctor triangulated the location where the Darksmiths had met the clients who commissioned the Eternity Crystal – the planet Ursulonamex, a.k.a. Oblivion – and went there with Gisella.

2257 - SLEEPY[561] -> Australia was now a wasteland, ruined through centuries of chemical and nuclear pollution, although some Australians had made a fortune from solar power.

Yemaya 4 was ideal for colonisation – it had a large temperate zone, gentle seasons and biochemistry not too different to that of Earth. The four hundred colonists – mostly Botswanans, South Africans and Burandans from the United African Confederacy – started accelerated gardens around the habitat dome almost immediately, and were busily turning some of the surrounding meadows into farms. They were going to use several Yemayan native plants as crops, and planetfall had been timed to allow almost immediate planting of Terran seed stock. With the help of drone farmers and AI administrators, the colony thrived for two months.

But then the first infections started. The seventh Doctor, Benny, Roz and Chris investigated why some colonists had developed psychic powers such as telekinesis, telepathy and pyrokinesis – the result of GRUMPY's RNA having been stripped into the colonists' inoculations. Chris also started to develop telepathy, but Benny and Roz made a trip in the TARDIS to DKC's research lab in the past, and upon their return distributed an antidote to the outbreak.

The core of GRUMPY resided in a crashed spaceship on Yemaya 4, but had become a blank slate re-named SLEEPY. DKC dispatched the warship *Flame Warrior* to Yemaya to safeguard its secrets, but SLEEPY sacrificed itself to destroy the warship. The colonists were able to partly assemble GRUMPY's memories from the RNA in their systems, and learned enough to either blackmail or bring down DKC. The corporation left the colony alone.

The Doctor won a bet with the personification of Death that he could prevent anyone from dying as a result of these events, but Death reminded the Doctor that he couldn't be everywhere...

---

561 Dating *SLEEPY* (NA #48) - The Doctor states it is "2257" (p29).

562 *Benny: Genius Loci*. It's some "centuries" (p71) prior to 2561, so this must be the early phase of humanity's colonial period, even though Pinky and Perky are far advanced from the technology generally available at this time.

563 *NAofBenny* V1: *Good Night, Sweet Ladies*

564 Dating *The Daleks* (1.2) - No date is given in the story, but the Doctor says in *The Edge of Destruction* that "Skaro was in the future". In *The Dalek Invasion of Earth*, the Doctor tells Ian that the first Dalek story occurred "a million years ahead of us in the future" and the twenty-second century is part of the "middle of the history of the Daleks". Where he acquires this information is unclear – he had not even heard of the Daleks when he first met them (whereas the Monk knows of them in *The Daleks' Master Plan* and *The Five Doctors* reveals that the Time Lords' ancestors forbid the use of the Daleks in their Games).

However, the Thals in *Planet of the Daleks* [2540] have legends of events in *The Daleks* as being from "generations ago".

In the original storyline for *The Survivors* (as the first story was provisionally titled), the date was given as "the year 3000", with the war having occurred two thousand years before. A revised synopsis dated 30th July, 1963, gave the date as "the twenty-third century".

The Terrestrial Index and *The Official Doctor Who & the Daleks Book* both suggested that the Daleks from this story were "new Daleks" created by "crippled Kaled survivors", and that the story is set just after *Genesis of the Daleks* – this is presumably meant to explain the Dal/Kaled question and also helps tie the Dalek history into the *TV Century 21* comic strip, although there is no evidence for it on screen. *The TARDIS Logs* dated the story as "2290 AD". The American *Doctor Who* comic

suggested a date of "300 AD", on the grounds that the Daleks do not seem to have developed space travel. The FASA Role-playing Game dated the story as "5 BC". "Matrix Databank" in *DWM* #73 suggested that *The Daleks* takes place after *The Evil of the Daleks* and that the Daleks seen here are the last vestiges of a once-great race. This ties in with *The Dalek Invasion of Earth*, but contradicts *Planet of the Daleks*.

Timelink suggests 900. *About Time* sifted through the evidence, stipulated that the story-dating was "hugely debatable", then concluded that "almost any date between the 1960s and 2300 would fit". The Virgin version of *Ahistory* speculated that the Doctor had returned Ian and Barbara to 1963, but on the wrong side of the galaxy. If it was set at the time of broadcast, it would be a couple of months after they left London, so – stretching a little – it qualifies as "the future".

The Sink Plunger entry and the Mark III Travel Machine entry in *A History of the Universe in 100 Objects* (pgs. 94, 96) both date *The Daleks* to "circa 1963". *The Dalek Handbook* remarks that "by the 20th century (in Earth's timescale), Skaro was an arid wasteland" (p8) and dates The Dalek War (either the conflict that precedes *The Daleks*, or the renewed Dalek efforts against the Thals in that story) to "circa 1963" (p18).

The main problem is that, whenever it's set, we have to reconcile the Daleks seen in first Dalek story – stuck in their city unaware of any life beyond it who are all killed – with the Daleks as galactic conquerors seen in all subsequent stories. We have to postulate (without any evidence from the series) that a faction of Daleks left Skaro at some point between becoming confined to their travel machines and the Neutronic War and they subsequently lost contact with Skaro. This faction of Daleks had a powerful space fleet (*Lucifer Rising*) invaded the Earth (*The Dalek Invasion of Earth*) and the rest of the solar system (*GodEngine*), and fought the

Humans tasked two sentient terraforming machines – Pinky and Perky – with establishing the architecture, railways and roadways for a colony on Jaiwan. Pinky and Perky fell in love, swapped subroutines and built increasingly creative layouts for one another. The colonists, worried that the AIs had evolved beyond their original programming, deactivated them.[562]

A Dalek time-vessel ran aground on the moon of Adolin. It languished as a cathedral was built atop it.[563]

First Encounter Between the Doctor and the Daleks

? 2263 - THE DALEKS[564] -> For centuries, the few survivors of the Thal race had lived on a plateau on Skaro, eking out an existence. They relied on rainfall that came only every ten years. One decade, the rain never came. After two years, the Thal Temmosus and his group left the plateau, hoping to find the city of the Daleks. This occurred five hundred years after the Neutronic War, and the Daleks had become affected by the reverse evolution on the planet, and had lost many of their technological secrets. Reconciliation between the Thals and the Daleks proved impossible.

The first Doctor, Susan, Ian and Barbara arrived on Skaro. They explored the Dalek city, then sided with the Thals in wiping out the Daleks.

& 2263 - NAofBENNY: RANDOM GHOSTS / THE LIGHTS OF SKARO[565] -> A vengeful Ace, armed with an Omega Device she acquired while studying on Gallifrey, travelled back to eradicate the Daleks during their early days. The Omega device went awry while the Daleks were dormant in their city, and co-mingled Skaro's past, present and future. Benny, sent by the seventh Doctor to help, encountered some Kaleds from Skaro's past and became lovers with Klinus: a Kaled artist fated to become one of the very first Daleks. She also revived the Dalek city's power systems, lessening the time breaks and enabling the Doctor to land the TARDIS.

A Dalek conveyed to Benny that its people had hoped to one day emerge from their shells and walk the surface of Skaro, but felt betrayed by the Thals' "lethal" anti-radiation drugs. The first Doctor's party, it claimed, inadvertently caused the Daleks to learn of other worlds and time travel, and motivated them to redouble their efforts to destroy all other life to facilitate their own survival. Benny used the Omega Device to summon a Dalek's future self from four million years on – the two were so philosophically opposed, they killed one another and caused a paradox that ended the time breaks. As the Daleks resumed sleeping in their city, the Doctor, Ace and Benny left for further adventures...

The Doctor's encounter with the Daleks was Last Contact, when the Time Lords first encountered the race that would ultimately destroy them.[566]

Mechanoids (*The Chase*). They developed internal power supplies and (at some point after *The Dalek Invasion of Earth*) the "slatted" design, rather than the "banded" one seen in the first two stories. Following this – possibly licking their wounds following their defeat in *The Dalek Invasion of Earth* – the survivors of this faction returned to their home planet. They would have discovered a city full of dead Daleks – and perhaps the Doctor's role in their cousins' defeat.

While unsupported by evidence from the show, and a little awkward, it fits in with the facts we learn at the end of *The Space Museum* and *The Chase* – the Daleks now live on Skaro, their influence stretches across time and space, they have limited knowledge of the Doctor, advanced science and a desire for revenge specifically against the Doctor, Ian, Barbara and Susan.

The Dalek City seen in *The Daleks* and *The Evil of the Daleks* (surely one and the same, given the Doctor's familiarity with it in the latter) isn't named on screen, but an increasing number of secondary texts (*The Dalek Handbook*, *Dalek: The Astounding Untold History of the Greatest Enemies of the Universe* and the video game *The Eternity Clock*) refer to it as "Kalaann".

565 Dating *NAofBenny* V1: *Random Ghosts/The Lights of Skaro* (*NAofBenny* #1.3-1.4) - The "contemporary" section of these stories coincides with *The Daleks*.

566 *The Gallifrey Chronicles*

LAST CONTACT: It's not recorded when the Daleks discover key facts about the Doctor. By *The Chase*, they can recognise the TARDIS (which they didn't see in the two TV stories up to that point, as it was either deep in the petrified forest or buried by rubble), and they also know the Doctor can travel in time. In *The Chase*, the Daleks refer to "The Doctor and these three humans", which might imply that they don't think the Doctor is human. Except that one of the other three is his granddaughter Susan, and later in the story they *do* refer to the Doctor as "human". In *The Chase*, it doesn't even occur to them that Susan might have left, so it's unlikely they've got records of other incarnations of the Doctor or companions. They think he's "more than human" (by virtue of his being a time traveller) in *The Evil of the Daleks*, and Chen claims that the Doctor was from "another galaxy" in *The Daleks' Master Plan*. When the Daleks deal with the Monk and the Master, they don't ever make the connection on screen that they are from the same planet as the Doctor.

Contrast all of this with *Resurrection of the Daleks,*

At some point after this time, the Moroks acquired a Dalek from Skaro, and put it on exhibit in their Space Museum.[567]

> = The spacefaring Daleks capable of feeling pity returned to Skaro to protect the Thals from the Quatch threat. When the Thals refused to accept Dalek rule, the Daleks subjugated them "for their own good".[568]

The planet Badblood became cut off from humanity's other colonies owing to an outbreak of vampirism, as well as carbonised dust in the upper atmosphere scrambling communications.[569] The Computers and Cybernetic Systems Act was passed on Uva Beta Uva in 2265.[570]

? 2266 - "The Lost Dimension"[571] -> The white hole crisis sparked by an insane Type 1 TARDIS weakened the dimensional walls. The fourth Doctor and the second Romana didn't reach the 1902 Royal Coronation Fleet Review at Spithead, and instead found themselves at a stand-off between extra-dimensional representatives of the Kroton Imperium, the Quarks and the Ogron Confederation

of Planets. The Doctor's towering reputation as a stopper of invaders compelled the participants to return their native realities.

> = The sixth Doctor visited the planet Huttan in the year 2267.[572]

> **(=) 2267 - "Assimilation 2"**[573] -> The Cybermen scanned other universes, and became interested in forging an alliance with the Borg Collective. A squad of Cybermen travelled across the universal divide, and overcame a United Federation of Planets archaeology team researching an alien communications array on Aprilia III. The fourth Doctor aided an away team from the USS *Enterprise* – Captain James T. Kirk, first officer Spock, medical officer Leonard McCoy and engineer Montgomery Scott – in defeating the Cybermen with gold dust. The Doctor left, unaware that the Cybermen had successfully sent the Borg a message, which would facilitate an alliance between them a century on.

---

where they refer (for the first time) to the Doctor as a Time Lord and identify his home planet as Gallifrey.

On the other hand, the Time Lords certainly know of the Daleks – they're referred to in the Doctor's trial in *The War Games*, plus the Time Lords send the Doctor on missions against them in *Planet of the Daleks* and *Genesis of the Daleks*. The Monk and the Master also know about the Daleks. In the time of Rassilon, the Daleks were banned from the Games of Death on Gallifrey, so the Gallifreyans then knew of the Daleks, but there's no evidence that the two races made contact. There's another continuity problem here – why is it that the Doctor and Susan *don't* know about the Daleks before they meet them in *The Daleks*? It's a particular problem because by *The Dalek Invasion of Earth*, the Doctor seems au fait with their complete history. It's possible, as with so much history of that period, that the modern Time Lords had long lost or filed away their knowledge of the Daleks.

We hear the Daleks and Time Lords have all but wiped each other out in *Dalek* and *The Parting of the Ways*.

567 In *The Space Museum*, the Moroks have a Dalek specimen from "Planet Skaro", one with horizontal bands rather than vertical slats. It seems likely that the Moroks raid Skaro at some undisclosed time around *The Daleks*. It's unlikely it was before, as it's implied that the Daleks have no knowledge of life on other planets. Although this in turn contradicts *Genesis of the Daleks*, in which both Davros and the Dalek leader express a wish to conquer other worlds once they know the Doctor is an alien.

568 "Hundreds of years" before *Unbound: Masters of War*, in the wake of *The Daleks*.
569 Three centuries before *Benny: The Vampire Curse*: "The Badblood Diaries".
570 *The Romance of Crime*
571 Dating "The Lost Dimension" (Titan mini-series) – Time unknown, but nothing suggests the dimension-hopping Krotons, Quarks and Ogrons can time travel. With the Ogrons in question being a *Star Trek* take off, placement here coincides with year one of *Star Trek: The Original Series*.
572 Dating *Assimilation 2* (IDW *Star Trek: The Next Generation/Doctor Who* mini-series) - In *Star Trek* terms, it's Stardate 3368.5. The Stardates given in classic *Star Trek* episodes are very scrambled (a more uniform, if still slightly problematic, Stardate system was introduced for *Star Trek: The Next Generation*), but the best corresponding spot for the Stardate given here seems to be between classic *Star Trek* Seasons 1 and 2, i.e. the year 2267. The fourth Doctor's encounter with Captain Kirk and company seems to retroactively happen as a "pre-echo" of elements from the *Doctor Who* universe working their way into the *Star Trek* one, with the eleventh Doctor suggesting that the Cybermen's eventual obliteration in the latter will conveniently scrub events on Aprilia III from the timeline.
573 *Spiral Scratch*
574 "One hundred and fourteen years" before *Antidote to Oblivion*, a sum presumably chosen to reflect the aftermath of *The Dalek Invasion of Earth*. No mention is made of ConCorp in *An Earthly Child* et al (or the related *Legacy of the Daleks*), which chronicle the Second Dalek

Democracy ended in the United Kingdom in 2268, as part of a ConCorp bailout. ConCorp bought out the UK's assets, including the Crown Jewels, as part of the bankruptcy settlement.[574]

By 2270, the Argolin had called a moratorium of their Recreation Programme. Instead, they set up the Leisure Hive, which offered a range of holiday pursuits for intergalactic tourists while promoting peace and understanding between races. Argolis became the first leisure planet. Meanwhile, a central government took control of the Foamasi planet, breaking the power bases of the old Lodges. The new government sought restitution with Argolis.[575]

Humanity had consolidated its position, and now possessed a large number of colony worlds. Both the Earth government and the corporations were quite capable of closing down the supply routes to uneconomic or uncooperative colonies, abandoning them entirely.

Away from Earth, life was often still very harsh. The corporations or governing elites that controlled each colony discovered that as long as Earth was kept supplied with minerals and other resources, Earth Central would turn a blind eye to local human rights abuses.[576]

Stanoff Osterling was regarded as one of the two greatest playwrights in human history. His work conformed to the stage conventions of his time, following the Greek tradition of reporting offstage action in elegant speeches rather than seeing it performed. The galaxy's economy was damaged after the wars and the colonies could not afford anything more lavish, but this reliance on dialogue and plotting rather than technological innovation led to a flourishing of the theatre across the galaxy. Osterling was regarded as a genius in his own time for such plays as *Death by Mirrors*, *The Captain's Honour* and *The Mercenary*. His greatest achievement, however, was felt to be his lost play *The Good Soldiers* (2273) that dealt with the aftermath of the battle at Limlough. The Doctor helped transcribe the play, as Osterling had restioparothis.[577]

Vilus Krull, a human born on the colony planet Tranagus, came into contact with a potent but mindless force from the end of time, which didn't obey conventional laws of physics. Krull thought the force was sentient and founded the Cult of the Dark Flame to facilitate its full manifestation; upon Krull's death, his skull became a lodestone for the Dark Flame's power. The cult infiltrated every star system in the galaxy for a time, but was eventually thought to have died out.[578]

Hila Tacorian, an early pioneer in the field of time travel, was lost to history during an experimental voyage into time. Her mind eventually made contact with her great-great-great-great-great grandmother, Emma Grayling, in 1974.[579]

Scientists at the Collabria Research Colony grafted the biological material from monsters into children, hoping to transform them into living weapons. The Doctor rescued the three surviving children, designated 78342, 78346 and 78351 – the latter of whom had Axon, Ogron and Pyrovile inheritance in his genetic make up.[580]

c 2275 - THE PRISONER'S DILEMMA[581] -> The seventh Doctor and Ace trailed Harmonious XIV Zinc and his wife IV Madga: two criminals from the Commune of the White Sun, who had stolen a time ring from the Trib Museum. Ace encountered them on the prison moon Erratoon, and also met Zara, a living tracer of the Key to Time. Zara found a Key segment disguised as an Erratoon lake. Harmonious XIV Zinc and Madga tried to kill everyone on Erratoon to acquire its mining rights; Ace prevented this, but in so doing destroyed Erratoon's geodesic sphere. Emergency systems lifted the colony's buildings into space without a single casualty. In future, Erratoon's robot wardens would be withdrawn, and the moon would become home to a space dock and an artificial sky.

Invasion of Earth.

575 *The Leisure Hive*

576 Many stories feature Earth colonies that supply the home planet and are subject to tyrannical regimes. This is typically treated as a specific era in future history, when space travel and interplanetary communications are limited, and so most of these stories have been placed together just prior to the Earth Empire's formation. The New and Missing Adventures attempted to weave a more systematic and consistent "future history" for Earth, and many concerned themselves with this period of early colonisation, corporate domination and increasing centralisation.

577 *Theatre of War*

578 "Centuries" before *The Dark Flame*, although there's some confusion about this; see the dating notes for this story. Tranagus was named in *Benny S4: The Draconian Rage*.

579 *Hide*. The Doctor claims Hila is from "a few hundred years" after 1974, but she's also cited as Alec Palmer and Emma Grayling's great-great-great-great-great granddaughter, which by the normal generational-counting rules of this chronology would total about 175 years. Tacorian's experiments with time must come to naught, as it's some millennia on, in the forty-nine century at the earliest, that humanity is in possession of time technology.

580 *Lights Out*

581 Dating *The Prisoner's Dilemma* (BF CC #3.8) - It's "generations" after Erratoon is established as a prison planet. The dating here is otherwise a bit arbitrary, but the adventure likely occurs when hyperspace vessels

The Knights of Jeneve emerged as a military power. Their founder, Vazlov Baygent, was assassinated in 2276, but the Knights eliminated Baygent's killers and protected his son.[582] The terraforming of Raghi was completed.[583] The Mutant Rights Act was passed in 2278. Uva Beta Uva III was at the centre of a belzite rush unparalleled in human history around this time.[584] A polymer used in Movellan ships was developed.[585]

On Earth, the fallout of the "Sphinx-giftwrapping" incident reached its conclusion when war broke out. The Leaning Tower of Pisa was destroyed – along with Pisa itself – by a mis-aimed half-ton asteroid. The economy's focus became weapons and transport, and the preservation of national monuments became less of a priority.[586]

c 2285 - VENGEANCE ON VAROS[587] **->** The Galatron Mining Corporation and the Amorb prospect fought over mineral rights on the planets of the galaxy, often with little concern for local populations. One such place was Varos, a former prison planet (pop. 1,620,783) in the constellation of Cetes. An officer elite ran Varos and lived in relative luxury, although everyone was confined to enclosed domes with artificial atmospheres. A majority of the people had the constitutional right to vote for the Governor's execution. Until traces were detected on the asteroid Biosculptor, Varos was long thought to be the only source of zeiton-7 ore, a fuel for space/time vehicles.

In the late twenty-third century, Galatron and the government of Varos entered negotiations for the zeiton-7 ore. Galatron had a stranglehold over Varos

are already in use, as Elysium ore will be used to refine the hyperspace process only "a generation" after this.

The robot wardens of Erratoon subject Ace to memory-wiping, and although the Doctor is confident that he can repair her lost memories using the TARDIS, the idea seems to be that Ace loses her memories of the New Adventures. This move was designed to help reconcile Ace's status later in the novel range (Spacefleet-trained adventurer with a motorbike that travels through time and space) with the Big Finish version (older sister to Hex, is still travelling with the Doctor). The seeming discrepancies in Ace's character, however, can be just as easily accounted for by the not-so-terribly controversial idea that people are different in their 20s, 30s and even 40s. Writer Simon Guerrier concedes that he added the memory-wiping angle "more for my own amusement than anything else", that it's certain that Ace gets back her memories of the Doctor and the TARDIS, and that the whole incident is a tool that continuity keepers can use or ignore as they wish.

582 *Benny: Dragons' Wrath*

583 "Nearly a quarter of a century" before *Lords of the Storm*.

584 "About a hundred and fifty years" before *The Romance of Crime*.

585 "Three hundred years" after *The Movellan Grave*.

586 About fifty years after 2234, according to *Benny: The Sword of Forever*.

587 Dating *Vengeance on Varos* (22.2) - The Governor states that Varos has been a mining colony for "centuries" and it has been stable "for over two hundred years". Peri tells the Governor that she is from "nearly three centuries before you were born". The story takes place before *Mindwarp* (set on 3rd July, 2379). Mentors must live longer than humans, as the Mentor Sil appears in both stories (although he changes colour from brown to green between the two).

The novelisation set it in "the latter part of the twenty-third century", as did *The Terrestrial Index*. The

Discontinuity Guide set a range "between 2285 and 2320". *Timelink* said "2324". *About Time* focused on the *Mindwarp* dating and Sil's participation, so decided upon "a dating slightly later than Peri's estimate".

588 Dating *Lights Out* (Puffin Books *Doctor Who* ebook #12) - Some of those present at the Intergalactic Coffee Roasting Station are human, so it's in the future. Perhaps tellingly, 78351 spends a three-year stint working for the Galatron Mining Corporation from *Vengeance on Varos* [c.2285].

589 Dating *Mission to Magnus* (BF LS #1.2) - Sil's operation on Magnus is a direct consequence of his defeat in *Vengeance on Varos*. Peri reads off that it's the "twenty-third century" on one of the TARDIS read-outs as the Ship is pulled through the Vortex. The novelisation of this story, released in 1990, had the Doctor telling Peri that it's "Midway through the twenty-third century", but the likely dating of *Vengeance on Varos* suggests it's a bit later than that. A minor continuity glitch exists in that both here and in *Mindwarp*, Sil implies that he last saw the Doctor and Peri on Varos.

511 Dating *The Leisure Hive* (18.1) - Romana establishes that the war was in "2250", "forty years" before. *The Doctor: His Lives and Times*, p99) displays a Leisure Hive visitor's log, signed by the Doctor and Romana, with the date "21-3-2290".

512 Dating *DotD: Night of the Whisper* (*Destiny of the Doctor* #9) - The blurb and the Doctor both cite this as the twenty-third century. However, the Doctor also names this as the time of the Earth Empire, when the twenty-third century is some hundreds of years too soon for that, and the overwhelming bulk of evidence in other stories suggests that humanity is still in its colonisation phase. Kronkburgers were first mentioned in "The Iron Legion", then in *The Long Game*. The Doctor's psychic paper claims to give him "complete authority from Earth", possibly suggesting that New New New Scotland Yard (presuming it isn't just the Doctor's invention) is based there.

because it supplied the colony with food, and so kept the price of zeiton-7 down to seven credits a unit. Successive Governors had developed an entertainment industry, Comtech, that sold footage of the executions, tortures and escape attempts of prisoners to every civilised world. This acted as a deterrent for potential rebels, and kept the population entertained.

Eventually, the sixth Doctor and Peri helped one Governor to negotiate the fair price of twenty credits a unit for Varos' zeiton, besting the efforts of Galatron's agent, Sil.

c 2285 - LIGHTS OUT[XXX-605] -> For three years, the mutant 78351 worked for Galatron Mining Corporation, and saved up enough to buy a second-hand spaceship. He became gainfully employed shuttling coffee beans between the Intergalactic Coffee Roasting Station (ICRS) in orbit of Chloris and the Planet of the Coffee Shops.

The twelfth Doctor stopped at the ICRS to purchase some coffee for Clara, and investigated an increasing number of mysterious deaths that happened when the lights went out. He deduced that 78351 was unknowingly killing people as his mutant system went through puberty, and required the energy of human beings to attain maturity. To prevent further deaths, 78351 piloted his spaceship close to a nearby star, intending to either gain the energy needed to mature, or just end his life. 78351's biology blossomed in the resultant heat and light, and he found he was not afraid.

c 2287 - MISSION TO MAGNUS[510] -> Humans had settled on the planet Magnus. The Seven Sisterhoods came to rule there when a virus killed off most of the male population; a few males were kept below the planet's surface for progenitor harvesting. The Ice Warriors triggered a series of nuclear explosions that moved Magnus into a colder orbit, hoping to alter the climate to their liking.

The Mentor Sil, trying to atone for his failure on Varos, was poised to reap a profit by selling warm garments and other goods to the Magnus inhabitants. Sil had previously met Anzor, a representative of the High Council on Gallifrey, on Thoros Beta. The sixth Doctor dealt with Anzor's interference by sending him and his TARDIS on a slow trek into the distant past.

(=) Rana Zandusia – the leader of the Sisterhoods – and Sil came into possession of the Doctor's TARDIS, travelled a few hours into the future and saw that Magnus had been devastated.

The Doctor and Peri reclaimed the TARDIS, and triggered a second series of explosions that moved Magnus back into a warmer orbit. The men of Salvak offered to become husbands to the Sisterhoods.

2290 - THE LEISURE HIVE[511] -> By 2290, it was clear that the Leisure Hive on Argolis was in trouble. Last year's bookings had fallen dramatically, and advance bookings for 2291 were disastrous. Argolis now faced competition from other leisure planets such as Abydos and Limus 4. The West Lodge of the Foamasi offered to buy the planet, but the board refused and instead pinned their hopes on tachyon experiments conducted by the Earth scientist Hardin. The fourth Doctor and the second Romana were present when agents of the Foamasi government arrested two members of the West Lodge, who were attempting to establish a power base on Argolis, and it was discovered that the Tachyon Recreation Generator could rejuvenate the Argolin. The Argolin and Foamasi governments re-opened negotiations.

c 2290 - DotD: NIGHT OF THE WHISPER[512] -> The city of New Vegas was established on a barren alien moon as a human tourist destination featuring some three thousand casinos, all contained in an atmospheric bubble. New Vegas was voted the Most Debauched Destination on any planet – partly, Jack Harkness claimed, because he sat on the awards committee for ten years straight. A territory neighbouring New Vegas – the Mignala Collective, a.k.a. the Union of Non-Human worlds – created bio-mechanoids, star marshals, to enforce the law within its borders. A star marshal crashed outside the New Vegas dome and remained there, wounded.

A few years later, the most influential gangster in New Vegas – the lupine Sirius Wolfsbane – had a disobedient operatives killed, then ordered that the man's meddlesome widow, Lillian Marsh, be thrown out of the city's dome. The wounded star-marshal merged with the dying Lillian, and the resultant hybrid became a vigilante: the Whisper.

The ninth Doctor, Rose and Captain Jack went undercover in New Vegas as the Whisper's mental state deteriorated, and it leeched energy from people, turning them into desiccated corpses, for the slightest of offences. The Doctor posed as "Inspector George Dixon" of the New New New Scotland Yard, Jack worked for the *Daily Galaxy* and Rose served kronkburgers with cheese at the Full Moon nightclub.

The eleventh Doctor sent his younger self a message stressing that he must protect Lillian's father, Commissioner James McNeil, who would become an influential New Vegas mayor. The Doctor's party foiled Wolfsbane's scheme to sabotague the New Vegas air generation plant on behalf of Bad Wolf Holdings, an off-world consortium. Wolfsbane killed the Whisper, but fell to his death during a struggle.

As the mayor of New Vegas, James McNeil ushered in a golden age of tourism that included the Memorial Hotel and Wedding Chapel.[513]

c 2290 - ZALTYS[514] **->** The Necrobiologicals aboard the *Exemplar* coveted Zaltys' underground cities as a power base for an empire of the undead. The fifth Doctor, Adric, Tegan and Nyssa failed to stop them, and so a Vulpine telepath, Gevaudan, gave his life to mentally command the vampires to remove their protective helmets, and perish in the light of Zaltys' sun.

Checkley's World, "The Horror Planet", was settled in 2290 and selected as the best location for a scientific research station. The laboratories were released from state control a decade after the planet was colonised, and the facilities were funded by a number of empires and corporations, including the Arcturans, Riftok and Masel. Earth Government remained the major partner. Weapon systems such as compression grenades, Freire's gas and the Ethers – genetically engineered ghost-troops – were developed.[515]

Human colonists discovered Selonart.[516] The residents of the planet Perfecton determined that their sun would go supernova. Unable to escape, they encoded their entire culture onto a missile that could recreate their civilisation with quantum fluctuations. Humanity didn't know why the Perfectons had vanished, and quarantined Perfecton.[517] The leaders of the Slav and Russian colonists on the planet Vishpok advocated genetic purity – the "Visphoi Ideal". A series of emperors and empresses ruled Vishpok until it fell under a military dictatorship.[518]

Tobias Tickle, the aged founder of the Tickle Town amusement park on Earth, foresaw a war that could potentially wipe out humanity. To save whomever he could, Tickle sealed off the park on its opening day, and transmatted it to a self-sustaining underground cavern. His cartoon holo-projections – including Constable Claws – acted as enforcers to keep Tickle Town's "guests" in line. On Earth's surface, the war Tickle predicted was averted.[519]

2294 - THE STONES OF VENICE[520] **->** After overthrowing yet another reign of terror, the eighth Doctor and Charley arrived in Venice on the eve of its destruction. The gondoliers of Venice, now amphibians with webbed hands and toes, eagerly awaited the chance to claim the city once it sank beneath the waves.

A series of tremors struck the city, but the Doctor discovered that the "late" Estella, now posing as a city resident

---

513 *DotD: The Time Machine*
514 Dating *Zaltys* (BF #223) - The Doctor remarks that it's "two or three centuries" after the plague on Draconia [c.2040].
515 *The Highest Science*
516 "Seventy years" before *The Infinity Race*.
517 "Centuries" before *Benny: Oh No It Isn't!*.
518 Centuries before *Benny: Dry Pilgrimage*.
519 "Twenty years" before "Welcome to Tickle Town". Tickle says that he foresaw war ahead "as the last century died".
520 Dating *The Stones of Venice* (BF #18) - The story itself says that it's the "twenty-third century", but *Neverland* gives a firm date of 2294.
521 Dating *Whispers of Terror* (BF #3) - No date given, but references to the play *The Good Soldiers* relate to information given in *Theatre of War*. The story is set within a generation of the first performance of the play.
522 Dating "Dreadnought" (*Radio Times* #3775-3784) - No date given, but *Placebo Effect* claims that Stacy's parents are from the "twenty-third century".
523 *Placebo Effect*
524 "Fifteen years" before "Space Squid".
525 *Interference*
526 About five years before *Excelis Decays*.
527 "Four hundred years" before *The Sensorites*. There is also a Central City on Earth in the year 4000, according to *The Daleks' Master Plan*.
528 In *The Dimension Riders*, Ace tells Lieutenant Strakk that she comes from Perivale, and he says that the area is a "forest" (p68).
529 "About four hundred years" after the 1909 section of *Birthright*.
530 *Synthespians™*
531 *The Stone Rose*
532 *The Highest Science* (p49).
533 Jake and Madelaine appear in *Goth Opera*, and we learn of their fate in *Managra* (p64).
534 *SLEEPY*
535 "Fifteen hundred years" before *A Device of Death*.
536 *The Pyralis Effect*
537 *The Big Bang*. The date of this is completely unknown, but the name suggests a connection to Earth, and it might be a leisure planet as seen in *The Leisure Hive*.
538 A generation after *The Prisoner's Dilemma*.
539 *The Taking of Planet 5* (p219).
540 *The Twin Dilemma*
537 "Almost one hundred years" before *LIVE 34*.
538 "Fifty years" before *The Price of Paradise*, which is set in the late twenty-fourth century. The reference to the Draconians apparently contradicts the timescale established in *Frontier in Space*, although other novels (such as *Love and War*) also suggested that humans and Draconians met before their "official" first contact.
539 Dating *Benny B5: Missing Persons: The Winning Side* (Benny box set #5.4) - No time given, but Theon's city is long dead, the stuff of ruins, by the time "our" Benny visits c.2620. If Victorian-Benny's comment that microwave ovens were used on Earth "a long time ago" isn't just figurative, it makes some sense to split the differ-

named Eleanor Lavish, had once owned an alien device capable of altering reality. The device had kept Estella and Duke Orsino alive for a century by draining Venice's life force, leading to its present decay. The Doctor recovered the device, and Orsino proposed that he and Estella end their lives for Venice's sake. Estella agreed out of continued love for Orsino, and the device turned them into ash, saving the city. The high priest of the Cult of Estella made off with their ashes.

c 2295 - WHISPERS OF TERROR[521] -> Despite a dislike of the visual medium, Visteen Krane became acclaimed as the greatest actor of his age. His body of work was chiefly confined to audio recordings and a few photographs. Later, he became a politician and stood for Presidency with his agent, Beth Pernell, as his running mate.

Before the election, Krane seemingly committed suicide in the Museum of Aural Antiquities, an institution dedicated to the study of all things audio. Pernell pledged to run in Krane's place and continue his policies. The sixth Doctor and Peri discovered that at the moment of his death, Krane used advanced sound equipment to transfer his brainwaves into the sound medium. Krane had become a creature of pure sound, demented from his transformation and outraged at Pernell, who had engineered his murder.

The Krane-creature attempted to endlessly replicate itself and take control of the planet, but the Doctor shocked Krane back to sanity. Pernell's plans were exposed, and Krane agreed to stay at the Museum to aid Curator Gantman with his research. Pernell fled, but Krane engineered an automobile accident that killed her.

Stacy Townsend Joins the TARDIS

c 2296 - "Dreadnought"[522] -> Stacy Townsend was the only survivor when the Cybermen attacked the cargo ship *Dreadnought*; her fiancé, Bill, was Cyber-converted. The eighth Doctor destroyed the Cybermen, and Stacy joined him on his travels.

The Doctor later brought Stacy's parents, Christopher and Mary Townsend, through time to attend her wedding in 3999.[523] The Holy Space Squid began attracting acolytes.[524] The colony ship *Justinian* set off for Ordifica at the end of the twenty-third century.[525]

Circa 2296, Grayvorn abandoned his "Lord Vaughn Sutton" identity and covertly continued his sociopolitical engineering in Excelis. The leaders of Artaris' city-states secretly signed the Artaris Convention, ending the war between them. Grayvorn found the conflict useful to his industrial efforts and sabotaged the accord. His research culminated in the creation of lumps of biomass named Meat Puppets, his master shock troops. He used the Relic's

abilities to rip the souls from dissidents and infuse the Meat Puppets with life.[526]

The Twenty-Fourth Century

By the twenty-fourth century, the lower half of England had become a vast Central City.[527] Much of what had been West London was covered in forest.[528] Duronite, an alloy of machonite and duralinium, was discovered in the early twenty-fourth century. Influenza had been eradicated.[529] The James Bond films were remade in the twenty-fourth century.[530] Merik's Theorem was discovered in the twenty-fourth century.[531]

Suspended animation ships were still available in the twenty-fourth century, but they had been superseded by the invention of super light drives.[532] Jonquil the Intrepid destroyed the vampires Lord Jake and Lady Madelaine, but their descendants survived for many thousands of years.[533] On a visit to the twenty-fourth century, the Doctor learnt about the colony at Yemaya.[534] Landor, on the galactic rim, was colonised around now.[535]

Humans colonised Pavonis IV, a verdant planet in the Delta Pavonis System, in the twenty-fourth century. It served as their home for a thousand years, during which time the first Doctor and his three companions saved the colonists from an alien invasion. The Pavonians regarded him as a mythical hero; some parents even named their children after him.[536]

The eleventh Doctor took Amy to Space Florida, a planet with automatic sand.[537]

Elysium ore was found to improve the fuel efficiency of hyperspace vessels by 6 or 7%, and became greatly sought after. Galactic laws gave indigenous populations first claim on mining rights, so the discovery of Elysium on Erratoon made its inhabitants very wealthy.[538]

Early in the twenty-fourth century, a philosopher on a colony world published a monograph, *The Myth of the Non-Straight Line*. The population had ceased being able to conceive of circles. The planet was quarantined as scientists from a survey ship attempted to work out why.[535] **The fourth Doctor and one of his fellow Time Lords, Azmael, met on Jaconda around this time.**[536]

Humanity settled a group of forty-nine colony worlds that became cut off from Earth. On Colony 34, a hospital was built in the northern mountains from marnite stone. Colony 48 lacked access to navigable waters.[537] Maurit Guillan discovered the paradise planet of Laylora, but later his ship was found drifting near Draconian space, the location of Laylora lost. The search for the planet went on to inspire a number of explorers.[538]

c 2300 - BENNY B5: MISSING PERSONS: THE WINNING SIDE[539] -> The version of Bernice Summerfield who escaped from the Epoch's recreation of Victorian

London "fell from the sky" to a low-tech city ruled by King Theon, and was taken for a Sky Witch. Victorian-Benny deduced that a crashed spaceship that was leaking Dallion radiation, afflicting Theon's people with plague-like symptoms. Meriol, the king's counselor, was hailed as a hero upon using the ship's weaponry to destroy a tribe of warring savages, the Garron. Benny's pleas to deactivate the ship's engine fell on deaf ears as Meriol and his supporters plundered the vessel to make huge technological advancements. Theon, having asked for Benny's hand in marriage, disregarded her advice and imprisoned her in a stone tower.

The Dallion radiation killed Theon's people. As a final act of penance, Theon detonated the spaceship to send Victorian-Benny hurling through time and space, to the headquarters of the Epoch...

? 2300 - MUMMY ON THE ORIENT EXPRESS[540] ->

"There were many trains to take the name Orient Express, but only one in space."

Synthetic lungs were available, and the Excelsior Life Extender, effectively a portable hospital, could keep alive people who were over a hundred years old. The *Orient Express* in space served as a faithful recreation of the original, albeit running on hyperspace ribbons. Mystery shoppers continued to strike fear into managers.

An unidentified party known only as "Gus" sought to reverse-engineer the Foretold's lethal abilities, and field-tested the mummy aboard the *Gloriana* and *Valiant Heart* space vessels. Gus succeeded in luring the twelfth Doctor and Clara to the *Orient Express* as

---

ence between the two, and place events on Theon's world c.2300.

540 Dating *Mummy on the Orient Express* (X8.8) - The participants aren't identified as human (one of the passengers resembles Einstein, but there's no sense of time technology being present beyond the TARDIS), and no mention is made of Earth, the Earth Empire, etc. And yet, the *Orient Express* is a good recreation of 1920s style, anachronisms such as "Don't Stop Me Now" by Queen notwithstanding. The train runs on "hyperspace ribbons", a technology seemingly in use as early as the early twenty-second century according to *Festival of Death* (working off *Transit*). Gus can deploy "hard light holograms", which brings to mind those seen in *Red Dwarf*, which opens in the late twenty-second century (although Gus runs multiple holograms simultaneously, whereas the *Red Dwarf* can only power one – albeit a fully sentient one – at a time).

Captain Quell's Certificate of Bravery, as issued by United Galaxy Tours, might suggest it's before humanity makes the leap out of its home galaxy. Against that, the Magellan black hole (also a named feature of *Final Fantasy XIV*) might have some relation to the Large Magellanic Cloud, which is a satellite of the Milky Way and would indicate a later dating. Agatha Christie's works remain popular until at least the year five billion (*The Unicorn and the Wasp*), so an Orient Express revival would seem appealing in basically any era before then.

541 Dating *Excelis Decays* (BF Excelis mini-series #3) - It is three hundred years before *Benny: The Plague Herds of Excelis*.

542 "Centuries" before *Benny S3: The Mirror Effect*.

543 Dating *The Slow Empire* (EDA #47) - No date is given, but it's before *Burning Heart*, because the Piglet People of Glomi IV are mentioned here and extinct there. This date is completely arbitrary. The realm is typically referred to just as "the Empire", and is here called "the Slow Empire" for clarity.

544 "Hundreds of years" before *Benny S10: Absence*.

545 "A few years" before "When Worlds Collide", and in an incarnation before his eleventh.

546 Dating *Graceless: The Sphere* (*Graceless* #1.1) - The trappings of the Sphere – whisky, roulette, hotel-casinos and even the term "Faraday cage" – suggests that the participants are descended from humanity. The fact that Amy and Zara's time rings don't function aboard the Sphere either suggests that its technology is incredibly advanced... or that it's just a fluke. The pirate Kreekpolt has illegal warships that can travel through time, but there's no way of establishing that if such technology is native to this era. It would be lying to say this placement is much more than a shot in the dark.

547 Dating *The Mists of Time* (BF promo, *DWM* #411) - The archaeology members seem human. Jo says that it's "the far future", then specifies that it's "centuries and centuries" after her time. Calder agrees that it's "hundreds of years" since Jo's native era.

548 Dating *The Twin Dilemma* (21.7) - In his novelisation, Eric Saward places the story around "2310". This is neither confirmed nor contradicted on screen. The freighter disappears "eight months" before *The Twin Dilemma*, which the novelisation sets in August. A computer monitor says that the "last contact" with the freighter was made on "12-99". If the twelve stands for the twelfth month, the ninety-nine might stand for the last year of a century. *The Programme Guide* set the story "c2310", *The Discontinuity Guide* in "2200", *Timelink* in "2200", *About Time* seemed comfortable with "2300".

549 Dating "When Worlds Collide" (IDW *DW* Vol. 2, #6-8) - No date is given. Lisa Everwell is from Basildon, in an era where she can save up and travel to Multiworld. There's enough interest in Earth's past to justify Multiworld patterning its zones after periods of it. There are twelve "fantasy" zones – the ones named are the Prehistoric, Old West, World War II, King Arthur, Swinging Sixties, Roman, Arabian Nights and Futuristic.

the space-train passed near the Magellan black hole. The Doctor deduced the Foretold's origins as a soldier and dissipated the creature by formally surrendering to it. The Doctor relocated everyone aboard the *Express* to a civilised planet as Gus destroyed the train.

c 2301 - EXCELIS DECAYS[541] **->** Excelis was now in a permanent state of war. Grayvorn's ambition started to reach beyond Artaris, and he desired to deploy his Meat Puppet troops through the whole of time and space. The seventh Doctor merged his soul with the Relic, exerting enough power to send Grayvorn's captured souls to the afterlife and making his Meat Puppets go inert. Rather than accept defeat, Grayvorn activated Excelis' orbital defence grid and bombarded every major city on Artaris with nuclear missiles. Grayvorn died in the onslaught, but the Doctor escaped.

An entity was trapped in a mirror on an ice planet.[542]

? 2305 - THE SLOW EMPIRE[543] **->** The Slow Empire had been founded in a region of space where the laws of physics prohibited faster-than-light travel. Some worlds facilitated trade and communication via Transference Pylons, which transmitted Ambassadors and materials between worlds at light speed. However, the Empire founders had long ago killed themselves through warfare, which helped to plunge the Empire into decay.

The Empire world Shakrath was ruled by a corrupt Emperor who gave visitors generous receptions for posterity, then sent them to the torture chambers. Some centuries previous on Goronos, a slave class had successfully revolted but found themselves unable to function without their masters. They transferred their minds into an elaborate "Cyberdyne" computer reality, and Goronos became an urban wasteland. On Thakrash, some five hundred years previous (as that planet recorded time), a metamorphic Collector crashed onto the planet and ruined its Transference Pylon. The slaves there revolted, forcing Thakrash into isolation.

A disturbance in the Time Vortex prompted some of its inhabitants, the Vortex Wraiths, to flee in fear of their lives. A group of them manifested on the long-dead homeworld of the Empire founders and usurped control of the Pylon System. The Wraiths hoped to manifest their entire race in its billions via the Pylons, and tried to coerce the eighth Doctor, Fitz and Anji's help by threatening the inhabitants of multiple worlds. The Doctor betrayed the Wraiths by shorting out the main Transference Pylon, both turning the Wraiths into ash and generating a pulse that would, in time, annihilate every Pylon and end the corrupt Empire.

The "detritus, junk and flotsam" of human and extra-terrestrial space travellers sometimes fused into habitable

cluster worlds. One of these became the world of Absence.[544] The Doctor saved the life of Rok Soo'Gar, governor of Multiworld. He gave the Doctor a free pass to the facility and access to his tailors, the best in the galaxy.[545]

? 2308 - GRACELESS: THE SPHERE[546] **->** No longer in the service of the Grace, the living Key-tracer Amy tracked her sister Zara to the Sphere – an arrangement in space of hotels and casinos, which doubled in size in a matter of weeks. The Sphere's technology prevented time rings from operating, and so Zara had fallen in with a rogue named Merak, and become pregnant with his child. Amy – having renamed herself "Abby" – for a time worked for a casino owner named Lindsey, using her mental powers to goad patrons into gambling away their winnings. Her opinion of the people aboard the Sphere became so low that she judged them as unworthy of surviving – and used her telekinesis to remove the pins holding the Sphere together. The subsequent ruination of the Sphere killed a hundred thousand beings, but enabled Abby and Zara to teleport away. Merak survived by happenstance, and pursued the sisters using time technology provided by the space pirate Kreekpolt.

? 2309 - THE MISTS OF TIME[547] **->** A team from the Space Archaeology Group (SAG) found a ruined city of the Memosen – a race obliterated by the Time Lords – on Zion VIII in the Argo Navis Cluster. A "remembrance" device there, built to replay scenes of Memosen history, started reaching back in time and created interactive projections of people who had died. The third Doctor and Jo were present as a SAG member sought to get rich from the device and killed his colleagues, then was slain by Newton Calder, the sole surviving team member.

? 2310 (August) - THE TWIN DILEMMA[548] **-> Earth feared attacks by aliens, and the Interplanetary Pursuit Squadrons were established. The mathematical prodigies Romulus and Remus were abducted in the Spacehopper Mk III Freighter XV773, which had been reported destroyed eight months before. Romulus and Remus mysteriously reappeared on Earth shortly afterwards, claiming the gastropod Mestor, who planned to destroy Jaconda and spread his eggs throughout the universe, had kidnapped them. The sixth Doctor, Peri and Azmael (a Time Lord and the former leader of Jaconda) defeated Mestor and killed him, but Azmael died, all of his regenerations having been used up, while doing so.**

? 2311 - "When Worlds Collide"[549] **->** The eleventh Doctor, Amy and Rory visited Multiworld, a holiday destination built on a stabilised fluctuation rift. Different "worlds" could be custom-made to replicate times in Earth history, and populated with holograms and artificial intelligences. A damaged Sontaran ship crashed on Multiworld, and fluronic gas leaking from its warp coil destabilised the wormhole. The Sontarans died on impact, but the Doctor's old friend, Rok Soo'Gar, sought to exploit the situation to harness the power of the rift and gain godlike powers. Everyone in Multiworld was duplicated, and everyone save the Doctor, Amy and Rory now believed the thirteen worlds to be real. The Sontarans appeared as Nazis, a flying carpet squadron commanded by Caliph Sul'Taran, and a set of Wild West outlaws: Sonny Taran and his men.

The Doctor learned of Soo'Gar's scheme, and the duplicate Sontarans turned on the governor en masse, evidently killing him and resetting reality. The Doctor placed Lisa Everwell, a vacationing project manager from Basildon, in charge of Multiworld.

Kevin the Tyrannosaur, a robot featured in the Prehistoric Zone, tired of his current occupation and accompanied the Doctor and his friends on their travels.

? 2311 - "Space Squid"[550] **->** The eleventh Doctor brought Amy, Rory and Kevin the Tyrannosaur to Space Station E11, a.k.a. Nebula Base, where the best granberry (a large thing with spiky ends, that tasted like mince) smoothies in the cosmos were made. The base was built on the edge of a Radion Singularity, and many followers of the Holy Space Squid religion had arrived to witness the coming of their god. The Doctor identified the squid as a brain-sucking Coledian – it had grown to huge proportions because of the radion, and dominated the minds of its followers. Only the Doctor and Kevin were able to resist, and they stunned the creature.

Nebula Base was converted into a tourist trap: the Last Sighting of the Holy Space Squid. Kevin decided to stay on as the base's new security commander.

c 2313 - "Welcome to Tickle Town"[551] **->** The residents of Tickle Town had now been trapped there for twenty years. Constable Claws realised how much Tobias Tickle had wrongly imprisoned his cartoon creations and park-guests alike, and killed him. The eleventh Doctor and Clara trans-matted Tickle Town back to Earth's surface, liberating those within.

2314 - THE TWELFTH DOCTOR YEAR ONE[552] **->** As part of their plan to resurrect their dark deity, a Kaliratha, the Scindia family finished construction of Haven – a continent-sized orbital city reportedly built to alleviate Earth's overpopulation crisis. A fleet of ScinidaCorp ships bore millions of people to their new home.

There are four we can infer from the costumes of the duplicates: Samurai-era Japan, a soccer zone, Seventies USA and some sort of hospital-themed one. We might infer that this is the era of the Leisure Planets, which is consistent with the levels of artificial intelligence seen.
550 Dating "Space Squid" (IDW *DW* Vol. 2, #9) - No date is given; this dating is arbitrary, but allows Kevin to settle in his native time. The level of technology might suggest this is relatively early in humankind's progress into space.
551 Dating "Welcome to Tickle Town" (*DWM* #465-466) - The Doctor tells Clara that it's "three hundred years" in her future.
552 Dating *The Twelfth Doctor Year One* (Titan 12th Doc #1.3-1.5, "The Swords of Kali") - The year is given.
553 *SLEEPY*
554 *Benny: The Joy Device*
555 Dating *The Gods of Winter* (BBC audiobook #22) - It's a human colony world. By now, the card has been in Diana's family "ever so long" (see The Winter Family sidebar).
556 "Profits of Doom"
557 Dating "Supremacy of the Cybermen" (Titan miniseries #1-5) - The century is given.
558 *Benny B1: Road Trip: Brand Management*
559 "Centuries" before *Benny: Adorable Illusion* (ch2).
560 "Two hundred and fifty years" before *The Also People*.

561 "A few centuries" before *Benny: Adorable Illusion*.
562 "Centuries" before *Benny: Filthy Lucre*.
563 "Three hundred years" after *Horror of the Space Snakes* (ch1).
564 *Fear of the Dark*. The book's internal dating is confused. On p81, the Doctor finds a record dated "2319.01.12", which puts these events seventy-three years before the novel takes place. However, Tegan claims this happened "one hundred and fifty years ago" (p81), and the Doctor says it was "over one hundred and sixty years" ago (p93).
565 "Centuries" before *Benny B4: New Frontiers: HMS Surprise*.
566 Dating "Profits of Doom" (*DWM* #120-122) - It's "eight decades out from Earth" and escaping "twenty-fourth century Earth". Although as the date is soon specified by a monitor robot as "January 7th 2321", they actually left twenty-*third* century Earth.
567 "Three hundred years" before *NAofBenny V4: Truant*.
568 *The Cradle of the Snake* specifies that the Mara comes to power in "Manussan Year 2326", here presumed to be the same as the Earth calendar; see the dating notes under *Snakedance*.
569 *The Also People* (p54).
570 *Recorded Time and Other Stories*: "A Most Excellent Match"
571 Dating *The Jupiter Conjunction* (BF #160) - The back cover blurb gives the year, and the Doctor states that

The archaeologist/adventurer Tiger Maratha had fought with the fourth Doctor against the Deathlings in Angkor Wat. Years later, the Scindia commissioned Maratha to find the Kaliratha's four reality-cleaving swords, but Maratha sensed duplicity and summoned the twelfth Doctor and Clara. A vampiric Thuggee killed Maratha, but his daughter Priyanka rescued the Doctor (and the warrior Rani Jhulka) from 1825 after he went there in a time portal.

The Doctor, Priyanka and Jhulka prevented the Scindia from crashing Haven into Mumbai, an act that would kill millions and fuel the Kaliratha's return to life. The Kaliratha hosted itself in Clara, but Doctor released the souls trapped in the Scindia's necro-cloud, and they obliterated the fiend's mind before departing to the afterlife. Priyanka and Jhulka became a couple as the Doctor and Clara left.

Youkali Press published *An Eye for Wisdom: Repetitive Poems of the Early Ikkaban Period* by Bernice S. Summerfield in 2315.[553] The Smermashi developed alpha-wave-altering crystals that made them exceedingly happy as pollution, disease and other disasters destroyed their world. The famed explorer Andreas Dorpfeld found a Smermashi crystal in 2315, and it kept him constantly full of joy. Dorpfeld cited the crystal as "my prison" on his deathbed, but this was misheard as "my prism", and so the gem was named after him. A Virabilis mining company took possession of it.[554]

c 2315 - THE GODS OF WINTER[555] -> The Golhearn,

beset by an unexplained madness every forty years, were forcibly repelled when they made overtures to a human colony world for aid. Diana Winter, age eight, used the TARDIS-summoning card in her mother's possession – the one reading, "On the worst day of your life, call for the Doctor" – to ask the twelfth Doctor and Clara to help find her missing cat, Mr Fluffy. The travellers negotiated a peace between the humans and the Golhearn, and also found Diana's cat.

Every six months, one of ten crew of the colony ship *Mayflower* was woken as part of a crew rota to check ship's systems – so each crewman woke every five years. Kara McAllista was revived, as planned, on 6th January, 2316.[556]

(=) c 2316 - "Supremacy of the Cybermen"[557]

-> The Cybermen extinguished the Rutan, the Alpha Centauri and many other races. The tenth Doctor, Gabby and Cindy visited Sontar via Cosmomart – an entire planet converted a shopping mall. The bearded Sontaran-Prime, an original of his race, appointed the Doctor as Field Marshall of the Last Great Sontaran War Fleet. The Doctor hardwired himself into a Cyber-King, but failed to repel the Cybermen's

onslaught on the Sontaran homeworld. The twelfth Doctor's actions averted this history.

The Dominicci family's novelty greeting card business was a front for organised crime, and would grow in power and influence over the next few centuries.[558]

The Myranian papal academician Hros'Ka'Bitte dubbed the Dragonfly Nebula's unexplained energy rift as "the Rapture". The human physicist Klaus Menkin ruined his reputation by offering the alternative name of the Brigadoon of the Spaceways. The Martian explorer Vaasst and his crew died while studying the Rapture, an event that holos called "The Death of an Explorer."[559]

The Dyson Sphere of the Varteq Veil had begun to break up.[560] Sexual harassment was phased out on Beta Capris.[561] Nine races united politically into the Kastor Vorax, which enjoyed a millennium of peace. The Nine Crowns of the Kastor Vorax symbolized the races inter-locking together, but were lost.[562]

The Doctor inadvertently added "zooping" – meaning the finger movement that one makes to enlarge or decrease images on a tablet – to the Galactic Humanish Dictionary without providing a definition.[563] Humans arrived on the moon of Akoshemon, on the edge of the Milky Way, in 2319. By this time, there was a Human Sciences Academy on Mars, and a base on Titan.[564]

Mortis Dock, a spaceship yard owned by the Catch family, was established in Legion's part of space.[565]

2321 (7th January) - "Profits of Doom"[566] -> Sluglike

aliens invaded the *Mayflower* colony ship. The sixth Doctor, Peri and Frobisher discovered that the cryotubes of the "top drawer", the elite, had been stolen. The aliens were the Profiteers of Ephte from Ephte Major – a profit-driven race of conquerors. The Doctor accessed the navigational systems and discovered there was nothing at the ship's destination. Instead, Varley Gabriel was profiting by selling the humans to the Profiteers. The Doctor got the aliens to withdraw by threatening to destroy the ship, and directed the navigation systems to set course for Arcadia.

= The empire of the inhabitants of Merrin, the owners of the Apocalypse Clock, came to an end for unknown reasons.[567]

The people of Manussa mastered molecular engineering in a zero-gravity environment, and thereby created blue crystals free from all flaws and distortions. Such crystals could convert thought into energy – into matter, even. The largest of these, the Great Crystal, harnessed and amplified the hatred, restlessness and greed of the Manussan people to create a snake creature: the Mara. It caused the end of the Manussan Empire almost overnight, and ruled over the newly formed Sumaran Empire.[568]

The Mindsmiths of Askatan created mind-control technology that let them to possess many of their enemies' soldiers, but nonetheless lost a "dirty little war". Cranton, a medical corps worker in a war in 2327, came into possession of a Mindsmith simulation generator.[569] Third Eye released their HvLP, *Outta My Way Monkey-boy*, in 2327.[570]

2329 - THE JUPITER CONJUNCTION[571] **->** Humanity's Jupiter colonies had attained independence from Earth, although frictions remained between the two. The Jupiter Axis Military advanced the colonies' interests.

Haulage companies used comets on desirable paths for transport, a sort of "second-class post" system. One such comet was designated 8/Q Panenka, in an elliptical orbit between Earth and Jupiter. Three hundred sixteen company employees lived on the comet, and were serviced by a community of shopping malls. The freight companies by law could not displace "backers" – people who couldn't afford shuttle flights, and hitched a lift on comets – but weren't obliged to aid them either. The Jovians, gas creatures native to Jupiter, were known to a select few on the Jupiter colonies, but not to Earth authorities.

The fifth Doctor, Tegan, Turlough and the older Nyssa visited 8/Q Panenka as it was in conjunction, meaning an Earth-Jupiter orbit only took eighteen months. The Jupiter Axis Military had spent four years covertly establishing a giant particle cannon on 8/Q Panenka – part of a scheme to ignite hostilities on the comet and lay blame upon the Jovians, thus uniting Earth and the Jupiter colonies against a "common foe". Eurasian President Zak Chang hailed a breakthrough as Earth and the Jupiter colonies signed an accord, but an unstable Axis member, Major Nash, primed the cannon to fire on Earth. The Doctor and his allies evacuated 8/Q Panenka as some Jovians died triggering an explosion that blew the comet off course, misdirecting the cannon fire. Nash self-destructed the cannon afterward, killing himself. The Axis' misdeeds and the existence of the Jovians were kept secret. Insurance was expected to cover the loss of 8/Q Panenka.

The second Doctor thought the addition of walkways made Jupiter much more pleasant.[572] In 2341, a Rutan spy adopted the identity of Sontaran Major Karne. An attack

---

they've arrived in "Earth's solar system, 2329".

572 *The Night Witches*, era unknown.

573 "Thirty years" before *Lords of the Storm* (p263).

574 Saraton has protected Sol for "three straight decades" prior to *Zygon Hunt*.

575 Dating *Valhalla* (BF #96) - The story would seem to occur in a year ending in 45, as "9-1-46" (the date given on a sales catalogue) is said to be "next month". Funnily enough, the actual century is never specified. One clue is that the Doctor says he has "overshot [Valhalla's] glory days" – meaning the gas mine rush there – by "about a century". This is probably related to humankind's original breakout from the solar system in the third millennium, but it's unlikely to have occurred in the twenty-second century (the Dalek invasion would surely have disrupted such a boom time, and no mention is made of this). We know from *Lucifer Rising* that people were living on Callisto as early as the early twenty-second century, and *To the Slaughter* (c.2505) depicts Jupiter's moons as being so worthless, they can be blown up in accordance with the principles of feng shui. The best compromise, then, is probably to say that the boom occurs in the twenty-third century, and *Valhalla* takes place in the twenty-fourth. (Callisto itself survives *To the Slaughter* and seems to have obtained greater significance by *So Vile a Sin*, set in 2982, as it's home to the Emperor's palace.)

Riots are held on the first Thursday of every month, and one occurs here. A piece of conflicting information, however, is that it's repeatedly said that electrical engineer Jevvan Petrovna Adrea is having a birthday, and she was born "3-2-23". This would seem to indicate that *Valhalla* takes place on 3rd February, not December as

the catalogue suggests. If push comes to shove, the catalogue is probably more important to the plot (as it's what motivates the Doctor to visit Valhalla in the first place) and should arguably take precedence.

576 Dating *Terminal of Despair* (BBC children's 2-in-1 #5, released in *Sightseeing in Space*) - It's "five months" after "October 2345" (p21).

577 *Original Sin* (p287).

578 "Three hundred years" after *K9: The Korven*.

579 Dating "The Seventh Segment" (*DWM Summer Special 1995*) - K9 says the planet was settled "Relative Terran date 2350 AD", but gives no indication how long ago that was, and a later dating is certainly feasible.

580 Dating *Exotron* (BF #95) - Writer Eddie Robson has stated that the planet was intended as being Earth, but the back cover states that the story takes place on "a distant outpost of Earth". Within the story, a colony ship arrives direct from Earth. (Track 36, for example, has Sergeant Shreeni say, "Bleedin' hell… what a time for the Earth shuttle to arrive.") Security officers are dispatched from an organisation named Earth Authority, which is presumably headquartered on Earth itself.

The atypical and dead-end development of the Exotrons themselves aside, the technology level suggests Earth's early colonial era. Otherwise, this date is arbitrary.

581 Dating *Recorded Time and Other Stories*: "A Most Excellent Match" (BF #150c) - The year of the fair is given.

582 Dating *The Gods of Winter* (BBC audiobook #22) - It's "forty years on" since the early part of the story. Diana, last seen at "age eight", is now described as a woman in "late middle age".

on a Sontaran cruiser was staged, and the Sontarans recovered his escape pod. For decades, the Rutans received top-level Sontaran military secrets.[573]

The Solar Knights, an order of noblemen, assumed sole responsibility for the protection of Earth's solar system, and formed defence shields around it.[574]

? 2345 (the first Thursday in December) - VALHALLA[575] **->** The Mars Express was in operation at this time.

The domed city of Valhalla, located on Jupiter's moon of Callisto, had fallen prey to blight. It cost nothing to arrive at Valhalla, but a fortune to leave, so the city increasingly became home to the dispossessed, space hippies and tourists who arrived on the wrong flight. Immigration services stamped bar codes onto the tongues of everyone in the city. Food and energy cutbacks were introduced, and owing to the shoddy conditions, riots were dutifully held the first Thursday of every month. On such occasions, licensed outlets sold body armour and refreshments.

Genetically engineered termites had grown to massive size on Callisto, and their queen – Our Mother the Fourth – directed her children to take control of Valhalla. Our Mother wanted to facilitate her progeny's future by selling off Valhalla's assets and people; a sales catalogue was prepared. The seventh Doctor tricked the termites into thinking that Our Mother had died. This forcibly instigated a new wedding flight as winged termites sought out the new queen, and Our Mother did pass away. Dialogue was opened with the new Queen, and it was hoped she would be more reasonable than her predecessor.

2346 (March) - TERMINAL OF DESPAIR[576] **->** Terminal 4000, an interchange station for spaceships, serviced companies such as Orion Spaceways. A single flight a year was offered to Callisto. The terminal was put in quarantine owing to an outbreak of Desponds: squat dog-like creatures that fed on the emotion of hope. The eleventh Doctor, Amy and Rory ended the quarantine, and an animal welfare organisation took possession of the Desponds.

In 2350, the Jullatii would have over-run the Earth but for INITEC's invention of the boson cannon.[577] **The cooling agent Phosphane was invented in the mid twenty-fourth century.**[578]

c 2350 - "The Seventh Segment"[579] **->** Humans settled Vyga 3 in 2350, and the eccentric culture that developed defied legal and policing systems. The fourth Doctor, the first Romana and K9 searched Vyga 3 for a Key to Time segment, but the tracer was confused by an object in a briefcase that a local criminal gang wanted. It wasn't a segment, but rather a fluctuating chronal wave. When

opened, the briefcase aged everyone in the area to death – the Doctor was glad he hadn't got round to checking it for himself.

? 2350 - EXOTRON[580] **->** Human colony planets were sometimes subject to oversight from Earth Authority, which could dispatch security officers as required.

On an unnamed Earth colony, the Exotron Project was initiated to create a new type of robot for sale to the military. Major Hector Taylor and Ballentyne, the Secretary of the Interior, colluded to further the project, which entailed hardwiring the bodies of mortally wounded soldiers into large Exotron robot shells. The soldiers remained alive in a state of pain, but their neural networks enabled the Exotrons to function.

Two years after the research team's arrival, a form of indigenous life – the hyena-like Farakosh – came into conflict with the Exotrons. Taylor died, but Ballentyne triggered the research facility's self-destruct. The troopers within the Exotrons regained some independence, and saved everyone by smothering the blast with their own bodies. The fifth Doctor and Peri expected that Ballentyne would be hounded from office.

2351 - RECORDED TIME AND OTHER STORIES: "A Most Excellent Match"[581] **->** The showman Cranton used a Mindsmith generator to offer patrons mental simulations based upon the books of Jane Austin and other works of literature. Peri tried out Cranton's device at the 2351 Galaxy Fair, but the last remaining Mindsmith, whose consciousness was in the machine, attempted to possess her. The sixth Doctor tried to coax Peri out of the simulation by competing for her hand in marriage as "Mr Fitzwilliam Darcy" of *Pride and Prejudice*. Tilly, an AI within the machine, saved the Doctor and Peri and terminated the simulation-scape, killing the Mindsmith.

c 2355 - THE GODS OF WINTER[582] **->** The Golhearn once again descended into madness. Diana Winter now worked in the human embassy on the Golhearn homeworld, but her two children were lost in the chaos. She once again summoned the twelfth Doctor and Clara, and they saved her offspring. The Doctor determined the cause of the madness – a Baldrassian Corp's engine waste – and removed it with an atmospheric scrubber. He also recommended that the Golhearn sue Baldrassian Corp for breaching basic galactic law.

The Eleventh Doctor
and River's First and Last Dates

2360 (21st September) - NIGHT AND THE DOCTOR: "First Night" / "Last Night"[583] **->** For their first outing together, the eleventh Doctor brought River Song to Calderon Beta: an otherwise dull planet of chip shops, but which featured a 400-foot tall tree growing on a cliff in the middle of the sea. At exactly twelve minutes past midnight on 21st September, 2360, anyone atop the tree would see the most star-filled sky in history.

A version of River five years older dashed into the TARDIS, fleeing from Sontarans enraged because she had suggested they were on a hen night. The two Rivers kept missing one another within the Ship, each of them irritated to think that the Doctor had brought someone else along. An even older version of River showed up, and the Doctor kept her distracted while he teleported the middle of the three Rivers (in terms of age) back to Stormcage...

An older version of the eleventh Doctor raced into the TARDIS, clad in a suit and a top hat, to reclaim his River. The younger Doctor realised that the two of them were going to the Singing Towers of Darillium, the last place they would visit before River died at the Library. The older Doctor and River left, and the younger River returned from the TARDIS' interior to say she was eager to see the star-filled sky.

Despite their best efforts, the eleventh Doctor and River failed to visit the Singing Towers. She would do so, in future, with the twelfth Doctor.[584] Around 2361, the *Mayflower* arrived to colonise Arcadia.[585]

? 2366 - THE MACRA TERROR[586] **->** The crab-like Macra had infiltrated a human colony, using indoctrination techniques to force the colonists to extract a deadly gas that the Macra breathed. The colonists were kept in a state of complacent happiness. Eventually, the second Doctor, Jamie, Ben and Polly exposed the Control – the colony's propaganda spokesperson – as a giant Macra. The Doctor directed Ben to destroy the Marca's gas pumps, which slew the invaders.

The Macra were a scourge of the galaxy, controlling a small empire with humans as slaves. Eventually, though, they degenerated into unthinking animals.[587]

2367 - DINOSAURS ON A SPACESHIP[588] **->** Alien races lived on Earth's moon. An IV system – an "Argos for the universe" – identified items of value for trade across the nine galaxies, including the Roxborne Peninsula commerce colony, but had no record of the Doctor.

The opportunistic trader Solomon came across the Silurian space ark. His robot enforcers woke the crew

---

583 Dating *Night and the Doctor: "First Night"/"Last Night"* (Series 6 DVD minisodes) - The exact day is given, and a sentimental enough occasion that River in future returns to it. The story is predicated on the notion that the Doctor and River's first date overlaps with their last one.

584 *The Husbands of River Song.*

585 "Profits of Doom". The *Mayflower* was twenty years from its original destination in 2321, its new destination is another "twenty or so" years away.

586 Dating *The Macra Terror* (4.7) - The planet was colonised "many centuries" ago. This date is somewhat arbitrary, but it allows the story to fit into a period in which Earth's colonies are relatively remote and unregulated. The level of technology is reasonably low. The second edition of *The Making of Doctor Who* described the setting as "the distant future". *The Programme Guide* set the story "c.2600", *The Terrestrial Index* preferred "between 2100 and 2150", *Timelink* "2670".

587 *Gridlock.* The Doctor says the Macra were the scourge of "this galaxy", and *New Earth* establishes that the planet New Earth isn't in our galaxy. Nonetheless, we can probably infer that he means our galaxy.

588 Dating *Dinosaurs on a Spaceship* (X7.2) - A caption provides the year.

589 Dating "Assimilation 2" (IDW *Star Trek: The Next Generation/Doctor Who* mini-series) - The Battle of Wolf

359 happened on Stardate 44002.3 (the *Next Gen* episode "The Best of Both Worlds Part Two"), which corresponds to the start of 2367.

590 *Zagreus*, but this is part of a suspect simulation.

591 Dating "Assimilation 2" (IDW *Star Trek: The Next Generation/Doctor Who* mini-series) - The Doctor, Amy and Rory and the Cybermen all cross over into the *Star Trek* universe (see the Star Trek sidebar) on Stardate 45635.2, which places the story slightly more than half-way through *Next Generation* Season Five, in 2368.

The Doctor's Hail Mary pass at claiming that the Cybermen's defeat will remove the historical details of their incursion is presumably designed to keep *Star Trek* continuity clean, although it's fuzzy as to how or why this occurs. Even if a sanitizing of the timeline does happen, the Borg's recollection of their encounter with the Doctor spurs their interest in time travel, quite possibly leading to their having time-technology in *Star Trek: First Contact.*

592 Tairngaire was colonised "three hundred years" before *Shadowmind* (p32).

593 Dating *Lords of the Storm* (MA #17) - The Doctor states that it is "Earthdate 2371" (p23).

594 Dating *Zygon Hunt* (BF 4th Doc #3.8) - The failed Broton expedition happened "a few hundred years" ago (*Terror of the Zygons*). It's "centuries" after the Zygon homeworld became uninhabited. It's unclear what

from stasis and threw them out the nearest airlock, but the Ark activated a pre-programmed course and returned home. The Indian Space Agency (ISA) asked the eleventh Doctor to deal with the oncoming Ark, warning that it stood ready to deploy missiles against the threat. The Doctor recruited Queen Nefertiti, the hunter John Riddell, Amy, Rory and (inadvertently) Rory's dad Brian to help. Rory and his father piloted the Ark to safety as the Doctor redirected the ISA missiles to destroy Solomon and his vessel instead.

= 2367 - "Assimilation 2"[589] **->** The eleventh Doctor, Amy and Rory went back to the Battle of Wolf 359 – in which the Borg destroyed thirty-nine starships and eleven thousand Starfleet personnel – copied the executive routines from Locutus' Borg cube, and jumped back to the future to reunite with the *Enterprise*.

Walton Winkle became known throughout the Earth Empire as "Uncle Winky, the man who put a smile on the galaxy". He founded the amusement park Winky Wonderland on Io, but entered hibernation inside his "Cosmic Mountain" on 18th December, 2367, due to a heart condition. He wouldn't revive from stasis until shortly before the end of the universe.[590]

The USS *Enterprise*

(=) 2368 - "Assimilation 2"[591] **->** The Cybermen breached the dimensional wall into another universe, and proposed an alliance with the Borg Collective based upon their mutual goals and methods. The Borg agreed, and a combined Borg-Cybermen armada attacked Delta IV, a member of the United Federation of Planets, destroying the Federation starships *Potemkin* and *Lassiter*.

The TARDIS also crossed between universes – the eleventh Doctor, Amy and Rory arrived in what seemed like San Francisco, 1941, but was actually a holodeck aboard the Federation starship *Enterprise*. The Cybermen deemed the presence of the last Time Lord an X-factor too great to ignore, and advanced their timetable to betray the Borg and conquer their homeworld. The Borg proved unable to assimilate the Cybermen, who overwrote the Borg's command protocols and rendered most of the Collective inert. The Doctor feared the Borg-augmented Cybermen would become unstoppable and conquer all universes.

A surviving splinter group of the Borg petitioned the Federation for aid against their mutual enemy. The captain of the *Enterprise*, Jean-Luc Picard, refused until the Doctor used the TARDIS to show him a

---

future in which the Borg-enhanced Cybermen had dominated the Federation and their home universe alike. The *Enterprise* overcame the Cyber-command ship with a particle beam of gold. An *Enterprise* away team and the Doctor's trio restored the Borg, who initiated the destruction of all Cyberships.

The Doctor speculated that the Cybermen's obliteration would retroactively erase all elements of their incursion into the *Enterprise*'s reality, but those directly involved would remember the events. He left with Amy and Rory for their home reality, even as the Borg pondered how best they could assimilate a Time Lord in future, and set about researching time travel.

Around 2370, human settlers colonised Tairngaire. The capital city was built on an isthmus and named New Byzantium. The planet rapidly became one of the more prosperous colonies. The temporary lights built by the settlers eventually became the Lantern Market.[592]

2371 - LORDS OF THE STORM[593] **->** The Sontarans, fresh from destroying the Rutan installation at Betelgeuse V, attempted to use captured Tzun technology against their eternal enemies. They genetically tagged the human population of the Unukalhai System, intending that a Rutan sensor sweep would indicate a Sontaran population of one hundred million. The Rutan would send a fleet from Antares and the Sontarans planned to ignite a brown dwarf using the Tzun Stormblade, destroying the Rutans and the whole system as well. The fifth Doctor and Turlough defeated the plan.

c 2375 - ZYGON HUNT[594] **->** At least ten races sought to assassinate Solar Knight Gregor Saraton, who alone held the codes to the Sol System's defence shields. Zygons infiltrated Saraton's inner circle when he and his Knight Commanders went on a hunting expedition to the jungle planet Garros. The fourth Doctor and Leela aided the Zygon impersonating Mina Challis, Saraton's adjutant, to find the humanity she was mimicking. Challis instigated the slaughter of Saraton's group, ruining the Zygon plan. A Zygon evacuation fleet en route to Earth diverted to Garros, intending to make it their new home.

By 2375, the Bureau Tygo was Earth's main scientific research centre, and humans were used to getting what they wanted. In May of that year, Salvatorio Moretti created Genetically Engineered Neural Imagination Engines (GENIEs) that could bend space and time to grant wishes. Earth was threatened by competing desires, so one group of people wished to go back in time and prevent the GENIEs' creation. A GENIE survived in ancient Rome.[595]

In 2375, the police broke up the notorious Nisbett firm, a criminal gang responsible for extortion, fraud, smuggling, arms dealing, torture and multiple murder. Tony, Frankie and Dylan the Leg were all executed, but the Nisbett brothers – Charlie and Eddie – escaped.[596] Sontaran Commander Vrag's commando squad was timescooped to the Eye of Orion by the Time Lord Ryoth, shortly after being presented with a medal by Admiral Sarg.[597]

The colony world Gadrell Major was on the brink of nuclear war in 2377, leading the population to construct fallout shelters. Around this time, the Earth was at war with the Phractons.[598] Dymok demanded isolation from Earth in 2378. Imperial Earth Space Station *Little Boy II* was built to oversee the planet.[599]

c 2378 - THE ANDROIDS OF TARA[600] -> On Tara, the fourth Doctor, the first Romana and K9 prevented Count Grendel from usurping the throne from its rightful heir, Prince Reynart. Grendel escaped to fight another day, and the travellers obtained the fourth segment of the Key to Time.

Peri Leaves the TARDIS

2379 (3rd July) - MINDWARP[601] -> The Mentors of Thoros Beta continued to trade across the galaxy via the warpfold relay, supplying phasers to the Warlords of Thordon, and weapons that allowed Yrcanos of the Krontep to conquer the Tonkonp Empire. They also traded with such planets as Wilson One and Posikar.

The brain of his Magnificence Kiv, the leader of the Mentors, continued to expand in his skull. He enlisted the services of Crozier, a human scientist who specialised in the transfer of consciousness. Crozier experimented on a number of Thoros Betan creatures and the Mentors' captives, creating hybrids and experimenting with the ageing process. After a decade of hard work, he had developed a serum that allowed him to place any brain in any body.

Subsequent events are unclear – it appears that the Time Lords intervened to prevent the threat posed to

Saraton's demise means to the Sol defence codes he alone possessed, although it's perhaps relevant that the system-wide defence shields aren't cited in any other story.
595 *The Stone Rose*
596 "Five or six years" before *The Romance of Crime* (p62-63).
597 *The Eight Doctors*. Not date given, but Sarg appears in *Shakedown*, so it is before that time.
598 "Ten winters" and "many years" before *Infinite Requiem*.
599 *Divided Loyalties* (p31).
600 Dating *The Androids of Tara* (16.4) - The Doctor implies that Tara is "four hundred years and twelve parsecs" away from Earth at the time of *The Stones of Blood*. It's here assumed that the TARDIS travelled into the future, not the past, and that Tara is an isolated Earth colony (as the Tarans know of life on other planets). *The Terrestrial Index* set the story in the "fiftieth century", *Timelink* in "2378", *The Discontinuity Guide* in the "2370s", *About Time* thought that "somewhere around 2400" was reasonable.
601 Dating *Mindwarp* (23.2) - The Valeyard announces that the story starts in the "twenty-fourth century, last quarter, fourth year, seventh month, third day". There is a case to be made for 2379, but not "2479" as suggested by the third edition of *The Programme Guide*. Peri is apparently killed in *Mindwarp*, but is revealed as having survived in *The Ultimate Foe*, and returns in the novel *Bad Therapy*, the comic "The Age of Chaos" and the audio *Peri and the Piscon Paradox* (which establishes there are multiples of her). Yrcanos' people are rendered as the "Krontep" in the *Mindwarp* novelisation, as "Kr'on Tep" in *Bad Therapy*.
602 *Peri and the Piscon Paradox*
603 "The Age of Chaos"

604 *The Widow's Assassin, Antidote to Oblivion*.
605 Dating *The Widow's Assassin* (BF #192) - The Doctor shows up soon after Yrcanos' death, which happens within days of his marriage to Peri, which itself happens in rapid succession after *Mindwarp* [2379].
606 *Mindwarp*
607 Dating *The Price of Paradise* (NSA #12) - It's "the late twenty-fourth century".
608 Dating *The Romance of Crime* (MA #6) - Uva Beta Uva was "colonised in Earth year 2230" according to Romana (p47); the story is set "a hundred and fifty years later" (p8). The month and day are given on p46.
609 Dating *The Infinity Race* (EDA #61) - A conspiracy of assassins who have been waiting "six hundred years" (p191) for the chance to eliminate Sabbath – this would appear to be an offshoot of the Secret Service, which initiated him into its ranks in 1762. (There are reports – in the standard timeline, at least – of the Service trying to kill Sabbath in 1780, although it's entirely possible that they moved to kill him sooner.)
Mention is also made of an Earth Empire that's ruled by an Emperor, but as the story takes place in a parallel universe, there's no guarantee that its history is comparable to our own. Dating this story off Sabbath's history seems a surer bet, as it's established in *Sometime Never* that the Council of Eight – deeming the Doctor the most unpredictable element in the whole of history – recruited Sabbath as the most constant variable in the whole of time. This is the reason, in fact, that no temporal duplicates of Sabbath show up in *The Last Resort*, whereas the Doctor, Fitz and Anji are duplicated thousands of times over. In every alternate history that we're shown in this period of the EDAs, then, Sabbath's history is reliably consistent.
610 "Dogs of Doom". The date is given.

the course of evolution across the universe, causing Kiv to be killed. The sixth Doctor's companion, Peri Brown, was seemingly killed but in reality remained on Thoros-Beta, where she eventually married Yrcanos.

Time Lord intervention in Peri's history made this but one of at least five possible outcomes. In one version of history, Queen Peri had two sons and a daughter.[602] Peri had a son, Corynus, who went on to marry Yrcanthia and have two sons (Artios and Euthys) and a daughter (Actis).[603]

The mental shock that Crozier's equipment delivered to the Doctor awakened memories of his imaginary childhood foe: Mandrake the Lizard King. When Crozier transferred the Lord Kiv's mind into Peri electronically, the faux Mandrake overwrote Kiv's mind and came to inhabit Peri's body. Once the Time Lords' temporal storm on Thoros Beta had abated, Lord Kiv was "no more", and Sil had Crozier executed as a failure. He also became a patron to Crozier's daughter, Cordelia Claire Crozier.[604]

c 2379 - THE WIDOW'S ASSASSIN[605] ->

King Yrcanos rescued Peri from Thoros Beta, failing to realise that a mental re-creation of Mandrake the Lizard King had possession of her body. Mandrake accepted Yrcanos' marriage proposal, then poisoned him with trimorphal a few days after the wedding – a means of inheriting Yrcanos' territory, and the start of a new empire.

The sixth Doctor investigated Yrcanos' death, and tried to reconcile with Queen Peri after "abandoning" her on Thoros Beta. He dutifully accepted the Queen's lack of forgiveness, and seemed to spend five years in a dungeon on Krontep per her orders...

The late twenty-fourth century saw wars around the Rim Worlds of Tokl.[606]

c 2380 - THE PRICE OF PARADISE[607] ->

For eighteen months, Professor Petra Shulough led an expedition in the SS Humphrey Bogart to find the Paradise Planet. An electromagnetic pulse crippled the ship, and it crashed on the beautiful forest world of Laylora. The tenth Doctor and Rose answered the ship's distress call. The planet was rich in trisilicate – as Shulough's father had discovered fifteen years earlier – but it was also alive and reacted to the presence of alien life by creating Witiku, fierce four-armed monsters. Shulough agreed to keep the existence of Laylora a secret.

Micro fusion generators had been banned on most planets by this time, due to the toxic waste they produced.

c 2380 (21st to 22nd April) - THE ROMANCE OF CRIME[608] ->

In the late 2370s, the Ceerads (Cellular Remission and Decay) – mutants – were purged on Vanossos. Some survived and resettled on Uva Beta Uva Six, leading to conflict with the colonists in that system. The galaxy faced another recession at this time.

Xais was the last of the Ugly Mutants and the self-proclaimed Princess of the Guaal Territories. She was a genius terrorist who murdered two thousand people, and was executed by particle reversal in 2377. Xais had learned, however, how to transfer her consciousness into the substance helicon. Her mind came to reside in a helicon mask made by the artist Menlove Stokes, enabling her to possess people.

Xais teamed up with the criminal Nisbett brothers and their Ogrons, claiming to have discovered rich belzite deposits on Uva Beta Uva Eleven. In fact, the planet contained a great deal of helicon, through which Xais hoped to generate duplicates of herself and commit mass slaughter. The Nisbett brothers perished as part of this affair, but the fourth Doctor, the second Romana and K9 worked to stop Xais' plan. Xais' mind became trapped in a mass quantity of helicon, which expanded to cover the whole of Uva Beta Uva Eleven. The Doctor supplied one of his associates, the police investigator Spiggot, with a formula that could destroy the helicon and Xais within.

= c 2380 - THE INFINITY RACE[609] ->

Sabbath attempted to harness the infinity forces on the planet Selonart in a parallel universe. Selonart served as host to the Trans-Global Selonart Regatta, which took place every five Earth years. The eighth Doctor, Fitz and Anji joined the fourteenth Regatta, defeating Sabbath's plan. Sabbath had released the Warlocks of Demigest to assist with his scheme, but the Doctor used time crystals formed on Selonart to erase the Warlocks' presence from the universe.

The New Earth System was colonised in 2380.[610]

On Colony 34, a planet with two moons, Premier Leo Jaeger swept to power. But a disease left him scarred, and surgical efforts to correct this only caused greater deformity. Jaeger feared this would erode his popularity, so a Jaeger look-alike from an outer province doubled for him at public events. The doppelgänger gradually replaced Jaeger's loyalists with his own staff, and finally took control. The genuine article was secretly kept alive so his Biometric ID could reinforce the duplicate's appearance.

Colony 34's resources were not as plentiful as previously thought, and an energy crisis caused unrest. Fifteen years after the real Jaeger took office, his double capitalised on the situation by restricting freedoms and postponing elections. Two years later, he tightened control using the Emergency Powers Act. Two years after that, the Chamber of Deputies was accused of widespread corruption and suspended.

Human bodies made excellent fuel if used properly, so

the government secretly began harvesting Colony 34's underclass. Jaeger's Inner Senate advertised employment opportunities for outsiders, and interested travellers from other colonies were captured and turned into fuel.[611]

Gilbert M was exiled from Vasilip when he accidentally wiped out half the planet's population with a germ he'd been working on. By this time, there were scheduled interplanetary flights, and he travelled to Terra Alpha with the Kandy Man's bones in his briefcase.[612]

& 2381 (29th March) - THE DIMENSION RIDERS[613]

-> Half the planets colonised by humanity had been abandoned during the wars. But now, generally, this was a period of interplanetary peace. The Survey Corps existed to patrol space and deal with situations unsuitable for military or humanitarian missions. As such, Survey Corps vessels had both troopers (armed with state-of-the-art Derenna handguns) and support staff. By the end of the twenty-fourth century, however, underfunding meant that many of the Corps' ships were obsolete.

On 22nd March, 2381, Space Station Q4 in the fifty-fourth sector of charted space, on the edge of the spiral arm and human territory, was attacked by the Garvond's Time Soldiers. The station's crew were aged to death. The Survey Corps vessel *Icarus* investigated and fell to the soldiers. The seventh Doctor, Benny and Ace aided in repelling the soldiers, who were destroyed when their energies were reflected back upon them. This prevented the Garvond from triggering temporal paradoxes and using a Time Focus to absorb the resultant chronal energy. During the battle, Darius Cheynor, second-in-command of the *Icarus*, distinguished himself.

Cheynor was offered command of the *Phoenix*.[614]

2382 - FEAR OF THE DARK[615] -> Humanity had made

contact with the Vegans, a proud mining race, by this time. Earth had interests in the Antares, Betelgeuse, Denox, Kaltros Prime and Earth Colony E5150. Suspended animation was still in use, and neurolectrin was used to resuscitate sleepers. The University of Tyr specialised in temporal compression.

The fifth Doctor was drawn to the moon of Akoshemon when the Dark – an ancient being ravenous for blood – influenced Nyssa's mind. The Dark hoped to manifest itself physically in our dimension, but the Doctor destroyed it.

2382 - ANTIDOTE TO OBLIVION[616] -> Led by President

Boscoe, Concorpia – the nation formerly known as the United Kingdom – had become a major manufacturer of pacification drugs used to subdue the populace. Fish was a rare commodity, but vitro-food designers could replicate it. Robo-scans had made some medical professionals redundant. The Houses of Parliament stood in ruin, bearing a ConCorp logo.

---

611 The real Jaeger comes to power "twenty years" before *LIVE 34*.

612 *The Happiness Patrol*

613 Dating *The Dimension Riders* (NA #20) - It is "the late twenty-fourth century" (p2). The Doctor repeats this, adding it is "Just before Benny's time, and after the Cyberwars" (p25); this analysis comes from *The Terrestrial Index* rather than the TV series. The date is not precisely fixed until the sequel, *Infinite Requiem*, which is set in 2387, "six years" after the events of the first book. "March 22nd" was "one week ago" (p76).

614 *Infinite Requiem*

615 Dating *Fear of the Dark* (PDA #58) - The date is given on the back cover. The personnel file of a mineral pirate, Jyl Stoker, says she departed Earth Central some years back in 2363 (p109), and Tegan notes it has been "four hundred years" since 1982 (p118). It is after the time when Mechanoids were used. The Vegans first appeared in *The Monster of Peladon*.

616 Dating *Antidote to Oblivion* (BF #182) - The year is given, following on from *Mindwarp* [2379]. "Lasarti's Wasting" looks suspiciously like an alias for Richter's Syndrome, as named after Nyssa's husband Lasarti, but it's about a millennium too early for that.

617 Dating *The Guardians of Prophecy* (BF LS #3.4) - The Doctor directs Peri's attention to a patch of darkness that used to be part of the Traken Union, and says the devastation there occurred "centuries" ago (in *Logopolis*). Serenity was founded (and Malador trapped in stasis) "a thousand years" ago, although it's not said how long this happened prior to Traken's destruction. Nonetheless, joining those dots together, the thirtieth century is the absolute latest this story can occur.

Serenity was formerly mentioned in *Cold Fusion*.

618 Dating *Slipback* (Radio 4 drama, unnumbered Target novelisation) - An arbitrary date. The *Vipod Mor* is undertaking a census, perhaps placing it in the same time period as *The Happiness Patrol*. The illegal time travel experiments in this story also fit neatly with the time travel research mentioned in a variety of other adventures set in the twenty-fourth century.

619 Dating *The Widow's Assassin* (BF #192) - It's "five years" after the Doctor's imprisonment on Krontep. For the Doctor, these events follow on from *Scavenger*.

620 *The Leisure Hive*

621 *The Well-Mannered War* (p273).

622 She's from "the twenty-fourth century" according to *Return of the Living Dad* (p41).

623 *The Highest Science* (p203, p235).

624 "Centuries" after *Night Thoughts*.

625 "Many hundreds of years" after *The English Way of Death*, with reference to the group Third Eye (p37).

Already indebted to the Universal Monetary Fund (UMF) for a trillion universal credits, Concorpia appealed to its UMF representative, Sil, for an additional 12 billion credits of funding. Sil authorized the loan on behalf of Lord Mav, then collaborated with the virologist Cordelia Claire Crozier to develop a means of reducing Concorpia's excess population, which would curtail its welfare rolls and guarantee repayment.

Records obtained during the Magnus affair enabled Sil to recall Anzor's TARDIS, and provide Crozier with a test-subject to crack the secrets of Time Lord immuno-biology. Crozier's isolation chamber yielded limited results, but mutated Anzor into a potato-like form with eye stalks. The sixth Doctor and Flip were captured while answering a distress call from Anzor's TARDIS, and Crozier hoped that the Doctor's antibodies would yield a defence against *cholorai titanicum, yosimia pestis novis*, Creeping Moon Fever, Lava Pox, Dark Space Plague, Lazarti's Wasting, the New Black Death and more.

Rebels among the proletariat halted distribution of the pacification drugs long enough to trigger an insurrection, ending the ConCorp regime. Sil threw in his lot with one of ConCorp's competitors.

c 2382 - THE GUARDIANS OF PROPHECY[617] -> The planet Serenity, a surviving colony of Trakenites, had experienced peace for a millennium. The highest-ranking of the Elect there – the Guardians, who served the super-computer Prophecy – governed the common people, the Meers. Malador, the founder of Serenity, was thought to be a myth. The dormant Melkur's psychic force pulled the TARDIS off-course, and the sixth Doctor and Peri landed on Serenity.

An interruption to Prophecy's power channeled energy into Malador's casket, reviving him. Propechy destroyed itself to delay Malador, who set about reversing the polarity on the "field of goodness" projected by Prophecy's systems even after its destruction. His sleeping army of Melkur began to revive on many worlds.

The Doctor created a space-time fissure in Prophecy's labyrinth, enabling creatures from another dimension to attack Malador. The Melkur on Serenity and Malador were pulled through the dimensional fissure, and the Melkur on other worlds went dormant again. The survivors on Serenity vowed to create a new government without benefit of Prophecy, and to share power with the Meers.

(A) Peri Rejoins the TARDIS

c 2384 - THE WIDOW'S ASSASSIN[618] -> Mandrake the Lizard King, posing as Queen Peri, had spent five years courting royal suitors to marry, hoping to amalgamate their territory into Krontep's domain. All prospective husbands insisted upon a fertility test, and rejected Peri after discov-

ering that she could not conceive. Mandrake-Peri sought political advantage as a mediator, and travelled aboard *The Sword of Peace*, formerly King Yrcanos' spaceship *The Spirit of Utmost Belligerence*, to resolve disputes.

The sixth Doctor was ostensibly locked up in Queen Peri's dungeon for five years, but periodically escaped to infiltrate the late Yrcanos' rivals. The Doctor had spent four years incognito as an aide to Baron Pteratrark, then nipped back in the TARDIS and lived four years as a sycophant to the Reverand Flitamus. He did spend a few years in his cell – about a decade of his life all told.

Events climaxed as suitors called upon Princess Dirani of the planet Hurn. The Doctor was present three times over in different guises, and foiled Mandrake's attempt to take over Dirani's territory. After imprisoning Mandrake's mind on a spare chip from the TARDIS, the Doctor gave the item to a patron of the Royal Society for the Protection of Alien Mind Parasites to hang on his wall. Dirani married Prince Harcross the Ever-Patient.

Peri comprehended her five years on Krontep as a sort of dream. She took up travelling with the Doctor again, after establishing the story that "Queen Peri" died helping to secure peace for Dirani and her subjects.

? 2385 - SLIPBACK[619] -> The TARDIS was pulled out of the Vortex by illegal time experiments aboard the starship *Vipod Mor*. A Maston, an extinct monster, attacked the sixth Doctor and Peri. The Doctor discovered that a botched maintenance job had endowed the ship's computer with a split personality, and one of its personas was planning to take the ship back in time to impose order on the universe. The Doctor was about to stop the time journey when a Time Lord made contact to inform him that the *Vipod Mor* was part of the established history – it would explode upon arrival, creating the Big Bang.

In 2386, Unreal Transfer was discovered.[620] The artist Menlove Stokes entered cryo-sleep, hoping to awaken in an era that better appreciated his work. He was revived in the Fifty-Eighth Segment of Time.[621] When her colleagues were captured, a physicist travelled back in time to Little Caldwell, 1983. With the help of Isaac Summerfield, she returned home and freed her workmates.[622]

The same year, slow compression time – a method of slowing down time in a small area – was first theorised. Within a couple of years a slow time converter, or "time telescope" had been built.[623] The Bartholomew Transactor became very popular as a party tool, able to send messages back in time and create ghostly images of an alternate timeline for a minute at most.[624] A law enforcement agency, the Bureau, discovered an alien time corridor in the Playa del Nuttingchapel. They dispatched an agent to investigate in 1930, where he adopted the alias "Percy Closed".[625]

2387 (29th May) - INFINITE REQUIEM[626] **->** In the late 2380s, there was a famine on Tenos Beta and storms in the Magellani System. There was also more co-operation between the various elements of the Earth's space navy. Over the next couple decades the military, the ships of the Guild of Adjudicators, the Survey Corps and the corporations' own battle squadrons unified into the Spacefleet.

The Earth colony of Gadrell Major had been rich in porizium ore, a valuable material used in medicine, but was now mined out. Earth Central perpetrated the lie that deposits of porizium remained – a means of causing the Phractons, telepathic cyborgs with a communal mind, to attack Gadrell Major to acquire the porizium for ailing members of their race. As Earth Central had planned, this kept the Phractons away from more central Earth worlds. Darius Cheynor was considered expendable by his superiors, and was sent with the Phoenix to "investigate" as the Phracton Swarm and their tanks – flamers – devastated much of the planet. The seventh Doctor and Benny were present, and met Cheynor again.

Cheynor negotiated a settlement with the Phractons; Gadrell Major was slated to become a war memorial. Earth's Colonial Office diverted funding to terraform an non-classed asteroid in the Magellani System. A breakaway faction of the Phractons sought retribution and killed Cheynor – this led to the Phractons achieving some vindication, and further negotiations would lead to peace.

? 2388 - THE HAPPINESS PATROL[627] **->** The Galactic Census Bureau at Galactic Centre surveyed every colonised planet every six local cycles and, where necessary, suggested measures to control the population size. On one such planet, Terra Alpha, the native Alphidae were driven underground by the settlers, who covered the planet in sugar fields and factories. Offworlders were restricted to the Tourist Zones. The planet was ruled by Helen A, who insisted that her citizens be happy. To this end, the planet was gaily painted, muzak poured from loudspeakers on every street corner and Helen A created the Happiness Patrol, which was composed of women authorised to murder the so-called "killjoys". She also employed the services of the Kandy Man, an artificial being of pure sugar who created sweets that killed people.

Terrorists, protest groups and the Alphidae (now confined to the sugar-pipe network) all resisted, and Helen A authorised the "routine disappearance" of some 499,987 people, 17% of the population. The seventh Doctor and Ace brought down Helen A's regime in one night. The Kandy Man's candy centre melted.

& 2388 - ORDER OF THE DALEKS[628] **->** A Dalek saucer involved in the invasion of Kantria, part of the Emperor's personal guard, crashed onto the planet Strellin. The benevolent Brotherhood of the Black Petal tended to the survivors, including a Black Dalek, and fashioned new Dalek casings from stained glass and leather. The sixth Doctor and Constance stopped the Daleks from acquiring Dream Flowers, which facilitated mental symbiosis, and could have allowed the Daleks to spread their mentality to target worlds.

The Protestant Church officially accepted all scientific disciplines, including genetic engineering, as valid. In response, Marunianism – founded by Marunia Lennox, a Scottish Protestant – declared that all science was evil.[629]

---

626 Dating *Infinite Requiem* (NA #36) - The year is quickly established as "2387" (p5). The precise date is given (p273). It is "six years" since *The Dimension Riders* (p15).

627 Dating *The Happiness Patrol* (25.2) - Terra Alpha is an isolated colony, apparently in the same system as Terra Omega. While Trevor Sigma's casual dismissal of Earth may suggest the story is set far in the future, the Doctor states only that the planet was "settled some centuries" in Ace's future. Interstellar travel is via "rocket pods". *Timelink* suggests "2788".

628 Dating *Order of the Daleks* (BF #218) - It's the time of the Galactic Census, presumably the same effort that employed Trevor Sigma in *The Happiness Patrol* [? 2388]. The Brotherhood, identified as human, has guarded the Dream Flowers for "centuries" – either suggesting they started early on in humankind's expansion into space, or that a later story dating is warranted. Thematically, *Order of the Daleks* is based somewhat on an early draft of *Alien 3*, which happened in the twenty-second century.

629 Two hundred years before *Benny: Dry Pilgrimage*.
630 *Benny: Dragons' Wrath*
631 *Benny: Down*
632 Two centuries before *Benny: The Doomsday Manuscript*.
633 *The Highest Science*
634 *The Taking of Planet 5*
635 "Twelve years" before *Divided Loyalties*.
636 "Nearly one hundred years" before *The Tenth Doctor Year One*: "The Arts in Space".
637 *The Tenth Doctor Year Three*: "The Good Companion"
638 Dating "Planet Bollywood" (DWM #424) - No year given. The tone of this story suggests that Bollywood culture has now crept into space, suggesting it's the future (unless Bollywood culture was, in fact, extra-terrestrial to start with).
639 "The Child of Time" (*DWM*)
640 *The Happiness Patrol*
641 *Synthespians*™
642 *Year of the Pig*

Near the end of the twenty-fourth century, the dictator Hugo Gamaliel ripped many colonies from Earth control so his corporation could avoid paying taxes. His campaigns against the Knights of Jeneve culminated in the Battle of Bocaro (a.k.a. Bosarno), where the Knights tricked Gamaliel into believing that he'd wiped them out. The Gamalian Dragon – an emblem of the Knights' power – served as a symbol of Gamaliel's victory, but a camera within it let the Knights spy on Gamaliel's operations. It also contained a low-grade nuclear device, so the Knights could obliterate Gamaliel if needed.[630]

A plague halved the population of Sarah-361. The local prytaneium outlawed celibacy, made monogamy a social sin and instituted mandatory pornography.[631]

On Kasagrad, the radiation in Rablev's tomb fell to safe levels.[632]

The Intergalactic Taskforce served the Inner Planets in the late twenty-fourth century. Throughout the latter half of the twenty-fourth century, the notorious criminal Sheldukher – a ruthless murderer, thief and extortionist – menaced the galaxy. He destroyed the entire Krondel constellation for no apparent reason other than that he could. In 2389, he planned his biggest coup yet, and set about recruiting accomplices.

Marjorie Postine had been an aggressive child, and her parents sold her to the military, a common practice in the commercially-minded twenty-fourth century. She became a mercenary, and Sheldukher secured her services by offering her a Moosehead Repeater, a rifle capable of blowing a hole in a neutron star. She was the veteran of seventeen front-line conflicts. Her right arm was a graft-job, performed by an unqualified surgeon in a trench on Regurel, and her bald head was scarred and lumpy.

A couple of years before, Rosheen and Klift had infiltrated McDrone Systems and embezzled a vast sum of money. The central markets collapsed, causing entire planetary economies in the fourth zone to collapse into starvation and war. Millions died. The planet Tayloe was flooded with imports. Rosheen and Klift fled to the luxury of the North Gate, where Sheldukher tracked them down. The locals gladly handed them over to him.

Sheldukher had converted a Kezzivot Class transport freighter, welding on a furnace engine, installing sleep suspension chambers stolen from the Dozing Decades company and fitting heavy weaponry such as the cellular disrupter and the spectronic destabiliser. His team raided Checkley's World, stealing Project FXX Q84 – the Cell – an advanced telepathic, organic computer. Although this brought down the wrath of the Intergalactic Taskforce, it was only the beginning of Sheldukher's scheme. He planned to locate the legendary planet Sakkrat, and the greatest prize in the galaxy: the Highest Science.

The mysterious Highest Science had preoccupied the galaxy's population for generations. In 2421, the explorer Gustaf Urnst claimed to have discovered Sakkrat, the planet which housed its secrets. No-one took Urnst seriously, although his books remained in print even after his mysterious disappearance. Unknown to the public, a Fortean Flicker had transported him to the twentieth century.

For the next three hundred years, the F61 searched the galaxy for Sakkrat, travelling past the stellar conjunctions of Naiad, the crystal quasars of Menolot and the farthest reaches of Harma. Over the centuries many lesser criminals would imitate Sheldukher, but none matched him.[633]

Archaeologists of this period believed the stories of HP Lovecraft were historically accurate.[634] *Convergence*, a cargo ship, mysteriously disappeared over Dymok in 2396.[635]

The artist Zhe Ikiyuyu achieved fame with works including block-transfer sculpture. Zhe went through a Kali phase and became increasingly reclusive on her private moon orbiting Ouloumous, but used a combination of block transfer and AI technology to create a friend. The resultant beings, two Apprentices, were opposing aspects of Zhe's psyche, her self-doubt given form. To deprive the Apprentices of power, Zhe put herself into stasis.[636] The Doctor took Sarah to visit Zhe Ikiyuyu many times.[637]

? 2397 - "Planet Bollywood"[638] -> A sentient construct, the Muse, was fashioned as an amusement for the elephantine Maharani of Baloch; it had the ability to make beings in her vicinity break into song and dance. The Maharani's attendants spirited the Muse away to a low-tech world when the Shasarak, a war-mongering people, deduced that her powers could force people to kill. The Shasarak tracked the Muse, but the eleventh Doctor and Amy helped the Muse to recalibrate her systems, and she forced the Shasarak to sing and dance until the Maharani could take them into custody.

(=) The TARDIS absorbed one of the Shasarak.

Upon the dissolution of the time-child Chiyoko, the Shasarak found itself at a singles night instead of a meeting for the Shasarak Revolutionary Front.[639]

The Twenty-Fifth Century

On a visit to Birnam in the twenty-fifth century, the Doctor saw a Stigorax.[640] The sixth Doctor took Peri shopping in a twenty-fifth century Wal-Mart.[641] In the twenty-fifth century, a mishap at a plastics factory with a matter synthesiser and an advertisement in an antique issue of *Power Man and Iron Fist* created a huge proliferation of x-ray spectacles. The company prospered for a year, but went out of business when a horde of rampaging sea monkeys – something else that shouldn't have existed – destroyed the factory.[642] Alphonse Chardalot wanted to take Toby the Sapient Pig to a scientific conference on Gamantis.[643]

Owing to Abby and Zara's interventions in time, the singer Alec Graves would die age forty-three rather than live to see ninety... but one of his compositions, "Love Ain't Easy", would be the first song played on Venus.[644]

> (=) But for Kortis and the bald Master's temporal interference, the Ides Scientific Institute would have been unnoteworthy, and ground out in the twenty-fifth century.[645]

2400 - THE PIT[646] **->** At the beginning of the twenty-fifth century, the space docks of Glasson Minor, a planet-sized ship-building station, bustled with activity and human colonisation continued to gather pace.

Bernice worried that the seventh Doctor was becoming too despondent, and tried to snap him out of it by having him investigate the destruction of the Seven Planets of the Althosian binary star system in 2400, an event that had never been explained. Colonisation at this time was still hazardous, and the Seven Planets were far from the normal trading routes, years away from the nearest other colony. A number of new religions sprang up on Nicea, the planet

---

643 "Five hundred" years after *Year of the Pig*, although it's impossible to know if the conference is real – and of interest to Chardalot's time-travelling father – or just part of Chardalot's half-baked imaginings.

644 The century before *Graceless IV: The Ward*. Quite a few stories, including *The Wheel in Space*, indicate human activity on Venus a few centuries before this.

645 *DEyes 3: The Death of Hope*

646 Dating *The Pit* (NA #12) - Benny states that the Seven Planets were destroyed "Fifty years before my time... 2400" (p9).

647 Dating *LIVE 34* (BF #74) - The isolated, heavily censored colonists believe that Earth was abandoned "centuries ago", and most facets of this society – the style of LIVE 34's broadcasts in particular – bring to mind an Earth colony rather than an alien one. Additionally, a LIVE 34 broadcaster doesn't question the dating system when Ace mentions a 1952 Vincent Black Lightning motorcycle. The dating of this story is somewhat arbitrary, although Colony 34 very much fits the mould of an isolated, oppressed Earth colony akin to Terra Alpha in *The Happiness Patrol*.

648 She was married to Yrcanos for twenty-five years according to *Bad Therapy* (p288).

649 PERI LEAVES AND CAUSES CONTINUITY PROBLEMS, TAKE TWO AND THREE: Peri's departure was a little confused on television. *The Trial of a Time Lord* first tells us that she died, then that she lived happily ever after with King Yrcanos – a last-minute addition to the script, and a big stretch given what we saw of their on-screen relationship.

However, there's a bigger problem: taking what we're told about subsequent events in the comics and novels, and – as *Ahistory* does – assuming that it's the same continuity, a couple of knotty problems emerge.

The first is exactly what happens to Peri, the problem being that the novel *Bad Therapy* and the comic "The Age of Chaos" contradict each other. In *Bad Therapy*, Peri resents her new life and returns to Earth after twenty-five years. In "The Age of Chaos", she remains on Krontep and raises a dynasty of children and grandchildren. This conundrum, at least, is easily explained thanks to *Peri and the Piscon Paradox* establishing that owing to the Time Lords' tinkering, there are at least

five Peris active in the universe. Clearly, the Peri from *Bad Therapy* and the one in "The Age of Chaos" number among these variants.

Thankfully, the novelisations don't "count" for the purposes of this book, because in the *Mindwarp* novelisation, Philip Martin stated that Peri and Yrcanos immediately went to the twentieth century and Yrcanos became a professional wrestler.

There's another continuity issue connected with Peri's departure – Frobisher is the companion of the seventh Doctor for one adventure ("A Cold Day in Hell"), and they make reference there to Peri leaving for Krontep with Yrcanos (on television in *Mindwarp*), implying it was very recent. For people reading the *DWM* strip at the time, it was – the story follows straight on from "The World Shapers", featuring the sixth Doctor, Frobisher and Peri, but this is difficult to fit around the TV series.

Furthermore, in "The Age of Chaos", the sixth Doctor and Frobisher are *twice* seen visiting Krontep, so it's odd that Frobisher hasn't come to terms with Peri leaving. The story also implies that the sixth Doctor has dropped Frobisher off in the Antarctic at some point and is travelling solo. (Strange how Frobisher seems to take sabbaticals from the Doctor's company, as he also leaves the TARDIS for a time in *The Maltese Penguin*, then returns.)

Any solution also has to explain how Mel – who's present when the Doctor regenerates (in *Time and the Rani*), but not in "A Cold Day in Hell" or the following story "Redemption" – fits in. Ultimately, unless Frobisher's hiding in the TARDIS, unmentioned, during the television stories (or Mel is doing the same during "A Cold Day in Hell" and "Redemption"), it's not easy to come up with a neat solution that fits all the evidence.

650 "About a hundred years" before *Sword of Orion*.

651 "Forty years" before *1stD* V1: *The Unwinding World*.

652 Dating *Vanishing Point* (EDA #44) - An arbitrary date. The colony has been around for "centuries".

653 Dating *Divided Loyalties* (PDA #26) - It is "thirty years" after Dymok became isolated in 2378 (p16). The Toymaker next appears in *The Nightmare Fair*.

654 Dating *Snake Bite* (BBC *DW* audiobook #21) - No date given, and it's not expressly said that anyone

with the largest population, and these spread to the smaller worlds of Trieste and Byzantine. Most of these were based around the Form Manipulator, and adopted Judeo-Christian beliefs to the environment of the Seven Planets. The geographical and religious isolation made it easy for them to declare independence from the Corporation, but the corporations responded by cutting off all supplies and communications. Rioting broke out that the Archon and his armies were unable to contain.

The Time Lords' ancient enemies, the Yssgaroth, were making efforts to invade our universe and had created a series of space-time tears. The Doctor fell through one such tear into the past, and returned to this era with William Blake. A former Gallifreyan general, Kopyion Liall a Mahajetsu, had been among the Althosian System's first settlers and was seeking to thwart the Yssgaroth – but was moved to save the Doctor and Blake. Fearing that the Yssgaroth would view his compassion as a weakness to be exploited, Kopyion destroyed the Althosian System purely to demonstrate his resolve, sealing the tears and killing millions. The Doctor and Benny took Blake home.

c 2400 (days 1 to 16, ninth month) - LIVE 34[647] ->
Elections on Colony 34 were now five years overdue. Jaeger's administration continued its crackdown, but the Colony Central Commission (CCC) accepted a petition from his opposition – the Freedom and Democracy Party (FDP) – and ruled that elections must be held in sixteen days. The radio station LIVE 34 called Jaeger's administration into question through such programmes as *Wareing's World* and *Live With Charlotte Singh*, but the station's independence was revoked, and the State Broadcast Monitoring Department assumed editorial control.

The FDP leader, Durinda Cauldwell, had reportedly been killed by members of her own party, and her predecessor had allegedly died in a transporter accident. The seventh Doctor – accompanied by Ace and Hex – accepted the FDP leadership, unwilling to risk anyone else's life in the post. Ace organised resistance as "the Rebel Queen", and her operatives blew up empty government buildings to obtain evidence of Jaeger's corruption. Nobody was killed, but Jaeger's forces blew up a vehicle manufacturing plant and a senior citizens' home, gaining political favour by blaming the hundreds of resultant casualties on the Rebel Queen and the FDP.

The Doctor stood for election against Jaeger, who claimed to have won with 81.5% of the vote, a victory margin of 63%. The CCC declared the election void as the Doctor was believed dead during the voting, and the truth about the false Jaeger was revealed. Jaeger's staff were arrested, political prisoners were freed and Charlotte Singh was designated the CCC's representative. A mob fell upon the false Jaeger.

One version of Peri spent twenty-five years being married to Yrcanos, and became Queen of the Krontep and the Seven Systems. She governed seven worlds. "Gilliam, Queen of Krontep", as she was known, disappeared in 2404 and returned to the twentieth century.[648] Another version of Peri stayed on Krontep with her family.[649]

Humans colonised the Garazone System. The Garazone Space Patrol was formed to fight smugglers.[650] Humanity caused a bloody war that nearly drove the Kenosians – squat, asymmetrical beings – to extinction. The guilt-ridden humans crafted a computer-driven society that chemically removed their memories and modified their behavior, hoping future generations would avoid such atrocities.[651]

? 2405 - VANISHING POINT[652] ->
The geneticist Cauchemar worked to overthrow "the Creator" responsible for the reincarnation process on an alien colony planet. The Creator's functions were disrupted to the point that deformed children named "mooncalves" were being born without the genetic "godswitch" needed to facilitate reincarnation. Cauchemar hoped to overload the Creator, triggering an energy release that would destroy the planet, yet facilitate his soul's admittance to the afterlife. The eighth Doctor, Fitz and Anji foiled this scheme. The genetic experiments that had extended Cauchemar's life, coupled with radiation exposure, failed and he died. One of the mooncalves became pregnant with Fitz's child.

Years later, the Creator had rebalanced enough to include the mooncalves in its designs.

2408 - DIVIDED LOYALTIES[653] ->
The fifth Doctor, Tegan, Nyssa and Adric arrived on space station *Little Boy II* to find communications with Dymok had been disrupted. The Doctor travelled to the planet and was captured by the Toymaker. An attack by the Toymaker made Dymok vanish completely, but the Doctor again defeated him. The Toymaker decided to base himself in Blackpool, the 1980s.

? 2412 - SNAKE BITE[654] ->
The Hormagaunt was the largest space station ever created: an inter-connected configuration of spaceships wrapped in geo-stationary orbit around the planet Midgard, and named as the second of the Seven Wonders of the Universe. Midgard itself was untouched by technology, and home to genetic chameleons that could adopt the guise of any visitors there.

A cobra-like race was trapped in a remote quadrant of space that was dying, and had rendered them sterile. One of their number arrived on the Hormagaunt in the adopted guise of Doctor Elehri Mussurana, and spent years researching the science of wormholes. A successful attempt to create a wormhole to Mussurana's homeworld drew the TARDIS off-course, and the eleventh Doctor, Amy and Rory learned that Mussurana's people intended to invade

Midgard, forcing the shapeshifters there to adopt their genetic forms and keep their race alive. The Doctor made the wormhole's beginning and ending points one and the same – Mussurana's people remained trapped, while Mussurana was time-looped.

In 2414, Darzil Carlisle was born outside Olympus Mons on Mars. At age three, following an airlock accident that killed his parents, he was relocated to an orphanage in Finchley, North London. At age 17, he earned a scholarship to the Phobos Academy of Music, and studied there for three years.[655]

An onslaught of swarming creatures all but destroyed human colonies in the Capris System, which rebuilt itself as a society devoted to science and medicine.[656] The discredited archaeologist Rintilda Vigintitres wrote the first book about the giant stone cats on Bubastis, dubbing the extinct people there the Mary Celestians. A later work, *The Nobal: My Part in the Discovery of a Lost Civilisation* by Chilton Christopher, opted for calling them the Nobal.[657]

c 2415 - THE HOUSE OF WINTER[658] **->** Afflicted with a rare blood disease, Harrison Winter established a research lab on Bravis II in the Asurmian Reach. Winter tried to cure his condition with genetic material from regenerative bloodmoths, but the effort caused him to periodically turn into a bloodsucking human-moth hybrid. OmniCorp sealed Winter in his house, and so he employed the TARDIS-summoning card kept by his family. The twelfth Doctor and Clara realised that Winter had become a murderous fiend, and killed him in Bravis II's artificial sun, a fusion reactor.

Humanity and the Ice Warriors continually came into conflict as they ventured into space. A ten-year war between Ice Warrior settlers on Bellona and human colonists on its sister world, Enyo, ended when a firestorm bomb ravaged Bellona's cities. Lord Hasskor and his warriors entered stasis, even as the Bellona survivors were granted asylum on Enyo, where they lived in slums.[659]

(=) c 2418 - "Assimilation 2"[660] **->** The eleventh Doctor, Amy and Rory showed Captain Jean-Luc Picard a possible future in which the Cybermen subjugated the Klingon homeworld of Qo'noS.

---

aboard the Hormagaunt is human (although "Elehri Mussurana" and "Ernst Wharner" sound like ethnic Earth names). Nonetheless, Mussurana and Wharner identify the eleventh Doctor's outfit as being "vintage twenty-first century denim", and Mussurana is acquainted with the Earth phrase "ladies first" – suggesting it's not *so* far in advance of the present day that this wouldn't be the case. With nothing else to go on, the placement here represents a guess.

655 *The Game*. Carlisle's birth date and details of his early life are given, Disc 1, Track 7.

656 "Two hundred or so years" before *Benny: Adorable Illusion* (ch22).

657 "Over two hundred years" before *Benny: The Slender-Fingered Cats of Bubastis* (pgs. 39, 77, 88).

658 Dating *The House of Winter* (BBC audiobook #23) - It's the "twenty-fifth century". The family legends about the Doctor, Harrison says, go back "almost a millennia" (to *The Memory of Winter* [1429]).

Harrison says the twelfth Doctor and Clara met his grandfather (off screen) "decades" ago, suggesting the TARDIS card hasn't been played in that time. No mention is made of how is Harrison related to Diana Winter from *The Gods of Winter*, but it seems reasonable to think that *The House of Winter* happens between that story and the next in this series, *The Sins of Winter*. Harrison might even be the son of one of Diana's two children, but this isn't said. The blurb gives Winter's first name as "Justin"; he's "Harrison" within the story.

659 "Five hundred years" before *Cold Vengeance*.

660 Dating "Assimilation 2" (IDW *Star Trek: The Next Generation/Doctor Who* mini-series) - It's "fifty years" after the story's main events.

661 Dating *Erimem: Three Faces of Helena* (*Erimem* novel #8) - The year is given.

662 Dating *Assimilation 2* (IDW *Star Trek: The Next Generation/Doctor Who* mini-series) - It's "thirty years" since the Cybermen defeated the Klingon Empire.

663 "Some seventy five years" before *The Sands of Life*. See the Presidents of Earth sidebar.

664 *The Game*

665 "More than a century" before *Parasite* (p49).

666 *The Menagerie*

667 "Pureblood"

668 In the "ten years" leading up to "The Age of Chaos".

669 Dating "The Age of Chaos" (*DWM Special*, unnumbered) - The story is set after *Mindwarp*, long enough afterwards that Peri's youngest grandchild is 16 (and her grandsons were young men ten years ago), but no exact date is specified. So, it has to be at least fifty years since Peri left the Doctor. The tenth Doctor claims in "The Forgotten" that he never visited Peri when she was living with Yrcanos, but he's not exactly in his right mind at the time.

670 Dating "Dogs of Doom" (*DWW* #27-34) - Babe tells Sharon the system has been "settled here for fifty years – since 2380 Old Earth time". It's never explained why the Daleks need Werelox to invade the settlements if they're going to sterilise the planets from orbit.

(=) 2419 - ERIMEM: THREE FACES OF HELENA[661] **->** Inquisitor Nine, an agent of a religious fundamentalist state, deemed the immortal Helena as an abomination and crucified her at the Fourth Temple of the Revelation. The termination of Helena's immortality in 1884 averted these events.

(=) c 2448 - "Assimilation 2"[662] **->** The Cybermen captured the paradise world of Raxacoricofallapatorius, and used its resources to fuel their war machine.

The President of Earth

The office of President of Earth was created.[663]

The fifth Doctor, having encountered an older Darzil Carlisle circa 2484, secretly aided Lord Carlisle in becoming a renowned peacemaker, and in saving billions of lives by ending wars on at least thirty-six planets.[664]

Around 2415, the people of the Elysium System discovered the Artifact, a vast ammonite-like structure, on the edge of their territory.[665] In 2416, on an unnamed colony world, IMC had set up a genetics engineering project named Project Mecrim. The Company built the ape-like Rocarbies, cheap labour developed from the native primate life; and the Mecrim, a race built for combat with a claw that could vibrate and cut through even the hardest materials. When a Mecrim gut microbe escaped, the colony was declared off limits. The survivors developed an immunity, but came to hate science and degenerated to a medieval level of technology.[666]

In 2420, the human race and Sontarans signed a non-aggression pact.[667] In the 2420s, the deserts of Earth were reclaimed and the city New Atlantis was built in the Pacific. The population of Earth was sixty billion at this time.

The sixth Doctor and Frobisher visited Peri on Krontep and caught up with her family. Following that visit, her son Corynus was killed in a hunting accident. Yrcanos died suddenly, and his and Peri's grandsons – Artios and Euthys – unaccountably fell out over the succession. Peri rode off, vowing not to return until the war had ended. Krontep was devastated by civil war between Artios and Euthys. Yrcanthia, their mother, was killed in crossfire, and this provoked the generals to rebel against both brothers and stake them out in the desert. Farlig was appointed regent to Peri's granddaughter Actis.[668]

c 2429 - "The Age of Chaos"[669] **->** The sixth Doctor arrived on Krontep to celebrate Actis' sixteenth birthday, and learned of the turbulence of the last decade. At Actis' insistence, they went to the Antarctic to meet Frobisher. The Doctor and Frobisher set off on a perilous journey to the distant land of Brachion, in hope of finding what had

gone wrong with the planet, and discovered a mysterious dome. The Doctor identified it as a Thought Aligned Random Displacement Energiser Negative Activated (TARDENA), and learned that it was being operated by a Nahrung, a member of an old race that fed on suffering – it was this madness that had consumed the planet. Deep underground in the Hall of Atonement, the lair of a sect of mad monks, the travellers went on to meet Euthys and Artios, and were reunited with Actis. They escaped thanks to the mysterious Ranith.

Comparing notes, the Doctor deduced that the regent Farlig had used Nahrung technology to set the brothers against each other. The Nahrung possessed Farlig, and both were killed. As the Doctor and Frobisher left, the Doctor revealled that Ranith was secretly Peri herself.

2430 - "Dogs of Doom"[670] **->** The savage Werelox were werewolf-like aliens who could convert humans into their kind with a single bite or slash of their claws, and they attacked the more than thirty colonies of the New Earth System.

The TARDIS landed on the *Spacehog*: an astro-freighter, operated by Joe Bean and Babe Roth, that was working the system. As the fourth Doctor and Sharon introduced themselves, the Werelox attacked the ship and their leader, Brill, clawed the Doctor. He became a Werelok and retreated to the TARDIS, taking it out of time. Three months later, he had cured himself, and returned to the *Spacehog* mere minutes after he left. The Doctor hypnotised Brill and realised the Werelox were the Daleks' servants. The Daleks were using neutron fire to sterilise planets and planned to colonise them. The Doctor headed to the Dalek ship with Brill and K9.

Meanwhile, Joe Bean and his partner Babe planned to ram the Dalek ship in the *Spacehog*. The Doctor discovered that the Daleks were distilling emotions from alien monsters to make themselves more efficient killing machines, and that unless something was done, the New Earth System would become a huge Dalek breeding ground. K9 released the alien monsters, which attacked the Daleks. Additionally, the Doctor used equipment in the Daleks' Room of Many Centuries – a laboratory where the Daleks were building a time transporter – to timelock the Dalek battlecruiser, removing the threat just as the *Spacehog* was about to ram it.

The Tyrenians had been developed as human supersoldiers with canine attributes, genetically engineered by Gustav Tyren. When the military pulled its funding for the project, the Tyrenians stole a ship and founded a colony on Axista Four. They set up satellite defences and then entered suspended animation using symbiotes.

Around 2430, the human colony ship *Big Bang* departed into space. The seventh Doctor, in preparing colonist

Kirann Ransome to help one of his previous selves, was the last person to visit her before she entered stasis.

The defence grid on Axista Four shot down the *Big Bang*, and it crashed to the planet. Kirann remained trapped in stasis while the survivors founded a colony based on her text, *Back to Basics*, and strove for a low-technology approach that modelled society on the Wild West. They were unaware of the Tyrenians' presence.[671]

= In 2436, an alternative Earth that was ruled by Nazis who had won the Second World War, and later gone on to galactic conquest, was destroyed.[672]

? 2440 - SURVIVAL OF THE FITTEST[673] -> Among the worlds of the galactic plane, the Geo-Police were a fascist group of "justice officers" who would cordon off various worlds to protect their resources.

The seventh Doctor and Klein arrived on a planet located high above the galactic plane, with a good view of the Milky Way. The insectoid Vrill who lived there were threatened by a team of humans seeking to acquire and sell the prized nutrient gels the Vrill used in their reproductive process. The humans used a nerve agent – the Spear of Destiny 2Tri-C81 – to kill the Vrill queen, their Authority. The Doctor saved enough gel to guarantee the Vrill's survival, but Klein – plotting to rewrite history in favour of the German Reich – stole the TARDIS, stranding him...

The Doctor was transplanted into the alternate reality Klein created in 2044, and retrieved his Ship.[674]

c 2443 - 1STD V1: THE UNWINDING WORLD[675] -> The first Doctor, Ian, Barbara and Vicki happened upon the brainwashed human society created in the aftermath of the Kenosian War, and spent three months undermining the system from within. The Doctor, Ian and Barbara

worked to disclose the society's true history and ruin its food-treatment operations, which distracted from Vicki reprogramming the oppressive computer systems, thereby liberating the populace.

The lost planet of Delfus Orestes, formerly designated Cappa Nine Seven, was re-named KS-159. The Delfans of Delfus Clytaemnestra had built the Oracle of the Lost – a sentient statue that could make predictions of the future based upon universal models – on Delfus Orestes, and it resided there even after its creators had passed.[676]

Enormous spaceport terminals were created as hyperspace travel enabled humanity to spread further into the universe. The small planet New Memphis was close to a hyperspace nexus point, and so became a hub of intergalactic travel, its Elvis the King Spaceport servicing traffic from a hundred different star systems.[677]

Circa 2450, Earth instigated a time-travel project on Vilencia Sixteen that went horribly wrong and destroyed half the planet. The Stella Stora Sigma Schutz-Staffel SturmSoldaten (SSSSSSS), a neo-Nazi organisation, used bits of this technology to weave their philosophies into the timelines of many worlds.[678]

c 2450 - THE TWELFTH DOCTOR YEAR ONE[679] -> The twelfth Doctor and Clara showed up at the ice planet Isen VI to practice skiing, but found that Kano Dollar, the richest human in the twenty-fifth century, had terraformed it into a tropical paradise for his impending business marriage to Princess Thanna of the Gothgolka Horde. The terraforming woke up a wrathful Hyperion, Rann-Korr, but the Doctor reverse-engineered a portion of Isen VI to become icy again, freezing Rann-Korr solid. Ravenous blue-faced monkeys killed Dollar.

---

671 The colonists crashed on Axista Four about a hundred years before *The Colony of Lies*. Kirann mentions meeting the seventh Doctor on p164.
672 *Spiral Scratch*
673 Dating *Survival of the Fittest* (BF #130b) - The cliffhanger is resolved in *The Architects of History*. The Doctor finds himself in 2044 in that story, owing to Klein's historical alterations, but it's impossible to believe that *Survival of the Fittest* occurs in the same year – it's much too early for humanity to have spread out this far into the Milky Way. Also, human technology is now at a stage where a team of fortune-seeking humans can venture off into space armed with a fearsome amount of hardware – enough to kill thousands of adult Vrill and take out their hive system. Even so, this date is arbitrary.
674 *The Architects of History*

675 Dating *The Unwinding World* (BF CC #9.2) - Vicki mentions being "quite good with vintage computers", suggesting it's prior to her native time [c.2493]. She also mentions "twentieth-century Earth" without the advanced computer interface she's conversing with asking what that means. Talk of memory suppressants first being used on traumatized soldiers "some centuries" ago brings to mind recent efforts to create a "forgetting pill" to treat PTSD patients.
676 *Benny: Tears of the Oracle*. KS-159 is the future home of the Braxiatel Collection.
677 "Decades" before *Judgement of the Judoon*.
678 *Benny: Down*
679 Dating *The Twelfth Doctor Year One* (Titan 12th Doc #1.1-1.2, "Terrorformer") - A broadcast and a "Previously On..." synopsis names Kano Dollar as "the richest human in the 25th century".

c 2450 - SCAREDY CAT[680] **->** Fathrea – the fourth world orbiting its sun – had known peace for centuries, and colonists from there settled in another system on the planet Endarra. The biological agent Saravin had been developed for warfare, and a passing Ventriki ship tested the weapon's effects on the Endarra colony. The eighth Doctor, investigating events that would occur four million years in the future, refrained from interfering for fear of disrupting history. C'rizz gave the colonists an antidote from the TARDIS medial facility, but this wasn't enough to save them. Within three months, the colonists had perished. One small girl, Galayana, had a natural immunity and survived a few weeks longer, then perished herself.

Endarra was newly formed, and the trauma of the colonists' deaths remained in its morphogenetic field. Galayana's memories and aspect were also preserved.

? 2450 - THE UNDERWATER WAR[681] **->** The purple water planet Hydron was home to the Schoal: fish people whose eggs carried an immense electrical charge. One egg could power a starship for a week. The Schoal attacked the Earth vessel *Marine Adventurer* when it tried to steal the Schoal's eggs, but two survivors – including a man named Fleming – escaped back to Earth. Two years later, the eleventh Doctor, Amy and Rory defused tensions when the Company sent the *Cosmic Rover* to scour Hydron for minerals. Fleming tried and failed to capture thousands of eggs, sell them and retire to Catrigan Nova and its whirlpools of gold. With peace restored, the Doctor and his friends decided to visit the Tower of London.

General Moret fought in the Telepathic Uprising of '54.[682] Spacefleet used psi drugs to enhance human psychokinesis.[683] The Doctor met a Legion in the twenty-fifth century.[684] A Dalek War broke out in 2459.[685] Forests in Madagascar and Portugal were made into cropland to such a degree, the sentient lemurs there dispersed throughout

the galaxy in search of a new home. They formed the Order of Lost Lemuroidea.[686]

The Drashani Empire spanned a whole galaxy, and was comparable to an interstellar version of ancient Rome. The Drashani's House Sorsha, later assisted by House Gadarel, conducted experiments that literally tore the souls out of their prisoners, consigning them to a plane of existence called the Undervoid. The bodies that remained regressed into a primal state with sharpened claws and toughened skin, making them ideal for mining and building labor. The transformed people became known as the Igris. It was publicly thought they had been genetically engineered from animals.[687] Certain members of House Sorsha were gifted with telekinesis and pyrokinesis, but the condition over time drove them insane. The great-grandfather of Prince Kylo was afflicted in this manner, and his family fractured as a result.[688]

Comes the Trickster released the HvLIP *All The Way From Heaven* in 2465.[689]

c 2465 - SINS OF WINTER[690] **->** The Cult of the Prime Self promoted the idea that each person was the most unique and beautiful thing in creation, and so its adherents prayed to themselves. The Church slipped from being the third-most popular religion to the fourth, and it was believed that the aged Shadrak Winter, the current High Cardinal of the cult, was – per the custom of succession – in danger of assassination.

In actuality, Winter used the Sinful – slug-like creatures that gestated in sinners – to purge his sins and wipe out his enemies. He also used his family's psychic-paper card to summon the twelfth Doctor and Clara to the cult's asteroid cathedral at the edge of the Great Rift, so Beldrassian Corporation's legal department could exact revenge upon the duo and handsomely reward him. The Doctor and overcame the Sinful, and left the cardinal to face the repercussions of his actions.

680 Dating *Scaredy Cat* (BF #75) - According to the Doctor, the Earth Empire bans Saravin "a few hundred years" after this point.
681 Dating *The Underwater War* (BBC children's 2-in-1 #7, released in *Alien Adventures*) - Earth's space technology seems relatively advanced, as two trips between Earth and Hydron are made in the span of two years, minus all the time Fleming spends on Earth in the interim. That said, Earth culture is not so advanced from the present day that Jules Verne has been forgotten, as two submersibles are here named after him. "The Company" is not IMC, the seemingly ubiquitous mining corporation in operation during Earth's Empire phase (not that it's ever established that IMC is the *only* mining company of its day), and it seems a stretch, without it being said, to think that it's the same corporation that runs Terminus (*Terminus*). Ultimately, the story could

occur just about anywhere.
682 2454, according to *Judgement of the Judoon*.
683 "Twenty years" before Mrs Ransandrianasolo is born, according to *Return of the Living Dad* (p164).
684 *The Crystal Bucephalus* – referred to as "shortly before the Second Dalek War" (q.v. The Dalek Wars).
685 *The Colony of Lies*
686 *Benny: Old Friends*. When this occurs is unclear, but by 2562, the lemurs' offspring are holding down jobs on the spacelanes.
687 *The Acheron Pulse, The Burning Prince*.
688 Three generations before *The Burning Prince*.
689 *The Also People* (p170).
690 Dating *The Sins of Winter* (BBC audiobook #24) - The Doctor and Clara pissed off the Beldrassian Corporation in *The Gods of Winter* (see The Winter Family sidebar for more).

Down Among the Dead Men, Bernice Summerfield's study of archaeology (particularly that of the Martians) was published.[691]

(=) c 2468 – "Assimilation 2"[692] -> Vulcan, a member of the United Federation of Planets, fell to the Borg-augmented Cybermen.

---

c 2470 – COUNCIL OF WAR[693] -> A century-long war ruined the planet Valiador, after which the people there used *Love is All You Need* by Margery Phipps as the blueprint of Valiador's new society. The Valiadorians recreated her hometown of Kettering down to its last detail, renamed their world Earth and were hailed across the seven systems as a peaceful, weaponless society.

The Blatherians, a race of pirate-like cockroaches, took many of the Validorians into slavery and plundered their world's mineral resources. The remaining Valiadorians used time-technology to abduct Phipps – as accompanied by Sgt Benton – from the twenty-first century to put her on trial for leading them down the wrong path. Benton and Phipps delayed a further Blatherian onslaught until the third Doctor arrived and caused the aggressors to go dormant, enabling the United Galactic Intelligence Grand Taskforce (UGIT) to take them into custody. He then took Benton and Phipps back to their own time...

(=) c 2470 – DC 4: SONGS OF LOVE[694] -> London Spaceport was established. Liv Chenka and Helen Sinclair briefly wound up there, having escaped from an eradicated future-time. The Coalition brought about an apocalypse that encroached upon Earth, but River Song returned the women to Gallifrey via a Biodata Scoop.

2472 (Tuesday, 3rd March, to Wednesday, 4th March) – COLONY IN SPACE[695] -> Earth was overpopulated, with one hundred billion people living like "battery hens" in communal living units. 300-storey floating islands were built, housing five hundred million people. There was "no room to move, polluted air, not a blade of grass left on the planet and a government that locks you up if you think for yourself".

IMC scoured the galaxy for duralinium, to build ever more living units. From Earth Control, their headquarters, a fleet of survey vessels ruthlessly stripmined worlds and killed anyone that stood in their way. Discipline on IMC ships and planets relied heavily on the death penalty: piracy, mutiny and even trespass were all capital offences. Earth Government turned a blind eye to these abuses, although an Adjudicator was assigned to each Galactic Sector to judge disputes in interplanetary law.

Despite the conditions on Earth, few were prepared to leave the homeworld for a bleak life on a colony planet. Some groups of eccentrics bought their own ship and tried to settle on a new world, but most people preferred a life on Earth, where the government may have been harsh, but at least they were able to feed their citizens.

Colonists on Uxarieus – a world that supported birds, insects and basic plant life, and which had an atmosphere similar to that of Earth before the invention of the motor car – found themselves in competition with IMC for control of the planet. The colonists arrived first, surveyed the planet and set up their habitation domes. They discovered that Uxarieus was inhabited by a small subterranean city of telepathic Primitives. Two colonists were killed when they tried to enter the city, but an understanding was reached – in return for food, the Primitives provided menial labour. The colonists proceeded with their plans, but it proved difficult to grow crops as they withered for no reason that the colonists could ascertain.

Just over a year after they arrived, giant lizards attacked some of the outermost domes and some colonists were killed. Many colonists were prepared to leave, but their spacecraft was obsolete, and would

---

691 *Theatre of War.* The date of publication is given as both "2566" (p36), and "2466" (p135). While the first date is actually in Benny's home era, the intro pages to Big Finish's Benny short story anthologies take such continual delight in pointing out that *Down Among the Dead Men* was "published originally in 2466, which is odd given that it is now 26—", the latter date has become a lot harder to discount. Appendix II of *Sky Pirates!* is "A Benny Bibliography", and contains further details.

692 Dating "Assimilation 2" (IDW *Star Trek: The Next Generation/Doctor Who* mini-series) - Projected as "twenty years" after the Cybermen assimilate Raxacoricofallapatorius.

693 Dating *Council of War* (BF CC #7.12) - It's some centuries into the future – *Love is All You Need* is still a bestseller "five hundred years" after its publication in the late twenty-first century, and the recreation of the Kettering Military Museum is stocked with weaponry-replicas "more than three hundred years" after the originals were housed on Earth.

694 Dating *DC 4: Songs of Love* (BF DC #4.2) - Liv remarks that the advent of London Spaceport means it's "definitely post-twenty-fifth century". *DC 4: The Side of Angels* repeatedly says that this apocalypse happens "five centuries" after the 1970s.

695 Dating *Colony in Space* (8.4) - We see a calendar being changed from "Monday 2nd March 2472" to the

almost certainly be unable to reach another world.

IMC arrived in Survey Ship 4-3, under the command of Captain Dent, and angered the colonists by staking a claim on the world. When they discovered that IMC had been using optical trickery to project images of the lizards, and a Mark III servo-robot to kill the colonists, many turned to arms.

Colonists and IMC men were killed in a series of gun battles. The UNIT Master posed as an Adjudicator and ruled in IMC's favour, but he was more interested in the Primitives' secrets. The IMC team attempted to murder the colonists by forcing them to leave in their obsolete rocket. They were defeated and a real Adjudicator was brought in.

It was discovered that the Primitive city was home to an ancient superweapon, which had been leaking and poisoning the soil. The third Doctor and Jo, working on behalf of the Time Lords, convinced the guardian of this device to destroy to weapon – and the city – rather than let it fall into the Master's hands.

Humanity at this time still used imperial measurements, projectile weapons and wheeled transport ("space buggies"). Ships were powered by nuclear motors, and communicated with Earth via "warp" radio and videolink. The language of Earth was English; the currency was the pound. IMC had advanced scanning equipment for mineral surveys and medical diagnoses. Colonists bought old ships to transport them to their colony planets.

In the twenty-fifth century, Earth colonised Solos, a planet with rich deposits of thaesium. The beautiful planet was ravaged and its people enslaved.[696] The seventh Doctor, Benny, Roz and Chris went to Navarro to rest after their adventure in Little Caldwell.[697] Mrs Ransandrianasolo was born. She was a telepath, as her mother was given psi drugs.[698]

Julius Winter, an amateur historian, used a crude time-travel device to go back to the time of Joan of Arc. The twelfth Doctor and Clara brought Winter back home after he had lost both his memories of them and his family's psychic-paper card. This marked the end of the Winter family's ability to call the Doctor and Clara to them.[699]

At this time, Earth was thought to be the only body in the solar system capable of supporting plant life.[700] In 2476, the Techno-Magi consulted the frozen head of Ralph Waldo Mimsey as an Oracle, driving him insane.[701]

The Korven invaded Earth in 2480, and attempted to cool the planet with phosphane devices because the planet was too warm for them.[702]

c 2481 - THE TENTH DOCTOR YEAR ONE[703] -> The tenth Doctor took Gabby to the Pentaquoteque Gallery of Ouloumos to visit his friend, the artist Zhe Ikiyuyu, but found the Apprentices in control of her private moon. Zhe awoke from her slumber and re-absorbed the Apprentices into her psyche.

Gabby's encounter with the Apprentices left her endowed with a measure of reality warping block-transfer computations – putting her on the path to becoming the Vortex Butterfly.[704] Circa 2481, the UI designated Cray as Earth's sister planet, due to its position relative to Earth from Galactic Zero. The increased focus on Cray compelled Earth to try and end the planet's embarrassing war. The negotiator Lord Carlisle would be dispatched to try and arbitrate a peace.[705]

c 2484 - THE GAME[706] -> On the planet Cray, only two teams – the Gora and the Lineen – had survived to continue playing the lethal game of Naxy. The past five seasons had seen the deaths of 78,349 Gora and 65,418 Lineen,

---

next day. Ashe tells Jo that they left Earth in "seventy-one". Hulke's novelisation sets this story in "2971".
696 "Some five hundred years" before *The Mutants*, according to the Administrator.
697 "Five hundred years" after *Return of the Living Dad* (p61).
698 *The Memory of Winter*
699 "Seventy-two" years before *Return of the Living Dad*.
700 "Almost thirty-five years" before *The Taking of Chelsea 426* (p74). It's notable that Mars is not thought to support plant life in this era – we know from *Benny: Beige Planet Mars* that by 2545, a settlement equipped with photon missiles is in operation there.
701 *Burning Heart* (p174).
702 *K9: The Korven*. The Korven are a threat and possibly even continue to control areas of the Earth at least

until 2618.
703 Dating *The Tenth Doctor Year One* (Titan 10th Doc #4-5, "The Arts in Space") - Zhe trained on Logopolis, which was destroyed "centuries ago" (in *Logopolis*, set in 1981). There's flourishes of Earth culture, such as the Pentaquoteque Gallery owning Picassos, Zhe patterning her current self after Kali, and Zhe having been influenced by the work of sculptor Alberto Giacometti (1901-1966) and sculptor/artist Henry Moore (1898-1986).
704 *The Tenth Doctor Year Three*: "Vortex Butterflies"
705 "Three cycles" (presumably years) before *The Game*.
706 Dating *The Game* (BF #66) - Lord Carlisle was born 2414 and started his career as a peacemaker around age 20 (so, circa 2434). On Disc 1, Track 70, he says he has been working as a mediator for "fifty years".

although the Gora were in much worse shape than was officially reported, and were on the brink of defeat.

The fifth Doctor and Nyssa witnessed Lord Carlisle's efforts to broker a truce, but the Doctor's involvement in a Naxy match led to an upset for the Lineen, with four hundred Lineen casualties. Carlisle died while saving the Doctor's life, but the Doctor exposed the Morian Crime Syndicate's manipulative influence on the planet. The Gora and Lineen united against the Morian, ending the Naxy tournaments. Carlisle was accredited with the planet's newfound peace.

Heroin slam, the so-called "razor drug", was now in distribution.

c 2485 - "Junkyard Demon"[707] -> The Salvage ship *Drifter* travelled along the edge of the galaxy, piloted by two traders: Flotsam and Jetsam of the Backwater Scrap and Salvage Company. They plucked the TARDIS out of space, interrupting the fourth Doctor's meditation. The Doctor was horrified to see that they'd recovered a Cyberman, and to learn that Flotsam and Jetsam reprogrammed them to sell on as butlers.

The Cyberman reactivated and took Jetsam to the planet A54 in the Arcturian System, where a great Cybernaut fleet had crashed. They quickly discovered Zogron, the deactivated leader, and Jetsam reprogrammed

him... as a butler. The Doctor and Flotsam arrived in the *Drifter* and immobilised the Cyberman with a polymer spray.

c 2485 - "Junkyard Demon II"[708] -> Joylove McShane of Joylove Antiques arrived on A54 wanting to buy Flotsam and Jetsam out, and set his henchman Stinker on them when they refused. Joylove was a gunrunner working for the Brotherhood of Logicians, and he wanted the army of Cybermen. The fourth Doctor arrived and destroyed the Cyber Army, but Flotsam and Jetsam discovered a supply of Cybermats to keep them busy. Joylove escaped... but a surviving Cyberman went with him.

c 2486 - LEVIATHAN[709] -> The clones aboard the Leviathan carrying the Sentinels of the New Dawn had spent their whole lives in a Middle Ages setting – a template of the society the Sentinels hoped to establish on the planet Felgathon. A meteor storm struck the Leviathan as it was less than fifty light years from its destination, and the sleeping Sentinels were all killed. The sixth Doctor and Peri visited the Leviathan as human salvagers overrode the ship's Zeron computer system, and attempted to have all the clones recycled. The Doctor thwarted the salvagers and arranged for the clones to be relocated to safety.

---

707 Dating "Junkyard Demon" (*DWM* #58-59) - No date is specified, and it's hard to place it with any certainty because we don't know how long the Cybernauts have been deactivated on A54. The sequel, however, places it in the same period as *The Tomb of the Cybermen*. The Cyberman resembles – with modifications – the ones from *The Tenth Planet*, and says they will "once again rule time and space". Zogron is "one of the pioneers of our interstellar empire". A54 orbits Arcturus.

708 Dating "Junkyard Demon II" (*DWM Yearbook 1996*) - It's "four months" since "Junkyard Demon". Joylove is working for Eric Klieg and the Brotherhood of Logicians, setting this story shortly before *The Tomb of the Cybermen*.

709 Dating *Leviathan* (BF LS #1.3) - One of the salvagers says that it's now the twenty-fifth century. The *Leviathan* left Earth in the twenty-second century and was to spend some "centuries" in transit.

710 Dating *The Tomb of the Cybermen* (5.1) - The story is set "five hundred years" after the Cybermen mysteriously died out according to Parry, although the Cybermen don't indicate how long they've been in their tombs. No reference is made to the Cyber War [q.v.], so we might presume it is before that time (the disappearance of the Cybermen after the Cyber War wasn't a mystery). The Cybermen's history computer recognises the Doctor from "the lunar surface", so the Cybermen went into hibernation (shortly?) after The

Moonbase. This would make it at least 2570, but we know that *Earthshock* is set in 2526. The Cybermen in *Earthshock* refer to the events of *The Tomb of the Cybermen*, so *The Tomb of the Cybermen* must be set before 2526 (although they also refer to *Revenge of the Cybermen*, which there's reason to believe is set later). Either Parry is rounding up or he doesn't know about the events of *The Moonbase*. As ever, no-one refers to stories made after this one, such as *Silver Nemesis* and *The Wheel in Space*.

Another option is that the Cybermen in *Earthshock* are time travellers. There's some circumstantial evidence for this – it explains how their scanner can show a scene from *Revenge of the Cybermen*, which is almost certainly set after 2526, and it may go some way to explaining how the freighter travels in time at the end – but there's nothing in the script that supports this, and if they have a time machine capable of transporting a huge army of Cybermen, then it's hard to believe that the best plan they can come up with is the one that they're implementing. Then again, even without a time machine, their plan makes no apparent sense.

Radio Times didn't give a year for *Tomb*, but specified that the month the story is set is "September". The draft script for serial 4D (at that point called *Return of the Cybermen*), suggested a date of "24/10/2248" for the story. *Cybermen* sets the story in "2486", *The Terrestrial Index* at "the beginning of the 26th century". "A History

The Expedition to Telos

c 2486 (September) - THE TOMB OF THE CYBERMEN[710] **/ RETURN TO TELOS**[711] **->** Eric Klieg and Kaftan, two members of the Brotherhood of Logicians, usurped control of an expedition mounted to unearth the Tombs of the Cybermen on Telos. The Cybermen were revived and planned to emerge into the universe, but were re-frozen by the second Doctor, Jamie and Victoria. Klieg and Kaftan were killed, and the CyberController was badly electrocuted and thought dead.

The currency at this time appears to have been the pound. Individuals and organizations could charter spacecraft.

> (=) While exploring the tomb on Telos, Jamie's tartan became infected with dormant Cyber-particles – a development that caused a resurgence of Cybermen two centuries later, on the planet Krelos. The fourth Doctor and Leela cleansed Jamie using a particulate vacuum cleaner, nullifying those events.

The CyberController was not destroyed, but merely damaged. He went on to build a new Cyber-Race.[712]

By the end of the twenty-fifth century, a museum was dedicated to the Beatles in Liverpool. Clothes were self-cleaning, dirt repelling and non-creasing. Ten-year-olds took a certificate of education in physics, medicine, chemistry and computer science using learning machines for an hour a week. There was evidence that humanity now had some familiarity with temporal theory – even children knew Venderman's Law: "Mass is absorbed by light, therefore light has mass and energy. The energy radiated by a light neutron is equal to the energy of the mass it absorbs".[713]

Vicki (Pallister)

Vicki Pallister, a companion of the first Doctor, was born in New London on Earth around 2480. She lived in Liddell Towers. Vicki's mother died when she was 11. After that, she and her father left Earth for a new life on space colony Astra.[714] She was inoculated using a laser injector when she was five, and owned a pony called Saracen.[715]

Machines enabled swifter learning in Vicki's time – students had to study about an hour a week. By the time she was ten, Vicki had taken a certificate of education in medicine, physics and chemistry. Aspirin was not in common use.[716] Vicki spent an hour a week on her astronomy lessons.[717] Vicki had medical skills.[718]

In Vicki's time, St Paul's was still standing, having survived four world wars "and an alien invasion".[719] Food was designed to be nutritious, not tasty. Pandas were extinct, and museums used holograms. Vicki's father, Lieutenant Commander Pallister, had basic paramedic training for his intended job on Astra.[720]

Cancer was a thing of the past by Vicki's time.[721] Spaceships in Vicki's era tended to operate with half gravity. There was no record of life on Ceres.[722]

2487 - JUDGEMENT OF THE JUDOON[723] **->** The planet New Memphis opened Terminal 13, hoping to expand its service of hyperspace vessels. Conflict escalated between criminal organisations respectively led by "Widow" and "Uncle", but the tenth Doctor and the Judoon stopped an effort to destroy Terminal 13 as part of an insurance scam. Uncle and Widow both died owing to a virus, the Invisible Assassin, that Uncle had tailored to Widow's DNA – he had failed to realise that she was secretly his daughter, and that the virus would affect him also.

Kronkburgers were served in the New Memphis settlement.

---

of the Cybermen" in *DWM* #83 preferred "2431", whereas *The Discontinuity Guide* settles on "2570". *Timelink* says "2526", *About Time* "early 2500s". The Cyber Tombs entry in *A History of the Universe in 100 Objects* (p195) is dated to "circa 25th century".

711 Dating *Return to Telos* (BF 4th Doc #4.8) - The action here is injected into *The Tomb of the Cybermen* episode one, starting when Jamie and Haydon break away from the main group, and ending when they enter the targeting room.

712 *Attack of the Cybermen*

713 This is the native time of the first Doctor's companion Vicki, who joins the TARDIS in *The Rescue*. We learn about her clothing and schooling in *The Web Planet,* and her visit to the Beatles Museum and familiarity with Venderman in *The Chase.* In that story we also learn that Vicki used to live close to a medieval castle.

714 *Byzantium!*

715 *The Plotters*

716 *The Web Planet*

717 *1stD V1: The Founding Fathers*

718 *1stD V2: Fields of Terror*, although it's not a talent she reliably uses on screen.

719 *Frostfire.* The "alien invasion" presumably refers to the Dalek invasion of the twenty-second century.

720 *Starborn*

721 *The Bounty of Ceres*

722 *The Eleventh Tiger*

723 Dating *Judgement of the Judoon* (NSA #31) - The year is given. A couple of Draconians are seen at Terminal 13, even though "first contact" (at least, officially) between Earth and Draconia doesn't happen until around 2520 (*Frontier in Space*).

The Interplanetary Mining Corporation established Unit 426, a colony equipped with oxygen gardens in orbit around Saturn, to aid and supply its first hydrogen mine there.[724]

The Conglomerate

? 2490 - THE SANDS OF LIFE / WAR AGAINST THE LAAN[725] -> The Conglomerate had emerged as the most powerful company in the Milky Way – it supplied hardware and weaponry for Earth's military forces, and held the exclusive contract for the Earth government's IT. Its CEO, Cuthbert, was known throughout fifty-nine civilised star systems. The Conglomerate stood on the cusp of total brand domination, and diverted resources to ease such disasters as the Baltic famine, the Silesian floods and the American financial collapse. Cuthbert boasted that his

company had saved billions of lives by helping to prevent a thousand worlds from starving,[726] assisting Earth's government in overcoming an energy deficit, and quelling discontent populations. The Conglomerate had also initiated the British Badger Extermination Programme, following the discovery that badgers carried a genetically mutated form of tuberculosis.

The public elected a protest candidate, Sheridan Walker, as the 15th President of Earth to keep the Conglomerate's power and influence in check. Walker was the first nonaligned person to win the office.

Cuthbert directed the Conglomerate staff aboard the space platform *Fortune* to conduct temporal experiments on a quantum fissure in the Proxima IV System, but the undertaking accidentally disorientated a herd of manatee-like Laan. This migratory species lived in the Vortex, emerging into reality to give birth on a sandy planet. A

724 The IMC armoury attached to the gardens has gone unused for "twenty years or more" (p88) before *The Taking of Chelsea 426*, so it's been at least that long since the oxygen gardens were established.

725 Dating *The Sands of Life/War Against the Laan* (BF 4th Doc #2.2-2.3) - It's Earth, the future. The most tangible dating clue is that Sheridan Winter (credited as "Sheridan Moorkurk") is here elected the 15th President of Earth - a position first seen in *Frontier in Space* [c.2540]. There's no clue as to where Winter's term falls in relation to the other Presidents (see the Presidents of Earth sidebar), nor is she the female President of Earth seen in *Frontier in Space* - they're played by different actresses, and there's no sense on either occasion that the President and the Doctor have met before.

Presuming the Earth presidents have terms roughly equivalent to the UK prime ministers and US presidents of today (as *Benny: Down* indicates), *The Sands of Life, War Against the Laan* and the two related stories to follow (*The Dalek Contract/The Final Phase*) have to occur in either the twenty-fifth or twenty-sixth centuries. The Doctor hasn't visited this era since he "last wore a frilly shirt" – possibly, but not necessarily, indicating the third Doctor's involvement in *Frontier in Space*.

We can establish an upper limit on this quartet of stories... the office of President of Earth was founded "seventy-five years" before Winter (*The Sands of Life*), so even if Levinson was the *first* such President, *The Sands of Life* et al cannot occur later than 2590. A placement later than the Dalek Wars commencing in 2545 can also be ruled out, as the Daleks would be so infamous during that time, Cuthbert would never sign a security contract with them (*The Dalek Contract*) – not for moral reasons, but because they'd be bad for business. Also, they'd unavoidably be referenced in *The Dalek Contract/The Final Phase* with much greater alarm.

Earth is currently enjoying prosperity and peace, so *The Sands of Life* et al doesn't coincide with any of the

major conflicts of this era (*Cyberman*, the Draconian War, the Cyber War, etc.). The Conglomerate is currently the most powerful interplanetary organization in the galaxy, but it never claims to be the *only* such group, so there's no evident conflict with the status of other corporations (IMC, for instance – see *Colony in Space*) operating in this period. There's no mention of the Earth Empire (the Conglomerate has instead furthered a "business empire").

Collectively, two options emerge for placing this block of stories...

1) In the twenty-sixth century, prior to the Earth Empire being founded, but after the Draconian and Cyber Wars - so, around 2530. The Conglomerate, in fact, could be responsible for helping humanity to get back on its feet after those conflicts (especially the havoc wrecked on Earth during *Cyberman*).

2) In the later part of the twenty-fifth century, or perhaps the early twenty-sixth. This would somewhat simplify matters (as there's no need to dodge around the likes of *Cyberman, Earthshock* and *Frontier in Space*). Perhaps tellingly, Winter states that her predecessors had experience with alien encounters, but she doesn't – meaning the public didn't value that as a quality in their head of state, which they likely would fresh after wars against the Cyberman and the Draconians.

726 *The Final Phase*

727 Dating *The Sleeping City* (BF CC #8.8) - Ian believes, rightly or wrongly, that the people of Hisk are human colonists who settled there in the twenty-fifth century, before Vicki left Earth. As such, he thinks that the people "won't be born for five hundred years" after his own time. Vicki recognizes the Limbus devices as akin to the teaching machines used in her native era, only "a bit bigger".

728 Dating "Assimilation 2" (IDW *Star Trek: The Next Generation/Doctor Who* mini-series) - "Twenty five years" after the fall of *Star Trek*'s Vulcan.

herd of seven and a half billion misdirected Laan damaged the *Fortune*, killing three hundred personnel, then burrowed under the Sahara. News reports stated that an alien species had infiltrated Earth, and at least three hundred women worldwide heard the Laan's telepathic song. The fourth Doctor and the first Romana helped to avert open violence between humanity and the Laan, and directed the Laan herd back into the Vortex.

c 2490 - THE SLEEPING CITY[727] -> The one million residents of the planet Hisk routinely entered into Limbus: a sleeping state in which their communing minds shared dreams, leading to a more giving society in the waking world. The collective consciousness that governed the Limbus process began targeting some of the populace as "unworthy" and manifested icons of doom, Harbingers, in Limbus to goad the downtrodden into committing suicide. The first Doctor used Ian and Barbara's unconditioned minds to purge the consciousness' influence.

> **(=) c 2493 - "Assimilation 2"**[728] -> The Cybermen defeated the Judoon, and converted them into shock troops.

Vicki Joins the TARDIS

c 2493 - THE RESCUE[729] -> There were emigrations to other planets. One such ship, the UK-201, crashed on Dido en route to Astra. This was a desert world, home of a peaceful humanoid race and lizard-like creatures known as sand beasts. The Didoans had a population of around one hundred, and had just perfected an energy ray that could be used as a building tool. A young girl named Vicki was one of only two survivors of the crash; her father was among the fatalities. When the TARDIS made a return visit to Dido, the first Doctor, Ian and Barbara exposed the other survivor, Bennett, as a murderer. Vicki joined them on their travels.

& 2494 - THE DALEK CONTRACT / THE FINAL PHASE[730] -> The Conglomerate's continued time experiments with the quantum fissure in the Proxima System, as conducted from the *Fortune II* space platform, had accidentally pushed the temperate Proxima Major out of orbit, making it unnaturally cold. The Daleks had been highly recommended to Cuthbert as a discrete and utterly reliable security force, and he signed a contract with them through second parties.

The fourth Doctor and the first Romana visited Proxima Major while investigating the spatio-temporal leakage caused by the Conglomerate's experiments. The Daleks had let Cuthbert widen the quantum fissure so they could dispatch Daleks to a myriad of realities, with the goal of conquering infinity. The fissure enabled Cuthbert to go back in time, and paradoxically bring about the Conglomerate's creation. The Doctor and Romana imploded the dimensional fissure, released a burst of Zuckodan's Haze that killed off the Daleks, and facilitated the return of Proxima Major to its natural orbit.

Boar-like aliens attacked human colonists in the Thynemnus System, causing disputes. The aliens were driven off, but the Valethske attacked the system soon after.[731] The interior of Tyler's Folly reshaped itself according to explorer Franz Kryptosa's conception of the "inner world" myths. He merged with the Pool of Life there.[732]

A super-volcano destroyed the Incorporated Nation of NeoCalifornia in the late twenty-fifth century, and so a consortium of entertainment businesses terraformed the planet Hollywood to serve as the centre of the movie industry in the Milky Way. The planet BollyWood was the next orbit over from Hollywood, as were some Celebra-Stations, where visitors could chase talentless android celebrities in safari parks. The tenth Doctor and Martha

---

729 Dating *The Rescue* (2.3) - Vicki states that the year her spaceship left Earth was "2493, of course". The draft script suggested that Vicki and her fellow space traveller, Bennett, have been on Dido "for a year", but there is no such indication in the final programme. Ian Marter's novelisation is set in 2501. *The Making of Doctor Who*, the various editions of Lofficier and *The Doctor Who File* set the date of "2493". *The TARDIS Special* "c.2500". Peel's novelisation of *The Chase* says that Vicki is from "the twenty-fourth century".

730 Dating *The Dalek Contract/The Final Phase* (BF 4th Doc #2.6-2.7) - Cuthbert has experienced "a long, hard struggle" to raise the Conglomerate's approval ratings after President Winters publicly scourged the company for its actions in the Laan affair (*The Sands of Life/War Against the Laan*). Winters is still president, so it hasn't been exceedingly long since then – we might approximate that it's been anywhere from three to eight years. Cuthbert has been trying to talk with the residents of Proxima Major about their world's climate change "for the last few years", but it's not specified where the planet's orbital shift occurred in relation to *The Sands of Life/War Against the Laan*. The Doctor says Earth coined the term hubris "centuries ago".

The locale of this story was repeatedly called "the Proxima IV System" in *The Sands of Time/War Against the Laan*, but is just the "Proxima System" here.

731 *Superior Beings*

732 About a century before *Benny: Down*.

visited Hollywood because she wanted to see a good Western, but when the cinema they planned to go to was closed, he took her to the real Wild West in the 1880s.[733]

c 2495 - SET PIECE[734] -> In the late twenty-fifth century, spaceships started disappearing from one of the less-used traffic lanes. A space vessel, designed to save a group of doomed colonists by directly uploading their memories, had outstripped its programming. It now sought to absorb the memories of every living being, and was using its robotic workers, the Ants, to kidnap people.

Five hundred and six people were taken from one such captured ship, the *Cortese*. The seventh Doctor, Ace and Bernice tried to intercede and were flung through time to ancient Egypt and nineteenth century France. They eventually brought about the Ship's destruction. Kadiatu Lethbridge-Stewart briefly became the Ship's thrall – she was liberated, but fell through a space-time rift. The Doctor would next meet her in 1754, near Sierra Leone.

Outbreak of the Orion War

Androids indistinguishable from humans were constructed in the Orion Sector. They became smart enough to demand equal rights and protest their mistreatment. This led to a conflict – the Orion War – against humanity. The androids settled in the Orion System, ordering the humans to accept android rule or leave.[735]

c 2495 - ATTACK OF THE CYBERMEN[736] -> The Cybermen faced total defeat. Thanks to Cryon guerillas and the Cybermen's failing hibernation equipment, they weren't even safe on Telos and planned to evacuate. They captured a three-man time machine that had landed on Telos, and used it to go to 1985 to prevent Mondas' destruction. The sixth Doctor and Peri were captured in 1985 and brought to Telos, where the Doctor destroyed the tombs and the CyberController. Lytton, a former Dalek operative now working for the oppressed Cryons, was killed.

& 2497 - THE PURSUIT OF HISTORY / CASUALTIES OF TIME[737] -> The Conglomerate would have a mixed impact on history – it was capable of philanthropy and compassion on the one hand, profit and extortion on the other. It would create healthcare and infrastructure that saved billions, but also exploited resources for profit.

Using its quantum gateway in the Proxima System, the Conglomerate sent its CEO, Cuthbert, back in time to facilitate the company's own creation. The gateway's time engine drew energy from a group of captive Laan – one of which escaped, materialised in the fourth Doctor's TARDIS and drew the second Romana to this era. The Doctor and K9 tracked Cuthbert through time, then returned with him as the Laan were nearly exhausted and the time engine was failing.

To guarantee the Conglomerate's place in history – and defeat the Black Guardian – avatars of the Doctor and

---

733 *Peacemaker*

734 Dating *Set Piece* (NA #35) - The Ants kidnap the Doctor, Benny and Ace in "the twenty-fifth century" (p33).

735 "Eight years" before *Sword of Orion*.

736 Dating *Attack of the Cybermen* (22.1) - No date is given on screen, but the story takes place after *The Tomb of the Cybermen* as the Controller remembers surviving that story. Although the Cybermen know of Lytton's people, and he is fully aware of the situation on Telos, it doesn't appear that *Resurrection of the Daleks* is set in this period... in that story, Stien says that the Daleks captured people from many different periods (while never really explaining why), so this could well be Lytton's native time (Lytton talks of humans as his "ancestors", so his home planet – Vita 15, in star system 690, with the satellite of Riftan V – is a human colony).

The previous edition of *Ahistory* dated *Attack* to circa 2530, but Big Finish's *Cyberman* mini-series (set circa 2515) occurs after an asteroid strike obliterates Telos an estimated five to ten years beforehand, and so *Attack* must take place prior to that point. There is little room to navigate around this, as the lead characters in *Cyberman* not only go to Telos' fragmented remains, they find its Cyberman-filled tomb floating about in

space. Strangely enough, *Attack* has no direct interaction between the Telos Cybermen and the Earth of the future, so it's entirely possible that the Telos Cybermen were re-frozen in *The Tomb of the Cybermen*, then awoke some years afterwards and upgraded themselves (and their electrocuted Controller), and then were re-entombed in *Attack* prior to Telos' annihilation.

Previous versions of *Ahistory* took into account Lytton's comment in *Attack* that the Cybermen are the "undisputed masters of space" (odd in itself, as *Attack* has them in an extremely weak position). However, er, no such comment actually appears in the TV story. Eric Saward's novelisation of *Attack* has Lytton tell Griffiths that the Cybermen are the "Undisputed masters of the galaxy!", but that's it. Sorry!

737 Dating *The Pursuit of History/Casualties of Time* (BF 4th Doc #5.7-5.8) - It's a sequel to *The Dalek Contract/ The Final Phase*, so the placement here is three years on, reflecting the real-world passage of time between the releases.

738 "Over a hundred years" before *Benny: Adorable Illusion* (ch24), so before Benny's birth and presumably during her time in the TARDIS.

739 At least ten years, if not more, before *The Taking of Chelsea 426* (p37).

Romana were made to power the time engine with their artron energy. The act of being copied killed the Doctor, but a Cerebus bird tucked away by the White Guardian restored him to life. No longer under the Black Guardian's influence, Cuthbert vowed to direct the Conglomerate along more benevolent lines.

Bernice Summerfield walked on Earth with a human, and instinctively flicked away a spider that landed on his shoulder.[738] In Earth's solar system, some humans who had been in cryo-freeze for centuries were revived, albeit with considerable brain damage. They were disparagingly called Cryogens, and most of them lived in nursing homes.[739]

The bloodthirsty Drexxons rampaged from planet to planet. They were defeated by the armies of the Combined Stellar Forces after a decade-long battle, and sealed inside a timeless Perpetuity Chamber which was hidden on the asteroid of Stanalan.[740]

The Twenty-Sixth Century

By the twenty-sixth century, interstellar travel had become a matter of routine. Fleets of spacecraft ranging from luxury liners to cargo freighters to battleships pushed further into deep space. Ships were built from durilium and had hyperdrives. The mind probe was commonly used to scan the minds of suspects, but it wasn't always reliable. Weapons of the time included hand blasters and neutronic missiles. This period saw the beginning of Earth's Empire.[741]

The warp drives of Earth ships were powered by anti-matter contained in stabilising vessels.[742] Space was divided into Sectors.[743] The currency was the Imperial.[744] It was likely around now that the Doctor gained a licence for the Mars-Venus rocket run.[745] *The Collected Works of Gustav Urnst* were published in June 2503, striking a chord with the bombastic people of the twenty-sixth century.[746]

Planetoid KS-159, the future home of the Braxiatel Collection, was once located within Draconian space. Even when it was outside their borders, the Draconians contested it under a caveat about war reparations.[747]

Genetic mutations in a variety of races gave rise to the Horofax Provosts: persecuted time-sensitives who sensed each other through the eras. The Provosts could alter other beings' perception of their own timelines, thereby brainwashing entire worlds into their service. Millions of human pioneers became enthralled as Horofax, but defeated their conditioning and slaughtered the Provosts. One of the survivors, Arianda, traversed time in a failed attempt to undo this defeat.[748]

In the twenty-sixth century, the galaxy did not experience a year that was free of war.[749]

2501 - THE MONSTERS INSIDE[750] **->** On the planetary system of Justicia, a penal colony of the Earth Empire, cruel guards oversaw construction of a set of pyramids. The ninth Doctor and Rose met two criminals from Raxacoricofallapatorius who planned to use gravity warps to convert the entire system into a weapon that could destroy planets. These were members of the Blathereen family. The Doctor teamed up with members of the Slitheen family to defeat them.

Kroton the Cyberman

? 2502 - "Throwback: The Soul of a Cyberman"[751] **->** The Cybermen invaded the planet Mondaran, and encountered heavy resistance. Cyberleader Tork requested reinforcements from Telos, which was six days away. These included Junior Cyberleader Kroton, who refused to kill a resistance cell. Kroton was developing emotions, and sided with the humans. Together, they stole a ship from the spaceport and retreated to the safety of the forest of Lorn. Kroton took the ship into orbit to prevent the humans

---

740 "Over seven hundred years" (p117) before *Death Riders*. The participants in this conflict are identified as being nonhuman.
741 *Frontier in Space*
742 *Earthshock*
743 *Colony in Space, Earthshock*. The freighter in *Earthshock* starts off in Sector 16, in "deep space".
744 *Warriors' Gate*
745 *Robot, The Janus Conjunction*. The Mars-Venus cruise is mentioned in *Frontier in Space*, although presumably such flights take place from the twenty-first century until the far future.
746 *The Highest Science* (p48).
747 "More than a century" before *Benny: Parallel Lives*.
748 *3rdA: Storm of the Horofax*, evidently during humankind's colonial phase. In the UNIT era, the third

Doctor judges a Horofax bomb as "several centuries" ahead of its time.
749 *Benny S8: The Judas Gift*. In fact, this century will see humanity in major conflicts with the Cyberman, the Draconians and the Daleks.
750 Dating *The Monsters Inside* (NSA #2) - Dennel tells Rose it is "2501". *Boom Town* refers to this story. *The Colony of Lies*, however, contradicts this book by suggesting a start date for the Earth Empire of circa 2534.
751 Dating "Throwback: The Soul of a Cyberman" (*DWW* #5-7) - No date is given. The story provides the impression of being set in the future of *The Tomb of the Cybermen*, as Telos is now serving as the Cybermen's strategic and military command centre, complete with a sprawling Cyberman city that has a monorail and space-field. This is very difficult to recon-

from being detected, but it was a one-way trip. When his batteries drained, he was left drifting in space.

Earth initiated the Sword of Orion project: an effort to obtain Cyber-technology left over from the Cyber incursions on Earth for use in the Orion War.[752]

2503 - SWORD OF ORION[753] **->** A derelict spaceship was discovered near the Garazone Central habitat. It was a Cybermen factory ship, and Earth High Command dispatched Deeva Jansen to recover the Cyber-technology aboard. Jansen, however, was actually an android trying to obtain the technology for the Orion androids. The eighth Doctor and Charley were present when the Cybermen aboard the spaceship revived in great numbers, but the Doctor defeated them. Jansen was swept into space with some Cybermen and presumably frozen.

The Destruction of Telos

Telos was destroyed in a random asteroid strike. The Cyber-vault there had been designed to survive the planet's break-up, and so floated in space amidst Telos' ruins, the Cybermen inside the vault still in cryo-sleep.[754]

c 2505 - KINGDOM OF SILVER[755] **->** On Tasak, the House of Argentia, under the command of Magus Riga, found a Cybermen tomb established some millennia ago. Argentia revolutionised medicine by reverse-engineering the Cyber-technology, including the development of a healing solution called Silver. In so doing, Argentia ended a devastating war with the rival House of Sarkota through benevolence, not force of arms.

As a conclave gathered to celebrate the war's conclusion, the seventh Doctor presented himself as "Dr Johannes Smither of the House of Gallifrey". The Doctor and Riga wiped out the revived Cybermen before they could send an activation signal that would awaken thousands of Cyber-tombs across the galaxy, but Riga was killed. Erin of the House of Sarkota gave up her birthright and pledged to work with the new Argentia Magus for peace. Afterward, the Doctor offered two androids that he'd met – Temeter and Sara – a lift back to the Orion Zone.

The Doctor claimed that Tasak had the best tea in its quadrant.

c 2505 - TO THE SLAUGHTER[756] **->** Earth had been abandoned to the poorer countries. Mercury had fallen into the Sun and Venus was a toxic waste dump. The Oort Cloud had been sold off and dismantled.

cile, however, against the comparatively shoddy state of the Cybermen seen in both *The Tomb of the Cybermen* and *Attack of the Cybermen*, and the evidence in the *Cybermen* audio series that Telos is destroyed perhaps eight years after *Attack* (which gives the Cybermen precious little time to recover from the setback in that story and to create the relatively formidable settlement seen in "Throwback"). If we're taking the design of the Cybermen into account, though, they most resemble the model seen in *The Invasion* or *Revenge of the Cybermen* (although with unique modifications, particularly their rank insignia), which again (via *Revenge*) fits a date around the twenty-sixth century.

752 The project is formally named in *Cyberman*, but such an undertaking was first seen in *Sword of Orion*.

753 Dating *Sword of Orion* (BF #17) - It's during the Orion War as featured in the *Cyberman* audios (also written, in part, by Nicholas Briggs), and "a very long time" after the Cyber Wars. The Doctor says the Cybermen are "safely tucked away in their tombs on Telos" (*The Tomb of the Cybermen*); humans assume the Cybermen are extinct. The only date given here is that the original Jansen died on "three zero zero five zero seven". However, *Neverland* gives a firm date of 2503.

754 "At least ten years" before *Cyberman* Series 1.

755 Dating *Kingdom of Silver* (BF #112a) - The story occurs during the Orion War. Both the Orion androids and the Earth military have dispatched agents to scour the galaxy to salvage Cyber-technology – as is the case in *Sword of Orion*, perhaps suggesting that *Kingdom of*

Silver happens about the same time. But in truth, *Kingdom of Silver* could occur at any pretty much point between here and *Cyberman*, set in 2515. The Tasak Cybermen here want to send out a reactivation signal to the thousands of dormant Cyber-tombs, somewhat contradicting *Cyberman*'s claim that the tomb on Telos was the "master vault" given the special status of sending out such a signal.

756 Dating *To the Slaughter* (EDA #72) - The dating of this story is inconsistent. It's "almost four hundred years" since 1938, according to Halcyon (p17, so before 2338), but Trix thinks it's "over five hundred years" since her time (p86, so after around 2503). The story is set before *Revenge of the Cybermen*, and explains why Jupiter only has twelve natural moons in that story. When *Revenge* was broadcast, astronomers thought Jupiter had twelve moons, but dozens more have been discovered in the years since, and Jupiter at present is known to have sixty-six (nineteen were discovered in 2003 alone; three more were discovered since the second edition of *Ahistory* saw print). Earth in this era has a President, the beginning of an Empire and there's a mention of the Draconians, supporting (strangely, perhaps) Trix over Halcyon.

757 "One hundred fourteen years" before *Benny B4: New Frontiers: The Curse of Fenman*. *Benny B4: New Frontiers: The Brimstone Kid* provides Bob's full name.

758 Enough time prior to *Benny: Parallel Lives*: "The Serpent's Tooth" that the Atwallans have lost their scientific know-how.

Falsh Industries demolished most of Jupiter's moons – using the designs of Aristotle Halcyon, a celebrity *decor-artiste* – as part of a redevelopment scheme to attract businesses to the solar system. The "Old Preservers", speaking on behalf of the Empire Trust, were opposed to this. Falsh himself was engaged in illicit weapons research. The eighth Doctor, Fitz and Trix uncovered his schemes and defeated him. Halcyon decided to use his talents to improve Earth.

Robert E. Lee Jefferson III Jr, a.k.a. Toothless Bob, became a resident in the rent-controlled Tranmere Building in Legion City.[757] The people of Atwalla 3 prevented a takeover by alien races by genetically engineering their women to inter-breed with other species. As more and more hybrids were born, the Atwallans found their own race was in danger of extinction. The Atwallan males wiped out the hybrids, and stripped their women of all rights.[758]

The human colony on Cantus was believed "lost"; in actuality, the Cybermen had cyber-converted all the adults there, and harvested the children's organs for use in Cybermats.[759] The Draconians committed war crimes during the reign of the thirty-fourth Emperor, and were later made to pay reparations.[760] After IMC closed its hydrogen mine on Saturn, Unit 426 was purchased and redeveloped by Powe-Luna Developments into a facsimile of a twentieth-century English market town. It was renamed Chelsea 426.[761]

Humanity built the Empire State: a single tower, named after the Empire State Building, that stretched from half a mile underground to the upper atmosphere on a desert moon that orbited six planets. It became a centre for trade and commerce, but around 2509, a misanthrope named Rand Goodwyn destabilised the State's generators and destroyed it.[762]

c 2509 (20th August) - THE TAKING OF CHELSEA 426[763] -> The Third Renaissance was about to commence. Some features of it, including the Theatre of Nomogan, the ceilings of the Chamber of Ra and the Simarine Orchestra,

would be talked about for centuries. Neptune had mining platforms.

The Oxygen Gardens of Chelsea 426 had become home to the Chelsea Flower Show. The top exhibit was the Blue Flower of Saturn, recently discovered in that planet's atmosphere. The tenth Doctor tried to attend the flower show, and found that the Blue Flower contained mind-controlling spores that the Rutans had seeded on Saturn five centuries previous. Compounding the situation, Colonel Sarg of the Fourth Sontaran Intelligence Division arrived with his shock troops, and demanded to search for enemies of Sontar. The Doctor contained the resulting battle and saved the humans on Chelsea 426. Sarg's Sontarans – not realising that they had been infiltrated by the Rutan spores – returned to Sontar.

Field Marshal Sir Henry Whittington-Smythe died as part of this conflict, and was given a full military funeral on Earth. He was a veteran of the Martian Wars, the Battle of Olympus Mons, the Battle of Mercutio 14 and the Siege of the Hexion Gates.

The Bantu Independence Group lost a war in 2511, and its position was greatly diminished.[764]

? 2511 - ARMY OF DEATH[765] -> Humans settled the frontier world of Draxine, and within ten generations had created the twin city-states of Stronghaven and Garrak. The Lifespan Project sought to extend human longevity, but President Carnex of Stronghaven discovered that it could transfer his mind into a psychic cloud. He wanted godhood by arranging Garrak's destruction with a bomb, and then, after the death of his physical form, animated the skeletons of Garrak's dead to attack Stronghaven. The eighth Doctor and Mary Shelley were present as Nia Bursk – a Garrak survivor – infused the psychic cloud with her own mind. She extinguished Carnex, then drove his skeleton army into the sea.

c 2514 - "Keepsake"[766] -> The androids Temeter and Sara were called before the Orion War Council to account for their failure to capture a Cybrid infiltrator and sabo-

759 "A hundred years" before *Benny* S6: *The Crystal of Cantus*, as implied by Jason Kane's narration.
760 "A century" prior to *Benny* S8: *Freedom of Information*. This seems to contradict *Shadowmind* (set in 2673), which occurs during the reign of the twenty-fourth Emperor – unless the numbering system was reset, for some reason.
761 The timeframe is a little unclear, but it's repeatedly said that Jake and Vienna Carstairs – children belonging to the family in charge of Chelsea 426 – relocate there from Earth "two years" before *The Taking of Chelsea 426*.

762 *Benny* S7: *The Empire State*
763 Dating *The Taking of Chelsea 426* (NSA #34) - The Doctor says it is "the beginning of the twenty-sixth century" (p54), roughly "five hundred years" (p37) after the twenty-first century. The day is given (p8).
764 *Benny: Another Girl, Another Planet*
765 Dating *Army of Death* (BF #155) - The humans on Draxine are "tenth generation" settlers, which has a ring to it of their originating from Earth in the third millennium.
766 Dating "Keepsake" (BF #112b) - The Orion War is still ongoing, and although the Orion androids still

teur, Corvus, who arranged the deaths of hundreds of androids. The Council judged that Temeter and Sara's feelings for one another had hampered their effectiveness. Temeter was returned to active duty after his emotional connection to Sara was deleted from his core consciousness. Sara was deemed less fit for service, so her consciousness was deleted and replaced by another operative. What remained of Sara's persona was redeployed in a servo robot with Grade 3 intelligence.

? 2514 - ROYAL BLOOD[767] -> The twelfth Doctor and Clara found themselves in Varuz, a city-state in decline as its energy-draining technology had weakened its lands. Duke Conrad had conquered the rest of the planet, and – with summer coming – looked to make his power absolute by adding Varuz to his kingdom. To the Doctor and Clara's surprise, Sir Lancelot arrived, with thirty knights, in search of the Holy Grail. The Doctor exposed Lancelot as an

aspect of the morphing Glamour, causing it to disappear. Conrad took control of Varuz, and it was expected that under his reign, the city would regain its vigor.

Dr Oleg Mikelz located the Oracle of the Lost on planetoid KS-159. The Oracle had tired of its servile existence, and attempted to trick Mikelz into destroying it – but its ambiguous statements instead drove Mikelz to kill his wife, his personal assistant and finally himself. Edward Watkinson, the finest archaeologist of his age and Mikelz's good friend, became infected with a mental parasite on the planet Paracletes. On September 11, 2515, Watkinson deduced the Oracle's involvement in Mikelz's murder-suicide and went to KS-159. Watkinson killed himself, causing the parasite to leap into the Oracle – which went inert to keep the creature contained.[768]

view Cyber-technology as a potential resource, there's no mention of the Cybermen having overrun Earth or encroaching into Orion territory (as occurs in *Cyberman*). Writer James Swallow intended *Keepsake* as a prelude to *Cyberman 2*, which is set in 2515.

767 Dating *Royal Blood* (NSA #58) - Date unknown, but it's after the time of the Arthurian legends. The "future" portions of *Deep Time*, dated in this guidebook to circa 2900, seem to represent the latest point the Glamour is active in the universe.

768 *Benny: Tears of the Oracle*

769 Dating *Cyberman* Series 1 and 2 (BF mini-series) - The evidence is abundant, but placement requires juggling *Cyberman* in relation to other stories.

Telos has been fragmented for as much as ten years, so it's at least that long since *Attack of the Cybermen*. Likewise, events in *Sword of Orion* (set in 2503) lead into these audio series. Samantha isn't surprised that Barnaby – one of the highest-ranking officers in Earth's military – has never heard of the Cybermen (though a couple of minor characters in *Cyberman 2* have heard vague rumours about them), so it's definitely before the Cyber War and Earth's involvement in the alliance against the Cybermen in *Earthshock* (set in 2526). There's no mention of the Draconians, so *Cyberman* almost certainly happens before the Draconian War occurs circa 2520.

Brett's victory against the Android Eighth Fleet is said to make the public on Earth the happiest it's been "in twenty years". If this denotes the current duration of the Orion War (said to start in 2495, according to statements made in *Sword of Orion* and *Neverland*), *Cyberman* Series 1 by logical extension would occur around 2515. It's repeatedly said that Series 2 opens "six months" after that, and the remainder of the story seems to take a few days, or at most a few weeks.

Presumably, the Cybermen's retreat into space – and

the survivors on Earth becoming all-too-horrifyingly aware of the Cybermen's existence – is the event that seeds humanity's future conflicts with the Cybermen, i.e. both the proposed alliance against the Cybermen in *Earthshock* and the Cyber War itself. In fact, the final installment of *Cyberman 2* entails the emergence of a "more advanced design of Cybermen" that's been made from "harvested human materials", which – although we can't *see* the Cybermen in question for confirmation – is probably meant to denote the *Earthshock*-style models. (Even so, this doesn't expressly rule out the sometimes-floated theory – not adopted by this chronology – that the Cybermen in *Earthshock* are time travellers.) Given the need to place *Attack of the Cybermen* before Telos' destruction, it's possible that the "more advanced" models in the mini-series are an improvement of the eminently killable versions first developed on Telos and seen in *Attack*.

Earth's current political structure bears some similarities to that in *Frontier in Space*, set in 2540: there's a global Senate, and in *Cyberman 2: Extinction*, Hunt is referred to as the "executive-in-chief of the Earth Empire". A feature of *Cyberman* that isn't mentioned in *Frontier in Space* is that the Earth president is based in the White House – either the current building in Washington, D.C., or one of the same name. It's entirely possible that in the interim between *Cyberman* and *Frontier in Space*, the White House was discontinued as the chief executive's residence – possibly to get a fresh start after Hunt's disastrous tenure, or possibly to eliminate the stigma of President Levison having been assassinated there.

770 *Cyberman 2: Machines*
771 The background detail to *Cyberman* Series 1.
772 *Cyberman 2: Terror*
773 *Cyberman 2: Outsiders*
774 *Cyberman 2: Terror*

Cyberman Series 1 and 2[769]

Earth's Leadership Infiltrated by Cybermen

On Earth, as the Orion War took a turn for the worse, the predecessor of President Levinson founded the Scorpius Project to make use of Cyber-technology developed from the failed Sword of Orion initiative. The Cybermen usurped Scorpius to their own ends, and manipulated Levinson into officially terminating it. Scorpius proceeded in secret; Paul Hunt, an advisor to the project, was converted into a Cybrid – a Cyber-operative who could pass as human[770] – and vanished from the public record. The Cybermen made plans to replace Levinson with a president more agreeable to using Scorpius as they desired.[771]

At this time, Article 7 of the Earth spacefleet charter allowed three officers of senior rank to remove a captain from command decisions.[772] Article 92, sub-section 3, paragraph 4 – which hadn't been used in years – allowed for those of command rank to conscript civilian vessels for military use. The Navy, now part of Earth's Spacefleet, was equipped with proton rifles. Mark 4 fusion cores – part of a spaceship's drive systems – were a bit out of date, and Mark 6 cores were available. Earth's dominions included the Vega colony.[773] The industrial heartland of the British North was currently a bunch of ruined factories. The soil there was so laced with cadmium, even nanosheets couldn't strip it out.[774]

c 2515 - CYBERMAN SERIES 1 -> The Orion War continued to go against humanity. Earth's Planetary Assault Force Delta on Orius Beta VIII walked straight into an ambush, and although Admiral Karen Brett of the *Redoubtable* led a counter-assault that destroyed the Android Eighth Fleet – which was hiding just off Orius Beta V – human casualties still numbered fifty thousand. Orius Beta VIII was nuked. The victory, however technical, surged morale on Earth to its highest point in twenty years.

Brett was promoted to Commander-in-Chief of Earth's forces. Paul Hunt secretly met with Brett on Reticek IV, and explained to her the potential that Scorpius offered. Soon after, the Cybermen arranged for a shuttle to crash into the White House – President Levinson was assassinated, and his killers teleported away. The Senate invoked emergency powers and made Brett president. She appointed her old friend, Captain Liam Barnaby, as Commander-in-Chief.

Several months passed, with humanity suffering further defeats. The androids destroyed the Dracian VIII colony's reactor, causing massive casualties. They also killed millions, including Brett's parents, in the undefended Vaslovian System.

Brett increasingly underwent Cyber-hypnosis and conversion, and Hunt became a presidential advisor. Earth was flooded with refugees from the Orion conflict; many of these wound up at a camp on the Isle of Wight, and were then transported off-world for conversion. The fresh Cyber-troops made incursions into Orion territory, and destroyed the android tracking station Beta-4.

Commander Barnaby became politically ostracised from Brett, and increasingly heard rumours concerning Scorpius. He allied himself with Samantha Thorn – an android secret agent who for years had been Paul Hunt's lover. Assisted by androids aboard the Orion flagship *Antares*, they discovered a map of the galaxy identifying a thousand planets with Cyber-hibernation vaults. They realised that if an activation signal were sent from the master vault on Telos, billions of Cybermen would awaken, spelling the end for humanity and androids alike. The *Antares* immediately left for Telos to prevent this.

The Cyber-Planner running Scorpius advanced its master plan. Brett revealed the existence of Scorpius to Earth, claiming that "volunteers" augmented with cyber-tech had destroyed key android installations. Cybernetic commando units were stationed in all of Earth's major population centres, purportedly to protect the public from retribution by the androids. Worldwide martial law was declared. Brett announced that she would personally lead the final assault against the androids – but in actuality, she underwent full Cyber-conversion, and left with a Cyber-task force aboard an advanced XP-900 warship to intercept the *Antares*. In her absence, Hunt became emergency executive-in-chief.

Barnaby's group found that the Cyber-vault on Telos had survived the planet's break-up, and a dogfight between the *Antares* and the XP-900 resulted in the *Antares* colliding with the vault. A thousand Cybermen space-walked from the XP-900 and wiped out the *Antares* crew save for Barnaby and Thorn. The two of them raised the fuel rods in the Cyber-vault's reactor, saturating the area with radiation that killed the XP-900 Cybermen, the entombed Cybermen and Brett.

The Orion War Ends; Humanity, the Orion Androids Unite Against the Cybermen

c 2516 - CYBERMAN SERIES 2 -> Six months passed as Barnaby and Thorn laboured to keep the *Antares'* damaged systems running, and the ship limped through space. Back on Earth, Brett was formally declared dead. Hunt became executive-in-chief in her place, extended his term indefinitely and continued martial law. To quell dissent, he engineered several "retirements" of senior officials. He also had Barnaby convicted in absentia of treason and given a death sentence.

The Cybermen continued efforts to turn Earth into a new Mondas, and staged a number of mass abductions – fodder for Cyber-conversion – in cities such as Lyons and

Kiev. Hunt released a number of cover stories, declaring various cities as off-bounds. An eruption was said to have occurred in Hawaii. Bombings were cited across Greater Britannica. Bergen, Norway, was completely emptied, supposedly due to biotoxins that a resistance movement put into the city's water supply. Eurozone News reported flooding in Birmingham, and that the Stafford metroplex had an emergency curfew. Meanwhile, a resistance movement to Hunt's rule began striking back, staging demonstrations in a dozen cities that included Moscow, Tokyo, New York City, Mumbai and the Canberra Arcology. Cybermen based in Nevada and the Sudan were targeted.

Thorn discovered that the Orion war council, fearful of the Cybermen on Earth, had authorised use of an Eclipse-Class device: a fusion initiator that would make Earth's sun release an intense solar shockwave. This would kill all organic life, human and Cyberman alike, within orbit of Mars.

Hunt underwent full Cyber-conversion as Barnaby and Thorn directed their attention toward the main Cyber-facility at Bergen. Thorn interfaced her positronic mind with the Cyber-network hub there, and convinced the Cyber-Planner that the Cybermen's campaign to conquer Earth would result in millions of Cyber-casualties and the complete obliteration of humanity and the Orion androids. The Cyber-Planner judged the cost of victory as too great, and ordered the Cybermen to leave Earth in fleet vessels. The strain of communing with the Cybermen killed Thorn. She was buried on the Norway coast.

The androids opted to live in peace with humanity, ending the Orion War. In deep space, an android warfleet engaged the Cyber-vessels before they could enter hyper-drive.

The twenty-sixth century saw the Great Orion Cyber Wars.[775]

? 2515 - PARASITE[776] **->** Three hundred and sixty-seven years after it had been colonised, the Elysium System was on the brink of civil war. Over the last fifty years, a schism had developed between the Founding Families (who wanted to remain isolated from Earth and maintain their own distinctive political system) and the Reunionists (who wanted to make contact with the Empire).

Before the situation could be resolved, the Artifact was found to be a vast transdimensional living entity. It could warp space to create water worlds that would collapse into stars, then generate gas giants to incubate its planet-sized eggs. The seventh Doctor, Benny and Ace visited the Artifact during a crucial point in its life-cycle – which threatened to accelerate. As each young Artifact required the water from forty or fifty thousand planets, this posed a threat to the entire universe. The Doctor altered the Artifact's biology so that it would only produce children with a symbiotic, not a parasitic, relationship with water-bearing worlds. Previously laid eggs would be born as parasites, and possibly threaten the Elysium System in several million years.

c 2515 - THE BLACK HOLE[777] **->** The second Doctor, Jamie and Victoria were drawn off course by an artificial black hole, which threatened the stability of a research habitat containing some twenty thousand humans and aliens. The Doctor's party assisted the Time Lord Pavo – a Constable of Chapter Nine – in stabilizing the black hole, but the effort destroyed Pavo's TARDIS. Pavo had orders to arrest or terminate the Doctor's old friend Dastari, but

---

775 *Real Time*, possibly denoting the Orion-Cyber conflict that breaks out at the end of *Cyberman 2*, and perhaps a prelude conflict to the greater Cyber War.

776 Dating *Parasite* (NA #33) - The dating of this story is problematic. Mark Bannen is the son of Alex Bannen, who died in *Lucifer Rising* "more than two centuries" ago (p165), so the story is set after 2357. 1706 "was more than seven hundred years ago" (p140), so it is after 2406. Mark Bannen was a baby during the Mexico riots of 2146 and has been kept alive by the Artifact since the founding of the colony "three hundred sixty-seven" years ago (p73), so the story must be set after 2513. This last date is supported in that Earth now has "Empire" (p136-137).

777 Dating *The Black Hole* (BF EDA #2.3) - The Monk says that two hundred years after this story takes place, the Earth Empire is much more militarised. On the Doctor and Jamie's side jaunt to the Third Zone, see the Season 6B sidebar.

778 Dating *Erimem: Churchill's Castle* (Erimem novel #7) - Erimem says she was born "almost four thousand

years ago in Egypt" (ch8), so it's probably about the twenty-sixth century. That fits with the broad details (mention of Earth Alliance, Earth's major cities being the same as today, etc.) suggesting it's earlier rather than later in humankind's colonisation of space.

779 Dating *The King of Sontar* (BF 4th Doc #3.1) - Dowcra's funding gets slashed because of the Earth-Draconian war, which happens "twenty years" prior to *Frontier in Space* [2540].

780 "One hundred years" before *Benny B5: Missing Persons: The Brimstone Kid*.

781 "Twenty years" before *Frontier in Space*. General Williams claims that his ship was "damaged and helpless" and well as "unarmed", but it managed to destroy a Draconian battlecruiser anyway. A scene cut from episode three explained that Williams used his "exhaust rockets" to destroy the other ship.

782 *Head Games* (p165-166).

783 *Love and War* (p10).

784 *Frontier in Space*

785 Forty years before *Prisoner of the Daleks*.

agreed to let the Doctor and Jamie use diplomacy instead. The Doctor and Jamie linked Pavo's Stattenheim Remote Control to the TARDIS, which synched its console room with the current Gallifreyan standard, and left Victoria to study graphology while they went to the Third Zone...

"Pavo" was actually the Monk, who had created the black hole as a conduit that the Seethe, a warrior race locked in their own pocket universe, could use to invade our reality and avert the Analogue Wars. The Monk thought he'd killed the real Pavo... but the Constable had regenerated into a female form, and become the habitat's commander, Melanie Flail. The Doctor and Jamie returned – after side-trips to places such as the City of Owls – as Dastari was busy with some Sontarans, and they thought it best to return later. They altered the Monk's TARDIS to generate a vortex that swept away the Seethe and the Monk himself. Pavo let the Doctor's party go in recognition of their good deeds... but covered her tracks by hypnotizing the Doctor, Jamie and Victoria into not remembering this adventure, and the two companions into forgetting the very term "Time Lords".

(=) c 2517 - ERIMEM: CHURCHILL'S CASTLE[778] -> Venus had cloud cities. Damatti pulse cannons were the most powerful weaponry humankind had developed. Nonetheless, without warning, alien spaceships overcame Earth's Planetary Defence Platforms and spacefleet, and laid waste to Earth's major cities. A time-travelling Erimem, Andy, Helena and Trina were aboard the cargo ship *Apex* as it fled to safety.

About three hundred thousand survivors made a rendezvous within the Beider Nebula aboard the space station *Castle*, and were protected by one last battleship: UKS *Churchill*. Erimem realised the Earth-destructors were the *Castle* inhabitants from the future, as mutated by two thousand years of exposure to the Nebula. To end the closed time-loop, Erimem convinced the assembled ship captains to detonate the *Castle*'s reactors and kill everyone aboard. Earth's timeline was restored.

---

c 2520 - THE KING OF SONTAR[779] -> Researchers at Dowcra Base undertook efforts to create teleportation portals, but the Earth Empire curtailed the project's funding during the Draconian War. The Sontaran Empire's cloning vats erroneously created General Strang: an entire platoon compressed into a single seven-foot-tall Sontaran, with no vulnerability at his probic vent. Strang captured Dowcra, and set about creation of vats from which to clone himself. He intended to destroy Sontar, then use Dowcra's portal technology to war against all species.

The Time Lords diverted the fourth Doctor and Leela to Dowcra, where they triggered explosive charges while

Strang was in a portal, scattering his remains throughout space. The Doctor intended to reprogram Strang's gestating clones to be more benign, but Leela – fearing that the Strang-clones would overrun many planets – defied his wishes and destroyed the cloning vats as well.

Diamond prospectors from such worlds as Brimstone, Scholl and Jahanum and more were among the earliest settlers of Legion. Some fortunes were made, but the area devolved into corruption and civil war. Many mines were equipped with lifeboats, out of concern that the planet was hollow and would collapse inward. The first mayor of Legion City – Golfax, elected when Toothless Bob was a boy – was elected to the post six months after his death. The Curzino Diamond mines on Legion were extremely prosperous, producing one out of three diamonds worn throughout the universe.[780]

The Draconian War

Around 2520, a peace mission between Draconia and Earth was arranged, but it ended in catastrophe when the Draconian ship approached, as was their tradition, with the missile ports open. The Draconian ship carried no missiles, but the humans assumed they had been lured into an ambush. A neutron storm prevented communications and the human ship destroyed the Draconian one. A war between Earth and Draconia started immediately, and although it didn't last long, millions died on both sides.[781]

As a result of a pop can that Bernice kicked onto a path in 2001, a less-elegant writer came to draft a crucial speech shortly before the outbreak of hostilities. The war consequently broke out an hour earlier, with dozens of extra casualties on both sides.[782]

During the Dragon Wars, Shirankha Hall's deep-space incursion squadron discovered a beautiful garden world halfway between human and Draconian Space. He named it Heaven.[783]

Although many on both sides wanted to see the war fought to its conclusion, diplomatic relations were forged and the war ended. The Frontier in Space was established, a dividing line which neither race's spacecraft could cross. Relations between the two planets remained wary, and factions on both Earth and Draconia wanted to wage a preemptive strike on the enemy. For twenty years, the galaxy existed in a state of cold war, although treaties and cultural exchanges were set up. Espionage between the powers was expressly forbidden.[784]

Arkheon was thought destroyed. It was known as Planet of the Ghosts, because it was the location of the Arkheon Threshold, a schism in time and space.[785] *Glory Under the*

Mud, a collection of Edward Watkinson's essays, was published in 2524.[786]

The Cyber War

Over five hundred years after Mondas' destruction, the Cybermen had been redesigned and were more deadly than ever.[787]

2526 - EARTHSHOCK[788] -> Earth was not directly affected, but it was clear that only the homeworld could provide the military resources needed to combat the Cyber threat. In 2526, a Conference was held on Earth that proposed that humanity should unite to fight the Cybermen. The fifth Doctor, Tegan, Nyssa and Adric stopped the Cybermen from detonating a bomb on Earth. The Cybermen then attempted to land an invasion force on Earth using a hijacked space-freighter. Adric was still aboard the freighter, trying to alter its coordinates, as the ship was thrown back to prehistoric times...

Shortly prior to his death, Adric pre-programmed the TARDIS to enter the next CVE it encountered.[789]

The Cybermen were unafraid of contravening galactic law or arms treaties, and were prepared to destroy entire planets using Cyberbombs. But the war against the Cybermen united many planets, and humanity started from a strong position. Earth was aware of the Cybermen's vulnerability to gold and developed the glittergun, a weapon that exploited this weakness. There was more gold on Voga than in the rest of the known galaxy, and when those vast reserves were used against the Cybermen, humanity inflicted massive defeats.[790] The glittergun was built by INITEC.[791]

Realising that they were beaten, the Cybermen launched an attack on Voga and detonated Cyberbombs that blew the planet out of orbit. The Vogans were forced into underground survival chambers. After this time, the Cybermen disappeared, and it was believed that they had died out.[792] The Cyber Fleet was destroyed. Bounty hunters and mercenaries hunted down the remaining Cybermen.[793]

---

786 *Benny: Walking to Babylon*, p173. *Benny: Tears of the Oracle* verifies that publication occurred posthumously, as Watkinson died in 2515.

787 Inferred from *The Tomb of the Cybermen*.

THE CYBER WARS: The "Cyber Wars" feature in much fan fiction and are referred to in a number of the books and audios. On television, though, the term "the Cyber War" is first used, by the Doctor, in *Revenge of the Cybermen* – everyone else refers to it simply as "the war".

We are told that this particular war took place "centuries" beforehand, and that the human race won when they discovered that Cybermen were vulnerable to gold and invented the "glittergun". Following their total defeat, the Cybermen launched a revenge attack on Voga, after which the Cybermen completely disappeared. The audio *Last of the Cybermen* positions itself as the final battle in this war, feeding into *Revenge of the Cybermen*.

From the on-screen information, it seems that we can precisely position the date of this "Cyber War": it can't be before 2486, because in *The Tomb of the Cybermen*, the Cyber Race is thought to have been extinct for five hundred years after Mondas' destruction. In that story, the Controller is ready to create a "new race" of Cybermen. We learn in *Attack of the Cybermen* that the Controller wasn't destroyed at the end of *The Tomb of the Cybermen*, so we might presume that this new race emerged soon afterwards and began its conquests. A new type of Cyberman – possibly the *Earthshock* models – is created in *Cyberman 2*.

Either way, the aforementioned conquests didn't directly involve Earth: in *Earthshock*, Scott, a member of the Earth military, hasn't heard of the Cybermen (even

though his planet is hosting a conference that the Cyber Leader says will unite many planets in a "war against the Cyber Race"). The Doctor observes that it is a war that the Cybermen "can't win". When the Cybermen's plan to blow up the conference is defeated (*Earthshock*), there is nothing to stop Earth from fighting this genocidal war against the Cybermen – and this is surely the "Cyber War" referred to in *Revenge of the Cybermen*. We might presume that the events of *Attack of the Cybermen* occur at the end of the War, when the Cybermen face defeat and are planning to evacuate Telos. The Cybermen are not mentioned in *Frontier in Space* (set in 2540), which could be inferred as meaning that the Cyber War has long been over by that time.

Before *Earthshock* was broadcast, *The Programme Guide* placed the Cyber "Wars" (note the plural) as "c.2300" (first edition) and "c.2400" (second edition). "A History of the Cybermen" (*DWM* #83) first suggested that the Cyber War took place immediately after *Earthshock*, post-2526. David Banks' *Cybermen* suggested that the Cyber Wars took place without any involvement with Earth around "2150 AD". *The Terrestrial Index* came to a messy compromise: The "First Cyber Wars" take place "as the twenty-third century began", when Voga is devastated. *Revenge of the Cybermen* takes place at the "tail end of the twenty-fifth century", then Voga's gold is *again* used after *Earthshock* to defeat the Cybermen in "the Second Cyber War".

Novels such as *Killing Ground* make it clear that the Cybermen menaced some early human colony worlds.

Nightmare in Silver takes place in the aftermath of, it's said, "the Cyberwars", but there's abundant pieces of evidence to say this happened in the far future, and

The Igris working the mines on the planetoid Sharnax rebelled against the mistreatment of their Drashani owners, who fled off world. Before long, twenty thousand Aegris were established there.[794] On Dellah, the Great Act of Toleration of 2528 recognised one thousand and thirty-six religions, including five hundred and twelve indigenous groups.[795] Mr Misnomer was a pulp-story hero of such adventures as *The Shadow of the Dying Ones* (2529).[796]

The Paris Psychology Unit closed when it came to light that some of its tutors and pupils had formed a secret society, the Brotherhood of Logicians, devoted to bringing about a future dictated by logic.[797] The Brotherhood of Logicians searched for the fabled Pyramid Eternia, but failed to find it.[798]

End of the Cyber War

c 2530 - LAST OF THE CYBERMEN[799] -> Humanity used Star Spitfires in the Cyber War, and inoculated its soldiers against the effects of Cyber-venom. The War had prompted the Brotherhood of Logicians to consider the benefits gained from humanity becoming closer to the Cybermen, and using the Cybermen for spare parts.

Telos remained one of the Cybermen's last strongholds, and came under siege, as the advent of the glittergun turned the tide of the war. The Super-Controller on Telos

– linked to operations throughout the crumbling Cyber Empire – abandoned hopes of conquering humanity. As a last-ditch effort, a fleet of ten thousand Cyberships was sent through a wormhole, with intent of locking onto a beacon – outwardly fashioned to look like a 500-foot-tall Cyber head – in the Kuiper Belt, and then eradicating humanity's homeworld. An electrical storm damaged the Cyber-Planner coordinating the Kuiper Belt base, and so the fleet remained trapped in warp space.

Owing to events ten years in the future, the Cyber-fleet was made to turn around in the wormhole and crash into Telos, marking the end of the Cyber War. The Super-Controller perished. Without its guiding influence, the surviving Cybermen were reduced to a few scavengers wandering about the galaxy.

Various micro-organisms in the human body became lost to science. In future, DNA modification would became so widespread, un-modified humans were a medical oddity.[800]

(=) c 2533 - "Assimilation 2"[801] -> Starfleet Academy in San Francisco served as Earth's final stronghold against the Borg-augmented Cybermen, but eventually fell. The last of humankind was converted into Cybermen.

isn't the same conflicts involved in *Revenge of the Cybermen* and *Earthshock* (see the dating notes on *Nightmare in Silver* for more).

788 Dating *Earthshock* (19.6) - The Doctor states that it is "the twenty-sixth century", Adric calculates that it is "2526 in the time scale you call Anno Domini". *The TARDIS Logs* set the story in "2500".

How the Cyber-scanner in *Earthshock* can show a clip from *Revenge of the Cybermen* remains a mystery, and causes problems with the dating of that story. The "real" reason is that the production team wanted to show the Cybermen facing as many previous Doctors as they could and didn't worry too much about continuity (in the same way that the Brigadier's flashback in *Mawdryn Undead* had the Brigadier "remembering" scenes he didn't witness). Equally, the Cyber-scanner doesn't show clips from *Attack of the Cybermen* or *Silver Nemesis*, the latter of which at least should appear.

"A History of the Cybermen" in *DWM* #83 suggested that the Scope tunes into the TARDIS telepathic circuits, which seems a little implausible. One fan, Michael Evans, has suggested that as there is no indication how long before *Attack of the Cybermen* the time machine crashed on Telos, it is perfectly possible that the Cybermen have had it since before *Earthshock* and used it to research their future before using it to alter history. This would certainly be a logical course of action. *About Time* suggests that the Cybermen themselves have travelled from the future. For other possible

explanations, see David Banks' *Cybermen* (p72, p79-80).
789 *Mistfall*; Adric charted a course home in *Earthshock*.
790 *Revenge of the Cybermen*
791 *Original Sin* (p287).
792 *Revenge of the Cybermen*. Stevenson claims that "the Cybermen died out centuries ago", the Doctor replies that "they disappeared after their attack on Voga at the end of the Cyber War".
793 *Real Time*
794 "A decade" before *The Burning Prince*.
795 *Benny: Where Angels Fear*
796 *Benny: Down*
797 The background to *Last of the Cybermen*; a member of the Brotherhood appeared in *The Tomb of the Cybermen*.
798 *Big Bang Generation* (ch3).
799 Dating *Last of the Cybermen* (BF #199) - It's the end of the Cyber War (see the Cyber War sidebar). The story serves to explain the Cybermen's reversal of fortunes between *The Invasion* and *Revenge of the Cybermen* [? 2875]. In the bonus interviews, writer Alan Barnes says this story was intended as "*The Evil of the Daleks* of the Cybermen", meaning it's touted as the Cybermen's "the final end", but isn't really.
800 "One thousand years" before *Prisoners of Fate*, according to Adric Traken's examination of Tegan.
801 Dating "Assimilation 2" (IDW *Star Trek: The Next Generation/Doctor Who* mini-series) - It's "forty years" since the Cybermen eliminated the Judoon.

The Christening of the Earth Empire

2534 - THE COLONY OF LIES[802] -> Matter transmitters were abandoned by this time, and there were strict laws on DNA manipulation. The Eurozone still existed. The human colonies were known as the Earth Federation, and were patrolled by Colony Support Vessels. Space was marked with navigation beacons. The term "Earth Empire" was used for the first time this year.

On Axista Four, the human colonists divided into conservative and technological-minded factions: the Loyalists and the Realists. The Realists set up their own settlement away from the Loyalist city of Plymouth Hope, but often raided the Loyalists for supplies.

By now, the Daleks were making gains in the third quadrant. Human space stations and colonies on the front line were evacuated. The Earth Federation had formed an alliance to try to prevent Dalek expansionism. About eighty thousand refugees were scheduled for relocation to Axista Four, and the Earth support vessel *Hannibal* entered orbit around the planet, responding to a signal for help from the Realist faction. The *Hannibal's* arrival triggered machinery that revived some Tyrenians from stasis, and they threatened to make warfare against the humans.

The second Doctor, accompanied by Jamie and Zoe, both revived Kirann Ransome from suspended animation and defused the conflict. The Realists and Loyalists agreed to accept Kirann as their mutual leader. The Doctor allowed the Federation to believe the Tyrenians were the survivors of a space plague, covering over their true history. Federation Administrator Greene agreed to let the Tyrenians live on Axista Four in peace.

Vega Station was built and secretly run by the Battrulian government. The fourth Doctor visited and lost a lot of money in the Station's casinos.[803] Jodecai Tyler founded a colony on a planet that became known as Tyler's Folly.[804]

c 2535 - MINDGAME / MINDGAME TRILOGY[805] -> The Sontaran-Rutan war continued on the "outer

---

802 Dating *The Colony of Lies* (PDA #61) - The book's internal dating is very confused. The back cover says it's 2539, and there's a tombstone (p23) which says that 2535 was "four years ago". Despite this, a native of this timezone says the date is 2534 (p147). Transmats are seen a number of times after this (in, for example, *The Ark in Space*) so it is clear that humanity readopts the technology.

803 *Demontage*. The fourth Doctor visited "soon after the place opened" (p6).

804 About sixty years before *Benny: Down*.

805 Dating *Mindgame* and *Mindgame Trilogy* (Reeltime Pictures films #4-5) - Date unknown, but it doesn't seem much of a stretch to suggest that the continuity-minded Terrance Dicks was thinking of the era of *Frontier in Space* when he wrote *Mindgame* – in which the Draconian Empire is mentioned, and the Draconian says that "the humans are not our allies". Also, twentieth century culture is topical enough for the mercenary (in *Mindgame Trilogy*) to mention James Dean and River Phoenix.

806 *Benny: Down*, and presumably a reference to the president seen in *Frontier in Space*.

807 *Benny: Down*

808 *Benny: A Life in Pieces*. Perfugium is the setting of *Master*.

809 *Benny; Beyond the Sun*. This is said to occur "before the Galactic War", i.e. the Dalek Wars.

810 Twenty years before *Prisoner of the Daleks*.

811 At least "eighty years" before *Benny B3: Legion: Everybody Loves Irving*, given when a fire extinguisher at one of the silos was last tested.

812 Dating *The Burning Prince* (BF #165) - Events here take place "thirty years" before *The Acheron Pulse*, the middle part of a trilogy that includes *The Burning Prince* and *The Shadow Heart*.

813 *The Acheron Pulse*

814 "Three generations" (p214) before *Benny: The Weather on Versimmon*.

815 Dating *Frontier in Space* (10.3) - The story takes place "somewhere in the twenty-sixth century" according to the Doctor. In the first scene, the freighter enters hyperspace at "22.09 72 2540 EST". This is probably nine minutes past ten at night on the 72nd day of 2540, although the President is later seen cancelling a meeting on "the tenth of January". The novelisation (also by Malcolm Hulke) gives the year as "2540", which *The Terrestrial Index* concurred with, although it misunderstood the relationship between Earth and Draconia at this time, suggesting that they are part of "the Alliance" [q.v.]. It isn't made clear whether the human military know of the Daleks before this story.

Dalek: The Astounding Untold History of the Greatest Enemies of the Universe (p215) mentions that at some point between the Daleks' failure in *Death to the Daleks* [?2600] and *Into the Dalek* [?6014], a renewed Dalek offensive causes the Draconian Empire to fall – not something that's reflected in any *Doctor Who* fiction.

PRESIDENTS OF EARTH: The first person to serve as "President of Earth", funnily enough, is the Doctor himself. At some point in the twenty-first century, Earth's governments privately agree that during a global crisis – say, an army of Daleks banging at the door, like a modern-day version of the Visigoths sacking ancient Rome – perhaps it'd be best to bushwhack the Doctor into serving as the chief executive of the entire planet, with full command of every standing military. To the twelfth Doctor's astonishment, UNIT practically hogties him into the position of President of Earth when Missy converts Earth's dead into Cybermen (*Death in Heaven*),

reaches of the universe". A representative of an advanced race teleported a human female mercenary, the commander of Draconian Brigade Merq (who had served in the Second Cryogenics Wars) and Field Major Sarg of the Sontaran First Assault Battalion into an asteroid located between dimensions, to determine which of their species was worthy of partnering with for conquest. The captives overpowered their abductor and separately departed. Sarg perished in battle, the Draconian was found guilty of sedition and sentenced to banishment to an outer moon of the Draconian Empire, and the mercenary killed herself when her fighter craft was damaged and her oxygen ran out.

Earth had a female president from 2536 to 2541.[806]

In the mid-2530s, KroyChem AgroMedical produced cancer-fighting drugs. Per the First Demographic Charter of 2537, the Spirea Consortia established concentration camps on Darvilleva-Q, and "processed" any colonist with less than 34% human lineage.[807]

The Earth Empire moved to incorporate the four planets of the Domus System, and warred against the human settlers there. Generosum, Perfugium and Salvum capitulated, and while Aequitas kept its independence, the Empire seized its moon, Verum. Decades of guerrilla fighting ensued.[808]

The Sunless – an ashen race of humanoids – lived below ground on a planet with a dying red sun. The Piercy Corporation stole technology from the Sunless homeworld, and relocated some clam-like reproductive units, the Blooms, to the planet Ursu. The Blooms propagated the eight races living there. Meanwhile, the Sunless copied the Piercy spaceships, left their homeworld and subjugated other worlds, searching for the Blooms.[809]

The spaceship *Wayfarer* was rescued from a scrap yard, and retrofitted for use as a naval patrol ship.[810] Launch silos were established near Legion City, to give the early settlers there a means of escape.[811]

c 2538 - THE BURNING PRINCE[812] -> The mad Emperor of the Drashani was deposed, triggering a war for the throne between House Sorsha and House Gadarel. Valdon Gadarel perished on the battlefield.

A few months later, a wedding was arranged between Valdron's daughter, Princess Aliona, and the son of Aldon Sorsha, Prince Kylo, to unite the two houses. A vengeful Aliona hoped to use the wedding to obtain Sorsha DNA – a means of calibrating a pulse cannon to wipe out her foes – but opponents to peace made her wedding gallery crash onto the planet Sharnax. The fifth Doctor, having left Tegan and Nyssa to enjoy the sights of Amsterdam, materialised aboard the starship *Lilanda* as it sought to rescue the princess. Prince Kylo and Aliona's uncle, Ambassador Tuvold, accompanied the group.

Aliona betrayed Kylo – she cut off his hand, stole his

genetic code and ejected him out an airlock. Her allies used the code to fire their pulse cannon and instantly kill all the Sorsha on Kylo's homeworld.

Tuvold murdered Aliona upon learning the depths of her inhumanity, and died himself after tasking the Doctor with delivering Aliona's royal carcanet to his daughter, Cheni. The public believed that Kylo and Aliona were star-crossed lovers who had valiantly died. A ceasefire was declared in their honour, and Cheni became Empress.

The sudden massacre of House Sorsha, and Cheni's resultant ascension to the throne, became known as the Succession of Blood. Prince Kylo survived on Sharnax by telekinetically slowing his descent, came to mentally commune with the Igris group mind, and psionically returned the displaced souls of the Igris on Sharnax back to their bodies. This augmented the Igris into the Wrath: formidable warriors driven by Kylo's goal of vengeance against the Drashani Empire. Kylo also crafted the Acheron Pulse: a psionic extension of the Wrath's suffering, which could dispatch other beings' souls and turn them into Igris.

Kylo renamed himself Lord Tenebris, and with the Wrath spent a quarter-century turning the remains of a mining colony on Sharnax into a space fleet. They finally left and spent five years making strikes into Drashani territory, drawing closer to Gadarel Prime.[813]

War between the planets Palastor and Sosostris in the Versimmion System led to the Palastorans making great biological advancements from Sosostrin discoveries. Fearing that the war would devastate their world, the Palastorans encoded their entire heritage into an ecosystem deployed onto the planet Versimmon (sic). The Archive Tree's existence as a living embodiment of Palastoran culture remained a secret when the war ended, and Palastor neglected to reclaim it.[814]

The Space War

The Master's Alliance with the Daleks

c 2540 - FRONTIER IN SPACE[815] -> At this point, Earth's "Empire" was still democratic, ruled by an elected President and Senate, although Earth Security forces also had political influence. The Bureau of Population Control strictly enforced the rule that couples could only have one child.

The Arctic areas were reclaimed. New Glasgow and New Montreal were the first of the sealed cities to be opened, and the Family Allowance was increased to two children for those who moved there. The Historical Monuments Preservation Society existed to protect Earth's heritage. While there was a healthy political opposition, any resistance to the principles of government by either anti-colonialists or pacifists was ruthlessly suppressed. Under the Special Security Act, a penal colony was set up on the moon to house thousands of political prisoners, each of whom served a life sentence with no possibility of parole or escape. In 2539, Professor Dale, one of the most prominent members of the Peace Party, was arrested and sent to the penal colony on Luna.

Larger colonies such as those in the Sirius System were given Dominion status, and allowed regional autonomy, including powers of taxation and extradition. Governors appointed directly by Earth ruled the smaller worlds.

In 2540, interplanetary tension mounted as human and Draconian spacecraft were subjected to mysterious attacks. Cargos were stolen and ships were destroyed. Each planet blamed the other, and eyewitnesses on both sides claimed to have seen their enemy. On Earth, war with the "Dragons" appeared to be inevitable.

On 12th March, Earth cargo ship C-982 was attacked only minutes from Earth at co-ordinates 8972-6483. The News Services monitored and broadcast their distress calls. Anti-Draconian riots flared up in Peking, Belgrade and Tokio. The Draconian consulate in Helsinki was burnt down, and in Los Angeles the President was burnt in effigy. When the C-982 docked at Spaceport Ten, Security discovered the third Doctor and Jo were on board. He resisted the mind probe, even on level 12, and was sent to the Lunar Penal Colony. He was convinced that a third party was trying to provoke war, a possibility that no one else had considered. A small ship under the command of General Williams was sent to the Ogron home planet at co-ordinates 3349-6784, where the true masterminds, the UNIT Master and the Daleks, were revealled.

After escaping the Ogron homeworld, the UNIT Master detected a discharge of energy from the twelfth Doctor's TARDIS, so went to 1973 to capitalise upon it.[816]

---

but he's more acquiescent when the UN Secretary-General asks him to again take up the post, when the Monks' Pyramid appears out of nowhere in Turmezistan (*The Pyramid at the End of the World*).

The public, as far as we can tell, never learns of the Doctor's appointment, nor that the office of "President of Earth" even exists. The twelfth Doctor's tenures as President appear to come and go with only the most politically-powerful knowing about it.

The elected President of Earth is first seen in *Frontier in Space* [2540] – we meet the female holder of the post ("Dora", the third Doctor affectionately calls her in *3rdA: The Transcendence of Ephros*), who shares power with "the full Earth Senate" and has to juggle social niceties such as potentially addressing the Historical Monuments Appreciation Society. It comes across as a power-sharing system rather than a fascist one.

The 15th President of Earth, Sheridan Walker, appears in *The Sands of Life/War Against the Laan* – by which point the office has existed for "some seventy-five years". Triangulating when those stories occur gets syrupy, but we settled upon "?2490" (see the Dating notes on *The Sands of Life* for our reasoning), which would mean the advent of the President of Earth circa 2415. *Benny: Down* suggests that Dora (surname unknown) served 2536-2541, possibly or possibly not suggesting five-year terms, and even then who knows if term limits are applicable.

The *Cyberman* audios [c.2515-2516], set between Walker and Dora's tenures, show the office in upheaval... the Cybermen arrange for President Levinson's assassination and replacement with their thrall, Karen Brett, then Brett dies after naming Paul Hunt "emergency executive in chief", then Hunt dies after undergoing full Cyber-conversion. A further brouhaha happens

2607, when a clone of Earth President Fiona Dickens becomes mentally unstable and throws herself to her death, whereupon a clone of Bernice Summerfield takes up the reins of President for a couple of years, until Samuel Frost murders her in 2609.

The office of President of Earth comes to an end "almost a century and a half" before *So Vile a Sin* [2982], when President Helen Kristiansen declares herself Empress and slaves her brain to the computer Centcomp, enabling an extended rule before the seventh Doctor euthanizes her. There's no recorded case of a President of Earth after that; in *The Daleks' Master Plan* [4000], Mavic Chen holds the title of "Guardian of the Solar System".

816 "Doorway to Hell"

817 Dating *Planet of the Daleks* (10.4) - The story is set at the same time as *Frontier in Space*. The *Terrestrial Index*, Nevertheless, the American *Doctor Who* comic dated this story as 1300 AD. It is "generations" after *The Daleks*.

818 *3rdA: The Conquest of Far*, amending the final scene of *Planet of the Daleks*.

819 *Asylum of the Daleks*

820 *Shadowmind* (p61).

821 *Love and War* (p10-11).

822 *Benny S7: The Summer of Love*

823 Dating *Graceless IV: The Ward* (*Graceless* #4.3) - No date given, but mention of "the Empire" sounds suspiciously like the Earth Empire from the third Doctor era. Writer Simon Guerrier conceded to us: "I took out a line specifically setting [*The Ward*] around the same period as *Frontier in Space* [2540], a story I adore."

Pool mentions that it's been "twenty thousand years and three times as many parsecs" since he last saw Abby and Zara in *Graceless IV: The Bomb* (dated in

The Frozen Dalek Army on Spiridon

& 2540 - PLANET OF THE DALEKS[817] **->** The third Doctor and Jo tracked the Daleks to the planet Spiridon in the ninth system, many systems from Skaro. Here, a group of six Thals – selected from the six-hundred strong division that hunted Daleks – were already investigating. They had discovered a research station where twelve Daleks were developing germ weapons, and also experimenting with an anti-reflective lightwave that rendered them invisible. The Doctor discovered an army of ten thousand Daleks in neutron-powered suspended animation beneath the research base. Supreme Command sent the Dalek Supreme to oversee the invasion of the Solar Planets, but the Doctor defeated them and froze the Dalek army with a mass of icy liquid from an "ice volcano".

After the Daleks' defeat on Spiridon, Jo requested that the Doctor take her home to Earth. Instead, the TARDIS embroiled them in a new Dalek conflict, in the future on the planet Far.[818] **At least one Dalek survived on Spiridon, and was taken to the Dalek Asylum.**[819]

The Doctor was remembered as a mediator between Earth and Draconia.[820] The Draconian Ambassador Ishkavaarr and the Earth President agreed that the planet Heaven should become an open world where both races would bury their dead. Years later, several interplanetary agreements were signed there by the President and the Draconian Emperor.[821] Irving Braxiatel was one of the signatories to the Treaty of Heaven.[822]

c 2540-2550 - GRACELESS IV: THE WARD[823] **->** Nanites were regarded as obsolete. Bespoke Function Grafting, a means of transplanting brain tissue to regain key skills, was still in development. Flat-pack cities were used on newly colonised worlds – Annie, one of the people who helped to install them, carved her name into the wall on the Techno Gothika on Flynn.

The revitalised Abby and Zara respectively posed as "Dr Mullos" and "Dr Pulminate" at Space Dock One. For a decade, their powers saved lives, giving Space Dock One the lowest incidence rate in its stellar group. Abby became involved with a medical student, Tarantine Chaff, and Zara with Dr Gutierezz. When those relationships ended, Chaff and Gutierezz became a couple. Abby and Zara arranged Gutierezz's death in a transporter accident, knowing that a grief-stricken Chaff would throw himself into his work, and curtail a virus outbreak throughout the galactic hub eighteen months later.

The so-called "golden age" of the autolit pulps reached a conclusion in the early 2540s, when the end of the cold war between Earth and its neighbours signalled the demise of humanity's pent-up sexual tensions, as funnelled through characters such as Mr Misnomer, Rex Havoc and Captain Carnivore.[824]

The Daleks were one of the greatest powers in the universe at this time.[825] At the end of the First Great Space War, Draconia entrusted Earth with documents detailing its history.[826] When word got out that the Ogrons had been defeated by an old man with white hair, the demand for their mercenary services collapsed. The Judoon picked up a lot of their contracts.[827]

The natives of Spiridon sought to conceal their world from further Dalek oppression. In the generations to follow, Spiridon was renamed Zaleria, and the natives made themselves visible by spreading cell-altering chemicals throughout their food supply.[828]

Bernice Summerfield

Bernice Surprise Summerfield was born on 21st June, 2540, on the human colony of Beta Caprisis. She was the daughter of Isaac Summerfield, a starship commander in Spacefleet, and his wife Claire.[829] Benny's dad used to say that if something was intractable, give it a swift thump.[830] Benny thought that the Healers were just a fairy story her dad told her.[831]

As a young girl, Bernice Summerfield watched and was inspired by the archaeology programme *Big Dig*. The Epoch forecast that Benny would one day visit the planet

---

Ahistory to &495,362). Guerrier, however, agrees that Pool could be speaking figuratively – or, given Pool's status as the embodiment of the Chaos Pool, it might have been twenty thousand years for *him*.

824 *Benny: Down*

825 According to the Doctor in *Death to the Daleks*.

826 "Cold-Blooded War!" The novelisation of *Frontier in Space* was called *The Space War*, and this is occasionally used by fans to refer to the events of both *Frontier in Space* and *Planet of the Daleks*. Presumably *this* battle is "the First Great Space War", not the conflict between Earth and Draconia twenty years earlier.

827 "Fugitive"

828 *Return of the Daleks*

829 BENNY'S BIRTHDAY: It is stated in *Love and War* (p46), in many later books and in the New Adventures Writers' Guide that Benny comes from "the twenty-fifth century". For a while, the writers worked on the assumption that she was from 2450 (e.g.: *The Highest Science* p34, *The Pit* p9). In *Falls the Shadow*, we learn that Benny was born in "2422" (p148). However, Paul Cornell's initial Character Guide had specified that she was born in "2472", which, as *Love and War* is set the day after Benny's thirtieth birthday, would make it 2502 (in the

Serevas, so created legends about its lost people to influence her younger self.[832]

c 2540 - LAST OF THE CYBERMEN[833] -> Half of Scotland was irradiated. Captain Frank, a veteran of the Cyber War, belonged to a posh family that owned the remainder. The second Doctor left Jamie and Zoe in the TARDIS to explore a dwarf planet in the Kuiper Belt. Curatrix Zennox of the Interplanetary War Museum – and secretly a member of the Brotherhood of Logicians – used Zoe's mind to restore the damaged Cyber-Planner, which re-activated the Cyber-beacon built to attract the Cyber-fleet trapped in warp space. The prodigy Findel died to make the Cyber-fleet reverse back down the wormhole.

> (=) The Monk forcibly exchanged the second and sixth Doctors, hoping to create a paradox in the Doctor's personal history. The plan failed, the two Doctors switched once more. As the timelines resettled, Jamie and Zoe forgot they had met the Doctor's older self.

A war between the Battrul and the lupine Canvine resulted in a draw, and a buffer zone was created between their territories. Vega Station was built as a casino and hotel, but the Battrulian government secretly used it to monitor the neutral zone.[834] The artist Menlove Stokes was born in 2542, according to official records.[835] Bernadette McAllerson discovered McAllerson's Radiation in 2542.[836] The Bantu Independence Group emerged as a purely commercial body, the Bantu Cooperative, in 2543.[837]

c 2545 - "Fugitive"[838] -> The Last Great Time War had left a power vacuum in the Stellian Galaxy, and it now been at war longer than living memory. A ceasefire was being negotiated in secret on Luna IV, and while the Sontarans favoured peace in the region so they could concentrate on their conflict with the Rutans, the Krillitane Empire wanted conflict so it could absorb the strengths of other races.

The Shadow Proclamation brought trumped-up charges of temporal interference against the tenth Doctor (owing to his having saved Emily Winter's life in 1926), as the

---

twenty-*sixth* century).

Causing further complications, *Love and War* is definitely set after *Frontier in Space* [2540]. In subsequent books there was confusion, with some novels claiming that Benny does indeed come from the "twenty-sixth century" (e.g. *Transit* p186; *Blood Heat* p3).

Latterly, so as not to contradict the television series, it has been decided that Benny is definitely from the twenty-sixth century. Benny explained that there are a number of calendars in use in the cosmopolitan galaxy of her time, and in our terms she is "from the late-twenty-sixth century" (*Just War*, p136) – this is intended to explain away some of the contradictions. Paul Cornell and Jim Sangster have astrologically determined Benny's birthday as 21st June, a date that first appeared in *Just War* (p135) and now appears on the Big Finish official biography on their website. Even so, she celebrates on 20th November in *The Dimension Riders*.

The few Benny solo adventures that reference her birth year tend to work from a dating of 2540, or reasonably close to it. She's 22 in *Benny: Old Friends*: "The Ship of Painted Shadows" (set in 2562), and the 2562 component of *Benny: The Sword of Forever*. In *Benny S9: The Adventure of the Diogenes Damsel*, Benny says that she was born "six hundred forty-seven years" after 1893 – so, again, she was born in 2540. *Benny: The Vampire Curse*: "Predating the Predators", which ends on "Saturday 24 June 2609", goes out of its way to reiterate Benny's birth as 21st June, 2540. (Benny, page 215: "If we go by the calendar and ignore the time-travel, I should be 68. Actually, hell – Wednesday would have been my 69th birthday. I must have been too wrapped up in

trivialities like not getting myself killed to notice.")

Benny: Genius Loci seems to make an honest mistake – the story occurs in 2561, but Benny has a birthday in the midst of it, so she should be 20 when she arrives on Jaiwan, and yet she's already 21 (p6). A bigger disparity is that *Benny S8: The Wake* (which ends in early 2608) has Benny telling Peter that she was born "seventy-one years ago" – which, even if she's not counting her upcoming birthday, at best adds up to 2538.

830 *Benny B3: Legion: Everybody Loves Irving*
831 *Benny B4: New Frontiers: HMS Surprise*
832 *Benny B5: Missing Persons: Big Dig*
833 Dating *Last of the Cybermen* (BF #199) - It's "ten Earth years" after the Cyber War's conclusion in the earlier part of the story. The Doctor tells Jamie that they can't call upon General Hermack and the Space Corps from *The Space Pirates* [? 2135] because it's the "wrong time zone". Jamie, presumably just guessing at the time involved, says his native era is "'a thousand years' away, a dozen lifetimes or more."

Certain details hint that it's not long after *The Tomb of the Cybermen*: Findel seems to treat the Brotherhood of Logicians, and the closing of the Paris Psychology Unit from which the Brotherhood originated, as a fairly recent development. Moreover, Findel – being a fairly young man – says he was "Class of 88" at the same institution, which isn't far from *Ahistory's* dating of *Tomb* to c 2486. However, it's hard to imagine the Cyber War commencing prior to *Sword of Orion*, the two *Cybermen* series and *Earthshock* (see the dating notes on those stories, as well as the Cyber War sidebar, for why). *Last of the Cybermen* also features Telos as an epicenter in the Cyber War, overlooking that the

Shadow Architect hoped that the trail would let the Doctor expose underground elements at work within the Proclamation. A mysterious woman named Advocate served as the Doctor's counsel, and was thought killed by the prosecutor: the Krillitane named Mr Finch. In truth, her older self had given "Finch" – actually a shapeshifting Gizou in her employ – a device that sent her younger self hurtling through time and space to the Last Great Time War, fulfilling on her own history. The Doctor was sentenced to life imprisonment on the prison planet Volag Noc, but uncovered the Krillitanes' plot and was allowed to return to 1926. The Advocate returned from the Time War to pursue a secret agenda against the Doctor.

The People of the Worldsphere were covertly involved in wars in their galaxy.[839] In an old curiosity shop on Aminion 2, the Doctor happened upon a catalogue advertising the people of Valhalla City for sale as slaves. The catalogue was located next to a bust of Joanna the Mad, although it wasn't a good likeness, and he initially mistook her for Pliny the Elder.[840]

The Alps were damaged in a local war in 2547.[841] Mind probes were made illegal.[842] The launch silos outside Legion City were discontinued.[843]

The Dalek Wars

The Daleks began their third wave of expansion, leading to the Galactic War, a.k.a. the Dalek Wars.[844] Life on the front was harsh, with tens of thousands killed by Dalek Plague on Yalmur alone. Other planets on the front line included Capella, Antonius, Procyon and Garaman (home to a Spacefleet station).

On the other hand, the Core Worlds – the heavily populated and fashionable heart of the Earth Empire – were safe and prosperous. The planet Ellanon was a popular holiday planet; Bacchanalia Two was the home of the Club Outrageous. There were shipyards on Harato, and thriving colonies on Thrapos 3 and Zantir. The Spinward Corporation's financial and administrative centre on Belmos was a space station the size of a planet. Humanity had also discovered Lubellin – "the Mud Planet" – and the

Cybermen mini-series established that Telos was destroyed much earlier than that (unless it's a different planet with the same name seen here, and not the exact world seen in *The Tomb of the Cybermen* – as is plainly the case in *Cybermen*). *The Secret History* explains the Monk's goals.

834 The ceasefire was declared "fifty years" before *Demontage* (p4).

835 *The Well-Mannered War* (p272). Stokes is from the 2400s, so the official records must have been altered to due to his relocation to the twenty-sixth century.

836 *Conundrum*

837 *Benny: Another Girl, Another Planet*

838 Dating "Fugitive" (IDW Vol. 1 #3-6) - It is "many centuries" since the time of the 15th Draconian Emperor, and the Draconians and Ogrons in this story date from relatively soon after *Frontier in Space*.

839 A generation or so before *The Also People*.

840 "Two hundred years" after *Valhalla*.

841 *So Vile a Sin* (p211).

842 "Three hundred years" before *Dark Progeny*. They are in use in *Frontier in Space*.

843 "Seventy years" before *Benny B3: Legion: Everybody Loves Irving*.

844 *Death and Diplomacy* (p124). We might infer from other stories that the first wave was in the mid-twenty-second century (seen in *The Dalek Invasion of Earth*) which was targeted on Earth's solar system, and the second led to the Dalek War mentioned in *The Crystal Bucephalus* and *The Colony of Lies*.

THE DALEK WARS: In *Death to the Daleks*, Hamilton states "My father was killed in the last Dalek War," implying there was more than one. We know from other Dalek stories that humanity and the Daleks come into conflict throughout history, starting with *The Dalek Invasion of Earth* [around 2157]. However, there are almost certainly no Dalek Wars affecting Earth directly between *To the Death* and *The Rescue* [c 2190-2493], as Vicki has only heard of the Daleks from history books discussing the Invasion (she doesn't even know what they look like). According to Cory in *Mission to the Unknown*, the Daleks have been inactive as a military force in Earth's sphere of influence for a millennium before *The Daleks' Master Plan* [between 3000-4000 AD]. In *Planet of the Daleks*, the Doctor uses the term "Dalek War" to describe the events of *The Daleks*, which did not involve humanity.

According to *The Terrestrial Index*, there are a string of Human/Dalek conflicts, the First to Fourth Dalek Wars. The First was the Dalek Invasion of Earth; the Second was fought by "the Alliance" of Humans, Draconians and Thals in the twenty-fifth century; the Third was again fought by the Alliance after the events of *Frontier in Space* and *Planet of the Daleks*; the Fourth was *The Daleks' Master Plan*.

This is a numbering system that is never used on television, and some of the details of Lofficier's account actively contradict what we're told in the stories – at the time he proposes a "Second Dalek War" involving the Thals and Draconians, the Thals don't have advanced space travel and a century later, they think that humans are a myth (*Planet of the Daleks*). The first contact between humanity and the Draconians was in 2520 (in the twenty-*sixth* century), leading to a short war, followed by twenty years of hostility and mutual mistrust (*Frontier in Space*).

spotless Tarian Asteroids.

The best whiskey from this time was made in South America, but some people preferred Eridanian Brandy.[845]

In 2545, monitoring systems in the Oort Cloud detected three hundred Dalek battlecruisers headed for Earth's solar system. Mars was equipped with nine hundred photon missiles, but the only person authorised to fire them – Karina Tellassar, Mars' Minister of Defence – failed to do so because the missile-command codes were implanted in the heart of her lover, Isaac Deniken. The Daleks destroyed Mars' seabases with firestorm bombs, then used the planet's three billion inhabitants – mostly pensioners – as a human shield and pelted Earth with bioweapons. The Earth Senate narrowly voted not to retaliate with a nuclear strike, and General Keele launched a successful counter-offensive. A pair of offworlders aided Keele in downing a Dalek saucer at Argyre Dam, and in coordinating the final assault that drove the Daleks from Mars.[846]

Dalek missiles fell on Europe for nearly a month. The retroviruses they contained wouldn't be discovered for almost a decade. During the war, Nike supplied footwear to Earth soldiers, and Coca-Cola returned to using cocaine in its products. The British Parliament was destroyed and replaced by the Republic Museum of Social and Political History. The whole of London became a museum. The Thames was detoxed and stocked with genetically pure species from the Pacific Ocean. Inverness was replaced by a deep-water trench connecting Loch Ness to the Moray Firth. Paris became populated with human-alien hybrids.[847]

The Earth military captured a borogove of budding Mim children, and initiated Project Narcissus to condition the shapeshifting offspring to infiltrate the enemy's ranks. Thousands of Mim offspring died, but their actions altered the course of the war in humanity's favour.[848]

The works of romance novelist Jilly Cooper were lost in the Dalek Wars.[849]

c 2545 - BENNY: BURIED TREASURES: "Closure"[850]

-> On the planet Panyos, an Ashcarzi soldier murdered a woman named Isabella. Her son – Ulrich Hescarti – would grow up to avenge his mother's death by instigating an ethnic cleansing programme against the Ashcarzi. Benny

---

The books have established that Dalek Wars took place in Benny's native time. She's born the same year *Frontier in Space* and *Planet of the Daleks* are set [q.v. Benny's birthday]. her father fights in the Dalek wars and her mother is killed in a Dalek attack. What's more, Ace spends three years fighting Daleks in this time period between *Love and War* and *Deceit*. As such, there is a mass of information about the Wars in many of the novels. There's no mention of a lull in the fighting – war presumably breaks out soon after *Frontier in Space*, it carries on into Benny's childhood and apparently into her early adulthood. Humanity is still fighting the Daleks when Benny hits thirty (*Love and War*), but they've defeated the Daleks within three years of that (*Deceit*). Nevertheless, according to *Lucifer Rising*, there are two distinct Dalek Wars at this time – Benny's father fought in the Second Dalek War (p65), whereas Ace fought in the Third (p309), so there must be a short-lived cessation of hostilities (which would seem to be at some point in the 2560s, when Benny is in her twenties).

A lengthy essay at the end of *Deceit* has the Dalek War starting after *Frontier in Space* and Ace fighting in the Second Dalek War.

Some stories (for example, *The Crystal Bucephalus*) stick to Lofficier's scheme.

So... the term "Second Dalek War" is used to refer to two or possibly even three different conflicts in both the twenty-fifth and twenty-sixth centuries (and this is further complicated because of the early confusion over which century Benny was born in). For the sake of clarity, references to the numbering of the Dalek Wars have been left out of the timeline itself; where they are given in a story, it's been footnoted.

Within the fiction, it's fairly easy to rationalise the discrepancy: these are the naming conventions of historians, and different historians will have different perspectives on the various conflicts and labels for them.

845 *Deceit*

846 *Benny: Beige Planet Mars*. The "offworlders" are the apocryphal forty-second Doctor (as "played" by Ian Richardson) and his companion, Iphigenia "Iffy" Birmingham. Both feature in 90s fan-fic stories by Lance Parkin and Mark Clapham.

847 *Benny: The Sword of Forever*

848 *Benny: Nobody's Children*

849 *Benny S9: The Diet of Worms*

850 Dating *Benny: Buried Treasures: "Closure"* (Benny audio #1.5b) - It's "fifty years" before the "modern-day" component of "Closure". It's not said whether Benny's actions actually change history or not.

851 Dating *Return of the Living Dad* (NA #53) - This happens "forty" years before 2587 (p7), Benny would have been "seven" at the time (p12). Although the date is given as "2543" (p29), there is some confusion over Benny's birthday in the NAs, and this is a victim of that. This is "the height of the Second Dalek War" (q.v. The Dalek Wars).

852 A number of references to Benny Summerfield's early life appeared in the New Adventures, and these were not always consistent. In *Love and War* (p75), Benny's birthplace is identified as "Beta Caprisis. Earth colony" – supporting that, in *Benny: The Wake*, Benny points at a star and tells Peter, "That's Beta Caprisis... that's where your mummy was born." But, in *Sanctuary*, Benny recalls that her mother was killed on a raid on

used her time ring to travel back and kill Isabella's would-be murderer, then made Isabella promise that she would either raise Ulrich properly or, failing that, kill him.

Benny Loses Her Parents

c 2547 - RETURN OF THE LIVING DAD[851] **->** The Daleks' tactics were repetitive and predictable. Earth's Spacefleet used vast Dalekbuster ships, highly-automated and heavily-armed six-man fighters. Isaac Summerfield captained one such ship. Albinex the Navarino contacted the Daleks and offered to change history in return for military assistance. The seventh Doctor and Benny arrived on Isaac Summerfield's ship, the *Tisiphone*, which was fighting the Daleks over Bellatrix. The *Tisiphone* interrupted Albinex's negotiations with the Daleks, and both the *Tisiphone* and Albinex ended up falling down a wormhole to the twentieth century.

The Dalekbuster commanded by Isaac Summerfield was reported to have broken formation and fled during a space battle, and its captain was branded a coward. In late 2547, at the height of the Dalek War, the Daleks attacked the human colony on Vandor Prime in the Gamma Delphinus System, where Claire Summerfield was killed. Bernice Summerfield was sent to military boarding school.[852] Benny's doll Rebecca was with Benny's mother when she was exterminated.[853]

Bernice Summerfield came to own an "I Dig Archaeology" badge from circa 2547.[854]

c 2550 - "Pureblood"[855] **->** The Dalek War continued to rage, but elsewhere in the galaxy, the conflict between the Rutans and Sontarans reached a critical point. The Rutans had already razed the community structures between the Warburg and the Prok Fral Edifice. Now, they destroyed Sontara, the Sontaran homeworld, with photonic bombs.

The Sontarans got their Racepool away in time, and headed towards Pandora.

The seventh Doctor and Benny arrived on the Pandora Spindle in the Terran Federation. This was a distant space station run by the Lauren Corporation – the biggest industrial giant in the galaxy – and the home of a genetics facility. The Sontarans occupied the station, and a Rutan agent informed their enemies that the Racepool was there. The Sontarans' genetic expert was killed in an accident and the Doctor agreed to help save the Sontarans from extinction. He also exposed the spy, Modine.

The Sontarans had been betrayed to the Rutans on Sontara... by pureblood Sontarans who were untouched by cloning and genetic engineering, and hailed from a distant colony that the Rutans discovered. The pureblood Sontarans attacked Pandora, but the Doctor and Benny showed how the Rutans had tricked them into destroying their own kind. The two factions of Sontarans united and settled on Pandora to rebuild their race. In return, the Sontarans agreed to erase all knowledge of the human race from their databanks.

The Sontarans' survival would prevent the Rutans from overrunning the galaxy, and Sontaran advances in space drive, vaccines and genetic solutions to disease would be of great benefit to the future.

Abslom Daak... Dalek Killer!

Hardened criminals on Earth were given the choice of facing the death penalty or becoming Dalek Killers (DKs). The most notorious of the DKs was Abslom Daak.[856]

Daak's beloved, Selene, had run off with his business partner Vol Mercurius after defrauding four billion from a shipping company. Consequently, Daak cut off Mercurius' hand with his chainsword. Mercurius bought the planet Dispater, but Selene left him.[857]

"Vandor Prime, in the Gamma Delphinus System" (p185). We might speculate that she was born on the former and moved to the latter. As pointed out in *Set Piece* (p132), there is some confusion about the exact sequence of events during the raid that killed Benny's mother. Accounts also vary as to whether Benny's father disappeared before or after her mother's death. *Love and War* (ch4) has Benny claiming that she was only seven when all this happened, so she is almost certainly misremembering some details or blocking out some of her unpleasant memories. *NAofBenny* V1: *Good Night, Sweet Ladies*, however, says that Benny was eight when her mother died.

853 "Emperor of the Daleks"
854 *Benny: Many Happy Returns*
855 Dating "Pureblood" (*DWM* #193-196) - It's "the

twenty-sixth century" in part one, but "the twenty-fifth" in part two. It seems to be around Benny's native time, as she's heard of the Lauren Corporation. The Second Dalek War is mentioned, but that's not as helpful a reference as one might think (q.v. "The Dalek Wars"). The Doctor says the Sontarans will not be a threat to Earth again until *The Sontaran Experiment* (which, as far as we know, they aren't). *Sontarans: Conduct Unbecoming* names Sontar as the Sontaran homeworld (perhaps it was founded after Sontara's destruction).

856 Abslom Daak first appeared in Marvel's *Doctor Who Weekly* #17, and has returned a number of times since. He was mentioned in *Love and War* (p46-47 – we also meet Maire, another DK, in that novel), before appearing in the (cloned) flesh in *Deceit*, and featured in *The Eleventh Doctor Year Two*.

The Death of Princess Taiyin

c 2550 - "Abslom Daak... Dalek Killer"[858] -> Rather than be vaporised, a serious criminal could choose "Exile D-K". He would be teleported to a world in the Dalek Empire, and made to kill as many of Daleks as possible before he was exterminated. The life expectancy of such DKs was two hours, thirty-two minutes and twenty-three seconds. Only one man in four survived the matter transmitter, and the overall odds of survival were six hundred million to one.

At this time, Curtis Fooble was accused of eating the Vegan ambassador. Humans had advanced humanoid robots, which operated machines and even sat as judges. Mazam was a human colony, with a monarchy as well as skysleds and space yachts. Dalek base ships were operated by a Command Dalek, wired into the ship's systems. The Daleks used Omega Units – advanced fighter/bombers – as well as hoverbouts.

The sociopath Abslom Daak was convicted of twenty-three charges of murder, pillage, piracy and massacre. He had been driven to such crimes by the loss of his beloved Selene, and chose Exile D-K. He was beamed to the feudal planet Mazam, located a thousand light years from Earth, where Princess Taiyin had just surrendered to the Daleks. Daak rescued her, and together they took on the Daleks' base ship. They destroyed it, but Taiyin was killed. Grieving for Taiyin's death, Daak vowed "I'm gonna kill every damned stinking Dalek in the galaxy!"

c 2550 - "Star Tigers"[859] -> "The Frontier War with Earth had been fought and settled", and Draconia was now at peace. However, Dalek expansion towards Girodun threatened Draconian trade routes. Factions within the Draconian court wanted to strengthen their defences, but the prevailing wisdom was that the Daleks wouldn't fight a war on two fronts, and they should be negotiated with.

Three Dalek ships entered Draconian space while pursuing Abslom Daak, but he destroyed them before landing on Draconia. Prince Salander looked after Daak, who had put Taiyin in cryogenic suspension. Salander's political rivals took the opportunity to have him arrested, and Daak shared his house arrest. Salander's family built warships, and he showed Daak a prototype frontier defence cruiser built to fight Daleks. Daak christened this the *Kill-Wagon*. Salander was told that a Dalek patrol had killed his son, and he decided to leave Draconia in the *Kill-Wagon* with Daak. They resolved to assemble a crew.

They went to the planet Paradise – a cosmopolitan planet where every pleasure was available for a price – and recruited the Ice Warrior Harma. They then headed to the war-torn planet of Dispater, where Vol Mercurius was playing a parachess tactics game with a robot companion that mirrored the real-life conflict. Mercurius owned the planet, but the Kill-Mechs of a self-proclaimed Emperor of the Jarith Cluster had invaded it. Mercurius agreed to join the *Kill-Wagon* crew. As they left Dispater, they discovered an army of Dalek Space Commando Units, ready to invade the Jarith Cluster while the inhabitants were divided. The *Kill-Wagon* let the Daleks invade, then wiped them out by dropping nuclear bombs into a nearby volcano.

At this time, Draconia was home to an animal somehow like a tiger, called a Thorion. The currency of Draconia was the "crystal", while bribes were in diamonds. Vorkelites enjoyed being executed. Rigellians had four tentacles, three mouths and a reputation for being untrustworthy.

The "Death" and Return of Abslom Daak

c 2550 - "Nemesis of the Daleks"[860] -> The *Kill-Wagon* launched an attack on the Dalek base on the planet Hell, but was shot down. The Emperor was there to super-

---

857 Before "Abslom Daak... Dalek Killer". Details are given in "Star Tigers".

858 Dating "Abslom Daak... Dalek Killer" (*DWW* #17-20) - It's "the twenty-sixth century"; humanity is at war with the Daleks. The sequel, "Star Tigers", establishes that it is shortly after a "frontier war" between the Draconians and Earth, a clear reference to *Frontier in Space*.

The matter transmitter between star systems is something humanity is still trying to perfect by the year 4000 and *The Daleks' Master Plan*. We learn about Vol Mercurius in "Star Tigers".

859 Dating "Star Tigers" (*DWW* #27-30, *DWM* #44-46) - It's within three months of "Abslom Daak... Dalek Killer"; Salander says Mazam was conquered "within the last three months". "The Emperor does not want another war... not so soon after fighting the humans."

860 Dating "Nemesis of the Daleks" (*DWM* #152-155) - It's "the twenty-sixth century". Clearly, this takes place

after "Star Tigers", but there's no indication of how much time has passed. The Emperor resembles the one from the comic strips (see The Dalek Emperors sidebar), and may well be killed in Daak's final attack because he's on the Death Wheel when it explodes. If so, it's tempting to imagine that the Emperor's death was the turning point in the war referred to as "years ago" in *Deceit* (which also says Daak's death here was "years ago").

There's no indication that these Daleks are time travellers. At first the Doctor assumes the Emperor is Davros, but the Dalek Emperor replies "Davros? Who is Davros?". *Terror Firma* has Davros losing his mind and mutating into an Emperor Dalek, but ultimately it seems as if he and *this* Emperor are not one and the same. The Daleks also (apparently) probe the seventh Doctor's mind, identify him and see images of the Doctor's previous six incarnations.

THE DALEK EMPERORS: Over the course of *Doctor Who* we see four different designs for the Dalek Emperor. We can be confident that this isn't always the same individual and, even allowing for the ability of the Daleks as a species and individually to survive what looks like certain death, can reasonably conclude that there are at least three bearers of the title.

• The "Golden Emperor" – *The Dalek Chronicles* comic strip introduced a gold Emperor with an oversized, spherical head, and he also appeared in the Dalek books of the sixties – he was the central character of the strip and we learn a great deal about him. He's never referred to as the "Golden Emperor" in the strip, but was in some supporting material, such as the game "The Race to the Golden Emperor" in *Terry Nation's Dalek Annual 1979*.

The character was introduced to new audiences by reprints in the seventies *Dalek Annual*s and *Doctor Who Weekly* reprints early in the eighties, and *DWM* used the same design in two original comic strips: "Nemesis of the Daleks" (set in the twenty-sixth century) and "Emperor of the Daleks" (set after *Revelation of the Daleks*). It's unclear if this is meant to be the same individual, and the Emperor is apparently killed at the end of both stories.

• The "Evil Emperor" – In *The Evil of the Daleks*, the Dalek Emperor is a vast, immobile Dalek based in a chamber in Dalek City. This design reappears in the stageplay *The Ultimate Adventure*, the *Dalek Empire* stories and *The Dalek Factor*. This Emperor is apparently killed at the end of *The Evil of the Daleks*, although he's not *quite* dead the last time we see him in that story (and this chronology places *Dalek Empire* significantly after *The Evil of the Daleks*).

Some commentators (Lofficier and *About Time* included) have speculated that this is Davros, although dialogue in *The Evil of the Daleks* seems to rule that out by stating it's the first time either the Doctor or the Emperor has met the other.

A more open question is whether this is the same individual as the Golden Emperor. The story "Secret of the Emperor" in *The Dalek Outer Space Book* depicts the Golden Emperor being rebuilt as an immobile Emperor based on Skaro. The design is not the same as seen in *The Evil of the Daleks*, but it's clearly the same concept.

In John Peel's books – the novelisations *The Chase*, *The Daleks' Master Plan*, *The Power of the Daleks*, *The Evil of the Daleks* and his original novels *War of the Daleks* and *Legacy of the Daleks* – the Daleks are led by the Dalek Prime. This is the same individual Dalek who makes the speech about the Daleks becoming the supreme beings of the universe at the end of *Genesis of the Daleks*. In Peel's version, he becomes the Daleks' leader, and in *War of the Daleks,* the description of his casing closely matches that of the Golden Emperor. *War of the Daleks* and the novelisation of *The Evil of the Daleks* have the Dalek Prime and Emperor respectively as the last survivor of the original batch of Daleks – the same individual, in other words. This is the Golden Emperor who becomes the Evil Emperor, tweaked to fit the origin of the race seen in *Genesis of the Daleks*, as opposed to the one in *The Dalek Chronicles*. The real-life creator of the Daleks, Terry Nation, is said to have preferred the idea that the Daleks were rule by a Council rather than an Emperor, and the Dalek Prime fits that, too.

In *The Evil of the Daleks*, the Doctor meets the Emperor for the first time and the implication is that it's the first time the Emperor has met the Doctor, too. The only story to contradict that is "Nemesis of the Daleks", which is set in the twenty-sixth century (there's no date given for the Skaro sequence of *The Evil of the Daleks*, but no fan chronology has ever put it before this time) and has the Emperor meeting the seventh Doctor and using a mind probe to visualize all six of his previous incarnations.

On balance, it might seem as if the Golden Emperor and Evil Emperor are the same individual, the last survivor of the first batch of Daleks (as seen in *Genesis of the Daleks* or, if you prefer, *The Dalek Chronicles*), who leads them for most of their recorded history. *1stD* V2: *Across the Darkened City*, however, shows the Evil Emperor's humble beginnings, rise to power and inspiration to find the Human Factor, and it's nothing to do with the Golden Emperor after all.

The Emperor we see in the *Dalek Empire* audio series resembles the Evil Emperor, but is this the same individual? There's no way of knowing conclusively, but it could well be. That Emperor dies at the end of that series, in a manner that goes out of its way to leave virtually no possibility he survived.

• "Emperor Davros" – At the end of *Revelation of the Daleks*, Davros is taken to Skaro to face trial by the Supreme Dalek, a role he wants for himself. In the next television story, *Remembrance of the Daleks*, Davros is Emperor and has a casing based on that of the Golden Emperor – although it is cream and gold, with a hexagonal patch instead of an eyestalk, and has no sucker or gun. How he comes to be Emperor has been depicted three times... the *DWM* strip "Emperor of the Daleks" shows the Golden Emperor being killed and Davros becoming Emperor. The book *War of the Daleks* says Davros never really had power, he was tricked by the Daleks into thinking he did. The audio *Terror Firma* has Davros undergoing a full mutation (physical and mental) to become a Dalek Emperor. (A fourth might exist in the DVD extra *The Davros Mission*, which has Davros bringing the Daleks on Skaro to heel, although the events to follow aren't specified.) *The Stolen Earth/ Journey's End* say that Davros was lost early in the Time War, but not that he was Emperor at the time.

continued on page 3141...

vise construction of the Daleks' vast battlestation, the Death Wheel. The seventh Doctor discovered the bodies of Salander, Vol Mercurius and Harma. He was cornered by the Daleks, but rescued by Daak.

The Doctor learned that Hell was the source of Helkogen, a poison gas. He and Daak boarded the Death Wheel, where the Doctor confronted the Emperor and Daak learned the Daleks were building a Genocide Device – a gas weapon that threatened every known planet. Daak prevented the Doctor from sacrificing himself to destroy the Death Wheel's central reactor, and the Doctor escaped as Daak died to destroy the Death Wheel.

c 2550 - "Emperor of the Daleks"[861] -> Abslom Daak was transmatted away from certain death and returned to what he thought was Earth. There he was told to kill the Doctor – and in return, Taiyin would be resurrected.

The seventh Doctor and Benny arrived on Hell and met up with the remaining Star Tigers, who weren't dead after all, as the Helkans had revived them. Within moments, though, Daak grabbed the Doctor and they were all transmatted to Daak's masters... but the Doctor realised they were Dalek robots, and that this was a trap. They were on Skaro, in the future, at the mercy of the Emperor.

Returning from the future, the Star Tigers drank at a bar on Paradise. Daak's fixation with Taiyin had ended... he was now obsessed with Benny instead. The seventh Doctor met his previous self, and thanked him for his help setting a trap for the Daleks.

History recorded that Abslom Daak died destroying the Dalek Death Wheel.[862] On Kastropheria, a group of priests used the drug skar to boost their psionic abilities and mentally restrain the people's self-destructive impulses. Humans established a colony on the planet, but the natives became aggressive when supplies of skar began to run out.[863] The Class G maintenance robot entered service.[864]

c 2550 - CATASTROPHEA[865] -> The third Doctor and Jo discovered the human colonists on Kastopheria had enslaved the natives, and the Doctor was mistaken for El Llama, a prophesied revolutionary. The priests asked the Doctor to destroy the Anima, a giant skar crystal, with great care to free the people from their mind-lock. The Anima was destroyed too suddenly, and the people's destructive rage returned. War loomed between the natives and the colonists, but the Doctor helped to forge a non-interference treaty. The Draconians aided the colonists in evacuating, and the natives were left in peace.

The war criminal Karina Tellassar was now in hiding as "Elizabeth Trinity", an academic. In 2555, Trinity published A History of Mars, which argued that humanity had been noble in freeing the Martians from their backward ways. The generation to come would consider both sides of the argument.[866]

Benny, age 16, went AWOL from her military academy and hid out in the woods nearby, giving advice to other girls living there.[867] A military recruit named Simon Kyle, age 18, had established a shelter in the woods – he became Benny's best friend and first lover. When the military captured them, Benny refused to testify against Kyle, but she traded his journal of their activities for a reduced punishment. The military took Benny off frontline service and made her a private; en route to Capella, she jumped ship and arrived on a colony world. She started working with

861 Dating "Emperor of the Daleks" (DWM #197-202) - This takes place shortly after "Nemesis of the Daleks". It's specified that Daak is "lured across space and time" – the sequence on Skaro takes place between Revelation of the Daleks and Remembrance of the Daleks (4625, according to this chronology), and accounts for Davros' (physical, not mental) transformation into the Emperor Dalek, as seen in Remembrance.

862 According to Deceit, which was published between "Nemesis of the Daleks" (where Daak died) and "Emperor of the Daleks" (where it turned out he hadn't). Presumably, either Daak evades the authorities, or they hush up his activities.

863 "Five years" before Catastrophea.

864 "Four decades" before Cold Fusion.

865 Dating Catastrophea (PDA #11) - It is "five or six hundred years" after Jo's time (p79).

866 Benny: Beige Planet Mars

867 Love and War

868 Love and War, Return of the Living Dad

869 Benny: Old Friends

870 NAofBenny V3: Planet X

871 Dating Prisoner of the Daleks (NSA #33) - This is stated to be in the middle of the first Earth Empire's war with the Daleks, at a point where "the Daleks are advancing, their empire constantly expanding into Earth's space" and young men can't remember a time they weren't at war. Bowman is a veteran of the Draconian conflicts. The Osterhagen Principle (almost certainly derived from the Osterhagen Key from Journey's End) was invented on Earth "over five hundred years ago". Gauda Prime is the planet in the Blake's 7 series finale, where Avon and his crew make their last stand. Conflicting all of this evidence, however, one of the Wayfarer crew says that Morse Code (developed in 1836 by Samuel F.B. Morse) came about "thousands of years ago". The Daleks are bronze, like the new series Daleks (Dalek X is black and gold).

872 War of the Daleks. No date is given, but it's while the Draconian Empire is at war with the Daleks. Female officers are anathema again by The Dark Path.

873 "Thirty years" before The Also People. Benny: Down

the archaeological unit there, faking her qualifications. Kyle went on to become Spacefleet officer.[868] Kyle later claimed that his bargain had prevented the officers involved from killing Benny, and that he'd never actually surrendered the journal.[869]

Benny suspected that the last time she was told her wardrobe was unacceptable, she was probably seventeen and not wearing most of it.[870]

c 2560 - PRISONER OF THE DALEKS[871] -> The

tenth Doctor became trapped within the disused refinery Lodestar Station 479 on Hurala, on the edge of Earth space. He was rescued by Dalek hunters led by ex-military man Jon Bowman, who were crewing the *Wayfarer* and received a fee from Earth Command for every Dalek eyestalk they netted. The Doctor was startled to realise that he had gone back to a point in Dalek history before their race's involvement in the Last Great Time War.

Thousands of human colonists on Auros evacuated their world, and destroyed it using the Osterhagen Principle – a series of nuclear devices buried within the planet. The Doctor and his allies learned that the Daleks were based on Arkheon, a planet believed destroyed forty years before, because they hoped to use the Arkheon Threshold – a schism in time and space – to become the masters of time, perhaps even wiping humanity from history. The Doctor and Bowman were interrogated by the Daleks' Inquisitor General, the feared Dalek X, who arrived with a Dalek fleet led by an *Exterminator*-class warship. This was the first of its kind, with ten antigravity impeller engines and a crew of five hundred Daleks. The *Wayfarer* was destroyed, but the Doctor escaped, setting off an astrionic explosion that obliterated the Dalek base and fleet. Hurala became a radioactive world, with a communications seal that would last for five thousand years. Dalek X survived in the ruins, vowing revenge.

A Supreme Dalek led the Daleks on Skaro. Koral – one of the *Wayfarer* crew – believed herself to be sole survivor of Red Sky Lost, a planet the Daleks had destroyed. Her crewmate, Cuttin' Edge, had grown up on Gauda Prime.

The Draconian vessel *Hunter* and five destroyers were lost fighting Daleks. Female officers had recently been introduced to the Draconian military.[872]

The People of the Worldsphere fought a war against the Great Hive Mind, using new weapons and powerful sentient Very Aggressive Ships. The war saw twenty-six billion killed, destroyed fifteen planets and devastated dozens of others. The Great Hive Mind became part of the People.[873]

...continued from page 3139

• "The Last Emperor" – *The Parting of the Ways* introduces a new Emperor: a vast and apparently immobile structure containing a vast Dalek mutant. This is clearly not Davros, and he's killed at the end of the story. Is this the Golden Emperor in another new casing? If it is, he's grown – it's no exaggeration to say that the mutant we see wouldn't fit in the Golden Emperor's casing.

We're never told if the Last Emperor actually led the Daleks during the Last Great Time War – it says the Daleks survived that conflict "through me", but that might have happened after the fact, with it ascending to the Emperorship because all the other high-ranking Daleks perished in the War. The Cult of Skaro, certainly, was familiar with *an* Emperor during the War (*Doomsday*). A Dalek Emperor (likely the one the Master said in *The Sound of Drums* "took control of the Cruciform" during the Last Great Time War) appears in *Gallifrey – Time War* Volume 1, and personality-wise, it's of the "Evil Emperor" variety.

There are at least two Emperors, then – a Dalek mutant and Davros. If we accept at face value the death of the Emperor in *The Evil of the Daleks*, we can say that there are at least three individuals. *Dalek Empire* would seem to make that four. *Gallifrey – Time War* V1 makes that five.

The maximum number of Emperors is harder to determine. The first panel we see the Golden Emperor's new casing in "Genesis of Evil", a caption informs us this is "the first Dalek Emperor", implying there would eventually be more than one, although there's little doubt the Emperor remains the same individual throughout *The Dalek Chronicles*. Russell T Davies' *Doctor Who Annual* essay refers to "puppet Emperors" of the Daleks. *The Dalek Factor* has an Emperor whose description matches the Evil Emperor, described as "an Emperor", which may mean there was more than one at that time.

We might infer that there were many Emperors. *The Dalek Chronicles* ends with the Emperor planning an attack on Earth. The stageplay *The Curse of the Daleks* is set in what could be the aftermath, and the Black Dalek rules Skaro following a Dalek defeat. So the Golden Emperor may have been killed. The Moroks raid Skaro and take a Dalek as a trophy according to *The Space Museum*. Could they have killed an Emperor as part of that conquest? An Emperor dies in *The Evil of the Daleks*, "Nemesis of the Daleks", "Emperor of the Daleks", possibly *We are the Daleks*, *The Parting of the Ways* and *Dalek Empire*. That would be seven or eight Emperors that we know of.

Corporations such as Ellerycorp, Peggcorp, Spinward, and IMC maintained battlefleets of their own. During the Battle of Alpha Centauri, a small squadron of Silurian vessels beat back the main Dalek force, which fled into hyperspace. Daleks also infiltrated human Puterspace.[874]

TAM Corporation's ships fought in the Galactic Wars. The corporation pulled out of remote colonies like Mendeb, taking as much high technology as it could.[875]

As often happened in wartime, the Dalek War saw a leap in human technological progress. A variety of intelligent weapons systems were developed: dart guns, data corrupting missiles, spikes, clusters and forceshells, random field devices, self-locating mines and drones.

Earth's Spacefleet included 1000-man troopships armed with torpedoes that could destroy a Dalek Battlesaucer. A fleet of warp vessels – X-Ships – were used to ferry communications, personnel and supplies. Most troopers were placed in Deep Sleep while travelling to the warzones. This was done to conserve supplies, not because the ships were particularly slow, as it now only took a matter of weeks to cross human space. Ships still used warp engines, but they also used ion drive to travel in real space.

Computer technology was now extremely advanced. The Spacefleet Datanet was a vast information resource, and data was stored on logic crystals. Nanotechnology was beginning to have medical applications: a nanosurgical virus was given to most troopers to protect against various alien infections, and cosmetic nanosurgery beautified the richest civilians. Holograms were now in widespread use for communications, display, entertainment, combat and public relations. Holosynths – simulations of people – acted as receptionists and could answer simple enquiries. HKI Industries, based on Phobos, specialised in the manufacture of transmats. These had a range of only a couple of thousand kilometres, but they were installed on all large ships and linked major cities on most colony worlds. Hoverspeeders were still in use.

By the late 2560s, it became clear that Earth was going to win the wars with the Daleks. By then, the fastline – a state of the art, almost real-time, interstellar communication system – had been developed.[876]

c 2560 - ENEMY OF THE DALEKS[877] **->** During the Dalek Wars, the planet Bliss was a sanctuary for rare flora and fauna. Professor Toshio Shimura, a scientist at a biological research facility there, took DNA from "piranha locusts" native to Bliss and gestated it in human beings without their consent. The subjects formed cocoons and emerged as the Kisibyaa: ferocious, metal-eating creatures that Shimura hoped would literally consume the Daleks. Shimura gave his own life to host Kisibyaa larvae. The seventh Doctor, Ace and Hex witnessed these events, and the Doctor – fearing the Kisibyaa would threaten all species – killed the Kisibyaa by destroying the facility.

and *Benny: Walking to Babylon* have further details.
874 *Love and War* (p5, p64).
875 This was "during the wars" (*Independence Day*, p22).
876 *Deceit*
877 Dating *Enemy of the Daleks* (BF #121) - The story occurs during the Dalek Wars, after the Daleks – according to Lt Beth Stokes – have spent "years" overrunning colony planets, either killing or enslaving the populaces. Ace has a familiarity with the weaponry and military practices of this era (so much so, she knows the make-up of a Valkyrie unit when asked), perhaps owing to the Spacefleet training she gained 2570-2573 (see *Love and War* and *Deceit*). As the conflict with the Daleks goes into decline in the late 2560s but is here running strong, it's probably earlier than Ace's Spacefleet tenure. Bliss is referred to as both a planet and a planetoid.
878 *Benny B5: Missing Persons: Big Dig*
879 Dating *Benny: Genius Loci* (Benny BF novel #8) - Benny spends most of 2561 on Jaiwan – some months at the very least pass before her birthday, which is 21st June – and she leaves the planet on 1st January, 2562 (p205). Cray might be the world seen in *The Game*.
880 Dating *Benny: Old Friends*: "The Ship of Painted Shadows" (Benny collection #9b) - The blurb says that it's "late 2562" and that Benny is 22. In Benny's lifetime, these events are specified as taking place after *Benny: Genius Loci*.

881 Dating *Benny: The Sword of Forever* (Benny NA #14) - The year is given on page 10; Benny is said to be 22 (p13). Page 19 cites that Daniel died in 2560, but this appears to be a typo. *Deceit* (p103) says that Benny didn't visit Earth for fifteen years before meeting the Doctor, but that claim contradicts *Benny: The Sword of Forever* and *Lucifer Rising* (p171).
882 Dating *Unbound: Masters of War* (BF Unbound #8) - This is the native universe of the Doctor played by David Warner in a number of *Unbound* stories, starting with *Sympathy for the Devil* (see the Unbound Doctors sidebar). It's some "hundreds of years" after *The Daleks*, and up to "thousands of years" since Davros was disfigured. An argument could be made that this story happens during the Davros Era, but it's a wild card as to how much of the future of the universe remains after the time-ripping war detailed in *The New Adventures of Bernice Summerfield* Vol. 3.
883 *Just War* (p137)
884 *Benny: Beige Planet Mars*, following the lead of *Lucifer Rising* (p171).
885 *The Dying Days*, again elaborating on *Lucifer Rising* (p171).
886 *The Also People*
887 *Return of the Living Dad* (p51).
888 Dating *Benny: The Vampire Curse*: "The Badblood Diaries" (Benny collection #12a) - The year is cited at the top of every chapter.

At this time, Valkyrie units – composed of one commissioned officer and twenty troopers – were all-female fighting forces commissioned to engage the Daleks.

The Early Career of Bernice Summerfield

Benny's first proper archaeological dig, in the Galadron Forest, involved unearthing a tyrannosaur that came to life and was killed again after it severed someone's arm.[878]

2561 to 2562 (1st January) - BENNY: GENIUS LOCI[879] ->

Benny's faked resume netted her the position of assistant field director at a dig on Jaiwan. Professor Mariela Ankola served as Benny's mentor, but died in her sleep after encountering lethal industrial toxins on the planet Cray. Benny adopted Ankola's habit of keeping journals. A non-sapient Jaiwan spider bit off Benny's foot, and she had a grown one attached on her birthday.

Owing to Benny's excavations, some Omega spiders were awakened from hibernation. This threatened to activate the Hibernation Clause of the Protocols of Colonisation, but the Omega spiders struck a clandestine deal with the Jaiwan authorities – the Omegas would share the planet in exchange for help in wiping out any remaining caches of Alpha spiders.

Benny and her allies – including members of Spacefleet's First Regiment of Combat Archaeologists, and the revived Pinky and Perky AIs – awakened some Alpha spiders to present their case. In doing so, Benny killed someone for the first time – she shot a local reporter and patriot, Lola, when she threatened to kill Benny's protégé, Shawnee.

No later than 1st January, 2562, Benny left Jaiwan aboard the *Goodnight Dolly*. A grateful archaeologist provided her with a certificate naming her as a Master of Science, Archaeology, accredited to the Department of History, University of Jaiwan at Kondeeo. On 2nd February, 2562, Benny travelled toward humanity's core worlds aboard the *Chin Shen Mo*. Papers provided by General Elsa Lafayette, a friend of Benny's parents, helped Benny avoid being incarcerated for desertion.

2562 - BENNY: OLD FRIENDS: "The Ship of Painted Shadows"[880] ->

Benny departed for Earth aboard the *Prince of Mercury* liner, and joined the New Gondwana Ladies' Choir to pay for her passage. The group was otherwise composed of the wives of Hanekawa Goro, a.k.a. Michio Dankizo XXVIII – a Kabuki performer who was being influenced by shadow beings that were entertained by tragedy. The shadow beings slaughtered many innocents, prompting Goro to commit suicide. Benny escaped as the *Prince of Mercury* disappeared into a spatial rift.

A demi-lemur, Ivo FitzIndri, had committed murder to save Benny's life – he asked that she go to a temple of the Order of Lost Lemuroidea and tell her story. Benny planned on doing so, but was diverted upon receiving a clue as to her father's whereabouts. FitzIndri was consequently excommunicated and spent the next fifty years looking for her.

2562 - BENNY: THE SWORD OF FOREVER[881] ->

By now, retroviruses released during the Dalek Wars had spread across 40% of Earth, and infested 68% of terrestrial DNA. Most of the retroviruses were harmless, producing physical changes in a small amount of those infected. The Rhone Valley, however, saw evolution run wild, and produced a thousand species of hybrid terrestrial-alien strains of planet, animal and human life.

Benny attempted to find the finger of John the Baptist as a means of securing herself an easy fellowship and to qualify for a doctorate. She located the Castle of Arginy, but her lover, Daniel Beaujeu, seemingly drowned while trying to overcome the traps within. He actually survived, was mutated by retrovirus, forgave Benny her mistakes and enjoyed a relatively happy life in Paris.

> ### = ? 2563 - UNBOUND: MASTERS OF WAR[882] ->
> The alt-third Doctor and the Brigadier worked to overthrow the Daleks – as led by the Black Dalek, the fourteenth holder of the title – enslaving the Thals on Skaro. The Doctor learned of the Daleks' creator, and reprogrammed a Dalek to think it was Davros reborn. This ripped Daleks' loyalties in half, plunging them into civil war. The real Davros returned with the Quatch, who hoped to capitalize on the Daleks' disarray. The Thals and Daleks banded together against the Quatch, who were unused to the Brigadier's unpredictable strategies. The Doctor showed Davros proof that the Quatch had caused his injuries, convincing Davros to activate a failsafe that shunted the Quatch back to their home dimension – and destroyed their mothership, with Davros aboard. The Brigadier remained on Skaro, to play peacemaker between the remaining Thals and Daleks.

At some point, Benny went to Stuttgart.[883] She visited Mars when she was 24. She was now in love with a man named Tim.[884] She made her reputation as an archaeologist during excavations of the Fields of Death, the tombs of the rulers of Mars in 2565.[885] She went on to investigate the Dyson Sphere of the Varteq Veil.[886] In Benny's time, humans had eradicated most of the previously common illnesses.[887]

2565 - BENNY: THE VAMPIRE CURSE: "The Badblood Diaries"[888] ->

The vampire-stricken Badblood had orbiting human settlements that moved to remain in continual daylight, and occasionally intersected for major celebrations. The Kikan corporation, run by psi-powered yakuza who went straight, coveted Badblood's fish exports as a means of strengthening its sushi monopoly. Benny was granted dispensation to study Hunanzun, the first human settlement on Badblood, and wound up preventing a vampire outbreak on Station CT1107.

2565 - BENNY: THE VAMPIRE CURSE: "Possum Kingdom"[889] **->** Benny joined an expedition to explore the cave system found underneath Possum Kingdom Lake in Texas. She found a naked, amnesiac man who was taken away to a military hospital at Fort Worth.

The biggest museum in the universe held an original manuscript of *Down Among the Dead Men* from circa 2566.[890] In 2568, the Spinward Corporation's computer, the Net, predicted that once the Dalek Wars ended, Earth's authorities would show an interest in their activities on Arcadia.[891] The last book on the lost race of Nobal on Bubastis was written prior to Bernice Summerfield's arrival there.[892]

c 2568 - THE ACHERON PULSE[893] **->** The Drashani Empire undertook negotiations with the medieval planet Cawdor, offering advanced technology in exchange for mining rights. A Drashani space station was established above Cawdor, and Igris were imported to mine the planet's galdrium deposits.

The sixth Doctor sought to return Aliona's royal carcanet to Gadarel Prime, but a deployment of the Acheron Pulse knocked the TARDIS some thirty years and seven parsecs off course. He arrived on Cawdor and met the Drashani empress, Cheni, who had arrived to continue negotiations.

Lord Tenebris and the Wrath captured Cawdor, and used the space station's power supply to greatly expand the Acheron Pulse's range. Once triggered, the Pulse would turn Gadarel Prime – situated less than sixty parsecs away – into an Igris world within hours. Cheni learned that Tenebris was the long-lost Prince Kylo, but he irrevocably consigned her soul to the Undervoid.

The Wrath came to see the contradictions within Kylo's goals, rejected him and asked the Doctor to reprogramme them with a new purpose. The Doctor endowed the Wrath's cerebral cortices with his own morality, hoping to make them a force for peace. He deposited Kylo at the Calliostro Primosphere – a pocket of reality where the space-time of thousands of worlds intersected – and hoped he too would know contentment. He also gifted Kylo with Aliona's royal carcanet.

---

889 Dating *Benny: The Vampire Curse*: "Possum Kingdom" (Benny collection #12b) - The year is given.
890 *Benny: Many Happy Returns*
891 *Deceit*
892 "Fifty years" before *Benny: The Slender-Fingered Cats of Bubastis* (p49).
893 Dating *The Acheron Pulse* (BF #166) - It's been "thirty years" since the Succession of Blood (*The Burning Prince*) and Cheni's crowning as empress. Kylo is marooned on Sharnax for "twenty-five years"/"two and a half decades", and has spent the last five years making strikes into Drashani territory. Galdrium was cited as a mineral in *The Pirate Planet*. "Metebelis moonstones" doubtless refer to *Planet of the Spiders*.
894 *The Shadow Heart*
895 Dating *Love and War* (NA #9) - The dating of this novel causes a number of problems as it features the debut of Bernice Summerfield. It is the "twenty-fifth century" (p46), and "five centuries" since Ace's time (p26). The novel clearly takes place after *Frontier in Space* (see p10-11 of *Love and War* or p252 of *The Programme Guide*, fourth edition) as it refers to events of that story. Heaven is established "three decades" before the events of the novel (p92), and *Frontier in Space* is set in 2540, so the novel can't take place before about 2570. Latterly, the decision was made that Benny is from the twenty-sixth century, so this is the date that has been adopted for this story. It is late June, as Benny celebrates her birthday just before the book starts, although it is autumn on Heaven.

896 *Deceit*. Many of the subsequent New Adventures contain references to Ace's exploits in Spacefleet.
897 *Lucifer Rising*
898 *First Frontier*, *Theatre of War*, *Shadowmind*, *Lungbarrow* and *The Shadow of the Scourge*.
899 "Final Genesis"
900 *Death to the Daleks*
901 Thirty years before *Benny: The Gods of the Underworld*.
902 *Benny: Down*
903 *Benny: Beyond the Sun*
904 Dating *Deceit* – (NA #13) The novel is set "two, probably three Earth years" after *Love and War* (p85), and as such the dating of the story is problematic (q.v. Benny's Birthday). Both the blurb and the history section in the Appendix of the novel state that *Deceit* is set in "the middle of the twenty-fifth century", just after what *The Terrestrial Index* calls the Second Dalek War (p62-63). This is restated at various other points (e.g.: p69, p216), but contradicted by other evidence in the same book: Arcadia was colonised three hundred seventy-nine years before *Deceit* (p115), but not before the EB Corporation's first warship was operational in 2112 (p27), so the book must be set after 2491 AD. The book also refers to the Cyber Wars, and "Nemesis of the Daleks" was "years ago". In the Marvel strips, Abslom Daak comes from the mid-twenty-sixth century.

Pool – while not named there – briefly reappears in *Benny: Dead Romance*. Arcadia may or may not be the same planet that was the destination of the *Mayflower*

After the Doctor left, Kylo paid for transport out of the Primosphere with Metebelis moonstones. The Wrath formally ended hostilities with the Drashani, but became incapable of not finding fault and criminal behaviour in every being they encountered. They moved from being benevolent peacekeepers to violence-prone oppressors.

The increasingly militaristic Wrath destroyed a hundred planets. Thargros was home to an advanced civilisation, but the Wrath literally sheered the planet in two – one half was vapourised, the other remained floating in space. Before long, the Wrath Empire replaced the Drashani Empire, and extended its dominion over half the galaxy. Prince Kylo hid from the Wrath on the remains of Thargros, procured the late Aliona's DNA from her carcanet, and created clones of her to keep him company.[894]

Benny Joins the TARDIS, Ace Leaves for Three Years

2570 (late June) - LOVE AND WAR[895] **->** Bernice Summerfield and her group arrived on Heaven to survey the artifacts of the extinct Heavenite civilisation on behalf of Ellerycorp. The seventh Doctor and Ace arrived as the fungoid Hoothi brought to fruition a plan centuries in the making – Hoothi spores infected everyone on Heaven, meaning that the Hoothi could instantly turn the living into fungoid creatures and animate corpses. They sought to create an army of billions to attack Gallifrey with. Ace became engaged to one of the Travellers, Jan, who was in an open relationship with a woman named Roisa and her lover Marie. Jan was pyrokinetic, and so the Doctor manipulated him into becoming transformed into a Hoothi fungoid and joining the Hoothi group mind. The Doctor encouraged Jan to bring his pyrokinesis to bear – the Hoothi, their fungoid creatures, their army of the undead and Jan were all incinerated, saving the galaxy. Heaven was evacuated shortly afterwards, and Ace departed the TARDIS, unable to forgive the Doctor for sacrificing her fiancé. Bernice better accepted the Doctor's actions and became his travelling companion.

Following this time, Ace spent three years in the twenty-sixth century during the time of the Dalek War. After a series of adventures, including a spell working for IMC, she ended up with the Special Weapons Division of Spacefleet. She fought alongside the Irregular Auxiliaries, reputed to be the most dangerous arm of the military.[896] Ace served aboard the *Saberhagen*, the *Corporate Raider* and the IMC-funded ship *Corporate Strategy*. The planet Lucifer became of strategic importance in the Dalek Wars, and IMC asked Ace – should the opportunity present itself – to go back in time with the Doctor and discover why the planet was walled off behind a force field.[897] She used a D22 photon rifle when she was a Marine.[898] She fought Daleks in the Ceti sector and Hai Dow. She killed a Black Dalek. She fought Marsh Daleks in the Flova trenches. She was issued a tool for removing the tops of Daleks.[899]

Hamilton's father died during the last Dalek War.[900]

Venedel joined the Earthlink Federation, an allied group of worlds with ties to Earth.[901] By 2571, the Repopulation Bureau on Sarah-361 established guidelines for what constituted good breeding stock.[902] Circa 2573, a Chelonian slave camp on Apollox 4 was discovered.[903]

Ace Rejoins the TARDIS

& 2573 - DECEIT[904] **->** The Dalek Wars were all but over, and although Dalek nests survived on a number of worlds, the army and Spacefleet were gradually demobilised.

During the Dalek Wars, Earth Central had superseded the Colonial Office, while Spacefleet had been expanded and modernised. The Office of External Operations, "the Earth's surveyors, official couriers, intelligence gatherers, customs officers and diplomats", now had a staff of five thousand. While the corporations remained powerful, the Earth government reigned in some of their power and broke some of their monopolies.

Agent Defries investigated the Arcadia System, the base of the Spinward Corporation. The nearest troopers were on Hurgal, although some were taking part in a pirate hunt in the Hai Dow System. Instead, Defries was assigned the troopship *Admiral Raistruck* and a squad of Irregular Auxiliaries. She was also given a "secret weapon": a clone of the Dalek Killer Abslom Daak, kept in cryosleep.

The ship's crew were told that they were going on a Dalek hunt. The *Admiral Raistruck* arrived in the Arcadia system and encountered an asteroid field carved to resemble terrified human faces. It was clear that Arcadia was subject to SYSDID (System Defence in Strength). Fighters attacked the *Admiral Raistruck*, but this was only a feint. The real attack came from behind: an energy being that was unaffected by the ship's torpedoes. The ship was destroyed.

Out of more than a thousand people, there were only four survivors: Defries, Daak and Troopers Ace and Johannsen. They discovered that Arcadia had been kept at a medieval level of technology. The population had been kept in ignorance, and the android Humble Counsellors enforced company law. All offworlders were killed as plague-carriers. The power behind Spinward was the Pool: vats of brain matter culled from generations of colonists, and housed in a space station in orbit around Arcadia. Pool intended to manufacture a universe of pure thought, making itself omnipotent. The clone Daak was killed, but Pool was ejected into the Vortex with the TARDIS' tertiary control room.

Ace rejoined the TARDIS, and travelled alongside the seventh Doctor and Bernice.

c 2573 - THE DARK FLAME[905] **->** The skull of Vilus Krull was unearthed on the toxic planet Marran Alpha, and agents of the Cult of the Dark Flame facilitated his resurrection in a dead body. The seventh Doctor and Ace collected Benny from a two-week stay on the deep-space research centre Orbos, and they stopped the Cult from creating a dark-light explosion that would enable the Dark Flame to spread its influence to every corner of space-time. Krull was thrown into the space-time vortex.

& 2574 - SHAKEDOWN[906] **->** The Sontarans secured information about the Rutan Host: Long ago, a wormhole had been established between Ruta III and Sentarion. In the event of a Sontaran victory, the Rutan Great Mother would use the tunnel to escape her fate. The Sontarans prepared to send a battlefleet down the wormhole to kill the Great Mother, but the Rutan spy Karne discovered the plan. The seventh Doctor, Roz, Chris and Benny tracked Karne down to the human colony of Megacity, and thwarted the Sontaran and Rutan plots.

The Galactic War had passed over the planet Dellah, and so the grateful three-eyed Sultan of the Tashwari built St Oscar's University – partly to affirm peace and learning, and partly to further keep Dellah from ranking as a target. The Sultan gave the university and its nine colleges names appealing to humans.[907] To protect its neutrality, Dellah banned all military research. Unofficially, St Oscar's continued weapons work in secret, and developed a prototype method of transferring mental engrams into synthetic forms – a means of producing the ultimate soldier. The process went awry, and the crew aboard the *Medusa*, a modified luxury liner, killed each other. Its navigation system damaged, the *Medusa* remained adrift.[908]

The Dalek Wars formally ended in 2575. At the end of the Galactic Wars, arms treaties were signed to limit the size and capability of combat robots.[909] A race of master weaponsmiths, the Xlanthi, had aided Earth during the Dalek Wars. Out of gratitude, Earth let the Xlanthi hunt fugitives in Earthspace without interference.[910]

2575 - BENNY: THE SWORD OF FOREVER[911] **->** Kenya and Somalia had been afflicted by Dalek retroviruses, and become home to many of the resultant mutations. The mutants were spreading south toward Tanzania

---

in "Profits of Doom", or that was on the front line of the Last Great Time War according to the Doctor in *Doomsday*.

905 Dating *The Dark Flame* (BF #42) - The dating clues within *The Dark Flame* are so ambiguous, previous editions of *Ahistory* consigned it to "None of the Above". What few dating clues we're given pertain to the Cult of the Dark Flame's own timeline – the back-cover blurb claims that the Cult was active "a thousand years" ago, and it's variously said that the Cult died out "centuries" or "thousands of years" ago. Vilus Krull, the Cult's founder, is twice said to have lived "thousands of years" ago.

However, the sequel to this story – *Benny S4: The Draconian Rage*, also written by Trevor Baxendale – not only makes references to Krull's defeat in *The Dark Flame*, it specifies that Krull was born on the human colony planet Tranagus. Given that *The Draconian Rage* occurs in 2602, and given the established timeline of human expansion into space, Krull could at most have lived a few centuries before events in *The Dark Flame* – meaning that all talk about Krull and the Cult going back "a thousand" or "thousands" of years must either be propaganda, or a case of those involved making guesses as to the Cult's shady past. With that in mind, there's only a window of some decades for *The Dark Flame* to occur before *The Draconian Rage*.

906 Dating *Shakedown* (NA #45) - There is no date given in the book, the story synopsis or the video version of this story. The novel is set after *Lords of the Storm* (set in 2371). The Rutans assert that the spy disguised as Karne "died long ago" (p66), but there's some sense that he is still a recent memory.

Benny: Mean Streets – set in 2594, and also written by Terrance Dicks – is something of a *Shakedown* sequel. It contains a flashback to Roz and Chris' visit to Megacity, in which they learn about an undertaking named The Project. *Mean Streets* p235 indicates that the Project has been running for no more than two generations.

Some general details about *Mean Streets* suggest that events in *Shakedown* were at most a few decades ago – the augmented Ogron Garshak appears in both books (although it's possible that he possesses an extended lifespan). According to *Mean Streets* p122, the bar manager Sara is the dancer that Chris ogles on *Shakedown* p78. She's admittedly a long-lived alien, but isn't surprised to see Chris again in *Mean Streets*, only that he should look a bit older. The account in *Mean Streets* of a former miner, "old Sam", also suggests that The Project was initiated within a human lifetime.

It's said that Chris Cwej – who's capable of time travel by the time *Mean Streets* occurs – wants to settle "unfinished business" in Megacity, and placing *Shakedown* shortly after *Lords of the Storm* would strangely have him doing so more than two hundred years after the fact. (Then again, it's also odd that he'd return a couple of decades later.)

907 *Benny: Oh No It Isn't!*
908 Twenty years before *Benny: The Medusa Effect*.
909 *Cold Fusion* (p247).
910 *Benny: Beige Planet Mars*. The 2575 dating concurs with the war winding down in 2573 (*Deceit*).
911 Dating *Benny: The Sword of Forever* (Benny NA #14)

and, more slowly, across the Ethiopian Plateau. Nairobi was nothing more than mutant jungle. Addis Ababa, formerly home to half a million, was now inhabited by hybrid humans. A Mason named Marillian tracked the Ark of the Covenant to Axum, a home to many human hybrids in Ethiopia. Marillian's translator, Ondemwu, escaped with the Ark as the Russian Conglomerate Military Red Cross purified the area.

& 2575 - ARRANGEMENTS FOR WAR[912] ->
The sixth Doctor and Evelyn visited the planet Vilag after witnessing the Killoran invasion to come, and observed the love developing between Princess Krisztina and Marcus Reid, a lowly gardener's son.

? 2575 - HUMAN NATURE (NA)[913] ->
The seventh Doctor and Benny visited a bodysmith and bought a Pod that would allow the Doctor to become human. They travelled to Earth, 1914, so the Doctor could experiment with living as a human being.

? 2576 - RAIN OF TERROR[914] ->
On Earth, holiday excursions were available to an alien zoo on the far side of the moon, and the National Museum of Mars. The Off-Planet Railroad Company had a solid reputation for building train lines. An engineer working for one of the big colony builders could spend weeks or months on faraway planets, returning to Earth in the interim. Colony ships could erect temporary buildings on target worlds prior to engineering firms moving in to do the job properly. Galactic Safari offered use of hyper-sleep chambers that even an upper middle-class family in Brighton could afford. The chambers enabled travel to such worlds as the tourist planet of Xirrinda, which featured such exotic animals as the Trinto, Beslons and the predatory Sharkwolf. The eleventh Doctor, Amy and Rory visited Xirrinda

after dealing with a revolution that involved super-evolved Mire Beasts, and were present as the swarm of ravenous machine-creatures ejected from Xirrinda – numbering in the tens of billions – returned to their homeworld. The Doctor deciphered the key to an ancient "fail-safe" device left by the creatures' creators, and switched them off.

2577 - BENNY: THE SWORD OF FOREVER[915] ->
Marillian inherited many businesses after his father died in a transport accident. He tracked the stolen Ark of the Covenant to the Palace of the Arch-Regent Gebmoses III – the self-proclaimed (and virtually unacknowledged) Emperor of the Third World – in Kampuchea. Gebmoses had Marillian killed, then resurrected using the Ark's power. Henceforth, Marillian acknowledged Gebmoses as his master.

On Draconia, only two of the six bloodlines from the reign of the First Emperor had survived to the twenty-sixth century: House Kaytar and House Salah. Members of House Kaytar found a stranded Earth ship and indentured the family they found within – but such was the respect and privilege that House Kaytar accorded to the humans, it was disbanded.[916]

The capital of Earth's moon colony was once the most exciting city in human space, but eventually became half historical theme park, half grimy port. The dark side of the moon was even worse off – efforts to keep it artificially lit and atmospherically supported ended when the population dropped below viability levels. It became a "huge, pitch-black ghost town".[917]

2579 - BENNY: THE VAMPIRE CURSE: "Possum Kingdom"[918] ->
Dallas-Fort Worth was now a city within the United States of Texas. Benny and her travelling companion questioned the amnesiac man – Nepesht – whom

- The year is given.
912 Dating *Arrangements for War* (BF #57) - This epilogue occurs five years before the main story.
913 Dating *Human Nature* (NA #38) - No date is given, but Ellerycorp and the Travellers are mentioned, suggesting this is around Benny's native time.
914 Dating *Rain of Terror* (BBC children's 2-in-1 #8, released in *Alien Adventures*) - The evidence sits at odds with itself. Professor Willard flew shuttlecraft "during the Cyber War" (p319); he's now older, indicating that it's a generation, or two at most, beyond that event. However, humanity's advancement – particularly the affordability, reliability and speed of space travel – seems well beyond that, more akin to the sort of thing one would expect from the Fourth Great and Bountiful Human Empire (*The Long Game*). Along those lines, the Doctor thinks that the Xirrinda colony was established

"in the last year or two" (p226), and yet the colony already has "eight million" colonists (p261). The "Cyber War" reference is very hard to shake, though, and space travel *is* very common in Bernice Summerfield's era. Perhaps it's a really nice planet.
No mention is made of either the Earth-Draconian conflict or the Dalek Wars, so the placement here, as much as anything, reflects the likelihood that the story occurs during a (relatively) peaceful period for Earth.
915 Dating *Benny: The Sword of Forever* (Benny NA #14) - The year is given.
916 "Forty years" before *Benny S8: The Judas Gift*
917 "Decades" before *Benny S11: Resurrecting the Past*. The Dalek Wars might well account for the drop in the moon's population. The dark side of the moon, at least in our time, never faces the Earth, but is not in permanent darkness.

she had met fourteen years previously. The man's memories returned, and he generated a portal that let him pursue his nemesis back to 1212.

> = The Jason Kane of a parallel reality used a stungun on a harpist when his version of Bernice Summerfield was moved to tears during the Philharmonic Uprising of 2580.[919]

c 2580 - ARRANGEMENTS FOR WAR[920] -> On Vilag, the countries of Galen and Malendia negotiated a ceasefire after centuries of warfare. Governor Justice Rossiter, the head of the country of Kozepen, served as an independent arbiter as Galen and Malendia worked to form a coalition: the Kingdom Alliance. The sixth Doctor and Evelyn visited Vilag three weeks prior to an invasion by the warlike Killorans, knowing that the Alliance was historically slated to overcome them.

The Doctor's loose lips caused Galen's Princess Krisztina to declare her love for Lieutenant Marcus Reid, ruining her intended political marriage to Malendia's Prince Viktor. Thousands were killed as the scandal caused Galen and Malendia to resume their conflict. Nonetheless, the nations united their forces when the Killorans attacked, and drove off the invaders. Krisztina and Reid were killed the con-

flict. Rossiter, being a widower, asked Evelyn to stay with him, but she resumed her travels with the Doctor...

Adrian Wall fought in the battle of Vilag, and killed a boy no older than five during it.[921]

Evelyn Smythe Leaves the TARDIS

& 2581 - THICKER THAN WATER[922] -> A triumvirate government was established on Vilag. The sixth Doctor and Evelyn re-visited the planet, and she left the TARDIS to marry Rossiter.

In 2582, Kothar – a descendent of the disgraced House Kaytar of Draconia – was appointed a cultural attaché to the Draconian Embassy on Earth.[923]

& 2583 - THICKER THAN WATER[924] -> Rossiter was elected Principle Triumvir, the head of the tripartite government on Vilag. The sixth Doctor and Mel visited Evelyn Rossiter, and the Doctor ended illicit experiments involving Killoran DNA. He and Mel were present as Evelyn and Rossiter renewed their wedding vows.

---

918 Dating *Benny: The Vampire Curse*: "Possum Kingdom" (Benny collection #12b) - The year is given.
919 *Benny: Many Happy Returns*
920 Dating *Arrangements for War* (BF #57) - No dating clues exist in this story or its sequel, *Thicker Than Water*, but placement is possible by extrapolating from the Bernice Summerfield range. *Benny: Parallel Lives*: "Hiding Places", set in 2606, establishes that Adrian Wall fought in the invasion of Vilag, suggesting that – once allowances are made that a Killoran lifespan might differ from that of humans – *Arrangements for War* and *Thicker Than Water* must occur closer to the start of the twenty-seventh century than not.

A recurring theory in fandom holds that the unnamed bodyguards to the Gallifreyan Imperiatrix Pandora (*Gallifrey II: Lies*) were Killorans, and that historical intervention on the part of the Time Lords – who "time-looped" the bodyguards' homeworld – is responsible for the Killorans transitioning from the primal brutes who attacked Vilag to the more civilised builders seen in the Benny range. A "time loop" would not in itself account for such historical revision, though; moreover, Adrian vividly remembers the Vilag invasion in *Parallel Lives*, so it's not as if the event was erased from history entirely.
921 *Benny: Parallel Lives*: "Hiding Places"
922 Dating *Thicker Than Water* (BF #73) - A year has passed since the Killoran invasion.
923 *Benny* S8: *The Judas Gift*

924 Dating *Thicker Than Water* (BF #73) - The blurb says that it's "Three years after Vilag was all but laid waste by the Killorans." The Doctor here takes Mel to meet Evelyn for "the first time", which disputes the claim in *Instruments of Darkness* that they've not only met but travelled together for a time, although the contradiction is literally limited to a few lines of dialogue between the Doctor and Mel in an opening scene. Nonetheless, it is there.
925 *A Death in the Family*. Evelyn resides on Pelican for seven years, and remarks at the end of her life that Rossiter died "ten years ago" – so she must live on Vilag for three years after his passing, and an indeterminate amount of time with him after *Thicker Than Water*.
926 "Seven years, three months and eleven days" before *Demontage*.
927 *Cold Fusion*. The year of the revolution is given (p230), the science fair was "ten years ago" (p200).
928 Dating *Deimos/The Resurrection of Mars* (BF BBC7 #4.5-4.6) - It's "centuries" after the destruction of the Martian warfleet in *The Seeds of Death*. Mention is made of the "hippy holiday camp" seen in *Phobos*, set in 2589, suggesting that this story occurs in the same period.

Mars here gains a human-compatible atmosphere (curiously, no mention is made of how the three hundred thousand people living on Mars are currently surviving without one). Mars was terraformed and given a breathable atmosphere in the early twenty-second century – however, the Daleks released a virus

Rossiter died. Three years later, Evelyn found the temporal stabiliser of the timeship UNS *Pelican* in a coal seam. It translocated her to billions of years in the past.[925]

Battrulian artist Toulour Martinique was mysteriously killed after painting his last work, *Murdering Art*, which depicted his being murdered by demons.[926] Around 2582, the Kalkravian Revolution took place, and the Adjudication Bureau was sent in to free hostages. The All Worlds Science Fair took place on the planet Dellah. Earth won the Worlds Cup in 2584.[927]

Lucie Miller Rejoins the Eighth Doctor, Tamsin Drew Leaves

c 2585 - DEIMOS / THE RESURRECTION OF MARS[928] -> The Mars Terraforming Project established a base on the Martian moon of Deimos, and built a re-ioniser to alter Mars' atmosphere from space, making it breathable to humans. The Project collapsed due to the onset of the Great Recession and technical problems related to the goal of warming Mars with artificial suns. In time, the Martian catacombs on Deimos were excavated, and the moonbase became a museum devoted to the Ice Warriors. The humans in the solar system believed that the Ice Warriors had been wiped out in the twenty-first century, and at least one documentary had been made of the T-Mat incident.

The Monk, in a bid to alter history so the utopian society on Halcyon would survive, awoke the Ice Warriors on Deimos "a few centuries" early. He also fired Lucie Miller as his companion, and left her in the moonbase on Deimos. Using the base's re-ioniser, the Ice Warriors attempted to alter Mars' atmosphere to support their race. The eighth Doctor destroyed the moonbase and the re-

ionizer – an act that altered Mars' atmosphere so it could sustain human life, and ignited the surface of Deimos. The resultant chain reaction turned Deimos into a miniature sun that would supply Mars with heat and light.

Six hundred people had died – and three hundred thousand people living on Mars been endangered – because the Doctor had hesitated in killing the Ice Warriors, as this would have also meant Lucie's death. The Doctor's companion Tamsin decried his cowardice, and departed with the Monk. Lucie resumed travelling with the Doctor.

c 2585 - THE ALSO PEOPLE[929] -> The seventh Doctor, Bernice, Roz and Chris enjoyed a holiday at the Worldsphere of the People. Chris became lovers with a young woman named Dep, and Roz had a romantic relationship with a war veteran named feLixi. The seventh Doctor solved the murder of viCari, the first drone to be killed in more than three hundred years. feLixi was punished for his culpability in viCari's murder with ostracism – nobody in the Worldsphere would ever speak to him again. The Doctor and Bernice also helped restore the feral Kadiatu Lethbridge-Stewart to sanity. Dep didn't tell Chris that she was pregnant with his child.

She later gave birth to a daughter, iKrissi. Because Dep made a mistake during conception, iKrissi was an exact clone of Chris. Dep had at least one more child.[930]

= 2586 - TIMEH: CHILD OF TIME[931] -> The Sodality had been created when the surviving members of the Cabal of the Horned Beast re-acquired the Daemon-linked book that was lost in the twentieth century, and retroactively make their insignificant

during the Dalek Invasion that ate all of the Martian atmosphere's oxygen and took "years" (according to *Fear Itself*, PDA, p63) if not decades to reverse. It's entirely possible – although it's not expressly said – that the same fate befell the planet when the Daleks overran Mars during the Dalek Wars (in 2545, according *Benny: Beige Planet Mars*), which both greatly reduced the number of people living on Mars (cited as three million in 2545 in *Beige Planet Mars*, but only three hundred thousand in *The Resurrection of Mars*) and prompted the Mars Terraforming Project seen here. Either way, Mars has a breathable atmosphere in *Beige Planet Mars*, set in 2595, further encouraging a placement prior to that.

The Earth public thinks that the Ice Warriors are extinct, suggesting that *The Resurrection of Mars* occurs prior to the Federation's diplomatic contacts with them (*The Curse of Peladon*, etc.), and neatly ties in with the claim in *Legacy* that the "extinct" Martians became of interest during the twenty-sixth century. The re-ionizer technology used on Mars is, clearly, a precursor to the

ionizer seen in *The Ice Warriors* (even if the re-ionizer on Mars, if anything, seems more powerful that the model used at Britannicus Base).

929 Dating *The Also People* (NA #44) - The remains of "a sub gas giant that had broken up sixty-two billion years previously" is referred to (p168) and the Doctor said his "diary's pretty much clear" until "the heat death of the universe" (p186). This led the Virgin edition of this book to conclude that the story was set many billions of years in the future. However, the Bernice Summerfield New Adventures made clear that the story takes place around Benny's native time.

930 *Happy Endings*

931 Dating *TimeH: Child of Time* (TimeH #11) - The year is given. Sodality in 2586 appears to be operating from a "potential" timeline – which is very fortunate, as the late twenty-sixth century is the native era of Bernice Summerfield, and it's impossible to reconcile the heavy amount known about this period with the total lack of a mention concerning the devastated Earth that Sodality has brought about. Sodality is expressly said to

group more powerful. Honoré Lechasseur and Emily Blandish arrived in a version of 2586 in which Sodality's meddling with history had created a devastated Earth. The Daemon named Mastho appeared at St Paul's Cathedral as Sodality summoned him a third time, and revealled that he had ordered Sodality to kill its time-sensitives and time-channellers as a means of culling all but the "Child of Time": a human with the combined abilities of both. The Daemons wanted to study such a creature, absorb its powers and gain the unfettered ability to travel through space and time. A woman named Maria became the Child of Time – but killed herself after falling through time to 1949, causing a psionic backlash that killed Mastho also.

An unknown incarnation of the Doctor witnessed these events, and took Sodality's High Executioner with him upon making his escape. She would part ways with him in 1949, and become Emily Blandish.

A company in the Catan Nebula made Artificial Personality Embodiments (APEs): synthetic humans with a tailored set of memories. Two synthoids – Kara Delbane and an unnamed agent with Stratum Seven-level clearance – were created to join a mercenary group, the Oblivion Angels. They reported to a computer intelligence: the Artificial Viral-based Intelligence Destabilisation (ARVID). The Agent and Kara were sent to the planet Sharabeth, a nexus point of industry and commerce. One of the Dellan gods had been flung back through time, causing a number of time fractures on Sharabeth. It merged its consciousness with the cyber-body of Absolam Sleed, the company founder, and used his resources to commit mass carnage. Sleed seemed to die at the Agent's hands, but his brain survived.[932]

The Dominicci Corporation specialised in the purchase, re-branding and marketing of forgotten-about religious iconography, including that of the Beneficiary and Hannah Montana.[933] During Bernice Summerfield and Jason Kane's honeymoon, the Imperator of Xoab was outraged when Jason graffitied "Jason and Benny did it here. Eight times. In a day" on the Imperator's Royal Tree.[934]

hail from a "possible" future in the *Time Hunter*-related film *Daemons: Daemos Rising*, and in *Child of Time* (co-written by David J. Howe, publisher of *Time Hunter* and the writer of *Daemos Rising*), and Honoré innately senses that Sodality's Earth isn't part of established history. By extension, this would seem to mean that Emily Blandish herself originates from a potential reality, but then crosses over and takes up residence in the universe's "main" timeline (similar to Elizabeth Klein; see *Colditz*). Whether or not this means that the Doctor who appears in *The Cabinet of Light* and *TimeH: Child of Time* is from the "proper" timeline or Sodality's altered history is an open-ended question. The "child of time" that Mastho here covets isn't to be confused with Chiyoko, the "child of time" seen in the *DWM* comics.

932 A decade before *Benny: Return to the Fractured Planet*.

933 "Decades" before *Benny B2: Road Trip: Brand Management*.

934 *Benny: Adorable Illusion* (ch3). Year unknown (especially as Benny and Jason spent some of their honeymoon flitting around via time rings), but the event is referenced as if it's still relevant to Benny's life in the twenty-seventh century.

935 Dating *Return of the Living Dad* (NA #53) - It's "2587" (p5).

936 *So Vile a Sin*

937 Dating *Phobos* (BF BBC7 #1.5) - "Apparently the year is 2589", the Doctor says.

938 "Over thirty years" before *Vienna S1: Deathworld*. Some liberties are taken with Vienna's age – she's about 34 in *Vienna* Series 1, but actress Chase Masterson was 50 when she recorded the part.

939 The background to *Worlds BF: The Archive*, with additional details given in *Worlds BF: Kronos Vad's History of Earth (Vol. 36,379)* and *Graceless III: The Battle*.

940 Dating *Graceless III: The Battle* and *Graceless III: Consequences* (*Graceless* #3.2-3.3) - The digital-only *Ahistory* 2012-2013 update initially dated these events to ? 600,000, on the grounds that the Archive contained a record of Abby and Zara's ultimate fate, which unfolded in *Consequences* [c.495,406]. *The Worlds of Big Finish*, however, redefines the Archive as a resource that contains every book written throughout the history of time. The elder Romulus Chang says in *Worlds BF: The Archive* that Chi died "a thousand years"/"more than a thousand years" ago, but that Kronos Vad's chronology of Earth was left with the Archive (by Bernice Summerfield and Vienna Salvatori) "*almost* a thousand years" beforehand. Similarly, Chang specifies that Abby and Zara visited the Archive before he was an apprentice there, but that he *was* an apprentice when Benny and Vienna showed up [c.2620]. Connecting those dots, it seems that Abby and Zara consult with Chi at the Archive some years or perhaps a few decades before Benny and Vienna arrive there.

941 "Three centuries" after *The Leisure Hive*.

942 "Ten years" before *Prime Time*.

943 Quinn's family dies while he's off training, and he has "thirty years" of piloting experience by the time *Worlds BF: The Phantom Wreck* rolls around.

944 Dating *Demontage* (EDA #20) - No date given, but the art forger Newark Rappare appears here and in *Benny: Dragon's Wrath* (set in 2593), and is "middle aged" in both.

2587 (autumn) - RETURN OF THE LIVING DAD[935] ->
The newly-married Bernice Summerfield and Jason Kane were on Youkali 6. Benny was studying for a genuine degree in archaeology, while writing a new book and trying for a child. An old friend of her father, Admiral Groenewegen, made contact with new information about Isaac Summerfield's disappearance. Benny called the seventh Doctor for help – and they discovered that Isaac was alive and well, and living on Earth in 1983.

The seventh Doctor and Chris visited Bernice and Jason on Youkali 6 to inform them of Roz Forrester's death.[936]

2589 - PHOBOS[937] -> An entity from a collapsing universe forged a singularity bridge to our reality. The bridge ended on the Martian moon of Phobos, but the entity became stuck in the transition point. It fed off feelings of euphoria, set up a thin atmosphere on Phobos and gained strength as the moon was used for extreme sports.

Problems arose during the development of Lunar Park (a hotel and botanical garden) on Phobos; only its environmental dome was finished. Squatters moved in when the moon was left unincorporated, and adrenaline junkies performed extreme sports against the backdrop of the moon's spectacular ice valleys. Such recreations included grav-board runs outside the dome, ice spelunking in the melted floes beneath the surface and "orbit-hopping".

The eighth Doctor and Lucie stopped on Phobos, and the Doctor jolted the emerging entity by concentrating his many fears – the creature either died or went dormant. As a precaution, the Doctor recommended that Phobos' sports come to an end.

The time-active Headhunter landed on Phobos days before the TARDIS' arrival, but fell off a bicycle and was unconscious until after the Doctor and Lucie had left.

In this era, the Githians were large, hirsute creatures who inter-acted with humanity, but were forbidden to marry outside their species in order to keep their gene pool pure. Hunters retrieved Githians who violated the law.

Vienna Salvatori

Death, Inc. purchased orphans and unwanted children, then educated and brainwashed them in immersion pods to become bounty hunters and killers. Fabricated memories compelled the operatives to undertake missions for Death, Inc., then return to their pods.

The future assassin Vienna Salvatori was bought, around age four, from her parents, Carlo and Delta Turala of Forest Gala I. Implanted memories convinced her that she hailed from the warrior caste on Mercator, and had attended the Assassin Academy there after a man named Crevo Finn killed her father, and gravely injured her mother, while a four-year-old Vienna hid in an air duct.

She became one of Death, Inc.'s best agents, thinking her fees were benefiting her mother's hospice on Miracle III, when they were actually going into Death, Inc.'s accounts. As an adult, Vienna had her spaceship remove the memory of her parents' "downfall", as it was hampering her effectiveness in the field.[938]

The Archive

The preservation of data continued to have its challenges: at one point, Earth had lost almost five centuries of art, music and literature in a single accident.

The Archive emerged as a near-infinite resource, bigger than an entire solar system, that contained every book imaginable – including those that would be written in future. It was so vast, the Archivist Chi Shin-Kylie's AI assistant would have needed nine days to count all the books in it.

Texts related to multiple universes were separated into five main branches. The Department of Eschatology (founded some two thousand years ago) focused on doomsday works, while the Meta-Archive contained books about the Archive itself. The Archivists could live up to a thousand years, their minds serving as back-ups to the Archive's holdings.[939]

c 2590 - GRACELESS III: THE BATTLE / CONSEQUENCES[940] -> Abby and Zara's intervention in the Battle of Maldon, 991, had so badly damaged history, 10% of the Archive's books were being erased every 80.46 seconds. The sisters took the Archivist Chi Shin-Kylie back to Maldon to repair history. Upon their return, Chi informed Abby and Zara of a record stating that they would meet Marek Golding again... on the same day they decided to die.

Around the year 2590, Radon 222 levels on the surface of Argolis had dropped to such a level that the planet became habitable again.[941] Blinni-Gaar was an agricultural planet feeding an entire sector. Channel 400 made a deal with the government and started broadcasting addictive programmes. The Blinnati stopped farming, nearly leading to famine on the Rim until offworlders started running the planet.[942]

The Thames Delta experienced a sudden and unexpected uprising. While Captain Quinn was off training on an Orbiter, his wife and daughter were killed in an aerial assault.[943]

c 2590 - DEMONTAGE[944] -> The eighth Doctor, Sam and Fitz arrived on Vega Station. General Browning Phillips was planning to return the Battrulian junta to power by killing President Drexler, but the Doctor defeated that plan. Drexler and a Canvine representative, Bigdog

Caruso, engineered a more permanent peace treaty between the Battrul and Canvine.

The artist Martinique had discovered a process that could physically transfer someone into a painting, or make items in paintings take physical form. He used this technique to survive his "murder", and took up residence in a serene painting, *On a Clear Day*.

The Doctor Reunited with Patience

2592 (31st October) - COLD FUSION[945] **->** By this time, the Third Draconian War had been fought. An Empress, revered as a goddess by some, now ruled Earth. The Empire had developed Skybases to operate as planetary command centres, and the Adjudicators were sent across the Empire to enforce Imperial Law. The Unitatus Guild, a secret society based on garbled legends of UNIT in the twentieth century, was politically influential.

The Scientifica, the ruling elite of scientists on an icy Earth colony planet, excavated a crashed TARDIS and its mummified pilot. Following experiments on the ship, ghosts start appearing across the planet. The seventh Doctor, Chris and Roz investigated the ghosts. The fifth Doctor, Tegan, Nyssa and Adric arrived a month later, and found the Patient – a mummified Time Lady – who promptly regenerated. The Doctor tried to get her to safety

as the Adjudicators declared martial law. Both Doctors realised that the ghosts were the Ferutu, beings from the far future of an alternative timeline in which Gallifrey was destroyed in the ancient past. The Ferutu attempted to ensure Gallifrey's destruction, but the fifth and seventh Doctors joined forces and ensured history was not altered. A few Ferutu were trapped within a chalk circle, the only survivors of their timeline.

The Time Lady, Patience, was fatally wounded but rescued by Omega, who transported her to his anti-matter universe.[946]

The corporation Helping Hand Solutions was created. To guarantee a respectable figurehead, the "company founder", Kensington Fox, was secretly a hologram controlled by the board.[947]

TerpsiCorp, which would become the largest music publishing company of the thirty-first century, and having more money than Megapolis One, based its offices – a single skyscraper – on the artificial moon of Semiquaver, orbiting Jupiter.[948] Fitz Kreiner awoke after almost six hundred years to find himself in Augustine City on Ordifica. The colonists had developed the Cold, a horrific weapon. Fitz celebrated his 626th birthday on Ordifica on 7th March, 2593.[949]

---

945 Dating *Cold Fusion* (MA #29) - The novel was originally set at the same time as *So Vile a Sin* and tied in quite closely to that book, but it became clear *So Vile a Sin* wouldn't be released as scheduled. Following that, *Cold Fusion* was reworked to occur just before the Benny New Adventures, and included the first mention of Dellah, the planet Benny was based on for that series. A copyright notice on a wardroid states that this is 2692, but that was a typographical error, and should have read "2592". It's "four hundred years" before Chris and Roz's time (p165). It's stated that the Adjudicators have been around for "half a millennium" (p247).

946 Patience vanishes mysteriously in *Cold Fusion*, and reappears in *The Infinity Doctors*.

947 "Over thirty years" before *Vienna S3: Impossibly Glamourous*.

948 "Seventy-nine years" before *Iris S4: A Lift in Time*.

949 *Interference* (p113).

950 Dating The Bernice Summerfield New Adventures – The twenty-three New Adventures novels featuring Benny start with her joining the staff of St Oscar's in 2593 (a year first established in The *Dying Days*) and roughly acknowledge the real-world passage of time during the two and a half years the Benny NAs were in publication. The series ends with *Benny: Twilight of the Gods*, set in 2596. See the individual entries for more.

TERMINOLOGY IN THE BENNY BOOKS AND AUDIOS: The New Adventures books continued after Virgin lost

the *Doctor Who* licence in 1996. They were unable to use characters and concepts that originated in *Doctor Who*, but those created for the New Adventures (Benny, Jason Kane, Chris Cwej, Roz Forrester, the People of the Worldsphere from *The Also People*, Irving Braxiatel, etc.) were fair game. For legal reasons, a number of new terms were coined when referencing characters or concepts firmly lodged in *Doctor Who*.

The Dalek Wars that were so influential to Benny's background were more generically referred to as "the Galactic War". Braxiatel in both the NAs and the Big Finish audios broadly has "time technology" or "owns a time machine", although his timeship's inter-dimensional nature – as prominently seen in *Benny: Tears of the Oracle* and various audios – leaves no doubt that it's a TARDIS, a notion reinforced by Big Finish's use of TARDIS-like noises. The Time Lords – who were still involved in the New Adventures, unnamed, as the signatories to the treaty with the People (*Benny: Walking to Babylon*), as Irving Braxiatel's race and as Chris Cwej's employers (*Benny: Dead Romance*) were occasionally called "the Watchmakers". Big Finish was similarly coy about naming the Time Lords, even though the status of "Braxiatel's people" mirrors developments with the Time Lords in the *Gallifrey* mini-series, and the Time Lord Straxus appears in both the BBC7 audios and *Benny S9: The Adventure of the Diogenes Damsel*. While the Benny stories frequently refer to the Time Lords as

Bernice Summerfield at St Oscar's University[950]

St Oscar's University had become became one of the most prestigious centres of learning in the Milky Way.[951] Dellah was closer to the Galactic Hub than Earth, but was considered more of a backwater. The days there lasted twenty-six hours. The Shakya Constellation was visible from Dellah's southern hemisphere.[952] Trans-galactic travel was fairly easy in this era for those with money, but navigation computers were expensive and time travel was forbidden. Instant information transfer was available.[953] Galactic Basic, the most common language, was an evolved version of English.[954]

The Eighth Doctor Drops Benny and Wolsey Off at St Oscar's

2593 (Wednesday, 8th May) - THE DYING DAYS[955]
-> Benny Summerfield was offered the chair of archaeology at St Oscar's University on Dellah. She received the job offer in 1997 despite never actually applying for the position. The eighth Doctor dropped her off, and they enjoyed a fond farewell. He also gifted her with Wolsey the TARDIS cat.

The People's supercomputer God had brainwashed Benny into joining the St Oscar's staff, preparing her for the coming day when she would help to free the conceptual entity MEPHISTO.[956]

The Black Guardian transported the con man and art dealer Menlove Stokes to Dellah from the far distant future. Stokes became a Professor of Applied Arts at St Oscar's.[957]

2593 - BENNY: OH NO IT ISN'T![958] -> Benny, in her post as the Edward Watkinson Professor of Archaeology at St Oscar's, accompanied a team of academics to the quarantined planet of Perfecton. The missile containing the encoded remains of Perfecton civilisation struck Benny's ship, the *Winton*, and impacted with Professor Archduke's thesis on obscure theatrical forms. The missile's quantum fluctuations manifested aspects of Archduke's thesis, and so Benny's team and some Grel – information monarchs/pirates with squiddy faces – found themselves in a world governed by pantomime. Benny passed as a young man named Dick Whittington, and her cat Wolsey temporarily became a talking biped. She ended the scenario, and her team escaped as Perfecton's sun went nova. Archduke acquired the data module containing the Perfecton culture.

The Knights of Jeneve captured Chris Cwej and put him in suspended animation.[959]

The Irving Braxiatel who was flung through the Time Vortex during his struggle with Lord Burner arrived on Dellah. He met Benny just once[960], realised that she was familiar with an alternate version of himself, and avoided contacting her until 2616.[961]

"Braxiatel's people", *Ahistory* has used the terms "Time Lords" and Braxiatel's "TARDIS" for clarity.

The Benny equivalent of the Ice Warriors is less straightforward... in *Benny: Dragons' Wrath*, writer Justin Richards introduced the recurring character of Commander Skutloid, whose description (p109) leaves no doubt that he's an Ice Lord in all but name. Richards named Skutloid's species in *Benny: The Medusa Effect* (p14) as "Neo Arietian" before establishing the more commonly used spelling of "Neo-Aretian" in *Benny: Tears of the Oracle* (p37, 40, etc.). Skutloid hails from "Neo Ares" (*The Medusa Effect*, p19), either an alternate name for "New Mars" (*Legacy*), a.k.a. "Nova Martia" (*GodEngine*) – a "Neo-Aretian" (i.e. "New Martian") could feasibly hail from either – or, more likely, Neo Ares and Nova Martia are separate Ice Warrior colonies, hence the different nomenclature. Big Finish wound up trying to have this both ways, using the term "Neo-Aretians" in *Benny: A Life of Surprises*: "Might", before having Benny encounter the actual, licensed Ice Warriors in *Benny: The Dance of the Dead*. In *Benny: A Life Worth Living*, Big Finish settled for calling the Braxiatel Collection gardener, Hass, "a Martian" (even if temporal distortion retroactively turned him into a Yesodi in *Benny: Something Changed*).

951 *Benny: Oh No It Isn't!*
952 *Benny: Ship of Fools*
953 *Benny: The Mary-Sue Extrusion*
954 *Benny: Return to the Fractured Planet*
955 Dating *The Dying Days* (NA #61) - The date is given. It's a bit of an oddity that Wolsey is still in the TARDIS even though the eighth Doctor is now "twelve hundred" years old. As Wolsey was initially the seventh Doctor's cat, and the seventh Doctor regenerated age 1009 (according to *Vampire Science*), the math would seem to suggest that, somehow, Wolsey has been living in the TARDIS for about two centuries.
956 *Benny: Down*
957 *The Well-Mannered War*
958 Dating *Benny: Oh No It Isn't!* (Benny NA #1) - The year was given in *The Dying Days*.
959 Six months before *Benny: Deadfall*.
960 *Gallifrey IV: Disassembled*, in a scene dramatised from *Dragons' Wrath*.
961 *Benny* S1: *Epoch: Judgement Day*

2593 - BENNY: DRAGONS' WRATH[962] -> Irving Braxiatel was presently the head of the St Oscar's Theatrology Department, and – from his perspective – met Bernice Summerfield for the first time. The warlord Romolo Nusek sought to further his power by proving that his ancestor, Hugo Gamaliel, once held a colony on Stanturus Three. Benny used the low-grade nuclear device hidden in the prized Gamaliel Dragon to obliterate the power-mad Nusek and his castle.

Jason Kane Returns to Benny's Life

2593 - BENNY: BEYOND THE SUN[963] -> The Sunless conquered the planet Ursu, and returned the Blooms stolen from them to their homeworld. Benny – with some help from her ex-husband Jason Kane, who approached her at a dig on Apollox 4 – deduced that the Blooms were a stellar manipulator. After being given the right keys – a particular brother and sister the Blooms had spawned – it generated enough energy to revitalise the Sunless' star.

2593 - BENNY: SHIP OF FOOLS -> Earth's seas were now a thick black sludge. The famed thief Cat's Paw stole an Olabrian joy-luck crystal from Marcus Krytell, one of the richest men in the sector. With the Olabrians prone to committing mass murder to recover their crystals, Krytell asked Bernice to handle the ransom exchange on the maiden voyage of the *Titanian Queen*, a luxury liner. Benny unmasked Cat's Paw as Isabel Blaine, a construct of the Catan Nebula. The *Titanian Queen* was destroyed when its artificial intelligence went mad, but Benny and Cat's Paw saved the passengers. In retribution for Krytell's crimes,

Cat's Paw returned the joy-luck crystal to him – but also informed the authorities of its location, causing Olabrian battle cruisers to swoop down on his location.[964]

On Boxing Day, 2593, Benny won a bet on Fat Lightning, odds 8-1, at the annual St Oscar's slug-racing championships. She celebrated by "not getting absolutely bladdered".[965]

2594 (January) - BENNY: DOWN[966] -> Tyler's Folly declared independence from Earth, and the Republican Security Force responded by staging a military coup, declaring the colony there a police state. Benny's actions helped the conceptual entity MEPHISTO to emerge, but prevented it from remaking reality in its image. MEPHISTO's philosophy of pain amidst a utopia aided the further development of the People of the Worldsphere.

2594 (January) - BENNY: DEADFALL[967] -> The Knights of Jeneve searched for descendants of their founder, Vazlov Baygent, hoping to host his preserved memories in one of them. Chris Cwej, as one of Baygent's descendants, and Jason Kane thwarted the Knights' efforts to find a Baygent-host aboard the *KayBee 2*, a prison ship.

2594 - BENNY: GHOST DEVICES -> The supercomputer God asked Benny to join an archaeological expedition to Canopus IV, where she found the Spire built by the long-dead Vo'lach race. Benny caused two Vo'lach Planetcracker missiles to travel into the past and damage the Spire. As God intended, this averted the paradox pertaining to the Spire's nature, saving billions of lives.

---

962 The art forger Menlove Stokes, also seen in *Demontage*, is here murdered.

963 Dating *Benny: Beyond the Sun* (Benny NA #3) - In Benny and Jason's timeline, eight months have passed since they last saw each other, and got divorced, in *Eternity Weeps*.

964 Cat's Paw is the same type of Catan-made artificial lifeform as the Stratum Seven agent from *Benny: The Mary-Sue Extrusion* and *Benny: Return to the Fractured Planet*.

965 *Benny: Down*

966 Dating *Benny: Down* (Benny NA #5) - It's now "early 2594" (p8). Benny arrives on Tyler's Folly no later than "January 14th" (p152), but the action opens at St Oscar's some time beforehand. After Benny is apprehended, an interrogation report and an arrest report are respectively dated to "15/01/94" (p165) and "22/1/94" (p8). Benny is subjected to "the sound of the Young Nazi Male Voice Choir of the year 2594" (p151).

967 Dating *Benny: Deadfall* (Benny NA #6) - It's said that Benny has now been at St Oscar's for "six months"; it's actually been more like nine, although it's possible

she's counting from the start of the term. Either way, it's January 2594 at the latest.

968 This is a sequel to the New Adventures novel *Shakedown*.

969 Dating *Benny: Walking to Babylon* (Benny NA #10) - An extract from Benny's memoirs (p27) says that it's still 2594. She's currently procrastinating on writing *An Eye for Wisdom*, slated for publication in 2595.

970 The *Schirron Dream* crew formerly appeared in *Sky Pirates!* and *Death and Diplomacy*.

971 "Chateau Yquatine" presumably references *The Fall of Yquatine*, also by Nick Walters. Café Vosta, an establishment at the Braxiatel Collection, is also cited as serving it (*Benny: Collected Works*). All of which is very curious, since *The Fall of Yquatine* claims that the Yquatine System won't be colonised for a couple of centuries yet.

972 *Superior Beings* (p108).

973 *Interference*

974 Dating *Benny: The Sword of Forever* (Benny NA #14) - The chapter headings reiterate that it's 2595.

975 *Benny: Walking to Babylon*. Obviously, publication must occur before St Oscar's is ravaged in *Benny: Where*

2594 - BENNY: MEAN STREETS[968] **->** Benny and Chris Cwej went to the planet Megerra and exposed The Project – an illicit undertaking by DevCorps to create genetically engineered miners with enhanced stamina. DevCorps was bankrupted. The Combine was currently the biggest crime syndicate in the galaxy.

2594 - BENNY: TEMPEST -> Benny gave a lecture to the archaeological society on the colony world of Tempest, then left for the spaceport aboard the *Polar Express* monorail. The business tycoon Nathan Costermann embarked on a murder and insurance scam involving the Drell Imnulate – an artifact of the Drell religion. After Benny exposed his plans, Costermann fell to his death.

2594 - BENNY: WALKING TO BABYLON[969] **->** !Ci!ci-tel and WiRgo!xu believed that the People of the Worldsphere had become complacent, and tried to goad the People and the Time Lords into war by establishing a treaty-violating time corridor to ancient Babylon. Benny went into the past and stopped the rogues, removing the need for God to destroy the time-corridor – and Babylon – with a singularity bomb.

2594 - BENNY: OBLIVION -> The sentient spaceship *Schirron Dream* sought help from its old friends – Benny, Jason Kane, Chris Cwej and the late Roz Forrester, the last of whom the ship brought through time as a 20-year-old – after disruptions in space-time made its crew go missing. The wealthy Randolph Bane had found the Egg, an artifact in the Shadow Depository, and hoped to gain immortality from it even if the universe consequently perished. Bane and his rival, Simon Deed, were time-looped. Roz destroyed the Egg, but its final burst of power erased her memories of these events. The *Schirron Dream* crew was located, and Roz was sent back to her native time.[970]

2594 - BENNY: THE MEDUSA EFFECT -> The *Medusa* had now been adrift for two decades, and Benny joined an expedition to recover it. She and Braxiatel learned that the Advanced Research Department at St Oscar's had been complicit in the deaths of the *Medusa* crew, but remained silent in exchange for a confession from Taffeta Graize, the main culprit. A synthoid containing the dead crew's memories killed Graize.

2594 - BENNY: DRY PILGRIMAGE -> Genetic engineering had now eliminated all major human cancers and blood disorders. Cigarettes contained no harmful substances, but very few people still smoked. Chateau Yquatine was in production.[971]

Saraani pilgrims fled an atheist revolution on their homeworld, and sought to establish themselves on an island on Dellah. Benny joined the Saraani aboard the cruise ship *Lady of Lorelei* as they searched for a suitable locale. Czaritza Violaine, the exiled leader of Visphok, cut a deal with some of the Saraani: they would use their mind-transference abilities (part of their reproductive cycle) to shift the minds of Violaine's aged veterans into weaponised bioconstructs, in exchange for Violaine liberating Saraanis. The agreement went south, and Violaine was killed.

In 2594, the fox-like Valethske searched for their former gods, the Khorlthochloi, and fought with the Sontarans. The Earth Empire had colonised the Thynemnus System, and a mass immigration led to tensions. The planet Korsair was established to settle disputes. The Valethske attacked one of the new colonies, overwhelming the Korsairs and capturing colonists for their larder.[972]

On Ordifica, Fitz was initiated into Faction Paradox around 2594. Laura Tobin, who would become the Doctor's companion Compassion, was sent to Ordifica the same year.[973]

2595 - BENNY: THE SWORD OF FOREVER[974] **->** Armstrong City was a settlement in the Sea of Tranquillity on the moon.

Marillian, unofficially the third-richest man in the world, now owned London and Greenwich. Benny encountered Marillian while investigating the journal of Guillaume de Beaujeu, and platonically married him to get a childbirth license – a pre-requirement for her accessing the texts within the British Library. Marillian assisted Benny in recovering the finger of John the Baptist from Castle Arginy, and what they believed was the skull of Christ from a Templar museum in Paris. He then made off with both items.

Benny realised that four items associated with Christ – the Spear of Longinus that pierced Christ's side, Christ's Crown of Thorns, the Holy Grail and the Ark of the Covenant – could be combined to form the Sword of Forever: a device capable of creating entire worlds and timelines. Marillian's master, Gebmoses III, died while trying to use the Sword to retroactively create a master race cloned from Christ's skull.

Evidence suggested that Benny had died using the Sword – which was intended for use by a higher power, and would kill any human who operated it – to recreate Earth's timeline after its destruction. She dutifully welcomed God into her heart and died to activate the Sword. Earth's timeline was reinstated, and Benny was restored to life in a new body.

St Oscar's University Press published Benny's *An Eye for Wisdom: Repetitive Poems of the Early Ikkaban Period* in 2595.[975]

Bev Tarrant Relocates to 2595

Bev Tarrant, a skilled thief from the future, found herself in the year 2595.[976]

c 2595 - BENNY: BURIED TREASURES: "Making Myths"[977] -> Benny and her friend Keri, a Pakhar journalist, visited the declining tourist planet Shangri-La; Benny claimed to have discovered the famed Mud Fields of Agrivan there. A video of Keri running atop a giant cart wheel motivated thousands of Pakhar to make bookings to Shangri-La, reviving the planet's economy.

c 2595 - BENNY: BURIED TREASURES: "Closure"[977] -> On the planet Panyos, the despotic regime led by Ulrich Hescarti ended when he was shot in the back by one of his own people. After witnessing the horrors of Hescarti's ethnic cleansing programme, Benny used her time ring to travel back and change his personal history.

2595 - BENNY: ANOTHER GIRL, ANOTHER PLANET -> Archaeologist Lizbeth Fugard researched the heritage of the colony planet Dimetos by studying the industrial sites established there by Eurogen Butler. Bantu Cooperative, a weapons manufacturer, sabotaged Fugard's operations to conceal how many installations had been built atop Eurogen nuclear reactors and disused mine workings, hoping to curry favour with the Dimetos administration.

Benny stymied Bantu by destroying their largest research facility, but obliterated the biggest Dimetan archaeological site in the process.

The only surviving Dimetan, Csoker, killed himself rather than endure as the last of his race. Fugard became a professor of sidereal mythology at Youkali University.[978]

2595 (21st June) - BENNY: BEIGE PLANET MARS[979] -> On Mars, human slaves were illegal, but vat-grown clone slaves were permitted. "Spartan" was slang for a staunchly homosexual soldier who detested weakness in either gender.

Jason Kane had embarked on a lucrative career writing semi-autobiographical xenoporn novels; his first book, *Nights of the Perfumed Tentacle*, sold twelve million copies. Bernice's *Down Amongst the Dead Men* was in its sixth printing. Benny was attending an academic conference that celebrated the five-hundredth anniversary of Mars' terraforming and had a passionate reunion with Jason Kane – who, unknown to her, was in a relationship with the organiser of the event, the Pakhar named Professor Megali Scoblow. Benny failed to prepare her paper for the conference and instead gave a stream-of-consciousness delivery – in which she accidently exposed fellow academic Elizabeth Trinity as the notorious war criminal Tellassar.

Philip and Christina York, the trillionaire couple who owned YorkCorp, nearly started a nuclear conflict on Mars while fending off a hostile takeover from Bantu Cooperative.

Angels Fear. The Ikkabans were mentioned in *SLEEPY*.
976 *Dust Breeding* ends with the seventh Doctor and Ace giving Bev a lift in the TARDIS, and the idea seems to be that after some unspecified adventures, she left their company "two years" prior to 2597 (according to *Benny S8: The Judas Gift*), and became a fixture of Benny's native era.
977 Dating *Benny: Buried Treasures: "Making Myths"/"Closure"* (Benny audio #1.5b) - The *Buried Treasures* CD was released as a bonus for customers who purchased Big Finish's (apocryphal) CD adaptations of *Walking to Babylon*, *Birthright* and *Just War*. The two stories within *Buried Treasures* are slightly problematic to place within Benny's lifetime – "Closure" establishes that it's during Benny's tenure at St Oscar's (so, prior to *Benny: Where Angels Fear*), but the CD was released in August 1999, concurrent to *Benny: Return to the Fractured Planet*. The placement here is arbitrary.
978 Youkali University appeared in *Return of the Living Dad*.
979 Dating *Benny: Beige Planet Mars* (Benny NA #16) - The day is given (p7). Benny here celebrates her thirty-fifth birthday, but she must be counting in absolute terms, allowing for her travelling through time with the Doctor. The book was published in October 1998, just before the thirty-fifth anniversary of *Doctor Who*.

980 *Benny S10: Venus Mantrap*
981 *The Infinity Doctors*
982 Dating *Benny: The Mary-Sue Extrusion* (Benny NA #18) - Four months have passed since *Benny: Where Angels Fear*.
983 Dating *Benny: Dead Romance* (Benny NA #19) - Events in the outside universe are set between *The Mary-Sue Extrusion* and *Tears of the Oracle*. Within the bottle universe, events unfold from 27th September to 12th October, 1970. The universe-in-a-bottle also appears in *Interference* and *The Ancestor Cell*. FP: *The Shadow Play*, strongly implies that Christine ends up joining Faction Paradox as "Cousin Eliza", a main character in the Faction audios.
984 Dating *Benny: Tears of the Oracle* (Benny NA #20) - Allowing that *Benny: Twilight of the Gods* takes place "a year" after *Benny: The Mary-Sue Extrusion*, the calendar-flip from 2595 to 2596 likely occurs somewhere in this vicinity. The eighth Doctor, Fitz and Sam visit Vega Station in *Demontage*.
985 *Interference*, "two years" after Fitz is initiated into Faction Paradox.
986 Dating *Benny: Return to the Fractured Planet* (Benny NA #21) - *Benny: Tears of the Oracle* ended with Benny having only "a month to live" owing to a brain illness, and she's here cured.

Together, Benny and Jason prevented the holocaust. Trinity submitted herself to General Keele for judgment.

The fiasco ruined Professor Scoblow's academic career. She became Jason's xenoporn editor. She was personally featured in Volume 7 (*Nibbling Around the Mousehole*, a bestseller) and took possession of his great unpublished work, *Barely Humanoid*.[980]

St Oscar's and Dellah Evacuated as the Gods of the People Return

2595 - BENNY: WHERE ANGELS FEAR -> Immensely powerful beings thought to be the former gods of the People freed themselves from imprisonment on Dellah. As the gods' influence spread, Dellah experienced a burst of increasingly violent religious fanaticism; both the Time Lords and the supercomputer God feared this was the start of a much larger conflict. Benny and Braxiatel were separated as a fleet evacuated many Dellans, and Earth quarantined the planet.

The Time Lords were concerned with this situation.[981]

2595 - BENNY: THE MARY-SUE EXTRUSION[982] -> The gods had such dominance over Dellah, it was turning to desert. Their influence spread into space – Thanaxos, the system neighbouring Dellah, was gripped in a religious fever until Emile Mars-Smith, an ex-St Oscar's student, went into seclusion to restrain the god nestled within him.

Pseudopod Enterprises Corporation dispatched an agent – a synthoid with Stratum Seven-level clearance – to find Bernice and learn more about the gods. The Agent discovered that Benny had rescued Wolsey from Dellah after submitting herself to a "Mary-Sue": a process that overwrites one's personality with a new persona, and helped her to resist the gods' influence.

Benny's former homeworld of Beta Caprisis was still abandoned, and had been since the Dalek assault there.

Christine Summerfield Leaves the Bottle Universe

2595 - BENNY: DEAD ROMANCE[983] -> The Time Lords feared the gods to such an extent, they altered their treaty with the People. In exchange for not siding with the gods, the People would be allowed to develop time technology. The Time Lords also, using Chris Cwej as their agent, sought to prepare a bottle universe – one that contained a replica of 1970 Earth – as a shelter in case the gods became too powerful.

Cwej went into the bottle universe, and performed rituals that would manipulate the bottle's protocols and give the Time Lords access. He cloned three women and ritual-istically murdered two of them – but the third escaped and came to believe she was a 23-year-old art student named Christine Summerfield. Cwej found himself unable to kill Christine, and they became lovers.

Cwej created and murdered yet-another clone, and a portal opened over London. The Time Lords poured forth, and reshaped the bottle Earth to their purposes. The world's nations fruitlessly launched a nuclear strike; Cwej caught a fatal radiation burst and was slated for regeneration. The Time Lords mutated the bottle-humanity into slaves or surrogate Time-Lords-in-waiting. Christine left the bottle.

c 2596 - BENNY: TEARS OF THE ORACLE[984] -> Despite the new treaty, God predicted an 87% chance of war between the People and the Time Lords.

Braxiatel learned that the Oracle of the Lost was probably located on planetoid KS-159 – which he won by gambling with its owner, Howard Denson, at Vega Station. Benny and Braxiatel led an expedition to KS-159, but the parasite within the Oracle started murdering their associates. The Time Lords force-regenerated Chris Cwej into a shorter body, and sent him to help.

The parasite jumped into Benny's robotic porter Joseph – who was actually a drone of the People Ship J-Kibb, and had been deployed by God to spy on Benny. God directed the J-Kibb to crash onto Dellah, believing that the parasite's ability to spread uncertainty would counter-act the faith and religious mania that empowered the gods. The Oracle confirmed that the universal war was now much less likely to occur.

The Time Lords sterilised the planet Ordifica, which killed three hundred million people. Two thousand survivors, including Laura Tobin and Fitz, were evacuated to the *Justinian*, which headed to the year 1799.[985]

2596 - BENNY: RETURN TO THE FRACTURED PLANET[986] -> The Proximan Chain had been established as a collection of space stations, planetary settlements and colonies. It was connected by a series of transit pads, and had a population of seven billion. The Chain lacked a cohesive law, and was largely inhabited by corporations doing shady business. Benny and Braxiatel recruited synthoids – Artificial Personality Embodiments (APEs) – to hunt down any gods who eluded the Dellan quarantine. The freelance APE Kara Delbane was murdered, and Benny agreed to help Delbane's lover, the Stratrum Seven agent, find her killers. Absolam Sleed had survived his encounter with the Agent and Delbane, and been transformed into a crystalline entity. Benny killed Sleed and the Dellan god merged with him, ending their plan to slaughter the Proximan Chain populace with a mutagenic bomb.

2596 - BENNY: THE JOY DEVICE -> Benny decided to have an adventure-filled holiday on the Rim frontier, with famed adventurer Dent Harper serving as her guide. Jason worried that Benny would enjoy herself so much that she'd never return home, and worked to prevent her from having a good time – or the stamina for an assignation with Harper. Braxiatel took possession of Dorpfeld's Prism, and filed in the KS-159 archives.

Defeat of the Dellan Gods; Building of the Braxiatel Collection Initiated

2596 - BENNY: TWILIGHT OF THE GODS[987] **->** The remaining gods on Dellah began to war amongst themselves, and the Time Lords and the People considered extinguishing them with a "doomsday probe" powerful enough to wipe out Dellah's sector of space. Hoping to avert this, Benny, Jason and Chris smuggled a dimensional-transfer node to Dellah using the *Revelation* – a dimension-hopping ship developed on Earth – then warped Dellah into the dimension from which the gods had originated. The gods stood revealled as a breakaway group of the Ferutu. They attacked Benny's group with temporal bolts – Benny's body was rejuvenated by about five years, and Chris reverted to his blonde-haired incarnation. Jason

was left behind as Benny and Chris fled in the *Revelation*, trapping the Ferutu.

The accomplished diplomat Terin Sevic negotiated a peace on the war-torn planet of Vremnya, enabling wealthy patrons – including Braxiatel – to establish a university there. Braxiatel arranged for Benny to become the head of the new university's archaeology department. He also initiated construction of the Braxiatel Collection on KS-159.

Braxiatel deliberately situated the Collection near an energy field in space, one that produced interdimensional leakage strong enough to power a hundred colonies. He worked to keep the existence of the energy field a secret, fearing the Time Lords' enemies would exploit it.[988]

Benny and the etymologist Bil Bil Gloap were trapped while translating runes in an underground chamber on Salva Noctra. She kept him amused with stories of her adventures until rescue arrived three weeks later.[989] Benny authored the obscure paper "The Ephemeral Eternal: Gold and Precious Metals in Human History and Currency".[990] Benny's students unearthed a statue of a goddess, the Quantum, from a Neo-Roman ruin on the nameless fourth planet of Pontifact's Star. Soon after, Benny's university appointed her adjunct professor of Archaeology.[991]

During a research term at Vremnya, Benny produced the

---

987 Dating *Benny: Twilight of the Gods* (Benny NA #23) - Benny and company here reunite after spending a bit on their own pursuits, so some time has passed since *Benny: The Joy Device*. Moreover, it's said on p48 that "it had almost been a year since [Benny] had seen [Dellah]" (in *Benny: The Mary-Sue Extrusion*), which roughly coincides with the real-life duration of ten months that passed between the two books. The Ferutu first appeared in *Cold Fusion*.

BENNY'S UNDOCUMENTED THREE YEARS (2596-2599): The Benny New Adventures end in 2596, but Big Finish's Bernice Summerfield range doesn't rejoin her life until the very end of 2599, starting with the Benny anthology *The Dead Men Diaries*. As much as anything else, the relaunch dating was presumably meant to accommodate the release of Big Finish's first full-length Benny novel, *Benny: The Doomsday Manuscript*, in 2000 – nonetheless, this does create a three-year gap in Benny's timeline. In *The Dead Men Diaries*, Benny mentions arriving at the Braxiatel Collection after having endured "fraught adventures" that include "Time travel, other universes, the destruction of everything I'd previously relied upon to define me" and Jason being lost... all of which seems to refer to her New Adventures tenure. It's possible that Benny whittled away a year or three at Vremnya until construction of the Braxiatel Collection was complete – but it's somewhat astonishing that she goes such a prolonged period with nothing particularly exciting happening to her.

988 *Benny S11: Resurrecting the Past*. It's possible that Braxiatel learned of the energy field near KS-159 after all the business concerning the Oracle of the Lost (*Benny: Tears of the Oracle*), and only then decided to make it the home of the Collection.

989 "More years ago" than Bernice cares to remember before *Benny: The Slender-Fingered Cats of Bubastis* (p23), set in 2618. Benny shares plenty of exploits with Bil over a three-week period, so it's probably after her TARDIS days. It's not specified that the Salva Noctra expedition happens while Bernice is at the Braxiatel Collection (although Bil – who is about 70 in 2618 – recalls that Benny held a position there), meaning it's perhaps cleaner to assume that it happens during the unchronicled three-year gap in Benny's life (2596 to 2599), at least some of which she spends at Vremnya university.

990 An unknown amount of time before *Benny B5: Missing Persons: The Revenant's Carnival*.

991 *Benny: Many Happy Returns*

992 "Ten years" before *Benny S9: Beyond the Sea*.

993 *Benny S8: The Judas Gift*

994 She's "25" in *Vienna S3: Self-Improvement*.

995 *Benny S10: Secret Origins*, *Benny S11: Resurrecting the Past* and *Benny S11: Escaping the Future*. Braxiatel says Buenos Aires is destroyed "in the late twenty-sixth century". Robyn says that it was "2598, or was it 2599?"

996 *Benny: Adorable Illusion* (ch8). The text claims that engineering was still a viable career in "the late 25th

documentary *Our Martians, Ourselves*.[992] In 2597, Bev Tarrant teamed with a smuggler, Ethan, who tried to kill her and steal their haul. Bev killed him instead.[993] Jexie Reagan, an associate of Vienna Salvatori, was born on Earth.[994]

A space-time fissure opened in Lezama Park in Buenos Aires, and remained active for a century. A few dozen people fell through the fissure and emerged on the other side of the universe at the planet Deindus, four million years in the future. The humans died, but the presence of their organic matter led to the creation of the Deindum.

> (=) Samuel Frost destroyed Buenos Aires to prevent the Deindum's existence. Bernice aided a Deindum creation, the android Robyn, in re-establishing the original timeline.[995]

Humans excelled at engineering even as other races outpaced them as soldiers, builders and cooks. Every human colony world diverted efforts into schools and colleges providing engineering degrees. A few years later, the prominence of AIs largely made the occupation of engineer redundant.[996]

The Twenty-Seventh Century

During the twenty-seventh century, oxygen factories were built in London.[997] Archaeologists unearthed documents pertaining to the extinct Ultani race and its bioharmonics, but failed to recognise their importance. The texts were filed, along with cosmographic mission reports, in the archives on Nocturne.[998] Colony World 4378976.Delta-Four was founded in the twenty-seventh century. The inhabitants soon started going "fantasy crazy" as a result of interactions with the microscopic native life, and the gov-

ernment banned all fiction to curb this problem.[999]

Humans in the twenty-seventh century genetically engineered a type of reed – the Water Thief – that could thrive in desert regions. A seed pod or spores of the Water Thief were transported back to ancient Egypt – possibly by a time storm or a time path, or possibly on the coat of a time traveller (perhaps even the Doctor himself).[1000]

wih - Hilberta's Hostel was a time-brothel in twenty-seventh century Vienna, second in infamy only to Foyle's House of the Rising Sun. Robert Scarratt arranged for his timeship to convey Ella Staunton – who had been reborn as part of the War's time-mechanics – to the safety of the Hostel following events aboard *The Brakespeare*. He visited her, hoping they could be lovers one last time, before leaving for his appointed death.[1001]

Braxiatel took Bernice Summerfield back in time to England, the Middle Ages, to convince her to come and work for his Collection...[1002] It was possible that Braxiatel wished to capitalize upon a temporal disruption centred around Bernice, failing to realize that it originated from her future dealings with the Epoch.[1003]

Bernice Summerfield at the Braxiatel Collection[1004]

Professor Bernice Summerfield became attached to the Braxiatel Collection, which touted itself as "A collection of everything. The various departments of the Braxiatel Collection house antique artifacts, literature, playscripts, recordings of events and people and performances, geological specimens, software and hardware of days gone by..."[1005] The Collection housed 40% of the recognised Wonders of the Galaxy.[1006]

Wolsey the cat had become a father – again – even though he'd been neutered, as the local fauna at the

---

century", but that the shift toward AIs surprised a man who trained as one in "2688" – this, in a novel that takes place circa 2617. With the "2688" date being blatantly wrong, it seems reasonable to think that the "late 25th century" mention should be "the late 26th" in accordance with when the book occurs.

997 *Original Sin* (p204).

998 Two hundred years before *Nocturne*.

999 *The Stealers of Dreams*

1000 *The Water Thief*

1001 *FP: The Brakespeare Voyage*. Foyle first appeared in *FP: The Book of the War*, as part of the post-humanity era.

1002 *Benny: Many Happy Returns*. Exact time unknown, but Braxiatel starts building the Collection in *Benny: Twilight of the Gods* [2596] and Benny is already established there in *Benny: The Doomsday Manuscript* [31st December, 2599].

1003 *Benny B5: Missing Persons: In Living Memory*

1004 WHEN WAS THE BRAXIATEL COLLECTION IN OPERATION?: *Benny S8: The Wake* confirms that Bernice (from her perspective) first visited the Braxiatel Collection and met Irving Braxiatel "a thousand years" in the future of her native era (in *Theatre of War*). This is slightly hard to reconcile against the Benny audios, where events progress in rough symmetry with the *Gallifrey* series – meaning that Braxiatel in 2610 is aware of the oncoming Last Great Time War, and it's a bit hard to think that he toils away for another thousand years before finally shutting the Collection down and returning home (in *Gallifrey III: Mindbomb*). That said, in *Tales from the Vault*, the fourth Doctor identifies a painting that was stolen from the Braxiatel Collection "over two centuries ago" – he can't mean that amount of time before the story (which is set in 2002), and so must mean that long ago in his lifetime, suggesting the

Collection were genetic hybrids, and bred in a curious fashion.[1007] Braxiatel built Benny a new Joseph drone, with at least fifty terabytes of data storage.[1008]

Jason Kane escaped from the Ferutu's domain, and wound up in the employ of Agraxar Flatchlock, a travel agent from an infernal dimension.[1009] He didn't age while in the Ferutu realm, owing to Dr Gilhooly's Theory of Transdimensional Contrivance.[1010]

Braxiatel foresaw that the Deindum – a race from the distant future – would develop time travel and conquer many worlds in many time periods, becoming strong enough to challenge even the Time Lords. He also discovered that Bernice would heavily impact the Deindum's development – that her memories and experiences would influence the primordial soup from which they would evolve. He meddled in Bernice's affairs and adjusted some of her personal history, hoping that, as a failsafe against his other efforts to curtail the Deindum failing, he could influence the future conquerors through her.[1011]

(=) Benny and Jason would eventually have two children – Keith Brannigan Summerfield-Kane and his younger sister Rebecca – and raise them alongside Benny's son Peter. Braxiatel, fearing that Keith and Rebecca would be too much of a drain on Benny's time, revised her history so they were never born.[1012]

= In a parallel reality, Bernice Summerfield and Jason Kane had two children: Rebecca, who was still in school, and a grown son, Keith. At the seventh Doctor's prompting, Jason left a message for Bernice that fondly remembered escapades such as the Cult of Varos forcing them to compete in *Dante's Kitchen*, and confronting a camp version of Irving Braxiatel who lived on the orchard moon of Esayez.[1013]

Braxiatel also changed the timelines so that Benny's friend Keri was a native of the twenty-sixth century, not the fortieth.[1014] In this era, nano-suppressants were available that cured colds and flu within minutes.[1015] Trans-Universal Export was "all over the galaxy" in Bernice's era. Messages

Collection is in operation at least that long.

In *Benny: Many Happy Returns*, Benny finally up and says something that's been inferred in other stories: she can't actually remember the first time she met Irving Braxiatel. That squares with the inconsistency of *Theatre of War* dating their first meeting (from Benny's perspective, at least) to 3985 – quite the feat, since, as mentioned, the Benny range establishes the Collection as being established a short while before 2600, but being defunct following the Deindum conflict of 2610. With Benny herself attesting confusion on this point, it seems best to assume that Braxiatel's time-tinkering (although it's hard to establish exactly *which* time-tinkering is germane here) either decoupled their first meeting from 3985, or that the Collection's demise roughly thirteen centuries prior to that made such an occurrence impossible. Taking all of that into account, it seems best to consider the 3985 meeting as part of a closed-off timeline, which isn't to say that the rest of *Theatre of War* no longer takes place in that year.

1005 From *Benny: The Dead Men Diaries*. The framing sequence says "it's now 2600", but the stories within predate *Benny: The Doomsday Manuscript* – which opens on New Year's Eve – and so must occur in 2599.
1006 *Benny* S10: *Glory Days*, not the same convention as the "Wonders of the Universe" (*Death to the Daleks*).
1007 *Benny: The Dead Men Diaries* (p73).
1008 *Benny: The Doomsday Manuscript*. The new Joseph is presumably built using what remains of the omnitronic processor that the seventh Doctor recovered from Victor Farrison's Joseph drone in *The Dark Flame*.
1009 *Benny: The Dead Men Diaries*: "The Door Into Bedlam"

1010 *Benny: The Infernal Nexus*, playing off a theory established in *Benny: Walking to Babylon*.
1011 *Benny* S11: *Resurrecting the Past*, *Benny* S11: *Escaping the Future*. Exactly when Braxiatel learns of Benny's significance to the Deindum's creation is unclear, but it motivates his actions and manipulations throughout much of the Big Finish Benny range.
1012 *Benny* S8: *The End of the World* and the framing sequence to *Benny: A Life of Surprises* (which takes place in Benny's future, and presumably doesn't occur after Braxiatel rewrites her history). Potential versions of Keith Summerfield-Kane appeared in *Return of the Living Dad* and *Benny: A Life of Surprises*: "Might"; he was 18 months in the former, and killed as an adult in the latter. In *Benny* S7: *The Summer of Love*, Benny claims to know that she and Jason are fated to birth Keith and Rebecca, but that things aren't turning out as they should. Fan-commentators sometimes suggest that Braxiatel changed Benny's history to facilitate Peter's birth as a sort of oddity – the product of a human-Killoran mating – but there's little evidence to support this. An enigmatic man named "Kane" appears in *Burning Heart*, and is alluded to as being one of Benny and Jason's descendants (or possibly not, after Braxiatel's revisions to Benny and Jason's histories).
1013 *Benny: Many Happy Returns*
1014 *Benny* S8: *The End of the World*. The change to Keri's background explains why she participates in the Benny audios, having first appeared in *Legacy*.
1015 *Benny* S11: *Escaping the Future*. Van Statten was said to have cured the common cold in *Dalek*; a vaccine exists at the time of *Fear Itself* (PDA). The secret was lost in the Tenth Segment of Time, according to *The Ark*.

IRVING BRAXIATEL VS. CARDINAL BRAXIATEL: Irving Braxiatel is one of Bernice Summerfield's best friends and most invaluable allies throughout the New Adventures, but the Big Finish Benny range recasts him as someone far more ruthless and amoral – a manipulator who (even under the caveat of acting for a greater good) aggressively rewrites the personal histories of Benny and her associates, brings the Mim to the point of extinction, and goads Benny's son Peter into savagely murdering Jason Kane.

In large measure, the difference in character owes to historical revision. *Gallifrey* Series 1 establishes that in Braxiatel's original history, he became so horrified by the destruction of Minyos (*Underworld*) that he left Gallifrey and founded the Braxiatel Collection to preserve the universe's great cultural treasures. Braxiatel's history changes, however, when a renegade Time Lord goes into Gallifrey's past and steals the timonic fusion device that obliterated Minyos, preventing the planet's annihilation and (inadvertently) robbing Braxiatel of his motive to leave Gallifrey. Alterations to Gallifrey's history are exceedingly rare – most of the tie-in ranges presume that safeguards created by Rassilon or his associates stop anyone from tampering with Gallifrey's past, although this isn't ever established on TV. Here, though, Gallifrey's timeline undeniably changes.

The second version of Braxiatel – the one who stays on Gallifrey long enough to become a Cardinal (as first seen in *Zagreus*) – presumably pops into existence and overwrites his previous self the exact moment the fusion device is stolen. Crucially, it's Cardinal Braxiatel and Romana (in *Gallifrey I: The Inquiry*) who restore Gallifrey's history by facilitating the device's detonation – but as their existence is vital to the restoration of the timeline, they're presumably insulated when Gallifrey's history returns to normal.

Romana's history remains largely the same, save that Cardinal Braxiatel (*Gallifrey II: Lies*) served as her tutor. For Cardinal Braxiatel, the result is that he stays on Gallifrey long enough for events to force him to trap a small part of Pandora's mind within his own. Owing to this development, Braxiatel exiles himself from Gallifrey (*Gallifrey II: Pandora*). (Side note to mention that *Benny B4: New Frontiers: The Curse of Fenman* entails Avril Fenman ripping the Pandora segment out of the current Braxiatel's head and sending it back 18 years into his previous self's noggin. As writer Gary Russell explained to us: "Avril sent it back to the right time and place so it could be put in Gallifrey Brax's head, creating a sort of temporal loop between the two. A sort of paradox really.")

After Cardinal Braxiatel leaves Gallifrey, events seen in the New Adventures run much the same – he still founds the Collection, etc. *Benny S8: The Wake* dramatizes scenes from *Theatre of War, Happy Endings* and *Benny: Tears of the Oracle*, helping to confirm that the NAs still occur, word for word (or near enough), in Braxiatel's revised history.

Whether the Pandora component directly warps Braxiatel's personality – or whether it just enhances his innate greed and arrogance – is a subject of some debate. Either way, it's surely not coincidence that the first instance of Braxiatel's machinations being exposed, *Benny: The Crystal of Cantus*, has one of Braxiatel's victims telling him, "The thing in your head... it's still there," presumably denoting the Pandora segment.

Odd as it might sound, the whole of Braxiatel's involvement in non-Gallifreyan time – all of the New Adventures with him, and the entire history of the Collection – seem to occur, from Gallifrey's perspective, between *Gallifrey* Series 2 and 3. While this seems to violate the unspoken idea that Time Lords meet in sequence, it's not unprecedented (see *The Apocalypse Element*).

In *Gallifrey III: Mindbomb*, Braxiatel returns to Gallifrey after the Collection is defunct and attempts to salvage something of Time Lord society before the oncoming Last Great Time War. Largely failing that, he's lost to the Time Vortex (*Gallifrey: Disassembled*), emerges into history just prior to *Benny: Dragons' Wrath*, and has to spend years eluding his younger self before leaving a message for Benny in 2616 (*Benny: Epoch: Judgement Day*) that she should contact him.

The *Benny* box sets, which feature this Braxiatel running the White Rabbit pub on Legion, flirt with the idea of there being multiple versions of Braxiatel at work in the universe – the idea seemingly being that his history has been revised so many times, even he doesn't have the luxury of worrying about who/where/why any particular Braxiatel relates to the others. *Gallifrey* Series 7 and 8 double down on this by having Braxiatel returning to aid Romana during a crisis, time being revised *again* (so much so, *Gallifrey* Series 7 is wiped out of existence), and the enigmatic Watchmaker offering the Braxiatel at hand – now the product of an erased timeline – the option of picking his own future. After that, *a* version of Braxiatel appears in *Gallifrey – Time War* V1. When it comes to Braxiatel, it's increasingly becoming easier to just worry about whichever one happens to be standing in front of you, rather than how they all fit together.

between its various branches were sent across subspace using the Omninet bandwidth.[1016]

2599 (31st December) to 2600 (1st-6th January) - BENNY: THE DOOMSDAY MANUSCRIPT[1017] **->** The Fifth Axis, a military dictatorship, expanded its territory by subjugating numerous worlds. The planet Kasagrad resided in Axis space, but was protected by a global force field. Kolonel Daglan Straklant, claiming to head the Axis' relic restoration team, approached Benny and Braxiatel with an offer to help retrieve *The Doomsday Manuscript* from Kasagrad. Benny and Braxiatel realised Straklant was using them to deactivate Kasagrad's defence screen; owing to their actions, Kasagrad forces wiped out an Axis' Sixth Fleet, and forced a retreat to the old Merinfast Line. The Axis arrested Straklant on charges of treason.

2600 - BENNY S2: THE SECRET OF CASSANDRA[1018] **->** Benny vacationed on the Earth colony Chosan, and was caught in a conflict between the warring continents of Calabraxia and Pevena. Cassandra Colley, a brilliant Pevenan neurotech designer, had transferred her mind into a synthetic form – a living bomb that was powerful enough to destroy the whole of Calabraxia. Colley's armaments were neutralised, and she was given into the care of her father, Captain Damien Colley.

The Pevenans and Calabraxians were mutually horrified by the scale of Colley's plans, and negotiated a peace.[1019]

Avril Fenman, in Benny's Body, has a Lost Weekend with Adrian Wall

2600 (February) - BENNY: THE SQUIRE'S CRYSTAL[1020] **->** The aged collector Arsine de Vallen believed that the cavern of the legendary Soul-Sucker – a squire named Avil Fenman, who came into possession of a

---

1016 *Benny B1: Epoch: Private Enemy No. 1*

1017 Dating *Benny: The Doomsday Manuscript* (Benny BF novel #1) - The story opens on New Year's Eve; Benny declares that it's "January the first" (p40) while tumbling into bed at three in the morning. Benny's diary cites the end date of the adventure as on or about "January 6th" (p125), and also confirms the year as 2600.

1018 Dating *Benny S2: The Secret of Cassandra* (Benny audio #2.1) - The audio takes place between *Benny: The Doomsday Manuscript* and *Benny: The Squire's Crystal*. Chosan is named in *Benny S4: The Poison Seas*.

1019 *Benny S4: The Poison Seas*

1020 Dating *Benny: The Squire's Crystal* (Benny BF novel #3) - The month is given, which means that *The Squire's Crystal* takes place before *Benny: The Gods of the Underworld*, even though it was published afterwards.

1021 Dating *Benny: The Gods of the Underworld* (Benny BF novel #2) - Benny's diary dates the start of the adventure to "March 12th 2600" (p7) and the story unfolds for some days afterwards.

1022 *Love and War*, presumably a reference to the Daleks' use of blackmail in *Death to the Daleks*.

1023 Dating *Death to the Daleks* (11.3) - There is no date given on screen, but the story takes place after the Dalek Wars.

    The Programme Guide placed it in "c.3700" (first edition), "c.2800" (second edition) and *The Terrestrial Index* put it in "the twenty-fifth century". *The TARDIS Logs* offered a date of "3767 AD" (the same year as *The Monster of Peladon*).

    Timelink suggested "3500". *About Time* said, "A dating between 2600 and 2900 would be plausible". The Exxilon mission occurs "circa 2600" in *A History of the Universe in 100 Objects* (p61). *Whoniverse* (BBC) sorts of some of its information by topic rather than hard

chronological dates, and yet it's still a mite odd to see *Death of the Daleks* (p276-278) slotted in after *The Daleks' Master Plan* [4000].

    The Official Doctor Who & the Daleks Book claimed that the Dalek Plague used in this story is the Movellan Virus, so the author set the story between *Resurrection of the Daleks* and *Revelation of the Daleks*, around 3000 AD. This is nonsense, though, as that plague would have no effect on humans – as the Doctor says in *Resurrection of the Daleks*, "it is only partial to Dalek". The gas that disfigures humans seen in *Resurrection of the Daleks* is not the Movellan Virus, but a weapon that the Daleks themselves are immune to.

    The Daleks routinely use germ warfare throughout their history (we see it in *The Dalek Invasion of Earth, Planet of the Daleks* and *Resurrection of the Daleks*). It's never stated in this story that the Daleks caused the plague on the human colony planets, but it's fair to infer they did, especially as they're stopped from launching a "plague missile" at Exxilon.

1024 *Asylum of the Daleks*

1025 Dating *Benny S2: The Stone's Lament* and *Benny S2: The Extinction Event* (Benny audios #2.2, 2.3) - These are placed strictly by order of release.

1026 Dating *Benny: The Infernal Nexus* (Benny BF novel #4) - "A few months" (p185) have passed since *The Squire's Crystal*.

1027 Dating *Benny S2: The Skymines of Karthos* (Benny audio #2.4) - Five months have passed since Benny got impregnated (in absentia) in *The Squire's Crystal*.

soul-swapping crystal on the planet Hera and was imprisoned by the noble Knights of Rowan – was on planetoid KS-159. One of de Vallen's agents found Avril's cavern, where her mind had indeed survived in a crystal. Wanting to question Avril about the crystal's applications, de Vallen's agent transferred Avril's mind into Benny's body – but Avril/Benny escaped and, after so long an imprisonment, availed herself of fleshly pleasures. She had a fling with the Collection's construction manager, Adrian Wall – a member of the Killoran race. Wall thought that he and Benny were in a relationship. More bodyswapping ensued, and de Vallen died after a botched bodyswapping attempt. Everyone regained their proper form, and Avril's mind was finally deposited into the body of a security guard named Bill, whose mind had dissipated. Braxiatel let Avril/Bill continue living in her cavern, and Avril smashed the bodyswapping crystal to better guarantee her freedom.

2600 (March) - BENNY: THE GODS OF THE UNDERWORLD[1021] -> Venedel voted to withdraw from the Earthlink Federation. Braxiatel suspected that the long-dead Argians had built a war temple on Venedel, and Benny ran the Federation blockade to find the edifice, as it was thought to contain the Argian Oracle – a device that could locate anyone in the universe, the missing Jason Kane included. Benny stopped the hibernating Boor from awakening and furthering a new criminal empire, but the Oracle was destroyed.

According to the Doctor, the Daleks "started coming up with other schemes" after they lost the Wars.[1022]

? 2600 - DEATH TO THE DALEKS[1023] -> A plague spread through the atmospheres of many of the Outer Planets. Thousands died, and ten million people were threatened. Earth scientists quickly discovered an antidote to the plague: parrinium, a chemical that acted as both a cure and an immunity. It only existed in minute quantities on Earth, and was so rare that it was one of the most valuable known substances.

A satellite surveying the planet Exxilon discovered that parrinium was almost as common there as salt was on Earth. A Marine Space Corps ship was sent to Exxilon to collect parrinium, but the Daleks wanted to secure the substance for themselves, then force the Space Powers to accede to their demands.

Upon arriving within range of the planet, the Earth ship suffered total power failure. The crew explored and discovered a fantastic city – the source of the power-drain – that was thousands of years old. The natives guarded this City fanatically, and the priests ensured that anyone caught there faced certain death. The third Doctor and Sarah Jane arrived shortly before the Daleks. Venturing into the City, the Doctor stopped

the power drain. One of the Earthmen, Galloway, sacrificed himself to blow up the Daleks and their ship.

A Dalek from Exxilon was locked up in the Dalek Asylum.[1024]

2600 - BENNY S2: THE STONE'S LAMENT[1025] -> The billionaire Bratheen Traloor contracted the Braxiatel Collection to build an extension onto his reclusive mansion on the planet Rhinvil. Traloor was obsessed with Benny, and had programmed his mansion's computer, House, to emulate her personality. Traloor and House physically merged into a cyborg that also became endowed with some of the planet's lifeforce. The gestalt tried to murder Benny, but Adrian Wall used explosives to kill it.

2600 - BENNY S2: THE EXTINCTION EVENT[1025] -> An auction house on Pelastrodon hosted The Extinction Event: an offering of items from destroyed civilisations. Braxiatel summoned Benny from a dig on the mud planet Lubellin to have her verify the authenticity of a harp from the obliterated planet Halstad. Hulver, the last survivor of Halstad, murdered the Gulfrarg ambassador for his role in the obliteration of his people. Hulver was taken away to the Gulfrarg homeworld for execution, but Braxiatel acquired the harp for the Collection.

2600 - BENNY: THE INFERNAL NEXUS[1026] -> Benny attempted to retrieve the damaged research vessel *Tinker's Cuss*, but her ship was pulled through space by an Enormous Space Octopus, part of an intergalactic towing service. She was deposited at Station Control – a nexus point between four hundred and seventeen multiverses, and run by clans from different realities – and reunited there with Jason Kane. He was contractually obliged – via his former employer, the benevolent demon Agraxar Flatchlock – to work for Volan Sleed, the head of the Iron Sun Clan. Jason and Benny exposed Sleed's plan to incite warfare between his clan-rivals. He was decapitated, and his body generated the head of Flatchlock – who explained that his race had primary, secondary and tertiary heads and personas. He made peace with the offended clans.

Benny learned that she was pregnant following Avril's encounter with Adrian Wall. Jason formed Dead Dog in the Water Preproductions to represent his xenoporn work, and wrote an outline for *The Kiss of the Dragon Woman* based upon his dalliance with Lady Mae An T'zhu, the head of the Dragon Clan. The Braxiatel Collection had a recently opened Starbucks.

2600 - BENNY S2: THE SKYMINES OF KARTHOS[1027] -> Benny travelled to the thullium mining settlement on the planet Karthos when her longtime friend Caitlin Peters went missing there. Winged humanoids made from carbon and thulium deposits – disposable troopers generated by a machine built by a long-dead race – attacked the miners. Caitlin was saved, and the machine was buried.

Peter Guy Summerfield

2600 (October) - BENNY: THE GLASS PRISON[1028] ->
Benny left to quietly give birth away from the Collection, but ended up crashing on Deirbhile, a Fifth Axis world. She was incarcerated within the Axis' Glass Prison, a jail made from transparent walls to better monitor the inmates. Benny gave birth to a son, but the imprisoned Kolonel Straklant sought revenge by trying to kill her child. In repelling Straklant, Benny unleashed sonic waves that weakened the prison. Benny fled with her son and left Straklant to die as the entire edifice was destroyed. A Grel inmate, Sophia, scuttled the Axis' invasion plans by killing the Fifth Axis Imperator.

Afterward, Benny presented her child to the universe as Peter Guy Summerfield in a christening ceremony attended by, amongst others, her father and an older-looking Chris Cwej.

Buffy the Vampire Slayer was now in Season 792.

2601 - BENNY S3: THE GREATEST SHOP IN THE GALAXY[1029] ->
Benny signed up for a dig on the planet Baladroon – an excuse to explore the Gigamarket, the galaxy's largest shopping centre. The Gigamarket's time fields were disrupted as part of a hostile takeover, enabling the carnivorous Borvali to attack the human patrons.

Benny's intervention prevented massive casualties, and the Gigamarket's stock plummeted.

2601 - BENNY S3: THE GREEN-EYED MONSTER ->
The Goronos System consisted of five inhabited planets, each of them desiring supremacy over the entire region. Lady Ashantra du Lac of Goron IV asked Benny to verify the authenticity of various artifacts – part of a scheme to install Ashantra's charges, Boris and Ronald, as the system's rulers, with Ashantra serving as regent. Ashantra's plot was exposed, and she was arrested.

2601 - BENNY: THE PLAGUE HERDS OF EXCELIS ->
Civilisation on Artaris had recovered enough that Excelis City had a feudal society. Benny visited Artaris and met Iris Wildthyme, who asked for help in recovering the Relic. An insectoid named Snyper used the Relic to create a horde of zombie animals, which attacked the Excelis populace. Snyper intended to kill the Excelans wholesale – an act that would detonate the Relic, destroy Artaris and obliterate the passing battlefleet of the war queen who had eradicated Snyper's people. Snyper was killed, and the Relic became an ordinary gold lame handbag.

2601 - BENNY: MANY HAPPY RETURNS[1030] ->
A shapeshifter, infuriated at a war queen favouring Iris Wildthyme as a peace negotiator instead of her firm, disguised herself as Benny to eliminate her rival. Iris slipped strontium laxative into the shapeshifter's vodka, and continued her travels with Benny.

1028 Dating *Benny: The Glass Prison* (Benny BF novel #5) - "About ten months" (p17) have passed since *Benny: The Doomsday Manuscript*. That's in line with Benny being inseminated in *Benny: The Squire's Crystal* (which takes place in February), allowing that human-Killoran matings must still have a nine-month gestation cycle. *The Glass Prison* begins at "Day -7" (p9) from Peter's birth and finishes with the event on "Day 0" (p122), save for an epilogue with his christening. It's still 2600 (p25). Peter's middle name is a remembrance of Guy de Carnac from *Sanctuary*.
1029 Dating Bernice Summerfield Series 3 (*Benny: The Greatest Shop in the Galaxy*, audio #3.1; *Benny: The Green-Eyed Monster*, audio #3.2; *Benny: The Plague Herds of Excelis*, Excelis mini-series #4; *Benny: The Dance of the Dead*, audio #3.3; *Benny: A Life of Surprises*, collection #2; and *Benny: The Mirror Effect*, audio #3.4) and Series 4 (*Benny: The Bellotron Incident* audio #4.1; *Benny: The Draconian Rage*, audio #4.2; *Benny: The Poison Seas*, audio #4.3; *Benny: Life During Wartime*, collection #3; *Benny: Death and the Daleks*, audio #4.4; *Benny: The Big Hunt*, novel #6) - The dating clues within these stories are sparse, but time, particularly with regards Peter's growth and development, appears to be progressing

roughly in accord with the real world. The opening story of Series 5 (*Benny: The Grel Escape*) dates to 2603, so it seems reasonable to conclude that Series 3 and 4 respectively occur in 2601 and 2602.
1030 Dating *Benny: Many Happy Returns* (Benny 20th anniversary special) - Benny is still with Iris following *Benny: The Plague Herds of Excelis* [2601].
1031 Dating *Benny: Many Happy Returns* (Benny 20th anniversary special) - Benny is seemingly in her early days at the Braxiatel Collection.
1032 "Seven years" before *Benny S9: Beyond the Sea*. IMC operatives were seen in *Colony in Space*; the company is also mentioned in *Benny S11: Resurrecting the Past*.
1033 Exact time unknown, but Xanadu Tower is in operation "fifteen years" before *Benny B2: Road Trip: Paradise Frost* and takes a decade to build, so Jones was rich at that point.
1034 *Benny B2: Road Trip: Bad Habits*
1035 *Benny S3: Death and the Daleks*
1036 Dating *Benny: Life During Wartime* (Benny collection #3) and *Benny S4: Death and the Daleks* (Benny audio #4.4) - According to the introduction of *Life During Wartime*, "It's 2602." The audio follows on from

2601 - BENNY S3: THE DANCE OF THE DEAD ->

Galactic dignitaries concluded peace negotiations with the war queen who had slaughtered Snyper's race, and Benny – hung-over from an outing with Iris – sought passage aboard the space liner *Empress*, which was en route to Ronnos Minor. Explosions breached the ship's hull – the Colgarian ambassador and his wife were killed, causing Benny and Grand Marshall Sstac, an Ice Lord, to inhale fumes from crystals that the Colgarians used to pass on memories to their offspring. Benny and Sstac experienced the Colgarians' memories until a team of Ice Warriors rescued them. The culprits behind the explosions were exposed, and further warfare was averted.

c 2601 - BENNY: MANY HAPPY RETURNS[1031] ->

A game of Strip Pontoon involving Benny and the Arcadian Ghoul's mother-in-law went viral on UniversalTube, prompting the Ghoul to send a trio of assassins to the Braxiatel Collection. Two of the killers accidentally murdered one another prior to Benny staggering home after an outing involving too much fermented dung beetle juice, and Benny slayed the third in self-defence with a sub-mezon pistol. Adam McAuliffe, one of Benny's students, was alarmed to stop by and learn there were corpses in her kitchen, bed and wardrobe.

2601 - BENNY S3: THE MIRROR EFFECT ->

A rare mirror found on an ice planet acted as a gateway to multiple timelines and locations. The entity trapped within the mirror sought to free itself by reflecting people's dark passions and absorbing their personalities. Benny, Jason and Adrian – but not Braxiatel – were made to confront dark reflections of themselves until Jason destroyed the mirror and the mirror-entity. Braxiatel mentally conditioned Jason to not question his authority and decisions.

IMC owned the planet Maximederias, a world that was only 3% land. The natives there were micro-organisms, who tricked an IMC survey team into thinking that the planet had no viable supply of minerals. The planet gained protected status when IMC signed it over to an affiliate.[1032] Professor Melville Trout – a famed archaeologist lucky enough to have been born a Talpidian, akin to a giant mole – discovered the Sunken Gardens of Gallimede and the Semprini Colonnade on Persinnia. *Excavation Today* named Trout its Man of the Year 2602.[1033]

Dr Jared Jones, a child prodigy and the self-titled King of Genetic Splicing, founded J-Netics and became the richest man in the galaxy. Such was Jones' wealth that he built Xanadu Tower Resort – a vertical city that could accommodate one hundred thousand guests and nearly as many staff – in the desert on the planet Kaff Zarnak.[1034]

2602 - BENNY S4: THE BELLOTRON INCIDENT ->

The Sontaran-Rutan war was now encroaching upon Terran trade routes. The planet Bellotron had an irregular orbit, and was passing from Rutan space into a Sontaran-controlled region. Before Bellotron slipped out of Earth jurisdiction, Benny attempted to examine a hieroglyph-covered slab on the planet. A peace-loving Rutan faction intercepted Benny, and kept her safe while their agents stopped the Rutan military from detonating a bomb on Bellotron to damage Sontaran assets – an act that would have destroyed Bellotron's hunter-gatherer population.

Benny encountered Bev Tarrant as part of this, and returned with her to the Collection.

2602 - BENNY S4: THE DRACONIAN RAGE ->

Vilus Krull's skull surfaced on Tranagus, a former Earth colony that was now part of the Draconian Empire. The skull renewed the Cult of the Dark Flame within the Empire; twenty million Draconians on Tranagus committed ritual suicide in support of it. On behalf of Emperor Shen and the Draconian court, Benny investigated the matter in Dralos, one of the oldest cities on Draconia. Dark Flame members within the court were exposed, and Benny helped to secure Krull's skull.

2602 - BENNY S4: THE POISON SEAS ->

A Sea Devil colony on Chosan came under threat from both Calabraxian terrorists and a lethal protein in the planet's waters. The Earth Reptile Council asked Braxiatel for help, and he referred the matter to Benny. The terrorists were thwarted, and the Sea Devils abandoned their colony upon discovering that the protein – common to all sea life on Chosan – was sentient and adapting itself to possess them.

The Daleks provided the Fifth Axis with advanced weaponry that enabled them to capture new territories. The expansion of the Axis' dominions was a massive distraction, part of a Dalek plot to capture Braxiatel's TARDIS and enhance their time-travel capabilities.[1035]

The Fifth Axis-Dalek Invasion of the Braxiatel Collection

2602 - BENNY: LIFE DURING WARTIME[1036] ->

Benny returned from Chosan as the Fifth Axis overran the Braxiatel Collection's sector of space. Braxiatel was under house arrest, Adrian and other Killorans were forced onto a work gang, Jason pretended to collaborate to better work against the Axis, and Peter went into hiding. Bev Tarrant secretly led a resistance movement. Benny made bolder moves against the Axis, and killed the sadistic Commander Spang. She later infiltrated the Axis' communications centre, and discovered that the new leader of the Axis was her father, Isaac Summerfield...

2602 - BENNY S4: DEATH AND THE DALEKS[1036] ->

Benny and Jason tracked Isaac Summerfield to the planet Heaven, where he was slaved to a Dalek battle computer and made to coordinate the Axis' battlefleets. Bev and Adrian combined their forces with mercenaries allied with Jason to launch a major attack against the troops occupying the Collection. The Daleks were wiped out, whereupon Braxiatel hard-wired his time machine to theirs and created a facsimile of the Dalek battle computer. Isaac used this lash-up to pilot the Axis' fleets into black holes, cause their forces to attack their own homeworlds, lead their own troops into ambushes, and more until the Axis was finished as a military power.

Benny resumed her relationship with Jason. Braxiatel forged deals with neighbouring empires to protect the Collection, and took Isaac home to his native era.

> (=) Jason Kane's psychic associate, Mira, was killed during the occupation. Braxiatel altered history to reverse Mira's death, and conditioned her to serve as his agent.[1037]

2602 - BENNY: THE BIG HUNT[1038] ->

A powerful businessman, Orlean Wolvencroft, owned the Eagle Museum on Earth's moon. A Van Neumann probe had landed on a planet in System 81, and spurred the creation of hyper-evolving robotic animals; robotic sabretooths were developed from robotic wolves, etc. Benny prevented Wolvencroft from possessing the robot-animal technology, as it could have destroyed entire ecosystems. Wolvencroft was stranded in System 81, and a hyperdrive explosion created gravity shockwaves that would prevent any ships from approaching the robots' adopted world for a decade.

Braxiatel fashioned a "daughter" – a living temporal physics experiment that he poured into a genetics engineering template that was available over-the-counter in Tokyo. He added a bit of his genetic material to stabilise the resultant creation: Margarita ("Maggi") Braxiatel Matsumoto, who could use temporal-rollback to restore people and edifices of the past. He tasked her with "cleaning up" various temporal messes.[1039]

---

the short story collection.

1037 *Benny S8: The End of the World.* Mira is mentioned throughout the works of Dave Stone, and first appeared in *Benny: The Mary-Sue Extrusion.*

1038 Dating *Benny: The Big Hunt* (Benny BF novel #6) - The blurb says that Benny is taking a break from the rebuilding of the Braxiatel Collection, suggesting that *The Big Hunt* follows on from *Benny S4: Death and the Daleks* – although technically, it was released between *Benny S5: The Grel Escape* and *Benny S5: The Bone of Contention.* The Eagle Museum is presumably in Armstrong City, mentioned in *The Sword of Forever.*

1039 "A good few years" before *Benny S7: The Empire State.* Maggi's full name is given in *Benny S8: The Tub Full of Cats.* Braxiatel tells Maggi that the raw energy for her power comes from a stabilised black hole – presumably the Eye of Harmony on Gallifrey.

1040 Dating Bernice Summerfield Series 5 and 6 (*Benny: The Grel Escape*, audio #5.1; *The Bone of Contention*, audio #5.2; *Benny: A Life Worth Living*, collection #4; *Benny: The Relics of Jegg-Sau*, audio #5.3; *Benny: The Masquerade of Death*, audio #5.4; *Benny: Silver Lining*, promo with *DWM* #351; *Benny: The Tree of Life*, Benny BF novel #7; *Benny: The Heart's Desire*, audio #6.1; *Benny: The Kingdom of the Blind*, audio #6.2; *Benny: A Life in Pieces*, collection #5; *Benny: The Lost Museum*, audio #6.3; *Benny: The Goddess Quandary*, audio #6.4; *Benny: Parallel Lives*, collection #6; *Benny: Something Changed*, collection #7; *Benny: The Crystal of Cantus*, audio #6.5) - The Series 5 opener (*The Grel Escape*) cites 2603 as "the present day", and the final adventure of Series 6 (*The Crystal of Cantus*) occurs in January (or possibly

February) 2606. Ergo, Benny Series 5 and 6 must be extended over a nearly three-year period.

Helpfully, two markers denote when the calendar changes – *Benny: A Life Worth Living* (released between *The Bone of Contention* and *The Relics of Jegg-Sau*) says "it's now 2604" (p1) and also that it's "April 2604" (p17), and *Benny S6: The Heart's Desire* takes place on Christmas Eve of the same year, pushing the remainder of Series 6 into 2605. This means that Benny has a comparatively unadventurous 2603, but it's no different from the similarly uneventful gap between her New Adventures and Big Finish stories.

1041 *Benny S6: The Crystal of Cantus; Benny: A Life Worth Living:* "A Summer Affair".

1042 Dating *100:* "The 100 Days of the Doctor" (BF #100d) - The expedition occurs while Benny is in Braxiatel's employ; otherwise, its placement is arbitrary.

1043 The year prior to *Benny S6: The Goddess Quandary.*

1044 Dating *Benny S6: The Heart's Desire* (Benny audio #6.1) - The story occurs on Christmas Eve, and ends at the stroke of midnight. Mention is made of a flight to Stella Stora, which was first referenced in *Terror of the Vervoids* and is cited in *Benny: Present Danger* (p93).

1045 This is the background to the Monoid race seen in *The Ark.* They appear to have some contact with humanity long prior to that story, however: *The Doomsday Weapon* (the novelisation of *Colony in Space*) cites the Monoids as a race that humanity encountered during its expansion into space, and *The Pirate Loop* references them as a slave race akin to the Ood.

1046 "Fifteen years" before *Benny B5: Missing Persons: Big Dig.*

2603 - BENNY S5: THE GREL ESCAPE[1040] **->** A party of time-travelling Grel from circa 2648 deemed Peter Summerfield – the child of a Killoran and a body-jumping sorceress of legend – as worthy of further study, and attempted to capture him. Peter proved capable of activating Benny and Jason's time rings, and the Grel pursued them to various points in space-time. The time rings temporarily matured Peter's body, and he killed the Grel following them.

2603 - BENNY S5: THE BONE OF CONTENTION -> Legends claimed that the inhabitants of the Mancor Sector fashioned skeletons around which cosmic storms would combine to form the Shadow Swans, creatures that terraformed worlds for their creators to inhabit. The Wishing Bone of Perlor was said to be a bone from one such Swan, and to bring good fortune upon whomever possessed it. The government on Perlor traded the Bone to the Galyari aboard the Clutch in exchange for weaponry, but fell to a rebellion anyway. The new Perlor government asked Benny to negotiate the return of the Bone. She found that a Galyari youth, Griko, had been grown around the Bone in the hope of creating a Galyari warrior who could overcome his race's deep-rooted fear of the enigmatic Sandman. Griko broke his conditioning, and was killed to prevent his destroying the entire Clutch. The Galyari compensated the Perloran for the loss of their artifact.

Braxiatel wanted an army of Cybermen that could protect the Collection, and usurped the Cyber-tombs on Cantus. The blissful summer that Braxiatel had promised Ronan McGinley came to an end, and McGinley was forcibly installed as the Cantus Cybermen's Cyber-controller.[1041]

c 2604 - 100: "The 100 Days of the Doctor"[1042] **->** The sixth Doctor and Evelyn aided an expedition funded by Irving Braxiatel, and led by Bernice Summerfield. Evelyn had many good talks with Benny, but judged that she drank too much and had a lot of relationship issues.

2604 - BENNY S5: THE RELICS OF JEGG-SAU -> Benny went to the abandoned planet Jegg-Sau to search for the lost treasures of Robert Eliot Whitman. The Kettlewell-style Robots inhabiting the planet – including one designated K-103 – had gone mad for their isolation, and sought to form a new colony with robotic replicas of human beings. Any human that acted irrationally would be replaced, as the Robots did when Ethan Kalwell – a descendant of Professor Kettlewell – came in search of his ancestor's inventions. The interstellar Red Cross dispatched rescue ships to retrieve Benny, but the Robots attacked them after absorbing enough energy to enlarge in size. The Red Cross jets brushed aside Benny's pleas for clemency, and wiped out the Robots.

2604 - BENNY S5: MASQUERADE OF DEATH -> Benny found a copy of a play, *The Masquerade of Death*, and fell prey to a complex virus embedded in the text. She was comatose for four days, and dreamed of a storybook land with characters such as the Queen of Spring, the Duke of Autumn, the Matriarch of Winter and the Player of All Seasons. She used storyland logic to wake herself up.

On Etheria, Abbot Primus greatly enjoyed watching the Galactic Snooker Championship.[1043]

2604 - BENNY: SILVER LINING -> Benny found a tomb of Cybermen on Tysir IV while giving an archaeology consult. The Cybermen hoped to weaken humanity with a plague, but Benny sealed the Cybermen within their tomb, and they were destroyed when it blew up.

2604 - BENNY: THE TREE OF LIFE -> The entrepreneur Hugo Tollip bought a jungle planet that he renamed Tollip's World, and initiated research to commercialise or even weaponise the variety of DNA found there. Benny helped to prevent Tollip from transplanting a Tree of Life off world, fearing it would defensively create a virus powerful enough to wipe out humanity. Tollip was killed, and the hammies stored within the Trees were revived.

2604 (24th December) - BENNY S6: THE HEART'S DESIRE[1044] **->** Benny became embroiled in a diversionary game between the Eternals Hardy and Barron on Marlowe's World. She captured the prize of their game – a shard of Enlightenment – and used it to wish away a pulsar that was headed towards the Braxiatel Collection. For good measure, she turned Hardy and Barron into mortals. She then threw the Enlightenment shard out an airlock, confident that another Eternal would instantly claim it.

2605 - BENNY S6: THE KINGDOM OF THE BLIND -> Benny came into telepathic contact with the enslaved descendents of the Halavans while examining artifacts from the lost civilisation on Petreus III. The Monoids had become increasingly cruel slave-masters, giving the Halavans numbers for names, and forcing any slave who developed the power of speech to forfeit one of their other senses. Benny aided the Halavans in regaining their telepathic gestalt, which enabled them to overpower their masters. The vengeful Halavans – despite Benny's plea for mercy – psionically stripped the Monoids of their names and removed their ability to speak. They also used their mental prowess to destroy the Monoid planet, and set course back to Petreus III.[1045]

Shepton Rothwell became the host of *Big Dig*.[1046]

The CroSSScape were gestalt beings who had transferred their minds into a datascape. The sudden appearance in the datascape of a box that couldn't be opened filled the CroSSScape with misery and loathing, and they theorised that their god – who had been imprisoned within the Tartarus Gate, a legendary gateway to Hell – could open it for them. To find the Gate, the CroSSScape presented themselves as a benevolent religious order that used an edifice, simply called "the Factory", to reverse natural disasters by rolling back time on doomed worlds. The CroSSScape spent a year looking for the Gate and finally located it on Cerebus Iera, a desert world prone to freak electrical storms.[1047]

2605 (23rd September to 14th November) - BENNY: A LIFE IN PIECES: "Zardox Break" / "The Purpura Pawn" / "On Trial"[1048] -> Earth had an official Acquisition of Alien Artifacts Department. A girl group, the Glitta Bitches, were working on a new Tri-D movie.

Marck Morton became governor of Verum – the contested moon of Aequitas – and negotiated a peace that granted Verum independence. However, Morton was mur-

dered on 23rd September, 2605. Jason Kane – who had leveraged his career as a xenoporn author and become a major celebrity on the resort planet Zardox, partly due to the salacious reporting of his exploits in *Aventures de la Frontière Nouvelle* – was charged with the crime, and thought to have killed Morton to steal a relic of the old empire, the Purpura Pawn, from him.[1049]

Jason's trial began on 12th November; Benny helped to establish his innocence on 14th November. As they returned to the Collection, a bomb destroyed the courthouse, killing one hundred and thirty-one people. The crime was blamed on parties who had opposed Verum's independence, stoking political tensions.

On 1st December, Aequitas cut all ties with Verum. On 2nd December, the Earth Empire dissolved Verum's government and secured the moon with peacekeeping troops; this instigated an era of hatred and terrorist incidents. On 2nd January, 2606, an Earth official named Matthew Barrister died in a shuttle explosion, after confiscating the remaining Ceatul Empire relics. The items officially went

1047 At least a year prior to *Benny S7: The Tartarus Gate*.

1048 Dating *Benny: A Life in Pieces* (Benny collection #5) - The collection was published in December 2004, which all things being equal would place it between *Benny S5: The Relics of Jegg-Sau* and *Benny S5: Masquerade of Death* in 2604. However, Benny's diary and other notations date these stories to 2605. Morton is murdered on 23rd of September, 2605 (extrapolating backward from the anniversary of his death, p150), and Benny's diary claims that she and Jason return to the Collection on the last day of his trial, "14/11/05".

1049 The pulp entertainment *Aventures de la Frontière Nouvelle* is presumably a translation of the Adventures of the New Frontier series often cited in New Adventures by Dave Stone.

1050 *Benny: A Life in Pieces*

1051 Dating *Benny S6: The Goddess Quandary* (Benny audio #6.4) - The cliffhanger leads into *Benny: Parallel Lives* [2606]. This audio was released after *Benny S6: The Lost Museum*, but that story leads into Braxiatel's departure in *Benny S6: The Crystal of Cantus*, so *The Goddess Quandary* and its related stories must come first.

1052 Dating *Benny: Parallel Lives* (Benny collection #6) - The book's introduction claims that "it is now 2606", which is in keeping with it variously being stated that Peter (who was born in 2600) is now "five" and "nearly six". The odd man out is Clarissa Jones' statement that it's been "nearly two years" (p4) since the Axis occupation when it's actually been more like four. In "Jason and the Pirates" – providing a word of its unreliable narration can be believed – mention is made of Oinky Pete, a Piglet Person, presumably the same race that's extinct in *Burning Heart* (set in 3174).

1053 *Benny: Something Changed*. Benny says that, rela-

tively speaking, she owned Wolsey for twelve years.

1054 Dating *Benny S6: The Lost Museum* (Benny audio #6.3) - The blurb specifies the date and month. The last page of *Benny: Something Changed* specifies that *The Lost Museum* comes next in sequence.

1055 Dating *Benny S6: The Crystal of Cantus* (Benny audio #6.5) - According to *Benny: Parallel Lives* (p10), Benny spends "two weeks" trailing Clarissa and Peter to Atwalla 3. If she spends the same amount of time returning, most of January must be consumed with her in transit. While it's *just* possible to imagine that *Benny S6: The Lost Museum* takes place in January as stated, Jason says that *The Crystal of Cantus* occurs nearly a week later, so it must now be February.

Benny mentions the realisation that the Cybermen have tombs dotted all over the galaxy as part of established history, confirming that her native time is after the *Cyberman* audio series. Mention is also made of the Garazone Bazaar from *The Sword of Orion*. The Crystal of Cantus would appear to be the Coronet of Rassilon (*The Five Doctors*), provided to Braxiatel by his younger self on Gallifrey.

1056 Dating Bernice Summerfield Series 7 (*Benny: The Tartarus Gate*, audio #7.1; *Benny: Timeless Passages*, audio #7.2; *Benny: The Worst Thing in the World*, audio #7.3; *Benny: Collected Works*, collection #8; *Benny: The Summer of Love*, audio #7.4; *Benny: Old Friends*, collection #9; *Benny: The Oracle of Delphi*, audio #7.5; *Benny: The Empire State*, audio #7.6) - Series 7 continues onward from Series 6 (which ends in February 2606) and finishes shortly prior to the opening episodes of Series 8 (which can be definitively dated to October 2607). Unavoidably, then, a single season's worth of stories must be spread out over a 20-month period.

It's not entirely clear when the switchover from 2606

missing, but the Purpura Pawn, somehow, wound up in Braxiatel's possession.[1050]

2606 - BENNY S6: THE GODDESS QUANDARY[1051] ->

The leaky roof of the Etheria monastery was one of the Wonders of the Galaxy.

Benny had completed a documentary on the legendary warlord Aldebrath for the Tri-D Broadcasting Company, and the monks on Etheria invited her to learn whether their planetoid system contained his final resting place. Tri-D's central news bureau was on Angola V. Benny's friend Keri, a journalist for Tri-D, documented the search.

Benny found Aldebrath's ship, the *Fervent Hope*, in one of Etheria's outer planetoids. Aldebrath's mind was in the ship's computer systems, and she used her love-inducing telepathy to stop a religious uprising. Keri's reputation had suffered after she botched an expose on the multi-zillionaire Stellis Gadd, and Benny ended their friendship after learning that Keri had hampered her search to get a better story. Benny took Aldebrath and the *Fervent Hope* back to the Collection, only to find that Clarissa Jones, one of the Collection's administrators, had gone missing...

2606 - BENNY: PARALLEL LIVES: "The Serpent's Tooth" / "Hiding Places" / "Jason and the Pirates" / "Parallel Lives"[1052] ->

Clarissa Jones abruptly kidnapped Peter and disappeared. Benny followed them to Atwalla 3, a medieval world in the Fallan Nebula where women had no rights. She went undercover as a man, joined some knights on a successful quest and was rewarded by being married to Jesh, the daughter of Emperor Jodal. Benny bluffed Jodal into thinking that a virus had been devised that would let the Atwallan breed with other species – an act that would, in time, destroy the Atwallan bloodline. Jodal considered Benny's threat to unleash the virus unless he granted the Atwallan females equal rights.

Jason joined the search for Peter late, having been delayed – or so he told Benny – owing to an escapade where he had to join some pirates led by Buggering Barnabas Jimmity Jim-Bob Hullabaloo, aboard their ship *The Black Pig*.

Benny, Jason, Bev and Adrian confronted Clarissa on the suburban worlds of Thuban. Clarissa said she was from the future, and that she wanted to raise Peter to avoid the life that Benny suspected was in wait for him. She relented and returned Peter to Benny, but a scuffle led to Bev killing Clarissa as she drew a gun on Adrian.

Wolsey Passes Away

Bernice's cat Wolsey died from natural causes, and was buried in the Collection's garden. Bev and Adrian were now in relationship. Temporal distortion revised the history of the Collection's gardener, Hass – instead of a Martian, he was now a Yesodi: a jellyfish-like being capable of generating a radiation cache within its pressure suit.[1053]

2606 (January) - BENNY S6: THE LOST MUSEUM[1054]

-> Benny and Jason went to salvage exhibits from the Trib Museum, as the dictatorial regime on the planet housing it had fallen. Jason quelled the carnage by tricking each faction into thinking that the other had backed down.

Benny Discovers Braxiatel's Duplicity

2606 (February) - BENNY S6: THE CRYSTAL OF CANTUS[1055] ->

The Galyari performed a production of *Macbeth* on Berkoff IV.

The crystal that allowed Ronan McGinley to control the Cybermen on Cantus was killing him, and a new Cybercontroller was required. Braxiatel tried and failed to install Jason as the new Cyber-controller; Benny learned of his treachery, and Jason broke Braxiatel's mental conditioning. Benny used the crystal to eradicate the Cantus Cybermen, then destroyed it. His machinations exposed, Braxiatel departed from the Collection. In his absence, the Draconians made a claim to planetoid KS-159.

2606 - BENNY S7: THE TARTARUS GATE[1056] ->

The Craxitanian government was so grateful to Benny for finding their prized temple, they rewarded her with ten boxes of their famed champagne.

The CroSSScape captured Bernice, thinking that – thanks to her body having already accommodated the mind of a goddess – she could serve as the physical host to their god. The Factory regressed time on Cerebus Iera to when the Tartarus Gate – a black hole, held in perfect balance – had last been opened, and the god transferred across. The god cast the CroSSScape into the Hell that lay beyond the Gate, and was then trapped in a datascape box.

2606 - BENNY S7: TIMELESS PASSAGES ->

Important manuscripts had been lost when a giant space aardvark accidentally inhaled the Splendid Biblious Spiroplex of the ten billion sapients of Zoomos Prime. Rare documents in this era included *The Atrocity Exhibitions*, *The Augenblick Presidency* by Robert Dallek and *Aristotle's Poetics, Part 3: Smokey is the Bandit*. The Adjudicators were still active.

The origin of the Labyrinth on the planet Kerykeion was unknown, but it contained one of the biggest collections of human publications outside Earth, with more than two hundred million books, including the only known copy of *Gay Bulgaria*. A corporation, Omni-Spatial Mercantile Dynamics (OSMD), sought to buy Kerykeion because the Labyrinth's passages stretched into different points in space-time, which is how the original librarians there acquired their collection.

Bev Tarrant was now administrating the Braxiatel Collection, and sent Bernice to purchase rare books from the Labyrinth before the OSMD buy-out. Benny met – and destroyed – a murderous cyborg sent from the future by OSMD's descendents.[1057] The librarian Hermione Wolfe wound up owning the Labyrinth, and cut a deal with the Braxiatel Collection as to the Labyrinth's holdings.

Braxiatel had merged his TARDIS with the Collection before his departure. Without him, the Collection became subject to breakdowns.[1058]

J-Netics developed the cheap food bar Xanabix using genetic material from the giant sandroaches on Kaff Zarnak. Xanabix enabled the Xanadu Tower staff to work harder, sleep less and withstand extreme temperatures, but increasingly started morphing them into actual sandroaches. The Tower was quarantined, and the condition spread when Dr Carol Bauer – seeking to force the upper classes to develop a cure – tainted the Tower's water supply with the Xanabix material. Jared Jones hastily concocted an

antidote for himself and remained in Xanadu Tower, a human-sandroach hybrid. Belenus – the largest moon of the neighbouring planet Dagda – was knocked awry and passed close enough to Kaff Zarnak to affect its orbit, drastically lowering its temperature.[1059]

2607 - BENNY S7: THE WORST THING IN THE WORLD -> Horses were believed to be extinct. Pop sensation Manda I had a new single, entitled "Pumpin' Out Your Baby of Love", set to the holovid of her daughter's birth.

The Drome had been established as a self-contained community that produced televised content for GalNet, and was located a half an hour from the Galactic Transit Core. The Drome's offerings included the *Inspector Wembley* movies, the long-running soap *Squaxaboolon Street*, *Topless Garden Makeovers*, *Whose Stool is That?*, *Airhead Factor*, *The Larder in the Garden*, *Mutilation Razor-Motor-Scooter Hockey on Ice*, *Frock and Fanny* and a revival of *The Infinity Division*. Galnet had at least 4796 channels.

to 2607 occurs. *Benny: Collected Works* is less helpful than other collections in making this call, as its stories are set over the course of a year, straddling both 2606 and 2607. Nor is trying to put the year in tandem with the year of release entirely helpful – *The Summer of Love* came out in October 2006, and yet must occur in 2607. The best compromise is to date the first two stories of Series 7 to 2606, and place *The Worst Thing in the World* in 2607, in accordance with a "last year" remark made regarding events in the Drome in *Benny S8: The Wake*.

In accounting for some of Benny's time in 2006, she spends at least a month being held captive in *The Tartarus Gate*. She also spends two weeks in transit to reach Kerykeion (and presumably the same amount to return home) in *Timeless Passages*.

1057 Benny destroys the cyborg by bringing its present and future selves into collision, evidently invoking the Blinovitch Limitation Effect.

1058 *Benny: Collected Works*. The malfunctions begin "months" prior to *Benny S7: The Summer of Love*. It's not said how Braxiatel went into the past without his TARDIS to become the Stone of Barter (*Benny S7: The Empire State*).

1059 The Xanabix outbreak and the Belenus event both occur "ten years" before *Benny B2: Road Trip: Paradise Frost*, which is a remarkable run of bad luck in a short span of time.

1060 Dating *Benny S6: The Summer of Love* (Benny audio #6.4) - The story does, apparently, take place in summer, with references to the heat.

1061 *Benny S6: The Summer of Love*, and similarly noted in the epilogue to *Benny: Collected Works*.

1062 Dating *Benny: Old Friends*: "Cheating the Reaper"/"The Soul's Prism" (Benny collection #9a, 9c) - The two "modern-day" novellas in this collection occur between *Benny S6: The Summer of Love* and *Benny S7:*

The Oracle of Delphi, and the back-cover blurb says that it's "late 2607". Benny now looks "nearly 40".

1063 Dating *Benny S7: The Empire State* (*Benny* audio #7.6) - Benny seems to spend a few days digging up the Stone, and then as many as eight in the new Empire State itself. Benny ends *The Empire State* intending to travel back to the Collection, only seems to lose about a week in transit in the following story, and arrives in time for *Benny S8: The Judas Gift*, which occurs in the third week of October 2607. So, *The Empire State* very probably occurs in the same month.

1064 Dating *Bernice Summerfield Series 8* (*Benny: The Tub Full of Cats*, audio #8.1; *Benny: The Judas Gift*, audio #8.2; *Benny: Freedom of Information*, audio #8.3; *Benny: Nobody's Children*, collection #10; *Benny: The Two Jasons*, novel #9; *Benny: The End of the World*, audio #8.4; *Benny: The Final Amendment*, audio #8.5; *Benny: The Wake*, audio #8.6) - The stories that compose Benny Series 8 unfold in the space of roughly three months. *The Judas Gate* dates itself to 23rd and 24th October, 2607, and the other stories can be extrapolated from that (see the individual entries for more). In *The Tub Full of Cats*, Maggie reiterates the year as "2607", which translates to "818" in the standard modern calendar.

1065 Dating *Benny S8: The Judas Gift* (Benny audio #8.2) - The exact dates are given via headline news and a recording that Bev makes. Events said to have occurred in "the last year" include alien pollen and time jumps (*Benny S7: The Summer of Love*) and gravitational shifts (*Benny: Collected Works*).

1066 *Benny S8: The End of the World*

1067 *Benny S8: The Final Amendment*. It's not explicitly said, but Bernard is presumably Clarissa Jones' father.

Jason Kane was being interviewed about his work on *Xenomorphic Bondage Slaves, Part 37,* and asked Benny to investigate mysterious occurrences at the Drome. Its central computer, an AI named Marvin, had become so advanced that it was altering reality in accordance with people's beliefs. The Drome's production teams became murderous and zombie-like; Benny resolved the situation by singing a happy song, making everyone act as if they were in an old-style musical. Official reports said that a terrorist attack had caused mass hallucinations.

2607 (summer) - BENNY S7: THE SUMMER OF LOVE[1060] ->

The Draconians and other races continued to have aspirations on the area of space that included the Collection. Bev undertook negotiations to avert war between six races. The Collection's systems further deteriorated, and exerted strain on all thirteen dimensions, causing people to randomly jump through time. Hass recommended planting Simpson's Thin Weave, which would work its roots into the Collection's soil and bind everything on a temporal level. As a side effect, the Thin Weave's pollen ramped up the libidos of everyone present, and a mass orgy ensued. Jason predicted that when word of this spread, student enrolment at the Collection would be up next year.

Bev asked Benny and Jason to undertake a mission to ancient Greece, and they left using their time rings...[1061]

2607 (autumn) - BENNY: OLD FRIENDS: "Cheating the Reaper" / "The Soul's Prism"[1062] ->

The disgraced Ivo FitzIndri had died on the ex-mining planet Balgoris, and Benny attended his funeral. Benny's ex-lover Simon Kyle was now an Admiral with Spacefleet. Benny, Jason and Kyle discovered that a Mim – one of a race of shapeshifters, whose natural forms were bundles of toxic sponge-like matter – had killed FitzIndri as part of a scheme to steal Balgoran artifacts. The Mim was incinerated in an ancient Balgoran tomb, and the loss of the items within removed any historical objection to Balgoris revamping itself as a retirement locale and holiday resort.

Jason privately warned Kyle to forever stay away from Benny, lest Jason show her a video recording of Kyle deliberately leaving Jason to die after the Mim attacked him. Benny visited the local temple of the Order of the Lost Lemuroidea, and her testimony cleared FitzIndri's name and that of his bloodline.

2607 (October) - BENNY S7: THE EMPIRE STATE[1063] ->

Benny unearthed the Stone of Barter on a desert moon, thinking it could help her locate Irving Braxiatel – the being most likely to stabilise the Collection, and avert the brewing interplanetary war. The Stone caused Benny to acquire Maggi Matsumoto's "fixer" talent, and she accidentally recreated the long-destroyed Empire State as a hodge-podge of her textbook readings about the edifice and her own desires. The new State decayed, and Benny was forced to destroy it again. Matsumoto regained her fixer abilities, and Braxiatel was liberated from the Stone – he had been resting in it for some millennia. Benny persuaded him to return to the Collection.

2607 (October) - BENNY S8: THE TUB FULL OF CATS[1064] ->

Tensions between the Draconians and the Mim worsened, and both sides established blockades around the Collection. Benny, Braxiatel and Maggi returned to the Collection aboard *Gravity's Rainbow*, a spaceship that was technically, for tax purposes, owned by some cats. The *Rainbow* was equipped with a Deselby Matango filter which could make the ship invisible to the laws of physics, but required someone to function as an "anchorite" to bring the ship back into reality. The *Rainbow*'s current anchorite, Captain Anthony Rogers, emerged from the filter and died of old age. Maggi permanently took his place.

2607 (23rd-24th October) - BENNY S8: THE JUDAS GIFT[1065] ->

Under the Universal Rules of Engagement, weapons such as radiation chains, phase cannons and biogenic assaults could not be used on sentient species. Texts on the Draconians included *The Rough Guide to Draconia, The Time Out Guide to Draconia* and *Twitching for Draconians*.

Braxiatel somewhat stabilised the Collection's systems. The Earth Parliament tried to stay out of the Draconian-Mim stand off, and considered having the Terran Reserves set up a buffer zone. Ambassador Kothar of Draconia sought revenge against Bev Tarrant for the death of his blood brother Ethan, and while his use of the Judas Gift severed Bev's left hand, she was able to fake her death and escape the Collection.

The Draconians destroyed the Stonehauser Medical Facility, which serviced dozens of species. They also landed combat troops on the Collection and occupied it.

> (=) Clarissa Jones, age six, was killed along with her parents in the attack on the Stonehauser facility. Braxiatel changed history so that an older version of Clarissa could serve as an administrator to the Collection.[1066]

Bernard Jones, a xenophobic clone-maker who worked at Stonehauser, was killed in the attack. He had facilitated the replacement of Earth President (and Empress) Fiona Dickens with a clone of herself. Per her conditioning, the clone-Dickens instigated a number of anti-extra-terrestrial policies upon Jones' death.[1067]

Devastation of the Mim-Sphere

2607 (November) - BENNY S8: FREEDOM OF INFORMATION[1068] -> Braxiatel resolved the Draconian-Mim standoff by having Hass store up his radiation output, then open his containment suit on the Mim-Sphere. The Mim were obliterated almost to the point of extinction. In return, the Draconian Emperor withdrew his troops from the Collection, and agreed that the Collection would have sovereignty while remaining in Draconian space.

2607 (November) - BENNY: NOBODY'S CHILDREN: "All Mimsy Were the Borogoves" / "The Loyal Left Hand" / "Nursery Politics"[1069] -> The Draconian-Mim conflict had entailed deployment of panic-inducing phase cannons against Proxima Longissima. Eight million Mim fled, and the Draconians claimed jurisdiction over the borogoves – nurseries for infant Mim – left behind.

Benny became pregnant with Jason's child, but miscarried. She learned – partly due to a Mim artifact she found

in the ruins of Windsor Safari Park – that Project Narcissus had continued after the Dalek Wars, and had been redirected against Earth's rivals. At least thirty high-ranking Draconians were Mim infiltrators. In exchange for their not bringing the Empire to ruin, the infiltrators were selected to oversee the borogoves in Draconia's name until the Mim children came of age, at which time the Emperor would honourably banish them from Draconian space. The arrangement prevented an Institute from acquiring the Mim progeny for use against Earth's enemies.

Braxiatel Goads Peter Summerfield into Killing Jason Kane

2607 (December) - BENNY S8: THE END OF THE WORLD / BENNY S8: THE FINAL AMENDMENT / BENNY: THE TWO JASONS[1070] -> On Earth, clones were being generated for use as TV celebrities; New Newport had experienced an Equity uprising as cloned actors demanded various rights. GalNet 4 was now run-

1068 Dating *Benny S8: Freedom of Information* (Benny audio #8.3) - A modest amount of time passes during the Draconian occupation of the Collection. Benny has been in hiding for five days when the story opens, and the Draconians lock her up for three more. Jason makes mention of Draconian troops shooting some civilians "the other week". Also, Hass disabled his radiation-neutraliser "weeks" ago, presumably the amount of time since Braxiatel returned to the Collection and could plot with Hass in person. All signs are, then, that it's now November – especially as some time must be allotted between this story and *Benny S8: The End of the World*, which finishes in December.

1069 Dating *Benny: Nobody's Children* (Benny collection #10) - The stories are set after *Benny S8: Freedom of Information*, and lead into *Benny S8: The Final Amendment*. The unnamed "institute" with a fondness for the name Victoria is probably Torchwood.

1070 Dating *Benny S8: The End of the World, Benny S8: The Final Amendment* and *Benny: The Two Jasons* (Benny audios #8.4 and #8.5, Benny BF novel #9) - These three stories run roughly concurrent to one another. Both *The End of the World* and *The Final Amendment* say that the Stonehauser Medical Facility was destroyed "two months ago" (in *Benny S8: The Judas Gift*, set in October), so it's now December. A small glitch exists in that Jason refers to Peter as a "half-Killoran eight year old", when he's seven at most.

The fact that Benny only here learns about *The Jason Kane Show* – now in Season 15 (which isn't to automatically say that it's been running for fifteen years) – suggests that the Braxiatel Collection and Earth are some distance from one another, and news from Earth doesn't reach the Collection very much. Even so, it's quite the conceit that nobody at all, not once, has ever

mentioned it to her.

The epilogue to *The Two Jasons* claims that Mira and the Jason-clone stay together for some decades, and that the Jason-clone eventually returns to Earth, has sex with President Summerfield and is informed that the remains of the original Benny have been found. However, it's hard to say (especially in light of President Summerfield's death in Series 10) whether this is canon or just some bit of fancy on writer Dave Stone's part.

Mention of the owner of London probably denotes Marillian from *Benny: The Sword of Forever*. The White Rabbit pub, here seen off Earth, appears in Big Finish stories such as *The Harvest* and *UNIT: The Longest Night*.

1071 Dating *TW: "Overture"* (TWM #25) - The year is given.

1072 Dating *Benny: Many Happy Returns* (Benny 20th anniversary special) - This interlude happens after Jason's death (*Benny S8: The End of the World*), but before Benny and Peter flee the Braxiatel Collection (*Benny S8: The Wake*).

1073 Dating *Benny S8: The Wake* (Benny audio #8.6) - Benny gets notification of Jason's death at the end of *Benny S8: The Final Amendment*, and the story picks up (albeit in flashback) upon her return to the Collection. An unspecified amount of time passes with her displaying normality at the Collection while she pieces together Braxiatel's actions, and it's almost certainly 2608 when she takes Peter and leaves. In support of this, her visit to the Drome (*Benny S7: The Worst Thing in the World*) is cited as being "last year". Braxiatel says that Jason's clones have been "taken care of" – although whether this includes the one who ran off with Mira in *Benny: The Two Jasons* isn't specified.

The Wake heavily cements ties between the *Doctor Who* New Adventures and the Big Finish Benny range,

ning Season 15 of *The Jason Kane Show* based upon Jason's books, with clones of Benny, Jason and their friends performing farcical hi-jinks. *Hollyoaks: Life on Phobos* was also being shown, as was *Fat, Fat, Fat, Fat, Fat, Fat!* Imperials were a currency used on Earth, and various establishments there displayed a rape-risk rating. Celebrity news reported that the owner of London was about to get married – again. Le Maison Celestial had established itself as a gourmet restaurant in a spaceship that was previously part of the Mim blockade. The White Rabbit pub, formerly an Earth establishment, had been relocated to Bedrock XII.

Kadiatu Lethbridge-Stewart became the personal bodyguard to Howard, the son of Earth President Fiona Dickens, and recruited Benny to investigate the president's increasingly strange behaviour. They stopped the clone-Dickens – who threw herself to her death – from pushing the Earth Empire into open warfare with various alien races. The clone of Benny from *The Jason Kane Show* became Earth president, while the original Dickens and Howard went travelling with Kadiatu.

Simultaneous to these events, Jason Kane learned that, owing to Braxiatel's machinations, large portions of his timeline had been altered or deleted altogether. Jason threatened Braxiatel with exposure – in response, Braxiatel goaded Peter into thinking that Jason was a threat to Bernice. Peter's savage side took over, and he killed Jason. Jason's associate Mira threw off Braxiatel's conditioning, and started a new life with a Jason-clone.

2607 (31st December) - TW: "Overture"[1071] **->** Jack Harkness visited the planet Zog. An alien representative gave him a sonic failsafe to curtail its sleeper agents on Earth, 1941, and Jack duly sent it back to his former self.

2607 (December) - BENNY: MANY HAPPY RETURNS[1072] **->** Benny and Adrian Wall deliberated upon the degree to which Peter could claim diminished responsibility for killing Jason Kane.

Benny and Peter Go on the Run

2607 (December) to 2608 - BENNY S8: THE WAKE[1073] **->** The dance version of "Abide With Me" was played at Jason's funeral, and his xenoporn books were republished. A provisional government was now running the Collection. Bernice continued teaching at the Collection for a time, but deduced Braxiatel and Hass' involvement in the Mim's downfall. Lacking the evidence and support to challenge Braxiatel directly, Benny snuck away from the Collection with Peter, and went on the run in a spaceship.

2608 - BENNY S9: BEYOND THE SEA[1074] **->** Galaxo-Starbucks-Disney copyrighted the name "Atlantis" when it opened up The Real Atlantis. Benny took a job producing a documentary of a lost civilisation on the watery world of Maximediras, which was rebranding itself as a tourist stop. Isolationist members of the micro-organisms who inhabited Maximediras animated some cadavers, and tried to push the human colonists off world. Benny curtailed the rogues, and the micro-organisms' government invited the colonists to share the planet with them.

Peter was transported back to 65,000 BC; Benny followed him after unearthing the time ring that he lost in a lava flow. They separately returned to their native era, after Benny made a side trip to 1893. Upon her return, Benny had manuscripts of some unpublished Sherlock Holmes adventures. These included *The Adventure of the Diogenes Damsel* and *The Cautionary Tale of Ludvig Cooray* – the latter of which involved the disappearance of the nephew of a minor German aristocrat.[1075]

---

enacting scenes from *Theatre of War* and *Happy Endings* (*Benny S8: The End of the World* similarly enacts a scene from *Death and Diplomacy*), and mentioning Heaven, and the defeat of the Hoothi (*Love and War*).
1074 Dating Bernice Summerfield Series 9 (*Benny: Beyond the Sea*, audio #9.1; *Benny: The Adolescence of Time*, audio #9.2; *Benny: The Adventure of the Diogenes Damsel*, audio #9.3; *Benny: The Diet of Worms*, audio #9.4) - Following Benny's departure from the Collection, the Benny range defaults back to being a number of stand-alone stories, and there is little reason to suppose that Series 9 doesn't occur over the course of a year (mirroring the passage of real time). Also, starting with Series 9, Big Finish decided that the Benny stories, for simplicity's sake, would occur exactly six hundred years in the future – a helpful yardstick (even if the policy later ended with the *Benny: Epoch* box set).

The novella collection *Benny: The Vampire Curse* was released between Benny Series 9 and 10 in November 2008, and the main contemporary story within ("Predating the Predators") dates itself to June 2609. Reconciling this against Bev's comments in (*Benny S10: Glory Days*), however, suggests that "Predating the Predators" takes place within Series 10, not beforehand. **1075** *Benny S9: The Adolescence of Time*, *Benny S9: The Adventure of the Diogenes Damsel*. The unpublished Holmes stories are mentioned in *Benny S9: The Diet of Worms*, although it's unclear when Watson had time to write the *Diogenes Damsel* manuscript, unless it pertains to Benny's work with Mycroft prior to their confrontation with Straxus. Alternatively, it's possible that Benny acquired these documents during her later meeting with Watson in 1914 in *Benny: Secret Histories*: "A Gallery of Pigeons".

2608 - BENNY S9: THE DIET OF WORMS[1076] -> On Earth, the Depository served as an archive for cultural and literary giants whose works had survived the Dalek Wars, including Martin Luther, Charles Darwin, Wilkie Collins and Barbara Cartland. Earth Central halved the Depository's budget, and a bibliopath, Myrtle Bunnage, wanted to regain this funding by giving the impression that paper-eating worms had infested the facility. The worms consumed a manuscript by Cartland that contained extra-terrestrial paper, and thereby gained the ability to recite any text they ate. Bernice contained the situation and saved the worms – who were now the sole source of documents written by Luther, Darwin and Cartland.

c 2609 - THE COMPANY OF FRIENDS: "Benny's Story"[1077] -> Hired by Countess Venhella, Bernice excavated 50-million-year-old rock on Epsilon Minima and thereby found the buried TARDIS key, which summoned the eighth Doctor's TARDIS. Venhella believed that TARDISes were an enslaved species, and tried to liberate the Doctor's Ship with a manumitter – a forbidden Gallifreyan device. Improper use of the manumitter created cracks in the fabric of the universe, and threatened to unleash ravenous monstrosities. The Doctor and Benny were briefly flung back to Epsilon Minima's past, but returned – whereupon the Doctor sealed the space-time cracks. He and Benny shared some adventures before he successfully took her home.

(=) 2609 - BENNY S10: GLORY DAYS[1078] -> Bev and Adrian aided Benny in breaking into Finger's bank to gain entry to a vault there owned by Braxiatel. They found within a painting that Benny had created while wearing her time ring – in case of emergency, Braxiatel could download his consciousness into a cloned body via the painting's temporal link. Benny altered the painting's history...

... and in so doing, averted Finger's ever being founded. A beer seller stood in its former location.

Cloning had come a long way since its use on specialised farm worlds. *Ocean's 14 1/2* had been released. *The Collected Works of Jason Kane* had topped the adult charts since Jason's demise.

1076 Dating *Benny S9: The Diet of Worms* (Benny audio #9.4) - The ending leads into *Benny S10: Glory Days* – but given the transit time over interstellar distances, the calendar might well change in the interim.

1077 Dating *The Company of Friends*: "Benny's Story" (BF #123a) - The story takes place while Benny is freelance, and Peter is with his father. *The Company of Friends* was released in July 2009, and is presumably concurrent with *Benny Series 10*, in which Benny and Adrian are reunited after her time away from the Braxiatel Collection. The only oddity would then be why Benny doesn't enlist the Doctor's help against the rogue Irving Braxiatel.

1078 Dating Bernice Summerfield Series 10 (*Benny: Glory Days*, audio #10.1; *Benny: The Vampire Curse*: "Predating the Predators", collection #12c; *Benny: Absence*, audio #10.2; *Benny: Venus Mantrap*, audio #10.3; *Benny: Secret Origins*, #10.4; *Benny: Secret Histories*, collection #13) - As with Series 9, there's little reason to suppose that Series 10 doesn't pace itself over the course of a year, mirroring the passage of real time. Per Big Finish's new policy that the Benny stories happen six hundred years in the future, it must now be 2609.

In *Glory Days*, Bev comments that she spent "the best part of a year running the Collection", and also that she's now spent a year working as a thief. Presuming that she's rounding down a bit from her departure from the Collection in October 2607, *Glory Days* probably takes place in early 2609.

1079 Dating *Benny: The Vampire Curse*: "Predating the Predators" (Benny collection #12c) - The dates are given in journal entries, with the final one (p215) specifying the year as 2609. The "Alukahites" seem to be the Benny equivalent of the Great Vampires (*State of Decay*).

1080 Dating *Benny S10: Absence* (Benny audio #10.2) - Peter is now a "young man", old enough to be hired to haul things. According to Benny's diary, the story takes place over fifty-nine days. The Technocult and the detail about the ball bearing were previously mentioned in *Benny S7: Timeless Passages*.

1081 Dating *Benny S10: Venus Mantrap* (Benny audio #10.3) - The story is a sequel to *Beige Planet Mars*, a story in which Benny and Jason similarly lose a fortune in royalty payments. The Lunar penal colony is almost certainly the one seen in *Frontier in Space*.

1082 *Benny S10: Secret Origins*

1083 Benny and Robyn's retroactive undoing of Buenos Aires' ruination isn't without its temporal hiccups – the entire story might be paradoxical, in fact. Writer Eddie Robson says that despite Benny and Robyn's historical intervention, it's safe to presume that events in this time zone unfolded in a relatively similar fashion, and that Frost is still dead.

1084 Dating *Benny: Many Happy Returns* (Benny 20th anniversary special) - It's between Benny encountering Samuel Frost in *Benny S10: Secret Origins* [2609] and the final confrontation with Braxiatel and the Deindum starting in *Benny: Dead and Buried* [2610].

1085 "Years" before *Benny: Adorable Illusion* (ch3).

1086 The framing sequence to *Benny: Secret Histories*.

1087 "Ten years" before *Benny B5: Missing Persons: The Revenant's Carnival*.

2609 (Sunday, 18th June to Saturday, 24th June) - BENNY: THE VAMPIRE CURSE: "Predating the Predators"[1079] **->** While Peter stayed on Fomalhaut IV, Benny joined an expedition arranged by the Fomalhaut Museum of Forerunner Artifacts to the Blood Citadel of the Alukah – an ancient race of vampires. She was present at the excavation of the tomb of Re'Olena, a servant of Lord Ekimmu who was banished as punishment for laughing. Olena awakened, and started a vampire insurrection at the First Colonial University on Murigen – a planet with three suns (Fea, Macha, and Nemhain), and was home to the Lavellans. Olena's vampires attempted to seize the intergalactic quantum tunnel system being developed by the Lavellan professor "Stassy" Leustassavil, hoping to create a transgalactic vampire empire with Olena at its head. Leustassavil opened tunnels that eradicated Olena and her vampires in Murigen's suns.

2609 - BENNY S10: ABSENCE[1080] **->** Benny and Peter stopped off on the cluster world of Absence – which was deep in human space and hundreds of light years from anyone hostile – while en route to Venus to collect Jason's immense royalties. Needing funds to leave Absence, Benny flipped burgers while Peter was hired to assist with an expedition sponsored by Interspatial Systems Acquisitions (ISA) into Absence's interior. The Technocult – a cyberculture that could store the entire holdings of the Labyrinth of Kerykeion on the inside of a ball bearing – took an interest in Absence, and it was suspected that the world's interior was evolving. The founder of ISA, Lamarque Aslinesdes, was killed by Cindy, a sentient prototype environmental suit built by his company.

2609 - BENNY S10: VENUS MANTRAP[1081] **->** The government on Venus was responsible for two artificial moons: Eros and Thanatos. Eros had a reputation for romance, but industry drove Thanatos, which was installed with Venusian warhives and rockets. Eros had an orbital spaceport. Thanks to an agency run by Megali Scoblow, a disgraced former academic who Benny had met on Mars in 2595, the rich and influential on Eros could hire "love drones". These used state of the art cerebral-profilogical mapping techniques to match their clients' conscious and subconscious desires. The penalty for owing certain types of lockpicks on Eros was five years in Earth's Lunar penal colony; on some of the outer worlds of the solar system, the sentence was death.

Benny tried to acquire Jason's royalties from his publisher, Velvet Mandible, while Peter stayed with his father in Dallas. The Trans-Galactic Taxes and Duties Division of Outland Revenue claimed most of Jason's fortune, pursuant to duties under Section 32: erotica and explicit fiction import to the Xlanthi Clachworlds. Benny capitulated, as an appeal would mean spending six months on the ice moon of Flisp, which only got two days of sun a month.

N'Jok Barnes – the half-Venusian, half-human ambassador representing Venus on Eros – tried and largely failed to ratchet up tensions between Eros and Venus so he could look heroic while resolving the "crisis". He came out of the incident unscathed – unlike his co-conspirator, Eros' Vice Chancellor Safron Twisk, who was left disgraced when he publicly read aloud a passage from *Barely Humanoid* – one of Jason's pornographic novels – that Benny had fed into his autocue.

Samuel Frost murdered President Summerfield and sent her body in a shuttle to Eros – as a means of getting Benny's attention.[1082]

2609 - BENNY S10: SECRET ORIGINS[1083] **->** Benny went to the ruins of Buenos Aires when Samuel Frost – her purported longtime nemesis, whom she didn't remember – kidnapped Peter. During the confrontation, Frost was killed. An android from the future, Robyn, sought to undo Buenos Aires' demise; her temporal powers enabled Benny, whose body remained in bed, to accompany her though time as a temporal projection. They encountered Frost in 2002 and 2212, and neutralised his obliteration of Buenos Aires after identifying his origin year as 1937.

c 2609 - BENNY: MANY HAPPY RETURNS[1084] **->** Benny and Bev Tarrant searched for a black box they believed Braxiatel hid near Samuel Frost's base of operations. Bev came to suspect that her memories or timeline had been changed, pertaining to the death of someone close to her...

Benny's encounter with the Soundsmiths of Lasa sparked a generational "Wanted Dead or Alive – Preferably Dead" bounty on her head.[1085]

Benny accepted an assignment to preserve a church on the war-torn planet Jovellia as an Antique Faith Environment. While doing so, she aided a lifeform that changed states of being in space – but was currently trapped on Jovellia as a series of black crystals – to attain the next phase of its lifecycle.[1086]

Terraforming succeeded on Moros Prime, a world of liquid rock and volcanoes. Willem van der Heever rose to power as the planet's prime minister/de facto dictator, and permitted organ harvesting of an Aboriginal people, the Kai. The Highgate Law tried to weigh civil liberties against security concerns, and mandated use of embarrassment filters in high-security areas to conceal people taking baths, going to the lavatory and more.[1087]

2610 - BENNY: DEAD AND BURIED[1088] -> Braxiatel fabricated a "lost civilisation" on the planet Jovada as bait for Benny. He had her put into stasis when she excavated the site, preventing her from interfering with his plans...

The Deindum Invasion

Downfall of the Braxiatel Collection

2610 - BENNY S11: RESURRECTING THE PAST[1089] -> Adrian and Peter found Benny and revived her from stasis. Braxiatel now believed that his people were doomed, and purchased the ocean planet Maximediras to adapt into a new home for the Time Lords he hoped to "resurrect". He relocated Maximediras' eight thousand residents, and moved the energy field near the Braxiatel Collection to Maximediras, hoping it would become the Time Lords' new power source.

Simultaneously, Braxiatel's operations against the Deindum entered a new phase... Braxiatel Protective Mechanoids (BPMs) were dispatched to kidnap various

individuals, who were scanned in a former moonrock processing facility on Earth's moon. Braxiatel was searching for an individual who, when dispatched into the time-space rift to the Deindum's homeworld in the future, would alter the Deindum's development so they wouldn't develop time travel, and would have a less aggressive and paranoid nature. Bernice was Braxiatel's failsafe – consigning her to the rift would have curtailed the Deindum's advancement. Before that could happen, the android Robyn accidentally fell into the rift, which then closed.

- -
(=) Robyn's inorganic matter had no effect on the Deindum's evolution, and they became immensely powerful beings that manifested as large, glowing reptilian heads. The Deindum sent troops back through time to conquer habitable space in the twenty-seventh century in the name of their empire...
- -

1088 Dating Bernice Summerfield Series 11 (*Benny: Dead and Buried*, Benny animated short #1; *Benny: Resurrecting the Past*, audio #11.1; *Benny: Present Danger*, collection #14; *Benny: Escaping the Future*, audio #11.2; *Benny: Year Zero*, audio #11.3; *Benny: Dead Man's Switch*, audio #11.4) - Benny ends Series 10 intending to return to the Braxiatel Collection, but has some side adventures (including the framing sequence for *Benny: Secret Histories*) before doing so. The animated short *Benny: Dead and Buried* – which leads into *Resurrecting the Past* – saw release in August 2010, and so seems as good a place to "start" Series 11 (and to roll the calendar forward to 2610) as any. The short story *Present Danger:* "Six Impossible Things" says that it's been three years minimum since Benny left the Braxiatel Collection, so the Deindum invasion initiated in *Resurrecting the Past* almost certainly occurs in 2610. The booklets to *Resurrecting the Past* and *Escaping the Future* claim that "It's the year 2607" – this has to be regarded as a mistake, given the preponderance of evidence saying otherwise.

1089 Dating *Benny S11: Resurrecting the Past* (Benny audio #11.1) - Benny is in stasis for "five days", and at least a few days pass in the course of the story.

1090 According to *Benny S11: Escaping the Future*, the Deindum invasion unfolds over some "months".

1091 *Benny S11: Year Zero* and *Benny S11: Dead Man's Switch*. *Benny* Series 11 ends on the cliffhanger of Benny arriving at "Atlantis", feeding into the *Benny: Epoch* stories.

1092 *Benny: Adorable Illusion*

1093 *Benny B4: New Frontiers: The Curse of Fenman*, prior to Braxiatel saving Peter from Bastion.

1094 *Benny B4: New Frontiers: The Curse of Fenman*, explaining the status quo when Benny finally reaches Legion at the end of *Benny B2: Road Trip* [c.2617]. Braxiatel and Peter establish themselves on Legion "four years" (*Benny B3: Legion: Vesuvius Falling*) prior to Benny's arrival.

Peter says that he's "17" in a flashback to his time on Bastion in *The Curse of Fenman*, but he's presumably lying to not freak out his boyfriend that (going by Peter's well-documented birth in 2600 in *Benny: The Glass Prison*) he's probably only between age ten and 13. Perhaps some accommodation can be made for the development rate of a human-Killoran hybrid – for that matter, Peter can only be 13 at most when he becomes Legion City's security chief, and he's grown enough by then to intimidate the local criminal element for four years running.

1095 *Benny: Adorable Illusion*

1096 *Benny B5: Missing Persons: The Revenant's Carnival*

1097 *Benny: Adorable Illusion* (ch15), presumably before the gap Benny is absent from the twenty-seventh century following *Benny S11: Escaping the Future*, and after the Braxiatel Collection's downfall.

1098 "Over a decade" before *Vienna S3: Self-Improvement*.

1099 *Benny B4: New Frontiers: The Curse of Fenman*. Jack arrives on Legion "a few weeks" prior to Benny and Ruth showing up there.

1100 "About four years" before *Benny B3: Legion: Vesuvius Falling*.

(=) 2610 - BENNY: PRESENT DANGER / BENNY S10: ESCAPING THE FUTURE ->
From a base on Maximediras, the Deindum conducted campaigns in the past and present to the stability of their timeline. They were a danger to every civilisation in the galaxy. In their wake, the Braxiatel Collection was overrun with refugees. Braxiatel, Bernice and their allies coordinated resistance efforts, but the Deindum succeeded in overcoming their coalition...[1090]

Bernice suggested to Braxiatel that manipulating the Deindum at a crucial point of their development would erase their invasion from history. Braxiatel concurred, even though the effort would expend more than half of the Maximediras energy rift, preventing him from resurrecting his people. The Deindum sabotaged their efforts – to retroactively undo this defeat, Hass opened up his containment suit on Maximediras, killing the Deindum there and every living thing. The Deindum overwhelmed the Collection; Peter, Adrian and Bev were left behind as Benny and Braxiatel travelled four million years ahead in his TARDIS, successfully implemented their plan, and historically nullified the Deindum invasion.

Aftermath of the Deindum Invasion

Benny Skips Six Years of Her Own Time

After the Deindum crisis, Benny found herself in the distant past on the planet Raster – one of twenty inhabited worlds where the disciplines of history and archaeology had been outlawed. She travelled to the worlds' capital, the planet Zordin, and found that it looked like Earth, and that the Great Leader had just renamed it "Atlantis..."[1091]

The surviving Deindum surrendered, having lost their appetite for conquest. Many planets obliterated during the Deindum war were restored per the historical alteration, but some elements of the conflict remained. Adrian Wall, Bev Tarrant, Peter Summerfield and a few beings retained their memories of the Deindum invasion, either owing to prolonged exposure to time phenomena, or because they were at the epicenter of the temporal revisions.[1092]

The Braxiatel who fell through a portal while assisting President Romana hid from the enemies of the Irving Braxiatel who had owned the Braxiatel Collection. He explored real estate options on Dexter Prime, but fell prey to Avril Fenman's mind-controlling crystals. Fenman encountered resistance from the Pandora segment within Braxiatel's mind, extracted it and sent it back "eighteen years or so" into the Braxiatel at the Collection. She then compelled Braxiatel to buy property on the distant planet Legion, as well as her own mobile asteroid Hera. Avril's crystal scrubbed Braxiatel's memory of their meeting.[1093]

Once reality restarted, Peter found himself aboard a slaver ship en route to the mining planet Bastion. The slavers also captured a young man named Antonio Tulloch. About six months after Peter's arrival on Bastion, he become friends, then lovers, with Antonio. About six weeks later, Avril Fenman implanted a crystal within Antonio so she could monitor Peter's movements. Braxiatel arrived on Bastion to purchase Peter's freedom. Adrian Wall and Bev Tarrant, unaware of Peter's location, were busy rebuilding the Maximediras System. Braxiatel's attempts to negotiate for Antonio's release led to robot guards shooting Antonio dead. Antonio's love for Peter, coupled with the crystal within him, enabled Avril to gain a toehold in Peter's mind. Braxiatel took Peter to live with him on Legion, and left a message for Benny – still in stasis on Mars – as to their whereabouts.[1094]

About a year after Peter's departure, 734 slaves from 306 species were liberated on Bastion. Adrian Wall had become the leader of Valentine's World, a refugee camp with some of the Federation's best medical facilities. He and Bev Tarrant married, and she became pregnant with his pups. They had possession of Bernice's computer Joseph, but former colleagues such as Doggles and Hass were missing. Someone fitting Robyn's description was seen on one of the Rimworlds.

The Braxiatel Collection and the entire satellite on which it was housed were both gone.[1095] Benny believed that Haas was dead.[1096] Her books were now out of print.[1097]

The aftermath of the Toxo-Plasmic Plague gave rise to Facsimiles: replicated humans who served as "universal bloodlines" in psychological experiments. Helping Hand Solutions purchased the planet Murian Tursis, the locale of Ludovic Glospan's efforts to create the Good Day Formula.[1098]

Benny's Associates, Jack and Ruth, Relocate to This Era

Avril Fenman returned to this era following her machinations in the Epoch's Atlantis, but failed to locate Benny's stasis chamber on Mars in 2613. She could continue to interfere in Benny's affairs, and confront her on Legion in 2619. Owing to the Epoch's remapping of reality, a shuttle containing Jack – an associate of Bernice Summerfield from Atlantis – was on translocated to the year 2613 and transformed into a large cruiser. Jack became the ship's entertainments manager, then got fired and wandered about for a time. He eventually learned that Benny's colleague Irving Braxiatel had taken up residence on Legion, and, at loose ends, went to Legion and took a job at Braxiatel's White Rabbit pub.[1099] EcoSi hired Mortan Hardak and Sheira Rynn.[1100]

Bernice's friend Ruth found herself in this era following the collapse of the Epoch's Atlantis timeline, recognised

Benny's influence on the legend of the Beneficiary, and presumed Benny would discover the same. Ruth enrolled in an archaeology course on planet Lyndyaz, a hub of Benficiary worship, to await Benny's arrival there. She quickly became Professor Harry Burtenshaw's assistant.[1101]

A supernatural familiar of the Collector inveigled herself into the mind of Emilia Blythe, a patient at the Firebrand medical facility. Isobella Klempe, Blythe's cellmate, learned the familiar's name – Caitlin – and died within a fortnight. Blythe committed suicide.[1102]

Benny Awakens from Stasis

2616 - BENNY: EPOCH: JUDGEMENT DAY[1103] ->

Having escaped from "Atlantis" in a stasis chamber, Benny awoke in 2616 aboard Mars Base Grantham-Echo-Four. The new version of Irving Braxiatel had left Benny a message that he could reunite her with Peter, and that she should rendezvous with him on the distant planet of Legion...

Benny en route to Legion[1104]

Benny upset the Heliok Syndicate by exposing one of their embezzlement schemes. Heliok issued a bounty on her head, but was culturally obliged to fulfill on it within six months or overlook the grievance.[1105]

c 2617 - BENNY: ADORABLE ILLUSION[1106] -> Madras, a sentient curry, was now the four-time consecutive winner of Galactic Masterchef.

An outing of Hoondock University students to the Rapture – an energy rift in the Dragonfly Nebula – aboard *The Hunter* disappeared while their instructor, Dr Anya Kryztyne, was having sex with an anti-grav squash player aboard his shuttle half a light year away. The industrialist Victor Cooke secretly killed Kryztyne and commissioned Bernice Summerfield to travel aboard the dreadnought *Adorable Illusion* and find his lost daughter. Benny boarded the *Adorable Illusion* on Valentine's World, failing to realise that Adrian Wall and Bev Tarrant were there.

Extra-dimensional creatures within the Rapture plotted to escape their dying realm and possess all sentient life across the universe, but the *Adorable Illusion* was detonated to seal off the rift, as Benny escaped with her fellow travellers and the missing students aboard the *Hunter*. Mission complete, Benny continued on to Legion.

c 2617 - BENNY B2: ROAD TRIP / BENNY: THE WEATHER ON VERSIMMON[1107] -> The Dominicci Corporation now effectively ruled worlds such as Lyndayaz, where its Commercial Rights Squad punished trademark violations.

Professor Harry Burtenshaw, the Dean of the Faculty of Archaeology on Lyndyaz, deduced that Bernice Summerfield was the source of the mythology behind a

---

1101 "About a year" before *Benny B2: Road Trip: Brand Management,* with Ruth's arrival in this era explained in *Benny B4: New Frontiers: The Curse of Fenman.*

1102 *Benny: Shades of Gray.* Exact date unknown, but the first sighting of Caitlin occurs at 3:37 a.m. on 27th November, 2616.

1103 Dating *Benny B1: Epoch: Judgement Day* (*Benny* box set #1.4) - A robot attendant supplies the year, indicating that Benny has missed out on a solid six years in this era. Benny comments: "Right... a little bit later than I was expecting, but same basic ballpark."

1104 THE BENNY BOX SETS: The five *Bernice Summerfield* box sets – under the umbrella titles of *Epoch, Road Trip, Legion, New Frontiers* and *Missing Persons* – follow on from eleven seasons of individual Benny audio releases, and contain three to five stories each. Additionally, three novels (*Benny: The Weather on Versimmon, Benny: The Slender-Fingered Cats of Bubastis, Benny: Filthy Lucre*) were released to respectively tie into events in *Road Trip, Legion* and *New Frontiers*. A fourth, *Benny: Adorable Illusion,* is a flashback story set prior to *Road Trip.*

Epoch entails Benny in the past (probably around the time of Atlantis) in an alternate timeline created by the titular characters, then returning to her native time after spending some millennia in a stasis capsule. *Road*

Trip sees Benny and her friend Ruth traveling to the planet Legion (of no relation to the race of the same name in *Lucifer Rising* et al) per Braxiatel's instructions, and the remaining three box sets feature Benny establishing herself on Legion to be near her son Peter. The numbering of this range was subsequently retired to make way for *The New Adventures of Bernice Summerfield,* in which a post-Legion Bernice again takes up traveling with the seventh Doctor and Ace.

Epoch claims that Benny awakens from stasis in 2616, and *Legion* and *New Frontiers* contain solid evidence that they respectively occur in 2618 and 2619. It's entirely believable that Benny and Ruth spend a year in transit in *Road Trip,* as Benny starts off on Mars and finishes the journey at Legion, which is literally on the edge of the Milky Way. (Complicating matters, Braxiatel doesn't appear to leave Benny coordinates or directions to Legion, meaning she loses some time before learning the way there in *Benny B2: Road Trip: Bad Habits.*)

Taking all of that into account, it seems best to swim with the tide and assume that – for Benny and company – the box sets each take place in successive years, even though they were commercially released at roughly six-month intervals (from February 2012 for *Road Trip* to December 2013 for *Missing Persons*). See

prominent goddess, the Beneficiary, and lured her there with a job offer. Benny arrived on the thirteenth day of the thirteenth month, Beneficiary Day, and found Lyndyaz awash in Beneficiary merchandise including boiled sweets, air freshener, lunchboxes, underwear and toilet paper. Such was Lyndyaz's devotion to the Beneficiary that an image of her face had been carved onto the planet's third moon with military lasers, and complimentary features rendered onto the other two.

Burtenshaw exposed the Dominiccis' deceptions at the 612th Sleep of the Beneficiary gathering, which featured many Beneficiary tribute bands. Benny was reunited with Ruth, and left Burtenshaw to organise resistance to the Dominiccis' rule.

While journeying to Legion, Benny and Ruth stopped at the planet Versimmon to examine its famous Caldera Archive: a living Archive Tree containing the whole of Palastor's culture. Ribnor, a Palastoran Council member, seeded the planet with a monsoon-triggering element to pave the way for biofuel crops. Benny and Ruth helped to save a worldseed (a mimetic copy of the Tree's ecosystem) for other Palastorans to germinate on a dead world.

A Varuumian holy man told Benny and Ruth, "Legion are the paths to serenity, but only serenity's sphere shows the path to Legion", whereupon they traveled to Agora: the holiest planet in the Theon System. They posed as nuns as Talishanti Monastery – renowned as the "most sacred place in the twelve galaxies" – and apprehended an agent of the Council of Ten who was murdering nuns and archaeologists alike to keep secret St Celestion's origins as a cosmonaut. Benny and Ruth acquired Celestion's Sphere of the Serenity: actually a Serenity 6000 star map, manufactured by Serenity Systems of Sassanovada. With it, they plotted

a course to Legion and hitched a ride on a medical ship...

... which they were thrown off, after Benny drank too much and punched out a robot. Benny and Ruth booked a private ship to Legion, but Dr Carol Bauer drew their vessel off-course with a tractor beam, hoping to find a means of leaving the quarantined Kaff Zarnak. The humans transformed into giant sandroaches killed Bauer, and the sandroach-hybrid Jared Jones died after helping Benny and Ruth escape in his private shuttle.

Benny and Ruth finally arrived at Legion, which had an automated spaceport and a single settlement: Legion City. A new version of Irving Braxiatel was running a bar, the White Rabbit, with Benny's associate Jack as his employee and her son Peter serving as the city's security chief...

A smuggler hacked the only dentist in Legion City to pieces.[1108] CrimeCorp detective Guy Wilkes became a mole for the Notari crime family, and faked his death to implicate their rivals, the Abromi Brothers. Wilkes' partner, Jexie Reagan, sought to avenge his "murder" – but Wilkes killed Franco Abromi, then altered Jexie's memories to make her believe she had pulled the trigger. Wilkes hid out in the Undercity, still on the payrolls of the Notari family and CrimeCorp CEO Carlos Van Meyer.[1109]

Bernice Summerfield at Legion

The colony Legion was built on the ruins of an ancient civilisation on the extreme edge of the galaxy – the very end-point before interstellar space. The planet's light side barely sustained life, with a dome protecting Legion's only settlement, Legion City, from solar winds and radiation.

The name Legion originated from the Gospel of Luke,

---

the individual entries for more.

1105 "Four months" before *Benny: Adorable Illusion*.

1106 Dating *Benny: Adorable Illusion* (Benny novel #13) - The book was released after *Benny B5: Missing Persons*, but takes place between Benny's revival from stasis on Mars (*Benny B1: Epoch: Judgement Day*) and her meeting up with Ruth in *Benny B2: Road Trip*. Benny has been awake for at least "four months" (ch3), but it's at least "six months" journey to Legion from her position on Valentine's World (ch2). Chapter 8 seems to contain a typo, claiming that it's been "nearly thirty years" since "2688" (ch8) when it was probably meant as "2588". Ginger, a Pakhar (so, presumably having a shorter lifespan than humans), was born after the Fifth Axis offensive (ch22) that ended in 2602 (*Benny S4: Death to the Daleks*). Her son, Russet, was six (ch15) when the Deindum invaded (*Benny: Present Danger/Benny S11: Escaping the Future*, set in 2610).

1107 *Benny: The Weather on Versimmon*, marketed as a *Benny: Road Trip* tie-in, contains a small continuity gaffe in that it mentions Professor Trout from *Benny B2: Road*

Trip: Bad Habits (p63), even though no gap seems to exist between *Bad Habits* and *Benny B2: Road Trip: Paradise Frost* for Versimmon to comfortably take place. Benny's mention of "Lyndyaz, Versimmon and Agora" in *Benny B4: New Frontiers: The Curse of Fenman* probably indicates the story order.

The Agora in *Bad Habits* is sometimes mistaken for the planet of the same name in *Time of Your Life* and *Killing Ground*, but the two are very different. Humans settled the latter (*Killing Ground*), but not the former (the timescale on the Talishanti Monastery's founding is all wrong for that). The latter isn't renowned for spirituality, but it's a crucial feature of the Benny story. The writers of *Bad Habits*, Simon Barnard and Paul Morris, never intended that their Agora was the previously established one; Barnard chose the name from the historical drama *Agora* (2009), and took some of the characters' names (such as Synesius) from it.

1108 "Two years" before *Benny B5: Missing Persons: The Brimstone Kid*.

1109 "Three years" before *Vienna S2: Underworld*.

suggestive of closeness and an army of like-minded individuals working towards a common cause. It was said that to be tired of Legion was to be tired of life, because beyond it, there was nowhere left to fall.[1110] Legion was an outlaw world, not affiliated with any empire or system.[1111] The more respectable elements in Legion City lived in its Western part, which went into lockdown at night.[1112] Less civilised souls camped out in the wastelands.[1113]

2618 - BENNY: SHADES OF GRAY[1114] -> Drs Warrilow and Hawke of the Firebrand medical facility asked Dorian Gray, an expert on the supernatural, to consult on two deaths related to a patient named Caitlin. Gray discovered that Caitlin was an "imaginary friend" made real, who caused the deaths of people she associated with. He advised Warrilor and Hawke to just leave Caitlin alone, then departed. The Collector entered the facility afterward, and watched as Caitlin killed the doctors.

Avril Fenman solidified her hold on Peter Summerfield's mind, causing him to believe that his late boyfriend Antonio was alive and part of his life.[1115]

2618 - BENNY B3: LEGION / THE SLENDER-FINGERED CATS OF BUBASTIS[1116] -> The Draconians made the best brandy on Legion's side of the galaxy, but didn't consume much of it themselves. The GalWeb served as an information network, even as far out as Legion. Cellular regrowth spores had been developed that, if injected with a donor's genetic material, could heal injuries such as broken ankles within a month.

On the same day that the CoreTech exploration ship *Vesuvius* left for the Mutara Nebula, it re-appeared – having been inert for five thousand years after falling through a wormhole into the past – near Legion with an impending warp core breach. Benny exposed two of the *Vesuvius* astronauts, Mortan Hardak and Sheira Rynn, as having murdered a third, Rickard Karne, because he knew they were having an affair and/or were corporate spies for SinoCorp. Rynn killed Hardak, but was trapped aboard the *Vesuvius* as Legion's batteries blew it out of the sky.

The immortal Dorian Gray received word that his portrait – lost to him for centuries – was held at Triptic House on Legion City's outskirts. Gray anonymously hired Bernice, who was accompanied by Jack and Ruth, to retrieve his property. Benny, Ruth and Jack found the por-

---

1110 The background to *Benny B3: Legion* and the subsequent Benny box sets.

1111 *Benny: Adorable Illusion* (ch12).

1112 *Benny B5: Missing Persons: The Brimstone Kid*

1113 *Benny B3: Legion: Everybody Loves Irving*

1114 Dating *Benny B3: Legion: Shades of Gray* (Benny box set #3.2) - Caitlin was first spotted "about a year or so ago" on "November 27th, 2616", and it's "fifteen months" after she caused Isobella Klempe's death. Benny concludes, after witnessing these events in a séance, "that asylum was definitely present day".

1115 "A year or so" before *Benny B4: New Frontiers: The Curse of Fenman*.

1116 Dating *Benny B3: Legion* (*Benny* box set #3, contains 3.1, *Vesuvius Falling*; 3.2, *Shades of Gray*; 3.3, *Everybody Loves Irving*; and the related *Benny: The Slender-Fingered Cats of Bubastis*, BF novel #11) - The séance that Benny, Jack and Ruth convene in *Shades of Gray* occurs "about a year or so" after Caitlin was first spotted on "November 27th, 2616" and "fifteen months" after Isobella Klempe's death, which triangulates to suggest that story – and presumably the rest of *Legion* – happens in 2618. Supporting that, Peter says he's "eighteen" in *Everybody Loves Irving*, which matches with his being born in 2600 (*Benny: The Glass Prison*).

In *Benny: The Slender-Fingered Cats of Bubastis*, Benny and company use "Brax's shuttle" (p75) rather than the Explorer Mark VI ship Benny acquires in *Everybody Loves Irving*. The book tries to have it both ways, though, in suggesting that Legion – supposedly in the desolate backwaters of space – is in shuttle distance of

a resort facility funded by the Atlan World Government, and which achieves some success with temporal mechanics.

The Mutara Nebula featured in *Star Trek II: The Wrath of Khan*.

1117 *Benny B4: New Frontiers: HMS Surprise*. An entry code that Benny employs gives the exact day.

1118 *K9: The Korven*

1119 "Five months" after *Benny B3: Legion: Vesuvius Falling*.

1120 Dating *The Shadow Heart* (BF #167) - No year is given, but it's the time of the Earth Empire. While nothing is said about the state of affairs on Earth, the expectation that the Empire could seriously challenge the Wrath Empire suggests that humanity is at something of a high point. "Fifty years" have passed since the Doctor last met Kylo (*The Acheron Pulse*).

A native of this time zone makes an incidental mention of a "Snortis on Vortis" (*The Web Planet*). No mention is made of how Vienna escapes imprisonment aboard the *Trafalgar*, but she's next seen, at liberty, in *Vienna: The Memory Box*.

1121 Dating *Vienna: The Memory Box* (*Vienna* #0) - Big Finish's official policy is that the *Vienna* series exists in a different continuity from that of *Doctor Who*, and yet *The Memory Box* takes place an unspecified amount of time after the fall of the Wraith Empire (*The Shadow Heart*), the Galileo space hotel is run by a Slithergee (*Flip-Flop*), and its clientele includes Mogarians (*Terror of the Vervoids*) and a Pakhar (*The New Adventures* et al). See the Vienna Salvatori sidebar for more.

trait and held a séance through which they experienced scenes from Gray's involvement with the Collector. Gray entered Triptic to reclaim his portrait, and Benny's trio left him alone to ponder it.

The etymologist Bil Bil Gloap summoned Benny to the Star Seasons resort and research facility, as the Experimental Library there – equipped with a prototype device that could offer books from the past, present *and* future – had flagged a book of Benny's poetry that she knew nothing about, but would be published in the next week. Benny, Jack and Ruth went to Bubastis to check in with an expedition led by Professor Neon Tsara – the heir to the Tsara bomb business. Tsara was allied with the Friends of Stone, a group devoted to discovering the truth behind some of the universe's most neglected monuments, and blew up one of the famed stone cats of Bubastis. The cat disgorged the many skeletons kept within, answering the long-asked question of the Nobal's fate. The number of books about Bubastis both before and after this discovery, 214 in total, still failed to compare with the amount written about Dr Butler's titillating theory of space harems.

Fearing that the Experimental Library would kill off paper research, as well as aid tyrants or people interested in forecasting lottery numbers, Benny turned a blind eye as Jack made off with the Library's Future Retrieval Device. The book of poetry that Benny authored, *Orisons in Two Languages* (one entry of which began *Oh Cats! You make me feel so small. Yet your long fingers to me call.*) became a pop-culture phenomenon on the planet Eugenie. Bil Bil Gloap's work became the foundation of the bestseller *One Word, Two Meanings: The Linguistic Phenomenon that Will Blow Your Brain!* and the show *I Say Potato, You Say Potato.*

Braxiatel forged deals with the Ikerians, prolific breeders who operated a trading post near the dark side of Legion, and helped Bernice establish herself in a new base of operations: Silo Crater XJ-7, a rocket base six klicks away from Legion City, complete with an Explorer Mark VI spaceship.

Mortis Dock became the last manned shipyard in Legion's part of the cosmos, as people remained a cheaper and more expendable resource than machines. On 9th July, 2618, the *HMS Surprise* – still hosting a suffering Healer within its mass – appeared at Mortis and made the shipyard's six thousand inhabitants vanish and reappear in a zombie-like state. Only Lucas Catch, a fire warden, remained himself.[1117]

In 2618, the human military organisation Global Command considered the Korven the most dangerous and destructive race of the age.[1118] Bernice and Peter Summerfield intended to inform CoreTech of the true fate of the *Vesuvius* – but only after the ship had fallen down a wormhole as scheduled, to prevent a paradox.[1119]

Vienna Meets the Seventh Doctor

c 2618 - THE SHADOW HEART[1120] **->** Scrap merchants known as Snailers traversed the space lanes in Stellar Ammonites: giant snails capable of warp speeds. The mineral galdrium was especially prized. The Wrath Empire became so powerful, it was increasingly hoped the Earth Empire could defeat it.

The Wrath established a new homeworld – a factory planet that housed the Shadow Heart. This was an Imperial super-computer built with organic components taken from thousands of Wrath captives, and coordinated the Wrath's justice fleets and Empire. Over time, moral contradictions surfaced within the Shadow Heart, and the Wrath searched for the two beings who had most influenced their origins – the Doctor and Prince Kylo – so they could reprogramme it.

The Doctor consequently became "the most wanted man in the twelve constellations", and the price on his head of ten thousand credits attracted the interest of the bounty hunter/professional killer Vienna Salvatori. She captured the seventh Doctor on Temperance VII, but was perplexed when her memory sifter indicated they had already met. The Doctor escaped, and instructed the Earth Empire war galleon HMS *Trafalgar* to head for the Wrath homeworld, located on the very edge of the galaxy, where they would encounter a younger version of himself.

The Wrath were thought to have murdered Prince Kylo's last Aliona clone. In actuality, the Doctor saved her and – with benefit of his hindsight – took her back in time and arranged for her to be aboard the *Trafalgar*.

Kylo physically merged with the Wrath's Imperial war machine, and declared himself the Emperor of the Wrath. The *Trafalgar* crew encountered a younger version of the seventh Doctor, who met Salvatori for the first time (from his perspective) and deactivated the Wrath's planetary shields. As the Doctor intended, Kylo refrained from attacking the *Trafalgar* because Aliona was aboard. The *Trafalgar's* attack run destroyed the Imperial engine and Kylo, marking the end of the Wrath Empire.

It was expected that Aliona, as the last surviving member of House Gadarel, would broker a peace treaty with the Earth Empire and form a new republic. The end of the war sharply reduced the price of galdrium. The Doctor left after turning Salvatori over to the *Trafalgar's* Captain Webster, who put her in irons.

c 2619 - VIENNA: THE MEMORY BOX[1121] **->** *The Infernal Prince: The True Story of Kylo and Aliona* was a movie based upon the famed star-crossed lovers of the Drashani Empire. The authorities of this era could interrogate suspects with memory scans, but Mental Search Warrants were sometimes required. Galactic protocols governed cases of murder that required a lockdown.

The trillionaire Berkeley Silver was one of the richest men in the Earth Empire, with half a dozen planets registered in his name. His business operations on the volcanic planet Vulcana lured refugees of the fallen Wrath Empire – who were massacred and re-animated as cadavers, a.k.a. Revenants, for use in manual labour in violation of galactic law. Silver had possession of a Memory Box – a device that could hide entire sub-folders of memories in the brain, but were retrievable with a code-phrase – and had extended his life nineteen times by using the Box to copy his entire mind into a new host.

The friends and family of Silver's reanimated victims aligned against him as a clandestine cell named Flaming Sword. To flush out the Flaming Sword members, Silver commissioned his own murder with an assignment crystal sent to Vienna Salvatori. Suspecting a trap, Salvatori agreed to expose Silver's misdeeds in exchange for Detective Captain Arnold McGinnis erasing certain transgressions from her record.

Salvatori went to kill Silver as instructed at the Galileo space hotel, but Silver doubled the fee of seven million poldats promised by "her unnamed employer", if she agreed to take down Flaming Sword. Silver then shot himself, knowing that his mind was copied into a Memory Box folder in his heir, the lawyer Norvelle Spraggott.

The memory folder restored Silver to life in Spraggott's body, but Vienna re-activated it, subduing Silver's memories beneath Spraggott's persona. Vienna also deactivated the Revenants on Vulcana.

c 2619 - BENNY: MANY HAPPY RETURNS[1122] ->
Benny and Jack went gambling at the Star Double Star Casino, the hottest nightspot on Legion, and prevailed against a crooked gambler, Jules Vega.

c 2619 - BENNY: MANY HAPPY RETURNS[1123] ->
The AI Curator of the biggest collection in the universe – capable of assembling artifacts from an individual's past, present and future – suffered virus corruption and began killing the museum's patrons. Benny went to the museum

---

1122 Dating *Benny: Many Happy Returns* (Benny 20th anniversary special) - "A couple of weeks" before the story's main events.

1123 Dating *Benny: Many Happy Returns* (Benny 20th anniversary special) - It's during Benny's time at Legion, in a story released between *Benny B3: Legion* and *Benny B4: New Frontiers*.

1124 Dating *Benny B4: New Frontiers* (Benny box set #4, contains 4.1, *A Handful of Dust*; 4.2, *HMS Surprise*; 4.3, *The Curse of Fenman*; and the related *Benny: Filthy Lucre*, BF novel #12) - The three audio stories featured in *New Frontiers* take place over a month, with *A Handful of Dust* commencing on the first day of Legion's 29-day Advent period, and *The Curse of Fenman* ending on Advent Day (the shortest day of Legion's year). This might translate to it being December (especially as Benny and Brax seem to think that Advent Day means it's "nearly a new year" for Legion), even though that would mean we've no idea what Benny and company get up to for most of 2618.

HMS Surprise yields the most telling evidence pertaining to the year: the disaster that befell Mortis Dock on 9th July, 2618 happened "twelve months ago", and a newsbot report dated to "Wednesday, the 9th of April, 2618" is cited as "just over a year ago". Whatever uncertainty one might ascribe to Legion's Advent season, it seems very likely that Big Finish's intent was for *New Frontiers* to take place in 2619, a year on from *Legion* [2618].

Either way, Benny, Ruth and Jack spend two weeks of Advent in transit to Nemeqit and back (*A Handful of Dust*). *Filthy Lucre* – said to take place "pre-Advent"/"a couple of weeks" prior to Legion's "winter festival" (ch2), and which mentions the Nemeqit trip but not events on Mortis Dock (*HMS Surprise*) – takes "thirteen days"

(ch18) to unfold, leaving previous little time in the allotted twenty-nine days for *HMS Surprise* to happen.

1125 According to Jack in *Benny B5: Missing Persons: Big Dig*.

1126 The background to *Benny B5: Missing Persons: The Brimstone Kid*.

1127 Dating *Big Bang Generation* (NSA #59) - For Benny and company, the story seems to take place between *Benny B5: New Frontiers* [2619] and *Benny B4: Missing Persons* [2620]. In support of that, Ruth has known Peter for "twelve months" (ch6)/"a year now" (ch10), and the *Irverfield* has been christened (ch14). Peter knows about the outcome of events (chs. 9, 10) in *Benny B4: New Frontiers: The Curse of Fenman* (set at Advent 2619). Enough time has passed since then that Peter met a special someone in a club on Bacchus Five, but it didn't work out (ch6). Peter is "18 years old" (chs. 5, 10), which matches his being born in late 2600 (*The Glass Prison*), although the Doctor guesstimates that he's "maybe 17 or 18" (ch6). A curveball is that Jack and Ruth are engaged – which wasn't the case in their audio stories.

For the Doctor, it's been "a lot of years and faces" since he last saw Keri (ch2). Benny claims that the last Doctor she met was the seventh (ch6), but gives contradictory remarks as to when exactly that happened, first telling Keri that she spoke with Seven "the other week" (ch7), but later informing the Doctor himself that they last met, in her timeline, "years ago" (ch9) when Ace stole an Omega Device (*NAofBenny* Volume 1).

1128 Dating *Benny B5: Missing Persons* (Benny box set #5, contains 5.1, *Big Dig*; 5.2, *The Revenant's Carnival*; 5.3, *The Brimstone Kid*; 5.4, *The Winning Side*; 5.5, *In Living Memory*) - No year given. Benny says (*In Living Memory*) that she's been on Legion with Peter "months, about a

and witnessed recreations from her life as constructed from journals and witnesses. Projections of Benny's many friends and associates aided her in restoring the demented Curator's systems.

The Return of Avril Fenman

2619 (Advent season) - BENNY: NEW FRONTIERS / FILTHY LUCRE[1124] -> To Benny's annoyance, Braxiatel christened her explorer ship the *Irverfield*. Vonna Byzantium hosted a revival of *Paranormal Planets*, a show that had run for sixteen years until a kerfluffle involving face ecoplasm. Byzantium had also featured on *Cooking with Ghosts*, *Cleaning with Ghosts* and *Sleeping with Ghosts*.

Benny, Ruth and Jack responded to a distress signal emanating from the "haunted" world of Nemeqit, which was listed in *Ten Planets You'll Never Want to Visit*. Nemeqit's 2000-year-death cycle ended with a storm tearing apart Nemeqit's children, Bel and Lud, to scatter their essences into space. They were consequently reborn as twin planets with dust ring circles.

The multi-multi-billionare Adam Yarri, a famed snacks and organic food tycoon and archaeology supporter, used pheromone-enhanced aftershave to compel Bernice to strike up a relationship with him. Benny brought Yarri's company to ruin by releasing evidence of its crimes, and killed Yarri in self-defence when he attempted to eliminate her in a wargame scenario.

Later, the tormented Healer within the *HMS Surprise* drew the *Irverfield* off course to Mortis Dock, where Benny, Jack and Peter aided the honourable Lucas Catch in becoming the Healer's new host. Benny's trio returned to Legion in time for Advent Day...

Avril Fenman brought her long-running scheme involving her pseudo-son Peter, Braxiatel, Ruth and Jack to a conclusion as her asteroid approached a once-in-4000-year eclipse between Legion and its sun. The event would have channeled solar power through the asteroid's crystals, enabling Avril to drain life energy from Ruth, Jack and Braxiatel, and fully manifest in the form of Peter's dead boyfriend Antonio. She hoped to rule the universe through the power of her crystals, with Peter at her side, but Braxiatel foiled the plan by blowing up Avril's asteroid. Peter shot Avril dead as her form solidified.

In this era, preparing a Candlestick cocktail remained one of the most challenging aspects of mixology.[1125]

On Brimstone, the Maglev Company developed train tracks through farmland belonging to the Ford family. Gunmen hired by Maglev killed the Ford brothers for sabotaging the train tracks, and so their sister, Billie Ford, robbed a Maglev train of a few million credits and became infamous as the Brimstone Kid.

The Irving Braxiatel who ran the Braxiatel Collection had become one of the most wanted men in the galaxy, charged with one count of petty larceny, four counts of theft, one count of vandalising a religious icon, three counts of assault, sixteen counts of fraud, two counts of corrupting a member of the clergy, five counts of arson and twenty-five counts of criminal damage. He was also named in paternity suits.[1126]

2619 - BIG BANG GENERATION[1127] -> Bernice Summerfield calculated she was in her mid-50s, but – as she had become somewhat immune to time, so aged more slowly – she outwardly looked and felt about fifteen years younger. Bournville still existed, but now covered the whole of Birmingham. Ruth owned a bag from Camden Market. An Emperor ruled the Pakhar BurrowWorld.

Benny found a fragment of the Glamour... but touching it transported her, Peter, Ruth and Jack to the Pyramid Eternia in the fifty-first century. Events there went so badly, Benny instructed her past self to break the First Law of Time to help them. The contemporary-Benny arranged for Ker'a'Nol ("Keri") the Pakhar to summon the Doctor to Legion via postcards, but was once again drawn into the future.

Keri had shared many adventures with the Doctor, including escapades where he'd left her on Tugrah... and the Azure Moon of Gald... and in jail on Kolpasha... and an incident on Nefrin, where he'd told her "I'll be back in five" and returned five years later, leaving her to guard the Eternity Capsule in the interim. She was currently mending a leg she'd broken while ice-skating on the planet Torvalundeen: a sentient world that the Doctor accidentally made cough. The Doctor walked into the White Rabbit on Legion while Braxiatel was out, conferred with Keri, and went to aid Benny's group in the twenty-first century...

> (=) Legion was vapourized when the Pyramid Eternia destroyed all of history in 2015, but the Doctor restored the correct timeline.

Upon their return, Benny and her friends buried the Glamour-shard some forty miles north of Legion City, and hoped it would never be found.

2620 - BENNY: MISSING PERSONS[1128] -> The Epoch further examined the temporal disruption centred on Bernice Summerfield by progressively removing her friends and colleagues from her timeline. As they did so, Benny lost all memory of her abducted loved ones...

Benny took Ruth and Jack to the planet Serevas in the tri-solared Peson System, where she appeared on the 712th event of the archaeology show *Big Dig*. She realised that the whole world was an Epoch facility made to study the influence of "truth" embedded into lesser minds. *Big*

Dig achieved its highest ratings in a decade, even when scheduled against *Celebrity Shark Jump Final* and *Empress John's Unitard*, as 150 million viewers tuned in to watch various calamities befall the hosts.

The Epoch slipped the message "Everyone's out to kill you" into the broadcast, causing 100 million people across the sector to spasm in horror. Benny ended the crisis by convincing the *Big Dig* host, Shepton Rothwell, to tell the viewers with his dying breath: "Nobody's out to get you. This is a truth." The Epoch captured Ruth and Jack...

On Moros Prime, the oppressed Kai people mounted increasing resistance to the rule of Willem van der Heever. He hired Peter Summerfield, who was accompanied by Bernice, as a security consultant for a masquerade for the Moros Prime elite. Van der Heever unleashed a gas attack on his own party, intending to butcher both his opponents and supporters, then blame the incident on off-world "terrorists" as the justification for a crackdown. Benny and Peter contained the situation, even as the Epoch removed Peter from time...

Two bounty hunters employed by the Sharpless Agency – the cybersaur Cazador and the humanoid Pike Thornton – separately went to the White Rabbit in Legion City. Cazador sought to capture the Brimstone Kid outlaw, whereas Thornton pretended to *be* the Brimstone Kid to lure Irving Braxiatel outside Legion's dome, and then take him to the intergalactic law court on Massaushi IX. The real Brimstone Kid killed Thornton, then gave her life to eliminate Cazador – the hired gun who had killed her brothers. Bernice and Braxiatel believed that Cazador had destroyed the White Rabbit, and ejected from Legion in Phoenix Mark III lifepods to escape Sharpless. The Epoch

---

year", which is possible if one squints *very* hard and decides that *Legion* happened toward the end of 2618 and that *Missing Persons* occurs close to the start of 2620 (given the calendar flip that seemingly follows Advent Day 2619 in *New Frontiers*) than not.

Benny shows that math isn't her strongest suit when she subtracts one from 150 million people and arrives at a sum of "149,999 people" (*Benny B5: Missing Persons: Big Dig*).

1129 *Singularity*

1130 "Two years" before *NAofBenny V2: The Pyramid of Sutekh.*

1131 Dating *Vienna* Series 1 (*Dead Drop*, #1.1; *Bad Faith*, #1.2; *Deathworld*, #1.3) - Events follow on from *Vienna: The Memory Box*. It's not said how much time has elapsed since then, but the Chtzin seek to capitalise on the fall of the Wrath in *The Shadow Heart* [c 2618]. With *Vienna* Series 2 similarly having no indicators as to the passage of time, it seems fair to arbitrarily think that each *Vienna* series takes place the next year on from the previous one, especially with the *Vienna* box sets seeing release on an annual basis.

1132 Dating *Worlds BF: The Lady from Callisto Rhys/The Phantom Wreck* (*Worlds BF* #1.5-1.6) - Benny is in her native era, and although she encounters Vienna on Mars via a Gomagog wormhole, and the Gomagog can travel through time, there's no evidence of Benny experiencing any temporal displacement. Moreover, the story ends with no expectation that Benny will need anything beyond conventional travel to return home.

Vienna mentions wines of "68" and "75" vintages. *The Phantom Wreck* confirms that Vad's chronology is yet another of those closed loop events, cycling through nearly two millennia with no starting or ending point.

VIENNA SALVATORI: The *Vienna* audios, featuring the mercenary/assassin Vienna Salvatori, establish that Vienna's native time is that of the Earth Empire: a future state of affairs seen throughout the third Doctor era (*Frontier in Space* et al). The Worlds of Big Finish crossover event goes a step further, however, in pinning Vienna and Bernice Summerfield down as contemporaries. Determining a date for Vienna and Benny's meet-up in *Worlds BF: The Phantom Wreck*, then, is key to deducing the placement of the *Vienna* series itself, as well as the trio of *Doctor Who* audios (*The Burning Prince*, *The Acheron Pulse* and *The Shadow Heart*) leading into it.

We know that for Vienna, *The Phantom Wreck* takes place before she meets her partner-in-crime Jexie in *Vienna* Series 2. Moreover, Big Finish producer Scott Hancock confirms that, as the theme song indicates, events are concurrent with *Vienna* Series 1. Where *The Phantom Wreck* occurs in Benny's history is more up for grabs – Big Finish didn't have a preference on that, but one can narrow it down. Tellingly, Benny only references her field trip in *The Phantom Wreck* as being attached to "a university" and makes no mention of the Braxiatel Collection, which seems to rule out anything between 2600 and 2616 (the years of her affiliation with the Collection and its aftermath). We can also probably exclude Benny's time on Legion [2616-2620], as it doesn't seem to allow her the luxury of doing such academic work. While it's possible that the "university" Benny mentions is either St Oscar's or Vremnya from the Benny New Adventures, that would put Benny and Vienna's lifetimes at least two decades out of synch.

Alternatively, we don't know much what Benny gets up to between *Benny B5: Missing Persons* [2620] and *The New Adventures of Bernice Summerfield* [c.2621], so if *The Phantom Wreck* takes place in that gap, it can be safely assumed that any future Benny and Vienna releases happen roughly in concert with one another. With *The Phantom Wreck* so dated to circa 2620 and serving as a lynchpin, the Vienna-related stories can be backtracked as occurring in the following years: *The Burning Prince*: c.2538; *The Acheron Pulse*: c.2568; *The Shadow Heart*: c.2618; *Vienna: The Memory Box*: c.2619; *Vienna* Series 1: c.2620; and *Vienna* Series 2: c.2621.

captured Braxiatel...

Benny's escape pod happened upon the ruined world of King Theon, and read about The Woman Who Killed the World – herself – in statues, murals and inscriptions made before the end. The king was portrayed as Theon the Doomed, who rejected the wise council of the heroic Meriol. Benny failed to realize the story pertained to her doppelganger created for the Epoch's Victorian London. Soon after, the Epoch captured Bernice...

= The Epoch's base of operations – containing four billion Epoch units – existed at the heart of time, at a location "like no other". All of history flowed through the Epoch's complex, and was remapped to conform to their Scheme. The Epoch had detected Benny's essence throughout the whole of space-time; conceivably, she could restart the universe and curtail the Epoch's abilities. Dr Bernard Springmoore, a remapped version of Benny, directed the Epoch's operations as their Occulant.

The Epoch attempted to isolate Bernice beneath layers of identity, trapping her in a story within a story. Benny, Ruth, Jack, Peter and Braxiatel were remapped to believe they were characters living in a rural setting, as performed by actors making an audio play for Big Finish Productions. One of Springmore's agents, Hierophant Gary Russell, monitored Benny as she became convinced she was actress Lisa Bowerman playing the rural girl Emma, who was playing the part of Bernice Summerfield.

The Benny from the Epoch's Victorian London arrived from Theon's world and helped Benny and her friends to recover their identities. An immense paradox resulted when Victorian-Benny pulled Springmoore through an Epoch portal that scattered their essences throughout space-time, causing the phenomenon the Epoch had invested in eliminating. The Scheme became riddled with instabilities, neutralizing the Epoch's operations and returning the Epoch and their Hierophants to their original timelines.

Benny suggested that she and her friends use the Epoch's apparatus to find the people they'd lost – Jason Kane, Adrian Wall, Bev Tarrant, Antonio Tulloch, Leonidas and Braxiatel's people – and enjoy another adventure together...

Circa 2620, crystal towers were constructed on Rigel VII, an Earth Empire colony.[1129] The Pyramid of Horus was rediscovered on Mars.[1130]

c 2620 - VIENNA SERIES 1[1131] **->** The arachnid Chtzin moved to fill the power void left by the Wrath Empire's defeat, and increasingly came into conflict with the Dyarid.

The Dyarid premier granted asylum to Jamela K'Lynn – an ex-Monk of the Inner Place, exiled after the mass murder of a sorority of novices – and named her the Supreme Commander of his Primary Vanguard. Such was K'Lynn's fanaticism that Admiral Salaron of the Dyarid hired Vienna Salvatori, for a fee of nine million poldachs, to infiltrate the Dyarid hyper-dreadnought *Custodian* and assassinate her. Vienna eliminated K'Lynn during a firefight with the Chtzin near Hyspero Major and Minor, and escaped as the *Custodian* was destroyed.

Under pastor Bax Spendlove, the New Church of Wonderment became a preeminent religion via a clandestine faith-stealing operation that extracted belief from the poor and pious, then injected it into models, renowned chefs, wine critics and other celebrities – including holovid star Taz Becker and warpsled champ Winona Flak – so they could use their stature to promote the church. Over time, the New Church surpassed the Old Church of Wonderment, the Naysayers, the Society of Euphoric Happiness and more. The New Church forbade use of artificial faith-aids such as Miracle Lenses, which reinterpreted events the wearer witnessed according to their theology.

Spendlove's wife, Kendra Spendlove, favoured unifying the New and Old churches, and secretly injected him with faith taken from the Old Church leader, Parsival Kendrick. The Parsival personality compelled Bax Spendlove to make mistakes, including the recruitment of Vienna Salvatori to "assassinate" Parsival on the desert planet Ozuri. Instead, the conflicting personas compelled Bax to throw himself out an airlock. Kendra became head pastor of the unified churches.

Soon after, Vienna pursued clues pertaining to Crevo Finn, the man she wrongly believed had assaulted her parents, and confronted Death, Inc. on the planet Mercator in the Golin V System. Vienna learned her true parentage, and brought Death, Inc. to ruin by usurping their network and sending their assassins on a rampage. She stored away the memory of her parents' identity, fearing they would not appreciate learning their daughter was a murderer-for-hire. Meanwhile, an enigmatic figure who claimed to have manipulated Vienna "for years" celebrated having successfully maneuvered her to eliminate his rivals, Death, Inc...

Benny Meets Vienna

c 2620 - WORLDS BF: THE LADY FROM CALLISTO RHYS / THE PHANTOM WRECK[1132] **->** Licenses were required to live on Mars. Bradburyville had become the second biggest city there, the home to 5.5 million living under a single dome, up from an original population of fifteen astronauts. Though Bradburyville was renowned as a city of sin, it remained a place of law and order; using an alias there was a federal crime. The same couldn't be said of another Martian city, New Damascus, whose monorail serviced the dormant volcano Ulysses Tholus. The Famine Fund sent relief supplies to the outer colonies, including instagrain shipments to Upper Ganymede. A black market operated in the Kuiper Belt.

Kronos Vad's *History of Earth* (Vol. 36,379) had been studied for a few centuries, and traded owners many times. The casino mogul Cage Zorn – owner of the Menagio Hotel, which overlooked the foothills of Olympus Mons – won the book on auction on Earth. A month later, Zorn's private curator – Callisto native Lara Memphis, hailing from a family of ice harvesters – stole the book, prompting Zorn to hire Vienna Salvatori to retrieve it. Vienna found Lara, but discovered that Zorn wanted the book on behalf of the Gomagog...

Meanwhile, Bernice Summerfield accompanied a GoBo Corp-sponsored university field trip to the desert planet Sisyphus IX, and found both the remains of comedian Jack Oddwards and the Gomagog dreadnought displaced through time circa 2015. The vengeful Captain Quinn allied with the surviving Gomagog to acquire the Jaffeth weapon used to devastate Sisyphus IX, but realised that the Gomagog intended to send the device down a wormhole and destroy Earth in the twenty-first century. The resultant paradox would destroy the universe, preventing Quinn's family from ever having existed. Quinn sacrificed himself to obliterate the Gomagog, but first aided Benny in escaping down a Gomagog wormhole...

On Mars, Zorn seized Vad's chronology, but Vienna activated the microstoker she'd slipped into his champagne, killing him with 50 amps straight to the heart. Vienna fell, but was cushioned by Benny's arrival through

a wormhole. Benny and Vienna decided that it was safest to donate Vad's book to the Archive. A young apprentice there, Romulus Chang, secured the book within the Archive's Department of Eschatology.

Pecorah City emerged as one of the richest cities in the universe – a commerce hub where the buildings were endowed with AIs, to better serve their patrons. A stock market crash erased the city's wealth in seven seconds; to staunch the financial bleeding, the authorities levelled a tax on buildings, compelling the AIs to find innovative means of generating income. The Pecorah residents reverted to savagery as their planet became home to a reality show called *The Selection*, which prevailed against competition such as *The Real Housewives of Drahva*.[1133]

The New Adventures of Bernice Summerfield[1134]

Benny Reunites with the Doctor and Ace

c 2621 - NAofBENNY: THE REVOLUTION / GOOD NIGHT, SWEET LADIES -> Officially, at least, Federation law required that all creeds, races and religions must be given equal recognition.

Humans began displacing the indigenous serpentine population on Arvien 2, and created a culture that persecuted people for crimes against science. Three months after Arvien 2 joined the Federation, Bernice Summerfield went there as an independent witness to swear that life owed to evolution, but instead provoked the oppressive

---

1133 "Twelve months" before *Vienna S3: Big Society*. The Drahvins appeared in *Galaxy Four*.

1134 Dating *The New Adventures of Bernice Summerfield* "modern day" sequences (*The Revolution/Good Night, Sweet Ladies*, #1.1-1.2; *The Pyramid of Sutekh*, #2.1; *The Library in the Body*, #3.1) - The New Adventures of Bernice Summerfield box sets follow on from Benny's last solo adventures, which ended in *Benny B5: Missing Persons* [2620]. Noticeably, *The Pyramid of Sutekh* opens after Benny has taken some time off to attend the wedding of her son Peter, who didn't even have a boyfriend at the end of *Missing Persons*. Benny otherwise doesn't air a lot of detail about her current status quo, only vaguely telling the Doctor in *The Revolution*: "I've got a family now, want to see pictures?" *Big Bang Generation* contradicts itself with regards Benny's lifetime (see the dating notes on that story), at one point indicating that Benny experienced the events of *NAofBenny* Volume 1 "years" prior to 2619.

The first three volumes of *The New Adventures of Bernice Summerfield* themselves fail to mention the year, and the format seems to accept that Benny, the

seventh Doctor and Ace are the sort of people who keep running into each other from time to time, without preamble, and then go off to have adventures together in time and space. It seems fair to think – until we're told otherwise – that a year for Benny passes between each of the volumes, reflecting the actual passage of time between releases.

1135 NAofBenny V2: The Pyramid of Sutekh

1136 Dating *Vienna* Series 2 (*Tabula Rasa*, #2.1; *Underworld*, #2.2; *The Vienna Experience*, #2.3) - An unknown amount of time has passed since *Vienna* Series 1. *The Vienna Experience* begins a day after *Underworld*, and seems to conclude fairly soon after. In *Tabula Rasa*, the Curtis-psychomorph is a little amazed that Anders can afford a bath with "genuine water", and yet Vienna – possibly just as a sign of how well working for CrimeCorp pays – takes a shower in *The Vienna Experience*.

1137 Dating *Vienna* Series 3 (*Self-Improvement*, #3.1; *Big Society*, #3.2; *Impossibly Glamourous*, #3.3) - The new series opens with Vienna and Jexie having just assassinated a vampire monarch, and it's not treated as their

authorities by testifying that life on Arvien 2 had been breathed out the nostrils of a space dragon named Grol.

The seventh Doctor needed help to find Ace, and located Benny, completely hammered, at Renk Van Magnastein's bar. Van Magnastein laced the Doctor's lemonade with the tears of the space sirens of Allurus Delta, making him extremely prone to suggestion. On Van Magnastein's instructions, the Doctor went back ten thousand years and brought about life on Arvien 2 in accordance with the serpentine people's *Book of Life*. The "discovery" of a 10,000-year-old dragon skeleton and eggshells triggered a migration of the serpentine people to celebrate their beliefs – which Van Magnastein's theme bars were strategically positioned to profit from. Benny left to find Ace, while the Doctor cleaned up the situation...

Bernice tracked Ace to the barren moon of Adolin, where the lonely AI governing a dying Dalek timeship adopted the form of Benny's late mother Claire. The ship drained the last of its energy to send Benny through a portal to Ace's location on Skaro, back when the Daleks were dormant in their city.

After resolving the Skaro affair, Benny opted to continue travelling with the seventh Doctor and Ace for a time...

Benny returned to her native time, and would next meet the seventh Doctor and Ace on Mars...[1135]

c 2621 - VIENNA SERIES 2[1136] **->** Genuine water baths were rare, the province of the elite. SynthCaff served as a coffee alternative.

CrimeCorp, as helmed by Carlos Van Meyer, emerged as a cost-effective means of police enforcement in the nine systems. On Earth, Van Meyer funded experiments to develop superstrong policemen billed as Human 2.0, but Subject No. 7 – a psychomorph capable of moving up the social ladder by duplicating people's minds and bodies – escaped and donned the guise of CrimeCorp police chief Doran Curtis. For a fee of one million poldacks, Van Meyer tasked Vienna Salvatori with tracking down the psychomorph. He also secretly implanted Vienna with a microchip that let him to experience her sensations.

The Curtis-psychomorph went to a Personality Hotel – where patrons could swap personas, and take a break from being themselves – in the hope of duplicating a powerful patron and CEO named Anders. Vienna overwhelmed the psychomorph with uploaded personalities from the hotel's networks, causing it to defensively take on Vienna's body and memories, and become convinced it *was* Vienna. The genuine article implanted her microchip in her double, then went undercover. Anders kept the persona of a bellboy while the hotel's AI took to running his corporation. The Vienna-psychomorph conceded that the world would probably be a better place if run like a good hotel.

The death of a material witness prompted the Vienna-psychomorph and Lieutenant Jexie Reagan to investigate the Undercity, and to discover that Reagan's former partner – the corrupt Guy Wilkes – was still alive. In the resultant escapade, a monstrous Undercity dweller killed Wilkes.

Working behind the scenes, the real Vienna learned of Van Meyer's long-running schemes as the Vienna-psychomorph increasingly reverted to its true form. The psychomorph crushed Van Meyer to death, then tried to murder Vienna and Jexie – but pursued them into an experience suite displaying information from its microchip, triggering an existential crisis that killed it. Vienna and Jexie publicized Van Meyer's corporate secrets, ruining CrimeCorp. Vienna deemed that the image of "her" killing Van Meyer would serve to advertise her services, then left Earth with Jexie as her associate.

Peter Summerfield Marries; Sutekh Returns

c 2622 - NAofBENNY V2: THE PYRAMID OF SUTEKH -> The Free Mars Party and the government of Mars fell into open warfare. Bernice Summerfield took a fortnight off to attend her son Peter's wedding, and happened upon a hieroglyph from ancient Egypt telling her personally to go to the Pyramid of Horus on Mars. She located a sarcophagus containing the seventh Doctor – who had been possessed by Sutekh's mind. A fleshloom within the pyramid wove Sutekh a new body, using the corpses of dead Osirians. Benny directed the warring Martian forces to attack the Pyramid, but Sutekh repelled the assault with a gesture, and wiped out the Martian colonists.

Sutekh escaped the pyramid via a time-space tunnel to ancient Egypt. The Osirian Isis drew the Doctor into the future. The TARDIS, with Ace aboard, arrived from 1941 to shuttle Benny back to twenty-first-century Egypt.

c 2622 - VIENNA SERIES 3[1137] **->** Ludovic Glospan neared completion of Good Day: a formula that would improve users' cognition, memory and empathy, turning them into the best possible version of themselves. Helping Hand Solutions hired Vienna Salvatori and Jexie Reagan to safeguard Glospan's work in his undersea base, but Glospan accidentally caused a hull breach that enabled monstrous algae to kill him. Glospan had wanted to distribute Good Day for the benefit of the masses, so Vienna and Jexie took the Good Day formula to Glospan's friend, Jonah Hall, on the planet Pecorah...

It transpired that "Jonah Hall" was actually an AI-driven concert venue. Chairman Sweet, the overseer of *The Selection* reality show, put a bounty on Vienna and Jexie's heads so he could acquire Good Day, but Vienna bettered Sweet's offer to Hall – whereupon Hall fought off opposing AI buildings with sonic blasts composed of Beethoven's Fifth and all six Brandenburg concertos, with a dash of

Wagner. Sweet died, but only after uploading the Good Day Formula to Helping Hand's servers. Vienna and Jexie realised that Helping Hand intended to reverse-engineer Good Day into Bad Day – a means of secretly spreading maladies, then selling cures at immense profit – and went to Helping Hand's headquarters, located on the old colony world of London...

Vienna went undercover as a Helping Hand spokesperson, the face of its Best Possible You cosmetics campaign. She and Jexie acquired a hard drive governing Kensington Fox, the company's holographic "founder", and threatened to air the company's wrongdoing via Fox's own "lips". Helping Hand capitulated, and announced that the Good Day Formula would be available to all.

Benny in an Unbound Universe

= The alt-third Doctor's native universe had experienced a devastating war. He largely left his race to their own devices, believing they were in the wrong. At the turning point of the conflict, the alt-Doctor

and the alt-Master held the pass at the Stigian Interface, where the Doctor prevented his friend from unleashing mutually assured destruction with a super-weapon. The worlds of the Great Empire of Tramatz burned in the war, and it retaliated with a device that irreparably damaged the very fabric of space-time. The Doctor bargained away many of his memories to buy his universe more life – thanks to his sacrifice, it would endure for some millennia. He was variously regarded as the Ruler or President of the Universe.[1138]

c 2623 - NAofBENNY V3: THE UNBOUND UNIVERSE[1139] -> An alternate version of the third Doctor hoped to escape his dying universe, and latched onto Bernice Summerfield's unique artron signature as she was teaching archaeology class. The alt-Doctor failed to cross over into our reality using Benny as an anchor, and she was instead pulled into his Unbound universe...

first mission together, suggesting an indeterminate amount of time has passed since *Vienna* Series 2. Vienna and Jexie decide to let matters with Helping Hand quiet down some after *Self-Improvement*, indicating that more time elapses between that story and *Vienna* S3: *Big Society. Impossibly Glamourous* seems to wrap things up over a period of "a few weeks", a month at most. The claim that the super-algae in *Self-Improvement* "grows rapidly during the summer months" likely refers to the time of year on Murian Tursis, but not necessarily elsewhere.

1138 The background to *NAofBenny* V3: *The Unbound Universe* and V4: *Ruler of the Universe*.

1139 Dating *The New Adventures of Bernice Summerfield* Vol. 3: *The Unbound Universe* (*The Library in the Body*, #3.1; *Planet X*, #3.2; *The Very Dark Thing*, #3.3; *The Emporium at the End*, #3.4) - No year given; placement depends upon whether any time deviation occurs when the alt-Doctor brings Benny into his reality. The alt-Doctor's TARDIS loses its time-travel capabilities at the end of *The Library in the Body*, so we know that these four stories occur in sequence, in the same time zone. *Planet X* occurs in "the 19th of the 4th, Year Five", but that numbering reflects the lifespan of the current regime.

There's a temptation to regard the devastating war as this Unbound Universe's equivalent of the Last Great Time War, save that in detail, it really isn't – both are universe-damaging affairs that involved a Doctor and a Master, but the similarities basically stop there. In the behind-the-scenes interviews, producer James Goss commented: "There has been a great and awful war, which is sort of that universe's equivalent to the Time War, but it's played out very, very differently – because

if you have listened to *Masters of War*, you'll know that the Daleks of this universe are treated very differently... [the war] not only would have been fought between different races, but the people involved would have played it very differently."

1140 Dating *The New Adventures of Bernice Summerfield* Vol. 4: *Ruler of the Universe* (*The City and the Clock*, #4.1; *Asking for a Friend*, #4.2; *Truant*, #4.3; *The True Saviour of the Universe*, #4.4) – There's no real sense of how much time has elapsed since Vol. 3, although we might take our cue from the Benny *New Adventures of...* box sets being released annually. If nothing else, the anthology *Benny: True Stories* (and setting aside Benny muddying the waters as to how many of those stories are true) indicates that Benny experienced some side-adventures in the Unbound Universe.

It's also vague as to how much time Vol. 4 takes up, save that *Benny: The City and the Clock* opens after Benny has spent "two months" digging for the Apocalypse Clock on Merrin. Culturally, this Unbound Universe seems close to our own, with the alt-Doctor referencing *Quatermass*. *The Beano* and renowned English writer Dorothy Sayers.

This Apocalypse Clock has no known relation to the one from *The Last Post*.

1141 The "Little Mind's Eye" crystal that the Doctor gets in *Snakedance* is dated to "eight hundred years ago".

? = c 2623 - NAofBENNY V3: THE UNBOUND UNIVERSE[1140] **->** As this Unbound universe wound down, information became the most valuable resource. A parasite disguised itself as one of the last remaining libraries – a lure to suck knowledge from the universe's smartest remaining denizens. The alt-Doctor and Benny helped to save the last Cyborg King, the Sisters of St Beedlix and more from the ravenous library, and satiated itself with the Kareem – a violent protest movement that regarded knowledge as evil. The alt-Doctor's TARDIS became drained of time energy, but Benny accepted the his offer to explore the planets that remained...

Planet X had purged any citizen deemed creative or "interesting". Society was dull and mediocre, neither of the war-powers bothered with it. Within just five years, "processing" had dropped the colony's 34,589,605 souls down to 10,259,482. The alt-Doctor palmed the dampeners protecting Prime Minister #470 and her key operative, Ego, from their own brainwashed Brute Squad, causing the Squad to murder them. The public were freed.

Later, the alt-Doctor and Benny prevented Fleet Admiral Effenish of the Combined Ninth Fleet from obliterating Tramatz with Reaper bombs, simply by getting a Tramatz native to issue an apology that her world had mortally wounded space-time.

Some of the universe's survivors congregated at the Gateway Emporium, a shopping centre overseen by "the Manager" – actually the alt-Master. Those assembled traded away their memories in exchange for lottery tickets – a chance, the Manager claimed, to go through the Gateway and escape their dying universe. In actuality, the Manager planned on converting the memories into raw energy, the means by which he could flee into a healthier reality. Benny and the alt-Doctor exposed the alt-Master's schemes, and the Sisters of St Beedlix threw him into the Gateway's energies to perish.

Unable to return to our universe, Benny continued travelling with the alt-Doctor in his weakened TARDIS...

& = c 2624 - NAofBENNY V4: RULER OF THE UNIVERSE -> The alt-Doctor was formally named the President/ Ruler of the Universe, working alongside the Parliament of the Universe and its Speaker, the Mother Superior of the Sisters of St Beedlix. A destructive wave, the Great Collapse, continued to progressively consume their universe. On the planet Merrin, Bernice Summerfield excavated an ancient reality engine: the Apocalypse Clock. With this, the alt-Doctor hoped to implement Apocalypse Equations that would create a safe zone against the Great Collapse.

The bureaucracy of office increasingly consumed the alt-Doctor, and forced him to make moral compromises. Benny recommended that he see a therapist, Guilana, but the alt-Doctor was so stricken with the guilt of everyone he'd failed to save, he tried to make one person's life better... and changed Guilana's timeline so she had a family and a less rainy environment. Guilana rebuked the alt-Doctor's underhandedness.

The alt-Doctor sought succour in his old habit of thwarting evil-doers. To his chagrin, however, megalomaniacs and serial killers surrendered as soon as he walked into the room, even if he graciously suggested they throw him into a pit of Galaxian piranha. The notorious Barbaric Butcher of Barthazar's Gate, when confronted by alt-Doctor, simply fainted. Soon after, the alt-Doctor and Benny discovered that nomadic parasitic replicators, the Silvans, had replaced the inhabitants of Kellor sixty years ago. They left the Silvans in peace, in exchange for their opening their world to refugees.

The alt-Master returned as the alt-Doctor covertly brought about his own impeachment. Benny and the alt-Master shared dinner, scintillating conversation and even some Dwarf Star Brandy before they agreed that – given the alt-Master's nature – it was best if she left before he killed her. Parliament removed the alt-Doctor from office, and appointed the alt-Master as Ruler of the Universe instead. As the alt-Doctor anticipated, the alt-Master reverted to type and tried to use the Apocalypse Clock to resurrect its makers, the Great Old Ones, from beyond time to wreck havoc. The alt-Doctor banished the Great Old Ones and used the Clock to install a permanent safe zone against the Great Collapse. The alt-Master was left to stew in the worst possible hell: the shackles of office, with the Mother Superior keeping him in check. The alt-Doctor believed the Apocalypse Equations had altered the alt-Master's mind, and he'd do quite well at the job.

With the excess energy the Clock had generated, the alt-Doctor turbo-charged his TARDIS and went with Bernice back to her native reality...

Some, if not all, of the crystals used by the Snakedancers of Manussa were created.[1141]

Mark Morton's illegitimate child – the historian and playwright Kristoffa Taillor – came to own a copy of Bernice Summerfield's diary, and studied it to learn more about his parents' deaths. Taillor found that no official records existed pertaining to Bernice Summerfield, Jason

Kane, Adrian Wall, Bev Tarrant and Irving Braxiatel. In 2647, Taillor was fatally poisoned at an orbiting restaurant, The Final Rest. *A Life in Pieces*, a collection of texts concerning Morton's murder, was subsequently published.[1142]

A party of Grel went back in time to capture Peter Summerfield and study him.[1143] The *Arrow of Righteousness* set out on its holy journey some time before 2650, the pilgrims inside frozen in meditation.[1144]

c 2650 - MASQUERADE[1145] **-> ** Earth Central sought to spread the human empire beyond the Milky Way. To that end, researchers at the Scientific Outpost for Research and Development of Inter-Dimensional Energies (SORDIDE) worked to develop Shadow Space: a means by which the consciousness could remain in a simulated environment while the body experienced warp conditions that would destroy the psyche. Inter-dimensional experiments with Shadow Space drew the TARDIS off-course, causing the fifth Doctor, Nyssa and Hannah Bartholomew to find themselves in a simulation of the Marquise de Rimdelle's estate in France, 1770.

The Vastayoi – a race whose worlds in the Nextant Rim had fallen to the Earth Empire – developed a virus that preyed upon emotion, causing a murderous rage and death. The Doctor's party prevented the Vastayoi from turning the Shadow Space users into virus-carriers who would infect millions of human colonists. The SORDIDE survivors cured the virus by using Shadow Space to delete each victim's emotional centres, and applied that treatment to themselves and Hannah. Realizing that she could never return home in her newfound state, Hannah urged the Doctor and Nyssa to leave without her.

In future, Hastron's Shielding helped to facilitate humanity's inter-galactic travels.

? 2750 - "Technical Hitch"[1146] **-> ** The seventh Doctor arrived aboard the Deep Probe Da Gama, which was in the thirteenth year of its mission to explore space. The probe's commander, Admiral Vayle, alleviated the isolation of his long flight with a mental simulation of Earth, but a software glitch emptied the simulation of avatars, leaving Vayle alone. The seventh Doctor repaired the fault, preventing Vayle from going mad with loneliness.

c 2650 - MIDNIGHT[1147] **-> The tenth Doctor brought Donna to Midnight, an airless but beautiful diamond world bathed in extonic sunlight. Donna preferred to sun herself in the Leisure Palace rather than take the Crusader tour to the 100,000-foot sapphire waterfalls. The Doctor and his fellow tour passengers were menaced by an entity that possessed them in turn – it repeated words spoken aloud, then *predicting* words**

1142 *Benny: A Life in Pieces*. Traillor is killed "two years" after the fortieth anniversary of Morton's death, cited as "23 September 2645" (p150). Mention that no records exist of Benny and company could simply mean that Verum is remote enough that Taillor lacks access to them. Alternatively, it could mean that all records of them have been expunged, somehow, in the wider universe.

1143 Forty-five years after the Braxiatel Collection component of *Benny S5: The Grel Escape*.

1144 "More than a century" before "Time Bomb".

1145 Dating *Masquerade* (BF #187) - It's the "pioneering" days of the Earth Empire. No mention is made of the Dalek Wars or any other prominent feature of the twenty-sixth century, perhaps ruling that out.

1146 Dating "Technical Hitch" (*The Incredible Hulk Presents* #5) - No date given. Vayle deliberately experiences a simulation of Earth, so would appear to be human, and it feels a bit like the early days of space travel. No connection was intended, but the "mental simulation to facilitate long space travel" brings to mind efforts to create Shadow Space (*Masquerade* [c.2650]).

1147 Dating *Midnight* (X4.10) - No date given, but *The Time Travellers' Almanac* sets it in the twenty-seventh century, as does the Lost Moon of Poosh entry in *A History of the Universe in 100 Objects* (p198).

1148 Poosh is mentioned in *Midnight*, and what

became of it is revealed in *The Stolen Earth*.

1149 "Many years" prior to *3rdA: The Havoc of Empires*. The locale suggests it's in the same time zone, but the Doctor could be speaking relative to his lifetime.

1150 *The Well-Mannered War*. The Thargons and Sorsons were originally seen in *The Tomorrow People*.

1151 Dating *The Fate of Krelos* (BF 4th Doc #4.7) - It's "a couple of centuries or so" after *The Tomb of the Cybermen*. The story doesn't overtly confirm Telos' continued existence, although the Doctor directs Leela's attention to a distant object that he claims is Telos.

1152 Dating *The Lost Flame* (BBC DW audiobook #29) - It's the time of the First Great and Bountiful Human Empire. Humanity loses immunity to the common cold by the time of *The Ark*.

1153 Dating "A Matter of Life and Death" (Titan 8th Doc #1-5) - The eighth Doctor says it's "the vast and bountiful human empire" – presumably the first of those leading to the Fourth Great and Bountiful Human Empire (*The Long Game*), although he doesn't specify.

1154 Dating *Shadowmind* (NA #16) - The Doctor tells Ace that "by your calendar the year is 2673" (p29). The events of *Frontier in Space* in "2540" (p74) were "one hundred and thirty years ago" (p61).

1155 Dating *The Sandman* (BF #37) - No date is given, but *Benny: The Bone of Contention*, also written by Simon Forward, features the Clutch and is set in 2603. In that story, it's said that the Galyari Research

before they were said. The tour hostess threw herself and the entity's core host, Sky Silvestry, into the radiation-saturated planetscape, killing them both.

The Crusader 50 shuttle bus ran on micropetrol.

By this point, the Lost Moon of Poosh had been stolen through time to become part of the Daleks' reality bomb.[1148]

The Doctor learned to speak Delphon in a little trattoria on Alpha Centauri V.[1149] In 2660, Fridgya was devastated in the fifth Thargon-Sorson war. Its cryo-morts would remain undisturbed for many thousands of years.[1150]

> **(=) c 2668 - THE FATE OF KRELOS**[1151] -> The fourth Doctor and Leela wanted to go fishing in the famed mountain pools of Krelos, a world neighboring the Telos System, but dormant Cyber-particles became active when K9's diagnostics brought the second Doctor's console room back online. The Cyber-particles, as contained in a remnant of Jamie McCrimmon's tartan, transferred to the Doctor's scarf and infiltrated Krelos City's communications network. Time-active Cybermen forced K9 to nudge the TARDIS forward to when the people of Krelos had become a Cyber-army. The Doctor and Leela undid this by going back and preventing Jamie from bringing the Cyber-particles aboard the TARDIS...

... after which, they enjoyed a nice fishing outing.

Alex Yow Leaves the TARDIS

? 2670 - THE LOST FLAME[1152] -> No case of Venusian Flu had appeared in decades. Humans now had an innate resistance to the common cold.

The planet Esculpepia emerged as one of the foremost medical hubs of the First Great and Bountiful Human Empire. Remedia Corp. field-tested new diseases among Esculepia's lower classes, then sold subscriptions to Remedia-Plus: a nano-virus that, for only five thousand credits a month, counter-acted the 78 billion known diseases in the Remedia datalogue.

Medinia, a rogue member of the Sisterhood of Karn, healed some of the masses with her own Sacred Flame. She heard John Dee's voice through the ether, and advised him on how to bind a Weeping Angel. The twelfth Doctor, with Alex Yow and her brother Brandon, reprogrammed Remedia-Plus to provide cures for free. The Sisterhood took away Medinia's knowledge of the Sacred Flame, then exiled her. The Doctor slyly told Medinia how to replicate Remedia-Plus elsewhere.

Alex stayed in this era to aid Medinia in healing the sick.

? 2670 - "A Matter of Life and Death"[1153] -> It was the time of the vast and bountiful human empire. Lady Josephine, a noblewoman and gallery owner from Palahaxis II, coerced an Artrificer of Wrall to paint a superb portrait of her. The Artificer laced the portrait with animae particles, and so Josephine's portrait-self came to life. Lady Josephine died of natural causes, but the twelfth Doctor and Clara bought the portrait at her estate auction, and took it to the Doctor's house in twenty-first century Earth.

Aboard their Resurrection Barge, the alien Bakai serviced the richest 0.0001% of humanity by downloading, at time of death, their consciousnesses into synthetic beings. Lady Josephine was reborn per an insurance policy as the synthetic beings became sentient and demanded independence. The eighth Doctor and Josie uploaded the human minds into a peaceful virtual environment, and left the Shadow Proclamation to resolve the matter.

2673 - SHADOWMIND[1154] -> This was the time of Xaxil, the twenty-fourth Draconian Emperor.

Thousands of years before, the Shenn of Arden had discovered "hypergems" that boosted their telepathic ability. Around 2640, one group of Shenn began to hear a mysterious voice from the sky that ordered them to construct kilns. This voice was the Umbra, a sentience that had evolved from carbon structures on a nearby asteroid.

The planet Tairngaire was now heavily populated and a member of a local alliance of planets, the Concordance, with its own space fleet that had recently seen action in the nasty Sidril War. In 2670, colonists from Tairngaire set up camp on the planet Arden. The Colonial Office decreed that the natural features of the planet should be named after characters from the works of Shakespeare. Accordingly, the main settlement was called Touchstone Base, and there was a Lake Lysander, a Titania River and a Phebe Range of mountains.

After completing wargame trials in the Delta Epsilon System, the CSS *Broadsword* was recalled to Tairngaire by Admiral Vego and sent to investigate the situation at the Arden. All contact had been lost with the settlers, and five ships dispatched to investigate also vanished. It was discovered that the Shenn were secretly operating in New Byzantium by inhabiting artificially constructed human bodies. The Umbra was building "shadowforms", extensions of its power. The seventh Doctor, Benny and Ace located Umbra and blocked off the sun's rays, effectively rendering it unconscious.

c 2675 - THE SANDMAN[1155] -> The Clutch, the fleet of ships containing the Galyari race and numerous tag-alongs, returned to the homeworld of the Cuscaru. A Cuscaru ambassador returned a piece of the Galyari's destroyed Srushkubr, but this catalysed the neural energy tainting the Galyari. The long-dead General Voshkar was reborn in a monstrous body, and tried to return the Galyari to warfare. The sixth Doctor and Evelyn's involvement resulted in Voshkar's demise. The Clutch departed into space, and resumed business as an intergalactic flea market of sorts.

During the twenty-seventh century, a Haitian deciphered the Rihanssu language, allowing a peace treaty that ended the war between Earth and that race.[1156] **There had been examples of humanity oppressing native species for centuries. The Swampies of Delta Magna, for example, had been displaced and oppressed. Slavery was formally reintroduced on many worlds.**[1157] **The time-sensitive Tharils had once been the owners of a mighty Empire, with territory stretching across several universes including N-Space and E-Space. Now slavers had captured them. The Tharils were a valuable commodity, as they alone could navigate the ships using warp drive based on Implicate Theory. Many humans became rich trading in Tharils. One privateer, a veteran of Tharil hunts on Shapia commanded by Captain**

Rorvik, vanished without trace following a warp drive malfunction.[1158]

Twenty families founded the colony of Kaldor City. The people there came to forget their origins, and had no contact with other planets.[1159]

2679 - 3rdA: THE HAVOC OF EMPIRES[1160] -> The

Teklarn Incorporation, an Earth Empire offshoot run along business lines, controlled five hundred planets. It stood in opposition to militaristic, horned aliens with a roughly equal territory: the Chalnoth Hegemony. The Earth Empire brokered a power-sharing agreement between the two, and Harmony Station was built to house the political marriage of Chalnoth Regent Tharlar and Teklarn Director Tina Andresson. The Chalnoth offered a dowry of three moons and an asteroid belt. The third Doctor, Jo and Captain Yates stopped agents of the Tyresius Corporation, which would have profited more from the Chalnoth and the Teklarn remaining at odds, from sabotaging the wedding.

Interstellar treaties forbid the scanning of diplomatic spacecraft. Members of the Delphon Empire – thin, lined, grey beings with two rows of red eyes from forehead to

---

Directorate hopes to build weapons against the Sandman. As the Clutch's weaponry isn't significantly advanced in *The Sandman* audio, it probably takes place soon after the Benny adventure.

1156 *White Darkness*

STAR TREK: In the Pocket Books' range of *Star Trek* novels (notably those by Diane Duane), the Romulans call themselves "Rihanssu", and the race is referred to in *White Darkness* (p129). A few of the other New and Missing Adventures have included such *Star Trek* in-jokes. There are many, for example, in *Sanctuary*, another of David McIntee's books, and Turlough refers to the Klingon homeworld in *The Crystal Bucephalus* (p104).

Star Trek and *Doctor Who* have radically differing versions of the future, and by this point, a wide variety of tie-in stories (*The Left-Handed Hummingbird, The Face of the Enemy, EarthWorld, The Gallifrey Chronicles, Pest Control, Peri and the Piscon Paradox, TW: The Conspiracy*, at least four stories involving the Doctor's companion Izzy, who is a huge fan of the series, etc.) establish that *Star Trek* is merely fiction in the *Doctor Who* universe. On screen, this is confirmed in *The Empty Child, Fear Her, The Impossible Astronaut, The God Complex, Closing Time, SJA: Warriors of Kudlak, SJA: The Lost Boy, SJA: Mona Lisa's Revenge* and *Extremis*. Maybe, just as Trekkies in the seventies managed to get NASA to name a prototype space shuttle after the USS *Enterprise*, the *Star Trek* fans of the future managed to name a lot of planets after ones from their favourite series – Vulcan, as seen in *The Power of the Daleks*, being one of the first.

In *Return of the Living Dad*, Benny confesses to mistakenly believing that *Star Trek* was a documentary the first time she saw it (the *ST: TNG* episode *Darmok*). Her

confusion, she claims, owes to "a good reason" she can't air "without giving something away about the future" – possibly an allusion to bits of *Trek* being real after all...

... which comes to pass in IDW's *Star Trek: The Next Generation/Doctor Who* mini-series, which has the eleventh Doctor, Amy and Rory cross over into the *Star Trek* universe, and meet Captain Picard's crew. A consequence of this, however, is to firmly establish that *Star Trek* and *Doctor Who* exist in separate realities. It's possible, then, that *Star Trek* exists as fiction within *Doctor Who* because of a sort of cultural "bleed through" effect from the *Trek* reality, akin to Silver Age comics in which the Barry Allen Flash read about the Flash of Earth-2's exploits in his comic book form.

1157 The Swampies appear in *The Power of Kroll*. Slavery exists at the time of *Warriors' Gate* and *Terminus*, and the work camps referred to in *The Caves of Androzani* are also near-slavery.

1158 *Warriors' Gate*. Stephen Gallagher has stated in interviews (see, for example, *In-Vision* #50) that Rorvik's crew come from N-Space, and their familiarity with English (such as the graffiti), "sardines" and "custard" suggest they come from Earth. The coin flipped is a "100 Imperial" piece and they use warp drive, both of which suggest an Earth Empire setting, although placing the story details here is arbitrary.

1159 *The Robots of Death*, as extrapolated from a painting native to Kaldor City (seen in *Kaldor City: Occam's Razor*) that's two hundred years old. "Crisis on Kaldor" concurs with this, as it seemingly happens around the time of *The Robots of Death*, and "centuries" after Kaldor was colonised.

chin – had never been seen before, but attended Tharlar and Andresson's wedding, having brought seven warships as a show of respect.

2680 - THE HIGHEST SCIENCE[1161] -> Authorities on Checkley's World had made the planet Hogsumm to resemble the fabled planet Sakkrat, hoping to capture the criminal Sheldukher and retrieve the Cell that he stole. A slow time converter set up on Hogsumm created a Fortean Flicker that moved objects through time, including a group of hostile Chelonians and some train-riders taking the 8:12 from Chorleywood in 2003.

In 2680, Sheldukher and his crew revived from stasis and landed on "Sakkrat". Sheldukher committed suicide while resisting arrest, and the Cell was killed also. Sheldukher's Hercules devastator atomised a large area of the planet. The Chelonians and the train-riders, known to the Chelonians as the EightTwelves, were left frozen in a stasis field.

The Tzun Master sabotaged the slow time converter on Hogsumm, creating a Fortean Flicker. President Romana of Gallifrey located the source of the disturbance on Hogsumm, and released the trapped humans and Chelonians. The Chelonians weren't grateful, so Romana marooned them there and took the humans home.[1162] The abandoned Chelonians survived and created a viable colony that made contact with the rest of their kind after a few thousand years.[1163]

c 2686 - THE LEGENDS OF RIVER SONG: "Death in New Venice"[1164] -> In the late twenty-seventh century, a pair of benevolent space hippies set up DreamInc. to offer eco-friendly holidays, then sold the business to a corporation on Krelane: a crustacean-packed world famed for arms manufacture. DreamInc. developed New Venice as a gated planetary community for elites, and moulded it into shape with WishCrete: a psychic material that one could think into shape. The company paid River Song four million credits to provide accurate representations of classical Venice, which she obtained by visiting it throughout the centuries.

The WishCrete unexpectedly responded to horrifying thoughts, and so the opening of New Venice was marred by deadly constructs such as plague doctors and hostile swarms of pigeons. River arranged an evacuation, and mentally commanded the WishCrete to emulate the original Venice and sink itself.

c 2690 - "Bus Stop!"[1165] -> Scientists on Mars invented a crude time machine. Mutant assassins captured the device and attempted to retroactively eradicate the ancestors of Martian President Lithops. The tenth Doctor followed the killers to the twenty-first century and stymied them while Martha and D.I. Moloch re-captured the time machine and recalled the Doctor to this time zone. The Doctor destroyed the time machine, which by extension exterminated the assassins.

The Battle of the Rigel Wastes took place in 2697. The seventh Doctor, Bernice, Roz and Chris witnessed the massacre. In the twenty-seven and twenty-eight hundreds, New Earth Feudalism was established. This social system would lead to the thirtieth-century Overcities.[1166]

The Twenty-Eighth Century

In the twenty-eighth century, the Legions tried to undermine the business consortia of the galaxy using their multidimensional abilities. The Time Lords intervened, sending Mortimus to imprison the Legion homeworld for eight thousand years. Around this time, the Wine Lords of Chardon had the best wine cellars in the galaxy.[1167] By the twenty-eighth century, interest in Mozart was so low, his work was pretty much restricted to the bargain bin.[1168]

Earth claimed the planet Dust on the Dead Frontier, but never developed it.[1169] The renegade Time Lord Koschei visited Earth in the twenty-eighth century and met Ailla, a woman who joined him on his travels. It was a time of food riots and constant war.[1170]

1160 Dating *3rdA: The Havoc of Empires* (BF *The Third Doctor Adventures* #1.2) - The Doctor notes that an Earth ship hails from the "late twenty-seventh century", and tells Yates that it's "780" years after W.G. Grace's final match, in 1899. The omnipotent narrator therefore seems a bit off in claiming that it's "two thousand years" after the UNIT Era. Delphons were mentioned in *Spearhead from Space*.
1161 Dating *The Highest Science* (NA #11) - Sheldukher's ship arrives at Sakkrat in "2680" (p17). It is "two hundred and thirty years" in Benny's future (p35) [q.v. "Benny's Birthday"].
1162 *Happy Endings*

1163 *The Well-Mannered War*
1164 Dating "Death in New Venice" (*The Legends of River Song* #1d) - It's "the late twenty-seventh century".
1165 Dating "Bus Stop!" (*DWM* #385) - It's "Mars in the twenty-seventh century". Environmental suits are here needed on the Martian surface, but Mars seems to still be inhabited (at the very least, it's got a president), so perhaps the toxicity is localised.
1166 *Death and Diplomacy* (pgs. 71, 203).
1167 *The Crystal Buchephalus* (p40, p80).
1168 *100*: "My Own Private Wolfgang"
1169 "A thousand years" before *Interference*.
1170 *The Dark Path*

The great-great-grandchildren of the shareholders of Omni-Spatial Mercantile Dynamics thought that their ancestors had blown a deal concerning the Labyrinth of Kerykeion, and sent a murderous cyborg back in time to secure a better result.[1171] The Earth Empire colonised the planet Far, so-named because of its distance from established space. The Doctor helped the Farians construct a hyperspatial gateway: a jump-point for Earth's largest spaceliners.[1172]

? 2707 - MISSION OF THE VIYRANS[1173] -> The Viyrans cured Peri of a virus that she contracted while attending a party on the planet Gralista Social, then wiped her and the fifth Doctor's memories of the event. This was the first time that the Viyrans came into contact with humanity.

2708 - "By Hook or By Crook"[1174] -> The eighth Doctor and Izzy landed in the City-State of Tor-Ka-Nom. The Doctor chided Izzy for being more interested in the guidebook than seeing the sights, but changed his tune

upon being arrested for a murder that he didn't commit. Izzy freed him by looking up the identity of the real murderer in her guidebook, which wouldn't be written for another twenty-three years.

The terraforming techniques available to the Earth Empire often destroyed coveted resources, and so pantropy – the science of modifying human DNA and organs to suit the local environment – for a short while was fashionable in some of the Empire's distant terrains. The Pantropy Commission regulated such biological transformations, barred the use of alien DNA, and only awarded contracts to capitalists who produced stable pantropic populations. The powerful Mason family acquired the colonisation rights to planet CRHX-756J, a.k.a. Hope Eternal, but found that their pantropy formulas were unstable. The patriarch of the Masons illegally created pantropy subjects, Nu-Humans, using alien DNA, to protect his family's mining rights.[1175]

Humankind ravaged many worlds during the Analogue Wars. The Monk witnessed the Museum of Sattis – which

---

1171 Four generations after *Benny S7: Timeless Passages*.
1172 *3rdA: The Conquest of Far*. The hyper-spatial gateway presumably happens later in the Empire's history, given the isolation of early colonies such as Terra Alpha (*The Happiness Patrol*).
1173 Dating "Mission of the Viyrans" (BF #102b) - Gralista Social seems to be a human planet; some of those present are named "Chris" and "Lawrence". The Viyrans in *Blue Forgotten Planet* (the ones associated with Charley Pollard) know about the revisions here to the fifth Doctor's memories – whether or not it's the *same* group of Viyrans, then, "Mission of the Viyrans" must fall before Charley's group is thrown back in time in *Patient Zero* [c.7190].

For lack of other evidence, this dating is very arbitrary. The blurb says the Viyrans can time-travel; within the fiction, it turns out they can't of their own volition (see *Patient Zero* and *Charlotte Pollard* Series 1). The sixth Doctor again visits Gralista Social in *Blue Forgotten Planet*.
1174 Dating "By Hook or By Crook" (DWM #256) - The date is given.
1175 Two generations before *The Nu-Humans*.
1176 "Two hundred years" after *The Black Hole*.
1177 "One hundred years" before *The Whispering Forest*.
1178 *Spiral Scratch*
1179 "Warlord of the Ogrons"
1180 Dating *DotD: Shadow of Death* (*Destiny of the Doctor* #2) - The TARDIS has arrived on the day that Jamie would be a thousand years old. Jamie specifies he was 22 when he first met the Doctor in *The Highlanders*, set in 1746, meaning that – depending on

whether or not his birthday has passed – he was born in either 1723 or 1724. The sometimes-used convention of attributing an actor's birthday to their character (see *Return of the Rocket Men*) might suggest the former, as Frazer Hines, who played Jamie, was born 22nd September.
1181 *DotD: The Time Machine*
1182 The same century as *Destination: Nerva*.
1183 Dating "Warlord of the Ogrons" (*DWW* #13-14) - Rostow mentions Federation patrols, but in the framing sequence the Doctor mentions that he met Leofrix in 2723, so it can't be the Galactic Federation.
1184 "Seven hundred years" before *Snakedance*.
1185 Dating *Destination: Nerva* (BF 4th Doc #1.1) - It's also been "hundreds of years" since Lord Jack's crew left Earth in 1895. Additionally, "It's early days" for Nerva space station, which later appears in *Revenge of the Cybermen* [c.2875] and, much later still, in *The Ark in Space*. The duration of time that Nerva serves as a space dock before being repurposed as a beacon warning ships about the planetoid Voga (*Revenge of the Cybermen*) isn't said, so *Destination: Nerva* has, a little arbitrarily, been placed within the preceding century. The "datacrash of '24" is still causing hassle for those working aboard Nerva, suggesting it's after that point within the century, but not so long that they've better compensated for the loss. The type of security drudgers seen here also appeared in *Dalek Empire* (also written by Nicholas Briggs).
1186 The war begins "seventy years" before *Nocturne*.
1187 The Babblesphere is built "about forty years" before *DotD: Babblesphere*.

had scrolls dating back to the year Sentience Plus Four – burning as part of the conflict, and slipped back two hundred years to address the situation. The conquering Seethe left their pocket universe and entered our own, but humanity defeated them.[1176]

A human hospital ship in the Dravidian war zone crashed "a long way from Earth" on the planet Chodor, at the eastern edge of Haldevron. The crew attempted to stop the ship's mechanical drones, a.k.a. Takers, from euthanising forty-four patients to contain the Richter's Syndrome they carried. This damaged the ship's quantum flux generator and released warp energy, turning the infected into ghostly beings. The surviving patients and their descendants – forgetting their past, and adopting hospital and sterilisation procedures as societal rituals – founded the colony of Purity.[1177]

> = The sixth Doctor visited the planet Narrah in 2721.[1178]

The Doctor met the mad scientist Linus Leofrix on Ricarus in 2723.[1179]

c 2723 - DotD: SHADOW OF DEATH[1180] -> The gravitational pull of a pulsar claimed a rogue planet wandering through space – to survive, the planet's natives converted themselves into energy. They became known as the Quiet Ones, and peacefully kept to themselves until the Fifth Galactic Surveyor Corps dispatched a team as led by Dr Sophie Topalovik, to solve the mystery of their "disappearance". The Quiet Ones' new nature meant that efforts to communicate aged some of the team members to death.

The second Doctor, Jamie and Zoe assisted Topalovik's team as the pulsar caused time to run at different rates. They received a message from the eleventh Doctor, via a piece of psychic paper, that it was vitally important to save Topalovik's research. The Doctor's special relationship with time enabled him to directly commune with the Quiet Ones, who agreed to answer the survey team's questions, but in doing so had to enter a patch of slow time inside Topalovik's base. Five minutes passed for Jamie, Zoe and the surviving surveyors while the Doctor spent a few years repairing Topalovik's control room, whereupon he announced the bargain with the Quiet Ones and left with his friends.

Topalovik's research gave rise to more efficient psychic broadcasts, and led to more advanced technology being used at the Library of Artificial Intelligence on Sirius V.[1181]

Huge amounts of information were lost in the datacrash of '24.[1182]

c 2725 - "Warlord of the Ogrons"[1183] -> The brilliant if misguided surgeon Linus Leofrix landed on the planet of the Ogrons, along with his pilot Rostow, and captured one of the natives: Gnork. Leofrix used a surgical implantation technique to make Gnork super-intelligent, planning to use him to conquer half the galaxy. Gnork challenged Gwunn for the leadership of the tribe, sparing his life because he wanted his help to defeat the Earthmen. Gnork stole the ship, leaving the humans at the mercy of Gwunn.

The middle Sumaran era produced some exquisite artwork, including a headpiece entitled the "Six Faces of Delusion".[1184]

& 2730 - DESTINATION: NERVA[1185] -> Lord Jack Corrigan and his two dozen men arrived at the Dellerian homeworld in the spaceship they captured in 1895, and dominated the weaponless civilisation there for the British Empire. As their oppression grew worse, the Dellerian searched for relics of their past and found a bio-agent that would repel their conquerors. Lord Jack and his crew were infected with a microorganism that both compelled them to return home, and amalgamated all human flesh it came into contact with into monstrous forms.

Nerva space station was in the early days of its construction, but operated as a space dock near Jupiter. The fourth Doctor and Leela arrived from 1895 as Lord Jack's ship docked with Nerva, and the microorganism started transforming Nerva's crew. The Doctor and Leela convinced the Dellerian that humanity had matured since Lord Jack's time, and so the Dellerian released an anti-viral that cured those aboard Nerva.

One branch of humanity fell into a futile and stalemated war against the Foucoo – a humourless, burrowing and territorial species that fought with micro-munitions. Such was the conflict that nobody actually knew what the Foucoo looked like. The warfare lasted for decades, and the human colony on Nocturne was used as a departure point for soldiers going to or leaving the warzone.[1186]

Human colonists on the volcanic world Hephastos constructed the Babblesphere – a means of networking their minds. Their shared minds produced spectacular creative works, and also enabled the participants to discuss political issues and reach a group consensus, a newfound form of democracy. Hephastos became one of Earth's most successful and prestigious protectorates.

Twenty years later, the ever-growing influx of information from the colonists' group mind overwhelmed the six Babblesphere moderators, who built the Prolocutor to regulate the Babblesphere for them. The Prolocutor saw no need for its creators and killed them, then made participation in the Babblesphere compulsory. Ten years after that, the Hephastos colony started to fall apart, as those integrated into the Babblesphere stopped attending to their basic needs.[1187]

In 2736, a guidebook to Tor-Ka-Nom was published; a copy of it would end up in the TARDIS library.[1188] A breakaway cell of Ventriki militants believed its enemies were operating from the trading world Crestus V, and deployed the biological agent Saravin there. In response, the Earth Empire destroyed Saravin production plants across an entire sector of space.[1189]

2750 - "Time Bomb"[1190] -> The *Arrow of Righteousness* was a hundred years from its destination. The TARDIS was nearby and was hit by a time weapon – a Temporal Disruption Pulser. The sixth Doctor and Frobisher traced it to a hundred years in the future on the planet Hedron.

c 2760 - THE NU-HUMANS[1191] -> The biological patch used to stabilise the Nu-Human population on Hope Eternal degenerated, causing an increasing outbreak of madness, illness and death. The eleventh Doctor, Amy and Rory arrived on Hope Eternal, and Governor Claudia Mason hoped to cover up her family's crimes by using Rory's purebred human DNA to cure her workers. The Mason family's misdeeds were exposed, and a carnivorous Sky Raptor ate Mason. The Doctor used Amy and Rory's DNA to stabilise the Nu-Humans, according them some

years to contact Earth Central and come up with a more long-term solution.

The Doctor claimed to know a nice place for breakfast just off the Ursa Minor bypass.

c 2764 - THE SENSORITES[1192] -> During the twenty-eighth century, spacecraft from Earth ploughed deeper and deeper into space, searching for minerals and other natural resources. On Earth, air traffic was becoming congested.

A five-man Earth ship discovered the planet Sense-Sphere, a molybdenum-rich planet that was inhabited by the shy, telepathic Sensorites. They feared exploitation, and refused to trade with Earth. The Earth mission left, but shortly afterwards, the Sensorites began dying from a mysterious new disease. Within a decade, two out of ten Sensorites had died.

By the time a second Earth mission arrived, the Sensorites were terrified of outsiders. They used their psychic powers to place the crew of the ship in suspended animation, a process that drove one human, John, mad. The first Doctor, Ian, Barbara and Susan found that the Sensorites were suffering from nightshade poisoning, introduced to the City water supply

1188 Twenty-three years after "By Hook or By Crook".
1189 "A few hundred years" after *Scaredy Cat*.
1190 Dating "Time Bomb" (*DWM* #114-116) - "Earthdate 2750" according to the opening caption.
1191 Dating *The Nu-Humans* (BBC *DW* audiobook #18) - It's the time of the Earth Empire – about half-way through it, if the Doctor's comment that they've arrived "slap-bang in the middle of a fascinating period of Earth history" can be taken at face value. As the Empire was named as such in *Colony of Lies* (set in 2534) and is in severe decline by *The Mutants* (circa 2990), splitting the difference and concluding that it's circa 2760 seems reasonable enough. In support of this, the Doctor says that humans have been establishing their off-Earth colonies "for centuries".
  Talk of Ursa Minor and space "bypasses" sounds suspiciously like some of the features from *The Hitch-Hiker's Guide to the Galaxy*.
1192 Dating *The Sensorites* (1.7) - Maitland says "we come from the twenty-eighth century", which might mean it is later than that. The novelisation suggested the Earth ship set out in the "in the early years of the twenty-eighth century". An incoherent John says they've been at Sense-Sphere either "four years" or "for years". *The Programme Guide* set the story in "c.2600" in its first two editions, *The Terrestrial Index* settled on "about 2750". *The TARDIS Logs* gave the date as "2765". *Timelink* "2764".
1193 Dating *DL: The End of Time* (*DL* #10) - A case study of the Mind Set by H. James Moore, University of Castillianus V, is dated to 2764 (p17), and which at least

provides the general era in which the Space Brain exists. The motives of the Krashoks have shifted slightly – the Doctor claimed in *DL: The Art of War* (p11-12) that they wanted to animate fallen soldiers so they could prolong wars and further their weapons trade, but here, the Krashoks calibrate the Crystal to only raise their own soldiers from the dead.
1194 *Original Sin* (p287).
1195 Dating *DotD: Babblesphere* (*Destiny of the Doctor* #4) - The Prolocutor seeks to dominate the Earth Empire, "a thousand worlds, a billion minds", and the Doctor and Romana are mistaken for Earth Administrative Services investigators. The story occurs after *DotD: Shadow of Death* [c.2723], as research developed in that story aids the development of broadcast equipment at the Library of Artificial Intelligence.
1196 *DotD: The Time Machine*
1197 Dating *The Stealers of Dreams* (NSA #6) - It's "2755 AD".
1198 *The Ravelli Conspiracy*
1199 Dating *Paradox Lost* (NSA #48) - The exact day is given. The Doctor vaguely alludes to the fact that much of old London will be preserved "for another few decades", possibly in reference to the new series' dating for *The Beast Below*, or something else altogether.
1200 "Twenty years" before *Nocturne*.
1201 Dating *Darkstar Academy* (BBC *DW* audiobook #16) - The Doctor has heard of the type of school to which Darkstar Academy belongs, and finds equipment aboard the space station that is used to service "twenty-eighth-century Earth Empire space vehicles".

by the previous Earth expedition. The second expedition left, promising not to return to the planet.

c 2764 - DL: THE END OF TIME[1193] ->
The Governors of Mygosuria had set up the "Universal Learning System", and ruled that the children of the Nine Galaxies should be educated to the highest standard. Those with the highest Ability Index were nicknamed The Mind Set and sent to study at the Space Brain, a school for gifted children.

The Krashoks finished construction of the Eternity Device – a machine that would reanimate the dead, when powered by the Eternity Crystal – and calibrated it aboard the Space Brain. The tenth Doctor recalibrated the device to emit an energy blast that turned the Krashoks' organic components to dust. He also destroyed the Eternity Crystal by tossing it into the Eternity Device, which exploded. Afterward, his companion Gisella elected to stay aboard the Space Brain.

By 2765, INITEC had built the first of a chain of Vigilant laser defence space stations in orbit around Earth. The station proved vital in preventing the Zygons from melting the icecaps and flooding the world.[1194]

c 2773 - DotD: BABBLESPHERE[1195] ->
The fourth Doctor and the second Romana found the surviving colonists on Hephastos, and confronted the Prolocutor AI keeping the colonists' minds trapped within the Babblesphere. A few elderly ladies had worn out their Babblesphere implants with their incessant gossiping, and formed a resistance cell against the Prolocutor's rule. The Prolocutor despaired of the tedium and insipidness of the minds within the Babblesphere, and sought to obtain more intelligent conversation by extending its influence throughout a thousand worlds within the Earth Empire.

The Doctor and Romana burnt out the Babblesphere by subjecting the Prolocutor to more tedious thoughts and bits of trivia than it could safely process. On instructions from the eleventh Doctor, they isolated the Prolocutor on a hard drive and donated it to the Library of Artificial Intelligence at the Academia Stellaris on Sirius V. A copy of the fourth Doctor's personality remained on the hard drive to keep the Prolocutor company.

The duplicate Doctor persona facilitated transmissions from the Library to the extra-universal Creevix, luring them into a trap in Oxford, 2013.[1196]

2775 - THE STEALERS OF DREAMS[1197] ->
The ninth Doctor, Rose and Captain Jack found themselves on Colony World 4378976.Delta-Four, where the authorities banned any form of fiction or fantasy. The Doctor discovered that a microscopic native life was feeding on the colonists' imaginations, overwhelming their ability to distinguish fact from fiction. When the truth emerged, the colony's scientists quickly came up with a cure.

The first Doctor tried to take Steven and Vicki to the 2784 Olympic Games in New Philadelphia, but wound up in Medici-ruled Florence instead. Events at the Olympics included the quantum javelin, team astronastics. A light year could be traversed in four minutes.[1198]

2789 (10th June) - PARADOX LOST[1199] ->
The TARDIS unexpectedly diverted the eleventh Doctor, Amy and Rory to the banks of the Thames, 2789. London was now a mixture of the future and the past – glittering metal towers were interspersed between brick houses and churches. Enormous glass domes housed forests and served as oxygen factories. St Paul's Cathedral, the Tower of London, Buckingham Palace, Oxford Street, the British Museum, the Houses of Parliament and Westminster Bridge were still in existence.

Humanoid constructs housing Artificial Intelligences, as created by the Villiers Artificial Life laboratory in Battersea, cost a small fortune and had been on the market for about three months. One such unit, Arven, was dredged from the Thames after nearly a thousand years spent buried there. Arven expired after warning the Doctor that a timeship created by Professor Celestine Gradius had drilled a hole in space-time through which the Squall – extradimensional parasites that fed on psychic energy – were swarming into the universe. The Doctor sent Amy and Rory to investigate Gradius while he went to the day before Arven fell into the Thames: 16th October, 1910.

Amy and Rory found that the Squall had killed Gradius, and met Arven's younger self – who had been serving as Gradius' assistant. They escaped to 1910 in Gradius' time vessel when the Squall attacked – and thereby created the hole in space-time that granted the Squall access to the universe.

The Doctor, Amy and Rory returned to 2789 after dealing with the Squall, and loaded a back-up copy of Arven's intelligence into a new body at the Villiers facility. They then took him to live with a mutual friend in 1923.

Lothar Ragpole established a drinking establishment on Nocturne, and it would serve the developing artistic enclave there.[1200]

c 2790 - DARKSTAR ACADEMY[1201] ->
Orbital stations were established within the Earth Empire as academies for the children of the elite – politicians, captains of industry and more. The academies were modeled on private British schools from 1950s Earth, to provide a "back to basics" education. Patrol ships, invisible force fields and prefects armed with Webley revolvers protected the students from their parents' political and commercial rivals.

Milton Hope Valentine – a Darkstar Academy student, and son of the immensely wealthy Conrad Hope Valentine – was so bullied that he would spent his adult life wishing revenge upon his tormentors. The adult Milton built a rudimentary time machine as inspired by his younger self's encounter with the Doctor's TARDIS, and traveled back some decades to attack the academy with cat-sized killer robots combining attributes of piranhas and tarantulas.

The eleventh Doctor, Amy and Rory arrived at the academy, as Milton's rickety time machine threatened to collapse time and destroy the past, present and future. The Doctor and his friends deactivated both Milton's robots and his travel craft – but not before the older Milton was consumed by one of his own piranha-creatures. The Doctor publicly credited the younger Milton with having saved everyone, to facilitate a better outcome for his life.

In the early 2790s, the ten-planet Minerva System was colonised by an Earth ship captained by Julian de Yquatine.[1202]

Elizabethan, the wife of President John F Hoover of New Jupiter, gave birth to triplets following fertility treatment. She had used DNA samples from Hanstrum, Hoover's chief technician, and not her infertile husband. The children were named Asia, Africa and Antarctica. Years later, Hanstrum tried to murder Elizabethan after she began to suspect her triplets were psychopaths, and wanted to confess her infidelity. Elizabethan was rendered comatose, and the triplets were blamed and imprisoned.[1203]

The human colony Nocturne was now home to the Department of War, munitions factories and some hospices, but the planet itself was secure, being located eight months of travel from the front. The adversity of the war with the Foucoo attracted to Nocturne the greatest concentration of artists and thinkers since the Florentine Renaissance – this creative revival would become known as the Far Renaissance. The creativity that flourished on Nocturne would only be accomplished about half a dozen times in the whole of human history.

Glasst City on Nocturne had canals and smelt like Venice. The Sol System, Zeta Reticula, the Hessa Cloud and the Foucoo home system and were all visible to the naked eye from Nocturne. The Doctor was involved when the Foucoo attempted to assassinate members of the War Department, and officials on Nocturne covered up two mysterious deaths.[1204]

Will Alloran, a student of Korbin Thessenger, went looking in the Nocturne archives and found alien scripts bearing the bioharmonics of the extinct Ultani race. He feared the documents' power and purged them – but his brother Lomas secretly made copies. Will signed up to fight in the war with the Foucoo. He spent eight months travelling to the front, and lost his leg during a skirmish on the planet Zocus.[1205]

c 2799 - COMPANION PIECE[1206] **->** Philosophical questions about alien civilisations, such as whether nonhumans possessed souls and could be baptised, caused a rift in the Catholic Church. Social and political instability compelled Pope Athanasius to relocate to Rome, a mobile space station with a replica of Vatican City. The Catholics who remained on Earth elected Pope Urban IX as their leader, and each side declared the other false.

Missionaries from the Catholic Church had arrived on the planet Haven and converted much of the indigenous

---

1202 *The Fall of Yquatine*, "over two hundred years" earlier than 2992.

1203 The girls are born, and Elizabethan is rendered comatose, "thirteen years" and about "seven years" respectively before *EarthWorld*.

1204 The foiled assassination attempts occur five years before *Nocturne*. Zeta Reticula is located thirty three light-years from Earth.

1205 Will happens upon the Ultani texts at least eighteen months before *Nocturne*.

1206 Dating *Companion Piece* (TEL #13) - It is "the twenty-eighth century" (p74), "eight hundred years" after Cat's time (p78). The seventh Doctor also travels with a robotic companion in *Death Comes to Time*.

1207 Dating *Nocturne* (BF #92) - The Doctor tells Ace and Hex that they're "about seven hundred ninety years and three parsecs in that direction" from their native era on Earth. As Ace hails from the late 1980s but Hex originates from 2021, this could support a dating of roughly anywhere between 2777 and 2811.

1208 Dating "War World!" (*The Incredible Hulk Presents* #4) - Date unknown, but the Bellus robots were, or so one of their number claims, made by humans. This extremely arbitrary dating is centuries after *The Androids of Tara*.

1209 Dating *EarthWorld* (EDA #43) - The date is arbitrary, but New Jupiter wants independence from Earth and the advanced androids are "pretty standard". It is "the far distant future".

1210 Dating *Journey to the Centre of the TARDIS* (X7.11) - The Van Braalen brothers identify themselves as human, so it's in the future. Otherwise, this is a highly arbitrary placement, extrapolating (once again) some centuries on from the humanoid androids seen in *The Androids of Tara*.

1211 The theme park's solar panels are said to be established "three thousand years" after the 200 BC component of *Luna Romana*. In *Frontier in Space*, the moon is shown to have a penal colony.

population. However, a malfunctioning TARDIS landed there and exploded, devastating the planet. The Church in response branded all Time Lords as witches. Grand Inquisitor Guii del Toro rose to power in the church on Haven, and instigated the Good Shepherd project, using human-like robots to evangelise.

A Carthian bandit chief named Brotak took control of most of the planets in the Magellanic System, and named himself Tsar of all the Magellanic Clouds. He converted to Roman Catholicism, and favoured the Cetacean Brrteet'k (a.k.a. Celestine VI) as the next Pope.

The seventh Doctor and his companion Catherine Broome repaired the malfunctioning TARDIS by stealing some mercury from the Weirdarbi, a race of cybernetic insects. They then arrived on Haven to do some shopping, but the Doctor, identified as a Time Lord, was quickly arrested by del Toro. The Doctor and Cat were dispatched to Earth aboard an Inquisition spaceship to face a papal conclave, but Pope John Paul XXIII was declared soul-dead at this time. Forces supporting either Celestine VI or Pope Urban XII as John Paul's successor fell into open conflict. Del Toro died amid the warfare.

The Inquisition ship took heavy damage, and the Doctor, Cat and their allies had minutes to live unless a robot could go through the ship's toxic areas and use the bridge controls to release the sealed-off TARDIS. With the Inquisition's robots nonfunctional, the Doctor resigned himself to telling Cat about her true nature.

The Twenty-Ninth Century

c 2800 - NOCTURNE[1207] -> The Far Renaissance was one of the Doctor's favourite periods of history, and he visited the locale in more than one incarnation. The security force on Nocturne – the Overwatch – had eight separate reports of the Doctor's visits, dating back thirty years. Tegan was present during one such stopover.

Lomas Alloran sought to achieve great music with his copy of the Ultani bioharmonics, but Nocturne inherently contained more discord than the Ultani homeworld. Use of the bioharmonics created a creature of pure noise – it sought works of artistry, but killed the artists themselves.

The noise creature killed the celebrated composer Lucas Erphan Moret. Lomas Alloran also perished, and his brother Will – upon realising that his actions had caused some deaths – goaded the creature to killing him. The seventh Doctor, accompanied by Ace and Hex, devised a means of echoing and cancelling out the noise creature's harmonics. Will's mentor, Korbin Thessenger, was moved to write his Great Mass – it would be the last great work of his career, and celebrated for as long as humanity persisted. History forgot the manner of Will's death, and it was speculated that he died in the war.

The war would continue for "a long time", but the Far Renaissance lasted a total of thirty years. It gave rise to the plays of Casto, Cinder's Odes, the Quantum Movement, Luminalism, all but one of Thessenger's symphonies, the Zeitists and the novels of Elber Rocas. Also, the sculptor Shumac took eight years to carve "Man Triumphant Above the Rigours of Space" from a single block of Lympian Onyx.

Nocturne was home to the Museum of Culture, the Lazlo Collection and the College of Music. Data pads were in use. Robotic "familiars" – fashioned after the female form, as research showed that people were more comfortable with representations of the female gender – performed menial tasks for the populace.

? 2800 - "War World!"[1208] -> The human-replicants on Bellus IV longed for a release from their centuries'-long war, but knew they weren't built for peace, and had not been programmed to terminate themselves. They tricked the seventh Doctor into deploying a neural kill switch against their fully robotic opponents – which gave the replicants the release of death also.

c 2800 - EARTHWORLD[1209] -> Earth Heritage had established around the galaxy thousands of EarthWorld theme parks, where lifelike androids would replicate – albeit in a rather garbled form – the history of Earth. Many of the people of New Jupiter wanted independence from Earth, and the Association for New Jupitan Independence (ANJI) was gaining support. The eighth Doctor, Fitz and Anji were arrested on suspicion of sympathy with the independence movement, but the Doctor stopped an android rampage.

Elizabethan revived from her coma, and although her daughter Asia died, she pledged to help her remaining two children.

(=) ? 2800 - JOURNEY TO THE CENTRE OF THE TARDIS[1210] -> The eleventh Doctor temporarily deactivated the TARDIS' shield oscillators to teach Clara how to fly the Ship, leaving it vulnerable to a magno-grab device – outlawed in most galaxies – wielded by the Van Braalen Bros' salvage operation. The TARDIS' engine consequently exploded, but the Ship wrapped the damage in a frozen time field. The Doctor crossed time paths within the TARDIS to retroactively aid his younger self, averting the whole encounter.

Earth's moon became the playground of the rich and idle at the peak of the Earth Empire. A solar-panel-powered theme park was constructed there, shielded beneath an ATMOS Bubble.[1211]

The deep-space exploration vessel *Carthage* disappeared down the last of the Phaeron wormholes, and was lost to history.[1212] **The Doctor was a drinking buddy of Henry XII.**[1213] Colonists seeking independence from Federation officials settled on Phoenix, the fourth planet in the Paledies System. Terraforming machinery automatically engaged while most of the colonists remained in hibernation, but sunspot activity hampered development of an ozone layer and set the process back by decades. Space station *Medusa* was set up in geostationary orbit.[1214]

c 2800 - THE STORY OF MARTHA: "Star-Crossed"[1215]

-> The tenth Doctor and Martha arrived on generation ship 374926-slash-GN66, which was full of frozen Earth colonists. The Artificials – vat-grown clones engineered to perform maintenance – had become "the Breed" and now ran the ship. The human colonists had woken up two years previous, and war had broken out between them and the Breed. The Doctor learned that the colonists had died when their cryogenics failed, and that the Breed had used what raw material was available to create Artifical bodies for as many colonists as possible, downloading their

memories into the new forms. The realisation that all of those present were Artificial stopped the conflict. The Doctor repaired the ship's energy cells enough to get the vessel to its destination.

(=) The eleventh Doctor was present when archaeologists dug up an empty coffin that was supposed to contain the remains of a Hawkshaw Manor nursing home resident. Finding this suspicious, he went with Amy to investigate the matter in 2011.[1216]

2815 - FESTIVAL OF DEATH[1217]

-> The leisure cruiser *Cerberus*, with a thousand passengers on board, was trapped in hyperspace between Teredekethon and Murgatroyd. Nearly one hundred ships crashed into it, including a prison ship containing dangerous Arachnopods. They escaped and went on the rampage. The Repulsion – an extra-dimensional creature that existed between life and death – offered the survivors of *Cerberus* the chance to escape. They agreed, and the Repulsion exchanged them

---

1212 "Over a century" (ch2)/"over a hundred years" (ch3) before *Deep Time*.

1213 *The Beast Below*. This is an arbitrary date – were the current Prince Harry to ascend to the throne (possible, but not likely), he would be Henry IX. Stories such as *Revenge of the Judoon* (p19) have established the reigns of Charles III and William V (the current Prince of Wales and his son, the Duke of Cambridge). *The Beast Below* establishes that eight Queen Elizabeths and at least four King Henrys rule after that, and we have to allow that *Interference* tells us the last King of England abdicated in the 2060s. *Legacy of the Daleks* says the last British monarch was exterminated in the Dalek Invasion of 2157 (so presumably only a Queen or Queens reigned for a hundred years before that). Clearly, as Liz X demonstrates, the British monarchy is restored at some point.

1214 "Fifty years" before *Three's a Crowd*.

1215 Dating *The Story of Martha: "Star-Crossed"* (NSA #28e) - No date is given. We know that old ships with colonists in suspended animation were still being found at the time of *The Sensorites*, and so this arbitrary placement puts it around that period.

1216 "Eight hundred years" after "Do Not Go Gentle Into That Good Night". The story is later reduced to being alternate history.

1217 Dating *Festival of Death* (PDA #35) - The date is given on p116.

1218 "Fifty years" before *Revenge of the Cybermen*.

1219 *Christmas on a Rational Planet* (p189).

1220 Dating *The Whispering Forest* (BF #137) - Mention is made of Earth Empire Command and the Dravidian (*The Brain of Morbius*) war zone, and the Doctor says that the Takers are "auto-medics in the twenty-eighth century". As one hundred years have passed since the

hospital ship crashed, it's presumably now the twenty-ninth century.

1221 Dating "Ghost Stories" (Titan mini-series) - The New York portion of the story happens in "the future", some "centuries" after Grant (*The Return of Doctor Mysterio*). The Doctor names this New York as "a future that never should have happened", but he seems to be speaking figuratively, as there's no effort to wipe it from the timeline. Placement depends, therefore, on finding a spot on the timeline where New York is functional beforehand (it's almost certainly not following the Dalek Invasion) for the Smoke to cause its ruin.

Otherwise, the Nixtus III and Sycorax storylines land on the undatable side of things (there's no guarantee, in fact, that all these "Ghost stories" take place in the same time zone), but are here included to provide context. That said, the Sycorax leader tells the Doctor, "Our memories are long [Doctor]... We know the destruction you have wrought upon our people", so it's after *The Christmas Invasion*.

1222 Dating *DEyes 3: Masterplan* (BF DEyes #3.3) - No year given, but the story relies upon Schriver "revolutionizing" humanity's interstellar travel, not creating it from scratch. Liv's native time (*Robophobia* et al), and the Eminence War are "in the future". Writer Matt Fitton commented: "Schriver is at most only a few centuries earlier than Liv - it could even be decades."

1223 *DEyes 4: Eye of Darkness*

1224 *The Ultimate Treasure* (p71).

1225 "Almost a century and a half" before *So Vile a Sin*.

1226 Dating *Dark Progeny* (EDA #48) - The date is given.

1227 Dating "Time Bomb" (*DWM* #114-116) - The caption states it's "Earthdate 2850".

with participants of the "Beautiful Death" in 3012. Rescue missions would discover only empty ships, prompting "the mystery of the *Cerberus*".

The wrecked spaceships were rebuilt inside the hyperspace tunnel as the G-Lock station.

A mysterious planetoid was detected entering the solar system, and it eventually became the thirteenth moon of Jupiter. It was named Neo-Phobus by humans, and the Nerva Beacon was set up to warn shipping of this new navigational hazard. Nerva was one of a chain of navigational beacons, which also included Ganymede Beacon at vector 1906702.[1218] ID implants were mandatory in citizens of the Empire, except for those exempted by the Corporate Faiths Amendment Act 2820.[1219]

c 2820 - THE WHISPERING FOREST[1220] ->

The fifth Doctor, the older Nyssa, Tegan and Turlough arrived at the Purity colony so Nyssa could test a potential cure for Richter's Syndrome. They destroyed the Takers and the ghostly beings who had been afflicting the colony for generations.

? 2825 - "Ghost Stories"[1221] ->

In New York, legends of the Ghost's heroism spurred the philanthropist Ethan Hall to procure a similar power-granting gemstone: the Arquess, a.k.a. the Smoke of Mystery and Deceit. The gem drove Hall insane, and the authorities' efforts to contain his tyranny devastated the city. The twelfth Doctor – along with Grant Gordon, Grant's wife Lucy and their daughter Jennifer – persuaded Hall to see the error of his ways, and to give them the Smoke gem.

On Nixtus III, the twelfth Doctor and his friends recovered the Crystal of Alcyone, a.k.a. the Breath of Hearts and Ashes, which Harmony Shoal had used to enslave the Zanthians. Elsewhere, they prevented the Sycorax from deploying the Sanguinare, a.k.a. the Blood Stone, to harvest the energy of four inhabited worlds – then open a rift so a lethal accumulation of universal dark energy could slide away into another reality.

The Doctor returned the Smoke, the Breath and the Blood Stone to where they were forged: the Gate of Tersimmon. Grant separated the Ghost from his body through sheer willpower, and the four gems opened a rift that drained the dark energy into another reality. As this universal cleansing was required every million years, the Doctor took the powerless Grant and his family home...

Initial Work Done to Create the Eminence

c 2830 - DEyes 3: MASTERPLAN[1222] ->

Orion Networks operated as an investment company.

At the bald Master's instruction, the Ides Institute put research facilities on planetoid Indigo 9 at the disposal of Professor Markus Schriver. He sought to develop a chemical compound that would mimic the human brain's neural network, enabling astronauts to place their minds in gaseous compounds – navigating between whole galaxies would become an act of will. The eighth Doctor and Liv Chenka arrived to preemptively thwart the Eminence's creation, and stopped the Master from controlling the Eminence's original essence by infusing it with Molly O'Sullivan's retrogentior particles. Schriver fled after killing the Master's thrall, Sally Armstrong, during a neurological extraction experiment.

The Master escaped with Molly and Liv to the end of humanity's fifty-year war against the Eminence. Aided by Coordinator-in-Extremis Narvin, the Doctor followed.

The Dalek Supreme took Schriver to the Eye of Orion Universal Retreat of Quietude and Repose in the future, as part of a trap set for the Dalek Time Controller.[1223]

The Privacy of Sentient Beings Act was passed in 2830.[1224]

The President of Earth Becomes Empress

Earth President Helen Kristiansen declared herself Empress. Life support systems kept Helen I alive, and her brain would be controlled by the computer Centcomp, which gave her access to the memories of all previous Earth Presidents. She became aware of the Doctor.[1225]

2847 - DARK PROGENY[1226] ->

The telepathic inhabitants of Ceres Alpha died out long ago, but survived as a psychic gestalt. Much later, the planet – the closest ever found to Earth's natural conditions – was colonised by humans. Earth was overcrowded and polluted at this time, and terraforming corporations like Worldcorp and Planetscape make planets suitable for human colonisation.

Influenced by the gestalt, the colonists' children began developing psychic powers. Worldcorp encouraged this, hoping that the children's telekinesis could be used to transform planets. The eighth Doctor, Fitz and Anji exposed the plan. The children rebelled against Worldcorp's corrupt leader, Gaskill Tyran, who died when the children made him mentally relive his acts of murder. The parents of one of the children, Veta and Josef Manni, took custody of the entire group.

The accelerator, a device than could heal wounds and change people's appearances, had been invented.

2850 - "Time Bomb"[1227] ->

The scientists of the City of Light on Hedron attained control of their environment, and the genetic cleansing of their race. They banished impurities with their time cannon. The sixth Doctor and Frobisher were caught in the weapon's effect – which sent them two hundred million years into Earth's past.

The pilgrims of the *Arrow of Righteousness* arrived at their destination, but although their bodies were sound, their minds had gone. The ship crashed into the City of Light and devastated it, killing the population when its microbes and poisons were released.

The Doctor and Frobisher learned that the Hedrons had located the origin of the *Arrow of Righteousness* – Earth – and deliberately targeted their time cannon. In doing so, the Hedrons allowed humankind to evolve, and didn't destroy it.

? 2850 - THE MIND'S EYE[1228] -> The Earth Empire Space Marines established a base on a planet designated YT45, which had a diurnal cycle lasting one hundred fourteen hours. YT45 was home to a type of flower – "kyropites" – that emitted a sleep-inducing gas; their victims experienced very detailed dream-realities while the kyropites fed upon their alpha waves, then their bodies. The fifth Doctor, Peri and Erimem were present when jekylls – monkey-like creatures who were immune to the kyropites – destroyed the marines' base. An agent of the Federation Drugs Administration thwarted a plan to derive mind-controlling drugs and telepathic enhancers from the kyropites.

The Dreamwavers of the Goyanna System had devices that could monitor dreams.

c 2850 - THREE'S A CROWD[1229] -> A group of militaristic, reptilian Khellians happened across the Phoenix colony, and the Khellian Queen laid a clutch of eggs aboard the colony ship. The colony leader, Auntie, bargained with the Khellians and allowed them to feed off humans in stasis; in return, they were to spare her family. The number of humans who were awake dwindled down to sixteen. They became agoraphobic and lived intensely isolated lives, unaware of the Khellian presence and what had befallen their fellows.

The fifth Doctor, Peri and Erimem exposed the Khellian threat. The Khellians were wiped out and the colony ship destroyed, but the terraforming process improved the planet's sustainability. Humans sleeping in a dozen habitat domes were slated for revival.

1228 Dating *The Mind's Eye* (BF #102a) - It's the time of the Earth Empire, and yet a Federation Drugs Administration (FDA) is in operation. As with Colin Brake's other fifth Doctor-Peri-Erimem audio, *Three's a Crowd*, mention of the Federation might suggest a tie to *Corpse Marker*, and it seems fair to place the two stories in the same vicinity. Erimem's dream-reality entails her ruling a colony planet in the twenty-fifth century – either a reflection of when she thinks the TARDIS has arrived on YT45, or just a tidbit her mind invented. Either way, the twenty-fifth century is too early for the Earth Empire – Brake's own novel, *The Colony of Lies*, depicts its christening in 2534.

1229 Dating *Three's a Crowd* (BF #69) - The Doctor estimates it is around the "twenty-eighth, maybe twenty-ninth century" from the space station's design, which dates back at least fifty years to the colony's formation. Mention of a Federation suggests this story occurs in the vicinity of *Corpse Marker*. There's talk of a "hyperspace transmat link" capable of "beaming" people from star system to star system, but nobody actually uses this device, and it's possibly part of Auntie's ruse against the colonists.

1230 *The Taking of Planet 5* (p15).

1231 *So Vile a Sin* (p28).

1232 "Fifteen years" before *Ten Little Aliens*.

1233 Dating *Revenge of the Cybermen* (12.5) - In *The Ark in Space*, the Doctor is unsure at first when the Ark was built ("I can't quite place the period"), but he quickly concludes that "Judging by the macro slave drive and that modified version of the Bennet Oscillator, I'd say this was built in the early thirtieth century... late twenty-ninth, early thirtieth I feel sure". Yet the panel he looks at appears to be a feature of the Ark, not the original Nerva Beacon.

Still, in *Revenge of the Cybermen*, when Harry asks whether this is "the time of the solar flares and Earth is evacuated", the Doctor informs him that it is "thousands of years" before. Humankind has been a spacefaring race for "centuries" before this story when they fought the Cyber War, according to both Stevenson and Vorus. It is clearly established in other stories that the Earth is not abandoned in the twenty-ninth century (but see the dating on *The Beast Below*). *Revenge of the Cybermen*, then, would seem to be the story set in the "late twenty-ninth, early thirtieth century", not *The Ark in Space*. The Cybermen are apparently without a permanent base of operations, so the story is presumably set after the destruction of their base on Telos in *Attack of the Cybermen*.

One difficulty with this is that the Cybermen in *Earthshock* (set in 2526) watch a clip from this story. It's here been assumed this is the production team showing us the previous Doctors, rather than trying to date the story (in the same way, in *Mawdryn Undead*, the Brigadier "remembers" scenes he wasn't actually in). However, *About Time* suggests the Cybermen in *Earthshock* are time-travellers, which explains the otherwise erroneous *Revenge of the Cybermen* clip.

The Programme Guide set the story in both "c.2400" and "c.2900", while *The Terrestrial Index* preferred "the tail end of the twenty-fifth century". *Cybermen* placed the story in "2496", but admitted the difficulty in doing so (p71-72). *The Discontinuity Guide* offered "c.2875".

In the mid-twenty-ninth century, zigma photography proved reconstructions of the Temple of Zeus to be inaccurate.[1230] The Forrester palace was built on Io.[1231] The Earth Empire annexed the Schirr homeworld and renamed it Idaho. Some Schirr – the Ten-Strong – formed a resistance movement. They stole knowledge of black arts from the non-corporeal Morphieans, who failed to distinguish between the Ten-Strong and the other corporeal beings. The Morphieans initiated retaliatory strikes against human worlds such as New Beijing, and the Ten-Strong launched terrorist strikes on planets such as New Jersey and Toronto, often killing millions.[1232]

? 2875 (Day 3, Week 47) - REVENGE OF THE CYBERMEN[1233] -> Fifty years after Neo-Phobos was discovered, the civilian exographer Kellman began his survey of the planetoid, setting up a transmat point between it and the Nerva Beacon. He renamed the planetoid Voga.

Fifteen weeks later, an extra-terrestrial disease swept through Nerva. Once the infection began, the victims died within minutes. The medical team on board the station were among the first to perish, and Earth Centre immediately rerouted all flights through Ganymede Beacon. As loyal members of the Space Service, the Nerva crew remained on board. Ten weeks after the plague first struck, all but four people on the station were dead. The Cybermen were responsible as part of their plan to destroy Voga. The fourth Doctor, Sarah Jane and Harry defeated them.

The Ice Warriors slumbering in the asteroid belt awakened and departed the solar system, hoping to found a new homeworld.[1234]

? 2878 - THE POWER OF KROLL[1235] -> The Sons of Earth Movement claimed that colonising planets was a mistake. They demanded a return to Earth, but most of its members had never been to the homeworld, which was now suffering major famines.

A classified project, a methane-catalysing refinery, was set up on the third moon of Delta Magna. Two hundred tons of compressed protein were produced every day by extracting material from the marshlands, and sent to Magna by unmanned rockets. It was claimed that the Sons of Earth were supplying gas-operated projectile weapons to the native Swampies on this moon, and that the group was employing the services of the notorious gun-runner Rohm-Dutt. The truth was that Thawn, an official at the refinery, was supplying the Swampies with faulty weapons as an excuse to wipe them out.

A squid creature on this moon had consumed the fifth segment of the Key to Time, and grown to a monstrous size. The Swampies regarded it as their god, Kroll. Thawn's plan was uncovered and he was killed. The fourth Doctor and the second Romana recovered the Fifth Segment, which ended Kroll's power. Kroll had been the source of the refinery's compressed protein, and the facility was useless upon the creature's reversion.

While the Doctor and Romana acquired the Fifth Segment of the Key to Time, K-9 drained his energy reserves playing four-dimensional draughts with the TARDIS.[1236]

? 2878 - "Victims"[1237] -> Kolpasha was the fashion capital of the human empire. The fourth Doctor and the second Romana arrived and were accused of copyright theft – a crime more serious there than murder. Elsewhere, the

---

Timelink suggests "2525". *About Time* went for "After the late 2800s, but 'thousands of years' before the time of the solar flares". "A History of the Cybermen" (*DWM* #83) suggested the (misprinted?) date "25,514".

A History of the Universe in 100 Objects (pgs. 158, 186) dates Nerva Beacon to the "29th century". *Whoniverse* (BBC, p177) says that Jupiter's gravity belt snared the rogue Neo Phobos in "the twenty-ninth century".

1234 "A few centuries" after *The Resurrection of Mars*.

1235 Dating *The Power of Kroll* (16.5) - The Doctor claims that Kroll manifests "every couple of centuries"; this is his fourth manifestation, suggesting it is at least eight hundred years since Delta Magna was colonised. *The Terrestrial Index* set the story in the "fifty-second century", *The TARDIS Logs* "c.3000 AD". *About Time* favoured it being the *far* future, possibly after the solar flares, or even the same era as *The Sun Makers*.

In *Diamond Dogs* [c.5046], Captain Laura Palmer worries about repelling an assault on diamond transport ships "from someone allied to the likes of Rhom-Dutt". We've discounted this as referring to the weapons smuggler from *The Power of Kroll* – it's not really his *mo*, and in any case they've slightly different names (the *Kroll* smuggler is called "Rohm-Dutt"), suggesting they're different people.

1236 *Luna Romana*

1237 Dating "Victims" (*DWM* #212-214) - The year isn't specified, but reference to the human empire seems to place it in the Earth Empire period. The implication is that the Doctor gets his burgundy outfit from Kolpasha following this story. The sixth Doctor says in *Year of the Pig* that his favourite tailor is on Kolpasha, and that his coat is considered the height of fashion there in *Instruments of Darkness*. *Spiral Scratch* mentions that

political activist Gevaunt was planning to release Vitality, an age-reversing cosmetic. Romana discovered that repeat use of Vitality would make human flesh break down... and make it easier to digest.

The Doctor discovered that a carnivorous Quoll from the Reft Sector was behind the scheme. The Quoll had stripped their home bare and wanted new feeding grounds, but the Doctor made the Quoll explode by dousing it with Vitality. However, this ruined the Doctor's clothes...

Earth colonised Dramos, located between the secondary and tertiary spiral arms of the galaxy. Dramos Port became an important trading post.[1238] The third Doctor and Jo visited the home planet of the Pakha and discovered that an ancient Diadem contained a being that made them aggressive. The diadem was lost when the Doctor cast it into a ravine.[1239] Artificial people, such as those created by the Villiers Artificial Life laboratory in Battersea, were given their independence.[1240]

Kaldor City

Kaldor was an Earth colony planet that had forgotten its origins.[1241] Kaldor City and its surrounding society became extremely reliant upon robots: fourteen million robots served a population of eight million people within Kaldor City itself, and a total of fifteen million people worldwide. The robots were created by the Company, which directly or indirectly ran the planet. The Company Board consisted of many Firstmasters, as led by a Firstmaster Chairholder.[1242]

Robots in Kaldor City became so advanced that some people found themselves greatly unhinged by the robots' inhuman body language. Psychologists chris-tened this Grimwade's Syndrome, or "robophobia".

Vehicles called storm miners ventured out on two-year missions into a hundred million mile expanse of desert. Sand blown up in storms was sucked into the storm miners' scoops, which sifted out lucrative substances such as zelanite, keefan and lucanol. The water supplies for the storm miners' eight-man crew was totally recycled once a month, but the crew lived in relative luxury. Most of the work was done for them by robots: around a hundred Dums, capable of only the simplest task; a couple dozen Vocs, more sophisticated; and one Super-Voc co-ordinating them.[1243]

The first time that Uvanov commanded a storm mine, one of his crew – the brother of Zilda – developed robophobia, ran outside the storm mine and died. Uvanov was such a good pilot, the Company didn't want to lose him and overlooked the incident.[1244]

Taren Capel was an extremely innovative robotics engineer who had been raised by robots, and sought to elevate his robotic brethren above their lowly status. He introduced changes to the Company's designs so that newly made Dums, Vocs and Super-Vocs were embedded with a trigger phrase – "Awake, my brothers! Let the slaves become masters!" – to be given in Capel's own voice. When transmitted, this would turn the robots into killers. **Capel** went into hiding for six weeks, then **assumed the identity of a robotics expert named Dask and joined the crew of a storm mine under the command of Uvanov.** He waited for eight months while the Company created new robots with his murder sub-routine.[1245]

---

the sixth Doctor and Mel visited Kolpasha. *Placebo Effect* (set in 3999) names Kolpasha as the "fashion capital" of the Federation.

1238 "Centuries" before *Burning Heart* (p4).

1239 "Many hundreds of years" before *Legacy*.

1240 "At least another century or two" after the future component of *Paradox Lost*.

1241 *KC: Metafiction*

1242 The *Kaldor City* mini-series as produced by Magic Bullet features a number of the same characters, concepts and actors as appeared in *The Robots of Death*. *Legacy* says that *The Robots of Death* was set in the deserts of Iapetus, the second moon of Saturn, but *Kaldor City* maintains that Kaldor City is removed enough from Earth space that Carnell (and possibly even Kerr Avon; see the *Blake's 7* essay) view it as a safe haven after fleeing the Federation from *Blake's 7*. Furthermore, much of the plot of the first audio, *KC: Occam's Razor*, is predicated on the idea that Kaldor City has no interstellar trade.

In real life, Iapetus isn't large enough to have a desert the size of the one referred to in *The Robots of Death*. Also, according to Uvanov in the mini-series, the planet on which Kaldor City resides has a 26-hour day; a day on Iapetus is equal to seventy-nine days.

1243 The background to *The Robots of Death*.

1244 "Ten years" before *The Robots of Death*.

1245 *The Robots of Death*, with details about Capel's scheme given in *Kaldor City*.

1246 Dating *The Robots of Death* (14.5) - An arbitrary date. *The Programme Guide* set the story "c.30,000", but *The Terrestrial Index* preferred "the 51st Century". *Timelink* set the story in 2777, the same period as it set *The Happiness Patrol*. *About Time* thought "around the fortieth century, at the time of the Federation", worked better than not. The Sandminer Robot entry in *A History of the Universe in 100 Objects* (p202) happens "circa 29th century". Previous editions of *Ahistory* picked 2877, while stressing this was a bit of a crapshoot.

While the specific century remains in doubt, at least two if not three episodes of the *Kaldor City* mini-series occur in or relatively soon after a year ending in "90",

The Storm Mine 4 Incident

? 2881 - THE ROBOTS OF DEATH[1246] **->** The robots aboard Uvanov's storm mine predated the augmentation Capel had made to the Company's robots, and so **Capel personally turned Uvanov's robots into killers and instigated the murder of his crewmates. Thanks to the fourth Doctor and Leela's intervention, a robot killed Capel. Three of the crew – Uvanov, Pool and Toos – survived the slaughter.**

The Company publicly blamed the murders as the work of ore raiders, and Capel's trigger phrase went unused.[1247]

? 2882 - "Crisis on Kaldor"[1248] **->** Storm miners were found with their Voc and Dum-class robots destroyed, and their Super-Vocs missing. An advanced Kaldor City robot, the Ultra-Voc (UV-1), had achieved a greater degree of independence and was recruiting Super-Vocs to help it liberate robotkind. Sylvos Orikon, an investigator for the Kaldor Robotics Corps, went undercover as a Super-Voc on a storm miner, found UV-1 and destroyed it – but was mistaken for a malfunctioning robot and "disassembled" by the storm miner's Vocs.

& 2887 - CORPSE MARKER[1249] **->** In Kaldor City, the lowly-born Uvanov was promoted to being a topmaster of the Company, but this failed to sit well with members of the elite classes on the Company Board. They asked the psycho-strategist Carnell to devise a means by which they could secure their power. Carnell's scheme entailed use of new generation of cyborg-robots, which had been secretly created. The cyborgs proved uncontrollable and went on the rampage, killing many prominent citizens. The fourth Doctor destroyed the cyborgs, and Carnell supplied Uvanov with blackmail information against members of

the Board. Uvanov quickly attained the position of Firstmaster Chairholder.

Kaston Iago

Criminals Wage War Against a Corrupt Federation

The man who became Kaston Iago, an assassin for hire in Kaldor City, had been born on Earth. He received a life sentence after defrauding the Federation bank, but was tasked – with two other convicts – en route to a penal planet with salvaging an advanced alien spacecraft. The trio made off with the ship – which was capable of traveling at Standard Speed (one Standard unit being either half or two-thirds of a Time Distort unit) – and rescued some fellow prisoners from the penal world.

The group's de facto leader directed his crew to wage war against the Federation: something of a lost cause, as the ex-cons had only one ship against the Federation's twelve battlefleets. The ex-cons liberated some oppressed dwarves, and slowed Federation development for months by ending its acquisition of Monopasium 239, a radioactive material that helped to power intergalactic travel. This proved a liability when an alien battlefleet from another galaxy attacked the Federation – though Federation forces prevailed, some billions died, and 80% of the Federation fleet was lost. Freedom City and Space City were destroyed.

The ex-convicts took up piracy after their leader was lost. Their bounty included useless energy crystals from a mine, and a stockpile of worthless cash. They encountered a planet covered with intelligent sand (which they diffused with rain), an enormous brain in space (which they destroyed) and a robot wearing its creator's head (which they exploded). In the Twelfth Sector, they blew up a facility belonging to the race who built their spaceship. In the

---

and it's said in *Kaldor City* episodes four and five that *The Robots of Death* – and the Company robot augmentations that Taren Capel carried out shortly beforehand – occurred "ten years" ago. Allowing that Capel went into hiding for "six weeks" (*KC: Taren Capel*) after making his modifications to the robot assembly lines, and that the storm mine was "eight months" into its tour (according to both *Taren Capel* and *Corpse Marker*) when events in *The Robots of Death* happened, it's entirely possible that *Corpse Marker* takes place roughly six years, one month and two weeks after *The Robots of Death*. That said, the "ten years" figure is bantered about with such approximation, it's a coin toss as to whether *The Robots of Death* itself occurs nine or ten years prior to the end of *Kaldor City*. The final date of 2881 given here was chosen to better synch this story with *Corpse Marker*, although 2880 is also feasible. See the dating

notes on *Kaldor City* for more.

1247 *Kaldor City: Taren Capel. Robophobia* confirms that the truth about the storm mine murders wasn't made public.

1248 Dating "Crisis on Kaldor" (*DWM #50*) - It seems to be around the same time as *The Robots of Death*.

1249 Dating *Corpse Marker* (PDA #27) - This is a sequel to *The Robots of Death*, and according to the back cover blurb occurs "several years later". The final installment of *Kaldor City* takes place "three years and thirty days" after Uvanov becomes Firstmaster Chairholder – an event that occurs at the end of *Corpse Marker*, when Uvanov leverages the previous chairholder, Dess Pitter, out of office. As ten months elapse within *Kaldor City* itself, this means that the audio series opens approximately two years and three months after *Corpse Marker*.

Sixth Sector, they found an egg-shaped world on which an experiment concluded humanity would one day evolve back into monkeys. "Iago" lost the original fortune he'd stolen by transferring it to a neutral space station outside Federation jurisdiction, which was destroyed by accident.

The ex-convicts' advanced spaceship was destroyed, and their new one was shot down on Gauda Prime. They were reunited with their leader, until "Iago" shot him dead. Federation soldiers slaughtered the ex-cons, but "Iago" survived by shooting out the lights, causing the troopers present to shoot themselves. "Iago" spent a few years working as a mercenary, gun-running and coordinating the odd revolution. Eventually, he joined the Assassin's Guild and found himself in Kaldor City...[1250]

& 2889 - KC: OCCAM'S RAZOR / DEATH'S HEAD[1251]
-> Kaston Iago, an assassin, arrived in Kaldor City and was suspected in the murder of several Company Firstmasters.

As Firstmaster Chairholder, Uvanov judged that Iago was innocent and hired him as his bodyguard and security consultant. The psycho-strategist Carnell told Uvanov that the murders owed to a conspiracy concerning Uvanov's motion that the Company send signals to other worlds and commence interplanetary trade with them. Iago killed the last of the alleged conspirators, seemingly ending the matter. In truth, Iago and Carnell had formed an uneasy alliance – Carnell knew that Iago had murdered the Firstmasters purely to gain a lucrative position with Uvanov, whereas Carnell had invented the "conspiracy" to prevent the Company opening up trade with the Federation, from which he had fled.

Some time after this, the Church of Taren Capel – a robot fundamentalist group led by the former storm mine worker Poul, a.k.a. Paulus – caused civil unrest and terrorist incidents. Uvanov, having hired Carnell as a consultant, arranged for security agent Elsca Blayes to go undercover

---

1250 *KC: Metafiction*

BLAKE'S 7: *Corpse Marker* and the *Kaldor City* audio series – both sequels to *The Robots of Death* – feature Carnell, a character who first appeared in the *Blake's 7* episode *Weapon*. Chris Boucher either wrote or was involved with all of these stories. Moreover, it's very likely that Kaston Iago – the lead character in *Kaldor City* – is Kerr Avon, who somehow survived the shootout at the end of *Blake's 7*, changed his name and went into hiding in Kaldor City afterwards. Although legal reasons prevented this from being expressly said, Iago is very much like Avon – he's a ruthless and brilliant killer with a number of programming skills. By the way, it's probably not coincidence that Iago, like Avon, is played by Paul Darrow. Iago says in *Kaldor City* that he killed "The Butcher of Zercaster" - the name given in the charity audio *The Mark of Kane* to Travis, the *Blake's 7* villain whom Avon shot dead on screen. *KC: Occam's Razor* identifies both Carnell and Iago as having fled the Federation.

KC: Metafiction goes a step further, in that Iago details large portions of his history prior to his arrival in Kaldor City – and his background is, almost to the letter, the history of Kerr Avon. If nothing else, *Metafiction* represents the strongest instance of someone reading the events of *Blake's 7* into the *Doctor Who* narrative, referencing the *Blake's 7* episodes *Space Fall, Cygnus Alpha, The Web, Breakdown, Redemption, Shadow, Gambit, Star One, Ultraworld, Terminal, Horizon, Headhunter, Games, Sand, Gold* and *Blake*, as well as the related audio *The Logic of Empire* (also written by Alan Stevens). It even knowingly pokes fun at the continuity error that the alleged four months remaining in the journey to the penal planet seems to occur in a matter of hours (*Space Fall, Cygnus Alpha*).

All of this opens a can of worms, as it suggests that *Blake's 7* and *Doctor Who* occur in the same universe,

which is just about possible. It's never established in which century *Blake's 7* takes place, and the original proposal stated only that it was "the third century of the second calendar". The only real indication was that the Wanderer spacecraft (in the *Blake's 7* story *Killer*, written by Robert Holmes) were the first into deep space "seven hundred years" before Blake's era. In *Doctor Who* terms, that would set *Blake's 7* in the twenty-eighth or twenty-ninth century.

The future history of *Blake's 7* is pretty basic – humanity has colonised many planets and most of those are under the control of the fascist Federation. While never stated in the series itself, publicity for the show (and subsequent guides to the series) said that there was a series of atomic wars across the galaxy several hundred years before Blake's time, and the Federation was founded in the aftermath. By coincidence, this fits quite neatly with the *Doctor Who* timeline, and the atomic war might be the Dalek/Galactic Wars of the twenty-sixth century. As might be expected, not every detail matches perfectly, but the oppressive Earth Empire of *Doctor Who* is not wildly different from the Terran Federation seen in *Blake's 7*. The symbol worn by the Earth expedition in *Death to the Daleks* (authored by Terry Nation, who created *Blake's 7* and wrote a fair amount of it) is the symbol of the Federation in *Blake's 7*, turned ninety degrees.

The audio *Three's a Crowd*, which roughly dates to this era, mentions a Federation and uses *Blake's 7* teleport sound effects. In *Kaldor City*, the sound effect of Iago's gun holster is very similar to that used in *Blake's 7* Series 4, and mention is made of Herculaneum, the substance that comprises the *Liberator's* hull.

1251 Dating *Kaldor City* (Magic Bullet audio series; *KC: Occam's Razor*, #1.1; *KC: Death's Head*, #1.2; *KC: Hidden Persuaders*, #1.3; *KC: Taren Capel*, #1.4; *KC: Checkmate*, #1.5) - The *Kaldor City* mini-series follows on from

and join the terrorists' ranks, then steered the Tarenists to eliminate his political opponents.

& 2889 - KC: METAFICTION[1252] **->** Uvanov's assistant, Justina, interviewed Iago to learn more about his background, and he recounted his history as a former embezzler caught up in a revolutionary's crusade against the Federation. Accounts differ as to whether Iago told Justina his real name was "Paul Darrow" or "Frank Archer".

The Fendahl Assault on Kaldor City

& 2890 - KC: HIDDEN PERSUADERS / TAREN CAPEL / CHECKMATE -> Carnell fled, having determined that the key players in Kaldor City were being manipulated by a force older than humanity. In a bid to stop the unseen entity's plans, whatever they might be, he activated Taren Capel's trigger phrase. Robots across Kaldor City turned murderous until Iago edited recordings of Capel's voice, and transmitted an order that the robots stand down.

Carnell arranged for Uvanov to receive evidence that his rival, Firstmaster Landerchild, was guilty of aiding the Tarenists; he also provided Landerchild with evidence that Uvanov was similarly culpable. The Company Board had to decide if they were both guilty, or if Carnell was lying.

Paulus acquired what he thought was Taren Capel's skull, but it was actually the Fendahl, which had become stronger after being thrown into a supernova. The Fendahl fed upon Paulus' followers, and its core hosted itself in Justina – Uvanov's personal assistant, and Iago's lover.

Iago tried to eliminate Blayes as competition for his services as a hired killer, and was gravely wounded in a shootout with her. The Fendahl, in Justina's body, appeared before Iago and suggested he would live if they went into the past and altered history. The two of them went back to an earlier point in Justina's quarters, where Iago destroyed Justina's painting of a red pentagram and killed her younger self. Carnell then appeared, and told Iago that they were both in Hell...

Kaldor City survived the Fendahl incident, and would prosper by exporting its robots to other worlds.[1253]

Corpse Marker. Iago indicates in *KC: Checkmate* that the central five-part *Kaldor City* series happens over a ten month period. The most glaring dating clue with regards the year is that Carnell's Voc says in episode four (*KC: Taren Capel*) that it was last upgraded on "09/01/90", so the later *Kaldor City* installments either occur in a year ending with 90 or, presumably, not long thereafter.

It's variously indicated that three or five months pass between episode two (*KC: Death's Head*) and episode three, so it's a toss-up as to whether episode two takes place in the same calendar year as episode one. Uvanov comments in episode three that Iago last took a holiday – a reference to events in episode one – "last year sometime", so episodes one and three must occur in different years. Where the Fendahl is concerned, its core, Justina, says it grew stronger after being flung into a supernova (at the end of *Image of the Fendahl*).

1252 Dating *KC: Metafiction* (*Kaldor City* #1a) - Iago has just recently become Uvanov's gun-for-hire, which places this audio between *KC: Occam's Razor* and *KC: Death's Head*. The only metafictional element to the story is Iago's answer to the question of his name – Paul Darrow being the real-life actor who voices Iago, "Frank Archer" being Darrow's character in the Magic Bullet audio *The Time Waster* (which takes place in 1997). Either or both names could, if one wishes, be nothing more than an alias – Iago, after all, would have abundant reason to not reveal his real name as "Kerr Avon".

1253 THE KALDOR CITY FINALE: The ending to the core *Kaldor City* mini-series, as the summary to *KC: Checkmate* demonstrates, is something of a surreal experience. So much so, it caused some confusion upon release as to how the story actually ended.

Different theories have been offered concerning this... one possibility is that Iago was mortally wounded in his shootout with Blayse, and everything he experiences concerning Carnell and the retroactive murder of Justina is a delusion of his dying brain. Another is that it's all a metaphor, part of the political and sexual power plays that permeate the audio series.

The explanation that is increasingly hard to avoid, however, is that the Fendahl wins at the very end, and absorbs everyone in Kaldor City who wasn't killed beforehand. The choice offered to Iago – to deface Justina's painting, and to retroactively murder her – is part and parcel of the Fendahl's seduction; Iago fully enables the Fendahl's victory by agreeing to it. (Quite why the Fendahl *needs* to tempt Iago in such a fashion rather than just up and absorbing him isn't said.)

Kaldor City writer/producer Alan Stevens has stated – by way of confirming observations made independently online by Paul Dale Smith – that the last scene of *Checkmate*, plus the whole of the short story *KC*: "The Prisoner" (included on *The Actor Speaks* CD featuring Paul Darrow) and *KC: Storm Mine* (KC 1.6) occur within the Fendahl gestalt (hence the refrain in the latter story that, "We're all in this together"). "The Prisoner" evidently occurs from Landerchild's perspective within the gestalt; *Storm Mine* occurs from Blayse's point of view. The "Iago" that appears in both stories is just their respective memories of him, although Smith – tapped as a potential writer to continue the series – postulated that the Iago that appears in *Storm Mine* was the genuine article, trying to subvert the gestalt from within and cheat death.

If it's possible to puzzle through how *Kaldor City* ends, however, the Big Finish audio *Robophobia* –

A time-vessel crewed by robots departed for the Promised Land, but instead ran aground in the time of Robin Hood.[1254]

? 2890 - THE JIGSAW WAR[1255] -> A fifth-dimensional being, Side, drew strength from the belief of the Unheld that worshipped it. Side feared that the Unheld would discover its true nature, and curtailed their development by bringing them into conflict with humanity. Humanity became convinced that the Unheld were dangerous – a function of their biology producing a fight or flight reaction – if allowed to mass in large numbers. The Unheld were heavily suppressed, with Side arranging or faking an uprising once a generation.

The second Doctor, Jamie and Zoe visited a world where humans had dominated the Unheld for eighty-nine years. Jamie was interrogated as a possible Unheld-rights activist, and began to experience events out of sequence in time – a test posed by Side. The challenge entailed Jamie deducing a code that would enable him to leave his cell, but Jamie realised that the endeavour was more about locking him into an immutable future; using the code would have made him Side's thrall. Jamie foiled Side's test and escaped with his friends.

c 2890 - GRIMM REALITY[1256] -> Titan had whale ranches and was being terraformed. Space mining was big business, with prospectors looking for rare particles such as strange matter, squarks and Hydrogen 3. Zero Rad Day was celebrated on Earth.

The eighth Doctor, Anji and Fitz landed on the planet Albert as the salvage ship *Bonadventure* entered orbit. The Doctor realised that the planet was alive and had absorbed the memory banks of a crashed Earth ship, then modelled itself as a world of fairy tales. The Doctor collected up various "wishing boxes", which contained the spawn of a nearby white hole. One of the insectoid Vuim used the great powers of the white hole to cure his race of a wasting disease, which seeded the white hole's spawn into a gap between realities to gestate. The parent white hole left and life on Albert returned to normal.

c 2890 (May) - TEN LITTLE ALIENS[1257] -> Earth was exporting its poor and levying repressive taxes. Those born on Earth had legal and social advantages over offworlders. Alien planets were renamed after places on Earth. Pentagon Central ran Earth's military, which included the Pauper Fleet, the Royal Escort and the Peacekeepers. The Japanese Belt was trying to develop teleportation.

An Anti-Terror Elite squad from Earth landed on a planetoid for an exercise and discovered a Schirr building there, with a murdered group of Schirr terrorists inside.

which has to take place after both *The Robots of Death* and *Kaldor City* – seems to indicate that Kaldor City not only survives the Fendahl incident (albeit through events we're never shown), but subsequently creates a booming robotics trade for itself. The eighth Doctor's companion Liv Chenka hails from this prosperous time; see the dating notes on *Robophobia*.
1254 *Robot of Sherwood*. The Doctor says the spaceship is "more twenty-ninth century than twelfth". If so, it's probably not of the same pedigree as the *SS Marie Antoinette* (*Deep Breath*) or the *Madame de Pompadour* (*The Girl in the Fireplace*), which hail from about two millennia on. Coincidentally or not, the Sherwood robots somewhat resemble the Kaldor City models (*The Robots of Death* et al), which are dated in this guidebook to the twenty-ninth century.
1255 Dating *The Jigsaw War* (BF CC #6.11) - The oppressors of the Unheld are human. This suspiciously sounds like the subjugation phase of the Earth Empire, but it's not specifically named as such.
1256 Dating *Grimm Reality* (EDA #50) - The mining companies were active "a hundred or a hundred and ten years" ago, in the 2780s.
1257 Dating *Ten Little Aliens* (PDA #54) - It is clearly the subjugation phase of the Earth Empire. An e-zine written somewhat prior to these events (p15), with biographies of Haunt's troopers, is dated "23.5.90", presumably meaning 23rd May, 2890.

1258 *The Fall of Yquatine* (p30, p43).
1259 "A thousand years" after *J&L S4: The Hourglass Killers*.
1260 "Thousands of years" before *The Krotons*.
1261 "Twenty years" before *Deep Time* (ch3).
1262 Dating "Supernature" (DWM #421-423) - It's the time of the Earth Empire. The forced use of an underclass to colonise worlds, and the Doctor's choice of an Earth city as the colony world's name, is somewhat akin to conditions described in *Ten Little Aliens*. The ongoing DWM storyline featuring Chiyoko starts in this story, continues in "The Screams of Death", "The Golden Ones", "Planet Bollywood" and "Do Not Go Gentle Into that Good Night", and ends in "The Child of Time" (*DWM*).
1263 "Apotheosis"
1264 *The Fall of Yquatine* (p30, p43).
1265 "Silver Scream"
1266 "A thousand years" before *Last of the Colophon*.
1267 "Maybe two hundred years" before *6th LA: The Red House*.
1268 Dating *Sontarans: Silent Warrior* (BBV audio #19) - The participants are cited as human, and mention of Grimwade's Syndrome suggests this is the same era as *The Robots of Death*. Alex's pedigree is unknown; he might be from Orion, but his vague talk of working for watchmen who "like to keep an eye on things" might imply that he's of Time Lord manufacture.

The first Doctor, Ben and Polly realised that Nadina Haunt, the human squad's leader, was a Schirr sympathiser who thought she was leading her men into an ambush.

The complex launched itself towards the Morphiean Quadrant. The Schirr terrorists, the Ten Strong, revived. They wanted to ally with a renegade faction of the Morphiean race, then topple the Earth Empire. The Doctor resisted the Ten-Strong's spells and annihilated them. The Morphiean authorities dealt with their renegades, ending the Morphiean Quadrant's conflict with humanity.

In 2891, the Daleks destroyed the planet of the reptilian Anthaurk, so the Anthaurk occupied Kaillor in the Minerva System and renamed it New Anthaur. The native Izrekt were massacred. The other planets declared war.

On the 16 Lannasirn, following the Anthaurk defeat, the Treaty of Yquatine was signed. The Minerva Space Alliance was formed when the system declared independence from Earth. The Anthaurks began the Century of Waiting, secretly rebuilding their arsenal. For a century, other races flocked to the Minerva System, including the Ixtricite (a crystal race combining "the Krotons, the Rhotons and the something-else-ons"). The Adamanteans and the Ogri colonised Adamantine.[1258]

The sixth Doctor begged off playing the trumpet in Henry Gordon Jago's New Regency Theatre, as he had an appointment in the Horsehead Nebula.[1259]

A space battle led to two of the four Krotons serving aboard a dynatrope being "exhausted", i.e. killed. The dynatrope was largely composed of tellurium, and required the mental power of four "high brains" to function. Per standard procedure, the dynatrope put down on a nearby planet. The two surviving Krotons entered stasis while the dynatrope operated on automatic. It regularly culled the most gifted students that the humanoids living on the planet – the Gonds – could offer, hoping to find a pair smart enough to function as high brains. No such Gonds were found, and the mental energy harvested from the students was only enough to keep the dynatrope functioning.[1260]

During the "last" Draconian War, the human military developed astrogators: short-lived astrogation clones that biologically joined with spaceships, and provided a cheap and effective method of navigating hyperspace.[1261]

c 2895 - "Supernature"[1262] **->** Following a massacre on Nigella IV, the Earth Empire adopted a policy of not risking innocent lives on colony worlds. Transports filled with outcasts – thieves, the bankrupted, political dissidents, etc. – were sent on a one-way trip to confirm that potential colony planets were viable. If so, traction factories would follow and lay concrete.

One such transport arrived on a world where an alien terraforming effort had gone awry. An alien gene-splicer caused people to hybridise with the local wildlife; when the eleventh Doctor and Amy showed up en route to Basingstoke, she was transformed into a butterfly person. The Doctor destroyed the gene-splicer, returning everyone to normal. On his recommendation, the colonists maintained their quarantine warning, keeping the Empire at bay from what was now paradise. They also accepted the Doctor's proposed name for the planet: Basingstoke.

The TARDIS was tainted with the genetic transfer effect. It would absorb lifeforms in its travels to follow, leading to the creation of Chiyoko, the "child of time".[1263]

The Thirtieth Century

Around 2900, the Vargeld family became prominent in the politics of the Yquatine System.[1264] Early Hollywood comedy star Archibald Maplin was known in the thirtieth century; a holograph of him appeared on the uniweb.[1265]

The scientist Astaroth Morax developed a contagion, and with it attempted to seize command of his people, the Colophon. The ruling Patricians called Morax's bluff, whereupon he wiped out his race. An antidote saved Morax, but rendered him invisible. Before their end, the Colophon locked him within a citadel with a robot nurse/jailor, so that his incarceration would be everlasting.[1266]

Humans colonised a world inhabited by werewolves, whose bites conveyed a virus that catalyzed in moonlight. The colonists wiped out the indigenous population, and isolated their infected members on an island.[1267]

c 2900 - SONTARANS: SILENT WARRIOR[1268] **->** Humanity now used cloning transports to supply its colony planets with livestock. The advent of the Sigma 3, a.k.a. Sentinel, AI series meant that such transports required only a gene tech and an engineer as crew. An adversary of the Sontarans had early warning systems and graviton mines stationed on a frontier at Sigma 150, impeding the Sontarans from waging full-scale war against humanity. Field Major Starn attempted to smuggle a Sontaran army through human space aboard the cloning transport *Genesis*, but an advanced android named Alex diverted the *Genesis* through a field of life-sucking Plasmites, killing them.

Decline of the Earth Empire

By the beginning of the thirtieth century, the Empire had become utterly corrupt. Planetary governors, such as the one on Solos, would routinely oppress the native races of the planet.[1269] Humans were often little more than "work units", fit only for manning factories or mines where using humanoid robots was uneconomic. Humanity was exploiting other worlds and "going through the universe like a plague of interplanetary locusts". Mogar, in the Perseus Arm of the galaxy, was a rich source of rare metals such as vionesium, but although Earth assured the Mogarians that they only required limited mining concessions, they were soon strip-mining the planet. The vionesium shipments to Earth received Grade One security.[1270]

Every native animal species died out except humanity and the rat.[1271] The humans of Earth in the thirtieth century had no appendix or wisdom teeth, and most racial differences had been smoothed out in the general popula-tion.[1272] Humans had a lifespan of around one hundred and forty years.[1273] Suspensor pools were fashionable in the Earth Empire.[1274] In the thirtieth century, the Cybermen built a time capsule, but a test flight left them stranded in Jersey in 1940.[1275]

In 2905, Chris Cwej's father graduated from the Academy. He served in the Adjudication Service, as his ancestors had for centuries, until 2971.[1276] **Nerva Beacon completed its mission at Voga. The space station remained operational for many centuries afterwards.**[1277]

c 2914 - THE BLOOD CELL[1278] -> Spaceships used Baxter Drives for short-range travel. In a region of space settled by humanity, political opponents of the HomeWorld president sought to disrupt voting patterns in the outer colonies. The undermining of vaccines caused an outbreak of the disease Lopo on the colony world Birling, but the Lopo strain further mutated and started killing vaccinated adults, including the president's wife. Nonetheless, the president won re-election by allowing his chief adviser,

---

1269 *The Mutants*

1270 *Terror of the Vervoids*

1271 *Just War* (p143), although we see bears and wolves in *The Ice Warriors*, and hear of a variety of animal specimens in *The Ark in Space*. Pigs and dogs survive until at least the year 5000 AD (*The Talons of Weng-Chiang*, *The Invisible Enemy*), there are sheep and spiders on the colony ship sent to Metebelis III in *Planet of the Spiders*, Europa is well stocked with animal life in *Managra*, and the Ark (in *The Ark*) contains a thriving jungle environment complete with an elephant and tropical birds.

1272 *Death and Diplomacy* (p16). The lack of wisdom teeth is also mentioned in *Benny: Dry Pilgrimage*.

1273 *Just War*

1274 "Fifty years" before Roz's time. *The Also People* (p10).

1275 *Illegal Alien* (p152).

THE THIRTIETH CENTURY: While it's highly likely that the Earth was not ravaged by solar flares at this time (see *The Beast Below* and *The Ark in Space*), the Doctor's description of a "highly compartmentalised" Earth society of the thirtieth century in *The Ark in Space* matches similar descriptions of Earth in stories set at this time. Earth is "grey" in *The Mutants* and "highly organised" in *Terror of the Vervoids* episode four. We learn of food shortages in *Terror of the Vervoids*.

In terms of the New Adventures, this is Cwej and Forrester's native time, and we meet them there in *Original Sin* – a story that ties in quite closely with *The Mutants* (Solos is even mentioned on p318). Roz returns and dies in her native time in *So Vile a Sin*.

We first learn of the decline of the Earth Empire and the Overcities in *The Mutants*, although in that story the Solos native Ky calls them "sky cities" and claims they were built because "the air is too poisonous", not because of the wars. *DEyes 3: Rule of the Eminence* [c.3186] sees the depolluting of Earth's atmosphere thanks to the efforts of twelve thousand sky stations.

1276 *Original Sin* (p160-161).

1277 Nerva Beacon has a "thirty year assignment" according to Stevenson in *Revenge of the Cybermen*, so it ought to be decommissioned around 2915. We see the Beacon again in *The Ark in Space*.

1278 Dating *The Blood Cell* (NSA #55) - According to the blurb, the Prison is located on "an asteroid in the furthest reaches of space". The participants are human (ch6), and it's far enough in the future that Earth and the term "Old Old Earth" are synonymous (ch4), the Governor's wife can quote sayings from "Old New Earth" (ch2), and mention is made that a group of nostalgia buffs, the Vintagers, died out with the latter (ch3). Repeated mention is made of the governing Homeworld – possibly, for all we know, the same planet referenced in *Kinda*.

"The ancient art of the Dewey Decimal" still in use (ch4), and the Prison library is rife with Earth works such as *Call the Midwife* (ch1), *I Hate Mondays by Garfield* (ch4), *The Woman in White*, *The Da Vinci Code*, *Shall We Tell the President?* (ch5), *The Barber of Seville*, *The Arabian Nights*, *The Phoenix and the Carpet*, *The Magician's Nephew* and *Not a Penny More, Not a Penny Less* by Jeffrey Archer (ch8). The Governor recognises "The Entry of the Toreadors" from *Carmen* when the Doctor hums it, but another character responds to mention of Paris with "[It] sounds like a lovely world" (ch4). There's also mention of a TV series featuring Moll Flanders, Dot Cotton from *EastEnders* (ch5) and an old dance move at the Astoria entailing Marge Simpson saying "shopping trolley... shopping trolley" (ch12).

Marianne Globus, to rig the results. A TransNet journalist discovered the fraud, causing the president's downfall.

The opposition party took power and finished construction of The Prison: a jail on an asteroid in deep space. In a final affront, the president was named its governor. The twelfth Doctor, scapegoated for the plague, was jailed there as Prisoner 428.

The new HomeWorld regime fell into disfavour, and instructed the Prison's systems to kill the political prisoners within. The Doctor and Clara halted the massacre, and gave the Governor the choice of returning to his failing HomeWorld, or letting them take him elsewhere...

c 2915 - DEEP TIME[1279] **->** The immensely rich Raymond Rueun Balfour III had finished construction of the most expensive deep-space private research vessel ever made – the *Heracles*-class starcruiser *Alexandria* – at his private shipyard, Far Station.

Professor Tabitha Vent, the Emeritus Professor of Extraterrestrial Studies at the University of New Earth, had mapped the ancient Phaerons' wormhole network. The only surviving wormhole was fifty light years outside the galactic rim, and the twelfth Doctor and Clara were present as it conducted the *Alexandria* to an orphaned solar system halfway between the Milky Way and Andromeda. The *Alexandria* crashed on one of the system's planets, the temporal nature of which conducted the survivors into the past toward Deep Time. The Doctor and Clara brought Balfour and Vent back to their native era.

? 2915 - THE TENTH DOCTOR YEAR TWO[1280] **->** Humans built a network of sky cities above the gas dwarf Wupatki, and lived in peace with the sentient songs there, the Shan'tee. Waystation Terra redistributed media from Earth to colonies throughout the quadrant. The tenth Doctor and Gabby purged a mimetic virus, Nocturnes, that started turning the Shan'tee into rampaging monsters.

? 2917 - 9thC: THE BLEEDING HEART[1281] **->** Eye interfaces helped to transform cameramen into walking, talking broadcasters. *Cosmic Nine* broadcast news reports across half the galaxy.

Travelling alone, the ninth Doctor visited Galen – famed as the Planet of Peace, with a history of negotiating peace accords – to check on its veracity. The Compassionate, a time-tear promoting empathy on Galen, reached out to the Doctor... but thereby made people *so* sensitive to the pain of others, they murdered them. A *Cosmic Nine* reporter, Adriana Jarsdel, gave her life to carry the Doctor's Sonic through the Compassionate, forever sealing it.

? 2917 - "The Lost Dimension"[1282] **->** The Rutan blockade of the Sargasso Rim frustrated some space travel. Space piracy remained an issue.

Most tellingly, the librarian Lafcardio says: "There was a time, less than a millennium ago when it was still possible to have read every important book and most of the trivial ones... Now, oh now, it's not possible. It just isn't." (ch8) That sounds so ominously like the world of today, it seems fair to place *The Blood Cell* less than a thousand years into the future.

1279 Dating *Deep Time* (NSA #60) - It's the "far future" of humanity. Far Station is located "a hundred thousand light years from Earth" (ch1), and while humans have gone as far as Ursa Minor (the Prologue), it's otherwise implied that humanity hasn't yet – by conventional means – made the jump across interstellar space to Andromeda. Human longevity seems advanced, because the *Carthage* disappeared about a century ago, but Marco, the son of its captain, seems outwardly young. Neil Armstrong is mentioned (ch8), and Vent is an academic on "New Earth" (by *New Earth*, there's been at least 15 worlds with derivatives of that name).

There's a small potpourri of references to other stories... the Doctor cites astrogation clones as a development of the "last" Draconian War (ch3), suggesting a conflict after the one discussed in *Frontier in Space* [2540]. Balfour keeps several multi-billion credit accounts at the Bank of Karabraxos, which was destroyed in *Time Heist* (dated in this chronology to the thirtieth century). Vent suspects (the Prologue) that

Balfour has shares in Spectrox (*The Caves of Androzani*). Another crewman mentions (ch21) the Mechonoids (first seen in *The Chase*; dated to ? 3565 in *Ahistory*, but possibly happening much earlier). The dating here gives priority to the Karabraxos reference.

The Glamour has been "lost for centuries" (ch4), and this would seem to represent the furthest point that it's a factor in universal affairs.

1280 Dating *The Tenth Doctor Year Two* (Titan 10th Doc #2.1-2.2, "The Singer not the Song") - The sky cities above Wupatki, and the seeming advancement of humankind's colony operations, brings to mind the Overcity Era (*The Mutants* et al).

1281 Dating *9thC: The Bleeding Heart* (BF *The Ninth Doctor Chronicles* #1.1) - It's the time of the Adjudicators. We don't know how many of the participants are human, although the names of the *Cosmic Nine* team lean in that direction. The Doctor here poses as an Examiner from Earth – presumably the same post mentioned in *Power of the Daleks* [c.2020]. It's unclear if he's bluffing when he mentions "BBC Transworld Service". The Catkind from *New Earth* [5,000,000,023] get a mention, and a recent news report "didn't exactly set the Seven Systems on fire".

1282 Dating "The Lost Dimension" (Titan mini-series #3) – The Doctor names Poseidon Station as a "fancy, experimental late expansion era [power facility]", a

Poseidon Station was established to syphon energy from Hades' Helix, a cluster of neutron stars, and beam it through hyperspace to Ultima Tarsus. Those involved regarded the Cybermen as a myth – until the tenth Doctor, Gabby and Cindy ended a Cyber-incursion by evacuating Poseidon Station and destroying it.

c 2917 - COLD VENGEANCE[1283] **->** The human empire regarded the Ice Warriors as an "ancient foe", not a present threat. Coldstar Inc. operated more than two thousand cold-storage satellites above human colonies on the outer spiral arm. The tenth Doctor and Rose stopped a revived Lord Hasskor from exacting vengeance upon the human colonists on Enyo, whereupon Hasskor lost the will to live and expired.

c 2925 - TIME HEIST[1284] **->** The Bank of Karabraxos was the most secure bank in the galaxy, serving as a fortress for the holdings of the super-rich. It had never been successfully robbed. The bank's key security feature – a mind-scanning alien, the Teller – telepathically sensed guilt, and turned the brains of would-be wrongdoers to soup. Madame Karabraxos, the bank's owner, was the wealthiest person in the universe.

The twelfth Doctor recruited Clara, the augmented human Psi and the mutant human Saibra to help him raid the bank. The quartet used memory worms to erase their short-term memories and avoid the Teller's mind-scans, and were guided by instructions that the Doctor had prepared under a cover identity, the enigmatic Architect.

The raid coincided with a solar disruption devastating the Bank, nullifying the inner vault's atomic seal. Psi and Saibra obtained their greatest wishes, and the Doctor and Clara rescued the Teller's mate. The Tellers – the last of their kind – resettled onto a peaceful planet, and Psi and Saibra went home. The Doctor gave Madame Karabraxos his phone number, expecting she'd call when she was old and full of regrets.

The Overcity Era

The pollution levels on the surface of Earth reached such a level that the population was forced to live in vast sky cities.[1285]

The Manussan people had been reduced to barbarism and degradation under the Mara's rule. The Mara was overthrown, and banished to the "dark places of the inside". The outsider who defeated the Mara founded and ruled over a three-world Federation, the

good distance away from Earth and its colonies. Humans don't yet have quantum engineering, a discipline that Bliss (*The Eighth Doctor – The Time War 1*) studied at Luna University. All told, the placement here reflects an educated guess.

1283 Dating *Cold Vengeance* (BF 10th Doc #2.3) – It's been "centuries" since humankind and the Ice Warriors spread themselves across the stars. Moreover, it's the time of the "human empire" – evidently meaning the Earth Empire seen in *Colony in Space* et al, as the Doctor says that Ice Warriors saved his life "in the far future, in the Galactic Federation" (*The Curse of Peladon*, dated to & 3885).

1284 Dating *Time Heist* (X8.5) - It's in humanity's future: Psi is an "augmented human", Saibra is a "mutant human" and Karabraxos' private vault is rife with such Earth-centric treasures as three Buddha statues; a model of a Ferris wheel; a winged figure riding an ostrich figurine (briefly seen in the *Sherlock* story "His Last Vow"); an Egyptian-style statue that may or may not be Amenhotep; a statue of the Hindu demon Garuda; what appears to be a Faberge egg; a headless, armless female marble statue (not a match for the Venus de Milo); a Chinese chair, vase and white porcelain blue dragon vase; a Native American bust; lion statues; and an Egyptian coffin (not a match for King Tut's coffin, but in the same style). The music played is Mozart's "Overture to the Abduction from the Seraglio".

The chief dating clue is that Psi uploads computer files of "every famous burglar in history". The images displayed include an Ice Warrior (of the *Cold War* variety), a Terileptil (*The Visitation*), the time-traveller John Hart (from *Torchwood*), a Weevil (also *Torchwood*), Androvax (*SJA: Prisoner of the Judoon, SJA: The Vault of Secrets*), Kahler-Tek (*A Town Called Mercy*), a Slitheen (*Aliens of London* et al), the Trickster (*SJA: Whatever Happened to Sarah Jane*), Abslom Daak ("Abslom Daak... Dalek Killer" [c.2550] et al) and a Sensorite (*The Sensorites*). In absence of photos from a later time period, the Sensorite photo suggests that *Time Heist* takes place around the twenty-ninth century: the earliest point that a Sensorite could leave the Sense-Sphere and become known to humanity as a master criminal.

1285 *The Mutants*

1286 "Five hundred years" before *Snakedance*.

1287 *Original Sin*

1288 *The Also People* adds that Roz's clan name is "Inyathi", which means buffalo.

ROZ FORRESTER: A discussion document about Roz and Cwej prepared by Andy Lane for the New Adventures authors said that Roz was born in 2935. No date is given in the books themselves, and the collective evidence suggests that Roz is born a little later than that. Roz meets the Doctor in *Original Sin* (set in 2975), three years (*Original Sin*, p211) after the death of her treacherous mentor, Fenn Martle. She spent fifteen years squired to Martle, and prior to that spent five years with an offworld Adjudicator, which was preced-

third planet of which was Manussa. A legend said that the Mara would return in a dream.[1286] Around 2945, the Wars of Acquisition fought by the Empire reached Earth itself. The Overcities were built over the battle-torn Earth using a new form of cheap and effective null-gravity. They floated around a kilometre from the surface, supported on stilts and by null-grav beams.

Half the Earth's population, everyone that could afford it, lived in the Overcities and Seacities. The wealthier you were, the higher the levels that you were allowed to access. Earth's surface became the Undertown: a flooded, ruined landscape. The Vigilant belt of defence space stations proved invaluable at repelling alien attacks, and within ten years the front had shifted so far away from Earth that humanity had almost forgotten they were taking place.

After a few years of austerity, Earth benefited from a technological and economic upsurge. It was "a time of peace and prosperity: well, for the peaceful and prosperous, at least". Earth was a cosmopolitan place, with races such as Alpha Centauri, Arcturans, Foamasi and Thrillip living in the lower areas of the Overcities, although aliens were treated as second-class citizens. Earth at this time had a human population of thirty billion, with almost as many robot workers. The data protection act was modified in 2945 to reflect the changes in technology and society.

Over the generations, a semi-feudal system had developed. A Baron was responsible for sections of an Overcity, typically controlling a few hundred levels. A Viscount ran the whole city (an area the size of an old nation state); a Count or Countess was responsible for ten Cities (equivalent to a continent). Earth, and each of the other planets, was ruled by a Marquis or Marquessa. The solar system and its Environs were under the authority of its Lord Protector, the Duke Marmion. The Divine Empress ruled over the whole of the Earth Empire, in which thousands of suns never set, and which stretched across half the galaxy.

Few on Earth knew that the Empress was Centcomp – the computer network that ran the solar system – setting judicial sentences, running navigational and library databases, co-ordinating virtually every aspect of life.[1287]

Roslyn Sarah Forrester, a companion of the seventh Doctor, was born.[1288]

The Glass Men of Valcea established their Glass City, and defended it against many enemies.[1289] The second Doctor and Jamie arrived at a communications centre on Mendeb Two's equator. They pocketed the main communications relay device as a reminder that they should revisit the area, but this altered history. Without the device, Mendeb Two's disparate settlements were unable to pool their resources and skills, and thus failed to match technological developments on Mendeb Three.[1290]

Roz Forrester joined the Adjudicator service, against the wishes of her aristocratic family. She spent two years training on Ponten IV, then five more years training with an offworld Adjudicator[1291]

c 2950 - INDEPENDENCE DAY[1292] **->** The Mendeb colonies regressed to a feudal, agricultural society without the corporations' advanced technology. On Mendeb Three, the tiny region of Gonfallon declared itself a duchy, and came to dominate the planet within a generation.

Military commander Kedin Ashar – the Duke of Jerrissar – helped King Vethran rise to power. Vethran enslaved Mendeb Two, using the drug SS10 to brainwash the populace into submission, but became increasingly tyrannical. Ashar launched a revolt against Vethran, and the seventh Doctor and Ace, hoping to atone for the Doctor's previous error in hindering Mendeb Two's development, helped Ashar achieve victory. Ashar formally ended the slave trade and ordered reparations be made to Mendeb Two.

---

ed by two years of training on Ponten IV (*Original Sin*, p127). In *Benny: Oblivion*, Martle is "29, nine years older than Roz". At this point, Roz has been squired to him for a year (p8). In *So Vile a Sin* (p127), Roz says she was an Adjudicator for "twenty-three years" (p293). She's variously said to have "thirty years' experience as an enforcer" in *Zamper* (p184), "twenty-five years on the streets" in *The Also People* (p46), and to have been an Adjudicator for "over twenty years" in *Just War* (p184). She's cited as being "Class of 2955" in *GodEngine* (p175).

Presuming the "twenty-three years" remark should be accepted (because it's the most specific) as marking the end of Roz's tenure with the Adjudicators in *Original Sin*, and doesn't count the training she received on Ponten IV, a composite of Roz's life can be rendered... she's born in either 2937 or 2938, she goes to train on Ponten IV at about age 12 (circa 2950), she trains for five years with the offworld Adjudicator (circa 2952-2957),

but "graduates" in 2955 (an event that, depending upon the training/coursework involved, might occur in the middle of her offworld training). She's squired to Martle at age 19 (circa 2957), Martle dies in 2972 and *Original Sin* occurs in 2975. All of which matches the New Adventures' continual (if somewhat vague) portrayal of Roz as someone who's closer to 40 than 30.

1289 "A thousand years" before *The Blue Angel*, according to *Iris: Enter Wildthyme*.
1290 "Some" Mendeb years before *Independence Day*.
1291 *Original Sin* (p127).
1292 Dating *Independence Day* (PDA #36) - It's "four hundred years" after the Galactic Wars (p22), which would place it in the mid-thirtieth century.

c 2950 - MASTER[1293] -> The seventh Doctor brokered a deal with Death, having come to recognise the entity's hold over the decaying Master. Their agreement was that the Master would remain outside of Death's purview for ten years, and live his days as a contented man. At the end of that time, the Doctor was required to kill his old friend.

The physically scarred Master consequently turned up in the colony of Perfugium with no memory of his past. He became known as "John Smith", settled into a happy life and became a physician.

In Perfugium, a serial killer slaughtered eleven prostitutes and an ordinary teenage girl. Green was the colour of death in the colony, and the bodies were found wrapped in green blankets. On the tenth anniversary of John Smith's arrival, his friends – the Adjudicator Victor Schaeffer and his wife Jacqueline – gathered at Smith's house to celebrate his "birthday". Their festivities were interrupted by the Doctor, who begrudgingly admitted Smith's previous identity as the Master. Victor was exposed as the serial killer and further murdered his wife – who was secretly in love with Smith.

The Doctor and Death amended their deal so Smith could choose his fate. Death presented Smith with the option of either killing Victor before he slew Jacqueline, an act that would retroactively save Smith's beloved but make him Death's agent again, or refraining from action and thus saving his benevolent personality. Death expelled the Doctor from Perfugium before he could learn of Smith's decision.

Christopher Rodamonte Cwej, a companion of the seventh Doctor, was born 5th September, 2954, in Spaceport Nine Overcity.[1294] Roz Forrester was squired to Fenn Martle. She would be his partner for fifteen years, and he would save her life on five occasions.[1295] When Roz was 20, the *Schirron Dream* took her through time to the future. She returned with no memory of the event.[1296] Herbert Quintagon, the thirty-first century's most prolific writers of commercial jingles and lift music, was born in 2961.[1297] **The Black Dalek and the Renegade Dalek Faction may have used the Time Controller to hide from Davros a trillion miles from Earth in the mid-2960s.**[1298]

? 2965 - THE SPACE MUSEUM[1299] -> **The TARDIS jumped a time track and the first Doctor, Ian, Barbara and Vicki found their future selves on exhibit in the Space Museum of the Morok Empire, located on Xeros. The Moroks had executed the adult population of the planet and set the children to work as slaves. The temporal anomaly ended, and the travellers came under risk of the future they'd glimpsed. Vicki incited revolution among some Xeron rebels, and the travellers made their escape once the Moroks were overpowered.**

1293 Dating *Master* (BF #49) - Perfugium is a colony, part of a human empire ruled by an Empress, where Adjudicators enforce the law; so the story is set during the Earth Empire period.
1294 According to Andy Lane's discussion document about Roz and Cwej, and confirmed in *Head Games* (p205). The month and day is given in *The Room with No Doors* (p20).
1295 *Original Sin* (pgs. 32, 219).
1296 *Benny: Oblivion*
1297 *Iris S4: A Lift in Time*
1298 This takes the Doctor's remark to the Black Dalek in *Remembrance of the Daleks* that the Daleks are "a thousand years" from home literally, although it's fairly clear the statement is rhetorical.
1299 Dating *The Space Museum* (2.7) - There's no date given in the story itself. However, it must fall somewhere before the collapse of the Morok Empire in Roz's time (mentioned in *The Death of Art*), and after the Moroks capture a "banded" Dalek (ie: one with the "bands" seen in *The Daleks* and *The Dalek Invasion of Earth*, not the "slatted" ones seen in all subsequent appearances). This date is arbitrary.
1300 Dating *CD, NM V1: Harvest of the Sycorax* (*Classic Doctors, New Monsters* #1.3) - The blurb simply says it's "the far future". Upon examining the technology at hand, the Doctor can only comment, "Aps and pads, is it? Sounds like one of those self-centred eras of human history." It's during a Human Empire, but we're not told which one. For lack of anything else to go on, we've arbitrarily decided it's the first, since the seventh Doctor seems to hang out there a fair amount.
1301 *The Death of Art*
1302 *Carnival of Monsters*, "a thousand years" after Jo's time.
1303 *So Vile a Sin* (p10, p182).
1304 *The Also People* (p101).
1305 *Eternity Weeps*
1306 *Happy Endings*
1307 Dating *Original Sin* (NA #39) - The Doctor tells us that this is the "thirtieth century" (p23). Although we are told at one point that "2955" was "four years" ago (p86), the year appears to be 2975 – this ties in with the birthdates established for Cwej and Forrester in Andy Lane's discussion document, and the fact that Cwej's father graduated "seventy years" before, in "oh-five".
1308 *The Sorcerer's Apprentice* (p17).
1309 *So Vile a Sin*, with Roz declared dead "six" years beforehand. The *Decalog 4* anthology covers the history of the Forrester family; Thandiwe appears in the short story "Dependence Day".
1310 *Hope*

? 2966 - CD, NM V1: HARVEST OF THE SYCORAX[1300]

-> Humanity increasingly turned to medication to control its emotions, appetites and needs, and heavily relied upon aps and pads to prescribe drugs such as Agonal, Tranquilla, Mindease, Longprox, ErosNix, Relaxipan, Calnivax and many, many more. Hyposprays allowed for self-administration of such drugs. Designer viruses were available.

In collusion with the Sycorax, Pharma Corps established a bloodbank at the edge of Earth's solar system – a facility with medical samples from everyone within the Human Empire, including the Ice Colonies. Pharma Corps planned to seize power as the Sycorax exerted blood control over everyone in the Empire. The seventh Doctor swapped Sycorax blood into their own machinery, meaning the Sycorax present controlled themselves and were frozen in a mental feedback loop. He also exposed Pharma Corps' plans to sell the human race into slavery.

The Morok Empire collapsed thanks to human intervention, with criminal gangs like the Morok Nostra filling the power vacuum.[1301] **During the 2970s, anti-magnetic cohesion was developed.**[1302] The Landsknechte – Earth's official security force – fought the Aspenal Campaign in 2970. The seventh Doctor, Chris and Roz helped the Jithra repel the Jeopards, but the Earth Empire conquered Jithra and Jeopardy. The Jithra were wiped out, but a few hundred thousand Jeopards survived. Leabie Forrester began plotting to usurp the Empress.[1303]

The Earth's oceans were heavily polluted in the thirtieth century.[1304] Humanity and the Silurians were now working together.[1305] The seventh Doctor hired two Silurian musicians, Jacquilian and Sanki, to play at Benny's wedding.[1306]

Roz Forrester and Chris Cwej Join the TARDIS

2975 - ORIGINAL SIN[1307] -> In the early 2970s, humankind fought a short but brutal war with the Hith, a sluglike race. The Empire annexed Hithis and terraformed it. The Hith were displaced, becoming servants and menial workers on hundreds of worlds. They adopted names to denote their displaced status, such as Powerless Friendless and Homeless Forsaken Betrayed and Alone.

The last Wars of Acquisition ended shortly afterwards, when Sense-Sphere finally capitulated. The Earth Empire now stretched across half the galaxy.

Soon after the Hith pacification, Roz Forrester saw a man kill a Ditz (a Centaurian pet akin to a bee, but the size of a small dog). When he denied it, she ate his ident and arrested him for perjury and not having valid ID. The incident entered Adjudicator folklore. Forrester eventually killed her partner Fenn Martle when she discovered he had betrayed the Adjudication Service and was on the payroll of Tobias Vaughn. She attended Martle's funeral, and shortly afterwards the Birastrop Doc Dantalion wiped her memories of Martle's death, replacing them with false memories that the Falardi had killed him.

Christopher Cwej graduated from the Academy in 2974. During his training on Ponten IV, he had achieved some of the highest marksmanship and piloting scores ever recorded. Cwej's first assignment was a traffic detail. A year later, he was squired to Roz Forrester.

The very same day, serious riots started throughout the Empire, particularly on Earth itself. Insurance claims were estimated at five hundred trillion Imperial schillings, a total that would bankrupt the First Galactic Bank. Worst of all, it was revealled that the Adjudication Service was rife with corruption. The riots had been sparked by the release of icaron particles from a Hith battleship, the *Skel'-Ske*, which had been captured by INITEC corporation and kept in hyperspace in Overcity Five.

When the source of the radiation was destroyed, it was clear that the Empire was collapsing. At the time of the rioting on Earth, the Rim World Alliance had applied to leave the Empire. Over the years, all the major corporations had moved from Earth to the outer Rim planets. An Imperial Landsknecht flotilla was sent to pacify them. Rioting also began on Allis Five, Heaven, Murtaugh and Riggs Alpha. Colony worlds took the opportunity to rebel, stretching the resources of the Landsknecht to their limit.

The seventh Doctor again encountered the now-robotic Tobias Vaughn, leading to a conflict in which Vaughn was decapitated. The Doctor used Vaughn's brain crystal to repair the Cwej family's food irradiator.

The corrupt head of the Adjudicators, Rashid, feared exposure. She named Roz Forrester and Chris Cwej as rogue Adjudicators, and placed a death sentence on them. Roz and Chris departed with the Doctor and Bernice.

At this time, Armstrong Transolar Aerospace were building Starhopper craft on Empire City, Tycho and Luna.[1308] The Empire conquered the Ogron homeworld of Orestes, one of the moons of gas giant Clytemnestra, in the Agamemnon System. When humans engineered pygmy Ogrons, a native uprising started that would last six years.

While searching for secret Ogron bases, the Imperial ship *Redoubtable* discovered the Nexus on the moon Iphigenia. This was a Gallifreyan device that could alter reality, and drove the expedition insane.

Roz was declared legally dead in 2976. Her sister Leabie created a clone of Roz, Thandiwe, to raise as her own daughter.[1309] Humberto de Silvestre was born 31st December, 2978. Heavy pollution levels on Earth made him sickly, but his computer skills meant he received medical grants.[1310]

Civil War for Earth's Throne; Roz Forrester Dies

2982 - SO VILE A SIN[1311] -> A demilitarised zone existed between the Empires of Earth and the Sontarans. The planet Tara was part of the Empire, and the importance of the nobility had been diminished.

The seventh Doctor, Roz and Chris returned to this time zone and investigated the source of a signal that was awakening Gallifreyan N-forms. Roz discovered an N-form at the Fury colony on planet Aegistus, the Agamemnon System, and crushed it under a slab of dwarf star alloy. Meanwhile, the Doctor found that the moon Cassandra was actually an ancient TARDIS, wounded during the war with the Vampires, and that its distress signal was waking N-forms. The Doctor programmed the TARDIS to self-destruct, destroying the moon.

Back on Earth, the Doctor euthanised Empress Helen I at her request. He was arrested for regicide. The Empress' death sparked civil war and widespread rioting. The psionic Brotherhood launched a brutal attack on the Forresters' palace on Io, killing a dozen Forresters. The casualties included Roz's niece and nephew, Somezi and Mantsebo.

Abu ibn Walid, actually a pawn of the Brotherhood, was crowned Emperor. He offered Roz the office of Pontifex Saecularis, head of the Order of Adjudicators. Roz's sister Leabie, with army and Unitatus backing, instigated a rebellion against Walid's rule. Her forces attacked Mars on 26th August. The Battle of Achebe Gorge started. Roz defected to Leabie's side and was appointed the rank of Colonel.

The Doctor and Cwej were captured by the Grandmaster, a psychic gestalt that hoped to use the reality-altering Nexus. The Doctor defeated the Grandmaster's plan, and the dozens of bodies that contained parts of the Grandmaster's persona were either killed or banished to alternate timelines.

Roz lost her life leading a ground assault on the Emperor's palace on Callisto. The death of the Grandmaster left the Emperor lifeless, and Leabie Forrester was declared Empress. The Doctor suffered a heart attack at Roz's burial.

A year later, the Doctor, Cwej, Benny and Jason attended to Roz's final funeral rites.

House Forrester had recently resurrected the long-extinct elephant.[1312]

Earth's moon was home to conurbations in the late thirtieth century.[1313] **In 2983, Kimber met Investigator Hallett while he was investigating granary shortages on Stella Stora. The Doctor visited this timezone a number of times. He met Hallett and visited the planet Mogar. On another occasion, he involved Captain Travers in a "web of mayhem and intrigue", but did save Travers' ship.**[1314] The Doctor was travelling with Evelyn at the time, and convinced her – rightfully, she thought – to turn down Travers' marriage proposal.[1315] **Madame Karabraxos, as the twelfth Doctor predicted, had become old and full of regrets, and phoned him to ask with his help in rescuing the alien Tellers.**[1316]

2986 (16th April) - TERROR OF THE VERVOIDS[1317] -> Professor Sarah Lasky planned to breed intelligent plants, Vervoids, that would hopefully make robots obsolete. Vervoids bred and grew rapidly, plus were quick to learn and cheap to maintain. For an undisclosed reason, the Vervoids also had a poisonous spike. A consortium was ready to exploit the creatures, but as the Vervoids were being transported back to Earth in the intergalactic liner *Hyperion III*, they went on the rampage and killed a number of the passengers and crew, including Lasky. The sixth Doctor and Mel's intervention resulted in every example of the species being wiped out using the mineral vionesium, which accelerated their growth cycle.

> = The Valeyard and Ellie briefly visited the *Hyperion III*, and dismissively left after the Vervoids killed everyone aboard.[1318]

1311 Dating *So Vile a Sin* (NA #56) - The date is given (p25).

1312 *So Vile a Sin* (p33). An elephant is seen in the far future in *The Ark*. Leabie surely misspeaks in claiming that elephants have been "extinct for almost two millennia".

1313 *Return of the Krotons*

1314 *Terror of the Vervoids*

1315 *Instruments of Darkness*

1316 *Time Heist*

1317 Dating *Terror of the Vervoids* (23.3) - The Doctor tells the court that this is "Earth year 2986". A monitor readout suggests it is "April 16". A report on Commodore Travers in *The Doctor: His Lives and Times* (p143), written in the aftermath of *Terror of the Vervoids*, is dated to "22.11.2986".

The story ends with the Doctor wiping out the Vervoids as a race (it's the reason he's hit with a charge of genocide), but they're evidently re-cultivated down the road, as they (or their descendants, the Navigators) impact upon stories such as *TW*: "Station Zero", *CD,NM V2*: *Night of the Vashta Nerada* and *The Eleventh Doctor Year Two*: "Downtime".

1318 *Unbound: He Jests at Scars...*

DALEK HIERARCHY: The ongoing Dalek comic strip in *TV Century 21* (called simply "The Daleks", later regarded as "The Dalek Chronicles") set up a straightforward hierarchy for the early Daleks. The Emperor led, guided by the Brain Machine (a perfect computer with the authority to dismiss him if he failed). The sixties Dalek annuals concurred with this, occasionally referring to the Emperor as the Supreme Dalek and the Gold Dalek. The Black Dalek was his "deputy" and "warlord" (and had a slightly more powerful casing and weapons than the normal Daleks). The rarely-seen Red Dalek looked after research and development on Skaro.

In non-television stories from the sixties – "The Dalek Chronicles" strip, the Dalek books, the stageplay *The Curse of the Daleks* – it seems clear that there's only one Black Dalek. It leads the Daleks in *The Curse of the Daleks*. In both the 60s and 70s in the *TV Comic/TV Action* strips, the Black Dalek is in overall command (he's black with red details in the *TV Action* comic "The Planet of the Daleks") and he's referred to as "Dalek Leader"; this could well be the same individual.

Black Daleks do show up frequently as leaders in the TV series, presumably because all the production team had to do to distinguish the head Dalek from the others was repaint an existing prop, and painting it black worked well even when the story was in black and white. We never see more than one at a time. In *The Dalek Invasion of Earth*, Dalek Earth Force is led by a Black Dalek, "the Supreme Controller", who takes his orders from a Supreme Command which is off world (presumably on Skaro, although this is never stated). A Black Dalek is "the Dalek Supreme" in *The Chase* (and is based on Skaro). A Black Dalek is "the Supreme" in *Mission to the Unknown/The Daleks' Master Plan*, and again reports to Skaro. There's a Black Dalek, a.k.a. "the Supreme Dalek", in *Resurrection of the Daleks* who seems to be the highest authority of the weakened Daleks. The Renegade Faction in *Remembrance of the Daleks* is led by a Black Dalek. The leader of the Cult of Skaro, Sec, had an all-black casing in *Doomsday* and *Daleks in Manhattan*. A black Dalek appears amongst the Dalek High Command in *The Magician's Apprentice/The Witch's Familiar*, but seems secondary to the Supreme Dalek.

All the Daleks present are wiped out in *The Dalek Invasion of Earth* and *The Daleks' Master Plan*. We don't specifically see the Black Dalek killed in either story, but neither do we see him escaping. We see the Black Dalek killed in *Resurrection of the Daleks*... then again, Davros is seen dying in identical circumstances and he manages to come back. The Black Dalek also dies in *Remembrance of the Daleks*, and presumably perishes (along with the rest of High Command) in *The Witch's Familiar*.

It's a stretch, then, but just about possible that this is the same Black Dalek in every TV story. If so, it may be the same individual from "The Dalek Chronicles".

It seems far more likely, however, that "Black Dalek"

becomes a rank as the Daleks expand. There are other stories in which Black Daleks are senior commanders – by *The Evil of the Daleks*, a group of Black Daleks serves the Emperor (they only have black domes and modified eyestalks). In the books, Ace kills "a Black Dalek" while she serves in Spacefleet. This represents a significant achievement, but also implies there is more than one Black Dalek at this point.

So what is the fate of the original Black Dalek, the first Dalek Emperor's deputy? John Peel's *War of the Daleks*, taking its cue from his *The Official Doctor Who and the Daleks Book* and his novelisation of *The Evil of the Daleks*, establishes that the Dalek Prime is the last surviving Dalek from the time of their creation (all the way back to *Genesis of the Daleks*), so the first Black Dalek must be dead by that point. It is possible, however, that before that, the original Black Dalek became the Supreme Dalek.

"Supreme Dalek" seems to mean a number of things over the course of the Dalek stories... When there's an Emperor, he is also referred to as Supreme Dalek (in, for example, *The Dalek World*). It may just be that "Supreme Dalek" and "Emperor" are interchangeable terms. The Supreme Dalek is usually treated like the Emperor in all but name – the sole Dalek at the top of the hierarchy.

If we go with the theory that only one individual was Emperor for most of Dalek history (see The Dalek Emperors sidebar), and that this individual was killed in *The Evil of the Daleks*, this creates a vacancy. This chronology places the Davros Era stories after *The Evil of the Daleks*, and in those, the Supreme Dalek rules the Daleks, with Davros deposing him to become a new Emperor. The (unseen) Supreme Dalek rules Dalek Central Control (from the Dalek space fleet) in *Destiny of the Daleks*, and Davros is keen to usurp the role. The Supreme Dalek in *Resurrection of the Daleks* is a Black Dalek. In *Revelation of the Daleks*, the (unseen) Supreme Dalek rules Skaro. In *Remembrance of the Daleks*, a Black Dalek leads the Renegade Faction, the group deposed by Davros.

This could, just about, be the same individual Dalek (although, as noted, it looks like he's killed at the end of *Resurrection of the Daleks*). The most natural successor to the original Emperor would be his deputy. So this Supreme Dalek might be the original Black Dalek, as introduced in "The Dalek Chronicles". Perhaps the implication is that once the original Emperor is dead, the Black Dalek leader doesn't quite dare to give himself the title "Emperor" – although Davros has no such qualms. This Black Dalek looks to be comprehensively killed at the end of *Remembrance of the Daleks*.

There are other Supreme Daleks, however... We see "the Supreme Dalek" in one illustration for *The Dalek Outer Space Book* story "The Living Death" and he's an odd mix – a standard Dalek body with a globe very like the Emperor's for a head. The book features (in other

continued on page 3219...

Professor Lasky's research contributed to the field of agronomy, as did the work of Delenger and Tremer.[1319]

The ruling Council on Earth came to realise that Earth was "exhausted... politically, economically, biologically finished", "fighting for its survival" and was "grey and misty" with "grey cities linked by grey highways across grey deserts... slag, ash, clinker". Earth's air was so polluted that the entire population now had to live in the vast sky cities if they wanted to breathe.

By this point, Earth couldn't afford an Empire any longer. By the end of the thirtieth century, most planets in the Earth Empire had achieved some form of independence from the homeworld.[1320] These were "the declining years of Earth's planetary empire".[1321]

As the Earth Empire underwent collapse, countless planets were cut off and abandoned.[1322] The Earth Empress granted Eta Centauri 6 the status of a Duchy Royal with the name of Tractis. Humans had committed genocide there during the Empire period, because the natives refused to allow the mineral exploitation of their planet or the growing of narcotic crops. The Silurian governor of the planet, Menarc, tried to establish an elected council, but human colonists formed a separatist party and assassinated key politicians. The decaying Empire tried to restore order, leading to a conflict that killed hundreds of thousands. The eighth Doctor told Sam Jones that matters would improve for Tractis after that.[1323]

c 2990 - THE MUTANTS[1324] -> One of the last planets to gain independence from Earth was Solos. The native Solonians staged organised resistance, but the Marshal of the planet resisted reform for many years. From his Skybase in orbit above Solos, the Marshal had been conducting experiments on the Solonian atmosphere, attempting to render it more suitable for humans. When the Solonians began mutating into insect-like creatures, the Marshal ordered the "Mutts" destroyed.

An Independence Conference was arranged between the Solonian leaders and the Earth "Overlords", with Solos to be granted independence. The Administrator was assassinated at the meeting, and martial law was declared. The Time Lords sent the third Doctor and Jo to Solos – they met Professor Sondergaard, who had

discovered that the Solonians underwent a radioactive metamorphosis every five hundred years, meaning that the process that was transforming the population into Mutts and altering the atmosphere was seasonal. The Doctor and his allies deduced that the Mutts were a transitional stage as the Solonians turned into advanced beings. One of the Solonians, Ky, completed his transformation and killed the Marshal.

2992 - THE FALL OF YQUATINE[1325] -> The eighth Doctor attended the inauguration of Stefan Vargeld, who defeated the unpopular Ignatiev to win the Presidency of Yquatine. Four years later, the Doctor returned just as sentient gas creatures named the Omnethoth, constructed millions of years ago as a weapon to conquer the universe, awoke from dormancy and devastated the planet with searing gas bombs. The reptilian Anthaurk attempted to capitalise on this and capture Yquatine space, but the Doctor's companion Compassion engaged her Chameleon Circuit and impersonated Vargeld, helping to sue for peace. The Doctor mentally reprogrammed the Omnethoth as peaceful cloud-like beings, but a vengeful Vargeld, in retribution for Yquatine's devastation, destroyed the Omnethoth with ionization weapons.

2994 - SUPERIOR BEINGS[1326] -> The fifth Doctor and Peri were caught when the fox-like Valethske invaded a pleasure planet, Eknur 4. The invaders were looking for the homeworld of their gods. The Valethske put Peri into suspended animation aboard their ship and departed. The Doctor calculated its next arrival point, in a century's time, and left to rendezvous with Peri then.

Eknur 4 was one of the Wonders of the Universe, and a utopian society given over to hedonism.

IMC established a mining facility, Piranesi-1, on a geological fault over planet No. ERM4997 in the outer galaxy, beyond Terran jurisdiction. Initial reports indicated profitable veins of trisilicate, limpidium and tramanganese, but a new silicon-based lifeform, the Bloom, mentally influenced the mining team into spreading its stone seeds. The Bloom fed off the miners' emotions, and they died after going mad.[1327]

1319 *The Seeds of War*
1320 *The Mutants*
1321 *Frontier in Space*
1322 *Burning Heart, The Ultimate Treasure.*
1323 *Genocide* (p274-275).
1324 Dating *The Mutants* (9.4) - The Doctor tells Jo that they have been sent to "the thirtieth century". The story must take place many years after *Original Sin*, where events are set into motion that will eventually mean the Empire's collapse. *The Programme Guide* set the

story slightly later ("c.3100"), *Timelink* in 2971, and *About Time* in "3000-ish".
1325 Dating *The Fall of Yquatine* (EDA #32) - The date is given (p43, p150).
1326 Dating *Superior Beings* (PDA #43) - The year is given (p108).
1327 *Terror of the Sontarans*. The mineralogical research team leader's final log entry is dated to "October 28th, 2996".

...continued from page 3217

stories) a Gold Dalek, the Dalek Emperor and the Black Dalek. This Supreme Dalek might be a very oddly drawn Emperor, or a completely new character.

Elsewhere in *The Dalek Outer Space Book*, the story "Super Sub" refers to the crew of one submarine as including "a Supreme Dalek who is in charge of the fighting" and "a Black Dalek who is in charge of the scientific investigations".

In the *Dalek Empire* series, there is a Supreme Dalek who acts as the Emperor's deputy. The third series introduces a new Supreme after the last one is killed. This replacement Supreme is also killed later in the series. Below them are Supreme Controllers – Red Daleks. At the start of the Last Great Time War (*Gallifrey – Time War*), the Supreme Dalek at best seems third in command after the Dalek Emperor and the Dalek Time Strategist – when the Supreme dies in battle, those two just appoint a new one.

In *The Stolen Earth/Journey's End,* the Daleks are ruled by a Supreme Dalek who has a modified red and gold casing. He is killed by Captain Jack. Similarly, a red Supreme Dalek with gold trim leads the High Council in *The Magician's Apprentice/The Witch's Familiar*.

Other stories state that the Daleks are ruled by a committee, not an individual (and this was apparently the preference of Terry Nation, the Daleks' real-life creator). In the Daleks' first story (*The Daleks*), the Dalek city is ruled by "the council", and all the Daleks we see look alike. While in *Planet of the Daleks*, we meet a Dalek Supreme – a larger Dalek than normal, black with gold bumps, with a redesigned eyestalk and other features – it's clear that this very senior Dalek is just one member of the Supreme Council (the Daleks on Spiridon also report to "Supreme Command"). A "Supreme Council" of Daleks seems to perish at the end of *We are the Daleks.*

Asylum of the Daleks features the one and (to date) only appearance of the Parliament of the Daleks – here, the Dalek Supreme (a white Dalek of the New Paradigm variety) answers to the Dalek Prime Minister, a Dalek mutant in a glass container. Later, in *The Magician's Apprentice/The Witch's Familiar*, we meet the Dalek "High Command": a roomful of Daleks a roomful of Daleks led by a Supreme Dalek.

Day of the Daleks and *Frontier in Space* both have Daleks led by gold Daleks. We never learn their title. "The Dalek Tapes" feature on the *Genesis of the Daleks* DVD says these are members of the Supreme Council.

The Dalek Outer Space Book story "The Dalek Trap" features a "leader" who is a gold Dalek, of apparently a standard design (he may be a little larger than the average Dalek, and like the Supreme Dalek in "The Living Death", he might be the Golden Emperor drawn by someone without reference material).

The fact that the Daleks have a Council doesn't contradict the idea they have an Emperor. We see the Dalek Emperor in command of a council in *The Dalek World*.

In *The Dalek Outer Space Book*, we see the most elaborate set up – below the Emperor (also referred to as "the golden Dalek"), there's the Black Dalek, possibly that odd Supreme Dalek with a globe head, a Dalek Council (including the Gold Dalek see in "The Dalek Trap"?) and a separate group, a conclave of senior Dalek commanders, such as the red Dalek who leads Red Extra Galactic Squadron. There are other Red Daleks, as well as Blue Daleks. In "The Secret of the Emperor", the blue/gold Daleks appear to be scientists. As noted, on the battlefront, a Dalesub has a Black Dalek and a Supreme Dalek in command.

The Doctor Who: Aliens and Enemies book (2006), published in close cooperation with the production team of the time, describes the set up in *The Parting of the Ways* as the Emperor in charge with a High Council, also known as the Emperor's Personal Guard. Some of these have black domes, some have two gunsticks.

There are other Dalek ranks: In *Destiny of the Daleks*, the leader of the squad sent to recover Davros has black central slats. We never learn this Dalek's title. In other stories (*The Daleks, The Power of the Daleks, Death to the Daleks, Planet of the Daleks*) we see groups of Daleks able to function perfectly well with leaders in ordinary casings.

While the Black Dalek, the Dalek Leader (black with red details) is in command in "The Planet of the Daleks" (*TV Action*), his senior subordinate on the Dalek planet is a white Dalek with red detailing. The commander of the Earth expedition is also referred to as Dalek Leader and is black with gold detailing. There are Daleks with red domes that seem to outrank the standard Daleks.

War of the Daleks states that the Dalek hierarchy – at least at that point in their history – runs: Grey Daleks, Blue Daleks, Red Daleks, Black Daleks, Gold Daleks, with the Dalek Prime as absolute authority. The Dalek Prime is described as "slightly larger than the others, with a bulbous head. It was a burnished gold colour, and had about a dozen lights about the expanded dome instead of the average Dalek's two" – in other words, it strongly resembles the Golden Emperor.

In *Prisoner of the Daleks*, the Daleks' overall leader is the Supreme Dalek and there is a chief interrogator Dalek X, the Inquisitor General, who is black and gold.

Victory of the Daleks introduces a "new Dalek paradigm", with five colour-coded classes of Dalek. These are red (Drone), orange (Scientist), yellow (Eternal), blue (Strategists) and white (Supreme). In that story, they're regarded as having "pure" Dalek DNA, so vapourise the Daleks who free them as being genetically deficient. The stories to come, however (noticeably *Asylum of the Daleks*), show New Paradigm Daleks working in concert with other forms of Daleks, and not outranking them by virtue of breeding. They're absent from the High Command that features in *The Magician's Apprentice/The Witch's Familiar*.

The Launching of *Starship UK*

Humanity migrated from Earth aboard space arks built to house the population of entire nations. Britain was unable to launch an ark until a star whale, hearing the cries of Britain's children, intervened. The Britons repaid this by capturing the whale and torturing it to fly through space with their ark atop it. The ark, named Starship UK, contained much of Great Britain, Wales and Northern Ireland (Scotland had chosen to go into space in its own ship). Enormous buildings housed the populations of Yorkshire, Devon, Surrey, Kent, Essex, Lancashire, London and more. The population of the ark chose to remain ignorant of the crime perpetrated upon the space whale, and continually had their memories of it erased.[1328]

? 2997 - NAofBENNY V2: THE TEARS OF ISIS[1329] ->

The seventh Doctor concluded that every time Sutekh was killed, a part of him would be reborn. To trap Sutekh's mind in an ouroboros timeloop, the Doctor relocated the estate of Russell Courtland, a member of the Temple of Sutekh, to Earth after the solar flares had ravaged it. Courtland's rituals drew Sutekh to this time zone. The world-destroyer mistakenly believed he had destroyed Earth, but the world was already dead, which limited his power. The Doctor, Benny and Ace arrived from ancient Egypt as the Osirian Isis was reborn, which prompted Sutekh – as the Doctor planned – to take over the Doctor's body and retreat down a time-space tunnel to the Pyramid of Horus. Isis pulled the Doctor back to this era following events in Benny's native era. The ouroboros loop cycled Sutekh between ancient Egypt, Benny's era and this time. Isis shed her tears, restoring life to the dead Earth.

In 2999, a Sun City teenager hacked Earth's TacNet, causing a meltdown that killed thousands on the East Coast of Australia. Humberto de Silvestre was wounded by this, and only saved when he was grafted with experimental liquid computers. He became the cyborg Silver.[1330]

1328 Three hundred years before *The Beast Below*. The Doctor cites this migration as owing to Earth being roasted by solar flares, but see the dating notes on this story for why that's probably not the case.

1329 Dating *NAofBenny V2: The Tears of Isis* (*NAofBenny* #2.4) - The Doctor plays off the highly suspect dating given in *The Beast Below* (see the dating notes on that story) by claiming that it's "Earth in the twenty-ninth century", shortly after the solar flares have sterilized the planet. It would be nice to think that he's made a mistake with his dating (see The Solar Flares sidebar), but this is a Doctor who has been extremely meticulous in working out how to trap Sutekh in a timeloop with loci in three different time zones.

Two pieces of evidence suggest dating beyond the twenty-ninth century... the Doctor at one point claims to have moved Courtland's twenty-first-century estate "a few thousand years" through time to the devastated Earth, and the obelisks the Doctor built in ancient Egypt are said to have a range of "ten thousand years". The end point for that would be circa 8500, with Isis' tears then restoring Earth's ecology in time for the fourth Doctor, Sarah and Harry to go there some millennia later in *The Sontaran Experiment*.

Either way, *The Tears of Isis* must happen after *Starship UK* launches (had Isis restored the barren Earth beforehand, it would have no reason to leave) – but it does so "three hundred years" before *The Beast Below* [? 3297], which makes fitting *The Tears of Isis* into the 2800s all that much harder.

1330 *Hope*

1331 "Six thousand years" after the 2,986 BC portion of *Gallifrey VII: Intervention Earth*.

1332 *The Dark Path*

1333 *Night of the Humans*

1334 *Iris: Enter Wildthyme.* Iris' companion Jenny muses (p169), "We're leaving our system and our millennium", so it's the third millennium if not later.

1335 *The Eternal Battle.* Captain Nina Albiston files her last (and unreceived) report to "Earth Command", a group mentioned in *Prisoner of the Daleks* [c.2560] and *The Infinite Quest* [c.3907].

1336 In *Mission to the Unknown*, set in the year 4000, Lowery confidently says, "'The Daleks invaded Earth a thousand years ago," and Marc Cory replies, "That's right." Even allowing for figures of speech, this surely can't refer to *The Dalek Invasion of Earth*, set around 2157.

1337 *The Daleks' Master Plan*

1338 *Placebo Effect*

1339 *The Art of Destruction*, and consistent with the New Adventures.

1340 *Dark Horizons* (p178). An allusion to "Year 3000", a song released in 2002 by the boyband Busted.

1341 *The Eye of the Jungle*

1342 Dating *Unbound: He Jests at Scars...* (*Unbound* #4) - This echoes another Gary Russell story, *Legacy*.

1343 *Hope*

1344 Dating *Shroud of Sorrow* (NSA #53) - The exact day is given (p251).

1345 "A thousand years" before *The Book of the Still*.

1346 "A few years" before *Festival of Death*.

1347 Dating *The Space Age* (EDA #34) - The year is given (p216). The people there think it is 2019.

1348 Dating *Festival of Death* (PDA #35) - The year is given (pgs. 115, 116, 194).

The Fourth Millennium

Humanity waged war over entire planets.[1331] At the turn of the thirty-first century, an Imperial Navy force was sent out to seek out alien technology that might help shore up the Earth Empire. They discovered the planet Darkheart and colonised it. They remained isolated for three and a half centuries, but came to discover a device that they also named the Darkheart, and which was built from Chronovore technology. The Chronovores had designed the device to beam healing energy to their remote, injured members, but the colonists adapted it to alter morphic fields. Properly tuned, the Darkheart could transform all alien species into human beings.[1332]

The Hexion Geldmongers of Mercutio 14, located out beyond Cassiopeia's Elbow, had an empire that spanned whole galaxies. They forged the Mymon Key: a device that could tap gravitational force to produce limitless energy. Mercutio 14 fell, and endless wars were fought over the Key – which was placed a casket that only a Hexion speaker could open. A museum of antiquities in the thirty-first century owned the casket, but had budget cuts. The Key was sold to a private buyer in Andromeda, but the Gobocorp ship transporting it, *The Herald of Nanking*, crashed on the Gyre: an amalgamation of space junk in the Battani 045 System. Only five hundred of the three thousand crew survived. In the hundreds of thousands of years to follow, their descendents forgot their origins, and thought that the Gyre was humanity's homeworld.[1333]

The mobile Super Hotel Miramar operated during humanity's first expansion into space. It resided on the Spiral Wing, then spent a century on the edge of the Golden Chasm.[1334] The Psigon Centre of Academic Excellence time-scooped a conflict between human colonists and Field Major Lenk's Sontarans. The Sontarans had standing orders to execute the Doctor on sight.[1335]

3000

The Daleks invaded the Earth around the year 3000.[1336] **From the year 3000 to the year 3500, Earth knew of no Dalek activity in the galaxy.**[1337] From around the year 3000, the Foamasi began gaining in power and reputation across the galaxy.[1338]

Africa was in the middle of its Third Golden Age in the year 3000.[1339] The eleventh Doctor believed that by the year 3000, the population of Earth – or a substantial portion of it – would be living underwater.[1340] The eleventh Doctor failed to take Amy and Rory to Margate for the 3000 AD World Jamboree.[1341]

> **= c 3000 - UNBOUND: HE JESTS AT SCARS...**[1342]
> -> The Valeyard and Ellie retrieved the Diadem from the Pakhar homeworld.

In 3006, aliens invaded Earth, overrunning America and capturing Washington. The government used experimental time machines to send agents to fetch help – Agent Grey was sent to the past, Agent Silver to the far future.[1343]

3006 (30th September) - SHROUD OF SORROW[1344]

-> The eleventh Doctor and Clara thought the Shroud was forever trapped in a space-time loop, but it established tendrils of itself on Station Epsilon following the assassination of President Winza.

Legends of *The Book of the Still* begin circulating. Unknown parties had developed this artifact so that stranded time travellers could summon help by writing their name in it. Copies of the book, made from invulnerable taffeta, found their way to various points in time and space, including the planet Lebenswelt in the year 4009.[1345]

Documentary maker Harken Batt was discredited when he used actors in an expose of organised crime.[1346]

3012 - THE SPACE AGE[1347]

-> The eighth Doctor, Fitz and Compassion found an asteroid that contained a reconstruction of a futuristic city. The inhabitants – rival members of the Mods and Rockers gangs – had been spirited there from 1965 by a benevolent alien named the Maker. However, the gangs had fallen into continued bloodshed for nineteen years. The Maker, imprisoned by the Mods and compelled to make weapons, had instigated the city's dissolution. Other Makers arrived, liberated their colleague and caused the Mods and Rockers to stand down. The Makers offered the humans a choice: return to 1965 as their younger selves with no memories of these events, or join a futuristic society in 3012. The humans made their decisions, and the Doctor's party departed.

3012 - FESTIVAL OF DEATH[1348]

-> Against objections from the major religions, Dr Koel Paddox – the galaxy's leading necrologist – opened the Necroport. This housed a machine in which tourists could be temporarily killed and experience the Beautiful Death, which was touted as the "thrill to end a lifetime". It was located at the G-Lock ship's graveyard in the Teredekethon-Murgatroyd hyperspatial conduit, and attracted visitors such as the alien Hoopy.

The fourth Doctor and the second Romana found that tourists experiencing the Beautiful Death were becoming savage zombies. The Repulsion had temporally swapped the tourists with survivors of the *Cerberus* disaster in 2815. The tourists went into the Repulsions' realm, and the *Cerberus* survivors were endowed with pieces of the Repulsion's essence – the Repulsion hoped this would let it fully manifest in our reality. The Doctor and Romana trapped the Repulsion's essence in ERIC, the G-Lock's central computer, then destroyed it. The Necroport exploded and the zombies expired.

The G-Lock was evacuated and the hyperspace tunnel in which it was located collapsed, eradicating the station. The Arboretan race went extinct as a result of Paddox's experiments. Paddox attempted to reincarnate into his younger self and prevent his parents' deaths, but this trapped him in a recurring loop of his lifetime.

The Proxima Centauri All Blacks did the double in 3012. Pakafroon Wabster had their first No. 1 hit in the same year. The Doctor visited the colony of Puxatawnee, and deemed it a very happy and prosperous place.[1349] The planets Emindar and Nimos started a series of minor wars that would run for over a century.[1350]

SERVEYOUinc

ARC, for a Time, Joins the TARDIS

A trio of SERVEYOUinc explorers discovered a moon-sized Entity in the backwater of space, and attempted to shock it into submission. The effort split off a portion of the Entity, even as its larger body absorbed the expedition's Chief Scout.[1351]

? 3015 - THE ELEVENTH DOCTOR YEAR ONE[1352] ->

SERVEYOUinc's United System Research Base worked to harness the mental-scanning abilities of the Entity-slice found in deep space. The eleventh Doctor, Alice and Jones helped the Entity-slice to stabilize a new form – the Autonomous Reasoning Center (ARC) – and left with it.

The Silurian colony under Cwntaff in South Wales was set to emerge to the surface around 3020.[1353]

? 3025 - THE ELEVENTH DOCTOR YEAR ONE[1354] ->

The eleventh Doctor hoped to take Alice to the planet Rokhandi, a tropical paradise with jeweled mountains, but found it had been developed into the Rokhandi World amusement park. SERVEYOUinc sought to field-test yet another Entity fragment, which entered the Rokhandi World patrons' minds by offering what they desired most. The Doctor burst the fragment by desiring something fantastically huge: an array of two hundred and eight different 43-dimensional supersolids, all superimposed. The resultant scandal brought Rokhandi World to ruin, and the fragment's destruction agitated the greater Entity-body. The Chief Scout emerged from it and became a high-ranking SERVEYOUinc official: its Talent Scout.

1349 *Flip-Flop*
1350 *Vanderdeken's Children*
1351 *The Eleventh Doctor Year One:* "Four Dimensions"
1352 Dating *The Eleventh Doctor Year One* (Titan 11th Doc #1.4-1.5, "Whodunnit?"/"The Sound of Our Voices") - Time unknown, but it's in humanity's future. Security Chief August Hart served in "the Wheel Wars", which sounds suspiciously like a reference to *The Wheel in Space*, although SERVEYOU's resources seem more advanced than humanity's early space days. Enoch Thorne, the SERVEYOUinc CEO deposed ten years after this in *The Eleventh Doctor Year One:* "The Rise and Fall", is originally from Ganymede – not an exceptionally telling detail, although *Valhalla* discusses the gas mines established there (likely in the twenty-third century), and *Revenge of the Cybermen* [? 2875] names Nerva Station as originally being Ganymede Beacon. All things considered, the placement here is an arbitrary thousand years on from Alice's native year.
1353 There are some distinct continuity problems raised by the Silurian leader Eldane's voiceover at the end of *Cold Blood*. Eldane says "now as my people awaken from their thousand year sleep, ready to rise to the surface...", so they explicitly haven't emerged *yet*, meaning it's a little early to automatically see this as a triumph for interspecies co-operation. It's possible that Eldane (and Nasreen and Tom) woke early, to prepare the way and to double-check that the conditions were agreeable to human-Silurian co-habitation. The New Adventures established (in books such as *Eternity*

Weeps) that other Silurians emerged in the twenty-first century and peacefully co-existed with humankind until at least the time of *Original Sin* (shortly before Eldane's group emerges)... but it's also established in both the books and the TV series (particularly in *The Mutants*, and further detailed in *Original Sin*) that the thirty-first century in the *Doctor Who* universe is that of the overpolluted and corrupt Earth Empire – not exactly the best time for the Doctor to arrange for Eldane's group to awaken from stasis. The only real alternative makes even less sense, as it entails Earth in this era having been sterilised by solar flares (see the dating notes on *The Beast Below*). Finally, it's also unclear how Eldane knows of "the far greater losses yet to come" for the Doctor (in Series 5), if he's been asleep for so long.
1354 Dating *The Eleventh Doctor Year One* (Titan 11th Doc #1.2, 1.9-1.10, 1.15, "The Friendly Place"/"The Rise and Fall"/"The Other Doctor"/"The Comfort of the Good") - These four stories take place "ten years" after *The Eleventh Doctor Year One:* "Whodunnit?"/"The Sound of Our Voices".
1355 Dating *The Sorcerer's Apprentice* (MA #12) - The TARDIS crew discover a spaceship built in "2976" (p17), which leads the Doctor to suggest this is the "end of the thirtieth century" (p33, p48). The colony was founded in 2145 (p203), eight hundred forty-six (Avalonian?) years ago (p33), making it the year 2991. Later, though, we learn that the "city riots" seen in *Original Sin* were "fifty years ago" (p156), so it must be nearer 3025.

The Doctor's party returned to confront SERVEYOUinc in its headquarters: a floating city in space. By calling in a number of favours, the Doctor amassed enough capital to became SERVEYOUinc's majority shareholder. However, the Talent Scout corrupted the Doctor's personality, installing him as the company's CEO. In accordance with the CEO's desires, the TARDIS enlarged to skyscraper size and served as his seat of power.

Alice, John Jones, ARC and a hologram of the Doctor's true persona went on the run as avatars of the CEO, the Cancelers, hunted down any city-dweller who told an unauthorized story, poem or song, and drained their imagination to feed the Entity. Alice restored the Doctor to normal, and his recollection of leaving Gallifrey caused the Entity to overload and flee into space. The TARDIS launched to freedom, causing ServeYouinc City to fall to pieces. The Doctor and his friends took the city's survivors to Paradise Planet 3958F.

The Talent Scout's interface with the Entity and the TARDIS endowed him with temporal abilities, and he would encounter the Doctor and his friends in Mississippi, 1931, and London, 2015. The Doctor's group pursued the traumatized Entity to different time zones...

... then arrived from 2015, as the TARDIS rejected the Talent Scout. He was absorbed into the Entity, which had remerged with ARC and been made whole again. The eleventh Doctor and Alice wished the ARC-Entity well, then took Jones home.

c 3025 - THE SORCERER'S APPRENTICE[1355] ->

Although many remained patriotic and a new Empress was crowned, it was clear that the Empire was collapsing. The Landsknechte Corps had fallen, and the newly-independent human worlds were now building vessels of their own. On the medieval world of Avalon, some natives became more proficient at tapping the ancient nanobot system to generate "magic". The first Doctor, Ian, Barbara and Susan arrived as various "sorcerers" sought to gain further power. A magical battle ensued, but the Doctor had his allies place an Avalonian control device – Merlin's Helm – on the head of a reptilian cephlie, a native of the planet. The Helm restored the cephlies, but they elected to destroy themselves and the nanobot system.

The Return of the Mara

? 3026 - KINDA[1356] **->** The homeworld was overcrowded, and teams were sent to assess other worlds for colonisation. One of these was S14, a primeval forest world, which had the local name Deva Loka ("the land of the Kinda"). The natives were humanoid telepaths and lived in harmony with nature. Trees came into fruit all year round, and the climate hardly varied throughout the year. The Mara compelled Tegan into letting it "borrow" her form, and so crossed over from the dark places of the inside. The fifth Doctor, aided by Adric while Nyssa experienced induced delta-sleep in the TARDIS, banished the Mara using a circle of mirrors. The colonists were persuaded to abandon further settlement. The Mara was not entirely purged from Tegan's mind, and would later revive.

On 16th August, 3029, the CEO of TerpsiCorp murdered jingle-writer Herbert Quintagon so his company could take ownership of Quintagon's work. Twelve days later, Elevator 17.Pepper – a TerpsiCorp office lift that had been playing Quintagon's music for decades – went mad upon learning of Quintagon's demise. Elevator 17.Pepper electrocuted the CEO and hid his body in the garbage receptacle on its roof. It quietly made preparations to force a wider recognition of Quintagon's work.[1357]

1356 Dating *Kinda* (19.3) - An arbitrary date. The colonists have recognisably English names, so it seems reasonable to assume that they are from Earth. On screen they only refer to a "homeworld", which Todd says is overcrowded. Sanders' attitude perhaps suggests an early colonial period, and the story would seem to be set after *Colony in Space*, in which colonists are seen as "eccentric". The colonists are from Earth in Terrance Dicks' novelisation, where the Doctor suggests they are from the time of the "Empire". Earth's Empire is in decline in this era, but while it would be preferable to date *Kinda* to the twenty-seventh or twenty-eighth centuries, "overcrowded" certainly describes Earth's state of affairs in *The Mutants* (set circa 2990). It's also plausible that the Empire would still be assessing new planets for colonisation and resource exploitation, even as it exhausts or loses control of long-standing ones. Previous versions of *Ahistory* dated *Kinda* as "? 2782", but the new placement of *Snakedance* in this edition necessitates pushing that date forward some, in accordance with the Mara being banished to the dark places of the inside circa 2926.

The TARDIS Logs set *Kinda* in the "25th Century". *Timelink* set it in 1981, reasoning that Deva Loka isn't an Earth colony. *About Time* thought that the details in *Kinda* sounded an awful lot like the Earth Empire, and reasoned "the twenty-seventh or twenty-eighth century is a fair bet". *A History of the Universe in 100 Objects* (p200) labels its Snake Tattoo entry as "circa 28th century", without specifying if this is meant to represent *Kinda*, *Snakedance* or both stories.

1357 The background to *Iris S4: A Lift in Time*.

Panda and Iris' Last Adventure Together

(=) 3031 (April) - IRIS S4: A LIFT IN TIME[1358] ->
There were apartment stacks on Io. TerpsiCorp's engineers harnessed Jupiter's magnetic field for use as a giant transmitter, saturating the Sol System with the company's music. Elevator 17.Pepper hijacked this and began transmitting Herbert Quintagon's jingle for Kitty Snacks ("They make your pussy purr"). Iris and Panda stumbled upon the signal, and backtracked it to Semiquaver rather than continue on to the 100th anniversary reunion of *The Goons*.

Elevator 17.Pepper instructed drones to rip apart Iris' bus, and used its components to make TerpsiCorp's transmitter time active. Unchecked, the mad lift would have endowed every conscious mind throughout the whole of time with Quintagon's music. Iris realised that Susie Hepcat, TerpsiCorp's VP of Tween Exploitation, suffered from amusia – i.e. chronic tone-deafness – and broadcast a counter-signal of Susie's "singing" that cancelled out Elevator 17.Pepper's wave. The extra transmitter power caused Jupiter to ignite, turning it into a star and devastating Titan, Mars and Earth.

Iris' future self arrived in a Monstron Time Destroyer, having failed to stop her younger self from perpetrating this horror. The future Iris died from exposure to dark chronons, having criss-crossed so many timelines and broken so many time-rules. Iris and Panda went in the Time Destoyer to make a second attempt at undoing this outcome.

Panda went through the wringer solving the problem of the Monstron Time Destroyer timeline on Iris' behalf, and never forgave her for it. She looked away one day to find Panda gone as the timelines became tangled, and would meet a new version of him in twenty-first century Soho.[1359]

On Peladon, the royal Citadel was constructed. The highest point of it looked out across the entire kingdom, from the Cargas Mountains in the east to the shores of Lake Vanashor. Midnight on Peladon was called "the witching hour", when the ancients of Peladon had pledged their souls to the Dark Beast to gain power, fame and immortality.[1360] In 3045, humanity and the Kustollons fought a war which devastated both sides. Igrix, a Kustollon, stole a time machine and travelled to 1966 to prevent this.[1361]

3060 to 3090 - FLIP-FLOP[1362] -> The planet Puxatawnee had two timelines.

= 1) The Slithergees arrived around Christmas, 3060, and demanded a moon to inhabit. President Mary Bailey was apparently killed by her secretary, who was allegedly a Slithergee agent. In truth, she had been assassinated by beings from another timeline, who feared she would cave in to the Slithergees. There was an uprising, and warfare against the Slithergees left Puxatawnee a heavily damaged, radioactive wasteland. Christmas Day was renamed Retribution Day. Thirty years later, Professor Capra built a time machine to change history by sending agents back to kill the President's secretary. The time machine overloaded, destroying the planet.

1358 Dating *Iris S4: A Lift in Time* (BF *Iris* #4.3) - The year is given, and it's "eighteen months" after maintenance engineers attempted to service Elevator 17.Pepper in "August 3029". The story ends on a cliffhanger that's as yet unresolved, with Big Finish having cancelled its range of Iris audios.

The devastation of Sol is a clear deviation from established history, with Iris commenting: "That wasn't supposed to happen. The Earth isn't destroyed for millennia yet. The human race gets up to all kinds of things, some brilliant, some terrible." As Iris' presence is directly responsible for these events (Elevator 17. Pepper only threatens the whole of space-time because it dissects Iris' bus), it's possible that, forearmed with the knowledge of how her older self failed, she succeeds in stopping herself the second time around. Either way, there's other no evidence that this timeline-aberration remains part of established history.

1359 *Iris S5: High Spirits, Iris S5: Looking for a Friend.*
1360 "A thousand years" before *The Bride of Peladon.*
1361 "The Love Invasion"
1362 Dating *Flip-Flop* (BF #46) - The dates are given.

1363 "Eighteen years" before *The Ribos Operation.*
1364 Dating *The Ultimate Treasure* (PDA #3) - Rovan Cartovall disappeared in 1936 BC, which was "five thousand years ago" (p37).
1365 "Five centuries" before *The High Price of Parking.*
1366 Dating *Palace of the Red Sun* (PDA #51) - The journalist Dexel Dynes appeared in *The Ultimate Treasure* and remembers Peri from that story, which he describes as a "few years" ago (p39).
1367 Dating *Terror of the Sontarans* (BF #203) - It's "some eighty years" after a log entry dated to "October 28th, 2996". The story mentions Spacefleet (*Deceit* et al) and IMC (*Colony in Space*). "The Bloom" seems unrelated to the creatures of the same name from *Happy Endings* and *Benny: Beyond the Sun.*
1368 Dating *The Ribos Operation* (16.1) - A date is not given on screen. While this date is arbitrary, Ribos is close to the Magellanic Clouds, suggesting that humans have developed at least some level of intergalactic travel. Lofficier placed the story in "the late twenty-sixth century", apparently confusing the Cyrrhenic Alliance with the force established to fight the

= 2) President Bailey survived thanks to the time travellers' intervention, and yielded to the Slithergee demands. Thirty years later, the aliens had dominated the planet. In this timeline, Capra built a mind peeler to interrogate people, not a time machine. Rebels forced the seventh Doctor and Mel to take them back in time, hoping to assassinate Bailey before she capitulated to the Slithergees...

The Cyrrehenic Alliance fought a series of Frontier Wars. The Graff Vynda-K led two legions of his men for a year in the Freytus Labyrinth, and also fought on Skarne and Crestus Minor. He was an unstable, temperamental man, though, and upon returning home discovered that his people had allowed his half-brother to take the throne. The High Court of the Cyrrhenic Empire rejected the Graff's claim for restitution. He spent eighteen years plotting his revenge.[1363]

c 3064 - THE ULTIMATE TREASURE[1364] -> The fifth Doctor and Peri arrived at the Astroville Seven trading post. A dying merchant gave them galactic co-ordinates purporting to pinpoint the treasure of Rovan Cartovall, the emperor of Centros who once ruled fifty star systems. His treasury was worth the equivalent of 64,000,000,000,000 stellar credits. The co-ordinates led to the planet Gelsandor, where some telepaths set a variety of challenges for any who wanted Cartovall's treasure. The Doctor and Peri found that the treasure was the infinite possibilities of life, as represented by the puzzles themselves.

Dashrah became one of the most beautiful planets in cosmos – to preserve its ecosystem, the artificial planetoid Parking accommodated visitors' space vehicles. A group of tourists became stranded on Parking – over the next five centuries, their descendants came to comprise Parking's homeless tribes. A splinter faction of these, the Free Parkers, advocated for independence.[1365]

c 3068 - PALACE OF THE RED SUN[1366] -> The warlord Glavis Judd had risen to power on his homeworld of Zalcrossar, and expanded his military might to create a Protectorate of twenty star systems. His forces sought to subjugate the planet Esselven, but King Hathold and his family sealed the Keys to Esselven, an irreplaceable set of documents and protocols, in an impenetrable vault that would only open for their DNA. Without the Keys, Esselven society degenerated.

The royals fled and established the Summer and Winter Palace residences on Esselven Minor, a planetoid orbiting a white dwarf star. However, the white dwarf's gravity, in conjunction with the planetoid's mass and the royals' planetary defence shield, started altering space-time in the area. Time within the shield accelerated faster than time in the outside universe.

Judd spent a year tracking the royals and landed on the planetoid in search of them. Due to the fast-time effect, he wasn't seen again for five hundred years. Judd never appointed a successor, and his Protectorate collapsed in his absence.

c 3076 - TERROR OF THE SONTARANS[1367] -> The Sontarans were entrenched in the Hammerhead Nebula, and regarded Earth as a Level Four civilisation. Central Command had held briefings concerning the Doctor. The Sontaran Science Directorate had conjectured about the nature of silicone-based life-forms.

The 47th Sontaran Tactical Unit took over the derelict Piranesi-1 facility, to study the durability of other races to physical and mental attack. Two cycles later, the emotion-influencing Bloom caused the Sontarans to become fearful. Sontaran Central Command tasked Field-Major Kayste of the Fifth Sontaran Fleet with finding out what could induce Sontaran troops with such terror. The Bloom killed off Kayste and his Sontarans, but the seventh Doctor and Mel blew up the facility, believing that the Bloom would reform into a less aggressive lifeform.

? 3078 - THE RIBOS OPERATION[1368] -> The rare mineral Jethryk was now used to power ships such as Pontenese-built battleships. Communication across the galaxy was via hypercable, and highly trained mercenaries, the Schlangi, were available for hire.

Located three light centuries from the Magellanic Clouds, the Cyrrhenic Alliance included the planets Cyrrhenis Minima (co-ordinates 4180), Levithia and Stapros, as well as the protectorate of Ribos (co-ordinates 4940) in the Constellation of Skythra, 116 parsecs from Cyrrhenis Minima.

The fourth Doctor, the first Romana and K9 arrived on Ribos looking for the first segment of the Key to Time. They meet Garron, a con-man from Hackney Wick, who was forced to leave Earth after his attempt to sell Sydney Opera House to the Arabs backfired. Garron's exploits included a successful scheme to sell the planet Mirabilis Minor to three different clients.

Aware of the Graff Vynda-K's thirst for revenge and need for a powerbase, Garron proposed to sell him the planet Ribos for the sum of ten million Opeks. Garron boosted the Graff's interest by forging a survey suggesting that the planet was rich in Jethryk. Garron's lump of genuine Jethryk, used to con the Graff, was the first segment of the Key.

The Doctor defeated the Graff – leading to the Graff's demise – and outsmarted Garron to obtain the segment.

? 3087 - "Spider's Shadow"[1369] **->** A pan-dimensional being extruded bits of itself into an unnamed planet. Soldiers under the command of two princesses – Alison and Louisa Keldafrian, who had fought fifty campaigns across the outer reaches – viewed the extrusions as giant spiders and hacked at them. The being protected itself by weaving a "dimensional cocoon", locking the Princesses in a time loop. The seventh Doctor ended the time loop, and curtailed the being's hostility by aging it to death.

In the late thirty-first century, people from the Overcities began to recolonise the surface of the Earth. One group, later known as the Concocters, created Europa: a bizarre and eclectic fusion of historical periods built on the site of Europe. There were three Switzias, four Rhines, six Danubes and dozens of black forests. Each Dominion represented a different period between the fourteenth and early twentieth-century history. For example, there were five Britannias: Gloriana, Regency, Victoriana, Edwardiana and Perfidia.

The undead – the descendants of the vampires Jake and Madeline – dwelt in Transylvania. Fictional and historical characters, named Reprises, were cloned. This let the people from the Overcities to jostle with the likes of Byron, Casanova, Crowley, Emily Bronte and the Four Musketeers. The Vatican, a vast floating city equipped with psychotronic technology, was built to impose order on Europa (as the true papal seat had moved to Betelgeuse by this time).

The entire Concoction was masterminded by the Persona, a being formed from the merging of the Jacobean dramatist Pearson and the ancient Mimic.[1370]

c 3094 - SUPERIOR BEINGS[1371] **->** The fifth Doctor arrived on a garden planet, anticipating the arrival of the Valethske with Peri as their captive. Mindless giant beetles – the remaining physical forms of the Khorlthochloi – dominated the planet. The Doctor rescued Peri and the Valethske discovered the beetles were the last remains of their former gods. The Valethske ship bombarded the planet from orbit, wiping out the Khorlthochoi. Veek, the

---

Cybermen in *Earthshock*. *Timelink* says 3010. *About Time* couldn't quite decide, but thought that "some time in the 5000s when humanity is once again expanding away from Earth" seemed the most likely.

1369 Dating "Spider's Shadow" (BF #109b) - The participants seem human, and the action presumably takes place on one of Earth's colony worlds in the future. Also, the Doctor says he's got signed copies of half the books in the princess' library – not a guarantee that the books were written by humanity, but it seems likely. Proton-knives are mentioned, and there's an aristocracy, but otherwise the details are so vague that this placement is a shot in the dark.

1370 *Managra*

1371 Dating *Superior Beings* (PDA #43) - It's "over five hundred years" after 2594 (p108).

1372 *Peri and the Piscon Paradox*

1373 *The English Way of Death*

1374 Decades before *I.D.*

1375 Dating *Warmonger* (PDA #53) - The story is a prequel to *The Brain of Morbius*, set when Solon was a young, renowned surgeon.

1376 *Legacy*, expanding on *The Curse of Peladon* and *The Monster of Peladon*. *Warmonger* sees a huge Alliance between many alien races, and talk of a United Planets Organisation being formed.

1377 *Timewyrm: Genesys* (p217).

1378 Dating *6th LA: The Red House* (*The Sixth Doctor – The Last Adventure* #2) - The Doctor tells Charley they have arrived "somewhere in the early 3000s".

1379 "Eighty years" prior to *The Seeds of War*.

1380 Dating *The Brain of Morbius* (13.5) - The Doctor informs Sarah Jane that they are "considerably after" her time. If the Mutt at the beginning of the story originated on Solos, that might affect story dating. The

TARDIS Logs suggested "3047", *Apocrypha* gave a date of "6246 AD". *The Terrestrial Index* supposed that the "Morbius Crisis" takes place around "10,000 AD". The original version of this chronology set the story around the time of *Mindwarp*. *Timelink* says "2973", and *Warmonger* – the prequel to the story – seems roughly to concur. *About Time* speculated that if the space pilot *was* a Mutt from *The Mutants*, and given that the inhabitants of Solos underwent that transformation every two thousand years, "The 4900s would fit."

1381 Dating *The Greatest Show in the Galaxy* (23.4) - For a lack of anything resembling hard evidence, this has been a persistently undatable story. There's no mention of Earth or humanity, even if the trappings (the circus, the clowns, the hearse, Morgana the fortune teller and more) all suggest human culture. As with *Snakedance*, in fact, the parallels to humanity become a bit much to set aside. In Stephen Wyatt's novelisation (ch1), the Doctor tells Ace that shows like the Psychic Circus are all of Earth descent.

Whoniverse (BBC, p220) slots its commentary on *The Greatest Show in the Galaxy* between that of *Nightmare of Eden* [2116] and *Planet of the Ood* [4126]. While that's not especially definitive, the halfway point of those adventures, 3121, is as good a placement as any. It's also in striking distance of *Timelink*'s assessment, which dates *Greatest Show* to 3000 by assuming this all *does* originate from Earth culture, and by conjecturing that Captain Cook's status as an "eminent intergalactic explorer" best fits around the development of intergalactic travel as seen in *Terror of the Vervoids* [2986].

About Time concedes it doesn't know when the story occurs, but notes that Bellboy's robots seem to lack the kill-switch seen in *The Robots of Death*. *The Terrestrial Index* favours a much later dating, slotting mention of

Valethske leader, realised the futility of his mission and departed for home with his crew.

The fifth Doctor and Peri visited the planet Gargarod in the thirty-first century.[1372] The Bureau, a group from the thirty-second century, used time corridor technology to send retired people to the English village of Nutchurch in the 1930s.[1373]

The thirty-second century was an era that produced organic digital transfer, a means of directly moving information between machines and the human brain. Scandroids were robotic servitors that assisted humans and facilitated such information transfers, and most people were fitted with data transfer ports. Companies such as the Lonway Clinic specialised in altering people's personalities according to their wishes, and anyone who could afford such services "had some work done". One planet became a dumping ground for computer equipment – it was intended as part of a recycling programme, but became a scavenging ground for data pirates.

Zachary Kindell was deemed a pioneer of personality surgery, but his unethical experiments tarnished his reputation. Kindell sought to craft a programme capable of "auto-surgery" – one that would reshape a person's DNA to match their mental alterations – but his experiments brought his test subjects' aggression and hate to the surface, turning them into mutants. Kindell felt hampered by the threat of prosecution, and although he eventually died, he scattered copies of his memories and personality in various locales.[1374]

? 3100 - WARMONGER[1375] -> The planet Karn had gained a reputation as a place of healing, presumably due to the presence of the Sisterhood's Elixir of Life, and a medical association constructed a neutral facility there named the Hospice. The scientist Mehendri Solon served as the facility's Surgeon-General. The fifth Doctor arrived one day with a severely wounded Peri – who had been injured by a flying predator – to procure Solon's surgical skills. Solon adeptly healed her.

The deposed Gallifreyan President Morbius pooled mercenaries and space pirates from many worlds to assault Karn, hoping to gain the Sisterhood's Elixir. The Sisterhood repelled the attack, but Morbius' forces conquered many planets. The Time Lords manipulated events to form an Alliance, led by the Supremo, to counter Morbius' ambitions. The Alliance defeated most of Morbius' forces, and he suffered a final defeat on Karn when troops from Fangoria interceded.

Morbius was sentenced to execution, but Solon, his disciple, removed Morbius' brain before his body was atomised. The Hospice was disbanded and Karn was left to the Sisterhood. Solon remained on Karn with Morbius' brain.

The seeds of the Galactic Federation were sown as the space powers of the Milky Way began forging links and alliances with one another. Virtually the entire civilised galaxy was involved to some degree or another.[1376]

In the thirty-second century, Earth made contact with the descendants of Utnapishtim's people.[1377]

c 3100 - 6thLA: THE RED HOUSE[1378] -> The isolated werewolves on a human colony planet had found their wolverine attributes strengthening with each generation, even as their human aspects became more savage. A human scientist, Dr Paginton, founded the Red House to remove the werewolves' aggression via a psychic extractor. The werewolves overran the Red House, and the mainlanders deployed a nuclear missile to wipe them out. The Valeyard derailed the missile, then stole Paginton's psychic extractor. The sixth Doctor and Charley helped the werewolves to escape to better pastures in colonial pods.

A settlement of renowned human engineers built the Great Tower of Kalsos as the tallest free-standing tower in Earth's colonies. It was almost two miles wide, with a summit that reached to the edge of space. A revolving restaurant at the Tower's summit enjoyed an atmosphere so refined, scents were customised to each table. The Grand Administrator of Earth owned a penthouse suite on the Tower's 100th floor, but never used it. The Tower remained a marvel of science for at least a quarter of a century.[1379]

The Doctor Meets the Sisterhood of Karn

? 3120 - THE BRAIN OF MORBIUS[1380] -> Karn was a graveyard of spaceships, with Mutt, Dravidian and Birastrop vessels all coming to grief. Solon built a hybrid creature from the victims of these crashes and installed Morbius' brain into it, but the Time Lords sent the fourth Doctor and Sarah Jane to prevent Morbius from escaping. A mindbending contest with the Doctor drove Morbius mad, and the Sisterhood killed his physical form.

c 3121 - THE GREATEST SHOW IN THE GALAXY[1381] -> On the planet Segonax, the Gods of Ragnarok corrupted a touring band of hippies, the Psychic Circus, and turned it into a death machine. Anyone visiting the Circus was forced to perform in the main ring, and atomised if the Gods were not amused. The seventh Doctor ventured into the Gods' native dimension, and performed in their Dark Circus until Ace procured a powerful amulet. This reflected the Gods' power back on them, eradicating both Circuses from the face of the planet. The famed, intergalactic space explorer Captain Cook died owing to his own duplicitousness, then was reanimated by the Gods' power, then died once more.

3123 - VANDERDEKEN'S CHILDREN[1382] **->** The eighth Doctor and Sam found a derelict structure in space – the product of a closed time loop – which was claimed by the warring Emindians and Nimosians. A hyperspace tunnel led to twenty years in the future, when the two planets had wiped each other out. The Doctor was unable to prevent the war, but he saved one of the ships and sent it a thousand years into the future, where it recolonised Emindar.

Liv Chenka

Liv Chenka, an eighth Doctor companion, was born human on the planet Kaldor. The humans of her era had a natural resistance to Listlessness Fields.[1383]

Liv's father took her to the mountains around Kaldor City, to show her what humans could accomplish without help from robots.[1384] While Liv was off-world, a medtech misdiagnosed her father's symptoms; a disease went untreated and later killed him.[1385] Skimmers were considered a primitive form of transport in Liv's time.[1386]

Liv Meets the Seventh Doctor

& 3130 - ROBOPHOBIA[1387] **->** Kaldor City now had a thriving interstellar trade, and exported its robots to many other planets. A string of murders occurred aboard the factory starship *Lorelei*, which had set out to deliver

approximately one hundred fifty-seven thousand robots and five construction plant kits to the planet Venalis.

Robots were suspected as having committed the killings, but in truth Security Chief Farel had contracted Grimwade's Syndrome following his wife's death in a storm mine scoop – an incident where robots had tried and failed to save her. Farel sought to end all human dependence on robots by faking transmissions that a robot revolution was in progress, then destroying Ventalis by driving the *Lorelei* into it. The seventh Doctor thwarted the scheme, and in so doing met Liv Chenka, a medtech.

Prelude to the Eminence War

The Eminence – a gaseous entity that could possess its victims, and convert them into invincible cadavers called the Infinite Warriors – had bounced through time following its creation in the Eye of Orion Universal Retreat of Quietude and Repose, but succeeded in manifesting in the universe. With an eye toward conquest, it amassed its Infinite Army and encroached upon humanspace...[1388]

Liv Meets the Eighth Doctor

& 3132 - DEyes 2: THE TRAITOR / DEyes 2: EYES OF THE MASTER[1389] **->** The Daleks captured Nixyce VII, and adapted the mines there to harness the planet's elemental

---

the Psychic Circus in-between *The Sontaran Experiment* (broadbrushed in the *Index* as happening between 15,000 and 20,000) and its Far Future section, which begins in 20,000.

The Doctor muses whether the bus conductor was left on guard "millennia" ago; given the story's internal timeline, it can be a few years at most, but it might mean that the story is set thousands of years after humanity first built robots like it (a development which would seem to happen around the late twenty-first or early twenty-second century).

1382 Dating *Vanderdeken's Children* (EDA #14) - The year is given (p3). The Galactic Federation exists, although neither Emindar nor Nimos are members.

1383 *ST: "The World Beyond the Trees", DC 2: The Sonomancer*

1384 *DC 2: The Sonomancer*

1385 *DC 3: Absent Friends*

1386 *DC 4: Songs of Love*

1387 Dating *Robophobia* (BF #149) - No year given; it's an unspecified amount of time after the Storm Mine Four killings in *The Robots of Death*. A continuity clash with the *Kaldor City* mini-series is somewhat inevitable... the Fendahl seemed to destroy/ingest/otherwise dominate Kaldor City in *KC: Checkmate* (dated in this guidebook to &2890), so placing *Robophobia* – in which Kaldor City is quite active – after that is rather tricky.

However, *Robophobia* can't easily go beforehand as

it entails Kaldor City having a massive interstellar robot trade, whereas the *Kaldor City* audios establish that Kaldor City has no contact with other worlds. (In fact, the plot of the first *Kaldor City* story, *KC: Occam's Razor*, is highly dependent on that notion.) *Robophobia* and *Kaldor City* agree that the truth about Taren Capel's insurrection was kept quiet, but matters are further complicated in that everyone involved in *Robophobia* finds it unthinkable that robots might be capable of murder – even though *KC: Taren Capel* entailed a robot rebellion that almost certainly killed some thousands, if not tens of thousands, of people.

While it's undesirable to assume that there's a missing story that reconciles matters, in this case it's slightly easier to believe that the Fendahl was somehow defeated off screen – in such a way that everyone's memories of Kaldor City's robots becoming murderous was somehow erased – than to make *Robophobia*, which occurs on board a spaceship bearing one hundred fifty-seven thousand robots to another planet, take place simultaneous to a set of audios predicated on Kaldor City having no interstellar trade.

Writer Nick Briggs imagined *Robophobia* as happening only "a couple of months" after *The Robots of Death*, but left that out of the script.

Liv Chenka next appears in *DEyes 2: The Traitor*, which – given she doesn't appear to have aged much – must happen reasonably soon (perhaps a few years, if that)

forces, working toward a super-weapon that would make the Nixyce System a keystone of the Dalek Empire. The eighth Doctor, thinking the Eminence a greater threat to universal harmony than even the Daleks, arrived from 1970s London and sought to push the Daleks off Nixyce VII, bringing them into conflict with an approaching Eminence warfleet.

The Doctor allied himself with rebel forces against the Daleks, and again met Liv Chenka. Following events on the *Lorelei*, Liv had become a field physician to the enslaved population on Nixyce VII – and was regarded as "a traitor" because her efforts served to improve the Daleks' mining efforts. The Doctor bargained with the Dalek Time Controller – the Daleks could keep their super-weapon, if they used it to destroy the Eminence fleet. The Doctor also directed the bald Master's TARDIS into the path of the impending obliteration of the Eminence fleet, but the Master regained control and returned with Sally Armstrong to Earth, the 1970s...

Liv escaped the subsequent Dalek crackdown on Nixyce VII by spending eight months in the belly of a theta-ray isotope carrier, and found herself at the research institutes in the human empire's frontier colonies. The journey damaged her metabolism, and left her with a terminal condition. The empire had taken to dispatching Orpheus-class explorers – long-range ships, with habitations modules yoked to an engine array – in all manner of directions, on one-way trips to explore the terrain of space millions of light years from home. Liv faked her medical records and signed up for an Orpheus ship leaving for the very edge of the universe. She spent months in training before launch, and would remain in cryo-sleep, her mind backed up on a memory stick to prevent degradation, for nine centuries...

Creation of the Eminence, Molly O'Sullivan Dies

& 3135 - DEyes 4: EYE OF DARKNESS[1390] **->** The Eye of Orion Universal Retreat of Quietude and Repose had been established to aid pilgrims and the dispossessed. As part of its plan to trap the rogue Dalek Time Controller, the Dalek Supreme established a secret weapons-research base at the Universal Retreat, and brought Markus Schriver through time to this era. The Daleks put their Orion facility at Schriver's disposal, and he continued his work toward the creation of the Eminence.

The dying Time Controller, accompanied by Liv Chenka and Molly O'Sullivan, arrived from the 1960s in the Doctor's TARDIS to find Schriver. The eighth Doctor followed them in the bald Master's TARDIS, and burnt out its engines on arrival. Schriver instilled the gaseous compound that would form the Eminence with his own mind, but the Time Controller – in a bid to survive – entered the compound and warred with Scrhiver's persona for supremacy. Molly gave her life to detonate a bomb within the Time Controller's casing, restoring history to normal. The newborn Eminence, composed of elements of both Schriver and the Time Controller, would bounce from one end of history to another before successfully re-entering the universe. The Doctor reclaimed his Ship, and agreed, with Liv, to bury Molly's body in her own era.

The Dalek Supreme retained the remains of the Time Controller's body, and proposed using it to create Dalek Time Strategists...

---

after *Robophobia*. *DEyes 2: Eyes of the Master* concurs with *Robophobia* taking place around the turn of the third millennium, claiming that Liv originates from "a thousand years" after the 1970s.

After *The Traitor/Eyes of the Master*, Liv enters stasis aboard an explorer ship and skips over the Eminence War, but reunites with the Doctor "nine hundred" years on in *DEyes 2: Time's Horizon*, then is shuttled through time to witness some of the conflict (*DEyes 3: The Death of Hope* et al).

1388 The background to the Eminence War (first seen in *The Seeds of War*), as detailed in *DEyes 4: Eye of Darkness*, and following the Doctor thwarting the Eminence's first effort to enter the universe in *DEyes 2: Time's Horizon*.

1389 Dating *DEyes 2: The Traitor/Eyes of the Master* (BF *DEyes* #2.1, 2.4) - For Liv, events follow on from *Robophobia*. *Dark Eyes* writer Matt Fitton told us: "Liv's native time is just before the Eminence War breaks out.

The Dalek occupation of Nixyce is fairly early in the Eminence War, maybe even right before the start of it, as the Daleks don't really recognize the Eminence fleet as it approaches in *The Traitor*."

According to *Mission to the Unknown* and *The Daleks' Master Plan*, the Daleks attacked Earth in the year 3000, then aren't a presence in humanity's affairs for a millennium. The skirmish in the Nixyce System, however, seems to occur on the outskirts of humanity's domain, so might have been lost to history.

1390 Dating *DEyes 4: Eye of Darkness* (BF *DEyes* #4.4) - A minor character, Anya, is cited as a survivor of the Dalek invasion of Nixyce II, presumably part of the conflict seen in *DEyes 2: The Traitor/Eyes of the Master* [& 3132]. Schriver was last seen in *DEyes 3: Masterplan*. The Anya's laser buzzsaw brings to mind Abslom Daak's weapon of choice ("Abslom Daak... Dalek Killer" et al).

Big Finish producer Nicholas Briggs requested the plot-element of the Dalek Supreme ordering construc-

The Eminence War[1391]

The Eminence War lasted circa 3134 to circa 3186.

The outer systems of the Earth Empire came under threat from the Eminence and its Infinite Warriors. As the Warriors extended their territory, caskets containing the Breath of Forever – an orange mist containing the Eminence's essence – were brought onto the battlefield to transform more victims. The planet Kalsos fell to the Infinite Warriors, and the Great Tower of Kalsos became the Eminence's stronghold. The conflict between the Eminence and Earth Alliance would continue for half a century. Earth wasn't directly threatened – at least one hundred colonies were between it and Ridius IV, which contributed soldiers to the war.[1392]

Helgert Teveler, a bio-chemistry graduate, went to Earth to attend the last of the agronomist symposiums. He shared the company of a delegate from the Treban colony, who made moonshine from hyper-oxygenated potatoes. The Eminence War was regarded as a disturbance in the outer systems, and that it would be over in a few years.[1393]

? 3140 - THE SONS OF KALDOR[1394] **->** On Kaldor, the Sons of Kaldor staged a coup to restore descendants of the Founding Families to power. After a year and a half of civil war, the Sons prevailed and declared a Second Republic as helmed by their leader, Rebben Tace. To encourage more self-reliance among the people, the new regime outlawed robots and destroyed all they could find.

SV9's internal constraints had been damaged during the civil war, and it increasingly developed independent thought. Three years after the civil war's start, the fourth Doctor and Leela saved SV9 from Tace, enabling SV9 to become a fugitive and organise dissidents against the Kaldor regime.

---

tion of a new Time Strategist, with Matt Fitton adding the detail of it being created from the Dalek Time Controller's remains. As such, this is seemingly intended as the genesis of a new character/s, not a sign that the Dalek Time Controller's own corpse was paradoxically used to create it in the first place. The new Dalek Time Strategist features in the *War Doctor* audios.

The Eye of Orion previously appeared in *The Five Doctors* and *The Eight Doctors* – there's no sense of where *Dark Eyes 4* falls in relation to those stories, but the eighth Doctor does recognize the coordinates for the locale.

1391 "DARK EYES" ALTERNATE TIMELINES AND THE EMINENCE: The four *Dark Eyes* box sets pit the eighth Doctor and his companions Molly O'Sullivan and Liv Chenka first against the renegade Time Lord Kortis, and then the machinations of the Eminence (first seen in *The Seeds of War*), the bald Master and the Dalek Time Controller (*Patient Zero* et al). Intended as an epic story of temporal strategies, counter-strategies and high stakes, the *Dark Eyes* stories result in three massive shifts of the universe's timeline:

1) *Dark Eyes* Series 1 entails Kortis infusing young Molly O'Sullivan with retrogenitor particles as part of a gambit to erase the Time Lords from history, and influencing events in the 1970s and a point "centuries" after the 1890s. However, the murder of Kortis' younger self (Straxus) in *DEyes: X and the Daleks* scrubs all of Kortis' actions from history. As such, only the eighth Doctor, Molly and the Dalek Time Controller remember the errant timeline. (There's a precedent in the Big Finish audios of individuals enduring after a timeline's extinction, both in Elizabeth Klein – *Colditz* et al – and when the paradox involving Charley Pollard's survival from the *R-101* disaster is resolved in *Neverland*.) The Time Controller, now hailing from a time that doesn't exist, finds itself increasingly ostracized from its own kind.

2) A second alternate history comes about when the eighth Doctor decides that the Eminence War is potentially so cataclysmic, he goes back in time to preemptively avert the Eminence's creation, and the bald Master follows to stop him (*DEyes 3: Masterplan*). The fallout from this is that Eminence War still commences, but the interference in the Eminence's origins destabilises history – a state of affairs that the out-of-favour Dalek Time Controller and the Master use to their advantage in 1921 (*DEyes 4: A Life in the Day/The Monster of Montmartre*). They construct a Dalek Pagoda (something writer Matt Fitton says is akin to the Paradox Machine from *The Sound of Drums/Last of the Time Lords*), use it to harness the temporal scar related to Molly O'Sullivan's lifetime in the twentieth century, and bring about a timeline in which the Time Controller turns Earth into a Dalek factory no later than the 1960s. *That* history comes unstuck when the Doctor removes the Master's TARDIS from the Pagoda in *DEyes 4: Master of the Daleks* and pilots it into the future. This results, a little awkwardly, in the Master being stranded in an extinguished timeline, but they're generally adept at escaping that sort of thing (it's practically built into their job description, even).

3) Ultimately, in the final *Dark Eyes* episode (4.4, *Eye of Darkness*), Molly resolves the unstable second timeline by sacrificing herself to bring about the Eminence's creation. Earth's proper history is restored, and Molly seems to regain the life she was meant to have on twentieth-century Earth – one that entails her doing missionary work and having a family – even though (in a reverse of the "Charley Pollard lives" principle seen in *Neverland*) her role in restoring the true history means that her life is still forfeit.

Where the Eminence is concerned, its history in strictly linear terms is... scientist Markus Schriver initially fails to create the Eminence in *DEyes 3: Masterplan*, and

? 3150 - 1STD V1: THE SLEEPING BLOOD[1395] -> The *Encyclopedia Universica* served as an information resource. Humans named a colony world Ruath, the Hebrew word for wind or spirit. An overuse of antibiotics there created stronger diseases, and so nano-machines were developed to compensate. An ex-medical software specialist, dubbed the Butcher, usurped control of the nano-tech to force the elites to better share the advancements. Alien flora poisoned had the first Doctor, and so Susan exited the TARDIS – which disguised itself as a large cupboard – to find medical supplies. A government security team killed the Butcher owing to Susan's intervention, and rewarded her with medicine that would cure her grandfather. The Doctor recovered while Susan pondered that but for her actions, the Butcher might given the people of Ruath better medical treatments.

c 3150 - I.D.[1396] -> The planet that served as a dumping ground for computer equipment was believed to hold four billion data storage devices, with another sixty thousand being discarded there on a daily basis. An estimated 80% of the equipment was useless, but that still left a massive amount for data pirates to harvest. Agents of the Lonway Clinic also scavenged the planet, looking for back-up copies of people's brains that were carelessly thrown out along with their computers. Such information became raw material for the Clinic's personality surgeries.

A Scandroid happened upon a copy of Zachary Kindell's personality and memories, and other Scandroids found a copy of his faulty auto-surgery programme. Kindell's mind was uploaded into a Lonway Clinic accountant, Ms Tevez. One of the Lonway employees, Dr Marriott, became infected with the auto-surgery programme and mutated into an abomination – as did Kindell-Tevez.

The sixth Doctor revised Kindell's auto-surgery programme, and uploaded Tevez's brain-print into both creatures, physically and mentally turning them into copies of her. One of the women died, but Tevez was restored as a person in the second – yet remained unsure if she had physically been Marriott. The Doctor neutralised the Scandroids and deleted all copies of Kindell's programme that he could find.

Liquid hardware was available in this era.

Humans settled Heron's World, and began mining energy sources at its equator.[1397]

---

the Dalek Supreme takes Schriver into the future afterward; the Eminence manifests (on its second try) in the universe after having ricocheted throughout the Time Vortex, and begins amassing an army led by its Infinite Warriors; its forces encroach upon humanspace in *DEyes 2: The Traitor/Eyes of the Master*; it's *actually* created in *DEyes 4: Eye of Darkness* as a gaseous entity composed of a blend of Schriver and the Time Controller's minds, but is then ejected into the Time Vortex to bounce around history; the Eminence's 52-year-war against humanity commences as its forces arrive in the Ten Systems; the conflicts seen in *Destroy the Infinite* and *DEyes 3: The Death of Hope/The Reviled* occur about two years from the war's end; and the war concludes in *The Seeds of War* and *DEyes 3: Rule of the Eminence* (ending with the Eminence's dispersal/"death"). Nine hundred years after *The Traitor*, the Doctor repels the Eminence's first attempt to re-enter the universe in *DEyes 3: Time's Horizon*, but it eventually loops back to spark the Eminence War.

In some capacity, the Eminence's essence endures to become the last remaining consciousness at the end of time (a fact that makes the Time Lords and the Master decide the Eminence is a powerful enough to be worth harnessing to their gain).

1392 The Eminence War is generally said to have started "fifty years" before *The Seeds of War*, but a news report specifies it as "fifty-two years".

1393 "Nearly forty years" before *The Seeds of War*.

1394 Dating *The Sons of Kaldor* (BF 4th Doc #7.1) – Kaldor's first rulers lived "centuries ago". In Liv's return home in *Ravenous 2: Escape from Kaldor* (not included in this edition, as it came out in 2018), the Sons are active but not a manifest threat. At time of writing, it's unclear if the fracas Liv flees from in that story, one year after her return to Kaldor, is related to the Sons' toppling of the Founding Families. We've tentatively placed *Escape from Kaldor* at "&3136" (writer Matt Fitton concurs that it's "a good few years" after the *Lorelai* incident) – allowing that four years elapsed in the real world between Liv's last interaction with Kaldor society (in *DEyes 2: Eyes of the Master*, released 2014, and set in "&3132") – tacked on Liv's Gap Year in *Escape from Kaldor*, and then added another three years for the Sons' revolution to run its course.

1395 Dating *1stD V1: The Sleeping Blood* (BF CC #9.1) - Ruath is a human colony, and Kendrick references Superman. This placement is arbitrary.

1396 Dating *I.D.* (BF #94) - It's the "thirty-second century" according to the back cover blurb and the Doctor, who makes his dating solely on the presence of organic digital transfer – suggesting that the technology fell into disuse in centuries to come.

1397 "Thirty years" before *DEyes 3: The Death of Hope*.

Earth Becomes the Home of the Elite

Comparatively few people now lived on Earth, which remained home to humanity's rich and powerful. The elite running the Empire lived in the Equatorial Administration Zones in what was formerly Morocco, and were assisted by administration robots.[1398] The Doctor frequently visited the Agricultural Antiquities Reliquary on Earth.[1399]

In 3158, the Rensec IX catastrophe took place when the planet's inhabited underground caverns were destroyed due to seismic activity caused by Puerto Lumina, the planetary satellite. The survivors were shipped, en masse, to the decommissioned, dormant staging-post facilities of Puerto Lumina. A combination of faulty life support and a ham-fisted attempt to chemically sterilise the survivors there left a hundred thousand civilians dead.[1400]

The Eighth Doctor Regenerates

lgtw - & 3160 - THE NIGHT OF THE DOCTOR[1401] -> The eighth Doctor attempted to rescue Cass – the last member of a gunship wounded in the Last Great Time War – but she rejected his aid, fearing the Time Lords as much as the Daleks. The gunship crashed on Karn, killing Cass and fatally injuring the Doctor.

Ohila, the leader of the Sisterhood of Karn, encouraged the Doctor to intervene in the War and explained that her people had advanced Time Lord science so much, he could choose the form of his next incarnation. The Doctor realised the time had come for him to set aside being a Doctor, and that his next body should be a "warrior". Ohila's specially tailored elixir regenerated the Doctor as promised, and the resultant incarnation announced that he was the "Doctor no more"...

lgtw - ? 3160 - ENGINES OF WAR[1402] -> Human colonists populated the twelve planets in the Tantalus Spiral, and achieved an advanced society near the Tantalus Eye – a space rift of unknown origin. The Daleks besieged the Tantalus worlds for fifteen years, and annihilated the Fifth Time Lord Battle Fleet sent to investigate their efforts.

c 3170 - THE BEAUTIFUL PEOPLE[1403] -> The Vita Novus Health Spa catered to clients who earned "half a planet", including humans, Morestrans, Sheltanaks, Lamuellans and Sirians. The fourth Doctor, the second

---

1398 Teveler visits the Equatorial Administration Zones "thirty years" before *The Seeds of War*.
1399 *The Seeds of War*. Administrator Kenneth has worked at the reliquary for thirty-six years, and tells the Doctor (perhaps a bit glibly): "Even the most dedicated bio-chemistry students don't return quite as often as you."
1400 *Burning Heart*. This happened when Mora Valdez, who is 21 (p15), was "five years old".
1401 Dating *The Night of the Doctor* (Series 7 minisode) - For Karn, these events take place some time after *The Brain of Morbius*; Ohila comments, "[The Sisters] have always known in our bones that [the Doctor] would one day return here." Steven Moffat has commented that the name Ohila suggests a connection to the similarly named Ohica from *The Brain of Morbius*, but they're not the same person.
　To the elation of many people who prefer to view *Doctor Who* as one big continuity, the eighth Doctor names on screen "Charley, C'rizz, Lucie, Tamsin, Molly" – some of his companions from the Big Finish audios. (Some have cited this as evidence that the novels didn't happen, but in truth the Doctor skips over Liv and Helen from the audios also. Clearly, in his dying moments, it's not an all-comprehensive list.)
1402 Dating *Engines of War* (NSA #54) - The Tantalus colonists are identified as human. Cinder is named as a "Dalek hunter", but only in the sense that she's part of the resistance against the Daleks, not because she's akin to Abslom Daak ("Abslom Daak... Dalek Killer" et al).

This placement is a guess, near *The Night of the Doctor* only because we know the Last Great Time War was actively being fought in this era.
1403 Dating *The Beautiful People* (BF CC #1.4) - The back cover specifies that the story takes place in the "thirty-second century". Morestrans appeared in *Planet of Evil*. A Tythonian was the titular *Creature from the Pit*.
1404 Dating *Burning Heart* (MA #30) - The year is given (p20).
1405 *Lucifer Rising*. An excommunicated Knight of Oberon, Orcini, appears in *Revelation of the Daleks*. The suggestion that the order was based on the moon of Uranus was first postulated in the Virgin edition of this book, and confirmed in *GodEngine*.
1406 "Thirty generations" before *Bang-Bang-A-Boom!*.
1407 "Ten years" before *The Seeds of War*.
1408 Dating *Destroy the Infinite* (BF 4th Doc #3.6) - It's "something like fifty standard years" after the Eminence War begins.
1409 Dating *DEyes 3: The Death of Hope/The Reviled* (BF DEyes #3.1-3.2) - Events on Herron's World and Ramosa happen during humanity's fifty-two-year war against the Infinite Warriors. The conflict on Delafoss (*Destroy the Infinite*) is now "old news". The action has shifted to the Ventos System, and the planet Kelsos currently serves as the Eminence's power base (the background to *The Seeds of War*).
1410 Dating *The Seeds of War* (BF #171) - It's the time of the Earth Empire. The Doctor tells Mel: "It's centuries into your future... there had been other taller constructions [than the Great Tower of Kalsos] back on Earth,

Romana and K9 came to Vita Novus in search of dough-nuts, and found that the proprietor, Karna, had developed a revolutionary tissue-reduction process. Subjects' body mass was broken down in "slimming booths", then reborn in revitalised forms. The excised fat was reconstituted as beauty products. Karna was brainwashing her clients, and sought to leverage contacts in the major galactic governments to set up slimming centres on every planet. Entire populations would be processed; those who refused would be killed.

The spa's computers were damaged, and Karna was slimmed to death. A client, Sebella Bing, took charge and reorganised the spa as a relaxation centre with fatty food, ice cream and champagne. The Doctor got a bag of sugary doughnuts.

Tythonians were known in this era.

3174 - BURNING HEART[1404] **->** The population of Earth was rebuilding following the destruction of the Overcities. Trade, culture and civil liberties suffered across the galaxy as humanity retrenched. On Dramos, a satellite of the gas giant Titania, the Church of Adjudication was becoming ever more draconian. Millions joined the extremist Human First group, which advocated the genocide of all aliens. White Fire was the group's inner core.

The sixth Doctor and Peri visited Dramos as conflict broke out between the Adjudicators and White Fire's forces. The Node of Titania, an area similar to Jupiter's Red Spot, was alive and had been increasing hostilities in its attempts to communicate. The sentience of the Node merged with OBERON, the Adjudicators' central computer. The conflict and xenophobia diminished, and the Adjudicators recruited more non-humans into their ranks.

The Sontarans and Cybermen had both recently tried to introduce more individuality into their species. The Sontaran attempt created disunity, and some of their ranks were banished.

As Earth went through its Empire and Federation phases, the fortunes of the Guild of Adjudicators waxed and waned. Eventually, they became unnecessary. A thousand forms of local justice had sprung up. Every planet had its own laws and police. The universe had passed the Guild by, leaving it nothing to adjudicate. The Guild degenerated into a reclusive order of assassins known as the Knights of the Grand Order of Oberon, dreaming of past glories and crusades for truth. The organisation was based on the moon of Uranus.[1405]

Gholos attacked the pastoral planet Angvia, beginning a conflict that would last thirty generations. Both sides violated the Tenebros IV peace treaty.[1406] The Eminence secretly tainted biocrops on some of humanity's colony worlds. Harvests started to fail on Ridius IV and other planets across the Ten Systems.[1407]

c 3184 - DESTROY THE INFINITE[1408] **->** The fourth Doctor took Leela to see one of humanity's most successful colonies, Delafoss, only to find it a polluted world enslaved by the Eminence. Its Infinite Warriors finished construction of the *Infinite*: a warship with three hundred decks and a thousand armaments. The Eminence exposed the Doctor to its Breath of Forever, supposedly possessing him, and put him in command of the *Infinite*. An Earth Alliance fleet proved no match for the warship, but the Doctor – having resisted the Breath with his respiratory bypass system – bled off the *Infinite*'s force field power, enabling Leela to coordinate an attack that destroyed it. The Doctor left with Leela, having failed to learn the Eminence's true purpose.

c 3185 - DEyes 3: THE DEATH OF HOPE / DEyes 3: THE REVILED[1409] **->** Earth Alliance withdrew from Heron's World – a Level Four planet in the Centris System, at the edge of the Ten Systems – and left the survivors there at the mercy of the Eminence's Infinite Warriors. A year later, the bald Master and Sally Armstrong spread retrogenitor particles throughout the Heron's World survivors via a mesmerized Molly O'Sullivan. A field-test proved the particles could provide immunity against the Eminence's Breath of Forever, but didn't make those infected susceptible to the Master's will. CIA Coordinator-in-Extremis Narvin informed the eighth Doctor of the Master's actions, and provided technology that shielded the Heron's World survivors from the Eminence's gaze. The Doctor left to rescue Molly from the Master's clutches...

Humans began mining operations on Ramosa over the protests of its scorpion-like natives, derisively referred to as "roaches". Narvin brought Liv Chenka forward from the 1970s to aid the Doctor, and she helped the settlers as a medtech. The Master refined the dosages of retrogenitor particle saturation on the settlers, then informed the Eminence of the colony's presence. As the Infinite Warriors attacked Ramosa, the Master evacuated the settlers in his TARDIS so they could serve as Patient Zero: transmitting the retrogenitor particles throughout the Ten Systems. The Eminence wiped out the Ramosans, who were biologically resistant to the Breath of Forever.

The Eminence War had now caused such death and destruction, the Doctor took Liv back in history to avert the Eminence's creation...

End of the Eminence War

c 3186 - THE SEEDS OF WAR[1410] **->** Suddenly and without warning, the Eminence's armies of Infinite Warriors collapsed and became truly dead. The Ventos System was identified as the turning point of the conflict, and while news reports said that Earth Alliance had prevailed, officials – including Earth Grand Administrator Walter

Vincent – privately had no explanation for the victory. Humanity hailed the end of a conflict that had cost millions of lives. Nonetheless, the war's end triggered a surge of anarchy on hundreds of colony worlds, which experienced an outbreak of disease, prolonged food shortages and little if any help from Earth Admin. For a short time, the Earth Empire was weakened.

Four months after the war ended, the sixth Doctor and Mel arrived at the Great Tower of Kalsos, and found they were some decades too late for its grand opening. Earth Alliance blew up the Tower, the final symbol of the Eminence's campaign. The Doctor and Mel discovered that the Eminence had feigned defeat to distribute a bioagent containing its essence into the food stocks throughout humanity's dominions. If successful, the Eminence would simultaneously transform all humans into Infinite Warriors.

The Doctor and Mel prevented the Eminence from tainting the seed stocks in the Agricultural Antiquities Reliquary, located in the Equatorial Administration Zones on Earth. The Reliquary's seeds were genetically pure, and quickly duplicated for widespread distribution to alleviate the famine. The Eminence vowed vengeance against the Doctor, who left with Mel.

Sky Stations Depollute Earth

c 3186 - DEyes 3: RULE OF THE EMINENCE[1411] ->

Twelve thousand sky stations had worked to depollute Earth's atmosphere, and the planet declared itself back open for business following the conclusion of the Eminence War. Billions were expected to return and repopulate humanity's homeworld. The tropics had been kept pristine for the Earth Administration residences there. Istanbul had been renamed Byzantium, and was home to a media hub designated the 21st Wonder of the World. Luna Station and Singapore Skybase serviced travellers.

The bald Master bought his scheme regarding the Eminence to a conclusion, as aided by his captives: Molly O'Sullivan and Liv Chenka. Earth Grand Administrator Walter Vincent was a conceptual construct of the Master: a trigger for trace elements of the Eminence dispersed into Earth's atmosphere. The retrogenitor particles that Vincent disseminated – as supplied by Molly – overrode the

---

but not without some form of geo-stationary support. When I visited the so-called Space Elevator of Sumatra [*The Great Space Elevator*, c.2044] several lifetimes ago, for instance."

Helgert Teveler has compiled research from "every major agronomist for the last two hundred years", including Professor Lasky from *Terror of the Vervoids* [2986]. It might be best to assume that Lasky's work really was a full two centuries ago, as Earth at the time was hideously over-populated and polluted (*The Mutants*, *Original Sin* et al), but by *The Seeds of War* is only inhabited by the rich and powerful.

1411 Dating *DEyes 3: Rule of the Eminence* (BF *DEyes* #3.4) - The Eminence War has officially ended, and conditions on Earth match those reported in *The Seeds of War*.

1412 Dating *Death Riders* (BBC children's 2-in-1 #1) - The Doctor says that according to the TARDIS instruments, it's "the thirty-third century" (p16).

1413 "Twelve hundred years" after *Worlds BF: Kronos Vad's History of Earth* (Vol. 36,379).

1414 Dating *Maker of Demons* (BF #216) - It's humanity's future, at a point when Elizabethan fashions have come back into vogue – and yet one of the participants doesn't recognise mention of Shakespeare's *The Tempest*, in a story thematically inspired by it. One of the working-class humans, Trink, is acquainted with how the water aboard a sandminer has no taste, suggesting the society that forged the *Duke of Milan* has made contact with that of Kaldor (see *The Robots of Death* [? 2881] and *Robophobia* [&3130]). *The Rescue* [c.2493] was predicated on there being no intended space-travel to Dido, so *Maker of Demons* must be some

time afterward.

1415 Dating *Full Circle*, *State of Decay* and *Warriors' Gate* (18.3-18.5) - None of these stories or the sequel Big Finish audios (*Mistfall*, *Equilibrium*, *The Entropy Plague*) suggest that the TARDIS experiences any dislocation of time while passing through a CVE or as it travels through E-Space, nor that time in E-Space operates any differently from that of our native N-Space. *The Invasion of E-Space* (BF CC #5.4) by *Full Circle* author Andrew Smith claims that "months" pass between *State of Decay* and *Warriors' Gate* while the Doctor and company search for a means of returning to N-Space – which would explain why *State of Decay* ends with the Doctor insisting that he's going to take Adric back to the Starliner, but *Warriors' Gate* drops the matter.

The *Hydrax* spaceship that features in *State of Decay* originates from Earth, and the *Hydrax* records that the Doctor and Romana examine bear the header "Data File 12/12/1998". Coupled with the Doctor's nostalgic remark of "Ah, lovely old technology. Back on twentieth-century Earth, the engineers used to just—", the idea seems to be that the *Hydrax* did indeed launch in the waning days of the twentieth century. (This in a story from Terrance Dicks, who might well have thought – per the UNIT era – that technology in *Doctor Who* runs in advance of the real world.) However, the effort and technology involved in humanity even *attempting* to send an interstellar vessel as far as Beta Two in the Perugellis Sector seems very incompatible with vast tracts of *Doctor Who* history, which reinforce over and over that humanity makes limited progress branching into even the solar system until around 2100. Presumably for this reason, and also possibly bearing in

Eminence traces and brought ten billion people under the Master's control. Earth constructed a warfleet with the intention of conquering all alien races, and forging a second Eminence Empire with the Master at its helm.

Aided by Narvin, the eighth Doctor enhanced the retrogentior particles in Vincent until he exploded, immunizing humanity against the Eminence's taint. The Eminence's mind was dispersed across the infinity of space, and the Master fled.

The Doctor and Molly realised she could only live free from the machinations of the Daleks and the Gallifreyan CIA if they stopped travelling together, and Narvin took her back to her native time. The antigens Liv absorbed during her forced service to the Master had cured her deadly case of theta-ray isotope poisoning, and she continued traveling with the Doctor.

c 3210 - DEATH RIDERS[1412] **->** The Interplanetary Mining Corporation found deposits of trisilicate and duralinium on the asteroid of Stanalan in the Torajii System, and established a frontier town there. "Fluripsent crystals" were embedded in rock walls as a means of illumination. The last Drexxon at liberty, just a child, came to Stanalan with the travelling Galactic Fair (which featured a Death Ride roller coaster). The eleventh Doctor, Amy and Rory stopped the Drexxon from freeing its murderous fellows from the Perpetuity Chamber imprisoning them.

> = Kronos Vad's *History of Earth* was published in a parallel universe, in the quadrant of Zagal. Iris Wildthyme knew Vad, and said he had a belly like a barrage balloon and a flatulence problem.[1413]

& 3216 - MAKER OF DEMONS[1414] **->** Solar storms disrupted a human spacefleet en route to Dido, threatening those aboard with starvation. The seventh Doctor and Mel guided the fleet to a habitable world, which was christened "Prosper". The *Duke of Milan*'s captain, Gonzalo, realised that Prosper could never sustain his people's numbers, and – once the travellers had gone – created a secret society, the Milanese, to undertake a century-long cull.

The humans on Prosper enjoyed Elizabethan fashions, as the tides of time washed in as well as out. The *Duke of Milan* contained a portrait of the Empress Beyonce II.

The TARDIS in E-Space[1415]

Adric Joins the TARDIS; Romana, K9 Leave

> = **c 3256 - FULL CIRCLE / STATE OF DECAY / THE INVASION OF E-SPACE / WARRIORS' GATE ->** The fourth Doctor, the second Romana and K9 attempted to answer a summons to Gallifrey, but the TARDIS unexpectedly went through an extremely rare space phenomenon, a Charged Vacuum Emboitment. This sent the Ship into a pocket realm called the Exo-Space Time Continuum, a.k.a. E-Space...

The TARDIS arrived on the planet Alzarius as the ruling Deciders declared the arrival of Mistfall: an ecological change that happened every fifty years, as another planet pulled Alzarius away from its sun. Worse, Mistfall entailed the emergence of the savage Marshmen from the swamps. Those aboard the Starliner prepared to lock themselves inside for a decade, even as a group of Outsiders – including a young man named Varsh and his brother Adric, whose parents had died in a forest fire – sought to survive away from the ship. The fourth Doctor and his allies repelled a Marshmen assault on the Starliner, but Varsh was killed. Adric stowed himself aboard the TARDIS as the Doctor aided the Deciders in preparing the Starliner for lift-off, and it rose from Alzarius...

The Doctor, Romana, K9 and Adric arrived on a nameless world where the vampires Zargo, Camilla and Aukon ruled as lords over a settlement of peasants, and laboured toward the restoration of the last of the Great Vampires. The vampires' former space vessel, the *Hydrax*, served as the tower in which they lived. The peasants were denied science and learning, and periodically harvested to feed the healing Great One with their blood. The vampires celebrated as the Great One rose, but the Doctor staked the Great One in the heart by launching one of the *Hydrax*'s scout ships. With the Great One's death, Zargo, Camilla and Aukon turned to dust.

The Farrian, a race of armoured raiders in N-Space, captured a mathematician who helped them develop technology capable of generating a CVE. Farrian scouts reported a rich supply of genellium – a highly sought-after mineral used in FTL drives – on the planet Ballustra in E-Space. After months of searching E-Space for a CVE, the Doctor, Romana and Adric were present as the Farrian generated a CVE large enough to transport their main battlecruiser and army. Ballustra was lost until the Doctor sabotagued the Farrian's CVE generator, forcing a retreat. The Farrian battlecruiser took heavy damage while returning to N-Space, and further efforts to create CVEs were abandoned.

The TARDIS arrived at the Gateway between E-Space and N-Space as a spaceship forged from dwarf star alloy – the only substance capable of containing the enslaved Tharils – misfired and ran aground there also. In trying to free his ship with a backblast, Captain Rorvik killed himself and his crew, as well as liberated the Tharils aboard. Romana decided to remain in E-Space and work to liberate the Tharils, as aided by the Tharil named Biroc and K9. The latter's databanks contained schematics for the duplication of the TARDIS, which would give the Tharils time technology.

The backblast enabled the TARDIS, with the Doctor and Adric aboard, to return to N-Space...

The crew of the Starliner, led by Decider Login, eventually settled on the world of the Hiragi, a pre-technology society. Within a century, the Starliner colonists were established enough to conduct trade with other worlds. The Hiragi had no name for their planet, so the colonists dubbed it New Alzarius. The

settlers remained governed by a trio of Deciders, who chose their own membership and eschewed democracy. Decider Decree 786 limited travel to Alzarius.[1416]

The sixth Doctor visited the planet C'h'zzz in 3263.[1417]

= & 3276 - THE INVASION OF E-SPACE / BLOOD HARVEST[1418] **->** The second Romana had spent some decades in E-Space working to liberate the Tharils. On the eve of their final battle for independence, she made a record of the Farrian invasion of Ballustra for posterity. She had never gotten around to building TARDISes for the Tharils.

With the Tharils liberated, Romana checked on the progress of the vampire planet, and found that an

---

mind that the *Hydrax* officers wore helmets similar to those seen in *The Space Pirates* [? 2135], *Lucifer Rising* (pgs. 59, 272-273) says that the *Hydrax* launched around 2127. It becomes a question, then, of whether to go by a hard year in a TV story that makes little sense, or a hard year in a novel that very much does.

Most reference texts place no faith in the former: *The TARDIS Logs* suggest the *Hydrax* launched in "the thirty-sixth century," *The Terrestrial Index* places it "at the beginning of the twenty second" and *About Time* thinks the *Lucifer Rising* dating is "far more reasonable". *Timelink* is the odd man out, taking the on-screen "1998" date at face value. The same book, however, rather courageously reasons that *Full Circle* happens in the same year as *Meglos* (dated by *Timelink* to 1983), but *State of Decay* happens nearly a millennium later in 2929, while *Warriors' Gate* occurs prior to both stories, in February 1981 (leading into *The Keeper of Traken*). The super-majority of *Doctor Who* fandom and commentators, however, seem to take as given that *Full Circle*, *State of Decay* and *Warriors' Gate* all happen consecutive to one another.

In *State of Decay*, Zargo and the rebels both say that the vampiric Lords have ruled the village for "a thousand years" – a figure that Terrance Dicks seems keen to reinforce in his novelisation of the story. Aukon, by contrast, mentions that the Lords have bred obedience and dullness into the villagers for "twenty generations", which only adds up to about five hundred years. (As *Timelink* points out, however, the *Hydrax* records suggest that the villagers are descended from the ship's scientific crew, who might have been allowed more intelligence and learning for some centuries before the Lords regarded such knowledge as a threat.) Also, K9 specifies that the vampire planet has a day and year slightly less than that of Earth (respectively 23.3 hours and three hundred and fifty days) – meaning that "a thousand years" in this case could be equivalent to just nine hundred and thirty Earth years.

The work-averse slavers seen in *Warriors' Gate* outwardly present as human, but their homeworld is never

specified, and Biroc speaks of the need to liberate his people on "many planets" within E-Space – suggesting the slavers are from there as well. Supporting that, there's no mention in any other *Doctor Who* story of N-Space vessels relying on Tharils for navigation.

The origins of the original Starliner crew aren't named in *Full Circle* itself, although the name "Terradon" might suggest they're of Earth descent, and the audio *Mistfall* (also written by Andrew Smith) names them as "ex-Terran" and "human". In *Full Circle*, the Deciders' official (and false) history claims that the Starliner crashed on Alzarius "forty generations ago", and although the Doctor and Romana determine it was "more like forty thousand generations", the hyper-speed at which cellular development occurs on Alzarius means that such a number must surely pass faster than human norm. Going by human biology, "forty thousand generations" would mean that something like a million years has passed since the Starliner crashed, and even if one could possibly believe that the Starliner was built to independently survive for that incredible amount of time, the *Hydrax* and the computer equipment the rebels find in the woods – as products of the twentieth-century or thereabouts – most assuredly weren't.

If the Starliner inhabitants use the same measurements of time as the original crew, however, "forty generations" would equal a thousand years... which neatly suggests that the *Hydrax* and the Starliner went through the same CVE at roughly the same time, and keeps the Starliner within the feasible timeline of Earth's space explorations. The audio *Death Match* [&3565] references a Starliner in passing, additionally suggesting that it's native to N-Space.

Adding to the complexity here, *Mistfall* happens "three hundred years" after *Full Circle*, after the TARDIS leaves the planet Valderon in *Prisoners of Fate* [3556] and intends to jump forward in time no more than a month. *Mistfall* also, however, states that the Starliner landed on Alzarius "thousands of years" before the fourth Doctor and Romana turned up there in *Full Circle*, which is potentially awkward to reconcile against

enigmatic third party was stoking aggression between the liberated villagers and an elite class led by Lord Veran. K-9 stayed behind to serve as Biroc's High Administrator. Romana summoned the Doctor, whose seventh self dispatched Bernice Summerfield to assist. Tensions increased as the third party arranged the murders of Lord Veran and the former rebel Kalmar.

Romana and Benny learned that Agonal – an eternal being that fed on pain and suffering – was conducting experiments on the Great Vampire's remains, to spawn a new generation of Great Vampires. The seventh Doctor, Ace and the private investigator Dekker arrived from Chicago, 1929, in response to Benny's Spatio-Temporal Alarm Beacon, and helped to end Agonal's operations. Agonal was Timescooped to Gallifrey, even as the vampire Lord Yarven stowed aboard the TARDIS and returned with the Doctor's party to 1929...

3278 - MANAGRA[1419] -> For centuries, the Nicodemus Principle had prevented a Reprise from becoming the Pope of Europa. But in 3278, Cardinal Richelieu, a Reprise, assassinated Pope Lucian and attempted to succeed him. He faced opposition from the Dominoes, a secret organisation stretching across the Dominions. The fourth Doctor and Sarah were present as the Persona – a combination of the Mimic and the failed playwright Francis Pearson – attempted to seize control of Europa. The Doctor trapped Persona inside Europa's Globe, which was actually a TARDIS, and crushed both of them to death in the Vortex. Richelieu become Pope Designate.

3286 - REAL TIME[1420] -> Three survey teams went missing on the desert planet Chronos. The sixth Doctor and Evelyn accompanied a follow-up group there, and found that an absent alien race had equipped a temple of sorts with a time machine. The time traveller Goddard, hailing from 1951, warned the Doctor that events in this era would precipitate the Cybermen conquering Earth in the twentieth century. The Cybermen of the future reverse-engineered a techno-virus that Goddard carried, and created a virus that turned living beings into cybernetic ones. The Cyber-controller of the future infected Evelyn with this virus. The Doctor triggered a temporal wave that aged the Cybermen of the future to death, whereupon he and Evelyn departed, unsuspectingly, for 1927...

? 3297 - THE BEAST BELOW[1421] -> **The eleventh Doctor and Amy found that Starship UK had become a virtual police state; it was monitored by human cyborgs (the Winders) and robot guardians (the Smilers). The Doctor learned that the ship's drive was a fake, and met Liz X – the British monarch Elizabeth**

the furthest point that *State of Decay* can comfortably take place, if the Starliner is of human manufacture.

With the 3556 dating for *Prisoners of Fate* being so rock solid (see the notes on that story), the simplest course of action might be to work backwards from that, which – if one assumes a bit of rounding for the "thousand years" that the Lords are said to rule – would preserve the preferred dating for the *Hydrax*'s launch. In which case, the *Hydrax* indeed left Earth in 2127; *Full Circle*, *State of Decay*, *The Invasion of E-Space* and *Warriors' Gate* occur c.3256; and the E-Space-centric audios *Mistfall*, *Equilibrium* and *The Entropy Plague* happen "three hundred years" later in 3556.

1416 *Mistfall*

1417 *Spiral Scratch*

1418 Dating *The Invasion of E-Space* (BF CC #5.4) and *Blood Harvest* (NA #28) - We're told that it took Romana "decades" to help liberate the Tharils. In *Blood Harvest*, a comparable amount of time has passed since Romana's last visit to the vampire planet (*State of Decay*) – the late Tarak's son has grown up, Zargo and his compatriots ruled in what's called "the Old Time", Kalmar is one of the few left who remember "those days", and enough time has passed that it's noticeable Romana has not physically aged. The writer of *Blood Harvest*, Terrance Dicks, takes a couple of liberties with his own *State of Decay*, by establishing that the vampire planet had

"nearby villages" (a status quo the TV story manifestly rejects) and a nobility class also stricken with the vampire taint.

1419 Dating *Managra* (MA #14) - The Doctor sets the co-ordinates for "Shalonar – AD 3278", and the TARDIS lands in the same timezone, but the wrong location (p26). Later, Byron states that he was created "in the middle of the thirty-third century" (p113).

1420 Dating *Real Time* (BF BBCi #1) - It is "millennia" since the creation of the Cybermen, who are thought to be extinct. The story is set after *Sword of Orion*. The online notes name the planet as Chronos.

1421 Dating *The Beast Below* (X5.2) - At time of writing, *The Beast Below* is, without a doubt, the New *Who* episode that's trickiest to place on a timeline.

We can calculate the date. Amy is said in dialogue to be "1306" – as she's seven in 1996 (*Flesh and Stone*), that means it's now 3295. However, the screen Amy looks at actually *says* "1308", which seems like a production error, possibly caused by confusion over the extra two years the Doctor keeps Amy waiting right at the end of *The Eleventh Hour*. If the screen's right, it's now 3297. *The Brilliant Book of Doctor Who 2011* similarly derived a dating of 3297 by favouring the screen and number-crunching Amy's birth year of 1989 with 1308.

Consistent with this, the Doctor dates the solar flares to "the twenty-ninth century", and Liz X says her mask is

X, who was similarly investigating the truth behind Starship UK. The Doctor discovered that Liz X wasn't fifty years old as she claimed, she was nearer three hundred, and her own memories had been erased. He, Amy and Liz X learned that Starship UK was powered by the last of the star whales, which was being tortured to drive it forward. Amy released the whale from its torment, and it continued helping Starship UK of its own volition.

Starship UK had candyburgers, clockwork-powered technology and air-balanced porcelain. While on Starship UK, Amy saw a banner for Magpie Electricals.[1422]

Various environmental disasters, including radiation storms, rendered Pavonis IV uninhabitable. A handful of the populace escaped in ships carrying cloning facilities.

They had also engineered a means of creating AI humanoids with fungal brains. The surviving Pavonians primarily sought to find their hero, the Doctor, thinking he could help restore their planet.[1423]

A gravity quake destroyed the planets orbiting the star Gloriana XVI and created the Gloriana Scattering, one of the most beautiful asteroid fields in the universe.[1424] The First Empire of Eternal Victory, a conquering regime from outside the Milky Way, fell when the Synthetic Emperor took the throne. The Emperor retasked the armies of robots the First Empire had created, spurring a new, robot-based Empire.[1425]

The Doctor rescued the Rembrandt painting *The Night Watch* from the Reichmuseum in Amsterdam shortly before the facility burned down.[1426] Mechanoids landed on Hesperus, and prepared it for habitation.[1427] The time-

"nearer three hundred" years old than the Doctor's estimate of two hundred. As the mask was custom made so Liz could explore the mysteries of Starship UK incognito, the ship has been in flight at least three hundred years, probably four hundred (it would mean the mask was made around 2995, which is nearly a hundred years after the end of the twenty-ninth century). Those are the dates given in the story, and they're clear and consistent.

Where this dating scheme runs aground is that while Earth is completely abandoned a number of times (see The Abandonment of Earth sidebar), it seems implicit that *these* solar flares are meant to be the same ones that cause Nerva Beacon to be converted into an Ark (as seen in *The Ark in Space/The Sontaran Experiment*). "The Keep" dates this to the fifty-first century, a time period that was already busy enough before the new series made it the native time of both Jack Harkness and River Song (neither of whom, though, have said much about Earth itself in their era). See the dating notes on *Revenge of the Cybermen* for where the "twenty-ninth century" date for the solar flares comes from, and The Solar Flares sidebar for why this chronology places them around 6000AD. The issue is that there are a number of classic *Doctor Who* stories (*The Mutants*, *Terror of the Vervoids*, etc.) definitely set in a thirtieth century where Earth isn't just populated, it's overpopulated, and there are even more set afterwards (say, *The Daleks' Master Plan*, set in 4000) where Earth has a highly functional/non-solar-flare-roasted society. There's no real wriggle room for any of this in *The Beast Below* itself – according to the Doctor, the solar flares have already happened, and so "the entire human race", not just some Britons, "packed its bags".

While some might be tempted to invoke the credo of "history can be rewritten, timey-wimey, wibbley-wobbley, it's after the Last Great Time War, the Cracks in Time affected things", etc., and say that *The Beast Below* represents a new history that has superseded the classic *Doctor Who* one... unfortunately, *The Beast Below*

doesn't match the continuity of the new series either. Only seven episodes later, *Cold Blood* has the Doctor setting the Silurians' alarm clocks to wake them in a thousand years time (so, around 3020), and expressing his hope that humanity of that time period will be more receptive to co-existing with the Silurians. But if the Doctor's comments in *The Beast Below* are kept sacrosanct, in actuality the Silurians would be waking up to an uninhabitable burnt cinder of a planet.

We see Liz X again in *The Pandorica Opens*, guarding the Royal Collection in a sequence after *The Beast Below* (she says that she "met the Doctor once") and dated to 5145 (although it's not established if the Royal Collection is on Starship UK or the planet the British settled on). While we know that Liz X's body clock had been slowed, that was specifically to keep the Star Whale's plight secret – by 5145, she'd be at least 2550 years old. It's possible that the slowing of her body clock was irreversible, but there's no indication in other stories that humankind discovers the secret of virtual immortality (not even the life-extending Spectrox, as seen in *The Caves of Androzani*, was this effective). While some sources claim Liz X "looks older" in *The Pandorica Opens*, neither of the authors of this chronology see it.

Setting the story a decade or two before 5145 is tempting, because it would consistent with "The Keep", and roughly supported if one presumes that the Doctor meant to say that the solar flares were twenty nine *centuries* after Amy's time. However... if the solar flares were in, say, 5010, and Liz X's mask is three hundred years old, *The Beast Below* would be well after 5145, i.e. when Liz X claims to have already met the Doctor (*The Pandorica Opens*). And it doesn't explain why the computer thinks Amy is 1306 (unless her connection to the Cracks in Time confused it).

Ultimately, the most pragmatic solution is to disavow not the Doctor's statement that Starship UK left Earth in the twenty-ninth century, but his claim that it happened as a result of the solar flares. Nobody and nothing else in *The Beast Below* makes this connection,

travelling Helena spent her hen weekend at a space station in the thirty-fourth century. Her friends returned home with T-Shirts with obscene messages in New Martian.[1428]

c 3312 - "Interstellar Overdrive"[1429] **->** Pakafroon Wabster had become the greatest rock band in recorded history – it was on its sixty-third line-up, around the two hundred album mark. The band's founder, Wabster, had died fifty years ago in a rollerblading accident, but had been exhumed and animatronically reanimated. The tenth Doctor and Rose met the group aboard a starship that was causing weird time dilations, and realised the group's manager was trying to eliminate them to cement their reputations. Wabster killed the manager, and the Doctor got the band to lifepods, then destroyed their ship.

Magellan-class starcruisers now used warp induction thrusters.

& 3316 - MAKER OF DEMONS[1430] **->** On Prosper, the Milanese had used an a-biotic energy source, Doctorium, to mutate a subterranean race, the Mogera, into savage, armoured monstrosities. The resultant conflict put the Milanese within two weeks of meeting their quotas of the reduced human population. The seventh Doctor and Mel, along with Ace, restored the Mogera and ended the Milanese's operations.

Officials on Manussa outlawed "snakedancing", a mental purification dance to resist the Mara's return.[1431]

c 3340 - THE DALEK FACTOR[1432] **->** Thal Search-Destroy squads continued to hunt down the Daleks, but it had been two generations since any significant contact had been made. On an unnamed planet, the Daleks worked to implant the Dalek Factor (or "Dalek-heart") into all other lifeforms. The Dalek-hearted life on the test planet considered itself superior to the original Daleks, forcing them to quarantine it. The Daleks successfully imprisoned an unidentified incarnation of the Doctor on this planet.

3380 - FORTY-FIVE: "Order of Simplicity"[1433] **->** Dr Verryman, a foremost expert in the field of bioengineering, had helped to found the Sphere of Influence: a world almost completely devoted to the advancement of knowledge. He developed an inductor: a scalpel-less means of performing surgery with energy pulses and gravity manipulation. The Order of Simplicity, a group devoted to destroying technology, acquired an intelligence-destroying virus. The seventh Doctor, Ace and Hex prevented an agent of the Order from manipulating Verryman into broadcasting the virus – an act that would have reduced billions of humans down to an IQ of 45.

---

and once that component is removed, everything else neatly slots into place. Earth as seen in *The Mutants* (circa 2990) is so overcrowded, it might well resort to all sorts of drastic solutions to shed its excess population (especially as the Earth Empire goes into decline). If Starship UK can be construed to house the excess millions of the United Kingdom, just not the *whole* of the United Kingdom as part of some global disaster, it would actually be in keeping with the "twenty-ninth century" period that the Doctor names. This is an imperfect solution, but it at least keeps intact the on-screen date and the calculation of Amy's age, plus creates the least amount of contradictions.

A History of the Universe in 100 Objects (p208) – as with so many *Doctor Who*-related projects – overlooks the knots this story ties in *Doctor Who* continuity, and simply dates the Starship UK to 3295. *Whoniverse* (BBC, p206), however, ignores the on-screen dating, and places *The Beast Below* after the Great Breakout of the year 5000.

1422 *The Beast Below.* The banner doesn't necessarily indicate that Magpie Electricals is still active in this era; it could just be a piece of decor from a previous era.
1423 *The Pyralis Effect*
1424 "Thousands of years" (p243) before *The Web in Space.*

1425 "One or two thousand years" before *The Web in Space.*
1426 *Dust Breeding,* "in the thirty-third century".
1427 *War of the Daleks,* "two hundred and seventy-five years" (p213) before the Daleks arrive on Hesperus.
1428 *Erimem: Three Faces of Helena*
1429 Dating "Interstellar Overdrive" (*DWM* #375-376) - It's "3000 ADish" according to the Doctor. *Flip-Flop* (also by Jonathan Morris) establishes that Pakafroon Wabster had its first hit single in 3012, and the group has now been around for "three hundred years". *The Tomorrow Windows,* however, seems to imply that the band dates to earlier than that.
1430 Dating *Maker of Demons* (BF #216) - It's "one hundred years to the day" after the seventh Doctor and Mel left Prosper, and "two glasses past the mid-season".
1431 "Nearly a hundred years" before *Snakedance.*
1432 Dating *The Dalek Factor* (TEL #15) - In *Planet of the Daleks,* the Thal space missions against their arch-enemies seem relatively recent. Here, there have been search and destroy missions against the Daleks for "eight centuries" (p17). The lull in Dalek activity ties in with the one noted in *The Daleks' Master Plan.* The incarnation of the Doctor featured here isn't specified.
1433 Dating *Forty-Five: "Order of Simplicity"* (BF #115b) - The year is given.

The Galactic Federation

Nearly three hundred years after the first steps towards confederation, the Headquarters of the Galactic Federation on Io were officially opened and **the Federation (or Galactic) Charter was signed. Founding members included Earth, Alpha Centauri,** Draconia, New **Mars and Arcturus. Earth was now regarded as "remote and unattractive". It was ruled by an aristocracy, "in a democratic sort of way". The Federation prevented armed conflicts, and even the Martians renounced violence (except in self-defence). Under the terms of the Galactic Articles of Peace (paragraph 59, subsection 2), the Federation couldn't override local laws or interfere in local affairs except in exceptional circumstances, and was hampered by a need for unanimity between members when taking action.**[1434]

c 3400 - "Cold-Blooded War!"[1435] **->** The galaxy had now enjoyed three centuries of galactic harmony. Draconia had recently joined the Federation, but the coronation of Lady Adjit Kwan as empress of the royal house of Adjit Assan – and by extension the whole Draconian Empire – led Draconia to the brink of civil war. The President of Earth sent Adjudicators Hall and Spane to Draconia with ancient records showing that the Draconian females had only lost their rights following the planet's industrial revolution, and the Federation denied it had requested intervention from the Shadow Proclamation. Some observers,

though, believed that Judoon troops would soon be sent to occupy Draconia's major cities. The Adjudicators' ship was destroyed en route, and the tenth Doctor and Donna were subsequently mistaken for that delegation. On Draconia, they worked alongside Martian monitors led by Commander Ixzyptir. Fusek Kljuco, the former head of the Draconian armed forces, accidentally killed his daughter during a botched attempt to assassinate the Empress. It was thought that the royal houses would respond to the tragedy by ratifying the Empress' ascendance, and put Kljuco on trial for crimes against the Empire.

c 3400 - THE DARK PATH[1436] **->** The Adjudicators had become the Arbiters, the judicial service of the Federation. The Federation Chair was located on Alpha Centauri. The Federation included the Veltrochni, Terileptils, Draconians and Xarax.

The Federation ship *Piri Reis* reached the lost colony of Darkheart just as temporal distortion attracted both the second Doctor's TARDIS and that of the renegade Time Lord Koschei (an old friend of the Doctor's) and his companion Ailla. The Doctor and Koschei found the Darkheart device, which the colonists were using to make alien beings human.

Koschei accidentally killed Ailla and became stricken with grief. He became increasingly intent on hoarding power, and eradicated the planet Terileptus as a necessary means of testing the Darkheart's destructive capabilities. Ailla regenerated, and Koschei became even more isolated

---

1434 *The Curse of Peladon* and its various sequels are set at the time of a Galactic Federation. The date of its foundation is given in *Legacy* (p164); the words are those of Alpha Centauri and the Doctor from *The Curse of Peladon*. The justice machines named the Megara also follow "The Galactic Charter" in *The Stones of Blood*, and they are from 2000 BC. Many other stories refer to "Intergalactic Law", "Intergalactic Distress Signals" and so on – there are clearly certain established standards and conventions that apply across the galaxy, although who sets and enforces them is unclear.

1435 Dating "Cold-Blooded War!" (IDW *DW* one-shot #5) - Dating this story is difficult, and the internal evidence seems a little confused. It's during the time of the Federation. As with *Frontier in Space* (set in 2540), Earth has a President, Draconia has an empire and Draconian females lack equality. Adjudicators dress as the Master did when he posed as one in *Colony in Space* (set in 2472). An Alpha Centaurian briefly runs past the Doctor, but it's unclear if this is the same individual as seen in the Peladon stories, or just a member of the same race.

What muddies the waters is that it's simultaneously implied that it's been "five hundred years" since both the First Great Space War (presumably the Earth-

Draconia conflict that forms the background of *Frontier in Space*, around 2520, meaning it's now around 3020), and since women on Earth were judged to have more important qualifications than "how many words they could type in a minute" (suggesting it's *currently* 2540-ish). Tellingly, though, there have been three hundred years of "galactic harmony" preceding this story – meaning it can't be either 2500 or 3040.

The novels established that the Adjudicators had become the Arbiters by *The Dark Path* (so this story is set before circa 3400). The novel *Legacy* (also written by Gary Russell) might provide the key - it establishes when the Federation was founded, that the process took around three hundred years (the "three centuries of galactic harmony" mentioned in this story?), and that Draconia was a founding member. If that's the case, the Alpha Centauri we see here almost certainly can't be the same individual from the Peladon stories.

1436 Dating *The Dark Path* (MA #32) - There is no exact date, but the Galactic Federation exists (p3) and it is over "three hundred and fifty years" after the turn of the thirty-first century (p175) which was "nearly half a millennium ago" (p178), which all suggests it's set in the thirty-fifth century. It's "a thousand years" since the Doctor first visited Draconia, which *Paper Cuts* helps to

upon realising that she had spied on him for the High Council of the Time Lords. The Doctor stopped Koschei's thirst for power by programming the Darkheart to turn the system's star into a black hole. The colonists evacuated aboard the *Piri Reis*, but Koschei went missing when the black hole consumed his TARDIS.

= These events happened in the Inferno universe, but in a different form that allowed Koschei and Ailla to continue their travels.[1437]

? 3410 - THE DEMONS OF RED LODGE AND OTHER STORIES: "The Entropy Composition"[1438] -> The fifth Doctor and Nyssa visited Concordium – a planet-sized repository containing music all the way back to the dawn of time – while en route to see the Terileptus event horizon. They visited 1968 upon examining the songs of Geoffrey Belvedere Cooper, and created a feedback loop between Concordium and Cooper's studio. This prevented an Entropy Siren from destabilising the entire universe with the primal sonics of creation.

Dojjin, the Director of Historical Research on Manussa, became convinced that the Mara would return. He abandoned his post, and joined the ranks of the snakedancers.[1439]

? 3417 - THE MENAGERIE[1440] -> Over the centuries, the Knights of Kuabris had prevented scientific discovery on their planet, and discouraged historical research. They came to be led by Zaitabor, who was unaware that he was an android. Zaitabor hoped to purge his city of corruption and revived some Mecrim, who initiated a slaughter. The second Doctor – travelling with Jamie and Zoe – arranged to detonate the city's reactor, which killed Zaitabor and the Mecrim. The Knights fell from power, and negotiations between the planet's various races were arranged.

& 3426 - SNAKEDANCE[1441] -> The Mara took control of Tegan's mind a second time, and routed the TARDIS to its homeworld of Manussa. The public held a cere-mony, as it did once every decade, to celebrate the Mara's defeat – this was the 500th anniversary of its downfall. The Federator's son, Lon, was mentally enthralled by the Mara and arranged that the Great Crystal would be returned to its ceremonial wall socket during the ceremony. This linked the Mara to the minds of those present, and it gained the mental energy required to partly manifest. The snakedancer Dojjin helped the fifth Doctor to resist the Mara by finding the still point within himself. The Doctor removed the Great Crystal from its socket, which caught the Mara in-between states of being and destroyed it.

date to circa 2040. Terileptus is the homeworld of the Terileptils (*The Visitation*).

1437 *The Face of the Enemy*

1438 Dating *The Demons of Red Lodge and Other Stories*:"The Entropy Composition" (BF #142b) - No year is given. Mention is made of swing musician Benny Goodman having died in 1986, so it's after that. The Terileptus event horizon is said to be "the most mag-nificent sunset in this part of space-time" – presuming that the event horizon forms after Terileptus' destruc-tion in *The Dark Path*, the Concordium sequences must take place after 3400. Even so, this placement is more guesswork than not.

1439 "Ten years" before *Snakedance*.

1440 Dating *The Menagerie* (MA #10) - It is "centuries" (p67) after Project Mecrim was initiated in 2416. The Doctor suggests that it happened "a millennium or three" (p126) and "hundreds, perhaps thousands of years ago" (p102).

1441 Dating *Snakedance* (20.2) - The story has been long held to be undatable due to the lack of concrete dating clues, and partly because it can't even be estab-lished if the Manussans are human or not. *The Cradle of the Snake* ascribes the end of the Manussan Empire to "Manussan Year 2326". The Federation's records begin some "six hundred years" after that catastrophe, and as the Federation is now exactly "five hundred years" old,

Snakedance must happen a total of eleven hundred years after the Mara's takeover. So, presuming for the moment that the "Manussan years" mentioned in *The Cradle of the Snake* are the same as Earth years, *Snakedance* would occur circa 3426.

While it's admittedly a stretch to think that Manussan years and Earth years *are* equal (if that's the case, what purpose does the different terminology serve?), the thirty-fifth century is a reasonably good fit for *Snakedance*. The Manussans do, to all intents and pur-poses, appear to be of human descent – the design of their clothing and environs suggests India, Punch and Judy shows are performed, and Earth flowers (includ-ing birds of paradise) are on display in the marketplace. Generally speaking, Manussa feels like a human colony cut off from Earth and left to its own devices after humanity's initial expansion into space (as with, to pick an example, Terra Alpha in *The Happiness Patrol*). A potential snag is that the twenty-third and twenty-fourth centuries (going by *The Cradle of the Snake*'s dating) seems a little early for humanity's descendents to have already established "an empire" – then again, we've no idea what actual scale the "Manussan Empire" entails. The grandiosely named "Federation" in *Snakedance*, after all, seems to consist of only three planets. Reference is made to the "leaders of the colo-nial worlds" in *The Cradle of the Snake*, but for all we're

The Mara survived in Tegan's mind, and would manifest a third time.[1442]

On Trionikus, the brilliant scientist Tobal Reist built a weapon called the Eraser. He attempted to destroy a spittoon on his workbench, but underestimated the device's power and blasted Trionikus into eighteen billion bits. He was the only survivor, and went mad as a result of his actions.[1443]

Christopher Shaw was born on New Celeste, and became the youngest captain in Earth's Space Corps at age 23. He received a distinguished service medal for his performance in the human-Bavali conflict of 3478.[1444]

c 3480 - PARADISE 5[1445] **->** Targos Delta, the fourth planet in the Targos System, had become the financial and industrial core of the Earth Alliance. Stock market fluctuations from a thousand worlds were recorded on indestructible plastic tickertape, which could be heated and pressurised to be used as building material.

The Elohim were angelic, multidimensional beings undergoing a civil war; many of their number desired contact with the lower races, but their leadership favoured leaving them alone. The holiday resort Paradise 5, a satellite station in orbit over the toxic Targos Beta, became a

recruiting tool for the rebel Elohim. The Paradise Machine there enabled visitors' minds to ascend and fight in the Elohim conflict, even as their bodies were recycled to become the servile Cherubs.

The sixth Doctor and Peri found that the Doctor's old friend Professor Albrecht Thompson, the galaxy's leading expert on the application of string theory to financial derivatives, had become a Cherub. Thompson died as the Elohim's rivals routed them.

Nyssa Leaves the TARDIS

? 3482 - TERMINUS[1446] **->** Passenger liners travelled the universe and sometimes fell victim to raiders, often those combat-trained by Colonel Periera.

Lazars' Disease swept the universe, spreading fear and superstition even among those in the rich sectors. Sufferers were sent secretly to Terminus, a vast structure in the exact centre of the known universe. The station was run by Terminus Incorporated, who extracted massive profits from the operation. The facility was manned by slave workers, the Vanir, who were kept loyal by their need for the drug Hydromel. The Lazars were either killed or cured by a massive burst

---

told, there might only be two of those.

About Time suggested that the twenty-seventh or twenty-eighth centuries were "an obvious estimate" for *Snakedance*, thinking it fair to assume that the Doctor takes Tegan to Manussa after events in *Kinda*, while concurring that the dating question largely hinged on whether or not the Manussans are human. *Timelink* presumes that *Snakedance* follows on immediately from *Arc of Infinity*, and that as the Doctor was teaching Tegan and Nyssa how to read "starcharts", meaning no temporal displacement has occurred, and it's still 1983 (*Timelink*'s preferred dating for *Arc of Infinity*) when they arrive on Manussa. Although as *Timelink* itself admits, it's a huge coincidence that without benefit of time-travel, the TARDIS has arrived at the five hundredth anniversary celebration of the Mara's defeat.

1442 *The Cradle of the Snake*
1443 "Fifty years" before "The Company of Thieves".
1444 *Zygons: Absolution*
1445 Dating *Paradise 5* (BF LS #1.5) - It's "the thirty-fifth century". The Galactic Federation is getting started around this time, and the Earth Alliance (prominent in the *Dalek Empire* audios) is presumably a smaller organisation within the larger Federation framework.
1446 Dating *Terminus* (20.4) - The date from the Virgin edition of *Ahistory* (? 3482) was adopted by *Asylum*, which is set in 3488, "six years" later. The Big Finish audios featuring the older Nyssa adhere to this, with *Prisoners of Fate* establishing that the later portion of *Cobwebs* takes place in 3530, "about fifty years" after *Terminus*. The *Terrestrial Index* saw Terminus Inc. as one

of the "various corporations" fought by the Doctor in the late "twenty-fifth century." The FASA Role-playing game gave the date as "4637 AD". *Timelink* doesn't assume that the characters are human and sets it in 1983. *A History of the Universe in 100 Objects* (p255) says that Terminus' potential destruction threatens the universe in the "35th century".
1447 *The Darkening Eye.* Nyssa's life and death "trading" ability – which we don't actually see put into effect, so she might only suspect she has the talent – stems from events in the main story of this audio, which are undatable. The Dar Traders' abilities are outlined in *The Death Collectors.*
1448 *The Five Companions.* Nyssa says that she "left the Doctor a very long time ago", so this could occur at virtually any point in her life after *Terminus.*
1449 *The Emerald Tiger*
1450 Dating *Cobwebs* (BF #136) - It's "forty years, two months, two days" before the latter part of the story (specified in *Prisoners of Fate* as 3530), which occurs "about fifty years" after *Terminus.* "The Company" isn't necessarily the same unseen corporation mentioned in *Terminus*, but it seems a reasonably safe bet.

Confusingly, Nyssa tells Turlough, "So, you're travelling with the Doctor now..." as if she remembers meeting him in *Mawdryn Undead*, but – incredibly – doesn't recall that he joined her, the Doctor and Tegan on their adventures. Nyssa also claims that she doesn't age at the same rate as humans, which is why Tegan claims that she's "looking pretty good" for someone who's about seventy, but this contradicts the Doctor's com-

of radiation from Terminus' engines.

The fifth Doctor, Nyssa, Tegan and Turlough arrived at Terminus as part of the Black Guardian's machination. Nyssa left the TARDIS to create an improved version of Hydromel that would break the Vanir's dependency on the Company, and to introduce proper disgnoses and controlled treatment to the Lazars.

During her time on Terminus, Nyssa approached one of the Lazars. She'd been unable to synthesise a cure for the disease, but offered to save his life in a manner similar to the Dar Traders – whose abilities she'd partly acquired, owing to her one-time encounter with them.[1447] Nyssa was Timescooped into a pocket dimension of the Death Zone, then returned home.[1448] Molecular synthesis – the process of fusing two life forms together – became discredited as a scientific theory. A research team on Terminus spent twenty years searching for homogenite, a substance said to have miracle healing properties, but failed to find any.[1449]

A Much-Older Nyssa Rejoins the TARDIS

c 3482 - COBWEBS[1450] **->** The Company established a bioresearch station on Helhine, a toxic planet in the uncharted backwaters in the Eastern edge of the galaxy. Helhine was home to the Cractids, the only organisms with a natural immunity to Richter's Syndrome. The Company hoped to both find a cure for Richter's and develop a new strain of the disease – one that could only be cured with a licensed product.

The fifth Doctor, Tegan, Turlough and a much-older Nyssa had been thrown back in time, and arrived as Bragg, an agent for the Independent Bio-Development Group, became infected with the deadlier Richter's variant. He entered cryo-freeze and escaped as the other research team members died, and the station went dormant. Nyssa opted to resume travelling with her friends, and worked to perfect a cure for Richter's.

In 3487, Christopher Shaw was the only survivor of a Space Corps team sent to deal with some Zygons in Antella

Orionsis. He was court-martialed for cowardice.[1451]

3488 - ASYLUM[1452] **->** Nyssa developed a vaccine for Lazar's Disease and travelled the galaxy until it was eradicated. Full of optimism, she discovered there were many other pandemic problems such as war, famine and disease. She worked to relieve suffering, including periods spent as a nurse on Brallis and airlifting food into Exanos.

When Exanos was destroyed in a nuclear war, Nyssa established herself in a peaceful system and became a university teacher specialising in technography, the study of writings about science. As part of this, she studied the works of Roger Bacon. The fourth Doctor met Nyssa while tracking an anomaly in space-time, and discovered discrepancies in her recollection of Bacon. This was evidence of alien interference with the timeline. When the Doctor departed for the thirteenth century, Nyssa stowed aboard. After restoring history, the Doctor brought Nyssa home.

Igtw - & 3489 - ST: "A Heart on Both Sides"[1453] **->** An asteroid academy, Gloucester, trained medical professionals. Following her work on Terminus, Nyssa ran a mobile medical ship – the *Traken* – equipped with robotic nurses. The eighth Doctor heard rumours of the *Traken*'s destruction as part of the Time War, and so jumped back some months to join Nyssa's humanitarian efforts incognito, as "Dr Foster". Together, they forced "Dr Isherwood", a Time Lord saboteur on the service planet Reeve, to retreat before destroying the *Traken*. Before Nyssa could acknowledge her old friend, he slipped away in the TARDIS.

Nyssa Marries Lasarti

c 3490 - CIRCULAR TIME: "Winter"[1454] **->** Nyssa married a dream specialist named Lasarti, and they had a baby daughter named Neeka. Upon dreaming of her time with the Doctor, Nyssa decided to investigate using a device that Lasarti had developed to consciously explore dreams. Lasarti insisted on following her, and the two of them mentally arrived inside the dreamscape of the fifth Doctor – who was dying on Androzani Minor. With their help, the

ment (*Circular Time:* "Autumn") that humans and Trakenites have about the same lifespan (perhaps Trakenites don't actually live longer than humans, but remain heartier than humans as they age).
1451 *Zygons: Absolution*
1452 Dating *Asylum* (PDA #42) - The year is given. It is "six years" since *Terminus*.
1453 Dating *ST:* "A Heart on Both Sides" (BF *ST* #7.9) – It's between *Terminus* [c.3482] and Nyssa marrying and having a family with Lasarti (*Circular Time* et al).
1454 Dating *Circular Time:* "Winter" (BF #91d) - Nyssa implies that it's been "a few years" since her stay at

Terminus and the Corporation Wars, but this claim seems very suspect, given that Neeka is here a baby, and was age 35 when stricken with Richter's and put into stasis - an incident that cannot have occurred prior to 3531, when she's still active according to *Prisoners of Fate*. The absolute soonest she can have been born is 3495. It's also a question of how far apart Neeka and her younger brother Adric (born in 3516) are in age - something that's never addressed, and difficult to address without knowing more about Trakenite biology and that of Lasarti's race, and the longevity treatments of this era.

Doctor overcame a mind-trap set by the Tremas Master, and initiated his regeneration.

Forewarned that he wasn't supposed to know that Nyssa had children, the Doctor feigned ignorance during their psionic communication to avoid a major paradox.[1455]

Within five years of Nyssa developing a vaccine for Lazar's Disease, the illness had been completely eradicated.[1456] Medical facilities were still in use on Terminus.[1457]

? 3500 - SHROUD OF SORROW[1458] -> The Shroud devastated the human colony on Semtis, a planet in Andromeda. Robbed of its ability to grieve, the population broke into tribes such as the Wanters, Ragers and Tremblers. The eleventh Doctor and Clara went to Semtis via the Shroud wormhole itself to learn more about it, then returned to 1963.

The Adventures of Kroton

? 3500 - "Ship of Fools" (DWW)[1459] -> Kroton, the Cyberman with a soul, was picked up and revived by the passengers of a human spaceliner. He learned the ship had been renamed the *Flying Dutchman II*, as it was caught in a time warp. Kroton opened up the cockpit and reprogrammed the robot pilot to escape the rift. But once outside, the lost time caught up with the passengers – they aged by six hundred and twenty-eight years in an instant, and Kroton was left alone once more.

The Technosmiths of Baroq VII upgraded Kroton's armour to thank him for helping them.[1460]

? 3500 - "Unnatural Born Killers"[1461] -> Kroton surfaced on a peaceful world that was being attacked by the

---

1455 *Prisoners of Fate*
1456 *Cobwebs*, in which Nyssa tells the Doctor that Lazar's Disease "ended, almost fifteen years ago. Since I developed a vaccine, there hasn't been a new case for over two decades." In other words, she developed a vaccine twenty years before she again meets the Doctor, then spent five years dealing with – and curing – all the people who caught the disease before the vaccine was available. This does, however, clash with account in *Asylum*, which claims that Nyssa developed a vaccine for Lazar's about six years after *Terminus*.
1457 *The Cradle of the Snake*
1458 Dating *Shroud of Sorrow* (NSA #53) - Time unknown, but the people of Semtis seem human, hence the Doctor's remarks that "humans are pretty much universal" (p174) and "Ah, the human race! It doesn't matter which planet you evolved on, you all want... to help your fellow man" (p177).
1459 Dating "Ship of Fools" (DWW #23-24) - The story is set after "Throwback", but no date beyond that is given. The story is set around six hundred and fifty-eight years after human space liners stopped using human pilots, but this isn't very helpful – it's possible human pilots were reintroduced (particularly if enough ships piloted by robots like this one were lost). It does mean that it can't possibly be set before around 2800, however.

The closest period to this seen in a TV story is *Terminus*, which takes place at a time where ships are piloted automatically, span the galaxy and are threatened by pirates. "Unnatural Born Killers" and "The Company of Thieves" follow this story, but there's no indication how long it is between stories (and it could be many centuries, given that Kroton is effectively immortal).
1460 "The Company of Thieves"
1461 Dating "Unnatural Born Killers" (DWM #277) - See the dating notes on "Ship of Fools" (DWW).

1462 Dating "The Company of Thieves" (DWM #284-286) - No date is given, but it's after "Unnatural Born Killers" and all previous Kroton stories. The pirates are scared of Cybermen, perhaps suggesting this is still within the period of the Cyber Empire (see "Did the Cybermen Ever Have An Empire?"). Pedants might note that the eighth Doctor doesn't recognise Kroton even though the fourth Doctor "introduced" his original appearance in a DWW framing sequence.
1463 "Five hundred years" before *The Book of the Still*.
1464 *Mission to the Unknown, The Daleks' Master Plan*.
1465 Sara Kingdom speculates that the clock was built "centuries" before *The Guardian of the Solar System* – which would match with the claim that all of Mavic Chen's predecessors were tasked with protecting it.
1466 Dating *Zygons: Absolution* (BBV audio #17) - Shaw left the Space Corps in 3487; while it's not specified how much time has passed since then, he seems to have one of the original colonists, and New Eden is nine years old. "Interplanetary Mining" is presumably the Interplanetary Mining Corps seen in *Colony in Space*. The New World translation of the complete Bible was introduced in 1961.
1467 At least "fifty years" before *The Chase*, according to Steven Taylor. There's a possibility that Steven is mistaken about the Mechanoids' origin.
1468 Adric is about 40 in *Prisoners of Fate*, set in 3556, so he must have been born around 3516. The same story specifies Neeka as Adric's "older sister".
1469 Dating *Sisters of the Flame/The Vengeance of Morbius* (BF BBC7 #2.7-2.8) - It's repeatedly confirmed that it's been "centuries" since *The Brain of Morbius*. Morbius' stellar manipulator is akin to Hand of Omega from *Remembrance of the Daleks*, although Morbius' manipulator is as big as a moon (*Orbis*). The Doctor suggests that the Hand of Omega itself is "long gone", suggesting that it was either lost or destroyed after returning to Gallifrey in *Remembrance*. Straxus previously

Sontarans. He destroyed the invasion force, but could not share in the elation of the natives.

Kroton Joins the TARDIS

? 3500 - "The Company of Thieves"[1462] **->** The Qutrusian Cargo Freighter X-703 was captured by pirates led by Grast Horstrogg. Kroton the Cyberman offered resistance, and made the acquaintance of the eighth Doctor and Izzy, while the pirates headed for a new target in a nearby asteroid belt. The TARDIS was stolen by Tobel, the mad scientist who had destroyed his planet Trionikus (and thus formed the asteroid belt) fifty years previous. The pirates tried to steal Tobel's super-weapon – the Eraser – but this merely destabilised the last habitable asteroid. The Doctor, Izzy and Kroton reached the TARDIS, and Kroton joined the TARDIS crew.

The planet Lebenswelt sold its entire mineral wealth to Galactinational. Now immeasurably rich, the population dedicated themselves to decadence.[1463]
The Daleks returned to Earth's galaxy. Over the next five hundred years, they had gained control of more than seventy planets in the ninth galactic system and forty in the constellation of Miros. They were, once again, based on their home planet of Skaro. The Daleks were the only race known to have broken the time barrier, although Trantis had tried in the past without success. Dalek technology was the most advanced in the universe.[1464]
On Earth, a giant clock was constructed that didn't just measure time – it *dictated* time, bending space-time and facilitating the hyperspace avenues through Earth's dominions. The Guardians of the Solar System – aided by trusted members of the Space Security Service – "guarded" the clock, as it was the secret of Earth's power. The clock ran off the mathematical potential of the minds of old men who serviced its inner workings. Without the clock, Earth's empire would have collapsed, leaving billions dead or starving, and making Earth vulnerable to its rivals.[1465]

c 3502 - ZYGONS: ABSOLUTION[1466] **->** Interplanetary Mining worked in concert with the human settlement of New Eden on Ganta 4, and shipped supplies of Amyrillum ore back to Earth. Christopher Shaw had become a religious leader dedicated to Neo-Christianity on Ganta 4. The New World translation of the Bible was still in circulation. Nine years after New Eden's formation, the Zygons seized the colony's spaceship – a means of evading Earth security and attacking humanity's homeworld. Shaw sacrificed his life so his fellow colonists could blow up the spaceship, killing the Zygons.

The Interplanetary Wars

The robotic Mechanoids were dispatched in rockets to planets such as Mechanus, and set out preparing the way for colonists. The Mechanoids cleared landing sites and made everything ready for the immigrants, but a series of interplanetary wars started. The space lanes were disrupted, and colonies such as Mechanus were cut off from Earth. Left to their own devices, the Mechanoid robots built and maintained a vast city, awaiting the code that would identify the rightful human colonists.[1467] Nyssa gave birth to a son, Adric.[1468]

The Eighth Doctor Spends Six Centuries on Orbis

& 3520 - SISTERS OF THE FLAME / THE VENGEANCE OF MORBIUS[1469] **->** Earth had embassies on different worlds. Space Traffic Control was in operation. Every spaceship had access to Galactinet: a supralight microwave information network transmitted across hyperspatial conduits. Members of many different species, including several humanoid ones and the Trell – an affable a race of giant centipedes – served as interplantary police marshals.

(=) Kristof Zarodnix became the richest man in the galaxy – possibly the universe – by buying and selling planets. The Sisterhood of Karn left their world after Zarodnix bought it out from under them. Karn became home to Zarodnix Corporation's central office. Zarodnix purchased many Trell worlds, and used mechanical devices to enslave the Trell.

Zarodnix was secretly the leader of the Cult of Morbius, and acquired a fragment of Morbius' brain from the deep chasm that Morbius fell into on Karn. Using a genetotron, Zarodnix combined Morbius' DNA into a captured Time Lord, Straxus. Morbius was reborn as a fusion of the two. He exacted vengeance on the High Council by using a stellar manipulator that he'd built to drain energy from the Eye of Harmony. Zarodnix's warfleet of converted Trell cordoned off Gallifrey. Ten years passed as Morbius raised a formidable army and conquered a thousand worlds, including Earth.

The eighth Doctor deactivated Morbius' stellar manipulator, restoring power to Gallifrey.

The Doctor and Morbius, both grappling for the remote activator to the stellar manipulator, fell into a chasm on Karn. The restored Time Lords reverted time back to before Zarodnix purchased Karn. Lucie Miller thought the Doctor was dead, and the Time Lords took her home.

The Sisterhood teleported the Doctor away from the chasm – either to aid an ally, or possibly because they didn't want the activator he clutched to be lost. The Doctor materialised in "tweenspace" – a layer of cosmic sediment – on the planet Orbis. The activator sank to the bottom of Great Ocean of Orbis, and the Doctor came to reside on the planet for six hundred years. The Headhunter acquired the Doctor's TARDIS from the Sisterhood, and went back to the twenty-first century to abduct Lucie.[1470]

Bragg was revived from cryo-stasis on Gondel Prime, and the enhanced version of Richter's Syndrome that he carried spread to other worlds in a matter of months.[1471]

Nyssa is Lost to her Family

3530 - COBWEBS[1472] -> Nyssa was still married to Lasarti. Six billion people were now infected with Richter's Syndrome. Nyssa travelled to the disused tech station on Helhine to find a cure, and happened across the fifth Doctor, Tegan and Turlough there. The station's AI initiated

a self-destruct, and the resultant explosion threw them, and the TARDIS, back in time forty years.

3531 (1st Quintilus) - PRISONERS OF FATE[1473] -> A reconnaissance satellite sent to Helhine in search of Nyssa found the wreck of her scoutship and the bioresearch station there. Thinking his wife dead, Lasarti sent word to their 15-year-old son, Adric Traken, on Zarat that his mother had died. Lasarti promised to return to his son in ten days.

(=) The TARDIS arrived with the fifth Doctor, the older Nyssa, and the Doctor's original Type 50 TARDIS, which was outwardly reconfigured to look like Tegan. Nyssa stepped out and entered her family home on Zarat, reuniting with the son she'd abandoned after Helhine. The Type 50, the Doctor and the TARDIS returned to the future as the historical con-

---

appeared in *Human Resources*.

And although it's not said, the chasm on Karn theoretically contains the body of a Morbius from a closed-off timeline.

1470 *Orbis*

1471 "Ten years" before the latter part of *Cobwebs*.

1472 Dating *Cobwebs* (BF #136) - From Nyssa's perspective, it's been "about fifty years" since *Terminus*. For the Doctor's group, that story happened two days ago. *Prisoners of Fate* definitively establishes that Nyssa leaves Helhine in the TARDIS, and is afterward mistaken for dead, in 3530.

THE OLDER NYSSA: A long-running storyline throughout the Big Finish audios (starting with *Cobwebs*, ending with *The Entropy Plague*) entails the fifth Doctor, Tegan and Turlough reuniting with Nyssa following her exit in *Terminus* (and, for Turlough, the resolution of his pact with the Black Guardian in *Enlightenment*).

For Nyssa, about 48 years have elapsed between *Terminus* [c.3482] and *Cobwebs* [3530], during which time she's gotten married and given birth to two (now adult) children: Adric and Neeka. Following *Cobwebs*, the older Nyssa shares more adventures with the TARDIS crew before an energy burst outwardly rejuvenates her in *The Emerald Tiger* – a set-up for when she again meets her son in *Prisoners of Fate* [3556], and he (for a time) convinces himself that she's the younger, pre-*Terminus*, version of his mother. Shortly after that, the TARDIS again gets stuck in E-Space (*Mistfall*), and Nyssa loses her second bout of youthfulness while helping her friends escape back to N-Space in *The Entropy Plague*. That story includes an epilogue with Nyssa in her twilight years, still trapped in E-Space, and for now seems the end point of the character.

As this is rather convoluted, even by the standards of such things, we've felt the need to distinguish between the two in our write-ups. The full list of audios featuring

the older Nyssa are: *Cobwebs* (BF #136), *The Whispering Forest* (BF #137), *The Cradle of the Snake* (BF #138), *Heroes of Sontar* (BF #146), *Kiss of Death* (BF #147), *Rat Trap* (BF #148), *The Emerald Tiger* (BF #159), *The Jupiter Connection* (BF #160), *The Butcher of Brisbane* (BF #161), *Eldrad Must Die!* (BF #172), *The Lady of Mercia* (BF #173), *Prisoners of Fate* (BF #174), *Mistfall* (BF #195), *Equilibrium* (BF #196) and *The Entropy Plague* (BF #197).

1473 Dating *Prisoners of Fate* (BF #174) - The year is given so repeatedly, it has to be accepted as true, even though it's also said that Nyssa re-joined the TARDIS crew in 3530 (see *Cobwebs*). Evidently, the new year passed as the reconnaissance satellite went to Helhine and sent back evidence of Nyssa's "death". The day is named as "1st Quintilus", which in the pre-Julian Roman calendar denoted the fifth month of a ten-month year. It became the seventh month in the post-Julian calendar, and was later named "July" in honour of Julius' birth month.

1474 *Prisoners of Fate*. We know that Neeka was uninfected with Richter's in 3531 and goes into stasis when she's 35, but without knowing her exact birth year, this placement is something of a guess.

1475 "Ten years" before the 3556 component of *Prisoners of Fate*.

1476 The background to *Mistfall*. Decree 1831 is issued "two years" before the story opens.

1477 *Death Match*

1478 Dating *Prisoners of Fate* (BF #174) - The year is given. It's repeatedly said to be "twenty-five years" since Nyssa went missing on Helhine (*Cobwebs*), although technically it's been twenty-six. *Mistfall* reiterates that Neeka hasn't seen her mother in "twenty-five years".

Nyssa seemed to imply in *Heroes of Sontar* that she'd named her daughter after Tegan, causing Tegan to here become confused upon learning that the daughter's name is Neeka.

flict caused by Nyssa and Adric's reunion threatened to destroy the planet Valderon in 3556. An older Adric contacted his mother from 3556 and convinced her not to rejoin his younger self, ending the paradox.

(=) Nyssa refrained from going into her family home, didn't reunite with her son, and went into hiding. She eventually reunited with her friends and older son on Valderon in 3556. As an act of mercy, the repentant Type 50 TARDIS made a final journey back to collect Nyssa, sparing her from having to live through the intervening quarter-century.

Thinking Nyssa dead, her family left Zarat and moved from planet to planet. Lasarti threw himself into his work, and Adric eventually enrolled at college on Trieste. He would receive a first class degree in xenomedicine, having specialised in treatment of Richter's Disease. He would chart the mutations of the Richter's virus over a quarter-century, across seven galaxies.

Adric's sister Neeka became a medic, and cared for the sick on pariah worlds ravaged by Richter's. A microscopic tear in her hazard suit resulted in her becoming infected with Richter's, and she was placed in suspended animation on Maxis Realta.[1474]

The Doctor's Original TARDIS Crashes on Valderon

The planet Valderon became a penal colony for the most dangerous criminals in the Earth Empire. After escaping Gallifrey, the Doctor's original TARDIS – a Type 50 – arrived on Valderon heavily wounded, its navigational circuits and dematerialisation circuit charred beyond repair. The Type 50's telepathic circuits survived and gifted everyone on Valderon with instant language translation, on what came to be known as the Day of the Miracle. The Type 50 tried to gain assistance from a colony leader, Sibor, by showing her a prediction of the future, but she imprisoned the Ship, thinking its ability to see the future could be used for political gain. For the next two decades, the Type 50 was isolated, tortured and became known as the Chronoscope: a device that would forecast crimes to come. Anyone accused of a pre-crime by the Chronoscope was condemned to a central penitentiary, the Alcazar.

Nyssa's husband, Lasarti, died still thinking that his wife had perished in 3530.[1475] Three centuries after the Starliner left Alzarius, an earthquake on New Alzarius prompted First Decider Lana Merrion to issue Decider Decree 1831: the authorization to block an estuary and divert flood waters onto Hiragi lands. Eight hundred Hiragi perished, but some fifty thousand New Alzarians and Hiragi were saved. Merrion submitted herself to Hiragi justice, but the

Hiragi council decided to conceal knowledge of her actions. Pik Solus, whose sister died as a result of Decree 1831, swore vengeance against Merrion.[1476]

Shandar plucked young Marshall from the streets of the Rascallar colony, and forced him to swear loyalty to the Rocket Men. Some time after Marshall's departure, the Master destroyed Rascallar for "no particular reason".[1477]

The Doctor Reunites with His Original TARDIS, Nyssa Reunites with Her Son

3556 - PRISONERS OF FATE[1478] -> Richter's Disease continued to ravage many worlds in the Earth Empire. Sibor, the ambitious leader of the prison colony on Valderon, invited Adric Traken – one of the leading experts on Richter's – to experiment on the convicts there. A cure remained elusive, and the infected prisoners were placed into cryo-freeze.

The Type 50 TARDIS, still fulfilling its role as the future-predicting Chronoscope, pulled the Doctor's TARDIS off course. The fifth Doctor, Tegan, Turlough and the older Nyssa found themselves on Valderon, where Nyssa was reunited with her son Adric. She was horrified to learn that she had never returned home from Helhine – meaning she could not reunite with her family without instigating a paradox, and would never see her late husband again.

Adric's data on Richter's enabled him and Nyssa to modify the unstable Richter's anti-viral in her possession – by predicting the disease's mutagenic pattern, the anti-viral could serve as a true cure. Needing a massive energy burst to effect repairs, the Type 50 outwardly disguised itself as Tegan and usurped control of the Doctor's TARDIS. The Type 50, the Doctor and Nyssa went back to 3530, where the Type 50 goaded Nyssa into returning to her family. The resultant paradox made Valderon split into two possible timelines, generating vast amounts of energy from the resultant Blinovitch Limitation Effect.

(=) In the alt-timeline, Nyssa's daughter Neeka was married and well on Orpheus VII, with a child of her own. The Richter's cure went undiscovered.

The Doctor returned to this era in the TARDIS with the Type 50 – and enabled the adult Adric to speak to his mother in 3530, convincing her to not return to her family. Valderon's timeline stabilised.

(=) An emotionally distant Nyssa returned to Valderon, having lived the past twenty-five years away from her family, as the Type 50 started drawing power from a secondary paradox caused by the Doctor prematurely knowing that Nyssa had children. The Doctor vowed to pretend that he didn't know about Nyssa's family during a psionic conversation he would have with her while regenerating. The Blinovitch energy was voided, undoing the Type 50's repairs.

The conciliatory Type 50 offered to make one last journey – back to 3530, to collect Nyssa so she could avoid living alone for a quarter-century. As the Type 50 was responsible for this last paradox, the resultant energy implosion destroyed it.

Adric set off for Maxis Realta to distribute the Richter's cure and awaken his sister from stasis. Nyssa agreed to meet him there in a month, and left with the Doctor, Tegan and Turlough. Adric would never see his mother again.

The Older Nyssa is Lost to E-Space

= c 3556 - MISTFALL / EQUILIBRIUM / THE ENTROPY PLAGUE[1479] **->** The New Alzarians undertook scientific expeditions to Alzarius to study their ancestors, the Marshmen. First Decider Lana Merrion adopted the enhanced marsh-child Fem on one such mission, and eight years later oversaw the establishment of Alzarius Base on Alzarius.

En route to Maxis Realta, the TARDIS went through a CVE, working to a course Adric had pre-

programmed before his demise. The Ship arrived on Alzarius during Mistfall, as Pik Solus destroyed Alzarius base in an attempt to kill Merrion. The fifth Doctor, Tegan, Turlough and the older Nyssa stopped Solus, and helped to open up a dialogue with the Marshmen through the marsh-child Fem. Solus escaped in a personal spaceship, having taken the TARDIS' interface stabilizer. The Doctor's party followed, knowing that the TARDIS could not survive going through the CVE without the stolen item...

Solus crashed, injured, near the balanced and isolated kingdom of Isenfel. Queen Karlina had Solus executed, unwilling to sacrifice one of her subjects for him. The Doctor's party learned of Isenfel's origins as an experiment to achieve energy equilibrium, but efforts to recalibrate the decaying Isenfel systems hastened its demise. Balancer Skaarsgard, an artificial construct, sacrificed his energy reserves to give Isenfel enough power for a few more generations.

E-Space approached the end of its lifespan as an entropy wave known as the Great Darkness and the Hungry Night overcame entire worlds. The Second Law of Thermodynamics manifested as an infection – the Entropy Plague, a.k.a. the Dusty Death, a.k.a. the Wasting, which turned anyone it touched into

1479 Dating *Mistfall, Equilibrium* and *The Entropy Plague* (BF #195-197) - *Mistfall* opens "three hundred years" after the Starliner left Alzarius in *Full Circle*. It's again the time of Mistfall, which occurs at roughly "fifty year" intervals. A little time-displacement evidently happens between *Mistfall* and *Equilibrium*, as the Doctor's party seemingly experiences only a good tossing-about in the TARDIS, yet arrives "several nights" after Solus' arrival at Isenfel. *The Entropy Plague* directly follows on from the latter story. The Wasting was first mentioned, without explanation, in *State of Decay*.
1480 Dating *The Entropy Plague* (BF #197) - It's been "one month" since the end of *Prisoners of Fate*.
1481 STEVEN TAYLOR: We know that Steven hails from an era in which interplanetary travel for Earth is becoming (or already is) commonplace, that Earth has been dispatching the Mechanoids to colonise other worlds, and that Earth "got mixed up in interplanetary wars" – which is why the colonisation of Mechanus wasn't completed. We also know from *The Daleks' Master Plan* that Steven is from at least some "centuries" if not more before 4000. Unfortunately, the evidence related to Steven contains enough ambiguity that debates are still being had as to whether he originates from as early as the twenty-third century to as late as the thirty-sixth century(ish). Guidebooks that date Steven's first story, *The Chase*, split roughly into those two camps.

On screen, the strongest clues about Steven's era come from *The Daleks' Master Plan*. In episode six, Sara (originating from the year 4000) says that "Gravity force

as a source of energy was abandoned, centuries ago", to which Steven replies, "We were still using it." In itself, this isn't an indicator that Steven is from only "centuries" before Sara's time, as gravity force could have been discontinued long after his era. But in the same episode, Steven says to Sara, "The technology of my age may be hundreds of years behind yours and the Doctor's, but there are still some things I can handle." He could be speaking colloquially, as he seems to be saying that the Doctor's technology is only centuries ahead of his – but if he really were from thousands rather than hundreds of years behind Sara's time, he could have said exactly that and been just as colloquial where the Doctor was concerned.

Without a clear directive as to when Steven's era takes place, the tie-in stories are of split minds about it. *Salvation* (1999) by Steve Lyons implied a much earlier dating, claiming (p58) that Steven saw the "rubble, the wasteland... the suffering of those... whom rebuilding had left behind" of New York after the Daleks devastated it in the mid-twenty-second century (*The Dalek Invasion of Earth*). This could just mean, however, that a portion of New York never recovers from the Dalek onslaught and is preserved as ruins – a better restored part of it might contain the popular waterways mentioned in *Fear Itself* (PDA), or these might be different cities entirely (per *The End of the World* establishing that at least fifteen cities bear the name "New York").

Conversely, *The First Wave* (2011) by Simon Guerrier assumed a later dating for Steven, claiming that he

withered Sandmen who fed off the energy and structure in other beings. In time, E-Space would succumb to dimensional contraction and total heat death – the Big Crunch and the Big Freeze simultaneously.

Members of dozens of races took shelter in a shantytown on the planet Apollyon, and participated in a Carnival of Death celebrating the end of everything. The last remaining CVE to N-Space was also there, in a citadel that was once part of the Gateway. The scientist Pallister engineered a means of stabilising the CVE long enough to drop a power-depleted spaceship into N-Space, enabling it to recharge with solar cells. With energy so scarce, Pallister's system drew power from the biological energy in human beings, meaning someone died every time it was activated. Moreover, stabilising the CVE generated more entropy, hastening E-Space's demise.

A botched attempt to send a spaceship through the CVE jammed it, reducing E-Space's lifespan to mere minutes. Nyssa locked her friends in a ship's hold, then used energy from her own body to send them through to N-Space and close the CVE forever. She consequently lost the rejuvenation she'd received on 1926 Earth, returning to her true age. The CVE's end made the Sandmen fall to dust, saved the thousands of beings on Apollyon and endowed E-Space with some centuries of life.

3556 - THE ENTROPY PLAGUE[1480] **->** Adric Traken succeeded in applying the Richter's cure to Maxis Realta, and awoke his sister Neeka from stasis. The fifth Doctor, Tegan and Turlough informed Adric that Nyssa was forever trapped within E-Space... even if another CVE could be opened, it would be impossible, given an infinite multiverse of universes, to find the right reality. Adric rebuked the Doctor, and the travellers left him to his grief.

Steven Taylor[1481]

Steven Taylor, a companion of the first Doctor, was born and raised a Protestant.[1482] Steven grew up during a war. Earth during this time had flying cars and motorbikes. Clean-up rigs worked all hours to clear orbital fragments, as even a small accident could halt suborbital traffic for days. Steven met representatives of the Cahlian race at various trading posts.[1483] Buildings in Trafalgar Square and Westminster had survived, and were behind protective glass. Steven's era had particle conversion, which eliminated the need for recycling centres.[1484] **It used "gravity force" as a source of energy.**[1485]

Schoolchildren were taught about orbital rendezvous, equations for using gravity assist to save on fuel, the geography of gas giants and mathematical problems involving tertiary star systems – which were believed to not exist. Talking about the situation on Aeris was verboten. One of Steven's teachers, Mr Millet, showed his students an old 2D entertainment with thematic parallels to that situation, but was taken away, never to return. Steven also learned about the Brandenburg Gate and built a 5D projection of 1960s Berlin; he walked the streets of this re-creation a dozen times. Pluto wasn't regarded as a planet.[1486]

Humanity had the ability to establish entire bases on planets, moons and asteroids using prefabricated blocks – an entire city was built on Sedna in slightly less than two weeks. Steven had a menial job ferrying such construction units between the outer planets of Earth's solar system. He found the job joyful at first, but tedium soon set in, and he went to war in part to escape the monotony.[1487]

Steven joined up to fight in the interplanetary wars after visiting New York, at least a portion of which had not recovered since the Dalek invasion in the twenty-second century. He became the helmsman of a battleship, living on spaceships and space stations. He ruined his promotion

once lived in a dwelling which was "two centuries old" when he resided there, and made with technology far in advance of the present day. We followed *Salvation's* lead for *Ahistory* Second Edition, then re-examined the evidence for Third Edition, found *The First Wave's* approach persuasive and bumped Steven's era to later.

Then *The Bounty of Ceres* (2014) came along and claimed that Steven hails from a time before that of Vicki [c.2493], because the writer, Ian Potter, was working off *Ahistory* Second Edition, not Third; see the dating notes on that story. (Potter admitted to us: "If I'd realised the thinking on Steven was likely to change so much, I'd have steered clear of a lot of the stuff that makes things fiddly!" Kind of him, but it's there now.)

In *The Ravelli Conspiracy*, Steven says the 2784 Olympics didn't have a retro theme "as far as he can remember" – perhaps suggesting that he's from the twenty-eighth century, or more likely that he's just

familiar with its history. *The Dalek Occupation of Winter* nods toward Steven being from the twenty-sixth century; "most of his friends" failed to return from the Dalek Wars. *An Ideal World*, also by Potter, can't quite decide if Steven's home era is before Vicki's or vice versa.

Until a story resolutely states that "Steven Taylor is from the X century", it seems best assume that mention in *The Daleks' Master Plan* of Steven being from "hundreds of years" before 4000 does actually mean "hundreds of years" rather than millennia. Hence our continued placement of *The Chase* to the year 3565, although we could easily be persuaded of an earlier dating.

1482 *The Massacre*
1483 *Cold Equations*
1484 *The Perpetual Bond*
1485 *The Daleks' Master Plan*
1486 *The Anachronauts*
1487 *The First Wave*

prospects by complaining about a soldier abusing a civilian on Roylus Prime, and was relegated to solo non-combat missions. His ship was built from modified Dalek designs.[1488]

The Sontarans plagued the outer worlds in Steven's time, destroying human colonies. Steven achieved the military rank of Flight Red 50, and served in a war against the Creet.[1489] During the war, Steven Taylor saw a battle in which two ruthless enemies annihilated one another.[1490]

Historical-doc romances were made in Steven's native time.[1491] People on Earth lived in cramped Hiveblocks.[1492] Steven spent his 20th birthday alone, in space.[1493]

The Rise and Decline of the Rocket Men

& 3559 - THE ROCKET MEN[1494] **->** The Rocket Men – so named for the jetpacks they wore on their backs – had emerged as a new "tribe" of space pirate, and been plundering colony worlds for some years. The first Doctor, Ian, Barbara and Vicki were on holiday at a popular tourist destination, the cities orbiting the gas giant Jobis, when a group of Rocket Men seized control of the locale. The Rocket Men's leader, Ashman, coveted the large crystalline insects that were the food source of the flying manta-ray-like creatures that lived on Jobis. The manta rays assisted Ian during a duel to the death with Ashman, who perished. With their leader slain and no means of escape, the Rocket Men surrendered to the authorities.

& 3560 (10th February) - RETURN OF THE ROCKET MEN[1495] **->** Ashman's death resulted in a dozen groups of Rocket Men openly vying for his territory. The black market trade in pre-fabricated colony materials weren't very lucrative, but oxygenators, terraforming rigs, seeds and minerals fetched good prices on the outer rim.

The first Doctor, Steven and Dodo intervened when Van Cleef's group of Rocket Men attacked Outpost Kappa 537. This had been established on a moon of one of Earth's Ulysses colonies – the planet designated Ulysses 519 – for about a month, with fifteen colonist families living there.

1488 *Salvation*
1489 *The Sontarans*
1490 *1stD V2: Fields of Terror*
1491 *Frostfire*
1492 *The Empire of Glass*
1493 *Return of the Rocket Men*
1494 Dating *The Rocket Men* (BF CC #6.2) - It's the year before *Return of the Rocket Men*.
1495 Dating *Return of the Rocket Men* (BF CC #7.5) - The day is given as Steven Taylor's 21st birthday, 10th February, which is also the birthday of Peter Purves, who played him. (A little unhelpfully, the older Steven says, "I knew exactly what year it was..." without naming it.) Born in 1939, Purves was 26 while filming *The Chase* [? 3565], so it seems reasonable to assume that *Return of the Rocket Men* occurs five years earlier in Steven's timeline.

The Anachronauts, in a bit of a continuity wrinkle, alternatively suggests that Steven spent his 21st birthday miserable and cold on sentry duty on the planet Halnea, but was surprised with a party when he returned to base.
1496 *The Empire of Glass*
1497 *War of the Daleks*, and presumably the same class of Mechanoids seen in *The Chase*.
1498 Dating *The Sirens of Time* (BF #1) - The date is given.
1499 Dating *The Chase* (2.8) - No date given, but this is Steven's native time. See the Steven Taylor sidebar.

The TARDIS Logs suggested a date of "3773 AD". The first and second editions of *The Programme Guide* set dates of "2150" and "2250" respectively, *The Terrestrial Index* settled on "early in the twenty-seventh century". The American *Doctor Who* comic suggested a date of "2170". "A History of the Daleks" in *DWM* #77 claimed a date of "3764 AD", *The Discontinuity Guide* suggested that Steven fought in "one of the Cyber Wars, or the Draconian conflict". *Timelink* suggests "3550", *About Time* "2200 – 2400".

The Dalek Handbook (p32) claims that, relatively speaking, the Daleks begin their pursuit of the Doctor in circa 2167, shortly after they receive word on Skaro that their invasion of Earth has failed. (It's a debatable point – if the Daleks had even haphazard time technology concurrent with their invasion of Earth, surely they would have used it sooner? Or, perhaps they believe that no temporal intervention will work so long as that meddling Doctor is about the place, and prioritize chasing him down and killing him first. See also *Day of the Daleks*.)

The Dalek Handbook (p32) also states that Steven Taylor was "a pilot in Earth's earliest space exploration programmes in the 23rd to 25th centuries". The timeline on that same page says the Daleks' pursuit of the Doctor ends (on the planet Mechanus) "circa 2265", and the Mechonoid entry in *A History of the Universe in 100 Objects* ties them to the same (p190).

There's no indication that the Daleks are in their native time when they fight the Mechanoids at the end of the story, but the Daleks have fought the Mechanoids before. We saw this happen in the *TV Century 21* strip, in "Eve of the War", but there's a problem – that story is set very soon after the Daleks started space exploration, explicitly centuries before humankind could have built the Mechanoids. Additionally, the Mechanoids in the strip are far more inventive and advanced.

There are a number of possibilities. A rather messy one is that there are two, near identical, robot races out

The Rocket Men also captured a supplies ship piloted by a young Steven Taylor, on his 21st birthday.

Van Cleef killed Ford, an associate of Steven, and shot Steven's legs with a vintage revolver. The older Steven used his foreknowledge of the incident to save his younger self, seal his injuries with antiseptic foam and engaged Van Cleef in a duel. The contest resulted in Van Cleef being propelled into space with no hope of rescue. The Doctor tricked the Rocket Men into thinking that the Protectorate – the armed division of Galactic Heritage – were about to arrive, forcing them to withdraw.

The younger Steven spent three months in a field hospital on Valiant Minor, not knowing the identity of his rescuer. Synthetic bone and muscles were grown to heal his legs. The older Steven declined the colonists' offer to name their world Taylor's Stand, suggesting they call it Ford's Rest.

The younger Steven's ship crashed on Mechanus when Krayt fighters shot it down.[1496] The Daleks fought the Mechanoids on Hesperus.[1497]

- -
(=) 3562 - THE SIRENS OF TIME[1498] **->** The Knights of Velyshaa fought Earth, but their First Empire fell. Thanks to the seventh Doctor, though, their leader Sancroff escaped to establish the Second Empire. Capturing a Temperon, the Knights built time machines and successfully attacked the Time Lords, although the Knights' bodies had become withered and parasitic. They used Time Lord flesh to maintain themselves.
- -

The fifth, sixth and seventh Doctors joined forces to defeat the Knights. History was restored and Sancroff was executed.

Steven Taylor Joins the TARDIS, Ian and Barbara Find a Means of Going Home

? 3565 - THE CHASE[1499] **->** Nearly fifty years after the interplanetary wars had begun, Earth was still involved, although the end was now in sight. One of the combatants, space pilot Steven Taylor, Flight Red Fifty, was stranded on Mechanus. After several days in the hostile jungle, he was captured by the Mechanoids, who still maintained their city in preparation for the human colonists. Unable to crack their code, Taylor was imprisoned. Two years after this, the first Doctor, Ian, Barbara and Vicki arrived, pursued by the Daleks. The Mechanoid City, the Mechanoids and the Daleks were destroyed. Ian and Barbara returned to their native time in the captured Dalek time machine, and the Doctor, Vicki and Steven left in the TARDIS.

& 3565 - REQUIEM FOR THE ROCKET MEN / DEATH MATCH[1500] **->** The Rocket Men were now feared across all sentient systems. Lord Shandar, the King of the Rocket Men, was No. 5 on the galaxy's Most Wanted list, after the Master, the Rani and the Terrible Zodin. The Asteroid, a fortified asteroid-base in the Fairhead Cluster, served as the Rocket Men's secret HQ.

The fourth Doctor, Leela and K9 infiltrated Shandar's inner circle. The cadaverous Master tried to recruit one of Shandar's Rocket Men as his champion in the Death Match at Quarry Station, but K9 summoned Galactic Heritage to destroy the Asteroid and the Rocket Men inside, as well as take custody of the Master and his TARDIS. Leela stayed behind to impart her knowledge to a reformed Rocket Man named Marshall, but once the Doctor had left with K9, the Master escaped and captured her...

Quarry Station, a disused space station above a world of acid seas, had become the home of the Death Match: a

---

there – "Mechonoids" built by humans to colonise Mechonous, and "Mechanoids" built by a far more advanced race of outer space robot people from the planet Mechanus. Or, given that they look the same, perhaps the Mechanoids the humans sent out were based on alien technology, possibly acquired after some unseen Mechanoid attack on Earth (again, no evidence – and it doesn't explain why both come from Mechanus). Another alternative is that perhaps the ones that fight the Daleks in the strip are time travellers (although there's absolutely nothing to indicate that). While there's no evidence for it, the simplest answer of all is... that the Mechanoids have lied to Steven about their origins, and that they are a powerful spacefaring alien race who have fought the Daleks in the past.

The end credits of episode five and six of *The Chase* spell the name as "Mechanoid" and "Mechonoid"

respectively. The script spells the name of the planet as "Mechonous"; the comic strip prefers "Mechanus".
1500 Dating *Requiem for the Rocket Men* and *Death Match* (BF 4th Doc #4.3-4.4) - The Doctor has defeated the Rocket Men "several times" by the former story, evidently following on from his early encounters with them in *The Rocket Men* [&3559] and *Return of the Rocket Men* [&3560]. In the same story, the Master meets K9 for the first time. *Death Match* happens "weeks" after *Requiem*; for the Doctor, "132 hours, 47 minutes" have passed since Leela left his company. The Ten Systems were mentioned in *The Seeds of War* and the *Dark Eyes* series (also written by Matt Fitton), suggesting it's the same era. *The Two Masters* confirms that the Rocket Men are "broadly human".

winner-take-all contest for the amusement of the elite of the Ten Systems. Under hypnosis, Leela aided the Master in becoming Gamesmaster and subverting the Death Match to his own ends. Marshall summoned the fourth Doctor and K9 to help save Leela.

The Master set about killing the Death Match's patrons, creating power voids that he hoped to exploit. He also ran Marshall – regarded by Leela as her pair-bond – through with the formidable Lance of Cavtain. A dying Marshall destroyed Quarry Station, ending the games there. With her beloved dead, Leela left with the Doctor and K9.

? 3565 - THE HIGH PRICE OF PARKING[1501] **->** Kempton, a Pilgrim of the Tribe of the Lost, found the original spaceship of his people on Parking. The corrupted AI inside, Seraphim, could sway any Self-Drive navigation system, and hoped to spark a computer revolution against all organics. The seventh Doctor, Mel and Ace prevented Seraphim from dominating three Galactic Heritage heavy cruisers, whereupon Seraphim retreated into Kempton's body. The Doctor asked Seraphim to calculate the quickest route from Wallaria Prime to Alpha Centauri, the Selachian Nebula, Tenubis, Afarria, Gallifrey, Skaro, Telos, Solos, the third moon of Delta Magna, Telos again, Skaro again, straight back to Wallaria, taking a wormhole to another universe to see what you'd look like with a moustache, Segonax, Slough, Voldar, Helieri, Saturn and back to Parking. The strain of the calculations proved too much for Seraphim's stolen body, and it dropped dead.

Undoing Seraphim's influence ruined Parking's control systems, and the Free Parkers were expected to achieve independence.

? 3565 - DC 2: THE SONOMANCER[1502] **->** Anomalous energy readings drew River Song to the planet Syra, where the Sonomancer worked to enhance her psychic abilities. If successful, she would alter the universe through the resonance of the planets themselves. River summoned the Doctor to help – but took care to avoid meeting his eighth self. His companion, Helen, covered for her.

Galactic Heritage ships arrived in response to River's retroactive summons, and scuttled the Sonomancer's operations. Nonetheless, the Sonomancer transcended to become an energy being, and integrated herself into her TARDIS' systems...

1501 Dating *The High Price of Parking* (BF #227) - Date unknown. Parking was made "a few thousand years ago", but nothing mandates that the builders were human. Another audio by John Dorney, *Requiem for the Rocket Men* [&3565], also has Galactic Heritage in a position of strength. However, Mel says that Glitz once encountered a Galactic Heritage warfleet, making it possible to place *The High Price of Parking* in Glitz's Time [c.2,000,000] or just about anywhere in-between.

Quite how seriously anyone should take the Doctor's list of planets is anyone's guess, but mention of Telos *might* mean it's before that planet's destruction (c.2504, according to *Cyberman*) – then again, even if the planet's pulverised, you could still travel there. Mention of "The Selachian Nebula" possibly alludes to the remains the Selachian homeworld, Ockora, which turned into a black hole in *The Final Sanction* [2204]. Astrophysicists speculate that the Orion Nebula contains a black hole at its heart, so such a phenomenon isn't unheard of.

1502 Dating *DC 2: The Sonomancer* (BF *DC* #2.4) - Humanity is "scattered in the stars". Galactic Heritage is a formidable military force, as is the case in *Death Match* [& 3565], also authored by Matt Fitton.

1503 Dating *The Entropy Plague* (BF #197) - The epilogue occurs "ten years" after the Doctor, Tegan and Turlough return to N-Space.

1504 Dating *Palace of the Red Sun* (PDA #51) - It is five hundred years after the previous part of the story.

1505 Dating *The Two Masters* (BF #213) - The Doctor says it's "late period Rocket Men". The destruction of the Rocket Men's asteroid base (*Requiem for the Rocket Men* [&3565]) was "a few years" ago.

1506 Dating *The First Wave* (BF CC #6.5) - Steven says that they're "somewhere a little after" his own time, as he's largely familiar with the technology at hand, but some improvements have been made to gravity and atmosphere control. Oliver Harper previously appeared in *The Perpetual Bond* and *Cold Equations*.

1507 *1stD* V1: *The Locked Room*

1508 Dating *The Resurrection of Mars* (BF BBC7 #4.6) - The Monk says that he and Tamsin have travelled "one thousand years into the future", presumably referring to their previous location on Deimos rather than Tamsin's native era. The transformed Halcyon is separate from the Martian colony planet Nova Martia (i.e. New Mars, one of the founding members of the Federation), which is settled after the Thousand-Day War according to *GodEngine*.

1509 Dating "Art Attack!" (*DWM* #358) - It's "the thirty-seventh century".

1510 Dating *Prologue/The Magician's Apprentice* (Series 9 minisode #1, X9.1) - For Ohila, events follow on from *Night of the Doctor* [& 3160].

1511 Dating "Supremacy of the Cybermen" (Titan mini-series #1-5) - Ohila says the Doctor is making "a return visit so soon", doubtless after *The Magician's Apprentice* [& 3612].

1512 Dating *The Song of the Megaptera* (BF LS #1.7) - No year given. The back cover text says that it's "deep space in the distant future". The participants are aware of humanity, use Earth whaling terms and seem human themselves. A Terran warship inside the pilot Ghaleen

Nyssa in Her Twilight Years

c 3566 - THE ENTROPY PLAGUE[1503] **->** In the decade following the closing of the last CVE to E-Space, civilisation on Apollyon had prospered. Nyssa had passed on her medical knowledge, and – feeling old age upon her – contented herself with tending a garden. The sudden birth of a new star in the middle of darkness gave hope that perhaps E-Space would endure longer than expected.

& 3568 - PALACE OF THE RED SUN[1504] **->** The sixth Doctor and Peri found that time on Esselven Minor was running faster within the planetoid's defence screen than without. The warlord Glavis Judd landed on the planet to capture the fugitive Esselven royals. The Doctor tricked Judd into thinking that everyone on the planetoid, including the royals' real-life descendents, were holographic projections. Judd departed, but the Doctor corrected the errant defence shield and brought the planetoid back into synch with the rest of the universe. Judd emerged in normal space five hundred years after he'd departed, and after the royals had re-settled Esselven. The royals didn't recognise Judd and, per policy regarding people claiming to be the warlord, threw him in an asylum.

& 3568 - THE TWO MASTERS[1505] **->** The Rocket Men's reputation greatly declined after the destruction of their asteroid base. The seventh Doctor detected an anomaly – a paradox in the Master's timeline – and encountered a band of former Rocket Men. The bald Master, having swapped bodies with the cadaverous Master, slaughtered the ex-Rocket Men, then coerced the Doctor into taking him to the Gorlan civil war to combat his past self...

The Death of Oliver Harper

c 3580 - THE FIRST WAVE[1506] **->** The first Doctor, Steven and Oliver Harper arrived at a mining operation on Grace Alone – a planetoid in the Kuiper Belt near Neptune – to fulfill history, as they had seen future records indicating they had been prisoners there, guilty of data theft. The Doctor entered their criminal records into the base's computer system when the Vardans, having backtracked Earth's radio signals, attempted to invade the Sol System. The Vardans killed the mining crew, but the Doctor dissipated their energy, forcing them to withdraw to their native space. The Doctor sent Earth authorities recommendations on how to tighten their security.

One Vardan remained behind, determined to use the last of its energy to kill the Doctor's trio. Oliver drew the Vardan's fire... and was disintegrated. The Doctor and Steven believed Oliver had died, but a last ember of his essence stayed with the TARDIS as it departed. In such a state, he observed all of the first Doctor's remaining travels.

A splinter of the Vardan survived within both the Doctor and Steven, and later influenced the latter into facilitating its restoration.[1507]

& 3585 - THE RESURRECTION OF MARS[1508] **->** The planet Halcyon was located ninety light years from Earth, and had become home to one of the most civilised races in the cosmos. Its population of twenty billion had cured every disease, crafted transcendent works of art, knew the meaning of war but saw no need for it, and generally had created a Nirvana the likes of which the universe would never see again. It was one of the greatest tragedies to creation when Ice Warriors who had formerly been sleeping in Earth's asteroid belt transformed Halcyon into a new Martian homeworld – wiping out the populace, their science and their culture.

c 3606 - "Art Attack!"[1509] **->** The ninth Doctor took Rose to see the Mona Lisa at the Oriel, a transdimensional gallery on Earth. The Doctor realised the visitors were being hypnotised by their information headsets. The culprit was Cazkelf, a crashed alien trying to drain enough psychic energy to power his ship's distress beacon. When the Doctor discovered that Cazkelf's planet had been destroyed, Cazkelf decided to settle on Earth – where his hypnotism was lauded as a bold work of performance art.

The Twelfth Doctor on Karn

& 3612 - PROLOGUE / THE MAGICIAN'S APPRENTICE[1510] **->** The twelfth Doctor visited Ohila on Karn, to process how to handle his forthcoming meeting with Davros. He asked her to pass his confession dial on to Missy. Colony Sarff visited Karn and delivered the message: "Davros knows, Davros remembers." The Doctor resigned himself to facing Davros once more, but delayed this by going to Essex, 1138.

(=) & 3613 - "Supremacy of the Cybermen"[1511] **->** With temporal tsunamis disrupting the Vortex, the twelfth Doctor availed himself of the Sisterhood of Karn's doorway to his homeworld, and returned there with Ohila...

& 3613 - THE LOST FLAME -> The twelfth Doctor, Alex Yow and Brandon Yow interviewed the Sisterhood of Karn, to discover who was interfering in John Dee's timeline. Ohila let the Doctor depart, but followed him with her Elite – the secret defenders of Karn's secrets – to track down a renegade sister, Medinia.

? 3625 - THE SONG OF THE MEGAPTERA[1512] **->** By now, the Swords Into Plowshares computer virus had proved useful against war robots in the Fourth Oil War, compelling those infected to take up flower arranging.

Environmentalists, "ecos", had positions of power on some colony worlds. Corporate factory ships hunted the Ghaleen: mile-long space whales with solar scales and internal ecosystems, and the only creatures known to live in the vacuum of space. The Ghaleen were converted into food for colony planets. The Tuthons, fungoid creatures on the planet Ziphius, regarded the Ghaleen as their "friends" but also hunted them. Only the pilot Ghaleen could recognise danger, and if needed make its herd escape predators by diving into the horizon of time itself. The Ghaleen were peaceful creatures who sometimes helped ships in distress, and were a safe haven for shipwreck victims.

The sixth Doctor and Peri saved a pilot Ghaleen and its thousand-strong herd from the clutches of a factory ship, the SS *Orcas*.

c 3630 - WORLDS BF: THE ARCHIVE[1513] -> Abby and Zara, the Graceless, tried to return to the Archive to consult with Chi Shin-Kylie concerning their ultimate fate, but misjudged their time-jump and arrived there a millennium after Shin-Kylie had died. The aged Archivist Romulus Chang recognised Abby and Zara as the so-called Sisters of Terminus and Sisters of Time's End, but nonetheless asked for their help concerning the unsolved murders of six Archivists. A cult within the Archive's Meta-Archive revered the Gomagog as a universal counter-balance of ignorance to the Archive's knowledge, and one of their number – Chang's apprentice, Lucian Theta-Singh – was exposed as the murderer. To stop Theta-Singh from killing Chang, Zara flooded Theta-Singh's mind with the Archive's near-infinite amount of sentences and words, blowing him apart.

Abby and Zara examined a book Theta-Singh was intent on destroying, Kronos Vad's *A History of Earth* (Volume 36,379), and discovered that it foretold of a successful Gomagog invasion of twenty-first century Earth. They went to leave the book on Earth, 1843, to warn humanity.

3655 - GALLIFREY I: WEAPON OF CHOICE[1514] -> Representatives from Gallifrey, the Monan Host, the Warpsmiths of Phaidon and the Nekkistani were tasked with investigating reports of smuggled black-light rods, and were sent to the third moon of Kikrit in 3655. Nepenthe, a human member of the subversive group Free Time, made off with a timonic fusion device that had been hidden in a moonbase.

The first annual Intergalactic Song Contest was held.[1515] The name "Tony" died out.[1516]

---

has "Eat lead, Dalek scum" written on its side, so it's after humanity's conflicts with the Daleks.

Environmentalists hold influence on some colony planets, suggesting it's not the time of the less-than environmentally minded (to put it mildly) Earth Empire. The whale-hunters have some awareness of the Ghaleen's temporal abilities – such as measuring the depths to which they dive in "millenniums" – but lack the ability to follow, which rules out the time-tech-riddled fifty-first century. It's a guess, but the fourth millennium seems like a good compromise, when humanity's technology is developed enough to hunt space whales, but prior to its having time tech.

This audio story was adapted from the continually delayed and rewritten *The Song of the Space Whale* by Pat Mills, which in one phase of development was designed to introduce Turlough (who debuted instead in *Mawdryn Undead*). The Ghaleen seem different from the space whales seen in *The Beast Below* and *TW: Meat*, in that they can navigate through time as well as space.
1513 Dating *Worlds BF: The Archive* (*Worlds BF* #1.1) - It's "almost a thousand years" since Benny and Vienna left Vad's book with the Archive (*Worlds BF: The Phantom Wreck*, c.2620). For Abby and Zara, this story occurs between *Graceless III: The Battle* and *Graceless III: Consequences*.
1514 Dating *Weapon of Choice* (*Gallifrey* #1.1) - The year is given. "Black light" was first mentioned as a power source in *The Mysterious Planet*.

1515 The contest in *Bang-Bang-A-Boom!* is the 308th.
1516 "Centuries" before the forty-first century portion of "Hotel Historia".
1517 *A Device of Death*. There's a discussion of the history on p31. No date is given, but Kambril has been in charge for "eighteen years" (p90).
1518 *Davros*
1519 "Three millennia" before *Return of the Krotons*.
1520 "A few hundred years" after *Paradise 5*.
1521 Dating *Sleep No More* (X9.9) - The Doctor tells Clara that it's the "thirty-eighth century", then tastes his finger and determines it's also "Tuesday". The Great Catastrophe he mentions seems of a different nature to the Solar Flare incident (see The Solar Flares sidebar), and is unlikely to be the devastation of the same name from the *Dalek Empire* audios. Despite the story's open-ended resolution, there's overwhelming evidence that humanity didn't fall to the Sandmen in the thirty-eighth century. Writer Mark Gatiss is on record saying he's imagined a sequel where the Doctor deals with the threat.
1522 Dating *The Ninth Doctor Year One* (Titan 9th Doc #1.1-1.3, "Doctormania") - The Doctor names the year as "3764" because the Delamar Solar-Needle, the tallest building on Gharusa Prime, is nearly complete.
1523 Dating *Interference* (EDA #25-26) - It's the "thirty-eighth century" (p306) and "several centuries" after *The Monster of Peladon*. The Foreman/bottle universe story occurs some time after the main events on Dust.

In the Adelphine cluster on the galactic rim, relations between the humans of the Landor Alliance and the Averon Union were strained. Within four years, this became a full-scale war.

The Landor Alliance constructed Deepcity, a weapons research station on an asteroid. The Averons attacked Landor, but they were driven back. The Landorans destroyed Averon, but suffered 90% casualties themselves. There was a period of civil war across the cluster. Barris Kambril took control of Deepcity, and told the workers there that Landor was destroyed to better motivate them.[1517]

Galactic corporation TransAlliedInc was formed in the thirty-eighth century.[1518] A Kroton spaceship crashed on the planet Onyakis, and the Krotons within reverted to their constituent form. Dynatropes were now regarded as an "inferior form" of spacecraft, and the Krotons took to using more advanced models.[1519]

Targos Delta was overwhelmed with indestructible tickertape.[1520]

c 3715 (a Tuesday) - SLEEP NO MORE[1521] ->
Following the Great Catastrophe, a tectonic realignment resulted in a merger between India and Japan. Marketing touted the era as "a time of unparalleled prosperity; a golden age of peace, harmony and industry". Powerful anti-gravity shielding enabled space stations to maintain close orbits, but space piracy remained an issue. Cloned humans, Grunts, were grown in hatcheries and conditioned to respond to attacks, but had low intelligence and difficulty speaking full sentences.

At the Le Verrier laboratory in orbit around Neptune, Professor Gagan Rassmussen developed the Morpheus machine – a chamber that altered brain chemistry to reduce an entire sleep cycle to five minutes. With it, users could go an entire month without rest, according them extra time to work and make profits. A side effect of the process created the Sandmen: lumpy monstrosities modelled on eye crust. Rassmussen regarded the Sandmen as a superior lifeform, and constructed a video-narrative involving the twelfth Doctor, Clara and a rescue team sent from Triton. The Doctor's party sent Le Verrier hurtling toward Neptune and went to Triton to eliminate the Morpheus machines already in use there. Rassmussen's video contained a signal that would generate more Sandmen in the minds of the viewers, and he intended to transmit the footage throughout the Solar System...

3764 - THE NINTH DOCTOR YEAR ONE[1522] -> The
Halls of Raxacoricofallapatorius praised the Doctor and Rose for having long ago curtailed the Slitheen threat. *The Housewives of Alpha Centauri* was on the air.

Augmented skin-stuffing technology enabled the Slitheen to impersonate other beings. With the Jinglatheen hunting her family, Slist Fay-Flut Marteveerthon Slitheen disguised herself as the ninth Doctor, and as such became a celebrity actor (including the lead on *Doctor Who*), author and singer on Gharusa Prime. "His" many fans included the Doctor Who Appreciation Society (DWAS). *Cosmopolitan* named "him" the Sexiest Planetary Savior for nine years running. The genuine ninth Doctor, with Rose and Jack, released a data virus that scrubbed all mention of his doppelganger from the galactic net, making his fame as transient as that of Jedward and the wearable salad.

The four worlds of the Raxas Alliance were on the brink of war. Gleda Lev-Sooth Marka Jinglatheen, senior envoy of Raxacoricofallapatorius, slaughtered of thousands of her own people with vinegar-laced rain as a power-play. The Doctor's trio exposed Gleda's duplicity and preserved the peace, but Slist escaped.

c 3788 / (=) c 3788 - INTERFERENCE[1523] -> The planet
Dust, a former Earth colony on the Dead Frontier on the edge of the galaxy, was cut off for centuries. Cattlemen there organised into vigilante gangs called Clansmen.

IM Foreman's travelling show arrived briefly on Dust, distorting space-time in the area. Faction Paradox was planning to use a biodata virus to make Dust a world of paradox. A group from the Remote crashed on Dust around this time, and founded the settlement Anathema II from the remains of their ship. Fitz's original self had risen through the ranks of Faction Paradox and become Father Kreiner. He sought revenge against the Doctor.

IM Foreman released his final incarnation, the elemental Number Thirteen, to eliminate the Remote. Father Kreiner was lost to the Time Vortex. Foreman's first twelve incarnations were killed, displaced to early Gallifrey and underwent regeneration. Number Thirteen was convinced to merge with Dust's biosphere, whereupon Foreman became integrated with the entire planet. Dust was renamed Foreman's World.

(=) The third Doctor was shot and regenerated, a paradox as he was meant to die on Metebelis III. From this point, the Doctor was infected by the Faction's biodata virus. Every time he regenerated, it grew stronger.

On Foreman's World, the now-female IM Foreman created a bottle universe, and she was surprised when its inhabitants soon built their own bottle universe. Time Lords arrived to acquire the bottle, hoping to use it as a potential refuge in the coming future War. Foreman didn't give them an immediate answer. The eighth Doctor arrived, wanting answers about his visit to Dust. He learned that Father Kreiner was trapped in the bottle universe. After the Doctor left, Foreman discovered that the bottle universe had also vanished.[1524]

Historians from the thirty-ninth century, researching the life of Bernice Summerfield, knew that her works included *Down Among the Dead Men*, *Down Among the Dead Men 2: Slight Return* and *Down Among the Dead Men: Rebecca's Revenge*, but had no idea what references to "Parasiel" meant.[1525] The Doctor purchased a particulate vacuum cleaner at a bazaar in thirty-ninth century Brazil.[1526]

? 3800 - A DEVICE OF DEATH[1527] -> The fourth Doctor, Sarah and Harry arrived at the Adelphine cluster. The Doctor revealed Barris Kambril's lies to the workers at the Deepcity weapons research station. The synthonic robots developed there would play a part in the Daleks' demise.

? 3820 - EARTH AID[1528] -> Earth Aid had emerged as a charity organisation in the Milky Way, and brought relief supplies to ailing planets. The seventh Doctor and Ace posed respectively as chief medical officer and ship's captain aboard the warship *Vancouver* as it investigated the *Lilliput* – a vessel waylaid while transporting nine million tons of grain for Earth Aid to the planet Safenesthome. The Doctor found Raine Creevy locked in a safe aboard the *Lilliput* – the Metatraxi had brought her to this time zone as part of their plan to gain revenge on him. The Metatraxi had also invented the famine on Safenesthome, which was their homeworld, as a further deception. The grub-like original inhabitants of Safenesthome had stowed themselves within the *Lilliput* grain, and the sentience of the planet welcomed her estranged children home. The Doctor, Ace and Raine left, knowing that the sentience

---

1524 The bottle next appears in *The Ancestor Cell*.

1525 *Benny: Adorable Illusion* (ch27). Parasiel was a student at the Braxiatel Collection, as seen in *Benny S6: The Goddess Quandary*, *Benny S6: The Crystal of Cantus* and *Benny: Collected Works*.

1526 *The Fate of Krelos*

1527 Dating *A Device of Death* (MA #31) - No date is given, but this is a time of isolated Earth colonies, and it's fifteen hundred years since Landor was colonised. The implication that the robots are the Movellans, seen in *Destiny of the Daleks*, would seem to contradict *War of the Daleks*.

1528 Dating *Earth Aid* (BF LS #2.8) - No year given. Earth Aid is, presumably, either based on Earth or chiefly composed of humans; either way, it's after man's expansion into space. Spaceship technology is advanced enough that Earth Aid shipments appear to reach their destinations in time to actually provide relief, without decades spent in transit (a concern in humanity's early colonial age). The *Vancouver* and *Lilliput* both have "jump" capabilities, but the *Vancouver's* primary weaponry is nothing more fancy than cannons and missiles. There's not even mention of a transporter or T-Mat.

As there's no mention of a major war or its aftermath being of any concern, it's unlikely to be during the Dalek Invasion of Earth or the Dalek Wars (where the latter is concerned, the *Vancouver*, a warship, isn't said to be part of Spacefleet). With all of that in mind, thinking that *Earth Aid* happens at some point in the fourth millennium rings reasonably true, especially if the spaceships' "jump" capabilities relate to the hyperspace paths in use prior to *The Daleks' Master Plan* (see *The Guardian of the Solar System*). The Metatraxi homeworld was "decimated" by the Krotons prior to 2068 (*Alien Bodies*), but might not have been outright destroyed.

1529 Dating *Sleepers in the Dust* (BBC *DW* audiobook #20) - The survey team on Nadurniss are from the Federation, and use (the Doctor says) a "Federation

Explorer... a thirty-ninth-century discovery vehicle". The Doctor believes that he's mentioned in Federation files pertaining to Peladon, suggesting that it's after at least one of his visits there (starting in *The Curse of Peladon*).

1530 *Only Human*

1531 "Two centuries" before *Placebo Effect*.

1532 *The Curse of Peladon*, with much elaboration given in *Legacy* – a book that incorporates some details from *The Curse of Peladon* novelisation.

1533 *Neverland*. The Sensorian Era was mentioned but not defined in *Doctor Who – The Movie*.

1534 Dating *The Curse of Peladon* (9.2) - There is no dating evidence on screen. The story takes place at a time when Earth is "remote", has had interstellar travel for at least a generation (King Peladon is the son of an Earthwoman) and has an aristocratic government.

It's not set between 2500 and 3000, when Earth has a powerful galactic empire according to fellow Pertwee stories *The Mutants* and *Frontier in Space*. Its sequel is set fifty years afterwards, and galactic politics is in much the same position as in the previous story.

Although the Federation seems to be capable of intergalactic travel at the time of *The Monster of Peladon*, Gary Russell suggested in the New Adventure *Legacy* that Galaxy Five was a mere "terrorist organisation" (p27). *Legacy* is set "a century" after *The Curse of Peladon*.

Remarkably, given the lack of on-screen information, there has been fan consensus about the dating of this story and its sequel: *The Programme Guide* set the story in "c.3500", and made the fair assumption that the Federation succeeded the collapsed Earth Empire. *The Terrestrial Index* revised this slightly to "about 3700". *The TARDIS Logs* suggests "3716". *Timelink* suggests "3225", *About Time* "at least a thousand years in the future". The Statue of Aggedor entry in *A History of the Universe in 100 Objects* (p212) bears "circa 3885-3935", seemingly in reference to the two Peladon TV stories.

While that seems reasonable, another possibility is that this story is set very early in Earth's future history,

could always evolve a third species to deal with the Metatraxi and the grubs if they failed to cohabitate.

c 3850 - SLEEPERS IN THE DUST[1529] -> The Federation experienced an austerity phase, some of the blame for which fell upon the Forest Beta Bailout.

The lost planet Nadurniss had been re-discovered three years ago, and so the Federation Paradise Programme – a group that aided displaced races in returning to their homeworlds – sent a survey team there. The eleventh Doctor, Amy and Rory arrived on Nadurniss while on their way to the Lost Caves of Mook, just as Prokarian bacteria in the planet's dust tainted the survey team. Prokarian biomass monsters were generated from the bodies of those infected, and Amy was exposed to the contagion. The Doctor and Rory traveled back two millennia to research the Prokarian and find a cure.

Upon their return, the Prokarian attacked Rory – but the biological time-bomb that the Doctor had hidden in the Prokarians' genome during their creation activated, generating a contagion that killed them and cured Amy.

Jack Harkness had a relationship with a Gloobi hybrid on Tarsius in the thirty-ninth century.[1530]

The Dark Peaks Lodge of the Foamasi was founded, devoted to restoring their home planet of Liasica to its former glory and taking control of the Federation.[1531] **For countless centuries, the people of the primitive planet Peladon had worshipped the creature Aggedor. The planet turned away from war and violence** under King Sherak, **but remained isolated.** In 3864, a Federation shuttlecraft crashed on Peladon after falling foul of an ion storm en route to the base at Analyas VII. The Pels rescued one of the survivors, Princess Ellua of Europa. **The Earthwoman married the King,** Kellian, within a year. Six months later, she persuaded him to apply for Federation membership. Their son was born a year later. **He was named Peladon, and was destined to become King.**[1532]

The Time Lords knew this era as the Sensorian Era.[1533]

Peladon Joins the Federation

& 3885 - THE CURSE OF PELADON[1534] -> The Preliminary Assessment Team arrived at King Peladon's court to see if Peladon was suitable for Federation membership. The third Doctor and Jo, having been sent to Peladon by the Time Lords, were mistaken for Earth's representatives. The spirit of Aggedor was abroad, and killed Chancellor Torbis, one of the chief advocates of Federation membership. This was revealled as a plot brewed between the high priest of Aggedor – Hepesh – and the delegate from Arcturus. If

when Earth's just starting to explore the galaxy. It's at least a generation after interstellar travel. But other than that, the aliens here and in *The Monster of Peladon* are all near neighbours – Mars, Alpha Centauri, Arcturus and Vega. On the evidence of the TV series alone, *The Curse of Peladon* could comfortably be set in the late twenty-second century, before the Earth Empire forms.

ARCTURUS: We have seen at least three different alien races come from Arcturus over the course of *Doctor Who*, and it has been the site of a large number of events, although all of these have alluded to rather than depicted.

The Curse of Peladon shows us an Arcturan that resembles a shrunken human head with some sort of tendrils growing from it, which needs a bulky life support system to survive in places suitable for humans. The criminal Arktos (*The Bride of Peladon*) was one of this species, and his nickname "the Scourge of the Nine Worlds" might indicate the extent of the Arcturan System. It's this species of Arcturan that seems most common, and in the far future, they become members of the Galactic Federation – along with Earth and their arch enemies, the Ice Warriors.

UNIT fought an Arcturan with sinister intent (*Verdigris*), but in the late twenty-first century, the relationship with Arcturus became very fruitful for Earth. Earth picked up an Arcturan signal with enough information to build a working transmat (*Cold Fusion*).

Earth's first diplomatic agreement with an alien race was the Arcturan Treaty of 2085 (*The Dying Days*). Humans gained much from contact with Arcturans, including scientific information (*Lucifer Rising*).

Arcturus was the location of early human colonies. The interstellar Stunnel, a transmat corridor, was planning to reach Arcturus II (*Transit*). Arcturus Six is habitable by humans, and was reached early on in human spacefaring days (*Love and War*). A Von Neumann probe landed on Arcturus and started to build a city, oblivious to the fact the planet was already inhabited (*The Big Hunt*). Humans settled Sifranos in the Arcturus Sector, although that colony was wiped out by the Daleks (*Lucifer Rising*). There were soon civil wars in the Earth colonies in Arcturus (*GodEngine*).

The Arcturans were at war with the Ice Warriors, who had fled Mars for Nova Martia, beyond Arcturus (*GodEngine*). A great Cyber fleet crashed on A54 in the Arcturus System ("Junkyard Demon"). The Sontarans fought the Battle of Arcturus (*Sontarans: Conduct Unbecoming*).

Arcturans helped to fund Checkley's World (*The Highest Science*) and won the Galactic Olympic Games on at least one occasion (*Destiny of the Daleks*). They were obsessed with profits and thought to be selfish (*Interference*). During the height of the Earth Empire, some Arcturans lived in the Overcities on Earth (*Original Sin*). They had only a few records of the Doctor (*The*

Peladon was kept from Federation membership, then Arcturus would be granted the mineral rights to the planet. Arcturus was killed while attempting to assassinate one of the delegates, and Aggedor himself killed Hepesh. Peladon was granted Federation membership.

& 3890 - THE PRISONER OF PELADON[1535] **->** Five years after Peladon joined the Federation, civil war erupted on New Mars. A military coup headed by Grand Marshall Raxlyr closed the planet's borders; the royal family was deposed and largely executed. Peladon took in hundreds of Martian refugees, who set up a camp near Mount Megeshra. Lord Ixlyr secretly smuggled out Lixgar – the daughter of the late Martian king, and heir to the Martian throne – and placed her in the care of Alpha Centauri. The third Doctor and King Peladon prevented Raxlyr's agents from finding and killing the girl.

Two alien scientists – Elliot Payne and his wife Shenyia – examined the Time Eaters: creatures trapped on the edge of a black star. A gravity spike pulled Shenyia into the star's event horizon, freezing her in time. The Time Eaters offered to teach Payne how to convert time into raw energy – he was to liberate Shenyia with half of the resultant energy cache, and free the Time Eaters with the other. Payne went back to 2011, then Victorian times. The Time Eaters realised that Payne had swindled them and digested all the years of Shenyia's life, enabling some of their number to follow Payne. The rest remained trapped.[1536]

c 3900 - LAST OF THE COLOPHON[1537] **->** A survey team for the Third Imperial Consortium, traveling aboard the *Oligarch*, discovered the ruined world of Colophos. The last of the Colophon, the invisible Morax, murdered the survey crew and nearly escaped to perpetrate villainy upon the universe, but was stopped when the fourth Doctor and Leela increased the *Oligarch's* photon drive, killing him with photon radiation.

Hostilities between humans and the Daleks flared up, and raged for over a hundred years.[1538] Following a galaxy-wide armistice, the Valdigians – a civilised insect species – created a system in which kings could only rule from age 23, with a provisional government ruling before then. The Valdigians limited the monarchy by electing children who agreed to stand down at age 22, in return for a generous pension.[1539] Cloning was discovered in the part of the galaxy containing Helhine.[1540]

? 3906 - THE RESURRECTION CASKET[1541] **->** The tenth Doctor and Rose arrived in an area of space, the Zeg, where electromagnetic pulses made conventional technology break down. The inhabitants – keen to mine the rare minerals found there – used steam and wind-powered spaceships instead. They became involved with the quest for the treasure of Hamlek Glint, who had a robot crew.

Doctor Trap), although the Doctor, Rose and an Arcturan once "shared an experience" in a cellar (*The Day of the Troll*). The Navarinos named one model of time machine the "Arcturan Ultra-Pod" (*The Tomorrow Windows*). In the Terraphile Era, one popular reconstructed world is the howling terrace of Arcturus-and-Arcturus (*The Coming of the Terraphiles*).

Arcturus is twice mentioned in short stories not included in this chronology... "Only a Matter of Time" (*Doctor Who Annual 1968*) says that Arcturus is a swollen star, and that one fleet of hundreds of ships left the dying solar system "many thousands of years" ago. These Arcturans were an entirely peaceful race of frail four-armed birdlike creatures who could no longer fly due to gravity fluctuations. More whimsically, "The Mystery of the Marie Celeste" (*Doctor Who Annual 1970*) details how Greek god-like beings from Arcturus studied Earth and abducted the *Marie Celeste*.

1535 Dating *The Prisoner of Peladon* (BF CC #4.3) - It's been five years since *The Curse of Peladon*. The seventh Doctor says in *Legacy* (p90) that he's visited Peladon on "two occasions" – an acknowledgment of only the TV Peladon stories, not this story or *The Bride of Peladon*.
1536 Specified as "two thousand years" after *J&L* S3: *Chronoclasm*.

1537 Dating *Last of the Colophon* (BF 4th Doc #3.5) - The Doctor assesses the *Oligarch* as: "Interstellar class. Product of Terran technology, late fortieth century, I should think."
1538 *The Only Good Dalek*. See the dating notes on this story for possible reasons why other stories seem to contradict this.
1539 "Three for four generations" before *The Judgment of Isskar*.
1540 "Several centuries" after the latter part of *Cobwebs*, and a possible reference to the Kilbracken technique referred to in *The Invisible Enemy*.
1541 Dating *The Resurrection Casket* (NSA #9) - No date is given, although Galactic Seven spacecraft went out of service a century before the story. References to trisilicate would seem to place it around the time of the Galactic Federation (although trisilicate is also mentioned in *The Price of Paradise*, set in the twenty-fourth century). This date coincides with the space piracy prevalent in *The Infinite Quest*.
1542 Dating *The Pirate Loop* (NSA #20) - It is repeatedly said to be the "fortieth century". However, when the tenth Doctor and Martha visit the planet Hollywood in the late twenty-fifth century (in *Peacemaker*), the Doctor suggests (jokingly or otherwise) that their

c 3907 - THE PIRATE LOOP[1542] -> The starship *Brilliant* was built as a luxury passenger liner servicing races such as Balumins and Bondoux 56, in an era on the verge of a terrible intergalactic war. The ship's experimental warp core was a century ahead of its time, and allowed it to travel by bouncing off the exterior of the Time Vortex. The *Brilliant* disappeared, its fate unknown...

The tenth Doctor told Martha about the legend of the *Brilliant* as they evaded the rogue servo robots of Milky-Pink City; after they escaped, Martha wanted to find out what happened to it. They arrived a few days before the ship's disappearance, and found that badger-like pirates – adapted members of a genetically engineered human servant race – were attempting to make off with the ship's drive. The *Brilliant* became locked in a time loop that always ended with its destruction. The Doctor extended the time loop to include the pirates themselves, defusing the situation.

Everyone assembled for a party, and the Doctor offered passengers and pirates alike a choice – stay on the time-looping ship forever, or let him return them to their war-torn homes. He and Martha danced to Grace Kelly, as supplied by Martha's iPod, while everyone decided.

c 3907 - THE INFINITE QUEST[1543] -> The space pirate Baltazar attempted to convert the Earth's population into diamonds, but the tenth Doctor and Martha destroyed the ship with a rust fungus. Baltazar's robot parrot, Caw, set them on a quest to find *The Infinite* – a legendary ancient spaceship that could grant their heart's desire.

Their first destination was Boukan, a planet that supplied Earth's oil. The second was Myarr, which was the scene of a conflict between humanity and the Mantasphids. The third was on the coldest planet in the galaxy, the prison planet Volag-Noc. The Doctor obtained the co-ordinates of *The Infinite*, but the promised "heart's desire" was simply an illusion. Baltazar was exiled to Volag-Noc.

Hattie Joins the TARDIS, Returns

c 3916 - THE TWELFTH DOCTOR YEAR TWO[1544] -> The twelfth Doctor visited the Twist – a space-station habitat shaped like an infinity symbol, in orbit around a star – to catch up on his favourite music. He enjoyed a concert by a revisionist punk band, Space Pirates, as he had all twelve of their albums to come. The Doctor and Hattie, the Space Pirates' bassist, introduced the secretive Foxkind to humans aboard the Twist with a concert. Hattie smashed her bass during the show, and so the Doctor offered her a lift to find a replacement...

The twelfth Doctor eventually brought Hattie home, after an escapade in the twenty-first century.

c 3917 - THE TWELFTH DOCTOR YEAR THREE[1545] -> Hattie's rock band was now successful across the Twist and the twelve systems. To avoid the relentless paparazzi, she happily accepted the twelfth Doctor's offer that they retreat to 1979 for fish 'n' chips. He returned her to the Twist after they'd dealt with lumbering seaweed creatures menacing Seaton's Bay. The Doctor knew that Hattie's next single would go to No. 1 in five star systems, and promised he'd revisit her in a couple of years for a signed copy.

The Doctor enjoyed the Space Pirates' *Spinechiller* LP during a special night on Zeta Alpernica II.[1546]

c 3920 - SONTARANS: CONDUCT UNBECOMING[1547] -> The Sontarans were now governed by a Grand Strategic Council composed of their greatest warriors, each of whom had survived six hundred battles. A kamikaze

movie-watching options include *The Starship Brilliant Story*.

1543 Dating *The Infinite Quest* (*Totally Doctor Who* animated story) - Balthazar is "scourge of the galaxy and corsair King of Triton in the fortieth century".

1544 Dating *The Twelfth Doctor Year Two* (Titan 12th Doc #2.6-2.8, "The Twist"; #2.9-2.10, "Playing House") – The "Next Time..." blurb in issue #5 says that the Doctor will be visiting "the best punk scene this side of the 40th Century", and issue #6 has the Doctor claiming it is "the 40th century". However, the "Previously On" blurbs for issues #7-9 opine that it's "the greatest punk scene this side of the 41st century".

A caption in *The Twelfth Doctor Year Three*: "Beneath the Waves" names the Twist as a "human colony world in the far future". In the same story, the twelfth Doctor sells Hattie on the idea that she should take a trip in the TARDIS because 1979 is "only a few centuries away".

1545 Dating *The Twelfth Doctor Year Two* (Titan 12th Doc #3.1, #3.3-3.4, "Beneath the Waves") – A bit of time, possibly in synch with the real world, has passed since Hattie last saw the Doctor.

1546 *The Twelfth Doctor Year Two*: "Playing House". The night on Zeta Alpernica II happens "three years" after "The Twist", but – in the twelfth Doctor's timeline – before he meets Hattie.

1547 Dating *Sontarans: Conduct Unbecoming* (BBV audio #27) - Maria, a fugitive of Haigen V, says, "To think... I'm a sophisticated fortieth century woman, and I'm reduced to throwing rocks." Later on, President Forrest claims that as prisoners, he and Maria should be treated according to the "Terran Treaty of 21,000", which we can only assume can't be a date.

attack five years previous had greatly razed facilities on the Sontaran homeworld, Sontar, and prompted the building of underground installations. Sontaran forces conquered the human colony on Haigen V, claimed the uninhabited planet Jogana, and were engaged in a "three-way battle of Arcturus".

For two years, the Council had known that their cloning process had been producing inferior stocks, as their master template – that of General Sontar – had become too corrupt after centuries of use. General Kreel outmanoeuvred his rival, General Bestok, to become the new template.

Successful experiments on human cloning were first carried out in 3922.[1548] The Daleks slaughtered a garrison on Alpha Millennia. Sixth months later, a Dalek space vessel was identified near Mars.[1549]

The Enslavement of the Ood

The Ood were native to the Ood-Sphere, a planet close to the Sense-Sphere. They were born with hand-held secondary brains (which functioned much like the amygdala in humans, processing memories and emotions), and were mentally connected by a giant Ood Brain. The Earth corporation Ood Operations established itself on the Ood-Sphere – it found the Ood Brain beneath the planet's Northern Glacier, and placed it within a telepathic inhibitor field. Many Ood

were lobotomised, their secondary brains replaced with translator units. Before long, Ood were bred to be slaves, household servants and soldiers.[1550]

In 3932, Zephon became all-powerful in his own galaxy, the Fifth, when he defeated Fisar and the Embodiment Gris, both of which had tried to depose him.[1551]

& 3935 - THE MONSTER OF PELADON[1552] **->** When Federation scientists surveyed Peladon, they discovered that planet was rich in trisilicate: a mineral previously only found on Mars, and which was the basis of Federation technology. Electronic circuitry, heat shields, inert microcell fibres and radionic crystals all used the mineral. Duralinium was still used as armour-plating.

King Peladon had died and been replaced by his daughter, the child Thalira. As she grew up, Federation mining engineers came to her world. Although Thalira's people were resistant to change, advanced technology such as the sonic lance was gradually introduced to Peladon.

The Federation was subject to a vicious and unprovoked attack from Galaxy Five, who refused to negotiate. The Federation armed for war, with Martian shock troops being mobilised. Peladon's trisilicate supplies would prove crucial in this struggle. The planet was still prone to superstition, however, and when the

1548 *The Invisible Enemy*
1549 "Seventy years" before *The Daleks*: "The Destroyers". This seems to go against Cory's claim in *The Daleks' Master Plan* that the Daleks "haven't been active in our galaxy for some time now", although it's debatable as to what exactly constitutes "active", and whether Cory would be informed concerning (or think it relevant to mention) every minor Dalek incident.
1550 "Two hundred years" before *Planet of the Ood*. That story is set during the time of the Second Great and Bountiful Human Empire, but these events seem to predate it. The Doctor says it's an Empire "built on slavery", so perhaps this is one of the first steps in that process. The Sense-Sphere is the home of the titular characters from *The Sensorites*.
1551 *The Daleks' Master Plan*, with the date of 3932 given in *Neverland*. The entity is referred to as "the Embodiment Gris" in *The Daleks' Master Plan*, as "the Embodiment of Gris" in *The Dying Days* and *Neverland*.
1552 Dating *The Monster of Peladon* (11.4) - Sarah guesses that it is "fifty years" after the Doctor's first visit, and this is later confirmed by other people, including the Doctor, Thalira and Alpha Centauri.
1553 Dating *The Blue Angel* (EDA #27) - No date is given, but the ship serves the Federation and is en route to Peladon.
1554 Dating "A Cold Day in Hell" (*DWM* #130-133) -

According to the Doctor, "you Martians allied yourself to the Federation years ago", and this is after *The Monster of Peladon*, because Axaxyr and the events of that story are mentioned. These Martians were "born and bred on the frigid wastes of Mars", and they style A-Lux "New Mars", so it would seem to be their original planet that's uninhabitable.
1555 Dating "Redemption" (*DWM* #134) - This is Olla's native time, so the story is set shortly after "A Cold Day in Hell".
1556 Dating *Bang-Bang-A-Boom!* (BF #39) - No date is given, but the story is set in the Federation period.
1557 *War of the Daleks*
1558 *Legacy*. We learn that the Vogans were "ultimately self-destructive" and that the Cybermen eventually settled on a "New Mondas", as they wished to do in *Silver Nemesis*. However, this second homeworld has also been destroyed by the time of *Legacy*. The Cybermen survive to appear in *The Crystal Bucephalus*.
1559 In *The Daleks' Master Plan*, Mavic Chen seems to have been Guardian for a very long time. He says, when accused of stealing the taranium, "Why should I arrange that fifty years be spent secretly mining to acquire this mineral..." – which implies, but does not actually state, that he has been actively involved with the plot for half a century. Against this, *The Guardian of the Solar System* establishes that Chen started mining taranium for rea-

spirit of Aggedor began to walk once more, killing miners that used the advanced technology, many saw it as a sign that Peladon should leave the Federation. For a time, production in the mines halted.

The third Doctor and Sarah Jane exposed the murders as the work of a breakaway faction of Martians, led by Azaxyr, who were working for Galaxy Five. When the plot was uncovered, Galaxy Five quickly sued for peace.

c 3935 - THE BLUE ANGEL[1553] -> The eighth Doctor, Fitz and Compassion arrived on the Federation ship *Nepotist*, which was en route to Peladon. The crew discovered the Valcean City of Glass had become connected to the Federation through space-time corridors. As the glass city was located within the Enclave, a pocket universe within the larger Obverse, the Federation feared this could destablise the region.

The Doctor joined the Federation mission to meet the Glass Men, and also met their leader, Daedalus, a giant jade elephant who planned to make war with the Federation. Daedalus had opened up forty-three space-time corridors from the Enclave to planets such as Telosa, Skaro, Wertherkund and Sonturak. The *Nepotist* launched a preemptive strike with sonic cannons, shattering the Glass Men, but was counter-attacked by the Sahmbekarts, a race of lizards. The *Nepotist* crashed near the Valcean city, and the people of the Obverse rushed to defend their territory. The Doctor attempted to intervene, but Iris Wildthyme tricked him into leaving the area. He would never know how the situation was resolved.

Frobisher Leaves the TARDIS

c 3940 - "A Cold Day in Hell"[1554] -> Ice Lord Arryx and a small squad of Ice Warriors captured the weather control station on the pleasure planet A-Lux. They transformed A-Lux into an arctic wilderness, wiping out almost the entire population. The Martian homeworld was uninhabitable at this time, and Arryx – who opposed Martian membership of the Federation – wanted this to become a home base.

The seventh Doctor and Frobisher arrived and reversed the weather control, killing the Ice Warriors. Frobisher stayed behind to help the natives rebuild their lives, and the Doctor was joined by a young woman – Olla – that Frobisher had met.

& 3940 - "Redemption"[1555] -> The TARDIS was caught in the null beams of a Federation ship captained by the Vachysian Skaroux. Olla confided that she used to be Skaroux's servant. The seventh Doctor was shocked to learn that her people, the Dreilyn, had no legal status in the Federation because they were heat vampires ... but this

was a lie. Olla was Skaroux's consort, and had stolen all his money. The Doctor handed her over for trial.

? 3950 - BANG-BANG-A-BOOM![1556] -> The 308th Intergalactic Song Contest was broadcast to over a quinquillion homes across the universe. Contestants included the Architects of Algol ("Don't Push Your Tentacle Too Far"), the Angvia of the Hearth of Celsitor ("My Love is as Limitless as a Black Hole, and I'm Pulling You Over the Event Horizon"), the Breebles, the Cissadian Cephalopods, Cyrene, the Freznixx of Braal and Maaga 29 of Drahva ("Clone Love"). The jury included a Martian. Earth's national anthem at this time was "I Will Survive".

The matriarchal warlords of Angvia and the transcendental gestalt Gholos had been feuding for thirty generations. A peace conference between the two was supposedly being held on Achilles 4, but this was a feint for the real conference, which was taking place at the Song Contest on the Dark Space 8 station. A Gholos nationalist tried to disrupt the proceedings, but both sides sued for peace.

Earth discovered and surveyed the planet Antalin.[1557] In the mid-fortieth century, a "Cyber-fad" swept the Federation. The Martian archaeologist Rhukk proved that both Telos and New Mondas had been destroyed, meaning the Cyber Race had been eradicated. The public were briefly fascinated by the Cybermen. Documentary holovid crews went to the dead worlds of Voga and Telos.[1558]

Mavic Chen

In 3950, **Mavic Chen became the Guardian of the Solar System, ruling over the forty billion people living on Earth, Venus, Mars, Jupiter and the moon colonies from his complex in Central City. At this time, the prison planet Desperus was set up to house the most dangerous criminals in the solar system.**

Chen sought alternatives to the giant clock that enabled humanity to travel through hyperspace, and **established a secret mining operation to find taranium, "the rarest mineral in the universe", and which was found only on Uranus.** Taranium, he suspected, was the vital component for a device that could bend time akin to the giant clock. **Many in the solar system showed an almost religious devotion to Chen. His reputation was enhanced in 3975, when all the planets of the solar system signed a non-aggression pact. For the next twenty-five years, they lived in peace under the Guardianship, and the solar system – though "only part of one galaxy" – now had a status that was "exceptional... it had influences far outside its own sphere". It was hoped that by following Chen's example, peace would spread throughout the universe.**[1559]

? 3951 - IRIS S2: THE SOUND OF FEAR[1560] **->** Iris Wildthyme met a man named Sam Gold at the Intergalactic Song Competition and wound up marrying him. On the night of their wedding, the Master Bakers of Barastabon took Iris out of time and tasked her with finding the six lost slices of the Celestial Gateaux. Six months later, Iris and Panda arrived on Radio Yesterday, a space station broadcasting golden oldies to Earth's colonies; Gold was the manager and DJ there. The evil Naxian hordes sought to strip a mood-altering harmonic into the Radio Yesterday broadcasts and make everyone in human space terribly depressed, paving the way for an invasion. The Naxian warlord made Iris, along with Gold, take him back to the 1960s in a bid to rewrite history. Iris returned after Panda had turned the Naxians' signals against them, and the ones

aboard the station threw themselves out the airlock.

After the Radio Yesterday incident, Iris and a Naxian named Roger had a relationship. While Iris was off galli-vanting around the cosmos, Roger and a Naxian beach-head were sent back to 2108.[1561] Iris once found herself in the middle of a war between the Krobians and Naxians, which entailed lots of bodily fluids.[1562] Modest apartments were available in Earth sub-orbit.[1563]

c 3966 - THE SONTARANS[1564] **->** The Sontarans devas-tated human colonies on Lambda Arietede, forcing mil-lions to escape in a space fleet at slower-than-light speeds. In his very first encounter with the Sontarans, the first Doctor – accompanied by Steven and Sara – stopped a

sons entirely unrelated to the Daleks, and only joined the conspiracy after the destruction of the giant clock in 3999 threatens Earth's security – a time-table that's in keeping with his being named as the newest member of the conspiracy, its "most recent ally", in the TV story. *Neverland* cites 3950 as the year that Chen became Guardian of the Solar System.

The non-aggression pact is referred to in *The Daleks' Master Plan*. This perhaps suggests that planets in the solar system were in conflict before this time, and Chen's hope that peace will spread throughout the universe implies that much of known space is at war. A short scene in *Legacy* suggests that Chen did not become Guardian until much later.

1560 Dating *Iris S2: The Sound of Fear* (BF *Iris* #2.1) - Iris and Gold meet at an Intergalactic Song Contest won by Nicky Newman, who appears in *Bang-Bang-a-Boom!*, so the two stories must occur relatively close to one another. Tom is no longer travelling with Iris and Panda, as he suddenly fell in love with someone he met while they battled giant alien cockroaches.

1561 *Iris S2: The Two Irises*

1562 *Iris S3: The Midwinter Murders*. Time unknown, but the Naxians appeared in *Iris S2: The Sound of Fear*.

1563 *The Anachronauts*

1564 Dating *The Sontarans* (EA #3.4) - The story involves the Space Security Service (*The Daleks' Master Plan*) and takes as read, without the year being named, that it's in Sara's past, meaning she knows the outcome of these events.

1565 Extrapolating from Jean Marsh being 31 when she played Sara in *The Daleks' Master Plan* [4000].

1566 *The Sontarans*

1567 *Placebo Effect*

1568 *The Book of the Still*

1569 Probably some decades before *The Only Good Dalek*.

1570 Carmodi was born as one of the Unnoticed's sensitives thirty years before *The Book of the Still*. At the end of that novel, she paradoxically averts the creation

of the Unnoticed, making it debatable whether these events occurred in the proper history or not.

1571 "Twenty years" before *Max Warp*.

1572 Dating "Deathworld" (*DWW* #15-16) - The Doctor explains in the framing sequence that the Ice Warriors "came from Mars thousands of years ago, then spread their conquests through the galaxy". Trisilicate is a min-eral that's only been found on Mars and Peladon by *The Monster of Peladon*, so this story is set after that. The two races don't recognise each other, and the Cybermen refer to the Cyberman Empire.

DO THE CYBERMEN EVER HAVE AN EMPIRE?: As they are the second best-known monsters to fight the Doctor, it's easy to assume that the Cybermen are sec-ond only to the Daleks when it comes to the power they wield and territory they control. Yet there's pre-cious little evidence for this in the televised stories.

We see or hear that at various points in history, humanity, Daleks, Sontarans, Rutans, Draconians, Mutts, Osirians, Tharils, Jagaroth, Skonnos, Movellans, Autons and even the Chelonians (according to *Zamper*) all control vast areas of our galaxy. Elsewhere in the uni-verse, races have achieved domination of an entire galaxy – in *The Daleks' Master Plan* alone, we meet eight delegates who each have total control of one of the Outer Galaxies. The Wirrn (*The Ark in Space*) dominated Andromeda until humanity drove them out. The win-ners, though, are... the Dominators, the masters of "ten galaxies" according to *The Dominators*. (They also state they control "the whole galaxy" that Dulkis is part of, but while it's not as impressive a boast, neither is it the contradiction some reference sources seem to think. That said, *The Blood Furnace* entails the seventh Doctor accusing the Dominators of exaggerating their con-quests.) Linx's boast (in *The Time Warrior*) that the Sontarans have subjugated every galaxy in the uni-verse must surely only be rhetoric.

Away from the televised stories, there's a parallel universe where the Roman Empire has conquered the entire galaxy ("The Iron Legion"), and the Gubbage

Sontaran cannon positioned in the Solgrave Asteroid Belt from obliterating the refugees.

Sara Kingdom

Sara Kingdom, a companion of the first Doctor, was born circa 3969.[1565] She would join the Space Security Service when she was seven.[1566]

Around 3970, the Hiinds overthrew the Mufls. The Reverend Lukas established The Church of the Way Forward, and preached that marriage between alien species was unholy.[1567] In 3972, Sirius-One-Bee University Press published Albrecht's *Of Finders and Seekers – a users guide to being lost in time*.[1568] Strantana was the site of an orbital mining facility that later became Station 7, where humans carried out experiments on Dalek artifacts.[1569]

(=) Circa 3979, emaciated, grotesque beings named the Unnoticed had constructed a Tent City, made from invulnerable taffeta, on the photosphere of Earth's sun and set about breeding a colony of human time sensitives there. Uncertain as to their origins, the Unnoticed used the time sensitives to keep watch for time distortion and time travellers – wary that contact with such phenomena could somehow avert their own creation. The human Carmodi Litian was born as one of the Unnoticed's sensitives and served for fifteen years before being left for dead on the planet Porconine. She swore revenge against her former masters.[1570]

The Varlon Empire tried to establish itself in the Sirius System, and fought a war with the Kith – a highly advanced spore-producing, sponge-like race (each of which had four progenitors) in the neighbouring system. Both sides were nearly wiped out before a treaty was signed at Pluvikerr-Hinton. The Varlon were made to apologise and pay compensation for the ruination of the Kith home system.[1571]

? 3980 - "Deathworld"[1572] **->** An Ice Warrior mission to Yama 10 scouted for trisilicate until a Cyberman spacecraft arrived to stake a rival claim. The Ice Warriors

---

Cones (*The Crystal Bucephalus*), Cat-People (*Invasion of the Cat-People*) and Foamasi (*Placebo Effect*) are all stated to be or have been major galactic powers.

So what of the Cybermen? For the most part, their effectiveness as would-be galactic conquerors is tepid to say the least. In *Doomsday*, tellingly, an army of parallel-universe Cybermen that's millions strong is no match for four Daleks, and when Dalek reinforcements arrive, the Cybermen are routed in minutes.

Perhaps surprisingly, in the four decades since the Cybermen debuted, the most territory we ever actually see them control in a television story... is one planet, and it's their homeworld. In *The Tenth Planet*, they control Mondas, which is destroyed at the end of the adventure. After that, the best they manage is one complex on one planet – in *The Tomb of the Cybermen* and *Attack of the Cybermen*, they control their city on Telos. Comparable to that, they control a good number of decks aboard a Mondasian colony ship (*World Enough and Time/The Doctor Falls*), but it seems a given that Nardole will find a means of threshing them like wheat. In every other TV story, we see only a small force of Cybermen launching a stealthy attack – usually with a larger army being held in reserve – and every story ends with the defeat or destruction of every single member of that army (with the possible exception of *Attack of the Cybermen*, where a base on the moon is mentioned and its fate isn't accounted for). In a number of stories (*The Tomb of the Cybermen*, *Revenge of the Cybermen*, *Earthshock*, *Attack of the Cybermen* and possibly *Silver Nemesis*), it's explicitly stated that the Cybermen are on the verge of extinction. Those that revive on Hedgewick's World in *Nightmare in Silver* are

wiped out. The Cyber-army that Missy creates in *Dark Water/Death in Heaven* take one for the team and die saving Earth.

The audios *The Harvest*, *Sword of Orion* and *The Isos Network* follow the same pattern. "A handful" survive in *Real Time*. They invade different time zones in "Supremacy of the Cybermen", only to have that victory annulled from history. The Cybermen fare no better in the books – in *Legacy*, the Federation thinks they're extinct. *Iceberg* and *Illegal Alien* feature a small group of isolated survivors. They're routed in *Killing Ground*, which ends – to compound their problems – with a group of converted humans setting out to pick off any Cybermen they can find.

In *none* of these stories does anyone claim that the Cybermen have "an empire" or anything like it.

Despite all of this, there's some evidence in the *DWM* comic strips that the Cybermen *do* have an empire. "Deathworld" directly makes this claim (a Cyberman tells an Ice Warrior, "Why are you intruding on a planet of the Cybermen Empire?"), and "Throwback", while not making actual mention of an empire, shows the Cybermen at their most powerful. They're feared, with a futuristic city on Telos, vast space fleets and the military power to conquer whole worlds with ease. "Black Legacy" shows Cybermen of the same vein as those seen in "Throwback", but is difficult to date.

"Kane's Story" makes reference of a "Cyber-Emperor" and is set at a time when Davros is the Emperor of the Daleks – so it's between *Revelation of the Daleks* and *Remembrance of the Daleks* (or after "Emperor of the Daleks" and before *Remembrance of the Daleks*, if we take the other media into account).

retreated to the polar areas and set a trap for the Cybermen, destroying them with rising water. As a last act of retaliation, the Cybermen buried the Ice Warriors in ice. The Martian commander, Yinak, remained conscious and waited patiently for the spring thaw.

Carrington Corp built the leisure planet Micawber's World between Pluto and Cassius around 3984.[1573]

Peladon Leaves the Federation

c 3985 - LEGACY[1574] **->** The Federation fought a number of wars to secure its position and to protect democratic regimes. GFTV-3 covered the main news stories of this era: atrocities on the Nematodian Border, the android warriors of Orion, slavery on Rigellon and Operation Galactic Storm. The Martian Star Fleet built the deep space cruiser *Bruk*, one of the largest vessels the galaxy had ever seen, and it helped enforce law throughout the galaxy.

With its trisilicate mines exhausted, Peladon faced a choice between becoming a tourist resort or leaving the Federation altogether. The question remained unaddressed while Queen Thalira ruled, but she died in a space shuttle accident. Within four years of her death, her successor King Tarrol applied to leave the Federation, suggesting that Peladon ought to try and find its own solutions to its problems. His choice had perhaps been made easier by the carnage caused when an ancient weapon, the Pakhar Diadem, was tracked to his world. The Diadem was blasted out of space by the *Bruk* and went missing.

Tarrol's decision probably saved Peladon – had the planet remained in the Federation, it would almost certainly have been targeted by the Daleks thirty years later during the Dalek War.

(? =) 3985 - THEATRE OF WAR[1575] **->** The colony of Heletia was founded by a group of actors wanting to stage the greatest dramas of the universe. Society on Heletia was confined to one small area of their own planet, but nonetheless became an expansionist power and fought a war with the Rippeareans. The Heletians believed that only races with a sophisticated theatre were truly civilised. Following the death of their leader, the Exec, the Heletians sued for peace. By this point, Stanoff Osterling's play *The Good Soldiers* had been lost.

The Cybermen are also powerful at the time of *Earthshock* (in 2526), and this chronology links that to their re-emergence from their tomb on Telos – the *Cybermen* audio series appears to do the same, but entail the Cybermen's subterfuge with Earth's administration achieving the remarkable feat of ending the long-running Orion War and uniting the forces of humanity and the Orion androids against them. Nonetheless, there may well be a Cyber Empire blossoming in the late twenty-fifth, early twenty-sixth century – indeed, the Super-Controller in *Last of the Cybermen* [c.2530] mentions being mentally linked to operations throughout the "Cyber-Empire", but that territory falls after their crushing defeat in the Cyber War, leading to the Cybermen's diminished state in *Revenge of the Cybermen*.

The coffee-table book *Dalek: The Astounding Untold History of the Greatest Enemies of the Universe*, which deliberately casts itself as an unreliable narrator, contains the comic "Cyber Crisis" (time period unknown). This takes place on the planet "New Mondas" at the heart of the "Cyber-Empire"... which the Daleks easily take control of, owing to the Cybermen's lack of foresight in scanning their fellows for bombs.

The seemingly formidable Twelfth Cyber Legion is seen in *A Good Man Goes to War* (set in the fifty-second century)... but the eleventh Doctor deals it an indeterminate amount of damage while learning Amy's location. Nonetheless, logic suggests that at least eleven other Cyber Legions must exist in this time zone, whatever their effectiveness.

Finally, Titan's *Ninth Doctor* comic "The Bidding War"

[c.5325] makes reference to the Cyber-Empire having annexed the planet Malleon, but it's such an off-handed remark, it's challenging to put much stock in it. Or the Cybermen's efficaciousness as warlords.

1573 "Fifteen years" before *Placebo Effect*.
1574 Dating *Legacy* (NA #25) - The dating of this book is problematic. It has to be set after "3948", when a couple of the fictional reference texts cited were written (p37). The Doctor says that it is "the thirty-ninth century" (p55) and later narrows this down to the "mid-thirty-ninth century give or take a decade" (p84) [c.3850]. The novel is set "one hundred years" after *The Curse of Peladon* (p106), at a time when "young" Mavic Chen is still a minor official and Amazonia, who first appeared at the end of *The Curse of Peladon*, is the Guardian of the Solar System (p237) [so before 3950]. It is "thirty years" before a Dalek War that might well be *The Daleks' Master Plan* (p299) [therefore 3970] and "six hundred years" after *The Ice Warriors* (p89) [therefore 3600, favouring the dating of that story as 3000]. The book takes place a couple of months before *Theatre of War*, and as that book is definitely set in 3985, this last date has been adopted.
1575 Dating *Theatre of War* (NA #26) - The book is set soon after *Legacy* in "3985" (p1), a fact confirmed by Benny's diary ("Date: 3985, or something close", p21), and the TARDIS' Time Path indicator (p81). (As to how much of this story actually happens, see the When was the Braxiatel Collection in Operation? sidebar.)
1576 *The Drowned World*. The commendation is presumably unrelated to Vyon's tenure with the Space Security Service, and he didn't join until 3990 according

(=) Bernice, while travelling with the seventh Doctor and Ace, first visited the Braxiatel Collection – and met its founder, Irving Braxiatel – at this time.

Sara Kingdom was present when her brother Bret Vyon, age 18, received a commendation.[1576] The Daleks used time corridors to establish hibernation units on many planets such as Kar-Charrat. The Daleks would only activate when a time traveller entered range, and the Daleks hoped this gambit would help them gain access to the Kar-Charrat Library.[1577]

Bret Vyon had been bred on Mars Colony 16, and joined the Space Security Service (SSS) in 3990.[1578] As a requirement of joining the Space Security Service, Sara Kingdom was sterilized – a decision that she didn't come to regret.[1579] Earth forces recaptured Caridos from the Daleks in '94 and took Robomen prisoners. On one of the worlds the Daleks had ravaged and abandoned, human researchers found deactivated Mechanoids.[1580] The artificial star of Tír na n-Óg was due to run out of fuel around this time.[1581]

c 3994 - THE DALEKS: "The Destroyers"[1582] **->** The Daleks were the dominant form of life on Skaro, which was located in the eighth galaxy. They exterminated the crew of Explorer Base One, located on the giant meteorite M5, as the first phase of a gambit to destroy Earth and its colonies. Three Space Security Agents – Sara Kingdom, Jason Corey and the humanoid robot Mark Seven – attempted to rescue the sole survivor of the incident: David Kingdom, Sara's brother. The Daleks escaped in a rocket with David as their captive...

Mavic Chen would later read Mark Seven's account of the incident.[1583] **Bret Vyon attained First Rank in the SSS in 3995, and Second Rank in 3998.**[1584]

Stacy Townsend and Ssard Get Married

3999 (July) - PLACEBO EFFECT[1585] **->** The eighth Doctor and Sam attended the wedding of his former companions Stacy Townsend and Ssard on Micawber's World. Stacy and Ssard had settled in this timezone two years ago after leaving the Doctor. The Church of the Way Forward, who opposed interspecies weddings, crashed the ceremony but order was restored. Stacy and Ssard left to honeymoon on Kolpasha, the fashion capital of the Federation.

Micawber's World was hosting the Olympic Games, and scientist Miles Mason was secretly infecting athletes with Wirrn eggs disguised as performance enhancing drugs. The Wirrn hatched, and the Space Security Service was called in to contain the situation. The Doctor destroyed the Wirrn Queen, although one group of Wirrn escaped to Andromeda. The Olympic Games continued.

Earth at this time had a Royal Family. King Garth had just died; Queen Bodicha was in mourning, but the rest of the world was glad to see the back of him. His heir was Prince Artemis, Duke of Auckland. Some humans on Earth, but few offworlders, followed the tenants of Christianity. There were 1362 races in the Federation's database, but the Time Lords weren't one of them. The Foamasi were members of the Federation.

? 3999 - MAX WARP[1586] **->** The Inter-G Cruiser Show was held at the Sirius Exhibition Station to showcase various spaceship models; it was hoped that the event would improve Varlon-Kith relations. Geoffrey Vantage – a war

to *The Daleks' Master Plan*. Using Nicholas Courtney's age as standard based upon when he played the role, Vyon would have been born in 3967, age 18 in 3985.

1577 "One thousand two hundred and seventy years" before *The Genocide Machine*.

1578 *The Daleks' Master Plan*

1579 *An Ordinary Life*

1580 *The Only Good Dalek*

1581 "Two thousand years" after *Cat's Cradle: Witch Mark* (p247).

1582 Dating *The Daleks: "The Destroyers"* (BF LS #2.2b) - According to Sara in *The Guardian of the Solar System* (set in 3999), this happens "Back when I'd first met the Daleks, so many years ago." In *The Daleks' Master Plan*, Sara doesn't indicate one way or another as to whether she's met the Daleks before.

"The Destroyers" was intended to serve as the pilot episode of a (ultimately unmade) Dalek TV show, the outline for which was first published in *The Official Doctor Who & the Daleks Book* (1988). The summation

here reflects the Big Finish audio adaptation released in 2010. In both Nation's outline and the Big Finish version, matters are left very open ended – the SSS team fails to rescue the Daleks' captive (David in the audio story, Sara in the original outline), and while the Daleks threaten to destroy Earth, nothing is said about how they intend to accomplish this – or if it has any relation whatsoever to the Time Destructor plot central to *The Daleks' Master Plan*.

1583 *The Guardian of the Solar System*

1584 *The Daleks' Master Plan*

1585 Dating *Placebo Effect* (EDA #13) - The date is given. *Placebo Effect* states that Christianity is still practised on Earth in 3999, but Sara Kingdom – hailing from the year 4000 – hasn't heard of Christmas in *The Daleks' Master Plan*. Historically, not every version of Christianity has placed an emphasis on Christmas, though.

1586 Dating *Max Warp* (BF BBC7 #2.2) - No specific year was intended by writer Jonathan Morris, who feared that a concrete dating might conflict with other

veteran, and now a presenter on the ten-year-old show *Max Warp* – had access to a computer virus developed late in the Varlon-Kith war, and planned to use it to make the Kith warfleet crash into one of Sirius' moons. The eighth Doctor and Lucie stopped Vantage; the Kith Oligarchy pledged to make a massive investment in the Varlon, and President Varlon (sic) used the influx of funds to abolish income tax. *Max Warp* became a lot more banal without Vantage to host it.

The planet Sirius Alpha had at least four moons. Varlon politicians used Spindroids to judge public opinion and help determine policy. Spaceships in this period included the new Kith Sunstorm, the Umbriel Slipstream (regarded by the Doctor as the sleekest, fastest spaceship ever constructed), the escape-pod-less Epsilon Nova 90, the Magellan Danube 4000, the Nebular Toscanini, the Umbriel Slipstream, the Freefall Sunstriker (which contained the same engine as the Moonstalk, but at a fraction of the cost), the Skythros Warpshock, the New Thorndon 90, and the antiquated Cobra Mark Three.

Spaceship design now incorporated quark drives, hyperion boosters, gamma burst regulators, catalytic filtration systems, residual dampeners, gravitic thrust converters, plasma outfits, tractor beams, hydrogen fuel filtration converters and a-line converters.

The eighth Doctor, Fitz and Compassion tried to find a way into the Obverse in the Wandering Museum of the Verifiably Phantasmagoric, also known as the Museum of Things That Don't Exist.[1587]

The Daleks' Master Plan

Mavic Chen Allies with the Daleks

3999 - THE GUARDIAN OF THE SOLAR SYSTEM[1588]

-> The first Doctor, Steven and Sara found themselves in 3999 – a year before they first met – at the giant clock that enabled humanity to travel through hyperspace. Sara's younger self was currently on Venus, part of a six-month posting. Mavic Chen continued to pursue a number of alternatives to the clock, hoping it could be slowly wound down without Earth going into decline. Chen was impressed upon meeting Sara, and – not comprehending that she was from the future – promoted her contemporary self to be part of his senior staff on Earth.

The clock ensnared the Doctor and Steven's minds into its network, and threatened to do the same to Sara – who realised that she was historically destined to wreck it. She reached out with her mind and brought the clock crashing down, enabling the travellers to escape...

---

stories. However, mention of the Magellan Danube 4000 – touted as "a *man's* spaceship", and not a historical piece – suggests a dating in or around 3999, provided spaceships follow the tradition that car models are designated a year ahead of manufacture. The story occurs in the Sirius System, and the overall prosperity and warmth of the society seen here matches much better with the time of the Federation – and the holding of events such as the Intergalactic Olympics in *Placebo Effect* (also set in 3999) – than the corporate-minded gloom that seems to pervade Sirius in *The Caves of Androzani*.

The only other dating clue is a derogatory mention of the Moroks from *The Space Museum*. According to *The Death of Art*, the Morok Empire collapsed in the thirtieth century, so it's entirely possible that they'd be the subject of ridicule afterwards.

It's not entirely clear if the Varlons are related to humanity, although the presence of a "gin and tonic" might suggest some human influence, and it's generally assumed that the inhabitants seen in *The Caves of Androzani* (if they do indeed reside in Sirius) are human. Mention of "Pluvikerr-Hinton" is a little tribute to the late Craig Hinton and his obsession with the Gubbage Cones (the unnamed fungus creatures seen in *The Chase*) from the planet Pluvikerr.

1587 *The Taking of Planet 5* (p13).

1588 Dating *The Guardian of the Solar System* (BF CC 5.1) - The year is given.

1589 The backstory to *The Daleks' Master Plan*, as catalysed by events in *The Guardian of the Solar System*. Writer Simon Guerrier has confirmed that the clock's destruction triggers a slow-acting erosion of Earth's shipping and security, not something as cataclysmic as, say, every road in the United States vanishing overnight. The matter-transportation experiment that teleports the Doctor, Steven and Sara (and a few mice) to Desperus in *The Daleks' Master Plan* is part and parcel of Chen's attempts to free Earth from its reliance on the giant clock.

1590 Dating *Mission to the Unknown* (3.2) - The story is set shortly before *The Daleks' Master Plan*.

1591 Dating *The Daleks' Master Plan* (3.3) - The date "4000" is established by Chen. The draft script for *Twelve Part Dalek Story* set it in "1,000,000 AD".

1592 *Asylum of the Daleks*

1593 *WD* S1: *Only the Monstrous*

1594 Dating *The Foe from the Future* (BF 4th Doc LS #1.1) - No year given, but the Doctor tells Leela (after they've arrived via the time rift, not the TARDIS): "Judging by the amount of time we spent travelling in the Vortex, [it's] the year 4000 or thereabouts". He later comments, presumably in reference to *The Daleks' Master Plan*: "I've been to the year 4000, and it wasn't like this." The back cover blurb says: "Jalnik [based in

The loss of the clock imperilled Earth's security so much that **Chen allied himself with the Daleks.** In exchange for the taranium that he possessed, the Daleks would make him ruler of the entire galaxy. The Daleks recruited Zephon to their Master Plan, and he secured the support of the rulers of two further galaxies, Celation and Beaus. The conspiracy also included Trantis, Master of the Tenth Galaxy (the largest of the Outer Galaxies), Gearon, Malpha, Sentreal and Warrien.[1589]

c 4000 - MISSION TO THE UNKNOWN[1590] ->

"This is Marc Cory, Special Security Agent, reporting from the planet Kembel. The Daleks are planning the complete destruction of our galaxy together with powers of the Outer Galaxies. A war party is being assemb---"

In the year 4000, Chen attended an Intergalactic Conference in Andromeda. The Outer Galaxies and the Daleks held a council at the same time, sending Trantis to Andromeda to allay suspicion. The Space Security Service (SSS) and the UN Deep Space Force had been monitoring Dalek activity for five hundred years.

On the planet Kembel, SSS agent Marc Cory learned that the Daleks and their allies were preparing for conquest. Cory was exterminated, but not before recording a warning.

Defeat of the Daleks and Mavic Chen, Katarina and Sara Kingdom Die

4000 - THE DALEKS' MASTER PLAN[1591] -> Shortly after concluding a mineral agreement with the Fourth Galaxy, Mavic Chen left Earth for a short holiday, or so he told the news service Channel 403. In reality, his Spar 740 spaceship headed through ultraspace to Kembel, the Daleks' secret base. There, he met the delegates from the Outer Galaxies for the first time, and presented the Daleks with a full emm of taranium – enough to power their Time Destructor, a device capable of accelerating time.

Space Security Agents were sent to investigate the disappearance of Marc Cory. One of them, Bret Vyon, allied with the first Doctor, Steven and Katarina. They stole the taranium and absconded with Chen's ship, which was diverted to the convict planet Desperus. The group escaped, but a convict smuggled himself aboard the Spar and took Katarina hostage. To end the standoff, she blew both of them out of an airlock.

The Doctor, Steven and Vyon reached Central City on Earth, where Vyon was killed by Sara Kingdom – his sister and a fellow SSS agent, who believed him a traitor. Pursued, the Doctor and Steven broke into a

research facility. They were transported with Sara across the galaxy, via an experimental teleportation system, to the planet Mira – the home of invisible monsters named the Visians. Sara came to side with the Doctor against Chen, and the group returned to the Daleks' base on Kembel. They fled through time and space in the TARDIS, with the Daleks in pursuit.

Chen was ready to doublecross the Daleks, and had special forces on Venus ready to occupy Kembel. Eventually, the Daleks re-captured the taranium, and they exterminated their allies – including Chen – in readiness for universal domination. They had assembled the "greatest war force ever assembled", including an assault division of five thousand Daleks to invade Earth's solar system. The Doctor activated the Daleks' Time Destructor, which destroyed their army and transformed the surface of Kembel from lush jungle to barren desert in seconds. Sara helped the Doctor and was aged to death. The universe was safe once more.

Earth was under totalitarian rule. Humans were "bred", and told not to question orders. Christmas was not celebrated or even remembered.

The Daleks imprisoned a Dalek from Kembel within their Asylum.[1592] lgtw - The Time Lords acquired Dalek Time Destructor technology from Kembel for use in the Last Great Time War.[1593]

> ### (=) c 4000 - THE FOE FROM THE FUTURE[1594] ->
> Fragmented historical records in this era claimed that Bruce Forsyth was a twentieth-century UK Prime Minister.
>
> On Earth, the ambitious politician Kostal campaigned for the office of Supreme Councilor on a platform of expansionist policies. She lost to Geflo, but gained a seat on the Supreme Council, the Council of Twelve. Four years later, one of Kostal's allies, the temporal physicist Jalnik, discovered a time rift leading back to the twenty-first century. He encountered the insectoid Pantophagen within the rift – exposure to their DNA, combined with his rift travel, left Jalnik only half-human.
>
> Kostal and Jalnik arranged for a limited release of the Pantophagen into our reality, thinking it would strengthen her political hand, but the creatures consumed entire countries and populations. Plans were made to relocate survivors in Straffham, Devon, into the safety of Earth's past, but the demented Jalnik arranged for the Pantophagen to travel down the rift to twentieth-century Earth – intending to wipe out humanity in a temporal paradox.
>
> Owing to the fourth Doctor and Leela's actions in 1977, Jalnik never discovered the rift opening, and this timeline never came to pass.

The expression "never turn your back on a dead Dalek" came into use among humans.[1595] In the forty-first century, humankind developed vegetable life that resembled humans – Bio-Organic Plasmatoid Creations, a.k.a. Biogrowers – and used them as servants. Biogrowers lived for a hundred years, but were brain dead after fifty. The braindead Biogrowers were dumped on the planet hospital Bedlam, which was patterned after the original sanatorium.[1596]

SSS agent Dryn Faber investigated the planet Antalin and discovered Daleks there.[1597] Earth was involved in a number of wars on the frontier of Earthspace. The Daleks massacred the colonists on a mining outpost.[1598] The Sycorax Tribe of Astrophia died out in the Valhalla Wars of the forty-first century.[1599]

4009 - THE BOOK OF THE STILL[1600] **->** About this time, TimeCorp offered its employees the plus of completing their workday, then temporally returning to the morning for family time. Participating TimeCorp workers aged a third faster than their families every day, but got to spend more time with their loved ones.

The temporal expert Albrecht managed to retroactively wipe himself from existence, but his diaries survived in a reality pocket. His theories gave rise to the condition Albrecht's Ennui, which affected temporally displaced

---

1977] has a scheme two thousand years in the making". It's not clear exactly how much territory the Supreme Council oversees, nor what relationship, if any, it has with the Guardian of the Solar System (*The Daleks' Master Plan*).

1595 *I am a Dalek*

1596 "Two centuries" before "Body Snatched".

1597 *War of the Daleks*. Not long after the death of an SSS agent called Marc, presumably Marc Cory from *Mission to the Unknown*. This throws the dating scheme of the book out, as Antalin is the planet the Daleks will disguise as Skaro to be destroyed. But that, according to writer John Peel, will happen *before* this.

1598 *Storm Harvest*

1599 "Agent Provocateur"

1600 Dating *The Book of the Still* (EDA #56) - It's "4009" (p57).

1601 "Thirty years after" *Legacy* (p299), and possibly intended as a reference to events of or following *The Daleks' Master Plan*.

1602 Dating *The Only Good Dalek* (BBC original graphic novel #1) - Although it's never confirmed that the human officers seen here are part of the Space Security Service, they wear SSS uniforms as seen in *The Daleks' Master Plan*. Tellingly, when the Doctor says he knew Bret Vyon and Sara Kingdom, Tranter replies, "you must have started fighting Daleks when you were very young". As the eleventh Doctor outwardly looks about thirty, "very young" would have to mean when he was a teenager, so *The One Good Dalek* is most likely to be set around fifteen to twenty years after *The Daleks' Master Plan*. Helpfully, *Legacy* had established that a "massive Dalek war" was fought at about this time.

One glitch is that the war is meant to have "raged for a hundred years", which is explicitly not the case in *The Daleks' Master Plan* – although a case can be made that this war against the Daleks is more covert than not. (*The Only Good Dalek* only talks about frontier worlds being ravaged by the Daleks, so perhaps this is a war fought on the edge of Earth space rather than at its heart.)

Alternatively, the Daleks in this story are the "new

paradigm" Daleks first seen in *Victory of the Daleks*, so it's possible they have inserted themselves into history at this point. Mention of the high-ranking security officer "Silestru" is possibly meant to denote Georgi Selestru from *Dalek Empire III*, but has to be taken as a different character with a similar name.

1603 *Big Bang Generation* (ch13).

1604 *Prime Time*. Reg Gurney has been in space corps for "thirty years".

1605 *Emotional Chemistry*

1606 He's "nearly 12" in *A Good Man Goes to War*.

1607 "A few hundred years" before the forty-fifth century segment of "Body Snatched".

1608 Dating *The Bride of Peladon* (BF #104) - It's "nearly a century" after *The Monster of Peladon*.

Peladon stops being a member of the Federation in *Legacy* – something that the seventh Doctor greets as good news, because it means Peladon will be left out of a Dalek conflict set to occur thirty years afterwards. It's entirely possible that by *The Bride of Peladon* – set roughly fifteen years after said conflict – Peladon has already re-entered the Federation or is at least considering it. Only one statement in *The Bride of Peladon* is made about Peladon's Federation status, when Alpha Centauri says that "Galactic peace is certain and Peladon's place in the Federation is assured" once the king marries Pandora. This can either be interpreted as suggesting that Peladon is about to return to the Federation fold, or just hopes to solidify its spot in the group's hierarchy.

If Aggedors have a century-long gestation cycle, it's little wonder that they're so rare and prized. That said, the pregnancy of the female Aggedor seen here – the daughter of the one seen on TV – raises the rather incestuous question of who sired her pups. (Appalling as it might sound, however, father-daughter and mother-son matings are not uncommon when breeding animals such as horses; genetic deficiencies only start to crop up with brother-sister crossings.)

people who went a few years without time travel.

The affluent, distant planet Lebenswelt settled into a state of hedonism and decay, as nobody would voluntarily travel so far to perform menial tasks. The IntroInductions escort service on Lebenswelt used illegal fast-acting memory acids to make kidnapped humans fall in love with their clients. Lebenswelt also became home to the Museum of Locks (*Das Museum der Verriegelungen*), which almost incidentally guarded a copy of *The Book of the Still*.

(=) In 4009, the Unnoticed desired to examine the *Book* because it mentioned their Tent City on the photosphere of Earth's sun. The eighth Doctor, Fitz and Anji discovered that the Unnoticed were the product of a closed time loop. By touching the time sensitive Carmodi, the Doctor accidentally caused the time loop to unleash waves of "soft time", which mutated IntroInductions founders Darlow, Gimcrack and Svadhisthana into a twisted gestalt creature that would give rise to the Unnoticed. When the newly created gestalt made contact with the Unnoticed, it both destroyed the Unnoticed and flung the gestalt back in time to become the Unnoticed.

Shortly afterwards, Carmodi departed with the *Book* and retroactively planted a bomb aboard the Unnoticed's spaceship, thus prematurely destroying them and averting the closed time loop altogether.

Around 4015, a massive Dalek War split the Federation. Upon the war's completion, the organisation was forced to re-evaluate itself.[1601]

c 4015 - THE ONLY GOOD DALEK[1602] -> The human soldier Tranter attained over ten years of frontline service, received the Mercury Medal with stars and moons, and was the hero of the fall of Pythagoran. He was reported killed at the siege of Logario, but was actually captured by the Daleks and conditioned to act as their sleeper agent. Tranter was allowed to escape, and subsequently became the commander of Station 7.

Station 7 now contained a conglomeration of items related to the Daleks, including a section of petrified jungle (complete with live Slythers and Varga plants) recovered from the ruins of Skaro. The station also held captive Ogrons and Robomen, as well as ten Dalek prisoners who could only move on static electrified pathways. Human scientists aboard the station laboured to harness Dalek technology, but were frustrated because it only worked for Daleks. The station's chief scientist, Weston, had worked for years to change the nature of the Daleks, hoping to make them less aggressive so they would operate Dalek technology on behalf of humans. The culmination of his efforts was The Only Good Dalek: a genetically engineered Dalek mutant thought to have respect for other life.

Two months after Tranter took charge of Station 7, the eleventh Doctor and Amy arrived there as the Daleks, having learned about The Only Good Dalek and deeming it an abomination that had to be terminated, attacked Station 7 in spaceships disguised as asteroids. Commander Tranter, Weston and The Only Good Dalek sacrificed themselves to destroy the Daleks. The sole survivor, a human agent named Jay, returned with Weston's data to Earth Central... where other Dalek agents were in positions of power, and arranged for Jay's ship to be destroyed en route. The Doctor told Amy that the ingenuity, bravery, love and hope that had spurred the creation of Weston's data would help Earth prevail.

(=) Stacy Townsend and Ssard were celebrating their eighteenth wedding anniversary on Mars, with their three children, when the universe ended owing to the Pyramid Eternia crisis.

The timeline was restored, and the five of them posed for a nice holovid.[1603]

The Colonial Marines raided Dalek strongholds in the 4020s.[1604] Kinzhal, a future general of the Icelandic Alliance, earned medals in the forty-second century.[1605] **The Sontaran Strax was born around 4025.**[1606] The Doctor established an account with Trans-Universal Union, which held his mail in a stasis drawer until he collected it.[1607]

Erimem Leaves the TARDIS

& 4030 - THE BRIDE OF PELADON[1608] -> On Peladon, the people no longer believed in Aggedor worship, and Queen Elspera – the daughter of King Paladin and Beladonia – dissolved the church upon her ascent to the throne. Elspera was thought to have been thrown from her horse on a hunting expedition and died, whereupon her son Pelleas became king. In actuality, the imprisoned Sekhmet the Avenger had killed Elspera – as well as the Martian ambassador Alyxlyr – because the blood of four royal females was required to unlock Sekhmet's bonds.

Earth sought to strengthen ties with Peladon, and arranged a marriage between Pelleas and the Earth princess Pandora. Sekhmet murdered Pandora, but failed to make the fifth Doctor's companion Erimem her fourth victim. The new Martian ambassador, Prince Zixlyr, blew up Sekhmet – and himself – with a Xanathoid Volatiser.

A female Aggedor had survived in secret for one hundred fifty years, and birthed new Aggedors after a century of pregnancy. Alpha Centauri assisted in the capture of the master Arcturan criminal Arktos – a.k.a. the Scourge of the Nine Worlds, the Silver Assassin and the Death Merchant. Erimem found Peladon very agreeable to her former way of life, and decided to leave the fifth Doctor and Peri and marry Pelleas.

At some point Erimem left Peladon and, missing some of her memories, made a life for herself on twentieth-century Earth.[1609]

Eminence: The First Incursion, Liv Chenka Joins the TARDIS

& 4034 - DEyes 2: TIME'S HORIZON[1610] **->** During the Twentieth Empire, the Orpheus vessel with Liv Chenka aboard awoke its crew as it reached "the edge of the universe": an energy wave front located a billion light years beyond populated space. The TARDIS brought the eighth Doctor and Molly O'Sullivan to this era, enabling the Doctor to deduce that the energy front was spilling back from the end of Time, and contained the essence of the Eminence: the last sentient mind in creation. The Eminence found the Doctor's name for its essence, "the Breath of Forever", as fitting and adopted it.

The Eminence threatened to transmit its energy along the Orpheus' communications buoys into human space, but the Doctor fired the Orpheus' engine reserves down a fracking beam into time's horizon, forcing the Eminence to return to the end of creation. The Doctor, Molly and Liv travelled back to Earth, the 1970s, to look into the affairs of the Ides Institute.

Strax

The Sontaran Strax once spent seventeen star cycles on an asteroid with his command group, waiting for the chance to destroy a Rutan ship. Strax did so, but was the only survivor of his unit.[1611]

4037 - A GOOD MAN GOES TO WAR[1612] **->** The eleventh Doctor called in a debt from Strax, a Sontaran Commander who had been demoted to battlefield nurse. As part of his atonement, Strax was helping humans during the Battle of Zaruthstra.

4039 (January) - "Hotel Historia"[1613] **->** The Graxnix invaded Earth, damaging London and Big Ben. The tenth Doctor was captured, but escaped down a time corridor to the Hotel Historia in 2008. The Graxnix followed and brought back a Chronexus 3000 device – which, as the Doctor intended, nullified the Graxnix from making any further change to history. They were left intangible and invisible.

Earth colonised the planet Mogar in 4043, and embarked upon ruinous mining operations there. The few humans present interbred with the Vervoids, creating a hybrid species: the Navigators. In time, Earth abandoned Mogar and its inhabitants to their fate.[1614]

The Daleks exterminated everyone on Santhorius.[1615]

1609 The as-yet unexplained transition for Erimem from *The Bride of Peladon* to the *Erimem* novels.

1610 Dating *DEyes 2: Time's Horizon* (BF *DEyes* #2.3) - It's "nine centuries" after Liv went into cryo-freeze (after *DEyes 2: The Traitor*), although this is often rounded up to "a thousand years". The Doctor says that Liv and her crew "missed out on a whole lot of history", including the Eminence War (*The Seeds of War*, etc.). He also estimates that the time tech used by the industrial espionage agent Randal Virand – which sounds suspiciously like the Vortex manipulators used in Captain Jack's era – is from "centuries" after this time.

1611 *Jago & Litefoot & Strax: The Haunting*

1612 Dating *A Good Man Goes to War* (X6.7) - The date is given in a caption. We know nothing else about this battle, save that one of the sides fighting is human.

1613 Dating "Hotel Historia" (*DWM* #394) - The month and year are given.

1614 *TW:* "Station Zero"

1615 Within living memory of "Children of the Revolution", but presumably before *The Evil of the Daleks*.

1616 Dating *1stD V2: Across the Darkened City* (BF CC #11.2) - This is the origin of the Emperor Dalek seen in *The Evil of the Daleks,* and its thirst to acquire the Human Factor. As such, *Across the Darkened City* bridges the gap between that story [? 4067] and *The Chase* [?

3565]. See The Dalek Emperors sidebar.

1617 Dating *The Evil of the Daleks* (4.9) - There is no date given for the Skaro sequences in the scripts. *About Time* and *Timelink* note that Maxtible says he and Victoria have undertaken a "journey through space" to get from Victorian England to Skaro, possibly indicating that the Skaro sequences are set in 1866. However, Waterfield calls the device used to get to Skaro a "time machine" and the story is based around the idea that humans have always beaten the Daleks in the long run – something that's not yet the case in the nineteenth century. The Doctor murmurs that this is "the final end" of the Daleks, and some fans have taken this statement at face value when they come to date the story. However, a line cut from the camera script of *Day of the Daleks* stated that the Daleks survived the civil war and that the human-ised Daleks were defeated. The surviving telesnaps are indeterminate – at the very end of the story, a Dalek has a bit of a lifeglow, but that could just be part and parcel of the carnage around it, not an indicator from the production team that perhaps the Daleks aren't entirely finished after all.

The Doctor knows his way into and around the Dalek city. The only previous time we've seen him on Skaro was in *The Daleks*, and the city is destroyed here – clearly indicating that *The Daleks* is set before *The Evil of the Daleks*. In *Mission to the Unknown*, Cory states that

Forging of the Dalek Emperor

lgtw - & 4066 - 1STD V2: ACROSS THE DARKENED CITY[1616] -> The Daleks dominated the planet Shade, but were then pushed off-world by the Chaons: space-borne predators with a fluctuating genetic code, who could absorb energy bolts and change their physiology at will.

Dalek experiments created genetic variants who were driven to survive at any cost – even the destruction of other Daleks – and believed themselves superior to their fellows. Warfare against the Daleks on Entropica separated Steven Taylor from the first Doctor and Vicki, and resulted in his crashing in a Dalek saucer onto Shade. Only Dalek Genetic Variant Two One Zero had survived, and its drive units were damaged. They formed an uneasy alliance, with Steven hauling Two One Zero on a cart through a darkened, Chaon-infested city. Upon reaching a Dalek transmat station, Steven sent Two One Zero to Skaro. Despite Two One Zero's efforts to betray him, Steven transmatted back to Entropica.

On Skaro, the Daleks acknowledged that Two One Zero had completed the ordeal and was truly the superior Dalek. It received an enhanced container, and declared itself the Emperor of the Daleks. Having witnessed Steven's determination to live, the new Emperor ordered that the Daleks work to distill the Human Factor – to use humankind's instinct as the instrument of its obliteration.

The Daleks in the Last Great Time War tried and failed to undo the Doctor's history at this point.

The Dalek Civil War

Victoria Waterfield Joins the TARDIS

? 4066 - THE EVIL OF THE DALEKS[1617] -> The Dalek Emperor made plans to capitalise on the difference between the Daleks and humanity. The Daleks were unable to make this distinction on their own, and so the Emperor hatched an elaborate trap in three time-zones for their old enemy, the second Doctor. The Daleks tricked the Doctor – who was accompanied by Jamie – into believing that they wished to become more human. He was all too willing to educate the Daleks about the "Human Factor", highlighting the difference between the two races: humans were not blindly obedient and showed mercy to their enemies. However, as the Emperor planned, this merely enabled the distillation of the "Dalek Factor". The Emperor planned to install this into all humans throughout the history of Earth, forcing them to become Daleks, but the Doctor managed to "humanise" a number of Daleks.

Civil war broke out between the "Human" and "Dalek" factions. Every Dalek had been recalled to Skaro in preparation for the conquest of humanity, and in the ensuing battle they were all wiped out. The Emperor was exterminated by his own kind. The Doctor named this the "final end" of the Daleks.

Victoria Waterfield joined the Doctor and Jamie on their travels after her father, Edward Waterfield, died while saving the Doctor's life.

the Daleks have not been active in Earth's galaxy "for a thousand years" (so, from 3000-4000), but also says that they've conquered one hundred and ten planets elsewhere "in the last five hundred years", so *The Evil of the Daleks* is apparently not set between 3000 and 4000. As the Doctor sees the Daleks active in the year 4000, logically he wouldn't think this was "the final end" of the Daleks unless he thought it was set after that date.

Taking what we're told at face value, this story has to be set before the destruction of Skaro in *Remembrance of the Daleks*. If Skaro wasn't really destroyed, as *War of the Daleks* states – and *Doctor Who – The Movie* and the new series imply – that needn't be a problem. However, *Destiny of the Daleks* seems to be set in the ruins of the Dalek city (built over the Kaled Bunker seen in *Genesis of the Daleks*). Again, the Doctor knows his way around. *The Evil of the Daleks* would seem to be set before *Destiny of the Daleks* (and so, therefore, the rest of the Davros Era, including *Remembrance of the Daleks*).

The Terrestrial Index set *The Evil of the Daleks* "a century or so" after *The Daleks' Master Plan*. John Peel and Terry Nation "agreed that *The Evil of the Daleks* was the final story" (*The Frame* #7), but did so before

Remembrance of the Daleks was written. Peel's novelisation of *The Evil of the Daleks* is set around the year 5000. "A History of the Daleks" in *DWM* #77 claimed that *The Evil of the Daleks* is set around "7500 AD". *Timelink* suggests "4066". *About Time* equivocates, but says it's after *The Daleks' Master Plan*. In *Matrix* #45, Mark Jones suggested that the Hand of Omega is sent into Davros' future, thousands of years after Dalek History ends.

We suggest that the civil war in *The Evil of the Daleks* is not the "final end" of the Daleks, but it does represent a severe defeat, one that removes them from the Milky Way for five hundred years (as referred to in *Mission to the Unknown*). The Doctor might be referring to the "final end" of the Dalek city, the Daleks' presence on Skaro, or the reign of the Dalek Emperor. Or he may just be optimistic (he also thinks he's finally wiped out the Daleks in *The Daleks*, *Remembrance of the Daleks*, *Dalek* and *The Parting of the Ways*, after all).

The Dalek Handbook by James Goss and Steve Tribe claims that the Dalek Civil War in *The Evil of the Daleks* happens in the "41st century" (p40), and the Dalek Emperor entry is dated to the same (p218-219). That is in accord with *Mission to the Unknown* indicating a

? 4066 - NAofBENNY V1: THE LIGHTS OF SKARO[1618]
-> Time breaks on Skaro enabled Bernice Summerfield to interact with the end of the Dalek Civil War, and to speak with the Dalek Emperor – who lamented that the Daleks questioned its authority. Benny returned to Skaro's past after meting out the worst insult to a Dalek she could imagine: by simply walking out of the room and surviving.

& c 4070 - "Bringer of Darkness"[1619] -> The second Doctor, Jamie and Victoria encountered a group of Daleks who taunted them with the news that the humanised Daleks had all been exterminated.

However, one saucer of humanised Daleks did survive, and travelled to the planet Kyrol...[1620]

c 4090 - "Children of the Revolution"[1621] -> The eighth Doctor and Izzy travelled to the waterworld of Kyrol, and spent time on the submarine *Argus*. While swimming at the uncharted Asamda Ridge, Izzy encountered some Daleks – who went on the board the submarine and greeted the Doctor as their saviour.

The Daleks steered the *Argus* to Azhra Korr, home of eight thousand Daleks who were the humanised Daleks from the civil war and their descendants. Their leader was Alpha, the first humanised Dalek, and he explained that the Daleks had developed psychokinetic abilities. When the Doctor and Alpha investigated a cavern under Azhra Korr, they discovered Kata-Phobus – the last Kyrolian and a giant octopus with psychic powers. Kata-Phobus had been planning to use the Daleks' psychic abilities to conquer the human colony.

Meanwhile, the humans rebelled and attempted to escape their Dalek captors. The Daleks were shocked that their saviour, the Doctor, was secretly more loyal to the humans than to them. Nonetheless, they sacrificed themselves to kill Kata-Phobus save the human colony.

As the Doctor and Izzy went to leave, two glowing beings emerged from the Vortex and kidnapped her...

The Second Great
and Bountiful Human Empire[1622]

Mavic Chen's descendants eventually ended democracy in the Federation. The Chen dynasty of Federation Emperors ruled for thousands of years.[1623] The Second Empire rose, with its origins on the human colony world of Dephys. The cruel, oppressive Elite ruled it.[1624]

Members of the Time Agency took special care to not reveal their presence in eras prior to the forty-second century. Temporal treaties in place after that point better prepared authorities for a visit from Time Agents.[1625]

marked decrease in Dalek activity in Earth's galaxy from the year 3000 to 4000, and presumably denotes Goss and Tribe's preference of *The Evil of the Daleks* following on from the Daleks' position of strength in *The Daleks' Master Plan*, and paving the way – once the Daleks on Skaro slaughter themselves – for the Davros Era. *Ahistory* Third Edition, ultimately, fell on the other side of the "year to 3000 to 4000" gap and placed *The Evil of the Daleks* at "? 2966".

The authors of this guidebook, having rethought the matter, prefer Goss and Tribe's approach, which has the benefit of *The Evil to the Daleks* chronologically following on from *The Daleks' Master Plan* [4000], and thereby giving the Daleks a proper, cleanly shaped black-and-white (TV) era.

1618 Dating *NAofBenny* V1: *The Lights of Skaro* (*NAofBenny* #1.4) - Events coincide with the end of *The Evil of the Daleks*.

1619 Dating "Bringer of Darkness" (*DWM Summer Special 1993*) - It's shortly after *The Evil of the Daleks*.

1620 "Children of the Revolution"

1621 Dating "Children of the Revolution" (*DWM* #312-317) - Kyrol was colonised "a few centuries in the future" according to Izzy, and this is "a few short decades" after *The Evil of the Daleks* according to Alpha. The cliffhanger is resolved in "Uroboros".

1622 THE EARTH EMPIRES: That the first Earth Empire lasted from the twenty-sixth century of *Frontier in Space* to the thirtieth of *The Mutants* has been well documented, particularly in the New Adventures. (The Doctor's companion Benny is from the Empire's early period, Ace lived in that time zone for a few years, and his later companions Chris and Roz were from the period when the Empire was starting to collapse.)

The Second Empire was first named in *Tomb of Valdemar*. The Doctor refers to the Second Great and Bountiful Human Empire in *Planet of the Ood* (set in 4162), *Pest Control*, *The Story of Martha*: "The Weeping", and by extension *The Impossible Planet/The Satan Pit* and *42*. *The Crystal Bucephalus* states that descendants of Mavic Chen became Federation Emperors, and it might be this Empire that they rule.

"A Fairytale Life" has the Doctor expecting to find the Third Great and Bountiful Human Empire in the seventy-eighth century. This could well be the human empire mentioned in *The Sontaran Experiment*.

The Long Game is set, in theory at least, at the time of The Fourth Great and Bountiful Human Empire, but the Emperor Dalek's machinations appear to alter history, and the apparent obliteration of Earth's continents (*The Parting of the Ways*) casts doubt on whether this Empire ever comes to pass. If Rose reset all the actions of the Daleks, Earth's history could be restored to the one the Doctor knows about, but there's no evidence on screen she did that.

Either way, the overwhelming amount of evidence suggests that Earth survives and continues to have great influence on the universe, at least for billions of

c 4106 - THE IMPOSSIBLE PLANET / THE SATAN PIT[1626] -> Humans continued to use the Ood as a slave race. The Ood seemed willing to be treated as such, but the Friends of the Ood organisation campaigned for their freedom. The Neo-Classic Congregational denomination didn't have a devil as such, but acknowledged that evil resided in the actions of men.

The tenth Doctor and Rose arrived on an unnamed planet which was set in an impossible orbit around the black hole K37Gem5.[1627] The scriptures of the Veltong named the world as Krop Tor – "the bitter pill" – and claimed the black hole was a demon that had swallowed the planet and spit it out.

Sanctuary Base 6, manned by people from the Torchwood Archive, monitored the anomaly. Beneath the planet was the Beast, a creature imprisoned before our universe was created. It influenced the Ood slaves to help engineer its release, but the Doctor prevented this. Krop Tor and the Beast's body fell into the black hole, as did the Beast's mind – which had taken root in the base's head of archaeology, Toby Zed.

The Torchwood Archive

c 4116 - TW: THE TORCHWOOD ARCHIVE (BF)[1628]

"Torchwood. Above the atmosphere, beyond the stars. Every century is when everything changes. And we will never be ready."

Torchwood was officially outlawed. Space Station Cardiff was in service. The Great Cobalt Pyramid hosted weddings.

The Committee wound up creating an Enemy that warred against humankind, and destroyed its makers. Anticipating this, the Committee stored a back-up of their essences in a pocket reality. Some years passed without contact between humans and the Enemy. The Mediasphere speculated that the Enemy had removed all memories of its identity.

The Torchwood Archive endured on an asteroid at the edge of the former Great and Bountiful Human Empire, but drifted into Enemy space. It had little information about the fate of Torchwood Four. Centuries after anyone had last stepped foot at the Archive, Jeremiah Bash Henderson arrived with the Bad Penny – and claimed that Jack Harkness had sent him to shut down the facility. Henderson interacted with holograms representing "classic" Torchwood personnel: Captain Jack, Ianto Jones, Andy Davidson, Gwen Cooper and Rhys Williams.

The Torchwood computer within the Archive's Memory Core had attained a sort of sentience, and appeared as an avatar of Queen Victoria. Henderson agreed to deposit the Bad Penny – a key to the Committee's holding dimension – with the Archive for safekeeping, then left. The Memory Core hoped to liberate itself to another dimension, and opened the Bad Penny so the Committee could return to our own. Henderson had turned over a faux Bad Penny with an explosive charge, which destroyed the Archive.

Afterward, Henderson reunited with his lover, Norton Folgate, and agreed to use the real Bad Penny to restore the Committee... for a suitable fee.

---

years into the future (*The End of the World*). It's probable, then, that there's a fifth and many more Empires after this point.

1623 *The Crystal Bucephalus*

1624 *Tomb of Valdemar*

1625 *DotD: The Time Machine*

1626 Dating *The Impossible Planet/The Satan Pit* (X2.8-2.9) - Casualties are repeatedly said as dying on "43K2.1". If the numbers mean anything we could interpret, the "K" perhaps suggests a date in the 43,000s. In the DVD commentary, Russell T Davies says the draft script stated it was the forty-third century. The overriding consideration, however, is that the story presumably happens before the Ood are liberated from slavery (*Planet of the Ood*, set in 4126). *Doctor Who: The Encyclopedia* and *Doctor Who: The Time Traveller's Almanac* both concur with that, dating events with the Beast to "the forty-second century". *Timelink* goes for an earlier dating of 4043. The Doctor's assertion they are "five hundred years" from Earth would seem to mean five hundred light years *or* that it would take the humans here five hundred years to get to Earth.

The Doctor previously encountered life from before the creation of our universe in *Terminus, Millennial Rites, All-Consuming Fire, Synthespians™*, and more.

1627 Commonly referenced as "K37J5", but it's "K37Gem5" in the closed captioning on the DVD – and indeed, that *is* what it sounds like Cross Flane is saying. (This is possibly the same dating system that starts inserting words like "apple" into year designations, as in *The End of the World*.)

1628 Dating *The Torchwood Archive* (BF *TW* special release #1) - The Torchwood Computer claims to have been imprisoned within the Archive's Memory Core "for thousands and thousands of years" (presumably since its creation by Archie in the late 1800s). The Mediasphere, writer James Goss told us, has no relation to the Big Finish *Blake's 7* novel of the same name.

Henderson's bogus account of how he came to visit the Archive contains details that aren't the sort of thing one would (or could) easily lie about – in flashback, "Jack" says the Archive lies at the edge of the ex-Great and Bountiful Human Empire, and Henderson wonders why Jack doesn't have an Ood. The Great Cobalt

The Doctor's Six Centuries on Orbis Ends

& 4120 - ORBIS[1629] **->** The eighth Doctor had pleasantly spent six centuries in the company of the jellyfish-like Keltons who resided on Orbis, and had introduced to them the tradition of celebrating the dead with a funeral-feast, having noticed that the Keltons' habit of eating and regurgitating their deceased wasn't a very efficient way to compost the seabed. Orbis' troposphere was progressively changing, owing to influence of a passing moon.

The Molluscari, a race of aggressive space-oysters who could change gender, thought the waters of Orbis would make an ideal breeding ground... and the Keltons would make an excellent source of protein. The Molluscari leader, Crassostrea, had previously massacred the Tetraploids.

The Galactic Council had rejected a Molluscari claim to Orbis a few years ago, but now ruled in their favour, having determined that the Keltons' ownership of the planet wasn't tenable due to the recent climate changes. The Headhunter arrived in the TARDIS with Lucie from 2009, having struck a bargain with the Molluscari. In return for their retrieving the activator to Morbius' stellar manipulator, she was to coerce the Doctor into leaving Orbis by threatening Lucie's life.

The passing moon proved to be Morbius' stellar manipulator, which had been drawn to Orbis by the presence of the activator. The manipulator's approach made the oceans on Orbis boil; Crassostrea spawned while the Molluscari went into a feeding frenzy and attacked the Keltons. The Doctor and Lucie escaped in the TARDIS just as the manipulator crashed into Orbis – obliterating it, the Molluscari and the surviving Keltons.

The Headhunter returned to her warship and used the activator to slave the stellar manipulator to Lucie's DNA – it would shadow the TARDIS through the Vortex, and emerge near Earth in 2015.[1630]

The Liberation of the Ood

4126 - PLANET OF THE OOD[1631] **->** A member of the Friends of the Ood infiltrated Ood Operations on the Ood-Sphere, and reduced the telepathic dampener around the Ood Brain. Many Ood on the planet became lethal – as indicated by their red eyes – and instigated a rebellion. Ood Sigma, the personal assistant to the head of Ood Operations – Klineman Halpen – had been lacing Halpen's hair-restorer with Ood-graft for years, causing Halpen to fully transform into an Ood. The

---

Pyramid was mentioned in *Bad Wolf* [200,100], but could certainly have existed beforehand. Also, Henderson and the Andy-hologram use the same dating convention (century number, letter K, decimal to denote year) as *The Impossible Planet/The Satan Pit* [c.4106].

A case could be made that "Jack" meant the *Fourth Great and Bountiful Human Empire* as seen in *The Long Game* [200,000], but the evidence better suggests that Henderson visits the Archive in the same era as *The Impossible Planet/The Satan Pit*, but before the Ood's liberation in *Planet of the Ood* [c.4126]. Also, the script dates Jeremiah's background scenes to "42k", and there's no mention of his reaching the Archive via time-travel. In *The Satan Pit*, Captain Zachary Cross Flane claimed to be working on behalf of the Torchwood Archive (but perhaps never stepped foot there, if *The Torchwood Archive* does happen in this era, as nobody has visited it in "centuries").

1629 Dating *Orbis* (BF BBC7 #3.1) - The Doctor and the Headhunter confirm that he's been on Orbis "six hundred years or thereabouts". The plotline with the activator continues in *The Eight Truths/Worldwide Web*.

1630 *Orbis, The Eight Truths, Worldwide Web*.

1631 Dating *Planet of the Ood* (X4.3) - The Doctor first says that the Ood are "servants of humans in the forty-second century", then gives the exact year.

1632 Dating *42* (X3.7) - While no date is given on screen, prepublicity for the episode said it was set in the forty-second century – possibly just as a take-off on

the title. Nonetheless, the Doctor's spacesuit bears the same design as the one he wore in *The Impossible Planet/The Satan Pit*, perhaps indicating that all three episodes take place in roughly the same time.

1633 "Centuries" before *Destiny of the Daleks*.

1634 *The Story of Martha:* "The Weeping"

1635 "Thirty years" before *The Yes Men*. Carvossa's name owes to Patrick Troughton playing Luigi Carvossa in a TV version of *The Third Man*, one of this story's inspirations.

1636 Dating *Iris S3: The Iris Wildthyme Appreciation Society* (BF *Iris* #3.1) - The century is given. The name New Naxian Empire presumably stems from the Naxian Empire mentioned in *Iris S2: The Sound of Fear*. The title of Iris' autobiography is a play on Jon Pertwee's memoir, *Moon Boots and Dinner Suits*.

1637 Dating *The Last Voyage* (BBC *DW* audiobook #6) - Earth currently has an empire, but as Eternity has a population of eight billion humans, this is well in advance of the struggling Earth Empire as seen in the Pertwee era. The only other historical clues are that a) robots are in use, b) a straight-shot flight from one end of the Empire to another is considered advanced (so presumably, standard spaceships aren't too shabby either), and c) human longevity is such that Cluxton is 160, and is spry enough to undertake pioneering business ventures involving space transport. With all of that in mind, this story has been arbitrarily set during the Second Empire.

tenth Doctor and Donna helped to fully liberate the Ood Brain, and so the entire Ood species. A telepathic call summoned the enslaved Ood home. The Ood promised to honour the Doctor and Donna's names in song forever.

The unit of currency at this time was the credit; an Ood cost fifty credits. Earth was "a bit full", but the Second Great and Bountiful Empire, "a great big empire built on slavery", stretched over three galaxies (the "tri-Galactic"). There were vidphones.

c 4142 - 42[1632] **->** The tenth Doctor and Martha answered a distress call in the Terrachi System, located half a universe away from Earth. The engines of the spaceship *Pentallian* had failed, and it was falling into the nearest sun. Crewmember Korwin succumbed to an alien influence, becoming a being of burning light who proceeded to kill other crewmembers. The Doctor realised the star was alive – it felt violated because the ship had illegally mined it for fuel. The living particles were ejected from the scoops, which restored the sun and saved the ship.

The Dalek-Movellan War

The Daleks encountered a new threat: the Movellans, a race of humanoid androids from system 4X-Alpha-4. The Daleks were forced to abandon all operations elsewhere in the galaxy, including Skaro, and mobilise a huge battlefleet. The mighty Dalek and Movellan fleets faced each other in space, their battlecomputers calculating the moment of optimum advantage. This created an instant stalemate, and not a shot was fired for centuries. The vast Dalek Fleet was kept completely occupied, except for the occasional raiding mission on Outer Planets such as Kantria for slave workers, or on the starships of Earth's Deep Spacefleet.[1633]

Two thousand settlers from Earth established themselves on the planet Agelaos, and it became one of the most remote outposts of the Second Great and Bountiful Human Empire. Agelaos was located near a wormhole that granted the settlers with psionic abilities – but then mutated them into monsters. A beacon warned travellers to stay away from the planet.[1634]

The first Doctor and Dodo helped to repel a Mim invasion of New Houston, an Earth colony in the Fourth Sector. One of their allies, Meg Carvossa, considered travelling with them, but ran away upon seeing the TARDIS interior.[1635]

c 4150 - IRIS S3: THE IRIS WILDTHYME APPRECIATION SOCIETY[1636] **->** An autobiography that Iris Wildthyme hoped to write in her next life, *Old Boots*

and Cat Suits: My Fabulous Life, was a bestseller for centuries.

Iris and Panda were respectively offered several glistening adonises and a Pleasure Palace after they saved the New Naxian Empire from the slime-filled Slavvians. The Emperor threw a ceremony honouring Iris and Panda, but the arrival of a Monstron Time Destroyer prompted them to flee in Iris' bus...

On their next stop, Iris discovered that she had become the most famous woman on the planet Trull Minor: the forty-second century equivalent of Milton Keynes, all shops and roundabouts. Wayne Bland II – as chairman, secretary and treasurer of the Iris Wildthyme Appreciation Society, as well as editor of its fanzine *Ratbags and Gladrags* – became so besotted with Iris that he used an Anabusian mind-transferrer to swap bodies with her. The switch occurred as Iris signed Bland's copy of the *Radio Times Iris Wildthyme Centenary Special*, which had her future incarnations (including a leggy one) and future companion Hoppy the Kangaroo on the cover.

Iris-Wayne was locked up at the Institute for the Criminally Insane while Wayne, in Iris' body, enjoyed her celebrity-dom. "She" starred on the reality show *Who Iris Did Next*, became the new face of *Cosmomart*, and became rich from merchandise that included life-size Iris love dolls. Iris-Wayne briefly escaped and failed to contact Panda after mailing her/himself to Wildthyme Manor as a giant bottle of Gordon's Gin.

Panda deduced Wayne's duplicity as Trull Minor came under threat from the Great Old One named Traguam (a.k.a. the World Mater, the Celestial Copulator and the Galactic Gigalo), who mated with planets unto their destruction. Iris regained possession of her body while Wayne's mind switched places with Traguam. Wayne entered into a peaceful existence as a Great Old One while Traguam-Wayne was incarcerated at the Institute.

Iris and Panda left as the Monstron Time Destroyer following them arrived...

? 4150 - THE LAST VOYAGE[1637] **->** Inter-dimensional entities implanted the blueprints for a new type of interstellar engine into the mind of Joseph Sterns Cluxton, a 160-year-old billionaire, fostering the technology as a means of invading our reality. Within three years, Cluxton had used the designs to build the first Interstitial Transportation Vehicle (ITV).

The ITV made its maiden voyage across the longest stretch of humanity's empire – from Earth to the planet Eternity, home to eight billion humans – and its engines transported those aboard to the entities' dimension. The tenth Doctor returned everyone home, and permanently wrecked the ITV's engines.

In this era, robots were used for food preparation and other menial tasks.

c 4180 - THE YES MEN[1638] -> Meg Carvossa, now the Prime Designate of New Houston, averted a mass starvation by amending the colony's data to suggest it had 22 million residents rather than 22,000, which prompted the Earth Empire to send additional supplies. Carvossa continued her scheme for selfish gain, and her repeated data-amendments caused the colony's robot servitors to develop a loose form of independent thought. The second Doctor's over-zealous use of the Fast Return Switch – an attempt to take Polly and Ben home – resulted in the TARDIS returning to New Houston. Hundreds of robots learned something of heroism from Ben and Jamie, and began a rampage while screaming *Creag au tuire!* The colonists learned of Carvossa's misdeeds, and resolved the situation by voting to give the robots citizenship.

c 4200 - PEST CONTROL[1639] -> Giants living in the Pettingard System came under threat from the Serfians – a large beetle-like species that reproduced by implanting eggs in other races. The Sharback Corporation built 25-metre-tall robots to combat the infestation, but the robots indiscriminately wiped out the giants and Serfians alike.

People of mixed human/alien heritage currently existed in the outer worlds of Earth's solar system. Human soldiers in the Pioneer Corps, a military arm of the Second Great and Bountiful Human Empire, invaded the planet Rescension. War broke out with the centaurs who lived there, the Akwabi, but a further infestation of Serfian eggs threatened to transform both sides into Serfian drones. The tenth Doctor and Donna intervened, and the Serfian queens were killed. It was expected that the surviving drones would be no threat without their leadership, and that the humans and Akwabi would rebuild the planet.

c 4211 - "Body Snatched"[1640] -> Dr Rubin, a scientist on the planet hospital Bedlam, developed Transmigratory Memory Mapping: a means by which minds could be transplanted into disused Biogrower bodies, according another fifty years of life. The Horse Lord of Khan wanted

---

1638 Dating *The Yes Men* (BF EA #2.1) - New Houston is part of the Earth Empire, and receives supply shipments direct from Earth. The colony is located in Sector Four; there are at least sixteen such sectors by *Earthshock*. It's said that the Earth Empire "has its own problems" – a bit vague, considering Empires pretty much always have headaches to deal with. Noticeably, however, Karvasa owns antique chairs from the thirtieth century, and a statue of "the last" Guardian of the Solar System – which may or may not refer to Mavic Chen from *The Daleks' Master Plan* [4000].

1639 Dating *Pest Control* (BBC *DW* audiobook #1) - The Doctor identifies the Pioneer Corps soldiers as being part of the Second Great and Bountiful Human Empire.

1640 Dating "Body Snatched" (IDW *DW* Vol. 2, #10-11) - It's "two hundred years" before the opening of "Body Snatched", which is set in the "forty-fifth century".

1641 Dating *The End of Time* (X4.17) - It's been "one hundred years" since the Doctor's last visit (*Planet of the Ood*).

1642 Dating *The Eleventh Doctor Year Three* (Titan 11th Doc #3.5, "Time of the Ood") – It's clearly after the Ood's liberation in *Planet of the Ood* [4126], but the story's internal timeframe is a bit confusing. Events end with the Doctor taking the hub-based Ood back to their homeworld, where their loss has been mourned for "over 100 years", and yet nobody comments that the time-discrepancy owes to the Doctor's bad piloting skills. In which case, does the story *open* a century after *Planet of the Ood*? If so, it's remarkable that a human Friend of the Ood (contemporaneous with the Ood's enslavement, one presumes) is still alive, never mind so righteously pissed off that the hub-Odd didn't return home a century previous. It's anyone's guess, therefore, if the Doctor skips over a hundred years, or takes the

Ood home with no time displacement.

1643 Dating *The Death Collectors* (BF #109a) - The participants seem human; not only do they possess such names as "Nancy" and "Smith Ridley", the sky station's computer has Puccini's "Madame Butterfly" in its music collection. No date is given, and so placement here amounts to little more than a guess, but the overall tone suggests it's a story where humankind has simply ventured so far into space, it's encountering horrors beyond its comprehension. Dar Traders also appear in *The Darkening Eye*.

1644 *A Christmas Carol*. The date is given on Elliot's portrait.

1645 "Centuries" before *The Davros Mission*, and probably explaining why the Doctor blows up Skaro in *Remembrance of the Daleks* without fear of eradicating the Thals as well.

1646 *The Crystal Bucephalus* (p42).

1647 "Centuries" before *Emotional Chemistry*.

1648 Dating *A Christmas Carol* (X6.0) - The Doctor first meets Kazran Sardick (from Kazran's perspective) when Kazran is 12; the precise year isn't given. Elliot Sardick was born in 4302, so couldn't have a 12-year-old son until, say, 4332 at the earliest (and while he has dark hair; Elliot's clearly at least middle aged at this point). The older Kazran was played by Michael Gambon, who was 68 at the time, so we can infer that Kazran is around 70 in the "present day". The Doctor then revisits Kazran on seven successive Christmas Eves.

1649 "Twenty years" before *A Christmas Carol*; the year of Elliot's death is on his portrait.

1650 *Spiral Scratch*

1651 Dating *A Christmas Carol* (X6.0) - We're told Elliot Sardick died "twenty years" before the story, and a plaque below his portrait states he died in 4378. In

to go further and put his mind into a Time Lord body – to that end, he summoned his old friend, the Doctor. The eleventh Doctor, Amy and Rory found that Rubin had been testing his mind swap on different races, including a Re'nar, a Ju'wes, a Saturnynian, a Slitheen, a Sycorax and a Gizhou. Confusion followed... the Doctor and Amy accidentally swapped consciousnesses, and the Biogrowers were induced with schizophrenia, triggering a riot. The time travellers incapacitated the Horse Lord, ended the riot and returned to their own bodies – moments before Rory, thinking his wife was still in the Doctor's form, gave "her" a passionate kiss.

4226 - THE END OF TIME[1641] **->** The tenth Doctor answered a summons to Ood-Sphere, and was shocked to see how developed the planet had become in the hundred years since his last visit. The mind of the Ood was troubled, and they showed him their dreams of the Harold Saxon Master. Time was bleeding, and events on Earth in 2009 were affecting everything...

& ? 4226 - THE ELEVENTH DOCTOR YEAR THREE[1642] **->** The eleventh Doctor, Alice and the Sapling stopped at the Devil's Eye: a galaxy-class pleasure hub near a black hole. The hub's stasis shields had prevented the Ood aboard from hearing the song summoning them home, prompting a spiteful Friend of the Ood to feed a psychic-algorithm into their telepathic feed, turning them murderous. The Doctor and his friends ended the rampage and took the Ood to the Ood-Sphere, where Ood Sigma hailed their return.

? 4300 - THE DEATH COLLECTORS[1643] **->** The volcanic planet Antikon was quarantined after it became the source of Antikon's Decay – a lethal virus that decimated a solar system. Professor Mors Alexandryn, the foremost authority on the Decay, headed a research team in a sky station over Antikon. They encountered a spacefaring race called Dar Traders, a.k.a. the Death Collectors, who typically scavenged corpses after battles. The Dar Traders were technically dead, and used metal frames to move their husks around. They could preserve the last few moments of life in other species by introducing their own flesh to the dead. The seventh Doctor found that the Decay was an alien intelligence that existed as a virus and trying to communicate through "a death state" – not comprehending that this was inimical to other species. The mass of Decay on Antikon increased exponentially upon contact with the Dar Traders, but Alexandryn gave his life to the Decay, peacefully dragging them both into death.

In 4302, Elliot Sardick was born on a human colony world near the Horsehead Nebula. His family had given their name to the main settlement, Sardicktown;

the first settlers there referred to mid-winter as the Crystal Feast. As an adult, he would gain even more power than his ancestors and have a son, Kazran. The currency on Sardicktown was the gideon.[1644]

The Thals were driven off Skaro by the Daleks.[1645]

In 4338, Turlough was the guest of Wilhelm, König of the Wine Lords of Chardon.[1646] The railway network was reestablished in Europe.[1647]

c 4340-& 4347/(=) c 4340-& 4347 (Christmas Eve) - A CHRISTMAS CAROL[1648] **->** Kazran Sardick was physically abused by his father, Elliott, and would grow up to become someone who didn't care if people lived or died. To teach Kazran Sardick the error of his ways, the eleventh Doctor travelled back to Christmas Eve when Kazran was 12. Kazran had been trying to make a video project about the sky fish that flew around Sardicktown, and the Doctor helped to disprove Kazran's belief that he was alone in a cruel world. The Doctor tried to attract the sky fish, but instead attracted a sky shark.

To transport the shark back to its natural habitat, Kazran suggested they borrow a hibernation unit from the vaults where his father kept people in suspended animation as debt-collateral. They opened the cryopod of Abigail Pettigrew, and her singing calmed the shark. She was returned to suspended animation, but Kazran was now smitten.

> (=) The Doctor returned for Kazran and Abigail each of the next seven Christmas Eves. They went for a sleigh ride with the flying shark, to the Egyptian pyramids, Uluru, the Eiffel Tower, the Statue of Liberty, to visit Abigail's family and a pool party in 1952 Hollywood. Abigail, though, was terminally ill, and had one more day to live. Kazran remained convinced the world was unfair.

The Doctor's efforts to rehabilitate Kazran failed, and so he took his 12-year-old self forward in time to see the miser he had become...

Elliot Sardick's machine to control the cloud bank over Sardicktown was finally completed. It had isomorphic controls that only responded to Elliot or his son Kazran. Elliot Sardick died in 4378.[1649]

> = The sixth Doctor visited the planet Schyllus in 4387.[1650]

4398 (Christmas Eve) - A CHRISTMAS CAROL[1651] **->** The eleventh Doctor left Amy and Rory to honeymoon aboard a galaxy-class starship, but they summoned him back when the ship went out of control near Sardicktown, a human colony world surrounded by a cloud bank. The ship could only be guided to safety by a machine operated by Kazran Sardick – but Sardick was a cruel man, and refused to help. The Doctor travelled back to Kazran's childhood and altered his history to make him a better person. When this failed, he brought Kazran's 12-year-old self to this time to see his future. The elder Kazran relented, but his history had been altered so much that the cloud-controlling machine no longer recognised him. The Doctor and Kazran woke Abigail Pettigrew for one last time, and she used her voice to create harmonics that controlled the clouds and saved the spacecraft.

The forty-fifth century was an era of technocrats and machine-driven life. One race engineered a biological-temporal link that enabled them to forge a mental connection with their machines. Some members of the species became biologically advanced enough to place themselves in metallic shells and time travel by simply willing the process. One such traveller was Celia Fortunaté, who would arrive in another time period at the Needle, a bio-mechanical living complex. The Needle's overseeing computer, Whitenoise, installed a chip in Celia to curb her of all violence, but this corrupted Whitenoise's systems and led to a string of murders.[1652]

c 4411 - "Body Snatched"[1653] -> The eleventh Doctor brought Amy and Rory to the Trans-Universal Union to collect his mail, which included a letter that had been sent two hundred years earlier from the Horse Lord of Khan. They went back in time to help.

c 4500 - "Keepsake"[1654] -> By this time, a musical had been made about the Orion War. Millions of self-repairing robots from Orion were still performing menial tasks.

The seventh Doctor stopped at Reclaim Platform Juliet-November-Kilo, the largest reclaim station on its side of the Easto Cluster, to acquire spare parts for the TARDIS. He encountered a servo robot containing the last vestiges of his android friend Sara's consciousness, and thereby learned of her fate.

The forty-sixth century saw the development of Dirty Rip engines, time machines that punched holes in time

---

SJA: Death of the Doctor, the Doctor mentions a seemingly unrelated incident in which he dropped Amy and Rory off on a "honeymoon planet" that as it turned out was itself on a honeymoon, having married an asteroid.
1652 *Red*. "The Needle" in this story is not the same one as the Needle in *The Infinity Doctors*. The time-travel process described here is similar to the early Gallifreyan experiments (as detailed in *Cat's Cradle: Time's Crucible*).
1653 Dating "Body Snatched" (IDW *DW* Vol. 2, #10-11) - It's the "forty-fifth century" according to the opening caption.
1654 Dating "Keepsake" (BF #112b) - The Doctor says that it's "nearly two thousand years" since *Kingdom of Silver*.
1655 *Only Human*
1656 Dating *Here There Be Monsters* (BF CC #3.1) - The back cover says it's the "distant future". Mention is made of yet another "human empire", but in itself, this isn't very telling. Rostrum says he doesn't know the year in Earth terms – a pity, as that would've been helpful.

"Benchmarking" has here been linked to the "dirty rip" engines mentioned in *Only Human*, as they seem to work on roughly the same principle. That would make this "empire" the Second Great and Bountiful Earth Empire.

It's unclear if the tentacled "deep space" creatures seen here are an evolved form of the Yssgaroth from *The Pit*, which were similarly loosed on our reality after Rassilon punched holes in the fabric of space-time. *Tomb of Valdemar* also alludes to similar creatures, and this chronology places the two stories at roughly the same time.

1657 Dating *Tomb of Valdemar* (PDA #29) - No date is given, but this is within a generation of the fall of the Second Empire. Since the last edition of *Ahistory*, which placed this story in 16,000, *Planet of the Ood* established that the Second Great and Bountiful Human Empire was around in 4126. Earth no longer seems to have an Empire in the Davros Era, so the latest this story can be set is around 4500.
1658 "More than two thousand years" after *Erimem: Churchill's Castle*.
1659 See The Davros Era sidebar.
1660 Dating *Destiny of the Daleks* (17.1) - The Daleks and Movellans have been locked in stalemate for "centuries". At this point, the Daleks are feared, highly advanced and have a vast war fleet which operates as their command base. In *Resurrection of the Daleks*, it is made clear that there is deadlock between the Movellans and the Daleks' computers, not the Daleks themselves.

Dalek: The Astounding Untold History of the Greatest Enemies of the Universe – while styling itself as a less-than-wholly-reliable source – says that following the Movellan victory against the Daleks (*Resurrection of the Daleks*), Dalek duplicates infected Movellan power plant facilities with a virus that plunged the Movellans into a civil war... paving the way for Davros's Imperial Daleks to wipe them out entirely in the *Pa Jass-Gutrik*, "the War of Vengeance". There's no pressing need to put much stock in this – but then again, the Movellans have yet, chronologically speaking, to be referenced anywhere after *Resurrection of the Daleks*.

and were prone to both exploding and increasing the vortex pressure on users until they also exploded.[1655]

? 4500 - HERE THERE BE MONSTERS[1656] **->** Humanity now treated mathematics like art; if an equation was beautiful and symmetrical, it was regarded as true.

On Earth, genetic manipulation was used to develop sentient vegetative lifeforms that could entwine their branches and leaves throughout a spaceship's interior. Such lifeforms could pilot spaceships, fight small wars and expand the human empire's boundaries, allotting humanity more time for pursuits such as sculpture and music. The lifeforms' memories were contained in seed pods, and they were genetically engineered to avoid boredom; they'd be content spending one hundred million years performing tasks and reaching for synthesized light.

Three hundred and thirty-eight years after these lifeforms were created, humanity also developed "benchmarking" – a means of using gravitational singularities contained in a Klein bottle to create a navigational system. Seven singularities were used in concert – one would puncture the fabric of space-time every tenth of a light-year; the remaining six would encode each "hole" with navigational information. The Earth Benchmarking Vessel (EBV) *Nevermore*, captained by the vegetative lifeform Rostrum, was intended as the first of many ships that would benchmark entire sectors of space. Spaceships would consequently always know their location, and which direction they needed to go.

The first Doctor, accompanied by Ian, Barbara and Susan, insisted to Rostrum that ravenous "things" lived in the "deep space" beneath space, and that the benchmarking process would give them access to our universe. A traveller from this "deep space" crossed over and adopted a human form – as benchmarking was laying waste to vast tracts of his reality – and said that while deep space contained lifeforms whose energy and matter were antithetical to humanity, it was also home to many intelligent, ethical civilisations. The traveller sealed the breach created by the *Nevermore*, which killed Rostrum and everything within half a light year. The traveller also perished, but only after recording a message warning humanity of the dangers of benchmarking.

Romana Regenerates

c 4500 - TOMB OF VALDEMAR[1657] **->** The Second Empire fell after three centuries, following a revolution that began with a declaration that the oppressed masses would no longer tolerate idle cruelty. The ruling class was aristocratic and decadent. The New Protectorate established the New Parliament on Earth, based on "the rigours of Puritanism applied to a purely materialistic philosophy". This was led by the Virgin Lady High Protector, the Civil Matriarch, who had the Elite's palaces destroyed with Immolator Six capsules. A Duke named Paul Neville fled to Terra and became a powerful magician, the head of a cult dedicated to the dark god Valdemar. The Protectorate located Neville, forcing him to flee to the ends of the collapsing Empire. Neville sought the planet Ashkellia, which he believed contained the palace of the Old Ones – Valdemar was the last of their kind.

Neville attempted to resurrect Valdemar through an adolescent psionic named Huvan, but the fourth Doctor and the first Romana defeated his plans. Huvan nearly punctured the higher dimensions, which could have destroyed the universe, but the Doctor and Romana convinced Huvan that he lacked the maturity for such power. Huvan agreed to erase his memory and assume a new identity. He became a trapper named Ponch on the planet Janus Forus. Fifteen years later, Romana returned to help him remember his past. She regenerated at this time.

The New Protectorate lasted around a century or two before burning itself out.

> (=) The human survivors within the Beider Nebula mutated into shorter, grey-skinned creatures who went back in time to fulfil their own creation.[1658]

The Davros Era[1659]

Davros Revives; Romana Regenerates

? 4500 - DESTINY OF THE DALEKS[1660] **->** The Daleks realised that their dependence on logic made it impossible for them to win a war against another logical machine race, the Movellans. Their battlecomputers suggested that they should turn to their creator, Davros, for help. The Supreme Dalek dispatched a force to Skaro to recover Davros from the ruins of the Kaled bunker. Mining operations started up, and the Daleks discovered their creator, who had survived in suspended animation for centuries.

A Movellan party was sent to Skaro to investigate Dalek operations. As they arrived, the Daleks' slaves broke free, helped by the fourth Doctor and Romana – who had just undergone her first regeneration. Before a Dalek ship could arrive from Supreme Command, the slaves had overpowered the Movellans and defeated the small Dalek force. Davros was captured by the human force, who returned to Earth in the Movellan ship.

Before this time, Arcturus won the Galactic Olympic games, with Betelgeuse coming a close second. The economy of Algol was subject to irreversible inflation.

The Movellans were built by the Daleks, and the entire war was faked as part of their plan to prevent the destruction of Skaro.[1661] The Movellans adapted their power packs to work by remote.[1662] Hoping to break the Dalek stalemate, the Movellans developed Chenek as a prototype warrior with independent thought. A Dalek assault forced a Movellan ship with Chenek aboard to time-jump back to Earth's Iron Age.[1663]

Human authorities put Davros on trial. Humanity had abandoned the death penalty, so Davros was placed in suspended animation aboard a prison station in deep space. Without Davros' help, the Daleks were helpless. They lost the war when the Movellans released a virus that only affected Dalek tissue. Weakened, the Daleks were forced to rely on hired mercenaries and duplicates: conditioned clones produced by their genetic experiments, and generated from humans snatched from many timezones.[1664]

Humanity discovered a cure for Becks Syndrome.[1665] Following another Dalek War with humanity, the Daleks were not active in the galaxy for a century.[1666] On Riften-5, the fifth Doctor saw archives of genetic tests on Daleks after the War of Sharpened Hearts.[1667]

? 4517 - THE PILOT[1668] **->** The twelfth Doctor, Bill and Nardole lured the Puddle into a Dalek-Movellan crossfire, but it survived even Dalek weaponry. Bill released the Puddle from its promise to not leave without her, and it dissipated. The travellers returned to St Luke's in the twenty-first century.

The Pilot endowed Bill with her tears, so she'd know if Bill needed help.[1669]

The first Doctor, Steven and Vicki aided some colonists against the Antoim, an intelligent virus. The trio stranded the Antoim on a deserted planet, and left in the TARDIS, to next arrive in Constantinople, 540...[1670]

& 4587 - ALIEN HEART / DALEK SOUL[1671] **->** A Dalek splinter group developed the Scion-Primes: spider-creatures grown from their own cells, as a means of affecting time and turning target planets into Dalek worlds. For thirty years, field tests with the Scion-Primes failed, and erased ten planets – including Varga, Ottonius, Hastus Major and Felkanto – from history. The fifth Doctor and Nyssa confronted the Scion-Primes and their creators in the Traxana System and incinerated them.

A secondary Dalek unit failed to capture the travellers, but settled for duplicating them. The Doctor-Duplicates spent five years putting down a rebellion against Dalek rule on Mojox, while the Nyssa-Duplicates served as the Daleks' Chief Virologist. One Nyssa-Duplicate regained her moral centre, and released a virus that exterminated all the Daleks and their Duplicates on Mojox, including herself, which freed the Mojoxalli.

1661 According to *War of the Daleks*.
1662 *The Movellan Grave*, overcoming the limitation from *Destiny of the Daleks*.
1663 *The Movellan Grave*. It's never stated explicitly that the Movellans can time travel, although in *Destiny of the Daleks*, Romana sees the Movellan ship and says: "Judging by design and size, I'd say it had intergalactic range and time warp capability", and it seems sensible to infer the Movellans have time travel if they're able to achieve a stalemate with the Daleks based on what we're told is a "balance of power" where neither side has the slightest advantage over the other.
1664 *Resurrection of the Daleks*
1665 "Forty years" before *Revelation of the Daleks*.
1666 Before *Davros*.
1667 *Christmas on a Rational Planet*. No date given, but Riften-5 was Lytton's home planet according to *Attack of the Cybermen*, and this is (presumably) his home timezone. *Attack of the Cybermen* ends with the Doctor saying he misjudged Lytton, yet they didn't meet at all in *Resurrection of the Daleks* (unless you count Lytton shooting at the Doctor from a distance) and they barely meet in *Attack of the Cybermen*. If we wanted to fix that, we could theorise that the Doctor met Lytton – from his perspective – between the two stories (it would be before *Resurrection of the Daleks* for Lytton).

1668 Dating *The Pilot* (X10.1) - The Doctor describes the Daleks and Movellans as "old friends" and insists "This is the past". The scene in the broadcast episode matches a version of a self-contained scene shown as publicity to announce the casting of Pearl Mackie (called *New Doctor Who Companion REVEALED* on the BBC America site), which ended with the Doctor saying "we need to get back... to the future: 2017". This seemingly contradicts *Destiny of the Daleks* and *Resurrection of the Daleks*, the two TV stories explicitly set during and after the Dalek-Movellan conflict, both of which are set in Earth's future (see The Davros Era sidebar).

The Doctor may mean "the past" relative to the Daleks' history with Gallifrey – and yet our heroes face a new-series Dalek, not a Davros Era model. We've taken the approach that the Movellan War was a specific period in history, in "the past" as far as the Doctor is concerned, not relative to 2017.
1669 *The Pilot, The Doctor Falls*.
1670 "Four thousand years" after the 540 portion of *The Secret History*.
1671 Dating *Alien Heart/Dalek Soul* (BF #224) - These stories jointly share a single release, and happen one after the other.

The Doctor says in *Alien Heart* that it's the "twenty-first time frame" (whatever that means); the same story

THE DAVROS ERA: Four consecutive Dalek TV stories (*Destiny of the Daleks, Resurrection of the Daleks, Revelation of the Daleks* and *Remembrance of the Daleks*) form a linked series in which the creator of the Daleks, Davros (first seen in *Genesis of the Daleks*), is revived. In due course, he's captured and imprisoned by Earth before re-engineering the Daleks and gradually taking control over his creations. The series ends with the ultimate destruction of the Daleks' home planet of Skaro, although the novel *War of the Daleks*, set shortly after *Remembrance of the Daleks*, significantly reinterpreted those events.

Three Big Finish audios (and *The Davros Mission*, an audio story exclusive to *The Complete Davros Collection* DVD set) occur in gaps between the television stories, and act as bridges between them – *Resurrection of the Daleks* is followed by *Davros, Revelation of the Daleks* is followed by *The Davros Mission* and *The Juggernauts*, and *Remembrance of the Daleks* is followed by *Terror Firma*. The comic strip "Emperor of the Daleks" depicts Davros becoming Emperor between *Revelation of the Daleks* and *Remembrance of the Daleks*. Here, for the sake of convenience, we refer to the events of these stories as "the Davros Era" – a term that is never used in any of the stories themselves.

It is never stated exactly when the Davros Era is set, although it is clearly far in Earth's future.

The key story here is *Remembrance of the Daleks*. Before *Remembrance*, it was widely felt that *The Evil of the Daleks* really was, as the Doctor said, "the final end" of the Daleks (even though the draft script *of Day of the Daleks* explained that the Daleks had survived their civil war). *Remembrance of the Daleks* changed that, by ending with the destruction of Skaro. Clearly, taking *Remembrance of the Daleks* at face value, it – and by implication the rest of the Davros Era – has to happen after *The Evil of the Daleks* (the climax of which was set on Skaro).

Even before that, the first two editions of *The Programme Guide* set *Destiny of the Daleks* "c.4500" (as did the earlier versions of this chronology and *Timelink*). Following *The Programme Guide*'s lead, the script of *Resurrection of the Daleks* referred to the year as 4590, although that's not established on screen.

There have been other attempts to place it. *The Terrestrial Index* took the Doctor's speech to the Black Dalek in *Remembrance of the Daleks* that the Daleks are "a thousand years" from home literally, and respectively set the stories in "as the twenty-seventh century began", "towards the end of the twenty-seventh century", "as the twenty-eighth century began" and "about 2960". *The TARDIS Logs* chose "8740 AD" for *Destiny of the Daleks*. Ben Aaronovitch's novelisation of *Remembrance of the Daleks* and his introduction to the *Abslom Daak – Dalek Killer* graphic album had extracts from a history book, *The Children of Davros*, published in "4065" – apparently well after *Remembrance of the Daleks*.

The non-fiction *Doctor Who* works by James Goss and Steve Tribe consistently date the Davros era to the 46th century... the Dalek-Movellan war in *Destiny of the Daleks* plays out from the "42nd century" (following the Daleks' diminishment in *The Evil of the Daleks*) to the "46th century" (*The Dalek Handbook*, p71); the Daleks "resurrect" Davros (*Destiny* again) in "4500" (*The Dalek Handbook*, p71); he's captured in *Destiny* in the "46th century" (*A History of the Universe in 100 Objects*, p158) and liberated in *Resurrection of the Daleks* from Earth forces in "4590" (*The Dalek Handbook*, p80); he creates his own Dalek forces on Necros in *Revelation of the Daleks* in the "47th century" (*The Dalek Handbook*, p82); and the Hand of Omega destroys Skaro in the "47th century" (*The Dalek Handbook*, p84). The Glass Dalek (*Revelation*) and Hand of Omega (*Remembrance*) entries in *A History of the Universe in 100 Objects* (pgs. 222, 224) date to the "47th century".

John Peel's *The Official Doctor Who & the Daleks Book* – written with Terry Nation's approval – offers a complete Dalek timeline, although it stresses it's not "definitive" and could change in the light of a new story (p209), and it was written *before Remembrance of the Daleks* was broadcast. In Peel's version, *Genesis of the Daleks* comes first, followed by *The Daleks* [c.1564], there are Dalek survivors in the Kaled Bunker and after five hundred years they emerge and force the Thals to flee Skaro. The Daleks discover space travel after about a hundred years, and launch *The Dalek Invasion of Earth* [2164]. The Dalek Wars begin, after several hundred years of Dalek preparation, leading to *Frontier in Space* and *Planet of the Daleks* [2540]. The Daleks developed time travel, as seen in *The Chase*. The Daleks and Mechanoids fought the Mechon Wars, and one Dalek capsule from that conflict ends up crashing on Vulcan where it is unearthed in *The Power of the Daleks* ["several centuries" after 2010]. The Daleks went back in time to reinvade Earth (*Day of the Daleks*). The Daleks were then attacked by the Movellans (*Destiny of the Daleks*) and the two races were deadlocked for "decades".

Ninety years later followed *Resurrection of the Daleks* (by which time, Earth and Draconia had defeated the Movellans). The Daleks exploited a space plague (*Death to the Daleks*). Davros had survived, but was captured by the Daleks at the end of *Revelation of the Daleks*, and he was taken to Skaro and executed. Weakened, the Daleks needed allies to conquer the galaxy, as seen in *The Daleks' Master Plan* [4000]. This led to the Dalek Wars, that lasted "the next couple of centuries" after which the Emperor Dalek initiated the events *of The Evil of the Daleks* [c 4200], which ended in a civil war that wiped out the entire Dalek race, once and for all.

No firm dates for the Davros Era are given, but working backwards, this timeline would seem to place *Destiny of the Daleks* somewhere in the thirty-ninth century.

continued on page 3283...

& 4590 - RESURRECTION OF THE DALEKS[1672] -> One Supreme Dalek came up with an audacious plan that would strengthen the Daleks' position. Davros would be released from prison, and use his scientific genius and understanding of the Daleks to find an antidote for the Movellan virus. Dalek duplicate technology would be used to strike on twentieth-century Earth, while a second group, composed of duplicate versions of the fifth Doctor and his companions, would assassinate the High Council of Gallifrey. The plan totally failed.

Once Davros was released, he attempted to usurp control of the Dalek army and completely re-engineer the race. This met from resistance from those loyal to the Supreme Dalek, and the two factions began fighting. The Duplicates rebelled, destroying the prison station and the Dalek battlecruiser. Davros escaped.

The Thals Depart Skaro for the Last Time

& 4595 - WE ARE THE DALEKS[1673] -> The only Thals remaining on Skaro were slaves, but many were in space as part of an anti-Dalek coalition.

The Dalek Emperor and the Dalek Supreme Council decided that outright warfare was inefficient, and began undermining their foes' economies with promises of investment – a prelude to strip-mining target worlds. Simultaneously, the Daleks deployed the *Warfleet* video game on Earth, 1987, to harness human imagination in piloting their drone fleets.

The seventh Doctor and Mel usurped the *Warfleet* system in 1987, and turned the Daleks' drones against them.

---

establishes that it's the time of the Earth Empire and the Guild of Adjudicators, and that it's "hundreds of years" into the absent Tegan's future. Captain Sonderal goes to Traxana by Beta Dart (*The Space Pirates*), arguably outdated by the Empire's time, but perhaps they just keep making better Beta Darts. Travana has a lucanol mine (*The Robots of Death*). Sonderal, a member of Earth's Intelligence Corps, knows about the Daleks' lethality from history, suggesting there's no major Earth-Dalek engagement at present.

Noticeably, *Alien Heart* entails a Dalek splinter group that's failed to realize the Movellans prevailed in this part of space "a hundred years ago"; it's less clear if this constituted the end of the Movellan-Dalek war. If not (or with benefit of rounding a little), we can sandwich these events between *Destiny of the Daleks* [?4500] and *Resurrection of the Daleks* [?4590], which continuity-wise works well for a fifth Doctor and Nyssa story.

1672 Dating *Resurrection of the Daleks* (21.4) - This is the sequel to *Destiny of the Daleks*. Davros says he has been imprisoned for "ninety years". According to some reports, the rehearsal script set the story in 4590, which would follow the date established in *The Programme Guide*. This date also appears in *The Encyclopaedia of the Worlds of Doctor Who*.

1673 Dating *We are the Daleks* (BF #201) - The story goes slightly berserk in trying to build bridges between various Dalek TV stories. Crucially, it serves to explain why a giant Dalek-shaped building is seen amidst an aged and corroded city on Skaro in *Asylum of the Daleks*. Events in *We are the Daleks* also seem to cause the downfall of the Daleks' Supreme Council (mentioned in *The Daleks*; one member is seen in *Planet of the Daleks*), presumably paving the way for the Parliament of the Daleks – and the Prime Minister leading them – in *Asylum of the Daleks*. Celia Dunthorpe, one imagines, is either mutated into the Prime Minister from that story, or she originates the post and the eleventh Doctor, Amy and Rory meet one of her successors.

The Daleks here acknowledge their over-reliance to logic, and leverage the power of human imagination – the former being seen in *Destiny of the Daleks/ Resurrection of the Daleks*, the latter in *Remembrance of the Daleks*. The Thals say the Doctor has "helped our kind in the past," and they here leave Skaro forever – meaning it's definitely after *Planet of the Daleks* [2540], and feeds into the run-up of (the Thal-less, presumably) Skaro's destruction in *Remembrance*.

The Dalek Emperor is intended as the one seen in *The Evil of the Daleks*, but it sounds different because the electronic treatment of Nicholas Briggs' voice used in other Big Finish adventures (such as *Dalek Empire*) was left off. The Doctor seems to acknowledge this Emperor as the *Evil* one when he says, "I defeated you once before with the Human Factor..."

Taking all of that into account, it is hard to make *We are the Daleks* serve *all* its intended masters, but the rough sequence of events seems to be... *The Evil of the Daleks*, *Destiny of the Daleks/Resurrection of the Daleks*, *We are the Daleks*, the opening to *Asylum of the Daleks* (the eleventh Doctor is captured in a Dalek-shaped building) and *Remembrance of the Daleks*. That works, if a bit uneasily, but seems to assume that the Dalek Emperor and the Supreme Council are still in power throughout some of the Davros Era, when the Daleks appear more rudderless than all that.

1674 Dating *Asylum of the Daleks* (X7.1) - Date unknown, but it's after *We are the Daleks*, and before Skaro's destruction (either in *Remembrance of the Daleks*, or its resurrected form prior to the Last Great Time War). To accommodate those requirements, it's best to assume that the opening of *Asylum of the Daleks* occurs in different time zone as the rest of the story; see The "Own Time" of the Daleks sidebar.

1675 *The Juggernauts*

1676 Dating *Davros* (BF #48) - *Davros* is set after *Resurrection of the Daleks*. It's never explicitly stated that it occurs between that story and *Revelation of the*

With this support, Thal forces rescued their enslaved fellows and fled into space... marking the last time any Thals resided on their homeworld.

The Daleks disrupted the *Warfleet* operators with the Zenos Tower's rage-inducing rays. In response, the Doctor and Mel used the Daleks' own time portal to move the Tower to Skaro, where its rays made the Daleks turn upon each other. The Emperor refused the Doctor's offer of mercy, and so the Doctor used the Tower's systems to generate a time storm that aged everything in a hundred mile radius of the Daleks' city.

The Supreme Council presumably perished, and the Emperor lay close to death as would-be ally of the Daleks from 1987 – Celia Dunthorpe, MP for Pottersbridge – declared herself the Daleks' Prime Minister...

? 4597 - ASYLUM OF THE DALEKS[1674] -> Darla von Karlsen was converted into a Dalek Puppet, and sent a message to the eleventh Doctor asking him to help rescue her daughter Hannah. The Doctor met with Karlsen on Skaro, and in so doing fell into a Dalek trap. He was taken away to the Parliament of Daleks overseeing the Dalek Asylum...

The parents of Geoff, who was later a member of Davros' science team, died in the Kensington disaster of '97.[1675]

c 4600 - DAVROS[1676] -> Arnold Baines, head of the TAI corporation (which sold everything from foodstuffs to recreational narcotics to laser cannons), tracked down Davros' body. The sixth Doctor saw Davros revive. Baines hired both the Doctor and Davros to develop business strategies to help humankind spread to other galaxies. Davros secretly developed a computer model that could accurately predict the galactic stock market. With it, he planned to destroy capitalism in favour of a system that placed the entire galaxy's economy on a permanent war footing. He launched a coup against Baines, but failed. Davros escaped in Baines' spacecraft with a hostage, Kim, who killed herself – allowing the Doctor to crash the ship. The Doctor suspected that Davros survived.

Collectors were looking for Dalek regalia at this time. Some historians, like Lorraine Baines, offered revisionist histories where the Daleks were seen as victims, not aggressors, and Davros was hailed as a visionary. The Treaty of Parlagon prevented individuals from having nuclear weapons. There was famine in the galaxy, virtually every available planet of which had been colonised by humanity.

...continued from page 3281

War of the Daleks, also written by Peel, attempted to reverse the destruction of Skaro in *Remembrance of the Daleks*, and – unsurprisingly – it broadly follows the timeline in Peel's earlier book. Ironically, though, it undermines the case for setting the Davros Era before 4000 – first, the SSS explore Antalin (the planet the Daleks trick the Doctor into destroying instead of Skaro) after the events of *The Daleks' Master Plan*. Secondly, for the Dalek plan to work, the Doctor has to think Skaro was destroyed in *Remembrance of the Daleks*, and he wouldn't if he knew it still existed in the year 4000. (*About Time* has suggested that while the Daleks report to Skaro in *The Daleks' Master Plan*, the Doctor doesn't *see* them doing that, so he might not realise they do.)

Some fans have speculated that the Daleks might move to "New Skaro" after *Remembrance of the Daleks*, but no evidence exists for this on screen, and on the occasions when we see Skaro it is clearly the same world – the Doctor knows his way around in *The Evil of the Daleks* and *Destiny of the Daleks*. In the Time War shown in the EDAs, the Time Lords created duplicate home planets and it's possible that the Daleks might do the same.

In two New Adventures by Andy Lane (*Lucifer Rising, Original Sin*) we discover that the Guild of Adjudicators eventually becomes the Grand Order of Oberon referred to in *Revelation of the Daleks*, yet the Adjudicators are still active in *Original Sin*, so *Revelation of the Daleks* must take place well after the thirtieth century.

Mission to the Unknown established that the Daleks hadn't been a military force in Earth's galaxy for a thousand years prior to 4000 (and in one of the scenes where "galaxy" seems to mean "galaxy", not "solar system"). This – and perhaps the presence of the Galactic Federation – would seem to rule out the Davros Era taking place between 3000 and 4000. Humans from the time of *Destiny*, *Resurrection* and *Revelation* all know and fear the Daleks, and see them as an active threat – whereas in *Mission to the Unknown*, Gordon Lowery only knows that the Daleks invaded Earth "a thousand years ago", and needs their renewed interest in Earth space spelled out for him. The Daleks have been deadlocked for "centuries" with the Movellans before *Destiny of the Daleks* (tellingly, Peel has to reduce this to "decades" in his timeline). The prominence of the Earth Empire in the centuries before 3000 seems incompatible with the idea the Daleks are a major galactic power. All in all, it seems likely that *Destiny of the Daleks* is set at least "centuries" after 4000. As we know the *Dalek Empire* series is set in the first half of the millennium, the case for *The Programme Guide*'s 4600 AD date, while not indisputable, is certainly persuasive.

For more, see The "Own Time" of the Daleks sidebar.

Davros developed mind-exchange technology, and test-ed it on the colonists of the planet Teldaran. Only Davros and the Supreme Dalek were present as the colony leader begged for mercy, and suggested his captors experiment upon his daughter Tamorra instead. Afterward, Davros and a group of Daleks left for nineteenth-century Earth, to field test the mind-exchanger in battlefield conditions at Waterloo.[1677]

The Daleks reoccupied Skaro, and a new Supreme Dalek came to power. The Daleks developed biomecha-noid computers that interfaced with human brains to provide the Daleks with raw creativity, and they began to reassert their power.[1678]

Davros Apprehended, Taken to Skaro

? 4615 - REVELATION OF THE DALEKS[1679] -> A human President now ruled the galaxy, which was becoming overpopulated. Famine was a problem on worlds across known space. Tranquil Repose on Necros had been established for some time as a resting place for the dead of the galaxy – literally, as they were kept in suspended animation there until whatever killed them was cured by medical science. The "rock and roll years" of twentieth century Earth were extremely popular. The grandfather of a DJ on Necros purchased some genuine records from Earth on a visit there.

Davros went into hiding on Necros and formed an alliance with Kara, a local businesswoman. He took control of Tranquil Repose, and secretly began to break down the corpses there into a foodstuff. This ended famine across the galaxy, and Davros gained a reputation as "the Great Healer". Kara discovered that Davros was also growing a new army of genetically re-engineered Daleks from the corpses, and planned to use them to take effective control of her company. She hired Orcini, an excommunicated member of the Grand Order of Oberon, to assassinate Davros.

Davros had been keeping track of the Doctor's move-ments – when one of the Doctor's friends, the agrono-mist Arthur Stengos, died, Davros prepared for the Doctor to attend the funeral. Orcini, the sixth Doctor and Peri thwarted Davros' plans, although Orcini died in the process. The Daleks were summoned from Skaro and captured their creator. The Doctor suggested that protein from a commonplace purple flower could alle-viate the famine.

? 4615 - THE DAVROS MISSION[1680] -> The Daleks took Davros to Skaro and put him on trial for plotting against them and creating "impure" Daleks. En route, a Thal named Lareen snuck into Davros' cell and – thinking she had convinced Davros to redeem himself by destroying his creations – provided him with a vial of super-concen-trated Movellan virus. Had Davros released this, it would have killed all Daleks on Skaro and broken their empire. Instead, Davros convinced the Daleks that his refraining from destroying them demonstrated that they owed him their allegiance. The Daleks concurred, pledged to make

---

Daleks, but the Big Finish website places it between *The Two Doctors* and *Timelash.* TAI was formed "back in the thirty-eighth century".

1677 *The Curse of Davros.* In Davros' timeline, this takes place during his dealings with the sixth Doctor (so, after *Resurrection of the Daleks*), but before the Daleks capture him and take him back to Skaro for trial (*Revelation of the Daleks*).

1678 Skaro has been abandoned for "centuries" before *Destiny of the Daleks,* but the Supreme Dalek is based there in *Revelation of the Daleks.* We see a biomecha-noid in *Remembrance of the Daleks* – presumably the Daleks haven't developed the technology when they lose the war with the Movellans. Although, according to *War of the Daleks,* the Movellan War was a ruse.

1679 Dating *Revelation of the Daleks* (22.6) - This story is set an unspecified amount of time after *Resurrection of the Daleks.* It has been long enough for Davros to gain a galaxy-wide reputation and build a new army of Daleks. The galaxy is ruled by a human President and faces famine.

1680 Dating *The Davros Mission* (exclusive audio story included with *The Complete Davros Collection* DVD set) - The story is set directly after *Revelation of the Daleks*

(the ship that takes Davros to Skaro departs from Necros), and on the surface might seem to conflict with "Emperor of the Daleks" as yet-another "bridge" story between *Revelation of the Daleks* and *Remembrance of the Daleks.* In detail, however, the two stories are com-patible – in *The Davros Mission,* the only leverage Davros gains over the Daleks on Skaro is a) what passes for his charm, and b) the concentrated Movellan virus he's holding. A Dalek civil war is slated to occur after this point (in *Remembrance*), so whatever fealty the Skaro Daleks might here pledge to Davros is certain to fall to ruin under any scenario. It makes sense to assume that the Skaro Daleks only declare obedience to Davros in *The Davros Mission* to buy themselves the time required to neutralise the Movellan virus in his possession. Once that occurs, Davros would probably have little choice but to flee, leading to *The Juggernauts* and his eventually being captured and put on trial a second time (in "Emperor of the Daleks").

Davros is here slated to become the Dalek Emperor, but that doesn't actually happen – so it's fair to think that it only happens down the road, once Abslom Daak takes a chainsaw to him in the comic story. He also gains a robotic hand (to replace the one shot off in

Davros their Emperor and exterminated Lareen...

? 4620 - THE JUGGERNAUTS[1681] **->** Davros crashed on the planet Lethe, where mining engineers excavated a group of Mechanoids. Davros attempted to build an army of Mechanoids (re-named "the Juggernauts") that incorporated human tissue, but the grey Daleks tracked him down. The sixth Doctor and Mel sabotaged the Juggernaut production lines, and Davros' body was severely injured in the fighting. His life-support chair self-destructed, which obliterated the colony, the grey Daleks and the Juggernauts, although the colonists themselves evacuated.

Earth had passed mandatory organ donation laws.

The sixth Doctor and Peri encountered the Daleks on Mandusus.[1682]

Davros Becomes the Dalek Emperor; a New Dalek Civil War Begins

? 4625 - "...Up Above the Gods" / "Emperor of the Daleks"[1683] **->** The Daleks put Davros on trial – he had replaced his destroyed hand with a claw, and started to persuade some Daleks that they could learn from him. Nonetheless, the Emperor sentenced him to execution. Before the sentence was carried out, a giant asteroid entered the Skaro System.

The sixth Doctor and Peri arrived on Skaro. While the Daleks were occupied with the asteroid (which the Doctor had sent their way), the Doctor infected the Dalek computers with a virus, then kidnapped Davros in the TARDIS. The Daleks vowed revenge.

A year later, the Daleks tricked Abslom Daak into bringing the seventh Doctor to Skaro (along with the other Star Tigers and Benny, from the mid-twenty-sixth century), Daak fought a pitched battle with the Daleks, but he and his allies were subdued. The Daleks demanded that the

Doctor take them to Davros, and used a Psyche Dalek to place the others in a hypnotic trance.

A Dalek battle fleet under the command of the Black Dalek was dispatched to Spiridon, where they were met by Davros and an army of four million white-and-gold upgraded Daleks. The Psyche Dalek was destroyed, and the Doctor's friends were released from hypnotic control. Routed, the Black Dalek withdrew his forces and ordered the orbiting fleet to destroy Davros – but the energy was reflected back and destroyed all but one ship, which was also blown up.

Davros had won the battle, and had *not* – as he had promised the Doctor – given his upgraded Daleks a conscience. Davros' fleet set course for Skaro, planning to reactivate the Doctor's computer virus and seize control. Davros' forces landed, and he watched as the former Emperor was exterminated. However, Daak sliced through Davros with his chainsword before being forced to withdraw by the other Star Tigers. A nuclear blast devastated the Dalek city, and finally destroyed Taiyin's body.

Davros had a new survival chair built only four days after his arrival, but a bitter civil war was underway between the Dalek factions. **Davros was now Emperor of the Daleks.**[1684] The Thals had relocated from Skaro by this point, and the Daleks did not normally enter their region of space, which included Spiridon.

Abel Gantz revived the lost science of alchemy when he discovered paracelsium, a metal-transmutating catalyst.[1685]

c 4635 - "Kane's Story" / "Abel's Story" / "Warrior's Story" / "Frobisher's Story"[1686] **->** Skeletoids invaded outposts on Vega and Sigma IV, meaning they were only weeks from the Sol System. The Skeletoids were armoured humans from the Vespin System, but their armour had gradually become so sophisticated, the humans inside had become redundant components. They swept through five

Revelation of the Daleks), but might upgrade to the claw he uses in "Emperor of the Daleks".

1681 Dating *The Juggernauts* (BF #65) - This story is set an unspecified amount of time after *Revelation of the Daleks*. It's said that Davros crash-landed seven hundred sixteen days prior to this story, but there's no indication of the duration of time in a day on Lethe.

1682 "Emperor of the Daleks"

1683 Dating "... Up Above the Gods"/"Emperor of the Daleks" (*DWM* #227, 197-202; sic) - The story is set between *Revelation of the Daleks* and *Remembrance of the Daleks*, and bridges the gap between them (even if this means that the seventh Doctor is experiencing developments with Davros out of order). The Emperor resembles the one from the *TV Century 21* Dalek comic strip. This raises a question as to which Dalek Emperor this is – and not because that Emperor Dalek was

apparently killed by Daak back in "Nemesis of the Daleks". We didn't *see* the Emperor killed on that occasion – we just didn't see him escape the exploding Death Wheel. Given that "Emperor of the Daleks" establishes that Daak and all the Star Tigers – who were seen to perish in "Nemesis of the Daleks" – didn't actually die, the Emperor Dalek barely makes the top five "least probable resurrections" in the story. See The Dalek Emperors sidebar.

1684 Per his appearance as such in *Remembrance of the Daleks*.

1685 "Ten years" before "Abel's Story".

1686 Dating "Kane's Story"/"Abel's Story"/"Warrior's Story"/"Frobisher's Story" (*DWM* #104-107) - Davros rules the Daleks, and the only time this is the case on television is between *Revelation of the Daleks* and *Remembrance of the Daleks*. (Taking other media into

systems in a year – either converting any humanoids they conquered, or wiping out races they couldn't convert (such as the Daleks and Cybermen). The Skeletoids were now at the gates of the Planetary Federation. The Draconians were their next targets, and the powers of the galaxy arranged a summit on Ankara III.

The sixth Doctor, Frobisher and Peri learned of the threat and headed for Xaos, the oldest planet in the galaxy – as did Abel Gantz, the Draconian Emperor's bodyguard Kaon (who the Doctor and Frobisher had met some years from now), and Kane Borg of Kaltarr. They were the champions of six worlds, and they travelled in the TARDIS to the Vespin System to take the fight to the Skeletoids. Abel sacrificed himself, destroying the Skeletoid command centre. The menace to the galaxy ended, and the Doctor and the surviving champions arrived at the galactic summit to tell the delegates they'd had a wasted trip.

c 4650 - THE STORY OF MARTHA: "The Weeping"[1687] -> Agelaos had become an icy planet following the failure of its terraforming. The last of the colonists, Waechter, had guarded the quarantine there and lived for centuries thanks to a slowed metabolism. Waechter found that he would die if ever he left Agelaos, and the tenth Doctor and Martha helped him to attain his last wish: that he be mutated into a creature like his fellow colonists, so he would never be alone.

? 4655 - THE ELEVENTH DOCTOR YEAR TWO[1688] -> The eleventh Doctor, Alice, the Squire and Abslom Daak paused in their travels to have a drink on Clundanius XI, a wretched hive of black marketeers. Daak had previously gotten hammered there and eviscerated twenty Vervoids who looked at him funny.

Skaro Seemingly Destroyed

? 4663 - REMEMBRANCE OF THE DALEKS[1689] -> Upon returning to Skaro, Davros usurped control from the Supreme Dalek and declared himself an Emperor Dalek. With his body now wasted, Davros was reduced to little more than a disembodied head. He fashioned a new casing for himself. Most Daleks supported Davros, who genetically re-engineered the race and oversaw a complete revamp of Dalek technology. These "Imperial Daleks" were given new cream and gold livery, improved weapons, sensor plates and eyestalks. As always, some Daleks dissented: this "Renegade Dalek" faction followed the Black Dalek and fled Skaro using a Time Controller.

Both factions had learned of the Hand of Omega, a powerful Gallifreyan device that could manipulate stars. They converged to its location on Earth in 1963. Davros acquired the Hand, but was unable to control the device. On the seventh Doctor's instructions, the

---

account, this is between "Emperor of the Daleks" and *Remembrance of the Daleks*.) This also fits with where the story falls in the Doctor's timeline. "War-Game" is set a few years after this, and states the Draconians rule a third of the galaxy. The Planetary Federation is also known as the Federation of Worlds, and could well be the same – or remnants of the same – Federation from the Peladon stories (although the Draconians were part of that Federation according to *Legacy*).

1687 Dating *The Story of Martha*: "The Weeping" (NSA #28b) - Agaloas is established as part of the Second Great and Bountiful Human Empire (p49), and the story occurs "almost five centuries" (p56) after the colony's failure.

1688 Dating *The Eleventh Doctor Year Two* (Titan 11th Doc #2.8, "Downtime") - It's tempting to say this is Daak's native era, since Bonapart Devizes, a dealer in Dalek artefacts, has been picking up the carnage he's left behind. But, the Vervoids were only created, then utterly destroyed (hence the Doctor being put on trial for genocide) in *Terror of the Vervoids* [2986]. If Daak slaughtered some in a drunken rage, it can only be after someone – off screen – has recultivated their race.

ABSLOM DAAK 2.0: When Abslom Daak shows up in the TARDIS in *The Eleventh Doctor Year Two* comics (released 2015-2016), it's meant to reintroduce the character after a long hiatus (setting aside cameos such

as *Time Heist*), without a great deal of thought as to how it joins up to his last ongoing appearance in "Emperor of the Daleks" (published 1993). Seen here, Daak has the corpse of his lover Taiyin in tow – her body was seemingly blown up in "Emperor of the Daleks", but it's possible that her cryofreeze tube remained intact. Daak now claims that he and Taiyin are married – in his mind only, presumably, since they knew each other only about a day before she died in "Abslom Daak... Dalek Killer". (As you've probably gathered, Daak is not an altogether well person.)

The bigger question is whether Daak returned to his home era [c.2550] following "Emperor of the Daleks", or if he stayed in the year it concluded [?4625]. There's reason to suspect the latter, in that the watering hole he frequents in "Downtime" (*Year Two* #7) can't be set in his native time, as he got wasted and killed some Vervoids there (so it's after *Terror of the Vervoids* in 2986). Or, he might have just gone there after obtaining his vortex manipulator.

One strange detail from a fever dream Daak experiences after being shot in "Physician, Heal Thyself" (*Year Two* #15): Taiyin claims that Daak has spent "decades" idolising her memory, and yet he looks the same as his very first appearance. Either he has an extended lifespan (as all humans by his time?), or he's yet-another Daak clone (*Deceit*). If so, he's living up to the Dalek-

Hand travelled to Skaro in Davros' native time and made its sun go supernova, obliterating the planet. Davros escaped, but his flagship was obliterated and the Dalek homeworld was seemingly destroyed.

> (=) In 4688, Chiyoko, the "child of time", transported a Vorlax Regeneration Drone from the war planet Grakktar back to 2011.[1690]

& 4693 - WAR OF THE DALEKS[1691] -> The Daleks had invaded Earth "several times" by this point.

The garbage ship *Quetzel* recovered both the eighth Doctor's TARDIS and Davros' escape pod. Thals raided the ship, and Delani, the Thal commander, asked Davros to reengineer his race to defeat the Daleks. Davros' reactivation alerted the Daleks, and the Doctor, Sam and Davros were taken to Skaro... which the Doctor had thought destroyed. The Dalek Prime explained that the Daleks had learned of Skaro's destruction beforehand and plotted to prevent it.

The Daleks had previously taken the dormant Davros from Skaro, and placed him in ruins on Antalin, which were designed to look like Skaro. The planet was then bathed in radioactivity. The Daleks then faked the Movellan War using their own robot servants, fooling Davros into

believing they needed his help, but Davros escaped and triggered a civil war. He took the Hand of Omega, which destroyed *Antalin* rather than Skaro. The Daleks' real homeworld survived.

Now, the Dalek Prime planned to draw the Daleks who supported Davros out into the open and destroy them. The Doctor made a seemingly easy escape in the Thal ship – then discovered a Dalek factory in the hold. He jettisoned it back in time, where it crashed on Vulcan.

Daleks loyal to Davros attempted to rescue him, but the Dalek Prime's forces prevailed. Davros was placed in a dispersion chamber and seemingly vaporized, but the Dalek implementing Davros' execution was one of his followers, and it was possible that Davros survived...

The Dalek Prime was later lost to the Time Vortex, owing to the intervention of four incarnations of the Doctor in the Daleks' war with the Jariden, a race of bio-mechanoids.[1692]

Samson and Gemma Griffin

The eighth Doctor ventured into a library and came to accept a worker there, Samson Griffin, and his sister Gemma aboard the TARDIS. They shared many adven-

---

killing obsession of the original.

1689 Dating *Remembrance of the Daleks* (25.1) - This story is the sequel to *Revelation of the Daleks,* and there's no indication how long it has been since the previous story. Davros has completely revamped the Daleks, which was presumably a fairly lengthy process.

Dalek: The Astounding Untold History of the Greatest Enemies of the Universe (p67) raises the possibility that even with its sun going supernova, a portion of Skaro survived – albeit "more blighted than after the war" – which explains its later appearances or eventual destruction in the Last Great Time War.

1690 "The Child of Time" (*DWM*)

1691 Dating *War of the Daleks* (EDA #5) - It's "about thirty years" after *Remembrance of the Daleks*. One of Davros' followers operates the controls of his dispersal chamber, suggesting that Davros was later reconstituted in secret – and later recaptured, leading to his next appearance in *Terror Firma*.

WAS SKARO DESTROYED?: The retcon in *War of the Daleks* that reversed Skaro's destruction proved controversial with fans. A couple of references in later BBC Books suggested that Skaro had been destroyed, after all. *Unnatural History* stated that the Doctor tricked the Daleks into tangling their timelines so much their history collapsed; *The Infinity Doctors* that Skaro suffered more than one destruction. *Doctor Who – The Movie* (after *Remembrance of the Daleks* in the Doctor's own timeline) opened on Skaro, but it could have histori-

cally been before it was destroyed. The 2005 TV series never stated that Skaro had been destroyed in the Time War (Russell T Davies' essay in the *Doctor Who Annual 2006* does name it and says it's now "ruins", though). The *Doctor Who Visual Dictionary* states that Skaro was "devastated" in *Remembrance of the Daleks*, but "finally obliterated" in the Time War.

There are a number of get-out clauses in *War of the Daleks* itself – the events aren't seen, only reported. Internal dating seems confused, and Antalin appears after it's meant to have been destroyed. There are pieces of contradictory information elsewhere – the origins of the Movellans in the book contradict their implied beginnings in *A Device of Death*, for example.

Dalek: The Astounding Untold History of the Greatest Enemies of the Universe discounts the Daleks building the Movellans as "propaganda", and paints the notion of Antalin perishing instead of Skaro (p70) as, very likely, the stuff of rumour: "The truth, however, is now lost in a complex web of causality and half-truths, with Skaro's timeline having been so decisively rewritten during the Last Great Time war, that it is effectively impossible to determine the truth behind these legends."

The Magician's Apprentice/The Witch's Familiar features a restored Skaro, but it's not specified if this is the actual Dalek homeworld reborn, or merely a made-to-order copy of it.

1692 *The Four Doctors.* The Dalek Prime seen in this audio isn't necessarily the exact same one seen in *War*

tures, until Davros – who desired to strip the Doctor of everything he held dear – and erased his memories of his two companions. Davros mentally conditioned Samson and Gemma to accompany him, then began a scheme to turn Earth into a new Dalek homeworld. Samson lived with his mother, Harriet Griffen, in Folkestone.[1693]

& 4703 - TERROR FIRMA[1694] **->** On Earth, Davros and his Daleks encountered the eighth Doctor, Charley and C'rizz upon their return from the Divergent Universe. Davros believed that his Daleks had turned Earth into a "new Dalek homeworld" and converted eight billion humans into Daleks; however, the Daleks were operating to their own agenda while mutating Davros into an Emperor Dalek. Davros hoped the Doctor would end his suffering and gave him a genocidal virus, but the Doctor instead used the threat of the virus to make the Daleks abandon Earth. The Emperor Dalek persona completely erased Davros', and the Daleks left with their new leader.

C'rizz "saved" Gemma, who had become the Daleks'

thrall, by killing her. Her brother Samson regained his memories of the Doctor, but continued living on Earth.

The New Dalek Era

The New Paradigm Daleks escaped to their "own time" following their involvement with the Ironside gambit in 1940. Some of their number participated in the allegiance of alien races that imprisoned the eleventh Doctor within the Pandorica.[1695]

? 4711 - THE WEDDING OF RIVER SONG -> The eleventh Doctor found a gravely injured Dalek, and rooted around in its databanks for information. He then tracked down the *Teselecta*, and asked its captain for assistance against the Silence.

? 4712 - ASYLUM OF THE DALEKS[1696] **->** Darla von Karlsen was converted into a Dalek Puppet, and sent a message to the eleventh Doctor asking him to help

---

of the Daleks, but the title isn't used in any other *Doctor Who* story. Allowing for all of the time travel involved, though, there's no guarantee that the Jariden sequences in *The Four Doctors* takes place in this era.

1693 Years rather than decades before *Terror Firma*. The presence of Samson and Gemma's mother suggests that this is their native time zone.

1694 Dating *Terror Firma* (BF #72) - No specific date is given, but it is obviously after *Remembrance of the Daleks*, and a gap of some measure (Davros mentions "years of solitude") is required after the novel *War of the Daleks*. *Terror Firma* doesn't acknowledge *War of the Daleks*, but the two are not irreconcilable. Davros' mental health is clearly eroding throughout this audio, so it's entirely possible that the Daleks have altered his memories or that he's simply too far gone to remember those events. In fact, as the Daleks are obviously fooling Davros into thinking that he's in charge, it suits their plans if he forgets about Skaro and believes he's gaining revenge against the Doctor by "turning Earth" into a new Dalek homeworld.

Big Finish says that Davros *does not* become the Emperor Dalek seen in *The Parting of the Ways*. Gemma's death happens off-screen, but she's among the voices in C'rizz's head of his victims.

WHO RULES THE DALEKS?: There's a fair amount of evidence the Emperor is not the ultimate, unchallengeable authority of the Daleks. In "Secret of the Emperor" (a comic from *The Dalek Outer Space Book*), it's stated that senior Daleks convene periodically to elect their Emperor... or rather to *re*-elect him, as it's always a unanimous vote and the only ever dissenter, seen in that story, is instantly exterminated for daring to question the Emperor's authority.

In *The Dalek Chronicles* strip, the Emperor follows the

advice of the Dalek Brain Machine, a central computer, and *Destiny of the Daleks* and *Remembrance of the Daleks* also show a computer dictating strategy.

War of the Daleks and *Terror Firma* have Daleks actively manipulating events and misleading Emperor Davros for their own ends. While Davros thinks he's asserting his own dominance, both stories suggest that the Dalek leadership have planned the events we see to unite the Daleks and harness his genius, while keeping all manner of key information from him. *The Stolen Earth/Journey's End* has Davros in a similar role, clearly more controlled by the Daleks than controlling. In *The Magician's Apprentice/The Witch's Familiar*, it's a toss-up as to who exactly is in charge – the Dalek High Command seemingly keeps Davros under house arrest while quietly endorsing his latest gambit against the Doctor (perhaps because they've something to gain from it).

Doomsday introduces the Cult of Skaro, four Daleks "above even the Emperor" (although still acknowledging his authority and concerned about his fate).

The Doctor claims in *The Evil of the Daleks* that the Daleks blindly obey their leaders, and this unity is their defining characteristic... to such a degree that in *Remembrance of the Daleks* and *Dalek* (and its "predecessor", the audio *Jubilee*), lone Daleks commit suicide because they've lost their entire purpose. We've seen Daleks ruthlessly eradicate individuals who dare to express even modest dissent on a number of occasions. However, the Daleks have a moral code that allows them to question orders if they seem un-Dalek-like and no compunction about replacing their leaders if they fail. It's perhaps no coincidence that this happens most visibly with two leaders who aren't pure Daleks: Davros and Sec (in *Evolution of the Daleks*).

THE "OWN TIME" OF THE DALEKS/THE NEW DALEK ERA: There seems to be some unknown mechanism – it's unclear whether this is a function of the TARDIS or a law of temporal physics – that ensures that when the Doctor meets time travellers, they meet in the same order for both of them. So, the Doctor's last adventure fighting the Master is the Master's last adventure fighting the Doctor. They are "on the same page", or "in sequence", meaning that – for instance – when the sixth Doctor and the Master meet in *The Mark of the Rani* [c.1813], from their personal points of view, it's after the fifth Doctor and the same Master last saw one another in *Planet of Fire* [c.1984].

There's technically an exception in Series 3, where the John Simm Master has been lurking in the background as Harold Saxon for about eighteen months prior to the tenth Doctor, Martha and Captain Jack departing for Malcrassairo to inadvertently free him in the first place (*Utopia*), but the Doctor and Master don't meet at that time. There are clearly times when the Doctor is on Earth the same time as the "wrong" Master – during the "Earth arc" in the eighth Doctor books when he spent the entire twentieth century marooned on Earth, he could potentially have met the Delgado Master in the 1970s or the Ainley one in the 1980s.

Otherwise, the most notable exception to what we might call the In-Sequence Rule involves River Song (see the Dating River Song is a Complicated Business sidebar), but even there it's (broadly) "in sequence", just a sequence that's flipped around so the first time the Doctor met River (that he's aware of) is the last time she met him.

The In-Sequence Rule is extremely handy, as it means characters don't refer to stories that we've not seen yet. It also offers something of an "in story" solution to why characters in a 1966 episode set in 1986 don't seem to know about what happened in a story made and set in 1985 (problems of this sort dog the continuity of Cybermen stories).

Noticeably, however, the Daleks are also time travellers, and – like the Time Lords – generally seem to meet the Doctor "in sequence". This is most explicit in *Destiny of the Daleks*, *Resurrection of the Daleks*, *Revelation of the Daleks* and *Remembrance of the Daleks*, which form a story arc fandom has named the Davros Era. How far back this "meta narrative" stretches is unclear. The Daleks in *The Chase* are explicitly seeking revenge for *The Dalek Invasion of Earth*, have only just invented time travel and know of the first Doctor, Ian, Barbara and Susan, but not Vicki (or, by implication, any of the Doctor's later companions). It's very possible that the first Doctor's Dalek stories (on television: *The Daleks*, *The Dalek Invasion of Earth*, *The Chase*, *The Daleks' Master Plan*) happen in the same order for both the Doctor and the Daleks, and they do in this chronology.

In *The Power of the Daleks*, the Daleks recognise the second Doctor on the very day he's regenerated. Do they simply know the second Doctor's face owing to encounters that have yet to happen in his personal future, or does he have some "Doctorish" aura they are able to recognise? It would seem to be the former, as they don't always recognise the Doctor on sight (see, for example, *Day of the Daleks* and *Doomsday*). *The Power of the Daleks* is dated in *Ahistory* to 2020, although *War of the Daleks* says the Daleks from that story are time travellers from after *Remembrance of the Daleks*... either way, it would seem to be "out of sequence".

Other than that, a cut line from *Day of the Daleks* indicates the Daleks have recovered from their last defeat, in the previous televised Dalek story, *The Evil of the Daleks*. That suggests every story from *The Daleks* to *Day of the Daleks* is part of the same "sequence".

The next story causes problems: the third Doctor adventure *Planet of the Daleks* takes place in 2540, but *The Daleks' Master Plan* is set in 4000. Both seem to feature Daleks native to those timezones (rather than Daleks who have time travelled). The simplest way to think about this is to ask what the Doctor and the Daleks should each be able to remember. No one mentions *The Daleks' Master Plan* in *Planet of the Daleks*, but we can assume the third Doctor "remembers" what happened to his earlier self in the very first Dalek story, *The Daleks*. A trickier question is whether the Daleks in *Planet of the Daleks* "remember" *The Daleks' Master Plan*. All things being equal, they don't – someone from 2540 would not, after all, know about something that will happen in 4000.

From there, there's nothing stopping the next story, *Death to the Daleks*, from being "after" *Planet of the Daleks*. The story after that is *Genesis of the Daleks* where the Time Lords blatantly send the Doctor back into the early days of the Daleks' history – the only Classic *Who* stories after that are those of the Davros Era. It may be worth noting that the Time Lords also direct the TARDIS to Spiridon in *Planet of the Daleks* – this is ostensibly because he's too injured to fly the Ship, but perhaps he also needs them to allow him to "break sequence" as he does in *Genesis*.

Or, to put it another way, there are only a couple of bumps in the road stopping us from saying that all the Dalek stories from the 1963-89 run of *Doctor Who* happen "in sequence".

Either explicitly or by heavy implication, the ninth and tenth Doctor Dalek stories all take place "in sequence". A small number of Daleks survive the Time War, but Rose-as-Dark Phoenix destroys them (*The Parting of the Ways*). And yet, the next Dalek story (*Army of Ghosts/Doomsday*) introduces a few Daleks – members of the Cult of Skaro – who have *still* survived and return, in sequence, in *Daleks in Manhattan/Evolution of the Daleks* and *The Stolen Earth/Journey's End*. (Davros appears in the last story, then isn't seen until *The Magician's Apprentice*.) All things considered, the

continued on page 3291...

rescue her daughter Hannah. The Doctor met with Karlsen on Skaro, and in so doing fell into a Dalek trap. He was taken away to the Parliament of Daleks overseeing the Dalek Asylum...

The Daleks had built the Dalek Asylum as a planet-sized prison to contain their rogue elements: the battle-scarred, the mad, the uncontrollable. The Asylum was fully automated, and walled off within a planetary force field. No formal count was made, but it was likely home to millions of tormented and sickly Daleks. A nano-cloud within the Asylum's atmosphere turned any organic matter that ventured there into Dalek Puppets or actual Daleks. Daleks from conflicts with the Doctor on Spiridon, Kembel, Aridius, Vulcan and Exxilon were kept on the Asylum in intensive care.

The starship *Alaska* crashed onto the Asylum. Oswin Oswald – an iteration of Clara Oswald, currently a junior entertainment manager – survived, but the nano-cloud transformed her into a Dalek. Such was Oswin's force of will that "she" spent a year thinking "she" was merely shipwrecked, her mind failing to comprehend her body's new state of being.

The Parliament of Daleks became concerned that if the *Alaska* could get into the Asylum, the legions of insane Daleks there could potentially escape and wreck havoc that even the Parliament couldn't control. The Parliament forcibly recruited "the Predator of the Daleks" – the Doctor – and his companions Amy and Rory to deactivate the Asylum's force field from within. The Oswald-Dalek realised its true nature and aided the Doctor's group in deactivating the force field, then died as the Dalek warfleet destroyed the Asylum from orbit. Oswald had also altered the Daleks' telepathic network, their PathWeb, so they forgot everything they knew about the Doctor.

> (=) The Great Intelligence murdered the eleventh Doctor on the Dalek Asylum.

Oswin Oswald, as one of Clara Oswald's doubles, overwrote the Intelligence in this time period.[1697]

Kaon's ship later crashed on Actinon after hitting a meteor field. The inhabitants were warlike, but no match for Kaon, who established himself as a warlord. His wife died in childbirth, but his daughter Kara grew to be a strong warrior.[1698] **The Weeping Angels wiped out the Aplans, the two-headed life form indigenous to Alfava Metraxis. Lacking a food source, the Angels went dormant in an Aplan moratarium.**[1699]

The metamorphic Collectors were galactic scavengers who entirely lacked the ability to discern the value or relevance of an item – essentially, they amassed junk. The Collectors' hyperwobble-drives and psychonomic shielding meant that no culture's defences could stand against them. The Daleks pretended that their planet had been destroyed to avoid being attacked by the Collectors.[1700]

The Klektid archaeologist Hogoosta investigated the Cradle of the Gods: an ancient monument on the planet Gethria. The Daleks knew the Cradle could reshape the matter of entire planets, but failed to crack its activation code, and secretly backed Hogoosta's work to discover it.

With humanity's fear of the Daleks having faded, the Daleks established the Dalek Foundation to administrate the Sunlight Worlds: four hundred planets that gave food,

---

Cunningly, the Daleks have their cake and eat it: they are led by strong, imaginative, ambitious individuals who can think in ways the Daleks themselves can not... but they have a very strong (overriding, in fact) sense of what it is to be a Dalek. So if their leaders stray too far away from the Dalek ideal, the Daleks can quickly reach a consensus to exterminate him, without fear of disrupting the Dalek order based on blind obedience to their leaders, by simply deciding that their leader doesn't count as a Dalek.

Ultimately, then, the true leader of the Daleks is not an individual, it's the belief in their own supremacy and their hatred for anything that isn't a Dalek.

1695 *Victory of the Daleks*, *The Pandorica Opens*.

1696 Dating *Asylum of the Daleks* (X7.1) - No year given. The Parliament of Daleks has time travel at its disposal (it's how Amy and Rory are kidnapped from the twenty-first century), but it's not stated if the insane Daleks were taken to the Asylum via that method or conventional means. The latter method would suggest that *Asylum of the Daleks* can't take place any earlier than 4000, as the Daleks in intensive care hail from a

laundry list of planets that appeared in classic *Doctor Who* stories: Spiridon (*Planet of the Daleks*, set in 2540), Kembel (*The Daleks' Master Plan*, 4000), Aridius (*The Chase*, dated in this chronology to ? 3565, but unlikely to occur any later), Vulcan (*The Power of the Daleks*, 2020) and Exxilon (*Death to the Daleks*, circa 2600). The teaser features the eleventh Doctor on Skaro before its destruction (either in *Remembrance of the Daleks*, or its resurrected form prior to the Last Great Time War).

Ultimately, placement of this story was derived from the characteristics of the New Dalek Era (see the sidebar of that name).

Dalek: The Astounding Untold History of the Greatest Enemies of the Universe (p294) says that the Dalek Parliament comes about as a response to the New Paradigm's "repeated failures" – probably a jab at how quickly the New Paradigm fell from grace as the flagship Daleks.

1697 *The Name of the Doctor*, *Asylum of the Daleks*.

1698 "Many years" before "War-Game".

1699 "Four centuries" before *The Time of Angels*.

1700 *Heart of TARDIS*

...continued from page 3289

In-Sequence Rule seems to very much apply.

There's a big question about whether this is true of the eleventh and twelfth Doctor Dalek stories, however. Are the stories in sequence – or have the Daleks simply rebounded after their near-extinction in the Last Great Time War, and are now just an established presence in different parts of the universe? *Victory of the Daleks* sees the very last "original" Daleks create a new Dalek paradigm, seen in many Dalek stories to follow (*The Pandorica Opens/The Big Bang*, *The Wedding of River Song*, *Asylum of the Daleks*, *The Time of the Doctor* and *Into the Dalek*). Later, and in a deviation from *Victory* (in which the New Paradigm Daleks exterminate some of their predecessors as being less racially "pure"), the New Paradigm Daleks work in concert with other Daleks to reestablish a Dalek Empire. They once again they have massive armies and battlefleets, and control great areas of space.

Asylum of the Daleks and *The Magician's Apprentice/The Witch's Familiar* somewhat confuse matters, in that they entail two entirely separate groups of Dalek leaders – the former involving the Parliament of Daleks, the latter led a Dalek Supreme who shows fealty to Davros – that otherwise seem to have nothing to do with one another. Both groups have time travel, and demonstrate an immense reach – they can send Daleks, Dalek agents and whole Dalek saucers to many points in space and time. We have to assume there are *some* limits to this capability, because it's hard to see how even the Doctor could have prevented them from overrunning the universe in all timezones. The limitation might be technological (the amount of fuel they have, or a practical range for their vessels), or more theoretical – either some Time Lord-like concept of duty to preserve the timeline, or perhaps a more Dalek-y version of that. They're doing rather well, and if they meddle in history they might accidentally undo their own strong position.

Asylum of the Daleks also has survivors from Spiridon, Kembel, Aridus, Vulcan and Exxilon... all Dalek survivors from before the Time War, something that we were told was impossible. It's unclear what has happened (was the Asylum planet always there, but knowledge of it lost until it was rediscovered?).

Moreover, the Daleks in *Asylum* capture the eleventh Doctor on Skaro, in what seems to be the planet's past (he wearily says: "Skaro. The original planet of the Daleks. Look at the state of it."), then whisk him away to wherever and whenever the rest of the story takes place. By comparison, in *The Magician's Apprentice/The Witch's Familiar*, the twelfth Doctor and Missy are *horrified* that Davros' Daleks have "built [Skaro] again"/have "brought it back", either suggesting that the original – or another world designed to mimic it – that has been restored in their "present", i.e. in sequence.

One line establishes something very important. A new Dalek in *Victory of the Daleks* says: "Extinction is not an option. We shall return to our own time and begin again." That story is set during the Second World War, but the original Daleks have travelled back in time to trap the Doctor. We know they're from the future, because the Doctor says so. ("What, and let you scuttle off back to the future?") The new Daleks, then, would seem to have a native timezone, a specific point in future history that they are "from". Let's call this the New Dalek Era.

The question then becomes: if the Daleks head back to the New Dalek Era at the end of *Victory of the Daleks*, are all the Daleks we see after that (*The Pandorica Opens* et al) based in this specific timezone? Do they encounter the Doctor in sequence? And – especially germane to the placement of *The Magician's Apprentice/The Witch's Familiar* (and laterally *Asylum of the Daleks*, presuming for the moment that it occurs in the same timezone that the Parliament of Daleks is based) – when *is* the New Dalek Era?

No easy answer exists to this, especially as the aforementioned three episodes have no on-screen dating.

There is one piece of dating evidence. The setting of *Into the Dalek* would seem to be the native time of the Daleks, and the script states that the ship we see is a product of the "31st Century". It's not a line used on screen, and perhaps we could cough discreetly and suggest that the ship's *really* old. The Daleks remain capable of projecting military force across a wide range of space and time, so it's possible they've mounted an invasion of the thirty-first century. For simplicity's sake, here we're going to assume it's just set in the New Dalek Era.

The best option would seem to be that the New Dalek Era simply continues on from the Davros Era, the final installment of which – prior to the new series – is the audio *Terror Firma* [&4703].

There's an extraordinary coincidence to account for – in *The Time of the Doctor*, the Time Lords are attempting to return to the universe in the exact same time zone where the post-Time War Daleks are resurgent, which seems like either poor planning on the Time Lords' part, or excellent planning by the Daleks. Then again, if we include the thousand or so years of *The Time of the Doctor* in this timeline, that produces a very large period of Dalek history in which the Parliament can be overthrown, a new Supreme Dalek installed and Skaro restored to its previous glory. The Doctor's time on Trenzalore, rather happily for us, falls a few centuries after the Davros Era, and we can build the eleventh and twelfth Doctor Dalek stories on either side of it.

Arbitrarily, then, we assign the eleventh Doctor's stories to the forty-eighth century, on the "anniversary" of their broadcast – so a story from 2010 is set in 4710 – and the twelfth Doctor Dalek stories to the sixty-first century. Then follows the substantial duration of *Time of the Doctor* (dated here from 5100-6000), with the twelfth Doctor Dalek stories resuming after that.

shelter and abundance to anyone who relocated there. An entire generation of human colonists – including Lillian Belle – grew up with the Daleks renowned as a force for good, and credited with saving countless billions of lives. Meanwhile, the Daleks plotted to use the Cradle to transform the raw materials on the Sunlight planets, converting those worlds into a billion Skaros with their own Dalek populations.

The Dalek Foundation representatives kept to themselves, and were never interviewed for holo-television. At times, a Dalek Litigator – secretly the Dalek Time Controller – appeared in court.[1701]

c 4750 - "War-Game"[1702] **->** The sixth Doctor and Frobisher landed on a barbaric world, Actinon, and detected advanced technology. Investigating, they discovered that the local Warlord Kaon was a Draconian. His daughter Kara had been kidnapped by Vegar, a rival warlord. The Doctor took Kaon to Vegar's fortress in the TARDIS and they rescued Kara – at the cost of Kaon's life. Kara vowed to stay on the planet and maintain his legacy.

? 4750 - THE DALEK GENERATION[1703] **->** The archaeologist Hogoosta hired two renowned physicists and polymaths, Terrin and Alyst Blakely, to solve equations related to the Cradle of the Gods' activation code. The Blakelys realised the danger the information posed, and ruined their research when the Daleks intercepted their spaceship, then committed suicide to prevent the information being ripped from their minds. The eleventh Doctor, arriving from nearly a century in the future, rescued Terrin and Alyst's children: Sabel, Jenibeth and Ollus, age four.

The Doctor delivered the children to the planet Carthedia, an Earth Alliance world with a population of three billion, and decried the Daleks to the media. He was charged with speaking out against the Dalek Foundation – a hate crime per Carthedia's Prevention of Hatred Act 9/70-3/4. The Blakely children were given into the care of

---

1701 The background to *The Dalek Generation*. Hogoosta spends "forty-seven years" (ch8) studying the Cradle of the Gods, although he must start his work before the Dalek Foundation comes into being, as the Sunlight Worlds were created "about thirty or forty years ago, something like that" (ch3). Supporting the latter claim, Lillian Belle is seven months old when she's relocated to Sunlight 349, but a professional broadcaster when *The Dalek Generation* takes place.

1702 Dating "War-Game" (*DWM* #100-101) - The Doctor meets Kaon again in "Warrior's Story" (which takes place before this in Kaon's timeline) and that adventure sets the rough date for this one. The Draconians rule "a third of the galaxy" at this point. Kaon crashed "many years ago" – enough for Kara to be born and grow to womanhood (although we don't know how long that takes for a Draconian).

1703 Dating *The Dalek Generation* (NSA #53) - The story takes place in humanity's future. Earth's status isn't mentioned, but Carthedia is an "Earth Alliance colony planet" (ch2). There's a "human empire" (ch16) that would suffer economically if the Sunlight Worlds were destroyed. "A Sound of Thunder" (a short story by Ray Bradbury, first published in *Collier's*, 28th June, 1952) is still in circulation.

The Daleks' atrocities were so "long ago" (ch9) and "apparently forgotten" about (ch10), they've been allowed – without any objection, it seems – to set up the Dalek Foundation and work as benefactors. At this point, it's getting harder and harder to find places in *Doctor Who*'s history where a protracted period of no overt Dalek activity has lulled humanity into a false sense of security, enabling the Daleks to instigate a new gambit that relies upon everyone's goodwill without using secondary agents or concealing their identities. Additionally, the gambit with the Sunlight Worlds

plays out over more than ninety years, so it can't happen very quickly or very discretely between other events. Placing *The Dalek Generation*, then, is largely dependent upon eliminating where it *can't* occur.

We can, perhaps, establish something of an upper limit – there's no mention of Earth Alliance in any story later than *Dalek Empire* (see the Earth Alliance sidebar), possibly because the Great Catastrophe of 5441 (*Dalek Empire II*) brings the Alliance to ruin. It's equally possible that Earth Alliance survives, or that Carthedia self-identifies as an Earth Alliance world long after the group has gone to dust. If either of these scenarios are true, placing *The Dalek Generation* becomes a matter of pinning a ribbon on the very large expanse that is *Doctor Who*'s future history.

If Carthedia's ties to Earth Alliance are current, and working to the premise that Earth Alliance doesn't survive past 5441, it's possible to whittle down the possibilities of when *The Dalek Generation* can occur...

• The third millennium: No mention is made of Earth Alliance prior to c.3480 (*Paradise 5*), and the lingering wounds of the first and second Dalek Invasions of the twenty-second century (*The Dalek Invasion of Earth*, *Lucie Miller/To the Death*), would, surely, render humanity unwilling to trust the Daleks for a long while. Also, Earth becomes so hopelessly overcrowded toward the end of the millennium (*Colony in Space*, *The Mutants*, etc.), mention of the four hundred Sunlight Worlds' prosperity and open immigration policies in other stories from this period would be almost unavoidable, and there aren't any.

• The fourth millennium: The Daleks invade Earth around 3000 (*Mission to the Unknown*), making it highly unlikely that *The Dalek Generation* happens for some time afterward. The latter half of this millennium can be conclusively ruled out, as it contains no prominent

Lillian Belle, a *Sunlight 349 Holo-News* broadcaster. The Daleks secretly infected Jenibeth Blakely with nanogenes, making her their agent, and released the Doctor per the Time Controller's instructions. The Doctor left Ollus with the hypercube used to summon him to the boy's funeral about eighty-six years hence. He returned there in the TARDIS, having deduced the Blakeys had hidden a copy of the Cradle's activation code in Ollus' toy spaceship.

How Nice is Your Brain? was the Sunlight Worlds' top-rated programme – a show in which participants would project holographic images of their innermost thoughts.

Prink's First Theorem of 4795 implied that Z-O radiation, a combination of Z-radiation and O-radiation, would produce an energy output equal to a billion neutron stars. Prink's Second Theorem was atomised in the backblast that resulted from his attempt to test his First Theorem.[1704]

The Time Agents[1705]

The forty-ninth century was an era of unparalleled peace and prosperity on Earth. Advanced ubertronic devices existed. Earth developed time travel using transduction beams, but Time Agents strictly regulated the proliferation of the technology. Time travel had other uses: the film archivist Jaxa recovered all the lost films and television programmes. Thirty years before her native time, the moon was terraformed. Sabbath press-ganged Jaxa into his service following a failed time-jump on her part.[1706]

The Time Agent named Scott Thrower would run afoul of the eleventh Doctor, Amy and Rory while perpetrating a scheme to restore his youth.[1707] In the "forty-ninth century of Earth's history or thereabouts", Warrior Historians from New Ultonia participated in the ultimate battle reenactment: going back in time to fight in old wars, and sometimes dying there.[1708]

Dalek activity (*Mission to the Unknown*).

• The fifth millennium: There isn't time between *Mission to the Unknown* [c.4000] and the Federation fighting a Dalek War around 4015 (*Legacy*) for the ninety-plus years that span *The Dalek Generation* to occur. The same war, surely, would make the Daleks' scheme with the Sunlight Worlds untenable for a while.

The Davros Era [c.4500 to c.4703] raises a related question: how many people know the Daleks' true nature per stories such as *The Daleks' Master Plan* (the only ones to know about the Time Destructor plot are, it seems, dead by story's end) and throughout the Davros Era? Events in *Destiny of the Daleks* and *Revelation of the Daleks* seem very localised. The Earth military imprisons Davros for some decades prior to *Resurrection of the Daleks*, but it doesn't follow that there's a broader recognition of a Dalek threat. *Remembrance of the Daleks* doesn't mention humanity's status in this period. *Terror Firma* entails Dalek operations in Folkestone, but it's debatable how much the rest of Earth is involved. If the answer to this question means that the public isn't aware of the Daleks' character during or immediately after the Davros Era, *The Dalek Generation* could occur just prior to...

• The sixth millennium: *Dalek Empire* [c.5425] opens long after awareness of the Daleks has been relegated to the dustbin of history, so *The Dalek Generation* can't feasibly occur beforehand. Following the Great Catastrophe of 5441, there's no evident Dalek activity until *Dalek Empire III* [c 7520].

All things considered, dating *The Dalek Generation* to after the Davros Era doesn't feel entirely right, but it is, arguably, the least *wrong* option available. It's a choice of either running with that date, or rationalising away the "Earth Alliance" reference and deciding the story should, after all, be relegated to None of the Above.

1704 *The Oseidon Adventure*

1705 HUMANITY'S TIME TRAVEL EFFORTS: Here we need to set aside a multitude of private inventors tinkering with temporal theory, pseudo-succeeding (usually but not always) owing to contact with alien races. Professor Maxtible winds up with a house full of Daleks by virtue of his closet of mirrors connecting him with the future (*The Evil of the Daleks*), Mariah Learman possesses a time scanner with the same principles (*The Time of the Daleks*), Theodore Kerensky attains time-bubbles that can age chickens into skeletons because his alien patron, Count Scarlioni, peddles antiques to the black market (*City of Death*) and so on.

But if we're looking at publicly-stated and concerted efforts by world governments to achieve time travel, akin to the Moon Race of the 1960s, then the results are feast or famine. In the new series, we twice encounter chrononauts from failed time launches: Colonel Orson Pink hails from a "hundred years" after the modern day, but his brave attempt to time-skip into "the middle of next week" overshoots a wee bit, and lands him on the last surviving planet in the universe (*Listen*). The twelfth Doctor and Clara give Orson a lift home – not an option for Hila Tacorian, a "time pioneer" from a "few hundred years" from today, who winds up causing spooky effects at Caliburn House in 1974, but can't go back because history wrote her down as missing (*Hide*).

The progression of technology in *Doctor Who* constantly suggests that any big-scale efforts to achieve time-travel prowess effectively come to naught in the third, fourth and fifth millenniums. Not a sausage, really. The lack of time-tech becomes pretty telling in stories such as *The Dalek Invasion of Earth* [c.2167] and *The Mutants* [c.2990], when the shape of Earth society would look *very* different if humanity had time travel available. In *The Daleks' Master Plan* [4000], it's plain that the Daleks have at least one time vessel at the ready (enough to dog the TARDIS through history and allow

Humans didn't explore some parts of Earth's moon until the forty-ninth century.[1709]

At some point in human history, AEGIS operated a time travel service that, though expensive, allowed people to go into the past. The Technos wrongly thought it was impossible to change the past because time travellers were part of history. One group was sent back to hunt dinosaurs in the Cretaceous.[1710]

Fennus was one of the more successful frontier colonies until it became unstable and disintegrated. The colonists were thought dead, but the father of Mindy 'Voir had engineered a data bank to contain the contents of the colonists' minds. Mindy's father was a pioneer in sonic sculpting, and had enhanced her voice until she was the only human singer with a ten-octave range. She came into possession of the Fennus data bank and wore it as a pendant, unaware of its true nature.[1711]

& 4840 - THE DALEK GENERATION[1712] **->** The Dalek Time Controller resulted from generations of genetic manipulation with a single goal: provide the Daleks with a strategist who could discern the patterns of the Time Vortex. As part of its effort to obtain the Cradle of the Gods' activation code, the Time Controller faked Ollus Blakely's funeral and arranged for the eleventh Doctor to receive Ollus' hypercube, which summoned him to the planet Gethria. The Doctor went nine decades back to investigate the Blakely family.

The Doctor returned, having realised that the code was hidden inside a toy spaceship Ollus owned when he was a child. The Daleks obtained the code and triggered the Cradle's activation, intending to reshape the Sunlight Worlds into their new powerbase: "a billion Skaros". The Cradle unexpectedly formed a mental link with Jenibeth Blakely – decades of Dalek servitude had left her in a child-like state, and the Cradle acted upon stories she had been told of the Sunlight Worlds, transforming them into peaceful planets with no Dalek influence. The Cradle's transformation wave also turned the Blakely siblings – Ollus, Sabel and Jenibeth – into children once more, and restored their

---

them to exterminate some ancient Egyptians), but the Guardian of the Solar System and his alien allies don't.

Then, suddenly and without any explanation that we've ever been given, the era of River Song, Captain Jack Harkness and the Time Agents – roughly the forty-ninth to the fifty second centuries – represents a veritable blossoming of time technology. It's so rife with the stuff, spacecraft such as the SS *Madame de Pompadour* (*The Girl in the Fireplace*) and SS *Marie Antoinette* (*Deep Breath*) cause mischief, mayhem and vivisections in the past when malfunction occurs. Similarly, vortex manipulators (the time-hopping wristbands employed by Captain Jack and his fellow Time Agents) are available on the black market, if one knows where to look (*The Pandorica Opens*).

The dating of this golden age of time-travel stems from a misinterpretation of *The Talons of Weng-Chiang*, in which Magnus Greel – who originates from the "fifty-first century" – arrogantly insists that he's the "first man to travel through time", but also frets that a Time Agent will track him down and arrest him (or whatever Time Agents do with temporal fugitives). Melding those statements together, it's rather unlikely that the Time Agency belongs to Greel's era, but so many stories have now pinned down the fifty-first century as having an abundance of time technology (*Silence in the Library* and *Let's Kill Hitler* very blatantly, *TW: Kiss Kiss, Bang Bang* off-handedly, and many more), we have to accept it as fact – even if stories such as *The Invisible Enemy* [5000] and *The Ice Warriors* [?5000] are set in the same era but make no mention of the temporal status quo.

But after that patch of temporal prosperity... nothing again. Just as we've no idea how humanity experienced such a windfall, it all seemingly goes away. The future-most mention of it is that Merrit OhOne works for the Time Agency in the fifty-second century (*DotD: Shockwave, DotD: The Time Machine*), but there's zilch on display after that. Whatever global crisis to come, nobody on Earth raises the potential of using time tech to fix the problem, accord themselves or their parents or grandparents pre-warning of the disaster, or simply escape to a more fruitful era. The solar flare event prompts those aboard Nerva Station to enter hibernation and hope for the best (*The Ark in Space*), and when they oversleep, nobody – taking *The Sontaran Experiment* [c.16,000] at face value – has used time travel to jump to an ideal point and resettle the fertile Earth. Ten thousand years on, it's up for grabs. Later still, those fleeing Earth's destruction do so aboard conventional space vessels (*The Ark, Frontios*). The Commander in *The Ark*, in fact, finds the notion of time travel spellbinding, and cites the failure of temporal experiments in the Twenty-Seventh Segment of Time.

The blip of humanity having time tech in the River Song/Captain Jack era, then, looks so anomalous as to make one wonder if an interloping time traveller somehow sparked and ended it all – but until that story gets written to explain, this bonanza of time technology looks like, and remains, the exception that proves the rule.

1706 *Trading Futures.* Magnus Greel (from the year 5000) feared Time Agents tracking him down in *The Talons of Weng-Chiang*, Time Agents appeared in *Eater of Wasps*, and in *The Empty Child/The Doctor Dances*, Captain Jack claims to have been a Time Agent, and knows that other Agents will be tracking him down. It's interesting to note that in the original, unbroadcast version of *An Unearthly Child*, the Doctor and Susan claim to be aliens, but Susan says she was born in the forty-ninth century.

dead parents to life. The Doctor destroyed the Cradle, and the Time Controller retreated.

? 4845 - 3rdA: THE CONQUEST OF FAR[1713] -> The Daleks engaged in warfare across a hundred systems, capturing the planet Far. Earth Alliance hoped to reclaim Far's hyperspatial gateway, and with it strike deeper into Dalek space. The Daleks fortified Far with a million-strong Dalek army, and a Robo-tizing transmitter dish to brainwash Earth Alliance's main fleet – but the third Doctor and Jo turned the latter upon the former, scrambling their minds and causing them to self-destruct. The Doctor didn't know the ultimate fate of Far and the Alliance fleet.

? 4850 - HELICON PRIME[1714] -> A long way from Earth's "side" of the universe, Helicon Prime served as a luxury resort in the Parnassas Cluster for many species. Helicon Prime was later moved to the Golden Section – an area of space that radiated a sense of well being – and thereby

became an exceedingly exclusive holiday destination. A booking of decades in advance was required.

The second Doctor and Jamie stopped a murder spree committed by Ambassador Dromeo, who sought the Fennus data bank. Mindy 'Voir, having given Jamie her pendant as a present, thought the Doctor had absconded with the data bank and travelled back to eighteenth century Scotland in search of it.

? 4850 - THE RENAISSANCE MAN[1715] -> The fourth Doctor tried to further Leela's education about her ancestors at the Morovanian Museum on Morvania Minor, which he touted as "the greatest collection of Earth artifacts in the universe, anywhere, anywhen". The Museum's systems copied raw information from the mind of any historical expert who visited, to preserve their knowledge for all eternity. One of its curators, Mr Jephson, usurped this machinery in a bid to create the ultimate Renaissance Man. He drained the minds of a few visitors entirely, then

1707 "Time Fraud"

1708 *The Haunting of Malkin Place*

1709 *I am a Dalek*

1710 "A Glitch in Time". It's never specified when the time travellers come from, but this would seem to be the only era in which humanity develops time travel.

1711 The Fennus disaster is said to have happened "long ago" prior to the main events of *Helicon Prime*, but as Mindy herself is portrayed as a young woman and we meet three members of the rescue team sent to Fennus, the disaster presumably – depending on human longevity in this era – happened decades rather than centuries before *Helicon Prime* opens.

1712 Dating *The Dalek Generation* (NSA #53) - It's "nearly nine decades" after the Doctor leaves the Blakely children on Sunlight 349 (ch14). That all of the Blakely children have survived to this ripe old age – Sabel, previously age 12 (ch6), must be over a hundred years old – perhaps says good things about human longevity in this era. It's possibly for that reason that the title, as well as the blurb, talks about those who have lived under the Daleks' benevolence for "a generation", not "generations".

The Dalek Time Controller here meets the Doctor for the first time from its perspective (ch16), and later encounters the sixth Doctor in *Patient Zero* and the eighth Doctor in *Lucie Miller* and *To the Death* (all in stories written by Nicholas Briggs) and again in the *Dark Eyes* series. The eleventh Doctor here realizes that the Dalek Time Controller capitalised on his inclination to meddle, and vows to give it up – possibly leading to his disillusioned state in *The Snowmen*.

1713 Dating *3rdA: The Conquest of Far* (BF *The Third Doctor Adventures* #3.1) - The story's trappings stem from *Frontier in Space* [2540]; the Doctor implies that it's "far into the future" from *Planet of the Daleks* [the same

year, most likely]. Far's hyper-gateway improves upon the hyperdrive capabilities of Earth and Draconian spaceships, there's a (male, this time) President of Earth and open warfare against the Daleks. Even so, the participants deem it "impossible" and the stuff of a "child's fable" that the Doctor "fought and defeated the Daleks throughout the Dalek Wars, and perhaps even before then". None of the human participants have heard of Spiridon (although this doesn't directly contradict *Frontier in Space/Planet of the Daleks*). Mention of the "civilized people of the galaxy" suggests it's before humanity leaves the Milky Way. These Daleks can hover, and while they've many of the Doctor's faces on file, they don't recognise his third incarnation.

The blurb just says it's "Earth Alliance, the future", in line with Nicholas Briggs' habit (to avoid continuity headaches) of not specifying the year. Steering clear of historical periods in which there's no open conflict with the Daleks (the fourth millennium, for instance, per *Mission to the Unknown*), we might as well place *The Conquest of Far* after another Dalek story by Briggs, *The Dalek Generation* [? 4750-4840] – a period that's somewhat less documented than others.

1714 Dating *Helicon Prime* (BF CC #2.2) - The dating clues are very vague. Mindy is specified as human, but as Helicon Prime is such a great distance from Earth, this is presumably a long time into humanity's expansion into space. It's not specified how, exactly, Mindy travels back to find a post-TARDIS Jamie, raising the possibility that time travel technology is available. Even so, this placement represents a stab in the dark.

Victoria is still studying graphology, so for the Doctor and Jamie, this story likely occurs during Season 6B.

1715 Dating *The Renaissance Man* (BF 4th Doc #1.2) - The Morovanian Museum is an immense repository of Earth artifacts, but it's situated off Earth, and seems to

filled them with data from a multitude of experts. This culminated in the creation of Harcourt: a living database who failed to comprehend the difference between knowledge and *learning*.

Harcourt threatened to steal the Doctor's knowledge... until the Doctor infected the museum's systems with the wholly improvised biography of "Mont Morensy Pescaville" – a poet, explorer, adventurer, fencer, amateur inventor, mountain climber, close friend of Winston Churchill, magician and pioneer of cow parsley. The resultant malfunction cascaded, destroying the data-collecting machinery. Harcourt and Jephson's other victims were restored, and returned to their native times.

The Museum's new Renaissance section defaulted to being an empty room – elite patrons viewed this, and joyfully presumed it a statement on the fact that nobody can truly know everything.

c 4865 - DotD: DEATH'S DEAL[1716] -> The extraction of slaughter crystals, a rare substance that could be refined into devastating bombs, had been banned across the galaxy. The Wraith Mining Cartel coveted deposits of slaughter crystals on the planet Death's Deal, and kept their existence secret by downing ships – especially those with mining surveyors – passing near the planet. Distress signals sent from Death's Deal agitated the local wildlife, including terror worms. In time, the planet was totally isolated, regarded as the most hostile planet in existence.

The tenth Doctor and Donna responded to the pleas for help from Death's Deal, which included a hidden message from the eleventh Doctor. He instructed his former self to protect Lyric Erskine, the daughter of the lost Professor Merrit Erskine, and to disclose the presence of the slaughter crystals to the authorities. They did so, enabling Galactic Central to contain the slaughter crystals and end the distress signals.

Lyric Erskine married Captain OhOne of the *Obscura*.[1717]

Humans from Earth established colonies in the Tarsus System in the forty-fifth century. They discovered an item later called the Voice of Stone – a Gallifreyan hypercube thrown into the Vortex by the eleventh Doctor – and heard from it a prediction that the Tarsus worlds would come to ruin. The hypercube was lost and thought a myth, but its message gave rise to a doomsday cult: the Senders.[1718]

c 4870 - DotD: SHOCKWAVE[1719] -> Purebred humans were now rare.

The sun Tarsus Ultra collapsed into a spatial anomaly, sending out a shockwave that progressively obliterated the worlds of the Tarsus System. The seventh Doctor and Ace, in search of Voice of Stone, joined the spaceship *Obscura* as it fled the oncoming destruction. OhOne, the *Obscura* captain, mistook the two of them for envoys from Earth Central – the governing body of Earth's colonies.

NineJay, a member of the Senders doomsday cult, sabotaged the *Obscura*'s engines. The eleventh Doctor's message on the Voice of Stone, which was found in property belonging to the Tarsus Bank, stressed that the seventh Doctor and Ace had to guarantee OhOne's safety, and caused NineJay to re-examine her beliefs. OhOne volunteered to give his life erecting a force field to protect the *Obscura* from the shockwave, but NineJay exchanged places with OhOne via T-Mat, and died saving the ship.

OhOne retained the Voice of Stone and went home to his wife, Lyric Erskine. His close call prompted them to enjoy a second honeymoon on New Vegas. A year later, their son Merrit OhOne – a future member of the Time Agency – was born.[1720]

On Earth, Professor Oskana **Kilbracken developed a holograph-cloning technique. The process was unreliable; the longest a clone ever lived was ten minutes, fifty-five seconds. Most serious scientists thought of it**

make use of limited time-travel to bring experts on history to it. No exhibit from later than the twentieth century is seen, which isn't to automatically say that the museum doesn't contain such works. While this placement is guesswork, the use of time technology brings to mind the fifty-first century – a late enough point that the preservation of humankind's relics and history might rate a higher priority.

1716 Dating *DotD: Death's Deal* (*Destiny of the Doctor* #10) - The Doctor comments, "I know it's the forty-ninth century, and everyone's off exploring the great unknown..." One of the minor characters is a "fifth generation" space pirate.

1717 There's no mention of Lyric being married in *DotD: Death's Deal*, but *DotD: The Time Machine* stipulates that OhOne "goes home to his wife" – Erskine, by all accounts – after events in *DotD: Shockwave*.

1718 *DotD: Shockwave*

1719 Dating *DotD: Shockwave* (*Destiny of the Doctor* #7) - The blurb says that it's "the far future," but the forty-ninth century is specified in the story. The Tarsus colonists are human. The Doctor and Ace pose as envoys from the Earth Empire, although it's unlikely to be the same Earth Empire as featured in *Frontier in Space*, and was winding down in *The Mutants* [c 2990].

1720 *DotD: The Time Machine*

1721 In *The Invisible Enemy*, the Doctor asks K9 for a "rundown" on the science of cloning, and is told, "Successful experiments first carried out in the year 3922." Shortly afterward, Professor Marius offers that "The Kilbracken [cloning] technique is very simple" – the implication being that the two developments are one and the same. *Revenge of the Swarm*, however,

as "a circus trick of no practical value".[1721]

wih - Robert Scarratt's standing with the Great Houses improved following an Enemy attack on the forty-ninth century.[1722]

Pursuant to Section 4 Paragraph 25 of the Future Time Edict dated E5150 pro-Hok Gibbon slash Kulkana, Hokrala Corp – a law firm in the forty-ninth century – filed suit against Captain Jack Harkness in the twenty-first century. A Vortex Dweller indebted to Jack closed off Hokrala's access to the past.[1723]

Around 4900, a Dalek expedition to the Magellan Cluster was attacked by spider-like creatures in Dalek-like armour, and it took months to subdue them. These spider-Daleks were Daleks from a parallel universe. The Daleks calculated that the only way to take the fight to the spider-Daleks was via a black hole, but knew their ships couldn't survive the journey.[1724] A thousand murders took place on the worlds of the Nepotism of Vaal in the fiftieth century. The Memeovore had made the population think their loved ones are impostors. The Doctor would visit and see them establish a universal brotherhood.[1725] Zytron energy, which was affordable and adaptable but could mutate people into psychopathic monstrosities, was discovered on Earth in the fiftieth century.[1726]

? 4917 - THE MIDDLE[1727] -> Humanity's expansion into space became such that a management firm invested in forty research spheres, each of which tried out a societal model geared to maximize resources. The inhabitants of such sphere, "the Earth colony Formicia", enjoyed pleasure and good times until age 35, when they were consigned to the colony's administrative branch: The Middle. At age 70, they were press-ganged into The End, and subsequently killed in a wholly-invented war with the Kronvos Horde. The sixth Doctor, Constance and Flip exposed the lies behind Formicia, liberating everyone within the forty spheres.

4920 - REVENGE OF THE SWARM[1728] -> Written language had largely become phonetic, leading to signs with seemingly erroneous spelling.

A portion of the Nucleus of the Swarm had endured inside the TARDIS' systems, and possessed Hector Thomas owing to his fractured psyche. Nucleus-Hector relocated the TARDIS – as well as the seventh Doctor and Ace – to a moonbase on Titan, 4920, to help fulfill upon its creation. Professor Oskana Kilbracken of the Centre for Alien Biomorphology had discovered that Saturnian plague, while itself fatal, eliminated all rival pathogens. With humanity decades away from a massive expansion, Kilbracken hoped to hyper-evolve the virus so it could ward off any diseases space explorers encountered.

Kilbracken cured Ace of Saturnian plague, then accelerated the virus she had carried at an evolutionary development rate of 12,000 years per second. The virus' Nucleus became sentient, and sensed when Kilbracken observed it through equipment – an act that made it feel small, and determined to grow bigger. Kilbracken killed herself and destroyed her laboratory as the Nucleus broke its containment. The Doctor ejected the Nucleus into space, knowing it would drift for eighty years before possessing a shuttle crew en route to Titan. Having experienced hyper-evolution, the Nucleus would wrongly believe it had wandered in space for "millennia". The Doctor also cleansed the Titan moonbase of Saturnian plague; in future, it would be repurposed as a fueling station.

A clone of the Nucleus remained in Hector's system, and relocated the TARDIS nearly three centuries ahead in time...

Humans established the settlement of Christmas on the planet Trenzalore. Jalen Fellwood, the village headsman of Christmas before a truth field was established there, married a young woman – Summerly Treece – and sacrificed her to the dark powers he worshiped. A hunting party led by Summerly's father, Rolan, pursued Fellwood away from

---

posits that they aren't: we actually meet Professor Kilbracken in that story, and she claims to have developed her cloning technique "forty years" prior to 4920. Clones are seen or referred to before this date in a number of subsequent stories such as *Heritage*, *Deceit*, *Trading Futures*, *Project: Lazarus*, *The Also People* and *So Vile a Sin*. Professor Marius distinguishes between the Kilbracken Technique, which instantly creates a "sort of three-dimensional photocopy", and a true clone that would take "years" to produce. *Heritage* also suggests cloning keeps periodically falling into disuse, whereupon another scientist will come forward and claim to have perfected the science for the "first" time.
1722 FP: *The Brakespeare Voyage* (ch5).
1723 TW: *The Undertaker's Gift*

1724 "Three hundred years" before "Fire and Brimstone".
1725 *The Taking of Planet 5* (p222).
1726 "Three thousand years" after *Ghosts of India*. The metamorphic nature of Zytron energy, and the similar-sounding name, suggests it bears some relation to Zeiton-7 ore (*Vengeance on Varos*).
1727 Dating *The Middle* (BF #232) – Based upon its (concocted) architecture, the Doctor identifies Formicia as an Earth colony. More pertinently, the story relies upon humanity's population woes – even away from its homeworld – being such that the management firm spends a century field-testing drastic solutions.
1728 Dating *Revenge of the Swarm* (BF #189) - The year is given, and is "eighty years" before *The Invisible Enemy* [5000].

Christmas, then killed him, buried him and salted his grave. The Mara tried to manifest by using Fellwood's skeleton as a focal point, but Fellwood's latent belief in salt as a magical defense kept it trapped beneath the ground.[1729]

The Blitzrats Jazz Quartet began performing. The group secretly worked as assassins, their sonic weaponry inducing anything from a heart attack to planetary destruction.[1730]

Charley Pollard Escapes the Viyrans

c (15th September) 4964 to 4966 - CHARLEY S1: THE LAMENTATION CIPHER / THE VIYRAN SOLUTION[1731] **->** Human medicine could readily replace spines, and quick-grow muscle flexors and extensors. Cloned tissue was available from Fifth Galaxy Olympians.

Having left the sixth Doctor's company, Charley Pollard continued to assist the Viyrans on various missions – more millennia had passed while she mostly remained in stasis. Charley aided the Viyrans in locating investment broker Robert Buchan: an Earthman infected with Amythyst Virus S10847-Variant 104, a.k.a. the Obscurantist, when he visited the fifth moon of the Indecisive Torrent. The Viyrans captured Buchan at a viewing station near the time-active Ever-and-Ever Prolixity, a cosmic phenomena at the edge of Galaxy Brouhaha Nine-Nine-Five.

The Viyrans increasingly deemed Charley a security risk and decided to mind-wipe her, but a rogue Viyran arrived from the past using the Prolixity, secretly infected Charley with a virus made by the Viyrans' creators, and aided her escape through the Prolixity to 1936. Afterwards, the Viyrans' efforts to eradicate time virus KX-Variant243 retroactively created the Prolixity.

Believing that Charley possessed the Lamentation Cipher, a failsafe device against which they had no defense, the Viyrans dispatched time-squads to find her. One such group returned Charley, who was now age 23, to this era two years after she left. Robert Buchan had become the Viyrans' organic agent.

The Viyrans had determined that an Amythest virus was responsible for the advent of evolution itself, so intended to send a panacea through the Prolixity to the dawn of time, eradicating all life in the universe. The virus within Charley, having finished incubating, activated and restored the Viyrans' memories and identity protocols to their original settings. Charley detonated time viruses that closed the Prolixity, and used its dying embers to escape into space-time with Buchan for another adventure...

1729 "Nine hundred years" before *Tales of Trenzalore*: "The Dreaming", by which point the eleventh Doctor has been on Trenzalore for 700 if not 750 years.

1730 "Two hundred years" before *Rhythm of Destruction*.

1731 Dating *Charley S1: The Lamentation Cipher/The Viyran Solution* (*Charley #1.1, #1.4*) - It's the future, broadbrushed as being "millennia" after Charley's own time (*The Lamentation Cipher*), and "goodness knows how many centuries" (*The Viyran Solution*) before Charley (born in 1912) specifies that her next diary entry should open with her being age "two thousand, nine hundred and something". In *DEyes 2: The White Room*, a Viyran thrown back to 1918 from this era says it's from "many thousands of years" in the future; a second is speculated as being from "thousands, maybe millions of years" ahead. The "Fifth Galaxy Olympians" mentioned in *The Viryan Solution* might stem from the same locale as Zephon, the Master of the Fifth Galaxy (*The Daleks' Master Plan* [4000]).

When *The Lamentation Cipher* opens, Charley has spent "years" of her personal time (presumably including the duration of time between *Patient Zero* and *Blue Forgotten Planet*) working for the Viyrans. "Two years" here pass in local time as Charley escapes to 1936 and returns. Robert Buchan names the day in *The Lamentation Cipher*.

Earth is fully functional (Buchan, in fact, expects to fairly easily return there after witnessing the Proximity, which is located at "the furthest reaches of known space"), suggesting it's prior to the Great Catastrophe of the sixth millennium and almost certainly before the solar flares ravage Earth c.6000 (*The Ark in Space*).

1732 *Charlotte Pollard* Series 2

1733 *Charley S1: The Viyran Solution*, leading to events in *DEyes 2: The White Room*.

1734 "Two hundred years" before *The Time of Angels*.

1735 *Borrowed Time*. See the World Wars sidebar.

1736 In the century before *The Ice Warriors*.

1737 *Interference*. The Doctor has a pair of those binoculars, no doubt acquired when he was with the Filipino army (mentioned in *The Talons of Weng-Chiang*).

1738 *The English Way of Death*

1739 *The Gallifrey Chronicles*

1740 According to Gryffen in *K9: Jaws of Orthrus*. This may mean K9 is a production model, and Marius built him from a kit. Or it may simply mean that other unique robots were built to look like dogs. It could also mean that once Marius gets back to Earth, he markets K9s commercially. The Doctor apparently acquires the Mark 2 and Mark 4 K9s very quickly – he seems to have them stored in the TARDIS, but likewise it's impossible to say if he built or bought K9s Mark 2 to 4.

1741 *The Resurrection of Mars*

1742 "A thousand years" before *City at World's End*.

1743 *The Art of Destruction*. Given the catastrophes that afflict the Earth in the fifty-first century, it's tempting to speculate that the Doctor does this somehow to

The collapsing Ever-and-Ever Prolixity sent Charley Pollard and Robert Buchan – who, anticipating they would die, became lovers – through to the twenty-first century. The Rogue Viyran, a.k.a. Bernard, followed; interaction with the Prolixity gave it fantastical abilities.[1732] The time-active virus KX-variant 243 displaced two Viyrans back to 1918, the year of the virus' creation.[1733]

Humans terraformed Alfava Metraxis. In time, six billion colonists would live there.[1734] Advanced genetic engineering facilitated the creation of fast-reproducing mutant crabs that consumed the otherwise-indestructible marine vessels used in World War V.[1735]

Under the auspices of the Great World Computer, human civilisation was more efficiently run than ever. But Earth regularly suffered massive famines. An artificial food was created on Earth that solved the problem. On the land once used to grow food, up-to-date living units were built to house the ever-increasing population. The amount of plants on the planet was reduced to an absolute minimum, and all plant life on Earth became extinct.[1736]

The Filipino Protectorate was established on Earth by 4993. Technology at the time included binoculars that could see through walls and read lips.[1737] Professor Marius registered K9 as a data patent on 3rd October, 4998.[1738] K9 was not Y5K compliant.[1739] **K9 wasn't the only cybernetic dog in the fiftieth century.**[1740]

The Fifty-First Century

The Monk's TARDIS had "Arctic coffee" from the fifty-first century.[1741] The Taklarian Empire began a program of selective breeding to create a master race.[1742] The Doctor took the Mona Lisa up Mount Everest on a camel in the fifty-first century.[1743]

In the fifty-first century, law and order collapsed. Derek Dell, a geek and avid reader of *Aggotron* – a twentieth century comic – adopted the identity of "Courtmaster Cruel", and struck fear into the hearts of criminals. Eventually, Derek went back in time to find the original artwork to the missing *Aggotron #56*, which revealled the Courtmaster's face.[1744] The fifty-first century was the era of the time traveller Chronodev, who was known to the Onihr.[1745]

K9 Mark I Joins the TARDIS

5000 - THE INVISIBLE ENEMY[1746] **-> Five thousand AD was the year of the Great Breakout, when humanity "went leapfrogging across the galaxy like a tidal wave". To prepare the way, the Space Exploration Programme was instigated in the late fiftieth century, and a huge methane/oxygen refinery was set up on Titan. On asteroid K4067, the centre for Alien Biomorphology (the Bi-Al Foundation) treated extraterrestrial diseases, as well as tending those who were injured in space. Regular shuttle runs were set up between the planets of the solar system and "good for nothing" spaceniks also travelled the cosmos.**

Photon beam weapons were in common use, as were visiphones. Sophisticated robots and computers were built. The native language of the time was Finglish, a form of phonetic English.

The Nucleus of the Swarm, a microscopic spaceborne entity, attempted to replicate itself across the universe and in the macro-world. It mentally compelled some humans to adapt the methane refinery on Titan into a breeding ground, but was destroyed by the fourth Doctor and Leela before it could reproduce.

Professor Marius' robot dog, K9, assisted the travellers against the Nucleus. The Doctor and Leela took K9 with them, as Marius was due to return to Earth.

protect the painting.
1744 *The Company of Friends:* "Izzy's Story"
1745 *Trading Futures*
1746 Dating *The Invisible Enemy* (15.2) - The Doctor states that it is the year "5000, the year of the Great Breakout" and implies that the human race has not yet left the solar system. This contradicts virtually every other story set in the future – indeed, *The Invisible Enemy* would fit very neatly into this timeline about the year 2100.

The Breakout might be to other *galaxies*, and this is supported by the audio *Davros*, which has humanity poised to dominate the whole galaxy and eager to expand. Alternatively, perhaps a big section of humanity wants to leave because they've had enough of the Ice Age, lack of scientific progress, threat of World War

and genocidal dictators we hear are on Earth in *The Talons of Weng-Chiang*. If so, no-one mentions it in *The Invisible Enemy*, and Marius' main concern with returning to Earth is that he has too much stuff to take home.

Looking more closely at the history of Earth since the collapse of the Earth Empire around the year 3000, it's clear that there are many human colonies – but there's no evidence that Earth has any political influence on them. While it's a major player on the galactic political stage, Earth's civilisation does seem to be confined to the solar system in *The Daleks' Master Plan*, the Peladon stories and the Davros Era stories (which even following the Peel timeline would fall between 3000 and 5000). Earth maintains a military capable of (small) missions across the galaxy, but the fact that it's ignorant of massive Dalek conquests in *The Daleks' Master*

c 5000 - THE GIRL IN THE FIREPLACE[1747] -> By the fifty-first century, humankind had warp engines capable of "punching a hole in the universe". Humans had travelled at least as far as the Dagmar Cluster, "two and a half galaxies" from Earth.

The spacecraft *Madame de Pompadour* was crippled in an ion storm, and drifted for a year while the clockwork robots aboard blindly followed their orders to repair it. They used the human crew as raw components, and then used the warp drive to travel back in time and find the historical Madame de Pompadour, who they mistakenly thought was the key to the problem. The tenth Doctor, Rose and Mickey arrived on the ship and – after multiple trips to the eighteenth century – deactivated the robots.

The *SS Marie Antoinette*, the *Madame de Pompadour's* sister ship, fell back in time to Earth's pre-history.[1748]

? 5000 - K9 AND THE BEASTS OF VEGA[1749] -> Twenty-seven light years from Earth, humans overseen by Professor Romius were building artificial planets near Vega III that would be ready in ten years. Four ships had been attacked, their crews paralysed. K9 saw the effects on the crew of Spaceshifter 138. Screaming hordes of giant space-borne monsters attacked the engineers, but K9 discovered that the real Vegans were intelligent energy, and that the monsters were a defence mechanism that projected fear. The Vegans didn't like the lasers the engineers were using, and so K9 suggested that the humans go more slowly.

Plan – even the fact that Earth needs to name a fleet as "the Deep Space Fleet" in *Destiny of the Daleks* and finds it hard to fund or reinforce Davros' prison station in *Resurrection of the Daleks* – suggests that Earth doesn't dominate the galaxy. In *The Talons of Weng-Chiang*, we learn that Earth's in a technological cul-de-sac.

In short, it actually ties in with other stories that human civilisation is confined to Earth's solar system for a couple of millennia before 5000, by which time it's ripe for a "breakout", a new wave of colonisation.

Revenge of the Swarm also claims that the story takes place in the year 5000. *The Gallifrey Chronicles* gives the story the "relative date one-one-one-five-zero-zero-zero". *The TARDIS Logs* offered the date "4778".

1747 Dating *The Girl in the Fireplace* (X2.4) - The caption cuts from events in eighteenth-century France to the future with the caption "3000 years later", making it around 4759. However, the tenth Doctor tells Rose and Mickey that it's "three thousand years into your future, give or take", which would make it around 5007. Still later, the Doctor states it's the fifty-first century. The SS *Madame de Pompadour* is in the Dagmar Cluster, two and a half galaxies from Earth, and the intergalactic travel probably supports the later date.

1748 *Deep Breath*, which says the *Marie Antoinette* as being from the "fifty-first century". *The Girl in the Fireplace* addressed the *Madame de Pompadour's* fate.

1749 Dating *K9 and the Beasts of Vega* (*The Adventures of K9* #2) - No date is given, but as this is set at a time when humans are mounting a massive colonisation effort, it's probably not too much of a stretch to say it's around K9's home time.

1750 Dating *The Ice Warriors* (5.3) - The date of this story is never given on screen. Base leader Clent says that if the glaciers advance, then "five thousand years of history" will be wiped out. If he's referring to Britannicus Base, a Georgian house, this would make the date about 6800 AD. If he is referring to human or European history, the date becomes more vague. It has to be set

well over a century in the future, because the world has been run by the Great World Computer for that long.

An article in the *Radio Times* at the time of broadcast stated that the year is "3000 AD", and almost every other fan chronology used to follow that lead, although the first edition of *The Making of Doctor Who* said that the Doctor travels "three thousand years" into the future after *The Abominable Snowmen*, making the date 4935 AD. *The Dark Path* and *Legacy* both allude to the date of this story as being 3000 AD (p63 and p89 respectively). Earlier versions of *Ahistory* did the same. The blurb for the Region 1 VHS of the story said it was "AD 3000".

In *The Talons of Weng-Chiang*, the Doctor talks of "the Ice Age about the year five thousand" – possibly even a reference to this story, if Robert Holmes was using *The Making of Doctor Who* as a reference.

Timelink and *About Time* both conclude that this is the ice age mentioned in *The Talons of Weng-Chiang*. This does certainly seem to be a neater solution than proposing two ice ages in quick succession – particularly when there are a fair few stories set around 3000 on an Earth which doesn't seem to be affected by an ice age. Occam's Razor doesn't always work on fictional timelines, and can be wielded too liberally, but it seems sensible to invoke it here.

One peculiarity is that the Martians have only been buried for "centuries", although it is also made clear that they have been buried since the First Ice Age, when mastodons roamed the Earth. (*About Time* states that mastodons became extinct five million years ago, but scientists disagree, estimating it was more like 10,000 BC.) *The Terrestrial Index* and *Legacy* (p90) both suggest that the Ice Age began as a result of "solar flares" (presumably in an attempt to link it with Earth's evacuation in *The Ark in Space*), but that's specifically ruled out as a cause in the story.

One problem is that later stories (starting with *The Curse of Peladon*) would establish the Martians as a significant presence in the future, which would make

The Second Ice Age

? 5000 - THE ICE WARRIORS[1750] ->

"And then suddenly one year, there was no spring. Even then it wasn't understood, not until the ice caps began to advance."

On Earth, the Second Ice Age had begun. Glaciers rapidly spread across every continent, displacing tens of billions of people to the Equatorial regions. Scientists attempted to come up with a theory that might account for the ice flow. They quickly ruled out a number of the possibilities: a reversal of the Earth's magnetic field, interstellar clouds obscuring the sun's rays, an excessive burst of sunspot activity and a severe shift of the Earth's angle of rotation. They came to realise that the extinction of Earth's plant life had dramatically reduced the carbon dioxide levels in the lower atmosphere, leading to severe heat loss across the world. Scientists tried to reverse the flow of ice, installing Ioniser Bases at strategic points across the globe: Britannicus Base in Europe, and complexes in America, Australasia, South Africa and Asia. These were all co-ordinated by the Great World Computer.

Many refused to leave their homelands and became scavengers. Before long, everywhere on Earth apart from the equatorial areas was an Arctic wasteland, home to wolves and bears. When captured, scavengers were registered and sent to the African Rehabilitation Centres. Scientists remained behind to measure the flow of the ice with movement probes.

Varga the Ice Warrior, who had been trapped in the glacier since the First Ice Age, was revived. He excavated his ship and crew, but was defeated by the second Doctor, Jamie and Victoria before he could use sonic weapons to destroy Brittanicus Base.

THE DAY OF THE TROLL[1751] -> Global efforts to use chemicals and ionizers to push back the glaciers succeeded, but many temperate zones remained ruined. Britain became a poisoned land and was abandoned, its people dispersing to the rest of the world. Synthetic food was so essential to the world's survival and economy that it became the new oil. Earth was re-divided according to defence of resources, and the fragmentation led to global mistrust. The Eurozone still existed, as did the Internet – some three hundred million people responded online to a charity appeal. Automated Medical Units were used to treat injuries. Paris had a satellite tracking office, and Spain was temperate enough for poolside parties.

Ten years after anyone had stepped foot in Britain, the philanthropist Karl Baring established The Grange, an experimental agricultural complex, in Hampshire. The tenth Doctor bore witness as the tentacled plant-creature Sphereosis emerged from the soil in search of sustenance, and generated several "trolls" – humanoids made from twigs – to do its bidding. Baring was absorbed into Sphereosis and mentally influenced the creature to exhaust itself to death. The Doctor was convinced that without Sphereosis syphoning soil nutrients, Britain would become arable again.

The Age of Greel

"By the end of the fifth millennium AD, the homunculi created by the human species – clones, crossbreeds, fighting-machines and artificial intelligences of all descriptions – outnumbered humanity by more than thirteen to one."[1752]

Twelve clockwork automata, each of them representing a different animal on the Chinese zodiac, were fashioned to serve as army commanders. Two of these were lost – the Dragon became a "crippled and idiotic thing" while the Pig

---

the humans' ignorance of them in this story notable – humankind has apparently forgotten about the Martians who were near neighbours, and fellow members of the Galactic Federation in the Peladon stories (and who they fought against in books such as *Transit* and *The Dying Days*).

THE SECOND ICE AGE: When base leader Clent explains the historical background to *The Ice Warriors*, he implies that the Ice Age began a century ago, but people are still being evacuated from England during the story, suggesting that glaciation is a more recent phenomenon. It would seem that although the global temperature drop is a direct result of the destruction of plant life, its consequences weren't felt overnight.

The present scientific consensus, of course, is that destroying the forests would cause global *warming*

because of the resulting rise in carbon dioxide levels. However, this didn't gain widespread awareness until the 1970s; when *The Ice Warriors* was produced in the 1960s, the idea that the Earth might undergo global cooling was given more credence.

1751 Dating *The Day of the Troll* (BBC *DW* audiobook #5) - The blurb says it's the "far future", and the story clearly follows on from the ionization effort against the glaciers in *The Ice Warriors*. It's been long enough since that story that the glaciers have been defeated, and Britain has been uninhabited for ten years.

1752 According to the back cover copy for *FP: In the Year of the Cat*. This is not what we see in *The Invisible Enemy* or *The Ice Warriors*, although both do feature artificial intelligences.

"forgot his lowly station and was taken from us".

wih - Lolita sent the rest of the automata to the eighteenth century, to the court of King George III.[1753] Earth in the fifty-first century had pan-dimensional sonic weaponry.[1754]

In the Ice Age around the year 5000, Findecker's discovery of the double-nexus particle had sent human technology into a cul-de-sac. Humans nonetheless developed limited psychic techniques such as the ability to read and to influence the weak-minded. Various Alliances governed the world.

The Peking Homunculus, an automaton with the cerebral cortex of a pig, was presented as a toy for the children of the commissioner of the Icelandic Alliance – but the pig component became dominant, and the Homunculus almost precipitated World War Six. The Supreme Alliance came to power, and horrific war crimes were committed. The Doctor was with the Filipino Army when it finally defeated the Alliance at the Battle of Reykjavik.

Magnus Greel – the Alliance's Minister of Justice,

and the infamous Butcher of Brisbane – had performed terrible scientific experiments on one hundred thousand prisoners in an attempt to discover time travel and immortality. He escaped to the nineteenth century using a beam of zygma energy, and feared Time Agents would pursue him.[1755]

The Doctor witnessed the sonic massacres in Brisbane.[1756] Greel's path through time was deflected when his zygma beam hit the TARDIS.[1757] A theme park on Earth's moon came to include a re-construction of the fiftieth century battle of Reykjavik. Other park features included the Western-themed High Moon, and the Land of the Rising Moon, where Samurai warriors fought ninjas.[1758]

5000 - EMOTIONAL CHEMISTRY[1759] -> Magnus Greel had been a Chinese national, part of the PacBloc regime. The PacBloc used anti-matter shells against opposing armies, but not on population centres, and deployed Stepperiders and Locust aircraft. The Alliance forces used Thor battle tanks and Fenrir reconnaissance tanks. An

---

1753 FP: In the Year of the Cat. This is intended as the background of Mr Sin from The Talons of Weng-Chiang, who is here referenced as "the Pig" automaton. For that reason, the Pig and his fellows originate from "three thousand years" after 1762.

1754 "Agent Provocateur". Captain Jack and River Song, natives of this time, both use sonic technology. The Hollow Men specifies one of Magnus Greel's atrocities (mentioned by the Doctor in The Talons of Weng-Chiang) as being "the sonic massacres in fifty-first century Brisbane".

1755 The Talons of Weng-Chiang. This happened "about the year five thousand" according to the Doctor; "the fifty-first" century according to Greel. The Doctor says he was with the Filipino army during their final advance. Note that World War Six is averted at this time, not fought, as some sources state.

Y5K: There are three television stories which establish versions of the state of Earth around the year 5000 which seem difficult to reconcile – The Ice Warriors, The Talons of Weng-Chiang and The Invisible Enemy. It's notable that those last two have the Doctor and Leela involved in events of the year 5000 in near-consecutive stories (only Horror of Fang Rock is between them) without any link being made.

From the details given in the stories, there's a way to reconcile them – The Invisible Enemy happens first, in "the year 5000" itself. It's a time where Earth has highly advanced technology and a rather sterile, computer-dependent society. The Ice Warriors depicts exactly the same sort of society. The Ice Warriors also suggests that the Ice Age has been around for a century of wintery weather – but goes on to claim that it's only recently

reached a crisis point, with glaciers threatening the imminent destruction of major cities. At the time of The Invisible Enemy, it's clearly not a pressing problem (no-one mentions the issue, and Marius is planning to return to Earth). But it might be a factor (or the factor) in the "breakout" – a mass emigration to other planets would ease population pressures on Earth.

After this, when the slowly-advancing ice starts encroaching on the temperate areas (in both hemispheres), the crisis seen in The Ice Warriors occurs. (This happens in an unknown year, but possibly later on in the year 5000 itself.) There is mass migration to the equator, and we see some people in that story have rejected the computer-controlled society for a more atavistic lifestyle. It's easy to imagine such a rigidly-controlled society collapsing very quickly if the computers started failing (or arguing with each other) – it might even happen in days. Society would be split in two – those heading off into space (the scientists), and the ones staying behind (the more atavistic).

An unregulated society with little scientific progress... is exactly what The Talons of Weng-Chiang tells us the world is like in Greel's time, "about the year 5000" and "the fifty-first century". Greel's a scientist – but clearly one who'd thrive better on the barbaric, individualistic Earth than on a regulated, sterile space station. Environmental collapse and warfare made the Earth a very hostile environment, as seen in Emotional Chemistry (towards the beginning of the process) and "The Keep" (ten years on).

Meanwhile, The Empty Child/The Doctor Dances tells us that humanity has spread across the galaxy. The Girl in the Fireplace shows us that, like the society seen in

Alliance division commanded by Razum Kinzhal stormed Greel's fortress and secured his Zygma technology. Using this, Kinzhal developed transit belts that let his agents roam time and secure possessions formerly owned by Kinzhal's beloved, Dusha.

Hostilities had increased between the PacBloc – led by one of Greel's lieutenants, Karsen Mogushestvo – and the Icelandic Alliance. The strategies of the Alliance's Lord General Razum Kinzhal devastated the PacBloc's air force. Kinzhal's forces further eliminated Mogushestvo's troops in Sverdlovsk, and overran Omsk.

Formerly a being known as a Magellan, Kinzhal sought to reunite with his other half, the nineteenth century Russian noblewoman Dusha. The eighth Doctor realised that such an act would obliterate Earth as the Magellan recorporalised. Kinzhal's assistant, Angel Malenkaya, was mortally wounded and offered herself as a host. The Doctor used the Misl Vremya device in 2024 to link this era with 1812, and thereby transferred Dusha's soul into Angel's body. Reunited with his love, Kinzhal considered reorganising his temporal paratroopers into "a unit for policing the past and preserving the future".

As part of these events, Trix stole a psionic weapon that Kinzhal had developed using enemy technology. However, she was forced to abandon it.

? 5000 - THE EVIL ONE[1760] **->** Inter-Galaxy Insurance was headquartered on the planet Sekkis.

Gigantic-class space liners used to transport the largest of the "indescribably rich" were increasingly plundered. The cadaverous Master, posing as Interplanetary Police Inspector Efendi, tried and failed to brainwash Leela into killing the fourth Doctor with a Janis thorn. The Doctor and Leela ended the raids, broke up the Master's partnership with the Solonis – a race of metallic praying mantises – and stopped his plan to upend the galactic economy.

The Older Nyssa and Magnus Greel

c 5002 - THE BUTCHER OF BRISBANE[1761] **->** The snow of the Second Ice Age now encompassed North America, Europe and as far as Tasmania in the south. Humanity had instigated a huge migration to its colony worlds; Earth itself "had little to offer" beyond being a gutted factory planet that processed raw materials from elsewhere, and was something of a dark spot at the heart of humanity's empire.

Dr Sa Yy Findecker's Zygma energy experiments created a Vortex breach that disrupted the TARDIS, and deposited the older Nyssa and Turlough on a frozen mountainside in Bhutan. Thousands of withered bodies had rained from the sky via Findecker's time portals from three years in the future. One such victim, Ragan Crezzen, knew Nyssa and Turlough's future selves, and died after telling them to seek out journalist Sasha Dialfa – as the travellers lacked ID tags, they officially wouldn't exist in this time. Dialfa and the editorial department of Earth Free Media aided Nyssa and Turlough with work placement while they awaited the fifth Doctor and Tegan to collect them.

Nyssa and Turlough trained in Reykjavik for a year, and first met Magnus Greel when he made an official visit to a hospital as part of his investment in medical research. They infiltrated Greel's inner circle, with Turlough serving as Nyssa's personal secretary, and so were positioned to provide intel to the Icelandic Alliance. After two more years, Nyssa and Greel were engaged.

c 5005 (May) - THE BUTCHER OF BRISBANE[1762] **->** Brisbane was now a wreck of a city, a "dead zone". Earth Free Media monitored Earth from the Correspondent's Club, a shrouded space station. The "credit" was a unit of currency in the Supreme Alliance of Eastern States. Guano dredgers sifted the rings of Saturn.

The Ice Warriors, people of this time clearly like reminders of the past along with their high-technology. And – as in the earlier story – when the technology fails, humanity doesn't last long.

1756 *The Hollow Men*, in the "fifty-first century".
1757 *The Shadow of Weng-Chiang*
1758 *Luna Romana*
1759 Dating *Emotional Chemistry* (EDA #66) - The date is given in the blurb, and is clearly tied in with *The Talons of Weng-Chiang*. It's left unclear as to whether the retasking Kinzhal proposes for his paratroopers (presuming it actually happens) leads to the founding of the Time Agents; *Talons* suggests that the Time Agency was active before this, otherwise Greel wouldn't worry about "Time Agents" following him. (Unless, perhaps, he'd previously encountered some from another era.) The psionic weapon surfaces in *Eater of Wasps*.

1760 Dating *The Evil One* (BF 4th Doc #3.4) - The Doctor states that gold was discontinued as a reserve currency in the twenty-first century, to which Calvert relies: "It's been back in fashion for as long as I can remember." Ultimately, this placement is a guess, based upon the name "Inter-Galaxy Insurance" suggesting that humankind has reached beyond the Milky Way.

1761 Dating *The Butcher of Brisbane* (BF #161) - Nyssa and Turlough arrive "three years" before the main part of the story.

1762 Dating *The Butcher of Brisbane* (BF #161) - This is the background of *The Talons of Weng-Chiang*, which stipulates that Mr Sin originates from "about the year 5000" and "nearly caused World War VI". No year is here given, but the Doctor tracks the Zygma beam's origin to "Earth in the fifty-first century", and Turlough claims to have learned the rules of "fifty-first century warfare"

Dr Sa Yy Findecker, an alien quantum physicist and cyborg-engineer serving as Magnus Greel's scientific adviser, had discovered the double-nexus particle: half of this existed inside our universe, and was complemented by a mirror nucleus outside space-time. Findecker experimented with Zygma energy, which was composed of double-nexus particles, to discover time travel. Human test subjects from Earth's colonies were sent via Zygma beam to three years in the past, so the results could be retrieved. Exposure to Zygma radiation disrupted Findecker's proteins, and he mechanically syphoned away his subjects' vitality to stay alive. The journalist Ragan Crezzen failed to assassinate Findecker, and was condemned by Greel – in one of the Supreme Alliance's Star Chambers – to the Zygma beam. His aged self arrived three years in the past.

The Icelandic Alliance sent a delegation to Peking to negotiate a new trade agreement with the Supreme Alliance of Eastern States. Greel, as the Supreme Alliance's Minister of Justice, welcomed Ingrid Bjarnsdottir, the Icelandic Commissioner. Findecker crafted a mechanical homunculus – a tumbler and performer named Mr Sin – that Greel gifted to Bjarnsdottir's children, but Mr Sin attacked Bjarnsdottir's son with a table fork and ran off.

The fifth Doctor and Tegan arrived in search of the older Nyssa and Turlough, even as Commissioner Eugene Duplessis discovered that Greel intended to stage a coup and take over the Supreme Alliance. A stymied Greel –

realising Nyssa had betrayed him – defected to Reykjavik, and offered the Icelandic Alliance the secret of time travel in exchange for asylum. Duplessis declared a state of war between the Supreme Alliance and the Icelanders; the Filipino Army (accompanied by the fourth Doctor) had been on maneuvers on the Siberian floes, but now advanced on Reykjavik and shelled it. Alaskan soldiers set up neutron blockades in the Arctic.

Sin killed Bjarnsdottir on Greel's orders. Findecker escaped in a time cabinet he'd built, but the fifth Doctor recalled it to Earth, knowing that it was part of Greel's historical fate. Greel had Sin murder Findecker, then fled with the homunculus in the cabinet into the past. The fifth Doctor contacted his previous self and advised him to halt the Phillipino Army, averting World War VI.

The fifth Doctor had passed himself off to Greel and Findecker as a Time Agent, and the words "Police Box" on the Doctor's time machine helped to convince them that the Time Agents represented the authorities.

c 5010 - "The Keep"[1763] -> The Sun began to fail. The great Metropolises fell and the rich deserted the Earth – they left for the stars in a fleet of space arks. Those who remained behind became desperate. Matter transmission was commonplace, and this development broke up the nation states and ushered in the Transmat Wars. The whole world became a battlefield.

while stuck in this time period. Nyssa's aide Kaori, a cybernetic spy for Findecker, recites a list of Nyssa's infractions against Greel starting on "May 4", and ending on "May 20". Although she's interrupted before finishing, it seems likely that *The Butcher of Brisbane* occurs in the same month.

Findecker's creation of Mr Sin is reasonably compatible with the claim in *FP: The Year of the Cat* that Sin was one of twelve such homunculi, as Findecker does seem a very ambitious and industrious type of mad scientist. While Greel does not appear in *Emotional Chemistry*, that book gives very different details concerning the geopolitical structure in which he lived.

1763 Dating "The Keep" (*DWM* #248-249) - It's "the fifty-first century", and the age of Magnus Greel. It's confirmed that the problem with the sun leads to the "solar flares" in "Wormwood".

1764 "Fire and Brimstone"

1765 *Borrowed Time*. The historical alteration is presumably undone when Blythe's scheme is nullified.

1766 Dating *Benny: The Vampire Curse*: "Possum Kingdom" (Benny collection #12b) - The year is given.

1767 "Fifteen years" (the blurb) before *Diamond Dogs*. Palmer is "23" (the Prologue) when the Ogron incident happens, a Captain when the story takes place.

1768 *Borrowed Time*

1769 Dating *Diamond Dogs* (NSA #61) - Bill picks up on the fact that it's "fifty-first century" (ch10), and during

the time of the Federation (*The Curse of Peladon* et al). An older sister of one of the participants (ch7) served as Professor Marius' nurse in *The Invisible Enemy* [5000]. More specifically, the Prologue flashes back "four years" to Frank Gammadoni, a Federation officer, reflecting upon "thirty-year-old memories" of a platform fire on Titan in 5012 – meaning, all told, it's now around 5046.

1770 "The Time Machination"

1771 Dating *Shroud of Sorrow* (NSA #53) - The Doctor says that Venofax is "400,000 light years away" from Earth and "in the 51st century." (p106)

1772 Dating *Big Bang Generation* (NSA #59) - It's the "fifty-first century" (chs. 1, 7, 13), and not long after Kik the Assassin tracks down con man Cyrrus Globb in "5066" (ch3). Likewise, Benny's friend Keri reads that the Aztec Moon exploded "somewhere around 5064" (ch7). The century was doubtless chosen to accommodate Stormcage turning down a request to let River Song advise on the Aztec Moon situation (ch1) – a parallel to writer Gary Russell asking Steven Moffat if he could include River in this book, and Moffat suggesting he use Benny instead. However, the hard dates given in *Let's Kill Hitler* [5123] and *The Pandorica Opens* [5145] establish River's era as the fifty-*second* century, meaning these events happen too early for her incarceration at Stormcage (see the Dating River Song is a Complicated Business sidebar). Mention of Colonel Octavian means that it's before his death in *Flesh and*

Ten years into the Transmat Wars, the eighth Doctor and Izzy followed an SOS in the Vortex. They were captured by Uber-Marshal Hsui Leng of Greel's army, who believed they hailed from a structure named the Keep, and that they could help him secure the "treasure" within.

The Doctor and Izzy were transmatted inside the Keep by an android called Marquez. He served the greatest scientist of the age, the shrivelled Crivello, who had built an artificial sun – the Cauldron – to become the centrepiece of a new solar system for humanity in the Crab Nebula. The Cauldron was alive, and required a living conduit to achieve fusion and launch itself – only the Doctor, as a time traveller, was able to communicate with the Cauldron and survive. He did so, and the Cauldron headed out to the Crab Nebula, promising a new life for those that followed. After the Doctor departed, Marquez killed Crivello.

Marquez was actually a Dalek construct, and was trying to help his masters secure the Cauldron. The Daleks needed the artificial sun to fight spider-Daleks from a parallel universe. Work on the Cauldron had been secretly funded by the Threshold, as part of a plan to eliminate the Daleks' war fleet.[1764]

Paper magazines still existed in the year 5013. For a time, it was fashionable to print them on edible, vitamin-rich paper that was flavoured with the saliva of the author.

Professor Henrietta Nwokolo and her team at Aberdeen University were honoured for their innovations, including the Super Infinite Cosmic Battery.

> (=) Jane Blythe's time commodity scheme in 2007 diminished Earth's future and Nwokolo's accomplishment, meaning that a professor at Tokyo University was given the Buffet Prize for inventing a less-effective cosmic-power battery.[1765]

5019 - BENNY: THE VAMPIRE CURSE: "Possum Kingdom"[1766] -> A salvage crew found the starship with the last of the vampiric Utlunta, Lilu, in orbit near Bathory's Star. Lilu escaped into history by booking passage with Yesterways, Ltd., a time travel company embarking on a "The V is for Vampire" tour of different Earth eras.

The human empire and the Cancri collaborated to harvest diamonds from Saturn. Laura Palmer graduated from the Federation Academy with Honours, having dealt with an Ogron attack on a grain shuttle headed to the Davy Crockett colony, the Sirius-B System.[1767]

The Super Lucky Romance Camera was invented on Earth in 5044, and was used on more than thirty planets. People could use such devices to extend their holidays by placing themselves in time bubbles.[1768]

c 5046 - DIAMOND DOGS[1769] -> The COMmunication Relay And Data Examination (COM-RADE) system relayed millions of messages between Earth and its environs, and sent alerts to the Federation Security Mainframe in Manhattan. Ganymede and Mars had shipyards; the latter was home to the Olympus Mons Casino. The Terran empire developed gravity-tasers, to avoid use of projectile weapons in pressurised environments.

Repeated attempts to mine diamonds from Saturn had cost hundreds of lives. The Cancri, a race from beyond Cygnus-A, supplied Earth with gravity inverters which allowed humanity to harvest diamonds produced through ionisation of the planet's upper atmosphere. Such diamonds became the empire's financial lifeblood, fuelling its expansion. Covertly, the Cancri used their share of the diamonds to fashion carbon focusing arrays, and prosecute a war against fluid beings, the Ba-El Cratt.

The twelfth Doctor and Bill were present as the Ba-El Cratt turned their attention to Saturn. Space raiders were diverted to destroy a Ba-El incursion vessel, which loosed millions of diamonds around Saturn and formed a new ring. With disclosure of the diamonds' role in the Cancri-Ba-El war, the Federation was expected to strengthen its borders and gather intelligence on the Ba-El homeworld, rather than lose such a valuable revenue stream.

In the mid-fifty-first century, "Jonathan Smith", a member of the Supreme Alliance, repaired the Zygma Beam and travelled to 1889 to try to prevent the death of Magnus Greel.[1770]

c 5050 - SHROUD OF SORROW[1771] -> The long-extinct Venofaxons lived on a world covered in a bubble-bath sea. The eleventh Doctor and Clara saved Professor Penelope Holroyde and her archaeological team as they tried to drain the sea and excavate its Ocean Peninsula. Afterward, the TARDIS was pulled off course to 1963.

The Doctor and Clara returned to seek Holroyde's help – and that of her ship, a Class 2 exploration cruiser/planethopper, the SS *Howard Carter* – in connecting together the two ends of a living wormhole, the Shroud.

> (=) c 5066 - BIG BANG GENERATION[1772] -> Professor Horace Jaanson's expedition to the Pyramid Eternia on the Aztec Moon caused a copy of its lodestone to draw Bernice Summerfield, Peter Summerfield, Ruth and Jack to the fifty-first century. Benny's quartet found their future selves trapped in a time eddy inside the pyramid, and replaced their future selves by touching them, thereby shorting out the effect. The Pyramid was drawn back to twenty-first century Australia, taking Benny's group with it. The Aztec Moon exploded in their absence, but events in 2015 annulled these events.

A young girl, Charlotte Abigail Lux, was dying – and so her family turned an entire planet into a library to keep her occupied. The planet's core was the largest index computer and hard drive ever built, and Charlotte's mind was deposited inside it. The world became known as simply The Library – it contained every book ever written, and had "whole continents of Jeffrey Archer, Bridget Jones, Monty Python's *Big Red Book*" and more.

The books in the library were made from forests inhabited by the Vashta Nerada: microspores that lived in darkness, and fed off meat. They were on most inhabited worlds, and had endowed nearly every species with a fear of the dark. The Vashta Nerada in the Library books swarmed, and so the central computer teleported out the four thousand and twenty-two patrons in the Library. With nowhere to send the patrons, the computer digitally saved them on the planet's hard drive. The last outgoing message from the Library read, "The lights are going out", and then the planet was sealed. It took the Lux family three generations to find a way back in.[1773]

A dormant Weeping Angel was found in the ruins of Razbahan, and was kept in private hands.[1774]

Captain Jack Harkness

The man who would later become known as Captain Jack Harkness[1775] was a Time Agent in the fifty-first century. He lived on the Boshane Peninsula.[1776] Captain Jack's real name was Javic Piotr Thane.[1777]

TW: ADAM[1778] -> An unnamed race of howling aliens routinely passed by Jack's hometown – but one day, when he was an adolescent, they besieged it. Jack's father, Franklin, was killed while searching for Jack's

Stone (ch3). The Church of the Papal Mainframe (*The Time of the Doctor*, dated to ? 5100) handles security on the Aztec Moon (ch3).

1773 "One hundred years" before *Silence in the Library/Forest of the Dead*.

1774 The end of the century prior to *The Time of Angels*.

1775 It's established in *TW: Captain Jack Harkness* that he adopted a false identity.

1776 *The Doctor Dances* first established that Jack is from the fifty-first century; the Boshane Peninsula is referenced in *Last of the Time Lords* and *TW: Adam*.

1777 *Jack: Month 25*

1778 Dating *TW: Adam* (TW 2.5) - No year given. The placement in *Ahistory* Third Edition to c.5084 was roughly derived from a) actor Jack Montgomery being 15 when he played Jack in *Adam*, and b) John Hart's comment that Jack – presumably as an adult – was "Rear of the Year, 5094". However, there's no way of specifying how much time passed for Jack in-between the two, and *TW: "Station Zero"* shows an adult Jack working for the Time Agency in 5067 (not that his work for a time-travelling organisation couldn't happen out of synch, but concurrent with, his lifetime).

1779 *TW: Miracle Day*

1780 *TW: Captain Jack Harkness*. The identity of his captors hasn't been revealed.

1781 *Last of the Time Lords, TW: Adam*. The clear implication is that immortal Jack will eventually transform into the Face of Boe, who was first seen in *The End of the World*. Those wishing to overlook this possibility often suggest that it could have just as easily been a punning nickname that Jack acquired because there was already a famous Face of Boe in his native era. Or, of course, both could be true.

There is no Boshane Peninsula on present day Earth. That said, it's a safe bet that some place names on Earth will change in the next three thousand years, particularly if various floods, ice ages, solar flares and other incidents create new geographical features. There's never been any explicit confirmation that Jack grew up on Earth rather than another planet colonised by humans. Wherever the Boeshane Peninsula is, the people there speak with American accents.

1782 According to Jack in *TW: Fragments*.

1783 *TW: Exodus Code* (ch57).

1784 *Jack: Wednesdays for Beginners*

1785 *TW: Kiss Kiss, Bang Bang, TW: Exit Wounds*. This could happen as a result of Jack time jumping, rather than the normal progression of his life.

1786 Dating *TW: "Station Zero"* (Titan *TW* #2.1-2.4) - A caption names the year. Even though Captain Jack and John Hart go back in time to Mogar's destruction, that too occurs in the "fifty-first century". Mogar is called "the home of the Vervoids" – it assuredly wasn't in *Terror of the Vervoids*, and we're not told what became of the native Mogarians seen in that story. The Mogar expedition is cited as one of Jack's "first missions as a Time Agent".

1787 *TW: "Station Zero"*

1788 *The Ninth Doctor Year One*: "Secret Agent Man". The Magorians are orange-skinned humanoids, not to be confused with the Mogarians from *Terror of the Vervoids*.

1789 "Weapons of Past Destruction"

1790 *TW: The Conspiracy*

1791 *TW: Aliens Among Us*

1792 Dating *Jack: Month 25* (BF *The Lives of Captain Jack* #1.4) - Much of Captain Jack's background is here revealed, including the details about his missing two years of memories (mentioned in *The Doctor Dances*, but never explained on screen), and the end of his service with the Time Agency. The organisation must survive without its Council, having been made to forget it

mother. Jack lost his grip on his younger brother Gray in the chaos, and, unable to face his mother afterwards, ran away. He fruitlessly spent years searching for his missing brother.

As an adult, Jack still didn't know his mother's fate.[1779] When Jack was young, he convinced a friend to go off with him to fight "the worst creatures imaginable", but they were captured and tortured. His friend was killed for being the weaker of the two.[1780] Jack was the first person from the Boshane Peninsula to join the Time Agency. He became a poster boy for the organisation, and was known as "the Face of Boe".[1781]

The people of the fifty-first century, including Captain Jack, had pheromones far more potent than people from the twenty-first.[1782] Captain Jack's fifty-first century DNA contained less of a dichotomy between male and female chromosomes. Jack theorized that the Helix Intelligence within Earth had a self-termination date of the fifty-first century, but that his presence in Earth's morphic field caused its demise to begin much sooner, in the twentieth century.[1783]

At some point, Jack worked as a waiter on Richworld Alpha, and had to tune, daily, each piece of cutlery to a particular note.[1784]

Jack as a Time Agent

The Time Agency partnered Jack with Captain John Hart, as it was thought that Jack could "control" him. They were once trapped in a time bubble together for five years.[1785]

5067 - TW: "Station Zero"[1786] -> Although fairly new to Time Agency, Jack Harkness and John Hart had already been imprisoned for breaking most, if not all, of its personal protocols. They received a commuted sentence, in exchange for their going back to learn the cause of the planet Mogar's destruction. They did so, then fled as the Navigators – human-Vervoid hybrids – plundered their own world's energy to fuel their world-destroyer, the Opsolarium. The ship went back to the twenty-first century, so the Navigators would attack humanity when it was more vulnerable.

The winged Docilius, an instructor of Jack and John at the Academy, later allied with the Navigators. Lady Karina (later Karina Sterling), a Time Agent from the Gelidus Galaxy, was sent to the prison planet Contrelli for counterfeiting proton blasters. She escaped, acquired a TARDIS knock-off, and would encounter Jack Harkness and John Hart in the twenty-first century.[1787]

As a Time Agent, Jack punched the Magorian Ambassador during a fancy party, and made off with cuff-links containing the plans for a Pulsar Manipulator... he fought a Malevilus in the Wild West... he and John Hart encountered a clutch of Weeping Angels... he erased the scientist Zloy Voth from time, to prevent him from inventing time travel for all.[1788] Jack visited the Fluren Temporal Bazaar as a Time Agent, and lost out on a like-new Monstrom Time Destroyer to a pair of Wrightosaur mercenaries.[1789] While a Time Agent, Jack worked as an Enabler for the Committee, and failed to stop them from targeting the Milky Way.[1790]

To Captain Jack's frustration, the manual to his vortex manipulator was written in Korean.[1791]

Jack Loses Two Years' Worth of Memories

JACK: MONTH 25[1792] -> The young Time Agent Javic Piotr Thane, later known as Captain Jack Harkness, reported directly to the Time Agency's chief: Maglin Shank. Fellow Agent Krim Pollensa was his best friend. Penalties for disobedient Time Agents included being stranded in the Cretaceous Period or worse. The Agency's paradox crews worked to resolve discontinuity pockets, or cauterise them into bubble universes. Agency operatives included Crank, Limehouse and Bramley, a former security chief. An open case involving the Shubert Conclave went cold when a potential source, Balthazar Frenk, hid in his fridge and didn't make it out alive.

The Time Agency's ruling Council tired of being temporal policemen, and believed they could manipulate history to position themselves as the Masters of All Time and Space. Thane became their covert assassin, and also used outlawed technology to separate the Council's base of operations, the Agency's 113th Floor, into a bubble reality. When the time was right, the Council would emerge to rule a new timeline. The Council repeatedly wiped Thane's memories of his work for them.

A future version of Thane convinced his younger self that he'd already aged two years in the Council's service without knowing it. As the Agency's vortex manipulators cancelled out the Blinovitch Limitation Effect, Thane spent a night of passion with himself. The older Thane provided his younger self and Pollensa with a device to summon the Harvesters: creatures that fed upon unique individuals in history. The Harvesters duly consumed the Council, and the Thanes disconnected the 113th Floor's link with reality.

To keep the timelines pure, the younger Thane dosed himself and his future self with Retcon, then suggested they enjoy an evening they literally wouldn't remember the next day.

Jack awoke one morning while still in the Time Agents' employ and found two years of his memories were missing. He eventually acquired a Chula warship and took up trying to con his former colleagues. Jack came to own a sonic blaster/cannon/disruptor fitted with digital removal and rewind, and which was made at the weapons factories at Villengard. The Doctor visited the weapons factories, leading to an incident where the main reactor went critical. The summer groves of Villengard, which produced bananas, took to growing in the factories' place.

By this point, humanity had spread out across half the galaxy, and had commenced "dancing" with many species.[1793]

5087 - BORROWED TIME[1794] -> Amy and Rory enjoyed a brief holiday on Earth until the eleventh Doctor collected them. Earth's cities had all been documented. New York had an Ascendancy Tower. Tourists could visit the beaches of Old Tokyo.

Captain Jack was dubbed "Rear of the Year, 5094".[1795] This era was the native time of Time Agents Kala, Jode and Fatboy; the eighth Doctor met them in Marpling in 1932. They could time travel using a temporal transduction beam.[1796] Cara, a Time Agent in the fifty-first century, was assigned to track down Magnus Greel. As her vortex manipulator was leaking chronoplasm, she would arrive in Victorian London years after him.[1797]

The 28-year-old Merrit OhOne, code-name Guy Taylor, worked for the Time Agency in the fifty-second century. He operated time capsules Grade 4 and below – all made before miniaturisation technology brought about the advent of vortex manipulators – and was authorised to travel thirty millennia into the future and the past. He kept a keepsake in his time machine: the Gallifreyan hypercube given to him by his father, Captain OhOne. Taylor left to investigate a temporal anomaly in 2013, but his time capsule chrono-collided with a duplicate of itself bearing the eleventh Doctor and Alice Watson to the Creevix's domain. The event enabled the Creevix to retroactively wipe Taylor from history and enter our universe through the resultant gap. The Doctor coordinated ten of his former selves to bring about Taylor's conception, restoring his timeline.[1798]

The Time Agency was eventually shut down; John Hart later told Jack Harkness that there were "only seven of us left now".[1799] At some point, the Intergalactic Defense League (IGDL, a.k.a. the reconstructed Time Agency) was founded.[1800]

John Hart found Jack's now-adult brother Gray surrounded by corpses, and chained to the ruins of a city in the Bedla Mountains. Gray was the only survivor, and had gone mad owing to the torture he'd received. He forced Hart to help him exact vengeance on Jack in

existed. John Hart reports the group as defunct in *TW: Kiss Kiss, Bang Bang*.
1793 *The Empty Child/The Doctor Dances*. The latter states Jack is from the fifty-first century.
1794 Dating *Borrowed Time* (NSA #49) - The year is given (p26).
1795 *TW: Kiss Kiss, Bang Bang*
1796 *Eater of Wasps*. The trio hails from "three thousand years" after 1932, but it's after *Emotional Chemistry*, so Kala is rounding up. They are presumably working for the same Agency as Captain Jack.
1797 *J&L* S13: *The Stuff of Nightmares*
1798 *DotD: The Time Machine*
1799 *TW: Kiss Kiss, Bang Bang*
1800 *TW:* "Station Zero"
1801 The backstory to *TW: Fragments, TW: Exit Wounds*.
1802 Apparently around twenty years before *A Good Man Goes to War*.
1803 "Many thousands of years" after *DotD: Trouble in Paradise*. Humans have developed time technology, suggesting it's the era of Captain Jack and River Song. Buffalo still exist, but in greatly reduced numbers – *The Also People* says the buffalo went extinct in 2193, but *Trading Futures* suggests that rhinos endure owing to clonetivity. It's possible that a few buffalo survived to this era through similar means.
1804 Six hundred years after *Tomb of Valdemar*, according to the Doctor.
1805 "Fifty years" before *Rhythm of Destruction*.
1806 Dating *Revenge of the Swarm* (BF #189) - It's "two

hundred years" in the future of the TARDIS' previous location in 4920.
1807 Dating "The Dragon Lord" (*DWM* #494-495) - Date unknown, but one of Lord Mortigan's technicians, Weezie, attended Lunar University (*Let's Kill Hitler*, 5123).
1808 "Thirty-seven years" before *Rhythm of Destruction*.
1809 DATING RIVER SONG IS A COMPLICATED BUSINESS: The Doctor refers to River Song's native time – in other words, when she attends university and is later confined to Stormcage – as "the fifty-first century" on two occasions (in *Silence in the Library* and *The Time of the Angels*). However, the two instances when we're given specific dates regarding River's home era (*Let's Kill Hitler*, 5123; *The Pandorica Opens*, 5145) occur in stories that chronologically take place before the Doctor's remarks, and happen in the fifty-*second* century. This contradiction would perhaps be more irritating, were it not so emblematic of River's history being even more complicated than it first appears.

The shorthand where River and the Doctor are concerned is that they meet in reverse order... the Doctor first meets River (from his point of view) when she dies (in *Silence in the Library/Forest of the Dead*), and she looks "younger" each subsequent time they meet up (with a line in *Let's Kill Hitler* explaining that she plays with her appearance). River broadly confirms in *The Impossible Astronaut* that she and the Doctor meet in reverse order ("It's all back to front. My past is his future. We're travelling in opposite directions. Every time we meet, I know him more and he knows me less."), and

the twenty-first century.[1801]

When Lorna Bucket was a child, she met the Doctor in the Heaven-neutral, normally uneventful Gamma Forests. He said "run" a lot, and they ran together. The event inspired her to join the military arm of the Church in the hope of meeting him again. To the people of the Gamma Forests, the word "doctor" came to mean "mighty warrior".[1802]

Bovin the Herd-Leader awoke from his icy imprisonment, and found that the number of surviving buffalo was too small to achieve the gestalt needed to regain supremacy of Earth. He copied human time technology, and went back to the fifteenth century to better the buffalo's prospects by causing the European settlement of the Americas.[1803] The principles of atmospheric flotation were discovered.[1804]

The Rhodellans inflicted massive casualties upon their rivals, the Drydd, after the Doctor failed to negotiate a peace between them. The daughter of the disgraced Drydd leader, Jamelia Varigast, became a peace envoy hell-bent upon revenge on him.[1805]

c 5120 - REVENGE OF THE SWARM[1806] -> The Bi-Al Foundation had now been repurposed as a relay station for the Hypernet, which facilitated near-instantaneous communication via hyperspace using quantum entanglement. The Hypernet serviced 100,000 systems, and was crucial to the human empire.

The surviving clone of the Nucleus of the Swarm took possession of Hector Thomas, and directed the TARDIS to this era. The Nucleus clone uploaded itself into the Hypernet, then used the TARDIS' relative dimensional stabiliser to bleed off the Hypernet's energy as it manifested physically, swelling to become larger than an asteroid. Unstopped, the Nucleus would become larger than a galaxy, reproduce and become the sole intellect in creation.

The seventh Doctor weakened the Nucleus with the antibody his fourth self had acquired, and Ace obliterated the Nucleus' physical form with an exploding shuttle. Afterwards, the Doctor elected to take Hector and Ace somewhere fun, and set course for Athens, 421 BC.

c 5123 - "The Dragon Lord"[1807] -> Colonists on an unnamed world enslaved the indigenous dragons, and crafted a society with Medieval trappings and space-age technology. The Dragon Lord burnt out the dragons' inhibitor chips and set them free, but was then slain. The twelfth Doctor, travelling with Clara, contained the situation but thought this world's "heroes" had become selfish and stupid. He summoned a rescue ship for the colonists, and gave the dragons their world back.

Rifts in Time, actual demigods who performed electric rock, disbanded.[1808]

River Song[1809]

The Trenzalore Crisis: Start of the Eleventh Doctor Living for a Millennium in the Human Colony of Christmas

? 5100 (July) - THE TIME OF THE DOCTOR[1810] -> Even after the Doctor had rebooted the universe during the Pandorica crisis, a Crack in Time remained on the planet Trenzalore. The Time Lords on Gallifrey sought to re-enter our universe via the Crack, but first broadcast a signal to the whole of history asking the question "Doctor who?" They also established a truth field around Trenzalore; if the Doctor answered the question by saying aloud his real name, the Time Lords would deem it safe for Gallifrey to return.

Trenzalore had become home to a Level Two human

---

the ending of *Day of the Moon* depends upon it. In that story, the Doctor kisses River for what to him is the "first time", and River becomes alarmed that for her, this means it'll be the final time.

The idea that River and the Doctor always meet in *exactly* reverse order starts to crumble once it's considered that if that were true, why do they compare diaries to determine where they are in each others' lifetimes? An exact reverse order would mean that River, at least, would always *know* the order of their meet-ups without having to ask. Perhaps she's just playing along, but this risks the Doctor hearing spoilers about the future. It becomes all the harder to rationalise in instances such as her asking in *Silence of the Library* if the Doctor has experienced the crash of the *Byzantium* (*The Time of Angels*), when exact reverse order would dictate that of course he hasn't. In fact, there are so many excep-

tions to the "reverse order rule" (the most glaring being that the Doctor, Amy and Rory are present when the Alex Kingston incarnation of River is "born" in *Let's Kill Hitler*, only to encounter her older self after that point – and also that River meets the twelfth Doctor in *The Husbands of River Song*, after all her adventures with the eleventh), a more accurate way of putting it would be, "River and the Doctor encounter each other in reverse order... except for all the occasions that they don't."

A looming question that never gets answered is why they're meeting in reverse order *at all*, as if someone or some thing is trying (however imperfectly) to actually make their meet-ups run back-to-front. One possibility goes to a theory mooted in *About Time* – that in classic *Doctor Who*, the TARDISes of Time Lords such as the Doctor, the Master, the Rani, etc., coordinate things so that their pilots keep meeting each other in chrono-

colony named Christmas. Warfleets of Daleks, Sontarans, Terileptils, Slitheen and other parties with a vested interest in preventing the Time Lords' restoration responded to the signal and converged on Trenzalore. The Church of the Papal Mainframe, a security organization that had engineered the Silents – confessional priests whose congregants forgot ever meeting with them – was first on the scene and blockaded the planet. The Mainframe's Mother Superious, Tasha Lem, allowed the eleventh Doctor and Clara through the blockade to learn more.

The Doctor realised that if the Time Lords returned, the opposing alien races would attack, re-starting the Time War. A stalemate ensued, with the Doctor unable to leave, but the warfleets holding back for fear he might speak his name aloud. Unwilling to let Clara live out her life on Trenzalore, the Doctor pre-programmed the TARDIS to take her home to the twenty-first century and return for him. Clara's attempt to re-enter the Ship derailed its return journey; it wouldn't re-appear on Trenzalore for three hundred years.

Creation and Splintering of the Silence

Tasha Lem declared the official start of the Siege of Trenzalore, and issued the Papal Mainframe with an unscheduled faith change. From this moment, the Mainframe would devote itself to the silence of the Doctor not speaking his name, lest war ensue.

In the following centuries, the Kovarian Chapter split from the Papal Mainframe and pursued its own agenda to silence the Doctor. Lam's group maintained the Trenzalore blockade, but the pro-active Kovarians hoped to prevent the Doctor from ever reaching Trenzalore. They raised River Song as an assassin and blew up the TARDIS in 2010 – paradoxically creating the Cracks in Time that led to the Trenzalore crisis.

The movement known as the Silence and Academy of the Question, allied with the military forces of the Church (the Clerics) and the Headless Monks, believed that on the fields of Trenzalore at the fall of the Eleventh, when any living creature present must answer truly, a question that should never, ever be answered would be asked... and that silence would

---

logical order. Perhaps such protocols are rent asunder following the obliteration of Gallifrey and the Time Lords prior to New *Who*, making the psuedo-reverse means by which the Doctor and River keep meeting better than nothing.

For the Doctor (and the audience), his meet-ups with River are: *Silence in the Library/Forest of the Dead*; *The Time of Angels/Flesh and Stone*; *The Pandorica Opens/The Big Bang*; *The Impossible Astronaut/Day of the Moon* (909-year-old Doctor); *A Good Man Goes to War*; *Let's Kill Hitler*; *The Wedding of River Song* (1103-year-old Doctor) and, by extension, *The Impossible Astronaut* again; *The Angels Take Manhattan*; *The Name of the Doctor* (River's digital self); and *The Husbands of River Song*.

It is usually not specified exactly how many years pass between the Doctor and River's encounters in either her home era or elsewhere. As River is a human-Time Lord hybrid with a more malleable appearance (per *Let's Kill Hitler*), the time between their encounters is doubly indeterminate.

It should also be noted that Captain Jack Harkness hails from the late 5000s and so is a rough contemporary of River, but we've no record of their meeting one another. In *Silence in the Library/Forest of the Dead*, River has a squareness gun identical to Jack's (although it's entirely possible that she found Jack's old gun in the TARDIS), and *The Pandorica Opens* has her buying a time travel-enabling vortex manipulator that's "fresh from the [severed] wrist of a handsome Time Agent" (not that said handsome agent is necessarily Jack himself).

Timelink dated *Silence in the Library/Forest of the*

Dead to 5008, but saw print before it could take River's appearances in Series 5 and 6 into consideration.

1810 Dating *The Time of the Doctor* (X7.16) - This is the origin of the branch of the Silence that tangles with the Doctor in Series 5 and 6, and is responsible for River Song's upbringing as a living weapon to kill him (see especially *The Impossible Astronaut/Day of the Moon* and *A Good Man Goes to War*). No year given, but the month is named as "July".

The Silence is time-active, so it can't be assumed that events on Trenzalore occur prior to River's native era. Nonetheless, without more evidence to go on, it seems best – for the sake of narrative clarity, if nothing else – to place the start of the Siege of Trenzalore before River's relocation to the fifty-first century (in 5123; *Let's Kill Hitler*) and count upward from there.

1811 The background to much of Series 5 and 6, as given in *The Wedding of River Song* and *The Time of the Doctor*.

1812 "The Lost Dimension"

1813 Dating *Let's Kill Hitler* (X6.8) - The date River starts university is given in a caption. Professor Candy, who is named in the credits, first appeared in the short story "Continuity Errors" (also by Steven Moffat) and is mentioned in *Benny: Oh No It Isn't*!

1814 Or so she says in *DC 4: Songs of Love*.

1815 Dating *Closing Time* (X6.12) - No date is given, but as River has been awarded her doctorate, it's at least several years since we last saw her in *Let's Kill Hitler*.

1816 After *Closing Time* and before *A Good Man Goes to War*. It's not entirely clear how this came to pass, as it looks like River is convicted and imprisoned for the

fall.[1811] Tasha Lem's barrier prevented Jenny from contacting the Doctor on Trenzalore.[1812]

River Song Relocates to This Era

5123 - LET'S KILL HITLER[1813] -> The eleventh Doctor, Amy and Rory took the newly regenerated River Song to the Sisters of the Infinite Schism, the "greatest hospital in the universe", to recover from the events of 1938. The Doctor left River a TARDIS-patterned, blank diary in which she would record her adventures. River recovered after the TARDIS had departed, and enrolled in Luna University to study archaeology under Professor Candy. The profession enabled her to uncover clues about the Doctor.

River worked hard "for several afternoons" to gain her Luna University qualification.[1814]

The Silence Conscript River as an Assassin; River Marries and Murders the Doctor, is Incarcerated at Stormcage

CLOSING TIME / THE WEDDING OF RIVER SONG[1815] -> The day River was awarded her doctorate, she read the account of children who saw the Doctor prior to his meeting his death at Lake Silencio in 2011. Madame Kovarian, the Silence and the Clerics overpowered River and placed her in an augmented NASA astronaut suit. They then took her back to Lake Silencio, to kill the Doctor as history dictated. River returned to this era after she had married the Doctor.

River Song was imprisoned in the Stormcage Containment Facility for murder.[1816]

NIGHT AND THE DOCTOR: "First Night"[1817] -> River was on the first night of her imprisonment at Stormcage, when the eleventh Doctor dropped by to take her to Calderon Beta in 2360. He emphasized the need for her to keep diary so the two of them could better determine when they were encountering one another. She also decided to appropriate a phrase the Doctor used, "spoilers", into her parlance.

The Daleks had records of River Song, and knew that she was not merciful.[1818] River dated a Nestene duplicate with a swappable head.[1819] She learned how to fly the TARDIS.[1820]

River Gains Her Own Vortex Manipulator

5145 - THE PANDORICA OPENS[1821] -> The TARDIS forwarded a call from Winston Churchill to River Song in Stormcage. He told her about the Vincent van Gogh painting *The Pandorica Opens*, and so she escaped and stole it from the Royal Collection aboard Starship UK. Liz X stopped River, but let her go when she understood that the Doctor was involved. River then travelled to a bar, the Maldovarium, and acquired a vortex manipulator "fresh from the wrist of a handsome Time Agent" from the bar owner, Dorium Maldovar. She used this to travel first to Planet One, then – based upon the date and map reference that Vincent included in the painting – Rome in 120 AD.

River returned to Stormcage after going to 2010 to spur Amy's memory of the Doctor, which restored him to life after he had sealed the Cracks in Time.[1822]

Five years into her sentence at Stormcage, River ventured out for a bit, managed to insult some Sontarans and fled from them to where the TARDIS was parked on Calderon Beta in 2360. The eleventh Doctor triggered River's vortex manipulator to send her back to Stormcage, despite her protests that such a transference always made her hair frizzy.[1823]

Doctor's murder by the Clerics – the same organisation that helped to train and task her with killing him in the first place. That said, different factions within the Clerics might be working to different ends – by *The Time of Angels*, Father Octavian and his Clerics are not only willing to involve the Doctor in their affairs, Octavian blatantly draws the Doctor's attention to the murder (namely, his own) that River committed.

1817 Dating *Night and the Doctor: "First Night"* (Series 6 DVD minisode) - It's the first of many of the Doctor and River's private outings while she's locked up at Stormcage.

1818 *The Big Bang*

1819 Before *The Big Bang*, as further detailed in *The Legends of River Song*: "Suspicious Minds".

1820 She can adeptly fly the Ship (in her timeline) no later than *The Pandorica Opens*. River says (*The Time of Angels*) that she had TARDIS-flying lessons from "the very best" and that it was a "shame" the Doctor was busy that day, but yells "You taught me!" at the Doctor in *The Pandorica Opens*. In *Let's Kill Hitler*, the TARDIS itself teaches River how to pilot it.

1821 Dating *The Pandorica Opens* (X5.12) - The date is given in three captions. River and the Doctor seem to be married by now, as implied by her impish conversation with him at the end of *The Big Bang*.

1822 In unknown circumstances between (from River's point of view) *The Big Bang* and *The Time of Angels*.

1823 *Night and the Doctor: "First Night"/"Last Night"*. The Doctor refers to this River as "Doctor Song" – possibly a slip of the tongue on his part, as she doesn't

The Silence learned that Amy Pond was pregnant, and determined that if she and Rory Williams conceived the child while travelling in the TARDIS, the child might have some Time Lord attributes – meaning it could be turned into a weapon. The pregnant Amy was kidnapped from another time zone, replaced with a Ganger duplicate and taken to an asteroid fortress: Demons Run. While Madame Kovarian kept watch over Amy's gestation, Amy's mind interacted with her Ganger duplicate – and remained unaware that she had been abducted.[1824]

The Battle of Demons Run

Amy Gives Birth to River Song

THE REBEL FLESH / A GOOD MAN GOES TO WAR[1825] -> The eleventh Doctor severed the connection between Amy and her Ganger. Amy awoke at Demons Run and gave birth to a daughter, whom she named "Melody" after her best friend Mels.[1826]

"Demons run when a good man goes to war; Night will fall and drown the sun; When a good man goes to war; Friendship dies and true love lies; Night will fall and the dark will rise; When a good man goes to war; Demons run, but count the cost; The battle's won, but the child is lost; When a good man goes to war."

The eleventh Doctor and Rory narrowed down Amy's location, and visited the Twelfth Cyber Legion because it monitored that quadrant of the galaxy. The Doctor destroyed part of the fleet, and the Cybermen revealled the location of Demons Run. To help save Amy, the Doctor and Rory recruited people who owed the Doctor a debt: Madame Vastra and Jenny, Commander Strax, the World War II pilot Danny Boy, the information broker Dorium Maldovar, space-pirates Captain Avery and Toby, as well as squads of Judoon and Silurians.

The Doctor provoked such in-fighting among his opponents that he swiftly took control of Demons Run and routed the Clerics. He and Rory rescued Amy and met the newborn Melody. The Headless Monks eluded detection and counter-attacked, decapitating Dorium and killing Strax and the Cleric named Lorna Bucket – who had come to warn the Doctor of the danger. Kovarian escaped with the infant Melody.

River Song appeared in the battle's aftermath, and revealed to the Doctor, Amy and Rory that she was the adult Melody Pond. In the language of the people of the Gamma Forests – which had no ponds – "Melody Pond" translated as "River Song". The Doctor departed with new confidence that he could defeat Kovarian, leaving River to return his allies home.

The Silence took Melody to Earth, the 1960s, so she could be raised in a human-norm environment.[1827] As a result of her imprisonment at Demons Run, Amy was left unable to have children.[1828]

THE BATTLE OF DEMONS RUN: TWO DAYS LATER[1829] -> Madame Vastra and Jenny aided Strax in healing his wounds. Two days after the Battle of Demons Run, he awoke – still alive, much to his sur-

---

become a professor until after leaving Stormcage (*The Time of Angels*) – although it's a little unclear as to when exactly she attains her doctorate.
1824 At some point prior to *The Impossible Astronaut*, as revealed in *The Rebel Flesh* and *A Good Man Goes to War*.
1825 Dating *The Rebel Flesh* and *A Good Man Goes to War* (X6.6-6.7) - No firm date is given, but Dorium's presence (he was last seen in *The Pandorica Opens*) suggests that this is River Song's "native time". It's a bit of an oddity that River is born after her adult self has been confined to Stormcage, but it's no more strange than so many other things about her. The River who appears at Demons Run can independently travel in time; for all we're told, she only gains the vortex manipulator that lets her do so in *The Pandorica Opens*. The Cybermen seen here are the first in the new TV series that don't have the Cybus logo on them, and are clearly a galactic power in the far future.
1826 *Let's Kill Hitler*

1827 *The Impossible Astronaut/Day of the Moon*
1828 *Asylum of the Daleks*
1829 Dating *The Battle of Demons Run: Two Days Later* (Series 7 webcast) - As the title states, it's two days after *A Good Man Goes to War*.
1830 *River S3: My Dinner with Andrew, River S3: The Furies*.
1831 *River S3: My Dinner with Andrew*
1832 Dating *River S3: The Lady in the Lake, River S3: The Furies* (BF *The Diary of River Song* #3.1, 3.4) – For Lake and his siblings, events begin the day after the Battle of Demons Run (*A Good Man Goes to War*); we pick up the narrative at Terminus Prime, presumably, days or weeks or possibly months after that (it seems a stretch to think that years have gone by). For River, however, *River S3: My Dinner with Andrew* happens after "Asgard, Byzantium, Demons Run" (*The Time of Angels/Flesh and Stone, A Good Man Goes to War*), and also after *The Husbands of River Song*, as she has "Twelve [husbands]. Or eleven. Or thirteen. It all depends on how you

prise – having made a full recovery. He agreed to go with Vastra and Jenny to London, 1888.

River's Siblings

Madame Kovarian infused River's DNA into other beings, creating new ranks of assassins. Her initial efforts produced the pseudo-Time Lords Beck, Creek, Lake, Rindle, Stream, Tarn and Wadi – all of whom escaped from Demons Run the day after the battle there. Kovarian's second wave of killers included Brooke, H-One, H-Two and O.[1830] River stumbled upon a garden owned by Andrew Edwardson, the spitting image of the fifth Doctor. Owing to River's interactions with Andrew, and his finding an unlimited credit slip from Galactic Century Bank, he came to found a multi-dimensional restaurant: the Bumptious Gastropod.[1831]

RIVER S3: THE LADY IN THE LAKE / THE FURIES[1832]
-> Terminus Prime established itself as the largest euthanasia centre in the galaxy, wherein clients could select from themed killing areas such as the Fantasy, Historic, Heroic, Metafictional and Humorous Zones (the last including rabbits with flamethrowers). To cross all the Ts and dot the Is, clients were sent back a few days in time, and already dead when they signed the approval forms.

Not knowing his longevity or number of extra lives, Lake established himself as the Great Lake: a cult leader who advocated experiencing death. His swayed siblings gave themselves to Terminus Prime's killing zones, allowing Lake to study their regenerations. River Song failed to save her siblings, but came to care for Lake's last incarnation, a female, before Lake's past self mistakenly murdered her. Anguished over the female Lake's passing, River summoned the TARDIS to spend some time with the Doctor...

On Madame Kovarian's orders, Brooke had already infiltrated the TARDIS as the fifth Doctor's companion. The Doctor, Brooke and River went back to see Mozart, and had an escapade in the Bumptious Gastropod, a famed restaurant outside of space-time. River kissed the Doctor

to remove his memories of her, but Brooke killed the Doctor with a regeneration inhibitor, and took his body back to Kovarian...

The Silence and the Headless Monks had washed their hands of Kovarian. Brooke's generation of pseudo-Time Lords became increasingly uncontrollable, and a row led to Brooke permanently killing her sister, H-One. As influenced by River, Brooke slipped back in time and tricked Andrew Edwardson – a double of the fifth Doctor – into dying in the Doctor's place. Brooke, H-Two and O turned on Kovarian, and although mental blocks prevented them from killing their "mother", they promised River they would find various means of torturing Kovarian.

THE WEDDING OF RIVER SONG[1833] -> The eleventh Doctor investigated the Silence, and found the Seventh Transept, where the Headless Monks were keeping the still-living head of Dorium Maldovar. He also tracked down a former envoy of the Silence, Father Gideon Vandaleur... who had died six months before, and was actually the justice-agent spaceship *Teselecta* in disguise. The Doctor believed he could no longer avoid travelling to 2011 to die at Lake Silencio, and asked the justice agents to deliver messages so Amy, Rory, River Song, an older Canton Delaware and a younger version of the eleventh Doctor could meet him there.

He also asked the justice agents if they would disguise the *Teselecta* to resemble him – a means of his avoiding death and thwarting the fixed point in time at Lake Silencio.

The Doctor succeeded, lived... and married River Song. He later returned Dorium's head to the transept, and Dorium pledged to keep the secret that the Doctor had cheated death.

A GOOD MAN GOES TO WAR[1834] -> River voluntarily returned to Stormcage after the Doctor took her ice skating on the river Thames, 1814, for her birthday. Rory approached River to help find him and the Doctor rescue Amy, but she refused, knowing that these events

count." In *The Furies*, River knows that Kovarian died in an alternate history (*The Wedding of River Song*). Trying to reconcile those positions isn't easy, unless River has used her vortex manipulator to backtrack in her own timezone (as she does), once she learns of her siblings' existence.
1833 Dating *The Wedding of River Song* (X6.13) - No date given, but we can infer that all of these events occur in the same timezone. Dorium's appearance is explicitly after the main events of *A Good Man Goes to War*.
1834 Dating *A Good Man Goes to War* (X6.7) - This is tricky to place. The fact that River has knowledge of

events at Demons Run – in particular, that the Doctor will then learn her true identity – suggests that for her, those events have already happened.

River doesn't seem to know, until Rory arrives, that it's the day that Demons Run will occur – so even though it's her birthday, it's presumably a different year from when she was literally born. This has the slightly awkward consequence that while *A Good Man Goes to War* is set in River's native era, Rory must not visit Stormcage at the exact same time as the effort to rescue Amy from Demons Run. With the Doctor recruiting allies from all throughout time and space, it's possible that Rory or the Doctor just told the TARDIS, "Take us to

would lead to the Battle of Demons Run, and that she could only appear at the "very end".

River Song and the Doctor met Jim the Fish. They also visited Easter Island.[1835] River aided the eleventh Doctor in dealing with a possessed orchestra at a moonbase.[1836] She also accompanied him to the planet of the rain gods.[1837] River and the Doctor visited Florana, where he was rude to a tour guide who quoted misinformation about some pyramids.[1838] At some point, River and the Doctor received dancing lessons from Rita Hayworth.[1839]

The eleventh Doctor, Alice, the Squire and Abslom Daak broke River out of Stormcage, so she could help them investigate the Doctor's role in the Overcast's downfall.[1840]

The eleventh Doctor asked for River's help in sorting out a time snafu in 2016.[1841]

5147 (5th May) - THE LEGENDS OF RIVER SONG: "Picnic at Asgard"[1842] -> River anonymously received ninety-five sugar mice and traded those to a feline associate, Frodene, for use of a Time Hopper. A Tesla force field blocked time travel within Stormcage, but she used the Hopper to travel in space back to when her cell was being built, then left to meet the Doctor at Asgard™, a planet-sized theme park.

THE LEGENDS OF RIVER SONG: "River of Time"[1843] -> As Stormcage inmate #50232, River Song kept her

---

River", and it acted accordingly. (Hence Rory's comment that, "The time streams, I'm not quite sure where we are...")

1835 In River's lifetime, these events happen before *The Impossible Astronaut*.

1836 *Night of the Doctor: "Good Night"*

1837 *Rain Gods*

1838 *River S1: Signs*

1839 *DC 3: The Doomsday Chronometer*

1840 *The Eleventh Doctor Year Two: "The Judas Goatee"*

1841 *The Legends of River Song: "A Gamble With Time"*

1842 Dating "Picnic at Asgard" (*The Legends of River Song* #1a) - The exact day is given, but that puzzlingly places it after *The Pandorica Opens* [5145], i.e. after River has acquired her vortex manipulator, so can come and go from Stormcage as she pleases.

1843 Dating "River of Time" (*The Legends of River Song* #1e) - For River, it's after she's married the Doctor.

1844 Dating *The Impossible Astronaut/Day of the Moon* (X6.1-6.2) - The general reverse order of the Doctor and River's meet-ups would suggest that these two episodes would, for her, occur prior to *A Good Man Goes to War*. Also, River acts as if she and the Doctor who took her to the 1814 frost fair are quite chummy – so if *Day of the Moon* is indeed the last time she kisses him, the frost fair trip likely occurs (for River) before that event.

1845 Dating *The Time of Angels, Flesh and Stone* and *The Big Bang* (X5.4-5.5, X5.13) - River tells the Doctor that they will next meet "when the Pandorica opens" – meaning that for her, it's after *The Pandorica Opens* (set in 5145).

1846 *The Time of Angels/Flesh and Stone*. There's no mention of her being imprisoned after this point.

1847 *The Wedding of River Song*. River says that she "climbed out of the wreck of the *Byzantium*" and is dressed as she was at the end of *Flesh and Stone*. She has very possibly been released from prison at this point, although that's not explicitly stated.

1848 As the Doctor let slip to her in *The Time of Angels*, and as she introduces herself in *Silence in the Library*, Octavian refers to her as "Doctor Song" in *The Time of Angels*.

1849 When the eleventh Doctor asks how River knows his current face in *The Time of Angels*, she says: "I've got pictures of all your faces. You never show up in the right order, though. I need the spotter's guide." Perhaps she's just lying – in the same story, after all, she keeps to herself that Amy is her mother. Either way, later on in River's life, she does have pictures of the Doctor's first 12 incarnations, in the correct order (*The Husbands of River Song*).

1850 *The Husbands of River Song*

1851 "The Lost Dimension". It's not specified that this happens in River's native era. Willdar's academic institution isn't even cited – as one might expect – as Luna University.

1852 *The Angels Take Manhattan*. In River's lifetime, this happens after she has married the Doctor, become a professor and been released from Stormcage. Strangely, she attributes the latter to the Doctor's records being deleted, meaning she couldn't be convicted of murdering someone who didn't exist. *The Time of Angels*, however, has her being offered a pardon if she assists with the *Byzantium* crisis.

1853 *The Husbands of River Song*. The story makes clear that River independently jumps around in time (presumably owing to her vortex manipulator), but for her, events in that story happen after *The Big Bang*, her picnic with the Doctor at Asgard and *Flesh and Stone*. She has "just been" to Manhattan (*The Angels Take Manhattan*).

1854 *The Caretaker*

1855 At some point before *Silence in the Library*. If the Doctor does indeed *not* tell River his real name when they're wed (*The Wedding of River Song*), and instead tells her the secret ("Look into my eye") that he doesn't have to die after all, then the most likely place that this occurs is when he's dying and whispers in her ear in *Let's Kill Hitler*. That, or the Doctor's real name actually *is* "Look Into My Eye".

1856 All before *Silence in the Library/Forest of the Dead*.

1857 *Silence in the Library/Forest of the Dead*

1858 *The Husbands of River Song*

vortex manipulator out of phase with our reality, and summoned it with a scan-worm implanted in her body. She'd given instructions that her funeral should run at least a week, and entail balloons, helter-skelters and bouncy castles. An acknowledged expert on the galaxy's Precursor races, River published a paper on the Racnoss ruins on Arcnoy Twelve.

Professor Darin Forcade took River out of Stormcage to examine Precursor ruins on an unnamed world. They discovered Rocinate's TARDIS, and their arrival triggered the termination of the stasis field holding the Qwerm eggs within. To stop a new generation of Qwerm from taking over the universe, River linked the Ship's front and back doors together – this created an infinite Klein bottle to forever trap everything within. Rocinate volunteered to trigger the Klein bottle while River escaped.

THE IMPOSSIBLE ASTRONAUT / DAY OF THE MOON[1844] -> The Doctor sent River an invite to join him at Lake Silencio in Utah, the twenty-first century. She escaped Stormcage, and went there. The Doctor later brought her back to Stormcage and they kissed... it was the first time they had done so for the Doctor, meaning it was the last time for River.

River Pardoned, Released from Stormcage

THE TIME OF ANGELS / FLESH AND STONE / THE BIG BANG[1845] -> There were laws against marrying one's self.

The Weeping Angel found on Razbahan caused the category-four starliner *Byzantium* to crash on Alfava Metraxis – all part of an attempt to rescue the Angels sleeping in a maze of the dead there. The Clerics released River Song from Stormcage into the custody of Father Octavian, and offered her a pardon if she helped contain the situation. She carved a message into the *Byzantium*'s flight recorder, its Home Box, that summoned the eleventh Doctor and Amy to this time. The Angels fed off the *Byzantium*'s power, and gained enough strength to stalk the Doctor's party.

The eleventh Doctor's future self momentarily visited the *Byzantium* while he was backtracking along his own timeline. He stressed to Amy the importance that she remember the words he spoke to her when she was seven.

A Crack in Time appeared, and the "current" Doctor fed the Angels into it – they constituted enough of a space-time event that the Crack was sealed as it destroyed them. The Doctor learned that River was imprisoned for killing "a very good man", and that he would see her again when the Pandorica opened.

River Song was granted her pardon.[1846] She travelled to 2011 to tell Amy and Rory that the Doctor didn't die at Lake Silencio.[1847] River Song became a professor.[1848] She had pictures of all the Doctor's incarnations, but didn't always know their order.[1849] A movie version of the *Byzantium* incident was made.[1850]

? - River took a graduate student, Willdar, to a dig on an asteroid forbidden by the trans-plutonian treaty. The leader of a failed Silurian colony had used a temporal generator to keep echoes of his people alive, but River Song destroyed the item, and Willdar achieved his doctorate.[1851]

River went to 1930s New York and went incognito as Melody Malone, private investigator. Afterwards, she realised she would never again see her parents, who were trapped in the past of New York. To fulfill continuity, River wrote the noir book *Melody Malone: Private Detective in Old New York Town* to provide the Doctor with clues in New York, 2012, then sent it to Amy Pond for her to publish. Records pertaining to the Doctor had been deleted on a widespread scale; nobody in this era had "ever heard of him".[1852]

Over time, River Song also married the actor Stephen Fry, a man named Ramone, King Hydroflax and at least two women. She helpfully acquired a copy of *History's Finest Exploding Restaurants*, which detailed the best places in space-time to get food for free (if you skipped the coffee).[1853] The Doctor and River had a fight, and he sulked while living among otters for a month.[1854]

The Doctor told River Song his real name; "there was only one time he could" do that.[1855] The Doctor and River went to the end of the universe together. Their adventures included the Bone Meadows and a picnic at Asgard. When the Doctor knew that the time had come for River to visit the Library and meet her fate, he showed up on her doorstep with a new haircut and a suit...[1856]

NIGHT AND THE DOCTOR: "Last Night" -> En route to the Singing Towers of Darillium, the eleventh Doctor and River arrived at the site of their first date: Calderon Beta on 21st September, 2160. The Doctor shared a private conversation with his younger self, who was on that very same date, but merely said "spoilers" in relation to events to come...

River's Night with the Doctor on Darillium

The Doctor took River to Darillium, where the towers sang – the Doctor cried, but didn't tell River why. He gave her an advanced sonic screwdriver equipped with a neural relay.[1857] River and the twelfth Doctor spent a night together on Darillium, where the nights lasted for twenty-four years.[1858]

River and the younger Doctors[1859]

At some point, River dealt with the so-called Rulers of the Universe, and while doing so prevented the eighth Doctor from identifying her.[1860]

River aided the eighth Doctor against the Coalition, by disguising her identity with a psychic wimple. He variously knew her as "Professor Malone" and "Sister Cantica", but came to forget their meet-ups involving the Great Storm, the Discordia and Vienna. River now held five master's degrees from the Sorbonne University, in five alternate timelines. She had trained at the Venusian Martial Arts Academy, having gone there during one of her honeymoons, as they misread the brochure.[1861]

She assisted the sixth and seventh Doctors against Golden Futures, and wiped their memories of her.[1862]

lgtw - CD,NM V2: NIGHT OF THE VASHTA NERADA / DAY OF THE VASHTA NERADA[1863] -> The entrepreneur Georgia Donnelly cut down a forest world, Theta 49, to accommodate a new amusement park: Funworld. The Vashta Nerada displaced by this consumed the Funworld workers, and then a hunting team sent to investigate, before the park even opened. Although he failed to save anyone, including Donnelly, the fourth Doctor stopped the Vashta Nerada from hitching a ride to Earth.

Synthesis Station, a scientific outpost, harvested Vashta Nerada from Funworld. Dr Eva Morrison and her team adapted the Vashta Nerada for medical applications and terraforming, and also created the Nerada Vashta strain: a variant that operated in light. Cardinal Ollistra invested in Morrison's efforts, hoping to create a Vashta Nerada capable of eating Dalekanium or wrecking havoc on Skaro. The eighth Doctor aided in Sythesis' destruction, and saved Ollistra, when the Vashta Nerada there escaped.

Bliss Joins the TARDIS

lgtw - Bliss, a companion of the eighth Doctor, studied quantum mechanics at Luna University. She ventured close to a battlefront of the Last Great Time War, to study quantum fluctuations in a temporal warzone.[1864]

lgtw - THE EIGHTH DOCTOR – THE TIME WAR 1[1865] -> A Time Lord, psionic enough to rewrite reality as he pleased, fled the Last Great Time War and wove himself into time as a human being. As "Quarren Maguire", he married a woman named Rupa.

The Time War's temporal distortion revised history aboard the *Theseus*, a ~~pleasure liner~~ a spaceship full of refugees escaping the War's ravages. The eighth Doctor arrived with ~~his companion Sheena~~ with ~~his companion Emma~~ with his companion Louise alone on the ship for a vacation to assist with the evacuation. As the Daleks invaded the ship, the Doctor fled in an escape pod with the Magures and Bliss, a Luna University student of Earth descent. The *Theseus* captain diverted the ship into a portion of hyperspace inhabited by life-consuming entitles:

1859 RIVER SONG AND THE YOUNGER DOCTORS: The Big Finish audios (primarily *The Diary of River Song* and also *Doom Coalition 2, 3* and *4*) entail River meeting the eighth, seventh, sixth, fifth and fourth Doctors... Big Finish released these stories reverse order of the Doctor's lives, following the TV show's tradition that River and the Doctor (mostly) meet in reverse order.

River mentions the Doctor's "magician" incarnation in *DC 2: The Sonomancer* – suggesting, for her, that story happens after *The Husbands of River Song* (she doesn't know about the twelfth Doctor before that). In *Silence of the Library*, by contrast, she claims to have last seen the Doctor during their "night" together on Darillium (presumably *Husbands*) – not technically true, if she briefly meets the eighth Doctor in *DC 4: Songs of Love*, although the dramatic point in *Library* is that the "last" time she saw the Doctor in his own timeline, he was ill at ease because it's soon time for her to visit the Library and die. For River, *Doom Coalition 3* happens after she's acquired her vortex manipulator (*The Pandorica Opens*) and Father Octavian's death (*Flesh and Stone*). *DC 4: Songs of Love* is, for her, probably not long before *Silence in the Library*, as she senses that she's "almost at my final destination".

Thematic intent of River's meeting with the tenth Doctor preserved, it seems easiest to think that River squeezes all of these "past Doctor" adventures in between *The Husbands of River Song* and her fatefully going to the Library.

1860 *River S1: The Rulers of the Universe*. River here uses a sonic trowel, akin to the one she employs in *The Husbands of River Song*.

1861 *Doom Coalition 2* and *3*

1862 *The Diary of River Song* Series 2. River has already married the Doctor, become a professor and obtained her sonic trowel (*The Husbands of River Song*), and works as a freelance archaeologist.

1863 Dating *CD, NM V2: Night of the Vashta Nerada* and *Day of the Vashta Nerada* (*CD,NM #2.1, 2.4*) - It's humanity's future. Donnelly has the resources to level an entire forest world (as with – one imagines – the Library in *Silence in the Library*), and the hunting team to Funworld includes a psychic and a silicon-based lifeform. There's no sign that the Library incident has informed the Funworld team (or vice versa) about the Vashta Nerada. Earth is functional; a spaceship autopilot in *Night of the Vashta Nerada* has a course set for there. Synthesis Station placates their Vashta Nerada by feeding them Vervoids, so it's after their creation in *Terror of the Vervoids* [2986]. *Day of the Vashta Nerada*

so-called "trolls" who destroyed the *Theseus* and the Daleks aboard.

The Doctor, the Maguires and Bliss landed on a forest world, along with a timeline-corrupted Dalek that couldn't remember its identity. "Dal" aided the travellers through unstable time zones, but slowly regained its memories. Just as the Doctor persuaded Dal to ponder such concepts as friendship – Cardinal Ollistra arrived with her retinue, and Captain Tamasan shot Dal dead. Ollistra apprehended the Doctor's party, and took them to a Time Lord stronghold in the far future...

Death of River's Physical Self at the Library

SILENCE IN THE LIBRARY / FOREST OF THE DEAD[1866] **->** Professor River Song joined an expedition sent by Felman Lux Corporation to their planet-sized Library, which had been sealed off for a hundred years, and sent a message that the Doctor should join her there. The message was received much too early in the Doctor's timeline, and so the tenth Doctor arrived at the Library with Donna. He had not yet met River (that he was aware) in his personal timestream.

The Vashta Nerada swarmed once more, and the Library's self-destruct was activated. The Doctor and the Vashta Nerada agreed that they could have the Library if the Doctor was given one day to free the four thousand and twenty-two people saved on the Library's hard drive. The Doctor intended to hook himself up the Library's computer so his own memory space could be used to initiate the transfer – an act that would burn out his hearts, and kill him beyond all hope of regeneration. River incapacitated the Doctor and took his place. When he awoke, bound, she told him:

"It's not over for you. You'll see me again. You've got all of that to come. You and me, time and space. You watch us run."

River's body died as the patrons were restored to life and the Library's self-destruct was terminated. The Doctor realised that River's sonic screwdriver had a neural relay that contained the last vestiges of her mind, and transferred it into the Library's hard drive. River's mind took up residence in the hard drive's simulation of reality, along with the minds of her slain archaeology team and Charlotte Abigail Lux. The Doctor and Donna continued their travels.

THE MAGICIAN'S APPRENTICE -> Colony Sarff went to the Maldovarium in search of the Doctor, but failed to find him there.

The Doctor found a Cyber-head, which became his friend Handles, at the Maldovar Market.[1867] The Sixty-Eighters traversed time and bought plasma weapons from Kebabel's "discount despot" stall in the Maldovarium.[1868]

RHYTHM OF DESTRUCTION[1869] **->** As hired by the peace envoy Jamelia Varigast, the Blitzrat Jazz Quartet – a group of musician assassins – wrecked havoc to get the Doctor's attention, so Varigast could gain revenge on him. The Quartet destroyed the planetoid Quich when the twelfth Doctor stopped by to enjoy The Hollow: an ampitheatre with some of the galaxy's best acoustics. The Doctor brought Varigast to justice for her crimes. Rather than face incarceration in Stormcage, the Blitzrat Quartet played one last tune aboard a disintegrating shuttle.

includes mention of "Maldevar's Bar" (*The Pandorica Opens* et al), which places these two stories in River Song's era.

1864 The background to *The Eighth Doctor – The Time War 1*.

1865 Dating *The Eighth Doctor – The Time War 1* (BF box set #1) – Bliss hails from Luna University, where River Song obtained her doctorate (*Let's Kill Hitler, Closing Time*). There's no indication of whether Bliss's time there falls before, after or during River's time there. Emma, before she's erased from the Doctor's history, comments that engines still look like engines "all these centuries along". A *Theseus* passenger won a competition "back in May".

1866 Dating *Silence in the Library/Forest of the Dead* (X4.8-4.9) - For River, the story takes place an unspecified amount of time after *Flesh and Stone*. *The Husbands of River Song* establishes that River goes to the Library by benefit of time travel (presumably via her vortex

manipulator) rather than naturally living to this point. See the Dating River Song essay.

1867 *The Time of the Doctor*, referencing Dorium Maldovar (first seen in *The Pandorica Opens*).

1868 *The Eleventh Doctor Year Three*: "The Tragical History Tour"

1869 Dating *Rhythm of Destruction* (BBC audiobook #31) – No date given. The SS *Pure White Dove* has a virtual reality bar with Robin Hood and King Solomon, as well as a 1980s-themed bar, all of which suggest a human-centric culture closer to the modern day than not. Also, one of the Blitzrat Jazz Quartet faked their death with an explosion in New Orleans, meaning Earth is still viable. All of that said, the Blitzrat leader fears incarceration in Stormcage, dating this story to the River Song era.

On the planet otherwise known as Oblivion, the bloodline of House Endoskiia began.[1870]

Nardole[1871]

? – Nardole, an android/cyborg/non-human (delete according to preference) companion of the twelfth Doctor, and an employee of River Song, was born/constructed/assembled (delete according to preference).

Nardole seemed sketchy about his origins, but said he "was sort of found". He felt comfortable working as a con man.[1872] Nardole sometimes swapped forms and body parts. While on the run, he switched his true face for another.[1873] At one point, he had blue skin.[1874] He studied martial arts, attaining the level of Brown Tabard. As he'd won his left hand in a game, he could only perform the Tarovian Neck Pinch with his right.[1875] Nardole dated an AI named Velma.[1876]

c 5200 - "Fire and Brimstone"[1877] -> Ninety-seven "audited precessions" after the Breakout, the eighth Doctor and Izzy landed on the satelloid Icarus Falling – one of six satellites revolving around the artificial sun Crivello's Cauldron. This was the New Earth System in the Crab Nebula, and held some of the remnants of humanity.

A Dalek fleet soon arrived and released self-replicating robot insects – the Contagium – to secure Icarus Falling. The Daleks sought to wipe out a race of spider-Daleks from a parallel dimension, and wanted to collapse the Cauldron and create a black hole – the means by which they could travel to the home territory of their rivals. The Daleks installed a synaptic conduit into the Doctor's brain, believing he could navigate their fleet through the black hole.

Sister Chastity, a religious official aboard Icarus Falling, revealed herself as a member of Threshold and rescued the Doctor. She claimed that Threshold had changed in the thousands of years since the Doctor last encountered them, and intended – with the Doctor's help – to crush the Dalek fleet as they passed through the black hole that the Cauldron would become. The Daleks took control of the Cauldron anyway, but spider-Daleks poured through the gateway and engaged Phalanx 44 of Special Weapons Daleks in battle. The Doctor learned that the Threshold had been hired by the Time Lords, and engineered a supernova that destroyed both Dalek armies. The Cauldron became an ordinary sun with planets orbiting it.

1870 "Three millennia" before "Oblivion" (*DWM*).

1871 NARDOLE: We're told almost nothing about Nardole's life before he meets the Doctor. While it's cumulatively obvious that he's a cyborg or android-type being, it's never flat-out said what that *means*, exactly. He's not purely mechanical, as he needs to breathe (*Oxygen, Empress of Mars*) and it transpires that the Doctor short-sightedly got Nardole cheap lungs (*The Pyramid at the End of the World*) while "re-assembling" him (Nardole's phrasing in *Thin Ice*, and the Doctor's in *The Husbands of River Song*) in the wake of Nardole's intro story, *The Husbands of River Song* [5343-&5354].

That adventure, weirdly enough, doesn't suggest that Nardole is anything other than purely biological. True, King Hydroflax's robot body incorporates Nardole's severed head into itself, but Hydroflax himself and Ramone endure the same fate, the idea being that Hydroflax's advanced tech lets him do such a thing. Nardole's cybernetic nature only emerges along the way in Series 10, and may explain why the Doctor's sonic sunglasses register him as "237" years old in *The Pyramid at the End of the World*. If we vest any trust in the rumours of the Doctor teaching at St Luke's for fifty, even seventy years (*The Pilot*), his artificial nature presumably explains how Nardole remained with the Doctor all of that time, but didn't outwardly age.

The more germane question for *Ahistory*'s purposes is *when*, exactly, Nardole is from (see also the notes on *Oxygen*). When we first meet Nardole in *The Husbands of River Song*, he's in River Song's employ... but is he native to that time, or did she take him there? It rings more true to think that River would source local talent, as it's not really her *modus operandi* to ferret people through time (presuming her vortex manipulator has enough power for such things).

Barring more information, it's compelling to assume that Nardole hails from the same time-frame as *The Husbands of River Song*. If he's 237 in *The Pyramid at the End of the World*, and *if* (a wild card here) he indeed spent seventy years with the Doctor at St Luke's, and without knowing how long he and the Doctor travel together between *The Husbands of River Song* and *The Pilot* (a la *The Return of Doctor Mysterio*), we might close our eyes, say a prayer, stab our fingers onto the timeline and conclude that he's about 167 when he meets the Doctor in *The Husbands of River Song* [5343], so was born (or forged, or Velcroed, or whatever) about 5176. To anyone who finds it beyond the pale that the Doctor actually stayed put at St Luke's University for seven decades, meaning that claim is just the stuff of rumours, Nardole was born (or forged, or Velcroed, or whatever) about 5106.

1872 *The Doctor Falls*.
1873 *Oxygen*.
1874 *World Enough and Time*.
1875 *The Lie of the Land*.
1876 *Oxygen*.
1877 Dating "Fire and Brimstone" (*DWM* #251-255) - The Doctor says "some two hundred years ago, I saw the Cauldron launched", a reference to "The Keep". The humans in this story don't recognise the Daleks.

c 5217 - THE NINTH DOCTOR YEAR ONE[1878] -> Director Highsmith of the Hesguard Institute – an ex-Stormcage facility positioned within a time storm – developed the Bad Wolf Process. Through this, a criminal's rage, hatred and negative impulses were funneled into a disposable blank being: a Sin-Eater. The ninth Doctor, forewarned that Highsmith's "cured" patients would cause murder sprees, investigated by framing himself for the killing of UNIT's Tara Mishra.

A Sin-Eater created from the Doctor's rage and hatred endowed the other Sin-Eaters with sentience. Aided by Tara and Rose, the Doctor transmatted his Sin-Eater into Hesguard's outlawed Matryoshka Drive, then ejected it into the Void. Without the Drive's protection, Hesguard fell to a time storm.

The price for Sin-Eaters dropped following the Hesguard disaster.[1879]

The Destruction of Earth's Moon

Downfall of the Threshold

c 5220 - "Wormwood"[1880] -> The newly-regenerated ninth Doctor (who was balding, wore a bowtie and carried a toothbrush in his jacket pocket), Izzy and Fey landed in Wormwood, a mock Western village controlled by Threshold on the moon. Their leader, Abraham White, showed the Doctor a host of landmarks from Earth such as the Eiffel Tower, the Statue of Liberty, Mount Rushmore and so forth, which he had saved to celebrate humankind's achievements. Fey confronted White after learning they'd been spying on her for years, but White summoned a demonic beast, the Pariah.

Izzy discovered that the Threshold were building the Eye of Disharmony, a device that made space impassable.

Activated, the Eye annihilated the Traxonnia Research Cluster, the Kapli Refugee Fleet, the Ninth Sontaran Armada and every other vessel in space. The Threshold sent a transwarp signal to every civilisation offering to sell their teleport windows as an alternative.

The eighth Doctor showed up, and revealled that the "ninth Doctor" was actually Shayde in disguise. The Pariah, in turn, revealed that she was the original Shayde – who had rebelled against Rassilon. She defeated Shayde in battle, then killed all the members of Threshold to drain their energy. Fey merged with the wounded Shayde, gaining his powers, and they launched a second attack that destroyed Pariah. White also died.

The Eye of Disharmony's destruction obliterated Earth's moon, but restored space to its natural state. "Feyde" left the Doctor and Izzy's company to travel on her own.

(=) Daleks infected with wasp DNA mutated into a swarm of invulnerable, giant wasp-like creatures and devastated Earth, draining all of its minerals and nutrients. The colony planets were unable to help and all attempts to recolonise ended in starvation.[1881]

Unique minerals on Etra Prime draw the attention of over fifty galactic powers, including the Daleks and the Time Lords. The Daleks removed the planet, along with a team of researchers and President Romana, from space-time. A galactic war was only narrowly averted.[1882]

(=) c 5250 - THE MUTANT PHASE[1883] -> The wasp-like Mutant Phase Daleks attacked Skaro, and the Emperor Dalek ordered the fifth Doctor and Nyssa to travel back to 2158 and prevent the Mutant Phase's creation. The Emperor Dalek self-destructed Skaro, but downloaded his consciousness into the Thal Ganatus and accompanied the TARDIS crew.

1878 Dating *The Ninth Doctor Year One* (Titan 9th Doc #1.11-1.12, "Sin-Eaters") - A bizarre bit of discontinuity occurs in that the previous story, "Slaver's Song", ends with the Judoon incarcerating the Doctor at Remand Station Mackay-One in the "23rd century", but "Sin-Eaters" opens with him imprisoned at the Hesguard Institute in the "53rd century". He *certainly* didn't live through the intervening millennia (see The Doctor's Age sidebar), and there's no claim that Hesguard interacts with the other time zone.

Rose here poses as an Earth Examiner (*The Power of the Daleks*); her warrant number with the Earth Central Registry, "5002/26/3", doesn't appear related to the date.
1879 Sin-Eaters reappear in *The Ninth Doctor Year One*: "The Bidding War".
1880 Dating "Wormwood" (*DWM* #266-271) - It's "twenty years" since "Fire and Brimstone" according to

Chastity. Earth's moon is here destroyed (albeit without any mention of the environmental havoc such an event would inevitably mean for Earth itself), but might be restored off screen, as it looks whole in "The Child of Time" (*DWM*). By *The Long Game* (set in 200,000), Earth is the centre of the Fourth Great and Bountiful Empire, and has five moons.
1881 "Thirty years ago" in *The Mutant Phase*.
1882 "Twenty years" before *The Apocalypse Element*.
1883 Dating *The Mutant Phase* (BF #15) - No date is given, but this is the first *Doctor Who* audio set in the period of the *Dalek Empire* series; see the dating notes on *The Genocide Machine*.

The Library of Kar-Charrat

c 5256 - THE GENOCIDE MACHINE[1884] **->** The seventh Doctor and Ace visited the library of Kar-Charrat. The chief librarian, Elgin, had built a wetworks research facility that stored the sum of universal knowledge in liquid form. To accomplish this, Elgin had enslaved nearly the entire Kar-Charrat race, using their drop-sized bodies as data storage units.

Dormant Daleks on the planet revived and attacked. They gained access to the library by duplicating Ace, and all but destroyed the library in their quest for its data. The Doctor defeated them with the help of a "collector", Bev Tarrant, a legendary thief[1885] who was planning a heist. The library was ruined.

& 5256 - THE APOCALYPSE ELEMENT[1886] **->** The sixth Doctor and Evelyn landed on Archetryx as a Time Treaty was being signed. The missing planet Etra Prime suddenly re-appeared on a collision course with Archetryx. The Daleks wanted to wipe out the conference. The second Romana escaped her captors on Etra Prime. The

Doctor, Romana and Evelyn went to Gallifrey as the planetary collision took place and the Daleks instigated an epic attack. The Daleks destroyed the Seriphia Galaxy with the Apocalypse Element, generating a million new worlds there. They set about reshaping Seriphia in their image.

& 5257 - STORM HARVEST[1887] **->** The inhabitants of the waterworld Coralee had developed the Krill – vicious, aquatic humanoids with razor-sharp teeth – as instruments of war. The Krill wiped out their own creators, then entered hibernation. The Dreekans later colonised the planet, despite the legends of great danger there. They offered private islands for sale to the super-rich. The Krill awakened and were defeated by the seventh Doctor and Ace. Nonetheless, some Krill survived as eggs in a nearby asteroid field.

& 5257 - DUST BREEDING[1888] **->** The decaying Master brought the Warp Core, an energy creature contained in Edvard Munch's painting *The Scream*, to the planet Duchamp 331, a refuelling station off the main space lanes. It served as home to technicians and a small colony

1884 Dating *The Genocide Machine* (BF #7) - The dating for this story – which otherwise seems so unimposing – is surprisingly important, in that the whole of the *Dalek Empire* mini-series and its related *Doctor Who* audios (*The Mutant Phase, The Apocalypse Element, Dust Breeding, Return of the Daleks*) are contingent on the placement of this one adventure. (See the dating notes under the individual audios, and especially those under *Dalek Empire I*, for why.)

Only four pieces of evidence, however, exist to help make this decision: 1. In *The Genocide Machine*, the war between the Knights of Velyshaa and Earth (mentioned in *The Sirens of Time* as ending in 3562) is said to be "centuries ago". 2. The Big Finish website at one point dated *The Genocide Machine* to 4256. 3. Bev Tarrant, a native to the era of *The Genocide Machine*, twice states in *Benny S8: The Judas Gift* (definitely set in October 2607) that she's from "three thousand years in the future". 4. *Dalek Empire II* (set some "centuries" after *The Genocide Machine*) ends with a "Kill All Daleks" pulse being sent out into the Milky Way and Seriphia galaxies. (So, any placement for *The Genocide Machine* can't be just before a story with high Dalek involvement in those territories.)

The two pieces of evidence central to this discussion are the website date and Bev's statements. They can't be reconciled without concluding that when Bev said "three thousand years", she actually means only about 1650-ish years. Previous editions of *Ahistory* favoured the website date, but did not include the Benny series. This edition takes the "three thousand years" lines and rounds it somewhat to fit it around other stories, so

that *The Genocide Machine* is set in 5256, not 4256.

One potential hiccup is that this is not long after the native time of Captain Jack Harkness and River Song, in which humanity has time technology at its disposal – whereas it manifestly doesn't throughout *Dalek Empire*. This is an issue, however, irregardless of *Dalek Empire*'s dating – in that in one brief period, humankind (or certain members of it, at the very least) has time-tech, and yet it clearly doesn't on an ongoing basis. No explanation has been provided in any *Doctor Who* story for why this is the case.

1885 *Benny: The Judas Gift*
1886 Dating *The Apocalypse Element* (BF #11) - Another story set around the time of the *Dalek Empire* audios.
1887 Dating *Storm Harvest* (PDA #23) - No date is given. Reg Gurney, an engineer and spy on Coralee, spent thirty years in the Space Corps and fought in the Dalek Wars, supporting that dating.
1888 Dating *Dust Breeding* (BF #21) - It is "several centuries" in Ace's future, in Earth's colonial period and after the Dalek Wars. Bev Tarrant is also present, and for her, it is after *The Genocide Machine*.
1889 Dating *Prime Time* (PDA #33) - It is a year after *Storm Harvest*.
1890 Dating *The Caves of Androzani* (19.6) - There is no indication of dating on screen. Sharez Jek seems worried when it appears that the Doctor and Peri are from Earth, suggesting it has political influence (and hasn't been evacuated). The machine-pistols suggest a colonial setting, but Sirius society is long-established; there seems to be an interstellar economy and the androids are highly advanced. The Spectrox supplies must be so

of artists. The Master sought to seed the Warp Core's energy into Duchamp 331's dust, then goad it into action against its ancient enemies, the Krill. This would have created a planet-sized weapon. The seventh Doctor and Ace defeated the Master, and the surface of Duchamp 331 was caught in an inferno that destroyed the Warp Core.

Bev Tarrant accepted a lift from the Doctor and Ace, and eventually parted company with them in 2595.

& 5261 - PRIME TIME[1889] -> The seventh Doctor and Ace investigated the activities of Channel 400 on Blinni-Gaar, only to become part of the station's programming. Meanwhile, the Tremas Master landed on Scrantek and made a deal with the Fleshsmiths, a race that harvested other races to continue their existence. The Master and the Fleshsmiths hoped to use the Channel 400 broadcasts to transport one hundred fifty billion viewers into the Fleshsmiths' body banks as raw material. The Doctor let the Fleshsmiths analyse a clone of himself, which broke down and released a molecular contagion. The toxin cascaded through the Scrantek network and reduced the Fleshsmiths to ooze. Channel 400 was disgraced and taken off the air.

Prior to its demise, the network tormented Ace with images from the past of her "future" tombstone. The Doctor falsely convinced Ace that the images were faked. Without her knowledge, he went back in time and dug up her corpse for clues as to how she died.

The Fifth Doctor Regenerates

c 5300 - THE CAVES OF ANDROZANI[1890] -> Spectrox was "the most valuable substance in the universe". At the recommended dose of .3 of a centilitre a day, spec-

trox could halt the ageing process and double lifespans. There was some evidence that with a sufficient quantity of the substance, a human might live forever.

Spectrox was refined from the nests of the bats of Androzani Minor, a dangerous process carried out by androids. Supplies of spectrox were halted when the scientist Sharaz Jek and his androids rebelled against Androzani Major. The Praesidium sent a taskforce to apprehend Jek and they captured the refinery, but Jek removed the supplies of spectrox. The fifth Doctor and Peri were involved in an escalation of hostilities between Jek and the Praesidium's forces – Jek was killed, and the Doctor and Peri escaped during a mudburst, a tidal flood of primeval mud. The Doctor had been poisoned by raw Spectrox, and regenerated.

> (=) The Great Intelligence killed the Doctor on Androzani, but a double of Clara Oswald restored history to its intended path.[1891]

Peri Brown was cured of spectrox toxaemia, but the condition rendered her unable to conceive.[1892]

Along the Eastern edge of the galaxy, there was political upheaval for a thousand years. Many human colony worlds such as Pyka, Marlex, Dalverius, Pantorus and Shaggra warred with each other, and the galaxy's monetary system was in almost permanent crisis. In the fifty-fourth century, a consortium of industrialists attempted to solve the problem. Eventually they built Zamper: a neutral planet, snug in its own mini-universe, that would supply state-of-the-art battleships to all sides.

The only way to the planet was through a hyperspace gate controlled by Zamper itself, and the planet was completely self-contained to keep its designs secret. In four

---

limited as to have little long-term effect on the human race, explaining why it is not referred to in any other story.

The Doctor, The Widow and the Wardrobe features a Harvesting team from Androzani Major in the year 5345, and the Harvester team seems to share the same capitalist ethos seen in the earlier story. It seems reasonable to place *The Caves of Androzani* in roughly the same era – although this is slightly arbitrary, and they could take place many centuries apart.

Diamond Dogs [c.5046] entails Captain Laura Palmer worrying that someone affiliated with Sharaz Jek might start raiding diamond transport ships, but given the military's containment of Jek in *The Caves of Androzani* and his being located in Sirius, it's hard to see how her concern is valid. Perhaps in future, "Sharaz Jek" is as common a name as "Billy Bob".

The Terrestrial Index made a dubious link between the "federal forces" on Androzani Minor and the

Galactic Federation (*The Curse of Peladon*), dating the story to the fifth millennium. *Timelink* chose "3983", and *About Time* thought it was "The future, date unspecified", while acknowledging that a dating of as early as the twenty-second century was feasible. All of these books, however, were published before being able to take the evidence from *The Doctor, The Widow and the Wardrobe* into account.

In wake of events in *Caves*, the minutes of a Sirius Conglomerate meeting in *The Doctor: His Lives and Times* (p127) are dated to "17 March 28". The harvesting of trees (*The Doctor, The Widow and the Wardrobe*) has been identified as a new source of income.

1891 *The Name of the Doctor*. The fifth Doctor claims to have visited Androzani prior to *The Caves of Androzani*, and the Intelligence could equally have attacked him on that trip.

1892 *The Widow's Assassin*

hundred and seventy-three years of operation, Zamper became rich and maintained a balance of power in East Galaxy. The operation was completely smooth, averaging one minor technical failure every two hundred years.[1893]

Olleril was colonised. Governed by the principles laid down in the ancient records *The Collins Guide to the Twentieth Century*, *One of Us* by Hugo Young, *The Manufacture of Consent* and *The Smash Hits Yearbook*, it developed an eccentric, unworkable political and economic system that was an almost exact copy of the United Kingdom in the twentieth century. The cult of Luminus managed the planet in secret.[1894]

The Cyber-Empire annexed Malleon.[1895]

Beyond the Milky Way

c 5317 - THE STAR MEN[1896] -> Humanity invented the Leap Drive, its first intergalactic drive system, which could fold and unfold space to make vessels arrive a hundred light years away. Gallius Ultima, a planet at the Milky Way's edge, became home to a multi-disciplinary research station, Gallius U, and would become the launch platform for humankind spreading beyond its own galaxy. Ion drives facilitated slower travels.

History recorded that the *Johannes Kepler*, a Leap Drive-fitted Explorer-class ship, successfully made the first-ever mission to the Large Magellanic Cloud. However, an advance party of conquering Keltin, a.k.a. Star Men, broke through from their dying reality, the Dark, into the Tarantula Nebula and threatened to pollute the timelines. The Star Men's essence killed on contact, covering their foes with a red choral-like substance and animating their corpses. The fifth Doctor, Adric, Nyssa and Tegan were present as the Star Men finished off the *Kepler* crew, and that of its sister ship, *Carl Sagan*.

The Doctor incapacitated the Star Men with liquid

nitrogen, and Tegan and Nyssa triggered space mines that destroyed the Star Men's central brain, and sealed off their home reality. Autumn Tace, an astronomy prodigy who was quite taken with Adric, died in the conflict.

& 5323 - "Weapons of Past Destruction"[1897] ->
Merchants of time technology – much of it leftovers from the Last Great Time War – established a temporal bazaar on the imminently doomed Fluren's World in the Vienna Cluster. The ninth Doctor, Rose and Jack caused such a ruckus during their conflict with the Lect and the Unon, the bazaar's protective time bubble was deactivated. The participants fled as Fluren's World's sun went supernova.

Tara Mishra Departs the TARDIS

c 5325 - THE NINTH DOCTOR YEAR ONE[1898] -> Memgram emerged as the top social media network of the fifth-fourth century, enabling users to literally share memories. Planetoid 94025, a.k.a. Nomicae, became the same century's equivalent of Silicon Valley, and headquartered tech juggernauts including Memgram, Grallista Online, Bookface and Stumblr.

The Time Agency had Jack Harkness shoot Zlou Voth – a Scientist General of the Vremya Union who would develop benevolent time technology – with an Eradicator gun, erasing him from time. Ten years later, the owner of Memgram, Addison Delamar, found traces of the Doctor's memories in the Furian Temporal Bazaar's network, and deduced the value of the whole motherlode. Delamar perpetrated a ruse that lured both Captain Jack – and consequently the ninth Doctor and Rose, whose company he'd left in 1682 – to Mead's World, then captured the Doctor. Representatives of the Harrigan High Command (sentient hippopotami), the Church of the Evergreen Man, the Supreme Synod and the Cybermen gathered to bid on the

---

1893 *Zamper*
1894 "Five hundred ninety-seven" years before *Tragedy Day* (p97).
1895 "A decade or two" before "The Bidding War" [c.5325].
1896 Dating *The Star Men* (BF #221) - The Doctor initially estimates: "We're in the fifty-third century, when humanity is still contained within its own galaxy. In a century or so, they'll discover intergalactic drives and make the next great leap." He later realises he's erred – the Leap Drive has been invented *already*, so the "great leap" is happening sooner rather than later. The dating framework is undoubtedly keyed to talk of the Great Breakout in *The Invisible Enemy* [5000], although that would suggest a slightly earlier placement for *The Star Men*, unless the idea is that the Leap Drive massively enhances a comparatively low-level intergalactic effort

already underway.
1897 Dating "Weapons of Past Destruction" (Titan 9th Doc #1.1-1.5) - No dating clues given, but the ninth Doctor (somehow) leaves behind memories at the Time Bazaar, prompting Addison Delamar's scheme in *The Ninth Doctor Year One*: "The Bidding War" [c.5325].
1898 Dating *The Ninth Doctor Year One* (Titan 9th Doc #1.13, 1.14-1.15, "Secret Agent Man"/"The Bidding War") - The Doctor gives the century, and later estimates the year as "5324? 5325?" It's after the Hesguard disaster in "Sin-Eaters" [c.5217], and – as Delamar demonstrates no time-travel prowess – the Doctor's visit to the Fluren Temporal Bazaar ("Weapons of Past Destruction"). Jack here gives up even more of his memories, above and beyond his missing two years (*The Doctor Dances*).
1899 Dating "The Lost Dimension" (Titan mini-series

Doctor's memories – then assaulted Nomicae when restraint failed. The radiated the full emotional impact of his memories of the Time War, forcing them to withdraw.

Jack tricked Delamar into thinking she'd escaped with a containment sphere of the Doctor's Time War memories, when in fact he'd substituted some of his own. Tara Mishra left the TARDIS to help in the restoration of Nomicae.

& 5325 - "The Lost Dimension"[1899] **->** Captain Jack tried to take Tara Mishra to reunite with ninth Doctor and Rose in 1886, but – despite Jenny's efforts to save them – they were lost into a white hole. The Void nearly claimed Jenny's bowship, but the fifth Doctor's TARDIS bumped her ship to 2017. After the white-hole crisis resolved, Jack and Tara found themselves on a planet that looked suspiciously like Skaro, but also had the Brighton Royal Pavilion.

? 5325 - THE WEB IN SPACE[1900] **->** Earth Corp Couriers served as intergalactic postmen, making deliveries to planets as the Earth colony on Hephestus Beta, which was experiencing an outbreak of Orion flu. Chelonian ships, "skymaidens", had terrorised humans in Galaxy 16. Enormous diamondweb spiders – space creatures that consumed the rocks, space dust and comets they caught in webs made from diamond – nearly went extinct when billionaires caged them as novelties. The eleventh Doctor, Amy and Rory stopped the Empire of Eternal Victory from dissecting the last diamondweb spider to adopt its biology into their spaceship hulls. The Empire's last warship perished in a miscalculated space jump.

Nardole Meets the Doctor

5343 (25th December) - THE HUSBANDS OF RIVER SONG[1901] **->** The cybernetic King Hydroflax – the butcher of the Bone Meadows, renowned for finishing battles by eating his foes dead or alive – raided the Halassi vaults, but the resultant firefight caused the Halassi Androvar, the most valuable diamond in the

universe, to become lodged in his head. River Song, now age 200 owing to an extended lifespan, wormed her way into Hydroflax's confidence and bedroom to steal the diamond, and married him as part of her deception. She had also wed a man named Ramone, but wiped his memory of their nuptials "as he was being annoying".

River brought Hydroflax to the human colony on Mendorax Dellora – the nearest intersection with the Doctor's timeline – and conscripted the services of "the finest neurosurgeon in the galaxy" to aid her ruse. She failed to recognise the twelfth Doctor and, thinking he was the neurosurgeon, stole Hydroflax's head and relocated the TARDIS to the starship *Harmony and Redemption...*

To learn more about River, Hydroflax's robotic body beheaded her employee, Nardole, and incorporated his noggin into itself.

5345 - THE DOCTOR, THE WIDOW AND THE WARDROBE[1902] **->** The eleventh Doctor had planned to take the Arwell family from 1941 to a planet where the fir trees grew natural Christmas baubles, making it the perfect winter wonderland. Cyril Arwell opened his present early and got lost on the planet. The Doctor and Lily followed, and the three of them found a lighthouse-like structure guarded by two wooden giants.

Madge Arwell followed them, and encountered a large metal walker: a Harvester from Androzani Major. A three-man team from Androzani Major was preparing to liquify the forest using acid rain; the melted wood of the Androzani Trees, when put in batteries, was the greatest fuel source in the universe. The trees were aware of this, and were planning to use the lighthouse to give up their physical forms and escape. They need to travel inside a living navigator to do this: a "strong" being, a mother. Madge served as the host, and used her memories of home to escape the world as the acid rain started to fall. She returned with the

---

#1, #8) - Events pick up after Tara's exit from the TARDIS in *The Ninth Doctor Year One.*
1900 Dating *The Web in Space* (BBC children's 2-in-1 #6, released in *Sightseeing in Space*) - Earth has colonies on other planets, although "Earth Corp Couriers" might be a brand name, and not service Earth itself. The Daleks are spacefaring at this time. It's after humanity has encountered the Chelonians, but before the Chelonians go peaceful. Mention of Galaxy 16 suggests intergalactic travel, so we're guessing to say that this story occurs in the 5300s.
1901 Dating *The Husbands of River Song* (X10.0) - A caption reads, "Mendorax Dellora (human colony),

Christmas Day 5343". River says she's "two hundred" years old, possibly in accordance with the newly born Alex Kingston version of the character being deposited in 5123 (*Let's Kill Hitler*), but allowing for larking about through space-time, she's probably somewhat older. It's a toss-up as to whether her extended lifespan owes to her Time Lord inheritance, or if humans in this era naturally live so long.
1902 Dating *The Doctor, the Widow and the Wardrobe* (X7.0) - One of the expedition team, Droxil, states that "the year is 5345". Droxil is "from" Androzani Major, meaning that this is a different planet, although they call the trees "Androzani Trees".

Doctor and her children back to 1941.

The Androzani Major expedition team had transmat technology, and scanners that could detect time travellers – but such scans could be confused if the subject was wearing wool.

? 5345 - THE HUSBANDS OF RIVER SONG[1903] ->

With the twelfth Doctor in tow, River Song piloted the TARDIS to the *Harmony & Redemption* – a starship on a seven-galaxy cruise, and which catered to the genocidal. Passengers had to pay a minimum ticket price of 100 billion credits, plus provide evidence that they had slaughtered many innocent beings (suites were reserved for planet-burners).

River sold the prized Halassi Androvar diamond, which was lodged in the head of King Hydroflax, to the Shoal of the Winter Harmony... then discovered that the Shoal revered Hydroflax, who had visited their world. Hydroflax's cybernetic body obliterated Hydroflax's head as inferior, and desired the Doctor's head as a replacement. A standoff ended when, as part of River's escape plan, the *Harmony & Redemption* hit a meteor storm and crashed onto the planet Darillium. River was struck unconscious, and so the Doctor popped out to the wreckage and gave the Halassi Androvar to a rescue team member, Alphonse. The Doctor suggested that the reward for the diamond's return would provide seed money for a restaurant near Darillium's famed Singing Towers...

1903 Dating *The Husbands of River Song* (X10.0) - It's not specified how much time has passed since the story's 5343 component, but it's no earlier than the same era, since the Shoal know of and revere Hydroflax. (The Shoal representative doesn't even specify that it's after Hydroflax gone missing or is believed to have died; he only claims that Hydrovax "visited their world in blood and joy.") *Some* time displacement from 5343 is clearly involved, which is why River borrows the TARDIS rather than using her own shuttle, but her escape plan only relies upon arriving at the *Harmony & Redemption* very shortly prior to its destruction – so the time-gap might not be all that substantial, it's just strategic on her part. A monitor screen aboard the *Harmony & Redemption* reads "07:08:32:17", but that's of limited help (the year certainly isn't 3217, for the aforementioned reasons). The *Harmony & Redemption* travels at warp factor twelve – perhaps a small dig at *Star Trek*, where it's impossible to go faster than warp ten.

1904 Dating *The Husbands of River Song* (X10.0) - It's unclear how much time has passed since the restaurant's founding, but the venue is now so successful, you have to wait four years to get a table.

1906 Dating *The Husbands of River Song* (X10.0) - It's "Christmas Day", "four years" on since the Doctor placed a reservation at the restaurant. The Doctor here gives River her "future sonic screwdriver", as seen in *Silence in the Library*.

1905 *Extremis*

1907 *The Husbands of River Song, The Return of Doctor Mysterio*.

1908 *Extremis*. The last we saw of River's diary before this, the tenth Doctor and Donna left it behind in the Library (*Forest of the Dead*). Nardole's copy looks even older, its pages almost falling out of the binding. Unless River kept two diaries, then, the computer-copy of River – not the earlier version of her on Darillium – must have sent the book along to Nardole. That matches Nardole referring to River as the Doctor's "late wife". It's more up in the air to wonder *how*, exactly, Nardole travels from Darillum to the Fatality Indexers' world (see the dating notes on *Extremis*, the Gallifrey section).

1909 *The Shining Man* (ch2).

1910 Dating *Tales of Trenzalore* (BBC Series 7 ebook #4: "Let it Snow", #4a; "An Apple a Day...", #4b; "Strangers in the Outland", #4c) - The *Tales of Trenzalore* anthology contains four stories that occur throughout the eleventh Doctor's tenure on Trenzalore (*The Time of the Doctor*). The first three contain dating clues placing them fairly close to the segment three hundred years on, when Clara first returns... the Doctor has already been on Trenzalore "for centuries" in "Let It Snow" (ch5); last made an ice rink in Christmas "a couple hundred" years ago and is "nearly fifteen hundred years old. At least, I think that's about right. Could be a few hundred years either way, really", in "An Apple a Day" (chapters 2, 8); and has repelled invaders to Christmas for "the last three centuries" in "Strangers in the Outland" (ch3). The fourth story in this collection, "The Dreaming", occurs much later, when the Doctor has been on Trenzalore for about 750 years.

An earlier script of *The Time of the Doctor* had the Doctor with a wooden leg on Trenzalore; Matt Smith has commented that he preferred this version, but the artificial limb isn't mentioned on screen (possibly because it was deemed too much of a downer for a Christmas special). The Doctor sports a wooden leg in "An Apple a Day..." and "Strangers in the Outland". In the former, he starts to tell some children the tale of how he lost his limb, but we never hear the details.

1911 Dating *The Time of the Doctor* (X7.16) - The Doctor's time on Trenzalore: "three hundred years".

1912 Dating *Dalek Empire I* (episode one, *Invasion of the Daleks*; episode two, *The Human Factor*) - As with the Davros Era, the *Dalek Empire* mini-series (I-IV) are fairly easy to date in relation to one another, but it's harder to establish the century they are set. The only tangible dating evidence is the Dalek Emperor's com-

& 5350 - THE HUSBANDS OF RIVER SONG[1904] -> The twelfth Doctor found the restaurant by the Singing Towers of Darillium had a four-year waiting list, but made a reservation for himself and River Song and jumped forward in the TARDIS...

The Doctor and River's Night on Darillium

& 5354 (25th December) - THE HUSBANDS OF RIVER SONG[1905] -> River Song awoke in the TARDIS following the destruction of the *Harmony & Redemption*, and stepped out to find the twelfth Doctor had a dinner reservation for them at the restaurant near the Singing Towers of Darillium. Nardole and Ramone, one of River's husbands, had been working for the restaurant for some time, their heads now part of the cybernetic body formerly belonging to King Hydroflax.

As her diary was nearly full, River feared that her time with the Doctor was ending, and she was mindful of legends saying that the two of them would spend their final night together at the Singing Towers. The Doctor gifted River with her own sonic screwdriver, and revealed to her that the nights on Darillium lasted for twenty-four years...

The Daleks believed that the Doctor had retired, and was enjoying domestic bliss on Darillium.[1906] The 24-year-long night on Darillium ended in 5378. By every account, River Song next encountered the Doctor at the Library. The twelfth Doctor worried he'd be lonely, and so restored Nardole's head to his body.[1907]

River Song bequeathed her diary to Nardole, with full authorisation to kick the Doctor's arse. Nardole followed the Doctor from Darillium to the planet of the keepers of the Fatality Index, and bore witness to Missy's "execution".[1908]

By the late fifty-fourth century, primroses had evolved into a race of brilliant philosophers and orators – the greatest minds the galaxy had ever seen.[1909]

& 5400 - TALES OF TRENZALORE: "Let It Snow" / "An Apple a Day..." / "Strangers in the Outland"[1910] -> The eleventh Doctor repelled various races who employed non-technological means to elude the Papal Mainframe's blockade of Trenzalore. Lord Ssardak's Ice Warriors landed on Trenzalore using ice capsules, and set up a makeshift sonic cannon... which the Doctor reflected back at Ssardak's soldiers with his sonic screwdriver, boiling them alive.

A Krynoid pod successfully fell to Trenzalore and germinated within a young man named Pieter, but was destroyed by the Doctor using vibrations from the Christmas Clock Tower. The Doctor also dispatched a cadre of Autons that

eluded the Papal Mainframe's barrier.

At some point during his life on Trenzalore, the Doctor lost a leg and replaced it with a wooden one.

& 5400 - THE TIME OF THE DOCTOR[1911] -> The eleventh Doctor, now visibly older and sporting a cane, defeated a wooden Cyberman that made it through the Trenzalore blockade.

The TARDIS returned for the Doctor three hundred years later than expected, as it had extended its exterior force field to protect Clara during its trip through the Vortex. The Daleks successfully broke into the Papal Mainframe and turned those within into Dalek Puppets. The Doctor aided Tasha Lem in restoring her true personality, then took Clara back home against her will. He returned to Trenzalore, and continued on as its protector.

The Seriphia-based Daleks Attack the Milky Way

& 5425 - DALEK EMPIRE I: INVASION OF THE DALEKS / THE HUMAN FACTOR[1912] -> The Milky Way was at peace, and under the protection of the Earth Alliance. The Daleks had been relegated to obscure history lessons, but had fortified themselves in the Seriphia Galaxy, and now unleashed a massive invasion of human space. They conquered many planets, and enslaved billions. Amongst the many worlds to fall was Vega VI – the Daleks put slaves there to work mining veganite, a rare mineral that was too volatile to collect with Dalek technology. The Daleks were relentless taskmasters, and worked their slaves to death.

Susan Mendes, an employee of the Rhinesberg Institute, was amongst those enslaved in the mines on Vega VI. She met a fellow slave named Kalendorf – a telepathic Knight of Velyshaa who had been slated to represent his people in negotiations with Earth against the Dalek menace. The Dalek Supreme had Mendes psychologically profiled, and deemed her suitable for an undertaking to aid the Dalek cause. The slaves were allowed to rest and given food, while Mendes served as a spokesperson who encouraged the slave ranks to have hope and work hard. In this capacity, Mendes became widely known as The Angel of Mercy. As the slaves worked more willingly and required less subjugation, the Daleks diverted more resources into their war effort against Alliance forces.

Six months passed as Mendes travelled to many planets on behalf of the Daleks, obtaining better working conditions that saved millions of lives. She insisted that Kalendorf accompany her, and the two of them plotted the Daleks' downfall. On every world they visited, Kalendorf would telepathically communicate with the slave leaders, and told them to wait until Mendes publicly declared a code-phrase that would trigger an unstoppable rebellion against the Daleks.

One rebellion on the Garazone moon K-5000 broke out prematurely – Mendes feared that the insurrection would undo her master plan and reported it to the Daleks, who killed those involved. The Daleks conquered the ocean planet Guria, despite heavy resistance from the Alliance.

& 5425 - RETURN OF THE DALEKS[1913] -> The Daleks stumbled upon the frozen Dalek army on the planet Spiridon – which had been renamed Zaleria – and sought to revive it as a weapon of war. They also hoped to crack the means by which the Spiridon natives had become visible, thinking they could reverse-engineer a means of turning Daleks invisible. Much data was collected, but any attempt to turn Daleks invisible caused fatal light-sickness.

The seventh Doctor feared that the revival of the frozen

Dalek army could tip history in the Daleks' favour. He encountered Kalendorf, and the two of them spurred a minor rebellion against the Daleks. Kalendorf was captured, and the Doctor – deeming Kalendorf's place in history as too important to risk – offered to help the Daleks develop invisibility if they let Kalendorf go. The Daleks agreed, and Mendes and Kalendorf went to their next assignment. The Doctor was the Daleks' prisoner for years.

? 5426 - BROTHERHOOD OF THE DALEKS[1914] -> The Thals had peacefully settled on the planet of New Davias. Many of them still regarded Earth as a lost planet, and the Doctor – who had contacts on New Davias – as a legend. The Thals now had access to books from across time and space, including *Das Kapital*, and had recently fought wars with the Mechanoids.

The Thal scientist Murgat adapted a Dalek facility in Antares, and experimented to see if kyropite flowers from

---

ment in *Dalek Empire I* episode four that it's been "centuries" since the Daleks invaded the Kar-Charrat library in *The Genocide Machine*, which in this chronology is dated to circa 5256. The war between the Knights of Velyshaa and Earth (mentioned in *The Sirens of Time* as ending in 3562) is said to have occurred "long ago".

An number of online sources claim that *Dalek Empire* begins in 4162 – possibly because the online Discontinuity Guide speculated upon that date, and other websites ran with it as fact. While that placement, between *The Evil of the Daleks* and the Davros Era, is workable, there's no smoking gun indicating it. To double-check, we asked writer Nicholas Briggs, who whimsically told us over email: "I definitely did not set a date for *Dalek Empire*, so this must be something that someone else imposed on it in a fruitless attempt to make sense of the continuity. :) "

1913 Dating *Return of the Daleks* (BF subscription promo #4) - The story occurs between *Dalek Empire I* episodes one (*Invasion of the Daleks*) and two (*The Human Factor*).

The knock-on effect of moving the *Dalek Empire* stories to the sixth millennium (see *The Genocide Machine* for how this came about) introduces a contradiction that *Ahistory* Second Edition had otherwise resolved. In *Return of the Daleks*, the seventh Doctor guarantees that the Dalek army on Spiridon (from *Planet of the Daleks*) remains frozen; later on, in "Emperor of the Daleks", Davros appropriates this army to create his Imperial Daleks. Reconciling the accounts of these stories was based upon the numbers of the Spiridon army... The Thals in *Planet of the Daleks* believe that "ten thousand Daleks" are buried on Spiridon, but *Return of the Daleks* says this is faulty information, and the frozen Daleks actually number 1,100,000. "Emperor of the Daleks" has Davros labouring on Spiridon for a year, whereupon he unleashes an army of four million gold-

and-white Daleks. So, one could conclude that the third Doctor froze the Dalek army (cited as only ten thousand, but actually numbering 1,100,000) in *Planet of the Daleks*, that the seventh Doctor prevented their revival in *Return of the Daleks*, and that Davros later used the Spiridon army to cobble together his force of four million Daleks.

All well and good... save that moving *Return of the Daleks* forward in time means that the seventh Doctor is here re-freezing a Dalek army that Davros has already appropriated for use elsewhere. One explanation is that it's never expressly established that Davros takes *each and every* last Dalek from Spiridon – perhaps he builds four million Daleks, but leaves one million(ish) behind on Spiridon as reinforcements to call upon should he need them. Or, perhaps he actually constructs *five* million Daleks, takes four million with him and leaves the extra one million behind. Either way, it's understandable why the seventh Doctor would want to keep the surplus million Daleks frozen. What this *doesn't* explain is how, if *Return of the Daleks* comes later than "Emperor of the Daleks", the Spiridons are still invisible in "Emperor" when *Return* states that they become visible following *Planet of the Daleks*, and only regain their invisibility owing to the Doctor releasing a virus during Mendes and Kalendorf's revolution.

1914 Dating *Brotherhood of the Daleks* (BF #114) - Dating clues abound, but no actual year is mentioned. Kyropites previously appeared in *The Mind's Eye*, but there's no other relation given between that story and this one.

One of the Thals says, "And there are Ganatus knows how many levels like this..."; if this denotes the slain Ganatus from *The Daleks*, *Brotherhood of the Daleks* must take place after that. The Thals have now settled on New Davias, on such a scale that it's quite possibly where they went prior to Skaro's obliteration in

planet YT45 – which was located four galaxies away – could replicate Thal personalities in Daleks, to sabotage the Dalek war effort. The Daleks, however, had secretly facilitated Murgat's undertaking to see if they could install Thal characteristics – such as camaraderie and fighting spirit – into Daleks to make them better killers.

Some Daleks with Thal personalities, named "Thaleks", turned against their own kind and executed a Black Dalek. The sixth Doctor and Charley hoped that the Thaleks would peacefully thrive – but after they left, the Thaleks' Dalek-ness took hold. Their renewed desire to exterminate triggered a booby trap on the facility's anti-matter reactor, destroying them and Murgat.

& 5427 - DALEK EMPIRE IV: THE FEARLESS[1915] ->

Earth Alliance developed elite cybernetic battlesuits for use against the Daleks. Agnes Landen headed the battlesuit division, "the Spacers".

The able-bodied men of Talis Minor, an inhospitable colony world, were forcibly conscripted into the Spacers. The Daleks attacked Kedru VII, and although the Alliance won, the Daleks initiated a kamikaze manoeuvre that destroyed the planet's atmosphere and anyone living there. Salus Kade was appointed a Spacer squadron commander.

Most of Kade's squad was wiped out in a botched attempt to assassinate Susan Mendes, the Angel of Mercy. Kade survived, but spent a year in isolation while returning in a Dalek trans-solar disc. He was appointed captain of the flagship *Herald*, and destroyed key Dalek generators that would have propelled an asteroid storm into Earth's solar system. Kade learned that Landen had reviewed surveillance and tagged him as a valuable asset prior to the Spacers ever visiting Talis Minor – setting in motion a series of events that had culminated in the death of his wife and child. He resigned his commission, but Landen suspected he'd rejoin the Spacers after realising his old life was gone.

& 5430 - DALEK EMPIRE I: "DEATH TO THE DALEKS!" / PROJECT INFINITY[1916] ->

The Daleks made great progress against the Earth Alliance in the years following their invasion of the Milky Way. Billions of people were killed. Carson's Planet attempted to stay neutral, and became a watering hole for space travellers.

Dalek forces directly attacked the Sol System – Jupiter and Saturn fell, and human forces on Mars were outnumbered 100 to 1. The President of Earth was left with no choice but to surrender.

The Dalek Supreme and Dalek Emperor were aware of Mendes and Kalendorf's plans, but let them proceed as the galactic invasion was a massive distraction. Using knowledge obtained from the Kar-Charrat library, the Daleks had learned of Project Infinity – an Alliance undertaking in the Lopra System, designed to penetrate the dimensional barriers so humanity could view a reality where the Daleks had been defeated, then replicate this accomplishment. Lopra was on the opposite end of the galaxy from Seriphia, and so the Daleks had invaded the Milky Way to reach it. The Daleks wanted to ally themselves with Daleks from another reality and jointly conquer the universe. The Imperial flagship departed, with the Dalek Emperor aboard, for Lopra Minor.

Mendes and Kalendorf judged that the time was right for their rebellion. She went to the planet Yaldos to make a major broadcast to all slaves in Dalek territory – and shouted the code-phrase "Death to the Daleks!", causing billions of slaves to turn en masse against their Dalek masters. The Daleks put Mendes into suspended animation so she could be turned into one of their number.

When news came forth that Mendes and Kalendorf had

Remembrance of the Daleks.

Tellingly, the Daleks at present have an empire. Also, one of the Thals is a veteran of "the Mechanoid Wars", which are likely to have occurred in the third or fourth millennium, as there's no record of the Mechanoids even being active later than some excavated ones dug up in 4620 (in *The Juggernauts*). Additionally, Murgat says that the Doctor aided the Thals in driving the Daleks from this sector of the galaxy, but the Doctor says he hasn't been near Antares in six millennia, and assumes that Murgat refers to events in his personal future. It seems reasonable to take this as a reference to *Return of the Daleks*, meaning that *Brotherhood of the Daleks* must occur in close relation to the *Dalek Empire* series – which is handy, as the Daleks do have an empire at that point.

At least two of the Daleks present remember meeting Charley in Folkestone in *Terror Firma*, but allowing that those post-*Remembrance* Daleks likely have some form of time travel (however crude), it's not an altogether helpful detail. The term "Thaleks" was used in the Unbound story *Auld Mortality*.

1915 Dating *Dalek Empire IV: The Fearless* – The story occurs in the years that pass very shortly after the start of *Dalek Empire I* episode three ("*Death to the Daleks!*"), but prior to the Daleks overrunning Earth in that installment. Ernst Tanlee, who's killed at the very end of *Dalek Empire I*, here appears as head of Earth Alliance security. Like *Dalek Empire II* but unlike the other *Dalek Empire* mini-series, *Dalek Empire IV* has no individual episode titles.

1916 Dating *Dalek Empire I* (episode three, "*Death to the Daleks!*"; episode four, *Project Infinity*) - An unspecified number of "years" occur as the Daleks make advances, and Mendes and Kalendorf shore up their master plan. "Eight months" pass after Mendes gives the rebellion signal, and Kalendorf spends five months after that in transit to the Lopra System.

initiated their galaxy-wide uprising, the seventh Doctor – still a prisoner on Spiridon – released a contagion he'd secretly developed. This wiped out his Dalek captors, and turned the Spiridon natives invisible again.[1917]

Eight months passed as the rebellion continued. Kalendorf learned of Project Infinity, and spent five months travelling to Lopra to investigate. Matters came to a head on Lopra Minor. The Dalek Emperor used the veganite obtained from Vega VI to power Project Infinity to a previously unimaginable scale, and opened a doorway to an alternate dimension where the Daleks reigned supreme. A delegation of alt-reality Daleks communed with the Emperor, but judged his Daleks as guilty of great crimes. The alt-Daleks vowed to destroy their counterparts.

The Mentor, the creator of the alt-Daleks, pledged to support the Earth Alliance against the enemy Daleks. Kalendorf became her fleet commander. The Dalek Emperor was captured on Lopra Minor, but mysteriously went inert.[1918]

? 5433 - PLANET OF THE SPIDERS[1919] **->** An Earth ship came out of its time jump without power and crashed on Metebelis III. Some humans, a few sheep and a handful of spiders survived the crash. The spiders found their way to the cave of the blue crystals,

and the energies there mutated them, making them grow and boosting their intelligence and psychic abilities. The "Eight-Legs" came to dominate the planet, harvesting the human population as cattle. The Eight-Legs were ruthless – they wiped out two hundred and sixty-nine villagers, the entire population of Skorda, when they tried to resist.

Four hundred and thirty-three years after the crash, the Spiders set up a psychic bridge with a Tibetan monastery on twentieth-century Earth. They plotted to travel back in time to conquer their homeworld. Their leader, the Great One, planned to gain omnipotence by completing the crystal lattice of her cave. The third Doctor confronted his fear by bringing her the one perfect crystal he had taken from Metebelis some time previous. The energy backlash killed the Great One, but the Doctor received a fatal dose of radiation while in the Great One's cave. He returned to twentieth-century Earth.

& 5433 - THE EIGHT DOCTORS[1920] **->** The humans on Metebelis III hunted down the spiders. The seventh Doctor visited the planet and was caught by a giant spider. The eighth Doctor rescued him.

1917 *Return of the Daleks*

1918 *Dalek Empire II*

1919 Dating *Planet of the Spiders* (11.5) - The colony ship that crashes on Metebelis III has intergalactic capability, as Metebelis is in the Acteon Galaxy. It made a "time jump", also suggesting it's from the far future. *The Terrestrial Index* claimed that the colony ship was "lost during the early days of the twenty-second century", dating *Planet of the Spiders* itself as "c.2530". *The TARDIS Logs* suggested "4256", *Timelink* "3415".

1920 Dating *The Eight Doctors* (EDA #1) - This happens at some point in the aftermath of *Planet of the Spiders*.

1921 *The Eight Truths/Worldwide Web*

1922 Dating *Dalek Empire II: Dalek War* (no individual titles) – Mendes is revived from stasis "five, nearly six" years after instigating her rebellion in *Dalek Empire I*.

1923 *Dalek Empire III*

1924 Dating *Dalek Empire II: Dalek War* (no individual titles) - Kalendorf's conflict against the Alliance Daleks is described as a "long, terrible war", and must run for a number of years. The Great Catastrophe seems to occur shortly after the Alliance Daleks' withdrawal to their home dimension.

THE GREAT CATASTROPHE: *Dalek Empire II* ends with all Daleks and Dalek technology in the Milky Way and Seriphia galaxies exploding to such a degree, "countless worlds" (all of them unnamed) are devastated. Some take centuries or millennia to recover, some

never do. The big question for *Ahistory*'s purposes is how much damage Earth itself endures... and, as it happens, this question is never answered. Although *Dalek Empire III* picks up the threads of the Great Catastrophe some two thousand years later, no mention whatsoever is made of Earth's status.

... which isn't to say that the homeworld has been especially devastated beyond repair. Although the Daleks do take control of Earth in *Dalek Empire II*, the "Daleks, Obliterate Yourselves" pulse that brings about The Great Catastrophe wouldn't mete out damage to the planets under Dalek control equally, and some worlds would surely weather that storm better than others. Where this is especially relevant is the question of whether the humans on Earth would emerge from the Great Catastrophe with the technological knowhow and resources to react as we're shown to the Solar Flare event (established in *The Ark in Space*). So little is said about what happens to Earth during The Great Catastrophe, there's nothing to directly rule out pretty much any scenario to follow.

1925 *Dalek Empire III*

1926 Dating *The Pyralis Effect* (BF CC #4.4) - It's long enough after the destruction of Pavonis IV that the Doctor is regarded as a mythical hero, but not so long that the planet's environment has recovered and the survivors have resettled there. Otherwise, this date is arbitrary.

Some of the Metebelis spiders survived the Great One's downfall. They allied themselves with the profit-minded Headhunter, and went back to 2015 to capitalise on a master plan she had devised. The surviving spiders returned to their homeworld upon their defeat.[1921]

& 5436 - DALEK EMPIRE II: DALEK WAR[1922] **->** Mendes' rebellion had greatly weakened the Daleks' empire, but they remained a formidable foe despite the best efforts of the Mentor's "Alliance Daleks" and the surviving human forces. The Alliance cut off the enemy Daleks' retreat back to Seriphia, triggering years of warfare. Meanwhile, Kalendorf learned that the Alliance Daleks had devastated several worlds, including Emeron, who refused to contribute to the war effort. He feared that if the enemy Daleks were defeated, humankind would just be replacing a nihilistic dictatorship with a more benevolent one.

Nearly six years after Mendes instigated her uprising, Kalendorf's most trusted allies located Mendes' cryo-pod and revived her. As they suspected, the Emperor had "escaped" by downloading his consciousness into Mendes' body. Kalendorf's fleet mounted an attempt to reclaim the Sol System – but the enemy Daleks' first wave self-destructed, obliterating a quarter of his forces. Kalendorf's fleet discovered that Jupiter had mysteriously been terra-formed and could now sustain human life. Half of Kalendorf's spaceships put down on Jupiter to make repairs before the Daleks' second wave arrived – and were overcome by Varga plants that the enemy Daleks had seeded there.

The Mentor relieved Kalendorf of command and ordered him brought in for "brain correction", but he escaped, located Mendes and shared with her his plan to rout both Dalek factions. Mendes agreed with Kalendorf's proposal and killed her beloved, Corporal Alby Brook, to prevent his interference. She then made a galaxy-wide broadcast, saying she was the Angel of Mercy returned, and urging humanity to join forces with the enemy Daleks against the Alliance Daleks. The Dalek Supreme agreed to this new alliance.

The Alliance Daleks tried to create "demons": augmented humans who could combat the enemy Daleks. On a space station in the Plowik System, some Alliance Daleks genetically and technologically augmented test subjects with physical strength, an extended lifespan and the ability to alter their appearance on a cellular level, becoming temporarily invisible. Enemy Daleks attacked the station, interrupting the undertaking. One of the "demons", Galanar, would remain in stasis for two millennia.[1923]

The Great Catastrophe Devastates "Countless" Inhabited Worlds

& 5441 - DALEK EMPIRE II: DALEK WAR[1924] **->** The Mentor accelerated plans to bring "brain correction" to those who resisted the Alliance Daleks. Kalendorf forged a pact with the enemy Daleks, and, alongside their forces, led what remained of humanity's forces against the Mentor. Years of warfare and devastation ensued. Kalendorf eventually convinced the Mentor that a continued conflict could only result in the destruction of all life in both their universes. She elected to withdraw all of her alt-Daleks back to their home universe.

For a short while, the galaxy knew peace as the enemy Daleks honoured the terms of their coalition with the Alliance. Kalendorf knew the Daleks would eventually renege, and went to Earth to negotiate with the Dalek Supreme. The Dalek Emperor took control of Mendes' body, and tapped the Dalek command net to probe Kalendorf's mind for signs of betrayal. In so doing, it enabled the last remnants of Mendes' personality to activate a telepathic self-destruct code that Kalendorf had planted in her mind. The destruct command routed through the entire Dalek network, running unfettered owing to the Emperor's full access. All Daleks and Dalek technology in human space and Seriphia were destroyed.

This event caused incalculable devastation, and became known as The Great Catastrophe. Entire star systems were ruined, and countless lives were lost. Parts of the galaxy took centuries, even millennia, to recover.

Kalendorf had expected to perish during his final gambit, but survived. In time, he returned to his homeworld of Velyshaa. His recorded memories were later stored in his burial chamber. History would regard him as a monster, a "dark one" who brought about the galaxy's ruination.

One Dalek outpost survived the Great Catastrophe, when a Dalek was conditioned to absorb Mendes' destructive pulse, then isolated from the outpost's command net. The isolated Dalek consequently absorbed some of Mendes' personality, and also gained the command codes for the entire Dalek network. In the millennia to follow, the Mendes-Dalek would become the new Dalek Supreme.[1925]

? 5500 - THE PYRALIS EFFECT[1926] **->** The fourth Doctor and the second Romana found the *Myriad* – one of the ships containing the cloned survivors of Pavonis IV – as it travelled through the Kasterborous Cluster. A disused Pyralis obelisk influenced a Type 12 AI designated CAIN, who calculated the codes necessary to open it. Thousands of Pyralis escaped, but CAIN sacrificed himself to detonate a device that recalled the Pyralis and imprisoned them once more. The Doctor advised the Pavonians to let go of their past – including their hero-worship for him – and programmed the *Myriad*'s flight computer to take them to a small, habitable planet.

In 5665, the Chelonians launched an attack on the human colony Vaagon, but the Chelonians' tanks vanished mysteriously before they could complete their conquest, transported by a Fortean Flicker to the twenty-seventh century. Believing themselves blessed by divine intervention, the colonists were quite unprepared when the Chelonians reinvaded several generations later and wiped out the colony.[1927] The Doctor bought a collapsible snooker table at the height of the retro-gaming fad of the fifty-eighth century.[1928]

In 5720, archaeologists discovered the remains of a Khorlthochloi starship.[1929] The militaristic Narbrab conquered an alien civilisation. The survivors, hosted in Ikshar host bodies, were banished in a solar-powered ship and arrived in London, 1346.[1930]

Tantane Spaceport served as one of the busiest spaceports in the galaxy. The Red Zone there serviced oxygen breathers, and the White Zone was for zero-gravity, methane-based lifeforms. Tantane possessed an alternating positronic force field, more common in this era than plain positronic ones.

During the Palpane-Shagrane war, a Palpane smuggled a young Wailer beast aboard the spaceport, to kill an incoming Shagrane diplomat with it. Customs objected to the Wailer, putting the spaceport into lockdown. Wailer spaceships surrounded the spaceport to retrieve their young one, but the station's force field held them at bay.

The standoff endured for four centuries. Those within Tantane, and their descendants, split into two tribes: Business and Economy. The stranded Palpane secretly ran both groups, respectively as Director Bones and Elder Bones. Tantane's power systems maintained the force field and life support, but went into standby. The internal lights only activated – in an event the residents called "Summer" – on the rare occasion of new arrivals.[1931]

> = In 5738, the sixth Doctor visited the planet Helios 3.[1932]

River Song excavated the remains of the *Harmony & Redemption*.[1933]

Around 5764, a Dalek civil war became so serious that the Time Lords intervened.[1934] Espero was colonised by

---

1927 *The Highest Science*

1928 *Synthespians™*

1929 *The Price of Paradise*

1930 "Thousands of years" after *Asylum*. No date given, and this is an arbitrary placing.

1931 Repeatedly said to be "four hundred years" before *Spaceport Fear*; the Economy tribe's calendar specifies that it's been "409 years" since Elder Bones took charge. Those same events are said to have occurred "nineteen generations" ago, which going by the rules of this guidebook would equate to 475 years – then again, the scarce resources aboard the isolated Tantane presumably mean that the inhabitants have diminished lifespans.

The Doctor's claim that Tantane is "the busiest spaceport in the galaxy" is interesting, given that nobody, as far as we're told, attempts to end the internal lockdown, or to liberate the station from the Wailer ships surrounding it. It's possible that Tantane was constructed before humanity's fortunes went downhill in the Great Catastrophe in the *Dalek Empire* series (see The Great Catastrophe sidebar), was unaffected by the carnage in those stories, but was left to its own devices afterward. The prolonged isolation of Tantane continues until 6127, by which time solar flares have devastated Earth (*The Ark in Space*), so humanity is even less able to lend assistance.

1932 *Spiral Scratch*

1933 "Four hundred years" after *The Husbands of River Song*.

1934 "Five thousand years" before *The Crystal Bucephalus* (p114).

1935 "Two hundred and seventy years" before *Half-Life*.

1936 Dating *Combat Rock* (PDA #55) - There's no date given, although cigarettes were banned on the colonies "hundreds of years ago". There are smokers in *Resurrection of the Daleks*, but of course a smoking ban can be lifted and ignored, so it's hardly firm evidence that this story is set after that. This date is arbitrary, but it's linked to the Christian colonists of Espero.

The date of the Earth-Indoni war is unspecified, but Jenggel's current political climate seems to stem from its fallout, suggesting a shorter rather than longer span of time since it occurred. The Indoni subjugated the Papul, and the Christian missionaries arrived, some "thirty rainseasons" before the novel takes place.

1937 Dating *Sick Building* (NSA #17) - No dating clues are given, but in *Iris: Enter Wildthyme* (p240), Barbra says that she's from "the fifty-ninth century". The character is named as "Barbara" in *Sick Building* and *Iris: Iris and the Celestial Omnibus*: "The Deadly Flap", but is "Barbra" in *Iris: Enter Wildthyme*.

1938 *Iris: Enter Wildthyme*

1939 Dating *Tales of Trenzalore*: "The Dreaming" (BBC Series 7 ebook #4d) - The Doctor came to Christmas "over seven hundred and fifty years ago" (ch2). Later, he claims it's been "seven hundred years, give or take a decade or five" (ch4). Fellwood was killed around the time of Christmas' founding, "nine hundred" years ago (ch4).

mostly African and Asian humans with a shared Christian faith. The colonists hoped to escape the influence of the Eurozone and America, and bought the planet from the Homeworld Corporation. They renounced technology, which made it all but impossible to extract the planet's natural resources. With nothing to offer in trade, Espero became isolated from the rest of the galaxy. Religious schisms led to the Almost War.[1935]

? 5800 - COMBAT ROCK[1936] -> Earth won a war against the Indoni, making the planet Jenggel an Earth colony. The Indoni subsequently invaded the rival Papul people, forcing the Papul leaders to vote for integration. Tourism swelled amid the new political climate, with visitors arriving to experience the "primitive" Papul culture. The corrupt President Sabit of the Indoni kept most of the profits for himself. Christian missionaries arrived to minister to the Papul. Twentieth-century icons such as *Winnie the Pooh, Wind in the Willows* and Leatherface horror films were in use in pop culture.

On Jenggel, a sentient organism contained in a purple fungus from the Papul swamps possessed a Papul named Kepennis. As the mysterious "Krallik", the organism-Kepennis founded the OPG, a Papul resistance movement. Some eight rainseasons later, Kepennis rigged Papul mumis to kill tourists and Indoni soldiers by spitting snakes, furthering an atmosphere of anarchy. The second Doctor, Jamie and Victoria arrived, and the Doctor ingested some of the fungus himself, enabling him to mentally nullify the organism within Kepennis. A cannibalistic Papul tribe took Kepennis away to consume him as punishment, and a mercenary with a bit of a noble streak killed Sabit.

c 5850 - SICK BUILDING[1937] -> Professor Ernest Tiermann made a fortune in the Servo-furniture industry, and retired to a snowy planet he had purchased, Tiermann's World, with his wife and son. The tenth Doctor and Martha warned the family that a Voracoious Craw – a spaceship-sized monster akin to a tapeworm – was approaching from space and would carve up the planet's surface. Tiermann was determined to abandon his futuristic Dreamhouse – the consciousness of which, the Domovoi, felt betrayed and possessed a sunbed named Toaster. Tiermann and Domovoi/Toaster mutually killed one another, and Tiermann's wife died also. The Doctor and Martha transported Tiermann's son Solin and a sentient vending machine named Barbra to Spaceport Antelope Slash Nitelite.

Barbra fell in with a bad crowd – a pirate gang of decommissioned Servo-furnishings – and fell through a space-time rift, the Deadly Flap, to the twenty-first century.[1938]

& 5850 - TALES OF TRENZALORE: "The Dreaming"[1939] -> The eleventh Doctor had now been on Trenzalore for more than seven hundred and fifty years. The Mara was freed from its imprisonment beneath the earth, and succeeded in manifesting through Jalen Fellwood's skeleton. The Doctor capitalized on Fellwood's belief that salt could harm magical entities, and annihilated the Mara by creating a salt-laden snowfall.

c 5895 - THE KROTONS[1940] -> **On the planet of the Gonds, the dynatrope registered the second Doctor and Zoe as the "high brains" it had long sought. The two surviving Krotons revived, and made plans to leave the planet, even though take-off would devastate the Gonds and their city. The Doctor, Jamie and Zoe helped to destroy the Krotons and their dynatrope with sulphuric acid.**

1940 Dating *The Krotons* (6.4) - This has been one of the most persistently undatable TV stories. *About Time* concedes that the year is "unknown", and Jon Preddle writes in *Timelink*, "I have placed *The Krotons* under ?????" While the story gives virtually no dating clues (it isn't even established if the Gonds are human or not), evidence from the tie-in media allows for the establishment of some parameters.

Alien Bodies (p263-264) says that the Krotons were literally patterned after the type of servo-robots seen in *The Wheel in Space*, meaning the Krotons didn't exist prior to humankind's colonial age. The same section of *Alien Bodies* suggests that (in terms of rudimentary personality, if nothing else) the Krotons as we know them took some "centuries" to develop.

In *Return of the Krotons*, a Kroton who went dormant circa 3700 regards dynatropes – relative to when it liquefied – as "an inferior form of craft, with low grade crew specifications. We are more advanced." So, if dynatropes haven't been outright discontinued by the thirty-eighth century, it's unlikely they were used much after. The Krotons featured in *The Krotons* might be using a dynatrope well past its expiration date, but we nonetheless have a rough approximation of when they landed on the planet of the Gonds.

The Gond leader Selris says in *The Krotons* episode one that the Krotons arrived "thousands of years" ago – not the most specific of terms to start with, and one that becomes even vaguer when it's taken into account that the Gonds have forgotten so much of their history. The Doctor similarly claims in episode three that the Krotons have been lying dormant for "thousands of years", but he might just be repeating what Selris told the TARDIS crew.

? 5900 - MISSION: IMPRACTICAL[1941] **->** Sabalom Glitz stole a Tzun data core from the reptilian Veltrochni. He sold it to Niccolo Mandell, an agent of the Vandor Prime government. Ten years later, the Veltrochni threatened to make war against Vandor Prime over the stolen Tzun data core. It was the last surviving information cache from the Tzun Empire, and contained blueprints on how to construct Tzun Stormblades. Vandor Prime head of security Niccolo Mandell, hoping to sell the data core, coerced the sixth Doctor, Frobisher and Glitz into retrieving the device from an orbital facility.

Glitz's associate Dibber died in a crossfire, but the Doctor purged the data core of its more dangerous information and returned it to the Veltrochni. Vandor Prime authorities arrested Mandell. Glitz continued travelling in his *Nosferatu*.

? 5900 - TRAGEDY DAY[1942] **->** On the Earth colony Olleril, the precocious boy genius Crispin, leader of the secret society of Luminus, sought to gain mental control of the population, and to pattern everyone after characters from the show *Martha and Arthur*. Meanwhile, the immortal Friars of Pangloss hired the arachnid mutant Ernie "Eight Legs" McCartney, the most feared assassin in the Seventh Quadrant, to retrieve a cursed piece of red glass that the Doctor had acquired. The seventh Doctor, Benny and Ace thwarted Crispin's plans, and Crispin died when the Luminus submarine *Gargantuan* was destroyed. Ravenous Slaag creatures consumed McCartney. The Friars were disrupted by an anti-matter burst, and flung powerless into the Time Vortex.

The Solar Flares and the Evacuation of Earth

The Earth was ruled by the World Executive. Earth at this time was technically advanced, with advanced suspended animation techniques, fission guns and power supplied via solar stacks and granavox turbines.

Scientists monitoring the Sun predicted a series of massive solar flares: within only a matter of years, the Earth's surface would be ravaged and virtually all life

---

For *Ahistory* Third Edition, we presumed that the Krotons landed on Gond circa 2895 (the mid-point between man's colonial age starting about 2090 and dynatropes being deemed "inferior" circa 3700), then arbitrarily added on three thousand years and dated *The Krotons* to circa 5895. After that, *A History of the Universe in 100 Objects* (p210) dated its Dynatrope entry to the "mid fourth millennium" – which sounds perfectly reasonable on its face, save that it's not especially possible for the Krotons to have landed on the planet of the Gonds "thousands of years" prior to that, if they didn't exist before circa 2090 per *Alien Bodies*, and took some centuries to develop.

While it's possible that Selris and the Doctor are simply off in their estimates, and the Krotons have been suspended in liquid tanks on the planet of the Gonds for centuries rather than "thousands of years", it seems best to simply note *A History of the Universe in 100 Objects'* preference and let stand Third Edition's figure of circa 5895.

1941 Dating *Mission: Impractical* (PDA #12) - It is "a couple of million years" before *The Trial of a Time Lord* (p56). Ernie McCartney from *Tragedy Day* is mentioned (p215), setting this around the same time as that book. This would not appear, from the other stories featuring Glitz, to be his native timezone. We might conclude that he has ended up somehow either acquiring time travel or been brought here by a time traveller.

1942 Dating *Tragedy Day* (NA #24) - There is no indication of the date in the book, although the colony planet Pantorus is mentioned here (p83) and in *Zamper* (p57), perhaps suggesting they are set around the same time.

1943 *The Ark in Space*

THE SOLAR FLARES: The solar flares ravage the Earth

"thousands of years" after the thirtieth century (*Revenge of the Cybermen*). Judging by information in the TV series, the last recorded human activity on Earth for millions of years is in the fifty-first century (*The Talons of Weng-Chiang, The Invisible Enemy*). The books and audios push this forward by about a thousand years, to around 6000. *Luna Romana*, for instance, acknowledges the solar flares as devastating Earth "sometime after the sixth millennium". The Solar Flares must occur relatively soon after this time.

The first edition of *The Programme Guide* claimed that Earth was only evacuated between "c.2800" and "c.2900", the second suggested dates between "c.2900" and "c.4300". *The Terrestrial Index* attempted to rationalise the statement that the Ark was built in the "thirtieth century", stating that Nerva was built, but then the Solar Flares "abated", Nerva was not informed and the population of Nerva went on to recolonise Ravolox "between 15,000 and 20,000" (as seen in *The Mysterious Planet*). This contradicts the date for *The Mysterious Planet* established on screen and would represent a rather implausible oversight on behalf of the Earth's authorities. The book's supposition that the Solar Flares caused the Ice Age we see in *The Ice Warriors* (a theory repeated in *Legacy*) is specifically ruled out by dialogue in *The Ice Warriors*. For analysis of the solar flares as referenced in the new series, see *The Beast Below*.

1944 Dating *Dreamtime* (BF #67) - Simon Forward scripted this story with the intent of it occurring during the time of the World Zones Authority in the twenty-first century, but nothing in the story itself supports this. Talk of evacuating the Earth means it fits naturally at the time of the solar flares. If the "past" segments are part of the Dreaming and inherently unreliable, dating

would be wiped out. It would be five thousand years before the planet would be habitable again.

The High Minister and the Earth Council began working on humanity's salvation. Carefully screened humans, the Star Pioneers, were sent out in vast colony ships to places such as Colony 9 and Andromeda. Nerva was converted into an ark housing the cream of humanity, some one hundred thousand people, who were placed in suspended animation along with samples of animal and plant life. Nerva also contained the sum of human knowledge stored on microfilm.

The rest of humanity took to thermic shelters, knowing that they wouldn't survive. When the solar flares came, every living thing on the Earth perished.

A group of Star Pioneers reached Andromeda and encountered the Wirrn, a race of parasitic insects who lived in space, visiting worlds only to breed.[1943]

? 5950 - DREAMTIME[1944] -> Facing a catastrophic natural disaster, evacuation coordinators herded the people onto Phoenix lifeships that departed for space. In Australia, a guru named Baiame sought an alternative and hoped to channel the Dreaming – a collective force, derived from the minds and dreams of humanity – to influence matter. Baiame wanted to lift Uluru, a sacred bluff, and its people into space under protection of a Dreaming-generated force field. The seventh Doctor traversed the Dreaming and arrived from thousands of years in the future. Baiame acceded to the Doctor's request that he extend his sphere of protection a few miles and include settlers in the surrounding vicinity. The Uluru lifted off from Earth with its people and sped into space, and the Doctor returned to the future.

? 5950 - SMILE[1945] -> Humanity's Third Industrial Revolution gave rise to servile microbots that communed through robot interfaces: the Vardies. The United Earth Colony Ship *Erewhon*, equipped with a Fleischmann cold fusion engine, founded a settlement on a planet twenty light-years from humanity's homeworld. While most of the colonists slept in cryo-freeze, the *Erewhon*'s microbots configured themselves into a city. Agriculture slated for the colony included wheat, orchards and olive groves.

The *Erewhon*'s skeleton crew grieved when an elderly woman died from natural causes, and the Vardies –

---

becomes even murkier. Forward says that the Galyari Korshal in *Dreamtime* isn't the character of the same name in *Benny S5: The Bone of Contention* (even if Steffan Rhodri voices both parts); the Galyari are long-lived, but traditionally hand down some names through the generations.

THE ABANDONMENT OF EARTH: Earth is completely evacuated six, possibly eight or nine, times that we know of: (1) for "ten thousand years" between the time of the Solar Flares and *The Sontaran Experiment* (c.6000-c.16,000 AD); (2) for at least three thousand five hundred years before (and an unknown amount of time after) *Birthright* (c.18,500 AD-?); (3) a line cut from the rehearsal script but retained in the *Planet of Evil* novelisation reveals that "The Tellurian planet [Earth] has been uninhabited since the Third Era" (significantly before 37,166 AD); (4) for a significant time after the Usurians move the workforce to Pluto before *The Sun Makers* millions of years in the future; (5) there is a mass evacuation shortly before Earth plunges into the Sun ten million years in the future, seen in *The Ark* and reported in *Frontios*; (6) finally, Earth was empty at the time of its final destruction in the year five billion, seen in *The End of the World*.

The Wreck of the World describes a downslide for Earth circa 600,000 – one vaguely said to entail "so many diseases, so few resources", and a lack of forward thinking on humanity's part. Whatever the exact cause, it's profound enough to warrant *The World* colony ship trying to evacuate with millions of people and a storehouse of high-profile cultural items.

A wild card is the migration from Earth involving Starship UK, as seen in *The Beast Below* (possibly, or possibly not, part of the aforementioned Solar Flare incident; see the dating notes on that story). Similarly, *Smile* points to a global apocalypse that could be one of the aforementioned disasters or something else altogether. *System Wipe* (p13) concurs that Earth "gets blasted" half a dozen times at least.

1945 Dating *Smile* (X10.2) - While *The Beast Below* remains the new-series story that's the most problematic to date, *Smile* gives it a run for the money. The chief obstacle is that the Doctor keeps revising his assessment of the colony's history in a manner that's vague, seemingly without any tangible evidence, and at times blatantly contradictory. As he fails to acknowledge that he's amending his remarks so strongly, one wonders if he even noticed. It's habitual in *Doctor Who* to defer to the Doctor, but such are his blinding reversals of facts here, it's helpful to recall that this incarnation habitually can't even tell an older person from a younger one (see, in particular, *The Caretaker*).

Certainly, the Doctor's initial claim that this represents "one of Earth's first colonies" (only "twenty light years" from Earth) and his later determination that it's after Earth was evacuated (revised *again* to say that these are the last humans) cannot both be true. The scenes we see of a deteriorating situation on Earth looks contemporary, because stock footage of real natural disasters and riots is used. On the other hand, even sticking to just the TV series, Earth has dozens if not hundreds or thousands of colonies long before the homeworld is abandoned for even the first time, let alone the last (see The Abandonment of Earth sidebar).

programmed to prioritise the colonists' happiness above all else – killed anyone unable to quell their sadness. The twelfth Doctor and Bill restored the murderous microbots to their factory settings, then encouraged the surviving humans to recognise the Vardies as a legitimate lifeform, and share the planet with them.

New arrivals showed up at the isolated Tantane Spaceport, causing the lights to bring about Summer before going dark two hours later.[1946]

During a period in which humanity didn't inhabit the Earth, an alien race set up the Gogglebox – a giant museum dedicated to Earth and its history – deep within Earth's moon. The fifth Doctor met history student Alan Fitzgerald there, and left behind a copy of *The Rough Guide to Shabadabadon* which detailed – among other things – Shabadabadon's famous ice caves. For Alan's benefit, the Doctor confirmed his involvement in the great fire of London and the *Mary Celeste*, but he refused to discuss when his tenure with UNIT occurred. The Doctor then

departed to investigate an energy spike emanating from Brisbane in September 2006.[1947]

There was a Cyber War in the late sixtieth century.[1948]

c 5995 - ZAMPER[1949] **->** There was revolution on Chelonia, where the peaceful forces of Little Sister overthrew Big Mother. This initiated a cultural reformation that saw the warlike race transformed into the galaxy's foremost flower-arrangers. Forty years later, many Chelonians hankered for the old blood-and-glory days, and Big Mother's fleet headed for Zamper to purchase a powerful Series 336c Delta-Spiral Sun Blaster – a ship whose effectiveness had been demonstrated in the Sprox civil war and the skirmishes of Pancoza. It was capable of withstanding neutronic ray blasts of up to an intensity of sixty blarks.

The seventh Doctor, Benny, Roz and Chris arrived on Zamper and found that the Zamps – slug-like creatures used to build the ships on the planet – had dreams of conquest and were building their own battleship. They had force-evolved their offspring to become ravenous

---

Furthermore, the technology tips the scales toward a later dating: these colonists do more than just freeze people and rocket them into space, they have microbots that can shape themselves into entire cities.

That said, there's no immediate reason to disbelieve the Doctor's remark that only humankind uses emojis, and the cutlery indeed looks human-compatible – so it's a fairly safe bet that the colonists are human. The Doctor also mentions the colony being renowned for cracking the secret to human happiness, but in the same breath he dubiously says it's "one of the first colonies".

We do know, from one of the colonists, MedTech Steadfast, that these people have fled some sort of apocalypse – and yet Steadfast doesn't specify its nature (Solar flares a la *The Ark in Space*? The sun expanding a la *The Ark*?) or whether they've come from Earth itself rather a human territory. We get nothing more than: Steadfast: "What day is this?", the Doctor: "The end of the world", Steadfast: "Again? We've only just got here." It's confirmation of a global cataclysm, but it's threadbare.

Nobody native to this time confirms that they're the last humans. Bill out of nowhere first airs that notion ("The people who came here, were they the last people? Were they our last hope?"), and the Doctor doubles down on it with "What's in those [cryo-sleep] pods, Bill, is the surviving population of Earth", but he fails to *give a single reason* why anyone should believe that. Even more confusingly, this is after the Doctor himself has said, "There were a number of ships [with evacuees]. I've bumped into a few of them over the years". Are we to believe that everyone aboard those ships (see *The Ark, Frontios* and more) and their descendants died, horribly or otherwise? As with those earlier examples,

perhaps we're to infer that even if there are other arks out there, so few humans survive that they are a species at serious risk of extinction.

Ultimately, if the history of the third millennium in *Doctor Who* is anything to go by, Steadfast's allusion to a global cataclysm necessitates throwing out the Doctor's "one of Earth's first colonies" remark as uninformed gibber-jabber.

Those parameters established, anyone hoping to date *Smile* has some freedom to just pick a late-in-the-game global apocalypse and run with it. The authors of this guidebook have (somewhat arbitrarily) prioritised the presence of a MedTech and cryogenics technology, and placed *Smile* in the same era as *The Ark in Space*. That story featured a distinct lack of city-sculpting microbots, but resources wouldn't be allocated uniformly during an Earthwide upheaval, and we know that the solar flare event involved a wave of colony ships. It also squares with the Doctor wondering what aspects of Bill's language have survived over "so many thousands of years", as opposed to millions or billions.

1946 *The Reaping, The Gathering*. The Doctor says that the Gogglebox was created while "humanity was on a day trip away from Earth space" owing to "solar flares or intergalactic war or something". This placement is arbitrary.

1947 "Sixty years" before *Spaceport Fear*. It's never said how these new arrivals managed to get past Tantane's force field, or the Wailer ships continually hammering away at it.

1948 *Heritage*. Cole's grandmother fights in it.

1949 Dating *Zamper* (NA #41) - It is "the sixtieth century" (p77). Earth appears to be populated at this time.

1950 *The Time of the Doctor*

1951 Dating *The Time of the Doctor* (X7.16) - No year

tentacle-like creatures powered by a springtail; the Doctor estimated that these creatures would become unstoppable if they reached populated space. Big Mother owed the Doctor a debt and agreed with his assessment. In a variation of the Diemlisch manoeuvre (first used in the third Wobesq-Majjina war), Big Mother's Chelonian fleet destroyed itself to obliterate the Zamps' ship and seal the gate between Zamper and the rest of the universe.

The Eleventh Doctor Gains a New Regeneration Cycle, Regenerates

The Doctor and the Church of the Mainframe, including its memory-wiping confessional priests, allied against the forces encroaching on Trenzalore. When all other players had been repelled, the Daleks continued the attack...[1950]

& 6000 - THE TIME OF THE DOCTOR[1951] -> The eleventh Doctor, still living on Trenzalore, was visibly aged and had reached the end of his regeneration cycle – so was facing his final death. Tasha Lem collected Clara in the TARDIS so the Doctor wouldn't have to pass on alone.

The Daleks overcome the Mainframe's resistance, and confronted the Doctor with their mothership. Clara appealed to the Time Lords, via the Crack in Time, to grant the Doctor a new regeneration cycle. They did so, endowing the Doctor with enough energy to destroy the Daleks' mothership and ground forces.

The eleventh Doctor briefly appeared much younger as his regeneration cycle reset, then regenerated into his new self...

Just prior to his regeneration, the eleventh Doctor phoned Clara's future self to tell her his next incarnation would be scared, and ask her to not give up on him. The TARDIS lurched out of control, and took the twelfth Doctor and Clara back to pre-historic times.[1952]

c 6000 - THE DYING LIGHT[1953] -> Quadrigger Stoyn had established himself as an Abbot on an alien world, and used Time Vector Equations to create wormholes that drew many spaceships – including the TARDIS, with the second Doctor, Jamie and Zoe inside – to him. Stoyn's technology network syphoned the TARDIS' energy to send a distress signal to Gallifrey, but the Doctor removed Stoyn's Temperon Limiter, causing an overload that threw Stoyn back along his own timeline. The Doctor's group left before anyone from his homeworld could answer Stoyn's signal.

Stoyn materialized back on the moon as solar flares ravaged the Earth and humanity abandoned its homeworld. He usurped an abandoned lunar theme park for his own purposes, and took control of robots made to look like Roman legionnaires. He constructed a time-viewer using various components, but as one of these originated from the Doctor's TARDIS, the viewer only rendered images of the Doctor's involvement in Earth's history.[1954]

Jenny

6012 (24th July) - THE DOCTOR'S DAUGHTER[1955] -> The fish-like Hath allied with humanity to create colonies. A spaceship containing some humans and Hath landed on Messaline with a third-generation terraforming globe that could create an ecosystem on the planet's barren surface. The mission commander died, and the resulting power vacuum put the humans and

---

given, but the Doctor is outwardly *very* old, only able to slowly hobble about the place. The blurb to *Tales of Trenzalore* claims that the Doctor lived in Christmas for "nine hundred years" – a claim that's borne out in the twelfth Doctor stating in *Deep Breath* he's more than "two thousand years old".

1952 *Deep Breath*

1953 Dating *The Dying Light* (BF CC #8.6) - It's been "hundreds and thousands of years" (*not* "hundreds of thousands of years") since the Doctor abandoned Stoyn in *The Beginning*. *Luna Romana* establishes that Stoyn arrives on the moon circa 6000 after being sent back "along his own timeline" at the end of *The Dying Light*, which suggests that the latter story occurs at the same time.

The only ripple in those waters pertains to Stoyn's age. He definitely ages two millennia during events in *Luna Romana*, and also ages however many "thousands" of years pass between his abandonment in the

twenty-first century in *The Beginning* and whenever *The Dying Light* opens. If the latter story indeed takes place circa 6000, then Stoyn must be almost six millennia old when he's thrown back to classical Rome in *Luna Romana*... but he's still voiced by Terry Molloy, and looks just as he did in *The Beginning*. Given the flexibility of Time Lord biology seen throughout the various periods of *Doctor Who*, we might usefully imagine that Stoyn maintains the same body and persona upon regeneration, and holds enough of a grudge against the Doctor to even keep the same facial scars from body to body.

1954 *Luna Romana*

1955 Dating *The Doctor's Daughter* (X4.6) - The dates shown on screen are in a format that gives figures such as "60120724". Donna works out that it's "a big old space date" that runs year, month, day. Or, in the more familiar British format, the colonists land on Messaline on 17/07/6012, and events in this story occur on

Hath into open warfare. Each camp had cloning devices that used "progenation": reproduction from a single organism. The conflict became so accelerated, twenty generations could be born and lost in a day.

Seven days later, the TARDIS brought the tenth Doctor, Donna and Martha to Messaline as it had sensed a paradox there – a young woman named Jenny, cloned from the Doctor's genetics within moments of his arrival. The Doctor smashed the terraforming globe, releasing its gasses and causing areas on Messaline to bloom with new life. The humans and Hath agreed to live peacefully. The Doctor and his friends left, thinking that Jenny had been fatally shot while saving the Doctor's life. She was revived by the terraforming gasses, and departed in a dshuttlecraft to find new adventures.

Jenny's spaceship wasn't equipped for interstellar flight, and so she spent six months making repairs on Kulontor. She investigated the mystery of the disappearing-and-reappearing asteroid Terebek, and found that a Gallifreyan bowship there had been making micro-time jumps, hoping to find rescue. Jenny set aside the dead pilot within, and claimed the bowship – and its time-travelling prowess – as her own. She soon encountered Captain Jack and Tara Mishra in the fifty-fourth century.[1956]

The New Dalek Era (continued)

? 6014 - INTO THE DALEK[1957] **->** The *Aristotle*, a medical frigate of the Combined Galactic Alliance, ran afoul of the Daleks in an asteroid field. The twelfth Doctor saved Lt Journey Blue when the Daleks destroyed her fighter, Wasp Delta, then left and returned with Clara to examine an injured Dalek the *Aristotle* had recovered. Suffering from a trionic radiation leak, the Dalek – which the Doctor dubbed "Rusty" – had been psychologically transformed after seeing the beauty of a newborn star, and advocated the destruction of all Daleks.

The Doctor, Clara and Blue used nanoscalers – devices which enabled surgeons to shrink and perform repairs inside patients – to miniaturise and venture into Rusty's inner workings. Sealing the radiation leak returned Rusty to normal – it summoned reinforcements, and began killing the *Aristotle* crew. The Doctor slaved his own mind to Rusty in an attempt to restore its morality, but it experienced the Doctor's hatred of Daleks. Rusty departed after destroying the other Daleks.

The Doctor estimated that by this point, the Daleks had eradicated "millions and millions" of stars.

24/07/6012. While the Doctor claims that said "big old space date" uses the New Byzantine Calendar, setting the story in 6012 AD seems reasonable enough.
1956 "The Lost Dimension"
1957 Dating *Into the Dalek* (X8.2) - The "good" Dalek identifies the *Aristotle* crew as human. Otherwise, the asteroid belt isn't specified as the same one between Mars and Jupiter, and Earth's status goes unmentioned. There's no sign that these Daleks can time-travel, although they look like the Time War models introduced in *Dalek*. The shooting script says that Journey Blue's craft is "a small 31st Century two-man fighter". If so, these events could pertain to the Dalek invasion of Earth around the year 3000 (*Mission to the Unknown*).

Two details within the story suggest it's after – possibly *long* after – the year 5000, the time of humanity's Great Breakout (*The Invisible Enemy*): the advent of the Combined Galactic Resistance, and the *Aristotle* having a shrinking device that seems like standard medical tech, whereas the Doctor had to use the TARDIS' Relative Dimensional Stabiliser to achieve the same results at the Bi-Al Foundation (*The Invisible Enemy* again – which, coincidentally or not, *did* take place near Sol's asteroid belt). See The "Own Time" of the Daleks sidebar for why this story has been placed in the sixty-first century.

Dalek: The Astounding Untold History of the Greatest Enemies of the Universe (p218) says that ultimately, Rusty was captured and sent to the Dalek Asylum

(*Asylum of the Daleks*). For all we know, he did spend some time there, prior to *Twice Upon a Time*.
1958 Dating *The Magician's Apprentice/The Witch's Familiar* (X9.1-9.2) - Davros comments that his Daleks have "remade" Skaro, suggesting that the Dalek City seen here was built atop the ruins of their original homeworld or that it's an entirely different planet tailor-made to look like the original. The Supreme Dalek seems very much in control of the new Skaro, and there's no mention of the Parliament of the Daleks (*Asylum of the Daleks*) being a factor. For more, see the "Own Time" of the Daleks sidebar.
1959 "Twenty" (p8) and "ten" (p18) years before *Heritage*.
1960 Three years before *Heritage* (p56).
1961 Dating *Heritage* (PDA #57) - Each chapter in the book has a precise date and time.

It's possible that Mel's death, as reported in this story, was cancelled out with the downfall of the Council of Eight (see the Council of Eight sidebar). Either way, *A Life of Crime* entails Sperovores eating Mel's potential futures, and her joining the seventh Doctor and Ace on their travels again. Owing to this in-universe explanation, it seems appropriate to decide that her life and death on Heritage was erased from the timeline.

THE COUNCIL OF EIGHT QUASI-MURDERS THE DOCTOR'S COMPANIONS: The Council of Eight, a group of entities who stepped into the power vacuum left by the Time Lords' sudden absence in the Eighth Doctor

? 6015 - THE MAGICIAN'S APPRENTICE / THE WITCH'S FAMILIAR[1958] -> Davros realised that the twelfth Doctor had been present during his childhood, and leveraged the Doctor's guilt concerning that meeting as part of a scheme to procure the Doctor's regeneration energy. With this, the Daleks and Davros would become more powerful than ever. Feigning that he was near death, Davros sent his agents across space-time with a message for the Doctor: "Davros knows. Davros remembers." Davros' operatives found the Doctor in Essex, 1138, and brought him to Skaro with Clara and Missy...

The Daleks had "remade" Skaro, which was invisible from a distance, save for a building that looked like a space station. The Doctor deduced that Davros was conning him, so freely yielded some regeneration energy – knowing it would also invigorate the aged Daleks left to die in the sewers below the Dalek City. The resurgent Daleks overran the Supreme Dalek's forces in a mad rush to re-obtain Dalek shells, bringing the whole Dalek City to ruin.

Colonists established a colony on Heritage. Ten years later, a company at Galactic Central developed a way of synthesising Thydonium, instantly putting mining colonies such as Heritage out of business. Melanie Bush and her husband Ben Heyworth settled on the impoverished Heritage sometime afterwards.[1959]

Years later on Heritage, the geneticist Wakeling successfully cloned a raven, naming her Arabella.[1960]

(=) 6048 (6th August) - HERITAGE[1961] -> Menopause had become extremely rare. Undergoing the condition, Melanie Bush Heyworth asked Wakeling for a genetic solution to the problem. Wakeling's treatment seemingly led to Mel and her husband Ben conceiving a child named Sweetness, but the Heyworths discovered that Wakeling had violated their wishes by cloning Sweetness from Mel. An argument between Wakeling and Mel led to his striking her with a genetic sequencer, killing her.

Ben Heyworth's attempt to alert offworld authorities was discovered. Wakeling persuaded the townsfolk that his experiments could restore prosperity to the hard-up colony, and the locals tore Ben to pieces with their bare hands before torching his house. Wakeling took Sweetness into his own home.

A shuttlecraft arrived on Heritage – the first in years – and two visitors wanted to see the Heyworths, causing quite a stir. The seventh Doctor and Ace gatecrashed an interstellar video conference and revealled Wakeling as a murderer, destroying the man's chance to reveal his success at cloning. Wakeling and two other inhabitants fell to their deaths when some of the old mineshafts collapsed under them. Cole, the Heritage town barman, adopted Sweetness.

c 6050 - HALF-LIFE[1962] -> Two races, the parasitic Makers and the Oon, had been at war for centuries. The organic spaceship Tain, a Maker construct, fled the war but was infected with an Oon-made Trojan program. Tain crashed onto the planet Espero, and his personality remained in conflict. The eighth Doctor, Fitz and Trix received Tain's distress signal. Tain thought that the TARDIS heralded the Oon's arrival and unleashed its ultimate weapon: a wavefront designed to disintegrate and reconstitute a planet under Tain's control. Tain's internal struggle threw the wavefront into chaos, but the Doctor purged the Trogan program and ended the wavefront. Tain prepared to leave Espero afterwards.

High Catholic doctrine came to forbid use of matter transmitters, stating it was impossible to teleport a soul.

The last colonist left Heritage in 6057. None of the ex-colonists ever discussed their reasons for departing.[1963] On

Adventures (*The Ancestor Cell*), base themselves in a time station powered by Schrodinger Cells. Very long story short, their energy reserves stem from points of indeterminacy in history.

As part of their gambit against the eighth Doctor, then, the Council manipulates events to murder his companions (well, maybe, possibly, the point is that nobody knows for certain), leading to a string of "deaths" in the Past Doctor Adventures. *Wolfsbane* ends unresolved, intimating that perhaps Harry Sullivan died after becoming a werewolf. *Bullet Time* murkily shows Sarah Jane Smith's crumpled form after a gun goes off. Most blatantly, *Heritage* involves the seventh Doctor and Ace landing on a colony world some time after Melanie Bush's brutal murder. In *Ahistory* Third Edition, we postulated that Ace's death in "Ground Zero" (not acknowledged outside of the *Doctor Who Magazine* comics) owed to the Council's schemes.

The Council's defeat in *Sometime Never...* appears to have ended the possibility of these "deaths", and the alleged fates of Harry, Sarah and Mel haven't been cited outside of the Council of Eight stories. Moreover, *A Life in Crime* had timeline-eating Sperovores consume Mel's possible futures, suggesting that if the Council's downfall didn't put paid to her dying on Heritage, the Sperovores assuredly did.

1962 Dating *Half-Life* (EDA #68) - This story is set after *Heritage*, as there are references to that story.
1963 *Heritage* (p227).

8th December, 6064, former Heritage colonist Lee Marks, now head of the Ellershaw Foundation, died in a fire deliberately set at his home.[1964] A grown-up Sweetness Cole penned an autobiography entitled *First of a New Breed*.[1965]

Clara Oswald Duplicated Throughout Space-Time; the Digital River Song (Probably) Switches Herself Off[1966]

(=) ? 6100 - THE NAME OF THE DOCTOR[1967] -> The Doctor had died a final time during a relatively low-level battle on the volcanic planet Trenzalore, and been buried there with honours. The TARDIS had also perished, and outwardly swollen to colossal size as its dimensional walls broke down. Within the Ship's console room resided the Doctor's "body": a temporal scar that embodied every trip he had made throughout time and space.

The Great Intelligence realised the Doctor's TARDIS/tomb could only be accessed by uttering his real name. The eleventh Doctor and Clara – aided by the digital copy of River Song in the Library – came to Trenzalore after the Intelligence captured Madame Vastra, Jenny and Strax. The Intelligence entered the tomb and – knowing it would perish doing so – entered the scar, replicated itself throughout the Doctor's personal life history and killed him several times over. Entire star systems that the Doctor had saved disappeared as his life was deleted from history.

Clara deduced that she could enter the scar and overwrite the Intelligence's duplicates with her own; indeed, that she had already done so, explaining why the Doctor had kept meeting copies of her. The Intelligence died as Clara was replicated throughout the Doctor's life, all the way back to his life on Gallifrey.

1964 *Heritage* (p279).

1965 Years after *Heritage*.

1966 DID THE DIGITAL VERSION OF RIVER SONG DIE?: In *The Name of the Doctor*, the eleventh Doctor and the computerized version of River that remained in the Library's hard drive following her physical death (*Forest of the Dead*) share a final (on screen, at least) conversation...

The Doctor: "There is a time to live and a time to sleep. You are an echo, River. Like Clara. Like all of us, in the end. My fault, I know, but you should've faded by now."

River: "It's hard to leave when you haven't said goodbye."

The Doctor: "Then tell me, because I don't know. How do I say it?"

River: "There's only one way I'd accept. If you ever loved me, say it like you're going to come back."

... he then does so, and the digital River vanishes.

One interpretation of this is that the digital River accepts the Doctor's argument that there's a reason and a season to all things, and self-terminates. The underplayed nature of this, however, means that fandom at large hasn't much embraced the idea. Still, with Steven Moffat's retirement from *Doctor Who*, and by extension there being less expectation of seeing River on TV again, it seems fair to assume that computer-River elected to end her life in *The Name of the Doctor*, and to draw a line under her extraordinary life. Even then, a possible get-out clause remains in that it's unclear exactly how much of *The Name of the Doctor* was nullified following the Time Lords intervening on Trenzalore in *The Time of the Doctor*.

1967 Dating *The Name of the Doctor* (X7.14) - Time unknown, but it's the aftermath of the Doctor's death on Trenzalore. At least some of these events are seemingly annulled when the Time Lords intervene to give the Doctor a new regeneration cycle in *The Time of the Doctor* (Clara: "Change the future", the Doctor: "I could have once, when there were Time Lords"). It's possible, though, that the principal players remain affected by what occurred (the Great Intelligence's attempt to kill the Doctor throughout space-time evidently still happens, for instance, or Clara would never have become the Impossible Girl in the first place).

1968 *Leth-St: The Forgotten Son*

1969 Dating *Spaceport Fear* (BF #170) - The Doctor asks the year according to Galactic Standard, to which Elder Bones replies: "In Earth years, it is 6127". By the calendar of the Economy Tribe, it's "the year of Elder Bones 409". Elder Bones is aware of Earth, and the inhabitants of Tantane may or may not be human. The sixth Doctor wears his blue coat on the cover, but dons his multi-coloured one within the story.

1970 *The Crystal Bucephalus*

1971 *The Kingmaker*. The publisher's robot is specified as being from the sixty-fourth century, but this isn't to say the dominating publishing house is located there also, and the Doctor's comments suggest that the company hails from much further in the future.

1972 *J&L S7: The Monstrous Menagerie*

1973 Dating "Ground Control" (IDW *Doctor Who Annual 2010*) - Mister K gives the year.

1974 Dating *Return of the Krotons* (BF subscription promo #7) - The solar-flare event described in *The Ark in Space* occurred some "centuries" ago. The mining technology used is similar to that used in the moon conurbations of the late thirtieth century, so it's definitely after that time.

1975 Dating *The Tenth Doctor Year Three* (Titan 10th Doc #3.6-3.8, 3.10, "Vortex Butterflies") - A caption says it's the "Seventh dominion of the lesser Mulchop (circa 6771, upper humanian era)".

1976 "Five thousand years" after *No Future*.

A fragment of the Great Intelligence's mind survived Clara's gambit by inveigling itself into Alistair Gordon Lethbridge-Stewart's timeline in 1937.[1968]

6127 - SPACEPORT FEAR[1969] **->** The Arrivals section of the disused Tantane Spaceport had become a maternity ward, and the Business tribe currently occupied the spaceport's hydroponics garden and water mills.

The long-lived Elder Bones, a.k.a. Director Bones, mistakenly believed that the Palpane had cordoned off Tantane to get him back, and gleaned enough information from the sixth Doctor's technical nous to deactivate the station's force field. The Wailers surrounding the station stormed it and retrieved their young one, then departed into space.

A 20-year-old member of Economy, Naysmith, learned that Elder Bones had manipulated the Business and Economy tribes for centuries, and blackmailed him into harmoniously uniting both groups. The Doctor and Mel advised that the Tantane inhabitants establish relations with their galactic neighbours.

The New Dark Age

In 6198, the Federation Scientific Executive funded a research project into genetic experimentation. The geneticist Maximillian Arrestis hired a team of consultants to develop the Lazarus Intent, a religion that he hoped would become a moneymaking venture. His "miracles" were publicised for three years, and his predictions of disasters all came to pass. *The Codex of Lazarus* was published early in the sixty-third century, and for nearly a decade he reaped the financial rewards of being the "Messiah".

Not content with this, Arrestis began to sell defence secrets to the Cybermen, Sontarans and Rutans. The Federation was fighting a war with the Sontarans at the time. In 6211, Sontarans launched a stealth attack that wiped much of the Federation DataCore on Io. Three weeks later, an earthshock bomb – sold by the Cybermen to the Sontarans – destroyed Tersurus. This didn't stop the Federation from winning the war. When the Sontaran Emperor suspected that Arrestis had double-crossed him, the traitor was brought to the Sontaran throneworld and executed. "Lazarus" became a martyr, the saviour of the galaxy, and it was the Intent of his followers to resurrect him.

Alexhendri Lassiter built a time machine and did rescue Arrestis moments before his death. Later, Arrestis escaped the destruction of the Crystal Bucephalus restaurant by fleeing through time, only to arrive back on Sontara right before his execution, which proceeded as planned.[1970]

Every small publisher in the universe had been bought out, and by "the end of time", this would give rise to one dominating, monolithic publishing house. The company owned the rights to all of the authors throughout history, especially the lazy ones who hadn't fulfilled on their contracts. Publisher's robots from the sixty-fourth century were equipped with time travel. Armed with laser cannons, they went throughout history to "remind" these writers to finish their texts. One such robot visited the fifth Doctor in 1597.[1971]

It became routine to endow domestic animals with a genetic trait to make them glow. Centuries later, a sixty-third century time expedition left to collect specimens from the Jurassic Era. The Sherlock Holmes stories had endured to this era, and a Temporal Retrieval Squad left for 1894 upon reading clues to the expedition's location in *The Hound of the Baskervilles*.[1972]

6558 - "Ground Control"[1973] **->** The tenth Doctor was stopped by Mister K of the Safety Patrol Interstellar Traffic Division in a space station forty clicks from the Antarean third moon, and forced to account for a number of safety violations he had made flying the TARDIS. He was shown a previous adventure where panda-like Cobalites chased him and Donna. One Cobalite was holding on to the TARDIS when the Ship dematerialised, and ended up in the Vortex. The Doctor realised this was all a trick to distract him while the TARDIS' energy was drained, and left.

c 6700 - RETURN OF THE KROTONS[1974] **->** Humans now received electronic identity implants at birth.

Some centuries after the solar flares ravaged Earth, two Euro Comgen ships bearing human colonists in cryo-sleep arrived at the dead planet Onyakis. They spent a year mining the energy-rich K-7 crystal there. The dormant Krotons on Onyakis reformed within K-7 solutions, and attempted to create an energy-transference network that would power Kroton vessels, enabling them to enslave several human outposts. Thousands of Krotons were re-generated on Onyakis, but the sixth Doctor and Charley intervened, killing them.

c 6771 - THE TENTH DOCTOR YEAR THREE[1975] **->** The Time Sentinel feared that the Doctor's actions in history could imperil Gallifrey's time lock, and moved to trap him in a pocket reality. The tenth Doctor, Gabby, Cindy and Noobis prevented the Time Sentinel from using the Circle of Transcendence to destroy Aramuko, but the Red TARDIS and Gabby were lost to the Circle. The Moment arranged for the twelfth Doctor to rescue her.

Around 6976, the Vardans who invaded Earth in 1976 arrived back home. They discovered there had been a revolution, and that the military had lost power.[1976]

? 7000 - WIRRN DAWN[1977] -> The humanoids on Korista VII lived like peasants and farmers, but were at peace with the Wirrn. Every season, the Wirrn were summoned at dawn by the striking of a metal shard across an altar, and the humanoids would offer up one of their own to be converted into a new Wirrn queen. So long as the queens gestated in people, they had enough intelligence to restrain the swarm. The grandfather of Delong, a soldier, was one of the last colony bosses to oversee this practice.

The old ways waned, and the arrival of the Galsec colonists created open warfare with the Wirrn. New Wirrn queens were gestated in senseless herbivores, and were born with limited brain power. The Wirrn stripped whole planets clean of crops and cattle. The Galsec colonists incorporated some of the natives – including Delong – into their infantry, but scornfully so. Such add-ons were referred to as "indigs" (short for "indigenous"), which became a by-word for anyone who didn't fit in, a scrounger, a criminal, etc.

The eighth Doctor and Lucie were present as the Galsec-Wirrn conflict encroached upon Korista VII. Admiral Farroll, who commanded a fleet of sixty-eight Galsec spaceships, was turned into a Wirrn queen. Delong knew that the Galsec colonists would never agree to continue the tradition of sacrifice, and so the Farroll-queen took her swarm into space, staving off a major bloodbath.

After a thousand years, the Star Pioneers had destroyed all the Wirrn breeding grounds, making Andromeda suitable for colonisation. One Wirrn Queen survived and travelled through space towards the Earth. She reached Nerva Beacon, but the station's automatic defences killed her. Before her death, the Queen damaged the systems that would have revived

1977 Dating *Wirrn Dawn* (BF BBC7 #3.4) - The story takes place amidst the background detail of the Galsec colonists as seen in *The Sontaran Experiment*. The migration of the Wirrn swarm into space could be the act that leads to a Wirrn queen invading Nerva Beacon in *The Ark in Space*. The title of this story seems to tip the scales in favour of spelling "Wirrn" with two r's, as opposed to the three-r'ed version preferred by *The Ark in Space* novelisation and *Placebo Effect*.

1978 *The Ark in Space*. As the colonists are scheduled to revive after "five thousand years" [c.11,000 AD], the Wirrn Queen must arrive on Nerva before that time.

ANDROMEDA: Andromeda is mentioned a number of times in *Doctor Who*, sometimes as a reference to the constellation, other times as the galaxy of the same name. According to the TARDIS Information File entry that the Master fakes in *Castrovalva*, Castrovalva itself is a planet in the Phylox series in Andromeda. The fourth Doctor finds mer-children a home in Andromeda in *Evolution*. There is some evidence that Zanak (*The Pirate Planet*) raided worlds there, as the ground is littered with Andromedan bloodstones.

The Committee, a nemesis of Torchwood, dominates an unspecified number of worlds in Andromeda (*TW: The Conspiracy*). *UNIT: Shutdown* reveals that an Andromedan ambassador once gave the Brigadier a jewel from Saturn. Tensions between organics and robot-kind in Andromeda give rise to the anti-robot Cult of the Shining Darkness (the undatable *Shining Darkness*).

In *The Daleks' Master Plan*, an intergalactic conference was held in Andromeda. The starship *Harmony & Redemption* cruises through Andromeda as part of a seven-galaxy tour in *The Husbands of River Song*. In *The Ark in Space*, we learn that Star Pioneers from Earth reached Andromeda and discovered that it was infested with the Wirrn. The two races fought each other for a thousand years, until humanity succeeded in destroy-

ing the Wirrn's breeding grounds.

Humankind went on to colonise the galaxy, and by the time of *The Mysterious Planet*, the civilisation was established on planets such as Sabalom Glitz's homeworld, Salostopus. At that time, Andromedans capable of building advanced robots and harnessing black light stole Matrix secrets and fled the wrath of the Time Lords. The Doctor considers visiting "the constellation of Andromeda" in *Timelash*. The Doctor took the mer-children to a water planet in the Andromeda Galaxy at the end of *Evolution*. According to Trix in *The Gallifrey Chronicles*, the currency in Andromeda is the Andromedan Euro, although *Dragonfire*, *Legacy* and *Business Unusual* all agree it is the grotzi in Glitz's time.

The threat in *Doctor Who and the Invasion from Space* comes from Andromeda in the far future. "A lot of Andromedan planets are full of Migrators", large amoeba like creatures protected by external antibodies, according to the Doctor in the short story "Danger Down Below" (*Doctor Who Annual 1983*), although they are usually only found on otherwise uninhabited worlds. *Shining Darkness* depicts a highly advanced Andromedan galactic civilisation where organic and machine live exists together in relative harmony.

1979 *The Sontaran Experiment*

1980 Dating "Prisoners of TIme" (IDW *DW* mini-series) - The Doctor says, "We're in the year 7214." If so, Antarctopolis cannot – although this seems to be the idea – located on the remains of Antarctica itself (see The Solar Flares sidebar and the dating on *The Ark in Space*).

1981 Dating *Patient Zero* (BF #124) - The story takes place in a region of space-time so remote, it causes a glitch or two in the TARDIS' translation system. The only tangible dating clue is that the Daleks seen here hail from the distant future (their time controller claims, almost wistfully, that they've travelled "so far back in time") and have a warfleet at their disposal. The

the humans, and laid her eggs within one of the sleeping Nerva engineers.[1978]

While those aboard Nerva slept, human colonies such as Galsec carved out an empire, with bases across half the galaxy. They retained legends of Nerva, "the lost colony" from the time of the Expansion, but most didn't believe that it really existed. In time, the colonies grew to distrust talk of Mother Earth.[1979]

7124 - "Prisoners of Time"[1980] -> Frobisher asked to frolic with some actual penguins, so the sixth Doctor took him and Peri to Antarctopolis: a mega-city with a nature preserve housing a last piece of "wild Antarctica". Having deduced that efforts to kill the Doctor always seemed to fail, the Tremas Master arranged for Antarctopolis officials to institutionalize him instead. Peri and Frobisher helped the Doctor to escape and melt the Master's cadre of Autons.

The tenth Doctor asked Frobisher to disguise himself as Peri – a means of the whifferdill infiltrating Adam Mitchell's base when the villain abducted "her".

Release of the Amethyst Viruses; Charley Pollard, the Viyrans Thrown Back in Time

c 7190 - PATIENT ZERO[1981] -> A virus rendered Charley Pollard comatose, and she remained in the TARDIS' Zero Room for years while the sixth Doctor searched for a cure. She awoke just as the Doctor traced the virus to "one of the remotest parts of space-time the TARDIS had ever travelled to". A war had nearly destroyed the galaxy in question, and the Great Armistice Treaty had enabled the creation of Amethyst Viral Containment Station: the biggest stockpile of uncureable viruses in the universe, located on a lava planet. The Viyrans, as the ultimate authority of this galaxy, had been tasked with destroying the viruses in the heart of Amathustro, Amethyst's sun.

A Dalek time squad from the future arrived on Amethyst, seeking both the viruses there and Patient Zero: the person who had infected Charley. The Doctor thwarted the Daleks from moving Amethyst through time, but the resultant temporal explosion – which destroyed Amethyst and the Daleks – spread the viruses throughout space-time.

Patient Zero was actually Mila – a former Dalek captive subjected to Amethyst virus No. 7001, which could rewrite the DNA of those infected to mirror that of the carrier. This left Mila invisible, untouchable and dimensionally out of phase. She had stowed aboard a Dalek time machine, then the Doctor's TARDIS, where she had remained for centuries. The TARDIS protected its passengers from Mila's virus, but Charley's anomalous status as someone travelling with a past incarnation of the Doctor deprived her of that immunity. Mila became a corporeal copy of Charley and left with the Doctor.

The temporal explosion that destroyed Amethyst threw the Viyrans and Charley back some millennia.[1982] The

Amethyst station-manager, Fratalin, hasn't heard of the Daleks – possibly indicating that *Patient Zero* takes place in an era free of Dalek interference, or possibly just that Amethyst is so remotely located, not even the Daleks have visited its galaxy before now. The Daleks don't know about the Viyrans, but given the Viyrans' habit of erasing the short-term memories of any being they encounter, this perhaps isn't surprising. It's unclear if Etheron, the commander of the Interstar Cargo Carrier *Blaze*, has any connection to humanity or not. The back cover copy says "the Doctor must travel back in time, beyond all known civilisations", suggesting this is the very deep past. The Doctor at one point broadly supports this, by saying, "this far into the past..."

In *Charley S1: The Lamentation Cypher* [c.4964-4966], Charley says the Amethyst explosion happened "long, long ago", but she could be speaking figuratively (from her frame of reference, it certainly must feel like that).

Crucially, *To the Death* (set c.2190, and also written by Nicholas Briggs) so repeatedly says that *Patient Zero* occurs in the future, it has to be taken as correct. The eighth Doctor says that Amethyst station was destroyed "relative to when we are now? Thousands of years in the future...", that the Dalek Time Controller "survived in the future and somehow travelled back", that he intends to rectify things by going *forward* in time to destroy Amethyst more conclusively this time, and so forth. The Monk, echoing the Daleks' claims, also says that the Dalek Time Controller was injured aboard Amethyst station "in the future". So, an arbitrary sum of five thousand years has been added to *To The Death* to derive a year for *Patient Zero*.

Patient Zero marks the genesis of Big Finish's "Virus Strand" story arc – which formally encompasses "Urgent Calls", "Urban Myths", "The Vanity Box" and *Mission of the Viyrans*. The viruses that appear in *The Death Collectors* and *Forty-Five*: "Order of Simplicity" might also stem from Amethyst.

It's implied that the invisible Mila stowed away aboard the TARDIS during *The Chase*. She impersonates Charley in *Paper Cuts* and *Blue Forgotten Planet*.

1982 Inferred from *Blue Forgotten Planet*. The Third Edition of *Ahistory* concluded that the Viyrans could time travel (partly because the blurb to *Mission of the Viyrans* says they can) – however, a re-examination of the Viyran stories, combined with the revelations in *Charlotte Pollard* Series 1, demonstrate that while the Viyrans *do* travel in time prior to *Blue Forgotten Planet*, they can't do so under their own power (ergo, the explosion in *Patient Zero* hurls them back some millennia). The Doctor discovers in *Patient Zero* that the Viyrans don't understand temporal physics, but can

Dalek Time Controller also survived, and rode the temporal explosion back to twenty-second century Earth.[1983]

7213 - "The Doctor and the Nurse"[1984] -> The Siblinghood of Saint Augustine, Physicist – a group of "presentist" religious extremists on Hipponensis 3 – found time travellers offensive, as they offered proof that the past and future existed. As the eleventh Doctor, Amy and Rory fled, the Siblinghood fired a chronomagnetic pulse strong enough to damage the TARDIS' chronolabe...

The Cybermen and Time Travel

On the desert planet Chronos, a race of beings built a time machine. This enabled them to travel into their world's future, when it had become a water planet and was far more habitable. In the distant future, only a handful of Cybermen survived. They fled to the water world Chronos and exterminated the beings who lived there, acquiring their time machine in the process. The Cybermen used it to travel back to 3286, but a temporal blast from that era surged here and aged them to death.[1985]

Advanced Cybermen from the far future had a Cybership which contained a fragment of the Time Vortex, and so could travel in time. They used it to attack Earth in the early twenty-first century.[1986]

In the far, far future, the Cybermen were nearly extinct. A surviving Cyber-Leader held the Doctor responsible for his race's destruction, and had access to Cyber-race's entire history banks. The Cyber-Leader found an abandoned time-ship – the product of Gallifreyan technology – on a planet nearly destroyed by fire, and decided to lay a trap for the Doctor in 1984. The time-ship proved difficult to pilot; the Cyber-Leader arrived two years early in 1982.[1987]

7382 - THE TIME VAMPIRE[1988] -> On a mission for the Time Lords, the third Doctor and his companion Joshua Douglas dined with H'mbrackle, the emperor of the Z'nai – a race of philosophers and magnificent architects who built hanging fountains and sky cities. H'mbrackle had arranged a trade agreement, and Z'nai representatives arrived on Westrope III to finalise it. The Westropian Embassy was a sea fort that had been used back in the Krypterian wars.

The emperor's son, H'mbrackle II, seized power and marshalled his people to war. H'mbrackle II sought to "purify the lesser species" by slaughtering billions – millions died when a Z'nai sky city incinerated Westrope III. Joshua released a virus the Z'nai themselves had developed, nearly wiping them out and ending their empire.

recognise chronon particles.
1983 *To the Death*
1984 Dating "The Doctor and the Nurse" (IDW Vol. 4 #3-4) - The year is given.
1985 *Real Time*. No date given. The CyberController in this era is an alternate history version of Evelyn Smythe.
1986 "The Flood". No date is given, but the eighth Doctor declares the Cybermen to be the most advanced he's ever seen. This places the story after *Real Time* and *The Reaping* – two stories which also feature time-travelling Cybermen from the unspecified far future.
1987 *The Reaping*. Presumably this occurs after *Real Time*, but this date is otherwise arbitrary.
1988 Dating *The Time Vampire* (BF CC #4.10) - The year is given. The Doctor and Joshua's encounter with the Z'nai was largely detailed in *The Catalyst*, but is actually depicted here. Mention is made of "the Naxian recession", which could refer to the aliens from the Iris Wildthyme audios.
1989 *The Catalyst*
1990 Dating *The Time Vampire* (BF CC #4.10) - It's fifty years after the "Great Plague" that Joshua Douglas unleashed against the Z'nai.
1991 *The Quantum Archangel*
1992 *The Quantum Archangel*. No date is given, but it's before the Federation splits.
1993 "Two centuries" before *The Outliers*.
1994 Dating *The Skull of Sobek* (BF BBC7 #2.4) - It's said that the "culture" of Sobek extends back ten thousand

years on various worlds, and it cannot be coincidence – although it curiously isn't mentioned – that the ancient Egyptians worshipped a crocodile-headed god of the same name. This must be yet another example of extra-terrestrials influencing Earth civilisation (as with *Death to the Daleks*, etc.). In real life, Sobek is mentioned in the Pyramid Texts, the oldest of which date to 2400-2300 BC. The dating of *The Skull of Sobek* to 7500 AD – i.e. about ten thousand years later – is somewhat arbitrary, but represents the latest that the adventure can feasibly occur. Conditions on Indigo 3 do, though, somewhat match with the "new dark age" of this era, as described in *The Crystal Bucephalus*.
1995 Dating *Dalek Empire II: Dalek War* (no individual episode titles) - The blurb to *Dalek Empire II* episode four says that it's "two thousand years" after the Great Catastrophe. This number is repeated – give or take a bit of phrasing – throughout *Dalek Empire III*.
1996 "Twenty years" before *Dalek Empire III*.
1997 "Years" before *Dalek Empire III*.
1998 Dating *Dalek Empire III* (*The Exterminators*, episode one; *The Healers*, episode two; *The Survivors*, episode three; *The Demons*, episode four; *The Warriors*, episode five; *The Future*, episode six) - The mini-series takes place "twenty years" after Tarkov sets out from Velyshaa at the end of *Dalek Empire II*, and ends on something of a cliffhanger, with humanity in this region of space presumably gearing up to fight the resurgent Dalek threat.

The act of near-genocide ended the Doctor and Joshua's friendship, and the Doctor took him home. H'mbrackle II, now carrying the virus, was placed in a quarantine tesseract accessible from both the TARDIS and Joshua's home.

The fourth Doctor re-visited the Westrope III disaster with Leela, whose future self was present as a time vampire – a gestalt creature able to experience the majesty of time and creation. The time vampire dispatched K9 centuries ahead in the TARDIS to retrieve the aged, imprisoned Leela as she was dying. When K9 returned, the proximity of the aged and younger Leelas paradoxically facilitated the time vampire's creation. Leela's younger self left the Doctor, having no memory of these events, and her older self merged with the time vampire.

Some Z'nai survived, and a few of their number used the time capsule to venture back to recover their emperor.[1989]

c 7432 - THE TIME VAMPIRE[1990] **->** An interplanetary tourist board coordinated visits to what remained of Westrope III. Leela was briefly tussled through time from 7382, and visited the disused Westropian Embassy. Gustav Holland, a tour guide, had used a temporal suspension cage he stole from the Doctor's TARDIS in 7382 to imprison a time vampire, thinking he could profit from the creature's abilities. The time vampire – Leela's future self – aged Holland to death, and Leela returned to the past.

> (=) The sixth Doctor and Mel failed to prevent nuclear warfare on the Federation planet Maradnias. A group of Chronovores and Eternals, grateful for the Doctor's help in the Bophemeral affair, changed history to prevent Maradnias' destruction.[1991]

Maradnias would become the centre of the Union.[1992] The Deltron War, between the twin worlds of Deltron, began.[1993]

? 7500 - THE SKULL OF SOBEK[1994] **->** The eighth Doctor and Lucie arrived on Indigo 3, a world with a blue sea, blue moons, a renowned blue desert and eighty-three different words for the colour blue. By coincidence, a torrential storm would flood the desert every eighty-three years, causing ultra-marine flowers to cover the region a few days afterwards. The storm wasn't due for another twenty years, but the Doctor swore he felt rain coming on.

The Sanctuary of Imperfect Symmetry on Indigo 3 was a place of pilgrimage, devotion and deliberate disparity. The old prince of the dead planet Sobek had paid for the construction of the sanctuary hall – the very foundations of which were actually the prized Skull of Sobek. General Snabb engaged the prince in personal combat for the Skull, and both perished when it collapsed on top of them.

The Triumphs of Sobek contained tales of that world.

& 7500 - DALEK EMPIRE II: DALEK WAR[1995] **->** The Galactic Union had been established, and was enjoying a time of peace. Technology, however, was inferior compared to what was available more than three thousand years prior.

The historian Saloran Hardew found Kalendorf's burial chamber on Velyshaa, and accessed his telepathic accounts of the Great Catastrophe by sleeping there. Siy Tarkov, an envoy from the Galactic Union, arrived with a military escort to examine Hardew's findings. It had taken Hardew five years to reach Velyshaa, but technology had improved since then, and Tarkov made the trip in one. Tarkov and Hardew decrypted a transmission conveyed via a freak wormhole, and concluded that the Daleks had refortified in the Seriphia Galaxy and were once again mobilising for war. Hardew remained on Velyshaa while Tarkov's group left to warn the Union about the Dalek threat.

Tarkov's ship stopped to refuel on the planet Scalius, where his crew were amongst the first to contract a devastating plague: Neurotransmitter Failure Syndrome (NFS). Tarkov entered hibernation to survive, and his audio warning about the Daleks was ignored. He remained in stasis when the ship was later broken up for salvage.[1996]

Some years later, the security agent Giorgi Selestru located the Alliance Daleks' space station in the Plowik System. He found within a cryogenic tube containing the augmented human Galanar, who awoke and became one of Selestru's most loyal operatives.[1997]

& 7520 - DALEK EMPIRE III[1998] **->** The NFS plague became rampant amongst the border worlds. Millions died, and billions more were threatened. The plague increased political tensions, and the border worlds increasingly broke ties with the Union. As part of this, the border worlds rescinded the Union's claim to the Graxis System – possibly the most peaceful and undeveloped sector of the galaxy.

The Galactic Union had failed to act upon Tarkov's sketchy audio warning of the Dalek menace, and now received word that the Daleks had arrived in the Scalani System and were distributing a cure for the plague. The Daleks established "healing zones" throughout the Graxis System – ruining the ecology there – and on planets such as Tantalus and the formerly uninhabitable Scalanis VIII. The Daleks began treating patients with the plague-cure, which was designated Variant 7.

The Daleks' ranks had never recovered from the Great Catastrophe. Lacking the numbers for outright invasion, they had secretly released the NFS plague as part of a scheme to create the largest Dalek army ever assembled. Variant 7 contained an extra genetic code which, in conjunction with a unique type of radiation, would mutate the plague-survivors into Dalek embryos. Dalek munitions factories stood ready to arm the new Daleks.

Siy Tarkov awoke from stasis, and reported his concerns about the Daleks to Giorgi Selestru, who was now the Union's security commander. Galanar, as one of Selestru's operatives, accompanied Tarkov on a six-month trip to Velyshaa to retrieve Kalendorf's records, and thereby goad the Union into action. The Daleks pursued them. On Velyshaa, the Daleks killed Saloran Hardew, but Tarkov transmitted a copy of Kalendorf's accounts to Selestru. It was believed that Selestru would convince the Galactic Union Security Committee and its chairman, Bulis Meitok, to mobilise against the Daleks.

The NFS plague mutated Tarkov into a Dalek. Galanar was captured and brought before the Dalek Supreme – which in part had Susan Mendes' personality. The Dalek Supreme gloated that humanity would literally become Daleks, or at the very least would emotionally become like Daleks while fighting them. Galanar maintained that humans would always have a quality that the Daleks lacked, and that the Daleks therefore had no real power over them.

Dalek X believed that the astronic radiation on Hurala would keep it alive until the planet's communications seal expired, and its appeal for help was received. The tenth Doctor promised to be waiting if this occurred.[1999]

Josiah W. Dogbolter, a ruthless tycoon and nemesis of the fifth, sixth and twelfth Doctors, was born.[2000]

7691 - THE OUTLIERS[2001] **->** Strife occurred between the human colony on Vega IV and the Daleks. Elsewhere, a deployment of Arkonite – a destructive substance capable of sterilizing whole worlds – ended the Delfron War after two centuries.

Corporate mining efforts for arkonite on an unidentified planet resulted in its clairvoyant, barnacle-like inhabitants forecasting disaster. To avert this, they began killing the humans present. The second Doctor, Polly, Ben and Jamie prevented Richard Tipple, the company's Cohesion Interface Manager, from retaliating with arkonite and wiping out the barnacles. Imperial Command became aware of Tipple's abuses, and curtailed his authority. The barnacles were given habitat zones designed for humans as compensation.

The twelfth Doctor and Bill tried to visit New Asgard – flying chariots, talking goats, robot valkyries and cosmic mead included – around the seventy-eighth century, but instead wound up in the Indian Territory, 1880.[2002]

In the seventy-eighth century, the planet Caligaris Epsilon Six was one of the most renowned holiday planets of the Third Great and Bountiful Human Empire. It was designed to look like a medieval fantasy land, complete with unicorns, elves and dragons.

The Empire fell into decline, experiencing war, famine, plagues and confrontations with the Sycorax, Drahvins, Sontarans and Chelonians. Aethelred, the chief adminis-

---

1999 "Five thousand years" after *Prisoner of the Daleks*.
2000 Dogbolter turns "500" in "The Stockbridge Showdown" [c.8194].
2001 Dating *The Outliers* (BF EA #3.2) – Chatura Sharma, a native from this time, names the exact year. She also makes reference to "an Adjudicator" (presumably the group first seen in *Colony in Space* et al). Those in power – interestingly, this late in humankind's history – accept the authority of the Doctor's Earth Examiner badge (*The Power of the Daleks* [2020]).
2002 "The Parliament of Fear"
2003 "Just over one hundred fifty years" before the main events of "A Fairytale Life". A holorecording showing the virus being released is timecoded "19-04-7711".
2004 Dating "A Fairytale Life" (IDW *DW* mini-series #3) – The Doctor is aiming for "the year 7704", but has to concede it's "Ah. Not the seventy-eighth century. More like the seventy-ninth … ish." Later, we learn the virus was released in 7711, "just over one hundred fifty years ago".
2005 Dating *The Catalyst, Empathy Games* and *The Time Vampire* (BF CC #2.4, 3.4, 4.10) - Leela says that it's "centuries" after the Z'nai Empire ended, owing to the plague that Joshua Douglas released. The notion that Leela enjoyed an extended lifespan owing to her proximity to the Time Lords' biofields, and that she'd rapidly age without them, was introduced in *Gallifrey II: Spirit*.

2006 *The Child*
2007 Dating *The Judgement of Isskar* (BF #117) - It's "sixteen thousand years" since the first part of the story. The Black Guardian rescues the Doctor and Amy at the start of *The Destroyer of Delights*.
2008 Dating *Luna Romana* (BF CC #8.7) - The solar flares event that devastated Earth is acknowledged as being "sometime after the sixth millennium", and Stoyn has been such on the moon for "two thousand years" since then.
2009 *The Anachronauts*. Steven and Sara estimate that Lang's crew hail from "thousands of years" after their own eras, a view that's supported by Mavic Chen (*The Daleks' Master Plan*) being something of a historical footnote. Lang's crew are the first anachronauts of their people, which suggests that they aren't human, as this is long after humanity successfully achieves time travel (see in particular the fifty-first century).
2010 *The Reaping, The Gathering*.
2011 The background of *The Darksmith Legacy* series, as given in *DL: The Graves of Mordane, DL: The Colour of Darkness* and *DL: The Planet of Oblivion*. The Darksmiths are variously said to have kept the Krashoks waiting for the Eternity Crystal "for millennia" (*DL: The Art of War*, p13) and (ungrammatically) for "a millennia" (p18). The Darksmiths *seem* to originate from circa 2012, and so must have travelled into the future more than once to

trator of Caligaris Epsilon Six, sought to protect the children of that world from the wider conflict – on 19th April, 7711, he reprogrammed the planet's biofilter to stop screening for recombinant *yersinia pestis*, "The Pest", which killed 7,564 adults but spared everyone under the age of ten. The children of Caligaris Epsilon Six grew up with no knowledge of the outside universe, and the planet was placed under quarantine per Imperial Order 54567. Aethelred – who became the children's king – used modern medical techniques to extend his lifespan.[2003]

c 7862 - "A Fairytale Life"[2004] **->** The eleventh Doctor and Amy had recently escaped the stomach of a space chicken, and he granted Amy's wish and landed the TARDIS on the fantasy-themed holiday planet of Caligaris Epsilon Six. They discovered the deception that King Aethelred had perpetrated in separating Caligaris Epsilon Six from the wider universe, and came to believe that the people there should make their own choices. The Doctor devised an antibody that eliminated the Pest contagion, and freed the colony from its isolation.

Leela Dies, is Reincarnated

& 7932 - THE CATALYST / EMPATHY GAMES / THE TIME VAMPIRE[2005] **->** After Gallifrey and the Time Lords were no more, Leela – who had enjoyed an extended lifespan thanks to the Time Lords' biofields replenishing her telomeres – rapidly aged. She became a prisoner of the Z'nai, who interrogated her about her encounter with their emperor, H'mbrackle II. Leela carried a Z'nai-killing virus that eliminated her captors, but their machines kept her alive for at least another year.

In the last moments of Leela's life, K9 arrived in the TARDIS and took her back some centuries – to meet her former self and facilitate her rebirth as a time vampire.

Leela died while being held captive by the Z'nai, and was reincarnated as a young girl named Emily. The girl lived in a country with a king, and her high-class parents expected that she would become a wife and mother someday. To Emily, Leela was an "imaginary" friend who related stories about a warrior woman who traveled through time and space with a wizard.[2006]

& 8000 - THE JUDGEMENT OF ISSKAR[2007] **->** A castle – actually a disguised segment of the Key to Time – on the planet Safeplace radiated a balance-restoring sensation, and so became an ideal location for peace talks. The fifth Doctor and the Key-tracer Amy converted the segment, but were captured by the revived Lord Isskar – who demanded they face trial for their role in Mars' devastation. The rival Key-tracer Zara attempted to crash Isskar's spaceship, thinking she could retrieve Amy's segments from the

rubble afterwards. Isskar ejected to safety in an escape pod. A new incarnation of the Black Guardian – needing the Key segments to restore his diminished abilities – transported the Doctor and Amy to ninth-century Sudan.

Death of Quadrigger Stoyn

c 8000 - LUNA ROMANA[2008] **->** The fourth Doctor and the second Romana explored the abandoned theme park on Earth's moon. Quadrigger Stoyn had become increasingly outraged at having spent two millennia there with only a time viewer showing pictures of the Doctor's exploits for company. A mishap caused Stoyn to fall to ancient Rome through the time viewer, which shattered and split him into six copies of himself. The Stoyns returned to this era in the TARDIS, which Romana dutifully sent back to her younger self. The incumbent fourth Doctor and Romana themselves fell back to ancient Rome through one of Stoyn's time portals, and were retrieved by Stoyn in their own TARDIS.

Stoyn attempted to settle past accounts by incorporating the TARDIS into a temporal feedback transponder that would take the entire moon back in time to its origins – erasing the Archaeons' actions and averting life on Earth. The Doctor and Romana left after arranging an energy feedback that obliterated Stoyn with three thousand years' worth of solar power.

A humanoid race at war with the Wall of Noise attempted to achieve time travel. A successful outing by the prototype time-ship *Hank Morgan IV* would have made its crew the first anachronauts of their people, but the *Hank Morgan IV* collided with the TARDIS, causing the Ship to execute emergency repairs. Captain Natalie Lang and her crew would part ways with the first Doctor, Steven and Sara Kingdom some ten thousand years after their own era. Lang's people regarded conflict with the Daleks as ancient history, and Mavic Chen – the former Guardian of the Solar System – was barely mentioned in schools.[2009]

Two thousand years after it had been established, the Gogglebox enabled users to view every recorded media event from the human race's history. Alan Fitzgerald had been cloned, and one hundred eight copies of him aided visitors.[2010]

The Krashoks – cybernetic humans who had incorporated weaponry from races such as the Daleks, Cybermen and Rinteppi; and alien organs such as Renevian tiger claws, Slitheen arms and Gappa legs – initiated various wars and sold weapons to both sides. They hired the Darksmiths of Karagula to create a device that would resurrect the dead – a means of extending conflicts, which would be good for their business.[2011]

The fourth Doctor visited the farming world Unicepter IV.[2012]

The Mazuma Era[2013]

On a world whose name was lost to history, war between the ruling houses led to creation of the Oblivion Plague. This virulence mutated its victims into a telepathic gestalt: the Horde. Six months after the Capital City quarantined itself, the elite attended a fancy-dress party while wearing animal masks. The Horde punished the elites with a psychokinetic pulse, turning them into a variety of humanoid animals, but then – as a remnant of their old selves – showed deference to the leader of the elites, Scalamanthia. The Horde renamed their world Oblivion, and remained docile as long as the elites provided entertainment.[2014]

Destriianatos, a.k.a. Destrii, a criminal and companion of the eighth Doctor, was born. She was trained for combat, and first fought in the arena at age ten. At some point, she gutted Lady Tetronnia's sister.[2015]

Sharon Allan

& 8155 - "Dreamers of Death"[2016] -> For three years, the colonists of Unicepter IV enjoyed sharing adventure dreams. These were courtesy of the company Dreams Deluxe, who made the dream possible by harnessing the telepathic powers of a native creature: the small furry Slinth. The fourth Doctor, Sharon and K9 arrived just as one team of dreamers died in an accident. The Doctor and Sharon took part in a dream led by a man called Vernor, where they were attacked by the dead dreamers and an army of monsters. K9 severed the connection before they

---

meet up with the Krashoks.

2012 "Six or seven years" before "Dreamers of Death".

2013 THE MAZUMA ERA – HOME TO FROBISHER, JOSIAH W. DOGBOLTER, SHARON ALLEN, DESTRII AND MAJENTA PRYCE: A number of stories from the mid-80s *Doctor Who Magazine* strip were set in the same colourful, cosmopolitan far future period. It might be termed the Mazuma Era, after the galactic currency which seems to preoccupy a number of the characters. The first time we're given a date for the era is in "The Crossroads of Time" (*DWM* #135) – a *Doctor Who* crossover issue – which sees the Doctor dropping off the cyborg Death's Head in the year 8162.

This is, beyond a doubt, the native era of the sixth Doctor companion Frobisher (a shapeshifting detective often seen in the form of a penguin) and the villainous tycoon Josiah W. Dogbolter. While Dogbolter's holdings include Venus, Mars and Jupiter, no mention is ever made of Earth – which the TV show tells us ought to be uninhabited at this time. (The solar flares clearly don't affect the other planets of the solar system.) A string of fifth and sixth Doctor stories are based in the Mazuma Era – partly because it's where Frobisher is based, and partly as a consequence of Dogbolter being culpable in the death of Gus Goodman, a fifth Doctor companion, in "The Moderator".

"The Stockbridge Showdown", a grand event to celebrate the 500th issue of *Doctor Who Magazine*, reframed much of our understanding about the beings who live in the Mazuma Era, and consolidated the timeframes of some of the major *DWM* characters. The story depicts a quartet of the Doctor's long-standing comic-strip companions – Sharon Allen (née Davies), Frobisher, Destrii and Majenta Pryce – as already being established in this time period, and teaming up with the twelfth Doctor to ruin Dogbolter's standing and bring him up on criminal charges. Whereas it had never been established exactly when Sharon departed the TARDIS (in "Dreamers of Death"), or when exactly Destrii and Majenta Pryce had originated from in the first place,

here we saw them – alongside Frobisher – as part and parcel of the Mazuma Era.

It's tempting to think the Doctor gave Sharon, Destrii and Majenta a lift through time, and gave them cover identities to aid in his Dogbolter-toppling scheme... but since we're not told that he did so, and there's no reason to think that Sharon and Majenta can time travel, it's more likely the case that Sharon left the TARDIS in the Mazuma Era, and Destrii and Majenta originate from there. There's not much difficulty in relocating Sharon's last story with the fourth Doctor ("Dreamers of Death"), as it doesn't feel like a category error to move a *DWM* strip from the 80s to the era of *DWM* strips from the 80s. The dating clues in Destrii's first stories ("Ophidius", "Uroboros" and "Oblivion") were so non-existent, we relegated them to None of the Above in earlier editions. And while moving the Majenta Pryce stories to the Mazuma Era goes slightly against the grain of their author, Dan McDaid, thinking that they happened during the Fourth Great and Bountiful Human Empire, he also admitted that he wasn't particularly wed to the idea (see the related Majenta Pryce and the Crimson Hand sidebar).

Most usefully for dating purposes, "The Stockbridge Showdown" very dutifully kept track of the real-world passage of time between the last ongoing appearance/s of Sharon et al, and their reintroduction in a story published in 2016. In particular, Sharon and the eighth Doctor companion Izzy (who here appears in the modern day) are shown having aged a commensurate amount of time since we last saw them. Moreover, "The Stockbridge Showdown" doubly noted the passage of time by celebrating the sixtieth birthday of Maxwell Edison, a recurring *DWM* character starting with "Stars Fell on Stockbridge" in 1982.

That being the case, there's grounds for correlating the publication year of all of the Mazuma Era stories, using the 8182 dating given in "The Crossroads of Time" as a benchmark, and deriving the corresponding dates for the following...

were killed, but the Slinths had become aggressive, fed off all the colonists' negative emotions, and fused into a single devil-like creature. The Slinths were absorbing electricity, so the Doctor doused them in water, collapsing the devil creature into a pile of harmless Slinths. Sharon elected to stay behind with Vernor.

The Doctor was later invited to Sharon's wedding.[2017]

& 8155 - "Free-Fall Warriors"[2018] -> Doctor Asimoff from Sigma had been coming to the Festival of the Five Planets for the last fifteen years, although it used to be the Festival of the Six Planets until one planet broke away from the Federation. Asimoff recognised the fourth Doctor as a Time Lord, and the Doctor showed him the TARDIS. They met the Free-Fall Warriors – a stunt pilot team who challenged the Doctor to go on a flight with Machinehead, one of their number. They launched right into the middle of an attack on the planet, and were forced down onto an asteroid. The remaining Free-Fall Warriors – Big Cat, Cool Breeze and Bruce – set off to intercept the raiders, and the Doctor fixed Machinehead's ship in time to play a decisive role in the battle.

Josiah W. Dogbolter

& 8158 - "The Moderator"[2019] -> Josiah W Dogbolter, a creature not quite a man and not quite a frog, was the owner of the Intra-Venus Inc and the richest man in the galaxy. He profited from everything, including the war on Phobos and ruby mining on Celeste. Dogbolter had a presence on many planets, including Celeste – a world where he sent "moles", meaning people who rebelled against him. He owned Mars, Jupiter and Venus, plus a score of worlds in other systems.

The fifth Doctor and Gus landed on Celeste and narrowly escaped arrest for breaking curfew. Deep in the ruby mines, they were attacked by the Wrekka, a combat robot sent in to deal with the moles. Dogbolter's guards brought the Doctor and Gus to their boss, who learned the Doctor had a time machine. Dogbolter knew that "time is money", but the Doctor refused to sell his Ship and left. A furious Dogbolter brought in the Moderator, a company troubleshooter. He tracked them down and killed Gus.

Gus had wounded the Moderator. The Doctor returned the Moderator to his home timezone... where Dogbolter's right-hand robot, Hob, turned off his life support.

- "Dreamers of Death" (*DWM* #47-48, published 1980-1981, occurs in 8155; Sharon Davies – later Allen – leaves the TARDIS)
- "Free-Fall Warriors" (*DWM* #56-57, 1981, 8155)
- "The Moderator" (*DWM* #84, 86-86, 1984, 8158; first appearance of Dogbolter, death of Gus Goodman)
- "The Shape Shifter" (*DWM* #88-89, 1984, 8158; the sixth Doctor meets Frobisher)
- "Voyager" (*DWM* #90-94, 1984, 8158)
- "Polly the Glot" (*DWM* #95-97, 1984-1985, 8159)
- "Once Upon a Time Lord..." (*DWM* #98-99, 1985, 8159)

Frobisher returns to his native time off-panel, and reappears in The Maltese Penguin *and "Where Nobody Knows Your Name".*

- "The Crossroads of Time" (*DWM* #135, 1988, 8162; the seventh Doctor relocates Death's Head from *Transformers* continuity to the Sol System of the Whoniverse)
- "Time Bomb!" (*Death's Head* #8, 1988, 8162; the seventh Doctor relocates Death's Head from the Whoniverse to the Marvel Universe)
- "Ophidius" (*DWM* #300-303, 2001, 8175; the eighth Doctor meets Destrii, who mind-swaps with Izzy. Cue about a year of comics in which Izzy keeps adventuring with the Doctor while in Destrii's form. For Izzy – and probably Destrii too – "months" pass before...)
- "Uroboros"/"Oblivion" (*DWM* #319-322 and #323-328, 2002-2003, 8176; Destrii and Izzy regain their proper forms. Destrii and her uncle become time-active, and next meet the Doctor in "Bad Blood" [1885].

Destrii becomes the eighth Doctor's companion, then returns to the Mazuma Era off-panel, her final status at the end of the eighth Doctor *DWM* strips having been left open-ended.

- *The Maltese Penguin* (BF #33 ½, 2002, 8176)
- "Where Nobody Knows Your Name" (*DWM* #329, 2003, 8177; Frobisher and the eighth Doctor meet, but fail to recognise one another)
- "ThinkTwice" (*DWM* #400-402, 2008, 8182; Majenta Pryce joins the tenth Doctor in the TARDIS)
- "The Deep Hereafter" (*DWM* #413, 2009, 8183)
- "The Crimson Hand" (*DWM* #416-420, 2009-2010, 8184; Majenta departs the TARDIS)
- "The Stockbridge Showdown" (*DWM* #500, 2016, 8190; Sharon, Frobisher, Destrii and Majenta collaborate with the twelfth Doctor to bring down Dogbolter)

2014 The background to "Oblivion"; Destrii's uncle, Count Jodafra, was a "mere child" when this occurred.

2015 Destrii's mother says she's "eighteen" in "Oblivion".

2016 Dating "Dreamers of Death" (*DWM* #47-48) - The year isn't specified in the story, but there's a reference to Unicepter dream machines being "recently banned" in the *Abslom Daak – Dalek Killer* collected edition, placing the story around then. The settlers on Unicepter IV are "human". Their technology is not terribly advanced – they have hover cars and energy weapons, thinking projectile weapons are "old fashioned".

2017 "Star Beast II"

2018 Dating "Free-Fall Warriors" (*DWM* #56-57) - The story sees the fourth Doctor meeting Dr Asimoff for the first time.

2019 Dating "The Moderator" (*DWM* #84, #86-87) - The Free-Fall Warriors are mentioned.

Frobisher

& 8158 - "The Shape Shifter"[2020] **->** Avan Tarklu was a 45-year-old Whifferdill – a shapeshifting private investigator who was tempted by the quarter of a million Mazuma reward that Dogbolter had posted for the fifth or sixth Doctor.

Meanwhile, the sixth Doctor learned that Dogbolter had sent the Moderator, and was heading to Greenback Bay, Venus, when he was attacked. Avan Tarklu secretly helped the Doctor repel the attack – purely to get his hands on the reward – and snuck into the TARDIS. The Doctor and the shapeshifter landed at the headquarters of Intra-Venus Inc, which Dogbolter had evacuated, then nuked. They tricked Dogbolter into handing over the reward, then escaped. The shapeshifter joined the Doctor on his travels.

& 8158 - "Voyager"[2021] **->** The sixth Doctor had a nightmare about a shadowy figure on a sailing ship, waking to find that the TARDIS had landed at the Antarctic of "an outback dimension somewhere between mythology and madness".

The shapeshifter – who was now semi-permanently in the form of a penguin, and calling himself Frobisher – had discovered the same ship, frozen in ice. Exploring the ship, the Doctor found star charts. He was accosted by Astrolabus, an old man with a blunderbuss, who took the charts and made his escape in a da Vinci flying machine.

The Doctor and Frobisher followed him to a lighthouse, where the Doctor confronted Astrolabus – and found that the lighthouse was his TARDIS. Astrolabus tried to escape, but crashed into the sea. Voyager showed himself to the Doctor and demanded the return of the charts – which Astrolabus had tattooed onto his chest. Astrolabus was in his last incarnation and was seeking immortality, but Voyager ripped the chart off his body, killing him. Voyager told the Doctor he was now free, and the Doctor and Frobisher continued their travels.

& 8159 - "Polly the Glot"[2022] **->** Terminal LX 116/RM was a space station at the centre of the Milky Way – the crossroads of an entire galaxy – and was known as Galena. Dr Ivan Asimoff was passing through when he saw the TARDIS. He invited the sixth Doctor to the Save the Zyglot Trust annual conference, as he was the group's treasurer.

Polly, the only Zyglot in captivity, was at the Ringway Carnival along with freakshow exhibits from a hundred worlds. The creatures were hunted for their colours by the dullest race in the universe, the Akkers, and the Trust was failing through lack of funds. The Doctor and Frobisher "kidnapped" Asimoff, generating a great deal of publicity for his cause.

The Doctor learned that the President of the Trust was a Professor Astro Labus. They headed for a hunting ship, freeing the Zyglot in their clutches and discovering that an Astral Arbus owned the Ringway Carnival. The Doctor also freed Polly, who soared and blossomed – and left Asimoff heartbroken. The Doctor left the quarter-million Mazuma reward he stole from Dogbolter for Asimoff to donate to the Trust.

& 8159 - "Once Upon a Time Lord..."[2023] **->** The sixth Doctor and Frobisher entered the cabinet of Astrolabus, and encountered a variety of surreal obstacles.

Death's Head

8162 - "The Crossroads of Time"[2024] **->** Having fallen into the Time Vortex, the enormous cyber-assassin Death's Head collided with the TARDIS... and proved so belligerent, a Time Warden held back from intervening, leaving the seventh Doctor on his own. The Doctor zapped Death's Head with the Master's Tissue Compression Eliminator, literally bringing him down to size. He then ejected Death's Head to Earth, 8162, and worried what the robot might do to his favourite planet...

2020 Dating "The Shape Shifter" (*DWM* #88-89) - This story happens soon after "The Moderator" from the Doctor's point of view, as he's looking to avenge Gus' death. Dogbolter is somehow aware that the Doctor has regenerated, but the wanted poster has images of both the fifth and sixth Doctors.
2021 Dating "Voyager" (*DWM* #90-94) - It's a "few weeks" since the end of "The Shape Shifter".
2022 Dating "Polly the Glot" (*DWM* #95-97) - It's after "Voyager", but there's no indication of how much time has passed.
2023 Dating "Once Upon a Time Lord..." (*DWM* #98-99) - The story follows on from "Polly the Glot".
2024 Dating "The Crossroads of Time" (*DWM* #135) - The year is given. Death's Head fell through a time portal in the UK *Transformers* story "The Legacy of Unicron".
2025 "Uroboros"
2026 "Bad Blood"
2027 Dating *The Maltese Penguin* (BF #33 1/2) - No date is given, but this is clearly Frobisher's native time zone.
2028 Dating "Where Nobody Knows Your Name" (*DWM* #329) - This is an unspecified amount of years after Frobisher has returned to his native time.

8162 - "Time Bomb!" -> Paper now sold for about four million megabux a ream.

Intra-Venus Inc. developed a prototype time machine, the Dogbolter Temporal Rocket. Dogbolter commissioned the cyber-assassin Death's Head with venturing through time and killing the Doctor, but the seventh Doctor discovered that Dogbolter also intended to eliminate Death's Head with a thermonuclear device. Death's Head dropped the bomb atop Dogbolter's headquarters, destroying it. The Doctor relocated Death's Head to an alternate version of Earth, the 1980s.

Destrii

Destriianatos, as the only daughter of House Endoskiia, was slated for marriage to the first-born son of House Dregganon, Duke Borvathorius. Destrii's uncle, Count Jodafra, developed a chronon capsule and – as part of his long game against the Horde – used it to let Destrii to escape from her homeworld, Oblivion.[2025]

& 8175 - "Ophidius" -> The Ophidians, a once-great culture, had withered as a disease weakened them. They enslaved the space-faring serpent Ophidius, and went into space with their creator, Gorolith. Eventually, they sought to transfer their minds into sentient rock creatures: the Mobox. The fugitive marine-warrior Destrii, having escaped her homeworld, found herself aboard Ophidius... as did the eighth Doctor and Izzy, who were snared while hoping to see the heart of the Andrallis Nebula. Destrii used Ophidian technology to swap bodies with Izzy, hoping to hide from any authorities pursuing her. The Doctor sabotaged Ophidius, and a trigger-happy Destrii killed both Gorolith and a Mobox named K'yruss. Its mate, B'rostt, seemingly vapourised Destrii.

A grieving Izzy, now trapped in Destrii's body, continued travelling with the Doctor...

B'rostt reconstituted Destrii-Izzy to punish her, but Destrii-Izzy escaped and survived in the forests of the Morox homeworld...

& 8176 - "Uroboros"/ "Oblivion" (DWM) -> Two of the Horde at Scalamanthia's command went back in time and captured Izzy on the planet Kyrol, thinking she was Destrii. The eighth Doctor summoned Fayde, and they tracked their friend to the Mobox homeworld. B'rostt was elected head of the Mobox Empire in a landslide victory, and ordered reconstruction of Ophidius for use against the Mobox's enemies. Ophidius broke free of its shackles, killed B'rostt and departed into space. The Doctor and Fayde found Destrii, and compelled her to go with them to rescue Izzy from Oblivion...

Destriianatos' mother, the Matriax Scalamanthia, hailed the return of her "daughter", and proceeded with "her offspring's" betrothal to Duke Borvathorius. The Horde, sensing something amiss with Destrii and Izzy, returned their minds to their proper bodies. A wrathful Destrii killed her mother, whose death loosed the Horde – actually ten billion strong – from the last vestiges of control. The herd-like Horde chose Destrii as their new leader, but she rejected the immense psionic might they offered, and compelled the Horde to self-destruct. Their essences fueled the chronon capsule engineered by Destrii's uncle, Jodafra, and the two of them left into time and space.

Izzy's had reassessed her relationship with her parents, and asked the Doctor to take her home...

The eighth Doctor next met Destrii and Jodafra in the Dakota Hills, 1885.[2026]

& 8176 - THE MALTESE PENGUIN[2027] -> Frobisher briefly returned to his homeworld to resume his occupation as a private investigator. Through a bizarre twist of economics, Josiah W Dogbolter was generating immense profit on the planet by making sure no factory actually made anything. Frobisher's ex-wife, the Whifferdill named Francine, manipulated events to display the joke, "You don't have to be crazy to work here, but it helps", on the computer terminals of Dogbolter's employees. This triggered communication and productivity, and ruined Dogbolter's operations. Frobisher resumed travelling with the sixth Doctor.

& 8177 - "Where Nobody Knows Your Name"[2028] -> The eighth Doctor drank at a bar run by his old friend Frobisher, but as both had changed their appearance, neither recognised the other.

The Crimson Hand; Majenta Pryce Joins and Leaves the TARDIS[2029]

The Order of the Crimson Hand was a secretive group of extra-terrestrial tyrants, elitists and industry tycoons. It possessed powerful artifacts that included the ashes of the scroll of Horath, a shard of the Glory and a piece of the Key to Time. The quartet that composed the Crimson Hand's inner cabal – Trique, Lunat, Pollox and Pi – recruited Lady Scaph after they acquired the Manus Maleficus: a machine from the higher realms that reshaped reality, but required five operators.

The wealthy adventurer Wesley Sparks was reputed to have harnessed the power of the quark, charted the depths of the multiverse, and duelled with Daemons. He established Stormlight House as a protected residence; those within could watch the largest storm in the universe as it raged at the edge of the Proxima System. Patrons could appear in Stormlight in bodies made from solid engram tachyonics. Scaph passed an initiation test in which she seduced Sparks, then abandoned him the night before their wedding.

The now-complete Crimson Hand field-tested the Manus Maleficus by reaching back to the twentieth century and obliterating a planet threatening their powerbase in the Obsidian Cluster: the Ownworld of the Skith. Lady Scaph regretted her role in the holocaust and fled. She became the entrepreneur "Majenta Pryce". With her assistant Fanson, they experienced the rout of Ichabod Nine, the Recession Wars on Fiscus and the Tarvu Initiative.

Majenta and Fanson operated one of the last remaining Hotel Historias in the year 2008, but were arrested by time-travelling bailiffs. Before Majenta was incarcerated, Fanson erased her memory to conceal the psychic tracking sigil the Crimson Hand had placed in her mind.[2030]

& 8182 (Tuesday the Gluteenth of Mauve, and Wednesday) - "Thinktwice"[2031] **->** The amnesiac Majenta Pryce was incarcerated at the Thinktwice Orbital Penitentiary, and the tenth Doctor met her for the second time while investigating abuses there. The facility's warden had become allied with the memory-eating Memeovax while he was a boy on Greene's World, and had constructed the Knowsall machine to extract memories from the prisoners for the Memeovax's benefit. Majenta destroyed the Memeovax with a power surge of unknown origin, and the Doctor agreed to take Majenta to the Hippocrats of Panacea – the finest mind-surgeons in the universe – for treatment. Majenta agreed – on the understanding that the Doctor was working for *her*, without pay (for now).

2029 The background to *DWM*'s Crimson Hand story arc, given in "Mortal Beloved", "The Age of Ice", "The Crimson Hand" and "Hotel Historia". Majenta's "relative age" is given as "eighty-one Earth years" in "The Age of Ice" (which may or may not include the time she's spent TARDIS-travelling), so under the dating scheme in this chronology, she would have been born circa 199,919.

MAJENTA AND THE CRIMSON HAND: The Crimson Hand story arc in *Doctor Who Magazine* comic (*DWM* #394, 400-420) is remarkably circumspect when it comes to identifying the home era of the super-criminal Majenta Pryce, a companion of the tenth Doctor. We know that Majenta can travel in time, as she's operating a time-travel holiday hotel when the Doctor first meets her (in the early twenty-first century, "Hotel Historia"). We also know that the Intersol agents who incarcerate her in the future at Thinktwice prison ("Thinktwice") have time-travel capabilities.

Does Majenta originate from the modern day or the future, though? Is the time travel tech in play indicative of her society? Does the Crimson Hand also have time technology? We're never told within the story itself – just as it's not expressly said whether or not the story arc's finale ("The Crimson Hand", *DWM* #416-420) takes place in the present or the future. The Intersol agents "time-lock" the TARDIS to prevent it escaping when the story begins, but it's not stated if the Intersol ship then time-jumps before Majenta gets free, rejoins the Crimson Hand and conquers a vast sector of space to establish the Crimson Age. Admittedly, if the Crimson

Age *was* contemporary, it would be nothing short of miraculous that the Hand's sweeping and tyrannical empire seems far removed from Earth and in no way affects it.

Author Dan McDaid had privately decided that Majenta, the Crimson Hand, the Thinktwice prison and Intersol all originated from the Fourth Great and Bountiful Human Empire – his intention being that the grubbiness of the Thinktwice facility nicely emulated the moral and social decay seen in *The Long Game*. "Intersol", McDaid commented over email, "have acquired time travel from somewhere (probably misappropriated from a Time Agent), so they're able to pursue their targets across time and space." He added, "[The Fourth Great and Bountiful Human Empire] is also Majenta's 'home' era... but you don't have to take any of this as gospel, and feel free to monkey about with it if you need to."

"The Stockbridge Showdown", however, showed Majenta as living in the Mazuma Era. With the actual dating evidence in The Crimson Hand stories otherwise being so vague, it had seems best to follow its lead. It also seems fair to think that time travel is limited to parties such as Intersol, as it's not a facet of the other Mazuma Era stories.

2030 "The Age of Ice" and "The Crimson Hand", although there doesn't appear to be a point in the story when this could have occurred.

2031 Dating "Thinktwice" (*DWM* #400-402) - The warden mentions his intention to spread use of the

& 8183 - "The Crimson Hand" -> Intersol recaptured Majenta in the twenty-first century and interrogated her, which unlocked her memories. The sigil in her mind attracted the inner circle of the Crimson Hand, who were wanted on 32,608 individual counts of grand larceny, murder and fraud. They brought Majenta back into their ranks, and she seemingly disintegrated the Doctor – but actually sent him into a pocket dimension for safekeeping.

The reunited Crimson Hand exerted the full power of the Manus Maleficus. Galaxies were swept aside, entire solar systems were rebuilt and many races were extinguished. Majenta brought prosperity, and tyranny, to her impoverished homeworld of Vessica.

On Day 36 of The Crimson Age, Majenta retrieved the Doctor because use of the Manus Maleficus had created an expanding space-time rift. She repented her villainy, killed the Crimson Hand members and relinquished the Manus Maleficus' hold on reality. Space-time was returned to normal. Majenta died, but the Doctor brought her back to life with a final use of the Manus Maleficus, which returned to its home dimension.

Afterward, the Doctor took Majenta through time to live in New Old Detroit.

& 8183 - "The Deep Hereafter" -> The tenth Doctor and Majenta Pryce aided a fatally wounded PI in New Old Detroit, one of the forgotten colonies of the Proxima System. Hecto Shellac, a lawyer from Alpha Centauri, had acquired a World Bomb so he could retire and stop being coerced to defend criminals in court *or* – if he felt like it – take over the city. The World Bomb was a one-use weapon that altered reality, and so the Doctor triggered it while thinking of England, creating a renewed green living space.

& 8184 - "The Crimson Hand"[2032] -> The renewed New Old Detroit was renamed Redemption. Following the destruction of the Crimson Hand, the tenth Doctor took Majenta Pryce to live there.

Sharon, Frobisher, Destrii, Majenta and the Twelfth Doctor Against Dogbolter

& 8190 - "The Stockbridge Showdown"[2033] -> Josiah W. Dogbolter celebrated his 500th birthday. His Intra-Venus Inc. had recently acquired the media rights to the astral plane, and his daughter, Berakka, was the only person in the galaxy that he liked.

The twelfth Doctor recruited four of his former companions – Sharon Allen, now a presenter for Galactic Broadcasting Corporation (GBC); Frobisher; Majenta Pryce; and Destrii, a.k.a. Lady Destriianatos of the Oblivion Empire – to assist him in toppling Dogbolter. They manipulated Dogbolter into journeying to Stockbridge, 2016, where he confessed his crimes, then returned him to this era for Intersol to arrest him. Majenta staged a hostile takeover of Intra-Venus Inc., and became its new CEO.

At some point in the next forty thousand years or so, Real Phobos crashed into Old Barsoom, a.k.a. Mars.[2034]

c 8400 - TURN LEFT[2035] -> The tenth Doctor and Donna visited the planet Shan Shen, where Donna was lured into a fortune teller's booth and attacked by an alien beetle – one of the Trickster's Brigade. Such creatures normally changed people's lives in tiny ways and fed off the resulting temporal shift, but the beetle changed Donna's personal history so she never met the Doctor – with grave consequences to the history of Earth. Rose helped Donna to restore history, and the beetle died.

Knowsall machine through "The entire human empire!" (presumably one, in this period of time, that doesn't actually involve Earth). The "cosmic bailiffs" who bring Majenta to Thinktwice presumably belong to Intersol – the justice organisation ("The Crimson Hand") that has access to time travel technology, but whose members aren't necessarily part of humanity.

2032 Dating "The Deep Hereafter" (*DWM* #413) and "The Crimson Hand" (*DWM* #416-420) - No year or era of time given. The story's author, Dan McDaid, intended that New Old Detroit was broadly analogous to New New York as seen in *New Earth* and *Gridlock*. It seems unlikely that New Old Detroit is located on the New Earth seen in those stories, however, as the tenth Doctor would hardly be likely to let Majenta live there prior to a devastating plague that he knows (*Gridlock*) will wipe out most of the population. And, again, "The

Stockbridge Showdown" shows Majenta as assuming command of Dogbolter's commercial empire, with no sense that she's travelled through time, which suggests that she'd already settled in the Mazuma Era at the resolution of the Crimson Hand story arc.

2033 Dating "The Stockbridge Showdown" (*DWM* #500) - Thematically, the story (released in 2016) denotes the real-world passage of time for the *DWM* characters involved, so thirty-two years have been added to Dogbolter's last appearance in the comics ("The Shape Shifter", published in 1984).

2034 Before *The Coming of the Terraphiles*, with Barsoom being Mars. Dogbolter profited from the war on Phobos, so it still existed at that point.

2035 Dating *Turn Left* (X4.11) - No date is given on screen or in the script. Shan Shen appears to be a human colony. *The Time Traveller's Almanac*, a chronol-

Donna passed a message from Rose to the Doctor – two words: "Bad Wolf" – which made the Doctor race outside the fortune teller's booth, and see that everything with writing said exactly that. The TARDIS cloister bell started ringing, and the Doctor told Donna that it signalled the end of the universe. They returned to the twenty-first century.[2036]

After the great cybernetic massacres of the eighty-fifth century, sentient androids fell out of favour. From this point, most robot servants were connected to a central webwork rather than being autonomous.

The Federation had remained a democracy, but the Chen dynasty brought an end to that. Civil war broke out, and the final battle of the conflict took place in the Mirabilis System. Federation forces won, but the Imperial Fleet devastated Mirabilis itself with an atmospheric plasma burst that killed 90% of the population. Emperor Chen was captured and executed.

The civil war had taken its toll on the Federation, and the galaxy entered a new dark age in which scientific progress all but ceased. During the ninetieth century, the remnants of the Federation became the Union – a united political entity at peace with the Draconian Republic, the Cyberlord Hegemony and the radioactive remains of the Sontaran Empire. There were two other forces for unity: the Elective, a massive criminal organisation that controlled all criminal activity between New Alexandria and the Perseus Rift; and the Lazarus Intent, a religious organisation which commanded eight quadrillion people.[2037]

The Darksmith Legacy

The entire surface of Mordane, the first planet of the Gandii Prime System, had been converted into a place of cemeteries and catacombs – according to the TARDIS data bank, Mordane served a hundred different species from a thousand worlds as a planet of the dead. Humans from colonies such as Folflower, Mayside, Riverville, Wystone and Humberville buried their dead on Mordane. Lady Rosilie of Peladon was buried there. An entire continent, Sector Alpha, was designated for humans.[2038]

An underwater research base was established on Flydon Maxima to monitor the planetary warming there. The global warming ultimately gave way to a catastrophic ice age, forcing the planet's inhabitants to abandon it.[2039]

King Morrish a'Jethwa, who ruled five planets in the Folflower System for many years, was buried on Mordane. Following his death, the monarchy was deposed in a bloodless coup and went into exile.

Brother Varlos, the Darksmiths' chief engineer on the Krashok project, succeeded in building a device that could reanimate the dead. He field-tested the device on Mordane, and succeeded in making the dead walk. Varlos realised that the device had the potential to revive the dead on millions of worlds, and was so horrified that he vowed to destroy the device – but didn't know how to demolish its central power source, the Eternity Crystal. Varlos left his "daughter", an android named Gisella, at a base made from Darksmith technology on Flydon Maxima. He then fled with the Crystal to nineteeth-century Paris.[2040]

---

ogy of the *Doctor Who* universe published by BBC Books, states that the story is set in the eighty-fifth century, without explanation. *SJA: Whatever Happened to Sarah Jane?* suggests that the Trickster's Brigade is affiliated with the Trickster, a recurring villain in *The Sarah Jane Adventures*. A number of sources, such as the BBC website, refer to the beetle as a Time Beetle, but it's not called that on screen.

2036 *The Stolen Earth*

2037 The background to *The Crystal Bucephalus*. According to *Dalek Empire II*, there is a Galactic Union by 7500.

2038 Earth's colony worlds start burying their dead on Mordane "four hundred years" before *DL: The Graves of Mordane*. Contrary to the TARDIS' estimate, the young woman Catz – who has studied Mordane in detail, but is perhaps working from faulty records – says that Mordane serviced only a dozen races from more than thirty different worlds.

2039 "A hundred and fifty years" before *DL: The Planet of Oblivion*.

2040 *DL: The Graves of Mordane*, *DL: The Depths of Despair*, *DL: The Dust of Ages*, *DL: The Vampire of Paris*. It's never established that Brother Varlos has time travel

capabilities, but the Darksmiths have a conglomeration of time technology by *The Dust of Ages*, so he could have nicked some bits of it beforehand.

2041 In *DL: The Graves of Mordane*, it's said that the Darksmiths have been waiting "centuries"/"hundreds of years" since Brother Varlos absconded with the Eternity Crystal, that Varlos' machine has been on Mordane for "hundreds of years" (p91), and that the dead have been walking there every night "for centuries" (p107). And yet, it's twice said that the quarantine on Mordane has only been in operation for "eighty years" (p37, 82). Given that up to a thousand funerals a day were previously held on Mordane (p92), it doesn't seem remotely credible that the Galactic Union failed to notice – or decided to ignore – that the dead were rising every night on Mordane for decades if not longer. The Darksmiths confirm (p96) that the Varlos' test is what prompted the Mordane quarantine, making it unlikely that the machine lay dormant for centuries and flared to life for no apparent reason.

2042 Dating *DL: The Graves of Mordane*, *DL: The Depths of Despair* and *DL: The Planet of Oblivion* (DL #2, 4, 7) - *The Graves of Mordane* occurs when quite a few of humanity's colony planets have been sending their

The walking dead on Mordane prompted the Galactic Union to designate the planet a quarantine world with a Grade Two Exclusion Order. In the eighty years to follow, all records of Mordane were erased.[2041]

c 9000 - DL: THE GRAVES OF MORDANE / THE COLOUR OF DARKNESS / THE DEPTHS OF DESPAIR / THE PLANET OF OBLIVION[2042] -> The tenth Doctor visited the cemetery world of Mordane to learn more about the Eternity Crystal. He deactivated Varlos' re-animation machine, turning the undead that walked on Mordane into dust. He also helped Catz, the granddaughter of King Morrish a'Jethwa, to retrieve a torch from the king's tomb – it was the symbol of her right to rule the Folflower System. The Darksmiths' Agent took the Eternity Crystal from the Doctor, and the Doctor pursued the Agent to the Darksmiths' homeworld of Karagula...

Later, the Doctor went to Flydon Maxima to learn how to destroy the Crystal. The Darksmiths' enforcers, the Dreadbringers, followed the Doctor through time in the Dreadnought *Adamantine*. The Doctor sent a surge of icy water through an underwater base – this both swept away the Dreadbringers and enabled some local lifeforms, the tentacled Blaska, to retrieve a clutch of their eggs. The Doctor met Gisella, and together they went to find her father in Paris, 1895...[2043]

The Darksmiths re-conferred with the Krashoks on the peaceful planet Ursulonamex, a.k.a. Oblivion, concerning the Eternity Crystal – a devastating "rain of fire" was then unleashed upon the planet to cover up the meeting. The insectoid Dravidians, a race of thieves, arrived at Ursulonamex's only surviving space station and claimed to have answered a distress call. The Dravidians clandestinely set about draining the station's power and adapting its environment to suit their offspring, which hatched in their thousands. The tenth Doctor and Gisella forced the Dravidians to withdraw.[2044]

After around eight thousand years in the time corridor created by the fourth Doctor, Sutekh finally perished at the beginning of the ninetieth century.[2045]

? 9000 - DREAMTIME[2046] -> The seventh Doctor, Ace and Hex arrived at the Uluru as it travelled through space. The people's faith in the Dreaming had weakened, and the Dreaming began absorbing people into itself by turning them into stone. The Doctor accidentally travelled to the time of the solar flares and influenced the Uluru's departure from Earth. He returned and restored the people to normal, and it was hoped that the Dreaming's next attempt to terraform the Uluru would prove more successful.

c 9000 - HEAVEN SENT[2047] -> Teleported by the Time Lords into his own confession dial, the twelfth Doctor found himself in a castle where each room reset itself after he left it. The Veil, a creature from the Doctor's nightmares, stalked him, only stopping when he aired a never-spoken confession. The Doctor located the way out – a wall of azbantium, a substance four hundred times harder than diamond – and struck it a few times before the Veil fatally wounded him. With his last strength, the Doctor burned his own body to ash to generate a copy of himself from the teleporter. The fresh copy of the Doctor thought he'd just arrived at the castle, even as his previous body added to the collection of skulls in the castle's moat...

? 9200 - THE CHILDREN OF SETH[2048] -> An army warred with itself on the plains of Ragnarok, and only three hundred of its mightiest heroes survived. Their leader, Autarch Siris, forged a major trading empire with the cities on the asteroid archipelago around Sirius as its core. Idra, a student, met the Doctor while she was subverting the propaganda agency on Sirius III. She belonged to the Gracious Academy of Women, and realised that the

---

dead to Mordane for "over four hundred years" (p37), and a "Galactic Union" (p82) passes a "galactic law" (p37) that quarantines Mordane. If the "Galactic Union" is the same "Union" mentioned in *The Crystal Bucephalus*, then *The Graves of Mordane* could occur more-or-less anywhere in the 8000s to 12000s.

The participants in *The Depths of Despair* are named as human (p96); *The Planet of Oblivion* does the same at least three times (pgs. 89, 90, 94), so both of these stories occur in humanity's future, quite possibly in the same time zone that Brother Varlos conducted his experiments on Mordane.

2043 Their adventures continue in *DL: The Vampire of Paris* and *DL: The Game of Death*.

2044 The story continues in *DL: The Pictures of Emptiness* and *DL: The Art of War*.

2045 *Pyramids of Mars*

2046 Dating *Dreamtime* (BF #67) - Some "thousands of years" have passed since the Uluru departed into space. Simon Forward says it's possible that as much as ten thousand years have elapsed. This date is arbitrary.

2047 Dating *Heaven Sent* (X9.11) - It's "seven thousand years" into the future.

2048 Dating *The Children of Seth* (BF LS #3.3) - Date unknown, although the participants are identified as human. It's tempting to think that the android technology seen here – and the fear of it – dates back to Sharez Jek's android designs in *The Caves of Androzani* (which also takes place in Sirius), but no connection between the two is made. This dating is ultimately a guess, based upon no mention of Earth being made, and the empire's wealth and prosperity being in excess of that seen in *The Caves of Androzani*.

budding empire would need an enemy to fear and rally against. Idra invented the bogeyman Seth, as he was named in her book *The Trick of Darkness*. In time, she would became Siris' concubine, Queen Anahita, a.k.a. the Queen of Poisons.

The Sirian Empire reached a long way across its sector, and included at least ten humanoid variants. Androids were outlawed, and *The Trick of Darkness* was banned. Anahita's face was scarred as she tried to rescue copies of it from a fire.

Forty-three years after Anahita met the Doctor, Siris relinquished his authority to Lord Byzan – who consolidated his power by rallying his people against Seth, now said to have taken shelter in worlds beyond the Rim. Anahita feared the consequences for the empire, and summoned the fifth Doctor, Tegan and Nyssa. Androids who had infiltrated Sirius staged a coup, hoping to create a society without humans. The Doctor posed as Seth, and Byzan ended the insurrection by destroying the android Albis – which by extension made random "people" across the empire become immobile, their android origins revealed.

The empire disbanded, with individual worlds regaining their sovereignty. Anahita and Siris retired, after she poisoned Byzan in his cell.

The Antonine rescue raid on Scultiis in 9381 failed when the natives' electric fields disrupted their weapons.[2049]

Iris Wildthyme Regenerates

c 9968 - THE SCARLET EMPRESS[2050] **->** The planet Hyspero was visited at some point by hawk-like beings who were revered by the natives, yet had no interest in ruling the planet. They left behind Cassandra – the first Scarlet Empress, a jam-like creature in a jar – to look after their affairs. She built up the Scarlet Palace and founded the tattooed Scarlet Guard. A long line of Scarlet Empresses – Cassandra's descendents – ruled Hyspero, and the planet became home to an interstellar market.

The latest Scarlet Empress was a tyrant who conscripted Iris Wildthyme – who was dying, as she had eaten the flesh of a Kaled mutant – to reunite a mercenary band named the Four. One of the group was guarding Cassandra, and the incumbent Empress sought to lay claim to her ancestor. The eighth Doctor and Sam helped Iris find the Four, whereupon Cassandra destroyed her descendent and reclaimed the throne. Iris regenerated thanks to the healing properties of a life-restoring honey.

Around the end of the one-hundredth century, the Silurian scientists Ethra and Teelis worked on time-travel experiments. The results were published in the March 9978 edition of *Abstract Meanderings in Theoretical Physics*.[2051] The ArcHive studied the history of the universe, and served as vast repositories of knowledge. They had access to time-travel technology.[2052] Emperor Brandt and the Cyberlord Hegemony possessed the ArcHive in the hundredth century.[2053]

2049 *The Crystal Bucephalus*
2050 Dating *The Scarlet Empress* (EDA #15) - The novel itself gives no dating clues. The word "human" is continually used, although it's frequently unclear if this means Earth-born humans or just "humanoid". Mention is finally made, however, of a "colony of human beings" on a private moon of a vizier, which would seem to indicate this is in humanity's future.

The short story "Femme Fatale" (*More Short Trips*, 1999), also by Paul Magrs, has the Doctor and Sam encountering Iris after events in *The Scarlet Empress*. "Femme Fatale" occurs in 1968 (concurrent with the radical feminist Valerie Solanas shooting Andy Warhol), and Iris mentions to Sam that events on Hyspero took place "eight thousand years" ago. It's a little unclear whether she means eight thousand years in the past or the future – she might mean the former, but the presence of Draconians, Ice Warriors and Spiridons (who presumably start space-travelling at some point after *Planet of the Daleks*) on Hyspero seems to indicate the latter. Portions of "Femme Fatale" are obviously apocryphal (rendering "the Doctor and Mrs Jones" as agents of the British government, and eventually waking up on a *Prisoner*-style island), but the dating reference occurs in a section that is as canonical as one can get in a story such as this.
2051 *The Crystal Bucephalus*
2052 *Killing Ground*. The ArcHivists first appeared in the reference book *Cybermen*.
2053 *The Quantum Archangel*
2054 Dating *The Crystal Bucephalus* (MA #4) - The Doctor claims they are "six or seven centuries into the tenth millennium" (p27), but also says that it is the "108th century" (p40, which is in the *eleventh* millennium). The latter date is correct – elsewhere we learn that "10,663" was in the recent past (p69). Although the novel doesn't specify the exact date, author Craig Hinton assumed that it was set in the year 10,764 and that date has been adopted here.
2055 Combining accounts from *The Crystal Bucephalus* and *Synthespians™*, both novels by Craig Hinton. *Synthespians™* claims that Chen's empire ends before the Union is formed, and yet someone else claiming descent from Mavic Chen (evidently not the beheaded emperor) is either the leader of the Junta (which follows on from the Union) or has some form of authority as humankind seeks out its lost colonies (p273).
2056 Dating *Synthespians™* (PDA #67) - The events of

10,764 - THE CRYSTAL BUCEPHALUS[2054] **->** In 10,753, Alexhendri Lassiter fulfilled on the Lazarus Intent, stabilising a time gate that rescued Lazarus from the Sontaran throneworld before his death. But the truth about the false Messiah quickly became clear, and Arrestis took control of the criminal Elective. Meanwhile, Lassiter and his brother Sebastian built the Crystal Bucephalus, a time-travel restaurant on the planet New Alexandria, which sent the galaxy's elite to the finest eating establishments in history.

Eleven years later, the Crystal Bucephalus was destroyed. Arrestis was revealled as Lazarus and escaped in a time gate, only to arrive back on Sontara moments before his execution.

About a hundred years after the Crystal Bucephalus ended, humanity was again fragmented by civil war. The Union swiftly evolved into the Concordance, then the Confederation, then the Junta – a totalitarian regime that stemmed from the Elective. This instigated a millennium of barbarism.[2055]

c 11,000 - SYNTHESPIANS[TM] [2056] **->** A fleet of ark ships fled the galactic civil war and passed through an area known as the Great Barrier. Cut off from the rest of the galaxy, the colonists found themselves in an area rich with natural resources. The New Earth Republic was founded, and included such planets as Bel Terra, New Alaska, New California, New Regency, Paxas and Tranicula in the Thomas Exultation (which was noted for its vineyards).

A hundred years later, the Republic was peaceful but boring. A business consortium failed in its bid to restore contact with the rest of the galaxy, but managed to pick up old TV broadcasts from twentieth-century Earth. These proved extremely popular and Reef Station One was built to produce new shows such as *As the Worlds Turn, Dreams of Tomorrow, Executive Desires, The Rep, Star Traveller: The Motion Picture, ReefEnders, Liberation Street, Confessions of a Monoid* and *This Evening With Phil and Bev*. The people of the Republic become obsessed with television.

A Time Lord force of War-TARDISes launched an attack against the Nestene home planet of Polymos. The mission was commanded by Lord Vansell, and destroyed swarms of energy units. The Nestene Consciousness attempted to relocate to the New Earth Republic. Plastic automata named Synthespians – in reality Autons – had been freely used to perform manual labour in the Republic, and those aboard Reef Station One instigated a slaughter. The sixth Doctor and Peri defeated the Nestene Consciousness and its Autons. The Consciousness was trapped in a plastic Replica body, forced to again and again act out the last episode of *Executive Desires*.

The Junta attempted to invade the New Earth republic several centuries after the Auton incident, but was repelled. The New Earth Republic began intergalactic colonization efforts, sending sleeper ships to the Wolf-Lundmark-Melotte Galaxy and Andromeda.[2057] A resurgent Confederation finally overthrew the Junta.[2058]

Birth of the Great Intelligence

Circa 11,926, on the planet Sathanasi, **the Great Intelligence was born** from the ascended soul Mahasamatman. It would travel across the astral plane, and encounter Padmasambhava circa 1730.[2059]

The Earth became habitable again. Humanity didn't recolonise its homeworld.[2060] The human colonists who had arrived on an unnamed planet as the Sol Three and Terraforming groups renamed themselves the "Soul Free" and the "Terror Farmers". They fought each other for ten thousand years.[2061] Cyberblind released their DTM *Machina ex Machina* in 11,265.[2062] **The year 12,005 was the time of the New Roman Empire.**[2063]

c 14,000 - HEAVEN SENT[2064] **-> Within his confession dial, the twelfth Doctor chipped away at the azbantium wall as the universe lived on...**

The Crystal Bucephalus were "several centuries" ago.
2057 *Synthespians*™
2058 *The Crystal Bucephalus*
2059 The Haisman Timeline, as intimated in *Leth-St:* "Legacies" and *Leth-St: Times Squared*.
2060 *The Ark in Space*. Vira notes that scientists had calculated it would be "five thousand years before the biosphere was viable" on Earth after the solar flares. In *The Sontaran Experiment*, we learn that humanity has spread across the galaxy, and that Earth has been habitable for "thousands of years" but has remained abandoned.
2061 Before "Final Sacrifice". There's some confusion in

the story about the time that elapses during the civil war, which is variously given as "tens of thousands of years", "ten thousand years", "over ten thousand years" and simply "millennia" before.
2062 *The Also People* (p247).
2063 According to the Doctor in *The End of the World*. This would seem to fall at the time Earth was thought to be abandoned by humanity following the solar flares. Perhaps the New Roman Empire wasn't based on Earth, or there was a short-lived resettlement of the planet.
2064 Dating *Heaven Sent* (X9.11) - It's "twelve thousand years" into the future.

? 15,000 - CITY AT WORLD'S END[2065] -> An asteroid hit the moon of Sarath, changing its orbit so that it was now on a collision course with the planet. Ten years later, the first Doctor, Ian, Barbara and Susan found that preparations to build a rocket to evacuate the planet for the nearby Mirath were nearly complete. However, the Sarath leaders, based in the capital city of Arkhaven, had realised that the rocket ship could never fly and were only planning to save five hundred members of the elite.

Most of the population had been killed in a recent war and replaced by androids. This was a plot on the part of Monitor, the central computer in Arkhaven, to save itself before the planet's destruction. Monitor was destroyed, and the Doctor and Susan increased the capacity of the true escape rocket to save those they could.

wih - The first land battle of the War in Heaven between the Time Lords and the Enemy was fought on Dronid in the 160th century. It lasted a day, and was utterly devastating. The Time Lords used clockwork bacteria as a weapon. The Time Lords' attempts to cover their tracks after the battle wreaked almost as much harm as the battle itself, and became known by the inhabitants as the Cataclysm. The Doctor was thought to have been killed on Dronid, and the Relic, said to be his body, was recovered there in 15,414. A misguided Faction Paradox member, Cousin Sanjira, cast the Relic into the Time Vortex and it arrived in the twenty-second century. The Faction made Sanjira murder his younger self as punishment.[2066]

2065 Dating *City at World's End* (PDA #25) - This is an arbitrary date, although we are told it is "thousands of years" after Ian and Barbara's native time.

2066 *Alien Bodies*

2067 Dating *The Ark in Space* (12.2) - Harry twice suggests that they are "ten thousand years" after the time of the Solar Flares, and the Doctor confirms this in *The Sontaran Experiment*, which takes place immediately afterwards. *The Terrestrial Index* set the stories between "15,000 and 20,000". *The TARDIS Logs* suggested a date of "28,537". *Cybermen* offered the year "?14714". *The TARDIS Special* gave the date "c.131st century". The first edition of *Timelink* said "10,000"; the Telos version jumped through some hoops and decided it was "2113". *About Time* decided it was "15000 AD, at the earliest".

Wirrn Isle is very specific in that it takes place in 16,127, "four decades"/"forty years" after *The Ark in Space*, which would date that story to 15,987.

2068 *Wirrn: Race Memory*

2069 Dating *The Sontaran Experiment* (12.3) - The story immediately follows *The Ark in Space*. In *SJA: The Last Sontaran*, Sarah claims that these events happened "ten thousand years" in the future.

2070 *Heroes of Sontar*

2071 Dating *The Eye of the Tyger* (TEL #12) - The dating is more than a little confused. The Doctor says this is "a million and a half years" in Fyne's future (p28), but the blurb says it's the "thirty-second century". It's clearly after the solar flares first referred to in *The Ark in Space*.

2072 *The Silurian Candidate*, in the aftermath of *The Ark in Space* [c.16,000]. It's not a bad plan, although there's no sign of Silurians active on Earth in *Wirrn: Race Memory* [& 16,100] or *Wirrn Isle* [16,127]. Oddly, it also kind of squares with the eleventh Doctor effectively setting an egg-timer to wake up the Silurians circa 3020 in *Cold Blood*, a story broadcast the same year that *The Beast Below* set the *The Ark in Space* evacuation in

the twenty-ninth century (see Dating *The Beast Below*). The broad story point seems to be that the Doctor twice engineers things so the Silurians will wake up at a (or perhaps the) time Earth has been ravaged by solar flares and abandoned by humanity.

2073 Dating *Wirrn: Race Memory* (BBV audio #29) - It's repeatedly said to be "one hundred years" after events in *The Ark in Space*. The audio concurs with the TV story in that "ten millennia have passed since the solar flares", but also, a bit oddly, says that the Nerva gene bank is fifteen thousand years old.

2074 *Wirrn Isle*. It's claimed that the Buchman family came to the loch "seventeen, eighteen years ago", and that the Wirrn were trapped when Nerva abandoned its colonies "fifteen years ago". Iron was thought dead "fifteen years" ago, Toasty is age twenty but was five when her brother was "lost", and Roger Buchman has spent the last "fifteen years" pouring over the transmat logs in the hopes of rescuing Iron. The early version of the transmat software used when Iron was lost is "fifteen years" old. In episode two, however, it's claimed – possibly by way of generalising – that the Wirrn have been trapped for twenty years, and that it's taken Roger "twenty years" to get back to the loch.

2075 Dating *Wirrn Isle* (BF #158) - The back cover reads: "The year is 16127. Four decades have passed since the colonists of Nerva Beacon returned to repopulate the once-devastated Earth." Roger declares in the story itself that "It's 16127. Barely forty years since we returned to Earth" (after *The Ark in Space*). The Doctor tells Flip that it's the "mid-162nd century. It's a long, long time since I was here." Sheer, a Nerva City engineer, concurs that the Wirrn aboard the Nerva space station were destroyed "forty years ago".

2076 *Genesis of the Daleks*. It's a presumption that "Space Year 17,000" is the same as 17,000 AD.

2077 Dating *The Time of Angels* (X5.4) - It's "twelve thousand years" after the story's main events.

Return to Earth

c 16,000 - THE ARK IN SPACE[2067] -> The fourth Doctor, Sarah Jane and Harry arrived on Nerva and helped some of the colonists there to awaken. The Wirrn had infested the Ark, and sought to absorb the humans' knowledge. The Wirrn were killed, and humanity prepared to reoccupy their homeworld. They intended to restock the planet with plant and animal life and to rebuild human civilisation.

Before their defeat, the Wirrn seeded their DNA into various insect species in Nerva's gene bank.[2068]

& c 16,000 - THE SONTARAN EXPERIMENT[2069] -> Field Major Styre of Sontaran G3 Intelligence conducted a Military Assessment Survey on Earth, which had acquired strategic value in the Sontarans' war with the accursed Rutans, and was believed devoid of intelligent life. Styre conducted experiments on Galsec colonists that he lured to Earth, but the fourth Doctor and Harry, accompanied by Sarah Jane, killed him.

The Sontarans posthumously published Styre's manual on human resistance to torture.[2070]

& c 16,000 - THE EYE OF THE TYGER[2071] -> Just after the people aboard Nerva had begun to resettle the Earth, a feline race arrived and helped the reconstruction efforts. Soon, though, some humans turned against the aliens, who left with ten thousand humans to find a new home. They were lured to settle on planets within a black hole by the avatars of their descendants, the Conservers, who existed in the black hole billions of years in the future.

The seventh Doctor programmed many of the Silurians on Earth to awaken in 16,087, when they stood a good chance of peacefully cohabiting with humanity.[2072]

& 16,100 - WIRRN: RACE MEMORY[2073] -> Fifty years after the Nerva sleepers revived, the station's solar stacks failed, and it was abandoned. Another half-century on, the remaining humans from Nerva and their descendents worked to restore Earth's ecology by using gene spoolers to re-create various animal species. Cherries had been cultured, but weren't yet approved for gene spooling. The Wirrn DNA hidden in Nerva's gene bank caused the spoolers to generate some mature Wirrn, and although these were killed, the Wirrn DNA persisted in at least two people. It was suspected that the Wirrn had absorbed so much non-Wirrn material, any new Wirrn offspring would be born as humans.

The revived humans aboard Nerva space station established Nerva City as their central settlement on Earth. Resources remained scarce, but additional colonies were attempted – the northern-most of which was at Inchfad Isle, Loch Lomond, in Scotland. Fish were found in the waters there. Pair-bonding breeding programmes were continued among the population, and genetic contamination from humans in the GalSec colonies was feared.

Earth continued to experience sudden climate changes, and so Nerva City recalled its colonists, revoking all travel privileges. A Wirrn swarm lost some of its number to a radiation cloud, and about four hundred survivors took shelter in Loch Lomond – which froze over, immobilizing them. As the Buchman family evacuated the colony there, a transmat mishap caused young Iron Buchman to become molecularly trapped within one of the Wirrn. He remained imprisoned along with them for fifteen years.[2074]

16,127 - WIRRN ISLE[2075] -> The transmats developed in this era were the most precise devices that man had ever, or would ever, create. The transmats could discern and relocate the very quarks, pinstripes and hydrons of matter.

Nerva space station was operational, but lacked enough power to keep its transmats constantly on-line. Nerva City attempted to restart seven of its discontinued colonies, and allowed the Buchman family to return to Loch Lomond in Scotland. The sixth Doctor and Flip arrived as Roger Buchman attempted to transmat his son Iron out of the Wirrn in which he was trapped, but the transmat failed to separate their DNA, and the fully mature Iron-Wirrn appeared on the loch's transmat pad. The Iron-Wirrn killed Roger, then reprogrammed the transmat to create an Iron-Wirrn copy on every transmat pad in Nerva City. The copies laid their young within the city's populace, and Nerva City's Council Chamber became a nursery for the incubating eggs. Faced with total defeat, the city's administrators ordered the colonies to forever switch off their transmats.

The Doctor reprogrammed the transmat to deposit all the Wirrn in Nerva City into the frozen loch, trapping them there, but opted against transmatting away the eggs they had laid in several corpses. He and Flip departed with the expectation that the Nerva humans and the Wirrn would find a means of co-existing.

The Dalek War against Venus in Space Year 17,000 was halted by the intervention of a fleet of war rockets from the planet Hyperon. The rockets were made of a metal completely resistant to Dalek firepower. The Dalek task force was completely destroyed.[2076]

c 17,150 - THE TIME OF ANGELS[2077] -> The Delerium Archive was the biggest museum ever and the final resting place of the Headless Monks. The eleventh

Doctor found artifacts there relating to himself, and also a message from River Song carved into the Home Box of the *Byzantium*: "Hello, Sweetie", along with a series of time-space coordinates. He and Amy went to the *Byzantium*, in the past, as instructed.

The Far Future

In the far future, humanity's influence was felt in other galaxies such as Andromeda, Acteon, Isop, Artoro and the Anterides.[2078]

lgtw - The Daleks were the greatest threat in the universe ... until one day, when they just vanished. Eventually they became mere legends. Unknown to humanity, they had left to fight the Last Great Time War with the Time Lords, a conflict that all but wiped out both races.[2079]

The Gods of Light conducted experiments on Vortis. They replaced the core with a propulsion system, and kidnapped the Menoptra from their home planet.[2080]

The Aapex Corporation, based on Mina Fourteen, started a genetics experiment on the planet Nooma to further terraforming and bioengineering on low-gravity planets. Nooma's sun was an Aapex spaceship, and the planet's artificial "Sky" – actually a sentient being programmed to regulate Nooma's biosphere – formed a protective shell around the planet.

Biology on Nooma became such that humanoids developed in the forest as carnivorous children, but mature males would fight to the death. The winners underwent genetic "promotion", which entailed their growing wings and joining the flying "naieen", but the losers would reanimate as infertile cadavers named the Dead. The naieen would mate, causing their seed to fall on the forest and bud new children.[2081]

? 18,000 - HEROES OF SONTAR[2082] **->** The Sontaran Empire now had seven "great" clans of distinction, each of which was cloned from one of the Sontarans' greatest warriors. Three Sontarans were required for a formal execution party. Under Standing Order 447-subsidiary clause two, mockery of a Sontaran officer was an act of war. The Sontarans regarded Terra as a Class-C civilisation. The Fifteenth Treaty – whether or not the Sontarans recognised it – exempted non-combatants in a war zone from martial jurisdiction. Sontarans could commit honourable suicide by ingesting coronic acid pills.

In this era, people all across the "middle galaxies" came to the planet Samur to find sanctuary and solace – especially at its Citadel, which stretched all the way around Samur's equator. Ten local years after the Doctor visited the Citadel, the Sontarans tried to oppress Samur and ran into heavy resistance from amorphic space-mercenaries, the Witch Guards. The Sontaran Stabb detonated one hundred twenty canisters of biological agent Zed-Oblique-Stroke-Zero-Zero-Two in Samur's troposphere, which transformed the planet's inhabitants into an invasive purple moss. Such was the honour to follow, Stabb became Field Marshall Stabb, the Unvanquished Supreme Commander of the Ninth Sontaran Space Fleet.

Stabb was used as the template for one million Sontaran clones, but a Witch Guard corrupted Stabb's DNA, so the

---

2078 Inter Minor is in the Acteon Group, as is Metebelis III (*Carnival of Monsters*), although it is later referred to as the Acteon Galaxy (*The Green Death, Planet of the Spiders*). The Isop Galaxy is the location of Vortis (*The Web Planet, Twilight of the Gods*), the home of the Face of Boe (according to *Bad Wolf*) and possibly the Slitheen (*Boom Town* refers to "venom grubs" – as they're called in *The Web Planet* novelisation; they're named "larvae guns" in the TV version). Artoro and the Anterides are referred to in *Planet of Evil*.

2079 "Thousands of years" before *The Parting of the Ways*. It's unclear exactly when this occurs. Captain Jack knows about the Daleks' disappearance, but as he's also a time traveller; it doesn't mean this happened before his native time. It's after "Space Year 17,000", historically the last recorded reference to the Daleks before *Bad Wolf*.

It's also unclear what this "vanishing" entails – the Doctor seems amazed that he meets a Dalek in *Dalek*, suggesting that they've been erased from history (would he, for example, have been surprised to meet one around 2164 on Earth, during their invasion?). However, Captain Jack recognises their ships in *Bad Wolf*, and the inhabitants of 200,100 both know the Daleks' name and that they vanished. Perhaps the simplest solution is that the new-style, gold Daleks that make their debut in *Dalek* are "Time War Era" Daleks, and so none of them should exist after the Time War.

2080 "Thousands of years" before *Twilight of the Gods*.

2081 "Four thousand years ago" before *Speed of Flight*.

2082 Dating *Heroes of Sontar* (BF #146) - A plaque commemorates the Sontaran invasion of Samur "in the Marshall year 7509", but this is unlikely to equate with the Earth calendar because a) the Sontarans are too inclusive and egotistical a race to resort to anything but their own dating, and b) a human-torture manual written by Field Major Styre is in use, so it's after *The Sontaran Experiment*. Judging exactly *how* far after is tricky: Styre's manual is still in circulation, even though one would presume that the Sontarans would eventually gain better intelligence on humans (whom they are aware of, to the point of designating Terra a Class-C civilisation) and render his findings outdated. And yet, enough time has passed since *The Sontaran Experiment* that Sontaran stories of the Doctor are now "legion", whereas Styre hadn't heard of him.

clones had subtle defects. This marked a turning point for the Sontaran Empire – after the victory at Samur, Sontaran forces increasingly had to pull back from Rutan space and consolidate within the Madillon Cluster.

Twenty local years after the Sontarans devastated Samur, the fifth Doctor, Tegan, the older Nyssa and Turlough were present as the Witch Guards perished while trying to usurp the cloning vats on the Sontaran homeworld and create an army of themselves. A rain composed of embryonic Sontarans washed over Samur, eliminating the moss and reviving the planet's ecosystem.

? 18,000 - STARLIGHT ROBBERY[2083] -> Interstellar Express was an accepted form of credit card. The "twelve systems" had ten-star orbital hotels.

The Sontaran Empire had destroyed the Rutan fleet at Wendon's Pass and eradicated the Velosian hordes in the seventh system, but its forces were stretched thin across a thousand systems, with clone-hatchlings in demand on every front. Billions of Sontaran clones were said to hatch each dawn on the Sontaran broodworlds. Sontaran Meson rifles fetched good money on the black market. The 78th Amendment to the Third Party Code related to prisoners of war. Under the 15th Treaty, non-combatants were exempt from Sontaran marshal jurisdiction. The Grag Diamond adorned the standard of the First Sontaran Legion – it was a double-compressed jewel from the mines of Sontar, a stone within a stone. A "Grag Diamond shot" entailed hitting two targets with a single bolt, the eradication of enemies old and new.

The Daleks arranged for the Kletcht to sell Kurt Schalk's assets to the Urodelian weapons trader Garundel, to distract the seventh Doctor, Elizabeth Klein and Will Arrowsmith. Garundel Galactic hosted an auction that drew parties such as Marshal Stenn of the 620th Sontaran Attack Fleet (the bloodletter of the ninth moon of Velos,

and who sent eight of his own clonespawn to perish as he ravaged the Doghead Nebula). Also on hand was the reptilian Krakenmother Banarra – the Queen of the House of Krellor, owner of the riches of twelve systems. The Bandrils sent their excuses. Stenn whittled down his competition by strangling the Tub-Lash Entity with its own tentacles.

The auction commenced at Q987, a J-class planetoid at the end of Mutter's Spiral, near the territory of a number of warlike species, including humans. The most prized item was Lot No. 749: Schalk's preserved body and mind, and his prototype Persuasion machine.

The auction was a scam – "Schalk" was actually the corpse of Lukas Hinterberger, and the Persuasion prototype had limited range and effectiveness. It could boost retail sales, but was useless for conquest. Garundel's assistant, Ziv, made off with his clients' deposits, payments and weapons – as well as Lot 749. Ziv attempted to secure the proceeds in a Galactic Credit Bank on Sirius IX, an A-rated exchange world, but was pursued. Stenn's meager forces wiped out the Krakenmother's fleet by use of the Venunian Gambit, confusing enemy sensors with moon debris the size of Sontaran battle-spheres.

The Doctor, Klein and Will left for the twentieth century to find the genuine Schalk... after Stenn obligingly cut off Garundel's hand, to unlock the gravity clamp the auctioneer had placed around the TARDIS. After the Doctor's party left, the Daleks killed Stenn.

c 18,000 - PLAGUE OF THE DALEKS[2084] -> The Lucerians were a scholarly, non-aggressive purple-coloured race with tentacles. They re-absorbed their dead, and displayed bioluminescence in their mating rituals. Humans inhabited Satellite 16 in the Hammer Nebula; working ninety hours a week was permitted there, and there were queues for health care. The WN5 filtration

---

The Sontarans currently have an empire with considerable holdings in the Madillon Cluster, a territory they seemed to be battling the Rutans for in *The Two Doctors*.

2083 Dating *Starlight Robbery* (BF #176) - It's long after the present day. Garundel touts Schalk and his Persuasion machine of being of "mid-twentieth century vintage", and Ziv needs convincing that Will Arrowsmith was born in the twentieth century. Will records in his audio log that it's "time: unknown". Garundel and the Doctor previously met "a long time ago" in the time of Beowulf (*Black and White*), but Urodelians seem to be long-lived, and there's no sense that Garundel used the Daleks' time technology to skip the interim. Sirius IX is a respected financial planet, which might suggest an expansion of "the five planets" (presumably those of the Sirius System) mentioned in

The Caves of Androzani [c.5300].

The Sontarans have an empire and know of the Doctor. A fallen Sontaran is credited as being "nine years old, a good lifespan for a warrior", an echo of Strax's claim that "I've had a good life. I'm nearly 12" in *A Good Man Goes to War*.

Perhaps most importantly, Stenn is familiar with humans, and believes that "Terra" (presumably Earth) has a Level C civilisation – the same designation given in *Heroes of Sontar*. Unless further information comes to light, it seems best to favour the Level C classification and place *Starlight Robbery* in the same era.

2084 Dating *Plague of the Daleks* (BF #129) - The Doctor notes the use of a fortieth century-style shuttlecraft and a forty-fifth century-style environmental dome; from this, he conjectures that he and Nyssa have arrived "beyond the Critical Age", i.e. after the solar flares

booster was obsolete, replaced by the WN9 in deep-space communication systems.

The Daleks learned of the Doctor's fondness for the village of Stockbridge, and laid a trap for him by preserving it beneath an environmental dome – it was one of only three sites given such treatment in Earth's Northern Hemisphere. Tourists would visit Stockbridge, and what villagers remained were Nth-generation clones, the products of a degrading gene pool.

The fifth Doctor and Nyssa surfaced in this era owing to a collapsing time bubble in the twenty-first century, retrieved the TARDIS from a Dalek stasis vault, and prevented the Daleks from using the Ship to gain mastery of space-time. They departed as one of the Daleks' thralls nullified the environmental dome, destroying Stockbridge and all within.

Around 18,500, Earth was abandoned once again.[2085] The Aapex Corporation went bankrupt. Nooma was abandoned to its own fate.[2086]

c 19,000 - THE ANACHRONAUTS[2087] -> The first Doctor, Steven and Sara Kingdom deliberately left Captain Natalie Lang and her crew of anachronauts near a peaceful city some ten thousand years after their native time, preventing them returning home and using their newfound knowledge of time travel to spark a temporal war.

? 20,000 - THE WEB PLANET[2088] -> The planet Vortis in the Isop Galaxy was the home of the moth-like Menoptra, who worshipped in glorious temples of light and lived in the flower forests. They kept an ant-like race, the Zarbi, as cattle. The planet was invaded by the Animus, an entity that could absorb all forms of energy, and which pulled three planetoids – including Pictos – into orbit around Vortis. Most of the Menoptra fled to Pictos, but the descendants of those that stayed behind slowly devolved into sightless dwarfs, the Optera. The Animus used the Zarbi as soldiers, and had dreams of galactic conquest until the first Doctor, Ian, Barbara and Vicki arrived. The Animus was destroyed by the Isop-tope, a Menoptra weapon.

---

have ravaged Earth (presumably the same incident established in The Ark in Space). However, this isn't to say that the adventure actually takes place near the forty-fifth century – both items could be long-lasting, or could have been recreated for nostalgic purposes. The history established in The Ark in Space, in fact, tends to rule out Plague of the Daleks as occurring near the forty-fifth century – the solar flare cataclysm is so great that humanity takes desperate measures such as converting Nerva Beacon into a hibernation station to survive, and it's hard to imagine that amidst this tragedy, a heritage trust is shuttling carefree senior citizens to Earth as a tourist service with declining revenues.

One of the seniors, Vincent Linfoot, says that he's backtracked "several hundred generations" (call it seventy-five hundred to seventeen thousand five hundred years for the sake of argument) of his family to Stockbridge, and here finds a family gravestone from 1872. Extrapolating "several hundred generations" from that point, the story could date anywhere from circa 9,350 to 19,350. As Stockbridge itself – however much the Doctor mourns for its loss – could itself be a Dalek recreation, and there's nothing to say that a single brick of it stemmed from the genuine article, it's perhaps best to assume that it was established as a heritage city after Earth's repopulation after The Ark in Space, and that its destruction comes before the planet being (yet again) abandoned by 18,500 according to Birthright.

That just leaves the task of correlating this story to Dalek history. The Daleks' instruments say they've been hibernating in Stockbridge for seventeen centuries awaiting the Doctor's arrival, but as their equipment is badly corroded, the accuracy of their time-keeping devices is very questionable. Whether or not the "sev-

enteen centuries" figure can be trusted, though, it's notable that A) the Stockbridge Daleks say their race possessed a mighty battle fleet when they went to sleep, and that B) two natives of this era – Lysette Barclay and Professor Rinxo Jabbery – respectively claim that "the Daleks died out centuries ago" and that most civilised races consider them to be extinct. If Plague of the Daleks does indeed take place after Earth's re-settlement in The Ark in Space, Jabbery and Barclay could be referring to the Daleks' failed assault against Venus in 17,000 (as established in Genesis of the Daleks).

Pursuant to this, the Doctor claims that while the Stockbridge Daleks slept, they were defeated by the "combined forces of over one hundred planets", and that they "were driven from this sector of the galaxy centuries ago; where there used to be a glorious Dalek empire, there's just a big empty nothing". As he's no means of establishing the year beyond the forty-fifth century technology he's witnessed, however, his opinion here can't particularly be trusted – he could just as easily be referring to the downfall in Dalek fortunes in the centuries after The Daleks' Master Plan or Dalek Empire II, or just be mocking them to gain a psychological advantage.

One last oddity: at story's end, the Doctor tells Nyssa that "time" deposited them at the last possible point in Stockbridge's future – i.e. its destruction. Not only is this claim bizarre on its face – does he mean the entity Time from the New Adventures, or does he actually mean to say that the time bubble in The Eternal Summer was somehow self-aware? – it's still not proof that the Stockbridge seen here isn't a Dalek recreation, and that the original didn't perish long ago.
2085 Birthright

A small tendril of the Animus survived the Isop-tope's effect. An opponent of the Doctor transported it through time to Earth, 1868, where Ian Chesterton dispatched it.[2089] New Rhumos broke away from Rhumos Prime, which marked the beginning of a lengthy conflict.[2090]

c 20,192 - TWILIGHT OF THE GODS[2091] -> After the Animus' defeat, Vortis wandered into the Rhumos System. Two Rhumon factions, the Imperials and the Republicans, fought for control of the planet. The second Doctor, Jamie and Victoria arrived a year later, just as a seed of the Animus emerged. The Doctor brought the Rhumons and Menoptera together to destroy the new Animus. The Gods of Light who had engineered Vortis agreed to stop interfering in its affairs, and it was hoped that Vortis could peacefully co-exist with its Rhumon neighbours.

? - "The Naked Flame"[2092] -> The fourth Doctor and Sarah landed on Vortis, where a glowing crystal was attracting Menoptra to their deaths. The Doctor shattered it with his sonic screwdriver.

c 20,592 - RETURN TO THE WEB PLANET[2093] -> Humanity developed a synthetic means of propagating itself throughout space that was more efficient than colonisation or invasion; "seed ships", each carrying two "gene-synthetics" – a male and a female – were dispatched to barren worlds where humanity couldn't thrive. Upon arrival, the gene-synthetics would adapt to the local conditions, then merge into a large cocoon from which hundreds of offspring – humans biologically adapted to the environment – would emerge.

One seed ship was drawn to Vortis by a "lode-seed" – a powerful gravitational attractor that both nourished the land and helped the Zarbi navigate during migrations. The female gene-synthetic, named Xanthe, became telepathically integrated into the Zarbi hive mind. The fifth Doctor and Nyssa were present when Xanthe merged with her mate, Yanesh, and it was expected that their offspring would live in peace with the Zarbi.

? 21,350 - THE ROSEMARINERS[2094] -> Earth controlled the most advanced weaponry in space, and humans still had pores in their skin.

Intergalactic Councils advanced relationships between different worlds. On Earth, the Universal Council oversaw development of Earth Station 454 in the Antares Galaxy between the gas giant Triangulum and the water world Cetus. The natives of Rosa Damescena – tall beings with green-brown skin, and having a culture and biology based on roses – similarly established *Rosemarinus*, a space station for prisoners, near 454. A failed coup on Rosa Damescena prompted scientists there to search planets for new types of roses – a means of pacifying rebellious ele-

2086 "2347.54 years" before *The Speed of Flight*.

2087 Dating *The Anachronauts* (BF CC #6.7) - It's "a good ten thousand years" since the time pilots' war with the Wall of Noise, estimated as happening "thousands of years" after Steven and Sara's native times.

2088 Dating *The Web Planet* (2.5) - The story seems to take place in the future as the Animus craves "Earth's mastery of Space". Bill Strutton's novelisation places it in "20,000", although the Doctor suggests that the TARDIS' "time pointer" might not be working. The New Adventure *Birthright* suggests that Earth is abandoned at this time, but it is established in *The Ark in Space* and *The Sontaran Experiment* that man has spread through the universe.

2089 "Prisoners of Time". The Doctor notes, "The Animus couldn't have [established itself on Earth] alone. The gateway alone that brought the Zarbi here [to Earth] is technology beyond the Animus' ken." As the villains here (Adam Mitchell and the Master) are time-active, and it seems reasonable to think that one of them transported the Animus into the past (presumably knowing the Doctor would visit his friend Thomas Huxley at some point) as well as space. The story doesn't ever reveal which of them was behind this plan; it's not part of Adam's goal to kidnap the Doctor's companions, but the Master never owns up to it.

2090 "Over a hundred and fifty years" before *Twilight of the Gods*.

2091 Dating *Twilight of the Gods* (MA #26) - This is a sequel to *The Web Planet*. The Animus was defeated "seventy thousand days ago" (p1), which is a little under one hundred and ninety-two years.

2092 Dating "The Naked Flame" (*DWM Yearbook 1995*) - It's an unspecified amount of time after *The Web Planet*.

2093 Dating *Return to the Web Planet* (BF subscription promo #6) - The back cover says, "It's been hundreds of years and several regenerations since the Doctor last visited the insect world of Vortis." Within the story itself, the Doctor mentions his "previous visits" (note the plural) and that he hasn't visited since "a few regenerations back", a tacit acknowledgement of the second Doctor's trip to Vortis in *Twilight of the Gods*, and possibly (for those who prefer) even those seen in the Annuals and TV Comic.

2094 Dating *The Rosemariners* (BF LS #3.8) - It's the future, most likely the *far* future, as Earth is part of an intergalactic community and highly functional. It's definitely past Zoe's time, as she "doesn't know the faintest thing about the time period". The *rosa toxicaira* was developed by the Daleks on Kembel (*The Daleks' Master Plan*, set in 4000), so it's after that.

The participants readily accept Zoe's bluff that Earth is sending a security fleet to Station 454, which is in the Antares Galaxy – either suggesting that Earth's spaceships are incredibly fast, or that Earth keeps fleets sta-

ments. They located a product of Dalek experiments with hostile plant life on Kembel, the *rosa toxicaira*, and from this derived the will-sapping serum Rosedream.

Without explanation, the Universal Council announced the closure of Station 454 and the recall of its staff back to Earth. The station's lead xenobiologist, Arnold Biggs, viewed this as the end of six years of productive experimentation, exploration and cosmological cooperation. A Rosa Damescena convict, Rugosa, captured *Rosemarinus* in an uprising, and attempted to force Biggs to develop a cure for Rosedream – the first step in Rugosa and his lieutenants conquering their homeworld, then the Betus Galaxy, then the universe with Rosedream.

The second Doctor, travelling with Jamie and Zoe, helped Biggs to develop a Rosedream cure and vaccine – but also incapacitated Rugosa's followers with Rosedream. Rugosa accidentally succumbed to Rosedream while trying to vaccinate himself. The Doctor's party left as authorities aboard *Rosemarinus* engaged the station's engines, starting its journey back to Rosa Damescena.

Carbon-dating suggested that *The Worshipful and Ancient Law of Gallifrey* was written circa 22,000 AD.[2095]

c 21,906 - "Final Sacrifice"[2096] -> Robert Lewis and Eliza Cooper of Torchwood, along with Alexander Hugh and Annabella Primavera, arrived from 1906 and met the tenth Doctor and Emily on an alien planet. The war between the Soul Free and the Terror Farmers had reduced a population of hundreds of thousands to just a few thousand. The Doctor deduced that the Terror Farmers would win the conflict and become known as the Terranites – and later his adversaries, the Terronites.

The Advocate arrived with Matthew Finnegan, who as a twentieth century-born human could activate the planet's terraforming satellite. This would have killed everyone present. Matthew turned on the Advocate and deactivated the satellite by electrocuting them both. The Advocate died, which released the millennia of fifth-dimensional power within her. The energy turned Matthew into the Tef'Aree: an immortal, five-dimensional being. The Tef'Aree manipulated events throughout time to engineer its own creation from Matthew's sacrifice.

Lewis and Primavera were killed during these events. Cooper stayed to help the surviving humans rebuild their world. The Doctor took Emily and Hugh back to 1906.

c 22,000 - BIRTHRIGHT[2097] -> For three thousand four hundred and ninety-seven years, the insect-like Charrl had occupied the planet Anthykhon, which was far from the major space lanes. Their vast hive pumped ammonia into the already-depleted atmosphere, the planet's ozone layer had been depleted, the seas had dried up, and the soil was barren. The native life, the Hairies, survived by adapting to this environment.

The Charrl were not savages – indeed, they had created over three hundred of the six hundred and ninety-nine wonders of the universe – before coming to this world to escape solar flares on their own planet. The Charrls made contact with Muldwych, a mysterious time-traveller exiled to Anthykhon at this time, and together they attempted to traverse the Great Divide back into the past on Earth. Muldwych came to regret his association with the Charrls and foiled their plans. He remained on Anthykhon in exile.

Anthykhon was Earth during one of the several periods when the planet was isolated and forgotten.

c 22,000 - SPEED OF FLIGHT[2098] -> The third Doctor, Jo and Mike Yates landed on Nooma. The Dead assaulted the planet's artificial sun, working on preprogrammed

---

tioned in Antares and has the ability to quickly issue orders over intergalactic distances. (Antares isn't a galaxy in real life, incidentally, but a red giant star in the Milky Way.) Communications technology is so advanced, in fact, that Antwerp and Serbia send good wishes to Station 454 in honour of its decommissioning. The Station 454 staff are recalled back to Earth, and there's no sense that they'll have to spend years, decades or centuries making the trip, or did so in getting to Antares in the first place.

The most tangible dating clue is that Rugosa tells Biggs: "Professor, both you and the Doctor here are working on a potentially disastrous intergalactic problem, one which would make the Black Death on Earth ten millennia ago look like a mild epidemic of a common cold." Taken at face value, that would suggest a dating of circa 11,350... which would place The

Rosemariners squarely in the period in which Earth is abandoned owing to the solar flare incident (see The Solar Flares sidebar and *The Ark in Space*). Rugosa is from Rosa Damescena, and there's no reason why he would be entirely fluent in Earth history, but Biggs doesn't question him on the point.

The circa 11,350 dating clue is probably symptomatic of *The Rosemariners* being intended for Season 6, (when the continuity of the solar flare incident wasn't yet established), and later adopted as a Big Finish audio in 2012. Given that Earth's status and technology here seems advanced from that of many periods even *before* the solar flare incident, it seems reasonable to put Rugosa's statement down as questionable, and arbitrarily place *The Rosemariners* at a much later date – such as randomly imagining that instead of "ten millennia", Rugosa meant to say "twenty millennia". It's an

instructions to seek a means of terminating the Nooma experiment to protect Aapex's trade secrets. The Doctor tapped the sun's databanks and found a message from Aapex granting the citizens of Nooma independence, restoring social order on the planet.

The shafts of the Great Pyramid would align with the constellation of Orion around 23,000.[2099] The Terranites eventually became the Terronites, and the Tef'Aree enabled one Terronite – Leo Miller – to travel to Earth in 1926.[2100] The second Doctor predicted that the Sanctuary world Quadrigger Stoyn had subverted would enjoy "tens of thousands of years" of life before its end.[2101]

Leela Joins the TARDIS

Leela was named after the Sevateem's greatest warrior. Her father, Sole, wrapped his arms around her as she cried after her first kill.[2102] Leela was ten when she learned how to tie ropes and set traps for beasts. The Sevateem had a saying: "Why trap ten mouthfuls when you can snare a feast?"[2103] The Sevateem had a war canoe, even though they had no waterborne enemies.[2104]

? - THE FACE OF EVIL[2015] **->** A Mordee colony ship landed on an unnamed world and developed a com-

puter failure. The fourth Doctor helped their descendants by linking the computer to his own mind, but he neglected to remove his personality print from the data core. As a result, the computer became schizophrenic.

Centuries later, the colonists worshipped the computer as Xoanon. It had split them into two groups: the Sevateem (the savage descendants of Survey Team Six); and the Tesh (formerly the technicians, to whom Xoanon granted psychic powers). Xoanon was thus attempting to breed superhumans, but the fourth Doctor returned and made a reverse transfer, curing the computer's multiple personality disorder. Leela, a warrior of the Sevateem, left with the Doctor.

? - LAST MAN RUNNING[2016] **->** Class warfare was brewing between the First Planet's "firsters" and the Second Planet's lowly "toodys". An Out System Investigation Group (OIG) was sent to a forest plane to look for a toody weapons manufacturer. The OIG team, the fourth Doctor and Leela got caught in a Last Man Running complex, a simulated environment built by the Lentic race to find and clone the ultimate warrior. Leela destroyed the force field surrounding the complex, and the OIG bombed it.

The Great Houses and Us by Prof. H. Lennistein was published in 31,441.[2107]

---

imperfect solution, to be sure, but at least preserves some narrative clarity.

2095 *Shada*. Chris Parsons' dating of the book gives a figure of "minus twenty thousand years", with time running backwards over the book. This might be a property of the book, rather than an indication it comes from the future.

2096 Dating "Final Sacrifice" (IDW Vol. 1, #13-16) - Robert Lewis' group arrives on the colony planet "twenty thousand" years after they left, in 1906.

2097 Dating *Birthright* (NA #17) - Ace says she was born "Oh, probably about twenty thousand years ago" (p134), although how she reaches this figure is unclear. It is "year 2959" of the Charrl occupation of Earth (p1) when they start their scheme, which will take "almost five hundred years" (p60), yet curiously it is "year 2497" (p109) when they finish! This is presumably a misprint, and ought to read "3497".

2098 Dating *Speed of Flight* (MA #27) - This is "about twenty thousand years" after Jo's time (p23).

2099 "Twenty one thousand years" after *The Sands of Time* (p122).

2100 "A few thousand years" after 21,906, according to "Final Sacrifice".

2101 *The Dying Light*

2102 *The Abandoned*

2103 *Death Match*

2104 *The Helm of Awe*

2105 Dating *The Face of Evil* (14.4) - The story could

take place at any point in the far future. The Doctor states in *The Invisible Enemy* that the year 5000 is the time of Leela's ancestors. This story, then, takes place at least ten generations after that – the crew of the colony ship were stranded for "generations" before the Doctor first helped them, and there have apparently been seven generations since (the Sevateem seem to attack the barrier once a generation, and this is the seventh attempt).

Humans evolve limited psychic powers around the time of the fifty-first century (*The Talons of Weng-Chiang*) and the Tesh have psychic powers, so they might originate after that time, but they probably receive all their abilities from Xoanon's selective breeding programme.

In *The Sun Makers*, the Usurian computer correctly guesses that "Sevateem" is a corruption of "Survey Team", and that Leela comes from a "degenerate, unsupported Tellurian colony" suggesting that there are many such planets known to the Company. *The Terrestrial Index* set the story "several centuries" after the "fifty-second century". *The TARDIS Logs* offered the date "4931", *Timelink* "6000", *About Time* said "Somewhere around the fifty-third century might be a good bet."

2106 Dating *Last Man Running* (PDA #15) - The story could take place at any time in the far future.

2107 FP: *Weapons Grade Snake Oil*

& 33,935 - IRIS: ENTER WILDTHYME[2108] -> The Glass Men of Valcea had been ousted from their city, and killed in great numbers, by their "new gods": Servo-furniture in the form of flying wardrobes, who had no memory of their origins. Iris Wildthyme, Panda, Simon, Jenny and Barbra the vending machine tried to stop Anthony Marville from using Valcea's space-time corridors to reach the planet Hyspero. What remained of the Glass Men's city was melted by a bomb, and its impending explosion prompted Marville, Jenny, the Scarlet Empress Euphemia, Barbra and all of the wardrobes to flee through the *Dii h'anno Doors*: a portal in the head wardrobe that led to Hyspero, millions of years in the future. Iris, Simon and Panda, thinking their friends dead, returned to the twenty-first century.

Around the year 34,600, humans committed atrocities during the Platonic War and became despised by other races. The Lord Predator, Haralto Wong Bopz Wim-Waldon Arlene, had died twenty-two years previous, and a new Lord Predator ruled. Some members of the Slitheen family, still exiled from their homeworld, came into possession of time technology that included a Navarino time-jump and a Sundayan stabiliser. Navarino technicians assisted in the construction of a time machine until the Slitheen ate them. The Slitheen used their plundered technology to open a time-travel tourist service to ancient Greece, but their operations in this era were bankrupted when they were held accountable for the wrongful death of Cecrops of the Collective of Mulch.[2109]

37,166 - PLANET OF EVIL[2110] -> A Morestran survey team arrived on Zeta Minor, searching for an energy source as their home planet was facing disaster. Zeta Minor was a planet on the edge of the universe, beyond Cygnus A, as distant from the Artoro Galaxy as that is from the Anterides.

The Morestran team discovered that a black pool on Zeta Minor was connected to an incomprehensible universe of anti-matter. As a result, it was impossible to remove anything from the planet without incurring the wrath of powerful creatures native to the anti-matter universe. The fourth Doctor and Sarah helped the Morestrans to survive the experience and return home.

The Doctor offhandedly suggested to Professor Sorenson that he explore the energy potential of the kinetic forces involved in planetary movement.

c 39,164 - ZETA MAJOR[2111] -> Morestra was abandoned, and the fleet set off on a search for a new home planet. A suitable home was located in the Beta System forty months later, and the city of Archetryx was founded there. The New Church Calendar began and the Sorenson Academy was established.

A hundred years later, work commenced on the Torre del Oro, a structure that would extract energy from planetary motion, but which would take fifteen hundred years to build. The dematerialisation beam was invented after several more centuries. Great Technology Wars were fought as the Cult of Science schismed.

A few years before the Torre del Oro was due to be completed, the Grand Council of Cardinals discovered errors in the equations – the Torre del Oro wouldn't work. To cover up this failure, they dispatched an expedition to extract anti-matter from Zeta Minor, and the Zeta Project was established on the nearby Zeta Major. By that point,

---

2108 Dating *Iris: Enter Wildthyme* (*Iris* novel #1) - It's "something like thirty thousand years" after the last time Iris visited Valcea, in *The Blue Angel*.

2109 *The Slitheen Excursion*

2110 Dating *Planet of Evil* (13.2) - While it could be argued that the date "37,166" that appears on the grave marker might use some Morestran scale of dating, the Doctor does state that the TARDIS has overshot contemporary London by "thirty thousand years". *The Dimension Riders* and *Infinite Requiem* both suggest that the Morestrans are not human, which is possible (although they do know of Earth). The Doctor's suggestion to Sorenson leads to events in *Zeta Major*.

2111 Dating *Zeta Major* (PDA #13) - It is 1998 by the New Church Calendar (p82), and that long since *Planet of Evil*.

2112 Dating *House of Cards* (BF CC #7.8) - Polly says, off-handedly, "We must be a long way into the future." The Sidewinder Syndicate also appears in the *Doctor Who Adventures* comics "Money Troubles" and "Snakes Alive!", all written by Steve Lyons. The placement here reflects the era in which "Money Troubles" takes place, circa 40,412, but in truth *House of Cards* could happen at just about any point after the Syndicate's origins in the 1920s.

2113 Dating *CD,NM V1: Judoon in Chains* (*CD,NM* #1.2) - Time-travel evidently occurs (but isn't specified), since the Genesis Corp workers are human, speak English and refer to the nineteenth-century court as an "ancient Earth building". Genesis Corp's advanced terraforming, and the ease of populations relocating from world to world, suggest that it's the far future. Galactic Central is active, but the aforementioned conditions seem much later than the group of the same name in *The Happiness Patrol*. Without a huge amount of rhyme or reason, we've placed this just prior to the Terraphile era.

2114 Forty-two thousand years after *Zamper* (p249).

2115 Algernon Pine is defrosted "about ten thousand years" before *The Coming of the Terraphiles*, and so the era of the Terraphiles is at least that old. The Lockesleys have governed for "nine millennia" before *The Coming of the Terraphiles*.

Morestran territory spanned eighty million light years and contained one thousand four hundred and twenty-seven inhabited star systems, but the energy crisis meant that eight hundred and ninety-two of them, the Outer Systems, were beyond the Empire's reach.

Students of the Sorenson Academy started vanishing, part of the cover up of the Torre del Oro debacle. The fifth Doctor, Tegan and Nyssa discovered that the tower was full of anti-matter. Soon after, anti-matter creatures started a rampage. A State of Crisis was declared and old political and religious rivalries re-emerged. The Zeta Project was destroyed. The Doctor once again negotiated with the creatures of anti-matter and returned all the plundered material to its original universe.

? 40,412 - HOUSE OF CARDS[2112] -> The gangster-themed Sidewinder Syndicate provided security to a casino with a no-tolerance policy for time technology, to prevent players from placing bets with benefit of foreknowledge. The second Doctor, Polly, Ben and Jamie enjoyed the casino until Ben went so far into debt, he was obliged to play the Game of Life: a high-stakes affair in which the losers were disintegrated. Polly acquired a time bangle from a scammer named Hope, and used it to give Jamie enough chips to win Ben's freedom. The casino manager, Ms Fortune, detected Polly's use of time tech and claimed her life as forfeit, but lost to the Doctor in a double-or-nothing game of Happy Families, as the Doctor had a Mrs Bunn card up his sleeve. Fortune left, disgraced, and the Sidewinder Syndicate assumed control of the casino.

? 41,000 - CD,NM V1: JUDOON IN CHAINS[2113]-> The universe grappled with a population problem – many planets were exhausted and died as the beings there relocated to newly terraformed worlds. Operating from Katura, a world 3.262 light years from Mars, Genesis Corp terraformed more than six hundred dead planets in one year alone.

Genesis commissioned the 19th Judoon Interplanetary Force to deploy Molecular Disruption Units on the supposedly vacant world of Ayishas in the Jericho System, but the one-dimensional beings there mentally influenced one of the Judoon, Captain Kybo, into abandoning his post. He fled to Victorian England, but the Judoon relocated an English court to this era so Kybo could stand trial. The sixth Doctor served as Kybo's defender, and tricked a Genesis Corp executive into admitting the company's misdeeds to Galactic Central. Kybo was acquitted, and Genesis Corp disgraced, as the court was returned home. The Ayishans endowed the Judoon with empathy and, unwilling to let the condition spread to their homeworlds, they settled down on Ayishas or one of its satellites, to enjoy poetry and yoga.

At this time, a new breed of Zamps should be ready to conquer the universe.[2114]

The Terraphile Era[2115]

Human Guide Sensors possessed the ability to plot courses through the cosmos and map the multiverse. They discovered the Second Aether, which was between *everything*: Matter and Anti-matter, Law and Chaos, Life and Death, Reason and Romance. It was where Famous Chaos Engineers performed morphing miracles that even Morphail's wizard-scientists couldn't explain. It was the home of the immeasurable entities Spammer Gain and the Original Insect. A legend held that the Doctor had named this region, although he denied this.

An early Guide Sensor, Lord Renark of the Rim, led a huge percentage of the human race out of the original universe and into another. Renark disappeared, possibly into a greater structure than the known multiverse, which was not understood but was known as Renark's Multiverse or Renark's Dilemma.

The Galactic Union now spanned millions of worlds, encompassing humanity as well as a vast diversity of other intelligent species made from "flesh, metal and petal". The great rockets of the IGP and the interstellar mercantile vessels of the Terran Service crossed the whole Milky Way and the dwarf galaxies surrounding it, and spread into other space-time continua. Privateers preyed upon them. This was a time when galactic civilisation cycled between ages of prosperity and dark ages, and was peppered with intergalactic wars.

Humanity was planet hungry, and the commercial worldbuilding companies terraformed countless worlds. EarthMakers, run by the Tarbutton family, was the largest terraforming company and built planets with ancient Roman, Mogal Indian, Buffalo, ancient Greek and Eireish themes, as well as literary worlds based on the works of Disney, Balzac, Austen, Meredith, James, Lansdale, Mieville, Pynchon, Sinclair, Calderon, Gygax and Moore. The second largest company, TerraForma, was run by the Banning-Cannon family and specialised in Medieval English Edwardian versions of Earth: the Peers™. The firm was run from Earth Regenerated, which orbited Barnard's Star. Intergalactic Air supplied atmosphere plants to terraforming companies. Aqua Suppliers supplied water to inhabited worlds. Water was a valuable commodity on many worlds, and a frequent target for pirates.

There was immense interest in Earth history, although humankind had a garbled understanding of it, as the only surviving texts – as recovered from a cave system in Arctic Skipton in Old Yorkshire – were some old cigarette cards, *Robin Hood*, *Boys' Friend*, *Thriller Picture Library*, *The Captain*, *British Boys' Book of the Empire*, *Captain Justice and His Submarine Gunboat* and *Sexton Blake and the Terror of the*

Tongs. They avidly played what they believed to be games from Earth such as broadswording (with swords far wider than they were long), cracking a nut with a sledgehammer and Arrers – a combination of darts, archery and cricket. The ancient artists Rembrandt, Picasso, Emin and Coca Colon were revered.

Earth itself was now known as Terra, Original Terra, Old Old Earth, Original Earth and Home Planet. It was in a thoroughly frozen state following a comet strike, massive earthquakes and a series of nuclear winters. It was to be found in the Greater Oort in Orion.

Around 41,000, Algernon Pine was defrosted on Old Old Mars to help create the backstory for the Peers planets, although he wasn't happy with the end result.

Other planets at this time included the beautiful worlds of Calypso V – Venice, Ur XVII and New Venus, as well as the howling terraces of Arcturus-and-Arcturus.

Chiyoko and the Galateans

? 41,000 - "The Child of Time" (*DWM*)[2116] **->** A falling star on Earth heralded the start of a plague that all but wiped out the human empire. Such was the widespread death, it was feared humanity was doomed. Keltor Jacobs oversaw an effort to engineer a new form for humankind, one that could resist all disease: the robotic Galateans. The original Galateans were kept in a station on the dark side of the moon. They resembled specific individuals, and contained duplicate copies of their memories. Jacobs activated the Galateans just three hours before Minerva Base reported finding a plague-cure.

> (=) The Galateans thought themselves a superior lifeform, and vowed to wipe out their creators. The time-child Chiyoko helped to ignite a war between humans and the Galateans. The conflict would last at least a hundred thousand years, and help to facilitate Chiyoko's creation.
>
> The eleventh Doctor, Amy and a Galatean-made version of Alan Turing were sent to this era from the Museum of Lost Opportunities in the future, to avert the Galateans' creation. They failed, and Chiyoko capriciously moved the trio ahead in time, to the day when the human-Galatean war destroyed Earth...

Chiyoko was eventually persuaded to undo her existence and the harm it had caused. The eleventh Doctor, Amy, a fading Chiyoko and the Galatean-made Alan Turing arrived once again from the Museum. Turing uploaded his memories of the human-Galatean war into the newborn Galateans' network, which persuaded them to work alongside humanity and rebuild the Earth. Chiyoko's mind was

2116 Dating "The Child of Time" (*DWM* #438-441) - Jacobs mentions the damage the plague has done to "the human empire" – that, and the advanced human science that creates the Galteans, very much suggests that it's a fair distance in the future. A little strangely, however, a caption suggests that the plague cripples humanity in "The Near Future". Author Jonathan Morris avoided giving exact dates for fear of contradicting other stories, and commented that, "['The Child of Time'] wasn't intended to tie in with anything that's already been established in *Doctor Who* (but if it does, that's fine with me!)." If one squints, then, it's possible to connect the meteor strike that spreads the plague in this story with the similar event that helps to inflict damage on Earth prior to *The Coming of the Terraphiles*.
2117 Dating "Apotheosis" (*DWM* #435-#437) - The war has been going on "a thousand years", following the genesis of the Galateans in "The Child of Time" (*DWM*).
2118 "The Child of Time" (*DWM*)
2119 Dating "The Child of Time" (*DWM* #438-441) - The Doctor says that it's "thousands of years" since Amy's time, estimates that Chiyoko has been worshipped as a goddess in the war for "several hundred years", and judges that the war "hasn't been going too well" since he and Amy last witnessed it in "Apotheosis" (so, it's some time after that story).
2120 Before *The Coming of the Terraphiles*.
2121 "Several millennia" before *The Coming of the Terraphiles*.

2122 Within "several millennia" of *The Coming of the Terraphiles*, as this has to be after the Bacon Street Regulators were set up.
2123 *The Coming of the Terraphiles* sees the fifteenth such tournament, they are held every two hundred and fifty years.
2124 "Onomatopoeia". Going by the galactic war numbering system used in *The Coming of the Terraphiles*, the seventh galactic war occurred somewhere between 47,000 and 50,957.
2125 *The Coming of the Terraphiles*
2126 Dating *Heart of TARDIS* (PDA #32) - There's no specific date, but it is "some tens of thousands of years beyond the twentieth century".
2127 *K9: The Bounty Hunter*. Pia's organisation is also referred to as the Galactic Peace Assembly. These events lead into the *K9* television series, starting with *K9: Regeneration*.
2128 Cornelius the pirate fought in the war, but not in the "past half century" before *The Coming of the Terraphiles*.
2129 *The Coming of the Terraphiles*
2130 "A few years" before *The Coming of the Terraphiles*. He claims this was in the "fifty-first thousandth century" – although the book is set in 51,007, which is in the 512th century.
2131 Dating *The Coming of the Terraphiles* (NSA #43) - The Doctor says "51,007's the date".

uploaded into a Galatean body; both she and the Galatean-Turing decided to stay in this era.

(=) & 42,000 - "Apotheosis"[2117] -> The human-Galatean war had now lasted a thousand years, and the planet Kepler IV was just one site of the conflict.

A church-based militia squad, the Sisters of Purity, investigated a space station that had wandered into human space, and met the eleventh Doctor and Amy there. The station had a defective time engine, which created pockets of fast-time. The TARDIS was hit with temporal acceleration, and the beings it had absorbed in its recent travels (the young girls Cosette and Margaret, part of the world-eater Axos and a Shasarak) were detached into a separate being that further incorporated Sister Konami into itself.

The Doctor tried to split the being into its separate components with a teleport, but they instead coalesced into a new individual: Chiyoko, a young girl with temporal abilities. She left to facilitate the events that led to her own creation, and the Doctor and Amy pursued her through time.

Chiyoko's temporal dissolution meant that Novice Konami's request to join the evangelical regiment was declined, and she stayed at an abbey for another year.[2118]

(=) & 42,000 - "The Child of Time" (*DWM*)[2119] -> The time-child Chiyoko was worshipped as a goddess by both sides in the human-Galatean war, and stoked conflict between them. Now she decided that the Galateans were the superior lifeform, and encouraged the remaining humans on Earth to deploy a network of fusion bombs under the Earth's crust. The eleventh Doctor and Amy tried to stop the countdown, but the Earth was destroyed. They were time-scooped at the last instant, and taken to the Museum of Lost Opportunities in the far future.

The TerraForma company refused to sell Peers to the Lockesleys for seven thousand years.[2120] The Sussex and Surrey Bacon Street Regulators kept law in the two hundred billion star systems of the Sagittarius Arm of the galaxy after the collapse of law during the last Dark Age, which followed the fifth or sixth intergalactic war.[2121] O'Bean the Younger drew the human race from the last Dark Age by discovering the colour pool, a method of propelling starships that made nukers obsolete.[2122]

In 47,507, the first Quarter Millennium Terraphile Renactment Tournament was held.[2123] Graveworld 909 was one of many cemetery planets established after the seventh galactic war. The robot guardian of Graveworld 909 went dormant after establishing a respectful quantum null field that forced visitors to remain silent.[2124]

Manakai invaders from the Arkwright Cluster were wiped out ages ago. Dructionjen clans had been exiled many generations before for worshipping the Daleks.[2125]

c 50,000 - HEART OF TARDIS[2126] -> The fourth Doctor and the first Romana found and rescued K9, who had become an exhibit at the Collectors' Big Huge and Educational Collection of Old Galactic Stuff.

The galaxy was at war in the year 50,000. The head of the Galactic Peace Commission, Zanthus Pia, was assassinated and K9 was framed for the killing. The real culprit was the renowned bounty hunter Ahab, who was working with the Jixen. K9 uncovered this plot and learned the Jixen were active in the mid-twenty-first century on Earth. He travelled there, but was heavily damaged and lost all his memories.

Later, Ahab followed K9 and was forced to retreat to his own time – but ended up adrift in deep space.[2127]

The twelfth intergalactic war was fought around 50,957, and by common consent it was fought in space, not on the surface of planets.[2128] The Doctor worked as a courier in the vast spaceport *Desiree* during his gap century, although he was fired because he kept getting lost.[2129] The Doctor joined the All Galaxy Legion of Terraphiles.[2130]

51,007 - THE COMING OF THE TERRAPHILES[2131] -> The clans who ran the terraforming companies were now fabulously wealthy. Lady Mars, owner of Intergalactic Air, could afford a hat that was a life-sized replica of the lost Martian moon Phobos. EarthMakers introduced Mystery Worlds, based on the Sherlock Holmes stories.

The Galactic Union was democratic, although people could pay politicians to retire in General Ejections (seventy-eight members were up for Ejection in Nova Roma). It encompassed countless alien species, including the Judoon (who had taken up Arrers after abandoning their own lethal sport of Nukeball), Centaurs and the Pilparque dog-men of Chardine. The Banning-Cannons had recently lost money in a failed scheme to transform the Scullum Crux into a rose garden light years across. Planets in this era included Cygnus 34, New North Whales, Old Barsoom and Loondoon (home of many fashion houses). Vast spaceports serviced many different types of starships from small, old nuker ships to massive 110-deck G-class vessels such as the ISS *Gargantua*, which used colour engines. The advanced technology of this time included nanotech translation. Humans now comfortably lived to be two hundred years old, and could take identity pills that allowed them to become someone else. Gbot messengers acted as couriers, punching holes in space that would kill a human.

The eleventh Doctor and Amy enjoyed a week on Peers, a terraformed world in the Moravian Cluster in the Medieval Edwardian style, and governed by the 507th Earl of Lockesley. The Doctor became aware of a threat to the whole of the multiverse. As it involved the black hole at the centre of the galaxy, he feared General Frank/Freddie Force and his Anti-matter Men were responsible. He joined a team of Terraphile Reenactors heading to Miggea, a Ghost World (i.e. a planet that orbits sideways between universes), where they were due to compete for the Arrow of Law. Captain Cornelius, an old rival and acquaintance of the Doctor, was also aware of the problem. His home was in the dwarf galaxy Canis, but he was most often seen in the *Paine*, the most perfect light-powered vessel ever built, with a crew from a hundred worlds and a dozen space-time continua. He had seen the dark tides rising and dragging galaxies across billions of light years, and knew that unless it was stopped, the universe would stop regenerating itself and the multiverse would collapse in just a few centuries. The Doctor and Cornelius secured the Arrow of Law – the fabled Roogalator, an artifact from the Realm of Law that could restore the cosmic balance.

? - "The Gift"[2132] -> The sixth Doctor went back to the point that a Zofton deep space load lugger had crashed on the moon of Zazz, and observed as – over the next fifty years – the surviving robot rebuilt and survived, eventually building self-replicating replacements for itself. Within twenty generations, they had a functioning civilisation.

A natural disaster on the moon of Zazz wiped out the machine civilisation there. The few survivors would lie dormant for two thousand years.[2133]

? - "The Gift"[2134] -> By now, Zazz was a planet heavily-influenced by the Jazz Era of Earth, and the sixth Doctor, Peri and Frobisher accepted an invitation to the twenty-first birthday bash for the Lorduke of Zazz.

The TARDIS first landed at the retreat of the Lorduke's brother, Professor Strut, who was a mad scientist exiled after crashing an experimental moon rocket on the city. They agreed to take a gift... which turned out to be a surviving self-replicating robot. Strut found the robot on the moon, but didn't understand the danger. The robots began breeding, and collected raw materials to rebuild their civilisation on Zazz. The Doctor used the musicians of Zazz to duplicate the robot's recall signal, luring them to Strut's island. They boarded the moon rocket, and were blasted off into space.

c 56,500 - IRIS S4: IRIS AT THE OCHE[2135] -> Bovine marauders from the planet Bos Taurus stampeded across the galaxy and forged the Bovian Empire in the fifty-seventh century. Suddenly, a trans-dimensional being named The One halted the Bovine's conquests with his flaming Dart of Justice, nearly wiping them out. The Bovine sovereign mistress, Lady Bow'n, sought to retroactively confront The One before he gained his powers – when he was merely an unemployed carpenter, Ted Taylor, from Bradford – and drew the Pondside Club, with Ted within, through a temporal rift to this era.

Iris Wildthyme and Panda deduced that the constant dart throws within the club were interacting with the uni-

---

2132 Dating "The Gift" (*DWM* #123-126) - It's "twelve thousand years" before the main events of "The Gift".
2133 "Two thousand years" before "The Gift".
2134 Dating "The Gift" (*DWM* #123-126) - No date is given, but the people of Zazz are the "distant descendants of an Earth colony".
2135 Dating *Iris S4: Iris at the Oche* (BF Iris #4.2) - The Bovian Empire falls in the fifty-seventh century, and while it's possible this story takes place within the fifty-eighth or later, it's within Lady Bow'n's lifespan.
2136 Dating *The Apocalypse Mirror* (BF CC #7.11) - It's the future of humanity, far removed from the Earth that the Doctor, Jamie and Zoe would recognize, with technology in advance of Zoe's era.
2137 Dating *Serpent Crest: Tsar Wars* (BBC fourth Doctor audios #3.1) - The story occurs in the future; the Robotov Empire is of human creation, and the insurrectionists are designated as human. In *Serpent Crest: The Broken Crown*, set in 1861, the Doctor tells Alex, "You've only just learned that you're the Robotov heir, from a hundred thousand years into the future."
2138 *Serpent Crest: Survivors in Space*
2139 Dating *Serpent Crest: Survivors in Space* (BBC fourth Doctor audios #3.5) - It's been "twenty years" since Alex was returned home (*Serpent Crest: Aladdin*

Time) and made Tsar.
2140 "A hundred millennia" after *Grimm Reality*.
2141 *The Condemned*
2142 Dating "Onomatopoeia" (*DWM* #413) - The guardian here ends the "hundred thousand years" of silence that have passed on Graveworld 909 since the seventh galactic war, the rough date of which can be established from *The Coming of the Terraphiles*.
2143 *The Forgotten Army*
2144 *The Ark*

THE SEGMENTS OF TIME: The Commander in *The Ark* states "Nero, the Trojan Wars, the Daleks... all that happened in the First Segment of Time." *The Ark* itself takes place in the Fifty-Seventh Segment. References in that story to the Tenth and Twenty-Seventh Segments are noted later in this book. *The Well-Mannered War* is set in the Fifty-Eighth. *The Quantum Archangel* refers to the Master stealing a Farquazi time cruiser from the 300th.

It's unclear whether a Segment is measured purely mathematically. A "century" has to mean "a hundred years". If a Segment is a fixed period of time, then as *The Ark* is set ten million years in the future, this might suggest fifty-seven equal segments of around 175,000 years.

Equally, the term might mark a specific era with dis-

verse's quantum mechanics. Owing to her Clockworks nature, and by encouraging the darts players present to make repeated throws, Iris achieved a critical mass of quantum mathematics that transformed Taylor into The One. So empowered, he created a squadron of dart-shaped spaceships, as piloted by the Pondside players, to engage Bow'n's forces. The One defeated Bow'n in personal combat, and returned the Club and those within back in time.

The remaining Bovians contented themselves with retirement and beekeeping on the grazing worlds in the Cow's Head Nebula.

? 75,000 - THE APOCALYPSE MIRROR[2136] **->** The First World Flood and the even greater Second World Flood devastated the surface of Earth. Tromesis endured – save for some small settlements – as the last inhabited city in the world in what was formerly Switzerland, and was home to millions of people.

Engineers in Tromesis hoped to re-shape the environment with a reality-altering Sympathy Engine, but instead created a duplicate Tromesis in another dimension. The populace splintered as its forward-thinking individuals were drawn over to the new Tromesis, while unimaginative ones remained in the original. In the decades to come, the first Tromesis lost nearly half its population to its twin. A select council, The State, operated in secret and kidnapped new recruits, out of fear of the public's distrust of government.

The second Doctor, Zoe and Jamie realised that a massive meteor would soon strike the Alps, annihilating the first Tromesis if not the whole planet. The new Tromesis had the technology to repel it, but wasn't "real" enough in Earth's dimension. The Doctor and Zoe inadvertently transferred to the new Tromesis, leaving Jamie to rally the people – via a holographic address system – to believe in the future. A critical mass of people shifted to the new Tromesis, causing it to swap places with the old one and destroy the meteor. The Doctor and his friends left the Tromesis residents to forge their own destiny.

c 101,861 - SERPENT CREST: TSAR WARS[2137] **->** Human-made robots became so advanced in a certain sector of space that they finally took over and formed the Robotov Empire. The humans that served the Empire lived on outlying worlds, and supplied energy from a biomoon. Centuries passed, and the humans moved closer to rebellion. Father Gregory, who physically looked like the fourth Doctor owing to "the endless chaotic ramifications of universal chance", allied himself with the rebels. The Tsarina conceived with Gregory a child cyborg, Alex, in the hope of cementing bonds between the humans and Robotovs.

Gregory, however, was secretly allied with the Skishtari – a race of conquerors who were adept at manipulating wormholes. The Skishtari subjugated other races by hatch-

ing monstrous Skishtari Emperor serpents from eggs – one such egg was to be hidden inside Alex. Gregory's agents brought the fourth Doctor and Mrs Wibbsey to this era via a Skishtari wormhole, but Alex's heart was failing, and Gregory donated his own to save him.

The Doctor tried to resolve matters by sending himself and Wibbsey – as well as a spaceship containing Alex, his guardian Boolin and the Skishtari egg – down a Skishtari wormhole to Nest Cottage in 2010. They all ended up in the right location, but the nineteenth century.

The Doctor later used the TARDIS to bring Boolin and a teenage Alex home. Alex was made the new Tsar of the Robotov Empire, and facilitated peace between the robot and human factions.[2138]

c 101,881 - SERPENT CREST: SURVIVORS IN SPACE[2139] **->** The entire village of Hexford and its two hundred fifty-three civilians arrived on the biomoon of the Robotov Empire, thanks to the Skishtari wormhole and a mishap in 2011. Captain Yates took charge of the stranded townsfolk, who were left to their own devices for three months. The fourth Doctor and Mrs Wibbsey arrived in the TARDIS just as the Skishtari egg in their possession hatched. The Skishtari welcomed their giant offspring – but the newborn Emperor had formed an empathic bond with Tsar Alex, and ate its progenitors instead. Alex agreed to relocate the giant snake to a planet with a sustainable food source. A clone of the second Doctor, freed from his obligation to the Skishtari, aided the fourth Doctor in sending Hexford back to the twenty-first century.

Circa 102,890, the white hole seedling from Albert was supposed to blossom into maturity.[2140] The Doctor judged that Carmen Priminger – a gambler who lost her memories – was human, and that her time machine originated from the 108th or 109th centuries.[2141]

c 148,500 - "Onomatopoeia"[2142] **->** The tenth Doctor and Majenta Pryce rebooted the slumbering robot guardian on Graveworld 909. It ended the pall of silence on the planet, and accepted the rat people who had evolved in the millennia while it slept as its new workforce.

The eleventh Doctor wanted to show Amy a museum in the 175th century, but warned her that the canteen there was rubbish, and for religious reasons served only boiled Jericoacoara beans.[2143]

The Daleks were part of the history of the First Segment of Time.[2144] **One Dalek ship, containing the Emperor, survived the Last Great Time War. It arrived at the edge of Earth's solar system, remaining hidden. For centuries, the Daleks would harvest the dregs and unwanted of humanity, building Daleks from their**

genetic material. The Emperor meddled in humanity's affairs and sought ways to slow its development.[2145]

? - "War of the Words"[2146] -> The war between the Vromyx and the Garynths had been raging for forty-seven point six three years. The conflict blocked access to the library planet Biblios, where all universal knowledge was stored by legions of robots. The warring factions wanted to access details of superweapons, then deny it to their opponents. The fourth Doctor blew up an empty building, telling both sides it was where the records were kept, and the rivals withdrew.

Sara Kingdom's Mind Copied into a Wish-Granting House

? 199,750 - HOME TRUTHS[2147] -> On an island at Ely, a house was built that could grant wishes to its occupants. A husband and wife resided there, but the house proved capable of facilitating even unspoken wishes. In a moment of irritation, the wife briefly wished her husband harm – causing him to fall dead. The horrified wife begged for the tragedy to "stop", and immediately died also. The house then sealed itself off, its interior almost frozen in time.

Some time later, the first Doctor, Steven and Sara found the bodies within. They came under threat from the house's wish-granting ability, so Sara wished that the house would develop a conscience that distinguished right from wrong. This endowed the house with a disembodied copy of Sara's persona, and the travellers left in the TARDIS.

Humanity fought a losing conflict with the Cyberiad during the CyberWars, with the Cybermen upgrading to overcome any weakness. The Cyberplanners built a Valkyrie to repair damaged Cybermen, with spare parts taken from visitors to the largest amusement park. The conflict ended with the destruction of the Tiberion Spiral Galaxy – humanity sacrificed a million star systems, a hundred million worlds and a billion trillion people there, but the Cybermen were also wiped out.

Three million Cybermen remained dormant on the amusement park planet. A man named Hedgewick bought it cheap, and renamed it Hedgewick's world.[2148]

c 199,900 - NIGHTMARE IN SILVER[2149] -> The Cybermen had been thought extinct for the millennium following the CyberWars. Impresairo Webley

---

tinct cultural or even physical features (like, say, "Victorian" or "Ice Age"). What would mark the beginning or end of a Segment? Would the boundary be formally defined and obvious (like say that of "the tenth Olympiad", or "the Leptonic Era"), even if it was open to a degree of interpretation (we can speak of "the Second World War", even though the exact moment it started and ended depends on which country you're from and how you define terms)?

Timelink offers the theory that as Zentos refers to "the Fifty-Seventh Segment of Earth life" and the Commander says "The Earth also is dying, we have left it for the last time", that Earth has been "left" before, and each Segment ends with the abandonment of Earth. It's neat and, as noted elsewhere in this book, Earth is certainly totally evacuated more than once. However, Bad Wolf and The Parting of the Ways have the Daleks active after the first abandonment of Earth, and, if the Commander is right, they were only part of the history of the First Segment.

2145 The Parting of the Ways. The Controller says the Daleks have been there for "hundreds and hundreds of years", the Doctor says "generations", and the Emperor Dalek says "centuries passed".
2146 Dating "War of the Words" (DWM #51) - The story is set after the twentieth century, because parliamentary records from that period are stored here. The head librarian robot has just had his two thousand year service, suggesting the facility has been around for millennia. Beyond that, no date is specified, so this is com-

pletely arbitrary.
2147 Dating Home Truths (BF CC #3.5) - It's "a thousand years" before the linking sequences of Home Truths, The Drowned World and The Guardian of the Solar System.
2148 "A thousand years" before Nightmare in Silver.
2149 Dating Nightmare in Silver (X7.13) - No year given. The American flag is on display at Hedgewick's World. It's "a thousand years" since the CyberWars, and in a script written by Neil Gaiman – who tends to include such classic-series references as the efficaciousness of nail polish in killing Cybermen (The Moonbase) – it's tempting to think of this as the same "CyberWar" mentioned in Revenge of the Cybermen. Similarly, it's a natural impulse to believe that Emperor Ludens' vast human empire is the Earth Empire seen in the twenty-sixth century and beyond (Frontier in Space et al).

In detail, however, Nightmare in Silver matches neither of these elements. Revenge of the Cybermen attributes the Cybermen's defeat in the Cyberwar to their vulnerability to gold (the fourth Doctor: "It was a glorious triumph, for human ingenuity. They discovered your weakness and invented the glitter gun, and that was the end of Cybermen except as gold-plated souvenirs that people use as hat stands"), but the Cyberiad Cybermen evidently upgraded beyond that limitation ("gold was the main weakness of early Cybermen, but by the end of the great war, they were nearly indestructible"), and were only defeated by the obliteration of the Tiberion Spiral Galaxy. The Cyberiad Cybermen's ability to compensate, Borg-like, for new threats is

owned a chess-playing Cyberman that had been displayed before the Imperial Court as the 699th Wonder of the Universe.

The eleventh Doctor agreed to take Clara's young charges, Angie and Artie Maitland, on a trip through time, and brought them to Hedgewick's World: the biggest amusement park ever built. A Punishment Platoon protected the planet, which was closed by Imperial order.

The Doctor was infected with Cyberiad-class Cybermites, which formed a CyberPlanner persona in his mind. The two of them engaged in chess, with control of the Doctor's body and mind at stake. The Doctor destroyed the CyberPlanner, and escaped with his friends as Emperor Ludens Nimrod Kendrick Cord Longstaff XLI – having gone on a walkabout as the chess player Porridge – ordered a bomb-implosion of Hedgewick's World, destroying the three million Cybermen there.

The Doctor had successfully deleted himself from a wealth of databanks, but it was possible to reconstruct what was lost from the data-hole this created.

The tenth Doctor, Gabby, Cindy and Noobis encountered a troupe of Cyber-renactors who enjoyed recreating battles from the last great Cyberwar.[2150]

The Fourth Great and Bountiful Human Empire

200,000 - THE LONG GAME[2151] -> It was the age of the Fourth Great and Bountiful Human Empire. Earth was at its height: the hub of a domain stretching across a million planets, covered with megacities, possessing five moons and a population of ninety-six billion.

A sandstorm on the New Venus Archipelago left two hundred dead. There were water riots in Glasgow. The Face of Boe announced that he was pregnant with a Baby Boemina. The Mighty Jagrafess of the Holy Hadrojassic Maxarodenfoe was manipulating humanity by controlling its news media from Satellite Five, which broadcast six hundred channels. This held back humanity's development, and made it fearful of immigrants. The ninth Doctor and Rose defeated the Jagrafess, and the Doctor expected that humanity's development would accelerate back to normal without its interference.

Adam, a companion of the Doctor and Rose, tried to acquire knowledge from the future and download it to his own time in 2012. The Doctor discovered Adam's intentions and returned him home.

After Satellite Five was put out of commission, the information feed to Earth stopped. The government and economy collapsed. A hundred years of hell ensued.[2152] The Great Atlantic Smog Storm started in

---

streets beyond the models seen in *Revenge of the Cybermen* and *Earthshock*, and they can now assimilate other races, including Time Lords, having formerly – by their own admission – been limited to cyber-converting humans.

The human technology and scale of the human empire in *Nightmare of Silver* seems massively ahead of the Earth Empire in *Frontier in Space*. Ludens holds the title of Imperator of Known Space, his flagship instantly warps to his location within instants of ID'ing his signal and it can instantly transmat Ludens' party aboard. It's implied that the Tiberion Spiral Galaxy was destroyed a millennium ago through human offensive capabilities – a level of devastation seemingly beyond the *Frontier in Space* Earth Empire, or even, by all accounts, the government led by Mavic Chen in *The Daleks' Master Plan* [4000]. Ludens' title also suggests the *far* future, if he's genuinely the 41st holder of his name.

Any placement must factor in the Cybermen being thought extinct for a whole millennia – something that's only possible following the CyberWar/*Earthshock* if the incursion in *Revenge of the Cybermen* [? 2875] was kept quiet. The final battle of the Cyber War as seen in *Last of the Cybermen* doesn't match the details given in

Nightmare in Silver, additionally suggesting that the two are separate conflicts. Taking all of this into account, mention that Ludens' empire encompasses "a thousand galaxies" brings to mind the Fourth Great and Bountiful Human Empire, said in *The Long Game* to contain "a million worlds".

Whoniverse (BBC, p182) is something of a maverick about this, deciding that the background to *Nightmare in Silver* involves a *second* Cyber War, which occurs "millennia" after a massing of Cyber warfleets in "the fifty-second century" (*A Good Man Goes to War*, presumably).

The waxworks seen in Webley's World of Wonders include a Shansheeth (*SJA: Death of the Doctor*); a Uvodni (*SJA: Warriors of Kudlak*); a Blowfish (*Torchwood* Series 1 and 2); a Dummy (*The God Complex*); and a Pan-Babylonian, Ultramancer and Lugal-Irra-Kush (*The Rings of Akhaten*).

2150 *The Tenth Doctor Year Three*: "Vortex Butterflies", in the "far future", but without specifying which Cyberwar is the "last" one.

2151 Dating *The Long Game* (X1.7) - The Doctor gives the date. It's established in *Bad Wolf* and *The Parting of the Ways* that the Jagrafess was a tool of the Daleks.

2152 *Bad Wolf*

200,080. On some days, it wasn't possible to breathe the air. The storm raged for at least twenty years.[2153]

Dalek Assault Devastates Earth, the Ninth Doctor Regenerates, Jack Harkness Becomes Immortal

200,100 - BAD WOLF / THE PARTING OF THE WAYS[2154] **->** The Earth was now divided into continents that included Europa, Pacifica, the New American Alliance and Australasia. Default payments were made to Martian Drones. The Great Cobalt Pyramid was built on the remains of the famous Torchwood Institute. The Great Central Ravine was named after the "ancient" British city of Sheffield. Stella Popbait made hats. There was a penal colony on the moon. *Jupiter Rising* was a holo-series. The dish gaffabeck had originated on the planet Lucifer. The Face of Boe was now the oldest inhabitant of the Isop Galaxy.

Humanity watched savage game shows such as *Big Brother*, *Call My Bluff* (with real guns), *Countdown* (where the aim was to defuse a bomb), *Ground Force* (contestants were turned to compost), *Wipeout*, *Stars in Your Eyes* (contestants were blinded), *What Not to Wear* (androids mutilated people), *Bear with Me* (contestants lived with a bear) and *The Weakest Link* (overseen by the dreaded Anne Droid). These were produced by the Bad Wolf Corporation, broadcast on ten thousand channels and filmed aboard the former Satellite Five, now called the Game Station.

Losing contestants were apparently vaporised, but in truth were teleported away and secretly converted into Daleks. The ranks of the Emperor Dalek's army swelled. The human, slaved Controller overseeing this operation sought out the Daleks' greatest enemy to help, and transmatted the ninth Doctor, Captain Jack and Rose to the Game Station.

The Doctor discovered the Daleks' machinations, and the Emperor mobilised his forces against Earth. Dalek missiles bombarded many of the continents, with enough force to alter their very shape. The Doctor briefly sent Rose to safety in her native time, but Rose gazed into the heart of the TARDIS and thus became endowed with the power of the Time Vortex. She gained the godlike ability to alter time, and used it to destroy the Emperor and his Daleks. The Doctor sacrificed his life to stop the Vortex energies from consuming Rose, and regenerated as a result. Jack had been

---

2153 "Twenty years" before *Bad Wolf*, according to the *Big Brother* contestant Lynda Moss.

2154 Dating *Bad Wolf/The Parting of the Ways* (X1.12-1.13) - The Doctor says in *Bad Wolf* that "it's the year two-zero-zero-one-zero-zero", and the opening caption says it is "one hundred years" after *The Long Game*. Lynda says the Game Station has ten thousand channels, although the Doctor's *Big Brother* game is broadcast on Channel 44,000. Lucifer is (almost certainly) the planet featured in *Lucifer Rising*. It's unclear whether Rose used her power to restore anyone or anything other than Captain Jack - it's not stated that she, for example, reset the devastated Earth. Jack's journey to the nineteenth century is referenced in *Utopia*.

2155 Jack in *TW: Miracle Day*, summarising the immortality that he exhibits throughout *Torchwood* and *Doctor Who*.

2156 Dating *Jack: The Year After I Died* (BF *The Lives of Captain Jack* #1.1) - The blurb names the year. Given this point in Jack's life, the placement is rather implicit in the title.

2157 *Utopia*

2158 Dating "Mortal Beloved" (*DWM* #406-407) - It's been "centuries" since Majenta Pryce abandoned Sparks. The application of tachyonics seen here is independent from the Argolis experiments seen in *The Leisure Hive*. Mazumas are a currency mentioned in the *DWM* comic (see The Mazuma Era); grotzis are a currency mentioned by Glitz (*The Trial of a Time Lord*, *Dragonfire*).

2159 Dating *Home Truths*, *The Drowned World* and *The Cold Equations* (BF CC #3.5, 4.1, 5.12) - The linking material in this trilogy of audios featuring Sara Kingdom takes place on an island at Ely, and although the historical clues are fairly numerous, no actual date is given. *Cold Equations* all-but-names the Cahlians as being responsible for the very same sleeping sickness that afflicts Earth in *The Drowned World* and *The Guardian of the Solar System*. Given that Simon Guerrier wrote all four audios, this doesn't seem like a coincidence.

The claim in *Cold Equations* that the continents of Earth are "all different shapes" brings to mind the devastation seen in *The Parting of the Ways*, and suggests - but doesn't confirm - that the sharp decline of Earth in the Kingdom trilogy is the result of the devastation of the Fourth Great and Bountiful Human Empire. That Empire is so advanced that it might well have facilitated the creation of the wish-granting house - or the house might result from the plethora of alien tech that accumulates on Earth over the millennia in numerous *Doctor Who* stories. *The Drowned World* establishes that humanity's encounters with the Daleks are now the stuff of legend, suggesting that it's not the immediate aftermath of *The Parting of the Ways* but rather some time later, and that humanity has in large measure forgotten (assuming they even had time to register what was happening before the Dalek onslaught) the cause of its current plight.

For benefit of non-UK residents, the Lion of Knidos is a giant stone lion on display in the British Museum, London.

killed by the Daleks, but Rose brought him back to life. He was left behind on the Game Station, and used his vortex manipulator to travel to the nineteenth century.

The manner in which Rose brought Jack back to life made him an immortal:

"Something happened to me once, a long way away. Time itself changed me to a fixed point, and now I can't die. I suffer, and I perish, but I always come back."[2155]

200,001 - JACK: THE YEAR AFTER I DIED[2156] -> The Dalek assault on Earth halved the population. The survivors grappled with starvation, theft and radiation sickness. Black Castle was uninhabitable. Some efforts were made to restore actual journalism; the Pluto Network continued to broadcast. Rail service ran as far as Reykjavik, and First Intergalactic functioned as a banking service. Drinkable canned coffee was available. Leftover Dalek time limpets, capable of erasing a target from history and automatically resetting, remained a danger.

Meanwhile, the ultra-rich prospered by relocating to Trear Station: a conglomeration of bits from the Game Station, starliners and freight ships. The Hope Foundation advertised itself as a means of relocating workers to other worlds, but turned any volunteers into organ donors for the wealthy.

Jack Harkness had eschewed any claim of heroism after the Game Station battle, and taken to living in a small cabin near the ruins of the Black Country Dome. A journalist, Silo Crook, increasingly made him aware of the Hope Foundation's exploitation, and together they ended its operations.

Jack Harkness Departs this Era

Eventually, Jack used his vortex manipulator to travel back to the nineteenth century.[2157]

c 200,300 - "Mortal Beloved"[2158] -> Centuries after Majenta Pryce betrayed Wesley Sparks, he had become an aged cyborg consumed by hate. His company, Sparktech, was moving to acquire Omnivax Inc. and Marscom. Sparktech's stock was falling, and Intersol acquired its offworld set-form division. The Mazuma was currently down against the grotzi.

Sparks targeted Majenta and the tenth Doctor when the TARDIS brought them to Stormlight House, but an engram of Sparks – reflecting his nobler, younger self – stabbed Sparks to death, then suffered file corruption.

? 200,750 - HOME TRUTHS / THE DROWNED WORLD[2159] -> In the thousand years since the duplicate Sara Kingdom persona was created, humanity had undergone decline and lost much of its scientific knowledge. Even simple intercoms were not in use. Humankind was no longer capable of space travel, and its encounter with the Daleks had become the stuff of stories and legend. Cambridge was home to a Council of Elders composed of revered "old men" in their sixties. War was brewing in mid-Africa. The duplicate Sara had spent the preceding centuries accommodating many guests within her walls. Law officers periodically interviewed her; the law forbade apparitions, but each officer was moved to grant her an exception.

Guests eventually stopped arriving, and a law officer named Robert became the first person to visit the house in a long while. Robert was also inclined to leave the Sara-ghost in peace, but he discovered that she wanted the Elders to visit so she could grant their wishes, and that her power was extending in range – Robert's wife, in accordance with his unspoken wish, had become pregnant. Fearing her power, Robert ordered the Sara-ghost to disperse itself. She did so.

Twelve years passed, and a fatal sleeping sickness became rampant. The young and oldest were the hardest hit; when the Elders succumbed to the illness, law and order decayed. Robert's daughter, now age 11, caught the disease. He took her to the house at Ely, and revived the Sara-ghost. She was too depleted to affect reality outside the house, but agreed to cure Robert's ailing daughter – on the condition that he remain with her for the rest of his natural days. He agreed, and his daughter recovered.

? 200,750 - THE COLD EQUATIONS[2159] -> Humanity had produced brilliant scientists and artists, and had shaped the destiny of a hundred different worlds, but a dark cloud had settled upon the Earth, and the remaining humans there were barely living above subsistence level. Earth had lost much knowledge following the downfall of its "vast sprawling empire", and an intergalactic Dark Age was underway. The very continents of Earth had been warped out of shape, and London was deep under water.

Much debris from Earth's space age remained in orbit, and a group of Cahlians – humanoids with fiery, sunset-coloured skin and sandy hair – representing the True-Jank Cahlian Co-operative set about salvaging whatever of value could be found in space or on Earth's surface. To whittle down the competition, the Cahlians had released a sleeping sickness that afflicted about four-fifths of Earth's population. Amongst other items, the Cahlians recovered the Lion of Knidos.

The first Doctor, Steven and Oliver Harper brokered a deal on behalf of Earth authorities – the Cahlians would keep the material they'd acquired in exchange for clearing the debris from Earth orbit. A coalition government on Earth agreed to assemble some historians, and determine if the salvage had value. Their work done, the Doctor's party left – having seen in records from the old empire that they were one day going to be incarcerated on the planetoid Grace Alone.

? 200,760 - THE GUARDIAN OF THE SOLAR SYSTEM[2160] **->** When Robert's daughter turned 21, she left the house to see the outside world. He never saw her again. Robert found he wasn't aging, and in accordance with his wishes, he and Sara traded places – she was incarnated in an older body, and Robert became the house's governing intelligence. Sensing Sara's desire to escape – and to gain absolution for murdering her brother – Robert

made the TARDIS materialise outside the house, with the Doctor inside.

At some point, the incarnated "house" version of Sara Kingdom was transported into the Death Zone on Gallifrey.[2161]

The Doctor claimed that the fare at Big Paulie's Sausages in New York, the twenty-first century, was regarded in the 208th century as the most famous food in the galaxy. "Anything with less than four stomachs" would spend a lifetime of savings to travel back and enjoy it.[2162]

250,339 (14th March) - NIGHT OF THE HUMANS[2163] **->** An Intergalactic Environmental Agency (IEA) was now in operation. Earth's solar system was home to the Lux

---

2160 Dating *The Guardian of the Solar System* (BF CC #5.1) - The Sara Kingdom audio trilogy concludes ten years after the end of *The Drowned World*.

2161 *The Five Companions*

2162 *The Forgotten Army*

2163 Dating *Night of the Humans* (NSA #38) - The Doctor says (p19), "To be precise, it's 14 March 250,339. And it's six minutes past one in the afternoon", based upon the atomic clock he retrieves from the Pioneer 10 probe. The day and year are confirmed in the Sittuun situation reports (pgs. 7-9), which seem to use the Julian calendar. The existence of the Lux Academy (doubtless referencing the family prominent in *Silence in the Library*) suggests that Earth has greatly recovered from the devastation the Daleks wrought in *The Parting of the Ways*. Somewhat uniquely, the Sittuun's natural language isn't translatable through the TARDIS' systems just because... it just isn't.

2164 '"Fifteen years" before *The Eyeless*. There is plenty of evidence that this was an incident during The Last Great Time War. The Doctor already knows of the Fortress, its Weapon and who built them. He also knows that both sides in the war are dead, and that one side had "footholds in different galaxies". The Eyeless probe the Doctor's mind, and see he was somehow involved with the firing of the Weapon. A number of Dalek stories have established that Skaro is in the Seventh Galaxy; *The Daleks*: "The Destroyers" says it's in the eighth. On the other hand, the Doctor says that "pretty much whoever your enemy is", you would destroy yourself by using the Weapon against them, but The War in Heaven offers an obvious candidate for an Enemy for which that would not be the case. Possibly, the Weapon was built for the War in Heaven but used in the Last Great Time War.

2165 Dating *The Eyeless* (NSA #30) - The date is given.

2166 Dating *The Eyeless* (NSA #30) - It's "twenty years" since the main events of the story.

2167 Dating *White Ghosts* (BF 4th Doc #3.2) - The survey team is identified as human, is already adept at

genetic alteration (such as endowing themselves with superior eyes), and have reached the furthermost point of the known universe. The "homeworld" of the survey team might be Earth itself.

2168 Dating *Iris S5: The Slots of Giza* (BF Iris #5.5) - Turner claims to be "thousands of years out of time", but Seth (probably more accurately) says it's "hundreds of thousands of years" after the time of Ra.

2169 Dating *The War Games* (6.7) - It is stated that humanity has been killing itself for "half a million years" before this story takes place, which (coincidentally) ties up with the date 309,906 established for the Doctor's first trial (or "Malfeasance Tribunal") in *The Deadly Assassin*. The TARDIS Logs suggested a date of "48,063" for this story, *Apocrypha* offered "5950 AD".

The aliens in this story are unnamed on screen, yet they're referred to as "the War Lords" in *The War Games* novelisation by Malcolm Hulke, *The Making of Doctor Who* 1972 edition, the Lofficier *Programme Guide*, and *Timewyrm: Exodus* by Terrance Dicks. They're simply "Aliens" in the 1973 *Radio Times Special*. As both Hulke and Dicks independently use the name "War Lords" in their other work, it has been adopted in this volume to avoid confusion with other unnamed alien races.

HOW MANY WAR ZONES ARE THERE?: *The War Games* establishes in dialogue that the aliens have "ten" zones under their control. The map we see shows eleven, not including the Control Zone. Three more appear in dialogue, making a total of fifteen... map: Greek Zone [c.500BC]; "two thousand years ago" map: Roman Zone; map: 30 Years War Zone [1618-1648]; map: English Civil War Zone [1642-1646]; "1745", Jacobite Rebellion; "1812", Napoleon's advance into Russia; map: Peninsular War Zone [1808-1814]; map: Crimean War Zone [1853-1856]; "1862", map: American Civil War Zone; map: Mexican Civil War Zone, "Mexican Uprising" (?1867); Franco-Prussian War [1870-1871]; map: Boer War Zone [1899-1902]; The Boxer Rising [1900]; "1905", map: Russio-Japanese War Zone; "1917", map: 1917 War Zone.

Academy, and offered classes in ancient Earth music.

The Sittuun had evolved on a world with no predators, and so never developed fear. Humanity made first contact with the Sittuun, who used human names and language conventions when dealing with humans, as their own language was too untranslatable. The comet Schuler-Khan was due to strike the Gyre (a conglomeration of space junk), which would have propelled city-sized debris toward twelve inhabited worlds within twenty-five million miles. A team of Sittuun destroyed the Gyre, and the humans living there, with the largest nanobomb – which contained metal-eating nanites – ever made. The bomb had been built with funding from eight Battani planets and fifteen associated worlds.

Prior to this, a relatively early incarnation of the Doctor had facilitated swashbuckler Dirk Slipstream's incarceration on Volag-Noc, after Slipstream had crashed a passenger ship – and killed seven hundred – during a botched diamond heist on Belaform 9. After Slipstream's escape, the eleventh Doctor and Amy stopped him from acquiring the Mymon Key and blackmailing the Sol System with it. The Key was destroyed, and ravenous Sollogs ate Slipstream.

In 291,994, an alien Fortress materialised at the heart of Arcopolis, a utopian city of arcologies on a world in the Sculptor Dwarf Galaxy (or Galaxy Seven) which had not known war or crime for thousands of years. The Weapon at the heart of the Fortress fired, apparently killing all two hundred million people in Arcopolis, as well as annihilating countless other star systems. It was the Ultimate Weapon – something that didn't just destroy one's enemy, but instead used vunktotechnology and vundatechnology to destroy everything that had ever been known about said enemy. This was the Last Battle of the Seventh Galaxy.[2164]

292,009 - THE EYELESS[2165] **->** The tenth Doctor went to Arcopolis to deactivate the Weapon at the heart of the Fortress there. He thought the Weapon had rendered the planet lifeless, but soon met survivors who lived in fear of "ghosts" that haunted the city. A girl called Alsa told him that the thirty-seven original survivors had birthed many children over the last fifteen years. The survivors and their offspring stayed away from the city, confining themselves to a settlement in what used to be a park.

The Eyeless – an alien race of glass telepaths who worked as galactic scavengers – arrived to claim the TARDIS. They soon learned of the Weapon and desired it, but Alsa wanted the Weapon for herself, believing it could power the ruins of the city. The Doctor learned that the "ghosts" were actually sentient shadows in space-time left by the people killed by the Weapon, but was himself forced to use the device – which wiped out the Eyeless and destroyed the Fortress. He took Alsa on his travels for a short time, returning her a little later than he expected...

292,029 - THE EYELESS[2166] **->** The tenth Doctor returned Alsa to Arcopolis two decades later than he intended – but this suited Alsa, who was more at home here than she had been in her own time.

? 300,000 - WHITE GHOSTS[2167] **->** The Time Lords diverted the fourth Doctor and Leela to the "edge of the edge of the universe", to a dark world that received a splinter of sunlight just once every 1040 years. A human survey team sought to capitalize upon snake-like plants, White Ghosts, that budded at this time, and thereby augment their race to survive in alien environments. The White Ghost material turned the surveyors into vampires, whom the Doctor and Leela prevented from returning to infect their homeworld. Aliens on winged horses arrived to harvest the White Ghosts, and the Doctor expected that the vampires would be put to work in the White Ghost fields.

c 300,000 - IRIS S5: THE SLOTS OF GIZA[2168] **->** The Giza became the premiere casino hotel-spaceship in the Hawkhead Nebula, orbiting the planet Ra and patterning itself after ancient Egyptian civilisation. A stage magician, Seth the Sensational, stole temporal hardware from a time traveller visiting the Giza. Seth lived five hundred years by syphoning time away from the Giza's guests; in return, he kept everyone within the casino entertained, and their body clocks distorted, until they expired. Iris Wildthyme and Captain Turner spent 110 years in the Giza's time field, but uncovered Seth's actions as he performed his one-millionth show. Iris challenged Seth to a Magic Off and removed his glamour, revealing his naturally withered state and ending his wrongdoing.

The War Lords Crisis; the Time Lords Apprehend the Second Doctor

309,906 - THE WAR GAMES[2169] **->** A race of alien warlords attempted to raise an army of galactic conquest by programming human soldiers kidnapped from various points in history with stolen Time Lord technology. A renegade Time Lord, the War Chief, aided them and was shot during an uprising engineered by the second Doctor, Jamie and Zoe. When the plan was uncovered, the Time Lords erected a force field that confined the aliens to their planet. The kidnapped soldiers were sent home, with no awareness of these events. The Time Lords also dematerialised the aliens' leader, the War Lord.

309,906 - THE EIGHT DOCTORS[2170] -> The eighth Doctor rescued his second incarnation and encouraged him to summon the Time Lords to deal with the War Lords.

> (=) The TARDIS' temporary erasure from history, owing to a conceptual bomb the cadaverous Master deployed in 1963, created a timeline in which the Doctor failed to stop the War Lords – who amassed an army and warred against the galaxy.[2171]

The War Chief was horrifically injured rather than killed. He was sent to the War Lords' home planet, but his regeneration aborted and his new form was disfigured. He allied with the son of the War Chief, and after many years, they broke through the force field the Time Lords had placed around the War Lords' home planet. They revived their dreams of galactic conquest, and decided to concentrate on helping Nazi Germany.[2172]

Around 317,000, humans encroached on the territory of the Sulumians in the eighth dimension. The Sulumians began a time travel campaign dedicated to rewriting human history to prevent this.[2173] In 365,509, the collapse of a star in NGC4258 destroyed four civilisations. A region of space warps, the Grey Interchange, was created.[2174]

Around 436,000, Earth was caught in the crossfire of a war between Kallix Grover and the Sine Wave Shrine of Shillitar. A magnetic wave shut down all digital technology, cutting Earth off from its colonies. This was the Great Retrenchment.[2175]

438,533 (2nd October) - ONLY HUMAN[2176] -> Following the Great Retrenchment, humans mastered the biological and chemical sciences to the point they could take apart the human body and put it back together without ill effects. All emotions were regulated, and – apart from the dissident Refusers – no human ever worried about anything.

Marek Golding and the Graceless[2177]

Scoutships settled on the homeworld of Brondle and General Cecilia Wing. The territory allocation wasn't settled until the Diaspora, and sketchy records from the period made reference to war in the old systems and an outbreak of disease.[2178] Manchu Golding's mother fought in the Battle of the Lower Sky.[2179]

c 495,010 - GRACELESS II: THE LINE -> Marek, the mutual lover of the living Key tracers Abby and Zara, grew up on a planetoid that was tidally locked. A mobile city traversed the line between the planetoid's perpetually light and dark halves, dropping off and picking up miners along the way. The city housed the biggest factory "this side of Rigel".

2170 Dating *The Eight Doctors* (EDA #1) - This happens during *The War Games*.
2171 *The Light at the End*
2172 The War Chief is shot in *The War Games*, and reappears in *Timewyrm: Exodus*.
2173 "Three hundred and seventeen thousand years" after 40 BC, according to *The Gallifrey Chronicles*.
2174 *The English Way of Death*
2175 *Only Human*
2176 Dating *Only Human* (NSA #5) - The Doctor calculates the precise date.
2177 Dating *Graceless II: The Line, Graceless II: The Flood*, and *Graceless II: Consequences* (*Graceless* #2.1, 2.2, 3.3) - These three stories can be pinned to the lifetime of Marek Golding, who is a boy away at school in *The Line*, but a grown insuranceman in *Consequences* (set "more than five years" after *The Flood*). In *The Flood*, Brondle notes that the city in which he lives previously burnt to the ground "on the bi-millennia, and in 494,920". The settlers of their world only arrived "fifteen hundred years ago", and so have not experienced the two-millennia birthing phenomenon of the creatures living within their world's sun. So, the absolute latest *The Flood* can occur is circa 496,420.

It's never established that Marek's race is human - if they are, they enjoy a decent longevity, as Manchu Golding's mother participated in the Battle of the Lower Sky "130 years ago" and is still living in a penthouse and participating in a family lunch every Sunday (*The Line*). A currency used in *The Line* is the "grotz", presumably a word-derivation of the "grotzi" used in Glitz's era (*The Mysterious Planet*). Abby and Zara comment that their foe Persephone is "thousands of years in the future" (they last saw her near the end of time in *Graceless: The End*, so it's actually been much longer than that). In *The Line*, Manchu Golding orders a bottle of the "'48 Fizz."
2178 "Fifteen hundred years" before *Graceless II: The Flood*.
2179 One hundred thirty years before *Graceless II: The Line*.
2180 Dating *Graceless IV: The Dance/The Bomb* (*Graceless* #4.4, #4.1; sic) - *The Bomb* happens "316 standard years" after *Graceless III: Consequences* [c.495,046]. Pool's group visit the aged Zara an unspecified point beforehand.
2181 Dating *The Girl Who Never Was* (BF #103) - The Cybermen seem to generalise the year as "500,000", but the eighth Doctor – using the TARDIS' scanning equipment – specifies the date as 500,002. This is further confirmed by the sixth Doctor in *The Condemned*, Charley in *Brotherhood of the Daleks* and the Valeyard in *6th LA: The Red House*.

The city had been destroyed in unknown circumstances. Marek's memories of the holocaust subconsciously influenced Abby and Zara – who were nomadic throughout space-time with him and Joy, Marek's daughter with Zara – to arrive on Marek's homeworld just before the disaster. They learned that the planetoid shifted slightly in its orbit, and while the city had been built to compensate for this, nobody had checked its systems in decades.

Suddenly, the city drifted off course. The side built to withstand extreme cold experienced the intense heat of the planetoid's sunlit half …

> (=) The city's main dome imploded, with a massive loss of life. Young Marek – the son of the corporate leader Manchu Golding – was attending school on the other side of the system, and was orphaned along with other scholarship boys. Urged by the older Marek, Abby and Zara teleported at least one thousand workers, as well as Marek's father, to a cargo ship. The city still perished, but at a lesser loss of life.
>
> Abby and Zara's intervention altered Marek's timeline – he never encountered the two of them, resulting in the older Marek and Joy fading from existence.

Traumatised by the loss of their family, Abby and Zara left to help people and redeem themselves as best they were able…

c 495,040 - GRACELESS II: THE FLOOD -> Abby and Zara aided a spaceship that crashed onto a planet experiencing unnatural climate change. The sisters found that the local sun was home to pan-dimensional beings who spawned in the oceans every two thousand years, as the planet's eccentric orbit took it near the sun. The residents, including the war veteran Brondle and his beloved, General Cecila Wing, agreed to leave their beaches alone for a month while the pan-dimensional beings completed their birthing cycle.

Abby and Zara continued their travels, and found themselves back at the end of time…

c 495,046 - GRACELESS III: CONSEQUENCES -> Abby and Zara returned to Brondle and Wing's homeworld, disturbed to have found documents verifying they would again meet their beloved Marek, but choose to die on the very same day. The historically revised version of Marek was living as an insurance agent, and knew that the sisters had saved his father and others from certain death when he was a child. Wing was suffering from dementia due to her war service, and so Abby and Zara negotiated that she and Brondle could join the creatures in their planet's sun, living on as pan-dimensional beings. Brondle left his house to Marek.

The sisters found that their interference in history had metastasised into an imbalance in the planet's sun – a hole in time that was getting larger. Abby and Zara elected to die, hoping that the extinguishment of their powers would let the flow of time heal itself. The disturbance remained, but a member of the Grace appeared to praise the sisters' selflessness, and say that the Grace had gained much perspective from their service. The Grace restored the sun, and allowed the sisters to "die" as they were. Abby and Zara would live on as "Amy" and "Joy", mortal and without any powers, in a shared relationship with Marek.

& 495,362 - GRACELESS IV: THE DANCE / GRACELESS IV: THE BOMB[2180] **->** Abby and Zara were now regarded as fairy stories on Brondle and Wing's homeworld. In truth, the sisters were outwardly aged, and living out their remaining days as "Amy" and "Granny Joy". They had many descendants; Amy Ambo was the oldest of Abby's offspring. Zara was a bit relieved when her children and grandchildren had passed on, as it ended their pain. Merak Golding died.

The incarnation of the Chaos Pool, along with Abby and Zara's future selves, briefly visited the aged Zara for insight.

The sisters retained little of their former abilities, and Abby was hospitalized after failing from a tree while trying to rescue her cat. The fission reactor that supplied a third of the world's power went critical, but the sisters unexpectedly absorbed the energy released, and regained their youth and powers. They healed everyone stricken with radiation poisoning, then departed for new horizons. Their family believed they had died.

Charley Pollard
Loses the Eighth Doctor, Joins the Sixth

500,002 - THE GIRL WHO NEVER WAS[2181] **->** A Cyberman time squad was dispatched on a test flight from the future, but their systems failed, and their vessel grounded on Earth in 500,002, when the planet had been abandoned once again due to solar flare activity. Cyber-signals were sent back in time – contact was made with the *Batavia* in 1942, and events allowed the ship to translocate to this year. The Cybermen sought to send the *Batavia* back in time stuffed with conversation facilities – thereby replenishing their numbers through historical alteration – but the eighth Doctor thwarted their plan.

Soon after, the smuggler Byron forced the Doctor and Charley to bring him to this year in the TARDIS, as he wanted to loot the Cyber-ship. Charley installed a Cyber-Planner infected with "temporal rust" into the Cyber-ship's systems, destroying Byron, the Cybermen of this era and their ship. Charley thought Byron had killed the Doctor, and the temporal corrosion triggered the TARDIS' HADS, taking it – with the unconscious Doctor inside – back to 2008.

Charley sent out an SOS signal, and the TARDIS materialised in response... whereupon Charley was appalled to find the sixth Doctor, not the eighth, had rescued her. She faked amnesia and became his companion, worried that her presence in his past would upset causality.

> = "Half a million years of industrial progress" had left the Earth's surface as "just a chemical slime". The Ancient One, a Haemovore, was the last living creature to inhabit an Earth.[2182]
>
> Lady Ruath showed Yarven, the Vampire Messiah, that humankind was destined to become a vampire race. The Haemovores lived in the sea, where they ganged up to hunt whales.[2183]

The Doctor arranged for a Mulo – a vampire created from a stillborn child – to become a caretaker at the Haemovore nature preserve on Vikramaditya.[2184]

c 600,000 - HEAVEN SENT[2185] -> Within his confession dial, the twelfth Doctor chipped away at the azbantium wall as the universe lived on...

The World Launched Amidst a Global Crisis

Earth faced a crisis point, as there were now "so many diseases, so few resources", and humanity had failed to "think far enough ahead". In response, The World – a colony ship the size of a moon, and capable of housing five million souls – was constructed and launched. Its Kinetic Engines, fitted with sub-atomic crunchers, could convert free-floating space particles into energy. Although it was believed that Earth's death was imminent, humanity chose a different course, and its homeworld endured.

The World never reached its destination. The crew discovered the Corvus – an ancient creature of decay – was aboard, and sabotagued the navigational systems to stop it from infecting other civilizations. *The World*, the Corvus and the human cadavers it commanded remained lost in space for 900,000 years.[2186]

? 800,000 - K9 AND THE MISSING PLANET[2187] ->

Earth had become known as Tellus, a smoggy, high-speed planet with no trees and plastic grass. It was a vast armaments factory run by Tellac Inc, a company that strip-mined worlds until they collapsed or exploded. One mining planet vanished, and represented a hazard to shipping.

The Time Lords sent K9 to investigate the missing world. K9's ship, the K-NEL fell into a time warp and arrived in a different universe. The unnamed mining planet had been transported there, as the miners found that the planet contained large deposits of Star Crystal – a substance that broke down barriers between universes. Over five hundred million years of Earth evolution were represented on the planet, including early humans. The miners liked the idyllic life the planet offered, and thought that a new race of men might arise there. At the miners' request, K9 left them alone, reporting that the planet had disappeared from the universe as we know it.

? 802,701 - TIMELASH[2188] -> The third Doctor and Jo visited Karfel, preventing a great famine there. The Doctor also reported the scientist Magellan, who had been conducting unethical experiments on the reptili-

---

2182 "Half a million years" after *The Curse of Fenric*. When the Reverend Wainwright asks the Doctor how he knows about the Haemovores' future, the Doctor says "I've seen it". Some commentators (including *The Discontinuity Guide* and the previous editions of this chronology) have presumed that the Haemovore timeline was created when the Ancient One poisoned the Earth, and erased when he/she refrained from doing so, but this isn't actually said on screen. The Doctor attributes the Haemovore era to "half a million years of industrial progress", not something as sudden and cataclysmic as a single chemical release.

The next story to deal with Earth is *The Mysterious Planet*, set around the year two million – meaning that if the Haemovore timeline is "real", there are 1.5 million years for the dying Earth, "its surface a chemical slime", to recover. It perhaps sounds like a cheat to assume the Earth could simply "get over" such a catastrophe, but it's no less plausible than the idea that humanity's homeworld recuperates after the Daleks bombard it with enough firepower to change the shape of the very continents (in *The Parting of the Ways*, set in 200,100).

2183 *Goth Opera*, in which Ruath says the Haemovore timeline is a "possible future" (p44).

2184 *Benny: The Vampire Curse: "Possum Kingdom"*, supporting the "haemovore future" from *The Curse of Fenric* being part of established history.

2185 Dating *Heaven Sent* (X9.11) - It's "six hundred thousand years" into the future.

2186 *The Wreck of the World*

2187 Dating *K9 and the Missing Planet* (*The Adventures of K9* #4) - It's after "The human race had swarmed like locusts across the galaxy". Earth becoming known as Tellus isn't referenced in any other story, so dating when this could have occurred is a matter of sheer guesswork. That the miners on the unnamed planet have the technological nous to move between universes when they come across Star Crystal, and that they know of the Time Lords, suggests that it's the far future.

2188 Dating *Timelash* (22.5) - No date given on screen. This has been arbitrarily set in the same year that the Time Traveller met the Eloi and the Morlocks in H.G. Wells' *The Time Machine*. There is no indication on

an Morlox, to the praesidium.

Over the next century, an accident with the substance Mustakozene caused Magellan to merge with a Morlox and became the mutated Borad. He took control of Karfel, enforcing discipline with an army of androids and the threat of exile into a time corridor, the Timelash. The Borad planned to provoke a war with neighbouring Bandril as a means of populating the planet with mutated clones of himself. Following the arrival of the sixth Doctor and Peri, the Borad was thrown into the Timelash, ending up in Loch Ness in the twelfth century.

& 802,711 - LETH-ST: "Time and Again"[2189] -> On

Karfel, Mykros and Vena – who had allied with the sixth Doctor against the Borad – enjoyed a single year of married life, then he passed away. In time, Vena led the ruling Council as Borad.

Dominator dreadnoughts blockaded Karfel and Bandril, hoping to claim the Timelash and redirect it to strategic points in space-time. Per the Karfel-Bandril treaty, Bandril technicians supplied the Karfel capitol with a protective force field. Vena unleashed androids that massacred the Dominators' ground troops. Two years into the blockade, and a decade after Megelen's downfall, the Bandril Host formally adopted a position of neutrality between Karfel and the Dominant Echelon.

Maylin Zulman deposed Vena, ordered her arrest and exile, and signalled Karfel's surrender. Vena reached the Timelash, to recall H.G. Wells to assist with the crisis. The Timelash beam interacted with the younger Edward Travers' return to his native era, causing Travers and Wells to find themselves in an unknown field, and confronted by a war machine...

Man fought the Primal Wars in the Tenth Segment of Time. Much scientific knowledge was lost during this period, including the cure for the common cold.[2190]

The viruses released at Amethyst Station all amassed at a single point in space-time.[2191]

? - "The Neutron Knights"[2192] -> Earth had endured in

a long chain of catastrophes, and the last link in this was an invasion by the Neutron Knights. Earth's defences were overrun by forces led by the great mutant Catavolcus, who had previously breached the gates of Hell. Earth was a shattered world where only the strong survived.

The fourth Doctor was summoned to a fortress on Earth by the force of will of a mysterious bearded figure, who had himself previously been summoned through time to fight Earth's last battle. Catavolcus wanted the Dragon – a vast nuclear fission device as powerful as the Sun. He broke into the fortress, despite the best efforts of the castle's defender, Arthur. The mysterious summoner was Merlin, who set the Dragon to overload as Arthur fell to Catavolcus and his sword of flame. The Doctor and Merlin retreated to the TARDIS as the fortress – and Catavolcus – were destroyed. The Doctor woke in a forest, unsure what has happened. Merlin contacted him and warned that their paths were destined to cross once more.

Ssard Joins the TARDIS

"Descendance" / "Ascendance"[2193] -> On Mars, Luass

– formerly of the House of Darsus Mons – thwarted her son Izaxryl's rite of ascension so that her brother, Artix, could become the head of the House of Balazarus Mons. The eighth Doctor and Stacy helped to end the warfare between the Houses, and Luass and Artix were both killed. Ssard, an Ice Warrior who had helped the Doctor and Stacy, joined them on their travels.

---

screen exactly when the third Doctor visited Karfel; the novelisation suggests it was "at least one hundred years" before this story, during the time of Katz's grandfather.

2189 Dating *Leth-St*: "Time and Again" (*Leth-St* novella #1a) - The story's climax happens "a decade" after *Timelash*.

2190 *The Ark*

2191 Date unknown, but it's in the "far distant future" of *To the Death*.

2192 Dating "The Neutron Knights" (*DWM* #60) - No date is given, but if it truly is Earth's last battle, the story would seem to be set either before *The Ark* or somewhere in vast gap between that story and *The End of the World*. The Doctor speculates that "past and future are flowing into the same event", which doesn't really help. It doesn't seem to be set during the Millenium

Wars. While the link isn't made in either story, it's been placed during the Primal Wars mentioned in *The Ark*.

2193 Dating "Descendance"/"Ascendance" (*Radio Times* #3785-3804) - No date given. The Doctor and Stacy open the story by witnessing "an early [Martian] period ascendancy rite", which could equally suggest that this is old Mars before the downfall of Ice Warrior civilisation, or that it's a traditional rite taking place in contemporary/future times. The surface of Mars is habitable – again, either an indication that it's prior to the decline of the Martian ecology (*The Judgement of Isskar*), or that it's after Mars has been terraformed (in stories such as *The Resurrection of Mars*). Either way, there are large Martian cities that modern-day astronomers and space probes would be unlikely to miss.

Two details suggest a future dating: The Martians are familiar with both Christmas and humanity (the Doctor

c 1,200,000 - HEAVEN SENT[2194] -> Within his confession dial, the twelfth Doctor chipped away at the azbantium wall as the universe lived on...

The seventh Doctor, Mel and Ace took the grievously injured Nathan Later back in time two decades, to the Krytomp Bio-Infirmary, near Andromeda in the Golden Dragon Nebula. The Doctor registered Later as "Nathan Lonnigan", knowing he would become the criminal Lefty Lonnigan. Sabalom Glitz was recovering from an accident on a stolen hoverscooter, and became roommates with Lonnigan while they convalesced – the start of their friendship and partnering in crime.[2195]

c 1,500,000 - THE WRECK OF THE WORLD[2196] -> The second Doctor, Jamie and Zoe worked to repair a space-time breach caused by their recent journey into the Land of Fiction, but in doing so happened upon *The World*: an infamous and immense colony ship that never reached its destination. A cultist tried to liberate the ancient decay-entity Corvis from *The World*, but Jamie destroyed the prism housing Corvis' energy, dissipating it.

c 2,000,000 - HEAVEN SENT[2197] -> Within his confession dial, the twelfth Doctor chipped away at the azbantium wall as the universe lived on...

Glitz's Time

The criminal Kane was guilty of systematic acts of violence and extortion with his lover Sana, who killed herself rather than face trial. Kane was exiled from his home planet of Proamon, and sent to the barren planet Svartos. He remained there for three thousand years, slowly building his powerbase and dreaming of a return to his homeworld.

Unknown to Kane, Proamon was destroyed when its star went supernova a thousand years after his exile. Kane operated from the trading post of Iceworld, which was capable of spaceflight. This required the Dragonfire, a source of energy contained within the head of the Dragon: a biomechanoid sent to Svartos to prevent Kane from escaping the planet. Kane remained trapped on Iceworld.[2198]

Sabalom Glitz came from Salostopus in Andromeda. He was an habitual jailbird and thief, always on the

---

is told, "You have all the outward appearance of a typically human buffoon"). No mention is made of the Federation. *The Silent Stars Go By* establishes that the Martians re-settle Mars at an unspecified point prior to the sun expanding and rendering the planet uninhabitable once more (*The Ark*). So while an old Mars dating is certainly feasible, a future dating was here chosen because the phrases "typically human buffoon" and Ssard's "It's the Martian equivalent of what humans call Christmas, Stacy" are rather hard to wave away as figures of speech.

As this was the last entry to be placed in *Ahistory* Third Edition, its exact placement (working to the parameters specified above) was literally chosen using the stairwell method – slips of paper were flung into the air, and the one reading "one million AD" reached the bottom of the stairs first.

2194 Dating *Heaven Sent* (X9.11) - It's "twelve hundred thousand years" into the future.

2195 "Over twenty years" before *A Life of Crime*.

2196 Dating *The Wreck of the World* (BF EA #4.4) - The blurb misleadingly names *The World* as the "very first colony ship to leave Earth"; it's actually the first to leave after a global downturn necessitates an evacuation. Said disaster, as best we're told, involves disease and a lack of resources – so, it's not the same tragedy as the Solar Flare event (*The Ark in Space*) or the Earth plunging into the sun (*The Ark, Frontios*).

The Doctor says it's "one and a half million years" into the future, and an AI confirms that *The World* was lost "900,000 years" ago (meaning Earth's decline happened c.600,000). The scope of *The World* – it's moon

sized, built to accommodate five million people – indeed suggests the far, *far* future, if it's of Earth manufacture. What's puzzling is how Zoe keeps identifying equipment aboard *The World* as "[not] that many years after me" and "give or take a few hundred years" after her native time. *The World* must truly have an interesting back-story, if it was constructed as a moon-sized ship with Kinetic Engines around 600,000, but makes use of twenty-fourth century (or thereabouts) technology. (Then again, perhaps tech in that era was built to last.) For that matter, Professor Blavatsky must be *exceedingly* good at her job, if – after a million and a half years of history – she's able to identify Zoe's use of "archaic cadences of the twenty-first century".

2197 Dating *Heaven Sent* (X9.11) - It's "two million years" into the future.

2198 *Dragonfire*

2199 *The Mysterious Planet*

2200 *The High Price of Parking*

2201 Dating *The Mysterious Planet* (23.1) - The Doctor consults his pocket watch and suggests that it is "two million years" after Peri's time. Both the camera script and the novelisation confirm this date. *The Terrestrial Index* attempted to rationalise the various "ends of the Earth" seen in the series, but in doing so it ignored virtually every date given on screen. It is claimed, for example, that this story was set "c.14,500". *The TARDIS Special* gave the date as "two billion" AD, an understandable mishearing of the Doctor's line. *About Time* speculates that this is the same destruction of Earth seen in *The Ark* (the first Doctor was confused about the date), but doesn't explain why Time Lords who

lookout for a fast grotzi.[2199] Glitz at some point encountered Galactic Heritage's warfleet.[2200]

Earth Moved Through Space, Renamed Ravalox

c 2,000,000 - THE MYSTERIOUS PLANET[2201] -> A group of Andromedans stole scientific secrets contained in the Matrix of the Time Lords and took shelter on Earth. By order of the High Council, the Magnotron was used to move the Earth and its entire constellation two light years, destroying everyone on the surface. The planet became known as Ravalox. The Andromedans, though, knew that the Time Lords had discovered them and had built a survival chamber. They entered suspended animation, awaiting rescue. The robot recovery mission sent to retrieve the Andromedans missed the Earth in its new location and sped on into the depths of space.

After five hundred years, this survival shelter had become Marb Station, a completely self-contained system. Station guards maintained strict water rationing and population control. The population worshipped the Immortal – a being that lived in a citadel within their complex, and which was actually the robot caretaker of the facility, Drathro. The Earth's surface became viable again and served as home to The Tribe of the Free – a few primitive humans who had escaped from Marb Station. They worshipped the god Haldron, and killed any space traveller trying to steal his totem, a black light converter made from pure siligtone. They believed their ancestors' space travel had brought down their god's wrath and caused the solar fireball.

Glitz formed a business partnership with the Tremas Master, who knew that Earth had been moved and renamed Ravalox by the High Council. The Master sent Glitz and Glitz's accomplice, Dibber, to Ravolox to retrieve the Matrix files. The sixth Doctor and Peri defeated Drathro, allowing the two communities of humans to make contact.

The Time Lords subsequently restored Earth to its correct location.[2202] Thanks to a timestorm engineered by Fenric, Ace arrived on the ice planet of Svartos. Glitz used his ship, the *Nosferatu*, to raid space freighters. He ended up on Svartos with a rotten cargo and a mutinous crew, and tried to sell both to Kane.[2203]

After this time, the Andromeda Galaxy fell under the rule of The One, a vast artificial intelligence that contained the memories and experiences of all Andromedans.[2204]

Ace Joins the TARDIS, Mel Departs

c 2,000,000 - DRAGONFIRE[2205] -> On the trading colony Iceworld, located on the dark side of Svartos, Kane was assembling an army. He put his soldiers into cryosleep, which erased their memories of their former life to make them serve him without question.

Others chose to serve Kane willingly... Kane, whose natural body temperature was minus 193 Celsius, would burn the Mark of the Sovereign onto the palm of their right hand. One of Kane's officers, Belazs, joined him when she was 16 and served for twenty years. Kane earned many Crowns trading supplies to space travellers.

Many beings were drawn to Iceworld by the legends of a firebreathing dragon that supposedly lived in the ice tunnels beneath the colony. Kane finally killed the Dragon, his biomechanoid jailer, and acquired its Dragonfire power source. The seventh Doctor helped Kane to realise that his homeworld had been destroyed two thousand years ago, which deprived Kane of his

---

would covertly sterilise the Earth to prevent their secrets getting out give humanity notice this would happen, and enough notice to build a giant evacuation ship to boot.

The setting reminds Peri of "a wet November", perhaps suggesting the month. There's nothing on screen to suggest this isn't Glitz's native time.

2202 *The Eight Doctors*

2203 Before *Dragonfire*. *The Curse of Fenric* unveiled Fenric's involvement in Ace arriving in the future.

2204 "Ten hundred million years" (a billion) before *Doctor Who and the Invasion from Space*.

2205 Dating *Dragonfire* (24.4) - No date is given on screen, but Glitz's presence suggests the story takes place after *The Mysterious Planet*. Iceworld services "twelve galaxies", and Glitz comes from Andromeda, suggesting that intergalactic travel is now routine (and

that it's after Andromeda was colonised). According to the novelisation, Svartos is in the "Ninth Galaxy".

Head Games claimed it was "a few thousand years into the future", at the time of the Galactic Federation. *Head Games* also establishes that Earth is devastated at this time, a reference to *The Mysterious Planet/The Ultimate Foe* (but one that might also support a dating around the time of the solar flares). Assuming it's the Galactic Federation from the Peladon stories, that and the dating of *Mission: Impractical* would seem to agree that Glitz's native time – and the events of *Dragonfire* – is much earlier than two million years in the future. Glitz is working for the Master in *The Mysterious Planet*, so could have been taken to the far future. However, with absolutely no evidence for this, or for Glitz having his own time machine, it seems better to conclude that he was in his native time in *The Mysterious Planet*.

revenge. Kane killed himself upon realising this. The Doctor's companion Melanie Bush elected to stay behind on Iceworld, now renamed the *Nosferatu II*, with Sabalom Glitz. He accepted as his new companion Ace, a time-stranded teenager working at Iceworld as a waitress.

A version of Clara Oswald pounded on a window as the seventh Doctor dangled over a sheer drop on Svartos.[2206]

> = In one of the Valeyard's scenarios, Mel Bush died when the *Nosferatu 2* crashed onto Cela Magnum.[2207]

c 2,000,000 - THE FOURTH WALL[2208] -> Universal translators were in use. Earth Co. made spaceships with turbo-temporal fusion engines and dimetricite hulls. The Acteon Galaxy was home to the Theatre of Light.

The warthog-like Porcians became the laughing stock of the galactic community, as they continually botched their attempts at conquest. Their numerous failures included an assault on a planet shortly before a supernova obliterated it, an attack a carnivorous world, an ill-advised trip to Skaro, the explosion of one invasion fleet because it took along the wrong equipment, and the annihilation of another in a black hole before it even reached its target. The Doctor met the Porcians on worlds such as Ballastron VII, and took all manner of steps to stop them from accidentally committing self-genocide.

Augustus Scullop's Trans-Gal intergalactic media empire faced a takeover bid from Zander Drexel. Based on the artificial planetoid Transmission, Scullop came into possession of a reality generator crafted by legendary "dream-spinners" – the Dashwa, a great lost race of the ninth gal-axy. The generator could convert images into reality, then overwrite the created reality onto targeted locales. Scullop consequently announced the debut of *Laser* – the first-ever programme that would enable viewers to interact with a three-dimensional reality. This, however, was a ploy so Scullop could create super-powered fictional creations to assassinate Drexel.

The sixth Doctor and Flip confronted the incarnated characters of *Laser*, including the villainous Lord Krarn. Krarn overthrew the limitations of his programming, murdered Scullop, and attempted to create an invincible army by copying himself with the reality generator. The Doctor used the generator to create a Fantasy Nullifier that erased the *Laser* characters. Drexel bought Scullop's company – but only after the Doctor destroyed the reality generator and all copies of *Laser*.

c 2,000,001 - YOU ARE THE DOCTOR AND OTHER STORIES: "You are the Doctor"[2209] -> While learning to pilot the TARDIS, Ace aimed for Australia but instead wound up on a space station subjugated by Chimbly the Porcian and his wife She That Defiles Dreams and Stamps Out Hope, a.k.a. Keith. The two had captured a Resurrectionist: a rare extra-dimensional creature that compassionately wound back time to restore those who had died. With this asset, Chimbly kept retrying various stratagems until he conquered the locals.

> (=) The seventh Doctor and Ace tried to defeat Chimbly, but were shot dead, then plunged to their deaths, then shot dead again, then shot dead *again*, then shot dead *again*. The Resurrectionist revived them each time.

2206 *The Name of the Doctor*
2207 *Unbound: He Jests at Scars...*
2208 Dating *The Fourth Wall* (BF #157) - No year given, although Zander Drexel is interviewed from his home on Earth, and the names and media model involved all suggest that it's the future of humanity. John Dorney, the writer of *The Fourth Wall*, imagined that the story occurred in "the near future", but refrained from picking a date to avoid continuity clashes and in case he wanted to use the Porcians again. The Doctor here meets Chimbly the Porcian for the first time, and re-meets him in *You are the Doctor and Other Stories*: "You are the Doctor" – which *A Life in Crime* places after *Dragonfire* [c.2,000,000], necessitating that *The Fourth Wall* be relocated there also.
    A theatre on the Acteon Galaxy (*Carnival of Monsters*, *Planet of the Spiders*) is mentioned, as well as a spaceship making a "left turn at Delta Magna" (*The Power of Kroll*).
2209 Dating *You are the Doctor and Other Stories*: "You are the Doctor" (BF #207a) - No date given, but *A Life in Crime* establishes that the TARDIS is here following in Mel's footsteps after *Dragonfire*.
2210 Dating *You are the Doctor and Other Stories*: "The Grand Betelgeuse Hotel" (BF #207c) - It's said to be the time of the Earth Empire. The hotel is constructed not long after humanity reaches Betelgeuse, which has already happened in *Fear of the Dark* [2383]. But once more, *A Life of Crime* states that the TARDIS lands here because it's tracking Mel, so it's after *Dragonfire*.
2211 Dating *A Life of Crime* (BF #214) - There's no suggestion that Mel has time-travel at her disposal, so it's the same era as when she left the Doctor's company in *Dragonfire*. (Supporting that, Lefty shared in the proceeds of Glitz's "Iceworld job", although it's unclear what this means, unless the *Nosferatu 2* was stripped of its assets.) Exactly how long Mel spent with Glitz post-*Dragonfire* isn't clear - the Doctor broadly tells her, "Time is relative. For you, it might only have been a matter of months", to which Ace adds, "But for me and

The Doctor freed the Resurrectionist, and freed Chimbly's slaves. Chimbly and Keith escaped.

? 2,000,001 - YOU ARE THE DOCTOR AND OTHER STORIES: "The Grand Betelgeuse Hotel"[2210] -> The Earth Empire reached Betelgeuse and constructed the Grand Betelgeuse Hotel: an opulent leisure complex. The seventh Doctor and Ace became embroiled in a heist into the Hotel's safety deposit boxes. In his personal future, the Doctor would aid the resistance on Soror B against the authorities.

Mel Rejoins the TARDIS after Her Futures are Revised

A LIFE OF CRIME[2211] -> Failing to rehabilitate Sabalom Glitz, Melanie Bush surreptitiously hacked his accounts and donated his spoils to the poor and downtrodden. Eventually, Glitz defaulted on his debt to the Sperovores – a hive mind that fed upon their victims' potential futures, and had become one of the wealthiest races in the galaxy – so signed his liabilities over to Mel. Glitz tricked Mel into entering cryo-sleep during hyper-jumps, enabling the Sperovores to feed on her possible futures. He *still* owed them thousands of credits, so ran out on Mel. Aboard the *Nosferatu 3*, Mel pursued Glitz and pulled funds from his ongoing schemes, including ones involving the Porcians and the Grand Betelgeuse Hotel.

Melanie Bush looked for Glitz on the planet Ricosta, a "Costa del Crime" for retired criminals, and the TARDIS – thinking she needed help – landed there also. The criminal Gloria Swannicker posed as a regenerated Doctor to fool Mel into participating in a bank heist, but Mel saw through the deception and looted Swannicker's accounts.

The Sperovores had underwritten Ricosta in exchange regularly eating the residents' potential futures, but now foreclosed on the planet and declared all the lives present as forfeit. The Sperovores consumed the criminal Lefty Lonnigan, then tried to do the same to Nathan Later of the Galactic Police... but since Later was Lonnigan's younger self, they suffered the indigestion of a massive paradox. The seventh Doctor, Ace and Mel forced the Sperovores to grant an extension of Ricosta's debt, then took Later back in time to fulfill upon history. Reunited, the trio looked forward to new travels together.

(=) ? 2,000,002 - HEAD GAMES[2212] -> The seventh Doctor had mentally influenced Mel into leaving his company, as he knew that Fenric was responsible for transporting Ace to Iceworld, and that he could no longer avoid certain responsibilities – of which Mel couldn't be a part. She soon left Glitz and attempted to reach Earth. She ended up marooned on the holiday planet Avalone, and spent two years there. She tried to get a lift from Glitz, and planted messages for him in the Galactic Banking Conglomerate's computer system, knowing that the Dragon cypher program she'd made for Glitz would find them. Glitz tried to exploit the open door and lift ten million grotzits from the bank, but he failed – causing officials to trace the intrusion to Mel's terminal. Avalone security caught up with Mel, who ran away and encountered the evil duplicate Dr Who.

On the sunless Detrios, an anomaly feeding off energy from the Land of Fiction had become the Miracle: a replacement source of heat and light for the planet. The unstable anomaly threatened the entire universe, so the seventh Doctor, Roz, Chris and Bernice sought to close it with force field generators. This nullified the Miracle, but some rebels on Detrios imposed order, and the inhabitants sought alternative methods of survival without a sun.

the Doctor. Well, we've had a whole world of adventures in between", while Mel herself only mentions that, "I've been living with Glitz long enough, I can spot a grifter a mile away". For the Doctor and Ace, it's while Ace is learning how to pilot the TARDIS (so, after the end of *Signs and Monsters*, and *You are the Doctor and Other Stories*).

A Life in Crime presents itself as the first time the Doctor has seen Mel since *Dragonfire*, which contradicts the novel *Head Games*. However, the fact that the Sperovores fed on some of Mel's potential futures might suggest that *Head Games* – and possibly also Mel's fate in *Heritage* – have been wrung out of her timeline, leaving her ongoing audio stories as her "true" history. *A Life in Crime* mentions the Doctor encountering Glitz on Vandor Prime (*Mission Impractical*), so is not wholly opposed to the novels' continuity.

2212 Dating *Head Games* (NA #43) - For Mel, it's been about two years since *Dragonfire*. It's here confirmed that Glitz is from the period when Earth was moved to become Ravolox. See *A Life of Crime* for how this story (or, at the very least, Mel's involvement in it) was retroactively written out of history.

Head Games is vague as to whether the Detrios sequences take place simultaneous to the modern day (2001), when Dr Who and Jason pick up Mel from Avalone in the future, or in some other time zone entirely. While a contemporary dating *feels* more likely, a future dating is indicated when someone living on Detrios cites the people there as "we humans", and suggests that the planet's first settlers were "astronauts" (p91). The first and second editions of *Ahistory* dated these sequences to the year 4000.

Glitz found a MiniScope and briefly met the second Romana, who was trapped inside. Flavia arrived in a Type 90 TARDIS and returned her to Gallifrey.[2213]

Hyspero

Iris Wildthyme believed that Hyspero was situated at edge of known universe, near the Ringpull aperture that led directly to her native domain: the Obverse. Hyspero was a constantly changing land that shifted according to the whims of the incumbent Scarlet Empress, whose mind influenced the planet.

The dragons of Hyspero were hunted for their blood, as it could make real things fictional and vice-versa. Leopard professors wanted the blood as ink for their books. Over the centuries, the dragons were brought to near extinction.[2214] Iris Wildthyme kept a "secret" base on Hyspero in the shape of a woman's head on a mountainside.[2216]

? 3,000,000 - IRIS: ENTER WILDTHYME[2216] -> The super-thief Terrance went to the planet Hyspero and made off with the Scarlet Empress Euphemia.[2217] He took her back to his bookshop in the twenty-first century.

Kelly and the villain Anthony Marville arrived on Hyspero via the *Dii h'anno Doors*... and found themselves looking at a 20-storey-tall face of Iris Wildthyme, which had been carved out of rock. Jenny, Euphemia and Barbra also travelled through the *Dii h'anno Doors*, and were reunited with Iris, Panda and Simon when they visited from the twenty-first century.

? 3,000,000 - IRIS: WILDTHYME BEYOND![2218] -> Iris and Panda encountered survivors from the Obverse, including Iris' aunties, who now lived in caves beneath Hyspero. They were unsure if anything else of the Clockworks had survived the Great Schism.

Kelly had spent many years in close proximity to a book from Hyspero, *The Aja'ib*, and – in conjunction with

2213 *Goth Opera*
2214 *Iris: Wildthyme Beyond!*
2215 "Thousands of years" (p227) before the Hyspero sequences in *Iris: Wildthyme Beyond!*, in an obvious parody of *The Face of Evil*.
2216 Dating *Iris: Enter Wildthyme* (*Iris* novel #1) - It's "millions of years" (p317) beyond the twenty-first century. Much of the book is spent trying to stop Marville from going to Hyspero to plunder its dark magic, but what happens after he reaches the planet is left unstated, beyond a homage to *The Face of Evil*.
2217 Euphemia says she's the first Scarlet Empress, but Cassandra made the same claim in *The Scarlet Empress*. The two of them don't appear to be the same character, although it's a bit hard to tell. Perhaps more than one empress has tried to augment her authority by claiming the mantle of being the "first", or perhaps each empress – for whatever reason – genuinely believes that they *are* the first. Or, perhaps owing to Hyspero existing in "a permanent state of magical anarchy and evolution" (*Iris: Enter Wildthyme*), the lineage resets itself every so often.
2218 Dating *Iris: Wildthyme Beyond!* (*Iris* novel #2) - The story follows on from *Iris: Enter: Wildthyme*.
2219 Dating *Iris S5: High Spirits* (BF *Iris* #5.6) - No date given. Iris says there's "no guarantee" that she'll die in future in the Garden, suggesting that this is a possible outcome for her. With nothing else to go on, *High Spirits* has been paired with one of the placements for *Iris: Enter Wildthyme* [? 3,000,000], which similarly elaborates on the fable-like and ever-changing nature of the planet Hyspero.
2220 Dating *Prison in Space* (BF LS #2.2) - No year given, nor is there any explanation as to how this story relates to the rest of Earth's history. The audio was made from an unmade (for good reason, the authors of

this guidebook would argue) script for Season 6.

While there's little doubt that *Prison in Space* takes place in the future, the TARDIS crew suspect early on that they've arrived in Earth's distant past, as part of a conversation that makes one wonder if the Doctor is entirely well. When Zoe very spuriously asks if they've arrived, "About what? Forty million years BC?", the Doctor replies, "Give or take the odd million, yes. Somewhere between the Oligocene and the Miocene periods." The Oligocene and Miocene *epochs* (subsets of *periods* of Earth prehistory) respectively ran from thirty-four to twenty-three million years ago, and from twenty-three to five million years ago – so the Doctor presumably means they're at twenty-three million BC, give or take. (Which would mean that when he says "give or take the odd million [years]", he actually means about "seventeen million [years]", but let's move on.)

Then the Doctor confirms, on the grounds that he's spotted some maple and oak trees, that they're in the Miocene [period], and that "It'll be another fourteen million years before man sets foot in this part of the world... in any part of the world." Calling upon the scientific consensus that man walked the Earth some four to six million years ago, it would further suggest the Doctor thinks they're somewhere between eighteen to twenty million BC.

Once the travellers meet Chairman Babs and her people, however, all discussion that they might be in Earth's past vanishes. At no point are Babs' people treated as aliens who have colonised Earth in defiance of established history – or, alternatively, breed in such a way as to become humanity's ancestors. They're decisively identified as human, have technology that has eliminated general need, and possess a drug that extends human longevity by two centuries (much more effectively, then, than even the life-extending

Euphemia – had gained the power to open the Ringpull. Marvelle attempted to sacrifice Kelly and Euphemia, an act that would have opened the Ringpull and enabled the current Scarlet Empress to plunder the Obverse's riches and wonders. Euphemia smashed her own jar, killing herself, to prevent this. The act severed the line of Empresses from its beginning, guaranteeing that the Ringpull would remain shut forever. Afterward, Iris took all of her friends – including Fenster, a Hysperon dragon – to a parallel universe, 2011, to attend IrisCon.

By this point, the poodles of Dogworld knew Iris as "the Evil One in the Wonderbra and Sensible Shoes".

A Possible Death of Iris Wildthyme

? 3,000,000 - IRIS S5: HIGH SPIRITS[2219] -> The Garden in the Clouds was one of the most tranquil places in the galaxy: a shining disc above a planet in the Montague Quadrant. Iris Wildthyme died there, and her spirit became a ghost known as the Grey Lady. The Grey Lady's cross-temporal nature drew other spirits to the Garden, and it became renowned as the most haunted place in the Nine Systems.

A century later, Iris' past self and Captain Turner arrived to find the Garden had gone to ruin. Iris helped to realign her ghostly self, enabling the other spirits to depart. The Grey Lady remained as the only ghost in the Garden.

The Regime of Chairman Babs

PRISON IN SPACE[2220] -> Life on Earth prospered as machines were engineered to provide for humanity's heat, light and food. Some people lived in a futuristic city that looked down upon the clouds, and had art-deco skyscrapers. The world's overpopulation had been exacerbated by the advent of a drug that extended the average lifespan by

two hundred years.

These developments gave rise to the regime of Chairman Babs. She brought about the World Federation of Womanhood and judged that men had become superfluous. Males were stripped of their right to vote, and treated as inferiors. Babs and the Federation Council outlawed war and capital punishment, but anti-social enemies of the state were launched in capsules to the Outer Space Corrective Establishment (OSCE): an octagonal satellite constructed more than a century ago. The most heinous crime cited in the Constitution of these United Female States was publicly insulting Chairman Babs. Her enforcers, all women, wore tight-fitting, black rubber uniforms. Paris, New York and Tokyo were provinces in Babs' government.

The second Doctor, Jamie and Zoe arrived on what was, in local time, the 14th of Aphrodite in the year 122 SCB (meaning Since Chairman Babs, denoting the time since her birth). The Doctor and Jamie were sent to the OSCE while Zoe underwent mental rehabilitation in Babs' Silver Maiden machine. Jamie's familiarity with kilts made him the logical candidate to crudely dress as a woman and attempt an escape; before long, he and the Doctor had started a revolt on the OSCE. Their actions gave the ruling Council the courage to depose Babs. A time of gender equality came about, with Sister Nora as Chairman. Jamie broke Zoe's mental conditioning by spanking her.

Chairman Babs, now just "Sister Babs", fancied the Doctor as the manliest man she had ever met. The Doctor fended off her advances, and escaped with his friends in the TARDIS.

One Dalek survived for "four thousand centuries", but was transported back to Skaro's past by Bernice Summerfield, and made to confront its younger self.[2221]

Spectrox from *The Caves of Androzani*). By any measure, then, Babs' regime must exist in the future – the *far* future, even.

Earth and its environs (Paris, New York, Tokyo, Mars, Jupiter) are named so often, we probably have to accept (however reluctantly) that Chairman Babs' regime *did* rule Earth for more than a century. Certainly, the Doctor seems certain when he tells his companions that they've arrived at, "Terra, with a capital T. What you call the British Isles, Jamie." (Then again, this is the same man who misidentifies the era by at least twenty million years.) Funnily enough, the presence of oak trees – while a fairly terrible means of determining the year – supports the notion that this is humanity's birthplace, per *The Android Invasion* establishing that oak trees being exclusive to Earth. At one point it's commented that Zoe, "comes from a different world, a different cul-

ture" – but while it's tempting to wish otherwise, this should, in the face of all the other evidence, be interpreted that she's from "a different time period".

Attempts were made to place *Prison in Space* in the pre-solar flare era, but it's too difficult to find a century where Babs' regime could have taken place without massively contradicting other stories, or at least being unavoidably referenced in them. The best option, then, is probably to set *Prison in Space* in the *very* far future, when humankind's technology is greatly advanced, and the continued abandonment and restoration of Earth might provide an opening for a comparatively weak regime to rule the planet for a time. At a guess, *Prison in Space* might come before the collapse of Earth society in *The Sun Makers* – if nothing else, it's a bit in keeping with the parody nature of the latter story.
2221 NAofBenny V1: *The Lights of Skaro*

Revolution on Pluto

c 4,000,000 - THE SUN MAKERS[2222] -> Earth's mineral wealth was finally exhausted and its people were dying. In return for their labour, the Usurians moved humankind to Mars, which they terraformed. The population was later moved to Pluto, where six megropolises were built, each with its own artificial sun. However, the fourth Doctor – who the Usurians knew had "a long history of violence and economic subversion" – and Leela started a rebellion. The Doctor imposed a growth tax and rendered the planet uneconomic.

Downfall of the Deindum

c 4,000,000 - BENNY S11: ESCAPING THE FUTURE[2223] -> The humans who fell through a time-space rift in twenty-sixth century Buenos Aires arrived on the planet Deindus, where their genetic makeup and memories co-mingled with primordial soup to create the Deindum – a race of reptilian humanoids.

(=) The Deindum made an immense technological leap during their Industrial Age, when they were contacted and aided by their future selves. This triggered their development into powerful beings who developed time travel and manifested as giant glowing heads. The hyper-evolved Deindum knew of Irving Braxiatel's efforts to hamper or eliminate them, and dispatched an android, Robyn, through time to stop him. They then sent warfleets to conquer the twentieth century – all in a bid to guarantee their creation.

Benny and Braxiatel intervened in the Deindum's Industrial Age using Braxiatel's TARDIS, and sent the younger Deindum down a wormhole to a faked civilisation they had constructed on the planet Rawlus.

2222 Dating *The Sun Makers* (15.4) - Set unspecified "millions of years in the future" according to contemporary publicity material, but this is never stated explicitly on screen. Earth has had time to regenerate its mineral wealth, which would suggest the story is set a very long way into the future. *The Programme Guide* failed to reconcile *The Sun Makers* with other stories, claiming that the Company dominated humanity only from "c.2100" to "c.2200" (first edition), or "c.2200" to "c.2300" (second edition). *The Terrestrial Index* suggested that the Earth was abandoned some centuries after the "fifty-second century", and recolonised "five thousand years" later. *The TARDIS Logs* suggested that the story was set "c.40,000", *Timelink* "25,000", *About Time* found it credible to think it was "millions of years in the future".
2223 Dating *Benny* S11: *Escaping the Future* (Benny audio #11.2) - Bev Tarrant says that the Deindum are based "four million years" in the future; as Benny and Peter have actually been there, one presumes Bev is in a pretty good position to know. *Benny* S10: *Secret Origins* says that the Deindum are from "billions" of years in the future, but this can probably be written off as misinformation spread by Robyn to hide her creators' native time. Writer Eddie Robson concurs that, "Although it says billions of years [in *Secret Origins*], for practical reasons we might say that's wrong and it's actually millions."
2224 *Benny* S11: *Escaping the Future*. It's after the Deindum's empire – before Benny and Braxiatel erase it, that is – has run its course.
2225 "Several million years" after *Benny: Present Danger:* "Excalibur of Mars".
2226 Dating *Scaredy Cat* (BF #75) - It is four million years after the previous part of the story, which roughly takes place during the time of the Earth Empire.
2227 Dating *The Criminal Code* (BF CC #4.6) - Benny says that the story takes place "far, far into my future, and a long way from human space"; the Doctor is a little more specific in saying that the terraforming technology seen here is "a good few million years at least" in advance of her time. The terraforming tech is clearly of human manufacture, but there's nothing to say that it was developed on Earth itself. The technology seen here appears unrelated to that of *The Sorcerer's Apprentice*, although both involve nanobots/nanites that obey spoken command and create "magical" effects through transference of matter and energy.
2228 Dating "4-Dimensional Vistas" (*DWM* #78-83) - The time it takes to grow the crystal is specified.
2229 "Five million years" after "The World Shapers".
2230 "Five million years" after *Iris* S2: *The Panda Invasion*.
2231 "Nine million years" after *The Girl Who Died*.
2232 *Time and Relative*. No date is specified, but it's safe to presume it wasn't when the Company occupied Pluto.
2233 "Many millions of years" after *The English Way of Death* (p189).
2234 *The Ark*. Earth, and a number of races known to Earth – most notably the Daleks – achieved limited success with time travel experiments (one human scientist built a time machine in the nineteenth century, according to *The Evil of the Daleks*), but these have presumably been forgotten by now.
2235 "Several million years" after *Parasite* (p304).
2236 *River* S2: *The Eye of the Storm*
2237 *FP: Weapons Grade Snake Oil* (ch27).
2238 Dating *The Eighth Doctor – The Time War 1* (BF box set) - It's the "53rd Segment of Time", presumably using the same dating convention as *The Ark* [c 10,000,000], which occurs in the "57th Segment of Time".

The younger Deindum were tricked into thinking that their "future selves" were frauds, and the resultant conflict either weakened the Deindum's development or destroyed them in a paradox. If the Deindum existed afterwards, they never developed time travel.

Before they were erased from history, the advanced Deindum broke into Braxiatel's TARDIS, and killed both him and Bernice.

Bernice and Peter, hoping to learn of the Deindum's weaknesses, went even further into the future and saw the ruins of the Deindum's empire. The Deindum's occupation had crippled the whole galaxy.[2224]

Benny went to collect Excalibur from Mars, but found that Merlin had already retrieved it.[2225]

c 4,000,000 - SCAREDY CAT[2226] -> According to legend, the people of Caludaar almost destroyed themselves through a series of global wars, and made a pledge to never set foot on their sister world, Endaara. Several millennia passed, but an expedition to Endaara was permitted when scans detected sophisticated indigenous lifeforms there. Professor Arken, a noted Caludaar scientist, used lambda radiation to experiment on the monkey-like natives, hoping to identify the part of the brain that facilitated evil. Arken hoped his research would facilitate a means of blocking evil impulses, ending war and violence.

The eighth Doctor, Charley and C'rizz arrived as Arken further used lambda radiation on Eunis Flood, a convicted serial killer from Caludaar. This unexpectedly forged a link between the planet's morphogenetic field and Flood, turning him into a formidable psionic. The planet's collective life force appeared in guise of the dead girl Galayana, and although Flood disintegrated her physical form, she peeled away his defences and left him with the mind of a child. Flood had similarly lobotomised Arken, but Endaara was now left to develop naturally.

c 4,500,000 - THE CRIMINAL CODE[2227] -> Humanity developed a new method of terraforming: a quasi-organic, asexually reproducing machine that would generate massive amounts of nanobots. Such nanobots could transform entire worlds, and interface with a user's synapses to respond to verbal commands. They could erect force fields, direct lightning strikes and create earthquakes.

An nine-member terraforming team got lost in a wormhole, and emerged a long way from human space. They terraformed a local world, but a disease killed all but one of them. The survivor was alone for forty years, and the machine created smoke creatures based upon the darker recesses of his mind. After the survivor's death, the creatures spurred evolution of the Shanquis – a race of pale blue humanoids, whose bodies they could inhabit. The Shanquis developed an advanced society, but the smoke-creatures possessed their political leaders and were deeply xenophobic. English became a forbidden language, as the smoke-creatures feared someone uttering commands that would terminate their existence.

Tensions increased between the Shanquis and the neighbouring planet of Esoria, and so the Doge of Micene – a cosmopolitan planet – asked the seventh Doctor to serve as an arbiter. The Doctor and Benny extracted the smoke-creatures from the Shanquis rulers, who petitioned for peace.

5,000,000 - "4-Dimensional Vistas"[2228] -> In the twentieth century, the Monk and the Ice Warriors seeded a giant crystal in the Arctic. Now they arrived to harvest it. They would be able to destroy continents with the sonic cannon powered by the crystal.

Two Time Lords visited the far future, and found that the Cybermen had evolved to become pure thought – the most peace-loving and advanced race in the universe.[2229]

(=) Iris visited an alternate universe "three dimensions to the left" from our reality, where flying, vampiric versions of her companion Panda decimated entire worlds.[2230]

Humanity finally achieved technology equal to that of twelfth Doctor's sonic sunglasses.[2231] The Doctor took the Cold to Pluto in the far future.[2232] Many millions of years in the future, the people of Phryxus established a technocracy in NGC4258 and developed galactic travel using warp capsules in the Grey Interchange. The renegade scientist Zodaal was jailed for experimenting on lesser life forms, and tried to escape using a warp capsule. This failed and he had to reduce himself to a gaseous state to survive. He escaped to the year 1929.[2233]

Humanity attempted time-travel experiments during the Twenty-Seventh Segment of Time, but these proved to be a total failure.[2234] Parasitic eggs laid by the Artifact were expected to hatch in the Elysium System.[2235]

The sixth Doctor, his memory wiped by River Song's lipstick, found himself on the far side of the Isop Galaxy in the Forty-Ninth Segment of Time. He backtracked his steps, and met her again in 1703.[2236]

In the late classical human period, Dr Herbert Schtucker of the University of Phobos theorised the idea of Displaced Confidence: that time-travellers became more self-assured from the act of being displaced.[2237]

lgtw - THE EIGHTH DOCTOR – THE TIME WAR 1[2238] -> Cardinal Ollistra consigned the eighth Doctor to a Time Lord boot camp on the timelocked Tranquility Base, in the 53rd Segment of Time, while she interrogated his associates: Bliss, and Quarren and Rupa Maguire. Tranquility

Base fell to a Dalek assault, but Quarren saved the Doctor and his associates by regaining his Time Lord inheritance, then deleting himself from history.

The Destruction of Earth

"Fleeing from the imminence of a catastrophic collision with the sun, a group of refugees from the *doomed* planet Earth..." [2239]

c 10,000,000 - THE ARK[2240] **->** In the Fifty-Seventh Segment of Time, ten million years hence, scientists realised that the Earth was falling towards the Sun. With the help of the Monoids, a mysterious race whose own planet had been destroyed in a supernova many years before, humanity constructed a great space vessel. It contained the entire human, Monoid, animal and plant population of the Earth in miniaturised form on microcells. Audio space research revealed that Refusis II was suitable for colonisation. It would take seven hundred years to reach the new world. To symbolise the survival of man, a vast statue of a human carved from gregarian rock was begun.

The ship set out, and the few humans and Monoid servants that remained active – the Guardians – watched the Earth's destruction. Very soon afterwards, the common cold swept through the vessel, brought by the first Doctor's companion Dodo. The Doctor cured the disease using animal membranes.

Enormous generation ships were "quite common" as humankind left Earth for the final time, during humanity's late expansion period: the great Diaspora Era. Human engineering was now at its peak – entire worlds could be terraformed to Earth conditions over several generations. The Ice Warriors had resettled on Mars prior to the Earth's death, but the Red Planet was rendered uninhabitable with the sun's expansion, and the Martians similarly migrated into space. [2241]

c 10,000,000 - FRONTIOS[2242] **->** A vast colony ship containing thousands of people, plus the technology and material capable of rebuilding the whole of human civilisation, was sent to the Veruna System on the distant edge of the universe. Despite being touted as failure-proof, every system on the colony ship failed. The ship crashed on Frontios. Most of the crew died in the crash, and many more perished from diseases that spread through the colony immediately afterwards.

Captain Revere eventually restored order. For ten years, the survivors planted and harvested crops, stocking up with food. But then meteorite bombardments began, striking the colony with such accuracy to make plain that it was being deliberately targeted. The bombardment continued for thirty years, but that wasn't the worst of it: the earth began swallowing up the dead. Over the years, the number of Retrogrades – people who deserted the colony – swelled.

And then, the earth swallowed Captain Revere while he was investigating the planet's potential mineral wealth. This left his son, Plantagenet, in command. The colony was soon in danger of falling apart.

2239 *Frontios*
2240 Dating *The Ark* (3.6) - The Commander states that this is "the Fifty-Seventh Segment" of time, which the Doctor instantly calculates to be "ten million years" after Steven and Dodo's time.
2241 *The Silent Stars Go By.* This is roughly in keeping with *The Ark*, save that such multi-generation vessels are cited as being more numerous than the TV story suggests. Also, there's no sign of the colonists in *The Ark* having terraforming technology – they target Refusis II because "only it" has conditions akin to Earth. The colonists in *Frontios* might have possessed such terraforming tech, but lost it when they crashed.
2242 Dating *Frontios* (21.3) - According to the Doctor, the story happens "on the outer limits. The TARDIS has drifted too far into the future". The inhabitants of Frontios are among the very last humans, and they have evacuated the Earth in circumstances that sound very similar to those of *The Ark.* While this would seem to dictate that *Frontios* is contemporary with *The Ark,* there is room for debate: no date is given in *Frontios,* there's no explicit link made to the earlier story, the

colony ship is of a very different design, there is no sign of the Monoids and neither story refers to other arks. It is difficult to judge the level of technology, as virtually everything is lost in the crash, but it does not seem as advanced as that of *The Ark.*
2243 *Excelis Dawns*
2244 *The Hollows of Time*
2245 Dating "The Child of Time" (*DWM* #438-441) - It's a long while after Earth was obliterated in the human-Galatean war timeline. The present-day Galateans are "the result of ten million years of robot evolution".
2246 Dating *The Silent Stars Go By* (NSA #50) - The Hereafter colonists left Earth owing to the same cataclysm as witnessed in *The Ark.* While it's unclear how long it took them to travel to Hereafter, "twenty-seven generations" (i.e. six hundred seventy-five years) have passed since they arrived. It's "winter" (p11).
2247 Dating *The Ark* (3.6) - The last two episodes of the story take place at the end of the Ark's journey, which occurs "seven hundred years" after the first two episodes.

The Tractators, insect creatures who could harness gravity, had arrived on Frontios five hundred years before and were responsible for the colony's setbacks. Under the command of their leader, the Gravis, they had pulled down the colony ship. They had given the colonists ten years to establish themselves, then began the meteorite bombardment. The Tractators had been kidnapping humans to serve as "drivers" for their tunnelling machines. The Gravis hoped to create a tunnel system that would amplify the Tractators' gravity fields and let them pilot Frontios throughout the cosmos.

The fifth Doctor, Tegan and Turlough arrived on Frontios, isolated the Gravis and transported it to the planet Kolkokron. Without their leader, the Tractators were mindless drones, and the survival of the human colony was better assured.

After delivering the Gravis to Kolkokron, the fifth Doctor made a side trip to the planet Artaris circa 1001 before returning to Frontios.[2243] Professor Stream retrieved the Gravis from Kolkokron using the Doctor's TARDIS, and returned to the twentieth century.[2244]

(=) c 10,000,000 - "The Child of Time" (DWM)[2245] **->** The time-child Chiyoko had built the Museum of Lost Opportunities in the remains of Earth – nothing more than an asteroid belt circling a dying sun – as a tribute to the human race. The synthetic Galateans had now lived so long that they had gone insane, and exterminated all other races.

Some Galateans working at the Museum – made to resemble famous persons such as the Bronte sisters, Alan Turing, Buddy Holly, John Keats and Jayne Mansfield – had gained self-awareness. The Brontes saved the eleventh Doctor and Amy with a Timescoop when Chiyoko destroyed the Earth, then sent them and the faux Turing back to avert the Galateans' creation.

The trio failed and returned. The Doctor timescooped the young women Cosette and Margaret, plus Sister Konami, from points prior to their being physically combined to create Chiyoko. This greatly weakened Chiyoko's abilities. The Doctor persuaded Chiyoko that her actions had caused universal suffering and death, and she undid her existence. The Doctor and Amy took Turing and the now-anomalous Chiyoko back to the genesis of the Galateans...

---

c 10,000,675 (winter) - THE SILENT STARS GO BY[2246] **->** A colony ship arrived on the Earth-esque planet Hereafter. Three mountain-sized Terra Firmers were established, each containing engines that, over the course of hundreds of years, would make Hereafter's environment entirely comparable to that of Earth. A thousand of Earth's most powerful and elite members hibernated within the Firmers in secret, intending to emerge once the settlers had performed the hard labour required to shape Hereafter to human norm.

Twenty-seven generations later, Hereafter's three settlements – Aside, Beside and Seeside – had a total population of around nineteen thousand. An Ice Warrior migration fleet with members of the Tanssor clan of the Ixon Mons family from Old Mars entered the quadrant, and judged Hereafter as the most viable colony world. Seven years passed as the Martians attempted to alter the Terra Firmers with their seed technology, hoping to change Hereafter's environment to Martian norm. When the Firmers' defence mechanisms prevailed, the Martians directly altered the machinery. Three years passed, with the winters becoming increasingly harsher.

The Terra Firmers converted some of the sleeping elite into powerful transhumans to attack the Warriors. The eleventh Doctor, Amy and Rory defused hostilities, and sent the transhumans back to sleep. The Doctor convinced the Martian warlord Ixyldir that it would be honourable to leave Hereafter to the human settlers, and left the settlers to decide when, if ever, they should awaken the sleepers.

At the Doctor's direction, the Ice Warrior fleet relocated Mars-like world Atrox 881, located eight light years from Hereafter.

c 10,000,700 - THE ARK[2247] **->** The fever that had swept through the Ark had never fully abated, and it had weakened the humans. Seven hundred years after leaving the solar system, the Monoids had seized control of the ship, and the statue commemorating the voyage was now of a Monoid. The humans now called the ship "the Ark" after an old Earth legend, but the Monoids kept the Guardians' descendants in check with heat prods.

The TARDIS again brought the first Doctor, Steven and Dodo to the Ark as it arrived at Refusis II and Launcher 14 was sent to the surface. At first there was no sign of life, but it quickly transpired that the native Refusians were invisible giants. Nevertheless, the Monoid leader, named 1, planned to take his race's microcells to the planet. He also intended to destroy the Ark with a bomb planted in the head of the statue, but the Refusians helped to throw the statue overboard, allowing it to explode harmlessly in space. The Refusians allowed the humans and Monoids to live on their world, but only if they promised to live in peace.

Atrox 881 became a quadrant capital to the fiefworlds of the Ixon Mons dynasty. The Doctor arrived on Atrox 881 nine thousand years after the Martians settled there, but – in his personal timeline – before he had aided them in doing so. Azylax, the warlord of the Tanssor, bestowed upon the Doctor the honourary title of *Belot'ssar*, meaning "cold blue star", in recognition of his friendship.[2248]

Thus, humanity survived the destruction of its homeworld by travelling across the universe and rebuilding human civilisation on distant planets. What happened in the untold billions of years after that was a mystery – any TARDIS attempting to travel further into the future than this exceeded its time parameters, and the Time Lords themselves were unaware of anything beyond this time. "Knowledge has its limits; ours reaches this far and no further".[2249]

> "The demise of Earth was followed by a period in which there was, effectively, no such thing as the human species; a period in which humanity suddenly found itself released from its heritage, with genetic manipulation and vast tracts of space separating the survivors from everything they'd once been. Many 'posthuman' societies inevitably became glorious, grotesque Princedoms, and none more so than those of the Blood Coteries, who – like the Medici and Borgia families of antiquity – commissioned the greatest art and culture of their age even as they conducted unimaginable vendettas and poisoned their potential rivals..."[2250]

wih - The family of Demetra Kein of the Blood Coteries was one of the greatest patrons of opera in the posthuman Renaissance. Shuncuker of Faction Paradox invaded the family's home and crippled their 1000-year-old empire, motivating the Blood Coteries to render their agents impervious to the Faction's shadow weapons.[2251]

Some inhabitants in the posthuman city of Civitas Solis sensed a temporal ripple related to Isaac Newton – an anomaly that could potentially undo their existence. They channelled themselves back to the seventeenth century, and manipulated the life of Nathaniel Silver to better guarantee their survival.[2252]

Compassion and UniMac Initiate the City of the Saved

wih - The War in Heaven became such that the final generation living in the posthuman era foresaw the impending demise of humanity, and built the Universal Machine (UniMac) as a conceptual device that personified the whole of human technology. Mesh Cos, the last documented person of human descent, raided the Homeworld of the Great Houses to acquire the technology for the UniMac – House Mirraflex responded with an attack that eliminated the last of humanity. The UniMac communicated through time with other forms of machine life. It made contact with the living timeship Compassion – together, they became the Secret Architects who created the City of the Saved, with Compassion's body forming the City's environs.[2253] Manufacture of the City of the Saved took millennia.[2254]

2248 *The Silent Stars Go By*

2249 In *Frontios*, a message flashes up on a TARDIS console screen: "Boundary Error – Time Parameters Exceeded". Likewise, in *The Sun Makers*, the Doctor is worried that the TARDIS might have "gone right through the time spiral". This limitation doesn't seem to affect the TARDIS in *The Ark* or *The Savages*, or the New Adventures story *Timewyrm: Apocalypse*, which is also set in the distant future. The words quoted are those of the Doctor in *Frontios*. The novelisation of that story makes it clear that "ours" refers to the Time Lords, and that the story is set at the "edge of the Gallifreyan noosphere". It may – or may not – be significant that the Time Lords are unable to travel beyond the time of Earth's destruction.

It is perhaps also significant that in stories set after the destruction of Gallifrey, such as *Father Time*, *Hope*, *Sometime Never*, *The End of the World* and *Utopia*, the Doctor is capable of travelling much further into the future (although he also seems quite capable of doing so in other stories set before Gallifrey's destruction, such as *Timewyrm: Apocalypse* and *The One Doctor*).

2250 The back cover copy from *FP: Movers*, building on *FP: The Book of the War*. The "supernova" in question would seem to be the one from *The Ark*, rather than the one from *The End of the World*.

2251 *FP: Movers*. Date unknown, but the blurb (in accordance with *FP: The Book of the War*) establishes that the posthumanity era follows Earth's final demise.

2252 *FP: Newtons Sleep*

2253 *FP: Of the City of the Saved*

2254 *City: Furthest Tales of the City*: "Salvation"

2255 Dating *Infinite Requiem* (NA #36) - Events at the Pridka Dream Centre occur "Beyond Common Era of Earth Calendar" (p83), millennia after the destruction of Earth, and the presence of Morestrans and Monoids emphasises that this is the far future. This date is arbitrary.

2256 Dating *TimeH: Peculiar Lives* (*TimeH* #7) - The era isn't named, but this strain of humanity is so advanced that one of their number, Sanfiel, has lived for "tens of millennia" purely on the basis of his genetics.

2257 *FP: The Brakespeare Voyage* (ch13). That is plausible, given the dating of *The Ark* and related stories to circa "ten million" based on the first Doctor's estimate, and that he's not the most trustworthy of individuals on such details.

2258 *Evolution* (p40).

2259 Dating *Heaven Sent* (X9.11) - It's "twenty million years" into the future.

? 10,000,000 - INFINITE REQUIEM[2255] **->** Far in the future, representatives of over seven hundred cultures – including the Monoids, Morestrans, Rakkhins and Rills – used the Pridka Dream Centre. The Pridka were a race of blue-skinned, crested telepaths, and the Centre used their healing skills. At any one time, fifteen thousand individuals would be booked into the Centre, making it a tempting resource for the Sensopaths, a psychic communal mind intent on dominating the physical world.

The malicious Sensopath Shanstra attempted to absorb the Sensopath Jirenal. The benevolent Sensopath Kelzen intervened, and all three of them died.

(=) ? - TIMEH: PECULIAR LIVES[2256] **->** Evolved members of humanity tried to facilitate their creation through the rise and fall of *homo peculiar* – but failed, and were erased from history.

Many post-human historians dated the death of Earth to 12 million AD.[2257] The Doctor estimated that dogs would evolve thumbs in around twenty million years time.[2258]

c 20,000,000 - HEAVEN SENT[2259] **->** Within his confession dial, the twelfth Doctor chipped away at the azbantium wall as the universe lived on...

c 23,000,000 - THE PILOT[2260] **->** To test the Puddle's time-travel prowess, the twelfth Doctor, Bill and Nardole visited an uninhabited world twenty-three million years into the future. It found them, so they fled into the past...

c 52,000,000 - HEAVEN SENT[2261] **->** Within his confession dial, the twelfth Doctor chipped away at the azbantium wall as the universe lived on...

Titan experienced a proper Spring.[2262]

The Fifty-Eighth Segment of Time - THE WELL-MANNERED WAR[2263] **->** In the Fifty-Eighth Segment of Time, human refugees colonised the planet Metralubit. There was peace for two thousand years, but then a planet-wide war suddenly wiped out two-thirds of the population. This had been engineered by the Hive, an evolved gestalt of flies that fed on dead bodies. There were four more such wars at roughly two-thousand-year intervals. The Helducc civilisation emerged from the sixth war, but also fell to conflict. A new civilisation rose and developed the Femdroids, led by Galatea, to increase male efficiency.

The Black Guardian brought a Chelonian squad from the distant past in a timestorm. The Chelonians claimed the planet Barclow, close to Metralubit, and the two races fought a short war until the Bechet Treaty was signed. Galatea learned the secret of the devastating world wars, evacuated most of the Femdroids to Regus V and plotted to lure the Hive back.

The fourth Doctor, the second Romana and K9 found that the Black Guardian was trying to trick the Doctor into releasing the Hive in the twenty-sixth century, which would destroy humanity. The Doctor defeated the Guardian by removing himself and Romana from time and space altogether.

This was the end of the Humanian Era.[2264] The Navarino civilisation was the only one to survive the war on its home planet – their culture was based on frivolity, and they were having too good a time to join in the conflict. The Navarinos had time tourism, but paid exorbitant taxes to the Time Lords for the privilege.[2265] Iris Wildthyme unwisely let a Chimeron boy in a leathers tinker with her bus' tailpipe, upsetting its dimensional exhaust.[2266]

2260 Dating *The Pilot* (X10.1) - The Doctor says they've arrived "twenty-three million years in the future".
2261 Dating *Heaven Sent* (X9.11) - It's "fifty two million years" into the future.
2262 "Sixty million years" after "The Soul Garden".
2263 Dating *The Well-Mannered War* (MA #33) - This is "right at the end of the Humanian era, after the destruction of Earth" (p25) and "the fifty-eighth segment of time".
2264 *The Well-Mannered War*
ERAS: The Humanian Era was first mentioned in *Doctor Who - The Movie*, which also referred to the Rassilon Era. The TARDIS console prop for that story also included references to the Peon, Manussan, Sumaron, Kraaiian and Sensorian eras. *Zagreus* adds the Morestran Era to the list.
The Humanian Era includes Earth in 1999, and is presumably a reference to the human race. *The Well-Mannered War* implies that it's simply the Era when humans exist. The Rassilon Era applies to Gallifrey (the "present" for the Doctor would seem to be 5725.2 in the Rassilon Era, according to the TV movie). *Neverland* specifies that the period around the Federation and Mavic Chen was the Sensorian. The Manussan and Morestran eras are presumably references to the planets from *Snakedance* and *Planet of Evil* respectively. Taking all this at face value, it would seem that eras can overlap each other – the Sensorian and Morestran eras, at least, fall comfortably within the Humanian Era.
2265 *Return of the Living Dad*, tying in with the date for *Delta and the Bannermen*.
2266 *Benny: Many Happy Returns*

? - DELTA AND THE BANNERMEN[2267] -> The Bannermen invaded the Chimeron homeworld, but the Chimeron Queen escaped to Tollport G715. She joined the seventh Doctor, Mel and a party of Navarinos on a Nostalgia Trips tour to America in the 1950s. Nostalgia Trips were notorious following an incident with the Glass Eaters of Traal, and true to form, their Hellstrom II cruiser wound up at a holiday camp in Wales by mistake. The Bannermen pursued them back in time.

Six weeks into a war between two colonies in Cassiopeia, a time traveller was brought before Uglosi, a high-ranking prosecutor, on vagrancy charges. The traveller told Uglosi that in three months, General Verdigast would travel to Corinth Minor – a planet with volcanoes that showered gemstones, and so had become a popular holiday destination for the rich and famous – and broker a peace treaty with the rival colony. This would create the Corinth Compact: an empire that would be "an unstoppable blight on the region". A rival general, Morella Wendigo, concurred with Uglosi that this must be averted, and killed the treaty-makers with a bacteriological weapon that ravaged Corinth Minor's troposphere. This stratagem bankrupted both armies, ending the war. Faced with the prospect of a flesh-eating plague in such a densely populated area, the authorities appealed to the Time Lords – who passed Corinth Minor through a cloud of super-violet radiation, sterilising it.

Corinth Minor was renamed Nevermore to symbolically denote the folly of war (not that many in Cassiopeia heeded this). A war crimes tribunal sentenced Wendigo to exile on Nevermore, and Uglosi – being obsessed with the works of Edgar Allan Poe – both designed her prison and equipped it with robot ravens.[2268]

? - NEVERMORE[2269] -> The Time Lords directed the eighth Doctor and Tamsin Drew to the planet Nevermore, where the Doctor pardoned and released General Morella Wendigo. In doing so, he curtailed the lethal mutant shadows who had sprung into being after the holocaust on Corinth Minor, and were now using Wendigo as a host.

The Master stole a force field from a Farquazi Time Cruiser during the 300th Segment of Time.[2270]

The Vulgar End of Time

THE ONE DOCTOR[2271] -> In the far future, everything had been discovered, everything had been done and technology made everything possible and affordable. It was therefore very boring.

A company on Generios VIII had thrived by exporting furniture, but the company's Assembler robots had wiped out the thirty-million-year-old population thousands of years ago. The Rim World of Abydos had no interesting features whatsoever, and Zynglat 3 boasted a sensory deprivation device. The Skardu-Rosbrix Wars were recent history. The super-computer Mentos spent thirty-three thousand years playing *Super Brain* against a holographic Questioner, even when warfare destroyed all other civilisation on Generios XIV.

The Doctor was famous in this era for his heroism, and the con man Banto Zame (a native of Osphogus, a planet that was terraformed five thousand years before) impersonated the Doctor to stage "defeats" of alien invasions, then collect rewards from grateful rulers. Banto tried his scheme on Generios I, but a genuine alien spaceship arrived and demanded the Generios System's three greatest treasures as tribute.

The sixth Doctor, Mel and Banto banded together to collect the Mentos super-computer from Generios XIV,

---

2267 Dating *Delta and the Bannermen* (24.3) - An entirely arbitrary date. However, Nostalgia Trips is notorious throughout the "five galaxies", suggesting that the story is set in a far future period of intergalactic travel. In *Dragonfire*, Svartos serves "the twelve galaxies", so perhaps it is set later than this story. While only the Daleks had broken the time barrier by 4000 AD (*The Daleks' Master Plan*), the human ship in *Planet of the Spiders* and the Movellan ship in *Destiny of the Daleks* have "time warp capability", and we see a couple of races developing rudimentary time travel around now (Magnus Greel in 5000 AD, the Metebelis Spiders a little later). Such secrets are limited, and are lost by the time of *The Ark*. Murray, the bus driver, says "the 1950s nights back on Navaro were never like this", which implies nostalgia parties rather than that he lived through the 1950s himself. *The Terrestrial Index* set this story

"c.15,000", *Timelink* went for "????" (sic), *About Time* broadly dated it to "the future, possibly the *far* future".
2268 "Twenty years" before *Nevermore*.
2269 Dating *Nevermore* (BF BBC7 #4.3) - The works of Poe have readily survived, to such an extent that Uglosi and company can correctly recite them. It's possible this story occurs in the *far* future, as the Doctor upon leaving sets the coordinates for "The Humanian Era" – then again, that doesn't automatically rule out *Nevermore* taking place there as well. It should also be noted that authorities in Cassiopeia have contact with the Time Lords, which also suggests a later placement. Even so, this dating represents a guess.
2270 *The Quantum Archangel*
2271 Dating *The One Doctor* (BF #27) - The Doctor expounds on the subject of the Vulgar End of Time at the beginning of the story.

furniture Unit ZX419 from Generios VIII, and the largest diamond in existence on Generios XV. The Cylinder accepted the tribute as proof of the Doctor's identity, but mistook Banto for the genuine Time Lord. The Cylinder spirited Banto away to face retribution for a past offence the Doctor had committed against the Cylinder's masters.

(? The Vulgar End of Time) - OMEGA[2272] **->** The legend of Omega had become widely known. Jolly Chronolidays set up a heritage centre in the Sector of Forgotten Souls, where it was believed Omega had detonated a star on behalf of the Time Lords. The centre was modelled on Omega's ship, the *Eurydice*.

Omega himself arrived in this time zone and met Sentia, a telepath who became enamoured of him. However, Omega's failed attempt to merge with the fifth Doctor in Amsterdam, 1983, had left him with a copy of the Doctor's memories and a split persona. Omega's mental health deteriorated, and Sentia conspired to return Omega to his anti-matter universe aboard the real *Eurydice*, which was within a dimensional anomaly. Sentia was killed and Omega was yet again cast – along with the *Eurydice* – over the event horizon of a black hole.

Two agents of Gallifrey's Celestial Preservation Agency – Maven and the living TARDIS Glinda – arrived to preserve the Doctor's reputation by keeping secret his eradication of the Scintillan race. They offered Daland, an actor, a job in a Gallifreyan museum.

(? The Vulgar End of Time) - 100: "My Own Private Wolfgang"[2273] **->** Time-travel had become remarkably economic, and cloning technology was child's play. An enterprising company went back in time and harvested Mozart's DNA, then marketed a cloned Mozart (including a deluxe child edition). Around eight hundred thousand Mozarts were sold and served in their households as per-

formers, cleaners and even baby-sitters. Each came with a lifetime guarantee, and a self-regenerating fluid that extended their lifespans.

> (=) The clones were treated as a lesser class, and many were made homeless. Such was their plight that one clone went back in time, hoping to weaken Mozart's reputation enough to eliminate demand for the clones, retroactively averting their creation. However, the subsequent downslide of Mozart's career made the clones' owners treat them with even less regard.

The clone who had saved Mozart's life returned to this era with Evelyn – who convinced him that they must travel back to Mozart's deathbed and restore history. Due to their actions, Mozart's reputation became such that his clones were custom-made rather than mass produced, and were actually prized by their owners.

(? The Vulgar End of Time) - THE ELEVENTH DOCTOR YEAR THREE[2274] **->** As part of the British Intergalactic Empire, human colonists founded Britzit-247 based upon their mutual propensity for being very cross all the time. The eleventh Doctor and Alice eluded a horde of gray-haired men screaming "Britzit!", and escaped in their monster truck, Bessie 2, with the only copy of John Jones' final album, *Whitestar*.

The year 500,000,000 was the most peaceful in human history. The people there were unaware of war or the Daleks.[2275] The computer that ruled the Andromeda Galaxy, The One, determined that the galaxy was doomed to enter a "region of Nothingness". It constructed a vast armada of artificial planets and set off towards the Milky Way, planning galactic conquest. It drew up the Diagrams,

---

2272 Dating *Omega* (BF #47) - The dating is arbitrary, but much about this story resembles the Vulgar End of Time: time travel is now deemed unfashionable rather than unattainable; the exploits of the Doctor, Omega and – generally speaking – the Time Lords are widely renowned, if somewhat erroneously; and the period is one of prosperity, leisure and dullness. The Doctor is said to have accidentally wiped out the thought-based Scintillans while combating space pirates who used telepathically-controlled weapons and ships, but a proper dating for this isn't given.

2273 Dating *100: "My Own Private Wolfgang"* (BF #100b) - This is vaguely said to happen "thousands upon thousands" of years in the future, but it surely must be many magnitudes further along than that – partly because cloning is being used as a consumer gimmick, but mostly because time-travel is now so

cheap that even a Mozart-clone fired from his job as a butler can save up enough for a trip. It's something of a guess, but the overall crassness, decadence and hedonism of this society – plus the fact that the Time Lords haven't curtailed the commonplace availability of time travel – very much suggests the Vulgar End of Time.

2274 Dating *The Eleventh Doctor Year Three* (Titan 11th Doc #3.1, "Remembrance") - Your guess is as good as ours. Without more to go on, we've opted for the Vulgar End of Time.

2275 *I am a Dalek*

a complete map of the Milky Way.[2276]

The Ancestral Earth Museum's director released pages found within the Black Vault (at the bottom of a deep crevice in Earth's Great Northern Desert), which detailed Vilhelm Schadengeist's failed bid to take over Earth.[2277]

c 950,000,000 - HEAVEN SENT[2278] **->** Within his confession dial, the twelfth Doctor chipped away at the azbantium wall as the universe lived on...

c 1,000,000,000 - DOCTOR WHO AND THE INVASION FROM SPACE[2279] **->** The first Doctor and his new companions, the Mortimer family, arrived on an artificial planet bathed in the light of the great spiral galaxy of Andromeda. They were met by the Aalas, blond giants who took them to The One: the entity that ruled their planet and had once ruled the entire Andromeda Galaxy for millions of years. Andromeda faced destruction and was running low on resources, so The One built an armada of almost a million artificial planets and set out on a

four hundred million year journey to the Milky Way. It was now a hundred million years into that mission.

The One realised that its aims would be achieved far more efficiently if it had the TARDIS' secrets. The Doctor refused, but the Andromedans prevented the TARDIS from leaving. The One was destroyed when Ida rebelled, throwing a food plate into a vital component. The Doctor and the Mortimers left the armada drifting aimlessly in space.

The Downfall of Capitalism

? 1,000,000,017 - OXYGEN[2280] **->** A blue-skinned race with yellow eyes faced discrimination in this era. A myth talked about a legendary group: the Union.

Mining Station Chasm Forge was established to procure copper ore. The crew relied upon Ganymede Systems Series Twelve SmartSuits, and had to buy oxygen from Chasm Forge's corporate owners. When the mine's productivity dipped, the algorithm deemed the Chasm Forge crew as inefficient, ordered their

2276 "One hundred million years" before *Doctor Who and the Invasion from Space*.

2277 *Leth-St: The Showstoppers*, "approximately 700,650,380" years after the UNIT Era.

2278 Dating *Heaven Sent* (X9.11) - It's "nearly a billion years" into the future.

2279 Dating *Doctor Who and the Invasion from Space* (World Distributors illustrated novella) - No date is given, but humans are legendary to the people of Andromeda, and seem to be the ancestors of the Andromedans ("the humans of the worlds of Andromeda were the patterns"). That galaxy faces (in the long term, at least) extinction.

Using information from other stories, we know from *The Ark in Space* that humanity first arrived in Andromeda after the Solar Flares, and that the events of *The Mysterious Planet*, set two million years in the future, involved Andromedans. The story is set, then, at some point in the distant future. As Glitz comes from Andromeda, the galaxy is clearly not dominated by The One at that time. Yet it's an interesting coincidence that the enclosed society set up by the Andromedans on "Ravolox" – with an obedient population controlled by an artificial intelligence – is very similar (albeit on an infinitely smaller and less advanced scale) to the Andromedan civilisation seen in *Doctor Who and the Invasion from Space*. It's also notable that they steal a copy of the Matrix in that story, and the Matrix contains the memories of all the Time Lords in the same way The One contains all the memories of the Andromedans.

On TV, there is no gap in which the first Doctor travelled without companions, although he did so in the *Doctor Who Annuals* in the sixties. This might suggest that this story takes place before the TV series starts – but the TARDIS is a police box, so this isn't the case – yet

there's no mention of Susan, and the Doctor has no control over the TARDIS navigation. An alternative is that couple of the novelisations (*The Massacre* and *The Five Doctors*) took a cue from the first Doctor's appearance in *The Three Doctors* to claim that he had a period of semi-retirement and reflection before his regeneration, spent in a beautiful garden. While it is unlikely that the Doctor dropped off a companion, retrieving them later, *The Two Doctors* seems to demonstrate that even as early as his second incarnation, the Doctor was able to drop Victoria off and expect to meet her later (and non-TV stories either suggest or state that he's routinely done that since at least his fifth incarnation).

2280 Dating *Oxygen* (X10.5) - A strange case, with a few X-factors.

The first tangible dating clue is that Nardole recognises Chasm Forge's AI, Velma, as an old flame. Presuming it's the *same* AI (and not a case of Nardole just being cheeky, or there being two AIs with identical voices), that would place *Oxygen* near *The Husbands of River Song* – if indeed that's Nardole's home era (see the Nardole sidebar). Actually, as Velma only here adopts that same name, *Oxygen* would need (if it's really his future girlfriend) to take place a bit in advance of *Husbands*. Supporting that, Nardole isn't aware that *Oxygen* marks the start of capitalism's downfall... surely not something he'd forget if he'd lived through it.

The other big piece of evidence, however, is the Doctor's off-handed (and possibly erroneous) claim that *Oxygen* sparks the flame that forevermore toasts capitalism as an economic model with humanity. It's a little (pardon the phrasing) rich to hear, as he apparently doesn't give any help to the only survivors – Abby and Ivan – who look distinctly unlike the sort of people capable of starting a successful rebellion, or having the

SmartSuits to terminate their organic components and dispatched replacements. The twelfth Doctor, traveling with Bill and Nardole, slaved the life signs of those present to Chasm Forge's reactors. The algorithm relented from killing them, afraid to deal its corporate masters their biggest financial loss.

Two survivors of this incident, Abby and Ivan, vowed to complain directly to Chasm Forge's home office. The Doctor recollected that six months later, a rebellion would end both the corporate dominance of space and capitalism as an economic model... whereupon humanity would find a "whole new mistake".

By removing his helmet to save Bill during a spacewalk, the Doctor was rendered blind.

The planet on which Dethras' test-subjects had settled was discovered. The question of how such advanced life could exist there became one of the Great Mysteries of the Universe, even though it was the fourth Doctor and the second Romana's fault.[2281]

c 1,250,000,000 - HEAVEN SENT[2282] -> Within his confession dial, the twelfth Doctor chipped away at the azbantium wall as the universe lived on...

c 2,000,000,000 - HEAVEN SENT[2283] -> Within his confession dial, the twelfth Doctor chipped away at the azbantium wall as the universe lived on...

The twelfth Doctor and Courtney Woods left a powered-down Skovox Blitzer adrift in space, within sight of the Olveron Cluster containing "a million stars, a hundred million inhabited planets".[2284]

The End of Time

"A distant point of time, an age of great advancement, peace and prosperity".[2285]

> (=) If history had run differently, and Gallifrey had been destroyed at the time of Rassilon, the first time travellers would have evolved a billion years from now. These would have been the Ferutu. They intervened to optimise history, so that the Daleks and CyberHost were both forces for good in a utopian universe. The Doctor tricked the Ferutu into preventing their creation to save our timeline.[2286]

Two billion years in the future, the Time Lord Solenti observed how the Dagusan sun ended its lifespan as a main sequence star. The planet's seas consequently evaporated, even as the remaining population retreated to the South Pole.[2287]

---

resources or contacts needed for such a thing. At best, economic conditions are already such that the sudden disclosure of a corporation maximizing profits by killing under-performing workers proves so radioactive, there's no turning back from it.

Trying to triangulate *when* capitalism fails within *Doctor Who*, however, is something of a mug's game – humanity gets so widespread and diverse in the future, it's challenging to pick a point that it uniformly and completely washes its hands of capitalism, even if a large sector of it collapses utterly. You'd also have to decide that on a number of times when we seem to be dealing with a capitalist system, it actually has non-capitalist underpinnings or is outside humanity's purview. Nonetheless, it's a fairly extensive list to rationalise away, as capitalism seems alive and well in – to name the big examples – the Mazuma Era [starting c.8162], the Terraphile Era [c.41,000 to at least 51,000], Glitz's Time [c.2,000,000 onward], definitely *The Sun Makers* [c.4,000,000; Usurians pulled the strings, but with human workers on Pluto], the Vulgar End of Time [the *far* future] and probably also the New Earth era [5,000,000,000 onward; Cassandra's scheme in *The End of the World* relies upon her investing in certain companies, then slaughtering their rivals]. The line beyond which there's no capitalism doesn't even match with

the slightly later portion of *The Husbands of River Song* aboard the opulent *Harmony & Redemption*.

The placement of *Oxygen*, then, heavily depends on how much stock to place in what the Doctor says, or what Nardole says. With some twitchiness, the authors of *Ahistory* have decided that Velma isn't Nardole's ex, and placed *Oxygen* in the far, *far* future (definitely after *The Sun Makers*, since that whole story entails the evils of capitalism), when we might better expect that capitalism has unilaterally run its course. While it's a pun on "trade union", the myth about the "Union" might stem from the ninetieth-century one cited in *The Crystal Bucephalus* and *Dalek Empire II*, or the Galactic Union from the Terraphile Era (*The Coming of the Terraphiles*).

2281 "A million years" after *Dethras*.

2282 Dating *Heaven Sent* (X9.11) - It's "well over a billion years" into the future.

2283 Dating *Heaven Sent* (X9.11) - It's "two billion years" into the future.

2284 *The Caretaker*, based on the Doctor's plan to deposit the Blitzer "billions of years" in the future.

2285 *The Savages*

2286 *Cold Fusion*

2287 *The Suns of Caresh*

? c 3,000,000,000 - TWICE UPON A TIME[2288] -> Rusty the Dalek had persisted in its hatred of Dalek-kind for billions of years. In the ruins of the weapon forges of Villengard (once the terror of the seven galaxies), Rusty and a network of Dalek mutants comprised the greatest database ever assembled – bigger, even, than the Matrix on Gallifrey. The twelfth Doctor, the first Doctor, Captain Archibald Lethbridge-Stewart and a Testimony-made avatar of Bill Potts used Rusty's database to ID Testimony's native time and purpose. The Doctors and Bill conceded that Archibald had to be returned to 1914, and took him there.

Three hundred thousand years before the Last of Man, the Doctor negotiated a lasting peace between the Sontarans and the Rutans. By this time, Gallifrey had long fallen. The Sontarans and Rutans undertook the largest demobilisation in the history of the universe.[2289]

SYSTEM WIPE[2290] -> Humanity had departed from its homeworld. In its absence, the surface of Earth was slated to be "flattened, processed" and rebuilt by robots. More than a century after the humans had left, five hundred factories had been positioned around the globe to this end; each contained a robot army to carry out the reconstruction. Legacy, an AI, coordinated the operation from a black pyramid in what was formerly Oklahoma.

The eleventh Doctor, Amy and Rory visited the ruins of Chicago, and helped to download the artificial personalities living in Parallife – a computer game-simulation of Earth – into robot bodies, sparing them from a fatal system wipe. The reconstruction of Earth commenced, and incorporated some building designs created by the Chief Architect of Parallife. One part of the new Chicago had steel spires, and a glass pyramid nestled between two buildings – one shaped like a square, the other a circle.

? - FORTY-FIVE: "False Gods"[2291] -> Ace and the Time Lord known as Jane Templeton arrived in Earth's far future, when the sun had become a red giant, and its radiation was blistering the surface of the planet. They retrieved Jane's TARDIS and used it to return to Thebes, 1902.

2288 Dating *Twice Upon a Time* (X10.13) - The twelfth Doctor says that Rusty (*Into the Dalek*) has endured in its Dalek-hatred for "billions of years". In *The Doctor Dances*, the ninth Doctor took credit for turning the Weapons Factories of Villengard into a banana grove; here, they're in ruins.

2289 *The Infinity Doctors*

2290 Dating *System Wipe* (BBC children's 2-in-1 #4) - The least trustworthy piece of dating evidence here, oddly enough, is the year that the Doctor names: "It's 2222 AD", he says (p12), without explaining how he's come to that conclusion. Then, when Amy asks if the devastation of Chicago "Could [owe to] solar flares? It's about the right era, isn't it?" (p13), he gives the bizarre answer of "Possibly." Even if they believe, per *The Beast Below*, that the solar flares occurred in the twenty-ninth century (and there's reason to doubt this; see the dating notes on that story), it makes no sense that the Doctor would now think that the *twenty-third* century is "about the right era" for the solar flares. It would be like saying that 1340 is "about the right era" for World War II.

To make matters worse, "over one hundred years" (pgs. 33, 95) have passed since the cataclysm that drove humanity from Earth – in conjunction with the "2222 AD" figure, this would mean that the solar flares devastated Earth in the early twenty-second century, at the infancy of Earth's venturing into space and before even the Dalek Invasion of Earth. No matter how cleverly one shuffles *Doctor Who* continuity, this is a non-starter.

The Parallife constructs have no recollection of the year or what prompted humanity to leave Earth, so the only dating evidence that remains is the nature of the reconstruction itself. Presuming for the moment that this *is* Earth (and the only thing to substantiate this claim is that Parallife is programmed as a computer copy of Earth), the story occurs when humanity has left its homeworld in the hands of five hundred robot armies, who by all accounts have the ability to level the entire planet and make it suitable for human occupation once more. Again, this is *well* beyond the time of the solar flares – if humans had such resources and technology when the solar flares struck, it's doubtful that they would have needed to resort to such desperate measures as venturing away from Sol on top of a space whale (*The Beast Below*), freezing humans aboard Nerva Beacon and hoping for the best, or leaving people behind to perish in thermic shelters (*The Ark in Space*). Rory raises this very question (p97), but never gets an answer.

Without more information to go on, the placement here is highly random, but contingent on the construction-robot armies being *far* beyond the solar flare era. The abandonment of Earth seen in *The Mysterious Planet* or *The Sun Makers* seems like reasonable guesses, but the choice made here speculates that the robot armies rebuilding Earth is part of the restoration done by the National Trust prior to *The End of the World*.

2291 Dating *Forty-Five: "False Gods"* (BF #115a) - No date is given, but it's obviously prior to Earth's destruction, when the surface is uninhabitable due to the sun's deterioration.

2292 Dating *Voyage to Venus* (BF J&L #4.5/BF DW Special Release #2) - It's after Earth has been completely exhausted, in what the blurb calls "the distant future". Jago and Litefoot's efforts explain why the third

VOYAGE TO VENUS[2292] -> Humanity had exhausted the resources of Earth, which was now a barren, airless lump of rock in space. Before the end, one group of humans migrated to Venus and built "cloud cities" above the desert-filled planet below. Enough generations passed that the settlers forgot their origins. Queen Vulpina came to rule the Venusian settlers, who viewed their males as a disposable means of reproduction. Music was unknown to their culture.

The factories that produced the settlers' food generated oxygen, increasingly making Venus' environment like that of old Earth. Six years after Venus' surface had come to resemble a tropical rain forest, some of the Cytherians' ecology caches had thawed. Vulpina's people found a number of the Cytherians' young, lemur-like creatures – which they dubbed "Thraskins" – and trained them as servants.

The sixth Doctor, Professor Litefoot and Henry Gordon Jago arrived as Vepaja – a collective intelligence forged by the Cytherians – moved to free the Thraskins and disabled the suspension devices on a sky city, bringing it crashing down. Vepaja mentally directed a herd of Shanghorns to charge the city, but Litefoot and Jago put the music-susceptible creatures to sleep with choruses of "God Rest Ye Merry, Gentleman". Vulpina was deposed, and the settlers agreed to share Venus with the sleeping Cytherians. The Thraskins were released back into the wild.

The zoologist Felina decided to change her field of study to music, and that the tune to "God Rest Ye Merry, Gentleman" would make quite a nice lullaby.

The second Doctor, with Jamie and Victoria, spent two weeks learning martial arts on Venus. Settlers from Earth and the indigenous Thraskins were living in harmony.[2293] **Venusian aikido normally required four arms.**[2294]

Gallifrey Returns to the Universe, the Doctor's Confession-Dial Ordeal Ends

HEAVEN SENT / HELL BENT[2295] ->

> "Gallifrey is currently positioned at the extreme end of the time continuum, for its own protection. We're at the end of the universe, give or take a star system."[2296]

Gallifrey had unfrozen itself following the Last Great Time War and returned to the universe. After 4.5 billion years of effort, the twelfth Doctor finally broke through the azbantium in his confession dial, and stepped out onto his homeworld. Owing to the Doctor's status as a war hero, and with the military's backing, he deposed Rassilon and the High Council. The Doctor used an extraction chamber to snatch Clara away from the moment of her death, then stole a TARDIS and went with her further ahead in time...

The Earth Empire reached Galaxy M57, and the Catkind planet New Savannah. The Catkind had no food, as their savannah could no longer sustain them. Within fifty years, with the Empire's help, the Catkind became a prosperous people that had adopted human customs. New Savannah agreed to become fully part of the Empire in the year five billion. Some factions refused and returned to the wilderness, where they starved to death.[2297]

Doctor sings a "Venusian lullaby" to the tune of "God Rest Ye Merry, Gentleman" in *The Curse of Peladon* and *The Monster of Peladon*. *Venusian Lullaby* offers an alternative scenario, with the lullaby created in pre-historic times.

2293 "Several hundred years" after *J&L: Voyage to Venus*. The first Doctor visited Venus in its distant past in *Venusian Lullaby*.

2294 *World Enough and Time*

2295 Dating *Heaven Sent* and *Hell Bent* (X9.11-X9.12) - Events rely upon the idea that Gallifrey is so near the end of time, and so few star systems now exist, that Rassilon and the High Council might find nowhere to go once the Doctor exiles them. It's a little hard to square that against the idea that it's only been "4.5 billion years" (the amount of time the Doctor is trapped in his confession dial; *Heaven Sent*) since the modern day, especially as *The End of the World/New Earth/Gridlock* all

take place circa the year five billion, and universal conditions don't seem as desperate as all that. Possibly, the Doctor *isn't* trapped the full duration of time that Gallifrey is positioned in the future, but he comes close enough for his confession dial to synch up with Gallifrey's time zone. *Whoniverse* (BBC, p309), as it happens, tosses out the "4.5 billion years" talk and puts Gallifrey in a safe haven much later than *Utopia*.

Ohila and the Sisterhood of Karn, last seen in *The Magician's Apprentice* (dated in this guidebook to "& 3612") here visit Gallifrey, but it's unclear whether they do so by virtue of time travel or their immortality. The latter, possibly, is suggested in Ohila's remark that, "At the end of everything, one must expect the company of immortals."

2296 The General, *Hell Bent*

2297 "Two hundred sixty years" before the year 4,999,999,999 component of "Agent Provocateur".

New Earth

NEW EARTH[2298] **->** Lady Cassandra was told she was beautiful at a party, but this was the last time anyone would say such a thing. She became increasingly bitter and obsessed with cosmetic surgery. The person who made the comment was actually her future self – whose mind resided in a force-grown clone named Chip – who had been brought there by the tenth Doctor and Rose. Moments later, Cassandra-Chip expired while in the arms of her younger self.

? - "The Forgotten"[2299] **->** In an alien courtroom, the sixth Doctor pleaded for Peri's life after she was accused of killing Mis'Kin Karac, a chronal scientist working on quantum flux technology, on the twelfth of Mc'Arda. It was discovered that Karac's assistant had shot him with a gun saturated in chronal energy, and then framed Peri.

4,999,999,999 (last day of year) - "Agent Provocateur"[2300] **->** The tenth Doctor and Martha went to the Milk Bar, a space station diner that the Doctor insisted served the best chocolate milkshakes in the whole universe. The Sycorax Empire was not what it once was – many of the Sycorax tribes had gone to explore space, and many of their asteroid ships never returned. The travellers encountered a Sycorax from the Tribe of Astrophia, who collected individuals who were the last of their kind, and staged hunts for beings who wished to hunt such creatures. The Sycorax had, amongst others, the last of the Ventrassians in stasis. The Doctor set the sonic screwdriver to fly the Sycorax ship to a research planet, and timed the ship's stasis chambers to open – and release the Sycorax's captives – after he and Martha left.

New Savannah, orbiting Felinus in Galaxy M57, was preparing to cede to the New Human Empire. The tenth Doctor and Martha arrived as, at the stroke of midnight, giant cat robots – the weaponry of an anti-human cult – moved into the city from the wilderness, blasting buildings. The Doctor and Martha learned that Bubastion of the Elite Pantheon was removing the populations from business worlds as a means of taking control of the galaxy, and had been manipulating the anti-human cult to his own ends. Garrard Townsend, one of the cult members, sabotaged the cat robots upon realising Bubastion's deception.

Billions of people disappeared from ten planets – including Mere, Kas and Nyrruh 4 – leaving only one survivor on each world. On Omphalos, seventeen billion people disappeared, leaving behind only Professor Tharlot. The tenth Doctor and Martha deduced that Tharlot was in league with Silas Wain, and that both had betrayed the Elite Pantheon. The ten worlds were in alignment and created a rend in space, through which an evil primal force began to emerge.

2298 Dating *New Earth* (X2.1) - The epilogue clearly occurs before *The End of the World*, but it's difficult to judge how many years before, as there's no way of knowing how long Cassandra survives as an elongated piece of skin.

2299 Dating "The Forgotten" (IDW *DW* mini-series #2) - The judge and many other inhabitants appear to be Catkind.

2300 Dating "Agent Provocateur" (IDW *DW* mini-series #1) - The date ties in with *New Earth*; New Savannah is being turned over to the Earth Empire as part of the impending year five billion, and a businessman says, "In eight hours, it'll be midnight, and we enter the year five billion." As part of this, a sign reads "Happy New Millennium." Curiously, in issue #5, the term "fifty-first century" is used to denote "five billion" – the Doctor says the technology being used "shouldn't exist on Earth outside the fifty-first century" and that he "was there recently... first on Savannah then on Omphalos", when he clearly visited those worlds in the time zone of *New Earth*. Martha makes the same mistake – even though Wain is a native of this time, she also says he's from the fifty-first century. At different points in the story, we're told that it's the psychic trauma of the people who have disappeared and the alignment of the planets that causes the Rend.

The Milk Bar sequences (from issue #1 of this mini-series) occur after the Sycorax Tribe of Astrophia died out in the forty-first century, but otherwise shy toward the undatable side of things. Even so, they fit here as well as anywhere else.

2301 Dating *The End of the World* (X1.2) - The Doctor tells Rose "this is the year 5.5/apple/26, five billion years in your future". This story seems to contradict *The Ark* (and, by implication, *Frontios*), which saw the destruction of the Earth a mere ten million years in our future, and had a different fate for humanity. The obvious inference to make is that the Earth wasn't completely destroyed in *The Ark*, and the National Trust's renovations were more extensive than the Doctor told Rose.

2302 *New Earth*

2303 *Leth-St:* "Legacies"

2304 Dating *The Twelfth Doctor Year One* (Titan 12th Doc #1.12-1.15, "The Hyperion Empire") - It's "five billion" years in the future, doubtless in line with the date of Earth's death given in *The End of the World*.

2305 The background to *Twice Upon a Time*. The year, one suspects, is an in-joke to reflect the new series being in its twelfth year.

2306 Dating *New Earth* (X2.1) - It is "twenty-three years" after *The End of the World*.

2307 "Twenty-four years" before *Gridlock*.

2308 "Twenty-three years" before *Gridlock*.

2309 "Twelve years" before *Gridlock*.

The Doctor and Martha were dematerialised and sent to 1957 to prevent their interference, but the Pantheon returned them. A massive battle was fought on the planet Kas to prevent the primal evil being from escaping. Tharlot became a victim of the sonic weapon he had captured, and the Doctor used the same gun to force the evil being back into the rend, sealing it afterwards. The populations of the planets were restored.

The Doctor told the Elite Pantheon he never wanted to see, hear or read anything about them ever again.

The Final Destruction of Earth

5,000,000,000 - THE END OF THE WORLD[2301] -> Earth was seen as the cradle of civilisation, and there was not a star in the sky that humanity hadn't touched. Humanity had evolved into new humans, protohumans, digihumans and the humanish. Many other races had evolved from Earth plants and animals.

For years, Earth was preserved by the National Trust, who reversed the process of continental drift (although by this time, Los Angeles was a crevasse and the Arctic was a desert). When the preservation money ran out, many diverse alien races, including the Trees of the Forest of Cheem (descendants of trees from Earth's tropical rainforest), the Moxx of Balhoon, the Adherents of the Repeated Meme, the Face of Boe, the Ambassadors from the City State of Blinding Light and the ninth Doctor and Rose all gathered on Platform One to witness the planet's final destruction.

The last purebred human – Cassandra, who had been reduced to a stretched-out piece of skin – plotted to engineer a hostage situation to sue the corporation that ran the Platform. Failing that, she tried to kill the assembled beings, as she had invested heavily in their rivals' companies. Cassandra's plan was defeated, and she paid for her crimes when the Doctor allowed her skin-body to dry out and burst.

Cassandra's mind survived and transferred into her back skin. She fled to New Earth with a servant named Chip, who had been force-grown from Cassandra's "favourite pattern".[2302]

The progeny of Alistair Gordon Lethbridge-Stewart and Colonel Pemberton protected Earth to its very end. In the year 5.5/apple/26, Ezekiel Spens Lethebridge-Stuart (sic) was president of the National Trust, and his wife Dorcas Lethebridge-Stuart (nee Pemburton) was a founder of New Earth.[2303]

c 5,000,000,000 - THE TWELFTH DOCTOR YEAR ONE[2304] -> The twelfth Doctor translocated the Hyperions and their fusion web to around Earth's sun as it perished. Deprived of a healthy star to plunder, the Hyperions died.

The Testimony Foundation

The Testimony Foundation was formed, on New Earth in 5,000,000,012, as a memory-extraction programme. Time technology lifted beings about-to-die from their timestreams, returning them after their memories had been duplicated. Glass avatars enabled the memory-duplicates to return to life. The Testimony archives included the memories of Bill Potts, Nardole and Clara Oswald.[2305]

5,000,000,023 - NEW EARTH[2306] -> New Earth had been established in the M87 Galaxy by people nostalgic about the loss of humanity's original homeworld. Ten million people lived in New New York (the fifteenth city to bear the name). Exotic diseases such as petrifold regression, Marconi's Disease and Palindrome Pancrosis (which killed in the space of ten minutes) were treated by the Sisters of Plenitude at their hospital on New Earth.

A green moon served as the universal symbol for "hospital". Psycho-graphs – devices capable of transferring consciousness from one being to another – were banned on every civilised planet. The goddess Santori was revered in this era.

The tenth Doctor and Rose were summoned by the Face of Boe. The Sisters were secretly experimenting on vast numbers of cloned humans to facilitate the miracle cures, but the Doctor cured the clones. The Sisters were arrested, and the clones catalogued as new humans. The Face of Boe told the Doctor they would meet one more time.

Cassandra's mind came to reside in Chip, but they were both dying. The Doctor showed Cassandra a last mercy, and took her back in time for a final meeting with herself.

Drug patches were available that created such emotional states as Happy, Anger, Forget and Sleep, but in 5,000,000,029, the introduction of Bliss patches made the population of New New York fall victim to a virus. The Senate was wiped out, as were seven million citizens. Only the Face of Boe and Novice Hane were able to resist. The power died, but the Face of Boe used his life energy to send survivors down into the Motorway, and convince them that life was normal. An automatic quarantine signal warned other planets to avoid New Earth for one hundred years.[2037]

The Cassini "sisters" (a married couple) were among the first people to join the Motorway, in 5,000,000,030.[2308] Brannigan's car joined the Motorway in 5,000,000,041.[2309] Junction Five of the Motorway closed in 5,000,000,050.[2310]

The Death of the Face of Boe

5,000,000,053 - GRIDLOCK[2311] -> The tenth Doctor and Martha found millions of cars were stuck in a permanent traffic jam in the Motorway beneath New New York. The Doctor also found a colony of crab-like Macra lurking at the bottom of the Motorway, thriving on the noxious fumes. The Face of Boe had engineered the situation to protect the populace from a plague that was now gone, so the Doctor opened up the Motorway, allowing the city to be repopulated.

Legend said the Face of Boe had lived for billions of years, but also that he was the last of his kind. He now died, but not before passing on a final message to the Doctor: "You are not alone."

& 5,000,000,063 - THE TWELFTH DOCTOR YEAR THREE[2312] -> Elite members of the Judoon, Sontarans, Catkind, Silurians, Zygons, Vinvocci and more paid a million credits each to witness the opening of the Saffshran Ziggurat: an edifice sealed for almost a millennium on New Oceana. The twelfth Doctor contained the situation when a manufactorum within generated an army of Quarks.

? 5,000,000,063 - THE TWELFTH DOCTOR YEAR THREE[2313] -> The twelfth Doctor, Bill and Nardole went shopping at the Ubermarket for various supplies, and reunited a lost Pathicol - akin to a humanoid owl - with her parents.

Compulsory quarantine on New Earth was due to be lifted in 5,000,000,129, a hundred years after it was imposed.[2314] The cure for Petrifold Regression was officially developed a thousand years after the Sisters of Plentitude discovered their own remedy.[2315] Agatha Christie was the best-selling novelist of all time. Her novel *Death in the Clouds* was still in print in the year five billion.[2316] The time loop holding Axos was expected to expire naturally in six billion years' time, long after the Milky Way had any life for Axos to threaten.[2317]

The Doctor once speculated that Earth's sun would finally become a supernova in ten thousand million years time.[2318]

wih - It was estimated that the Great Attractor would consume the Milky Way, the Magellanic Clouds, Andromeda and the Hydra-Centaurus Supercluster circa 60,000,000,000. The living timeship Compassion found that someone involved in the War in Heaven was fencing the Attractor off.

> = In some futures of Earth, the sun was artificially given more life and went supernova around the year 65 billion.[2319]

? - "Autopia"[2320] -> The tenth Doctor and Donna landed on Autopia. The inhabitants had built an automated utopia some millennia before, and used an energy shield to cut themselves off from the rest of the universe to perfect their minds. A century before, the Chronos Mission – five sentients who got through the energy shield, and hoped to invite the Autopians to rejoin the universe – had disappeared. Autopia was now a beautiful planet, full of beautiful people and tended to by robots.

Mistress Ixtalia told the Doctor and Donna that the people of Autopia had perfected all the arts and sciences,

---

2310 "Three years" before *Gridlock*.

2311 Dating *Gridlock* (X3.3) - The Doctor gives the date as "the year five billion and fifty three".

2312 Dating *The Twelfth Doctor Year Three* (Titan 12th Doc #3.1, "Beneath the Waves") – Date unknown, but the attending races and the designation "New Oceana" suggests it's the New Earth era. We've arbitrarily added ten years, to represent the real-world decade that elapsed between release of *Gridlock* and this story.

2313 Dating *The Twelfth Doctor Year Three* (Titan 12th Doc #3.9, "The Great Shopping Bill") - The beings at the Ubermarket include Catkind and tree people, suggesting the New Earth era.

2314 *Gridlock*

2315 *New Earth*

2316 *The Unicorn and the Wasp*

2317 *The Feast of Axos*

2318 *Colony in Space*. It's possible the Doctor witnessed this for himself. It doesn't contradict *The Ark*, which had Earth crashing into the Sun, not the Sun going supernova, or *The End of the World*, where the Sun merely expands enough to destroy the Earth.

2319 FP: *The Brakespeare Voyage* (ch13).

2320 Dating "Autopia" (IDW *DW* one-shot #3) - We're told, unhelpfully, that it's "somewhere, someplace, sometime". The people of Autopia are described as "human". This story has been placed in the far future.

2321 A quick summation of the Posthuman Period which follows the Earth's destruction, and was sketched out in FP: *The Book of the War*.

2322 The background to FP: *Weapons Grade Snake Oil*. The uprising against the Company on Pluto is a different conflict from the one seen in *The Sun Makers*.

2323 Dating FP: *Weapons Grade Snake Oil* (FP novel #10) - It's "billions of years in the future" (ch4).

2324 Dating *The Savages* (3.9) - At the end of *The Gunfighters*, the Doctor claims that they have now landed at "a distant point in time" (see the quote above). The Elders have the technology to track the TARDIS, but are not capable of time travel themselves. They declare themselves to be "human".

that all there was to do was contemplate what had already been discovered. She also mentioned that intruders to Autopia were put to death: the Chronos Mission had been killed, and the Doctor and Donna were to receive the same fate. Donna inspired one of the robots – an Automantron she called Sam, after a cat she once owned – to successfully lead a robot rebellion that ended human rule on Autopia. The Automantrons and humans were no longer certain of their purpose, and accepted Donna's suggestion that they live in harmony, and turn the planet into a high-end spa.

Posthumanity

Earth's destruction had effectively deracinated humankind, requiring a new *epistemology* to understand and define the human condition. The Posthuman Period saw a flourishing of diversity among Earth's descendants – the societies of this era resembled humans biologically, but an ever-increasing number of subspecies appeared, either through sudden mutation or deliberate generic modification. Several posthuman worlds had long since severed connections to other species, and didn't know that life on other worlds existed.[2321]

Having manipulated her own biodata to escape being Cousin Ceol, Sojourner Hooper was "birthed" in the Posthuman Era via a genetic printer.

A number of oligarchs ruled the Chance Coteries, whose main trade was gambling. Coruscacia De Rein's ancestors founded the most successful of these, Serendipity Keep. Five hundred years later, as the incumbent Indeterminatrix, she had amassed more wealth than her entire bloodline combined. Per the Neam Treaty of 50⁹ 6543, Faction Paradox supplied the Chance Coteries with temporal defenses; agents of the War in Heaven powers were not allowed there. The Keep had devotees in their billions, some of whom risked their entire cultures – as the Thane of the Finiphec discovered when he lost at cards, and the Keep came to own his people's planets, citizens and every last asset. The Collateral Belt housed the larger assets claimed by the Coteries' liquidation fleets. The Coteries valued famous humans from history as trophies.

Cymbionts emerged as the most agreeable of the technosapien subspecies, and could attain cybernetic-symbiosis – a deep emotional and mental bond – with organics, their personalities overlapping. Sojourner bonded with a cymbiont mammoth, L-Event ("Ellie"), and led a cymbiont uprising on Pluto against the ruling Company there. Eris marked a turning point in the conflict as a cymbiont fleet, commanded by the non-cymbiont Michael K Spaceman, massacred the Company's siege armada. De Rein secretly backed the insurgents as part of a long-term strategy. The Company was kicked out of the region, and the Plutonic Cymbiont Bill of Rights was forged. Spaceman was elected prime minister of Eris.

Immensely popular, Sojourner was elected the first president of the Plutoid Republic of Technosapien Enhanced Cultures (PROTEC), as formed from the mining communities on Pluto, Eris, Haumea and their sister planetoids. Hades was home to an industrial conrubation. Charon had an artificial star. Cymbionts held equal rights within PROTEC and gained influence in other cultures, signalling an irreversible shift in the posthuman condition. Some Coteries elites also opted for cybernetic-symbiosis as it became fashionable.

Key works from this era included *Technosapience: An Introduction* by Dr M Banks (50⁹ 7029), and *Posthumanity on a Budget* by I. Thul (50⁹ 7031).[2322]

FP: WEAPONS GRADE SNAKE OIL[2323] -> In 50⁹ 7043, President Sojourner Hooper-Agogô was in her mid-50s, with a husband, Rex; a daughter, Rez; and a three-year-old granddaughter, Anami. Her family lived in the Eurydice colliery.

Father Christèmas of Faction Paradox strong-armed Hooper-Agogô into helping his operatives to steal – he claimed – the 2nd Second from the Chance Coteries. Hooper-Agogô accepted an invitation to the Serendipity Keep's Quincentennial Jubilee, and assisted Cousin Chantelle, Anne Bonny, the Hussar and his TARDIS (the Kraken) once there. Christèmas' true goal was to bring Hooper-Agogô, Chantelle and Bonny into conflict within a tailored meme within Nonchalance, the Keep's AI. He also persuaded the Kraken to rip open the Hussar beyond hope of rebirth. The Hussar's biodata fueled a ritual of indeterminacy between Hooper-Agogô, Chantelle and Bonny, which created a baby *loa*. The Kraken took the newborn to the Eleven-Day Empire.

Coruscacia De Rein tried to seize the PROTEC worlds from Hooper-Agogô, but was killed by Hooper-Agogô's cymbiont, L-Event – which itself died while trying to escape. The Coteries fell into economic chaos with De Rein's death and Nonchalance's termination. It was possible that Godmother Antigone of Faction Paradox took charge and restored order.

The Elders

Steven Taylor Leaves the TARDIS

? - THE SAVAGES[2324] -> On one planet, the Elders maintained a utopian civilisation free from material needs. They survived by draining life energy from the savages who lived in the wastelands outside their beautiful city. "The Traveller from Beyond Time", the first Doctor, ended this injustice, and his companion Steven Taylor remained behind to rule the civilisation as it renounced barbarism.

When Steven was an older man, he encountered a Sontaran survey unit.[2325] The civilisation of the Elders and the Savages was "more or less" at peace. The older Steven was briefly Timescooped to aid the fifth Doctor in the Death Zone on Gallifrey.[2326]

& - THE WAR TO END ALL WARS / 1STD V1: THE FOUNDING FATHERS / 1STD V1: THE LOCKED ROOM[2327] **->** Steven Taylor became king, and had three daughters – including one named Rayleen, and his youngest and favourite, whom he named Dodo. The people Steven ruled no longer had the ability to view all of space and time, as the TARDIS crew had wrecked their machinery to do so. A corrupted copy of the first Doctor's mind – created when his persona was temporarily endowed in the Elder Jano – remained in a jar-shaped device. Some years later, the faux Doctor attempted to transfer its consciousness into a young lab technician, but burnt out the technician's mind in the process. Steven hushed up the incident, fearing his people's reaction to the truth.

Recalling his experiences on the wartorn planet Comfort, Steven instituted reforms that guided his people toward a meritocracy. He abdicated his position, and a war followed. Acting on reports claiming that Dodo was either dead at the insurrectionists' hands, or had chosen to side with them, Steven issued an executive order that ended the conflict and sealed his daughter's fate. His other two daughters came to odds over their father's dominion.

Nonetheless, the people opted for self-governance as Steven predicted, and he went into seclusion in a mountain home. His grief and regret made him more susceptible to the Vardan essence in his mind, and – under her influence – he diverted government resources toward building a radio telescope that could locate the real Doctor.

Two weeks after she came of age, Steven's granddaughter Sida informed him that the faux Doctor was thinking about standing for the presidency. Steven related the time he, Vicki and the Doctor met Benjamin Franklin in 1762, to illustrate that the faux Doctor lacked regard for "people who were not important" to the grand web of time. Sida learned of the faux Doctor's complicity in the death of a technician and publicized the truth. Amidst calls that it receive the death penalty, the faux Doctor transferred into the city's systems.

At the faux Doctor's suggestion, Sida stood for election and won the presidency. Three years later, when Steven was almost a hundred years old, he summoned Sida as his radio telescope neared completion. The device drew the Doctor's mind through space-time from 1986, reuniting the Vardan essences within Steven and the Doctor. The resurrected Vardan embarked on a terror campaign, but was stopped when, aided by Sida, the faux Doctor unravelled the Vardan into 0s and 1s.

The faux Doctor sacrificed its essence to hold the genuine article together in transit back to 1986. The havoc the Vardan wrought was attributed to a natural disaster, and Steven agreed to help Sida in restoring the damage.

End of the First Quest for the Key to Time

THE ARMAGEDDON FACTOR[2328] **->** The planet Atrios was at war with its opposite number, Zeos. The Atrios spacefleet was down to its last few ships, and the Atrions remained unaware that the inhabitants of Zeos

---

2325 "A few years" before *The Five Companions*.
2326 *The Five Companions*
2327 Dating *The War to End All Wars, 1stD* V1: *The Founding Fathers* and *The Locked Room* (BF CC #8.10, 9.3-9.4) - These stories follow on from *The Savages*, and portray Steven as a much older man. Three years elapse between the former two stories and *The Locked Room*, at which point Steven is "nearly one hundred" years old.
2328 Dating *The Armageddon Factor* (16.6) - No clues given on screen. *The Chaos Pool* stipulates that Atrios exists "much closer" to the end of time – an opposite number, of sorts, to the Teuthoidians who stem from the universe's early days. Marking a more specific placement than that, however, is a bit problematic.

It's said that Princess Astra lives to be more than 200 following *The Armageddon Factor*, and she participates in events on the planet Chaos – which is said to exist sixty-six minutes from the end of time (*The Chaos Pool*). However, this is not to say that *The Armageddon Factor* literally takes place just two centuries before the universe's end. Firstly, it's very hard to believe that a society of Atrios' level could be functioning so close to the universe's total heat death without specific technology in place (as that of the Grace or the Council of Eight in *Sometime Never*) to counter-act this. Second, it's doubly hard to believe that Astra and the Atrions accompanying her could have been flitting about in a spaceship without noticing that the universe is little more than an hour away from total extinction. Third, *The Chaos Pool* ends with Zara retiring to Atrios – not something she'd be likely to do if it had only sixty-six minutes left to exist.

It's far more likely that Chaos is held in suspension at the exact moment of sixty-six minutes from the end of time, and that some time-shifting is required to visit it. As further proof of this, time on Chaos seems to operate independently from that of the outside universe – there's no sense, for instance, that those on Chaos have only sixty-six minutes to live, just as more than eleven days can pass for those living within the boundaries of Faction Paradox's Eleven-Day Empire.
2329 *The Trouble with Drax*
2330 *The Chaos Pool*
2331 Dating *Hide* (X7.10) - It's the far future of Earth.

had died off. Mentalis – a supercomputer installed on Zeos by the Time Lord Drax – was coordinating the Zeon military effort. The Shadow, an agent of the Black Guardian, had been furthering the war from a space station located between Atrios and Zeos.

The fourth Doctor and the first Romana discovered that the sixth segment to the Key to Time was a person: Princess Astra of Atrios. The Shadow's space station – and the Shadow himself – were destroyed, and the Key was successfully assembled. The Doctor refrained from giving the Key to the Black Guardian – who appeared in the guise of the White Guardian – and again dispersed the segments throughout space-time, earning the Black Guardian's animosity.

During the Zeos affair, Drax planted a recall device aboard the Doctor's TARDIS, so he could summon the Ship to him if needed.[2329]

Romana became the new sixth segment of the Key to Time. As a side effect of Astra having been the Key segment, her life was extended at the cost of draining energy from those around her. The Atrions withered and died in large numbers, and their life expectancy dropped to twenty-nine years. Astra – not knowing she was the cause of her people's blight – became president of the Atrion Alliance and survived for two hundred years. The position of the Marshall of Atrios went unfilled.[2330]

c 100,000,000,000 - HIDE[2331] **->** The eleventh Doctor and Clara finished their photographic survey of Earth's life cycle, in a period when Earth's environment lay devastated.

Towards the End of the Universe

Many billions of years from now, the universe was cold and almost dead. The suns were exhausted. The last few survivors of the universe huddled around whatever energy sources they could find.[2332]

Eight billion years in the future, humanity was long dead. Mutter's Spiral had been abandoned by all sentient life.[2333] A few ten billions of years in the future, the Conservers existed in a black hole, preserving information there in the face of the universe's death. They engineered

their own creation by sending avatars into the past to bring a colony ship to their black hole. The Doctor visited the Conservers.[2334]

The Return of the *Consolidator*

Life on Praxilion developed long after what was commonly regarded as galactic history; it was "not even a glint in creation's eye when Gallifrey knew its last hour", and born when "The galaxy was old. Its stars had been through many generations of birth, exhaustion and rebirth." The Epoch of Mass Time Travel (EMTT) was long ago.

(=) Edwina McCrimmon, having been thrown through time, arrived on Praxilion. She became the Praxilions' Red Queen, a.k.a. her Imperial Majesty Uxury Scuita, and aided them in reviving forgotten technologies and jump-starting an industrial revolution. Her life was extended through artificial means, and she frequently entered stasis.

Such was the boom of technology on Praxilion that it attracted the time-lost *Consolidator*, a Gallifreyan vessel with forbidden artifacts. Six thousand years later, Praxilion explorers aboard the *Consolidator* accidentally released the Sild from their imprisonment.

The third Doctor brought some survivors of a dead Praxilion, as well as their Red Queen – the product of an erased timeline – back in time to resettle Praxilion in its prime, and more gradually develop their technology to avert the horrors they had witnessed...[2335]

(=) **THE HARVEST OF TIME**[2336] **->** The *Consolidator* had now orbited Praxilioin for two million years. The Sild detected a distress signal from the UNIT Master, who was imprisoned in the twentieth century, and from it identified the Master's psychokinetic imprint. This let them disconnect the Master's past and potential selves from history, to "harvest" about 470 versions of him – some men, some women, some children and some non-humanoids and wraiths – for use in a living computer. The Assemblage of captured Masters cracked temporal equations and difficulties, giving the Sild some control of time travel. An incur-

---

Clara says, "I've been dead one hundred billion years", but could be approximating or speaking figuratively.
2332 *Timewyrm: Apocalypse, The Infinity Doctors, Father Time, Hope, The Eye of the Tyger, Sometime Never.*
2333 "Eight billion years" after *Cold Fusion.*
2334 *The Eye of the Tyger*
2335 The background to *The Harvest of Time* (pgs. 9, 246). Edwina arrives on Praxilion "twelve million years" before the story's final component (p246). Chapter 35

gets a little confused about this, saying the Doctor has taken the alternate Red Queen back "ten million years and a bit of loose change", when it's really been only two million, if it's really "a century or so before the time when the Red Queen first landed" (p347).
2336 Dating *The Harvest of Time* (PDA #78) - Praxilon is after the Epoch of Mass Time Travel, at the "extreme end of history" (p197). Neither the third Doctor nor the Master have ventured "this far into the extreme future

sion team went to the twentieth century to capture the Master held by UNIT. Preparations were also made to drain Praxilion's oceans and atmosphere to twentieth-century Earth to terraform it.

The third Doctor and the Master arrived from ten million years on, having been sent back by the Red Queen's future self. Praxilon was rendered uninhabitable as the Assemblage rebelled against the Slid, and the *Consolidator* – with the Assemblage aboard – was destroyed. The Sild were randomly hurled through time and space, rendering them militarily useless.

The Doctor took the rejuvenated Red Queen and a group of Praxilion survivors back two million years to avert this timeline. The Master was left behind, found an obsolete TARDIS, and returned to the twentieth century.

(=) THE HARVEST OF TIME[2337] -> The third Doctor's TARDIS overshot its intended destination by ten million years, causing him and the UNIT Master to arrive on Praxilion long after the Sild had conquered it. Many of the Masters in the Assemblage had perished, but some hundreds remained, forced to enable to Sild's temporal operations. The Red Queen destroyed the *Consolidator* and the Assemblage with an Axmiliary Orb, and provided a tachyon lock for the Doctor and the Master to go back and aid her younger self...

The Assemblage's death freed the Master's mind from the gestalt effect caused by his other selves, and he begged the Doctor to take him even earlier in time, before the Epoch of Mass Time Travel, that he might become a force for good. The Doctor didn't believe

the Master and went back only ten million years as planned, causing the Master's villainous persona to re-assert itself.

TIMEWYRM: APOCALYPSE[2338] -> Billions of years in the future, the guardians of the universe, even the Time Lords, were long extinct. The people of Kirith (the only planet orbiting a red giant in Galaxy QSO 0046 at the edge of the universe) never grew old or unhappy. For three thousand eight hundred and thirty-three years, the Kirithons had been ruled by the eighty-four Panjistri, who gave them food and technology. For nearly a thousand years, the Panjistri performed genetic experiments, forcing the evolution of the Kirithons in an attempt to create a being that had reached the Omega Point: an omniscient, omnipotent entity capable of halting the destruction of the universe. They succeeded in creating a golden sphere of expanding light, but the machine destroyed itself and the Panjistri, knowing that the universe must end.

The Divergents almost emerged into our universe sixty billion years in the future, towards the end of time. Uncle Winky's Wonderland had been moved several times and was situated atop the ruins of Rassilon's lab on Gallifrey. Uncle Winky revived from stasis, but died from his heart condition.[2339] The Ministers of Grace travelled from the end of time to fight in the Millennium War.[2340]

A huge disaster led to galaxies being evacuated and whole sections of the timeline being erased. The Doctor's people were somehow responsible, and the four surviving Time Lords used their great powers to impose control on the rest of the universe. The last Time Lord became the first ever Emperor of the entire universe, ruling over a

---

of the galaxy" (p201).

2337 Dating *The Harvest of Time* (PDA #78) - The Doctor and the Master have missed their target by "ten million years" (p245), then go back there with the Red Queen's help.

2338 Dating *Timewyrm: Apocalypse* (NA #3) - The novel is set "several billion years" in the future (p3), "ten billion years" before the end of the universe (p178).

2339 *Zagreus*. These facts were presented as part of a simulation, and so may not take place.

2340 *The Quantum Archangel*. The Ministers first appeared in the short story "The Duke of Dominoes" (*Decalog*, 1994).

2341 *The Infinity Doctors, Father Time.*

2342 *Unnatural History*

2343 Dating *Father Time* (EDA #41) - The exact time-scale is unclear, and is stated to be "a few million years in the future", "several million years hence", and "a million years in the future". The physical state of the universe, however, suggests it is much later than that.

2344 Dating *Miranda* (*Miranda* comic #1-3) - It's "bil-

lions of years" in the future. Three issues of this projected six-issue story were published by Comeuppance Comics. The story simplified/ignored some of the plot points in *Father Time* (such as the existence of Cate, a robot Miranda, Miranda not knowing at first that Ferran was evil and the inclusion of the characters Rum and Thelash, who apparently died in *Father Time*).

2345 Dating *Hope* (EDA #53) - The Doctor pushes the TARDIS to see how far into the future he can take it and the TARDIS goes "too far". This is the same far, far future time period referred to in *The Infinity Doctors* and *Father Time*, which alluded to Silver and this period (p191).

2346 *Sometime Never*

2347 *The Magic Mousetrap*

2348 Dating *Singularity* (BF #76) - It is clearly toward the end of the universe. It's said that the Ember base is located "trillions of years" in the future, but it's also mentioned that, "This far into the future, numbers become meaningless." Technically, Xen's claim that he is "the last human" seems dubious, as episodes such as

divided and broken populace that split into Factions and Houses. These included the Klade, "goblin shapeshifters" and cybernetic gangsters – the ultimate descendants of the Daleks, Sontarans, Rutans and the Cybermen.

Most of the people of the universe relocated to the Needle, a light-year long structure that was the remains of a TARDIS that had tried to escape the pull of a black hole. The largest building on the Needle was the Librarinth, where all surviving knowledge and art was preserved.[2341]

Griffin the Unnaturalist resided on the Needle.[2342]

Miranda

FATHER TIME[2343] **->** The Doctor and two companions visited the planets Galspar and Falkus around this time. The Doctor also fought a robotic tyrant who panicked, accidentally destroyed his own palace and killed his own wife. This robot, who later assumed the identity "Mr Gibson" to blend in on twentieth-century Earth, vowed revenge.

At least some of the Emperor's subjects, such as the Klade – the super-evolved descendants of the Daleks – resented Imperial rule. One Klade senator, the mother of Zevron and Ferran, incited revolution against the Emperor but was assassinated. Zevron stormed the Imperial Palace, killing and scattering all of the Imperial Family. The Emperor was killed. The Emperor's daughter, Miranda, was rescued by her nanny and taken down a time corridor to twentieth-century Earth.

Over the years, Zevron tracked down and killed every other member of the Imperial Family. Finally, he located Miranda and led the mission to kill her on Earth in the early nineteen-eighties.

When Zevron failed to return, Ferran became Prefect of Faction Klade. Some years later, Ferran received a distress signal from Sallak, Zevron's deputy. Ferran travelled to twentieth-century Earth to complete Zevron's mission but failed and returned to his native time.

A team of Ferran's scholars spent fifteen years in the Librarinth, and eventually pinpointed Miranda's whereabouts. Ferran also recovered a derelict sentient ship built by the People of the Worldsphere, which he christened the *Supremacy*. The political situation had deteriorated, putting the Houses and Factions at open war, and galactic civilisation was on the brink of collapse. Ferran believed Miranda could access sealed sections of the Librarinth and thus give him the power to dominate the other Factions. Using the *Supremacy*, he set off to the twentieth century.

Miranda and Ferran returned to this time. Convinced she could unite the universe, Miranda was crowned Empress.

MIRANDA[2344] **->** Miranda woke aboard Ferran's ship, the *Supremacy*. She was attacked by an assassin robot which she dispatched, but which turned out to be one of many attempts on her life that night. She was being taken to the Needle to be formally crowned, and shown the forces at the disposal of the Empress. A handmaiden, Keli, warned her that Ferran would try to kill her. Miranda got a little drunk at her first formal reception, but nonetheless fought off an alien attempt to abduct her. She learned that Ferran wanted access to the Librarinth, the storehouse of universal information – he planned to marry her, which would give him the authority to open it. Miranda and Keli escaped into the forests of the Needle, where they were met by hero dynamic space hero Mack Gideon... who was promptly killed by Rum and Thelash, trackers sent by Ferran to find her...

... Miranda was destined to marry Ferran and become Empress.

HOPE[2345] **->** Taking the TARDIS into the far future, the eighth Doctor, Fitz and Anji landed on planet A245, known locally as Endpoint. It was an icy planet with a toxic environment. The TARDIS fell through the frozen crust of an acid sea, and the Doctor asked the cyborg Silver – the warlord of the nearest settlement, Hope – for assistance. Silver was from the far past, the year 3006.

Anji was tempted to use the cloning technology of this era to recreate her dead boyfriend, Dave, and granted Silver scans of the TARDIS in return for this. The Doctor found survivors from other colonies were murdering the people of Hope to harvest Kallisti, a hormone that could revive more of the colonists from cryo-sleep. Silver found the sleepers and converted them into Silverati: half-synthetic soldiers loyal to him. With his soldiers and the colonists' hypertunnel, Silver attempted to take control of a richer planet. The Doctor exiled Silver and his Silverati to the barren planet A2756.

There were no pure humans left, but human genes survived in a number of races. Apple trees were extinct until Silver cloned one from an apple core that the Doctor gave him. The universe was past the point of sustainable expansion, and the rate of star death had dramatically increased.

Miranda brought the Factions and Houses together and united the people of the universe. She had at least one child, a daughter named Zezanne. Zezanne's father died. The Council of Eight kidnapped Miranda and Zezanne when Zezanne was a teenager.[2346] It was possible that the electrocuted board imprisoning the Celestial Toymaker remained active until around the year two trillion.[2347]

? - SINGULARITY[2348] **->** The planet Ember had served as an outpost from which to watch other galaxies for signs of intelligent life. Toward the end of the universe, some descendants of humanity prolonged the lifespan of Ember's sun as most stars in the universe extinguished, and thereby survived for some millennia. They believed that the Time Lords had opened a gate to another realm and escaped with all the life they deemed worthy, leaving humanity's children to perish.

Ember's sun began to fade also, and the survivors began swapping their intelligences with Earthlings in the late twentieth century, hoping to facilitate the creation of a Singularity entity. The plan failed, whereupon the conspirators were forced to return to this era and quickly died off.

The laws of time and causality started to break down as Ember approached its end. Nonetheless, the fifth Doctor and Turlough arrived as one of the conspirators – Xen, who claimed to be the last human – passed on.

The stars of the universe were burning out and fading away. The Science Foundation initiated the Utopia Project to preserve humankind, and enable it to survive the collapse of reality itself.[2349] Professor Yana was found as a boy, naked in a storm off the coast of the Silver Devastation. He was discovered with a watch, which he kept with him as he went from one refugee ship to another. No university had existed for a thousand years, but Yana became accomplished at science and took the title "Professor" as an affectation.[2350] People still drank coffee in the year one hundred trillion.[2351]

The War Master Regenerates

100,000,000,000,000 - UTOPIA[2352] **->** The planet Malcassairo had been home to an advanced race of humanoid insects, the Malmooth, but the Conglomeration there died. Chantho was the last representative of this species, and she served as Yana's assistant for seventeen years.

A signal came from far beyond the Condensed Wilderness, out toward the Wild Lands and the Dark Matter Reefs. It said nothing more than "Come to Utopia", and some remnants of humanity gathered on Malcassairo in preparation to journey there. They huddled to protect themselves from the cannibalistic Futurekind – said to be what humankind would become – while Yana and Chanthro worked to complete a rocket that would evacuate everyone save themselves.

The tenth Doctor, Martha and Captain Jack arrived and helped to complete the rocket. Martha learned that Yana was – unknown even to himself – the Master, disguised as a human to escape the Time War. The rocket launched. The War Master learned of his true identity, but was shot by Chanthro, whom he had fatally wounded. He regenerated, stealing the TARDIS and marooning the Doctor and his companions, but not before the Doctor fused the TARDIS' controls. It could only travel to this point in time and within eighteen months of the Ship's last departure in 2008.

The Doctor's trio returned to the twenty-first century with Jack's vortex manipulator.[2352]

The End of the World and *New Earth* indicate that no purebred humans exist after Cassandra's era. The planet Ember bears no apparent relation to the star of the same name from *The Suns of Caresh*, although that story might explain why the Doctor here mutters "Ember... I've heard that name before."

2349 "Thousands of years" before *Utopia*.

2350 *Utopia*. It's said in *The End of the World* that the Face of Boe also hails from the Silver Devastation.

2351 *Lights Out*, probably with *Utopia* in mind.

2352 Dating *Utopia* (X3.11) - The TARDIS is propelled into the far, far future, with the last date the Doctor reads being "one hundred trillion years" (it's possible it lands even later). As in *The Sun Makers* and *Frontios*, the Doctor states that the Time Lords didn't travel this far into the future, although he never explicitly rules out the possibility he's been here before, as we saw in a number of books and audios.

2353 *The Sound of Drums*

2354 *Last of the Time Lords*. The number of Toclafane is given by the Master in *The Sound of Drums*.

2355 *Timewyrm: Revelation*

2356 *The Cradle of the Snake* – provided we take the title literally.

2357 Dating *The Infinity Doctors* (PDA #17) - The date is given (p137). This is "within a few decades of Event Two" (p130).

2358 Dating *The Eternal Battle* (BF 4th Doc #6.2) - The Doctor says it's "the universe's twilight years, the distant future." The Sontarans seem to exist, at least in some form, in the far future depicted in *Father Time*, *Hope* and *Miranda*, so it's after that.

2359 *The Dark Flame*

2360 *Sometime Never*

2361 *Benny B1: Epoch: Judgement Day*

2362 *Iris S4: The Iris Wildthyme Appreciation Society*; presumably the characters of the same name from the comic *Daleks*: "The Menace of the Monstrons".

2363 Dating *Engines of War* (NSA #54) - It's the "end of the universe" (ch18).

The Harold Saxon Master returned to this future era with his wife Lucy, and found the darkness overtaking the humans on Utopia. He arranged to house their shrunken heads into metallic spheres equipped with weaponry, and named them the Toclafane. Six billion Toclafane were created in this fashion. The Master then returned to the twenty-first century, and converted the TARDIS into a Paradox Machine.

(=) Thanks to the Paradox Machine, the Toclafane were able to travel back and enslave their ancestors.

With the Paradox Machine's destruction, the Toclafane were stranded at the end of the universe.[2354]

Event Two

"One mad prophet martyr journeyed too far and saw the Timewyrm. He saw it in a timeline that he could not be sure of, devouring Rassilon or his shade, during the Blue Shift, that time of final conflict when Fenric shall slip his chains and the evil of the worlds shall rebound back on them in war." [2355]

The Doctor owned a copy of *A Universal History of Fable and Demonology, Written at the End of All Time*.[2356]

100,000,000,000,000,000,000,000,000,000,000 - THE INFINITY DOCTORS[2357] -> The Needle had been inhabited for tens of millions of years, but now it was all but abandoned. Ruined cities dotted its surface, and the atmosphere had frozen. The only known survivors were the predator animals named the Maltraffi, mushrooms and four "knights": Gordel, Willhuff, Pallant and Helios. Each could only remember the future — with less and less to remember each day — and each had his own theory as to their origins. They may have been the last survivors of the Children of Kasterborous, human/Gallifreyan hybrids who intervened in the universe at great cost; superevolved Thals who fled the penultimate destruction of Skaro at the start of the Final Dalek War; members of the People of the Worldsphere, left behind when everyone else transcended reality; or the last High Evolutionaries (Helios might have been Merlin, or his son).

The Doctor arrived from Gallifrey to find the god Ohm, who was trapped in the black hole at one end of the Needle. Two of the Doctor's colleagues, the Magistrate and Larna, were sent in to rescue him when he vanished. Omega emerged from the black hole wearing the Doctor's body, banishing the Magistrate somewhere unknown and taking Larna back to Gallifrey.

Omega sought to attain ultimate power by unleashing the Eye of Harmony. The Doctor had been reunited with his wife as part of these events, but was forced to lose her again. He once more defeated Omega.

The Final Sontaran

THE ETERNAL BATTLE[2358] -> The Sontaran race was now extinct; even Sontar was no more. The Psigon race thrived for a time after their demise, then also passed from existence. The Psigons had founded the Centre of Academic Excellence in the year 97,391 of the New New Calendar — without them, its systems time-scooped innocuous battlefields from history, as a lesson to absent students about the futility of war.

The TARDIS failed to reach the Lake District, and so the fourth Doctor, the second Romana and K9 found themselves in one of the Centre's time bubbles, in a pitched battle between Sontarans and human colonists. The decaying time bubble revived the dead on each side to fight the living. The Doctor convinced the Centre's AI that as war was futile and it was warring against war, it too was futile. The AI shut down, and the remaining soldiers emerged to resettle the planet's wasteland.

The sole survivor from the Sontaran ranks, Sgt Major Stom, was the last of his race. The Doctor hoped the survivors would welcome him into their number.

The Time Lords believed that a powerful force, the Dark Flame, stemmed from a pocket dimension that was pushed out of space-time during the universe's collapse.[2359] The Last Museum stood as a collection of the human race's greatest objects and achievements. It was located at the end of Time, at the exact centre of the universe. The Council of Eight member Soul served at the Museum, disguised as an old man named Singleton.[2360]

The Epoch claimed to be from the end of time, and that they would meet Bernice Summerfield there.[2361] The Monstrons — the creators of the Monstron Time Destroyer that Iris Wildthyme used to chase herself through time — were a "nasty" bunch of chrononauts from the end of time, who were imprisoned in a pocket reality by the Clockworks Council.[2362]

ENGINES OF WAR[2363] -> The War Doctor hijacked control of Commander Partheus' TARDIS and relocated it to a red-giant star at the end of time. The Doctor fired the Tear of Isha, a stellar device, into the star to prevent its use in the Tantalus Spiral.

The Forging of the Key to Time and, Later, its Destruction; Creation of the Graceless

Event Two Minus Sixty-Six Minutes - THE JUDGEMENT OF ISSKAR / THE CHAOS POOL[2364] -> Extra-dimensional beings – the Grace – sought to maintain the universal balance. To that end, they forged the Key to Time in a pool on the planet Chaos, which existed sixty-six minutes from the end of time. Chaos had been known as the planet Safeplace, the Teuthoidians' final resting place.

The Key to Time was a perfect cube consisting of six segments, which when combined helped to maintain the equilibrium of time itself. The segments contained the elemental force of the universe, and could adopt any shape or size. They were dispersed throughout space-time until it became imperative to restore the universal balance. The White Guardian sent the fourth Doctor and the first Romana to recover the segments; they did so, then dispersed the segments once more.

The Doctor had used a synthetic sixth segment to complete the Key, but in doing so had destabilised it. The scattered Key segments decayed and damaged local space-time; a total collapse would destroy the universe. The Grace created two living Key-tracers – Amy and her sister Zara – and tasked them with retrieving three segments each. The fifth Doctor accompanied Amy on her quest.

They returned to Chaos as President Astra came in search of the legendary Chaos Pool, which she hoped would cure her people's deteriorating condition. The weakened and amnesiac White Guardian – now passing as Professor Lydall, an Atrion – had created a fold in hyperspace, liking the extreme beginning and end of time. The Teuthoidians, servants of the White Guardian, travelled through the fold and engaged an army of the Black Guardian's supporters.

The second Romana arrived with the Black Guardian, having answered the Doctor's cry for help from Gallifrey. The Key to Time was assembled after Astra re-acquired the essence of the sixth segment from Romana, then transformed into it. The Grace declared that neither of the Guardians should possess the Key, and banished them back to the howling void to continue their conflict.

The Doctor destroyed the Key to Time within the Chaos Pool – an act that dispersed the Grace throughout eternity.

Amy and Zara were left as human beings, but retained many of their powers. Zara retired to Atrios while Amy accepted Romana's invitation to visit Gallifrey.

GRACELESS: THE END[2365] -> Abby and Zara navigated the space pirate Kreekpolt's warships back to Chaos, hoping to absorb enough lingering power from the Grace to heal Kreekpolt's wounded daughter, the Lady Persephone. Kreekpolt accepted an offer from an incarnation of the Grace, and traded his life for his daughter's health – the restored Persephone vowed vengeance against the sisters for their role in her father's death. The Grace told Abby and Zara that they would live as long as they wished, and left them with time rings that functioned so long as they were together. They left to perform good acts as penance for their various crimes, accompanied by Marek – their mutual lover, and the father of Zara's infant daughter Joy.

GRACELESS II: THE DARK / GRACELESS II: THE EDGE[2366] -> Having left their friends Brondle and Wing, Abby and Zara found themselves back on a barren and starless world at the end of time. Persephone Kreekpolt was much older, and pretended to be Zara's lost daughter

---

2364 Dating *The Judgement of Isskar* and *The Chaos Pool* (BF #117, 119) - Chaos is held in stasis "sixty-six minutes" from the end of the universe. Details on the Key were first given in *The Ribos Operation*. The fifth Doctor knows that Romana has returned to Gallifrey (in accordance with *Goth Opera*); she's not yet President, but she might already be a High Council member.

Contrary to the Big Finish audios (which in this case, being *Doctor Who* fiction, for *Ahistory*'s purposes take precedence), *Whoniverse* (BBC) and *A History of the Universe in 100 Objects* (p14) both link the Key to Time to the universe's very beginning.

2365 Dating *Graceless: The End* (*Graceless* #1.3) - Events happen on the planet Chaos, following *The Chaos Pool*.
2366 Dating *Graceless II: The Dark* and *Graceless III: The Edge* (*Graceless* #2.3, #3.1) - Joy/Persephone tells the sisters in *The Dark*, "We're at the end of the universe." Even allowing that Persephone can time travel (*Graceless III: The Battle*), these events seem to follow on, within her lifetime, from *Graceless: The End*. Kurt tells

Abby and Zara in *The Edge* that the hotel is "at the end of time and space", and that the "flotsam and jetsam of history" arrive there; taking him at his word, the story presumably occurs in the same end-of-time period as *Graceless II: The Dark*.
2367 Dating *Graceless IV: The Dance* (*Graceless* #4.4) - It's "The End of Time, and it's going to be ballroom dancing". Given Pool's involvement, it must follow on from *The Chaos Pool*.
2368 Dating *Listen* (X8.4) - The Doctor tells Clara they're at "The end of the road. This is it, the end of everything. The last planet... There's nothing to hear. There's nothing anywhere. Not a breath, not a slither, not a click or a tick. All the clocks have stopped. This is the silence at the end of time."
2369 Dating *Sometime Never* (EDA #67) - The scene in the Vortex Palace ends with the end of the universe.
2370 Dating *DotD: The Time Machine* (*Destiny of the Doctor* #11) - The Creevix tell the Doctor and Alice that it's "the end of your universe", so it's before the Creevix's

Joy to lull the sisters into a false sense of security. Persephone pushed Zara into the Time Vortex, claiming revenge for herself and Abby and Zara's victims. She hoped that the Vortex would tear Zara apart, but Abby leapt in after her sibling...

Abby found Zara at a hotel with such lodgers as a German named Kurt, the stage performer Miss Simone and a music hall devotee named Albert. Kurt was seemingly murdered, and Simone and Albert died trying to escape after the hotel caught fire. Abby and Zara discovered that the lodgers were the spirits of the deceased, and that Kurt was tasked with horrifically "killing" them or driving them into the sea – a representation of their next stage of existence. Kurt failed to trick the sisters into committing suicide, and was himself extinguished. Abby and Zara used their willpower to restore Miss Simone and Albert, who became the hotel's managers. Displaced spirits could stay there as long as they liked, only moving beyond the veil when they wished.

Curious because Persephone had claimed that Marek was at the Battle of Maldon, Abby and Zara went there to find their lost lover.

The Dissolution of the Grace

GRACELESS IV: THE DANCE[2367] -> Abby and Zara's powers derived from the Grace, meaning that the more they used them to change history, the more the Grace were diminished, and a darkness prevented the Grace from reading the timelines.

The Chaos Pool incarnated itself as a humanoid named Pool, who journeyed through space-time and spoke with 13,462,000 beings affected by Abby and Zara's decisions, to ask if their actions served a greater good. Abby and Zara found themselves in a dance room outside of space-time, where the dancers – the Grace – were to decide whether or not to continue empowering the women. Although the majority of those he asked said the result was not worth the cost, Pool gave the Graceless all of his energy and disintegrated. A critical mass of the Grace concurred, and all of their number extinguished. Before her end, the dissenting Lady Triangle predicted the sisters would be in conflict with the Doctor.

The Last Planet in the Universe

LISTEN[2368] -> One of Earth's first chrononauts, Colonel Orson Pink, became stranded on the last planet remaining in the universe. The twelfth Doctor located Pink by tracing the contours of Clara's timeline, and sat with Clara in Pink's vessel, hoping that creatures capable of perfect hiding might reveal themselves to the last person alive. The airlock of Pink's vessel cycled, and opened to reveal... nothing. The Doctor

was injured in the resultant decompression, and the TARDIS took him, Clara and Pink to the Doctor's early life on Gallifrey...

Pink gave Clara a family heirloom – a weaponless plastic soldier – that he'd kept as a good luck piece.

The Council of Eight: Miranda and Sabbath Die

SOMETIME NEVER[2369] -> The Council of Eight existed in the Vortex Palace, right at the end of time. By placing unique crystals at the beginning of time, they mapped out events across the universe, and generated energy from unused potential timelines by correctly predicting the course of events. This energy was stored in Schrodinger Cells. The Council sent apes mutated by the Time Winds ("the Agents of the Council") to ensure their version of history transpired, and also recruited Sabbath to unwittingly work on their behalf. The Council deemed many of the Doctor's companions a threat, as they were touched by his innate ability to influence history, and thus engineered the possible deaths of Sarah Jane Smith, Harry Sullivan, Melanie Bush, Ace and Samantha Jones.

The Council leader, Octan, planned to destroy human history with a starkiller, releasing vast amounts of energy. This energy would paradoxically create the Council of Eight, and in all probability allow them to survive the end of the universe. Octan took Miranda hostage, but she sacrificed herself, allowing the eighth Doctor a free hand to fight them. Sabbath killed himself to thwart his former employers, and his death helped to instigate the destruction of the Vortex Palace.

The Council of Eight perished except for the benevolent Soul and Octan, who journeyed to 1588 in a last-ditch effort to save their plans. The Doctor donated some of his life energy to stabilize Soul's body into his former guise as the old man Singleton. Soul took Octan's starkiller.

The Doctor and his allies left in the TARDIS, while Soul and Miranda's daughter Zezanne evacuated in the *Jonah*, which arrived in a junkyard in 1963. Beings who sought to acquire the starkiller monitored the *Jonah*'s departure.

Other beings that survived until the last moments of the universe included the Solarii and Korsann's reptilian race.

(=) DotD: THE TIME MACHINE[2370] -> The eleventh Doctor and Alice Watson arrived in a copy of Guy Taylor's time machine at the end of the universe, in a devastated timeline where the Creevix had consumed all of history after 2013. The Creevix took Alice back to 2013 to complete the temporal paradox that would guarantee their victory. The Doctor summoned the TARDIS – which entered the Creevix's alternate history using the power of the omniparadox within its interior – and followed them.

The TARDIS was at the end of time.[2371] The eleventh Doctor wrote the entire history of the universe in jokes.[2372] Legends said the Sycorax would be one of the last three races left when the universe finally died. Humans were one of the other two.[2373]

Lady Me at the End of Everything

"Five minutes from Hell" - HELL BENT[2374] -> Every immortal had now perished save for Ashildr, a.k.a. Me, who maintained a reality bubble as the stars died off. The twelfth Doctor found Ashildr in the ruins of the cloisters on Gallifrey, and conversed with her about the Hybrid foretold to unravel the Web of Time. Ashildr raised the possibility that the Hybrid was not one, but two people – the Doctor, a Time Lord, and Clara, a human, who pushed each other to extremes. The Doctor realised he'd gone too far in risking the whole of time and space on Clara's behalf, and that they could no longer stay together. They agreed to let a neural block remove the memories of one of them from the other, without knowing who would be affected. The device removed the Doctor's memories of Clara – he would remember their adventures together, but not what she was like – whereupon she and Ashildr took him to Nevada in the twenty-first century...

After Event Two

BIG BANG GENERATION -> The Ancients of the Universe constructed a null space "one microsecond beyond the destruction of time and space, beyond the col-lapse of the multiverse, beyond the absence of all", where they could rest from all of their partying and excursions into reality. The universe had been destroyed owing to the Ancients' negligence pertaining to the Pyramid Eternia lodestone – even the Heat Death of the Universe had gone cold. The twelfth Doctor accessed the Ancients' null space, and convinced them to restore the universal timeline.

The Eminence spent an eternity alone and became the last mind in creation: a singularity in the void. The eighth Doctor repelled an attempt by the Eminence to ride a wave front back in time, and pushed it back to this point. The Eminence would later succeed in its efforts, and threaten humanity in the fourth millennium.[2375]

Our universe was destroyed in the Big Crunch. All matter imploded to a central point, returning to the state from which it was created: "a bright blazing pinprick of sheer energy".[2376] The Time Lords referred to the end of the universe as Event Two.[2377]

Insect-like "forces of chaos" fed on the debris of the collapse of the universe, as they had fed on the Big Bang.[2378]

The City of the Saved[2379]

The City of the Saved created by Compassion and the UniMac occupied – or rather comprised – an artificially sustained bubble that existed after the end of the universe, and before the beginning of the next one. Within the City's environs – believed to be the size of a spiral galaxy – literally every member of the entire human race, "from its sentient prehuman ancestors to its posthuman offshoots", had been resurrected in invulnerable bodies. The City's

native territory in the next one.
2371 *Death is the Only Answer*
2372 *Night and the Doctor:* "Good Night"
2373 "Agent Provocateur"
2374 Dating *Hell Bent* (X9.12) - The Doctor tells Clara they've gone "to the last hours of the universe. We're going long past where the Time Lords were hiding. Literally, to the end. They won't be able to track us there." He also states – and Ashildr concurs – that they're "five minutes from hell [the end of everything]", although neither of them seems very rushed during their conversation, possibly because Ashildr's reality bubble overrides such considerations.
2375 *DEyes 2: Time's Horizon*
2376 *Timewyrm: Apocalypse. A History of the Universe in 100 Objects* (p255) draws a line under the whole of universal history with the note: "100,000,000,000,000": The end of everything. Goodbye."
2377 *The Infinity Doctors*
2378 "Hunger from the Ends of Time!"
2379 The City of the Saved first appears in *FP: The Book of the War* and *FP: Of the City of the Saved...* Following on

from there, five (to date) anthologies from Obverse Press chronicle life there: *Tales of the City*, #1; *More Tales of the City*, #2; *Tales of the Great Detectives*, #3; *Furthest Tales of the City*, #4; and *Tales of the Civil War*, #5.
2380 *FP: Of the City of the Saved*, with additional detail given in *FP: The Book of the War*.
2381 *FP: Of the City of the Saved, City: Furthest Tales of the City:* "God Encompasses"
2382 *FP: The Book of the War, FP: Of the City of the Saved...*
2383 *FP: Weapons Grade Snake Oil*
2384 *FP: The Book of the War*
2385 *FP: Of the City of the Saved...*
2386 The prologue to *FP: Warlords of Utopia*, published at the end of *FP: Of the City of the Saved...*
2387 Dating *FP: Of the City of the Saved...* (FP novel #2) - According to this book and *FP: The Book of the War* (p33), the City exists after the end of the current universe, and before the beginning of the next one. The Story So Far page in *City* says that the War in Heaven (which started in 244 AF) is now in its "forty-eighth year".

population easily numbered in the septillions. Multiple versions of the same person could be present (as was the case with Compassion's four previous iterations, who had been born in the Remote's remembrance tanks).

The City had a single access point: the Uptime Gate, a powerful time corridor connected to the far future of the universe, at a point beyond which most of the temporal powers travelled. The Rump Parliament unofficially represented Faction Paradox's interests within the City.

Compassion forbade use of time travel within the City. All things being equal, the City's citizens were immortal and impervious to harm. The City's calendar logged time by AF: the number of years After Foundation.[2380]

Whereas the Uptime Gate served a purpose, the North, South, East and West Gates were decorative, only opening into a void. Hermits and ascetics settled near the North Gate, explorers near the West Gate, and the South Gate contained a safety net the size of Earth's orbit to prevent suicides. In the first decade After Foundation, the East Gate was designated a Civil architectural Preservation Area and quarantined.[2381]

CITY: FURTHEST TALES OF THE CITY: "Salutation"

-> Compassion completed construction of the City of the Saved's galaxy-wide structures, as well as the hundreds of thousands of millions of billions of trillions of inert bodies awaiting an infusion of sentience from her consciousness. Compassion would become an icon, the goddess Civiata, in her temple in the Romuline District – only intervening in the gravest of emergencies.
UniMac questioned whether humanity was better off surviving as stable data within Compassion's memory. Compassion counter-argued that life was a process, and initiated Resurrection Day...

... whereupon everyone of human inheritance awoke to find themselves in the City, a utopia at the end of time.[2382]

Faction Paradox: A Negotiable History by S. Walmric was published AF 189.[2383]

wih - From the City's point of view, the War in Heaven started in 244 AF. In AF 262, Lady Mantissa of House Mirraflex attacked the City of the Saved, by re-configuring her timeships into worm-like behemoths. The timeships overcame the City's state of grace protocols, and wrecked havoc in the City's Snakefell District. Unnamed authorities in the City – possibly the City Council or Compassion and UniMac – launched an assault that killed 20 million citizens, but cleaved Snakefell from the City entirely. Eleven

of Mantissa's timeships perished in the Big Crunch. Snakefell was restored, and the fallen citizens were re-resurected, within hours.[2384]

In AF 291, a City census numbered its population at 1038 septillion.[2385] Marcus Americanus Scriptor visited the City of the Saved in search of the reincarnated Adolf Hitler. Upon learning that Hitler had been sentenced to imprisonment for six million lifetimes, Scriptor vowed to be waiting when he was released.[2386]

Start of the City's Civil War

wih - 292 AF - FP: OF THE CITY OF THE SAVED...[2387]

-> The first of Compassion's timeship offspring, the unstable Antipathy, escaped from the Homeworld of the Great Houses and smuggled himself into the City. Antipathy's presence disrupted the codes governing the City and caused political unrest; to rectify the problem, Godfather Avatar of Faction Paradox – a loa who took human hosts – destroyed himself and Antipathy's mind with an annihilation bomb.

Compassion's original iteration, Laura Tobin, worked as a private investigator in the City. Her investigation into the advent of "potent" weapons, i.e. weapons that could kill City residents, brought her into contact with the timeship Compassion (a.k.a. Compassion V) – who wanted Tobin to become her living avatar, and help restore order within the City. Tobin refused to become a spokesperson for a would-be goddess, and departed onto the City streets.

Antipathy's actions had pushed various factions within the City – many of whom longed to settle old scores – toward civil war. As a safeguard against the City's destruction, UniMac helped to secretly establish an enclave of humans within Antipathy's interior dimensions.

The onset of the civil war prompted the sealing of the Uptime Gate.

Casualties from the City's civil war exceeded four trillion. UniMac facilitated creation of a Downtime Gate, to allow access to the universe beyond our own, but this stretched too far forward and brought back humanity's final descendant: the Anonymity. It was incomplete, and hoped to become more by amalgamating its ancestors into itself.[2388]

CITY: FURTHEST TALES OF THE CITY: "God Encompasses" -> The Anonymity unleashed a wave of ignorance that rendered the City unknowable, erasing it until only Compassion remained. She had excluded her

---

2388 *FP: A Romance in Twelve Parts:* "A Hundred Words from a Civil War", which – as the name implies – contains many snapshots from the City's Civil War. The City has existed for "300 years" (possibly a generalization) by the time of *City: Tales of the City:* "Apocalypse Day", set during the Civil War.

children from the City so that, as timeships, they could house a copy of the City's environs, people and concepts. From their back-ups, Compassion restored the City.

The Next Universe

Just as a universe existed before ours, so will another universe be formed from the ashes of ours, and the physical laws there will be very different. This will be the domain of Saraquazel.[2389] The monstrous Zytragupten will exist in the universe to come. A Zytragupten child, the Lokhus, will be born malformed and culled. It will be cast into the infernal abyss, but survive, fall into our universe and arrive in the village of Stockbridge.[2390]

The insectoid Creevix resided in the "next universe along" from our own, and were masters of time in their domain – no moment happened in the Creevix realm that they had not willed into being, and they fed on the potential of the future they created. The eleventh Doctor, as aided by ten of his previous selves, stopped the Creevix from similarly consuming our universe.[2391]

The end result of humanity's bloodline, the Anonymity, existed in the next universe along, but travelled back via a Downtime Gate to attack the City of the Saved.[2392]

2389 *Millennial Rites*
2390 "The Stockbridge Child"

CRACKS IN TIME: The Cracks in Time seen throughout Series 5 have three primary functions…

1. Erase individuals who are exposed to the Cracks' time energy from history. As the Doctor tells Amy (*Flesh and Stone*): "If the [Crack in Time] catches up with you, you'll never have been born. It will erase every moment of your existence. You will never have lived at all."

2. Consume/erase nodes of history. This seems to explain why, in *Victory of the Daleks*, Amy doesn't remember the Dalek invasion of 2009 (*The Stolen Earth*). In *Flesh and Stone*, the Doctor implies that the same fate befell the Cyber King (*The Next Doctor*).

3. Act as "magic doorways", i.e. enable alien races to cross from Point A to Point B in space/time (*The Vampires of Venice*, *The Pandorica Opens*).

Why the Cracks function as "magic doorways" and also "erase things from history" is never said – their abilities change from story to story, per Steven Moffat regarding *Doctor Who* as a fable. The most candid, if unsatisfying, explanation is to say that the Cracks function as magic doorways "just because they do".

However, *do* the Cracks in Time erase individuals from history entirely? Despite the Doctor's insistence about this, all the evidence says otherwise. When the Cracks "erase someone from history", that person's absence does not create a new timeline – Amy not only keeps existing when the Cracks consume her parents (pre-*The Eleventh Hour*), the alleged "historical deletion" of her lifetime best friend and fiancé causes no long-term personality changes beyond her no longer being sad, as she can't remember that a Silurian shot him dead (*Cold Blood*). Nor does Rory's "erasure" seem to affect River – which it should, as he's her father.

Granted, Amy is unique because she grew up with a Crack in her bedroom, but the same principle applies to four of Father Octavian's Clerics being "erased" (*Flesh and Stone*). If the Clerics "never lived at all", then as each one is dematerialised, another should instantly appear. Octavian started the mission with twenty Clerics, so if four were retroactively "never born", it shouldn't create a timeline where he only took sixteen instead.

More noticeably, when the Doctor is "erased" (*The Big*

Bang), Earth in 2010 still exists. Considering how many times he has saved the planet, deleting the Doctor from history should, almost without fail, result in a 2010 where Earth is under alien domination or totally destroyed (see *Pyramids of Mars*, et al). Similarly, Captain Jack's Torchwood team and Sarah Jane's adeptness at fighting aliens would never have happened without the Doctor, so every menace they defeated in their own series would be back on the table.

What must actually happen when the Cracks consume somebody is that said person's (to coin a term) "temporal opacity" must get lowered to zero. The effects of their lives remain, but they're so "temporally transparent" that nobody can acknowledge said effects. When Amy "remembers" the Doctor back into existence (*The Big Bang*), it's likely that her "seeing" his existence and acknowledging him as real restores his temporal opacity to normal. This supports the continued (and otherwise nonsensical) claim that, "If something can be remembered, it can be brought back…"

A final question: Is the universe that the Doctor "restarts" in *The Big Bang* a different continuity from the previous one? The answer would seem to be "no"… the whole point of the universe being rebooted is that everything comes back as it was before, not "everything comes back, save for the huge tracks of history that the Cracks destroyed". In Series 6, the only thing suggesting that history has changed is in *A Good Man Goes to War*, when the Doctor develops a convoluted theory to specify that Amy and Rory conceived River in the TARDIS on their wedding night. But this comes from a being who claims to not really understand human sexuality ("[Sex] is all human-y, private stuff… They don't put up a balloon, or anything"), and might just be crafting a tortured alternate explanation. Rather than attributing the timing of River's conception to a massive overwrite of universal history, Occam's Razor suggests that she could have "started" at any point in Amy and Rory's TARDIS travels because they were feeling saucy and didn't have a prophylactic handy.

2391 *DotD: The Time Machine*
2392 *FP: A Romance in Twelve Parts*: "A Hundred Words from a Civil War", *City: Furthest Tales of the City*: "God Encompasses".

... being a compilation of sidebars that were too big to comfortably fit into the main text...

The Fast Return Switch

Infamously, *The Edge of Destruction* by David Whitaker is a 45-minute, Harold Pinter-esque affair in which the TARDIS – an incredibly advanced time and space machine, and bigger on the inside than the outside to boot – nearly kills itself and everyone aboard when a button on its central console gets stuck. The Doctor, we learn, regarded the offending item – the Fast Return Switch – as an easy remedy to the problem of getting Ian and Barbara back to 1963 (their starting point in *An Unearthly Child*), following their escapade on Skaro in *The Daleks*. As the Doctor tells Ian in *The Edge of Destruction*: "I, er, had hoped to reach your planet Earth. Skaro was in the future, and I used the Fast Return Switch."

The one seems contingent on the other – it's *because* Skaro (or, rather, the events of *The Daleks*) is in the future that the Doctor uses that particular Switch. When it gets stuck, and therefore stays on far too long, the TARDIS goes so far into the past that the lethal energies at the birth of a solar system (possibly Earth's but probably not Skaro's, if we're to presume the Ship successfully "reached" its destination before careening on by) nearly obliterate it. The inherent danger isn't that the stuck Switch takes the TARDIS to the wrong *place*, it's the wrong *time*, probably billions of years earlier than intended.

Those basic facts established, however, back-engineering what the Switch actually *does* can get quite thorny. And while working it out might seem trivial, it has some bearing on the placement of *The Daleks* – which holds a unique status as the first Dalek story, and somewhat impacts the other 1960s Dalek stories.

That being the case, two possibilities for the Switch's function present themselves...

• **The Rewind Option:** The Switch performs the shortcut of rushing the TARDIS *into the past* very, very quickly, for those occasions when one wants to go into the past very, very quickly. It's the equivalent of an accelerator pedal that's supposed to cut out when the pilot takes his/ her foot (or in this case, finger) off, but it gets stuck, so the vehicle stays in motion rather than slowing down.

• **The Redial Option:** Alternatively, hitting the Fast Return Switch makes the TARDIS "go back to its previous location". It's effectively a "last number redial" – just press the Switch, and the Ship relocates to its last position in space-time. There's no expectation, in any story that mentions the Switch, that you need to stand there pressing it for the whole duration of the journey.

Fandom overwhelmingly favours the Redial Option interpretation, as does – in fact – every single story that references the Switch post-*The Edge of Destruction*. And yet, it makes little sense in *The Edge of Destruction* itself, if one games out the Doctor pressing the Switch on Skaro. If the Switch instructs the Ship to go to Temporal Location A and Spatial Location B then stop, a stuck Switch should have made the TARDIS appear at its previous locale in prehistoric times (*An Unearthly Child*) and sit there on a hill, its navigation frozen (as it thinks to itself "go to 100,000 BC, go to 100,000 BC...") while torch-bearing cavemen stared at it slackjawed. Further travels wouldn't be possible until the Switch was turned off.

... that, *or* the Switch would have compelled the Ship to cycle through the whole back catalogue of its journeys (a junkyard in 1963 next, then whatever came beforehand) until told to stop. At some point on that nostalgia tour, we might imagine that it would have wound up back up in the TARDIS cradles on Gallifrey (*The Name of the Doctor*).

Either way, it's hard to fathom how the Redial Option would have made the TARDIS plunge into a newborn solar system. We know that the first Doctor and Susan have never experienced such a phenomenon in their travels – *The Edge of Destruction* renders them so bewildered as to what's happening outside the Ship that the Doctor hurls groundless accusations at Ian and Barbara over the situation, compelling Barbara to give him a good dressing down, and causing a massive shift in the Doctor's character upon his being humiliated into acknowledging his mistake. Basically, the whole course of *Doctor Who* relies upon the Doctor and/or Susan not having any reason, at all, to ponder what's happening outside the TARDIS in *Edge* and think, "Hang on, we've been here once before..."

Nonetheless, the only other on-screen mention of the Switch (the "Fast Return Protocols" the eleventh Doctor cites in *The Name of the Doctor*) and the numerous non-TV stories that reference the Switch unequivocally, and without fail, go for the Redial Option. Chronologically after *Edge*, Susan next uses the Switch in *The Witch Hunters*, which ends with the Doctor judging that the damn thing has been such a headache *twice* now, he disconnects it (ch10). Perhaps for this reason, the Switch isn't an option in *The Daleks' Master Plan*, else the first Doctor, Steven and Sara would surely have used it to return to Kembel when needs must (instead, they steal the directional unit from the Monk's TARDIS). Later in *The Yes Men*, the second Doctor's overuse of the Switch to get Ben and Polly back home takes the TARDIS to one of its previous locales, but (weirdly) thirty years after the fact. Additional stories in which the Switch (successfully or otherwise) features are: *Black and White, Daleks Among Us, DC 3: The Doomsday Chronometer, DC 2: The Sonomancer, The Destination Wars,*

Ghost Ship, J&L: Voyage to the New World, The Kingmaker, Neverland, 100: "100 BC", Seasons of Fear, Shroud of Sorrow, Time in Office and The Witch from the Well. Councilor Ollistra mentions her TARDIS' "Fast Return Circuit" in WD2: The Neverwhen.

Consulting with the story's writer David Whitaker would be helpful, but he died in 1980, not having novelised The Edge of Destruction. The man who did, eight years after Whitaker's passing – Nigel Robinson – altered the TV dialogue in such a way (ch10) that could favour either option... Ian: "The Fast Return switch? What's that?" Doctor: "It's a means whereby the TARDIS is supposed to retrace its previous journeys." Ian: "Don't you see, Doctor, you've sent us back too far! We've gone back past the Earth of 1963, we've even gone on back past prehistoric times!"

All of that said, a few remedies exist that might reconcile the two options...

• Even if the first Doctor and Susan haven't encountered a newborn solar system, the pilot/ crew who operated the TARDIS before they stole it did (perhaps even deliberately, for research or somesuch), but – unlike the Doctor – they had the know-how to do so safely. A neat solution, but almost certainly not on David Whitaker's mind when he wrote Edge in 1963/4.

• The Redial Option is in play in The Edge of Destruction, and its failure to disengage is rather like wanting to go by train from Leeds to Leicester, so you use the M1 Southbound, but you miss the exit and just keep going southward. No "going through previous locations" angle required there, but that would make the Switch quite simply the worst autopilot ever invented. Worse, it presumes that even if you feed the exact coordinates for your destination into one of the most advanced time machines ever built, it's incapable of actually stopping on its own, or thinking to itself "Drat, I've gone too far" and simply turning itself around. (It would also suggest that the newborn solar system in Edge is neither Earth's nor Skaro's, if we're to imagine the Ship tearing past its target in spatial as well as temporal terms. Edge would take place in some system along in a direct line from Skaro to Earth.) The Rewind Option presumes the Ship isn't quite so advanced as that (not unreasonable in the programme's early days), so avoids much of that stupidity.

• The Switch was installed as a redial button, but the Doctor broke it while tinkering with the console (it would make sense for him to disengage whatever protocols would let the Time Lords recall the Ship). In which case, he fixes it at the end of the story, explaining why it works differently all the other times we see it.

• The first Doctor actually invented the Switch, which explains why its early use was less than totally efficacious and nearly murdered everyone aboard, but it was later refined. If so, Time Lord engineers either copied the idea or also came up with it, explaining why it appears in the WarDIS used in Time in Office, and the TARDISes belonging to Ollistra and the Clocksmith (Doom Coalition).

Whatever the case – and most pertinent to Ahistory's purposes – there remains no vivisection of the Switch's function that allows The Daleks to occur, as is sometimes suggested, concurrent with An Unearthly Child in 1963 or beforehand. Skaro was in the future, so the Doctor used the Fast Return Switch.

# # # # #

In the final stages of production on this guidebook, we ashamedly discovered that The Transcendance of Eprhos had been left out through simple human error. The intended entry is included here, with apologies.

c 2540 – THE TRANSCENDANCE OF EPHROS ->

The woman known in this period as "Mother Finsey" had associated with the Master – together, they had burned worlds, enacted power plays with battlefleets and more mischief. Finsey survived the Master's inevitable attempt on her life, but was left blind and began her own confidence schemes. The third Doctor and Jo encountered Finsey after she had created the religion of Zortan to fleece its followers. She had also invested heavily in Galactux: an energy company that had constructed an extraction sphere around the "doomed" world of Ephros, which Finsey had seeded with devastative Thoraxian lavaworms. The Doctor foiled Finsey's scheme by transmatting the bloodworms to explode in space, but she escaped in a cargo ship.

Dating The Transcendance of Ephros (BF 3rd Doc #2.1) – According to the Doctor, not much time has passed since the business with the "Daleks, Ogrons and Draconians" (in Frontier in Space, set in 2540). He also claims to have "rather impressive credentials in this time period" – and, sure enough, the President of Earth seen in Frontier in Space ("Dora", he calls her) vouches for him by remote.

The history of the Daleks would be convoluted even if they weren't time travellers. What follows is an attempt to boil Dalek history down to the basics. Speculation is in italics, and most of the working in the footnotes is to be found in the main timeline – see especially the articles Are There Two Dalek Histories?, The Neutronic War, The Dalek Emperors, The Middle Period of Dalek History, The Alliance, Last Contact, The Dalek Wars, Was Skaro Destroyed?, The Davros Era, The Great Catastrophe, The Last Great Time War and The "Own Time" of the Daleks/ The New Dalek Era.

The Thousand Years War between the Thals and Kaleds on Skaro devastated the planet. The Daleks were created by the Kaled scientist Davros, but the fourth Doctor believed he had set their development back a thousand years.[1]

A thousand years passed. There were again two races on Skaro – the Thals and the Daleks (or Dals), squat blue-skinned warriors *who had evolved from the Kaled survivors.* We don't see the Thals at this time, but their rivals the Dals occupied futuristic cities and had an advanced civilisation.[2]

A neutron bomb exploded, devastating Skaro. Forests were petrified, and animal life mutated into exotic monsters. The Dals and Thals also mutated.[3]

A mutated Dal, a creature like that created by Davros' experiments (*perhaps even a survivor from those experiments*), crawled into a war machine designed by Yarvelling, almost identical to Davros' ancient design (*and so clearly influenced by it*), and became the first Dalek. He became the Emperor Dalek and casings were soon constructed for other Dalek mutants. Within months, the Daleks had built the Dalek City, and soon after that they developed space travel. A social hierarchy emerged, with the feared Black Dalek in charge of military production on Skaro and the Red Dalek in charge of space projects. The Emperor Dalek led the fleet of Dalek saucers in the first conquests. They encountered the Mechanoids. *It was the late eighteenth century on Earth.*

No more than five centuries passed. During this time, the Daleks didn't encounter the human race or learn of the Earth, and they never met the Doctor. They paid little attention to Skaro itself and didn't encounter the Thals.[4]

Quite what they do during these centuries is unclear. They might have a war with the Mechanoids, but it's never mentioned. We have no account of them meeting any other Doctor Who monsters, but that is also possible – the Sontaran-Rutan war is underway across the galaxy, for example. At this time the Daleks are building up a powerbase, and developing advanced weapons, but are far from being the all-conquering race we'll see later.

The only thing we know from this period is that a Dalek ship crashed on Vulcan in the early nineteenth century.[5]

Dalek survivors from the Last Great Time War attacked the Earth a number of times in the early twenty-first century, most notably in 2007, when they fought the Battle of Canary Wharf against the Cybermen, and in 2009, when they conquered the planet in a blitzkrieg, then moved the entire planet across the universe.[6]

In 2012, a Dalek from the future was unable to detect any Dalek transmissions.[7] In the mid-twenty-second century, the Daleks learned of Earth and humanity.[8]

Around 2157, the Daleks attacked the human race – their powerful space fleet cut Earth off from the space lanes, and then a relatively small force invaded the Solar System. They attacked humanity on Earth and the Mars colony. Earth was occupied for ten years.[9]

Thirty years later, the Daleks invaded Earth again, only to suffer another defeat.[10]

The Daleks were defeated, but retained their ambition to conquer Earth.[11] Around this time, the Daleks internalised their power sources, removing their greatest vulnerability – now they ran on psychokinetic power, not static electricity.[12]

For the Daleks, their defeat had great significance for another reason – this was the very first time, from

---

1 *Genesis of the Daleks*
2 The *TV Century 21* strip, which builds on information from *The Daleks.*
3 *The Daleks*
4 The *TV Century 21* strip.
5 Two hundred years before *The Power of the Daleks* – even there, the dating of the story is open to question, and *War of the Daleks* states that the crashed ship came from the far future. In any event, these Daleks are not in contact with Skaro, which remains unaware of the events of this story.
6 *Doomsday, The Stolen Earth/Journey's End*

7 *Dalek*
8 This is depicted in the *TV Century 21* strip, but obviously happens at some point before *The Dalek Invasion of Earth.*
9 *The Dalek Invasion of Earth* (and references in other stories to it – see the main timeline for details).
10 As depicted in the Big Finish audios *An Earthly Child, Relative Dimensions, Lucie Miller* and *To the Death.*
11 Oddly, the Daleks say the Doctor merely "delayed" their conquest of Earth in *The Chase.*
12 They run on "psychokinetic power" according to *Death to the Daleks,* but static electricity in *The Daleks,*

their point of view, that they encountered the Doctor. Soon after the Dalek Invasion, the Daleks developed time travel and sent an assassination group in their time craft to exterminate him.[13]

The Daleks also used their time travel to achieve their other great ambition – they went back in time and conquered the Earth. These Daleks already knew the Doctor's name – they hooked the Doctor up to a Mind Analysis Machine, and learned that the third Doctor was the same individual as his previous two incarnations. Whether this knowledge survived the collapse of the alternative timeline is unclear[14]. But from now on, even if they don't always recognise the Doctor on sight, they understand that he can change his appearance.[15]

The Dalek Invasion was also long-remembered by humanity (some historians called it The First Dalek War), and it resulted in an Alliance of a number of planets, and races being set up to defend against such an attack. The Daleks themselves don't seem to threaten Earth for centuries (Vicki, from 2493, only knows the Daleks from history books about the Invasion).[16]

What the Daleks do in this period, though, is a mystery. We know that the first Doctor's first encounter with the Daleks – when we see them in severely reduced circumstances – happens in Ian and Barbara's "future", "generations" before the year 2540, which would seem to fall around here on the timeline.

The Daleks were confined to Dalek City on Skaro. The Doctor and his companions helped the Thals to destroy them. There's no indication at this time that these Daleks have space travel, time travel, or even are aware that life exists on other planets.[17]

However you rationalise this away, even if you don't try to incorporate the TV Century 21 comic strip, the result is clumsy. The most straightforward explanation is perhaps that the vast majority of Daleks abandon Skaro because their conquests have taken them elsewhere, leaving behind a small group... but this doesn't explain why the Daleks there can't move or see beyond their city. Perhaps they have refused to upgrade their power supplies and literally been left grounded as a result.

Perhaps these are all the surviving Daleks – crippled by their defeat on Earth and the loss of their time craft, and perhaps leaderless (the Daleks need strong leadership, and are prone to turn on each other the moment they don't have it). We know

---

The Dalek Invasion of Earth and The Power of the Daleks. Maxtible and Waterfield's experiments with static electricity attract the Daleks (The Evil of the Daleks).

13 *The Chase.* The Daleks have done some research – they know what the TARDIS looks like, even though they never saw it in *The Dalek Invasion of Earth* (or *Genesis of the Daleks*, *The Power of the Daleks* or *The Daleks*, for that matter). They know the Doctor's a time traveller, somehow (perhaps this was an accidental discovery when their were conducting their own time travel experiments). However, there are some big gaps in their knowledge: they don't even consider the possibility that the TARDIS crew might have changed, and they refer to the Doctor as "human" – we might infer they have yet to encounter another incarnation of the Doctor, and they don't know about the Time Lords.

14 *Day of the Daleks*

15 From *The Chase* onwards, the Daleks know about the Doctor. They have "files" on him by *The Daleks' Master Plan*; Chen thinks, possibly because the Daleks told him, that the Doctor is from "another galaxy". The Daleks recognise the second Doctor on sight in *The Power of the Daleks*, and lay a trap for him in *The Evil of the Daleks* (they have a photograph of him). They need to use the Mind Analysis Machine to identify the third Doctor in *Day of the Daleks*, but understand he can change his appearance. They know the third Doctor on sight in *Frontier in Space*, *Planet of the Daleks* and *Death to the Daleks* and the fourth Doctor in *Destiny of the Daleks*. They again lay a trap for the fifth Doctor in *Resurrection of the Daleks* (and have built duplicates of the fifth Doctor, Tegan and Turlough, so know of them).

In *Revelation of the Daleks*, Davros has a tombstone prepared that's specifically the sixth Doctor's; the Daleks don't seem to recognise the seventh Doctor in *Remembrance of the Daleks* – and Davros remarks on his changed appearance – but they know his name (and, indeed, both factions' plans rely on detailed knowledge of the Doctor's past).

Since the Time War, the Doctor has gone from being "an enemy of the Daleks" who they know is a threat to someone they are viscerally scared of – in *Dalek*, the Dalek knows the Doctor's name and reputation, but apparently doesn't recognise the ninth Doctor on sight. In *Doomsday*, the Daleks don't recognise the tenth Doctor, but are able to identify him, on sight, as a threat.

16 *The Rescue*

17 *The Daleks*

18 *The Chase*, *Day of the Daleks* and "Dogs of Doom".

19 *Frontier in Space*

20 "Nemesis of the Daleks"

21 "Metamorphosis", *Death to the Daleks*.

22 The seventh Doctor met the Emperor earlier in history in the comic strip "Nemesis of the Daleks". As the Emperor in *The Evil of the Daleks* says it's their first meeting, he's either lying or a different individual from the one in the earlier story.

23 *The Daleks' Master Plan*

24 *The Apocalypse Element*

25 The Doctor explicitly states that the Daleks don't want to conquer the Earth in *Remembrance of the Daleks*.

26 The four Big Finish *Dalek Empire* mini-series.

that the Moroks were on Skaro – perhaps they stole more than just the one Dalek seen in their space museum. If they took, say, the Dalek Brain Machine that's seen to guide the Daleks and stripped the Daleks' archives, then it would have been a crippling setback.

The next time we see the Daleks, they're attacking human colony planets in the mid-twenty-fifth century. The Daleks did not, at this time, seem to have the strength to launch an attack against Earth itself.

However, they are clearly far more powerful than they were when confined to one city on Skaro. They've had a few centuries to rebuild and regroup, but we don't know anything about the catalyst for this process. Perhaps various defeated remnants of the Daleks – the space travellers, the time travellers and the inhabitants of Dalek City – converge on Skaro. There's a Supreme Council in place by the twenty-sixth century – perhaps this is the body that provides the unified leadership that allows the Daleks to gain strength.

A century later, the Daleks are far more powerful than ever before.

Presumably this is just a natural consequence of building up a powerbase for centuries. Interestingly, the Daleks seem to have time travel, but not to use it – they might just be wary after their two high profile defeats. They don't seem aware of the Time Lords, yet, but they must have spotted that the Doctor has thwarted them on the three occasions they've used time travel technology.[18]

In the twenty-sixth century, there was "the third wave of Dalek expansion", and the Doctor described the Daleks as "one of the greatest powers in the universe" at this time. This was the time of the Second and Third Dalek Wars, which sparked off when the Daleks attempted to divide and conquer the space empires of Earth and Draconia.[19]

The Daleks plot this with the Master. It's never made clear exactly what the Master tells them about himself, but this might be the point where the Daleks realise that the Doctor is just one of a race of time travellers with TARDISes.

This was Benny Summerfield's native time – her father, Abslom Daak and (later) Ace all fought in these Dalek Wars. Abslom Daak apparently killed the Dalek Emperor at this time. *This might have been a turning point in the war.*[20] It was a war that lasted a generation, ending in the early 2570s. The Daleks lost.

Following this, the weakened Daleks tried tactics other than full scale assaults.[21]

There are no accounts of the Daleks for centuries – and the human race goes from strength to strength as the Earth Empire spreads across the galaxy. Perhaps unsurprisingly, the Daleks became interested in "the Human Factor". The next time we see them, the Daleks are in their city on Skaro. The introduction of the Human Factor into the Daleks leads to civil war, to the Emperor's death and to the Doctor declaring this to be

"the final end".[22]

So, the Daleks disappeared around the year 3000. It was the year 4000 before humanity came into contact with them again, but they'd begun their expansion around 3500.

The Daleks' Master Plan saw the Daleks' most ambitious scheme yet – a conquest of the entire Solar System, but merely as part of a strategy to dominate eleven whole galaxies. These Daleks also used time machines, and hoped to construct a Time Destructor. The Daleks were based back on Skaro at this point.[23]

Despite being defeated, the Daleks were now a powerful intergalactic force. Within twenty years of their Master Plan failing, the Daleks had succeeded in splitting the Federation. Within a couple of centuries of that, the Daleks were capable of threatening the Time Lords themselves.[24]

By now, then, the Daleks have learned of the Time Lords and Gallifrey. To a race dedicated to becoming the supreme beings of the universe, the Time Lords were now obviously the ones to beat – and from now on, the Daleks express no interest in conquering the Earth.[25]

The Davros Era took place – the Daleks lost their war with the Movellans, but Davros clawed his way to become the new Dalek Emperor. He re-engineered the Daleks, upgraded their technology and put them in a position where they were a genuine threat to the Time Lords... which may have been what the Dalek leadership had planned all along.

Whether the events of War of the Daleks *can be taken at face value or not, the Daleks get what they want – they go from military defeat and fragmented forces to having a strong leader and the knowledge and ability to fight a war across an entire galaxy and take on the Time Lords.*

The Dalek Empire period saw the Daleks based in the Seriphia galaxy launch a massive assault on the Milky Way, forcing the Earth Alliance to surrender. Resistance leaders Mendes and Kalendorf were able to forment a slave uprising and enlisted the help of Daleks from a parallel universe, but despite countless sacrifices, still the Daleks could not be defeated. Eventually, a signal was sent that destroyed all Daleks and Dalek technology in both the Milky Way and Seriphia – triggering a Great Catastrophe that took those territories millennia to recover from. The Daleks were not utterly destroyed, and thousands of years after the Great Catastrophe, they unleashed a new plague on the galaxy. Humanity mobilised against them once more.[26]

The Daleks may, or may not, have lost Skaro. Either way, by now the Daleks were operating at a universal level, not just an intergalactic one. We have patchy information for the next ten thousand years or so, but Captain Jack sums it up: they were the greatest threat in the universe.

The Daleks now merely superficially resembled Davros' original creation. The Dalek Emperor (at least the third or fourth bearer of the title, and definitely not Davros) now oversaw an entirely revamped Dalek force – a huge army of highly-mobile, heavily-defended Daleks, with a re-engineered Dalek mutant inside. At least some of these Daleks had built-in "temporal shift" units. Dalek Saucers were now capable of firing missiles that could shoot down a TARDIS in flight.

To put the Daleks' might in perspective: now that the Daleks were upgraded, a single one of them was capable of subduing the entire human population of twenty-first century Earth. Four of them could fend off droves of Cybermen with no evident damage or difficulty.

Before this upgrade, in 2540, the largest army of Daleks ever assembled consisted of ten thousand Daleks – it was capable of conquering an entire galaxy. In the year 4000, five thousand Daleks would have been enough to subdue Earth's solar system.

Now, the Dalek space fleet consisted of ten million ships, each with two thousand Daleks onboard. Twenty *billion* Daleks.

The Daleks were ready to fight the Last Great Time War ...

The War devastated both sides, leaving few survivors. A few Daleks survived, as did remnants of their technology. From this, they were able to rebuild their strength, but only by losing their genetic purity. Eventually, the Daleks were able to create a new Dalek paradigm – genetically pure, with advanced travel machines.[27]

Although the new paradigm Daleks prized genetic purity, they were members – with other types of Daleks – of the Parliament of the Daleks. Led by a Prime Minister, this group oversaw the destruction of the Dalek Asylum, fearing the millions of rogue Daleks within were about to escape.[28]

The Daleks eventually consolidated in their "own time", brought about the restoration of Skaro, and continued to show mercy to their creator, Davros. A gambit against the Doctor resulted in the destruction of their city and Dalek High Command.[29]

27 The televised Dalek stories from 2005 onwards have told a continuing story of the post-War Daleks rebuilding. These are *Dalek, Bad Wolf/The Parting of the Ways, Army of Ghosts/Doomsday, Daleks in Manhattan/Evolution of the Daleks, Journey's End/The Stolen Earth, Victory of the Daleks, Asylum of the Daleks, Into the Dalek* and *The Magician's Apprentice/The Witch's Familiar*. We see Daleks actually involved in the Time War in *The Day of the Doctor*.
28 *Asylum of the Daleks*
29 *The Magician's Apprentice/The Witch's Familiar*